W9-AVX-346

Exam 70-562: TS: Microsoft .NET Framework 3.5, ASP.NET Application Development

OBJECTIVE	CHAPTER	LESSON
CONFIGURING AND DEPLOYING WEB APPLICATIONS (10 PERCENT)		
Configure providers.	14	1,2
Configure authentication, authorization, and impersonation.	14	3
Configure projects, solutions, and reference assemblies.	1	3
Configure session state by using Microsoft SQL Server, State Server, or InProc.	4	2
Publish Web applications.	16	1
Configure application pools.	16	1
Compile an application by using Visual Studio or command-line tools.	16	1,2
CONSUMING AND CREATING SERVER CONTROLS (20 PERCENT)		
Implement data-bound controls.	8	2
Load user controls dynamically.	10	1
Create and consume custom controls.	10	2
Implement client-side validation and server-side validation.	3	1
Consume standard controls.	2	1,2
WORKING WITH DATA AND SERVICES (17 PERCENT)		
Read and write XML data.	7	3
Manipulate data by using DataSet and DataReader objects.	7	1,2
Call a Windows Communication Foundation (WCF) service or a Web service from an ASP.NET Web page.	9	2
Implement a DataSource control.	8	1
Bind controls to data by using data binding syntax.	8	1,2
TROUBLESHOOTING AND DEBUGGING WEB APPLICATIONS (16 PERCENT)		
Configure debugging and custom errors.	12	1
Set up an environment to perform remote debugging.	12	1,2
Debug unhandled exceptions when using ASP.NET AJAX.	12	1
Implement tracing of a Web application.	12	2
Debug deployment issues.	12	1,2
Monitor Web applications.	12	2
WORKING WITH ASP.NET AJAX AND CLIENT-SIDE SCRIPTING (15 PERCENT)		
Implement Web Forms by using ASP.NET AJAX.	6	1
Interact with the ASP.NET AJAX client-side library.	6	2
Consume services from client scripts.	9	1,2
Create and register client script.	6	2
TARGETING MOBILE DEVICES (5 PERCENT)		
Access device capabilities.	15	1
Control device-specific rendering.	15	1

Add mobile Web controls to a Web page.	15	1
Implement control adapters.	15	1
PROGRAMMING WEB APPLICATIONS (17 PERCENT)		
Customize the layout and appearance of a Web page.	5	1,2,3
Work with ASP.NET intrinsic objects.	11	2
Implement globalization and accessibility.	13	1,2
Implement business objects and utility classes.	1	2,3
Implement session state, view state, control state, cookies, cache, or application state.	2,4	Chapter 2: Lesson 1 Chapter 4: Lesson 1
Handle events and control page flow.	2,3	Chapter 2: Lessons 1 and 3; Chapter 3: Lessons 1 and 2
Implement the Generic Handler.	11	1

Exam Objectives The exam objectives listed here are current as of this book's publication date. Exam objectives are subject to change at any time without prior notice and at Microsoft's sole discretion. Please visit the Microsoft Learning Web site for the most current listing of exam objectives: http://www.microsoft.com/learning/en/us/exams/70-562.mspx.

Microsoft®

MCTS Self-Paced Training Kit (Exam 70-562): Microsoft® .NET Framework 3.5—ASP.NET Application Development

Mike Snell

PUBLISHED BY
Microsoft Press
A Division of Microsoft Corporation
One Microsoft Way
Redmond, Washington 98052-6399

Library of Congress Control Number: 2009920804

Printed and bound in the United States of America.

2 3 4 5 6 7 8 9 WCT 4 3 2 1 0

Distributed in Canada by H.B. Fenn and Company Ltd.

A CIP catalogue record for this book is available from the British Library.

Microsoft Press books are available through booksellers and distributors worldwide. For further infor-mation about international editions, contact your local Microsoft Corporation office or contact Microsoft Press International directly at fax (425) 936-7329. Visit our Web site at *www.microsoft.com/mspress*. Send comments to tkinput@microsoft.com.

Acquisitions Editor: Ken Jones
Developmental Editor: Laura Sackerman
Project Editor: Maureen Zimmerman
Editorial Production: nSight, Inc.
Technical Reviewer: Kurt Meyer; Technical Review services provided by Content Master, a member of CM Group, Ltd.
Cover: Tom Draper Design

Body Part No. X15-45849

Dedication

For my mom, Tonya Snell.

—Mike Snell

Acknowledgments

I would first like to thank the authors of the first edition of this book: Glenn Johnson and Tony Northrup. It has been a pleasure building on the foundation that you laid.

I would also like to thank the hard-working people at Microsoft Press, including Ken Jones for getting me involved in another great project and Maureen Zimmerman for her guidance on this work.

Many thanks to Chris Norton and his team at nSight (*www.nsightworks.com*) for keeping the book on schedule. This includes Teresa Horton for her great editing work.

Thanks also to Richard Kobylka and the team at GrandMasters (*www.grandmasters.biz*) for their help shepherding this book through the process.

Also, thanks go to my technical editor, Kurt Meyer. Thanks for working through the labs, getting the CD right, and challenging various technical anomalies.

Thanks to Kristy Saunders for her wonderful work on the sample questions for the CD.

Finally, I would like to thank my wife, Carrie, and my children, Allie and Ben. Thanks for your patience and understanding during this process.

—Mike Snell

Contents

Chapter 4 ASP.NET State Management 183

Chapter 5 Customizing and Personalizing a Web Application 229

Introduction

This training kit is designed for developers who plan to take Microsoft Certified Technical Specialist (MCTS) exam 70-562, as well as for developers who need to know how to develop applications using the Microsoft .NET Framework 3.5 and ASP.NET. We assume that before you begin using this kit, you have a working knowledge of Microsoft Windows and Microsoft Visual Basic or C#.

By using this training kit, you'll see how to do the following:

- Create a Web application using Web server controls, event handlers, application state, and session state.
- Create custom Web server controls.
- Develop accessible Web applications that can be used by a global audience.
- Write rich, Web-based user experiences using AJAX.
- Integrate a Web application with a back-end database.
- Create a Web application that stores user-specific information and preferences.
- Monitor, troubleshoot, and debug ASP.NET applications.
- Build service-oriented applications (SOAs) using Web services and Windows Communication Foundation (WCF).
- Add authentication and authorization features to your application to improve security and add multiple access levels.
- Create Web applications that can be used from mobile phones and PDAs.

System Requirements

We recommend that you use a computer that is not your primary workstation to do the practice exercises in this book because you will make changes to the operating system and application configuration.

Hardware Requirements

To use the companion CD, you need a computer running Microsoft Windows Server 2003, Windows Server 2008, Windows Vista, or Windows XP. The computer must meet the following minimum requirements:

- 1 GHz 32-bit (x86) or 64-bit (x64) processor (depending on the minimum requirements of the operating system)
- 1 GB of system memory (depending on the minimum requirements of the operating system)
- A hard disk with at least 700 MB of available space
- A monitor capable of at least 800 × 600 display resolution
- A keyboard
- A mouse or other pointing device
- An optical drive capable of reading CD-ROMs
- An optical drive capable of reading DVDs if you are installing the 90-day evaluation edition of Visual Studio 2008 Professional Edition included on the DVD with this book

Software Requirements

The computer used with the companion CD-ROM should also have the following software:

- A Web browser such as Microsoft Internet Explorer version 6 or later
- An application that can display PDF files, such as Adobe Acrobat Reader, which can be downloaded at *www.adobe.com/reader*
- Visual Studio 2008 (A 90-day evaluation edition of Visual Studio 2008 Professional Edition is included on the DVD with this book.)

These requirements will support use of the companion CD-ROM.

Using the CD and DVD

A companion CD and an evaluation software DVD are included with this training kit. The evaluation software DVD contains a 90-day evaluation edition of Microsoft Visual Studio 2008 Professional Edition, in case you want to use it with this book. The companion CD contains the following:

PRACTICE TESTS

You can reinforce your understanding of how to create ASP.NET applications using the .NET Framework 3.5 by using electronic practice tests that you customize to meet your needs from the pool of Lesson Review questions in this book. Or, you can practice for the 70-562 certification exam by using tests created from a pool of 200 realistic exam questions, which is enough to give you many different practice exams to ensure that you're prepared.

CODE

The chapters in this book include sample files associated with the lab exercises at the end of every lesson. For some exercises, you will be instructed to open a project prior to starting the exercise. For other exercises, you will create a project on your own and be able to reference a completed project in the event you experience a problem while following the exercise.

AN EBOOK

An electronic version (eBook) of this book is included for times when you don't want to carry the printed book with you. The eBook is in Portable Document Format (PDF); you can view it by using Adobe Acrobat or Adobe Reader. You can use the eBook to cut and paste code as you work through the exercises.

GLOSSARY

Key terms used in the chapters are included in a glossary on the CD.

SAMPLE CHAPTERS

The CD also includes sample chapters from other MS Press books for your review.

> ***MORE INFO*** **DIGITAL CONTENT FOR DIGITAL BOOK READERS**
>
> **If you bought a digital-only edition of this book, you can enjoy select content from the print edition's companion CD. Visit *http://go.microsoft.com/fwlink/?LinkId=144372* to get your downloadable content. This content is always up-to-date and available to all readers.**

How to Install the Practice Tests

To install the practice test software from the companion CD to your hard disk, do the following:

1. Insert the companion CD into your CD drive, and accept the license agreement. A CD menu appears.

> ***NOTE*** **IF THE CD MENU DOESN'T APPEAR**
>
> **If the CD menu or the license agreement doesn't appear, AutoRun might be disabled on your computer. Refer to the Readme.txt file on the CD-ROM for alternate installation instructions.**

2. Click the Practice Tests item, and follow the instructions on the screen.

How to Use the Practice Tests

To start the practice test software, follow these steps:

1. Click Start | All Programs | Microsoft Press Training Kit Exam Prep. A window appears that shows all the Microsoft Press training kit exam prep suites installed on your computer.
2. Double-click the lesson review or practice test that you want to use.

> ***NOTE*** **LESSON REVIEWS VS. PRACTICE TESTS**
>
> **Select the (70-562) Microsoft .NET Framework 3.5—Web-Based Client Development *lesson review* to use the questions from the "Lesson Review" sections of this book. Select the (70-562) Microsoft .NET Framework 3.5 — Web-Based Client Development *practice test* to use a pool of 200 questions similar to those in the 70-562 certification exam.**

Lesson Review Options

When you start a lesson review, the Custom Mode dialog box appears so that you can configure your test. You can click OK to accept the defaults, or you can customize the number of questions you want, how the practice test software works, which exam objectives you want the questions to relate to, and whether you want your lesson review to be timed. If you're retaking a test, you can select whether you want to see all the questions again or only those questions you missed or didn't answer.

After you click OK, your lesson review starts.

- To take the test, answer the questions and use the Next, Previous, and Go To buttons to move from question to question.
- After you answer an individual question, if you want to see which answers are correct—along with an explanation of each correct answer—click Explanation.
- If you'd rather wait until the end of the test to see how you did, answer all the questions, and then click Score Test. You'll see a summary of the exam objectives you chose and the percentage of questions you got right overall and per objective. You can print a copy of your test, review your answers, or retake the test.

Practice Test Options

When you start a practice test, you choose whether to take the test in Certification Mode, Study Mode, or Custom Mode:

CERTIFICATION MODE

Closely resembles the experience of taking a certification exam. The test has a set number of questions, it's timed, and you can't pause and restart the timer.

STUDY MODE

Creates an untimed test in which you can review the correct answers and the explanations after you answer each question.

CUSTOM MODE

Gives you full control over the test options so that you can customize them as you like.

In all modes, the user interface you see when taking the test is basically the same, but with different options enabled or disabled, depending on the mode. The main options are discussed in the previous section, "Lesson Review Options."

When you review your answer to an individual practice test question, a "References" section is provided that lists where in the training kit you can find the information that relates to that question; it also provides links to other sources of information. After you click Test Results to score your entire practice test, you can click the Learning Plan tab to see a list of references for every objective.

How to Uninstall the Practice Tests

To uninstall the practice test software for a training kit, use the Add Or Remove Programs option in Windows Control Panel.

How to Install the Code

To install the sample files referenced in the book's exercises from the companion CD to your hard disk, do the following:

1. Insert the companion CD into your CD drive, and accept the license agreement. A CD menu appears.

> ***NOTE*** **IF THE CD MENU DOESN'T APPEAR**
>
> **If the CD menu or the license agreement doesn't appear, AutoRun might be disabled on your computer. Refer to the Readme.txt file on the CD-ROM for alternate installation instructions.**

2. Click the Code item, and follow the instructions on the screen.

   The code will be installed to \Documents and Settings\<*user*>\My Documents \MicrosoftPress\TK562.

Microsoft Certified Professional Program

The Microsoft certifications provide the best method to prove your command of current Microsoft products and technologies. The exams and corresponding certifications are developed to validate your mastery of critical competencies as you design and develop, or implement and support, solutions with Microsoft products and technologies. Computer professionals who become Microsoft-certified are recognized as experts and are sought after industry-wide. Certification brings a variety of benefits to the individual and to employers and organizations.

> ***MORE INFO*** **ALL THE MICROSOFT CERTIFICATIONS**
>
> **For a full list of Microsoft certifications, go to *www.microsoft.com/learning/mcp/default.asp*.**

Technical Support

Every effort has been made to ensure the accuracy of this book and the contents of the companion CD. If you have comments, questions, or ideas regarding this book or the companion CD, please send them to Microsoft Press by using either of the following methods:

E-mail

- tkinput@microsoft.com

Postal Mail:

- *Microsoft Press*

  Attn: MCTS Self-Paced Training Kit (Exam 70-562): Microsoft .NET Framework 3.5—Web-Based Client Development Editor

  One Microsoft Way

  Redmond, WA 98052–6399

For additional support information regarding this book and the CD-ROM (including answers to commonly asked questions about installation and use), visit the Microsoft Press Technical Support Web site at *www.microsoft.com/learning/support/books/*. To connect directly to the Microsoft Knowledge Base and enter a query, visit *http://support.microsoft.com/search/*. For support information regarding Microsoft software, please connect to *http://support.microsoft.com*.

Evaluation Edition Software Support

The 90-day evaluation edition provided with this training kit is not the full retail product and is provided only for the purposes of training and evaluation. Microsoft and Microsoft Technical Support do not support this evaluation edition.

Information about any issues relating to the use of this evaluation edition with this training kit is posted to the Support section of the Microsoft Press Web site (*www.microsoft.com/learning/support/books/*). For information about ordering the full version of any Microsoft software, please call Microsoft Sales at (800) 426-9400 or visit *www.microsoft.com*.

CHAPTER 1

Introducing ASP.NET 3.5

The Web development experience continues to evolve with Microsoft Visual Studio 2008 and ASP.NET 3.5. These new tools enable you to build highly interactive, robust Web applications more efficiently than ever. This includes building sites that provide users with a high degree of interactivity with AJAX. There are also new and improved controls that both speed development and add to the user experience. Other enhancements include improvements in Web site security, integration with Microsoft Internet Information Services 7.0 (IIS 7.0), and a better Web service programming model. All of these enhancements were developed to give ASP.NET developers more control and increased confidence when building and deploying the next generation of Web sites.

This chapter introduces the basics of Web site development with ASP.NET. It starts by describing the key players in any Web site: the server, the browser (or client), and Hypertext Transfer Protocol (HTTP). This serves as a basis for understanding the architecture of an ASP.NET Web site. In Lesson 2, "Creating a Web Site and Adding New Web Pages," you will learn the key components that make up an ASP.NET development site. The chapter closes with a discussion on configuring the many aspects of an ASP.NET application.

Exam objectives in this chapter:

- Configuring and Deploying Web Applications
  - Configure projects, solutions, and reference assemblies.
- Programming Web Applications
  - Implement business objects and utility classes.
  - Handle events and control page flow.

Lessons in this chapter:

Before You Begin

To complete the lessons in the chapter, you should be familiar with developing applications in Microsoft Visual Studio using Visual Basic or C#. In addition, you should be comfortable with all of the following:

- The Visual Studio 2008 Integrated Development Environment (IDE)
- A basic understanding of Hypertext Markup Language (HTML) and client-side scripting
- How to make assemblies available to other applications
- Working with Visual Studio projects, files, classes, and designers

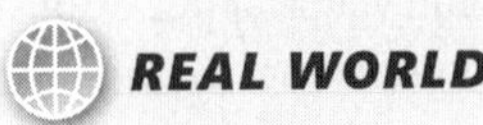

Mike Snell

A good Web application developer needs to know a lot more than just his or her favorite development language to be effective. In fact, C# or Visual Basic is just the starting point. You also must know how to handle page layout with HTML. You need to know how to create, manage, and implement interface styling with Cascading Style Sheets (CSS). JavaScript will also be required if you intend to write your own client-side functionality for your Web pages. You might also need to understand Extensible Markup Language (XML), Web services, and database programming. Of course, you also need to know how all of these things work together to form a single solution. The modern Web developer needs to know more technologies (and be able to easily switch between them) than any other developer in history. I think this is one of the reasons Web development is such a challenging, fun, and rewarding experience.

Lesson 1: Understanding the Players

A Web application is unlike a standard Windows application. It does not run in a single process on a single machine. Instead, it is typically hosted on a Web server and accessed via a Web browser on a client machine. The communication between the Web server and Web browser is sent using HTTP. It is imperative you have a basic understanding of how these items work and communicate together before you start writing much code. The typical communication process between browser and server can be generalized into the following steps:

1. A user uses his or her Web browser to initiate a request for a Web server resource.
2. HTTP is used to send a *GET* request to the Web server.
3. The Web server processes the *GET* request on the server (typically locating the requested code and running it).
4. The Web server then sends a response back to the Web browser. The HTTP protocol is used to send the HTTP response back to the Web browser.
5. The user's Web browser then processes the response (typically HTML and JavaScript) and renders the Web page for display to the user.
6. The user may then enter data and perform an action such as clicking a submit button that causes his or her data to be sent back to the Web server for processing.
7. HTTP is used to *POST* the data back to the Web server.
8. The Web server then processes the *POST* request (again, calling your code in the process).
9. The Web server then sends a response back to the Web browser. HTTP is used to send the HTTP response to the Web browser.
10. The Web browser again processes the response and displays the Web page to the user. This process is repeated over and over during a typical Web application session.

This lesson provides an overview of the responsibilities and boundaries of a Web browser and the Web server. You will also learn the basics of HTTP and how browsers and servers use it to process user requests.

After this lesson, you will be able to:

- Describe the Web server's role in responding to requests for resources.
- Describe the Web browser's role in submitting requests and presenting the response to the user.
- Describe the role of HTTP in communicating with the Web server.
- Describe how HTTP verbs are used to request resources from the Web server.
- Describe the status-code groups that are implemented in HTTP.
- Describe Distributed Authoring and Versioning.
- Describe *PostBack*, the common method of sending data to the Web server.
- Describe methods for troubleshooting HTTP.

Estimated lesson time: 30 minutes

The Web Server's Role

The first Web servers were responsible for receiving and processing simple user requests from browsers via HTTP. The Web server handled its request and sent a response back to the Web browser. The Web server then closed any connection between it and the browser and released all resources that were involved with the request. These resources were easy to release as the Web server was finished processing the request. This type of Web application was considered to be *stateless* because no data was held by the Web server between requests and no connection was left open. These applications typically involved simple HTML pages and were therefore able to handle thousands of similar requests per minute. Figure 1-1 shows an example of this simple, stateless environment.

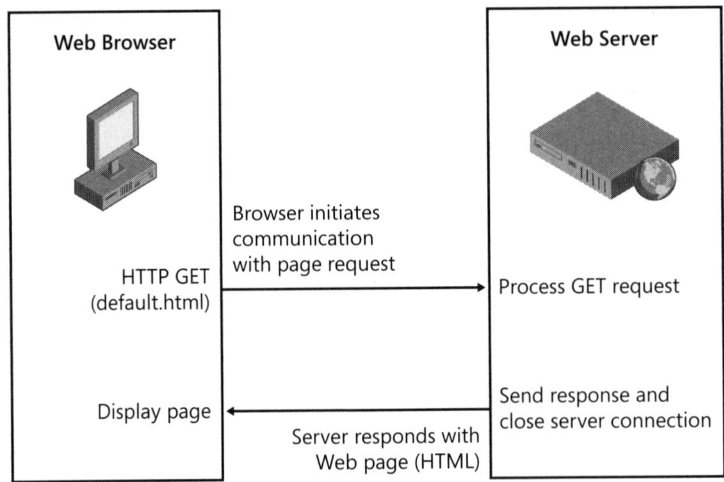

FIGURE 1-1 A simple request and response between browser and server in a stateless environment

Today's Web servers deliver services that go far beyond the original Web servers. In addition to serving static HTML files, modern Web servers also handle requests for pages that contain code that executes on the server; the Web server executes this code on request and responds with the results. These Web servers also have the ability to store data between requests. This means that Web pages can be connected together to form a Web application that understands the current state of each individual user's requests. These servers keep a connection open to the browser for a period of time in anticipation of additional page requests from the same user. This type of interaction is illustrated in Figure 1-2.

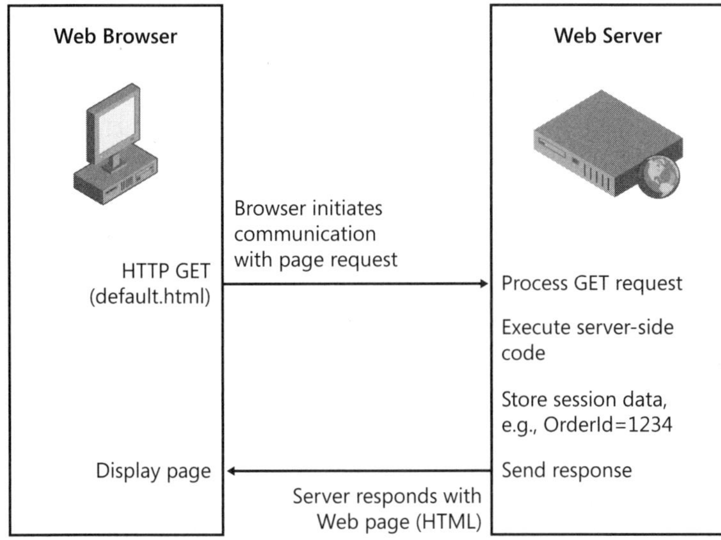

FIGURE 1-2 Modern Web servers store state between page requests to enable more sophisticated Web applications

The Web Browser's Role

The Web browser provides a platform-independent means of displaying Web pages that were written in HTML. HTML was designed to be able to render information on any operating system while placing no constraint on the window size. This is why Web pages are considered platform independent. HTML was designed to "flow," wrapping text as necessary to fit into the browser window. The Web browser also displays images and responds to hyperlinks to other pages. Each Web page request to the Web server results in the Web browser updating the screen to display the new information.

Although the Web browser's role is simply to present information and collect data from users, many new client-side technologies enable today's Web browsers to execute code such as JavaScript and to support plug-ins that improve the user's experience. Technologies such as Asynchronous JavaScript and XML (AJAX) and Microsoft Silverlight allow Web browsers to communicate with Web servers without clearing the existing Web page from the browser window. These technologies make the user experience more dynamic and interactive.

Understanding the Role of Hypertext Transfer Protocol

HTTP is a text-based communication protocol that is used to request Web pages from the Web server and send responses back to the Web browser. HTTP messages are typically sent between the Web server and Web browser using port 80, or port 443 when using Secure HTTP (HTTPS).

> ***MORE INFO*** **HTTP/1.1 SPECIFICATION**
>
> **For more information on the current HTTP standard (HTTP/1.1), you can review the specification at the following Web address: *http://www.w3.org/Protocols/rfc2616/rfc2616.html.***

Pages are typically requested by a user entering information in his or her browser by clicking on a favorite, conducting a search, or typing in a Uniform Resource Locator (URL). When a Web page is requested, a textual command is sent from the browser to the Web server. This command might look as follows:

```
GET /default.aspx HTTP/1.1
Host: www.northwindtraders.com
```

The first line in this command contains what is called the method, also known as the verb or command. In this case the verb is *GET*. The verb is followed by the URL of the Web page to be retrieved (/default.aspx). Following that is the version of HTTP to be used to process the command (HTTP/1.1). In this way, the method indicates the action to be performed by the Web server, the URL that is the target of that method, and the communication protocol.

The second line of the command (Host: *www.northwindtraders.com*) identifies the name of the host that should be used by the Web server. This is useful if a Web server is hosting more than one Web site. In this case, the Web server needs to pass on the request to the appropriate site for processing. This process is known as using host headers to identify the Web site that will handle the given request. There are other methods defined by HTTP. Table 1-1 contains a list of some of the common HTTP methods with a description of their uses. Note that if Distributed Authoring and Versioning (DAV) is enabled on the Web site, many more verbs are available, such as *LOCK* and *UNLOCK*.

What Is Distributed Authoring and Versioning?

Distributed Authoring and Versioning (DAV) is a set of extensions to HTTP/1.1 that simplifies Web site development when working in a team scenario. DAV is an open standard and is available on numerous platforms. DAV provides the ability to lock and unlock files and the ability to designate versions.

DAV is built directly on HTTP/1.1, so no other protocols, such as File Transfer Protocol (FTP) or Server Message Block (SMB), are required. DAV also provides the ability to query the Web server for various resource properties such as file names,

time stamps, and sizes. DAV also gives developers the ability to perform server-side file copying and moving. For example, you can use the HTTP *GET* and *PUT* verbs to retrieve files from the Web servers and save them to different locations, or you can use the DAV's *COPY* verb to simply tell a server to copy the file.

TABLE 1-1 Common HTTP/1.1 Methods

HTTP METHOD	DESCRIPTION
OPTIONS	Used by client applications to request a list of all supported verbs. In this way, you can check to see if a server allows a particular verb before wasting network bandwidth trying to send an unsupported request.
GET	Gets a URL from the server. A *GET* request for a specific URL, say, /test.htm, retrieves the test.htm file. Data retrieved using this verb is typically cached by the browser. *GET* also works with collections, such as those in directories that contain collections of files. If you request a directory, the server can be configured to return a default file, such as index.html, that may be representative of the directory.
HEAD	Retrieves the meta information for a resource. This information is typically identical to the meta information sent in response to a *GET* request, but the *HEAD* verb never returns the actual resource. The meta information is cacheable.
POST	Sends data to the Web server for processing. This is typically the result of users entering data on a form and submitting that data as part of their request.
PUT	Allows a client to directly create a resource at the indicated URL on the server. The server takes the body of the request, creates the file specified in the URL, and copies the received data to the newly created file. If the file exists and is not locked, the content of the file will be overwritten.
DELETE	Used to delete a resource at the Web server. Requires write permissions on the directory.
TRACE	Used for testing or diagnostics; allows the client to see what is being received at the other end of the request chain. Responses to this method are never cached.
CONNECT	Reserved for use with a proxy that can dynamically switch to being a tunnel, such as Secure Sockets Layer (SSL) protocol.
DEBUG	Not defined in the HTTP/1.1 specification, but used to start ASP.NET debugging. This method informs Visual Studio of the process to which the debugger will attach.

The communication from the Web browser to the Web server is referred to as a request. In ASP.NET, there is a *Request* object that is used to represent the Web browser's communications to the Web server. It wraps the resource request in an object that can be queried in code. This includes providing your code access to things like the cookies associated with your site, the query string parameters passed on the URL, the path to the request, and more.

The communication from the Web server back to the Web browser is commonly referred to as the response. In ASP.NET this information is wrapped in the *Response* object. You can use this object to set cookies, define caching, set page expiration, and more. When the Web server responds to a request, it uses what it finds in the *Response* object to write the actual, text-based HTTP response. This communication might look as follows:

```
HTTP/1.1 200 OK
Server: Microsoft-IIS/6.0
Content-Type: text/html
Content-Length: 38
<html><body>Hello, world.</body><html>
```

The first line indicates the communication protocol and version information. It also includes the status code for the response and the reason that explains the status code. The status codes are three digits and grouped as shown in Table 1-2.

EXAM TIP

Even if you don't memorize every status code, it is helpful to know the five status code groupings in Table 1-2.

TABLE 1-2 Status Code Groups

STATUS CODE GROUP	DESCRIPTION
1xx	Informational: Request received, continuing to process.
2xx	Success: The action was successfully received, understood, and accepted.
3xx	Redirect Command: Further action must be taken to complete the request.
4xx	Client Error: The request has a syntax error or the server does not know how to fulfill the request.
5xx	Server Error: The server failed to fulfill a request that appears to be valid.

In addition to the status code groups, HTTP/1.1 defines unique status codes and reasons. A reason is nothing more than a very brief description of the status code. Table 1-3 shows a list of common status codes and reasons. Reason text can be modified without breaking the protocol.

TABLE 1-3 Common Status Codes and Their Reasons

STATUS CODE	REASON
100	Continue
200	OK
201	Created
300	Multiple Choices
301	Moved Permanently
302	Found
400	Bad Request
401	Unauthorized
403	Forbidden
404	Not Found
407	Proxy Authentication Required
408	Request Time-out
413	Request Entity Too Large
500	Internal Server Error
501	Not Implemented

The second line of the response indicates the type of Web server (e.g., Server: Microsoft-IIS/6.0). The third line (Content-Type) indicates the type of resource that is being sent to the Web browser as part of the response. This indicator is in the form of a Multipurpose Internet Mail Extensions (MIME) type. In the case of this example (Content-Type: text/html), the file is a static HTML text file. The MIME type is a two-part designator type/subtype, in which the first part is the resource type (text in this example) and the second part is the resource subtype (html in this example). Some common MIME types are shown in Table 1-4.

TABLE 1-4 Common MIME Types

MIME TYPE	DESCRIPTION
Text	Textual information. No special software is required to get the full meaning of the text, aside from support for the indicated character set. One subtype is *plain*, which means that the text can be read without requiring additional software. Other subtypes are *html* and *xml*, which indicate the appropriate file type(s).
Image	Image data. Requires a display device (such as a graphical display or a graphics printer) to view the information. Subtypes are defined for two widely used image formats, *jpeg* and *gif*.

MIME TYPE	DESCRIPTION
Audio	Audio data. Requires an audio output device (such as a speaker or headphones) to "hear" the contents. An initial subtype called *basic* is defined for this type.
Video	Video data. Requires the capability to display moving images, typically including specialized hardware and software. An initial subtype called *mpeg* is defined for this type.
Application	Other kinds of data, typically either uninterpreted binary data or information to be processed by an application. The subtype, called *octet-stream,* is to be used in the case of uninterpreted binary data, in which the simplest recommended action is to offer to write the information into a file for the user. The *PostScript* subtype is also defined for the transport of PostScript material.

MORE INFO **MIME TYPES**

The Windows registry contains a list of MIME types/subtypes at the following location:

HKEY_CLASSES_ROOT\MIME\Database\Content Type

The next line is content length (Content-Length: 38 in this example). This simply indicates the size of the content that follows. After the content-length line, the response message is returned. This message is based on the MIME type. The browser attempts to process the content based on its MIME type. For example, it interprets HTML for HTML MIME types and renders an image for image MIME types.

Submitting Form Data to the Web Server

The HTML *<form>* tag can be used to create a Web page that collects data from the user and sends the collected data back to the Web server. The form tag is nested inside the *<HTML>* tags. The form tags typically include information for the user in the form of text and input tags for defining things like buttons and text boxes. A typical use of the *<form>* tag might look like this:

```
<form method="POST" action="getCustomer.aspx">
   Enter Customer ID:
   <input type="text" name="Id">
   <input type="submit" value="Get Customer">
</form>
```

This example form prompts the user for a customer ID, displays a text box that collects the desired customer ID, and also displays a Submit button that initiates the sending of data to the Web server. The method attribute of the form tag indicates the HTTP verb (*POST*) to use when sending the request to the server. The action attribute is the relative URL of the page to which the request will be sent.

There are two HTTP methods that can be used to submit the form data back to the Web server: *GET* and *POST*. When the *GET* verb is used, the form data is appended to the URL as part of the query string. The query string is a collection of key–value pairs, separated by an ampersand (&) character. The start of the query string is indicated by a question mark (?). The following provides an example:

```
GET /getCustomer.aspx?Id=123&color=blue HTTP/1.1
Host: www.northwindtraders.com
```

In this example, a *GET* request is made to the Web server for a Web page called get-Customer.aspx on the root of the Web site (indicated by the forward slash). The query string contains the form data following the question mark (?).

When using the *GET* method to send data to the server, the complete URL and query string can be seen and modified in the address bar of the Web browser. Keep in mind that, depending on the scenario, this can be a disadvantage or even a security risk. You do not want people manipulating this data in the query string and thus potentially seeing things they should not be seeing or corrupting your data. You also might not want users bookmarking pages that include query string information sent to the server and thereby causing the same information to be sent to the server every time a user requests a page. Another disadvantage is that the query string is limited in size by the Web browser and Web server being used. For example, when using Microsoft Internet Explorer and IIS, the limit for a given query string is 1,024 characters.

The *POST* method is the preferred means of submitting data back to the server as part of an HTTP request. When the *POST* verb is used, the data is placed into the message body of the request as follows:

```
POST /getCustomer.aspx HTTP/1.1
Host: www.northwindtraders.com

Id=123&color=blue
```

Using the *POST* verb removes the size constraint on the data. (As a test more than 10 megabytes of data were posted to see if the Web server would accept the data. It worked, but sending that much data across the Internet can cause other problems, primarily related to bandwidth, such as timeout errors and performance problems.) Additionally, the *POST* method prevents users from manipulating the request in the address bar of their browser. Instead, the data is hidden in the message body. Therefore, in most scenarios, the *POST* method is the more desirable way to send data to the Web server.

Sending data back to the server as part of your request is often referred to as a PostBack in ASP.NET. Although its name comes from the *POST* method, it is possible to perform a Post-Back using the *GET* method already described. An ASP.NET Web page contains a property called *IsPostBack* that is used to determine if data is being sent back to the Web server or if the Web page is simply being requested.

HTTP Troubleshooting

You can view the exchange of HTTP messages between browser and server by using a network sniffer application. The network sniffer captures all packets between the Web browser and the Web server, and you can simply view the packet data to read messages such as the requests and responses described in this section.

Glenn Johnson

I always keep Microsoft Network Monitor, which is a network packet sniffer that is included with Microsoft Server operating systems and Microsoft Systems Management Server (SMS), installed on my computer so I can readily run this application to see the packet-by-packet conversation between my computer and other computers on the network. This is probably the best way to understand what is happening because you see the raw data packets that were exchanged.

Another tool that you can use for HTTP diagnostics is Telnet. Telnet is nothing more than a terminal emulator that sends and receives textual data on port 23, but you can specify port 80 to communicate to the Web server. With Telnet, you can type the HTTP commands and view the results.

There are also many applications you can download from the Internet to troubleshoot and analyze HTTP. Simply type **HTTP** as the keyword in a search on the site *http://www.download.com* to get a list of such applications.

Quick Check

1. **What protocol is used to communicate between the Web browser and the Web server?**
2. **In ASP.NET, what does the *Request* object represent?**
3. **In ASP.NET, what does the *Response* object represent?**

Quick Check Answers

1. **HTTP is used for Web browser and Web server communication.**
2. **The *Request* object in ASP.NET wraps the communication from the Web browser to the Web server.**
3. **The *Response* object in ASP.NET wraps the data bound for the Web browser and sent from the Web server.**

LAB Exploring HTTP

In this lab, you explore HTTP by using Telnet, the terminal emulation application that is built into Microsoft Windows.

EXERCISE 1 Starting and Configuring Telnet

In this exercise, you start the Telnet client and configure it to work with HTTP.

1. Open a command prompt. You can do so by selecting Start | All Programs | Accessories | Command Prompt.
2. Clear the screen. Enter the following command to clear the screen:

   ```
   CLS
   ```

3. Start Telnet. In the command prompt window, enter the following command to start the Telnet client:

   ```
   Telnet.exe
   ```

   Note that you might get an error indicating that Telnet is not installed on your computer. It is not installed by default in Windows Vista. To install, navigate to Control Panel, Programs, Programs and Features. Click the Turn Windows Features On Or Off link. In the Windows Features dialog box, you should be able to select and install Telnet Client.
4. Configure Telnet to echo typed characters. Enter the following command into the Telnet window, which will cause locally typed characters to be displayed as you type them:

   ```
   set localecho
   ```

   Telnet will respond with the following:

   ```
   Local echo on
   ```

5. Set carriage return and line feed to On. Enter the following command to instruct Telnet that it should treat the Enter key as a combination of carriage return and line feed.

   ```
   set crlf
   ```

   Telnet will respond with the following:

   ```
   New line mode - Causes return key to send CR & LF
   ```

EXERCISE 2 Communicating with a Web Site

In this exercise, you connect to a Web site, request the default page, and observe the result.

> ***NOTE* TAKE YOUR TIME**
>
> **In this section, if you mistype a command, you will need to start over, so take your time entering each command.**

1. Open a connection to a Web site. Enter the following command into the Telnet command window to open a connection to *msn.com* on port 80:

   ```
   o msn.com 80
   ```

   Telnet responds with the following:

   ```
   Connecting To msn.com. . .
   ```

   Note that Telnet will not indicate that you are indeed connected.

2. Press Enter multiple times until the cursor is positioned on the next line.

3. Attempt to *GET* the default page. Enter the following lines. After typing the second line, press Enter two times, to indicate the end of message to the Web server.

   ```
   GET / HTTP/1.1
   Host: msn.com
   ```

   After pressing Enter two times, you will see the result shown in Figure 1-3. Notice that the status code is 301 with a reason of Moved Permanently. The message body contains HTML with a hyperlink to the new location.

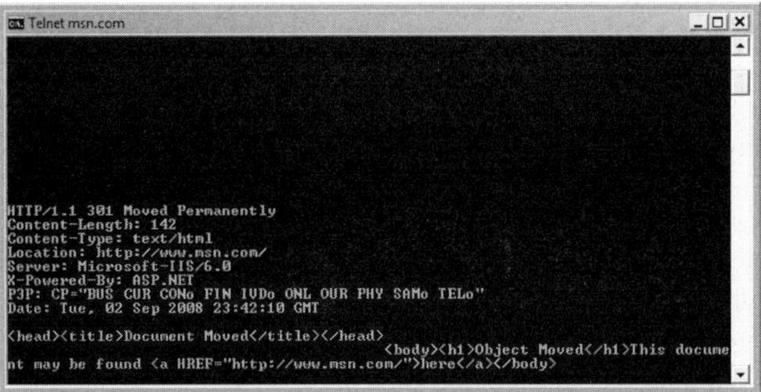

FIGURE 1-3 The response is a result code that indicates a redirect

4. Try other sites. After pressing Enter, you will be back at the Telnet command prompt. Repeat the steps in this exercise to connect to other Web sites.

Lesson Summary

- The Web server is responsible for accepting requests for a resource and sending the appropriate response.
- The Web browser is responsible for displaying data to the user, collecting data from the user, and sending data to the Web server.
- HTTP is a text-based communication protocol that is used to communicate between Web browsers and Web servers using port 80.
- Secure HTTP (HTTPS) uses port 443.
- Each HTTP command contains a method (also called a verb) that indicates the desired action. Common methods are *GET* and *POST*.
- Sending data to the Web server from the browser is commonly referred to as a Post-Back in ASP.NET programming.
- You can troubleshoot HTTP by using the Telnet application or a packet sniffer.

Lesson Review

You can use the following questions to test your knowledge of the information in Lesson 1, "Understanding the Players."

The questions are also available on the companion CD if you prefer to review them in electronic form.

> ***NOTE*** **ANSWERS**
>
> **An answer to this question and explanations of why each answer choice is right or wrong are located in the "Answers" section at the end of the book.**

1. What is the name of the *Page* object's property that you can query to determine if a Web page is being requested without data being submitted?
   - **A.** *IsCallback*
   - **B.** *IsReusable*
   - **C.** *IsValid*
   - **D.** *IsPostBack*
2. Which one of the following HTTP verbs indicates that you are creating and writing a file on the Web server?
   - **A.** *PUT*
   - **B.** *CONNECT*
   - **C.** *POST*
   - **D.** *GET*

Lesson 2: Creating a Web Site and Adding New Web Pages

Visual Studio 2008 provides a number of options for setting up Web projects. A Web project contains the folders and files that define a Web site. This might include HTML files, ASPX pages, images, user controls, master pages, themes, and more. Defining the initial structure correctly for your situation is paramount to being able to easily manage your site. This lesson presents your options for defining and organizing a new Web site project with Visual Studio 2008.

After this lesson, you will be able to:

- Create a new Web site within Visual Studio 2008.
- Understand the various configuration options available when defining a new Web site.
- Add new Web pages (or Web Forms) to a Web site.

Estimated lesson time: 45 minutes

Creating Web Sites

The Visual Studio 2008 project system allows you to define a new Web site project based on how you intend to access the site content from a Web server. You can create a Web project connected to a file-system–based server on your computer, an IIS server, or an FTP server. Selecting the right option depends on how you wish to run, share, manage, and deploy your Web site project. The following describes each option in further detail:

- **File system** The file-based Web site stores all of the files for the Web site inside a directory of your choosing. This Web site uses the lightweight ASP.NET development server that is included in Visual Studio 2008. A file system site is great when you wish to run and debug your Web site locally but do not want to run a local IIS Web server (or cannot due to security restrictions on your network).
- **FTP** The FTP-based Web site is useful when you want to connect to your site via FTP to manage your files on a remote server. This option is typically used when your Web site is hosted on a remote computer and your access to the files and folders on that server is through FTP.
- **HTTP** An HTTP-based Web site is used when you are working with a site deployed inside of IIS (either locally or on a remote server). This Web site may be configured at the root of the IIS Web server, or in a virtual directory that is configured as an application. Note that a remote server running IIS will have to provide access to your Web files using Front Page Server Extensions.

Creating a Web Site Project

You can create a new Web site project directly from Visual Studio 2008. The basic steps for doing so are as follows:

1. In Visual Studio 2008, use the File menu to create a new Web site (File | New | Website). This launches the New Web Site dialog box as shown in Figure 1-4.
2. Select the Web site type, location, and default programming language.
3. You might also wish to select the target framework for your project. New to Visual Studio 2008 is the ability to code against multiple versions of the Microsoft .NET Framework. You can choose among versions 2.0, 3.0, and 3.5.
4. Once defined, click OK to finish setting up your site. Depending on your type selection, you might be promoted to enter additional information.

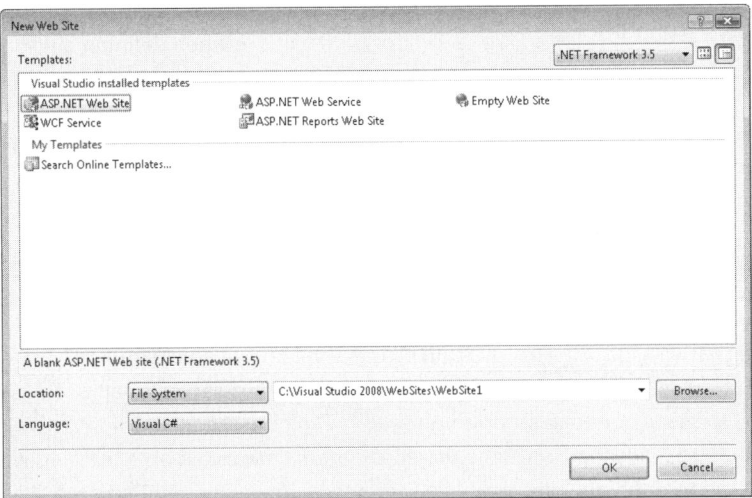

FIGURE 1-4 The New Web Site dialog box contains properties for setting the Web site type, location, .NET Framework version, and default programming language

Creating a File-System Web Site

A file-system–based Web site runs locally using the ASP.NET Web server that ships with Visual Studio. This option allows you to keep your development local until you are ready to publish code to a server for sharing. To create a file-system Web site, you again use the New Web Site dialog box. However, you select File System from the Location drop-down list box (refer to Figure 1-4). You then simply set a valid folder location for storing your Web site files locally on a hard drive.

Visual Studio 2008 creates the folder for your site and adds a new Web page named Default.aspx (and its code-behind file, Default.aspx.cs). The default Web site template also creates the folder App_Data, as well as a configuration file called Web.config. When the Web site opens, Visual Studio 2008 displays the Default.aspx page in HTML Source view, where you can see the page's HTML elements. Figure 1-5 shows an example of the IDE after creating a new Web site.

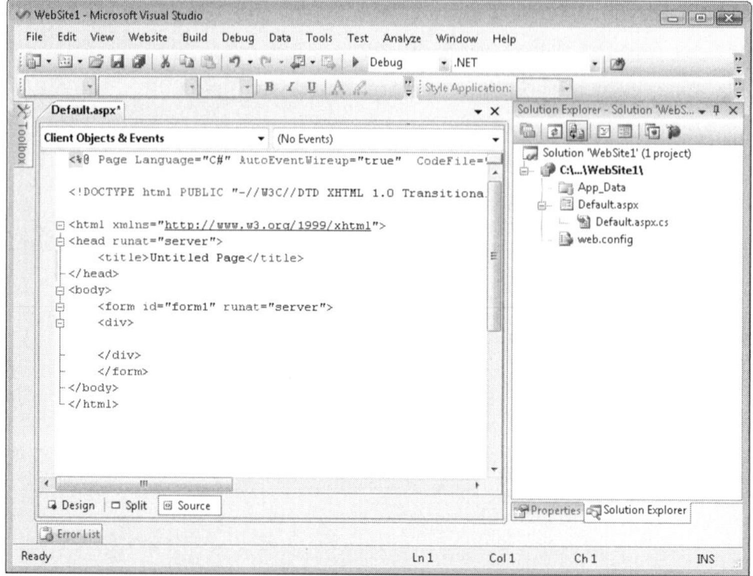

FIGURE 1-5 The structure of a newly created Web site

Creating an FTP-Based Web Site

An FTP-based Web site is one that communicates with a remote server over FTP. This can be useful if you are using a hosting provider's server, communicating to it over FTP, and wish to use Visual Studio to edit your files directly on the server. To create an FTP-based Web site project, in the New Web Site dialog box, from the Web Site Type drop-down list, select FTP. You then need to provide a valid FTP address for your site.

Once you click OK in the New Web Site dialog box, you are prompted for a set of additional FTP parameters. This includes choosing between active and passive mode and selecting login credentials. Figure 1-6 shows an example of the FTP Log On dialog box.

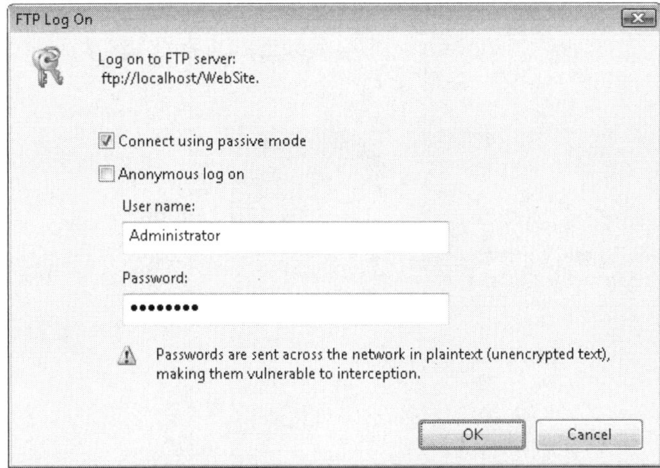

FIGURE 1-6 Configuring the FTP parameters for a new, FTP-based Web site

Note that FTP is, by default, not secure. When a user logs on to a server, his or her credentials are sent as plaintext. Therefore, you should avoid FTP connections where security is critical.

FTP Active Mode vs. Passive Mode

FTP is based on Transmission Control Protocol (TCP) and has a connection. It has no connectionless User Datagram Protocol (UDP) component. FTP requires two ports for communication: a command port and a data port. Port 21 is typically the command port at the server; port 20 is the typical data port when using active mode FTP.

Active mode FTP communications is the default mode and starts with the client selection of two ports: n and n+1. The client will use port n to initiate communications to port 21 of the server. When the server responds, the client sends a *port* command. This command instructs the server which port to use for data communications, as shown in Figure 1-7. It is the server that initiates data communications from port 20 to the client's data port (n+1). If the client has a firewall installed, the server may be blocked from initiating communications to the client on the data port.

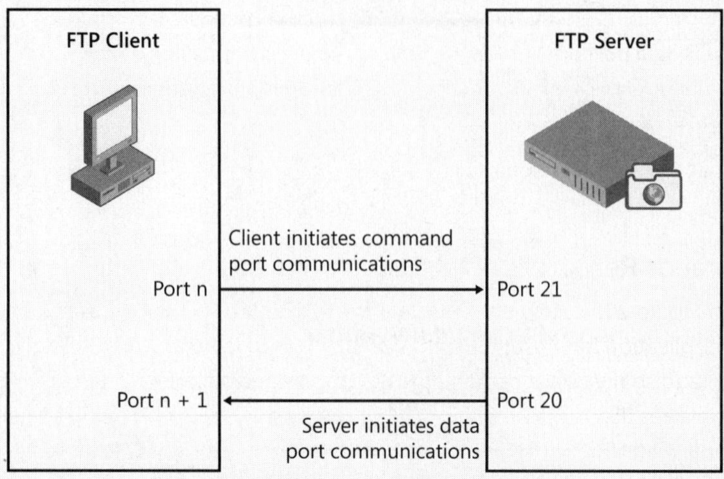

FIGURE 1-7 Active mode requires that the server initiate the connection on the data port

Passive mode FTP communications can be used to correct the problem with active mode communications. Passive mode starts with the client selection of two ports: n and n+1. The client uses port n to initiate communications to port 21 of the server. When the server responds, the client sends a *pasv* command to the server. The server selects a random port p to use for data communications and sends the port number to the client. The client then initiates communications on the data port (n+1) to the server's data port (p), as shown in Figure 1-8.

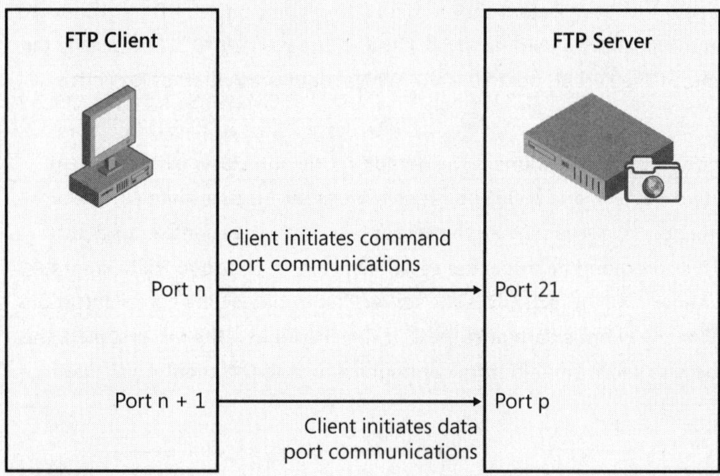

FIGURE 1-8 When using passive mode, the client initiates communications on the command and data ports

Notice that when using passive mode, the client initiates communications on the command and data ports. This fixes the problem of the client having a firewall installed that blocks the server's request to initiate communications on the data port.

Creating a Local or Remote HTTP-Based Web Site

You can use Visual Studio 2008 to create Web sites backed by IIS. This can be useful if you want to run your application against the full version of IIS (and not just a local Web server). In addition, you might do so if you are coding against a separate development server. To create a Web site that leverages IIS, in the New Web Site dialog box, select HTTP. You will then be prompted to enter a valid URL for the Web site. This could be localhost (for local versions of IIS) or a fully qualified remote location.

Note that if you are connecting to an HTTP server using Windows Vista you might need to run Visual Studio with the Administrator account. To do so, right-click the Visual Studio shortcut and select Run As Administrator. In addition, if you are using a remote server, the remote server must have Front Page Server Extensions installed and enabled to connect to it using Visual Studio. It must also have the .NET Framework and ASP.NET enabled.

Creating an ASP.NET Web Application Project

Visual Studio provides yet another means of creating a Web project. Instead of a Web site project you can create what is called an ASP.NET Web application project. This project uses the standard New Project dialog box and thus participates in the standard project structure of Visual Studio. This can be useful if you wish to add a Web application to an existing solution that contains other projects or if you wish to treat your Web application less like a Web site and more like a standard Visual Studio project. Figure 1-9 shows an example.

Notice that you do not have the option of selecting the Web site type. Instead, Visual Studio creates the project with the assumption that you will use the file system type and the ASP.NET server. You can modify this at a later point for ASP.NET Web applications only. To do so, right-click the project file in Solution Explorer and select Properties. This opens the property pages for your Web application as shown in Figure 1-10. Notice that you can configure the Visual Studio Developer Server. You can also connect your project to an IIS Web server. Finally, note that these settings can be shared (using the Apply Server Settings To All Users check box) with other users that might access this project through source control.

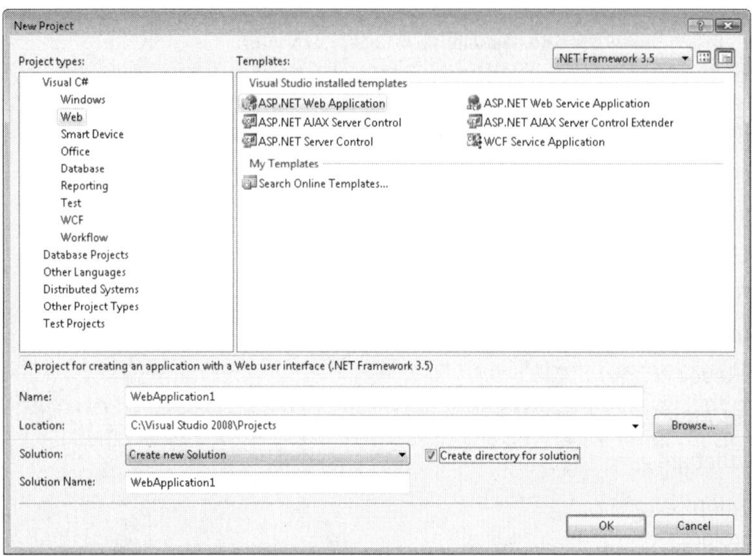

FIGURE 1-9 Creating an ASP.NET Web application project

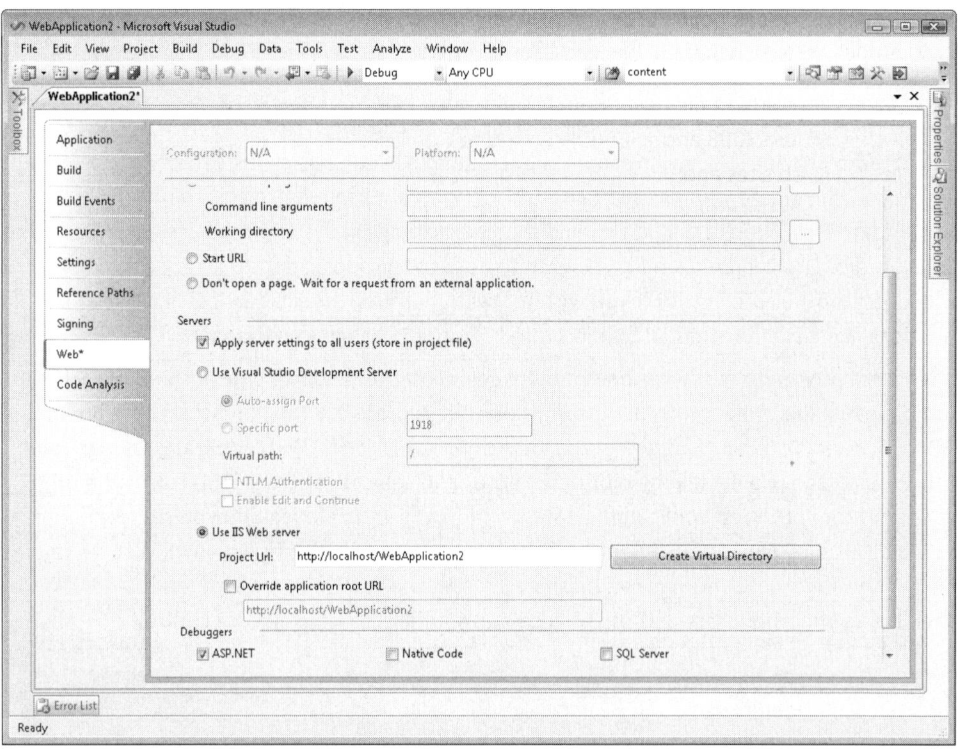

FIGURE 1-10 Configuring an ASP.NET Web application project

Web Site Solution Files

When a Web site is created, Visual Studio creates a solution file (.sln) and a hidden solution user options file (.suo). By default, these files are created in the Documents\Visual Studio 2008\Projects folder for Web sites. This includes those sites with an actual root folder that is stored elsewhere. The solution file is a text file that contains information such as the following:

- A list of the projects that are to be loaded into Visual Studio 2008 to make up the entire solution
- The target framework version for the solution
- The default language for the solution
- A list of project dependencies
- Source control information such as Microsoft Visual SourceSafe
- A list of add-ins that are available

The solution user options file is a binary file that contains various user settings related to the IDE for the given project. These files are not shared among developers (like a solution file would be). Settings this file contains include the following:

- The task list
- Debugger break points and watch window settings
- Visual Studio window locations

Note that the solution files are not located in your Web site's folder because they are specific to Visual Studio 2008 and are not required in the deployed Web site. Also, a solution can contain many Web sites and Visual Studio projects, so it is best to keep the solution files in an independent folder. Solution files also can be developer specific, meaning that developers might want to configure solution files based on their preferences.

A Visual Studio Web site also does not contain an associated project file. Again, this keeps the Web site simple and prevents users from deploying the wrong files to their site. However, a Visual Studio Web application does have a project file associated with it. Again, the Web application is useful to those developers who are used to building applications with Visual Studio and not just working with Web sites.

The Content of a Newly Created Web Site

The default Web site template in Visual Studio 2008 adds a special folder to your solution called App_Data. This folder is reserved for databases such as Microsoft SQL Server 2005 Express Edition .mdf files. Table 1-5 contains a list of special folders that exist in ASP.NET that can be added to your Web site. These folders are protected by ASP.NET. For example, if a user attempts to browse to any of these folders (except App_Themes), he or she will receive an HTTP 403 Forbidden error.

TABLE 1-5 ASP.NET 3.5 Special Folders

FOLDER NAME	DESCRIPTION
App_Browsers	Contains browser definition files (.browser) that ASP.NET uses to identify browsers and determine their capabilities. These files are often used to help support mobile applications.
App_Code	Contains source code for classes and business objects (.cs, .vb, and .jsl files) that you want to compile as part of your application.
App_Data	Contains application data files (.mdf and .xml files).
App_GlobalResources	Contains resources (.resx and .resources files) that are compiled into assemblies and have a global scope. Resource files are used to externalize text and images from your application code. This helps you support multiple languages and design-time changes without recompilation of source code.
App_LocalResources	Contains resources (.resx and .resources files) that are scoped to a specific page, user control, or master page in an application.
App_Themes	Contains subfolders that each define a specific theme (or look) for your site. A theme consists of files (such as .skin, .css, and image files) that define the appearance of Web pages and controls.
App_WebReferences	Contains Web reference files (.wsdl, .xsd, .disco, and .discomap files) that define references to Web services.
Bin	Contains compiled assemblies (.dll files) for code that you want to reference in your application. Assemblies in the Bin folder are automatically referenced in your application.

Special folders can be added to a Web site from the Visual Studio menu system. Typically this involves right-clicking the Web application project and selecting Add ASP.NET Folder.

Creating ASPX Pages

Once your Web site has been created, the next step is to begin adding pages to the site. An ASP.NET page is also known as a Web Form and can be composed of a single file or a pair of files. The steps for adding a new Web page to a Web site are as follows:

1. Using the Visual Studio 2008 menus, request a new Web Form. Typically this is done inside Solution Explorer by right-clicking the Web site and selecting Add New Item.
2. In the Add New Item dialog box (see Figure 1-11), assign a name to the Web Form.
3. Select the programming language for this Web Form.

4. Indicate if the page is self-contained or uses a pair of files using the Place Code In Separate File check box.

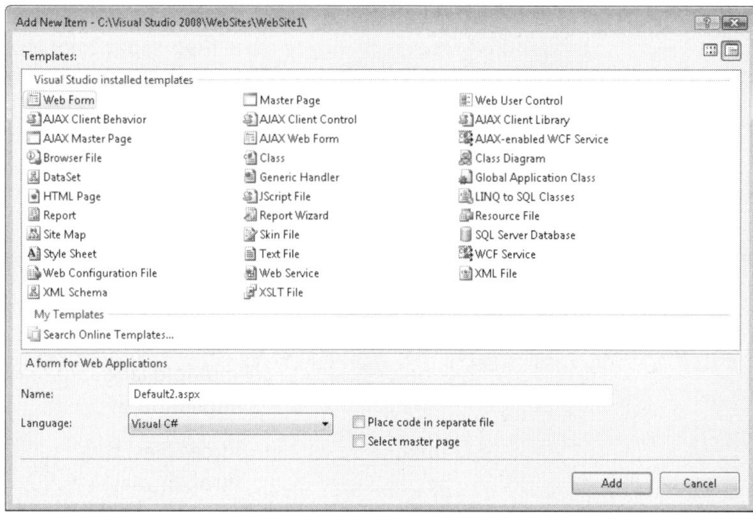

FIGURE 1-11 Adding a new Web Form to your Web site

The Place Code In Separate File check box allows you to indicate whether your page should be made up of a single, self-contained file or a pair of files (HTML layout and an associated code-behind file). Note that you can also select a master page on which to base the look of your page. Master pages allow you to create a consistent look and feel for your entire Web site. We cover master pages in more detail in Chapter 5, "Customizing and Personalizing a Web Application."

The Anatomy of an ASPX Page

A page in ASP.NET contains user interface layout information, code that executes on the server, and directives to both connect the layout with the code and to tell ASP.NET how the page should be processed. The standard ASP.NET page has an .aspx extension. The typical .aspx page includes three sections: page directives, code, and page layout. These sections are defined as follows:

- **Page directives** This section is used to set up the environment, specifying how the page should be processed. For example, this is where you can indicate an associated code file, development language, transaction, and more.
- **Code** This section contains code to handle events that execute on the server based on the ASP.NET page processing model. By default, Visual Studio creates a separate file that contains your code. This is called a code-behind file and is attached to the .aspx page. This file includes the .cs or .vb extension to indicate the file represents code (for example, Default.aspx.cs).

Code can be placed within the .aspx page itself (typically at the top of the file). To do so, you define *<script>* tags and place your code within them. The script tag should include the *runat="server"* attribute to denote server-side script. In this way you can create single files that contain your entire page.

- **Page layout** The page layout is written using HTML. This includes the HTML body, markup, and style information. The HTML body may contain HTML tags, Visual Studio controls, user controls, and simple text.

The code for a simple, single-file Web page might look like Listing 1-1.

Listing 1-1: A Single-Page Web Form

```
<!--page directives-->
<%@ Page Language="C#" %>

<!DOCTYPE html PUBLIC "-//W3C//DTD XHTML 1.0 Transitional//EN"
  "http://www.w3.org/TR/xhtml1/DTD/xhtml1-transitional.dtd">

<!--code-->
<script runat="server">
    private void OnSubmit(Object sender, EventArgs args) {
        LabelReponse.Text = "Hello " + TextBoxName.Text;
    }
</script>

<!--page layout-->
<html xmlns="http://www.w3.org/1999/xhtml">
<head runat="server">
    <title>Sample Page</title>
</head>
<body>
    <form id="form1" runat="server">
    <div>
        Enter Name: <asp:TextBox ID="TextBoxName"
          runat="server"></asp:TextBox>

        <asp:Button ID="ButtonSubmit" runat="server" Text="Submit"
          OnClick="OnSubmit" />

        <br />

        <asp:Label ID="LabelReponse"
          runat="server" Text=""></asp:Label>
    </div>
    </form>
```

```
</body>

</html>
```

Notice the *runat="server"* attribute is defined in the script block. This indicates that the code contained within the script block will run on the server (and not on the client). On execution, ASP.NET will create server-side objects that contain this code as well as an instance of the *Page* class to contain the controls defined inside the page as instances of their given type (*System.Web.UI.WebControls.Textbox*, for example). This server-side object will be invoked on user request and will execute code in response to events.

Single-File Versus Code-Behind Pages

In the previous example, the Web page contains both server-side code and markup in a single file. This is referred to as a single-file page in ASP.NET. You can create these types of pages by leaving the Place Code In Separate File check box cleared in the Add New Item dialog box. Some developers are more comfortable working with single-file pages than the code-behind model.

In the single-file model, the compiler generates a new class for your page. This class inherits from the base *Page* class. It is typically named with the format ASP.pagename_aspx. This class contains control declarations, event handlers, and related code you have written for your page.

The code-behind programming model physically separates your user interface layout markup and your server-side code into two distinct files. In this case the .aspx page contains your layout markup and the related .aspx.cs or .aspx.vb file contains the associated code. Developers who prefer to separate code from form layout will find this model easier to work with.

In the case of code-behind files, your code is stored in a partial class that inherits from the base *Page* class. Partial classes allow code-behind files to be dynamically compiled with their associated .aspx pages into a single class type. This means you no longer need to declare member variables in the code-behind page for each control, nor do you need this code getting in the way of your code. Instead, Visual Studio keeps control declaration and page initialization information in a separate partial class. This greatly simplifies maintenance of sites that are based on the code-behind model.

When your page gets compiled, the partial classes are merged to form yet another partial class. This class is then used by ASP.NET to generate another class (which inherits from the merged partial class) that is used by ASP.NET to build your Web page. Both these classes are then compiled into a single assembly similar to that of the single-file model.

Mike Snell

There is no real execution difference between the two page models. It is simply a matter of developer preference. I find that the single-page model is often preferable to Web site designers or Web-only developers. Often, these developers are used to working with a combination of markup and script and do not wish to be bothered with the mechanics of object-oriented programming. The opposite is true for those developers who have more of a programming background and need to create Web applications. These developers are much more comfortable in a code-only editor and often want to know (and see) how their code operates.

Web Site Compilation

Most Web applications are not precompiled. Instead, pages and code are typically copied to a Web server and then dynamically compiled by that Web server the first time they are requested by a user. On compilation, the code is placed inside an assembly and loaded into your site's application domain. Additional requests for the same code will be served by the compiled assembly.

This model is referred to as dynamic compilation. It has a number of pros and cons, including the following:

- **Pro** Changes to a file in the site will result in an automatic recompilation of a given resource. This allows for easier deployment.
- **Pro** The entire application does not need to be recompiled every time a change is made to a single page or component. This is great for large Web sites.
- **Pro** Pages that contain compile errors do not prevent other pages in the Web site from running. This means that you can test Web sites that contain pages still in development.
- **Con** This model requires the first user to take a compilation performance hit. That is, the first request for an uncompiled resource will be slower than subsequent requests.
- **Con** This model requires your source code to be deployed to the server (typically not a major concern in most ASP applications).

Visual Studio 2008 also allows you to precompile your Web site. In this case your entire site is compiled and error checked, and only the layout code and associated assemblies are deployed to the Web server. Precompilation has the following pros and cons:

- **Pro** Provides verification that all the pages and their dependencies can be compiled. This includes code, markup, and the Web.config file.
- **Pro** Performance for the first user requesting a resource is improved as he or she is not required to take the compilation hit.

- **Con** Precompiled Web sites can be more difficult to deploy and manage, as you have to compile and then copy only the necessary files to the server (versus simply copying your code files to the server).

Quick Check

1. Where are solution files created by default?
2. Which ASP.NET page model separates layout from code?

Quick Check Answers

1. By default, solution files are created in the My Documents\Visual Studio 2008\Projects folder.
2. The code-behind programming model separates user interface layout markup from code.

LAB Create a New Web Site and Add a Page

In this lab, you create a new Web site and explore its contents using Visual Studio 2008. After that, you add a new Web page to the Web site.

EXERCISE 1 Creating a New Web Site

In this exercise you create a new, file-based Web site using Visual Studio.

1. Start Visual Studio 2008.
2. Create a file-based Web site. From within Visual Studio, select File | New | Web Site to open the New Web Site dialog box.
3. In the New Web Site dialog box, make sure the Web Site Type drop-down list box is set to File System. For the location select **%Documents%\Visual Studio 2008\WebSites\MyFirstSite** as the site location on your local hard drive. Select your preferred programming language for the Web site and click OK. This creates a new directory and subdirectory for the new Web site.
4. Explore the new Web site. In the Solution Explorer window (View | Solution Explorer), notice the special folder called App_Data and the Web page called Default.aspx. Click the plus (+) sign beside the Default.aspx file to reveal its code-behind page.
5. Navigate to the actual folder that contains the solution file. This should be %Documents%\Visual Studio 2008\Projects\MyFirstSite. You can open this file and view it inside of Notepad. Also, notice that the actual Web project files are not stored in this location.
6. Navigate to the folder containing your Web site files. This should be %Documents%\Visual Studio 2008\WebSites\MyFirstSite. Here you can see your page, its code-behind file, the App_Data directory, and the Web.config file.

7. Next, compile the Web site. In Visual Studio 2008, select Build | Build Web Site. Return to your Web site directory. Notice it is unchanged. Visual Studio compiled your site but is hiding the results from you. Had this been a Web application project, you would see a Bin directory and the compiled code placed in that directory.
8. View the Default.aspx page inside a browser. In Visual Studio 2008, select Debug | Start Without Debugging. After a moment you should see a blank Web page.

EXERCISE 2 Adding a New Web Page

In this exercise, you add a new Web page to the Web site that you just created.

1. Add a new Web page. In Visual Studio 2008, from the Website menu, select Add New Item. In the Add New Item dialog box, select Web Form. In this case set the page name to **Page2.aspx**. Select your preferred programming language. Next, clear the Place Code In Separate File check box and click Add.

   Observe the result in Visual Studio 2008. There should be no code-behind file for the given file.
2. In the Solution Explorer window, add a new file called **Page3.aspx**. Make sure the Place Code In Separate File check box is selected.

   Observe the results in Visual Studio. Click the plus (+) sign next to Page3.aspx inside of Solution Explorer to reveal the code-behind page.
3. Reopen Page2.aspx. Edit the page to include the code shown in Listing 1-1. This code is included in both Visual Basic and C# versions in the sample files installed from the companion disc.
4. Run the page in a Web browser and observe the results.

Lesson Summary

- ASP.NET 3.5 supports the file system Web site type. This is a good option when IIS is not installed on the developer's computer and the developer wants to create a Web site without the use of a remote Web server.
- ASP.NET 3.5 supports the FTP Web site type. This option can be used when building a Web site that is being hosted on a remote computer that does not have Front Page Server Extensions installed.
- ASP.NET 3.5 supports the HTTP Web site type. This option is a good choice when IIS is installed on the developer's computer or on a remote server with Front Page Server Extensions installed.
- When using FTP in ASP.NET 3.5, active mode is the default. However, passive mode can solve communication problems when the client has to go through a firewall.
- ASP.NET 3.5 supports two programming models for Web pages: single-file and code-behind. With the single-file programming model, all of the Web page markup and

code are in a single file. With the code-behind model, the server-side code is separated from the markup and put into a separate file.

- In ASP.NET 3.5, dynamic compilation refers to the delayed compilation of Web pages that takes place when a user requests a Web page.
- ASP.NET 3.5 defines several special folders. When a new Web site is created, the App_Data folder is created by default; it can contain a SQL Server 2005 Express Edition database, another database, or an .xml data file that will be used in the Web site.

Lesson Review

You can use the following questions to test your knowledge of the information in Lesson 2, "Creating a Web Site and Adding New Web Pages."

The questions are also available on the companion CD if you prefer to review them in electronic form.

> ***NOTE*** **ANSWERS**
>
> **Answers to these questions and explanations of why each answer choice is right or wrong are located in the "Answers" section at the end of the book.**

1. If you want to create a Web site on a remote computer that does not have Front Page Server Extensions installed, which Web site type will you create?
   - **A.** Remote HTTP
   - **B.** File system
   - **C.** FTP
   - **D.** Local HTTP
2. If you want to create a new Web site on a Web server that is hosted by your Internet service provider and the Web server has Front Page Server Extensions installed, what type of Web site would you create?
   - **A.** Local HTTP
   - **B.** File system
   - **C.** FTP
   - **D.** Remote HTTP
3. If you want to separate your server-side code from your client-side layout code in a Web page, what programming model should you implement?
   - **A.** Single-file model
   - **B.** Code-behind model
   - **C.** Inline model
   - **D.** Client-server model

4. Joe created a new Web site using Visual Studio 2008, setting the Web site type to File, and the programming language to C#. Later, Joe received an elaborate Web page from his vendor, which consisted of the Vendor.aspx file and the Vendor.aspx.vb code-behind page. What must Joe do to use these files?

   A. Joe can simply add the files into the Web site, because ASP.NET 3.5 supports Web sites that have Web pages that were programmed with different languages.

   B. The Vendor.aspx file will work, but Joe must rewrite the code-behind page using C#.

   C. Both files must be rewritten in C#.

   D. Joe must create a new Web site that contains these files and set a Web reference to the new site.

Lesson 3: Working with Web Configuration Files

You use configuration files to manage the various settings that define a Web site. These settings are stored in XML files that are separate from your application code. In this way, you can configure settings independently from your code. Typically a Web site contains a single Web.config file stored inside the application's root directory. However, there can be multiple configuration files that manage settings at various levels within an application. This lesson presents an overview of configuring Web sites using configuration files.

> **After this lesson, you will be able to:**
>
> - Understand the configuration file hierarchy.
> - Use the graphical user interface (GUI) configuration tool to make changes to configuration files.
>
> **Estimated lesson time: 15 minutes**

Understanding the Configuration File Hierarchy

Configuration files allow you to manage the many settings related to your Web site. Each file is an XML file (with the extension .config) that contains a set of configuration elements. The elements define options such as security information, database connection strings, caching settings, and more. A given site might actually be configured with multiple .config files. Therefore it is important to understand how these files work together to establish and override various settings.

Configuration files are applied to an executing site based on a hierarchy. Generally this means there is a global configuration file for all sites on a given machine called Machine.config. This file is typically found in the %SystemRoot%\Microsoft.NET\Framework\<*versionNumber*>\CONFIG\ directory.

The Machine.config file contains settings for all .NET application types, such as Windows, Console, ClassLibrary, and Web applications. These settings are global to the machine. Some of the settings in the Machine.config file can be overridden by settings in Web.config files that are further up in the hierarchy, whereas other settings are more global in nature. The global ones are owned by the .NET Framework, so they are protected and cannot be overridden by the Web.config files.

The Machine.config file can define settings for all sites running on a machine provided another .config file further up the chain does not override any of these settings. Although Machine.config provides a global configuration option, you can use .config files inside individual Web site directories to provide more granular control. Between these two poles you can set a number of other .config files with varying degree of applicable scope. Figure 1-12 shows this hierarchy.

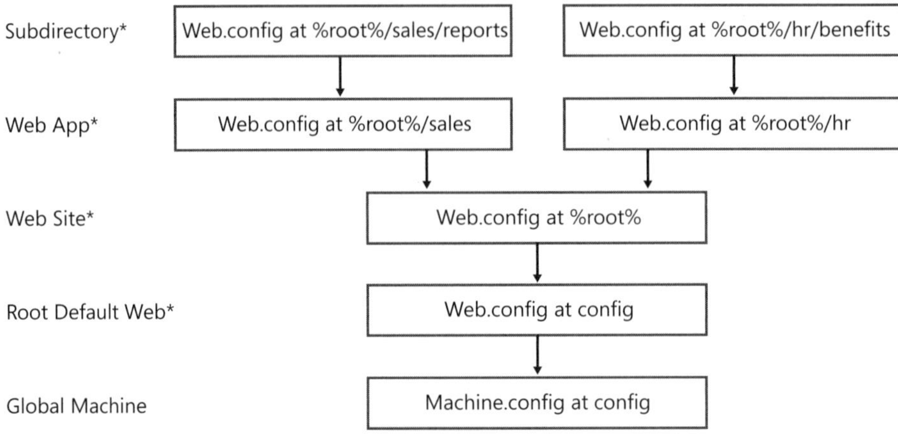

*Indicates an optional configuration file

FIGURE 1-12 The configuration file hierarchy

The next file in the hierarchy is the root default Web.config file, which is located in the same directory as the Machine.config file. This file contains default Web server settings, some of which can override settings in the Machine.config file.

At the root directory of each Web site, you have the ability to add a Web.config file. This optional file can contain additional settings for the Web site as well as overrides. Inside each Web application you can optionally have another Web.config file to provide more settings and to override settings set further down the chain. Finally, each subdirectory in a Web application can optionally have its own Web.config file in which only a subset of the settings are valid.

Processing the Configuration Files

When you initially run your Web application, the runtime builds a cache of the configuration settings for your Web application by flattening the layers of configuration files as follows:

1. The Machine.config file settings are retrieved.
2. The settings from the root Web.config file are added to the caches, overwriting any conflicting settings that were created earlier while reading the Machine.config file.
3. If there is a Web.config file at the root of the Web site, this file is read into the cache, overwriting existing entries.
4. If there is a Web.config file at the Web application, it is read into the cache, also overwriting any existing settings. The resulting cache contains the settings for this Web site.
5. If you have subdirectories in your Web application, each subdirectory can have a Web.config file that includes settings that are specific to the files and folders that are contained within the subdirectory. To calculate the effective settings for the folder, the

Web site settings are read (steps 1–4), and then this Web.config file is read into the cache for this folder, overwriting (and thereby overriding) any existing settings.

Editing Configuration Files

Because they are XML files, the configuration files can be opened and modified with any text editor or XML editor. You can also use the .NET Framework 3.5 Configuration snap-in with the Microsoft Management Console (MMC), which provides a GUI for modifying some of the configuration file settings that an administrator might want to change.

Visual Studio 2008 also provides the Web Site Administration Tool (WSAT), which can be used to modify many of the configuration file settings. You can access this tool by selecting Website | ASP.NET Configuration. The WSAT allows you to edit the following categories of the configuration files:

- **Security** This setting allows you to set up security for your Web site. In this category, you can add users, roles, and permissions for your Web site.
- **Application Configuration** This category is used to modify the application settings. Figure 1-13 shows the Application tab of the WSAT.
- **Provider Configuration** This configuration file contains settings that allow you to specify the database provider to use for maintaining membership and roles.

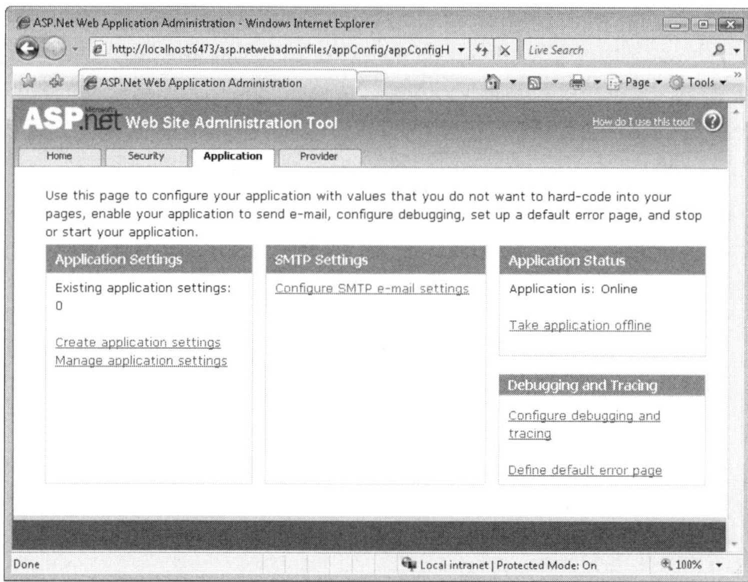

FIGURE 1-13 The Application tab of the Web Site Administration Tool

The WSAT lets you create and modify Web site settings that are not inherited. If a setting is inherited and cannot be overridden, it will appear, but it will be dimmed when the setting is disabled.

 **Quick Check**

1. Is the format of a configuration file .csv, .ini, .xml, or .doc?
2. If a setting exists in the root Web.config file and also in the Web.config file at the Web application but with a different value, which Web.config file takes precedence?

Quick Check Answers

1. The configuration file is formatted with XML.
2. The Web.config file at the Web application level takes precedence.

LAB Modifying a Web Site Configuration

In this lab, you use the WSAT to modify a Web site's configuration by enabling debugging on the Web site. After that, you view the changes in the Web.config file.

EXERCISE 1 Creating the New Web.config File

In this exercise, you start Visual Studio 2008 and open the Web site created in the previous lab.

1. Open the MyFirstSite Web site from the previous lab. Alternatively, you can open the completed Lesson 2 lab project in the samples installed from the CD.
2. Note that this project will most likely already contain a Web.config file. If the project does contain a Web.config file, delete it.
3. Open the WSAT by selecting Web Site | ASP.NET Configuration.
4. Click the Application tab to display the application settings.
5. Click the Configure Debugging And Tracing link to open the page shown in Figure 1-14.

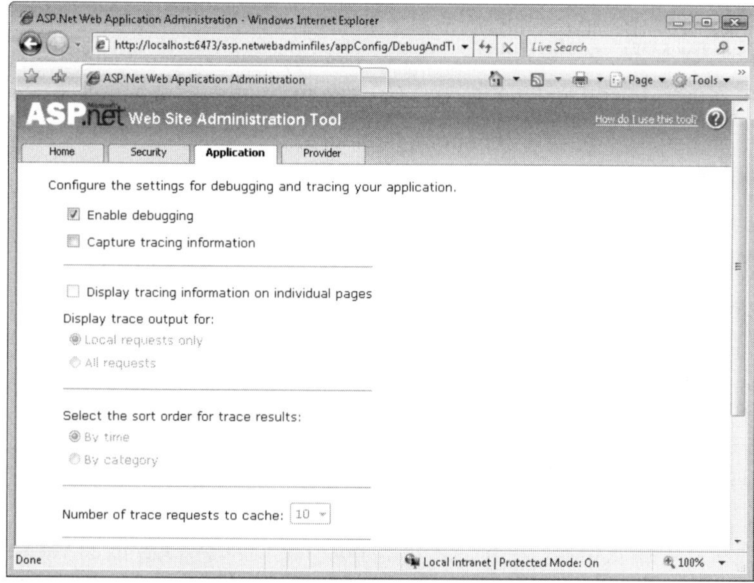

FIGURE 1-14 The Configure Debugging And Tracing page

6. Select the Enable Debugging check box to enable debugging for the current Web site. Notice that selecting this check box performs a PostBack to the Web server.
7. Close the WSAT.
8. A new Web.config file was created as part of the PostBack to the server. Click Refresh at the top of the Solution Explorer window to see the Web.config file.
9. Open the Web.config file. The new Web.config file will contain the following code:

```
<?xml version="1.0" encoding="utf-8"?>
<configuration>
    <system.web>
        <compilation debug="true" />
    </system.web>
</configuration>
```

Notice that the file contains the setting to set *debug* to *true*. This turns on debugging for the Web site.

Lesson Summary

- Web sites are configured based on a hierarchy of XML configuration files, starting with the Machine.config file, followed by the Web.config file that is in the same folder. After that, you might have a Web.config file in the root of the Web site, in each Web application, and in any subdirectory in a Web application.

- The configuration files can be edited with a text editor, an XML editor, the Configuration snap-in for MMC, or the WSAT.
- The WSAT is used to add and modify the Web site settings.

Lesson Review

You can use the following questions to test your knowledge of the information in Lesson 3, "Working with Web Configuration Files."

The questions are also available on the companion CD if you prefer to review them in electronic form.

> ***NOTE*** **ANSWERS**
>
> **Answers to these questions and explanations of why each answer choice is right or wrong are located in the "Answers" section at the end of the book.**

1. You want to make a configuration setting change that will be global to all Web and Windows applications on the current computer. Which file do you change?
   - **A.** Global.asax
   - **B.** Web.config
   - **C.** Machine.config
   - **D.** Global.asa
2. You want to make a configuration setting change that will affect only the current Web application. Which file will you change?
   - **A.** Web.config that is in the same folder as the Machine.config file
   - **B.** Web.config in the root of the Web application
   - **C.** Machine.config
   - **D.** Global.asax
3. You want to make a configuration setting change that will affect only the current Web application, and you want to use a tool that has a user-friendly GUI. Which tool should you use?
   - **A.** Notepad
   - **B.** Microsoft Word
   - **C.** Open directly with Visual Studio
   - **D.** WSAT

Chapter Review

To further practice and reinforce the skills you learned in this chapter, you can perform the following tasks:

- Review the chapter summary.
- Complete the case scenarios. These scenarios set up real-world situations involving the topics of this chapter and ask you to create solutions.
- Complete the suggested practices.
- Take a practice test.

Chapter Summary

- A Web browser is used to make requests to a Web server. It renders HTML to the user, collects data from the user, and sends data back to the Web server. The Web server is responsible for accepting a resource request and sending the appropriate response. The communication between browser and server is done via the text-based communication protocol HTTP.
- ASP.NET 3.5 supports three Web site types: file system, FTP, and HTTP.
- ASP.NET 3.5 supports two programming models for Web pages: single file and code-behind.
- Visual Studio 2008 allows you to select a programming language for each Web page.
- ASP.NET 3.5 uses a hierarchy of configuration files that can be modified to manage the settings of an application.

Case Scenarios

In the following case scenarios, you apply what you've learned in this chapter. You can find answers to these questions in the "Answers" section at the end of this book.

Case Scenario 1: Creating a New Web Site

You are assembling a group of developers to create a new Web site for a company named Wide World Importers. On each developer machine you will install Visual Studio 2008. You want each developer to be able to debug the Web application independently, but you do not want to install IIS on each of the developer machines.

1. What type of Web site will you create, and why does the Web site type fulfill the requirements?

Case Scenario 2: Placing Files in the Proper Folders

You have created a new Web site for a company named Wide World Importers. The new site will use a third-party component called ShoppingCart.dll to process customer purchases. This component requires a SQL Server 2005 Express Edition database. The database files are named Purchases.mdf (data file) and Purchases.ldf (transaction log file). In addition, you will add a new class file called ShoppingCartWrapper.vb or ShoppingCartWrapper.cs, which will be used to simplify the use of the ShoppingCart.dll component.

1. In what folder(s) will you place these files? What is the benefit of using these locations?

Suggested Practices

To help you successfully master the exam objectives presented in this chapter, complete the following tasks.

Create a New Web Site Using Visual Studio 2008

For this task, you should complete at least Practice 1. If you want a more well-rounded understanding of all of the Web site types, you should also complete Practice 2.

- **Practice 1** Become familiar with Web sites by creating a file-based Web site. Also create a local HTTP-based Web site and explore the differences.
- **Practice 2** You will need a remote computer with IIS, FTP, and Front Page Server Extensions installed. Create an FTP-based Web site and explore the options. Create a remote HTTP Web site and explore the options.

Add a Web Page to the Web Site

For this task, you should complete at least Practice 1. If you want a more well-rounded understanding of adding a Web page, you should also complete Practice 2.

- **Practice 1** Create any type of Web site. Add a Web page that has a code-behind page. Add a Web page that does not have a code-behind page.
- **Practice 2** Add another Web page, selecting a different programming language.

Program a Web Application

For this task, you should complete the previous two practices first.

- **Practice 1** In a Web page that you have created, add code to test the *IsPostBack* property of the Web page and display a message if the Web page is posted back.

Configure Settings for a Web Application

For this task, you should complete Practice 1 from the previous section.

- **Practice 1**
  - Locate the Machine.config file and open it with Notepad.
  - Explore the various settings that exist in the Machine.config file.
  - Locate and open the Web.config file that exists in the same folder as the Machine.config file.
  - Examine the settings that exist in this file.

Take a Practice Test

The practice tests on this book's companion CD offer many options. For example, you can test yourself on just the content covered in this chapter, or you can test yourself on all the 70-562 certification exam content. You can set up the test so it closely simulates the experience of taking a certification exam, or you can set it up in study mode so you can look at the correct answers and explanations after you answer each question.

> ***MORE INFO*** **PRACTICE TESTS**
>
> **For details about all the practice test options available, see the "How to Use the Practice Tests" section in this book's Introduction.**

CHAPTER 2

Adding and Configuring Server Controls

Users of Web applications want an experience that is similar to that of other applications. They want their Web site to behave seamlessly between their browser and the server. In fact, they do not even care to know there is a server involved. This means moving data back and forth between each user's browser and the Web server in a way that gives the impression that browser and server are one. This is a big challenge for developers. ASP.NET helps with this challenge by supplying server controls that already provide this level of communication. Developers use these controls to create great user experiences.

This chapter covers the many server controls available to the ASP.NET developer. The first lesson covers the basic underpinning concepts of working with server controls in a Web application. This includes the life cycle of an ASP.NET page and its controls. Lesson 2 covers many of the standard server controls you would expect to use on basic Web forms. Controls like the *Label*, *TextBox*, *Button*, *CheckBox*, and others are discussed. The last lesson in the chapter focuses on some of the more specialized server controls available to ASP.NET developers. This includes the *Image*, *Calendar*, and *Wizard* controls to name a few.

> ***NOTE*** **CONTROL COVERAGE**
>
> **There are many controls in ASP.NET. This chapter covers a large sample of the standard controls. If you are looking for information on a specific control and cannot find it here, please look elsewhere in the book, as controls like *Validation*, *Data*, *AJAX*, and others are covered in their respective chapters.**

Exam objectives in this chapter:

- Consuming and Creating Server controls
  - Consume standard controls.
- Programming Web Applications
  - Handle events and control page flow.

Lessons in this chapter:

Before You Begin

To complete the lessons in the chapter, you should be familiar with developing applications with Microsoft Visual Studio using Visual Basic or C#. In addition, you should be comfortable with all of the following:

- The Visual Studio 2008 Integrated Development Environment (IDE)
- Hypertext Markup Language (HTML) and client-side scripting
- Create a new Web site
- Adding Web server controls to a Web page

REAL WORLD

Glenn Johnson

On many occasions, I've seen developers select the wrong server control for the functionality that needed to be implemented. The problem was that these developers tended to use only a select few controls for most tasks. The end result is that they spent excessive amounts of time developing something that already existed in a different control.

Lesson 1: Understanding and Using Server Controls

An ASP.NET server control is a control that provides both user functionality and programmability through a server-side event model. For example, a *Button* control allows users to trigger an action, such as indicating they have completed a task. In addition, the *Button* control is posted back to the server where ASP.NET is able to match the control with its associated event code (an on-click event, for instance). The server controls that ship with ASP.NET allow you to write code against a well-defined object model. In fact, all server controls, including the Web page class itself, inherit from the *System.Web.UI.Control* class. Figure 2-1 shows the class hierarchy of the *Control* class with some of its key child classes like *WebControl*, *HtmlControl*, *TemplateControl*, and *Page*.

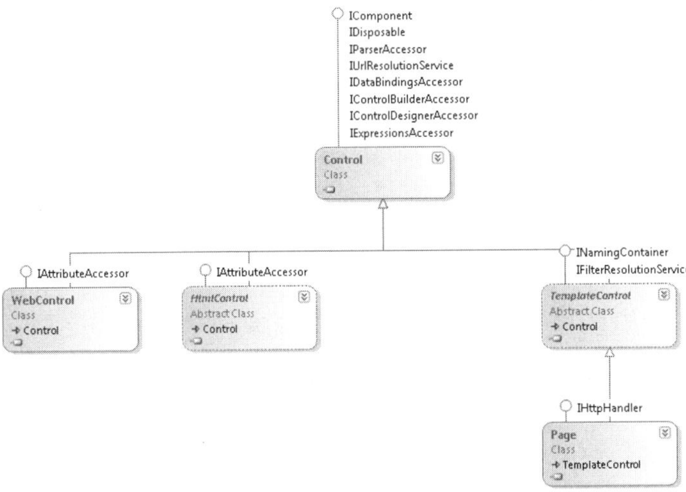

FIGURE 2-1 The *Control* class with its primary child classes

There are two primary types of server controls in ASP.NET: HTML and Web. The HTML controls provide server-side processing that generally maps back to an HTML input element like a text box or submit button. The Web controls are ASP.NET controls that focus more on their object model and less on their HTML rendering aspects. This lesson covers the major differences between these two control types. First, however, we start by discussing the life cycle of a Web page and its controls.

After this lesson, you will be able to:

- Describe the life cycle of an ASP.NET Web page and its controls.
- Describe the purpose and use of view state.
- Explain the principal differences between HTML and Web controls in ASP.NET.

Estimated lesson time: 30 minutes

Understanding the Life Cycle of an ASP.NET Web Page and Its Controls

To better understand how server controls operate, it is important to have a good understanding of the life cycle of an ASP.NET Web page and its controls. The life cycle starts when a user requests a Web page through his or her browser. The Web server then processes the page through a series of stages before returning the results back to the user's browser. These processing stages define the life cycle of a Web page. Understanding how ASP.NET processes a Web page on the server is key to being able to successfully develop Web applications. Figure 2-2 shows a high-level overview of the page processing life cycle.

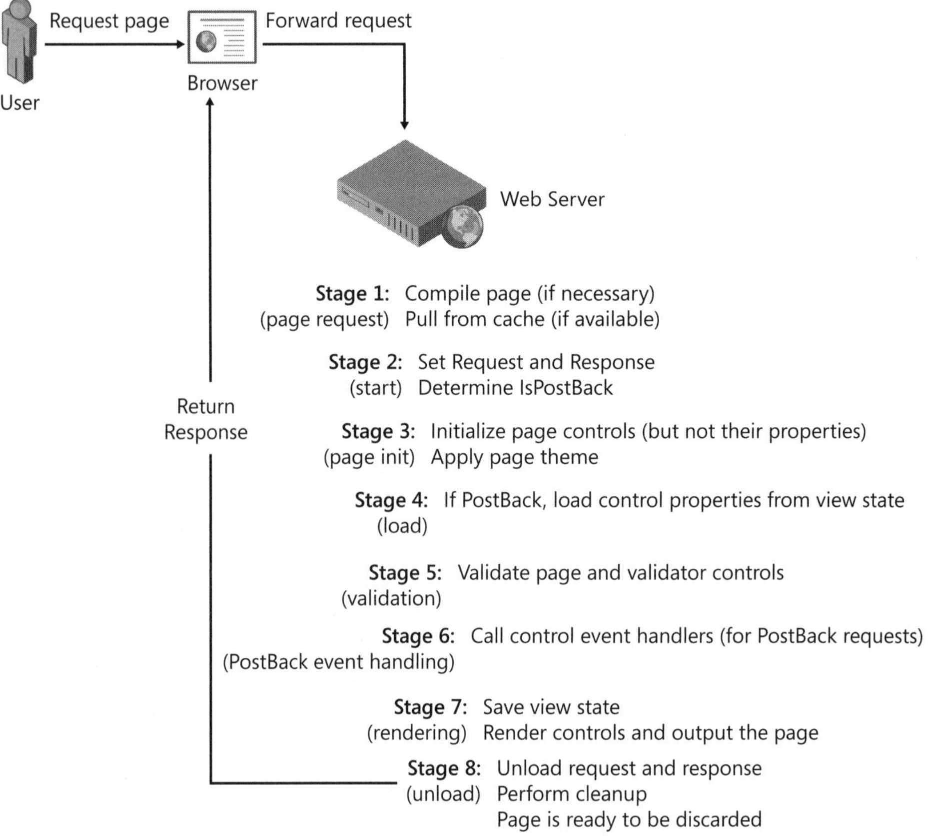

FIGURE 2-2 The life cycle of an ASP.NET page

When a Web page is requested, the server creates objects associated with the page and all of its child control objects and uses these to render the page to the browser. Once the final stage is complete, the Web server destroys these objects to free up resources to handle additional requests. This allows the Web server to handle more requests from more users. However, it poses problems for the developer in that there is no process that maintains the object data (called state) between requests. ASP.NET uses what is called view state to solve this issue. Refer back to Figure 2-2 and notice that a couple of the stages of an ASP.NET page involve both using view state and saving view state.

The Importance of *View State*

View state is a mechanism used by ASP.NET to store user-specific request and response data between page requests. The data being stored is typically associated with the server controls. This data is referred to as control state. Again, the view state data is not stored by the server. Instead, it is saved into the page's view state (stage 7, rendering) and sent in the page's response back to the user. When the user makes the next request, the view state is returned with his or her request. When the page processes, ASP.NET pulls the view state from the page and uses it to reset property values of the page and its controls (stage 4, load). This allows ASP.NET to have all the object data between requests without having to store it on the server. The result is a more scalable Web server that can handle more requests.

View state is just one of a few important state management techniques for Web applications. These techniques are covered in depth in Chapter 4, "ASP.NET State Management." Refer to this chapter for a much richer discussion on view state.

Page Life Cycle Events

As ASP.NET processes a page through its stages, various events are raised for the page and its related controls. You write code to handle these events and thus respond to various actions related to the processing of a page. For example, you might wish to write code that gets called when a page is first loaded (stage 4) to determine if the user is requesting the page or posting back to the server. This is a common scenario. When a page is first requested you often have to initialize data and controls. However, when it posts back you do not wish to run this code. Another common example is when a user clicks a button. You want to respond to the click event for that button only. Knowing which events are called in what order is important to making sure your code executes properly and can be debugged. Table 2-1 contains an ordered list of the more common events that are triggered when a page is processed by ASP.NET.

TABLE 2-1 Page Life Cycle Events

EVENT	DESCRIPTION
PreInit	This is the first real event you might handle for a page. You typically use this event only if you need to dynamically (from code) set values such as master page or theme. This event is also useful when you are working with dynamically created controls for a page. You want to create the controls inside this event.
Init	This event fires after each control has been initialized. You can use this event to change initialization values for controls.

EVENT	DESCRIPTION
InitComplete	Raised once all initializations of the page and its controls have been completed.
PreLoad	This event fires before view state has been loaded for the page and its controls and before PostBack processing. This event is useful when you need to write code after the page is initialized but before the view state has been wired back up to the controls.
Load	The page is stable at this time; it has been initialized and its state has been reconstructed. Code inside the page load event typically checks for PostBack and then sets control properties appropriately. The page's load event is called first. Then, the load event for each child control is called in turn (and their child controls, if any). This is important to know if you are writing your own user or custom controls.
Control (PostBack) event(s)	ASP.NET now calls any events on the page or its controls that caused the PostBack to occur. This might be a button's click event, for example.
LoadComplete	At this point all controls are loaded. If you need to do additional processing at this time you can do so here.
PreRender	Allows final changes to the page or its control. This event takes place after all regular PostBack events have taken place. This event takes place before saving *ViewState*, so any changes made here are saved.
SaveStateComplete	Prior to this event the view state for the page and its controls is set. Any changes to the page's controls at this point or beyond are ignored. This is useful if you need to write processing that requires the view state to be set.
Render	This is a method of the page object and its controls (and not an event). At this point, ASP.NET calls this method on each of the page's controls to get its output. The *Render* method generates the client-side HTML, Dynamic Hypertext Markup Language (DHTML), and script that are necessary to properly display a control at the browser. This method is useful if you are writing your own custom control. You override this method to control output for the control.
UnLoad	This event is used for cleanup code. You use it to release any managed resources in this stage. Managed resources are resources that are handled by the runtime, such as instances of classes created by the .NET common language runtime.

Control Life Cycle Events

Recall that the ASP.NET *Page* class inherits from the same *Control* class from which server controls inherit. Therefore it should not be surprising to learn that server controls share a common life cycle with the *Page* class. Each server control goes through the same life cycle as a page such as *init, load, render,* and *unload.* These events occur during the same event for their parent, so when a page executes the load event it then does so for each child control. Each child control that contains other child controls also executes the load events for each child control.

It is important to note that this synchronized event execution is true for all controls added to the page at design time. Those added dynamically during code execution will not have their events execute in a similar sequence to that of the page object. Instead, when they are added to the page dynamically, the control's events are executed sequentially until the events have caught up to the current stage of their container (typically the executing page).

Creating Event Handlers

Controls in ASP.NET have a default event you typically handle. For example, the *Page* object's default event is *Load*, and the *Button* object's default event is the *Click* event. Inside the Visual Studio page designer you can wire up an event handler for the default event of a control by simply double-clicking the design surface for the given control. For example, if you double-click a page you are taken to the *Page_Load* event handler in the code-behind file for the page. You can do the same for other controls you add to a page. Simply double-click a *Button* or *TextBox* to generate a default event handler in your code-behind file.

This double-click method works throughout Visual Studio. However, the Visual Basic.NET and C# designers differ when it comes to defining event handlers for other nondefault events.

WIRING UP A VISUAL BASIC.NET EVENT HANDLER

In Visual Basic.NET you use two drop-downs to define your events. This is a carryover from previous versions of Visual Basic. In the first drop-down you select an object on the page. The second drop-down is then used to generate the event handler. The following steps walk you through this process. Here you add the event handler *Page_Init.*

1. Inside Visual Studio's Solution Explorer, right-click a Web page and select View Code. This opens the code-behind page without inserting any code.
2. In the code-behind file, select the object drop-down list from the upper left part of the page and click Page Events, as shown in Figure 2-3.

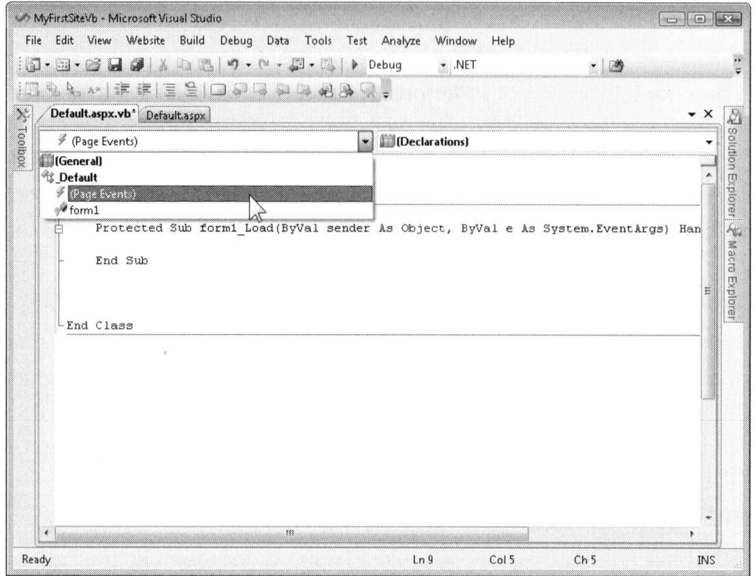

FIGURE 2-3 Select the object that contains the event you wish to handle

3. Next select the event drop-down list from the upper right part of the page. Notice that all the events for the page are listed. Those events that are already wired up on the page are listed in bold. Select the *Init* event as shown in Figure 2-4.

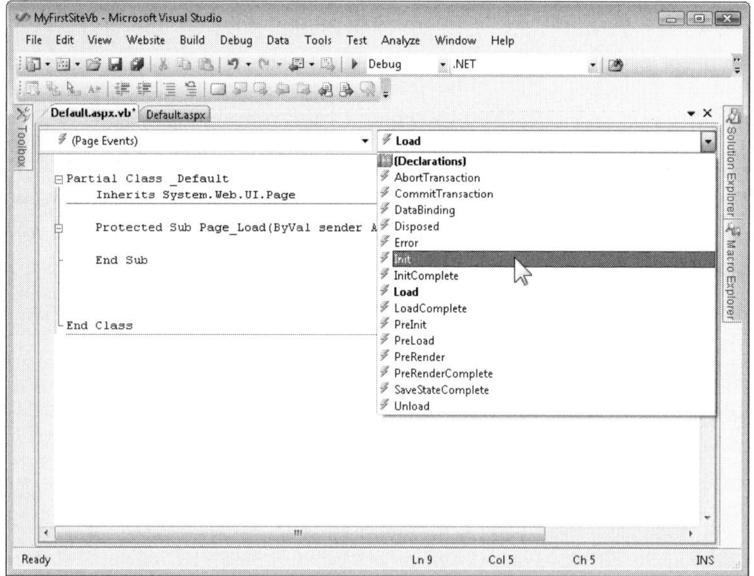

FIGURE 2-4 Select the *Init* event handler for a Visual Basic.NET Web page

4. Next, Visual Studio generates the following event stub for you. You can then add code inside this event that will be executed when this event is fired.

```
Protected Sub Page_Init(ByVal sender As Object, ByVal e As System.EventArgs) _
    Handles Me.Init

End Sub
```

WIRING UP A C# EVENT HANDLER

The code editor for C# also has an event handler drop-down list. However, it only contains access to events you have already wired up. The C# environment provides a tool for wiring up control events. However, it does not provide such a tool for the *Page* events. For these, you have to code the event manually. Follow these steps to add the *Init* event handler to a C# Web page:

1. Right-click a Web page from Solution Explorer and choose View Markup to open the design code (HTML) for a given page. Verify that the page's *AutoEventWireup* property is set to *true* in the *@Page* directive (this is the default). This simply means that the runtime will automatically connect event handlers it finds in your code that match the common form of *Page_EventName.*
2. Next, right-click the same page and choose View Code to open the code editor with the page's code-behind file loaded. From within the partial class brackets, add the handler code as follows. This code will automatically get wired up to the page's *Init* event at compile time.

```
private void Page_Init(object sender, EventArgs e)
{

}
```

Wiring events to individual controls in C# is a little easier. You are not required to recall the signature of each event. Instead, you can use the Property window for a control to generate an event stub in your code-behind file. The following procedure walks through defining a *Click* event for a *Button* control.

1. Open a page in Design view. From the Toolbox, add a *Button* control to the page.
2. Select the *Button* control and view its properties (right-click and select Properties).
3. In the Properties window, click the Events icon (yellow lightning bolt). This changes the Properties window to the events view. Figure 2-5 shows an example.
4. From here, you locate the event you wish to handle and double-click it in the Properties window. This will open the code-behind page and insert the event handler stub code.

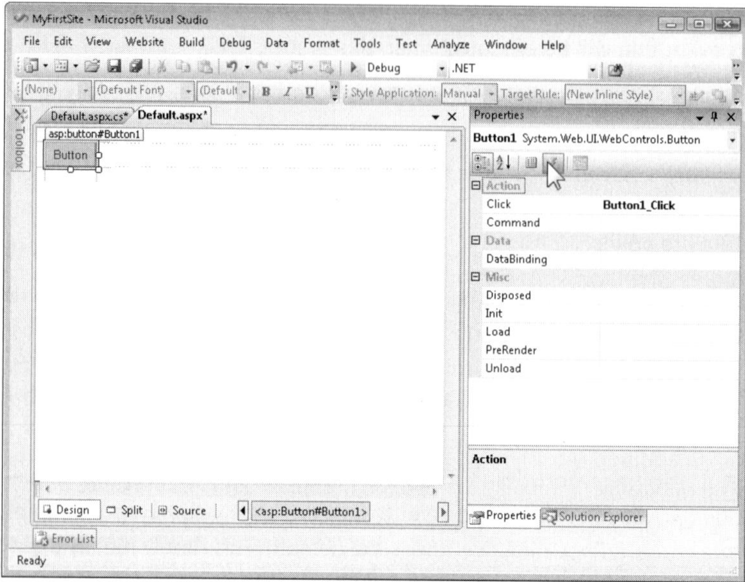

FIGURE 2-5 Adding an event handler to a C# server control

HTML vs. Web Server Controls

You have two options when creating many common user interface elements like buttons, text boxes, labels, and the like: HTML server controls or Web server controls. The following sections cover both types of controls. However, this question might arise: Which type of control should I use for my purpose? The following is some high-level guidance that can help you choose the proper control type for your situation.

Consider using HTML server controls when any of the following conditions exist:

- You are migrating existing, classic ASP pages over to ASP.NET.
- The control needs to have custom client-side JavaScript attached to the control's events.
- The Web page has lots of client-side JavaScript that is referencing the control.

In nearly all other cases, you should consider using the more powerful Web server controls. Web server controls follow a similar programming model and naming standard as that of Windows Forms. In addition, they do not map to a single HTML tag. Instead, they can generate multiple lines (or tags) of HTML and JavaScript as their rendered output. These controls also have other benefits such as multibrowser rendering support, a powerful programming model, layout control, theme support, and more.

> ***MORE INFO*** **HTML AND WEB SERVER CONTROLS**
>
> **For more information about the differences between HTML server controls and Web server controls, visit *http://msdn.microsoft.com/en-us/zsyt68f1.aspx*.**

HTML Server Controls

An HTML server control allows you to define actual HTML inside your ASP.NET page but work with the control on the server through an object model provided by the .NET Framework. Each HTML control is defined inside your page using standard HTML tag syntax. This means using the tags *<input />*, *<select />*, *<textarea />*, and the like. By default, these HTML tags are not connected to any server control. Therefore, it can be difficult to use them from the server in that there are no instances of related controls with properties and methods. Instead, you can simply access the tag values through the *Page.Request.Form* collection. This model is fine for very simple pages and was the only model for classic ASP.

Alternatively, you can apply the attribute *runat="server"* to these control tags. In this case, ASP.NET will wire up the HTML tag to a related, server-side object that provides properties and methods designed to work with the given tag. This can make your programming experience much easier. In addition, ASP.NET automatically maintains state for these items between calls for you (recall the view state discussion). Figure 2-6 shows the class hierarchy of many of the more common HTML server controls.

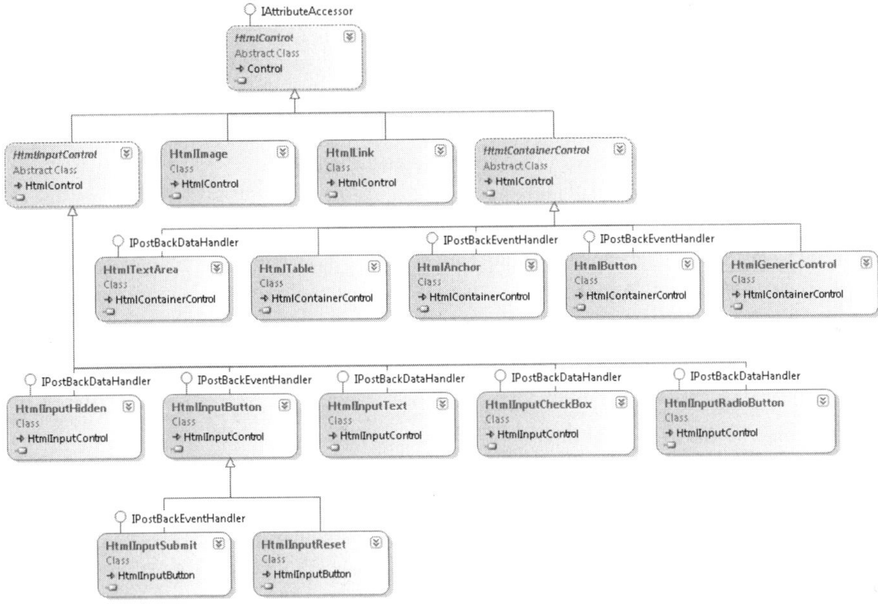

FIGURE 2-6 Class hierarchy of the common HTML server controls

Creating HTML Control Elements in an HTML Document

One of the best uses for HTML server controls is converting classic ASP pages over to a .NET Framework model. The classic ASP page typically contains a number of *<input />* tags nested inside a *<form />* tag. Consider the following classic ASP Web page.

Classic ASP Web Page

```
<html>
   <head><title>Customer Page</title></head>
   <body>
      <form name="Form1" method="post" action="update.asp" id="Form1" >
         <input type="text" name="CustomerName"
            id="CustomerName" >
         <input type="submit" name="SubmitButton"
            value="Submit" id="SubmitButton" >
      </form>
   </body>
</html>
```

This page contains a form with a text box and a submit button. The user can type a customer name and click the submit button to *POST* their entered data back to the update.asp page (the *action* attribute of the form) on the Web server. This page can be converted to use ASP.NET HTML server controls and thus simplify the programming model on the server. Consider the following code. It represents the same page converted to use ASP.NET.

Converted ASP.NET Web Page

```
<html>
   <head><title>Customer Page</title></head>
   <body>
      <form name="Form1" method="post" id="Form1" runat="server">
         <input type="text" name="CustomerName"
            id="CustomerName" runat="server" >
         <input type="submit" name="SubmitButton"
            value="Submit" id="SubmitButton" runat="server">
      </form>
   </body>
</html>
```

Notice that there is a one-to-one conversion from the HTML tag to the HTML server control. What changed is that the *runat="server"* attribute was added to each control. This attribute tells ASP.NET to create server control instances for each of these items. Also, notice that the same was added to the form tag. In addition, the *action* attribute was removed from the form tag, as with ASP.NET you typically send the data back to the same page.

It is also important to note that these tags are required to have a defined *ID* attribute value for you to reference it in code. The value of this *ID* attribute becomes the name of the control instance in your code.

Creating HTML Server Controls in the Designer

The HTML server controls are grouped together inside the Toolbox of the Visual Studio designer. You can simply drag and drop these controls onto your form. To create an HTML server control using the Visual Studio designer, follow these steps:

1. Open an ASP.NET page inside the designer.
2. In the Toolbox, click the HTML tab to expose the HTML controls (see Figure 2-7).
3. Drag an HTML element to either Design or Source view of the Web page.
4. Convert the HTML element to a server control by setting the *runat* attribute. In Source view, add the *runat="server"* attribute (see Figure 2-7).

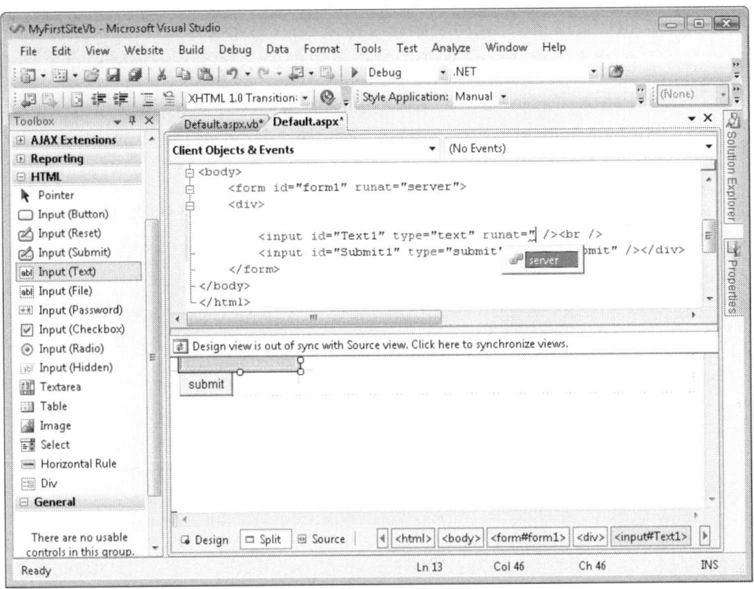

FIGURE 2-7 Setting the *runat* attribute of an HTML server control

> ***NOTE*** **LOCATION OF HTML SERVER CONTROLS**
>
> **An HTML server control must be located inside a form element that has the *runat="server"* attribute to operate properly.**

If you decide that you no longer need to program an HTML server control in server code, you should convert it back to a plain HTML element. Each HTML server control in a page uses resources, so it is good practice to minimize the number of controls that the ASP.NET page needs to work with on the server. To do so, open the page in Source view, then remove the *runat="server"* attribute from the control's tag. If the HTML element is referenced by client-side script, you should not remove its *ID* attribute.

Setting the HTML Server Control Properties

By default, HTML elements within an ASP.NET file are treated as literal text. You cannot reference them in server-side code until you convert the HTML element into an HTML server control. You should also set the element's *ID* attribute to give you a way to programmatically reference the control. Table 2-2 provides a list of the properties that all HTML server controls have in common. You can set the properties of the HTML server control by setting the attributes in Source view, by setting the properties in Design view, or by setting the properties programmatically in code. This section examines all three methods.

TABLE 2-2 Common HTML Server Control Properties

PROPERTY	DESCRIPTION
Attributes	A list of all attribute name-value pairs expressed on a server control tag within a selected ASP.NET page. This is accessible using code.
Disabled	A value that indicates whether the *disabled* attribute is included when an HTML control is rendered on the browser, which makes the control read-only when *true*.
Id	The programmatic identification of the control.
Style	A list of all Cascading Style Sheets (CSS) properties that are applied to the specified HTML server control.
TagName	The element name of a tag that contains a *runat="server"* attribute.
Visible	A value that indicates whether the HTML server control is displayed on the page. If this value is set to *false*, the control does not render any HTML to the browser.

SETTING PROPERTIES IN SOURCE VIEW

In Source view, you set the properties of an HTML control by adding the appropriate HTML attributes to the HTML server control's element. These attribute values will be connected to the server control's property values automatically by ASP.NET. Consider the following HTML server control button and its attributes:

```
<input type="button"
  id="myButton"
  runat="server"
  value="Click Me"
  style="position: absolute; top: 50px; left: 100px; width: 100px;" />
```

Notice that this server control has many of the same attributes that an HTML input button element has, except it has the *runat="server"* attribute and the *visible* attribute (not shown). The *ID* sets the programmatic identification to *myButton*, the *style* attribute sets the location of the control on the page, and the *value* of *Click Me* displays on the button's face. The HTML that is rendered by ASP.NET in a user's browser looks as follows:

```
<input name="myButton"
  type="button"
  id="myButton"
  value="Click Me"
  style="position: absolute; top: 50px; left: 100px; width: 100px;" />
```

Notice that the *name* attribute is not explicitly set in the ASP page. However, it is set inside the browser HTML. ASP converts the *ID* attribute's value to the *name* attribute value at the time of rendering.

SETTING PROPERTIES IN DESIGN VIEW

In Design view, the properties of an HTML control are set by selecting the server control and modifying the desired properties in the Properties window. Figure 2-8 shows the same button configured using the Properties window. Changes that are made in the Properties window are reflected in Source view, and changes in Source view are reflected in the Properties window in Design view.

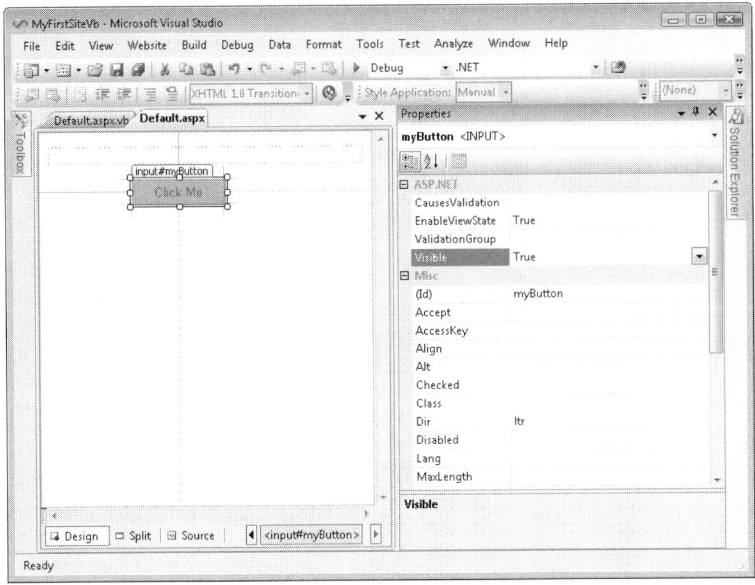

FIGURE 2-8 Setting HTML input button properties using the Properties window

Notice that there are two groups of properties for HTML server controls: ASP.NET and Misc. The ASP.NET properties group groups together a set of properties for the control that are processed specifically for ASP.NET purposes and not specific to the given control. For example, you can set a validation group, disable view state for the control, and tell ASP.NET not to show the control (Visible) from these properties. The Misc group contains properties that are specific to the selected server control.

SETTING PROPERTIES PROGRAMMATICALLY IN CODE

ASP.NET defines an instance variable for you to use in your code for each server control on the page. These variables are named relative to each control's *ID* property. These variables are then just available to you in your code. All properties of these controls are simply types like strings, integers, or Boolean. The exception is the *style* property, which is a key-value collection. The following shows example code added to the *Page_Load* event handler; it sets the *disabled* and *style* properties of the button that has the *ID myButton*:

```
'VB
myButton.Disabled = True
myButton.Style.Add("background-color", "Black")
myButton.Style.Add("color", "Gray")

//C#
myButton.Disabled = true;
myButton.Style.Add("background-color", "Black");
myButton.Style.Add("color", "Gray");
```

> ***NOTE* THE <DIV/> TAG**
>
> **You can run any of the HTML tags from the server. Again, you must indicate *runat="server"* to do so. When you apply this attribute to the *DIV* tag you have a couple properties with which to work. You can set the text that shows up inside the *DIV* tag by using its *InnerText* property. You can also insert (or read) HTML nested inside the *DIV* tag by using the *InnerHtml* property.**

Web Server Controls

ASP.NET provides programmers a set of Web server controls for creating Web pages that provide more functionality and a more consistent programming model than that of HTML server controls. Web server controls are specific to ASP.NET (and not part of the HTML standard). They each have a corresponding class in the .NET Framework. These classes offer a much richer set of features.

Web server controls are able to provide more functionality because they are not tied to a single HTML tag element. Instead, they typically render many HTML tags and may also include client-side JavaScript code. Web server controls also have the ability to detect the Web browser's capabilities and render the appropriate HTML based on those capabilities. This allows ASP.NET Web server controls to use a specific browser to its fullest potential. The programmer is also abstracted from the actual HTML and instead works with the Web server control to define the appropriate functionality for the page. This allows developers to use controls that would be very complex HTML, such as the *Calendar, Wizard, Login*, and *GridView* controls.

Most Web server controls inherit from the *WebControl* class. Figure 2-9 shows the class hierarchy of some of the more common Web server controls. Note that it does not include those controls typically associated with data binding. These are covered in Chapter 8, "Working with DataSource and Data-Bound Controls."

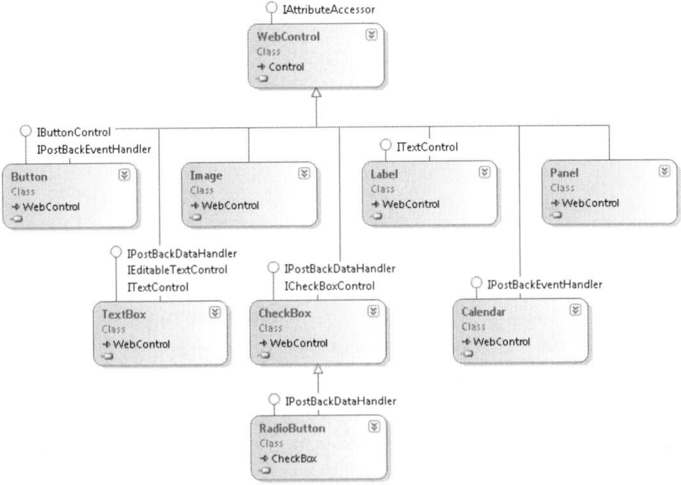

FIGURE 2-9 The class hierarchy of some common Web server controls

Adding Web Server Controls Using Design View

A Web server control can be added to an .aspx page using the Visual Studio Design view or Source view, or dynamically using code. First we look at adding Web server controls using Design view. Follow these steps to add a Web server control to a Web page using Design view:

1. Open a Web page in Visual Studio.
2. Click the Design tab at the bottom of the Web page.
3. Open the Toolbox and click the Standard tab.
4. Drag a Web server control from the Toolbox and drop it on the Web page.

   Figure 2-10 shows an example of dragging a *TextBox* control onto a Web page.

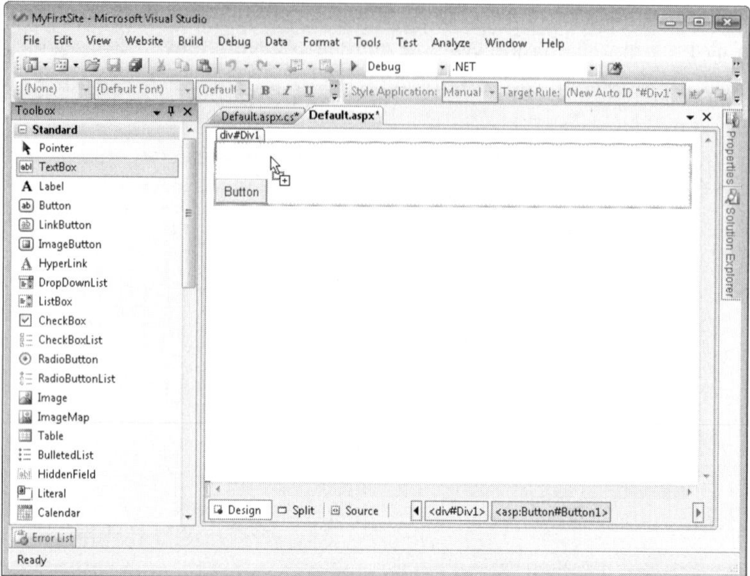

FIGURE 2-10 Adding a standard Web server control to a page from Design view

Adding Web Server Controls Using Source View

Follow these steps to add a Web server control to a Web page using Source view:

1. Open the Web page in Visual Studio.
2. Click the Source tab at the bottom of the Web page.
3. In Source view of the Web page, type the Web server control element and its attributes (see Figure 2-11).
4. Alternatively, you can drag a control from the Toolbox directly into the page source.

   Note that like HTML server controls, Web server controls must be located within an HTML form element that has the *runat="server"* attribute defined.

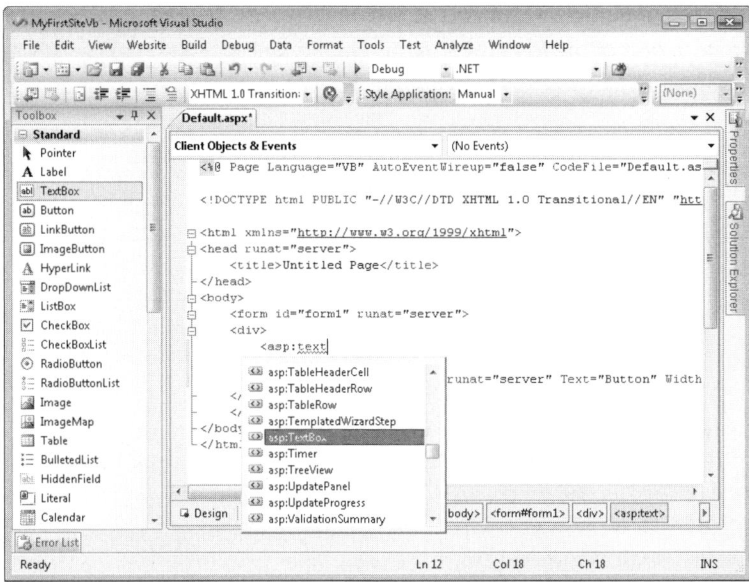

FIGURE 2-11 Adding a Web server control to a page in Source view

Adding Web Server Controls Dynamically Using Code

You can also programmatically add Web server controls to a page dynamically. When doing so it is imperative you understand the Web page and server control life cycle described in Table 2-1. Knowing this life cycle will assure that the control operates properly. Recall that the *PreInit* event is typically used to create dynamic controls prior to their initialization inside the *Init* event. The following steps demonstrate the implementation of dynamically generated Web server controls:

1. Open the Web page's code-behind page in Visual Studio.
2. Create a handler for the *Page_PreInit* event. Recall that defining these events is different for C# and Visual Basic (refer to "Creating Event Handlers" earlier in this lesson).
3. In the *Page_PreInit* method, add code to create a new instance of a *TextBox* Web server control. This *TextBox* would typically be created based on some logic. However, here we are simply creating the item dynamically.
4. After creating the instance, add code to set the control's *ID* property.

5. Finally, add the control to the *Controls* collection of *form1*. This will make sure the control is output as part of the form.

Your code should look similar to the following:

```
'VB
Protected Sub Page_PreInit(ByVal sender As Object, ByVal e As System.EventArgs) _
  Handles Me.Init
  Dim textBoxUserName As New TextBox
  textBoxUserName.ID = "TextBoxUserName"
  form1.Controls.Add(textBoxUserName)
End Sub

//C#
protected void Page_PreInit(object sender, EventArgs e)
{
  TextBox textBoxUserName = new TextBox();
  textBoxUserName.ID = "TextBoxUserName";
  form1.Controls.Add(textBoxUserName);
}
```

Setting Web Server Control Properties

Most Web server controls inherit from the *WebControl* class. All Web server controls must contain a unique (at the page level) *ID* attribute value to give you a way to programmatically reference the control. The other attributes and properties of a Web server control are used to control the look and behavior of the control. Table 2-3 contains a list of the attributes and properties that all Web server controls have in common.

TABLE 2-3 Common Web Server Control Properties

PROPERTY	DESCRIPTION
AccessKey	The keyboard shortcut key. It can specify a single letter or number that the user can press while holding down Alt. For example, specify "Q" if you want the user to press Alt+Q to access the control. The property is supported only in Microsoft Internet Explorer 4.0 and later.
Attributes	A collection of additional attributes on the control that is not defined by a public property, but that should be rendered in the primary HTML element of this control. This allows you to use an HTML attribute that is not directly supported by the control. This property is accessible programmatically; it cannot be set in the designer.
BackColor	The background color of the control, which can be set using standard HTML color identifiers, such as "red" or "blue," or RGB values expressed in hexadecimal format ("#ffffff").

PROPERTY	DESCRIPTION
BorderColor	The border color of the control, which can be set using standard HTML color identifiers, such as "black" or "red," or RGB values expressed in hexadecimal format ("#ffffff").
BorderWidth	The width of the control's border in pixels. Not fully supported for all controls in browsers earlier than Internet Explorer 4.0.
BorderStyle	The border style, if there is any. Possible values are *NotSet*, *None*, *Dotted*, *Dashed*, *Solid*, *Double*, *Groove*, *Ridge*, *Inset*, and *Outset*.
CssClass	The CSS class to assign to the control.
Style	A list of all CSS properties that are applied to the specified HTML server control.
Enabled	An attribute that disables the control when set to *false*. This dims the control and makes it inactive. It does not hide the control.
EnableTheming	The default is *true*, which enables themes for this control.
EnableViewState	The default is *true*, which enables view state persistence for the control.
Font	An attribute that contains subproperties that you can declare using the property-subproperty syntax in the opening tag of a Web server control element. For example, you can make a Web server control's text italic by including the *Font-Italic* attribute in its opening tag.
ForeColor	The foreground color of the control. It is not fully supported for all controls in browsers earlier than Internet Explorer 4.0.
Height	The control's height. It is not fully supported for all controls in browsers earlier than Internet Explorer 4.0.
SkinID	The skin to apply to the control.
TabIndex	The control's position in the tab order. If this property is not set, the control's position index is 0. Controls with the same tab index can be tabbed according to the order in which they are declared in the Web page. This works only in Internet Explorer 4.0 and later.
ToolTip	The text that appears when the user hovers the mouse pointer over a control. The *ToolTip* property does not work in all browsers.
Width	The width of the control. The possible units are *Pixel*, *Point*, *Pica*, *Inch*, *Mm*, *Cm*, *Percentage*, *Em*, and *Ex*. The default unit is pixels.

You can set the values of the of Web server control properties by setting their attributes in Source view, by setting their properties in Design view, or by setting their properties programmatically in code. This section examines all three methods.

SETTING PROPERTIES IN SOURCE VIEW

In Source view, the properties of a Web server control are set by adding the appropriate attributes and their values to the Web server control's element. Consider the following Web server control button:

```
<asp:Button ID="ButtonSave"
  runat="server"
  Text="Save"
  Style="position: absolute; top: 50px; left: 100px; width: 100px;" />
```

Notice that this server control has different attributes from its HTML counterpart. For example, the *Text* property on the Web server control coincides with the *value* property on the HTML server control. The difference is an attempt to provide a consistent programming model among Web server controls and Windows forms controls. As with HTML server controls, the *ID* property sets the programmatic identification. The *style* attribute sets the location of the control, and the *Text* property is used to display the text for the button's face. The rendered HTML in the user's browser looks like this:

```
<input type="submit"
  name="ButtonSave"
  value="Save"
  id="ButtonSave"
  style="position: absolute; top: 50px; left: 100px; width: 100px;" />
```

Notice that the rendered HTML creates an HTML *input* element that is configured as a submit button, and the *value* attribute is mapped to the *Text* property on the Web server control. Also, if the *name* attribute is not explicitly set, the *name* attribute is automatically set to the *ID* property value.

SETTING PROPERTIES IN DESIGN VIEW

The properties of a Web control can be set in Design view by selecting the server control and modifying the desired properties in the Properties window. Figure 2-12 shows the same button configured using the Properties window. Note that the *Style* property is not available in the Properties window. Changes that are made in the Properties window are reflected in Source view; changes in Source view are also reflected in the Properties window in Design view

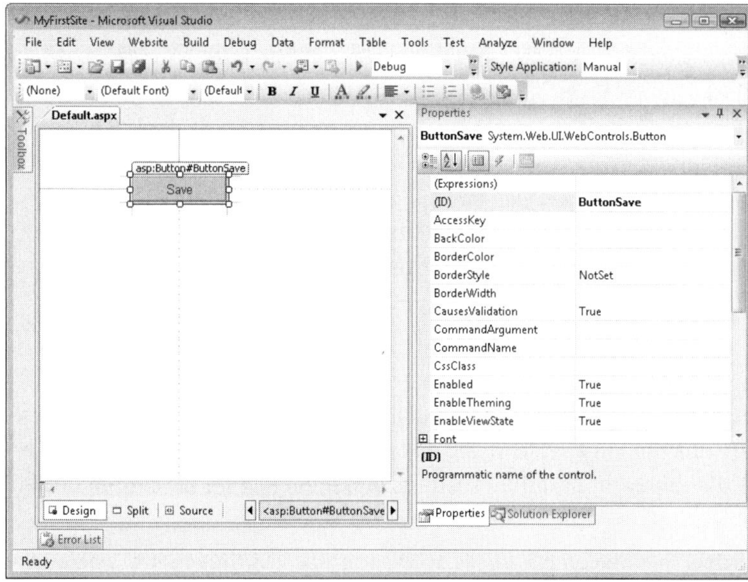

FIGURE 2-12 Setting the Web server *Button* control properties using the Properties window

SETTING PROPERTIES PROGRAMMATICALLY IN CODE

Web server control properties can be set programmatically in the code-behind files of a Web page. Like all server controls, you reference the Web server controls by an instance variable named after the control's *ID* property. The following code was added to a *Page_Load* event handler. It sets the *Style, Text,* and *Enabled* properties of the button that has the *ID* of *ButtonSave.*

```
'VB
ButtonSave.Enabled = False
ButtonSave.Text = "Click to Save"
ButtonSave.Style.Add("background-color", "Blue")

//C#
ButtonSave.Enabled = false;
ButtonSave.Text = "Click to Save";
ButtonSave.Style.Add("background-color", "Blue");
```

Controlling Automatic PostBack

Some Web server controls always cause a PostBack when a specific event occurs. For example, the *Button* control's *Click* event always causes a PostBack. Other controls, such as the *TextBox*, have events that do not cause an automatic PostBack to the server. However, they are configurable to do so if required. For instance, the *TextBox* contains a default event called *TextChanged*. By default, the *TextChanged* event does not cause an automatic PostBack. The event is not lost, however. Instead, the event is raised when another control's event that does cause a PostBack is triggered (such as the *Button* control).

When working with controls with events that do not cause automatic PostBack to the server, it is important to understand when these events are raised. Recall the Web page life cycle defined in Table 2-1. Any postponed event (an event triggered by a user that does not cause an automatic PostBack) executes before the actual event that caused the PostBack. For example, if the text is changed in a *TextBox* and a *Button* is clicked, the *Button* causes a PostBack, but the *TextChanged* event of the *TextBox* executes and then the *Click* event of the *Button* executes.

The *AutoPostBack* property for a control is used to change whether that control's default event causes an automatic PostBack to the server. You set its value to *true* to turn a postponed event to one that causes an immediate PostBack. You can do so in the Properties window, using code, or by adding the *AutoPostBack="True"* attribute to the Web server control element in Source view.

Working with Naming Containers and Child Controls

A Web page is made up of a hierarchy of controls. The *System.Web.UI.Control* class, which is the class from which the Web page and its controls inherit, has a *Controls* collection property. This property is used to work with the various controls that belong to a given page. In addition, each control in the collection also has its own *Controls* collection, and so on.

The Web page is a naming container for the controls that are added to its *Controls* collection. A naming container defines a unique namespace for control names. Within a naming container, every control must be uniquely identifiable. Typically, this is accomplished by assigning a unique value to the server control's *ID* property. The *ID* is the programmatic name of the control instance. For example, if you set the *ID* property of a *Label* control to *lblMessage*, you can reference the control in code as *lblMessage* and there cannot be another control in this naming container that has the *ID* of *lblMessage*.

Many data-bound controls, such as the *GridView* control, are containers for child controls. For example, when the *GridView* control is instantiated, it generates multiple instances of child controls to represent the row and column data. How can multiple *GridView* controls be added to a Web page, and then, when their child controls are created, each has its own unique *ID* property? This is because the *GridView* control is a naming container.

The naming container for a given child control is a control above it (parent or higher) in the hierarchy that implements the *INamingContainer* interface. A server control implements this interface to create a unique namespace for populating the *UniqueID* property values of its child server controls. The *UniqueID* property contains the fully qualified name of the control. The difference between this property and the *ID* property is that the *UniqueID* property is generated automatically by the *NamingContainer* and contains the *NamingContainer* information.

SEARCHING FOR CONTROLS

If you want to locate a child control within a given *NamingContainer*, use the *FindControl* method of the *NamingContainer*. The *FindControl* method recursively searches the underlying child controls, but the searches do not enter the *Controls* collection of any child control that is a *NamingContainer*. The following code sample shows how to find a control named *lblMessage* on the Web page:

```
'VB
Dim c As Control = FindControl("lblMessage")

//C#
Control c = FindControl("lblMessage");
```

This code might not have much value because you can simply access *lblMessage* directly by its *ID*. The *FindControl* method is most valuable when you need to locate a control that has been dynamically created. If a control is created dynamically, you are not able to directly reference it by its *ID* property. Instead, you need to find the control, based on its *ID* property, and assign the returned value to a control variable that you can use to access the control. For example, the *GridView* dynamically creates its child controls using the format "ctl" plus *n*, where *n* is a numeric index for each control. To access a child control called *ctl08*, use the following code:

```
'VB
Dim c As Control = GridView1.FindControl("ctl08")

//C#
Control c = GridView1.FindControl("ctl08");
```

 **Quick Check**

1. **What property do you modify on a server control to minimize the size of the *ViewState* data?**
2. **What happens in the *Init* event of a page?**
3. **If you are migrating classic ASP pages to ASP.NET, what type of server controls might you use?**

Quick Check Answers

1. Set *EnableViewState* to *false*.
2. Each child control of the page is initialized to its design time values.
3. Use HTML server controls for easily converting classic ASP pages to ASP.NET.

LAB Exploring the Web Page Life Cycle Events

In this lab, you explore the Web page life cycle to gain an understanding of the events and when they are triggered. If you encounter a problem completing an exercise, the completed projects are available in the samples installed from the companion CD.

EXERCISE 1 Configuring Web Page Event Handlers

In this exercise, you configure event handlers for some of the Web page and server control events. You then run the Web page to display the order in which these events are fired by ASP.NET.

1. Open Visual Studio and create a new Web site called **LifeCycleEvents** using your preferred programming language. This lab assumes you are using the code-behind model (and not the single-page model).
2. Your new Web site should include the page Default.aspx. Open its associated code-behind file. You can do so from Solution Explorer or by right-clicking the page in the designer and choosing View Code.
4. Add a *Page_Load* event handler to the page (the handler is there by default in C#). Recall this is a different process for Visual Basic and C# (see "Creating Event Handlers" earlier in this lesson).
5. In the *Page_Load* event handler, add code that will write to the Output window in Visual Studio through the *System.Diagnostics.Debug* class. The following code provides an example:

```
'VB
Protected Sub Page_Load(ByVal sender As Object, _
  ByVal e As System.EventArgs) Handles Me.Load

  System.Diagnostics.Debug.WriteLine("Page_Load")

End Sub

//C#
protected void Page_Load(object sender, EventArgs e)
{
  System.Diagnostics.Debug.WriteLine("Page_Load");
}
```

6. Add event handlers for the *PreInit*, *Init*, *PreRender*, and *Unload* events. In each, place a call to *Debug.Write*. Each call should write out the respective event name associated with the handler. These additional handlers should look like the following:

```
'VB
Protected Sub Page_PreInit(ByVal sender As Object, _
  ByVal e As System.EventArgs) Handles Me.PreInit

  System.Diagnostics.Debug.WriteLine("Page_PreInit")

End Sub

Protected Sub Page_Init(ByVal sender As Object, _
  ByVal e As System.EventArgs) Handles Me.Init

  System.Diagnostics.Debug.WriteLine("Page_Init")

End Sub

Protected Sub Page_PreRender(ByVal sender As Object, _
  ByVal e As System.EventArgs) Handles Me.PreRender

  System.Diagnostics.Debug.WriteLine("Page_PreRender")

End Sub

Protected Sub Page_Unload(ByVal sender As Object, _
  ByVal e As System.EventArgs) Handles Me.Unload

  System.Diagnostics.Debug.WriteLine("Page_Unload")

End Sub

//C#
protected void Page_PreInit(object sender, EventArgs e)
{
  System.Diagnostics.Debug.WriteLine("Page_PreInit");
}

protected void Page_Init(object sender, EventArgs"e)"
{
  System.Diagnostics.De"ug.WriteLine("Page_Init");
}

prote"ted "oid Page_PreRender(object sender, EventArgs e)
{
```

```
    Sy"tem.Diagnostics.Debug.WriteLin"("Page"PreRender");
}

protected void Page_Unload(object sender, EventArgs e)
{
    System.Dia"nostic".Debug.WriteLine("Page_Unload");
}
```

7. Run the Web application in Debug mode (click the Start Debugging button on the standard toolbar). You might receive a prompt stating that the Web site cannot be debugged without enabling debugging in the Web.config file. Allow Visual Studio to enable debugging and click OK to continue. The Default.aspx page should be displayed in a browser window (although it is blank because no controls were added to the page).

8. In Visual Studio, locate the Output window (View Output). You should see a list of events at the bottom of the Output window. This list is the result of the *Debug.WriteLine* calls in your code. Figure 2-13 shows an example. Notice the order in which the events fired.

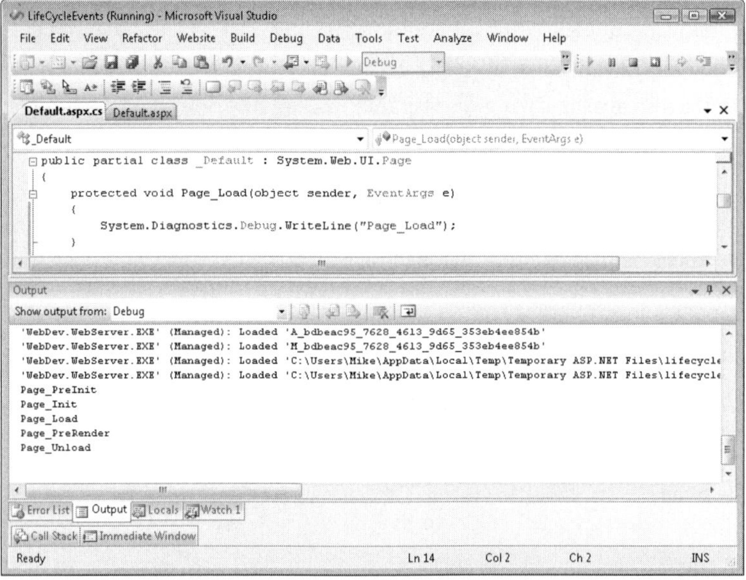

FIGURE 2-13 The Output window in Visual Studio showing the order in which the page events fired

Lesson Summary

- An ASP.NET page has a defined life cycle that determines how ASP.NET will process the page, call events, and connect data to the page.
- *ViewState* is the mechanism by which Web page object and child control object data can be maintained between page requests.
- A server control is a control that is programmable by writing server-side code to respond to events from the control.
- Server controls contain the *runat="server"* attribute.
- HTML server controls are useful when a classic ASP Web page needs to be migrated to ASP.NET.
- HTML server controls are also useful when you are working with a server control and you also need to write a lot of associated client-side JavaScript.
- Web server controls are more powerful than HTML controls. A single Web server control can render as many HTML elements and JavaScript code blocks. They also provide a more intuitive programming model for Windows developers.

Lesson Review

You can use the following questions to test your knowledge of the information in Lesson 1, "Understanding and Using Server Controls."

The questions are also available on the companion CD if you prefer to review them in electronic form.

> ***NOTE*** **ANSWERS**
>
> **Answers to these questions and explanations of why each answer choice is right or wrong are located in the "Answers" section at the end of the book.**

1. To add an HTML server control to a Web page, you must drag an HTML element from the Toolbox to the Web page and then perform which of the following tasks?
   A. Add the attribute *run="server"* to the control element in Source view.
   B. Double-click the HTML element to convert it to an HTML server control.
   C. Add the attribute *runat="server"* to the control element in Source view.
   D. Select the HTML element in Design view and set the *RunAt* property to *true* in the Properties window.

2. You noticed that clicking a *CheckBox* does not cause an automatic PostBack. You need the *CheckBox* to PostBack so you can update the Web page based on server-side code. How do you make the *CheckBox* cause an automatic PostBack?

   A. Set the *AutoPostBack* property to *true*.

   B. Add JavaScript code to call the *ForcePostBack* method.

   C. Set the *PostBackAll* property of the Web page to *true*.

   D. Add server-side code to listen for the click event from the client.

3. You need to dynamically create an instance of a *TextBox* server control in your code. In which page event would you create the server control to ensure that the view state is properly reconnected to the control on PostBack?

   A. *PreInit*

   B. *Init*

   C. *Load*

   D. *PreRender*

4. You need to write code to dynamically create a new instance of a *TextBox* server control. You want to make sure the *TextBox* control displays on the Web page. Which action do you take?

   A. Call the *ShowControl* method on the *TextBox*.

   B. Set the *Visible* property to *true* on the *TextBox*.

   C. Call the *Add* method of the *Page* class to add your *TextBox* instance to the page.

   D. Call the *Add* method of the *form1.Controls* collection to add your *TextBox* instance to the page.

Lesson 2: Exploring Common Server Controls

There are many Web server controls inside of ASP.NET. In fact, with each new release the number, power, and flexibility of these controls all increase. Having all these controls available ensures developers have the tools to create applications with great user experiences. Not all controls will be covered in this book. However, many of the controls have a similar programming model. This book exposes you to enough of these controls to ensure you have the knowledge to work with them all.

In the previous lesson we looked at how Web controls work and how to work with them inside of Visual Studio. Here we look at the controls in greater depth. This lesson covers many of the basic, standard Web server controls you will use for an application. Lesson 3 covers some of the more advanced or specialized controls in ASP.NET. This leaves many of the controls uncovered in this chapter. These controls are discussed in later chapters on topics such as data-bound controls, validation, navigation, AJAX, site membership, and more.

After this lesson, you will be able to:

- Use the following Web server controls:
  - *Label*
  - *TextBox*
  - *Button*
  - *CheckBox*
  - *RadioButton*

Estimated lesson time: 30 minutes

REAL WORLD

Glenn Johnson

A friend of mine asked me to review his Web site, so I navigated to his site and did some exploring to get acquainted with it. It didn't take long for me to see that I was able to enter *<script>* tags into some of the *TextBox* controls on the site, and that the script was then stored in the database. When someone else visited the site, the script I entered was loaded from the database to the page and executed. This Web site contained numerous cross-site scripting (XSS) vulnerabilities that could be exploited to allow hackers to steal users' identity information.

Fortunately, the site wasn't in production, so my friend was able to correct the problems and avoid the embarrassment that this could have caused him and his company.

The *Label* Control

The *Label* control displays text at a specific location on a Web page using the properties that the control has been assigned. Use the *Label* control when you need to use server-side code to change the label's text or another one of its properties. If you simply need to display static text, do not use the *Label* control, as it is overkill. It requires processing on the server and increases the amount of data sent back and forth across the wire. Instead, define your static text using standard HTML.

Labels can be used as the caption of a *TextBox* or other controls in a situation where using the access key for the *Label* moves the focus to the control to the right of the *Label*.

> ***SECURITY ALERT*** **Populating the *Label* control with data from an untrusted source can create XSS vulnerabilities. This is true for many of the controls that contain a *Text* property. This means the data applied to the *Text* property of the control can contain HTML code and script that will be executed by the page. To prevent this, use the *HttpUtility.HtmlEncode* or the *Server.HtmlEncode* method to encode the untrusted data prior to placing it in the *Text* property.**

To add a *Label* Web server control to a Web page, perform the following steps:

1. If you are in Source view of the Web page, type an *<asp:Label>* element. You will be given IntelliSense to help you complete the tag. Make sure you set the *runat="server"* attribute for the control.

   If you are in Design view, drag the *Label* control from the Standard tab of the Toolbox to the Web page.

2. You can set the value of the label's *Text* property in two ways. You can define *Text* as an attribute of the *Label* as follows:

   ```
   <asp:Label ID="Label1" runat="server" style="color: Blue" Text="Some
   Text"></asp:Label>
   ```

   Alternatively, you can nest text between the opening and closing elements as follows:

   ```
   <asp:Label ID="Label1" runat="server" style="color: Blue">Some Text</asp:Label>
   ```

   You can also set the value of the *Text* property from code. If you change the *Text* property in code it will override what is set on the page inside the designer. The following shows an example of this code:

   ```
   'VB
   Label1.Text = "Some Text"

   //C#
   Label1.Text = "Some Text";
   ```

The *TextBox* Control

The *TextBox* control is used to collect information from a user. The *TextBox* control's *Text* property gets or sets the contents of the *TextBox* control. Like the *Label* control, you can set the *Text* property as an attribute, in between the opening and closing of the tag, or from code.

The *TextBox* control contains a *TextMode* property that you can set to *SingleLine* (default), *MultiLine*, or *Password*. The *SingleLine* value allows the user to enter a single line of text. The *Password* value creates a single-line text box that masks the values entered by the user as they are entered. The *MultiLine* value indicates that a user is able to enter many lines of text. You use this value in conjunction with the *Columns* and *Rows* properties to provide a large *TextBox* for the user to enter a larger amount of data. The *Columns* property sets the width of the *TextBox in terms of the number of characters on a given line.* The *Rows* property sets the maximum height of a multiline *TextBox* in terms of the number of lines a user should be able to see at any given time. Figure 2-14 shows an example of defining a multiline *TextBox* control using the Properties window in Visual Studio.

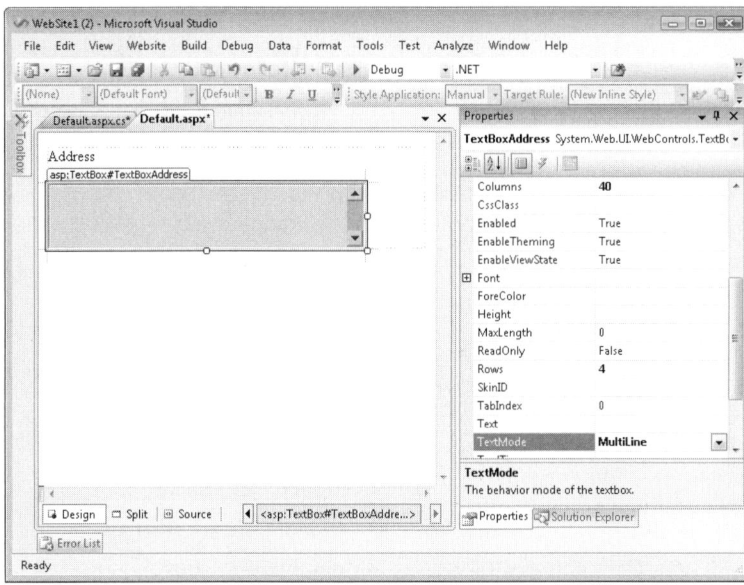

FIGURE 2-14 A multiline *TextBox* control in the Visual Studio designer

The *TextBox* control also has a *MaxLength* property that limits the number of characters that can be entered by a user. This helps constrain the user's entry to what you can store in a database field. The *Wrap* property (default value is *true*) automatically continues the text on the next line when the end of the *TextBox* width is reached.

The *TextBox* control contains the *TextChanged* event. This can be trapped by the server to respond to when the user has changed the text of a given *TextBox*. This event does not automatically trigger a PostBack.

The *Button* Control

The *Button* control displays a button on the Web page that a user can click to trigger a PostBack to the Web server. A *Button* control can be rendered as a submit button (default) or a command button. A submit button simply performs a PostBack to the server. You provide an event handler for the button's *Click* event to control the actions performed when the user clicks the submit button.

A *Button* control can also be used as a command button, which is one of a set of buttons that work together as a group, such as a toolbar. You define a button as a command button by assigning a value to its *CommandName* property. For example, you might create a set of buttons to allow a user to control video playback on your page. You might include back, pause, play, and forward buttons. You would define each to have a unique *CommandName* value. Figure 2-15 shows an example.

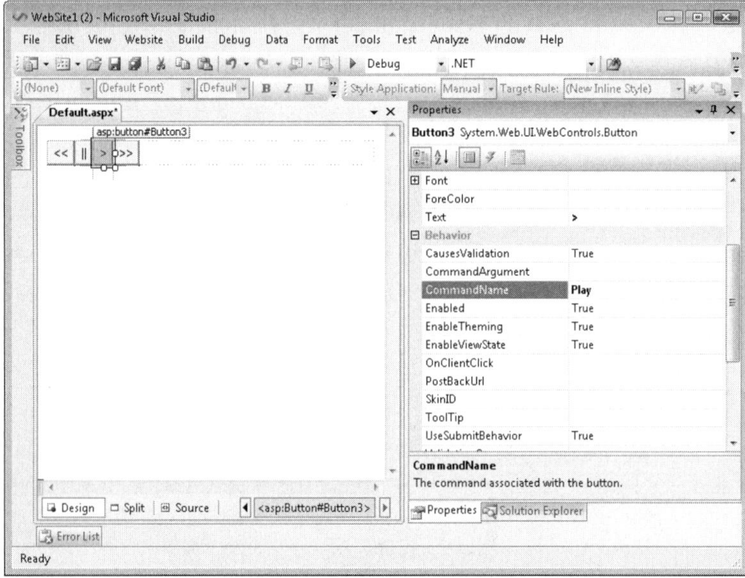

FIGURE 2-15 A set of command buttons on a Web page

When a user clicks one of the command buttons, its *Command* event is called on the server. This event is passed an instance of *CommandEventArgs* as a parameter. You can use these arguments to find out which button was clicked and respond accordingly. A common pattern is to create a single command event handler and wire up each button to it. Inside the event handler you can determine the button selected and take the appropriate action. The following code provides an example:

```
'VB
Protected Sub Playback_Command(ByVal sender As Object, _
```

```
  ByVal e As System.Web.UI.WebControls.CommandEventArgs) _
  Handles Button2.Command

  Select Case e.CommandName
    Case "Back"
      Response.Write("back")
    Case "Pause"
      Response.Write("pause")
    Case "Play"
      Response.Write("play")
    Case "Forward"
      Response.Write("forward")
  End Select

End Sub

//C#
protected void Playback_Command(object sender, CommandEventArgs e)
{
  switch (e.CommandName) {
    case "Back":
      Response.Write("back");
      break;
    case "Pause":
      Response.Write("pause");
      break;
    case "Play":
      Response.Write("play");
      break;
    case "Forward":
      Response.Write("forward");
      break;
  }
}
```

You can also use the *CommandArgument* property of the *Button* control to provide additional information about the command to perform. This property is also available from the *CommandEventArgs* object.

The *Button* control also contains a *CausesValidation* property. This property, set to *true* by default, causes page validation to be performed when a *Button* control is clicked. Set the *CausesValidation* property to *false* when you want a *button* control to bypass page validation. Reset and help buttons are examples of buttons that typically bypass validation. See Chapter 3, "Input Validation and Site Navigation," for more details on page validation.

The *CheckBox* Control

The *CheckBox* control gives the user the ability to select between true and false. The *CheckBox* control's *Text* property specifies its caption. Use the *TextAlign* property to specify on which side of the check box the caption appears. The *Checked* property is used in your code to both set and get the status of the *CheckBox* control.

The *CheckedChanged* event is raised when the state of the *CheckBox* control changes. By default, the *AutoPostBack* property of the *CheckBox* control is set to *false*. This means that changing the checked state does not cause a PostBack. However, the *CheckChanged* event will still be raised when another control causes a PostBack.

EXAM TIP

If you need to create groups of *CheckBox* controls, consider using the *CheckBoxList* control. The *CheckBox* provides more granular layout control, but the *CheckBoxList* control is easier to use when binding with data.

The *RadioButton* Control

The *RadioButton* control gives the user the ability to select between mutually exclusive *RadioButton* controls in a group. This is useful when you are asking a user to select a single item from a group of items. To group multiple *RadioButton* controls together, specify the same *GroupName* for each *RadioButton* control in the group. ASP.NET ensures that the selected radio button is mutually exclusive within the group. The *RadioButton* control's *Text* property specifies its caption. The *TextAlign* property is used to specify the side on which the caption appears. Figure 2-16 shows an example of working with two groups of radio buttons on the same page.

You determine which button is selected in your code by reading the *Checked* property of each control. The *RadioButton* control also exposes the *CheckedChanged* event for responding when a user clicks a given radio button. This event does not automatically cause a PostBack to the server.

EXAM TIP

Be sure to also consider using the *RadioButtonList control.* The *RadioButton* provides more granular control over layout, but the *RadioButtonList* control is easier to use when binding with data.

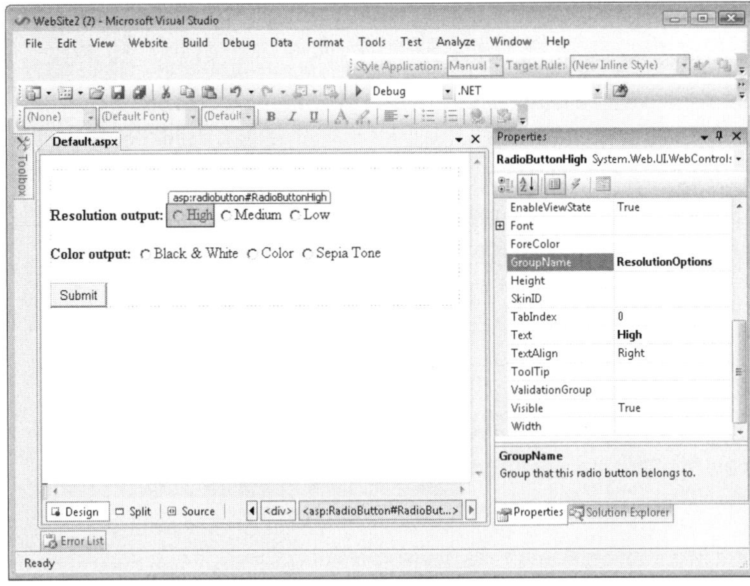

FIGURE 2-16 Defining properties of the *RadioButton* control on a Web page

Quick Check

1. What are the two types of Web server *Button* controls that can be created?
2. How do you create a *TextBox* for retrieving a password from a user?
3. How do you make a *CheckBox* cause immediate PostBack to the server?

Quick Check Answers

1. The two types of Web server *Button* controls are submit and command buttons.
2. You can mask the user's entered password by setting the *TextMode* property of the *TextBox* control to *Password*.
3. You can force an immediate PostBack for a *CheckBox* control by setting its *AutoPostBack* property to *true*.

LAB Working with Web Server Controls

In this lab, you work with the Web server controls that are defined in this chapter.

If you encounter a problem completing an exercise, the completed projects are available on the companion CD in the Code folder.

EXERCISE 1 Adding Controls to the Web Page

In this exercise, you add Web server controls to a Web page.

1. Open Visual Studio and create a new Web site called **WebServerControls**.
2. Open the Default.aspx Web page in Design view.
3. Drag a *Label, CheckBox, TextBox*, three *RadioButtons, and a Button* control onto the Web page. Change the *Text* properties of these controls to match Figure 2-17.

   In addition, name these items **LabelInformation**, **CheckBoxAdmin**, **TextBoxUser-Name**, **RadioButton1**, **RadioButton2**, **RadioButton3**, and **ButtonSave**, respectively. Also, set the *GroupName* for the radio buttons to **ApplicationRole**.

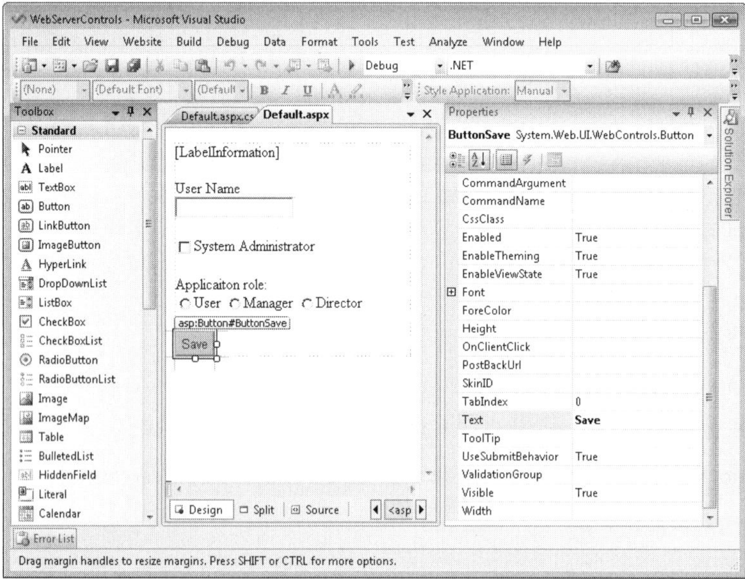

FIGURE 2-17 Drag Web server controls onto the page as shown

4. Right-click the Web page and select View Code to open the code-behind page. Notice that no additional code was added to the code-behind page.
5. Run the Web application. Click the *Button*, *CheckBox*, and *RadioButton* controls. Observe the behavior of these controls. Notice that the *Button* is the only control that performs a PostBack to the server. Also notice that the *RadioButton* controls are not mutually exclusive.
6. Open the page in Design view. Select the *TextBox* control and set its *MaxLength* property to **12** to restrict user input.
7. Run the page and type in the *TextBox* control. Notice that you cannot type more than 12 characters into the control.

8. Double-click the *CheckBox* control to add the *CheckedChanged* event handler. Add code to replace its *Text* property based on whether or not the user has selected the check box. Your code should look like the following:

```
'VB
Protected Sub CheckBoxAdmin_CheckedChanged(ByVal sender As Object, _
  ByVal e As System.EventArgs) Handles CheckBoxAdmin.CheckedChanged

  If CheckBoxAdmin.Checked Then
    CheckBoxAdmin.Text = "System Administrator"
  Else
    CheckBoxAdmin.Text = "Check to set as system administrator"
  End If

End Sub

//C#
protected void CheckBoxAdmin_CheckedChanged(object sender, EventArgs e)
{
  if (CheckBoxAdmin.Checked)
  {
    CheckBoxAdmin.Text = "System Administrator";
  }
  else
  {
    CheckBoxAdmin.Text = "Check to set as system administrator";
  }
}
```

9. Run the page. Notice that changing the *CheckBox* control has no effect. Click Save and notice that the text changes as the button causes a PostBack. Return to the page and set the *AutoPostBack* property of the *CheckBox* control to *true*. Rerun the page and select the *CheckBox* to see the results.
10. To make the *RadioButton* controls mutually exclusive, these controls must have the same *GroupName* property setting. Assign *ApplicationRole* to the *GroupName* property of all three *RadioButton* controls.
11. Run the page and select each of the radio buttons. Notice that they are now mutually exclusive.
12. Open the page in Design view. Double-click the *Button* control to add the button's *Click* event handler to your code-behind file. Add the following code to populate the *Label* indicating the page's data has been saved:

```
'VB
Protected Sub ButtonSave_Click(ByVal sender As Object, _
  ByVal e As System.EventArgs) Handles ButtonSave.Click
```

```
    LabelInformation.Text = "User information saved."

End Sub

//C#
protected void ButtonSave_Click(object sender, EventArgs e)
{
  LabelInformation.Text = "User information saved.";
}
```

13. Run the page, click Save, and notice the results.

Lesson Summary

- The *Label* control displays text at a specific location on the Web page using the properties that have been assigned to the *Label* control.
- The *TextBox* control collects text from the user.
- The *Button* control displays a push button on the Web page that can be clicked to trigger a PostBack to the Web server.
- The *CheckBox* control gives the user the ability to select between true and false.
- The *RadioButton* control gives the user the ability to select between mutually exclusive *RadioButton* controls in a group.

Lesson Review

You can use the following questions to test your knowledge of the information in Lesson 2, "Exploring Common Server Controls."

The questions are also available on the companion CD if you prefer to review them in electronic form.

> ***NOTE*** **ANSWERS**
>
> **Answers to these questions and explanations of why each answer choice is right or wrong are located in the "Answers" section at the end of the book.**

1. If you want multiple *RadioButton* controls to be mutually exclusive, what property must you set?

A. *Exclusive*

B. *MutuallyExclusive*

C. *Grouped*

D. *GroupName*

2. You are creating a Web page that has several related buttons, such as fast forward, reverse, play, stop, and pause. You want to create a single event handler that processes the PostBack from these *Button* controls. Other than the normal submit button, what type of button can you create as a solution?

   A. OneToMany

   B. Command

   C. Reset

   D. ManyToOne

3. In Design view, what is the simplest way to create an event handler for the default event of a server control?

   A. Open the code-behind page and write the code.

   B. Right-click the control and select Create Handler.

   C. Drag an event handler from the Toolbox to the desired control.

   D. Double-click the control.

Lesson 3: Exploring Specialized Server Controls

It was not long ago when creating something as basic as a calendar on a Web page was a time-consuming task involving the creation of HTML tables with hyperlinks on each date. You also had to create JavaScript to process the selection of a date, and more. With ASP.NET, common tasks such as creating a calendar involve simply dragging and dropping a feature-rich control on your Web page.

The previous lesson covered some of the more basic controls used to build Web pages. There are, of course, many more controls available for use. This lesson covers the more specialized Web server controls. These are controls that go beyond those basic controls but are not covered elsewhere in the chapter.

After this lesson, you will be able to:

- Use the following Web server controls:
  - *Literal*
  - *Table*, *TableRow*, and *TableCell*
  - *Image*
  - *ImageButton*
  - *ImageMap*
  - *Calendar*
  - *FileUpload*
  - *Panel*
  - *MultiView*
  - *View*
  - *Wizard*

Estimated lesson time: 60 minutes

The *Literal* Control

The *Literal* control is similar to the *Label* control in that both controls are used to display static text on a Web page. The *Literal* control does not inherit from *WebControl*, as shown in the *Literal* control's object model in Figure 2-18. The *Literal* control does not provide substantial functionality and does not add any HTML elements to the Web page, whereas the *Label* is rendered as a *<span>* tag. This means that the *Literal* control does not have a *style* property, and you therefore cannot apply styles to its content.

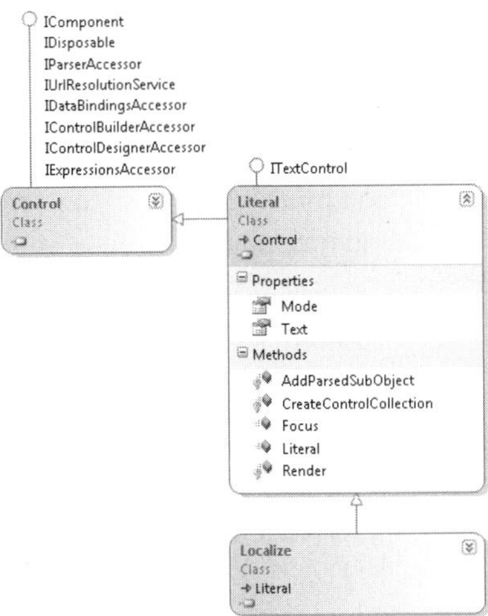

FIGURE 2-18 The *Literal* control object model

The *Literal* control is useful when you need to add text to the output of the page dynamically (from the server) but do not want to use a *Label*. If your text is static, you can simply add it to the markup of the page (you do not need a *Label* or a *Literal* control). The *Literal* control contains the *Mode* property, which is used to specify particular handling of the content of the *Text* property. The modes available and their descriptions are shown in Table 2-4.

TABLE 2-4 The *Literal* Control's *Mode* Property

MODE	DESCRIPTION
PassThrough	The *Text* content is rendered as is. This includes HTML markup and script. These items are output to the page and processed by the browser as HTML and script.
Encode	The *Text* content is HTML-encoded; that is, any HTML markup or script is actually treated like text and not HTML or script.
Transform	The *Text* content is converted to match the markup language of the requesting browser, such as HTML, Extensible Hypertext Markup Language (XHTML), Wireless Markup Language (WML), or Compact Hypertext Markup Language (cHTML). If the markup language is HTML or XHTML, the content is passed through to the browser. For other markup languages, invalid tags are removed.

As an example, consider a Web page with three *Literal* controls, one for each *Mode* property setting. Suppose the following code is added to the code-behind page to demonstrate the use of the *Literal* control and the effect of the *Mode* property:

```
'VB
Protected Sub Page_Load(ByVal sender As Object, _
  ByVal e As System.EventArgs) Handles Me.Load

  Literal1.Text = _
    "This is an <font size=7>example</font><script>alert(""Hi"");</script>"
  Literal2.Text = _
    "This is an <font size=7>example</font><script>alert(""Hi"");</script>"
  Literal3.Text = _
    "This is an <font size=7>example<script>alert(""Hi"");</script>"
  Literal1.Mode = LiteralMode.Encode
  Literal2.Mode = LiteralMode.PassThrough
  Literal3.Mode = LiteralMode.Transform

End Sub

//C#
protected void Page_Load(object sender, EventArgs e)
{
  Literal1.Text =
    @"This is an <font size=7>example</font><script>alert(""Hi"");</script>";
  Literal2.Text =
    @"This is an <font size=7>example</font><script>alert(""Hi"");</script>";
  Literal3.Text =
    @"This is an <font size=7>example</font><script>alert(""Hi"");</script>";
  Literal1.Mode = LiteralMode.Encode;
  Literal2.Mode = LiteralMode.PassThrough;
  Literal3.Mode = LiteralMode.Transform;
}
```

Figure 2-19 shows the rendered output of the *Literal* control when the Web page is displayed. The alert message was displayed twice: once for *Transform* and once for *PassThrough*. Note that this is a security risk if you are setting the *Text* property of the *Literal* control dynamically from user input. However, the encoded version of the *Literal* control encodes the HTML and script and displays it to the browser window.

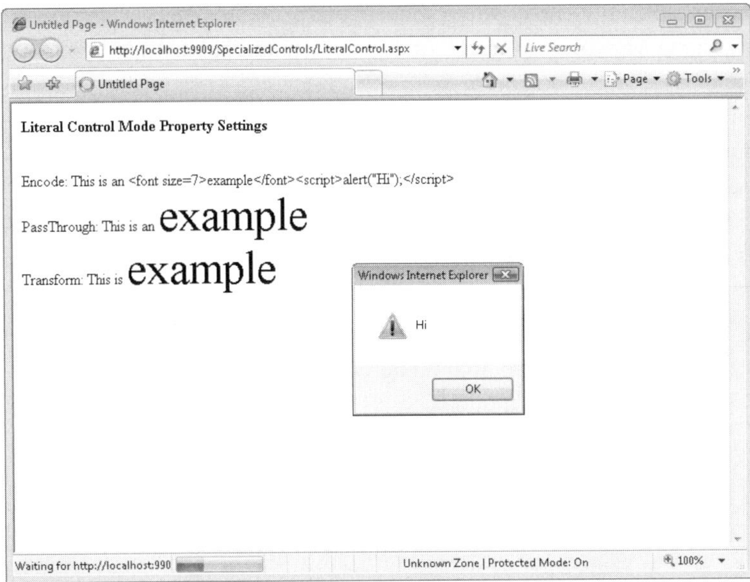

FIGURE 2-19 *Literal* controls rendered using different *Mode* settings

The *Table*, *TableRow*, and *TableCell* Controls

Web developers have been using tables to format information displayed on Web pages since the first HTML pages. Tables are useful for tabular data, but they can also help with the layout of graphics and controls on a form. The concept of columns and rows is a powerful layout technique for Web pages.

HTML provides the *<table>* tag for defining a table, the *<tr>* tag for creating a row, and the *<td>* tag for defining a column in the row. Web developers should be very familiar with these tags. ASP.NET provides the *Table* control for creating and managing tables without these tags. Like its HTML counterpart, the *Table* control can be used to display static information on a page. However, the *Table* control's real power comes from the ability to programmatically add *TableRow* and *TableCell* controls from your code at run time. If you only need to display static information, consider using the HTML tags instead.

EXAM TIP

There is also an *HtmlTable* control. It can be created from the HTML *<table>* tag by adding the *runat="server"* attribute to the tag and assigning an *ID* to the tag. However, the *Table* control is easier to use because it provides a programming model that is consistent with the *TableRow* and *TableCell* controls.

Again, the *Table* control is the right choice when you need to programmatically add rows and cells to a table at run time. The rows are added using the *TableRow* control and the cells are added using the *TableCell* control. You add these rows and cells in a similar manner as you would dynamically create other controls on a page. This also means the same rules apply to these dynamically created controls. That is, for them to be available at PostBack they need to be re-created when the page posts back to the server. Your page might only be for display or it might be simple enough to manage. In either case you should be fine to use a *Table* control. However, if your needs are more complicated, you have a lot of data, and you need it to survive PostBack, consider using the *Repeater, DataList,* or *GridView* controls. The *Table* control is also very useful for control developers who use a table as part of a custom control.

The *Table* control provides an object model that is consistent with other Web controls. Figure 2-20 shows the *Table* control's object model.

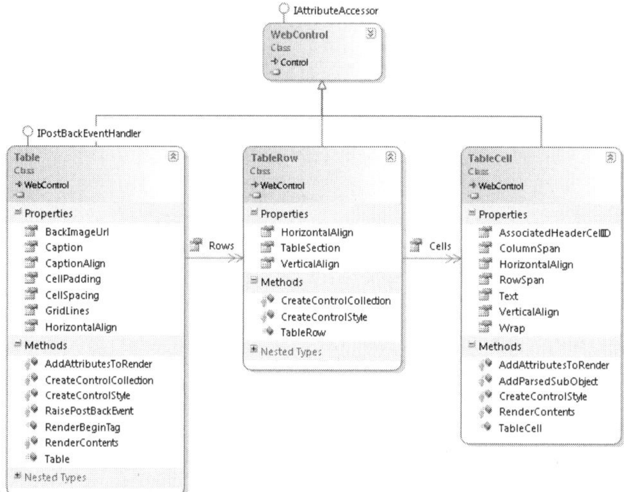

FIGURE 2-20 The *Table* control's object mode

Notice that the *Table* control contains a *Rows* collection property (shown as a collection association in Figure 2-20). This property is a collection of *TableRow* controls. It is used to add and access the rows of your table. The *TableRow* control contains a *Cells* collection property (also shown as a collection association). This property represents a collection of *TableCell* controls. These are the actual cells (or columns) within the given row.

The *Table, TableRow,* and *TableCell* all inherit from the *WebControl* class. This class provides base properties such as *Font, BackColor,* and *ForeColor.* If you set these properties at the *Table level,* you can override them in *TableRow instances*, and in turn, the *TableRow* settings can be overridden in the *TableCell instances.*

Adding Rows and Cells Dynamically to a *Table* Control

Visual Studio provides a designer for adding rows and cells to *Table* controls on your page. You access this design tool from the *Table* control's *Rows* property in the Properties window. From here you can add rows to your table. Each row also allows you to manage its *Cells* collection in a similar manner. Figure 2-21 shows this dialog box in action.

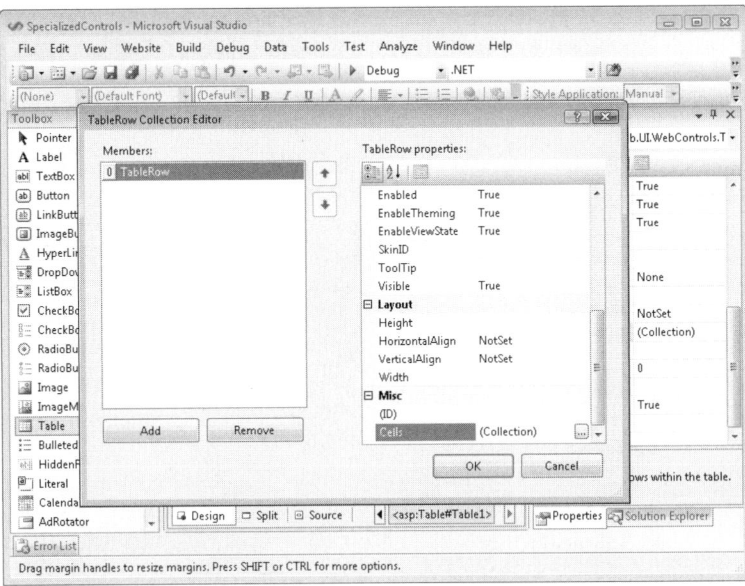

FIGURE 2-21 The *TableRow* collection editor in Visual Studio

The real power of the *Table* control, however, is being able to work with it from your code. The following steps show how to dynamically add *TableCell* and *TableRow* objects to an existing *Table* control.

1. Open a Visual Studio Web site or create a new one. Open (or create) a Web page with which to work.
2. From the Toolbox, drag a *Table* control onto your page.
3. Open the code-behind file for the given page and add a *PreInit* event to the page.
4. Inside the *PreInit* event write a *for* loop to create five new rows in the table.
5. Inside this loop, add another *for* loop to create three columns for each row.
6. Inside this loop, modify the *TableCell.Text* property to identify the row and column. The following code provides an example:

```
'VB
Protected Sub Page_PreInit(ByVal sender As Object, _
  ByVal e As System.EventArgs) Handles Me.PreInit
```

```
    Table1.BorderWidth = 1
    For row As Integer = 0 To 4
      Dim tr As New TableRow()
      For column As Integer = 0 To 2
        Dim tc As New TableCell()
        tc.Text = String.Format("Row:{0} Cell:{1}", row, column)
        tc.BorderWidth = 1
        tr.Cells.Add(tc)
      Next column
      Table1.Rows.Add(tr)
    Next row

End Sub

//C#
protected void Page_PreInit(object sender, EventArgs e)
{
  Table1.BorderWidth = 1;
  for (int row = 0; row < 5; row++)
  {
    TableRow tr = new TableRow();
    for (int column = 0; column < 3; column++)
    {
      TableCell tc = new TableCell();
      tc.Text = string.Format("Row:{0} Cell:{1}", row, column);
      tc.BorderWidth = 1;
      tr.Cells.Add(tc);
    }
    Table1.Rows.Add(tr);
  }
}
```

In the code example, notice that the code starts by setting the *BorderWidth* property of the *Table* control to 1, which causes the *Table* to have a line around its outside edges. The *TableCell* objects also have their *BorderWidth* set to 1, which causes each *TableCell* to be outlined as well. When the Web page is displayed, it will look like the page shown in Figure 2-22.

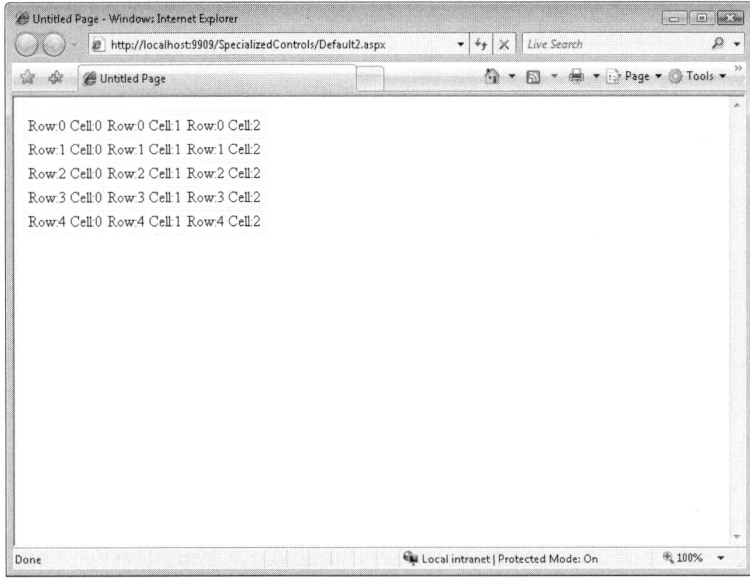

FIGURE 2-22 A Web page showing the result of dynamically creating *TableRow* and *TableCell* controls

The *Image* Control

The *Image* control can be used to display an image on a Web page. Again, this control should be used when you need to manipulate the properties of the control in server-side code. If you simply need to embed a static image on your page you can use the HTML *<img>* tag. In fact, when the *Image* control is rendered to a page it generates an *<img>* element.

The *Image* control inherits directly from the *WebControl* class. The *ImageMap* and *ImageButton* controls inherit directly from the *Image* control. Figure 2-23 shows the class hierarchy of the *Image* control.

The *Image* control is represented as the *<asp:Image>* element in the source and has no content embedded between its opening and closing tags. Therefore you can write this element as a singleton (closing the tag with /> instead of using a separate closing tag). It is important to understand that the *image itself* is not embedded in the Web page; instead, when the browser encounters the *<img>* element with the *href* attribute, the browser initiates a separate request for the image from the server.

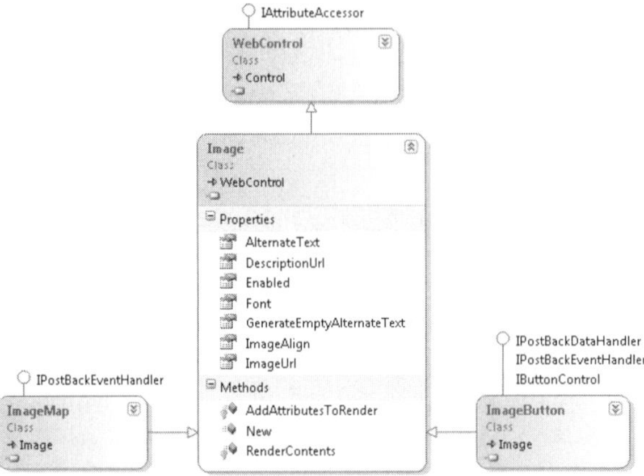

FIGURE 2-23 The *Image* control hierarchy

The *Image* control's primary property, *ImageUrl*, indicates the path to the image that is downloaded from the browser and displayed on the page. This property maps directly to the *href* attribute of the *<img>* element in HTML. Some additional properties to consider when working with the *Image* control are as follows:

- The *Image* control also contains a property called *AlternateText*. You can set this property to display a text message in the user's browser when the image is not available or the browser is set to not render the image.
- The *ImageAlign* property of the *Image* control can be set to *NotSet*, *Left*, *Right*, *Baseline*, *Top*, *Middle*, *Bottom*, *AbsBottom*, *AbsMiddle*, or *TextTop*. These settings specify the alignment of the image in relation to the other objects on the Web page.
- The *DescriptionUrl* property is an accessibility feature that is used to provide further explanation of the content and meaning of the image when using nonvisual page readers. This property sets the *longdesc* attribute of the *<img>* element that is generated. This property should be set to the Uniform Resource Locator (URL) of a page that contains details of the image in text or audio format.
- Setting the *GenerateEmptyAlternateText* property to *true* will add the attribute *alt=""* to the *<img>* element that the *Image* control generates. From the accessibility perspective, any image that does not contribute to the meaning of the page, such as a blank image or a page-divider image, should always carry this attribute; it causes the nonvisual page readers to simply ignore the image.

The following code provides an example of a Web page with an *Image* control. An image file called Whale.jpg is inside a folder called Images. An HTML page called WhaleImage-Description.htm, which contains a description that can be used by nonvisual page readers, was also created. The following code demonstrates setting the *Image* control's properties programmatically inside the page's code-behind file.

```
'VB
Protected Sub Page_Load(ByVal sender As Object, _
  ByVal e As System.EventArgs) Handles Me.Load

  Image1.ImageUrl = "images/whale.jpg"
  Image1.DescriptionUrl = "WhaleImageDescription.htm"
  Image1.AlternateText = "This is a picture of a whale"

End Sub

//C#
protected void Page_Load(object sender, EventArgs e)
{
  Image1.ImageUrl = "images/whale.jpg";
  Image1.DescriptionUrl = "WhaleImageDescription.htm";
  Image1.AlternateText = "This is a picture of a whale";
}
```

Figure 2-24 shows the rendered Web page. This includes the alternate text displayed as a ToolTip.

FIGURE 2-24 The rendered *Image* control displaying the *AlternateText* property as a ToolTip

The *ImageButton* Control

The *Image* control does not have a *Click* event. In situations in which a *Click* event is necessary, you can use *ImageButton* or *ImageMap* instead. These controls allow you to treat an image like a clickable button. In addition, you can retrieve the x- and y-coordinates of the user's click. This is useful for determining where on the given image the user has clicked. You can use this information on the server to perform different actions, depending on the area clicked by the user.

The *ImageButton* control is used to display a clickable image on a Web page that can be used to PostBack to the Web server when the image is clicked. This control generates an *<input type="image">* element when rendering to HTML. The *ImageButton* control inherits directly from the *Image* control class as shown in Figure 2-25.

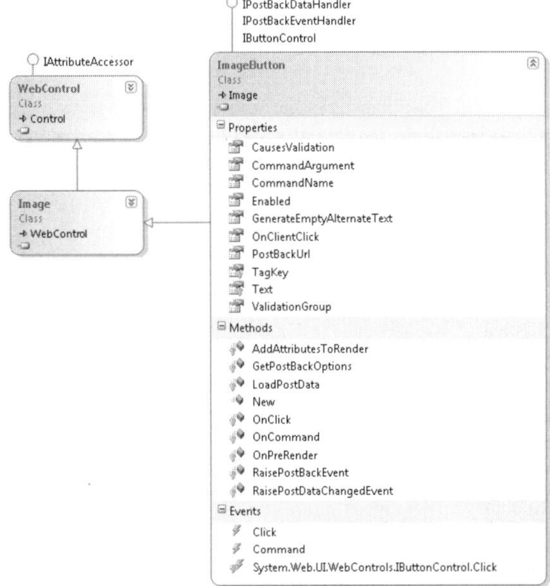

FIGURE 2-25 The *ImageButton* control hierarchy

The *ImageButton* control is represented as an *<asp:ImageButton>* element in Source view and has no content, so you can write this element as a singleton element. Like the *Image* control, the *ImageButton* control's primary property, *ImageUrl*, indicates the path to an image that can be downloaded from the browser and displayed. This property maps directly to the *src* attribute of the *<input>* element in HTML. Because the *ImageButton* inherits from the *Image* control, it also contains the *AlternateText*, *DescriptionUrl*, *ImageAlign*, and *GenerateEmptyAlternateText* properties.

The *ImageButton* control has a *Click* and *Command* event that functions like the *Button* control. The second argument of the *Click* event has a data type of *ImageClickEventArgs*, which lets you retrieve the x- and y-coordinates of the user's click.

Here's another example: A Web page was created and an *ImageButton* control was added to the page. This control uses an image that is both red and blue (redblue.jpg). The following code was added to the code-behind page to show how the *ImageButton* control's properties can be set programmatically and the *Click* event can be implemented.

```
'VB
Partial Class ImageControl
  Inherits System.Web.UI.Page

  Protected Sub Page_Load(ByVal sender As Object, _
    ByVal e As System.EventArgs) Handles Me.Load

    ImageButton1.ImageUrl = "images/redblue.jpg"
    ImageButton1.AlternateText = _
      "This is a button. The left side is red. The right is blue."

  End Sub

  Protected Sub ImageButton1_Click(ByVal sender As Object, _
    ByVal e As System.Web.UI.ImageClickEventArgs) Handles ImageButton1.Click

    ImageButton1.AlternateText = _
      String.Format("Button Clicked at {0},{1}", e.X, e.Y)

  End Sub

End Class

//C#
public partial class ImageButton_Control : System.Web.UI.Page
{
  protected void Page_Load(object sender, EventArgs e)
  {
    ImageButton1.ImageUrl = "images/redblue.jpg";
    ImageButton1.AlternateText =
      "This is a button. The left side is red. The right is blue.";
  }
  protected void ImageButton1_Click(object sender, ImageClickEventArgs e)
  {
    ImageButton1.AlternateText =
      string.Format("Button Clicked at {0},{1}", e.X, e.Y);
  }
}
```

This code sets the *ImageButton* control properties in the *Page_Load* event handler. In the *ImageButton1_Click* event handler, the x- and y-coordinates are retrieved and placed into the

AlternateText property, as shown in Figure 2-26. In this example you can use this information to determine the area (or color) on which the user clicked and make a decision accordingly.

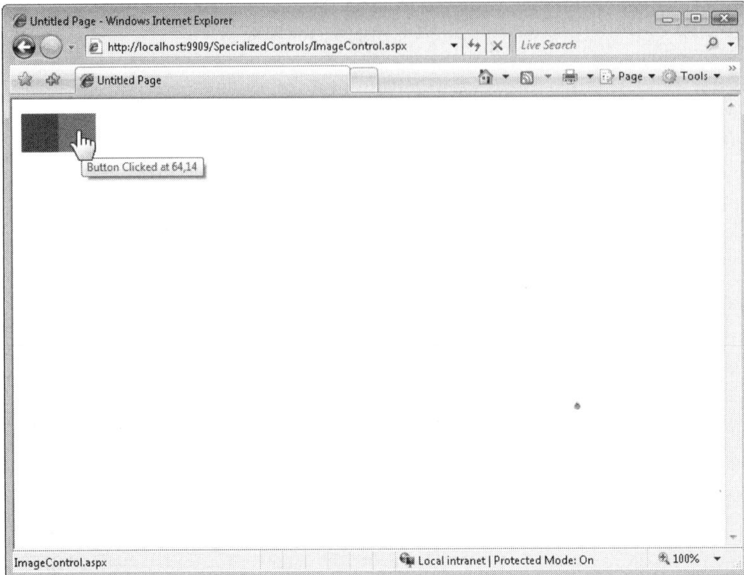

FIGURE 2-26 The rendered *ImageButton* displaying the *AlternateText* message after the *ImageButton* was clicked

The *ImageMap* Control

The *ImageMap* control is used to display a clickable image on a Web page that can be used to PostBack to the Web server when the image is clicked. This control differs from the *Image-Button* control in that the *ImageMap* control allows you to define regions or "hot spots" that cause a *PostBack*, whereas clicking anywhere on an *ImageButton* causes a *PostBack*.

The *ImageMap* control generates an *<img usemap="#myMap">* element in HTML. In addition, a *<map name="myMap">* element with nested *<area>* elements is also created when rendering to HTML.

The *ImageMap* control inherits directly from the *Image* control class. Figure 2-27 shows the class hierarchy.

Like the *Image* control, the *ImageMap* control's primary property, *ImageUrl*, indicates the path to the image that can be downloaded from the browser and displayed. This property maps directly to the *src* attribute of the *<img>* element in HTML. Because the *ImageMap* inherits from the *Image* control, it also contains the *AlternateText*, *DescriptionUrl*, *ImageAlign*, and *GenerateEmptyAlternateText* properties.

In Source view, the *ImageMap* control is represented as an *<asp:ImageMap>* element and has nested hot spot elements that can be *CircleHotSpot*, *RectangleHotSpot*, and *Polygon-HotSpot* elements.

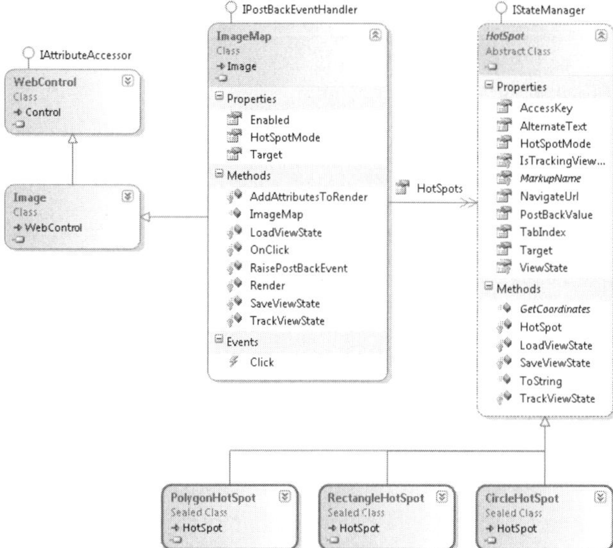

FIGURE 2-27 The *ImageMap* and *HotSpot* control hierarchy

The *ImageMap* control has a *Click* event that functions like the *ImageButton* control. The second argument of the *Click* event has a data type of *ImageMapEventArgs*, which lets you retrieve the *PostBackValue* of the associated hot spot that the user clicked.

Working with *HotSpot* Controls

A hot spot is a predefined area on an image that can be clicked to perform an action. Hot spots can be created to define areas on the image that are displayed by the *ImageMap* control. You can define many overlapping areas, with each layer based on the *HotSpot* definition order. The first *HotSpot* defined takes precedence over the last *HotSpot* defined. The *HotSpot* object model is also shown in Figure 2-27. The classes that inherit from the *HotSpot* are the *CircleHotSpot*, *RectangleHotSpot*, and *PolygonHotSpot*. Table 2-5 contains a list of *HotSpot* properties.

TABLE 2-5 *HotSpot* Properties

PROPERTY	DESCRIPTION
AccessKey	The keyboard shortcut for a *HotSpot*. You can place only a single character into this property. If this property contains "C," for example, a Web user can press Alt+C to navigate to the *HotSpot*.
AlternateText	The text that is displayed for a *HotSpot* when the image is unavailable or renders to a browser that does not support images. This also becomes the *ToolTip*.

PROPERTY	DESCRIPTION
HotSpotMode	The behavior of the *HotSpot* when it is clicked. Can be *NotSet*, *Inactive*, *Navigate*, or *PostBack*.
NavigateUrl	The URL to navigate to when a *HotSpot* object is clicked.
PostBackValue	The string that is passed back to the Web server and is available in the event argument data when the *HotSpot* is clicked.
TabIndex	The tab index number of the *HotSpot*.
Target	The target window or frame that displays the Web page and is linked to the *HotSpot*.

Understanding the *HotSpotMode* Property

The *HotSpotMode* property is used to specify how the *HotSpot* behaves when clicked. You can specify the *HotSpotMode* on either the *HotSpot* or the *ImageMap* control. If you set the *HotSpotMode* on the *HotSpot* and the *ImageMap*, the *HotSpot* takes precedence. This means that you can specify the *HotSpotMode* on the *ImageMap* control to set a default *HotSpot* behavior, but the *HotSpotMode* of the *HotSpot* must be set to *NotSet* to inherit the behavior from the *ImageMap*.

Specifying *Navigate* for the *HotSpotMode* causes the *HotSpot* to navigate to a URL when clicked. The *NavigateUrl* property specifies the URL to which to navigate.

> ***NOTE* *HOTSPOTMODE* DEFAULT**
>
> **If the *ImageMap* and *HotSpot* have their *HotSpotMode* set to *NotSet*, the *HotSpot* defaults to *Navigate*.**

Specifying *PostBack* for the *HotSpotMode* causes the *HotSpot* to generate a *PostBack* to the server when the *HotSpot* is clicked. The *PostBackValue* property specifies a string that is passed back to the Web server in the *ImageMapEventArgs* event data when the *HotSpot* is clicked and the *Click* event is raised.

Specifying *Inactive* for the *HotSpotMode* indicates that the *HotSpot* does not have any behavior when it is clicked. This is used to create an inactive *HotSpot* region within a larger active *HotSpot*, thus allowing you to create complex *HotSpot* zones within an *ImageMap* control. You must specify the inactive *HotSpot* before you designate the active *HotSpot* in the *ImageMap* control.

The following code presents an example of a Web page that contains a *Label* and *ImageMap* control. The *ImageMap* control is set to use a stoplight image (red, yellow, green). The following code was added to the code-behind page to show how the *ImageMap* control's properties can be set programmatically and how the *Click* event can be implemented to display the *HotSpot* that is clicked:

```
'VB
Partial Class HotSpotVb
  Inherits System.Web.UI.Page

  Protected Sub Page_Load(ByVal sender As Object, _
    ByVal e As System.EventArgs) Handles Me.Load

    ImageMapStopLight.ImageUrl = "images/stoplight.jpg"
    ImageMapStopLight.AlternateText = "Stoplight picture"
    ImageMapStopLight.HotSpotMode = HotSpotMode.PostBack

    Dim redHotSpot As New RectangleHotSpot()
    redHotSpot.Top = 0
    redHotSpot.Bottom = 40
    redHotSpot.Left = 0
    redHotSpot.Right = 40
    redHotSpot.PostBackValue = "RED"
    ImageMapStopLight.HotSpots.Add(redHotSpot)

    Dim yellowHotSpot As New RectangleHotSpot()
    yellowHotSpot.Top = 41
    yellowHotSpot.Bottom = 80
    yellowHotSpot.Left = 0
    yellowHotSpot.Right = 40
    yellowHotSpot.PostBackValue = "YELLOW"
    ImageMapStopLight.HotSpots.Add(yellowHotSpot)

    Dim greenHotSpot As New RectangleHotSpot()
    greenHotSpot.Top = 81
    greenHotSpot.Bottom = 120
    greenHotSpot.Left = 0
    greenHotSpot.Right = 40
    greenHotSpot.PostBackValue = "GREEN"
    ImageMapStopLight.HotSpots.Add(greenHotSpot)

  End Sub

  Protected Sub ImageMapStopLight_Click(ByVal sender As Object, _
    ByVal e As System.Web.UI.WebControls.ImageMapEventArgs) Handles ImageMapStopLight.
Click

    Label1.Text = "You clicked the " + e.PostBackValue + " rectangle."

  End Sub

End Class
```

```
//C#
public partial class HotSpotControl : System.Web.UI.Page
{
  protected void Page_Load(object sender, EventArgs e)
  {
    ImageMapStopLight.ImageUrl = "images/stoplight.jpg";
    ImageMapStopLight.AlternateText = "Stoplight picture";
    ImageMapStopLight.HotSpotMode = HotSpotMode.PostBack;

    RectangleHotSpot redHotSpot = new RectangleHotSpot();
    redHotSpot.Top = 0;
    redHotSpot.Bottom = 40;
    redHotSpot.Left = 0;
    redHotSpot.Right = 40;
    redHotSpot.PostBackValue = "RED";
    ImageMapStopLight.HotSpots.Add(redHotSpot);

    RectangleHotSpot yellowHotSpot = new RectangleHotSpot();
    yellowHotSpot.Top = 41;
    yellowHotSpot.Bottom = 80;
    yellowHotSpot.Left = 0;
    yellowHotSpot.Right = 40;
    yellowHotSpot.PostBackValue = "YELLOW";
    ImageMapStopLight.HotSpots.Add(yellowHotSpot);

    RectangleHotSpot greenHotSpot = new RectangleHotSpot();
    greenHotSpot.Top = 81;
    greenHotSpot.Bottom = 120;
    greenHotSpot.Left = 0;
    greenHotSpot.Right = 40;
    greenHotSpot.PostBackValue = "GREEN";
    ImageMapStopLight.HotSpots.Add(greenHotSpot);

  }
  protected void ImageMapStopLight_Click(object sender, ImageMapEventArgs e)
  {
    Label1.Text = "You clicked the " + e.PostBackValue + " rectangle.";
  }
}
```

In the sample code, clicking a *HotSpot* on the *ImageMap* causes a *PostBack* of the *PostBackValue* to the server. The *ImageMapEventArgs* contains the *PostBackValue*. Inside the click event, the *PostBackValue* is placed into the *Text* property of the *Label control*. Figure 2-28 shows the *page* after the image has been clicked.

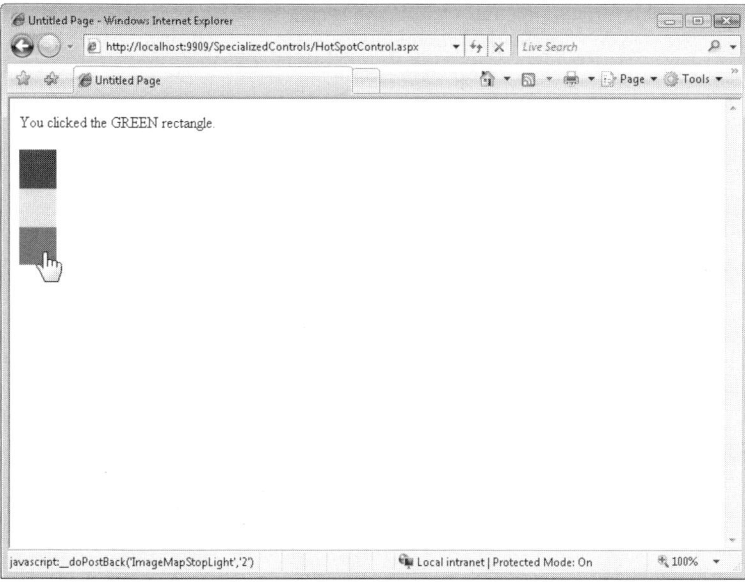

FIGURE 2-28 The rendered *ImageMap* displaying the *PostBackValue* message in the *Label* after the image was clicked

The *Calendar* Control

The *Calendar* control allows you to display a calendar on a Web page. The calendar can be used when asking a user to select a given date or series of dates. Users can navigate between years, months, and days. The *Calendar* control is a complex, powerful Web server control that you can use to add calendar features to your page. The *Calendar* control inherits directly from the *WebControl* class as shown in Figure 2-29.

The *Calendar* control is represented as an *<asp:Calendar>* element in Source view. It can contain style elements to change the look of the control. When rendered to a user's browser, the control generates an HTML *<table>* element and a set of associated JavaScript.

The *Calendar* control can be used to select a single date or multiple dates. The *SelectionMode* property controls this. It can be set to one of the following settings:

- ***Day*** Allows selection of a single date.
- ***DayWeek*** Allows the selection of either a single date or a complete week.
- ***DayWeekMonth*** Allows selection of single date, a complete week, or the whole month.
- ***None*** Does not allow you to select any date.

The *Calendar* control contains many additional properties that can be used to adjust the format and behavior of this control. Table 2-6 contains a list of the *Calendar* properties and their associated descriptions.

FIGURE 2-29 The *Calendar* control hierarchy

TABLE 2-6 *Calendar* Properties

PROPERTY	DESCRIPTION
Caption	The text that is rendered in the *Calendar*.
CaptionAlign	The alignment of the caption: *Top*, *Bottom*, *Left*, *Right*, or *NotSet*.
CellPadding	The space between each cell and the cell border.
CellSpacing	The spacing between each cell.
DayHeaderStyle	The style to be applied to days of the week.
DayNameFormat	The format for the names of the days of the week: *FirstLetter*, *FirstTwoLetters*, *Full*, *Short*, *Shortest*.
DayStyle	The default style for a calendar day.
FirstDayOfWeek	The day of the week to display in the first column of the *Calendar* control.

PROPERTY	DESCRIPTION
NextMonthText	The text to be displayed in the next month navigation control; ">" is the default. This only works if *ShowNextPrevMonth* property is *true*.
NextPrevFormat	The tool that sets the format of the next and previous navigation controls. Can be set to *CustomText* (default), *FullMonth* (for example, January), or *ShortMonth* (for example, Jan).
NextPrevStyle	The style to be applied to the next and previous navigation controls.
OtherMonthDayStyle	The tool that specifies the style for days on the calendar that are displayed and are not in the current month.
PrevMonthText	The text to be displayed in the previous month navigation control, which defaults as "<". This only works if the *ShowNextPrevMonth* property is *true*.
SelectedDate	The date selected by the user.
SelectedDates	A collection of *DateTime* values that represents all of the dates that were selected by the user. This property contains only a single date if the *SelectionMode* property is set to *CalendarSelectionMode.Day*, which allows only single date selection.
SelectedDayStyle	The style of the selected day.
SelectionMode	A value that indicates how many dates can be selected. Value can be *Day*, *DayWeek*, *DayWeekMonth*, or *None*.
SelectMonthText	The text displayed for the month selection column. The default value is ">>".
SelectorStyle	The style for the week and month selectors.
SelectWeekText	The text of the week selection in the week selector.
ShowDayHeader	An indicator that shows whether the day header should be displayed.
ShowGridLines	An indicator that tells whether grid lines should be displayed.
ShowNextPrevMonth	An indicator for whether the next and previous month selectors should be displayed.
ShowTitle	An indicator for whether the title should be displayed.
TitleFormat	A tool that sets the format for displaying the month (*Month*), or the month and year (*MonthYear*).
TitleStyle	The style for the title.

PROPERTY	DESCRIPTION
TodayDayStyle	The style of today's date.
TodaysDate	Today's date.
UseAccessibleHeader	A control that, when set to *true*, generates <*th*> for day headers (default), or, when set to *false*, generates <*td*> for day headers to be compatible with version 1.0 of the .NET Framework.
VisibleDate	A display that specifies which month to display in the *Calendar* control.
WeekendDayStyle	The style of weekend days.

The *Calendar* control also exposes a few events with which to work. The primary event, *SelectionChanged*, is triggered after a user selects a date on the control. The *SelectionChanged* event causes a *PostBack* when the user selects a new date. Inside the event handler you access the selected dates via the *SelectedDates* property. The *SelectedDate* property simply points to the selected date in the *SelectedDates* collection.

The *VisibleMonthChanged* event also causes a *PostBack* when the user selects a different month to be viewed. You can handle this event if you need to respond to the user changing months in the control.

The *Calendar* control is typically used as a date picker control. However, it can also be used to display a schedule. The trick to using the *Calendar* control to display scheduled items and special days such as a holiday is to make the control large enough to display text in each day. You can then add *Label* controls (or other controls) to the *Cell* object's *Controls* collection in the *DayRender* event handler. The *Calendar* control's *DayRender* event triggers when each day is being readied for output. This is not a PostBack but an event that fires on the server as the control renders its HTML. This allows you to add text or controls to the day being rendered.

The following code example shows how a *Calendar* control can be used to display a schedule. In this example, a Web page was created and a *Calendar* control was added to the page. The following code was added to the code-behind page to show how the *Calendar* control's properties can be set programmatically and the *Calendar* control events can be used to render individual days.

```
'VB
Partial Class CalendarControl
  Inherits System.Web.UI.Page

  Dim _scheduleData As Hashtable

  Protected Sub Page_Load(ByVal sender As Object, _
    ByVal e As System.EventArgs) Handles Me.Load
```

```
  _scheduleData = GetSchedule()

  Calendar1.Caption = "Personal Schedule"
  Calendar1.FirstDayOfWeek = WebControls.FirstDayOfWeek.Sunday
  Calendar1.NextPrevFormat = NextPrevFormat.ShortMonth
  Calendar1.TitleFormat = TitleFormat.MonthYear
  Calendar1.ShowGridLines = True
  Calendar1.DayStyle.HorizontalAlign = HorizontalAlign.Left
  Calendar1.DayStyle.VerticalAlign = VerticalAlign.Top
  Calendar1.DayStyle.Height = New Unit(75)
  Calendar1.DayStyle.Width = New Unit(100)
  Calendar1.OtherMonthDayStyle.BackColor = Drawing.Color.Cornsilk
  Calendar1.TodaysDate = New DateTime(2009, 2, 1)
  Calendar1.VisibleDate = Calendar1.TodaysDate

End Sub

Private Function GetSchedule() As Hashtable

  Dim schedule As New Hashtable()

  schedule("2/9/2009") = "Vacation Day"
  schedule("2/18/2009") = "Budget planning meeting @ 3:00pm"
  schedule("2/24/2009") = "Dinner plans with friends @ 7:00pm"
  schedule("2/27/2009") = "Travel Day"

  schedule("3/5/2009") = "Conf call @ 1:00pm"
  schedule("3/10/2009") = "Meet with art director for lunch"
  schedule("3/27/2009") = "Vacation Day"

  Return schedule

End Function

Protected Sub Calendar1_SelectionChanged(ByVal sender As Object, _
  ByVal e As System.EventArgs) Handles Calendar1.SelectionChanged

  LabelAction.Text = "Selection changed to: " _
    + Calendar1.SelectedDate.ToShortDateString()

End Sub

Protected Sub Calendar1_VisibleMonthChanged(ByVal sender As Object, _
  ByVal e As System.Web.UI.WebControls.MonthChangedEventArgs) _
  Handles Calendar1.VisibleMonthChanged
```

```
    LabelAction.Text = "Month changed to: " + e.NewDate.ToShortDateString()

  End Sub

  Protected Sub Calendar1_DayRender(ByVal sender As Object, _
    ByVal e As System.Web.UI.WebControls.DayRenderEventArgs) _
    Handles Calendar1.DayRender

    If Not _scheduleData(e.Day.Date.ToShortDateString()) Is Nothing Then

      Dim lit = New Literal()
      lit.Text = "<br />"
      e.Cell.Controls.Add(lit)

      Dim lbl = New Label()
      lbl.Text = _scheduleData(e.Day.Date.ToShortDateString())
      lbl.Font.Size = New FontUnit(FontSize.Small)
      e.Cell.Controls.Add(lbl)

    End If

  End Sub

End Class

//C#
public partial class CalendarCSharp : System.Web.UI.Page
{

  Hashtable _scheduleData;

  protected void Page_Load(object sender, EventArgs e)
  {
    _scheduleData = GetSchedule();

    Calendar1.Caption = "Personal Schedule";
    Calendar1.FirstDayOfWeek = FirstDayOfWeek.Sunday;
    Calendar1.NextPrevFormat = NextPrevFormat.ShortMonth;
    Calendar1.TitleFormat = TitleFormat.MonthYear;
    Calendar1.ShowGridLines = true;
    Calendar1.DayStyle.HorizontalAlign = HorizontalAlign.Left;
    Calendar1.DayStyle.VerticalAlign = VerticalAlign.Top;
    Calendar1.DayStyle.Height = new Unit(75);
    Calendar1.DayStyle.Width = new Unit(100);
    Calendar1.OtherMonthDayStyle.BackColor = System.Drawing.Color.Cornsilk;
```

```
  Calendar1.TodaysDate = new DateTime(2009, 2, 1);
  Calendar1.VisibleDate = Calendar1.TodaysDate;

}

private Hashtable GetSchedule()
{
  Hashtable schedule = new Hashtable();

  schedule["2/9/2009"] = "Vacation Day";
  schedule["2/18/2009"] = "Budget planning meeting @ 3:00pm";
  schedule["2/24/2009"] = "Dinner plans with friends @ 7:00pm";
  schedule["2/27/2009"] = "Travel Day";

  schedule["3/5/2009"] = "Conf call @ 1:00pm";
  schedule["3/10/2009"] = "Meet with art director for lunch";
  schedule["3/27/2009"] = "Vacation Day";

  return schedule;
}


protected void Calendar1_SelectionChanged(object sender, EventArgs e)
{
  LabelAction.Text = "Selection changed to: "
    + Calendar1.SelectedDate.ToShortDateString();
}

protected void Calendar1_VisibleMonthChanged(object sender,
  MonthChangedEventArgs e)
{
  LabelAction.Text = "Month changed to: " + e.NewDate.ToShortDateString();
}

protected void Calendar1_DayRender(object sender,
  DayRenderEventArgs e)
{
  if (_scheduleData[e.Day.Date.ToShortDateString()] != null)
  {
    Literal lit = new Literal();
    lit.Text = "<br />";
    e.Cell.Controls.Add(lit);

    Label lbl = new Label();
    lbl.Text = (string)_scheduleData[e.Day.Date.ToShortDateString()];
```

```
            lbl.Font.Size = new FontUnit(FontSize.Small);
            e.Cell.Controls.Add(lbl);

        }
    }
}
```

This code sets the *Calendar* control properties, such as style and size, in the *Page_Load* event handler. A method called *GetSchedule* is added to populate a collection of special dates. In the *Calendar1_DayRender* event handler, the *Date* and *Cell* of the day that is being rendered is available. If a special date is found, a *Label* is created that contains the special date, and it is added to the *Cell* object's *Controls* collection. When the Web page is displayed, the special dates are rendered on the *Calendar* controls, as shown in Figure 2-30.

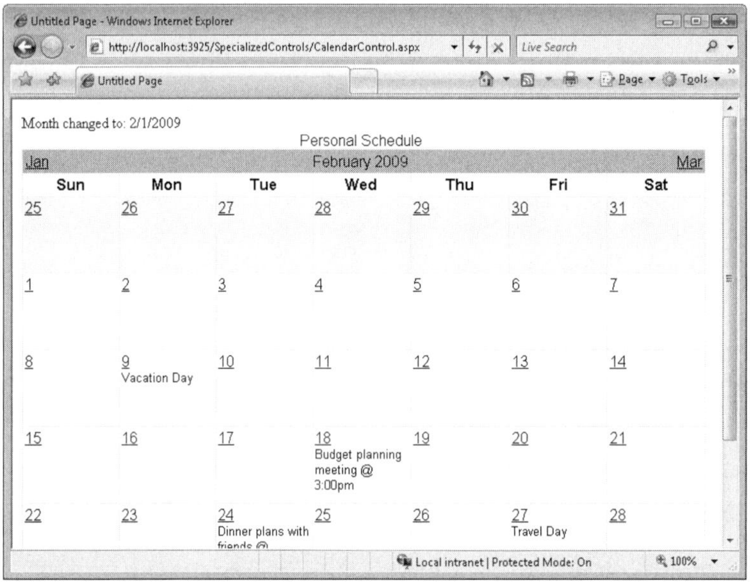

FIGURE 2-30 The rendered *Calendar* control displaying a schedule

The *FileUpload* Control

The *FileUpload* control is used to allow a user to select and upload a single file to the server. The control displays as a text box and Browse button. The user can either type a file name and path into the text box or click the Browse button and select a file. The *FileUpload* control inherits directly from the *WebControl* class as shown in Figure 2-31.

The *FileUpload* control is represented as an *<asp:FileUpload>* element in Source view. It has no content nested within its opening and closing tags, so you can write this element as a singleton element. This control generates an *<input type="file">* element when rendered as HTML to a browser.

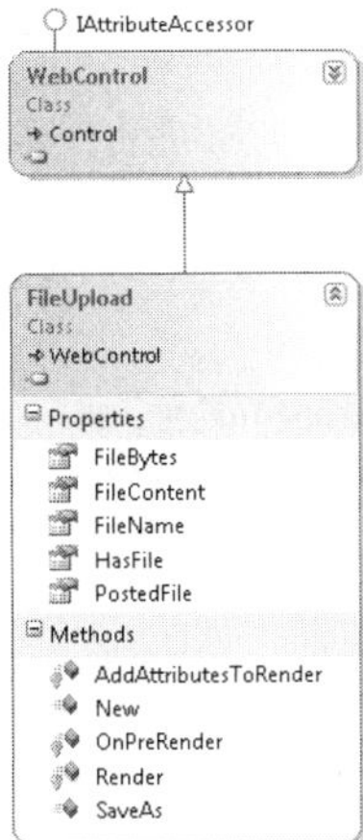

FIGURE 2-31 The *FileUpload* control hierarchy

The *FileUpload* control does not cause a PostBack to the Web server. After the user selects a file, the user needs to cause a PostBack using a different control, such as a *Button*. The PostBack causes the file to be uploaded to the server as posted data. At the server, the page code does not run until the file is uploaded to server memory.

The following properties give you flexible ways to access the uploaded file:

- ***FileBytes*** The file is exposed as a byte array.
- ***FileContent*** The file is exposed as a stream.
- ***PostedFile*** The file is exposed as an object of type *HttpPostedFile*. This object has properties, such as *ContentType* and *ContentLength*.

You need to examine any file that is uploaded to determine if it should be saved; you can examine characteristics such as the file name, size, and Multipurpose Internet Mail Extensions (MIME) type, which specifies the type of file that is being uploaded. When you are ready to save the file, you can use the *SaveAs* method on the *FileUpload* control or the *HttpPostedFile* object.

You can save the file in any location for which you have permission to create files. By default, the *requireRootedSaveAsPath* attribute of the *httpRuntime* configuration element in the Web.config file is set to *true*, which means that you need to provide an absolute path to save the file. You can get an absolute path by using the *MapPath* method of the *HttpServerUtility* class and passing to the method the tilde (~) operator, which represents the application root folder.

The maximum size of the file that can be uploaded depends on the value of the *MaxRequestLength* attribute of the *httpRuntime* configuration element in the Web.config file. If users attempt to upload a file that is larger than the *MaxRequestLength*, the upload fails.

SECURITY ALERT The *FileUpload* control allows users to upload files but makes no attempt to validate the safety of the uploaded files. The *FileUpload* control does not provide a means to filter the file types that can be uploaded by a user, but you can examine the file characteristics, such as the file name and extension, as well as the *ContentType*, after the file has been uploaded.

Although you can provide client-side script to examine the file that is being submitted, remember that client-side validation is a convenience for the honest user. A hacker can easily strip the Web page of client-side code to bypass this validation.

In this example, a Web page was created and a *FileUpload* control was added to the page. In addition, a *Button* was added to the Web page that is used to submit the file to the Web server via PostBack. A folder was added to the Web site called Uploads. The following code was added to the code-behind page to show how the *FileUpload* control's properties can be set programmatically and a file can be uploaded and saved.

```
'VB
Protected Sub Button1_Click(ByVal sender As Object, _
  ByVal e As System.EventArgs) Handles Button1.Click

  If (FileUpload1.HasFile) Then
    Label1.Text = "File Length: " _
      + FileUpload1.FileBytes.Length.ToString() _
      + "<br />" _
      + "File Name: " _
      + FileUpload1.FileName _
      + "<br />" _
      + "MIME Type: " _
      + FileUpload1.PostedFile.ContentType
    FileUpload1.SaveAs( _
      MapPath("~/Uploads/" + FileUpload1.FileName))
  Else
    Label1.Text = "No file received."
  End If
End Sub

//C#
protected void Button1_Click(object sender, EventArgs e)
{
  if (FileUpload1.HasFile)
  {
    Label1.Text = "File Length: "
       + FileUpload1.FileBytes.Length
       + "<br />"
       + "File Name: "
```

```
        + FileUpload1.FileName
        + "<br />"
        + "MIME Type: "
        + FileUpload1.PostedFile.ContentType;
      FileUpload1.SaveAs(
        MapPath("~/Uploads/" + FileUpload1.FileName));
    }
    else
    {
      Label1.Text = "No file received.";
    }
}
```

The Web page is shown in Figure 2-32. When a file is selected and the Submit button is clicked, the code checks to see if a file has been uploaded. If a file has been uploaded, information about the file is placed into the *Label* control for display. The file is then saved to the Uploads folder. The Web site requires an absolute path, and *MapPath* performs the conversion from the relative path supplied to an absolute path. Finally, the file is saved.

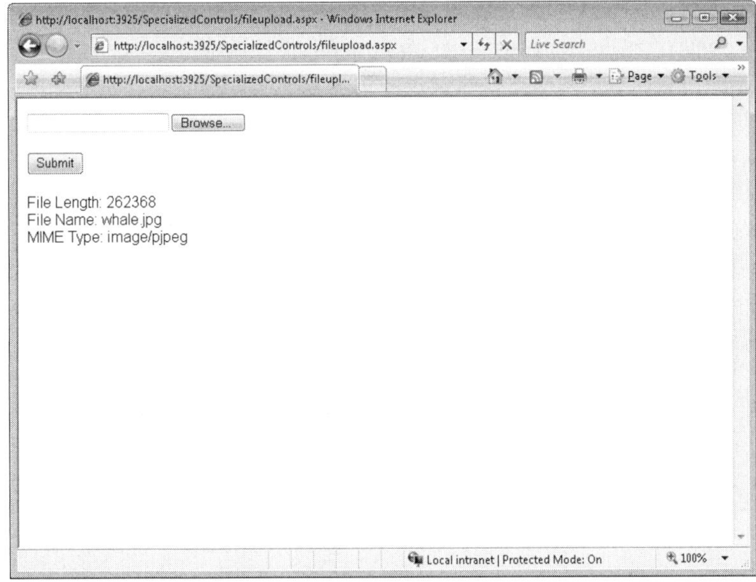

FIGURE 2-32 The *FileUpload* control after uploading a file

The *Panel* Control

The *Panel* control is used as a control container. It can be useful when you need to group controls and work with them as a single unit. A common example is the need to display and hide a group of controls. Panel controls are also useful for control developers who are creating features like tabs or show/hide toggle features. The *Panel* control inherits directly from the *WebControl* class as shown in Figure 2-33.

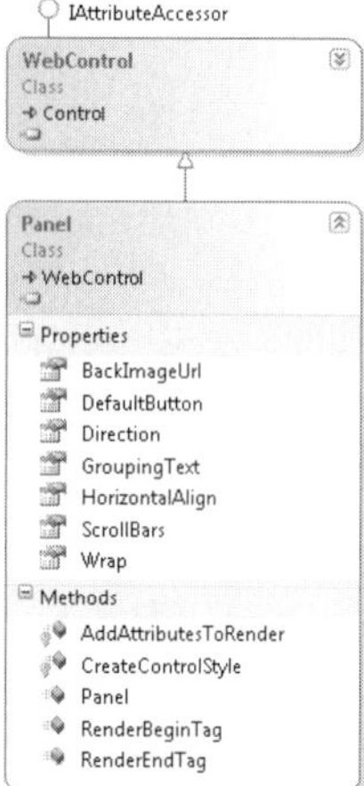

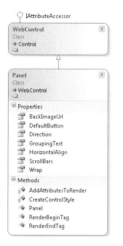

FIGURE 2-33 The *Panel* control hierarchy

In Source view, the *Panel* control is represented as an *<asp:Panel>* element. This element can contain many controls nested within it. These controls are considered to be contained by the panel. In HTML output, the *Panel* control generates a *<div>* element inside the browser.

There are a few properties that you need to be aware of when working with the *Panel* control The *BackImageUrl* property can be used to display a background image in the *Panel* control. The *HorizontalAlignment* property lets you set the horizontal alignment of the controls that are in the *Panel.* The *Wrap* property specifies whether items in the *Panel* automatically continue on the next line when a line is longer than the width of the *Panel* control. The *DefaultButton* property specifies the button that is clicked when the *Panel* control has focus and the user presses Enter on his or her keyboard. The *DefaultButton* property can be set to the *ID* of any control on your form that implements the *IButtonControl* interface.

As an example, consider a page with a Login form. You might wish to provide a button that allows a user to turn off the visibility of (hide) this form. The following shows the HTML body of the ASP.NET source:

```
<body>
    <form id="form1" runat="server">
    <div>
        <asp:Button ID="ButtonShowHide" runat="server" Text="Login: hide form"
            width="200" onclick="ButtonShowHide_Click"/>
        <asp:Panel ID="Panel1" runat="server" BackColor="Beige" Width="200">
            <asp:Label ID="Label1" runat="server" Text="User name: "></asp:Label>
            <br />
            <asp:TextBox ID="TextBox1" runat="server"></asp:TextBox>
```

```
            <br />
            <asp:Label ID="Label2" runat="server" Text="Password: "></asp:Label>
            <br />
            <asp:TextBox ID="TextBox2" runat="server"></asp:TextBox>
            <br />
            <asp:Button ID="ButtonLogin" runat="server" Text="Login" />
        </asp:Panel>
    </div>
    </form>
</body>
```

The code to show and hide this form is straightforward. You need to handle the toggle button's click event and set the *Visible* property of the *Panel* control appropriately. The following code demonstrates this:

```
'VB
Protected Sub ButtonShowHide_Click(ByVal sender As Object, _
  ByVal e As System.EventArgs) Handles ButtonShowHide.Click

  Panel1.Visible = Not Panel1.Visible
  If Panel1.Visible Then
    ButtonShowHide.Text = "Login: hide form"
  Else
    ButtonShowHide.Text = "Login: show form"
  End If

End Sub

//C#
protected void ButtonShowHide_Click(object sender, EventArgs e)
{
  Panel1.Visible = !Panel1.Visible;
  if (Panel1.Visible)
  {
    ButtonShowHide.Text = "Login: hide form";
  }
  else
  {
    ButtonShowHide.Text = "Login: show form";
  }
}
```

The example Web page is shown in Figure 2-34. Clicking the *Show/Hide* button hides the *Panel* and all of its controls, and clicking again displays the *Panel* and its controls.

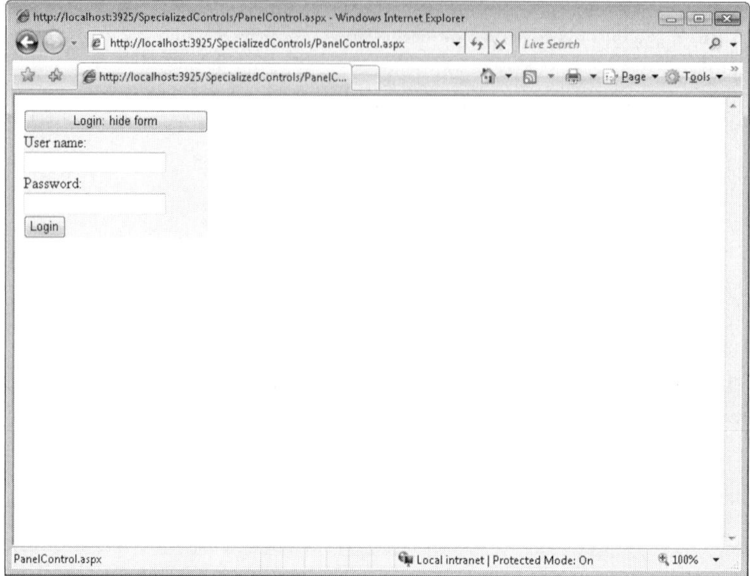

FIGURE 2-34 A *Panel* control with a button to toggle visibility

The *MultiView* and *View* Controls

Like the *Panel* control, the *MultiView* and *View* controls are also container controls; that is, they are used to group other controls. Again, this is useful when you want to treat and manage a group of controls as a single unit. A *MultiView* exists to contain other *View* controls. A *View* control must be contained inside a *MultiView*. The two controls are meant to work together. The *MultiView* is meant to contain many child *View* controls. It allows you to hide one and then show another *View* to the user. The *MultiView* control is also used to create wizards, where each *View* control in the *MultiView* control represents a different step or page in the wizard. The *MultiView* and *View* controls inherit directly from the *Control* class, as shown in Figure 2-35.

The *MultiView* and the *View* do not generate any direct HTML elements when rendering because these controls are essentially server-side controls that manage the visibility of their child controls. In Source view, the *MultiView* control is represented as an *<asp:MultiView>* element, and the *View* control is represented as an *<asp:View>* element nested inside a *MultiView*.

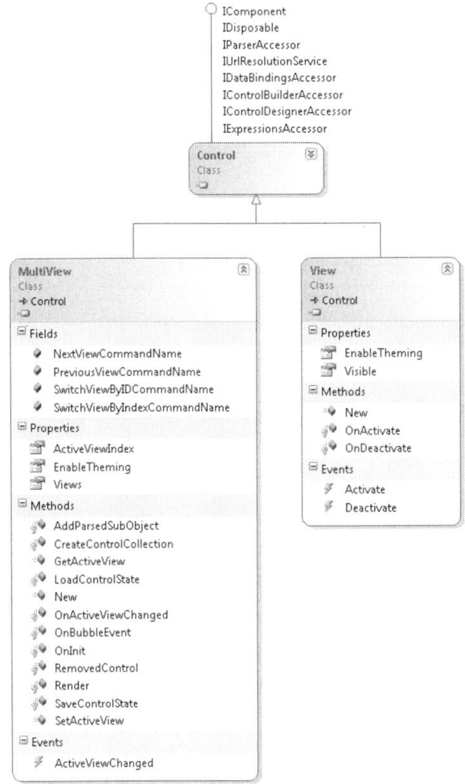

FIGURE 2-35 The *MultiView* and *View* control hierarchy

You can use the *ActiveViewIndex* property or the *SetActiveView* method to change the *View* programmatically. If the *ActiveViewIndex* is set to -1, no *View* controls are displayed. If you pass an invalid *View* or a *null* (*Nothing*) value into the *SetActiveView* method, an *Http-Exception* is thrown. Note that only one *View* control can be active at any time.

As an example, consider a user registration Web page where you need to walk a user through the process of registering with your site. You could use a single *MultiView* control and three *View* controls to manage this process. Each *View* control represents a step in the process. An example of the page's layout is shown in Figure 2-36.

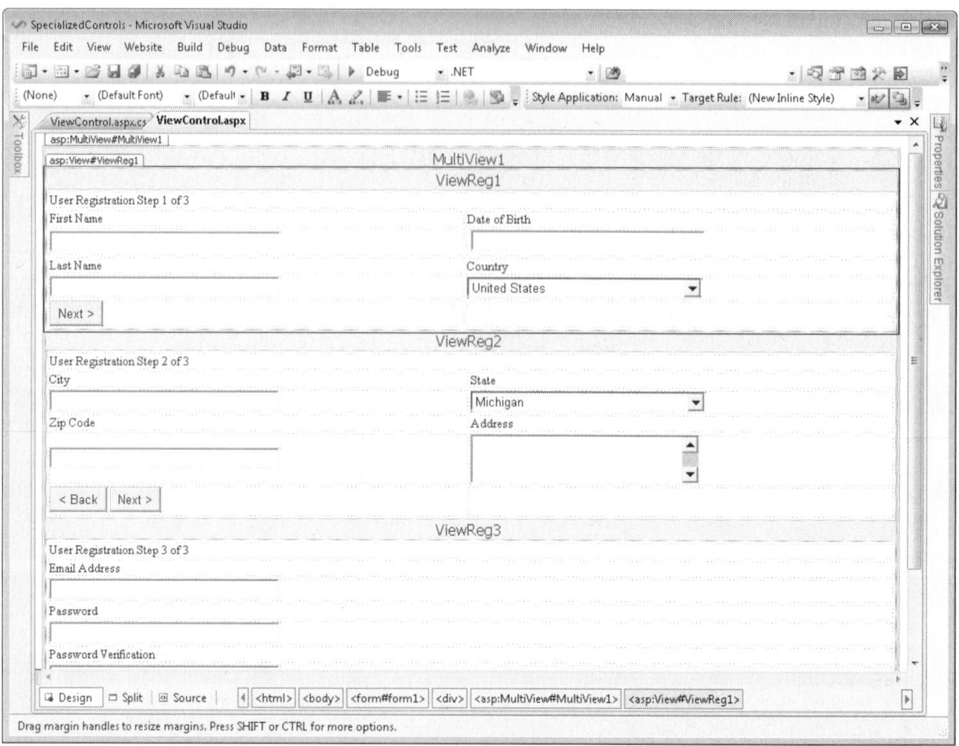

FIGURE 2-36 The *MultiView* and *View* control example Web page

To manage the page in this example, the buttons on the page are set to command buttons. When a user clicks a button, the *CommandName* property of *CommandEventArgs* is checked to determine the button pressed. Based on this information, the *MultiView* shows (and thereby hides) another *View* control. The following is an example of the code-behind page:

'VB

```
Partial Class ViewControlVb
    Inherits System.Web.UI.Page

  Protected Sub Page_Load(ByVal sender As Object, _
    ByVal e As System.EventArgs) Handles Me.Load

    MultiView1.ActiveViewIndex = 0

  End Sub

  Protected Sub Button_Command(ByVal sender As Object, _
    ByVal e As CommandEventArgs)
```

```
    Select e.CommandName
      Case "Step1Next"
        MultiView1.ActiveViewIndex = 1
      Case "Step2Back"
        MultiView1.ActiveViewIndex = 0
      Case "Step2Next"
        MultiView1.ActiveViewIndex = 2
      Case "Step3Back"
        MultiView1.ActiveViewIndex = 1
      Case "Finish"
        'hide control from user to simulate save
        MultiView1.ActiveViewIndex = -1
    End Select

  End Sub

End Class
```

```
//C#
public partial class ViewControl : System.Web.UI.Page
{
  protected void Page_Load(object sender, EventArgs e)
  {
    MultiView1.ActiveViewIndex = 0;
  }

  protected void Button_Command(object sender, CommandEventArgs e)
  {
    switch (e.CommandName)
    {
      case "Step1Next":
        MultiView1.ActiveViewIndex = 1;
        break;
      case "Step2Back":
        MultiView1.ActiveViewIndex = 0;
        break;
      case "Step2Next":
        MultiView1.ActiveViewIndex = 2;
        break;
      case "Step3Back":
        MultiView1.ActiveViewIndex = 1;
        break;
      case "Finish":
        //hide control from user to simulate save
```

```
            MultiView1.ActiveViewIndex = -1;
            break;
        }
    }
}
```

When the Web page is displayed, the first step is displayed to the user. When he or she clicks Next, the processing returns to the server and the *Button_Command* event is fired. The page changes to another *View* control based on the results of this event. Figure 2-37 shows the *MultiView* example in action.

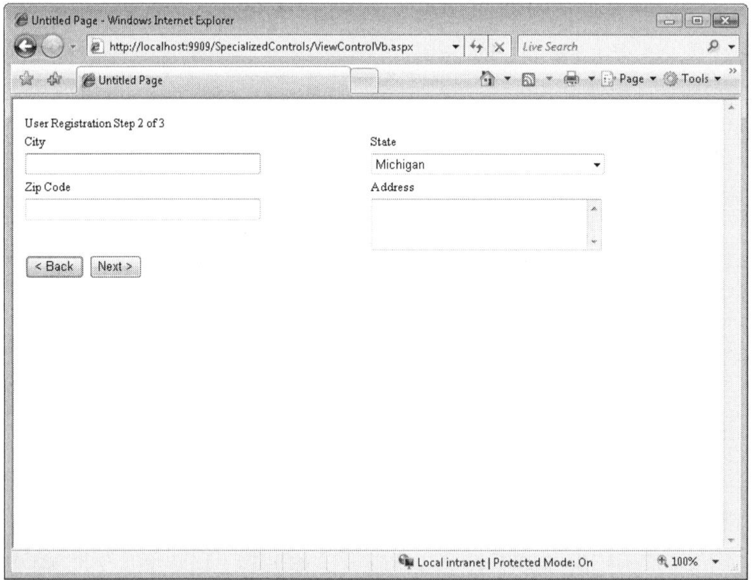

FIGURE 2-37 The *MultiView* is used to switch between the *View* controls on the server

The *Wizard* Control

The *Wizard* control is a complex control that is used to display a series of *WizardStep* controls to a user, one after the other, as part of a user input process. The *Wizard* control builds on the *MultiView* and *View* controls presented previously. It provides functionality to ensure that only one *WizardStep* control is visible at a time and provides the ability to customize most aspects of the *Wizard* and *WizardStep* controls. The most significant use of the *Wizard* control is to prompt the user for a large amount of data by breaking the data into logical chunks, or steps. The *Wizard* control presents the user with steps that can be validated, either at the end of the process or in between each step. You certainly can accomplish the same result by using separate Web pages for each logical chunk of data, but the *Wizard* consolidates the data collection process into a single Web page.

The *Wizard* control inherits from the *CompositeControl* class. It uses the *BaseWizardStep* control, which inherits from the *View control*. This model is shown in Figure 2-38. Notice that the *Wizard* control exposes a *WizardSteps* collection that contains the user interface for each step that is created by a developer. As you can also see from the many styles that can be assigned to parts of the *Wizard* control, the *Wizard* control can be significantly customized.

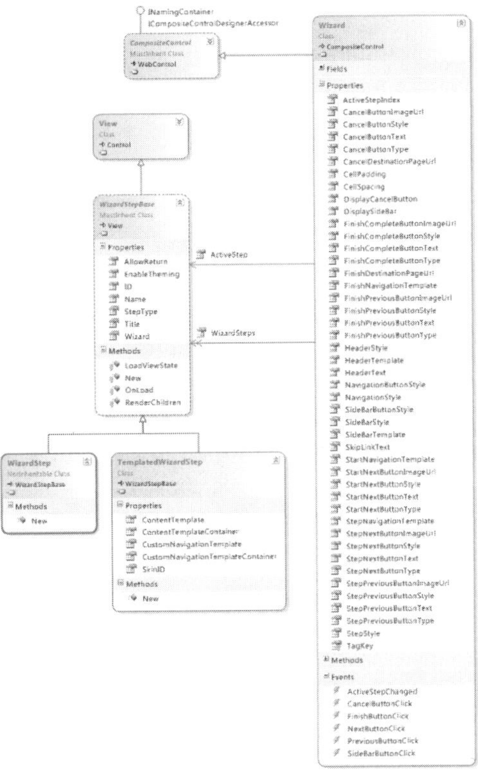

FIGURE 2-38 The *Wizard* and *WizardStep* control hierarchy

The *Wizard* control contains a header area that can be customized to display information specific to the step with which the user is currently engaged. The *Wizard* control also contains a sidebar area that can be used to quickly navigate to steps in the control. You can also programmatically control which step is displayed; you are not constrained to navigating through the steps in a linear fashion.

The built-in navigation capabilities determine which buttons are displayed based on the *StepType* value. The *BaseWizardStep* class contains the *StepType* property that can be set to one of the following values:

- ***WizardStepType.Auto*** This renders navigation buttons based on the location of the set within the WizardSteps collection property of the *Wizard*. This is the default.

- ***WizardStepType.Complete*** This is the last step to appear. No navigation buttons are rendered.
- ***WizardStepType.Finish*** This is the final data collection step; the Finish and Previous buttons are rendered for navigation.
- ***WizardStepType.Start*** This is the first one to appear, and only the Next button is rendered.
- ***WizardStepType.Step*** This is a step between the Start and the Finish steps. The Previous and Next buttons are rendered.

In this example, a wizard gives users the ability to select options on a vehicle. In a typical real vehicle selection scenario, many more options would, of course, be available. This, in turn, would dictate simplifying the option selection for the user (and thus justifying the use of the *Wizard* control).

To create the form for this example you add a *Wizard* control to a Web page. Inside the *Wizard* control are *WizardStep* controls, one for each selection step, as follows: exterior, interior, options, and summary. The exterior selection step contains three *RadioButton* controls for selection of red, blue, or black exterior. The interior selection step contains two *RadioButton* controls for selection of leather or cloth seats. The options selection step contains *CheckBox* controls for selection of AM/FM radio, heated seats, and an air freshener. The summary step contains a *Label* control that is populated with the selections that were made in the previous steps. The populated *WizardStep* controls were cut out of Visual Studio and put in a single graphic for you to view as shown in Figure 2-39.

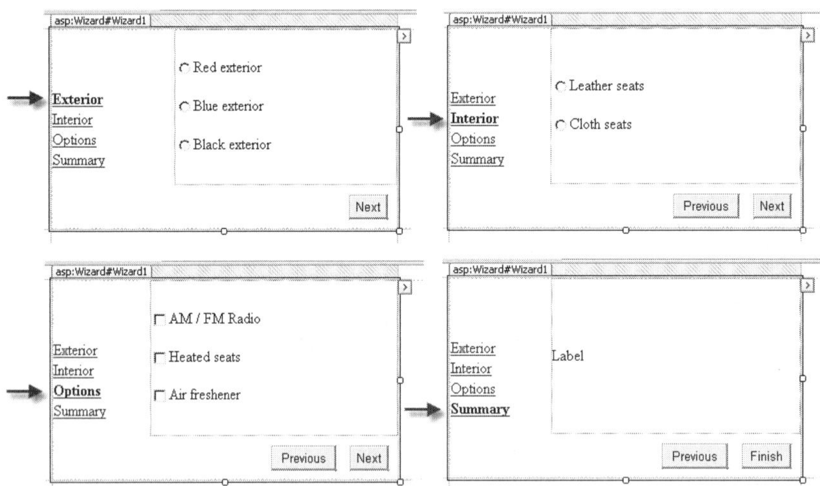

FIGURE 2-39 The *WizardStep* controls are populated with the controls to be displayed to the user

After the *WizardStep* controls were created and each step was populated, code was added to the code-behind page to populate the *Label* control in the summary step. Also, code was added to the *Form_Load* event handler to assure that the *Wizard* starts at the first step, and finally, code was added to the *Wizard1_FinishButtonClick* event handler to display the results. The code-behind page is as follows:

```
'VB
Partial Class WizardControl
  Inherits System.Web.UI.Page

  Protected Sub Wizard1_FinishButtonClick(ByVal sender As Object, _
    ByVal e As System.Web.UI.WebControls.WizardNavigationEventArgs) _
    Handles Wizard1.FinishButtonClick

    Wizard1.Visible = False
    Response.Write("Finished<br />" + Label1.Text)

  End Sub

  Protected Sub Wizard1_NextButtonClick(ByVal sender As Object, _
    ByVal e As System.Web.UI.WebControls.WizardNavigationEventArgs) _
    Handles Wizard1.NextButtonClick

    If (Wizard1.WizardSteps(e.NextStepIndex).Title = "Summary") Then
      Label1.Text = String.Empty
      For Each ws As WizardStep In Wizard1.WizardSteps
        For Each c As Control In ws.Controls
          If (TypeOf c Is System.Web.UI.WebControls.CheckBox) Then
            Dim cb As CheckBox = CType(c, CheckBox)
            If (cb.Checked) Then
              Label1.Text += cb.Text + "<br />"
            End If
          End If
        Next
      Next
    End If

  End Sub

  Protected Sub Page_Load(ByVal sender As Object, _
    ByVal e As System.EventArgs) _
    Handles Me.Load
```

```
    If Not IsPostBack Then
      Wizard1.ActiveStepIndex = 0
    End If

  End Sub

End Class

//C#
public partial class WizardCSharp : System.Web.UI.Page
{
  protected void Page_Load(object sender, EventArgs e)
  {
    if (!IsPostBack)
    {
      Wizard1.ActiveStepIndex = 0;
    }
  }

  protected void Wizard1_FinishButtonClick(object sender,
     WizardNavigationEventArgs e)
  {
    Wizard1.Visible = false;
    Response.Write("Finished<br />" + Label1.Text);
  }

  protected void Wizard1_NextButtonClick(object sender,
     WizardNavigationEventArgs e)
  {
    if (Wizard1.WizardSteps[e.NextStepIndex].Title == "Summary")
    {
      Label1.Text = String.Empty;
      foreach (WizardStep ws in Wizard1.WizardSteps)
      {
        foreach (Control c in ws.Controls)
        {
          if (c is CheckBox)
          {
            CheckBox cb = (CheckBox)c;
            if (cb.Checked)
            {
              Label1.Text += cb.Text + "<br />";
            }
          }
        }
```

```
            }
        }
    }
}
```

When the Web page is displayed, the user sees the first step (Exterior). The user can go from step to step, and on the final step, click Finish. In the Summary step, the *Label* control displays the current selections. After the user clicks Finish, the *Wizard* control is hidden and the summary information is displayed.

> **MORE INFO** ***WIZARD* CONTROL**
>
> **Take a look at MSDN for more information about the *Wizard* control at *http://msdn.microsoft.com/en-us/library/fs0za4w6.aspx*.**

The *Xml* Control

The *Xml* control is used to display the contents of an XML document. This control is useful if your data is stored in XML and you need to execute an Extensible Stylesheet Language (XSL) transform. The data can then be rendered for display to a user using the *Xml* control. The *Xml* control hierarchy is shown in Figure 2-40.

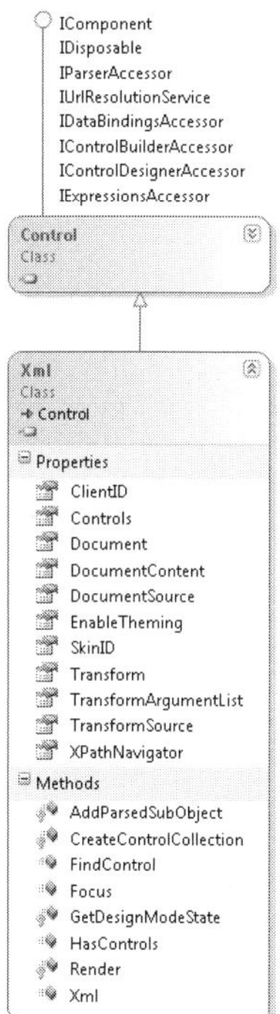

FIGURE 2-40 The *Xml* control hierarchy

The XML document you wish to display is specified by setting either the *DocumentSource* property or the *DocumentContent* property. The *DocumentSource* property accepts a string that specifies the location of an XML file to be loaded into the control. The *DocumentContent* property accepts a string that contains actual XML content. If the *DocumentContent* and the *DocumentSource* are both set, the last property that is set is the property that is used.

The *TransformSource* property accepts an optional string that contains the location of an XSL transformation file to apply to the XML document. The *Transform* property accepts a *Transform* object that can be used to perform the transformation as well. If both of these properties are set, the last property set is used. The *Xml* control also contains the *Transform-ArgumentList* property, which is used to pass arguments to the XSL transformation.

In the following example, an *Xml* control is used to display the contents of an XML file after applying an XSL transformation. This XML file and the XSL transformation file are as follows:

XML File: ProductList.xml

```
<?xml version="1.0" encoding="utf-8" ?>
<ProductList>
  <Product Id="1A59B" Department="Sporting Goods" Name="Baseball" Price="3.00" />
  <Product Id="9B25T" Department="Sporting Goods" Name="Tennis Racket" Price="40.00" />
  <Product Id="3H13R" Department="Sporting Goods" Name="Golf Clubs" Price="179.00" />
  <Product Id="7D67A" Department="Clothing" Name="Shirt" Price="12.00" />
  <Product Id="4T21N" Department="Clothing" Name="Jacket" Price="45.00" />
</ProductList>
```

XSL Transformation File: ProductList.xsl

```
<?xml version="1.0" encoding="utf-8" ?>
<xsl:stylesheet version="1.0"
xmlns:xsl="http://www.w3.org/1999/XSL/Transform"
xmlns:msxsl="urn:schemas-microsoft-com:xslt"
xmlns:labs="http://labs.com/mynamespace">
  <xsl:template match="/">
    <html>
      <head>
        <title>Product List</title>
      </head>
      <body>
        <center>
          <h1>Product List</h1>
          <xsl:call-template name="CreateHeading"/>
        </center>
      </body>
    </html>
  </xsl:template>
  <xsl:template name="CreateHeading">
    <table border="1" cellpadding="5">
      <tr >
```

```
        <th bgcolor="yellow">
          <font size="4" >
            <b>Id</b>
          </font>
        </th>
        <th bgcolor="yellow">
          <font size="4" >
            <b>Department</b>
          </font>
        </th>
        <th  bgcolor="yellow">
          <font size="4" >
            <b>Name</b>
          </font>
        </th>
        <th  bgcolor="yellow">
          <font size="4" >
            <b>Price</b>
          </font>
        </th>
      </tr>
      <xsl:call-template name="CreateTable"/>
    </table>
  </xsl:template>
  <xsl:template name="CreateTable">
    <xsl:for-each select="/ProductList/Product">
      <tr>
        <td align="center">
          <xsl:value-of select="@Id"/>
        </td>
        <td align="center">
          <xsl:value-of select="@Department"/>
        </td>
        <td>
          <xsl:value-of select="@Name"/>
        </td>
        <td align="right">
          <xsl:value-of select="format-number(@Price,'$#,##0.00')"/>
        </td>
      </tr>
    </xsl:for-each>
  </xsl:template>
</xsl:stylesheet>
```

For the Web page related to this example, an *Xml* control is added to the page. The following code was added to the code-behind file to display the XML file after applying the XSL transformation:

```
'VB
Protected Sub Page_Load(ByVal sender As Object, _
  ByVal e As System.EventArgs) Handles Me.Load

  Xml1.DocumentSource = "App_Data/ProductList.xml"
  Xml1.TransformSource = "App_Data/ProductList.xsl"

End Sub

//C#
public partial class XmlControlVb : System.Web.UI.Page
{
    protected void Page_Load(object sender, EventArgs e)
    {
       Xml1.DocumentSource = "App_Data/ProductList.xml";
       Xml1.TransformSource = "App_Data/ProductList.xsl";
    }
}
```

When the Web page is displayed, the XML and XSL files are loaded and the resulting transformation is shown in Figure 2-41.

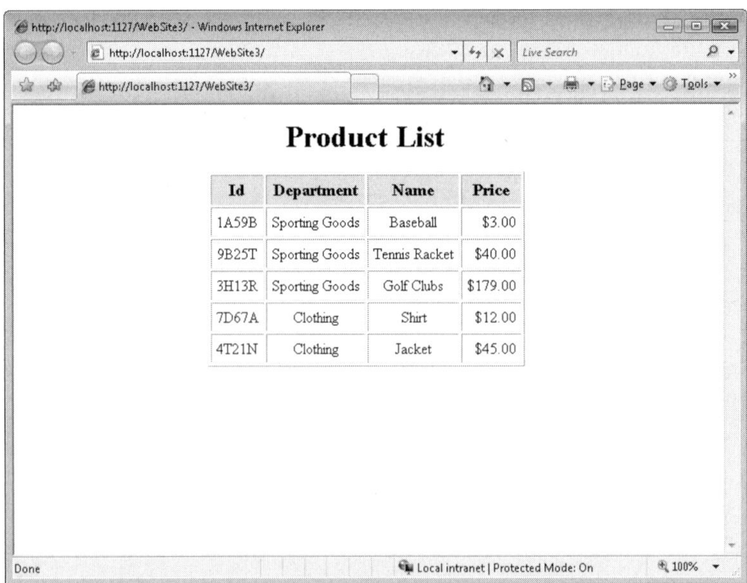

FIGURE 2-41 The result of applying the XSL transformation to the XML file

Quick Check

1. What control provides the best implementation of a schedule of special dates?
2. You want to create a Web page that prompts the user to input lots of data, and you want the data input to be spread across multiple screens. What is the best control to use to implement this solution on a single Web page?
3. Your customer wants the home page to contain an image of the world and require users to click their specific countries. This redirects the users to the Web sites for their respective countries. What control will you use?

Quick Check Answers

1. The *Calendar* control provides the best implementation of a schedule of specific dates.
2. The *Wizard* control would be the best control to use.
3. The *ImageMap* control should be used.

LAB Work with Specialized Web Controls

In this lab, you use the specialized Web controls that have been defined in this lesson to create a Web page for selecting an office on a floor plan that needs to be serviced.

If you encounter a problem completing an exercise, the completed projects are available on the companion CD in the Code folder.

EXERCISE 1 Create the Web Site and Add Controls

In this exercise, you create a Web site and add controls to the site.

1. Open Visual Studio and create a new Web site called **UsingSpecializedControls**. Use your preferred programming language. Open the Default.aspx page of the site inside the Visual Studio designer.
2. Add a *Wizard* control to the Default.aspx Web page. From the Properties window, select WizardSteps to display the WizardStep Collection Editor.
3. Use the collection editor to define three wizard steps. Set their *Title* properties to the following (in order): ***Select Office***, ***Service Date***, and ***Summary***. Figure 2-42 shows an example. When complete, close the WizardStep Collection Editor.

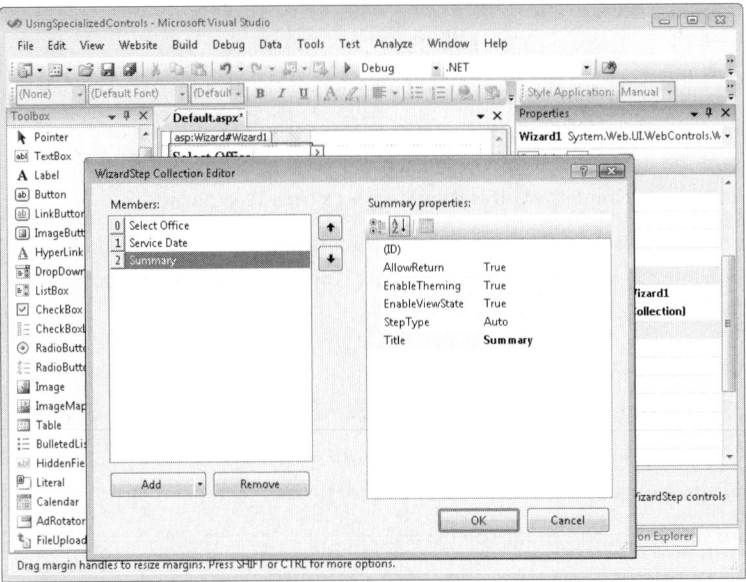

FIGURE 2-42 The WizardStep Collection Editor

4. Add a new folder to your project. Right-click the project node in Solution Explorer and select New Folder. Rename the folder **Images**.
5. Add the file Floorplan.jpg to the Images folder. This file is available in the sample code installed from this book's CD-ROM.
6. In Design view, select the *Wizard* control. Use the Properties window to set the *Height* property to **250px**, and set the *Width* property to **425px**.
7. In Design view, click the Select Office link in the *Wizard* control to assure that this is the current, selected step in the designer.
8. Add an *ImageMap* control to this step (drag and drop from the Toolbox). Set its *ID* to **ImageMapOffice**. Set its *ImageUrl* property to point to the Floorplan.jpg file.

   Under the *ImageMap* control, type **Office Selected:**. After this text, add a *Label* control and clear its *Text* property. Your ASPX source for this *WizardStep* control should look like the following:

ASPX Source: Select Office

```
<asp:WizardStep ID="WizardStep1" runat="server" Title="Select Office">
  <asp:ImageMap ID="ImageMapOffice" runat="server"
    ImageUrl="~/images/floorplan.jpg" ImageAlign="Middle">
  </asp:ImageMap>
  <br />
  <br />
  Office Selected:
  <asp:Label ID="Label1" runat="server"></asp:Label>
</asp:WizardStep>
```

9. In Design view, click the *Wizard* control's Service Date link to make this the active step.

   Inside this step, add the text **Select Service Date**. Under this text, add a *Calendar* control. Your ASPX source for this step should look like the following:

   ASPX Source: Service Date

   ```
   <asp:WizardStep ID="WizardStep2" runat="server" Title="Service Date">
     <br />
     Select Service Date<br />
     <asp:Calendar ID="Calendar1" runat="server"></asp:Calendar>
   </asp:WizardStep>
   ```

10. Next, in Design view, click the Summary link in the *Wizard* control to make this the active step.

    In this step, add a *Label* control and set its height to **200** and its width to **250**. Your ASPX source for this step should look like the following:

    ASPX Source: Service Date

    ```
    <asp:WizardStep runat="server" Title="Summary">


      <asp:Label ID="Label2" runat="server" Height="200px" Text="Label"
        Width="250px"></asp:Label>

    </asp:WizardStep>
    ```

11. In the Wizard Tasks window, click AutoFormat. Click Professional, and then click OK. The final result of each screen shown in the Visual Studio designer is shown in Figure 2-43.

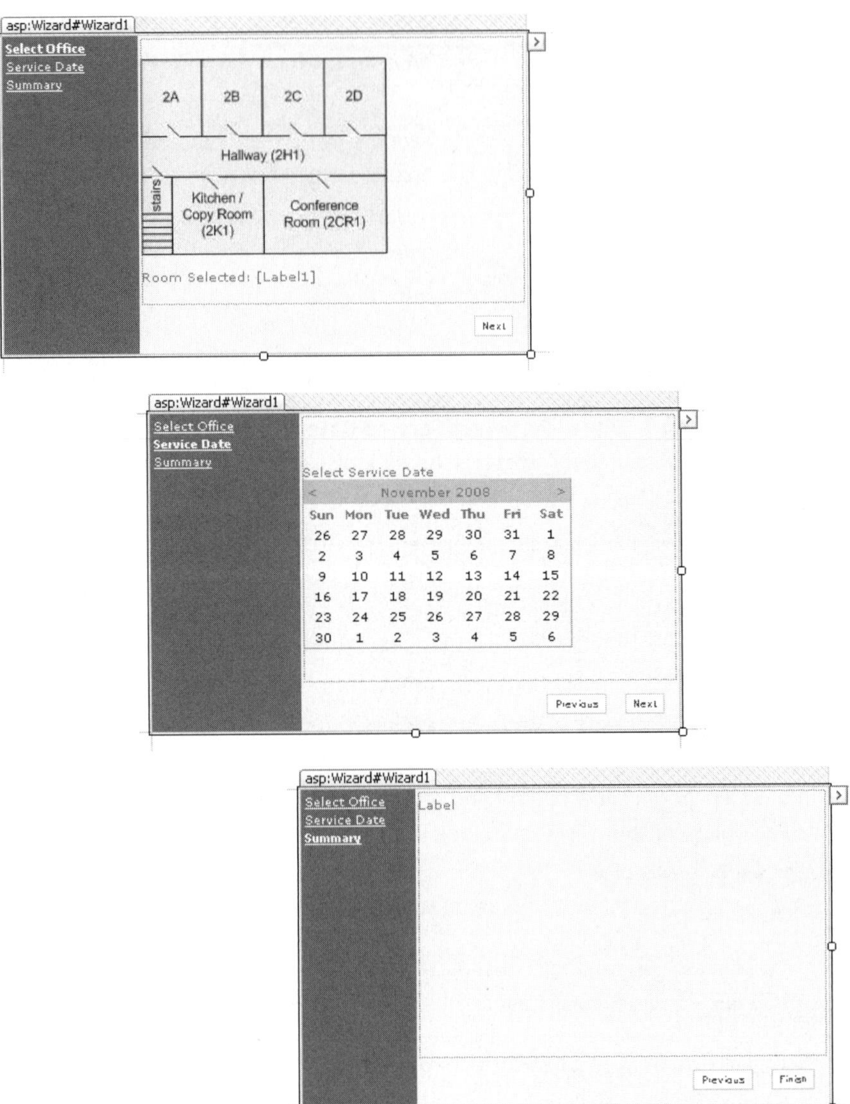

FIGURE 2-43 The completed wizard user interface

EXERCISE 2 Add Code to the Code-Behind Page

In this exercise, you add code to the code-behind page to initialize the *Wizard* control and the *ImageMap* hot spots. You also write code to display a summary after the wizard has completed its actions.

1. Open the Web page's code-behind file and add a *Page_Load* event handler.
2. In the *Page_Load* event handler, add an *if* statement that tests whether the Web page is being posted back to the server.

   Inside the *false portion of the if statement (no PostBack)* add code to set the *ActiveStepIndex* of the *Wizard* to the first *WizardStep (0)*.

   In the same block, add code to set the *HotSpot* mode of the *ImageMap* to perform a *PostBack (ImageMapOffice.HotSpotMode = HotSpotMode.PostBack)*.

   Finally, create a function that returns a *RectangleHotSpot* instance and takes the appropriate parameters. Add code to call this function and add the resulting *RectangleHotSpot* instance to the *ImageMap* control. Table 2-7 shows the dimensions of the various office hot spots.

   TABLE 2-7 RectangularHotSpot Values

POSTBACKVALUE	LEFT	TOP	RIGHT	BOTTOM
Office 2A	0	0	50	60
Office 2B	51	0	100	60
Office 2C	101	0	150	60
Office 2D	151	0	200	60
Hallway 2H1	0	61	200	90
Stairs	0	91	25	155
Kitchen / Copy Room 2K1	26	91	100	155
Conference Room 2CR1	101	91	200	155

3. Create an *ImageMap1_Click* event handler in the code-behind page. Add code to this event that places the *PostBackValue* from the *ImageMap* event arguments into the *Label1 control.*
4. Create an event handler for the *Wizard1_FinishButtonClick* event in the code-behind page. In this event, add code to hide the *Wizard* control and write out a thank-you message to the user.
5. Create an event handler for the *Wizard* control's *ActiveStepChanged* event. Add code to this method to find out if the active step is the summary step. If the summary step is the current step, populate the *Label2* control with a message that shows the current selection summary. Your final code-behind page should look like the following:

```
'VB
Partial Class _Default
  Inherits System.Web.UI.Page
```

```
Protected Sub Page_Load(ByVal sender As Object, _
  ByVal e As System.EventArgs) Handles Me.Load

  If Not IsPostBack Then

    Wizard1.ActiveStepIndex = 0
    ImageMapOffice.HotSpotMode = HotSpotMode.PostBack

    ImageMapOffice.HotSpots.Add(GetHotSpot("Office 2A", 0, 0, 50, 60))
    ImageMapOffice.HotSpots.Add(GetHotSpot("Office 2B", 51, 0, 100, 60))
    ImageMapOffice.HotSpots.Add(GetHotSpot("Office 2C", 101, 0, 150, 60))
    ImageMapOffice.HotSpots.Add(GetHotSpot("Office 2D", 151, 0, 200, 60))

    ImageMapOffice.HotSpots.Add(GetHotSpot("Hallway 2H1", 0, 61, 200, 90))

    ImageMapOffice.HotSpots.Add(GetHotSpot("Stairs", 0, 91, 25, 155))

    ImageMapOffice.HotSpots.Add( _
      GetHotSpot("Kitchen / Copy Room 2K1", 26, 91, 100, 155))

    ImageMapOffice.HotSpots.Add( _
      GetHotSpot("Conference Room 2CR1", 101, 91, 200, 155))

  End If

End Sub

Private Function GetHotSpot(ByVal name As String, ByVal left As Integer, _
  ByVal top As Integer, ByVal right As Integer, ByVal bottom As Integer) _
  As RectangleHotSpot

  Dim rhs As New RectangleHotSpot()

  rhs.PostBackValue = name

  rhs.Left = left
  rhs.Top = top
  rhs.Right = right
  rhs.Bottom = bottom

  Return rhs

End Function

Protected Sub ImageMapOffice_Click(ByVal sender As Object, _
```

```
    ByVal e As System.Web.UI.WebControls.ImageMapEventArgs) _
    Handles ImageMapOffice.Click

    Label1.Text = e.PostBackValue

  End Sub

  Protected Sub Wizard1_FinishButtonClick(ByVal sender As Object, _
    ByVal e As System.Web.UI.WebControls.WizardNavigationEventArgs) _
    Handles Wizard1.FinishButtonClick

    Wizard1.Visible = False
    Response.Write("Thank you! Your request is being processed.")

  End Sub

  Protected Sub Wizard1_ActiveStepChanged(ByVal sender As Object, _
    ByVal e As System.EventArgs) Handles Wizard1.ActiveStepChanged

    If (Wizard1.ActiveStep.Title = "Summary") Then
      Label2.Text = "Summary Info:<br />" _
      + "Room: " + Label1.Text + "<br />" _
      + "Delivery Date: " _
      + Calendar1.SelectedDate.ToShortDateString()
    End If

  End Sub

End Class
```

```
//C#
public partial class _Default : System.Web.UI.Page
{
  protected void Page_Load(object sender, EventArgs e)
  {
    if (!IsPostBack)
    {
      Wizard1.ActiveStepIndex = 0;
      ImageMapOffice.HotSpotMode = HotSpotMode.PostBack;

      ImageMapOffice.HotSpots.Add(GetHotSpot("Office 2A", 0, 0, 50, 60));
      ImageMapOffice.HotSpots.Add(GetHotSpot("Office 2B", 51, 0, 100, 60));
      ImageMapOffice.HotSpots.Add(GetHotSpot("Office 2C", 101, 0, 150, 60));
      ImageMapOffice.HotSpots.Add(GetHotSpot("Office 2D", 151, 0, 200, 60));
```

```
        ImageMapOffice.HotSpots.Add(GetHotSpot("Hallway 2H1", 0, 61, 200, 90));

        ImageMapOffice.HotSpots.Add(GetHotSpot("Stairs", 0, 91, 25, 155));

        ImageMapOffice.HotSpots.Add(
          GetHotSpot("Kitchen / Copy Room 2K1", 26, 91, 100, 155));

        ImageMapOffice.HotSpots.Add(
          GetHotSpot("Conference Room 2CR1", 101, 91, 200, 155));

      }

    }

    private RectangleHotSpot GetHotSpot(string name, int left,
      int top, int right, int bottom)
    {
      RectangleHotSpot rhs = new RectangleHotSpot();

      rhs.PostBackValue = name;

      rhs.Left = left;
      rhs.Top = top;
      rhs.Right = right;
      rhs.Bottom = bottom;

      return rhs;

    }

    protected void ImageMapOffice_Click(object sender, ImageMapEventArgs e)
    {
      Label1.Text = e.PostBackValue;
    }


    protected void Wizard1_FinishButtonClick(
      object sender, WizardNavigationEventArgs e)
    {
      Wizard1.Visible = false;
      Response.Write("Thank you! Your request is being processed.");
    }

    protected void Wizard1_ActiveStepChanged(object sender, EventArgs e)
    {
```

```
    if (Wizard1.ActiveStep.Title == "Summary")
    {
      Label2.Text = "Summary Info:<br />"
      + "Room: " + Label1.Text + "<br />"
      + "Delivery Date: "
      + Calendar1.SelectedDate.ToShortDateString();
    }
  }
}
```

6. Run the Web page and test it.

   Try clicking each room on the floor plan and observe the results.

   Click the Service Date link or click Next to display the *Calendar* control. Select a date.

   Click the Summary link or click Next to display a summary of your selections.

   Click Finish to see the thank-you message.

Lesson Summary

- The *Literal* control is used to display static text on a Web page.
- The *Table*, *TableRow*, and *TableCell* controls provide ways to format tabular and graphical information that is displayed on a Web page.
- The *Image* control is used to display an image on a Web page.
- The *ImageButton* control is used to display a clickable image on a Web page that can be used to PostBack to the Web server when the image is clicked.
- The *ImageMap* control is used to display a clickable image on a Web page that can be used to PostBack to the Web server when the image is clicked.
- The *Calendar* control displays a calendar for a user's month of choice and allows the user to select dates and move to the next or previous month.
- The *FileUpload* control is used to display a *TextBox* and Browse button that allows a user to either type a file name and path, or click Browse and select a file and path.
- The *Panel* control is used as a control container and is useful for controls that you want to display and hide as a group.
- The *View* control is a control container that is useful when you have controls that you want to display and hide as a group.
- The *MultiView* control contains a collection of *View* controls; the *MultiView* control provides behavior that allows you to switch between *View* controls.
- The *Wizard* control is a complex control that is used to display a series of *WizardStep* controls to a user, one after the other.
- The *XML* control is used to display XML data to a user.

Lesson Review

You can use the following questions to test your knowledge of the information in Lesson 3, "Exploring Specialized Server Controls."

The questions are also available on the companion CD if you prefer to review them in electronic form.

> ***NOTE*** **ANSWERS**
>
> **Answers to these questions and explanations of why each answer choice is right or wrong are located in the "Answers" section at the end of the book.**

1. Which of the following represents the best use of the *Table*, *TableRow*, and *TableCell* controls?
   - **A.** Creating and populating a table in Design view
   - **B.** Creating a customized control that needs to display data in a tabular fashion
   - **C.** Creating a table of static images stored in a folder on your site
   - **D.** Displaying a tabular result set
2. Your graphics department just completed an elaborate image that shows the product lines that your company sells. Some of the product line graphics are circular, others are rectangular, and others are complex shapes. You want to use this image as a menu on your Web site. What is the best way to incorporate the image into your Web site?
   - **A.** Use *ImageButton* and use the x- and y-coordinates that are returned when the user clicks to figure out what product line the user clicked.
   - **B.** Use the *Table*, *TableRow*, and *TableCell* controls, break the image into pieces that are displayed in the cells, and use the *TableCell* control's *Click* event to identify the product line that was clicked.
   - **C.** Use the *MultiView* control and break up the image into pieces that can be displayed in each *View* control for each product line. Use the *Click* event of the *View* to identify the product line that was clicked.
   - **D.** Use an *ImageMap* control and define hot spot areas for each of the product lines. Use the *PostBackValue* to identify the product line that was clicked.

3. You are writing a Web site that collects a lot of data from your users. The data collection spreads over multiple Web pages. When the user reaches the last page, you need to gather all of the data, validate it, and save it to the database. You notice that it can be rather difficult to gather the data that is spread over multiple pages and you want to simplify the development of this application. What control should you use to solve this problem?

   A. The *View* control

   B. The *TextBox* control

   C. The *Wizard* control

   D. The *DataCollection* control

Chapter Review

To further practice and reinforce the skills you learned in this chapter, you can perform the following tasks:

- Review the chapter summary.
- Complete the case scenarios. These scenarios set up real-world situations involving the topics of this chapter and ask you to create solutions.
- Complete the suggested practices.
- Take a practice test.

Chapter Summary

- A Web page in ASP.NET follows a standard life cycle of events. Data is stored between requests in the ViewState mechanism for the page.
- ASP.NET provides a number of server-side controls for exposing functionality to users and provides a familiar programming model to developers (writing event-driven methods on the server).
- Web server controls are more powerful than basic HTML controls. Both can be run on the server. However, a Web server control can render many HTML elements and JavaScript code blocks.
- The *Label*, *TextBox*, *Button*, *CheckBox*, and *RadioButton* are common Web server controls that can increase developer productivity. The *Table*, *ImageMap*, *Calendar*, *Panel*, and *Wizard* controls are examples of specialized server controls that ease the programming burden on developers needing to expose rich features to their users.

Case Scenarios

In the following case scenarios, you apply what you've learned in this chapter. You can find answers to these questions in the "Answers" section at the end of this book.

Case Scenario 1: Determining the Type of Controls to Use

You are creating a new Web page that collects customer data. This Web page needs to capture customer names and addresses, and an indicator of which customers are active. You also need to display several vertical market categories and give the data entry person the ability to place the customer into all matching categories. You also prompt the data entry person for the quantity of computers that the customer has, based on several ranges, such as 0–5, 6–50, 51–250, 251–1,000, and 1,001 or more.

1. Define the type of controls that you will use and indicate why.

Case Scenario 2: Selecting the Proper Events to Use

You need to create the controls for your page dynamically based on information from the database. The database also contains data that is used to set the properties of these controls.

1. In what event handler should you place code to dynamically create the controls? Why?
2. Where should you place code to set properties of the control? Why?

Case Scenario 3: Determining How to Prompt for Data

You are creating a new Web page that will be used to price a car insurance policy. There are many factors that go into pricing the policy, but the customer information can be placed into the following categories:

- Location
- Vehicles
- Other drivers
- Accident history
- Motor vehicle violations

You are concerned that a prospective customer might leave the site before all of the information is entered.

1. List some of the ways that you can prompt the user for this information in an organized fashion, keeping the displayed prompts to a minimum so the customer does not feel inundated with too many prompts.

Case Scenario 4: Implementing a Calendar Solution

You are a training provider who is creating a Web site that will be used to schedule training contractors to work at different locations. The application will prompt you for the contractor information and the training class dates. You can view a schedule showing all of your training classes and which contractors are scheduled for which times. Also, a contractor can log in and see the training classes that have been assigned to him or her.

1. Where can you use the *Calendar* control in this solution?
2. Would you need to use a *Table* control?

Suggested Practices

To help you successfully master the exam objectives presented in this chapter, complete the following tasks.

Create a New Web Page Using Server Controls

For this task, you should complete at least Practice 1. If you want a more well-rounded understanding of server controls, you should also complete Practice 2.

- **Practice 1** Create a new Web page and add the Web server controls that have been defined in this chapter.
- **Practice 2** Obtain an existing ASP page and convert this page to ASP.NET by changing all existing HTML elements to HTML controls.

Create Event Handlers for Pages and Controls

For this task, you should complete at least Practice 1.

- **Practice 1** Create a new Web page and add the Web server controls that have been defined in this chapter. Add event handlers for the default events and explore the other events that are available in each control.
- **Practice 2** Add event handlers for the Init and *Load* events on the Web page.

Program a Web Application

For this task, you should complete Practice 1.

- **Practice 1** Create a new Web page and add some of the HTML server controls that have been defined in this chapter. Practice converting the HTML server controls back to HTML elements.

Take a Practice Test

The practice tests on this book's companion CD offer many options. For example, you can test yourself on just the content covered in this chapter, or you can test yourself on all the 70-562 certification exam content. You can set up the test so it closely simulates the experience of taking a certification exam, or you can set it up in study mode so you can look at the correct answers and explanations after you answer each question.

MORE INFO **PRACTICE TESTS**

For details about all the practice test options available, see the "How to Use the Practice Tests" section in this book's Introduction.

CHAPTER 3

Input Validation and Site Navigation

Input validation on both the client and server is paramount to a quality user experience and a robust application. Users do not want to make unnecessary mistakes that increase the time it takes to do their job. Instead, they need visual cues, data input restrictions, and validation that happens as they enter the data, not after they have sent it to the server. Of course your Web page also needs to validate the data that is sent to it. It needs to verify that everything sent from the client is valid once it reaches the server. ASP.NET provides developers with a set of validation controls expressly for handling these issues.

Another hallmark of a usable and robust Web application is solid navigation. Developers need to know how to move users from page to page based on a request, PostBack information, and the overall context of the user's actions. In addition, users expect to be able to navigate through the taxonomy of a Web application as they see fit. You need to be able to manage the application as users move through it.

This chapter builds on what was covered in the first two chapters. The first lesson covers managing data input on both the client and the server. The second lesson is all about the various means of navigating from page to page and through a Web site.

Exam objectives in this chapter:

- Consuming and Creating Server Controls
    - Implement client-side validation and server-side validation.
- Programming Web Applications
    - Handle events and control page flow.

Lessons in this chapter:

Before You Begin

To complete the lessons in the chapter, you should be familiar with developing applications with Microsoft Visual Studio using Visual Basic or C#. In addition, you should be comfortable with all of the following:

- The Visual Studio 2008 Integrated Development Environment (IDE)
- A basic understanding of Hypertext Markup Language (HTML) and client-side scripting
- How to create a new Web site
- Adding Web server controls to a Web page

REAL WORLD

Mike Snell

In my experience, what users call good software is software that is easy to use, prevents them from creating errors, treats them intelligently, and does not make them feel frustrated. Often this means going the extra mile in the user interface (UI). I have seen many developers create middle-tier frameworks that other developers would drool over. They are proud of how their business rules are processed, the separation of their tiers, and the reuse of their code. And they should be, as these are hard things to get right. However, I have seen these same people create a UI that was, at best, utilitarian; in their mind all the magic happens on the server.

Unfortunately, users just don't appreciate back-end code. Instead, they want as many intuitive features as you can provide them while keeping the application responsive. Well-received applications have paid attention to this. They use things like client-side validation and good navigation to ensure a quality, responsive UI. This can go a long way toward creating an application that users love.

Lesson 1: Performing Input Validation

In this lesson, you learn how the validation framework operates and how you can use the validation controls that are included in ASP.NET to perform input validation.

After this lesson, you will be able to:

- Understand the validation framework.
- Add validation controls to a Web page.
- Configure validation controls.
- Implement the *CustomValidator* control.
- Test for valid user input.

Estimated lesson time: 60 minutes

Understanding the Validation Framework

A common problem for developers is ensuring that data entered by users is valid. That problem is made more difficult when your application exists in a Web browser. When the data is sent from the browser to the server you need to make sure that data is valid. In addition, users expect some feedback and assistance entering valid data before they spend the time sending it back to the server for a response. Thankfully, ASP.NET has a built-in data validation framework for handling this scenario. It provides a straightforward way to accomplish both client- and server-side validation with minimal coding.

The ASP.NET data validation framework includes a built-in set of validation controls that can be attached to user input controls to handle validation on both the server and the client. Figure 3-1 shows the data validation framework control hierarchy.

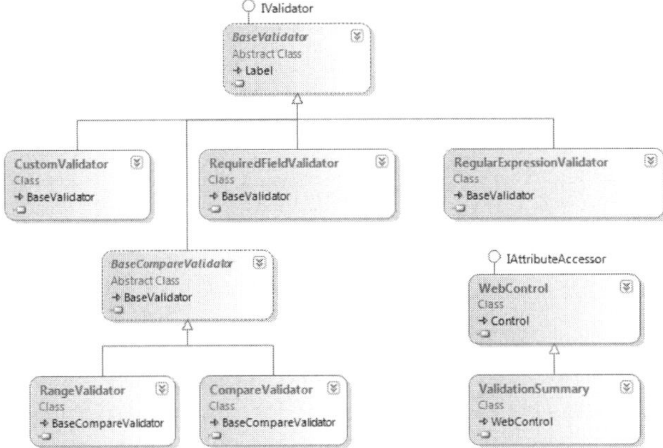

FIGURE 3-1 The validation control hierarchy

Client-side validation is a convenience to users. It improves performance by checking the data at the browser before sending the data to the server. This avoids unnecessary round trips to the server. However, client-side validation can be easily defeated by hackers. Server-side validation is the only secure means of validating the data that is posted back to the server. Using both client-side and server-side validation provides a better experience to the user and secure validation for your Web site.

Adding Validation Controls to Your Page

Validation controls are found in the Visual Studio toolbox and are added to a Web page like other controls. The following are the basic steps for using a validation control on a Web page:

1. Open a Web page in Design view and open the Visual Studio Toolbox. Navigate to the Validation tab of the toolbox.
2. Drag and drop the desired validation control next to (or near) the control you intend to validate. For example, you might drag a *RequiredFieldValidator* control next to a *TextBox* control to ensure a user enters data in the text box.
3. Next, you set the *ID* property of the validation control (from Source view or in the Properties window). Of course, it is important to name it similarly to the field it validates.
4. The next step is to set the validation control's *ControlToValidate* property. Here you can select another control already on the page. This is the control that the validation control will validate.
5. The *ErrorMessage* property of the validation control should also be set. The values set as the *ErrorMessage* will be displayed to users as assistance when they try to submit the form with invalid data. This message is typically put into a *ValidationSummary* control on the page.
6. It is a good idea to also set the validation control's *ToolTip* property to be the same as or similar to the *ErrorMessage* property. This value will display when the user hovers the pointer over the validation control's text (during an invalid operation).
7. Finally, you set the *Text* property of the validation control to a short string. This might be an asterisk (*), for example. Keeping this short minimizes the space that is required by the validation control but still offers a visual cue to the user that something is wrong with the given item.

Creating a Summary of Validation Errors

You should also consider adding a *ValidationSummary* control to your data input pages. This control is placed on a Web page to display all the validation error messages in one location after the user has triggered page-level validation by clicking a submit button. This is especially useful in scenarios where the Web page is crowded with other controls and displaying the validation error message next to the invalid control presents a difficult layout situation.

The *ValidationSummary* control can also be configured to display a pop-up message with the validation errors in lieu of, or in addition to, displaying the validation errors on the Web page.

Server-Side Validation

The validation controls work in concert with the *Page* object. Recall that the *Page* object is the base class for your Web page. ASP.NET uses the *Page* class and the validation controls together to ensure data coming from the client is still valid when it gets to the server.

The *Page* class has a *Validators* property that contains a collection of all the validation controls defined on the page. The *Page* class also has a *Validate* method. You call this method to ask the *Page* to check each of the validation controls and determine if anything on the page is not valid.

ASP.NET calls the *Validate* method automatically after the page's *Load* event handler method executes. Therefore, once the page has loaded, you can find out if the page is indeed valid on the server. To do so, you call the *Page.IsValid* property (set by the *Validate* method). This property is of type *Boolean* and is only true if all validation controls process correctly. Although the *IsValid* property is set automatically, you need to check the *IsValid* property in every event handler to determine whether the code should run; that is, your code will still execute when *IsValid = false* unless you tell it not to.

Client-Side Validation

Client-side validation code is written for you simply by using the validation controls on your page. ASP.NET renders the controls along with their JavaScript to the page. This JavaScript executes as users enter and leave focus of the controls on your page. Client-side validation is turned on by default. You can turn it off for specific validation controls if you wish, but this is not recommended. To do so, set the *EnableClientScript* property to *false*.

Again, when the user leaves focus of a control (tabs or navigates away from a control) the client-side validation for that one control fires. If validation fails, the validation control's *Text* property is displayed to the user.

You can also use the *Focus* method of a control to set the focus to a specific control when your page is loaded. The *Focus* method adds client-side JavaScript code that executes at the browser to set focus to the appropriate control. In addition to the new *Focus* method, a validation control has a similar property called *SetFocusOnError*. You can set this property to *true* to cause the invalid control to automatically receive focus. In this way, a user does not leave the control until it has valid data. This property is set to *false* by default.

Determining When to Cause Validation

Client-side validation is considered a convenience for users. Its primary benefit is that it prevents a page from being posted back to the server until all client-side validation has successfully occurred. Sometimes this can be a problem.

For example, suppose a user wants to click a cancel or help button and the page is not in a valid state. The default behavior of these buttons is to attempt a PostBack to the server. However, if the page is not valid, clicking the button will trigger client-side validation and not cause a PostBack to the server. There is a solution.

Controls that should be able to bypass validation can do so by setting their *Causes-Validation* property to *false*. This property defaults to *true*. For example, if you have a button called *ButtonReset* that triggers a reset on the page, you can set it to cause a PostBack even when the page is not valid by setting *ButtonReset.CausesValidation = false*.

Using Validation Groups

Often you do not want to treat your entire page as a single entity that is validated as a whole. Instead, you might want to break up sections of the page and have them validated independently. This is especially true for long data entry forms with multiple sections. You might not want the entire page's validation to fire when only submitting a single section of the page. Thankfully, ASP.NET allows for this scenario.

The validation controls in ASP.NET have the property *ValidationGroup* attached to them. This property can be assigned a string value to specify a section of your page (or group of controls to validate as a single unit). This property exists on the validation controls and on the controls that cause a PostBack. When a control performs a PostBack, the validation controls that have a matching *ValidationGroup* property value are validated. This allows for these controls to validate as a unit.

When you hit the server (following PostBack), the *IsValid* property on the *Page* object only reflects the validity of the validation controls that have been validated. By default, these are the validation controls that are in the same *ValidationGroup*, but you can call a validation control's *Validate* method to add that control to the set of controls on which the *IsValid* property reports.

There is also an overload method to the *Page* object's *Validate* method. This overload accepts a string used to specify the *ValidationGroup* to validate. This overload is executed when a PostBack that causes validation occurs. The *Page* object also has a *GetValidators* method that accepts a string containing the name of the *ValidationGroup*. This method returns the list of validation controls in the given *ValidationGroup*.

Understanding the *BaseValidator* Class

The validation controls inherit from the *BaseValidator* abstract class. This class contains most of the validation functionality exposed by the validation framework. Table 3-1 contains a list of the properties that the *BaseValidator* provides its child classes.

TABLE 3-1 *BaseValidator* Properties

PROPERTY	DESCRIPTION
ControlToValidate	Set this to the control that is to be validated.
Display	Set this to control the behavior of the validation message; it can be set to one of the following: ■ *None* (does not display the validation message). If a validation control is to supply information to the *Validation-Summary* control and not display its own information beside the invalid control, set the Display property of the control to None. ■ *Static* (displays the validation message and consumes the same space on the Web page even when the message does not display). ■ *Dynamic* (displays the validation message, but takes up no space if no message needs to be displayed).
EnableClientSideScript	Set to *false* to disable client-side validation. Default is *true*.
ErrorMessage	Set to the text that displays when validation fails. If the *Text* property is set, the validation control displays the contents of the *Text* property, whereas the *ValidationSummary* control displays the *ErrorMessage* contents.
IsValid	The valid status of a single validation control.
Enabled	Set the property to *false* to completely disable the control.

Understanding the *BaseCompareValidator* Class

The *RangeValidator* and *CompareValidator* controls inherit from the *BaseCompareValidator* control. This base class contains common comparison behavior used by these controls. The *BaseCompareValidator* contains the *Type* property, which you can set to the data type that the text is converted to before a comparison is made. The data types that are available are as follows:

- ***Currency*** The data is validated as *System.Decimal*, but currency symbols and grouping characters also can be entered.
- ***Date*** The data is validated as a numeric date.
- ***Double*** The data is validated as *System.Double*.
- ***Integer*** The data is validated as *System.Int32*.
- ***String*** The data is validated as *System.String*.

The *BaseCompareValidator* class is, of course, a base class and not an actual validation control. We look at its features more closely when discussing the child controls that inherit from *BaseCompareValidator*.

Understanding the *RequiredFieldValidator* Control

The *RequiredFieldValidator* is used to ensure that the user has entered a value into a control (excluding white space). The other validation controls do not validate for an empty field. Therefore you will frequently need to use the *RequiredFieldValidator* with one of the other controls to achieve the desired validation.

The *RequiredFieldValidator* provides the property called *InitialValue. It is* used when the control that you are validating defaults to an initial value and you want to ensure that the user changes this value. For example, if you set some default text in your control, you can set the *InitialValue* property to this text to ensure that it is not a valid user input. As an example, consider a drop-down list for selecting a state on an address entry form. The drop-down list might contain a value that is an instruction to the user such as "Select a state . . . ." In this case, you want to ensure the user selects a state and not this value. You can use the *InitialValue* of the *RequiredFieldValidator* to manage this scenario. Figure 3-2 shows the example in the Visual Studio designer.

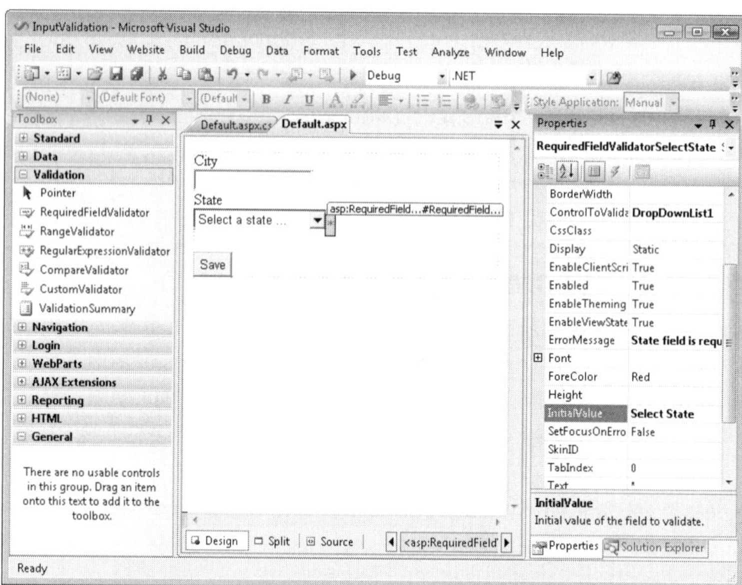

FIGURE 3-2 The *RequiredFieldValidator* and the *InitialValue* property

Using the *CompareValidator* Control

The *CompareValidator* control performs validation by using comparison operators such as greater than and less than to compare the data entered by a user with a constant you set or a value in a different control.

The *CompareValidator* can also be used to verify that the data entered into a given control is of a certain data type, such as a date or a number. To do so, you set the *Type* property to a valid data type. ASP.NET will then validate that the user's input can be cast into a valid instance of the given type. If all you intend is a data type check, you can also set the *Operator* property to *DataTypeCheck*. Figure 3-3 shows setting this property from the Property window for a *CompareValidator* control.

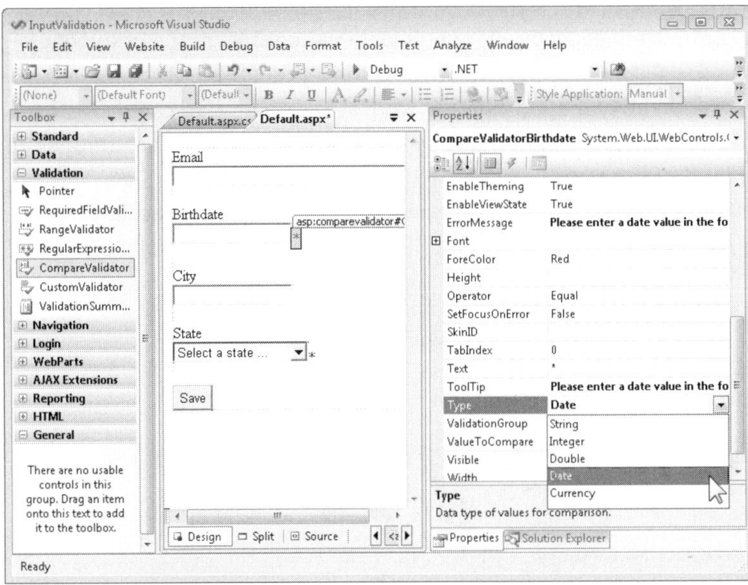

FIGURE 3-3 The *CompareValidator* control verifying the user has entered a date value

The *CompareValidator* control uses the property *ValueToCompare* to set a constant that is used to perform a comparison. For example, you might want to make sure users enter a birth date greater than 1900. You could do so by setting the *ValueToCompare* to 1/1/1900. You would then set the *Operator* property of the control. This property defines how to perform the comparison and can be set to *Equal*, *NotEqual*, *GreaterThan*, *GreaterThanEqual*, *LessThan*, *LessThanEqual*, or *DataTypeCheck*. In the case of the birth date example, you would set this value to *GreaterThanEqual*.

You can also use the *ControlToCompare* property to define another control that is used to perform the comparison. In this case, you are doing a comparison from one control to the next. For example, if you are asking a user to enter a range of dates you would want the second defined date to be greater than the first. You could use a *CompareValidator* to perform this check. You would set its *ControlToValidate* to the second date entry text box and its *ControlToCompare* property to the first date entry text box. You would then set the *Operator* property to *GreaterThan*.

Using the *RangeValidator* Control

You often need to validate that a value entered by a user is within a predefined range of acceptable values. For example, you might want to write a Web page that shows sales for the current year up through a specific date. You would then want to verify that the user has entered a date value that is within the range of the current year. To do so, you can use the *RangeValidator* control.

The *RangeValidator* control verifies that user input is within a specified range of values. This control has two very specific properties for managing the range of acceptable values: *MinimumValue* and *MaximumValue*. These properties work as their name indicates. The *RangeValidator* control also uses the *Type* property to determine the data type of the user's input. In the example of sales for the current year, you would set the *Type* property to *Date*. You would then set the *MinimumValue* and *MaximumValue* properties programmatically on the server to represent the current year and current date. The following code shows an example of what this might look like:

```
'VB
Protected Sub Page_Load(ByVal sender As Object, _
  ByVal e As System.EventArgs) Handles Me.Load

  RangeValidatorSalesDate.MinimumValue = _
      "1/1/" & DateTime.Now.Year.ToString()

  RangeValidatorSalesDate.MaximumValue = _
    DateTime.Now.ToShortDateString()

End Sub

//C#
protected void Page_Load(object sender, EventArgs e)
{
  if (!IsPostBack)
  {
    RangeValidatorSalesDate.MinimumValue =
      "1/1/" + DateTime.Now.Year.ToString();
    RangeValidatorSalesDate.MaximumValue =
      DateTime.Now.ToShortDateString();
  }
}
```

Using the *RegularExpressionValidator* Control

The *RegularExpressionValidator* control performs its validation based on a regular expression. A regular expression is a powerful pattern-matching language that can be used to identify simple and complex character sequences that would otherwise require writing code to accomplish. The control uses the *ValidationExpression* property to set a valid regular expression that is applied to the data that is to be validated. The data is validated if it matches the regular expression.

The regular expression language is not a subject for this book. Fortunately, however, Visual Studio does have a number of predefined regular expressions from which to choose. For example, you might simply need to validate that a user has entered a valid Internet e-mail address. You can do so by selecting the button next to the *ValidationExpression* property in the Properties window. Doing so opens the Regular Expression Editor dialog box shown in Figure 3-4.

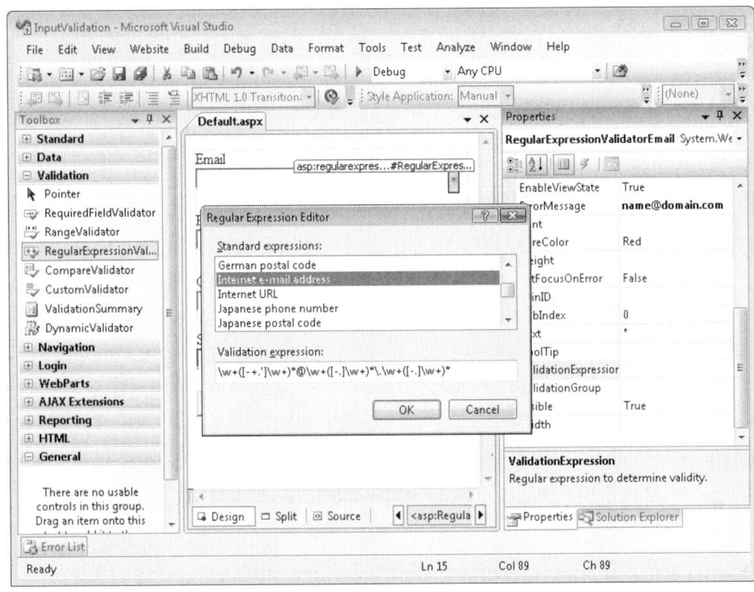

FIGURE 3-4 The Regular Expression Editor dialog box used for selecting predefined regular expressions for a *RegularExpressionValidator* control

> ***MORE INFO*** **REGULAR EXPRESSIONS**
>
> **For more information about regular expressions such as tutorials and sample regular expressions, refer to the following sites:**
>
> ***http://www.regexlib.com/***
>
> ***http://www.regular-expressions.info/***

The *CustomValidator* Control

Even with the robust set of validation controls provided by ASP.NET, you still might find yourself having another validation need. Thankfully, there is the *CustomValidator* control. You can use it to create your own validation and have that validation run alongside the other validation on the page. The *CustomValidator* control performs validation-based code you write. You can write validation code that will be executed on the client side using JavaScript; you can also write server-side validation code using your preferred .NET language.

Custom Client-Side Validation

Client-side validation provides users immediate feedback when they are working with your page. If you intend to write custom validation and are using other client-side validation, you should consider writing the JavaScript necessary for your custom validation scenario. Your custom validation JavaScript needs to participate in the data validation framework that the other validation controls use. Following this framework ensures your custom validation control works alongside the other validation controls.

The first step in writing your custom client-side validation is to define a JavaScript function inside your Web page (Source view, not code-behind). This function must have the following method signature:

```
function ClientFunctionName(source, arguments)
```

You can name your function to suit your needs. However, the parameters should follow the standard shown here. Your function will be automatically called by the data validation framework once it is attached to a *CustomValidator* control. When the function is called, the *source* parameter will contain a reference to the validation control that is performing the validation. The *arguments* parameter is an object that has a property called *Value;* this property contains the data to be validated by your client-side function.

Next, you need to write your validation logic. This logic should evaluate *arguments.Value* and determine if it is valid or not. Once you have determined this, you set the *arguments .IsValid* property to *true* (valid) or *false* (invalid).

Finally, you attach your client-side function to a *CustomValidator* by setting the *ClientFunctionName* property of the *CustomValidator* control to the name of your validation function.

Consider an example. Suppose you need custom validation for managing password rules at the client level. Your requirement might be that passwords are between 6 and 14 characters in length and must contain at least one uppercase letter, one lowercase letter, and one numeric character. Suppose your page includes a *TextBox* control for entering a new password, a *Button* control for submitting the password change, a *ValidationSummary* control for showing the long error message, a *RequiredFieldValidator* control to ensure the user has typed a password, and a *CustomValidator* control for validating the actual password. Your Web page source might look as follows:

Change Password Web Page Source

```
<%@ Page Language="VB" AutoEventWireup="false" CodeFile="NewPassword.aspx.vb"
Inherits="NewPassword" %>

<!DOCTYPE html PUBLIC "-//W3C//DTD XHTML 1.0 Transitional//EN" "http://www.w3.org/TR/
xhtml1/DTD/xhtml1-transitional.dtd">

<html xmlns="http://www.w3.org/1999/xhtml">
<head runat="server">
    <title>Change Password</title>
</head>
<body style="font-family: Arial">
    <form id="form1" runat="server">
    <div>
    <table width="400">
        <tr><td colspan="2" style="font-size: x-large">Change Password</td></tr>
        <tr>
            <td colspan="2">
                <asp:ValidationSummary ID="ValidationSummary1" runat="server" />
            </td>
        </tr>
        <tr>
            <td width="190" align="right" valign="middle">New password:</td>
            <td width="210" valign="middle">
                <asp:RequiredFieldValidator ID="RequiredFieldValidatorPassword"
                  runat="server" ErrorMessage="Please enter a valid password" text="*"
                  Tooltip="Please enter a valid password"
                  ControlToValidate="TextBoxNewPassword">
                </asp:RequiredFieldValidator>

                <asp:CustomValidator ID="CustomValidatorNewPassword" runat="server"
                    Text="*" ToolTip="Password must be between 6-14 characters and
include 1 capital letter, 1 lowercase letter, and 1 number"
                    ErrorMessage="Password must be between 6-14 characters and include 1
capital letter, 1 lowercase letter, and 1 number"
                    ControlToValidate="TextBoxNewPassword">
                </asp:CustomValidator>
            </td>
        </tr>
        <tr>
            <td></td>
            <td><asp:Button ID="ButtonSubmit" runat="server" Text="Submit" /></td>
        </tr>
    </table>
    </div>
```

```
    </form>
</body>
</html>
```

The next step is to add client-side validation code to the Web page source. You can do so before the *<body>* tag on the page. The following provides an example JavaScript function called *ValidatePassword*. Notice the function signature matches the one defined by the data validation framework. Also notice the setting of *arguments.IsValid*.

Validate Password JavaScript Client-Side Validation

```
<script language="javascript" type="text/javascript">
    function ValidatePassword(source, arguments)
    {
     var data = arguments.Value.split('');
     //start by setting false
     arguments.IsValid=false;

     //check length
     if(data.length < 6 || data.length > 14) return;

     //check for uppercase
     var uc = false;
     for(var c in data)
     {
        if(data[c] >= 'A' && data[c] <= 'Z')
        {
           uc=true; break;
        }
     }
     if(!uc) return;

     //check for lowercase
     var lc = false;
     for(c in data)
     {
        if(data[c] >= 'a' && data[c] <= 'z')
        {
           lc=true; break;
        }
     }
     if(!lc) return;

     //check for numeric
     var num = false;
     for(c in data)
     {
        if(data[c] >= '0' && data[c] <= '9')
```

```
        {
            num=true; break;
        }
    }
    if(!num) return;

    //must be valid
    arguments.IsValid=true;
  }
</script>
```

The final step is to set the *CustomValidator* control's *ClientValidationFunction* property to the function name *ValidatePassword*. You can then run the Web page to test the example. When the *TextBox* control loses focus, the custom client-side validation is executed, as shown in Figure 3-5.

FIGURE 3-5 The client-side validation causes the *ValidationSummary* control and the *CustomValidator* control's *ToolTip* to display the error message

Custom Server-Side Validation

The *CustomValidator* control can work client-side, server-side, or both. We recommend that you do validation on both the client and the server in the same way the other validation controls operate. This is good coding practice. In addition, you cannot totally rely on client-side validation only, as it can easily be defeated. As we have discussed, only implementing server-side validation does not always provide the best user experience.

To implement server-side validation with the *CustomValidator* control, you override its *ServerValidate* event. This server-side event can be trapped in your code-behind file to execute code that you write. You wire up an event handler for the given *CustomValidator* control the same way you would any other control's event. Like client-side validation, server-side validation also provides the same two parameters: *source* provides access to the source validation control, and *args* provides the *args.Value* property for checking the data that should be validated. You also use the *args.IsValid* property to indicate validation success or failure. The following code shows the password example using the *ServerValidate* event to perform server-side validation.

Validate Password Server-Side Event Handler

```
'VB
Protected Sub CustomValidatorNewPassword_ServerValidate( _
  ByVal source As Object, _
  ByVal args As System.Web.UI.WebControls.ServerValidateEventArgs) _
  Handles CustomValidatorNewPassword.ServerValidate

  Dim data As String = args.Value

  'start by setting false
  args.IsValid = False

  'check length
  If (data.Length < 6 Or data.Length > 14) Then Return

  'check for uppercase
  Dim uc As Boolean = False
  For Each c As Char In data
    If (c >= "A" And c <= "Z") Then
      uc = True : Exit For
    End If

  Next
  If Not uc Then Return

  'check for lowercase
  Dim lc As Boolean = False
  For Each c As Char In data
    If (c >= "a" And c <= "z") Then
      lc = True : Exit For
    End If
  Next
  If Not lc Then Return

  'check for numeric
  Dim num As Boolean = False
```

```
    For Each c As Char In data
      If (c >= "0" And c <= "9") Then
        num = True : Exit For
      End If
    Next
    If Not num Then Return

    'must be valid
    args.IsValid = True

End Sub
```

```
//C#
protected void CustomValidatorNewPassword_ServerValidate(object source,
  ServerValidateEventArgs args)
{
  string data = args.Value;
  //start by setting false
  args.IsValid = false;

  //check length
  if (data.Length < 6 || data.Length > 14) return;

  //check for uppercase
  bool uc = false;
  foreach (char c in data)
  {
    if (c >= 'A' && c <= 'Z')
    {
      uc = true; break;
    }
  }
  if (!uc) return;

  //check for lowercase
  bool lc = false;
  foreach (char c in data)
  {
    if (c >= 'a' && c <= 'z')
    {
      lc = true; break;
    }
  }
  if (!lc) return;
```

```
    //check for numeric
    bool num = false;
    foreach (char c in data)
    {
      if (c >= '0' && c <= '9')
      {
        num = true; break;
      }
    }
    if (!num) return;

    //must be valid
    args.IsValid = true;
}
```

The server-side validation you write does not need to provide the exact same validation as that of the client-side code. For example, the custom client-side script for a *CustomValidator* that validates a five-character customer ID might simply test to ensure that five characters are provided within the acceptable range (uppercase, lowercase). The server-side validation might perform a database query to ensure that the customer ID is that of a valid customer in the database. In this way, you can combine server- and client-side validation to provide a total solution for a user.

Quick Check

1. **Which validation control can be used to determine if data that is entered into a *TextBox* control is of type *Currency*?**
2. **What control can be used to display all validation errors on a page inside a pop-up window?**

Quick Check Answers

1. **You can use the *CompareValidator* control to do a data type check. Set its *Operator* property to *DataTypeCheck* and its *Type* property to *Currency*.**
2. **The *ValidationSummary* control can be used to show a summary of validation error messages for a given page. The control can also be used as a pop-up browser window.**

LAB Working with Validation Controls

In this lab, you create a Web page that simulates user registration with a site. This page will contain *TextBox* controls for users to enter their name, e-mail address, password, and password confirmation. The following are the validation rules for the page:

- All fields are required to contain data.
- The user name field must be between 6 and 14 characters in length. These characters can be uppercase, lowercase, numeric, or underscores.
- The user's e-mail address should be in valid e-mail address format.
- The password and confirm password fields will be 6 to 14 characters. A user's password must contain at least one uppercase letter, one lowercase letter, and one number (as described in the custom validation control example).

If you encounter a problem completing an exercise, the completed projects are available in the samples installed from the companion CD.

EXERCISE 1 Create the Web Site and Add Controls

In this exercise, you create the Web site and add the user input controls.

1. Open Visual Studio and create a new Web site called **WorkingWithValidation-Controls** using your preferred programming language.
2. Open the Default.aspx page and add an HTML table to the page. This table will start with six rows, two columns each. In the first row, set the title of the page to **User Registration**.
3. Add the data entry field descriptions in the first column of each of the next four rows. The descriptions are **User name**, **Email**, **Password**, and **Confirm Password.**
4. Add a *TextBox* control in the second column of these same four rows. Name the *TextBox* controls **TextBoxUserName**, **TextBoxEmail**, **TextBoxPassword**, and **TextBoxConfirmPassword**.
5. Set the *TextMode* property of *TextBoxPassword* and *TextBoxConfirmPassword* to **Password**.
6. Add a *Button* control under the table. Set the *Text* of the *Button* control to **Register**.

   Figure 3-6 shows the Web page in the designer.

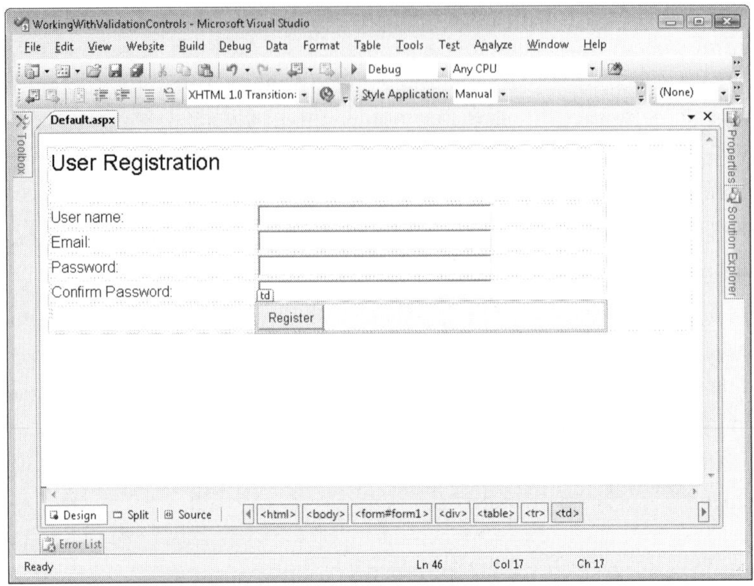

FIGURE 3-6 The registration page in Visual Studio prior to adding validation controls

EXERCISE 2 Add the Validation Controls

In this exercise, you add and configure the validation controls.

1. Continue with the project from the previous exercise, or open the completed Lesson 1, Exercise 1 project in the samples installed from the CD.
2. All of the *TextBox* controls require user input. Therefore, you will add a *RequiredFieldValidator* next to each *TextBox* control. Name each of these controls relative to the field it validates.

   For each of the *RequiredFieldValidator* controls, set the *ControlToValidate* property to the *TextBox* that is being validated.

   For each of the *RequiredFieldValidator* controls, set the *ErrorMessage* and *ToolTip* properties to **User name is required**, **Email is required**, **Password is required**, and **Confirm password is required**, as appropriate.

   For each of the *RequiredFieldValidator* controls, set the *Text* property to asterisk (*).
3. Next, you will define validation for the *TextBoxUserName* control. Recall the rule: The user name field must be between 6 and 14 characters in length and these characters can be uppercase, lowercase, numeric, or underscores.

   To process this rule, you will use a *RegularExpressionValidator* control. Add one next to the *TextBoxUserName* control and set the *ControlToValidate* property to **TextBoxUserName**.

Set the *Text* property to asterisk; set the *ErrorMessage* and *ToolTip* properties to **Please enter only alpha-numeric characters (and no spaces)**. Finally, set the *ValidationExpression* property to the regular expression, **\w{6,14}**. The table cell for the *TextBoxUserName* control should look similar to the following:

```
<td>
  <asp:TextBox ID="TextBoxUserName" runat="server" Width="250"></asp:TextBox>
  <asp:RegularExpressionValidator ID="RegularExpressionValidatorUserName"
    Text="*" runat="server" ControlToValidate="TextBoxUserName"
    ErrorMessage="Please enter only alpha-numeric characters (and no spaces)."
    ToolTip="Please enter only alpha-numeric characters (and no spaces)."
    ValidationExpression="\w{6,14}">
  </asp:RegularExpressionValidator>
  <asp:RequiredFieldValidator ID="RequiredFieldValidatorUserName" runat="server"
    Text="*" ErrorMessage="User name is required"
    ControlToValidate="TextBoxUserName"
    ToolTip="User name is required"></asp:RequiredFieldValidator>
</td>
```

4. The field you need to validate next is the user's e-mail address. To do so, you will use another regular expression validation control. Add it next to the *TextBoxEmail* control. Set its *Text, ToolTip, ControlToValidate*, and *ErrorMessage* properties. Use the Properties window to set the control's *ValidationExpression* property. Select Internet Email Address from the list of available regular expressions.
5. The next control you need to add validation to is the *TextBoxPassword* control. You will use the custom validation example defined earlier in the chapter.

   To start, add a *CustomValidator* control next to the *TextBoxPassword* control.

   Set the *ControlToValidate* property to **TextBoxPassword**.

   Set the *Text* property to asterisk (*).

   Set the *ErrorMessage and ToolTip properties* to **Please enter 6-14 characters, at least 1 uppercase letter, 1 lowercase letter, and 1 number**.

   Below the head section of the HTML source, add the client-side code from the listing "Validate Password JavaScript Client-Side Validation," shown earlier in this lesson.

   Set the *ClientValidationFunction* of the *CustomValidator* control to **ValidatePassword**.

   Add the *ServerValidate* event handler for the *CustomValidator* control to your code-behind page. In this method, add the code from the listing "Validate Password Server-Side Event Handler," shown earlier in this lesson.
6. The final validation you need to do is to ensure that both the password and confirm password fields contain the same data. To do so, start by adding a *CompareValidator* next to the *TextBoxConfirmPassword* control.

Set the *ControlToValidate* property to **TextBoxConfirmPassword**.

Set the *ControlToCompare* property to **TextBoxPassword**.

Set the *Text* property to asterisk (*).

Set the *ErrorMessage and ToolTip properties* to **Both password fields must match**.

7. Finally, add a *ValidationSummary* control to the top of the Web page in its own row. This will be used to display the long error messages when the user submits the form.

   The completed Web page is shown in Figure 3-7.

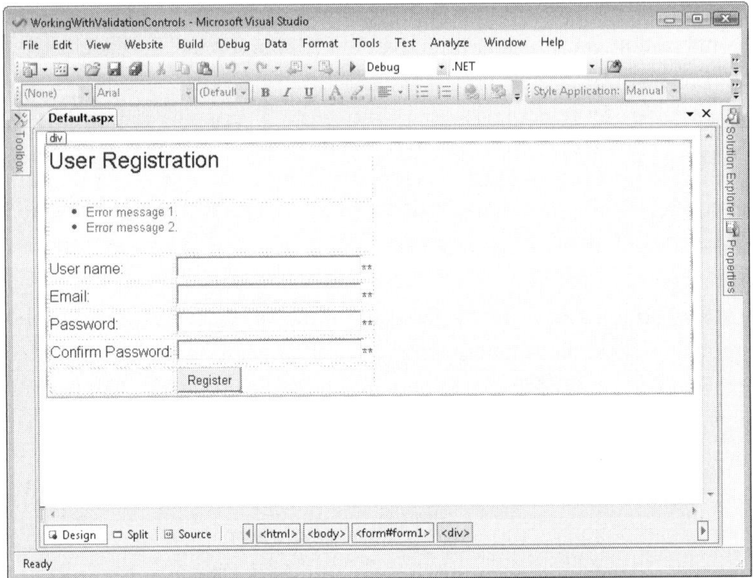

FIGURE 3-7 The completed Web page containing all validation controls

EXERCISE 3 Test the Validation Controls

In this exercise, you run the Web page and test the validation controls.

1. Continue with the project from the previous exercise, or open the completed Lesson 1, Exercise 2 project in the samples installed from the CD.
2. Run the Web page.
3. Before entering any information into the *TextBox* controls, click Register. Verify that the *RequiredFieldValidators* are displayed by noting the errors that are displayed in the *ValidationSummary* control and by hovering your pointer over each of the asterisks to see each *ToolTip*.
4. Test the user name validation by typing fewer than six characters into the *TextBox-UserName* control and clicking Register. Note the validation error. Also, try typing 15 or more characters. Next, type 10 characters into the field but use an invalid character

such as the apostrophe ('). Finally, type valid data into the text box to ensure the validation control works properly.

5. Test the e-mail field by entering an invalid e-mail address. Finally, test with a valid e-mail address.
6. Test the password field for the appropriate input by trying to input fewer than 6 characters or more than 14 characters. Also, attempt a password that is all lowercase, all uppercase, or all numeric. Notice that special characters, such as plus sign (+), minus sign (-), and percent sign (%), are allowed in the password, but not required. Finally, attempt to enter a valid password.
7. Test the confirmation password by typing a confirmation password that does not match the password. Test again with a matching password.

Lesson Summary

- The data validation framework provides a set of validation controls that bind to one or more Web controls to perform validation of the data that is input into those Web controls.
- The ASP.NET validation controls provide both client-side and server-side validation.
- Client-side validation can be disabled by setting the *EnableClientScript* property to *false*.
- The validation controls available in ASP.NET include *CustomValidator*, *CompareValidator*, *RangeValidator*, *RegularExpressionValidator*, and *RequiredFieldValidator*.
- The *ValidationSummary* control can be added to a Web page to provide a summary of the validation errors on the Web page and as a pop-up message.
- The *RegularExpressionValidator* is used to specify validation patterns.
- The *CustomValidator* allows you to provide your custom client-side and server-side code to perform input validation.
- The *Page.Validate* method can be explicitly called to force validation.
- The Web page's *IsValid* property can be queried to verify that the page is valid before running code.

Lesson Review

You can use the following questions to test your knowledge of the information in Lesson 1, "Performing Input Validation." The questions are also available on the companion CD if you prefer to review them in electronic form.

> ***NOTE*** **ANSWERS**
>
> **Answers to these questions and explanations of why each answer choice is right or wrong are located in the "Answers" section at the end of the book.**

1. You need to validate a vendor ID entered by a user. The valid vendor IDs exist in a database table. How can you validate this input?

   A. Provide a *RegularExpressionValidator* and set the *ValidationExpression* property to */DbLookup{code}*.

   B. Provide a *RangeValidator* and set the *MinValue* property to *DbLookup(code)* and set the *MaxVaue* property to *DbLookup(code)*.

   C. Provide a *CustomValidator* with server-side code to search the database for the code.

   D. Provide a *CompareValidator* and set the compare expression to the name of a server-side function that performs a database lookup of the code.

2. You created a Web page that contains many controls that are validated using validation controls. This page also contains *Button* controls that perform PostBacks. You disabled all of the client-side validation and noticed that when you clicked any of the *Button* controls, the code in the *Click* event handler was executing even when some of the controls did not have valid data. How can you best solve this problem to ensure code is not executed when invalid data exists?

   A. In the *Click* event handler method for each of your *Button* controls, test the Web page's *IsValid* property and exit the method if this property is *false*.

   B. In the *Load* event handler method of the Web page, test the Web page's *IsValid* property and exit the method if this property is *false*.

   C. Re-enable the client-side script to disable PostBack until valid data exists.

   D. Add the *runat="server"* attribute to all of the validation controls.

3. You have created an elaborate Web page that contains many validated controls. You want to provide a detailed message for each validation error, but you don't have space to provide the detailed message next to each control. What can you do to indicate an error at the control and list the detailed error messages at the top of the Web page?

   A. Set the *Text* property of the validator control to the detailed message and set the *ErrorMessage* property to an asterisk. Place a *ValidationSummary* control at the top of the Web page.

   B. Set the *ErrorMessage* property of the validator control to the detailed message and set the *Text* property to an asterisk. Place a *ValidationSummary* control at the top of the Web page.

   C. Set the *ToolTip* property of the validator control to the detailed message and set the *ErrorMessage* property to an asterisk. Place a *ValidationSummary* control at the top of the Web page.

   D. Set the *ToolTip* property of the validator control to the detailed message and set the *Text* property to an asterisk. Place a *ValidationSummary* control at the top of the Web page.

Lesson 2: Performing Site Navigation

Seamless navigation from one Web page to another is what makes a collection of Web pages feel like a Web application. You need to consider when and how you move a user between pages. You need to make this seem automatic and planned, putting the user in control. When doing so, you need to consider how you handle navigation following PostBacks and how you allow a user to navigate within your site.

When a page performs a PostBack, you typically end up posting data to the same Web page that originated the request. However, there are scenarios where you may post data from one Web page to another. You also need to consider where the user goes next as a result of a given PostBack.

All Web sites have some form of user navigation control. The sites that stand out are those that provide easy-to-use navigation. Of course, developers need to provide this navigation. They need to determine what happens as the result of user-driven navigation—especially when a user is in the process of a transaction such as purchasing a product.

This lesson covers how you navigate from the server and how you allow client-driven navigation. You will learn the many ways to navigate pages using ASP.NET.

After this lesson, you will be able to:

- Determine the correct method for navigating a user from one page to another in your site depending on your needs.
- Redirect users to pages using both client-side and server-side methods.
- Use the *SiteMap* Web server control to display a representation of a site's navigation structure inside the navigation controls *SiteMapPath*, *Menu*, and *TreeView*.

Estimated lesson time: 40 minutes

Is Page Navigation Necessary?

Page navigation is the process of moving between one actual page of your Web site and another. However, with controls like the *Wizard* control and technologies like AJAX you can embed a lot of functionality inside a single actual page in your site. In this way, navigation takes on a new meaning. You are no longer moving between pages. Rather, you are moving around your page. You might do so from the client and you might do so as a response from a PostBack to the server.

Embedding all the controls and data collection for a given process on a single page can make your work easier. Instead of moving data from page to page or storing it in the database or on the server you can rely on the page itself to manage the entire process. Of course, these solutions are not always suitable for each data collection scenario. Therefore, it is important to know what is involved when doing page-to-page navigation.

Choosing a Method to Navigate Pages

There are many ways to navigate from one page to another in ASP.NET. It's helpful to first identify these ways and then examine each in detail. The following are the methods for page-to-page navigation in an ASP.NET site:

- **Client-side navigation** Client-side code or markup allows a user to request a new Web page. Your client code or markup requests a new Web page in response to a client-side event, such as clicking a hyperlink or executing JavaScript as part of a button click.
- **Cross-page posting** A control and form are configured to PostBack to a different Web page than the one that made the original request.
- **Client-side browser redirect** Server-side code sends a message to the browser, informing the browser to request a different Web page from the server.
- **Server-side transfer** Server-side code transfers control of a request to a different Web page.

Client-Side Navigation

One of the easiest ways to navigate to a different Web page is to provide a *HyperLink* control on the form and set the *NavigateUrl* property to the desired destination. The *HyperLink* control generates an HTML anchor tag, *<a>*. The *NavigateUrl* property is placed into the *href* attribute of the *<a>* element. The following example shows both the source of a *HyperLink* control and its rendered HTML.

***HyperLink* Control: Source**

```
<asp:HyperLink ID="HyperLink1"
  runat="server" NavigateUrl="~/NavigateTest2.aspx">Goto NavigateTest2</asp:HyperLink>
```

***HyperLink* Control: Rendered HTML**

```
<a id="HyperLink1" href="NavigateTest2.aspx">Goto NavigateTest2</a>
```

In this example, if this control is placed on a Web page called NavigateTest1.aspx, and the *HyperLink* control is clicked, the browser simply requests the NavigateTest2.aspx page. This means that no data is posted to NavigateTest2.aspx. If data is required to pass to NavigateTest2.aspx, you need to find a way to get the data to the page. You might consider embedding it in the query string in the *NavigateUrl* property of the *HyperLink* control.

Another means of forcing client-side navigation is through JavaScript. In this case you write code to perform Web page navigation by changing the *document* object's *location* property to a new URL. The *document* object represents the Web page in client-side JavaScript; setting its *location* property causes the browser to request the Web page defined by the *location* property's value.

The following example contains an HTML button element with a bit of client-side JavaScript to request a new page when the button is clicked.

```
<input id="Button1" type="button"
        value="Goto NavigateTest2"
        onclick="return Button1_onclick()" />
```

Notice that the *onclick* event is configured to call the client-side method, *Button1_onclick*. The JavaScript source for the *Button1_onclick* method is added into the *<head>* element of the page as follows:

```
<script language="javascript" type="text/javascript">
function Button1_onclick() {
  document.location="NavigateTest2.aspx";
}
</script>
```

Once again, the NavigateTest2.aspx page is requested and no data is posted back to the Web server. Of course, you could send data into the function as part of a parameter and then append that data to the query string of the request.

Cross-Page Posting

Cross-page posting is frequently desired in a scenario where data is collected on one Web page and processed on another Web page that displays the results. In such a scenario, a *Button* control typically has its PostBack*Url* property set to the Web page to which the processing should post back. The page that receives the PostBack receives the posted data from the first page for processing. This page is referred to as the processing page.

The processing page often needs to access data that was contained inside the initial page that collected the data and delivered the PostBack. The previous page's data is available inside the *Page.PreviousPage* property. This property is only set if a cross-page post occurs. If the *PreviousPage* is set to *Nothing* (*null* in C#) no cross-page posting occurred. You can access the controls found in the previous page by using the *FindControl* method of the *PreviousPage* property (which is a *NamingContainer*).

In the following example, a Web page called DataCollection.aspx contains a *TextBox* control called *TextBox1* and a *Button* control that has its PostBack*Url* set to *"~/ProcessingPage.aspx"*. When the processing page is posted to by the data collection page, it executes server-side code to pull the data from the data collection page and put it inside a *Label* control. The code to do so is as follows:

```
'VB
Protected Sub Page_Load(ByVal sender As Object, _
  ByVal e As System.EventArgs) Handles Me.Load

  If Page.PreviousPage Is Nothing Then
    LabelData.Text = "No previous page in post"
  Else
```

```
    LabelData.Text = _
      CType(PreviousPage.FindControl("TextBox1"), TextBox).Text
  End If

End Sub

//C#
protected void Page_Load(object sender, EventArgs e)
{
    if(Page.PreviousPage == null)
    {
        LabelData.Text = "No previous page in post";
    }
    else
    {
        LabelData.Text  =
            ((TextBox)PreviousPage.FindControl("TextBox1")).Text;
    }
}
```

Accessing Posted Data as Strongly Typed Data

You can also provide access to cross-page posted data through strongly typed properties on the page. This eliminates the need to call *FindControl* and execute the type casting calls. You first define the public property (or properties) on your data collection page. You then set the *PreviousPageType* directive on the processing page to point to the data collection page. ASP.NET does the remaining work to wire up the properties to the *Page.PreviousPage* object.

In the following example, the DataCollection.aspx page performs a cross-page PostBack to ProcessingPage.aspx. However, it first defines a public property called *PageData* as follows:

```
'VB
Public ReadOnly Property PageData() As String
  Get
    Return TextBox1.Text
  End Get
End Property

//C#
public string PageData
{
  get { return TextBox1.Text; }
}
```

Like the previous example, the DataCollection.aspx page also contains a *Button* control on which the PostBack*Url* property has been set to *"~/ProcessingPage.aspx"*.

To access the newly created *PageData* property for the processing page, you need to set the *PreviousPageType* directive in the *ProcessingPage*.aspx page. This directive is added after the *Page* directive in the page's source and looks like this:

```
<%@ PreviousPageType VirtualPath="~/ProcessingPage.aspx" %>
```

The processing page contains a *Label* control that is populated from the *PageData* property. The following code demonstrates this:

```
'VB
Protected Sub Page_Load(ByVal sender As Object, _
  ByVal e As System.EventArgs) Handles Me.Load

  If Page.PreviousPage Is Nothing Then
    LabelData.Text = "No previous page in post"
  Else
    LabelData.Text = _
      PreviousPage.PageData
  End If

End Sub

//C#
protected void Page_Load(object sender, EventArgs e)
{
    if (PreviousPage == null)
    {
        LabelData.Text = "No previous page in post";
    }
    else
    {
        LabelData.Text =
            PreviousPage.PageData;
    }
}
```

Note that you might find IntelliSense does not show the *PageData* property when you code this example. Simply build the page that causes the data type of the *PreviousPage* property to be set and the *PageData* property will be visible to IntelliSense.

Client-Side Browser Redirect

Often you need to redirect users to another page based on the result of their request or PostBack to the server. For example, a user might click Submit Order on your page. After processing the order successfully, you might then want to redirect the user to an order details page. The *Page.Response* object contains the *Redirect* method for doing just that.

The *Redirect* method can be used in your server-side code to instruct the browser to initiate a request for another Web page. The redirect is not a PostBack. It is similar to the user clicking a hyperlink on a Web page.

Consider the following example code. Here the SubmitOrder.aspx page contains a *Button* control that performs a PostBack to the server. Once that PostBack processes, a call is made to redirect the user to the OrderDetails.aspx page:

```
'VB
Protected Sub ButtonSubmit_Click(ByVal sender As Object, _
  ByVal e As System.EventArgs) Handles ButtonSubmit.Click

  Response.Redirect("OrderDetails.aspx")

End Sub

//C#
protected void ButtonSubmit_Click(object sender, EventArgs e)
{
  Response.Redirect("OrderDetails.aspx");
}
```

The redirect is accomplished by sending a Hypertext Transfer Protocol (HTTP) response code of 302 to the browser along with the URL of the page to which to redirect. The address that is displayed in the browser is updated to reflect the new URL location. Note that this comes at the cost of performing an extra round trip to the server.

The *PreviousPage* property does not get populated when using the *Redirect* method. To access data from the original page, you need to resort to traditional methods of passing data, such as placing the data into cookies, placing the data into session state variables, or passing the data in the query string.

Server-Side Transfer

Sometimes you might need to transfer the server-side processing of an entire Web page over to another page. These scenarios are rare and tend to add needless confusion to your code and application. However, you might need to hide the name of the page processing the request from the user. You can do so using the *Page.Server.Transfer* method.

The *Transfer* method transfers the entire context of a Web page over to another page. The page that receives the transfer generates the response back to the user's browser. In doing so, the user's Internet address in his or her browser does not show the result of the transfer. The user's address bar still reflects the name of the originally requested page.

Like the previous redirect example, you execute a *Transfer* call from the server. This is typically the result of a PostBack. As an example, suppose you have a page called Order-Request.aspx. Suppose this page contains a button for submitting an order. When an order is submitted, your code on the server might transfer the entire request to another page called OrderProcessing.aspx. The following shows an example of making this method call:

```
'VB
Protected Sub Button1_Click(ByVal sender As Object, _
  ByVal e As System.EventArgs) Handles Button1.Click

   Server.Transfer("OrderProcessing.aspx", False)

End Sub

//C#
protected void Button1_Click(object sender, EventArgs e)
{
   Server.Transfer("OrderProcessing.aspx", false);
}
```

The *Transfer* method has an overload that accepts a Boolean parameter called *preserveForm*. You set this parameter to indicate if you want to keep the form and query string data. It is generally better to set this to *false*. You can also access the *PreviousPage* property during a transfer (just as you would with cross-page posting).

Using the Site Map Web Server Control

Thus far you have seen how to help push users from page to page using both client- and server-side techniques. Another key component of any Web site is providing a solid navigational structure for users. Users need to be able to navigate to the various features and functionality provided by your application. ASP.NET provides controls to help you both manage the navigational structure of your site and provide the display of that structure to users.

Managing and documenting your site structure can be done through the use of a site map. A site map in ASP.NET is an XML file that contains the overall structure and hierarchy of your site. You create and manage this file. This gives you control over what pages you want as top-level pages, the pages you want to be nested pages within that top level, and any pages to which you do not want users to navigate.

You can add a site map to your application by right-clicking your Web site and selecting Add New Item | Site Map. A site map is an XML file with the extension .sitemap. You add nodes to the site map by adding *<siteMapNode>* elements. Each of these elements has a *title* attribute that gets displayed to the user, a *url* attribute to define the page to which to navigate, and a *description* attribute for defining information about the page. A Web.sitemap for a small, order-entry site might look as follows:

```
<?xml version="1.0" encoding="utf-8" ?>
<siteMap xmlns="http://schemas.microsoft.com/AspNet/SiteMap-File-1.0" >
  <siteMapNode url="Default.aspx" title="Home"  description="">
```

```
    <siteMapNode url="Catalog.aspx" title="Our Catalog"  description="">
      <siteMapNode url="ProductCategory.aspx" title="Products"  description="" />
      <siteMapNode url="Product.aspx" title="View Product"  description="" />
    </siteMapNode>
    <siteMapNode url="Cart.aspx" title="Shopping Cart"  description="" />
    <siteMapNode url="Account.aspx" title="My Account"  description="">
      <siteMapNode url="SignIn.aspx" title="Login"  description="" />
      <siteMapNode url="PassReset.aspx" title="Reset Password"  description="" />
      <siteMapNode url="AccountDetails.aspx" title="Manage Account"  description="">
        <siteMapNode url="Profile.aspx" title="Account Information"  description="" />
        <siteMapNode url="OrderHistory.aspx" title="My Orders"  description="">
          <siteMapNode url="ViewOrder.aspx" title="View Order"  description="" />
        </siteMapNode>
      </siteMapNode>
    </siteMapNode>
    <siteMapNode url="AboutUs.aspx" title="About Us"  description="" />
    <siteMapNode url="Privacy.aspx" title="Privacy Policy"  description="" />
    <siteMapNode url="ContactUs.aspx" title="Contact Us"  description="" />
    <siteMapNode url="MediaKit.aspx" title="Media Relations"  description="" />
  </siteMapNode>
</siteMap>
```

This site map defines the hierarchy and navigational structure of your site. It determines which pages involve subnavigation of the outer top-level navigation. It also determines which pages are left out of your direct navigation. In this example, that might include pages for checkout, shipping, credit card processing, and such. You do not want users to navigate directly to these pages. Rather, you want them to start with their shopping cart and use the navigation techniques discussed previously to move the user through the buying process.

Using the *SiteMap* Class

The *SiteMap* class provides programmatic access to the site navigation hierarchy from within your code-behind page. Its two primary properties are *RootNode* and *CurrentNode,* and both return *SiteMapNode* instances. The *SiteMapNode* object represents a node in the site map and has properties called *Title*, *Url*, and *Description*. To access nodes in the hierarchy, you can use the *SiteMapNode* instance's *ParentNode*, *ChildNodes*, *NextSibling*, and *PreviousSibling* properties. For example, the following code snippet can be used to navigate to the Web page that is listed as the parent Web page in the Web.sitemap file.

```
'VB
Protected Sub Button1_Click(ByVal sender As Object, _
  ByVal e As System.EventArgs) Handles Button1.Click

  Response.Redirect(SiteMap.CurrentNode.ParentNode.Url)

End Sub
```

```
//C#
protected void Button1_Click(object sender, EventArgs e)
{
  Response.Redirect(SiteMap.CurrentNode.ParentNode.Url);
}
```

Displaying Site Map Information to Users

Of course, the site map information is just an XML file. To display this information, you need to put a navigational control on a Web page. These controls can take a site map file or a *SiteMapDataSource* control as their data source and display information accordingly.

A *SiteMapDataSource* control is simply a control designed to provide you with programmatic access to a site map file. This control can also be used by the navigation controls to provide a source for their data. You can use a *SiteMapDataSource* control by dragging it onto your page. It will automatically connect with the site map file you have defined for your site.

There are a couple of attributes you can use to configure the *SiteMapDataSource* control. The first is *ShowStartingNode*. You can set this value to *false* if you do not want the user to see the root node in your site map file. The second is *StartingNodeOffset*. This is useful if you are creating a subnavigational control and only want to show parts of the navigation. You can set this to the node at which you wish to start. The following shows this control added to a page:

```
<asp:SiteMapDataSource ID="SiteMapDataSource1" runat="server"
  StartingNodeOffset="0" ShowStartingNode="False" />
```

Like the site map file, the *SiteMapDataSource* does not have a visual representation to a user. Instead, it manages access to your site map data. To show the data to a user you must add a navigational control and connect it to the *SiteMapDataSource* control. There are three main navigational controls available in ASP.NET: *Menu*, *TreeView*, and *SiteMapPath*.

The *Menu* control is used to show the structure of your site in a menu-like format. It allows users to navigate both from the top level and to child levels within your site. There are many attributes for you to manage the *Menu* control; many of them have to do with the style and layout of the control. Two attributes to be aware of are *DataSourceId* and *Orientation*. You use the *DataSourceId* attribute to set the data source for the control. You can set it to the ID of a *SiteMapDataSource* control on your page. *Orientation* allows you to set whether you want the menu to be displayed vertically or horizontally. The following shows the markup source for a *Menu* control:

```
<asp:Menu ID="Menu1" runat="server" DataSourceID="SiteMapDataSource1"
  MaximumDynamicDisplayLevels="5" Orientation="Horizontal">
</asp:Menu>
```

Figure 3-8 shows a *Menu* control that uses the site map defined earlier. Notice this *Menu* control is expanded for the My Account child items.

FIGURE 3-8 A Menu control on a Web page

The *TreeView* control shows your site structure in a collapsible tree format. It allows a user to navigate to the hierarchy of your site and then select an item and navigate to the selected page. It works with the *SiteMapDataSource* the same way the *Menu* control does. Figure 3-9 shows the same site map file shown in a *TreeView* control.

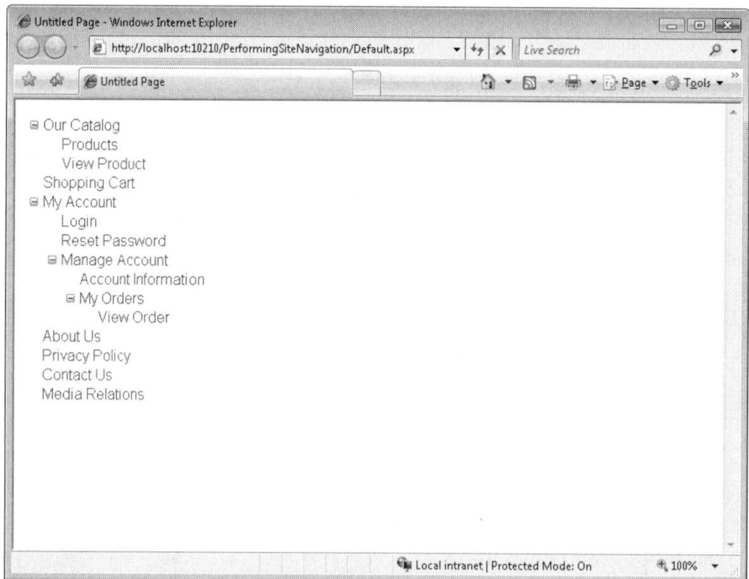

FIGURE 3-9 A *TreeView* control on a Web page

The last navigational control, *SiteMapPath*, allows users to see their current location within your site along with the path of pages they went through to get there. This is often referred to as the breadcrumb trail of site navigation. This is useful if users navigate many depths of your site and need to work their way back up from those depths.

The *SiteMapPath* can be added to a page or a master page file. It automatically picks up the site map file; you do not need to configure a data source. It then wires up the site map with the actual page being requested by the user. Based on this information, it provides navigation back up to the parent page of the shown child page. Figure 3-10 shows a *SiteMapPath* for the Profile.aspx page in the site map XML file example defined earlier.

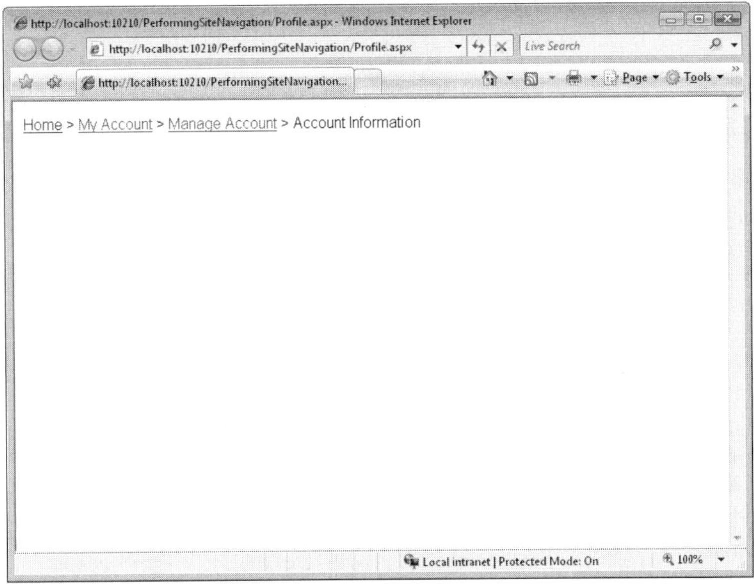

FIGURE 3-10 A *SiteMapPath* control on a Web page

✔ Quick Check

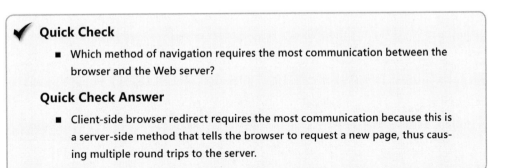

- **Which method of navigation requires the most communication between the browser and the Web server?**

Quick Check Answer

- **Client-side browser redirect requires the most communication because this is a server-side method that tells the browser to request a new page, thus causing multiple round trips to the server.**

LAB Working with Site Navigation

In this lab, you create the basis for the navigation of a Web application for managing customers and their calls.

EXERCISE 1 Create the Web Application Project

In this exercise, you create the Web application project. You also add a site map XML file and configure the layout of the navigation controls on the Default.aspx page. If you encounter a problem completing an exercise, the completed projects are available in the samples installed from the companion CD.

1. Open Visual Studio and create a new Web site project called **WorkingWithSite-Navigation** using your preferred programming language.
2. Add a site map file to the Web site by right-clicking the project and selecting Add New Item. Select the Site Map item from the Add New Item dialog box. Leave the name of the file as Web.sitemap.
3. Add a set of *<siteMapNode>* elements to the site map. Each node should represent a page in your fictitious customer service application. Your site map XML file should look as follows:

```
<?xml version="1.0" encoding="utf-8" ?>
<siteMap xmlns="http://schemas.microsoft.com/AspNet/SiteMap-File-1.0" >
  <siteMapNode url="Default.aspx" title="Home"  description="">
    <siteMapNode url="SearchCustomers.aspx" title="Search Customers"
        description="">
      <siteMapNode url="CustomerDetails.aspx" title="Customer Details"
        description="" />
    </siteMapNode>
    <siteMapNode url="NewCustomer.aspx" title="New Customer"  description="" />
    <siteMapNode url="CallLog.aspx" title="Log Call"  description="" />
    <siteMapNode url="ReportsList.aspx" title="Reports"  description="">
      <siteMapNode url="ReportIssues.aspx" title="Issues By Priority"
        description="" />
      <siteMapNode url="ReportCalls.aspx" title="Customer Call Report"
        description="" />
      <siteMapNode url="ReportActivities.aspx" title="Activities Report"
        description="" />
    </siteMapNode>
  </siteMapNode>
</siteMap>
```

4. Open the Default.aspx page in Source view. Start by adding an HTML *<table>* to the page. It should contain two rows. The first row should contain a single column that spans the table. The second row should contain two columns.

5. Above the table add two *SiteMapDataSource* controls to the page. You can do so from the Toolbox in the Data section.

   Configure one *SiteMapDataSource* to not show the first node in the source data; name this node **SiteMapDataSourceMenu**. Configure the second to show all of the site map data; name this node **SiteMapDataSourceTree**. These controls should look as follows:

```
<asp:SiteMapDataSource ID="SiteMapDataSourceMenu"
  ShowStartingNode="false" runat="server"  />
<asp:SiteMapDataSource ID="SiteMapDataSourceTree" runat="server"  />
```

6. Add a *Menu* control to the HTML table's first row. Configure this control to use the menu data source control. Set its display to show menu items horizontally across the top of your page. Your control's configuration might look as follows:

```
<tr>
  <td colspan="2">
    <asp:Menu ID="Menu1" runat="server"
      DataSourceID="SiteMapDataSourceMenu" Orientation="Horizontal"
      StaticMenuItemStyle-HorizontalPadding="10">
    </asp:Menu>
  </td>
</tr>
```

7. Add a *TreeView* control inside the first column of the second row. Set the *DataSourceId* attribute accordingly. This column should look as follows:

```
<td width="225">
  <asp:TreeView ID="TreeView1" runat="server"
    DataSourceID="SiteMapDataSourceTree" LeafNodeStyle-VerticalPadding="8">
  </asp:TreeView>
</td>
```

8. Add a *SiteMapPath* control to the second column of the second row. Set the *Data-SourceId* attribute accordingly. This column should look as follows:

```
<td width="375" valign="top">
  <br />
  <asp:SiteMapPath ID="SiteMapPath1" runat="server" Font-Size="Smaller">
  </asp:SiteMapPath>
</td>
```

9. Finally, add one of the child pages to the site. Add the CustomerDetails.aspx page to the site. Copy everything in the *<body>* section of Default.aspx and paste it into the CustomerDetails.aspx page. Normally you would not do such a thing. Instead you would create your navigation inside a master page. However, master pages are not

covered until later chapters. This page will be used to demonstrate the *SiteMapPath* control.

10. Build the Web application project.

EXERCISE 2 Test the Site Navigation

In this exercise, you test the site navigation on the Web application.

1. Continue with the project from the previous exercise, or open the completed Lesson 2, Exercise 1 project in the samples installed from the CD.
2. Right-click the Default.aspx page and select Set As Start Page.
3. Run the Web application to display the Default.aspx page. You should see the page as shown in Figure 3-11.

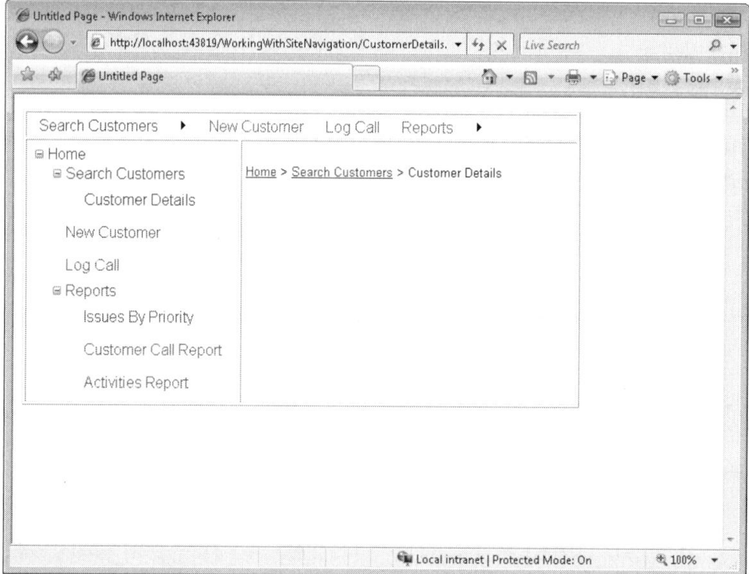

FIGURE 3-11 The CustomerDetails.aspx Web page with all the navigation controls

4. Try clicking the Customer Details link on both the *Menu* and *TreeView* controls.

Lesson Summary

- There are multiple ways to navigate from page to page in your site through code. You can write both client and server code to do so.
- You can send the entire processing of a given page over to another page using the server-side *Transfer* method of the *Page.Server* object. This is useful if you wish to hide the file name of the processing page.

- You can create a site map XML file to represent the navigational structure of your Web site. You can display this information using the *Menu*, *TreeView*, and *SiteMapPath* controls.

Lesson Review

You can use the following questions to test your knowledge of the information in Lesson 2, "Performing Site Navigation." The questions are also available on the companion CD if you prefer to review them in electronic form.

> ***NOTE* ANSWERS**
>
> **Answers to these questions and explanations of why each answer is right or wrong are located in the "Answers" section at the end of the book.**

1. Which of the following server-side methods of the *HttpServerUtility* class can be used to navigate to a different Web page without requiring a round trip to the client?
   A. *Redirect*
   B. *MapPath*
   C. *Transfer*
   D. *UrlDecode*
2. Which control automatically uses the Web.sitemap file to display site map information to a user on a Web page?
   A. *Menu*
   B. *TreeView*
   C. *SiteMapDataSource*
   D. *SiteMapPath*
3. You want to provide an Up button for your Web pages to programmatically navigate the site map. Which class can you use to access the site map content to accomplish this?
   A. *SiteMapPath*
   B. *SiteMapDataSource*
   C. *SiteMap*
   D. *HttpServerUtility*

Chapter Review

To further practice and reinforce the skills you learned in this chapter, you can perform the following tasks:

- Review the chapter summary.
- Complete the case scenarios. These scenarios set up real-world situations involving the topics of this chapter and ask you to create solutions.
- Complete the suggested practices.
- Take a practice test.

Chapter Summary

- You can use the data validation framework to ensure data integrity at both the client and at the server. This ensures both a good user experience and a robust application.
- You can provide site navigation using client-side code or markup, server-side code, and cross-page posting.
- The site map file can be used to define the structure of your site. It can be bound to navigational controls for the display of this information.

Case Scenarios

In the following case scenarios you apply what you've learned about input validation and site navigation. If you have difficulty completing this work, review the material in this chapter before beginning the next chapter. You can find answers to these questions in the "Answers" section at the end of this book.

Case Scenario 1: Determining the Proper Validation Controls to Implement on a User Name

You are creating a new Web page that collects various data from users. On the registration page, the user name must be a valid e-mail address.

- Which validation controls will you implement on the user name text box?

Case Scenario 2: Determining the Proper Password Validation Controls to Implement

You are creating a new Web page that collects various data from users. On the registration page, the user must supply a password and password confirmation. The password must contain at least one uppercase letter, one lowercase letter, and one number. The password must also be between 6 and 14 characters.

- Which validation controls will you implement on the password text box?

Case Scenario 3: Implementing a Site Map

You are creating a Web site for a customer and want to create a menu that contains a tree view of the locations to which the user can navigate. You also want to display a breadcrumb path to show the user the path to the page.

- Which controls will you use?

Suggested Practices

To successfully master the input validation and site navigation exam objectives presented in this chapter, complete the following tasks.

Create a Web Site and Program Redirection

For this task, you should complete Practice 1.

- **Practice 1** Create a new Web page that collects data from users. Add a submit button and configure the button to perform a cross-page PostBack. Add code to the destination Web page that retrieves the data from the source Web page to prove that you can access this data.

Create a Data Collection Page with Validation

For this task, you should complete Practices 1 and 2. Complete Practice 3 to obtain extra experience with the *CustomValidator* control.

- **Practice 1** Create a new Web page that collects data from users. Practice adding the validation controls to restrict data entry to the known set of good data.
- **Practice 2** Disable all client-side validation and test server-side validation.
- **Practice 3** Add at least one *CustomValidator* and supply client-side and server-side validation code.

Implement the *HyperLink* Web Server Control

For this task, you should complete Practices 1 and 2.

- **Practice 1** Create a new Web page and add several *HyperLink* Web server controls to the page.
- **Practice 2** Configure some *HyperLink* controls to navigate to different Web pages on the same Web site, and configure other *HyperLink* controls to navigate to a Web page on a different Web site.

Take a Practice Test

The practice tests on this book's companion CD offer many options. For example, you can test yourself on just the content covered in this chapter, or you can test yourself on all the 70-562 certification exam content. You can set up the test so that it closely simulates the experience of taking a certification exam, or you can set it up in study mode so that you can look at the correct answers and explanations after you answer each question.

MORE INFO **PRACTICE TESTS**

For details about all the practice test options available, see "How to Use the Practice Tests" in this book's Introduction.

CHAPTER 4

ASP.NET State Management

A common challenge in application development is tracking the user state, or data, that is relevant with respect to your application. This is true of both Windows and Web-based applications. You often need to know (and remember) information about users, about the requests they are working on, and about data they have entrusted you to keep. This state data ranges from things like a user's role within your application (like manager or employee) to data that exists as part of a transaction (like a Web shopping cart) to data that you store (like a transaction history). You need to effectively manage this state to provide a good user experience on your site and to gain user confidence with respect to your application.

ASP.NET provides multiple ways for you to manage user state in your applications. These features can be split across two major lines: client-side and server-side state management. Client-side state management stores information on the client's computer by embedding the information into a Web page, a Uniform Resource Locator (URL), a browser cookie, or the browser's cache. Server-side state management tracks the user with a cookie or a URL but stores the information about a user in the server's memory or a database. This chapter explores both server and client state management techniques.

Exam objectives in this chapter:

- Configuring and Deploying Web Applications
  - Configure session state by using Microsoft SQL Server, State Server, or *InProc*.
- Programming Web Applications
  - Implement session state, view state, control state, cookies, cache, or application state.

Lessons in this chapter:

Before You Begin

To complete the lessons in the chapter, you should be familiar with developing applications with Microsoft Visual Studio using Visual Basic or C#. In addition, you should be comfortable with all of the following:

- The Visual Studio 2008 Integrated Development Environment (IDE).
- A basic understanding of Hypertext Markup Language (HTML) and client-side scripting.
- How to create a new Web site.
- Building a Web form by adding Web server controls to a Web page and programming against them on the server.

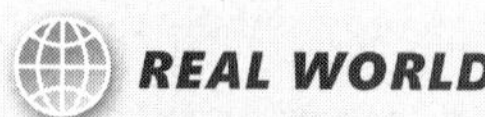

Mike Snell

The decisions you make regarding state management can greatly impact the ability of your application to scale. When we talk about application scalability, we are typically asking how many users and how many requests a given application can service. The answer to this question lies in the application's use of the resources found on its hosting server. The fewer resources tied up on a per-user, per-request basis, the more users can be satisfied by the application and its host. If, however, you consume a lot of server resources on a per-user basis, you are limited in your scalability. For this reason, you need to make trade-offs in terms of ease of programming, location of state storage, and need for scalability.

This single issue has plagued many applications with which I have had the chance to help. These applications often start out with the right intentions: Throw a few simple forms up on a site as quickly and easily as possible to solve a specific business problem. These same applications then morph into larger and larger solutions following the original, unintentional architecture. Of course, these applications suffer from their ability to scale. Fortunately, there are more options available these days to solve these issues (like moving the large amounts of session data to a database or another caching server). However, often the only solution is to take a hard line with respect to state management and rewrite much of the application. Understanding these issues before putting together "easy and quick" solutions can often prevent the issues from occurring.

Lesson 1: Using Client-Side State Management

If you intend to maximize your application for scalability, then you need to strongly consider using the client for storing application state. Removing this burden from the server frees up resources, allowing the server to process more user requests. ASP.NET provides several techniques for storing state information on the client. These include the following:

- **View state** ASP.NET uses view state to track values in controls between page requests. You can also add your own custom values to the view state.
- **Control state** Control state allows you to persist information about a control that is not part of the view state. This is useful to custom control developers. If view state is disabled for a control or the page, the control state will still function.
- **Hidden fields** Like view state, HTML hidden fields store data without displaying that data to the user's browser. This data is presented back to the server and is available when the form is processed.
- **Cookies** Cookies store a value in the user's browser that the browser sends with every page request to the same server. Cookies are the best way to store state data that must be available for multiple Web pages on an entire Web site.
- **Query strings** Query strings are values stored at the end of the URL. These values are visible to the user through his or her browser's address bar. Use query strings when you want a user to be able to e-mail or instant message state data within a URL.

In this lesson, you first learn when to choose client-side over server-side state management. Then, you learn how to implement all of the client-side state management techniques just listed: view state, control state, hidden fields, cookies, and query strings.

After this lesson, you will be able to:

- Choose between client-side and server-side state management.
- Use view state to store custom data values.
- Use control state to store values for custom controls even if view state is disabled.
- Use hidden fields to store values in a Web form.
- Use cookies to track state management data as a user browses multiple pages in a Web site.
- Use query strings to pass values embedded within the URL to another page.

Estimated lesson time: 30 minutes

Choosing Client-Side or Server-Side State Management

State management information, such as user name, personalization options, or shopping cart contents, can be stored at either the client or on the server. If the state management information is stored on the client, the client submits the information to the server with each request. If the state management information is stored on the server, the server stores the information, but tracks the client using a client-side state management technique. Figure 4-1 illustrates both client-side and server-side state management.

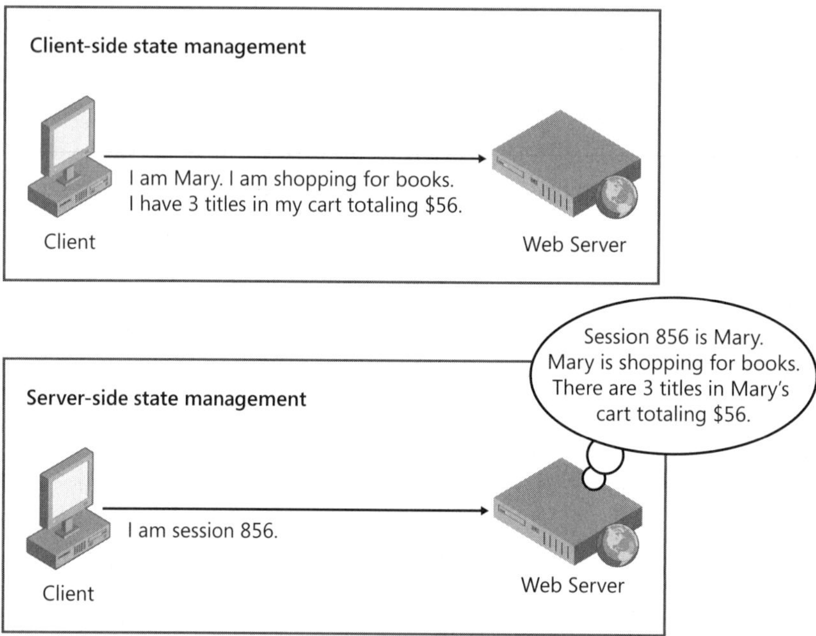

FIGURE 4-1 Client-side state management stores data on the client, whereas server-side state management requires the server to store the data

Storing information on the client has the following advantages:

- **Better scalability** With server-side state management, each client that connects to the Web server consumes memory on that server. If a Web site has hundreds (or thousands) of simultaneous users, the memory consumed by storing state management information can become a limiting factor. Pushing this burden to the clients removes that potential bottleneck and frees the server to use its resources to serve more requests.
- **Supports multiple Web servers** With client-side state management, you can distribute incoming requests across multiple Web servers (or a Web farm). In this scenario each client provides all the information any Web server needs to process a request. With server-side state management, if a client switches servers in the middle of the session, the new server does not necessarily have access to the client's state

information (as it is stored on a different server). You can use multiple servers with server-side state management, but you need either intelligent load balancing (to always forward requests from a client to the same server) or centralized state management (where state is stored in a central database to which all Web servers have access).

Storing information on the server has the following advantages:

- **Better security** Client-side state management information can be captured (either in transit or while it is stored on the client) and maliciously modified. Therefore, you should never use client-side state management to store confidential information such as a password, authorization level, or authentication status.
- **Reduced bandwidth** If you store large amounts of state management information, sending that information back and forth to the client can increase bandwidth utilization and page load times, potentially increasing your costs and reducing scalability. The increased bandwidth usage affects mobile clients most of all, because they often have very slow connections. Instead, you should store large amounts of state management data (say, more than 1 KB) on the server.

The choice you make for managing application state should be decided based on these trade-offs. If you are writing an application with relatively few users and high security requirements, you might consider leveraging server-side state. If you want to maximize for scalability but potentially slow down requests across slower bandwidth connections, you should rely on a heavy mix of client-side state.

Of course, there is also persisted state, or data stored in the database. You need to factor this into your decision, too. You can decide to store all user information in the database and thus rely on it for state management. However, this often puts too much pressure on your database server. In this case it is best to store real, transactional data and rely on other techniques for managing more transient state.

Finally, there is the concept of shared state. This is information common to many users of your application. In this case you can often use the caching features of ASP.NET to optimize for the heavy usage of this data. You might use application data caching to store commonly accessed data from the database between user requests. You can also use page-level or fragment-level (partial page) caching to cache commonly accessed pages on the server. Again, the key is to get the right mix for your environment, application requirements, usage, and hardware. ASP.NET makes many tools and techniques available for you to manage state in your application.

View State

As discussed in Chapter 2, *"Adding and Configuring Server Controls,"* view state is the default mechanism used by ASP.NET to store user-specific request and response data between page requests. The data being stored is typically specific to the controls on the page. View state stores object data that is not already represented as HTML in the page response. This ensures that data set on the server is preserved between round trips to the client and the server.

Unless disabled, view state is part of every ASP.NET page. As an example, suppose a user requests a Web page that allows him or her to edit his or her own profile information. When processing the user's request on the server, you might have to go out to a database and get the user's profile information. You then use this information to set property values of the data entry fields on the page. When this page is sent to the user, these property value settings are wrapped up and stored in the view state. When the user then clicks a button to submit his or her changes back to the server, the user also sends back the view state as part of the PostBack. ASP.NET uses this view state information to again set the property values of the server controls on the page back to what they were as part of the request. It then checks to see if any of these values were modified by the user as part of the PostBack request. Next, suppose there is an issue with processing the page on the server and therefore the server must return the same page back to the user. In this case, it again wraps the server control state (including any data changed by the user) back into the view state and sends it back to the client. You did not have to write this code; it just happens for you because of the ASP.NET view state client-side state management feature.

The *Page.ViewState* property provides a dictionary object for retaining values between multiple requests for the same page. This object is of the type *StateBag*. When an ASP.NET page is processed, the current state of the page and its controls is hashed into a string and saved in the page as an HTML hidden field called *__ViewState*. If the data is too long for a single field (as specified in the *Page.MaxPageStateFieldLength* property), ASP.NET performs view state chunking to split it across multiple hidden fields. The following code sample demonstrates how view state adds data as a hidden form field within a Web page's HTML:

```
<input type="hidden" name="__VIEWSTATE" id="__VIEWSTATE"
  value="/wEPDwULLTEzNjkxMzkwNjRkZAVvqsMGC6PVDmbCxBlPkLVKNahk" />
```

Notice that the view state values are hashed, compressed, and encoded for Unicode implementations. This provides better optimization and more security than just simple HTML hidden fields.

The sections that follow describe how to work with ASP.NET view state. For most scenarios, it can be taken for granted. However, you might need to secure your view state data, disable view state data to increase performance, or add your own custom values to the view state.

View State Security Considerations

You need to be aware that view state can be tampered with, as it is simply a hidden field in the user's browser. Of course, you should profile your application to better understand what risks you might face. An Internet application that works with private, personal information has a higher risk profile than that of an internal application that solves simple problems without using private (or secret) information.

For most situations, you can rely on the fact that view state is hashed and encoded before being sent to the user's browser. The view state also includes a message authentication code (MAC). This MAC is used by ASP.NET to determine if the view state has been tampered with.

This helps ensure security in most situations without having to go to a fully encrypted view state.

If you do have very sensitive information that is stored in the view state between page requests, you can encrypt it using the *ViewStateEncryptionMode* property of the *Page* object. This will secure the view state but will also decrease overall performance of the page processing due to the encrypting and decrypting of data. It will also increase the size of the data being sent between the browser and server.

To enable view state encryption for your entire site, you set a value in your Web site configuration file. The *viewStateEncryptionMode* attribute of the pages element can be set to *Always* in the Web.config file. This tells ASP.NET to always encrypt your view state information for the entire site. An example of this setting in the configuration file is as follows:

```
<configuration>
  <system.web>
     <pages viewStateEncryptionMode="Always"/>
  </system.web>
</configuration>
```

Alternatively, you can control view state encryption at the page level. This is useful for scenarios in which sensitive information is confined to a single page or set of pages in your site. To do so, you again set the *ViewStateEncryptionMode* attribute to *Always*. However, you do so inside the individual page's directive section. The following is an example:

```
<%@ Page Language="C#" AutoEventWireup="true"  CodeFile="Default.aspx.cs" Inherits="_
Default" ViewStateEncryptionMode="Always"%>
```

Because *view state* supports encryption, it is considered the most secure(able) method of client-side state management. Encrypted *view state* is secure enough for most security requirements; however, it is more secure to store sensitive data on the server and not send it down to the client, where it has the potential to be manipulated and sent back to the server.

Disabling View State Data

View state is enabled by default for your page and all of the controls on the page. This includes controls like the *Label* control that you might never need to be part of view state. In addition, lots of view state data can cause performance problems. Remember, the view state data is sent back and forth between browser and server. A larger view state means more information going across the wire and consequently longer waits for users. This includes processing time to package the view state, processing time to unpackage it, and bandwidth to transmit it to and from the client.

You can minimize the data that gets stored and passed with the view state by setting the *Control.EnableViewState* property for each control on your page. Setting this property to *false* will instruct ASP.NET to not wire this control into the view state. This is useful if you do not need the control's exact state between requests. Doing so will reduce server processing time and decrease page size. However, if you do need this state, you will either have to reenable view state for the control or code the repopulation of its data yourself.

For most scenarios the view state size is not a big concern. It can be, however, for very large forms with a lot of data entry. It can also be overused when putting your own data into view state. If you think you have run into a bloated view state issue, you can use ASP.NET trace to examine the page and find the culprit. Trace allows you to see the size of the view state for each page and each control on the page. For more information on working with ASP.NET tracing, see Lesson 2 in Chapter 12, "Troubleshooting a Running ASP.NET Application."

EXAM TIP

Controls in ASP.NET have the ability to separate data state and control state. Previous versions of ASP.NET stored data and control state together. When a control's *EnableViewState* property was set to *false*, the control lost its appearance data along with the view state data. In the latest versions of ASP.NET (beyond 2.0), you can set a control's *EnableViewState* to *false* and you will turn off the property value data but not the control's appearance information. Of course, this also means that a control might still be contributing to the size of the view state even when the *EnableViewState* property is set to *false*.

Reading and Writing Custom View State Data

You can use view state to add and retrieve custom values that you need persisted between page requests. These values might not be part of a control but simply something you want to embed in the page to be returned as part of the next request. Adding a value to the view state collection is an efficient and secure way to accomplish this task.

The reading and writing of these collection values is as straightforward as working with the *Dictionary* collection. The following code demonstrates simple calls to write data into the view state and retrieve it from the collection.

```
'VB
'writing to view state
Me.ViewState.Add("MyData", "some data value")

'read from view state
Dim myData As String = CType(ViewState("MyData"), String)

//C#
//writing to view state
this.ViewState.Add("MyData", "some data value");

//read from view state
string myData = (string)ViewState["MyData"];
```

Adding data to the view state is great when you need the information passed back to the server as part of the page post. However, *the content of the view state is for that page only. The view state does not transfer from* one Web page to another. Therefore, it is useful only for temporarily storing values between requests to a single page.

You can store a wide variety of object data inside *the view state*. You are not limited to just string values as you are with cookies. Instead, any data that can be serialized can be embedded in the view state. This includes classes in the .NET Framework that are marked serializable as well as classes you write and mark serializable. The following code shows an example of storing a *DateTime* object instance inside the *ViewState* without converting it to a string.

```
'VB
'check if ViewState object exists, and display it if it does
If (Me.ViewState("lastVisit") IsNot Nothing) Then
  Dim lastVisit As DateTime = CType(Me.ViewState("lastVisit"), DateTime)
  Label1.Text = lastVisit.ToString()
Else
  Label1.Text = "lastVisit ViewState not defined!"
End If

'define the ViewState object for the next page view
Me.ViewState("lastVisit") = DateTime.Now

//C#
//check if ViewState object exists, and display it if it does
if (ViewState["lastVisit"] != null)
  Label1.Text = ((DateTime)ViewState["lastVisit"]).ToString();
else
  Label1.Text = "lastVisit ViewState not defined.";

//define the ViewState object for the next page view
ViewState["lastVisit"] = DateTime.Now;
```

View State and Control State

Recall that you can disable view state for a given control. This can be problematic for control developers. If you write custom controls (see Chapter 10, "Creating Custom Web Controls"), you might need view-state-like behavior that cannot be disabled by a developer. ASP.NET provides control state for just this purpose.

Control state allows you to store property value information that is specific to a control. Again, this state cannot be turned off and therefore should not be used in lieu of view state.

To use control state in a custom Web control, your control must override the *OnInit* method. Here you call the *Page.RegisterRequiresControlState* method, passing an instance of your control to this method. From there, you override the *SaveControlState* method to write out your control state and the *LoadControlState* method to retrieve your control state.

Quick Check

1. How do ASP.NET Web forms remember the settings for controls between user requests?
2. Is the view state lost if a user refreshes a Web page? What if the user e-mails a URL to a friend?

Quick Check Answers

1. View state, which is enabled by default, is used to embed control property values to be sent to the client and back again to the server.
2. View state is embedded inside the HTML of a single instance of a Web page resting in the user's browser. It is lost and rewritten when a user refreshes his or her page. If the URL is copied and sent to another user, the view state does not go along. Instead, when new users request the page, they get their own view state instance.

Hidden Fields

As discussed, ASP.NET view state uses HTML hidden fields to store its data. Hidden fields in HTML are simply input fields that are embedded in a page's HTML, not displayed to the user (unless the user chooses to view the page's source), and then sent back to the server on the page post.

ASP.NET provides a control for creating your own custom hidden fields in a similar manner as you would create and use other ASP.NET controls. The *HiddenField* control allows you to store data in its *Value* property. You add *HiddenField* controls to your page the way you would any other control (drag from the Toolbox).

Like view state, hidden fields only store information for a single page. Therefore, they are not useful for storing session data that is used between page requests. Unlike view state, hidden fields have no built-in compression, encryption, hashing, or chunking. Therefore users can view or modify data stored in hidden fields.

To use hidden fields, you must submit your pages to the server using *HTTP POST* (which happens in response to a user pressing a submit button). You cannot simply call an *HTTP GET* (which happens if the user clicks a link) and retrieve the data in the hidden field on the server.

Cookies

Web applications often need to track users between page requests. These applications need to ensure that the user making the first request is the same user making subsequent requests. This type of common tracking is done with what are called cookies.

A *cookie* is a small amount of data that you write to the client to be stored and then passed with requests to your site. You write persistent cookies to a text file on the client machine. These cookies are meant to survive the user shutting down the browser and reopening it at a later time. You can also write temporary cookies to the memory of the client's browser. These cookies are used only during the given Web session. They are lost when the browser closes.

Again, the most common use of cookies is to identify a single user as he or she visits multiple Web pages within your site. However, you can also use cookies to store state information or other user preferences.

Figure 4-2 illustrates how a Web client and a server use cookies. First (Step 1), the Web client requests a page from the server. Because the client has not visited the server before, it does not have a cookie to submit. When the Web server responds to the request (Step 2), the Web server includes a cookie in the response; this cookie is written to the user's browser or file system. The Web client then submits that cookie with each subsequent request for any page on the same site (Steps 3, 4, and any future page views).

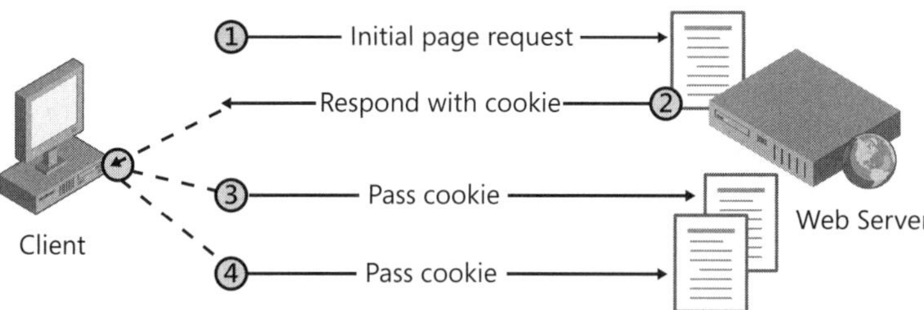

FIGURE 4-2 Web servers use cookies to track Web clients

> ***NOTE*** **ASP.NET SESSIONS AND COOKIES**
>
> **By default, ASP.NET uses cookies to track user sessions. If you have enabled session state, ASP.NET writes a cookie to the user's browser and uses this cookie to identify his or her server session.**

Cookies are the most flexible and reliable way of storing data on the client. However, users can delete cookies on their computers at any time. You can set cookies to have long expiration times but that does not stop users from deleting all their cookies and thus wiping out any settings you might have stored in them. In addition, cookies do not solve the issue of a user moving from computer to computer. In these cases, users' preferences do not always go along with them. Therefore, if you allow a lot of personalization for users of your site, you need to allow them to log in and reset their cookies. Doing so should then reenable their customizations provided you have them stored elsewhere.

Reading and Writing Cookies

A Web application creates a cookie by sending it to the client as a header in an HTTP response. Of course, ASP.NET makes writing to and reading from the cookie collection a relatively straightforward task.

To add a cookie to the cookies collection and have it written out to the browser, you call the *Response.Cookies.Add method.* The *Cookies* property of the *Page.Response* property is of the type *HttpCookieCollection*. You add instances of *HttpCookie* to this collection. The *HttpCookie* object simply contains a *Name* property and a *Value* property. The following code shows how you might add an item to the cookies collection:

```
Response.Cookies.Add(New HttpCookie("userId", userId))
```

To retrieve a cookie sent back by the Web browser, you read the values in the *Request. Cookies collection*. The following shows an example of this code:

```
Request.Cookies("userId").Value
```

As a larger example, the following sample code in a *Page_Load* event handler demonstrates both defining and reading cookie values by setting a cookie named lastVisit to the current time. If the user already has the cookie set, the code displays in the *Label1* control the time the user last visited the page.

```
'VB
'check if cookie exists, and display it if it does
If Not (Request.Cookies("lastVisit") Is Nothing) Then
  'encode the cookie in case the cookie contains client-side script
  Label1.Text = Server.HtmlEncode(Request.Cookies("lastVisit").Value)
Else
  Label1.Text = "No value defined"
End If

'define the cookie for the next visit
Response.Cookies("lastVisit").Value = DateTime.Now.ToString
Response.Cookies("lastVisit").Expires = DateTime.Now.AddDays(1)

//C#
//check if cookie exists, and display it if it does
if (Request.Cookies["lastVisit"] != null)
  //encode the cookie in case the cookie contains client-side script
  Label1.Text = Server.HtmlEncode(Request.Cookies["lastVisit"].Value);
else
  Label1.Text = "No value defined";

//define the cookie for the next visit
Response.Cookies["lastVisit"].Value = DateTime.Now.ToString();
Response.Cookies["lastVisit"].Expires = DateTime.Now.AddDays(1);
```

The first time the user visits the page in the previous example, the code displays "No value defined" because the cookie has not yet been set. However, if you refresh the page, it displays the time of the first visit.

Note that the code sample defines the *Expires* property for the cookie. You must define the *Expires* property and set it for the time period you would like the client to store the cookie if you want the cookie to persist between browser sessions. If you do not define the

Expires property, the browser stores the cookie in memory and the cookie is lost if the user closes his or her browser.

To delete a cookie, you overwrite the cookie and set an expiration date in the past. You cannot directly delete cookies because they are stored on the client's computer.

> ***NOTE* VIEWING AND TROUBLESHOOTING COOKIES**
>
> **You can use Trace.axd to view cookies for every page request. For more information, see Chapter 12, "Monitoring, Troubleshooting, and Debugging."**

Controlling Cookie Scope

Cookies should be specific to a given Web site's domain or a directory within that domain. The information in cookies is typically specific to that site and often private. For this reason a browser should not send your cookie to another site. By default, browsers will not send your cookie to a Web site with a different host name (although, in the past, vulnerabilities in browsers have allowed attackers to trick a browser into submitting another Web site's cookie).

You have control over a cookie's scope. You can limit the scope to either a specific directory on your Web server or expand the scope to the entire domain. The scope of your cookie determines which pages have access to the information embedded in the cookie. If you limit the scope to a directory, only pages in that directory will have access to the cookie. You control cookie scope on a per-cookie basis. To limit the scope of a cookie to a directory, you set the *Path* property of the *HttpCookie* class. The following shows sample code for doing just that:

```
'VB
Response.Cookies("lastVisit").Value = DateTime.Now.ToString
Response.Cookies("lastVisit").Expires = DateTime.Now.AddDays(1)
Response.Cookies("lastVisit").Path = "/MyApplication"

//C#
Response.Cookies["lastVisit"].Value = DateTime.Now.ToString();
Response.Cookies["lastVisit"].Expires = DateTime.Now.AddDays(1);
Response.Cookies["lastVisit"].Path = "/MyApplication";
```

With the scope limited to "/MyApplication", the browser submits the cookie to any page in the /MyApplication folder. However, pages outside of this folder do not get the cookie, even if they are on the same server.

To expand the scope of a cookie to an entire domain, set the *Domain* property of the *HttpCookie* class. The following code demonstrates:

```
'VB
Response.Cookies("lastVisit").Value = DateTime.Now.ToString
Response.Cookies("lastVisit").Expires = DateTime.Now.AddDays(1)
Response.Cookies("lastVisit").Domain = "contoso.com"
```

```
//C#
Response.Cookies["lastVisit"].Value = DateTime.Now.ToString();
Response.Cookies["lastVisit"].Expires = DateTime.Now.AddDays(1);
Response.Cookies["lastVisit"].Domain = "contoso.com";
```

Setting the *Domain* property to *"contoso.com"* causes the browser to submit the cookie to any page in the *contoso.com* domain. This might include those pages that belong to the sites *www.contoso.com*, *intranet.contoso.com*, or *private.contoso.com*. Similarly, you can use the *Domain* property to specify a full host name, limiting the cookie to a specific server.

Storing Multiple Values in a Cookie

The size of your cookie is dependent on the browser. Each cookie can be up to a maximum of 4 KB in length. In addition, you can typically store up to 20 cookies per site. This should be more than sufficient for most sites. However, if you need to work around the 20-cookie limit, you can store multiple values in a single cookie by setting the given cookie's name and its key value. The key value is usually not used when storing just a single value. However, if you need multiple values in a single named cookie, you can add multiple keys. The following code shows an example:

```
'VB
Response.Cookies("info")("visit") = DateTime.Now.ToString()
Response.Cookies("info")("firstName") = "Tony"
Response.Cookies("info")("border") = "blue"
Response.Cookies("info").Expires = DateTime.Now.AddDays(1)

//C#
Response.Cookies["info"]["visit"].Value = DateTime.Now.ToString();
Response.Cookies["info"]["firstName"].Value = "Tony";
Response.Cookies["info"]["border"].Value = "blue";
Response.Cookies["info"].Expires = DateTime.Now.AddDays(1);
```

Running this code sends a single cookie to the Web browser. However, that cookie is parsed to form three values. ASP.NET then reads these three values back in when the cookie is submitted back to the server. The following shows the value sent to the Web browser:

```
(visit=4/5/2006 2:35:18 PM)  (firstName=Tony)  (border=blue)
```

Cookie properties, such as *Expires*, *Domain*, and *Path*, apply for all the values within a single cookie. You cannot control these at the individual key value. Rather, they are controlled at the cookie (or name) level. You can access the individual values of a cookie using *Request.Cookies* in the same way you define the values (using both name and key).

Query Strings

Query strings are commonly used to store variable values that identify specific context for a requested page. This context might be a search term, page number, region indicator, or something similar. Query string values are appended to the end of the page URL. They are set off with a question mark (?) followed by the query string term (or parameter name) followed by an equal sign (=) and the given parameter's value. You can append multiple query string parameters using the ampersand (&). A typical query string might look like the following real-world example:

```
http://support.microsoft.com/Default.aspx?kbid=315233
```

In this example, the URL identifies the Default.aspx page. The query string contains a single parameter named *kbid*. The value for that parameter is set to "315233." In this example the query string has one parameter. The following example shows a query string with multiple parameters. In this real-world URL the language and market are set as parameters and the search term for searching the *Microsoft.com* Web site is set as a parameter:

```
http://search.microsoft.com/results.aspx?mkt=en-US&setlang=en-US&q=hello+world
```

Values sent to your page via the query string can be retrieved on the server through the *Page.Request.QueryString* property. Table 4-1 shows how you would access the three values in the preceding query string example.

TABLE 4-1 Sample Query String Parameter Access

PARAMETER NAME	ASP.NET OBJECT CALL	VALUE
mkt	*Request.QueryString["mkt"]*	en-US
setlang	*Request.QueryString["setlang"]*	en-US
q	*Request.QueryString["q"]*	hello world

Query strings provide a simple but limited way to maintain state information between multiple pages. For example, they are an easy way to pass information from one page to another, such as passing a product number from a page that describes a product to a page that adds the item to a user's shopping cart. However, some browsers and client devices impose a 2,083-character limit on the length of the URL. Another limitation is that you must submit the page using an *HTTP GET* command for query string values to be available during page processing. You also need to be aware that query string parameters and values are visible to the user in his or her address bar. This often invites tampering.

IMPORTANT **ALWAYS VALIDATE USER INPUT**

You should expect users to modify data in your query strings. For that reason, you must always validate data retrieved from a query string.

One big advantage of query strings is that their data is included in bookmarks and e-mailed URLs. In fact, it is the only way to enable a user to include state data when copying and pasting a URL to another user. For that reason, you should use query strings for any information that uniquely identifies a Web page, even if you are also using another state-management technique.

> ***IMPORTANT*** **PRACTICAL QUERY STRING CHARACTER LIMITS**
>
> **Browsers have 2,083-character limits on URLs, but you'll start to have problems with much shorter URLs if users e-mail them using plaintext e-mail or send them to other users using instant messaging. To allow a URL to be e-mailed, limit the length to 70 characters (including the *http://* or *https://*). To allow a URL to be sent through instant messaging, limit the the length to 400 characters.**

REAL WORLD

Tony Northrup

Although only the most sophisticated users are comfortable modifying cookies or hidden fields, many casual users know how to change query strings. For example, the first interactive Web application I ever wrote allowed a user to rate pictures on a scale from 1 to 10, and the user's rating was submitted as a query string value. For example, if the user rated a picture 7, the query string might read "page.aspx?pic=342&rating=7." One day I noticed a picture with a rating above 100—a clever user had manually changed the query string to include a very large value, and my application had added the rating to the database without validation. To fix the problem, I added code to reject any request with a rating more than 10 or less than 1.

A common mistake I see is that developers use query strings to allow users to navigate search results but do not validate the query strings properly. Often, query strings for search results have query strings for the search terms, the number of results per page, and the current page numbers. If you don't validate the query string, the user can set the number of results per page to a huge number, such as 10,000. Processing thousands of search results can take several seconds of your server's processing time and cause your server to transmit a very large HTML page. This makes it very easy for an attacker to perform a denial-of-service attack on your Web application by requesting the search page repeatedly.

Don't ever trust values from a query string; they must always be validated.

Adding Query String Parameters to a URL

To create your own query string parameters, you modify the URL for any hyperlink a user might click. This is a simple process, but always getting it right can be time-consuming. In fact, there are no tools built into the .NET Framework to simplify the creation of query strings. You must manually add query string values to every hyperlink that the user might click.

For example, if you have a *HyperLink* control with *NavigateUrl* defined as "page.aspx," you can add the string "?user=mary" to the *HyperLink.NavigateUrl* property so that the full URL is "page.aspx?user=mary."

To add multiple query string parameters to a page, you need to separate them with ampersands (&). For example, the URL "page.aspx?user=mary&lang=en-us&page=1252" passes three query string values to page.aspx: user (with a value of "mary"), lang (with a value of "en-us"), and page (with a value of "1252").

Reading Query String Parameters in Your Page

To read a query string value, access the *Request.QueryStrings* collection just like you would access a cookie. To continue the previous example, the page.aspx page could process the *"user"* query string by accessing *Request.QueryStrings("user")* in Visual Basic or *Request.QueryStrings["user"]* in C#. For example, the following code displays values for the *user, lang,* and *page* query strings in the *Label1* control:

```
'VB
Label1.Text = "User: " + Server.HtmlEncode(Request.QueryString("user")) + _
  ", Lang: " + Server.HtmlEncode(Request.QueryString("lang")) + _
  ", Page: " + Server.HtmlEncode(Request.QueryString("page"))
```

```
//C#
Label1.Text = "User: " + Server.HtmlEncode(Request.QueryString["user"]) +
  ", Lang: " + Server.HtmlEncode(Request.QueryString["lang"]) +
  ", Page: " + Server.HtmlEncode(Request.QueryString["page"]);
```

> ***SECURITY ALERT*** **You should always encode cookie or query string values using Server.HtmlEncode before displaying the value in an HTML Web page to any user. Server.HtmlEncode replaces HTML code with special characters that a Web browser cannot process. For example, Server.HtmlEncode replaces a "<" sign with "<." If you display the value in a browser, the user sees the "<" sign, but the browser does not process any HTML code or client-side scripts.**
>
> **To provide extra protection, the runtime throws a *System.Web.HttpRequestValidationException* if it detects HTML or client-side scripting in a query string. Therefore, you cannot pass HTML code in a query string. This can be disabled by an administrator, however, so you should not rely on it for protection.**

LAB Store State Management Data on the Client

In this lab, you use different client-side state management techniques to track the number of pages a user opens. It helps you gain a better understanding of how each of the techniques works.

If you encounter a problem completing an exercise, the completed projects are available in the samples installed from the companion CD.

EXERCISE 1 Store Data in View State

In this exercise, you explore how data is stored in the view state and returned to the server during page processing.

1. Open Visual Studio and create a new ASP.NET Web site named **ClientState** in either C# or Visual Basic.
2. Add a second page to the project. Name this page **Default2.aspx**.

   Add a label named ***Label1*** to the page.

   Add a hyperlink control named ***HyperLink1*** to the page. Set the property *HyperLink1.NavigateUrl* to **Default.aspx**. This will access the other page without sending view state to that page.

   Add a button control named ***Button1*** to the page. This control will be used to submit the page back to the server.
3. Open the Default.aspx page. Add the same set of controls to this page as follows:

   Add a label named ***Label1*** to the page.

   Add a hyperlink control named ***HyperLink1*** to the page. Set the property *HyperLink1.NavigateUrl* to **Default2.aspx**. This will access the other page without sending view state to that page.

   Add a button control named ***Button1*** to the page. This control will be used to submit the page back to the server.
4. Inside the *Page_Load* method for both Default.aspx and Default2.aspx, add code to store the current number of user clicks in the view state object. Also, add code to display the number of times a user has clicked inside the *Label* control. The following code sample demonstrates what this code would look like:

```
'VB
Protected Sub Page_Load(ByVal sender As Object, _
  ByVal e As System.EventArgs) Handles Me.Load

  If (ViewState("clicks") IsNot Nothing) Then
    ViewState("clicks") = CInt(ViewState("clicks")) + 1
  Else
    ViewState("clicks") = 1
  End If
```

```
  Label1.Text = "ViewState clicks: " + CInt(ViewState("clicks")).ToString

End Sub

//C#
protected void Page_Load(object sender, EventArgs e)
{

  if (ViewState["clicks"] != null)
  {
    ViewState["clicks"] = (int)ViewState["clicks"] + 1;
  }
  else
  {
    ViewState["clicks"] = 1;
  }

  Label1.Text = " ViewState clicks: " + ((int)ViewState["clicks"]).ToString();

}
```

5. Build the Web site and visit the Default.aspx page. Click the button several times and verify that the clicks counter increments.
6. Click the hyperlink to load the Default2.aspx page. Notice that the counter value is not passed to this page. It is lost because a different page is opened.
7. Click the hyperlink to return to Default.aspx. Notice that the counter is again reset. Switching between pages loses all view state information.

EXERCISE 2 Store Data in a Hidden Field

In this exercise, you add a *HiddenField* control and use it to store client-side state.

1. Continue editing the project you created in the previous exercise. Alternatively, you can open the completed Lesson 1, Exercise 1 project in the samples installed from the CD.
2. Open the Default.aspx page in Source view. Add a *HiddenField* control and name it ***HiddenField1***.
3. Open the code-behind file for Default.aspx. Edit the code in the *Page_Load* method to store the current number of user clicks in the *HiddenField1* object. Also display the clicks in the *Label* control. The following code demonstrates this:

```
'VB
Protected Sub Page_Load(ByVal sender As Object, _
  ByVal e As System.EventArgs) Handles Me.Load
```

```
    Dim clicks As Integer
    Integer.TryParse(HiddenField1.Value, clicks)
    clicks += 1
    HiddenField1.Value = clicks.ToString

    Label1.Text = "HiddenField clicks: " + HiddenField1.Value

End Sub

//C#
protected void Page_Load(object sender, EventArgs e)
{

    int clicks;
    int.TryParse(HiddenField1.Value, out clicks);

    clicks++;
    HiddenField1.Value = clicks.ToString();

    Label1.Text = "HiddenField clicks: " + HiddenField1.Value;

}
```

Notice that *HiddenField.Value* is a *String*. This requires converting data to and from the *String* type. This makes it less convenient than other methods of storing data.

4. Build your Web site and visit the Default.aspx page. Click the button several times and verify that the clicks counter increments.

   Notice that if you browse to other pages, the *HiddenField* value is lost.

   View the source of the Default.aspx page in your browser (right-click, then select View Source). Notice that the hidden field value is displayed in plaintext.

EXERCISE 3 Store Data in a Cookie

In this exercise, you use a cookie to track user clicks.

1. Continue editing the project you created in the previous exercise. Alternatively, you can open the completed Lesson 1, Exercise 2 project in the samples installed from the CD.
2. In the *Page_Load* method for both Default.aspx and Default2.aspx, add code to retrieve the current number of clicks from a cookie named clicks. Also add code to increment the number of clicks and store the new value in the same cookie. Display the clicks in the *Label* control. The following code demonstrates this:

```
'VB
Protected Sub Page_Load(ByVal sender As Object, _
```

```
  ByVal e As System.EventArgs) Handles Me.Load

  'read the cookie clicks and increment
  Dim cookieClicks As Integer
  If Not (Request.Cookies("clicks") Is Nothing) Then
    cookieClicks = Integer.Parse(Request.Cookies("clicks").Value) + 1
  Else
    cookieClicks = 1
  End If

  'save the cookie to be returned on the next visit
  Response.Cookies("clicks").Value = cookieClicks.ToString

  Label1.Text = "Cookie clicks: " + cookieClicks.ToString

End Sub

//C#
protected void Page_Load(object sender, EventArgs e)
{

  //read the cookie clicks and increment
  int cookieClicks;
  if (Request.Cookies["clicks"] != null)
  {
    cookieClicks = int.Parse(Request.Cookies["clicks"].Value) + 1;
  }
  else
  {
    cookieClicks = 1;
  }

  //save the cookie to be returned on the next visit
  Response.Cookies["clicks"].Value = cookieClicks.ToString();

  Label1.Text = "Cookie clicks: " + cookieClicks.ToString();

}
```

3. Build the Web site and visit the Default.aspx page. Click the button several times and verify that the clicks counter increments.
4. Click the hyperlink to load Default2.aspx. Notice that the counter is not reset. Remember, these are cookies. They are available to any page in the site. You can browse to any page on the same site and access and write to the cookie.

EXERCISE 4 Store Data in a Query String

In this exercise, you use a query string to track user clicks.

1. Continue editing the project you created in the previous exercise. Alternatively, you can open the completed Lesson 1, Exercise 3 project in the samples installed from the CD.
2. In the *Page_Load* method for both Default.aspx and Default2.aspx, add code to retrieve the current number of clicks from a query string parameter named clicks. Also add code to increment the value of clicks and store the new value back in the query string via the *Hyperlink1.NavigateUrl*. Display the value of clicks in the *Label* control. The following code demonstrates how to do this:

```
'VB
Protected Sub Page_Load(ByVal sender As Object, _
  ByVal e As System.EventArgs) Handles Me.Load

  If Not IsPostBack Then
    'read the query string
    Dim queryClicks As Integer
    If Not (Request.QueryString("clicks") Is Nothing) Then
      queryClicks = Integer.Parse(Request.QueryString("clicks")) + 1
    Else
      queryClicks = 1
    End If

    'define the query string in the hyperlink
    HyperLink1.NavigateUrl += "?clicks=" + queryClicks.ToString

    Label1.Text = "Query clicks: " + queryClicks.ToString
  End If


End Sub

//C#
protected void Page_Load(object sender, EventArgs e)
{

  if (!IsPostBack)
  {
    //read the query string
    int queryClicks;
    if (Request.QueryString["clicks"] != null)
    {
      queryClicks = int.Parse(Request.QueryString["clicks"]) + 1;
    }
```

```
    else
    {
      queryClicks = 1;
    }

    //define the query string in the hyperlink
    HyperLink1.NavigateUrl += "?clicks=" + queryClicks.ToString();

    Label1.Text = "Query clicks: " + queryClicks.ToString();
  }


}
```

> ***IMPORTANT*** **WHY DOES THIS EXAMPLE NOT USE *SERVER.HTMLENCODE*?**
>
> **Earlier, this lesson warned you to always use *Server.HtmlEncode* to encode cookies or query strings before displaying them in an HTML page. These exercises don't seem to practice what they preach, however. Instead, the exercises use strong typing to ensure there is no malicious code contained in the values before they are displayed. By converting the values from strings to integers and back to strings, there is no possibility that HTML code or client-side scripts can be displayed. If the user inserts malicious code in a cookie or query string, the runtime throws an exception when it attempts to parse the value, preventing the malicious code from being displayed. However, you must always use *Server.HtmlEncode* before directly displaying the string value of a cookie or query string.**

3. Build the Web site. Visit the Default.aspx page and click the hyperlink to load Default2.aspx. Notice that the counter is incremented as values are passed back and forth between the pages using the query string.
4. Click the hyperlink several times to switch between pages. Notice that the URL includes the number of clicks, and it is visible to the user.

If the user bookmarks the link and returns to the page later, or even uses the same URL on a different computer, the current clicks counter is retained. With query strings, you can e-mail or bookmark Web pages and have the state information stored in the URL. However, you must include the query string in any link the user might click on the page, or the information is lost.

Lesson Summary

- Use client-side state management when scalability is the top priority. Use server-side state management when data must be better protected or when bandwidth is a significant issue.

- ASP.NET uses view state by default to store information about controls in a Web form. You can add custom values to view state by accessing the *ViewState* collection.
- Use control state when a custom control cannot function with view state disabled.
- Use hidden fields to store data in forms when view state is disabled. Hidden fields values are available to users as plaintext in the HTML.
- Cookies store data on the client that the Web browser submits with every Web page request. Use cookies to track users across multiple Web pages.
- Query strings store small pieces of information in a hyperlink's URL. Use query strings when you want state management data to be bookmarked, such as when displaying multiple pages of search results.

Lesson Review

You can use the following questions to test your knowledge of the information in Lesson 1, "Using Client-Side State Management." The questions are also available on the companion CD if you prefer to review them in electronic form.

> ***NOTE* ANSWERS**
>
> **Answers to these questions and explanations of why each answer choice is right or wrong are located in the "Answers" section at the end of the book.**

1. You need to store a user's user name and password as he or she navigates to different pages on your site so that you can pass those credentials to back-end servers. Which type of state management should you use?
   - **A.** Client-side state management
   - **B.** Server-side state management
2. You need to track nonconfidential user preferences when a user visits your site to minimize additional load on your servers. You distribute requests among multiple Web servers, each running a copy of your application. Which type of state management should you use?
   - **A.** Client-side state management
   - **B.** Server-side state management
3. You are creating an ASP.NET Web page that allows a user to browse information in a database. While the user accesses the page, you need to track search and sorting values. You do not need to store the information between visits to the Web page. Which type of client-side state management would meet your requirements and be the simplest to implement?
   - **A.** View state
   - **B.** Control state

C. Hidden fields

D. Cookies

E. Query strings

4. You are creating an ASP.NET Web site with dozens of pages. You want to allow the user to set user preferences and have each page process the preference information. You want the preferences to be remembered between visits, even if the user closes the browser. Which type of client-side state management meets your requirements and is the simplest to implement?

   A. View state

   B. Control state

   C. Hidden fields

   D. Cookies

   E. Query strings

5. You are creating an ASP.NET Web form that searches product inventory and displays items that match the user's criteria. You want users to be able to bookmark or e-mail search results. Which type of client-side state management meets your requirements and is the simplest to implement?

   A. View state

   B. Control state

   C. Hidden fields

   D. Cookies

   E. Query strings

Lesson 2: Using Server-Side State Management

Often, it is just not practical to store your state on the client. Your state might be more involved and thus too large to be transmitted back or forth. Perhaps you have state that needs to be secured and even encrypted and should not be passed around a network. Additionally you might have state that is not client specific but global to all the users of your application. In all of these scenarios you still need to store state. If the client is not the right choice, you must look to the server for state management needs.

ASP.NET provides two ways to store state on the server and thus share information between Web pages without sending the data to the client. These two methods are referred to as application state and session state. Application state information is global to the application. It is available to all pages regardless of the user requesting the page. Session state is user-specific state that is stored by the server. It is available only to pages accessed by a single user during a visit to your site. This lesson explores these two server-side state management techniques.

> ***IMPORTANT*** **CHOOSING SERVER-SIDE STATE MANAGEMENT**
>
> **It is important to note that you do not need to use server-side state management for your application. Your application can rely on a mix of client-side and database state management. This frees up valuable server resources for processing more page requests (and thus increases your server's scalability).**

After this lesson, you will be able to:

- Use application state to store and share information that is accessible to all Web pages in a given Web site.
- Use session state to store user-specific information on the server and share that information across pages within your site.
- Understand the purpose and use of profile properties in ASP.NET.

Estimated lesson time: 30 minutes

Application State

Application state in ASP.NET is a global storage mechanism for state data that needs to be accessible to all pages in a given Web application. You can use application state to store information that must be maintained between server round trips and between requests for pages. Again, application state is optional; it is often not required. You should consider it a form of application-level caching of data that is too time-consuming to obtain on each request.

You store application state in an instance of the *HttpApplicationState* class that is provided through the *Page.Application* property. This class represents a key–value dictionary, where each value is stored and accessed by its key (or name). You can add to and read from the application state from any page on the server. However, you have to keep in mind that the state is global and accessible by all pages executing on your server.

Once you add application-specific information to the application state, the server manages it. This state stays on the server and is not sent to the client. Application state is a great place to store information that is not user-specific but is global in nature. By storing it in the application state, all pages can access data from a single location in memory, rather than keeping separate copies of the data or reading it every time a page is requested.

> ***IMPORTANT*** **CHOOSING APPLICATION OR SESSION STATE**
>
> **You should not store user-specific information in application state. Instead, you should use session state to store user-specific information (as described later in this lesson).**

Data stored in the *Application* object is not permanent. It is temporarily held in memory on the server. Therefore, it can be lost any time the application is restarted. The host server of your application, such as Microsoft Internet Information Services (IIS), might restart your ASP.NET application. In addition, the application is also restarted if the server is restarted. To work with this constraint, you should understand how to read, write, and sometimes persist application state using the application events described later in this lesson.

The ASP.NET Application Life Cycle

It is important to have a solid understanding of the life cycle of an ASP.NET application when working with server-side state management. This life cycle defines how the application server starts and stops your application, isolates it from other applications, and executes your code.

Your ASP.NET application runs based on the server application that hosts it. This typically means IIS. There are multiple versions of IIS that can run your ASP.NET application, including IIS 5.0, 6.0, and 7.0. IIS 5.0 and 6.0 execute relatively similarly. IIS 7.0 has a classic mode that also executes in a similar fashion. However, IIS 7.0 by default processes pages a little differently from earlier versions.

This section outlines how your pages are processed by these servers to give you a basic understanding of how you can affect application state management. The following stages constitute the application life cycle of an ASP.NET application:

1. The life cycle of an ASP.NET application begins when a user first makes a request for a page in your site.
2. The request is routed to the processing pipeline. In IIS 5.0, 6.0, and classic mode of IIS 7.0, requests for .aspx pages (and related extensions like .ascx, .ashx, and .asmx) are passed to the Internet Server Application Programming Interface (ISAPI) extension for ASP.NET. It executes its pipeline for these requests.

   In IIS 7.0 integrated mode, a common, unified pipeline handles all requests for a resource in a given application. This allows resources such as .html files to be passed through the same pipeline as .aspx pages. This allows managed code to support these resources, too (such as securing their access).

3. An instance of the *ApplicationManager* class is created. The *ApplicationManager* instance represents the domain that will be used to execute requests for your application. An application domain isolates global variables from other applications and allows each application to load and unload separately as required.
4. Once the application domain is created, an instance of the *HostingEnvironment* class gets created. This class provides access to items inside the hosting environment like directory folders and the like.
5. The next step is for ASP.NET to create instances of the core objects that will be used to process the request. This includes *HttpContext*, *HttpRequest*, and *HttpResponse* objects.
6. Next, the application is actually started through the creation of an instance of the *HttpApplication* class (or an instance is re-used). This class is also the base class for a site's Global.asax file (if you use it). This class can be used to trap events that happen when your application starts or stops (more on this in the coming section).

   In addition, when an *HttpApplication* instance is created, it also creates those modules configured for the application such as the *SessionStateModule*.
7. Finally, requests are then processed through the *HttpApplication* pipeline. This pipeline also includes a set of events for doing things like validating the request, mapping URLs, accessing the cache, and more. These events are of interest to developers extending the *Application* class but are outside the scope of this book.

Responding to Application Events

The *HttpApplication* class provides a number of events that you can trap to do things when certain events fire at the application level. This includes things like initializing variable values when your application starts, logging requests to your application, handling application-level errors, and more. Again, these events fire based on your application starting, stopping, handling a request, and so on. They are application-level events that do not work on a per-user level.

The principal way you write code against these events is to use the ASP.NET file, Global .asax (also known as the Global Application Class). An application can have one instance of this file. It derives from the *HttpApplication* class and allows you to extend a number of the events on that class. You trap the event for the stage of the application life cycle you intend to intercept. Events are mapped automatically provided you follow the *Application_* naming structure. The following are some of the key events you might need to trap:

- ***Application_Start*** The *Application_Start* event is raised when your application is started by IIS (typically as the result of a user request). This event is useful for initializing variables that are scoped at the *application level*. This event, along with *Application_End*, is a special event in ASP. They do not map back to the *HttpApplication* object.

- ***Application_End*** The *Application_End* event is raised when your application stops or shuts down. This event is useful if you need to free application-level resources or perform some sort of logging. This event, along with *Application_Start,* is a special event in ASP. They do not map back to the *HttpApplication* object.
- ***Application_Error*** The *Application_Error* event is raised when an unhandled error occurs and bubbles up to the application scope. You might use this event to perform worst-case, catch-all error logging.
- ***Application_LogRequest*** The *Application_LogRequest* event is raised when a request has been made to the application. You can use this event to write custom logging information regarding a request.
- ***Application_PostLogRequest*** The *Application_PostLogRequest* event is raised after the logging of a request has completed.

These are just some of the *Application_* events. Others include *Application_BeginRequest, Application_EndRequest, ResolveRequestCache,* and many others. These events map to the application processing pipeline. You can get a full listing by looking up the *HttpApplication* class inside the MSDN library.

You can implement these events by adding a Global.asax file to your project. This file does not have a code-behind file. Instead, it has a script block that you use to add code for these events. Follow these steps to use the Global.asax file:

1. Open your Web site in Visual Studio. Right-click your Web site project file and select Add New Item to open the Add New Item dialog box.
2. In the Add New Item dialog box, select the Global Application Class item, and then click Add to add the file to your project.

   Visual Studio will add a Global.asax file to your project that already contains stubbed out method signatures for *Application_Start, Application_End,* and *Application_Error.* It also includes method signatures for *Session_Start* and *Session_End.* These are described later in this lesson.

   The following code demonstrates an example of a Global.asax file. In this example, the application-level variable *UsersOnline* is defined at application start. The variable is incremented when a new user comes to the site and starts a session. The variable is decremented when a session ends. (The session end code is only called for *InProc* session state management, which is covered later in this chapter.)

```
'VB
<%@ Application Language="VB" %>

<script runat="server">

  Sub Application_Start(ByVal sender As Object, ByVal e As EventArgs)
    Application("UsersOnline") = 0
  End Sub
```

```
  Sub Session_Start(ByVal sender As Object, ByVal e As EventArgs)
    Application.Lock()
    Application("UsersOnline") = CInt(Application("UsersOnline")) + 1
    Application.UnLock()
  End Sub

  Sub Session_End(ByVal sender As Object, ByVal e As EventArgs)
    Application.Lock()
    Application("UsersOnline") = CInt(Application("UsersOnline")) - 1
    Application.UnLock()
  End Sub

</script>


//C#
<%@ Application Language="C#" %>

<script runat="server">

  void Application_Start(object sender, EventArgs e)
  {
    Application["UsersOnline"] = 0;
  }

  void Session_Start(object sender, EventArgs e)
  {
    Application.Lock();
    Application["UsersOnline"] = (int)Application["UsersOnline"] + 1;
    Application.UnLock();
  }

  void Session_End(object sender, EventArgs e)
  {
    Application.Lock();
    Application["UsersOnline"] = (int)Application["UsersOnline"] - 1;
    Application.UnLock();
  }

</script>
```

Writing and Reading Application State Data

You can read and write application-level state data using the *Application* object instance. This object is an instance of the *HttpApplicationState* class. The object works like the *ViewState* object—as a collection. However, because multiple Web pages may be running simultaneously on multiple threads, you must lock the *Application* object when making calculations and performing updates to application-level data. For example, the following code locks the *Application* object for a single thread before incrementing and updating an application-level variable:

```
'VB
Application.Lock()
Application("PageRequestCount") = CInt(Application("PageRequestCount")) + 1
Application.UnLock()

//C#
Application.Lock();
Application["PageRequestCount"] = ((int)Application["PageRequestCount"]) + 1;
Application.UnLock();
```

If you don't lock the *Application* object, it is possible for another page to change the variable between the time that the process reads the current value and the time it writes the new value. This could cause a calculation to be lost. You do not need to lock the *Application* object when initializing variables in *Application_Start*.

The values of an *Application* variable are of the *Object* type. Therefore, when you read them you must cast them to the appropriate type. There is no need to lock a variable for a read as multiple threads can read the same data without issue.

Session State

Most Web applications need to store user-specific data between individual requests. For example, if a user is going through a multistep process to register for your site, you might want to temporarily store this data between pages until the user has completed the process. Of course, Windows applications do this all the time. These applications run in a process that stays alive on the client during a given user session. Therefore, they can simply store this data in memory on the client. ASP.NET applications have the disadvantage that they share a server process and do not own a process on the client. Lesson 1 already explored how you can leverage the client machine to store this type of data between requests. However, this is often not practical. Often, the data is too large or requires additional security. In these cases you can leverage the shared ASP.NET process to store this data in memory, on the server. This is referred to as *session state* in ASP.NET.

Session state can be thought of in a similar way as application state. The big difference is that session state is scoped to the current browser (or user) session and only available to that session (and not the entire application). Each user on your site then has his or her own isolated session state running in your application's process on the server. This state is available to different pages as they make subsequent requests to the server. Session state is, however, lost if the user ends his or her session (or times out). In most cases, however, session state is not needed between sessions. Data that is needed from one session to another should be persisted in a data store.

By default, ASP.NET applications store session state in memory on the server. However, they can be configured to store this information in client-side cookies, on another state server, or inside of SQL Server. These other options support centralized session management for Web farm scenarios (multiple front-end Web servers in your application).

Reading and Writing Session State Data

You store user-specific session state in the *Session object*. This is an instance of the *HttpSessionState* class and represents a key–value dictionary collection. Items are added, updated, and read in a similar manner as working with any .NET dictionary collection.

The following code demonstrates how to write to and read from the *Session* object. In this example, each time a user requests a page the time is written into his or her *Session* instance. The last time the user requested the page for the given session is also displayed in a label control. Although this code performs a similar function to the *ViewState* in Lesson 1, the *Session* object is available to any page the user visits.

```
'VB
'check if Session object exists, and display it if it does
If (Session("lastVisit") IsNot Nothing) Then
  Label1.Text = Session("lastVisit").ToString()
Else
  Label1.Text = "Session does not have last visit information."
End If

'define the Session object for the next page view
Session("lastVisit") = DateTime.Now

//C#
//check if Session object exists, and display it if it does

if (Session["lastVisit"] != null)

{

  Label1.Text = ((DateTime)Session["lastVisit"]).ToString();

}

else

{

  Label1.Text = "Session does not have last visit information.";

}
```

```
//define the Session object for the next page view

Session["lastVisit"] = DateTime.Now;
```

NOTE SESSION STATE AND COOKIES

ASP.NET writes a cookie to the client's machines to track their session. This cookie is called *ASP.NET_SessionId* and contains a random 24-byte value. Requests submit this cookie from the browser and ASP.NET maps the cookie's value to the session on the server.

Disabling Session State

If you don't use session state, you can improve performance by disabling it for the entire application. You do so by setting the *sessionState* mode property to *Off* in the Web.config file. The following shows an example:

```
<configuration>
  <system.web>
    <sessionState mode="off"/>
  </system.web>
</configuration>
```

You can also disable session state for a single page of an application by setting the *EnableSessionState* page directive to *False*. You can also set the *EnableSessionState* page directive to *ReadOnly* to provide read-only access to session variables for the given page. The following code sample shows how you set a page directive to disable session state for a single page:

```
<%@ Page Language="C#" AutoEventWireup="true" CodeFile="Default.aspx.cs"
  Inherits="_Default" EnableSessionState = "False"%>
```

NOTE STORING VALUES IN SESSION STATE

Values stored in *Session* must be serializable.

Configuring Cookieless Session State

By default, session state uses cookies to track user sessions. This is the best choice for the vast majority of applications. All modern Web browsers support cookies. However, users can turn them off. Therefore, ASP.NET allows you to enable cookieless session state.

Without cookies, ASP.NET tracks sessions using the URL by embedding the session ID in the URL after the application name and before any remaining file or virtual directory identifier. For example, the following URL has been modified by ASP.NET to include the unique session ID lit3py55t21z5v55vlm25s55:

```
http://www.example.com/s(lit3py55t21z5v55vlm25s55)/orderform.aspx
```

You enable cookieless sessions through the Web.config file. Set the *cookieless* attribute of the *sessionState* element to *true*. The following example shows a Web.config file that configures an ASP.NET application to use cookieless sessions.

```
<configuration>
  <system.web>
    <sessionState cookieless="true"
      regenerateExpiredSessionId="true" />
  </system.web>
</configuration>
```

Responding to Session Events

Many times you want code to run when a user initiates a session or a session is terminated. For example, you might want to initialize key variables when a session starts or do some user-specific logging.

You can trap session events using the Global.asax file (as discussed in the previous section). There are two special events that ASP.NET provides for responding to session activities:

- ***Session_Start*** Raised when a new user requests a page on your site and thus begins a new session. This is a good place to initialize session variables.
- ***Session_End*** Raised when a session is abandoned or expires. This event can be used to log information or free per-session resources.

Again, to implement these events, you use the Global.asax file as discussed earlier in the section "Responding to Application Events."

> ***NOTE*** **THE *SESSION_END* EVENT**
>
> **The *Session_End* event is not always raised. When your state mode is set to *InProc*, ASP.NET will raise the *Session_End* event when a session is abandoned or times out. However, it does not raise this event for other state modes.**

Choosing a Session State Mode

Memory on the server is not always the best or most scalable place to store session state. For example, you might have a load-balanced server farm that routes requests between front-end Web servers based on server load. In this case you cannot guarantee a user will always be routed to the same server and thus you might lose his or her session information. One solution to this issue is a smarter loadbalancer that allows for "sticky" sessions that assign users to servers and keep them there throughout a session. However, this can also be problematic if a server fails or you need to take one down.

Fortunately, ASP.NET provides a few different session management modes for your application. These modes are configurable. You can, for example, start out using an in-memory (*InProc*) mode and, as your site grows, switch session state to a database or a state server. ASP.NET provides the following session storage options:

- ***InProc*** Stores session state in memory on the Web server. This is the default mode. It offers much better performance than using the ASP.NET State Service or storing state information in a database server. However, it is limited in load-balanced scenarios where you might make a performance trade-off to increase scalability. The *InProc* mode is a good choice for simple applications. However, applications that use multiple Web servers or persist session data between application restarts should consider using the *StateServer* or *SQLServer* modes.
- ***StateServer*** Stores session state in a service called the ASP.NET State Service. This ensures that session state is preserved if the Web application is restarted and also makes session state available to multiple Web servers in a Web farm. ASP.NET State Service is included with any computer set up to run ASP.NET Web applications; however, the service is set up to start manually by default. Therefore, when configuring the ASP.NET State Service, you must set the startup type to Automatic.
- ***SQLServer*** Stores session state in a SQL Server database. This ensures that session state is preserved if the Web application is restarted and also makes session state available to multiple servers in a Web farm. On identical hardware, the ASP.NET State Service outperforms *SQLServer*. However, a SQL Server database offers more robust data integrity and reporting capabilities. In addition, many sites run their SQL Server databases on powerful hardware. You will want to performance test for your scenario.
- ***Custom*** Enables you to specify a custom session state storage provider. You also need to implement (code) the custom storage provider.
- ***Off*** Disables session state. You should disable session state if you are not using it to improve performance.

Configuring Session State Modes

You can specify which mode you want ASP.NET session state to use by assigning *SessionStateMode* enumeration values to the mode attribute of the *sessionState* element in your application's Web.config file. Modes other than *InProc* and *Off* require additional parameters, such as connection-string values. You can examine the currently set session state by accessing the value of the *System.Web.SessionState.HttpSessionState.Mode* property in code.

The following example shows settings in a Web.config file that cause the session state to be stored in a SQL Server database identified by the specified connection string.

```
<configuration>
  <system.web>
     <sessionState mode="SQLServer"
        cookieless="true "
        regenerateExpiredSessionId="true "
        timeout="30"
        sqlConnectionString="Data Source=MySqlServer;Integrated Security=SSPI;"
        stateNetworkTimeout="30"/>
  </system.web>
</configuration>
```

Configuring session state for an application is typically the responsibility of the systems administrators who are responsible for hosting and supporting your application. For example, a systems administrator might initially configure a Web application on a single server using the *InProc* mode. Later, if the server gets too busy or requires redundancy, the systems administrator might add a second Web server and configure an ASP.NET state service on a separate server. They would then modify the Web.config file to use the *StateServer* mode. Fortunately, the session state mode is transparent to your application, so you won't need to change your code.

Quick Check

1. **Which typically consumes more server memory: application state or session state?**
2. **Which might not work if a user has disabled cookies in his or her Web browser: application state or session state?**

Quick Check Answers

1. **Session state tends to use much more memory than application state because application state is shared among users, whereas session state exists on a per-user basis.**
2. **Session state, by default, won't work if a Web browser that supports cookies has cookies disabled. Application state is not user-specific, though, and does not need to be tracked in cookies. Therefore, application state works regardless of cookies.**

Profile Properties

ASP.NET offers yet another state management tool called profile properties. These property values are per-user settings. You use profile properties to set user-specific profile information for your site such as a user's location, his or her favorite layout options, or any other profile information your application requires. The significant difference is that profile properties are persisted in a database on a per-user basis and not stored in memory on a server.

The concept of profiles is built into ASP.NET. These profiles can be configured, set, and automatically stored and maintained in a database by ASP.NET. This database can be SQL Server or SQL Express. The property values are associated with individual users. This allows you to easily manage user information without having to design a database or write code to work with that database. In addition, the profile properties make the user information available using strongly typed classes that you can access from anywhere in your application. This allows you to store objects of any .NET type in the user's profile.

To use profile properties, you must configure a profile provider. ASP.NET includes the *SqlProfileProvider* class, which allows you to store profile data in a SQL database. You can also create your own profile provider class that stores profile data in a custom format and to a custom storage mechanism such as an XML file or a Web service.

Data placed in profile properties is preserved through IIS restarts and worker-process restarts without data loss. Additionally, profile properties can be persisted across multiple processes such as in Web farms.

> ***MORE INFO*** **PROFILE PROPERTIES**
>
> **Refer to Chapter 5, "Customizing and Personalizing a Web Application," for more information about profile properties.**

LAB Store State Management Data on the Server

In this lab, you use different server-side state management techniques to track the number of pages a user has opened.

If you encounter a problem completing an exercise, the completed projects are available in the samples installed from the companion CD.

EXERCISE 1 Store Data in the Application Object

In this exercise, you create two pages that link to one another. Each time a user accesses the site, the application variable will be incremented and displayed on the page. This demonstrates how to add custom values to the *Application* object and how to use the Global.asax file.

1. Open Visual Studio and create a new ASP.NET Web site. Name the site **ServerState**. Select either C# or Visual Basic as your programming language for the site.
2. Add a new page to the site and name this page **Default2.aspx**.
3. Open the Default.aspx page in Source view. Add the text **Default Page 1** to the page. Add a label to the page and name it ***LabelApplicationClicks***. Also add a *HyperLink* control to the page and name it ***HyperLinkPage2***. Set the *HyperLinkPage2.NavigateUrl* property to **Default2.aspx**.
4. Open Default2.aspx in Source view. Add the text **Default Page 2** to the page. Add a label to the page and name it ***LabelApplicationClicks***. Also add a *HyperLink* control to the page and name it ***HyperLinkPage1***. Set the *HyperLinkPage1.NavigateUrl* property to **Default.aspx**.
5. Add a Global.asax file to your project by right-clicking the site and selecting Add New Item. Select the Global Application Class item.
6. Inside the Global.asax file, add code to the *Application_Start* method to initialize an *Application* variable named *clicks* as follows:

```
'VB
Sub Application_Start(ByVal sender As Object, ByVal e As EventArgs)
  Application("clicks") = 0
End Sub
```

```
//C#
void Application_Start(object sender, EventArgs e)
{
  Application["clicks"] = 0;
}
```

7. In the *Page_Load* method for both Default.aspx and Default2.aspx, add code to increment the number of clicks in the *Application* object. Don't forget to lock the application object before updating the value. Then add code to display the value in *LabelApplicationClicks*. The following code demonstrates this:

```
'VB
Protected Sub Page_Load(ByVal sender As Object, _
  ByVal e As System.EventArgs) Handles Me.Load

  Application.Lock()
  Application("clicks") = CInt(Application("clicks")) + 1
  Application.UnLock()

  LabelApplicationClicks.Text = "Application clicks: " + _
    Application("clicks").ToString

End Sub

//C#
protected void Page_Load(object sender, EventArgs e)
{
  Application.Lock();
  Application["clicks"] = ((int)Application["clicks"]) + 1;
  Application.UnLock();

  LabelApplicationClicks.Text = "Application clicks: " +
    Application["clicks"].ToString();
}
```

8. Build your Web site and visit the Default.aspx page. Click the hyperlink several times to switch between pages and verify that the click counter increments.
9. As an optional step, open the same page from a different computer. Of course, this requires that you are running your code under IIS or you deploy the code to a server. It also requires you to have access to another machine. If you do, you will notice that the click count includes the clicks you made from the first computer because the *Application* object is shared among all user sessions.
10. Restart your Web server and visit the same page again. Notice that the click count is reset; the *Application* object is not persisted between application restarts.

EXERCISE 2 Store Data in the Session Object

In this exercise, you explore using the *Session* object.

1. Continue editing the project you created in the previous exercise. Alternatively, you can open the completed Lesson 1, Exercise 1 project in the samples installed from the CD.

2. Open the Global.asax file. Add code to the *Session_Start* method to initialize a session variable named *session_clicks*. This variable should be set to zero when the session is first initiated. The following shows an example:

```
'VB
Sub Session_Start(ByVal sender As Object, ByVal e As EventArgs)
  Session("session_clicks") = 0
End Sub

//C#
void Session_Start(object sender, EventArgs e)
{
  Session["session_clicks"] = 0;
}
```

3. Open Default.aspx in Source view. Add a new *Label* control under the existing one. Name this control ***LabelSessionClicks***. Do the same for Default2.aspx.

4. In the *Page_Load* method for both Default.aspx and Default2.aspx, add code to increment the number of clicks for the given user's session. Also, add code to display the value in *LabelSessionClicks*. The following code shows how your *Page_Load* event should now look (the new code is shown in bold):

```
'VB
Protected Sub Page_Load(ByVal sender As Object, _
  ByVal e As System.EventArgs) Handles Me.Load

  Application.Lock()
  Application("clicks") = CInt(Application("clicks")) + 1
  Application.UnLock()

  LabelApplicationClicks.Text = "Application clicks: " + _
    Application("clicks").ToString

  Session("session_clicks") = CInt(Session("session_clicks")) + 1

  LabelSessionClicks.Text = "Session clicks: " & _
    Session("session_clicks").ToString()

End Sub
```

```
//C#
protected void Page_Load(object sender, EventArgs e)
{
  Application.Lock();
  Application["clicks"] = ((int)Application["clicks"]) + 1;
  Application.UnLock();

  LabelApplicationClicks.Text = "Application clicks: " +
    Application["clicks"].ToString();

  Session["session_clicks"] =
    (int)Session["session_clicks"] + 1;

  LabelSessionClicks.Text = "Session clicks: "
    + Session["session_clicks"].ToString();

}
```

5. Build your Web site and visit the Default.aspx page. Click the hyperlink several times to switch between pages and verify that both the *Application* and *Session* click counters increment.
6. From a different computer (or a different browser on the same computer) open the same page. Notice that the *Application* click count includes the clicks you made from the first computer (or browser) because the *Application* object is shared among all user sessions. However, the *Session* click counter includes only clicks made from one computer (or browser).
7. Restart your Web server. If you are running locally, you can right-click the server instance in the system tray and choose Stop. If you are running in IIS, open the admin console and start and stop the server. Now visit the same page again. Notice that both click counts are reset; the *Application* and *Session* objects are not persisted between application restarts.

Lesson Summary

- You can use the *Application* collection to store information that is accessible from all Web pages but is not user specific. To initialize *Application* variables, respond to the *Application_Start* event in your Global.asax file.
- You can use the *Session* collection to store user-specific information that is accessible from all Web pages. To initialize *Session* variables, respond to the *Session_Start* event in your Global.asax file. You can store session information in the server's memory using the *InProc* session state mode, store it in an ASP.NET State Service server using the *StateServer* mode, store it in a database using the *SQLServer* mode, implement your

own custom session state storage using the *Custom* mode, or turn session state off completely.

Lesson Review

You can use the following questions to test your knowledge of the information in Lesson 2, "Using Server-Side State Management." The questions are also available on the companion CD if you prefer to review them in electronic form.

> ***NOTE*** **ANSWERS**
>
> **Answers to these questions and explanations of why each answer is right or wrong are located in the "Answers" section at the end of the book.**

1. In which file should you write code to respond to the *Application_Start* event?
   - **A.** Any ASP.NET server page with an .aspx extension
   - **B.** Web.config
   - **C.** Global.asax
   - **D.** Any ASP.NET server page with an .aspx.vb or .aspx.cs extension
2. You need to store state data that is accessible to any user who connects to your Web application. Which collection object should you use?
   - **A.** *Session*
   - **B.** *Application*
   - **C.** *Cookies*
   - **D.** *ViewState*
3. You need to store a value indicating whether a user has been authenticated for your site. This value needs to be available and checked on every user request. Which object should you use?
   - **A.** *Session*
   - **B.** *Application*
   - **C.** *Cookies*
   - **D.** *ViewState*
4. You need to log data to a database when a user's session times out. Which event should you respond to?
   - **A.** *Application_Start*
   - **B.** *Application_End*
   - **C.** *Session_Start*
   - **D.** *Session_End*

5. Your application is being deployed in a load-balanced Web farm. The load balancer is not set up for user server affinity. Rather, it routes requests to servers based on their load. Your application uses session state. How should you configure the *SessionState* mode attribute? (Choose all that apply.)

   A. *StateServer*

   B. *InProc*

   C. *Off*

   D. *SqlServer*

Chapter Review

To further practice and reinforce the skills you learned in this chapter, you can perform the following tasks:

- Review the chapter summary.
- Complete the case scenarios. These scenarios set up real-world situations involving the topics of this chapter and ask you to create solutions.
- Complete the suggested practices.
- Take a practice test.

Chapter Summary

- State management enables you to access data between multiple Web requests. Client-side state management offers the best scalability. ASP.NET includes five ways to store client-side state management data: control state, cookies, hidden fields, query strings, and view state.
- Server-side state management offers improved security and the ability to store larger amounts of both user-specific and shared data. ASP.NET includes three server-side state management techniques. Application state is the best choice when you need to store information relevant to multiple users. Choose session state to store information about a single user's visit to your Web site.

Case Scenarios

In the following case scenarios, you apply what you've learned about how to implement and apply ASP.NET state management. If you have difficulty completing this work, review the material in this chapter before beginning the next chapter. You can find answers to these questions in the "Answers" section at the end of this book.

Case Scenario 1: Remembering User Credentials

You are an application developer for Contoso, Ltd., a business-to-business retailer. You are writing an e-commerce Web application that retrieves inventory and customer data from a back-end database server. Recently, your marketing department has received requests from customers to provide enhanced account management capabilities. Your manager asks you to interview key people and then come to his office to answer his questions about your design choices.

INTERVIEWS

Following is a list of company personnel you interviewed and their statements:

- **Marketing manager** "We recently had a session with our most important customers to identify potential areas of improvement. One of the comments that we heard frequently was that they want a way to log in to our Web site and view past order information. I know I hate having to log in to Web sites every time I visit the Web page, so if we could remember their login information, I think the customers would be happier."
- **Development manager** "This seems like a fair request; however, we need to keep security in mind. Don't do anything that would allow an attacker to steal a user's session and view his or her orders."

QUESTIONS

Answer the following questions for your manager.

1. What state management mechanism would you use to remember a user's login credentials?
2. How can you reduce the risk of a user's credentials being stolen?
3. How should you store information about previous orders?

Case Scenario 2: Analyzing Information for Individual Users and for All Users

You are an application developer working for Fabrikam, Inc., a consumer Web-based magazine. Recently, your marketing department personnel requested the ability to see a snapshot of what users are doing on the Web site in near real time. Additionally, they would like to display advertisements to those users based on the content viewed in the current session. Finally, they would like the ability to analyze multiple different articles that users might have read during a given visit.

You discuss the needs with the Marketing Manager, who says, "We have great tools for analyzing Web site logs, but we often want to know what's happening on the site in real time so that we can make instant decisions. For example, if we post a new article, we'd like to see how many users are currently viewing that page. Also, I think we can better cater our advertisements to customer needs by analyzing a user's path through our Web site. Is there any way to track what a user does during a visit to our site?"

QUESTIONS

Answer the following questions for your manager.

1. How can you present data for all users to be analyzed by the marketing department?
2. How can you analyze and track an individual user through the site?

Suggested Practices

To successfully master the ASP.NET state management exam objectives presented in this chapter, complete the following tasks.

Manage State by Using Client-Based State Management Options

For this task, you should complete Practice 1 to get a better understanding of how to implement control state. Complete Practices 2 and 3 to explore how real-world Web sites use cookies.

- **Practice 1** Create a custom control and implement control state management.
- **Practice 2** View your Temporary Internet Files folder (typically located in C:\Documents and Settings*username*\Local Settings). Examine cookies that Web sites have stored on your computer and open the files in a text editor to view the information they contain.
- **Practice 3** Disable cookies in your Web browser. Visit several of your favorite Web sites to determine if the Web site behavior changes at all.

Manage State by Using Server-Based State Management Options

For this task, you should complete all of Practice 1 to get experience using the *Application* objects. Complete Practices 2 and 3 to gain experience working with user sessions.

- **Practice 1** Using a Web application that you previously developed, add real-time application activity analysis functionality described in Case Scenario 2 so that you can open a Web page and view which pages users are currently viewing.
- **Practice 2** Using a Web application that you previously developed, enable Web site personalization using the *Session* object. Allow a user to set a preference, such as background color, and apply that preference to any page the user might view.
- **Practice 3** Disable cookies in your Web browser and visit the Web application you created in Practice 2. Attempt to set a preference and study how the application responds. Think about how an application might determine whether a browser supports sessions and what to do if the browser does not support sessions.

Maintain State by Using Database Technology

For this task, you should complete Practices 1 and 2.

- **Practice 1** Configure a Web application to use a SQL state server.
- **Practice 2** Configure a Web application to use the ASP.NET State Service.

Respond to Application and Session Events

For this task, you should complete Practices 1 and 2.

- **Practice 1** Using a Web application that you previously developed, add code to initialize variables in the *Application_Start* event. Add code to release resources in the *Application_End* event.
- **Practice 2** Using a Web application that you previously developed, add code to initialize variables in the *Session_Start* event. Add code to release resources in the *Session_End* event.

Take a Practice Test

The practice tests on this book's companion CD offer many options. For example, you can test yourself on just the content covered in this chapter, or you can test yourself on all the 70-562 certification exam content. You can set up the test so that it closely simulates the experience of taking a certification exam, or you can set it up in study mode so that you can look at the correct answers and explanations after you answer each question.

MORE INFO **PRACTICE TESTS**

For details about all the practice test options available, see "How to Use the Practice Tests" in this book's Introduction.

CHAPTER 5

Customizing and Personalizing a Web Application

The demands on Web applications have been steadily increasing. Developers are asked for applications that are flexible to change, personalized to the individual user, and highly customizable to support different situations. A quick look at many consumer-based Web sites will demonstrate this. Content is customized based on who you are and what you are doing. Users are also given control over the content they wish to see. They are also often given features to change the page layouts, the site colors, and various sizing options. These demands are, of course, also being made of business applications. Single applications might be made customizable to different departments. For example, users might want control over the company's intranet to show different information in a different format depending on the user's role (such as the sales department versus the quality control department).

Thankfully, the tools are keeping pace with demand. ASP.NET provides a number of features for developers to better manage and control the layout, styles, and personalization of their applications. This chapter discusses four of these ways: master pages, themes, user profiles, and Web Parts.

Exam objectives in this chapter:

- Programming Web Applications
  - Customize the layout and appearance of a Web page.

Lessons in this chapter:

Before You Begin

To complete the lessons in the chapter, you should be familiar with developing applications with Microsoft Visual Studio using Visual Basic or C#. In addition, you should be comfortable with all of the following:

- The Visual Studio 2008 Integrated Development Environment (IDE).
- A basic understanding of Hypertext Markup Language (HTML) and client-side scripting.
- How to create a new Web site.
- Building a Web form by adding Web server controls to a Web page and programming against them on the server.

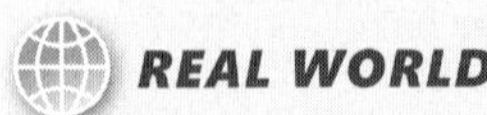

Tony Northrup

In the early 1990s, having any Web site at all was an accomplishment, and all it took to impress people was an animated GIF. Near the mid-1990s, developers started adding simple scripting to create static Web sites that incorporated a few dynamic Web components, such as e-mail forms.

Over time, the Web development community has continued to raise the bar. Today, almost all Web pages incorporate some dynamic content. Almost all e-commerce and other business Web sites enable users to identify themselves to get permissions to view personalized versions of the Web site and maintain their own accounts.

Creating a large personalized Web site like this would have been next to impossible with the Perl scripts most of us used in the early to mid-1990s. Today, with the Microsoft .NET Framework, you can build dynamic, personalized Web sites with very little code. The Web sites are not only easier to create, but more secure, reliable, and manageable. That means that, unlike some of the Perl scripts I wrote in the 1990s, I probably won't have script kiddies hacking my site just for the fun of it.

Lesson 1: Using Master Pages

Developers by trade tend to focus more on functionality and less on aesthetics. As a result, some available complex Web applications have wonderfully structured code but are often inconsistent when it comes to the user interface (UI). This problem is exacerbated by the fact that these applications often have their UI spread out across the many pages of the site. This makes it very difficult to make comprehensive changes to update the UI.

Master pages are one way ASP.NET helps to solve this problem. Master pages allow developers to isolate the shell of the UI from the many forms in the application. This shell often contains the site's header, its navigation, any subnavigation, and the footer information for the site. The pages a developer then creates are housed within the master page. In this way, designers can provide updates to the UI and developers can easily apply them to the entire site in a consistent manner. When users request a Web page, ASP.NET merges the content of the individual page with that of the master page and shows a single page to the user.

This lesson describes how to create and use master pages in your applications.

REAL WORLD

Tony Northrup

All Web sites require consistency. Before master pages were available, I used to create custom controls for every component that would be repeated throughout a Web site, including the logo, the navigation bar, and the page footer. This way, if I needed to change an aspect of one of the common components, I could make the change in one place and have it reflected throughout the site.

That worked great, unless I wanted to add or remove a component, or change the layout of the components. Then I'd have to go into every single Web page and make the change. After that, I'd have to test every page to make sure I hadn't made any mistakes.

Now master pages allow me to make centralized changes to the entire site by editing one file. It speeds up the development of content pages, too, because I don't have to worry about copying and pasting the structure for the shared controls.

After this lesson, you will be able to:

- Explain the purpose of master and content pages.
- Describe the process of creating master and content pages.
- Use different techniques for attaching content to a master page.
- Reference controls and properties on a master page from a content page.
- Explain how event handling works in master pages.
- Create nested master pages.
- Programmatically switch between master pages to provide user-selected templates.

Estimated lesson time: 45 minutes

Overview of Master and Content Pages

An ASP.NET master page defines the core layout of the pages in your site. This information is common to all pages that use the same master page. Advantages of using master pages include the following:

- They allow you to centralize the common functionality of your pages so that you can make updates in just one place.
- They make it easy to create one set of controls and code and apply the results to a set of pages. For example, you can use controls on the master page to create a menu that applies to all pages.
- They give you fine-grained control over the layout of the final pages by allowing you to control how the placeholder controls are rendered.
- They provide object models that allow you to customize the master pages from individual content pages.

A master page is defined with the file extension .master. Master pages are very similar to regular .aspx pages. They contain text, HTML, and server controls; they even have their own code-behind files. One difference is that a master page inherits from the *MasterPage* class. Another is that instead of an @ *Page* directive at the top of the page source, master pages contain an @ *Master* directive. Following this are the common things you would expect to see in the source of an ASP.NET page like *<html>*, *<head>*, and *<form>* elements. You can then embed your own source inside the master page, such as a company logo, navigation elements, footer, and more.

You use master pages in conjunction with content pages. Content pages contain page-specific content while inheriting their shell from their master page. To enable pages to insert content into a master page, you must add one or more *ContentPlaceHolder* controls. This defines an area for content pages to add their page-specific text, HTML, and server controls.

At run time, master pages and content pages are processed as follows:

1. A user requests a page by typing the Uniform Resource Locator (URL) of the content page.
2. When the page is fetched, the @ *Page* directive is read. If the directive references a master page, the master page is read as well. If this is the first time the page has been requested, both pages are compiled.
3. The master page with the updated content is merged into the control tree of the content page.
4. The content of individual *Content* controls is merged into the corresponding *ContentPlaceHolder* control in the master page.
5. The resulting merged page is rendered to the browser as a single page.

There has been a great need for something like master pages for a long time. Developers have been finding a way to provide similar features. Master pages take the place of functionality that developers have traditionally created by:

- Copying and pasting existing code, text, and control elements repeatedly.
- Using framesets.
- Using include files for common elements.
- Using ASP.NET user controls.

Creating a Master Page

You create a master page through the Add New Item dialog box. You lay out a master page in a similar manner as you would any .aspx page. You can use tables, styles, controls, and so forth, to define your page. The following code shows a sample master page:

```
<%@ Master Language="VB" CodeFile="SiteMaster.master.vb" Inherits="SiteMaster" %>

<!DOCTYPE html PUBLIC "-//W3C//DTD XHTML 1.0 Transitional//EN"
 "http://www.w3.org/TR/xhtml1/DTD/xhtml1-transitional.dtd">

<html xmlns="http://www.w3.org/1999/xhtml">
<head runat="server">
    <title>Contoso Inc.</title>
    <asp:ContentPlaceHolder id="head" runat="server">
    </asp:ContentPlaceHolder>
    <link href="SiteStyles.css" rel="stylesheet" type="text/css" />
</head>
<body>
    <form id="form1" runat="server">
    <div class="header">
        <img src="images/contoso.jpg" alt="Contoso" />
```

```
            <a href="products.aspx" class="topNav">Products</a>
            <a href="services.aspx" class="topNav">Services</a>
            <a href="about.aspx" class="topNav">About Us</a>
            <a href="contact.aspx" class="topNav">Contact Us</a>
          <hr />
        </div>
        <asp:ContentPlaceHolder id="ContentPlaceHolderMain" runat="server">
        </asp:ContentPlaceHolder>
        <div class="footer">Copyright <%=DateTime.Now.Year.ToString()%>, Contoso Inc.</div>
        </form>
</body>
</html>
```

In this example, the master page connects to a style sheet for the site, defines the top-level navigation for the site, and defines the site's footer. In addition, notice the *ContentPlaceHolder* controls. The first is used to allow child pages to add information into the *<head>* section of the master page. The second placeholder is used to define the actual page content. Figure 5-1 illustrates how this master page looks in Design view.

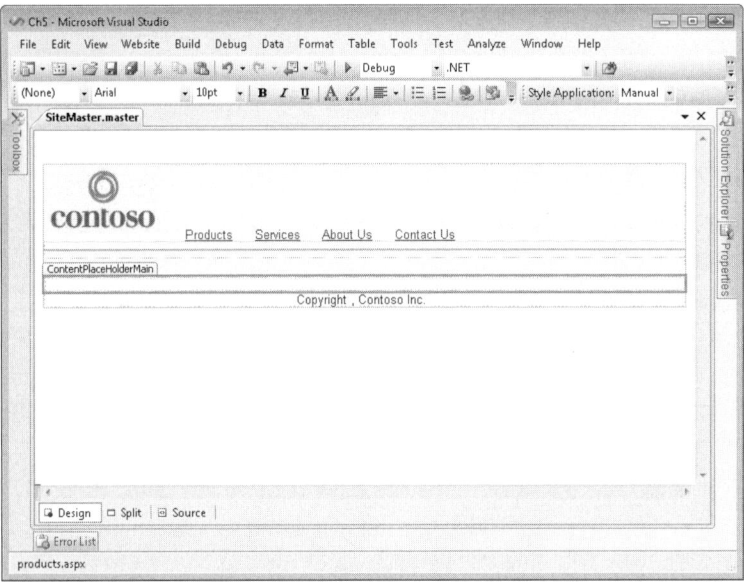

FIGURE 5-1 A master page in Design view

Creating Content Pages

You add content pages to your site the same way you add any .aspx page. However, in the Add New Item dialog box, you select the Select Master Page check box. This allows you to select a master page for your .aspx file. Alternatively, you can associate an .aspx page to a master page using the *MasterPageFile* attribute in the *@ Page* directive.

A content page defines the *ContentPlaceHolder* controls in a master page. When you define a new page from a master page, you are given an .aspx page that contains the content placeholder elements for the master page. You are then left to nest page-specific information inside the content placeholder controls.

The following page source demonstrates a content page derived from the master page defined earlier. Note that all text and controls must be within a *Content* control or the page will generate an error. Otherwise, the page behaves exactly like a standard ASP.NET page.

```
<%@ Page Language="VB" MasterPageFile="~/SiteMaster.master"
  AutoEventWireup="false" CodeFile="Login.aspx.vb" Inherits="Login"
  title="Contoso Login" %>

<asp:Content ID="Content1" ContentPlaceHolderID="head" Runat="Server">
</asp:Content>

<asp:Content ID="Content2"
  ContentPlaceHolderID="ContentPlaceHolderMain" Runat="Server">

  <asp:Login ID="Login1" runat="server">
  </asp:Login>

</asp:Content>
```

Notice that in the *@ Page* directive, the *MasterPageFile* attribute is set to the master page, *SiteMaster.master*. Inside this same directive is the *title* attribute. This allows you to set the actual title for the content page. This title will be used when the master page and content page are merged and output to the browser.

You can also use Design view to add content to a master page. In Design view, you drag controls onto the page and place them inside the placeholder controls. The rest of the page is actually grayed out and disabled in the Designer. Figure 5-2 shows the content page defined in the source given earlier, inside the Visual Studio Designer.

> ***NOTE*** **MASTER PAGE SETTINGS**
>
> **In general, the master page structure has no effect on how you construct your content pages or program against them. However, in some cases, if you set a page-wide property on the master page, it can affect the behavior of the content page. For example, if you set the *EnableViewState* property on the content page to *true* but set the same property to *false* in the master page, view state is effectively disabled because the setting on the master page takes priority.**

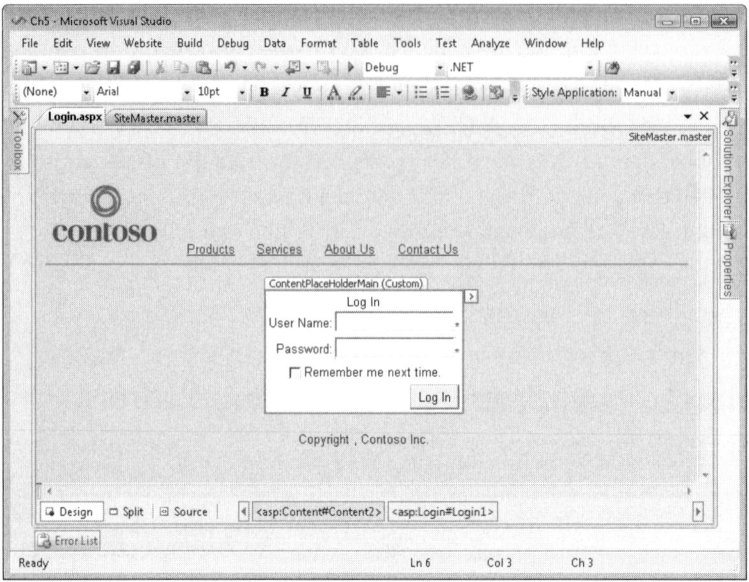

FIGURE 5-2 A content page in Design view

Attaching Master Pages to Content Pages

There are three levels at which you can attach master pages to content pages in your site. The first is at the page level using the *@ Page* directive as discussed previously and shown in the following code example:

```
<%@ Page Language="VB" MasterPageFile="MySite.Master" %>
```

You can also define a master page for your entire site by setting this in the *<pages>* element of the application's configuration file (Web.config). Here you can specify that all .aspx pages in your site automatically bind to a master page. If you use this strategy, all ASP.NET pages in the application that have *Content* controls are merged with the specified master page. If an ASP.NET page does not contain *Content* controls, the master page is not applied. The following shows an example of the *<pages>* element in the Web.config file:

```
<pages masterPageFile="MySite.Master" />
```

Finally, you can define a master page to work at the folder level within your site. This strategy works like binding master pages at the application level, except that you make the setting in a Web.config file that is added to a folder in your site. The master page bindings then apply to the ASP.NET pages in that folder.

 **Quick Check**

1. Which control is required inside a master page?
2. Which control is required inside a content page?

Quick Check Answers

1. You must have at least one *ContentPlaceHolder* control on a master page.
2. You must have a *Content* control on a content page. One *Content* control is added to the page for each *ContentPlaceHolder* control inside the master page.

Referencing Master Page Properties and Controls from Content Pages

You can leverage master pages to define application-specific settings on which child pages depend. For example, if many content pages need something like a user's login ID, you can set this value inside the master page and then make it available to content pages as a property of the master page. This saves you from having to look the value up or track it on all pages or in the session state.

The basic process to reference master page properties from a content page is as follows:

1. Create a property in the master page code-behind file.
2. Add the @ *MasterType* declaration to the .aspx content page.
3. Reference the master page property from the content page using the syntax *Master.<Property_Name>*.

The sections that follow describe this process in more detail. You can follow a similar process if you need to expose and reference properties of control values. In this way, you can map a property to a control's value.

Creating a Property in the Master Page

Content pages can reference any public property declared in the master page code-behind file. For example, the following code sample defines the property *UserId* in the master page code-behind file. In this example, the master page provides strong typing for the session variable, *UserId*:

```
'VB
Public Property UserId() As String
  Get
    Return CType(Session("UserId"), String)
  End Get
  Set(ByVal value As String)
    Session("UserId") = value
```

```
  End Set
End Property

//C#
public String UserId
{
  get { return (String)Session["UserId"]; }
  set { Session["UserId"] = value; }
}
```

Connecting to Master Page Properties from Content Pages

You must add the @ *MasterType* declaration to the .aspx content page to reference master properties in a content page. This declaration is added just below the @ *Page* declaration. The following code demonstrates this:

```
<%@ Page Language="VB" MasterPageFile="~/SiteMaster.master"
  AutoEventWireup="false" CodeFile="Login.aspx.vb" Inherits="Login"
  title="Contoso Login" %>
<%@ MasterType VirtualPath="~/SiteMaster.master" %>
```

Once you add the @ *MasterType* declaration, you can reference properties in the master page using the *Master* class. For example, the following code sets the Login control's *UserName* property to the *UserId* property exposed by the master page:

```
'VB
Login1.UserName = Master.UserId

//C#
Login1.UserName = Master.UserId;
```

If you later change the master page associated with a content page, make sure you implement the same public properties to ensure the content pages continue to function correctly.

If you are creating multiple master pages that might be referenced by the same set of content pages, you should derive all master pages from a single base class. Then specify the base class name in the @ *MasterType* declaration. This enables the content page to reference the same properties, regardless of which master page is being used.

Referencing Controls in the Master Page

In addition to properties, you can also reference and update controls in the master page from an individual content page. One way is to encapsulate the control's property in a property of the master page (as demonstrated earlier). This is often a clean solution, as the master page developer is exposing these properties on purpose and thereby creating a contract with the content pages.

The other means of referencing a control on the master page from a content page is through the *Master.FindControl* method. You need to supply this method with the name of the control you want it to find. This approach requires the content page to have knowledge of the master page. *Master.FindControl* returns a *Control* object, which you then need to cast to the correct control type. Once you have this reference, you can read or update the object as if it were local to the content page.

The following code (which belongs in the *Page_Load* method of the content page) demonstrates this method by updating a *Label* control in the master page named *Brand*:

```
'VB
Dim MyLabelBrand As Label = CType(Master.FindControl("LabelBrand"), Label)
MyLabelBrand.Text = "Fabrikam"

//C#
Label MyLabelBrand = (Label)Master.FindControl("LabelBrand");
MyLabelBrand.Text = "Fabrikam";
```

In this example, a local variable named *MyLabelBrand* is set to reference a *Label* control on the master page. Once you have this reference, you can use it to customize information in a master page's *LabelBrand* control.

Handling Events When Working with Master Pages

Responding to events in master pages works the same as responding to events in other ASP.NET pages. Events in the master page are executed in the same order as those in the content page. The major difference is that events execute in their order trading off from master page to content page. Events occur in the following sequence for a content page that is part of a master page:

1. Master page controls *Init* event.
2. Content controls *Init* event.
3. Master page *Init* event.
4. Content page *Init* event.
5. Content page *Load* event.
6. Master page *Load* event.
7. Content controls *Load* event.
8. Content page *PreRender* event.
9. Master page *PreRender* event.
10. Master page controls *PreRender* event.
11. Content controls *PreRender* event.

Developers typically do not have to be too concerned about this. They can simply add event code to the master page that belongs in the master page and event code in the content page that belongs there. For example, if you need to write code that has to respond to a button's click event and that button is on the master page, add that code to the master page's code-behind file.

Creating Nested Master Pages

A common scenario for Web applications is to define an overall master page for the site. This page typically includes the structure and overall navigation for all pages. As users navigate to subareas of the site, these subareas might also have many things in common. In this case you can define a second master page for these subareas. This second master page can be nested inside the content placeholder of the first master page. Content pages can then derive themselves from the nested master page and take on the features of both master pages.

A child master page also has the .master extension. However, the child master page also has the attribute *MasterPageFile* set in the *@ Master* declaration. This attribute points to the parent master page. The following example demonstrates a child master page with a parent master page named *SiteMaster.master*:

```
<%@ Master Language="VB" MasterPageFile="~/SiteMaster.master" AutoEventWireup="false"
  CodeFile="SubMasterPage.master.vb" Inherits="SubMasterPage" %>

<asp:Content ID="Content1" ContentPlaceHolderID="head" Runat="Server">

</asp:Content>
<asp:Content ID="Content2" ContentPlaceHolderID="ContentPlaceHolderMain" Runat="Server">

  <h2>Sub Department</h2>
  <asp:panel runat="server" id="panel1" backcolor="LightBlue">
    <asp:ContentPlaceHolder ID="ContentPlaceHolderSubDept" runat="server" />
  </asp:panel>

</asp:Content>
```

The child master page typically contains content controls that are mapped to content placeholders on the parent master page. In this respect, the child master page is laid out like any content page. However, the child master page also has one or more content placeholders of its own. This defines the areas where its content pages can put their content.

Dynamically Changing Master Pages

You define the master page in a content page's *@ Page* declaration. However, that doesn't mean you cannot switch to a different master page programmatically. Changing master pages allows you to provide different templates for different users. For example, you might give users a choice of different colors and styles (you can also do this with themes, as discussed in the next lesson). You could also use different master pages to format data for different browsers or different mobile devices.

> ***MORE INFO*** **MOBILE DEVICES**
>
> **For more information about creating Web pages for mobile devices, read Chapter 15, "Creating ASP.NET Mobile Web Applications."**

To dynamically change master pages, follow these high-level steps:

1. Create two or more master pages with the same *ContentPlaceHolder* controls and public properties. Typically, you create one master page, copy it to create the second master page, and make any necessary modifications. Note that, from this point forward, you must make any changes to the *ContentPlaceHolder* controls or public properties to all master pages to ensure compatibility.
2. Optionally, provide a way for users to switch between master pages. If the master page should be the user's choice (for example, if color and layout are the primary differences), add links to your master pages to enable users to switch between pages. You need to define the current master page within the content page, however, so you can choose to store the setting in the *Session* variable or in another object that is accessible to both the master and content pages.

   For example, the following code can be called from a link or button on the master page to set a *Session* variable to the name of a different master page. After you define the master page within the content page, reload the page.

   ```
   'VB
   Session("masterpage") = "Master2.master"
   Response.Redirect(Request.Url.ToString)

   //C#
   Session["masterpage"] = "Master2.master";
   Response.Redirect(Request.Url.ToString());
   ```

3. Define the master page in the content page's *Page_PreInit* method. *Page_PreInit* is the last opportunity you have to override the default master page setting, because later handlers (such as *Page_Init*) reference the master page. For example, this code defines the master page based on the *Session* object:

   ```
   'VB
   Sub Page_PreInit(ByVal sender As Object, ByVal e As EventArgs)
     If Not (Session("masterpage") Is Nothing) Then
       MasterPageFile = CType(Session("masterpage"), String)
     End If
   End Sub

   //C#
   void Page_PreInit(Object sender, EventArgs e)
   {
     if (Session["masterpage"] != null)
       MasterPageFile = (String)Session["masterpage"];
   }
   ```

When you switch master pages, you need to make sure both pages define the exact same content placeholder control names. Exercise 2 in this lesson's lab walks you through this process step by step.

LAB Using Master and Child Pages

In this lab, you create two different master pages. Each master page defines an alternative layout for the page. You then create content pages based on the master page. Finally, you add code to allow users to set their master page preference dynamically.

If you encounter a problem completing an exercise, you can find the completed projects in the samples installed from the companion CD.

EXERCISE 1 Create Master Pages and a Child Page

In this exercise, you create a new ASP.NET Web site with two master pages and a child page.

1. Open Visual Studio and create a new ASP.NET Web site named **MasterContent** in either C# or Visual Basic.
2. Add a new master page to your Web site and name it **Professional.master**.
3. Add top-level navigation and footer information to your master page. In the middle of the page make sure there is a content placeholder; name it **ContentPlaceholderMain**. Your page should look like Figure 5-3. Note that you can copy the Contoso logo and the style sheet used in this example from the samples installed from the companion CD.

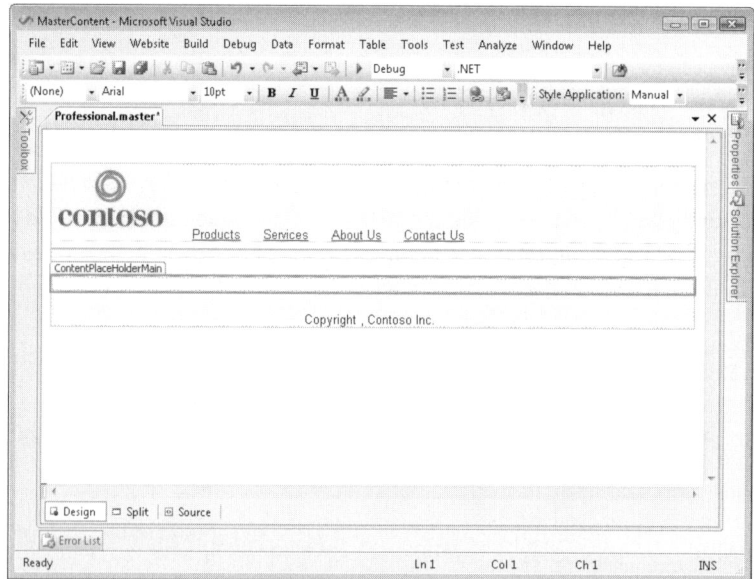

FIGURE 5-3 Create the Professional.master page

4. Create a second master page that mimics the first. Name this page **Colorful.master**. Set the body tag to show the background color of yellow.
5. Add a new Web page to your site and name it Home.aspx. In the Add New Item dialog box, select the Select Master Page check box, then click Add. In the Select A Master Page dialog box, select Professional.master.

6. Open Home.aspx in Source view. Inside the *ContentPlaceholderMain* add a *TextBox* control and name it **TextBoxUserName**. Add a *DropDownList* named **DropDown-ListSitePref**. Add two *ListItem* elements to the *DropDownList* and name them **Professional** and **Colorful**. You can do so by clicking the smart tag in Design view and choosing Edit Items. This will launch the ListItem Collection Editor.

   Add a *Button* control named **ButtonSubmit**. Finally, add a *Label* control to show up under the navigation. Name this label control **LabelWelcome** but set its *Text* property to nothing for now. Figure 5-4 shows how your page might now look.

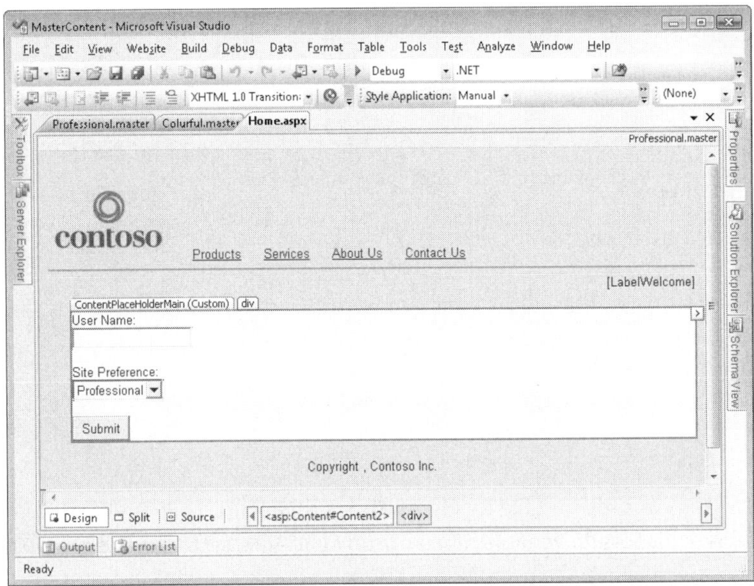

FIGURE 5-4 Define a content page

7. Build your project and open the resulting Home.aspx page in a browser. Verify that it displays correctly. Note that the page does not do anything yet. We will add code in the next exercise.

As this exercise demonstrated, master and content pages can be created in just a few minutes without writing any code.

EXERCISE 2 Modify Master Page Properties and Switch Master Pages

In this exercise, you add functionality to a content page to change the controls on a master page and to switch between two master pages dynamically.

1. Continue editing the project you created in the previous exercise. Alternatively, you can open the completed Lesson 1, Exercise 1 project in the samples installed from the CD.
2. In Design view double-click the submit button to open the button's event handler. Add code to the *ButtonSubmit_Click* method to determine whether the user provided a value in the *TextBoxUserName* text box. If the user did, use the name he or she typed

to define a *Session* variable named *UserName* and change the welcome message in the master page *LabelWelcome* accordingly. The following code demonstrates this:

```
'VB
Protected Sub ButtonSubmit_Click(ByVal sender As Object, _
  ByVal e As System.EventArgs) Handles ButtonSubmit.Click
  If Not (TextBoxUserName.Text = "") Then
    Session("UserName") = TextBoxUserName.Text

    Dim welcome As Label = CType(Master.FindControl("LabelWelcome"), Label)
    welcome.Text = "Welcome, " + TextBoxUserName.Text + "!"
  End If
End Sub

//C#
protected void ButtonSubmit_Click(object sender, EventArgs e)
{
  if (TextBoxUserName.Text != "")
  {
    Session["UserName"] = TextBoxUserName.Text;
    Label welcome = (Label)Master.FindControl("LabelWelcome");
    welcome.Text = "Welcome, " + Session["UserName"] + "!";
  }
}
```

3. Next, open the code-behind file for Home.aspx. Add a *Page_Load* method. Here, check to see if there is a *Session* variable named *UserName*. If there is, change the welcome message in the master page accordingly. The following code demonstrates this:

```
'VB
Protected Sub Page_Load(ByVal sender As Object, _
  ByVal e As System.EventArgs) Handles Me.Load

  If Not (Session("UserName") Is Nothing) Then
    Dim welcome As Label = CType(Master.FindControl("LabelWelcome"), Label)
    welcome.Text = "Welcome, " + Session("UserName") + "!"
  End If

End Sub

//C#
protected void Page_Load(object sender, EventArgs e)
{
  if (Session["UserName"] != null)
  {
    Label welcome = (Label)Master.FindControl("LabelWelcome");
```

```
    welcome.Text = "Welcome, " + Session["UserName"] + "!";
  }
}
```

Build your project and open the Home.aspx page. Type your name in the *TextBox-UserName* text box and then click Submit. Verify that the page successfully changes *LabelWelcome* in the master page. Browse to a different page and then come back. The page should pull your user name from the session.

Note that this solution only works within the Home.aspx content page. If a user loads a different content page on your site, the welcome message reverts to nothing. You would then have to add similar code to every page in your site. This is fine for a demo page. However, in reality you would add the code to set the label control from the session to your master page and not to each content page.

EXERCISE 3 Allow Users to Dynamically Select Their Master Page

In this exercise, you add functionality to a content page to change the master page dynamically in your code.

1. Continue editing the project you created in the previous exercise. Alternatively, you can open the completed Lesson 1, Exercise 2 project in the samples installed from the CD.
2. Open Home.aspx in Design view. Double-click the drop-down list control to generate the default event handler. In the event handler, define the session variable, *Template*. The following code demonstrates this:

```
'VB
Protected Sub DropDownListSitePref_SelectedIndexChanged( _
  ByVal sender As Object, ByVal e As System.EventArgs) _
  Handles DropDownListSitePref.SelectedIndexChanged

  Session("Template") = DropDownListSitePref.SelectedValue

End Sub

//C#
 protected void DropDownListSitePref_SelectedIndexChanged(
   object sender, EventArgs e)
 {
   Session["Template"] = DropDownListSitePref.SelectedValue;
 }
```

3. Add a *Page_PreInit* method to your code. In the *Page_PreInit* method, check to see if there is a *Session* variable named *Template*. If there is, use it to change the *MasterPage-File* object to the selected template's file name. The following code demonstrates this:

```
'VB
Protected Sub Page_PreInit(ByVal sender As Object, _
  ByVal e As System.EventArgs) Handles Me.PreInit

  If Not (Session("Template") Is Nothing) Then
    MasterPageFile = CType(Session("Template"), String) + ".master"
  End If

End Sub

//C#
protected void Page_PreInit(object sender, EventArgs e)
{
  if (Session["Template"] != null)
    MasterPageFile = (String)Session["Template"] + ".master";
}
```

4. Build your application and then open the Home.aspx page. Switch to the Colorful template and click Submit. Then reload the page. Notice that the page does not change templates until you reload it. This happens because the *Template_SelectedIndexChanged* method runs after the *Page_PreInit* method. Therefore, the *Page_PreInit* method cannot detect the *Session("Template")* variable until the second time you load the page.

Lesson Summary

- Master pages provide templates that you can use to create consistent Web pages throughout an application.
- To use master pages, first create a master page and add site layout information and other common elements. Then add one or more *ContentPlaceHolder* controls to the master page.
- To create the content pages, add standard Web forms to your site but select the Select Master Page check box when creating the page. You then add content to the page inside the content area defined by the master page.
- To reference public properties in a master page, add the @ *MasterType* declaration to the content page and reference the property using *Master.<Property_Name>*. To reference controls in a master page, call *Master.FindControl* from the content page.
- Nested master pages fit into the *ContentPlaceHolder* controls on a master page but can contain other content pages. To create a nested master page, add a master attribute to the @ *Master* page declaration and specify the parent master page.
- To programmatically change the master page for a content page, set the page's *MasterPageFile* property and reload the page.

Lesson Review

You can use the following questions to test your knowledge of the information in Lesson 1, "Using Master Pages." The questions are also available on the companion CD if you prefer to review them in electronic form.

> ***NOTE* ANSWERS**
>
> **Answers to these questions and explanations of why each answer choice is right or wrong are located in the "Answers" section at the end of the book.**

1. Which of the following statements about referencing master page members is true? (Choose all that apply.)
   - **A.** Content pages can reference private properties in the master page.
   - **B.** Content pages can reference public properties in the master page.
   - **C.** Content pages can reference public methods in the master page.
   - **D.** Content pages can reference controls in the master page.
2. You are converting an existing Web application to use master pages. To maintain compatibility, you need to read properties from the master page. Which of the following changes are you required to make to .aspx pages to enable them to work with a master page? (Choose all that apply.)
   - **A.** Add an @ *MasterType* declaration.
   - **B.** Add an @ *Master* declaration.
   - **C.** Add a *MasterPageFile* attribute to the @ *Page* declaration.
   - **D.** Add a *ContentPlaceHolder* control.
3. You need to dynamically change the master page of a content page. In which page event should you implement the dynamic changing?
   - **A.** *Page_Load*
   - **B.** *Page_Render*
   - **C.** *Page_PreRender*
   - **D.** *Page_PreInit*

Lesson 2: Using Themes

Many applications target multiple groups of customers. For example, imagine a business-to-business site that you create for each of your partners to leverage. They, in turn, might want to leverage portions of your site for their customers. It doesn't take long for someone to realize the need in this case for a different-looking version of the site for each of your partners. Each partner might want its own colors and styles. Partners might also need to change a number of graphics on the site if they intend to expose it to their customers. In this case, you need to create a separate theme for each of your partners.

An ASP.NET *theme* is a collection of styles, property settings, and graphics that define the appearance of pages and controls on your Web site. A theme can include skin files, which define property settings for ASP.NET Web server controls; Cascading Style Sheet files (.css files) that define the colors, size, and appearance of your site; and graphics. You apply a theme to your site. In this way, you can give the pages across your Web site a consistent appearance. You can also easily create a new theme to provide a different appearance.

This lesson describes how to create and leverage ASP.NET themes.

After this lesson, you will be able to:

- Use themes to easily change the overall appearance of a Web site or all the sites in a domain.
- Use themed skins to specify attributes for controls on a single page or an entire Web site.
- Create a style sheet that defines the styles used throughout your site's theme.
- Easily switch between themes for a page, a site, or programmatically based on a user preference.

Estimated lesson time: 35 minutes

Themes Overview

The Web pages that belong to the same Web site will invariably contain controls that have many properties in common across pages. This includes properties for setting things like background color, font size, foreground color, and other styles. You can manually set the properties for every control on every page in your site. However, that is time consuming, error prone (as you might overlook some settings), and difficult to change (as a change would have to sweep across your entire site). Instead, you can use ASP.NET themes.

Themes save you time and improve the consistency of a site by applying a common set of control properties, styles, and graphics across all pages in a Web site. Themes can be centralized, allowing you to quickly change the appearance of all the controls on your site from a single file. ASP.NET themes consist of the following set of elements:

- **Skins** Skins are files with .skin extensions that contain common property settings for buttons, labels, text boxes, and other controls. Skin files resemble control markups, but contain only the properties you want to define as part of the theme to be applied across pages.
- **Cascading Style Sheets (CSS)** These are files with .css extensions that contain the style property definitions for HTML markup elements and other custom style classes. A style sheet is linked to a page, master page, or entire site. ASP.NET applies the styles to the page.
- **Images and other resources** Images (such as a corporate logo) along with other resources can be defined inside a theme. This allows you to switch out the images when you switch themes for a site.

Not all of these items are required to define a theme. You can mix and match as necessary. The sections that follow further describe the usage of themes and demonstrate how you implement them.

Creating a Theme

You create themes inside the ASP.NET special folder, App_Themes. This folder sits in your ASP.NET application root. The folder contains separate folders for each theme in your site. You then add the corresponding skins, style sheets, and images to the theme folders. To define a theme for a single ASP.NET application, you can follow these steps:

1. Add an App_Themes folder to your Web application. In Visual Studio, right-click your Web site in the Solution Explorer, select Add ASP.NET Folder, and then select Theme.
2. Within the App_Themes folder you define individual folders for each theme in your application. For example, you could create a theme folder named RedTheme or BlueTheme. The name you set for the folder is also the name of your theme. You use this name when referencing the theme.

   You can have multiple themes in a Web application, as Figure 5-5 illustrates.

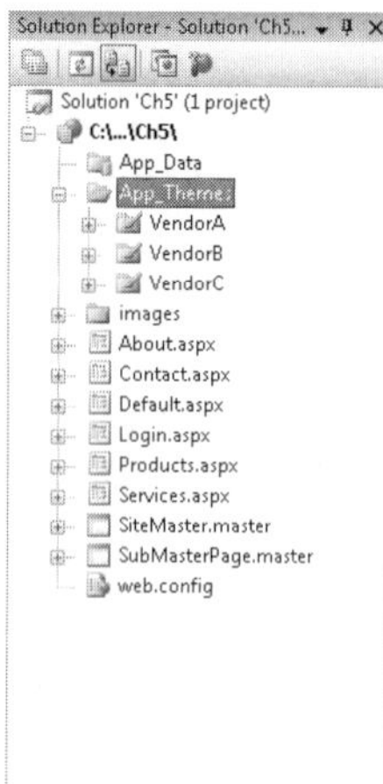

FIGURE 5-5 Create multiple themes by adding subfolders to the App_Themes folder

3. Next, you add skin files, style sheets, and images that make up your theme to your theme folder. Many times you define the first theme, copy it to the second, and then change the items as necessary.
4. You need to apply the theme to your site. You can do so at the individual page level by adding the *Theme* or *StyleSheetTheme* attribute to the @ *Page* directive and setting the attribute's value to the name of your theme (folder name).

   Alternatively, you can apply the theme to an entire Web application by adding the *<pages Theme="themeName">* element or the *<pages StyleSheetTheme="themeName">* element to the Web.config file. This will automatically apply the theme to all pages in your site.

Creating a Global Theme

ASP.NET also supports the concept of global themes. A global theme is one that you define for all sites in your domain. It is available to any application running on your server (and not simply application-specific). This can be useful if you run many sites that share a look and feel. You can define a global theme for your server by following these steps:

1. Create a Themes folder using a path on the server by defining it in the directory, *iisdefaultroot*\Aspnet_client\System_web*version*\Themes. This is the path for compiled Microsoft Internet Information Services (IIS) Web sites.

   If you are creating a file-system–based Web site inside your development environment or on your development server, you create the Themes folders in the path %windows%\Microsoft.NET\Framework*version*\ASP.NETClientFiles\Themes folder.

   As an example, if the default Web root folder on your server is C:\Inetpub\Wwwroot\ and the version of the .NET Framework is 2.0.50727, the new Themes folder should be created at C:\Inetpub\Wwwroot\Aspnet_client\System_web\2_0_50727\Themes.

2. Within the Themes folder, create a subfolder with your theme name (as you would with any other theme).
3. Within the theme subfolder, add skin files, style sheets, and images that make up your theme. You can't do this directly with Visual Studio; however, you can create a theme for a Web application and then move it to the global Themes folder.
4. You then apply the global theme as you would any other (see earlier or the Applying Themes section later in this chapter).

   Note that Visual Studio does not recognize the global theme name in the IDE; however, ASP.NET processes it properly when you retrieve the page in the browser.

Quick Check

1. **In which folder should you place themes for an application?**
2. **In which folder should you place global themes?**

Quick Check Answers

1. **Place themes for an application in the App_Themes folder.**
2. **Place global themes in the *iisdefaultroot*\Aspnet_client\System_web*version*\Themes folder.**

Creating a Skin File

Skin files serve to define default settings for server control appearance attributes. Each server control has attributes for things like font, background color, width, height, and more. Many of these appearance attributes are common among the controls on your site. Both style sheets and skin files allow you to set these properties once and apply them to multiple places in your site.

A skin file differs from a style sheet in that the skin file uses the attributes of the actual control and not just a set of standard HTML style elements. In addition, skin files will be applied at the control level automatically by ASP.NET. Style elements, on the other hand, can be applied automatically only to HTML items. For ASP.NET controls you must set the style class manually in your markup code.

You create a skin file by adding a .skin file in your theme folder. This can be done through the Add New Item dialog box in Visual Studio. You can create multiple .skin files for your theme. A common pattern is to create one skin file for each control you intend to skin. Alternatively, you can embed multiple control skins in a single file. The choice is yours.

Skin files contain two types of skins: default and named skins:

- **Default skins** A default skin automatically applies to all controls of the same type when a theme is applied to a page. A skin is considered a default skin if it does not have a *SkinID* attribute. For example, if you create a default skin for a *Calendar* control, the control skin applies to all *Calendar* controls on pages that use the theme.

Default skins are matched exactly by control type, so that a *Button* control skin applies to all *Button* controls, but not to *LinkButton* controls, or to controls that derive from the *Button* object.

- **Named skins** A named skin is a control skin with a *SkinID* property set to a specific name value. Named skins do not automatically apply to controls by type. Instead, you explicitly apply a named skin to a control by setting the ASP.NET control's *SkinID* property (like you would a style sheet class). Creating named skins allows you to set different skins for different instances of the same control in an application.

The following is a default control skin for a *Button* control. It defines the foreground and background colors as well as font information:

```
<asp:Button runat="server"
  BackColor="Red"
  ForeColor="White"
  Font-Name="Arial"
  Font-Size="9px" />
```

You can create a similar named skin by adding the *SkinId* attribute. The following shows another example:

```
<asp:Label runat="server"
  SkinId="Title"
  Font-Size="18px" />
```

Adding Images to Your Theme

Themes also allow you to switch out the images on your site. This is done through the skin file. To do this, you simply add a named skin of the *Image* control type to the skin file. You then set its *SkinId* appropriately.

For example, suppose you need to change the company logo for a site based on a specific theme. In this case, you would create a different theme for each company. Inside each theme's directory, you would add the appropriate image file. You could then create a skin file that contained the *Image* declaration as follows.

Company A's Skin File:

```
<asp:Image runat="server"  SkinId="CompanyLogo"
  ImageUrl="~/App_Themes/Contoso/contoso.jpg" />
```

Company B's Skin File:

```
<asp:Image runat="server" SkinId="CompanyLogo"
  ImageUrl="~/App_Themes/Fabrikam/fabrikam.jpg" />
```

Notice that in both skin files the *SkinId* is set to *CompanyLogo*. However, each defines a different logo file (ImageUrl). You can use this skin by first setting a page's *Theme* directive to either Contoso or Fabrikam (name of the theme folder). You then add an *Image* control to the page and set its *SkinId* attribute appropriately. The following code shows an example:

```
<asp:Image ID="Image1" SkinID="CompanyLogo" runat="server" />
```

ASP.NET will then grab the correct company logo based on the skin file. If you switch themes, the logo will automatically switch as well.

Adding a Cascading Style Sheet to Your Theme

A CSS contains style rules that are applied to elements in a Web page. CSS styles define how elements are displayed and where they are positioned on the page. Instead of assigning attributes to each element on your page individually, you can create a general rule that applies attributes whenever a Web browser encounters an instance of an element or an element that is assigned to a certain style class.

To add a CSS to your Web site, right-click the name of your theme in Solution Explorer and select Add New Item. You can then select the Style Sheet item template. Here you define styles for HTML elements and your own custom style classes (those preceded by a dot "."). The following are a few simple styles in a style sheet:

```
body
{
 text-align: center;
 font-family: Arial;
 font-size: 10pt;
}
.topNav
{
  padding: 0px 0px 0px 20px;
}
.header
{
  text-align: left;
  margin: 20px 0px 20px 0px;
}
.footer
{
  margin: 20px 0px 20px 0px;
}
```

When the theme is applied to a page, ASP.NET adds a reference to the style sheet to the head element of the page. In the HTML, this reference looks something like the following:

```
<link href="SiteStyles.css" rel="themeName/stylesheet" type="text/css" />
```

Visual Studio provides a number of tools for creating and managing style in your application. This includes the style builder, the style manager, IntelliSense in the style sheet, and more. Of course, style sheets are not reserved for just themes. They can be used for any of your sites regardless of whether they use themes.

EXAM TIP

CSS is not part of ASP.NET; CSS works for any type of Web site. It isn't specifically covered in the exam objectives and won't be covered in much detail in this book. However, CSS is still extremely useful, and all Web developers should be familiar with it. There are a number of good topics and discussion on MSDN regarding style sheets.

Rules for Applying Themes

We've already looked at the ways in which you can apply themes to your pages or to the entire site. However, your site might have multiple, often conflicting, style definitions for the same set of controls. That is, you might have a standard style sheet, a theme, and actual styles defined directly on the control. Which gets applied is based on a standard precedence order followed by ASP.NET.

Within ASP.NET, attributes and elements take precedence in the following order (first to last):

1. *Theme* attribute in the @ *Page* directive
2. *<pages Theme="themeName">* element in the Web.config file
3. Local control attributes
4. *StyleSheetTheme* attribute in the @ *Page* directive
5. *<pages StyleSheetTheme="themeName">* element in the Web.config file

In other words, if you specify a *Theme* attribute in the @ *Page* directive, settings in the theme take precedence and override any settings you've specified directly for controls on the page. However, if you change the *Theme* attribute to use the attribute *StyleSheetTheme*, you change the precedence and now control-specific settings take precedence over the theme settings.

For example, this directive applies a theme that would override control properties:

```
<%@ Page Theme="SampleTheme" %>
```

In other words, if *SampleTheme* specifies that *Label* controls use a red font, but you specify a blue font for a *Label* control, the labels appear with a red font.

The following directive changes the theme to a style sheet theme:

```
<%@ Page StyleSheetTheme="SampleTheme" %>
```

In this case, any changes you make to local control properties will override settings in the theme. Therefore, continuing the previous example, if *SampleTheme* specifies that *Label* controls are red but you override these to blue at the control level, the labels will show as blue. However, *Label* controls that do not have a color specified appear as red.

You can also disable themes for a specific page by setting the *EnableTheming* attribute of the @ *Page* directive to *false*:

```
<%@ Page EnableTheming="false" %>
```

Similarly, to disable themes for a specific control, set the control's *EnableTheming* property to *false*.

Applying a Theme Programmatically

Themes are useful for centralized management of the styles in your application. You might create a second theme as you experiment with changing the look and feel of your site. However, you might also need to create multiple themes that get switched based on the identification or preference of the user.

To apply a theme programmatically, set the page's *Theme* property in the *Page_PreInit* method. The following code demonstrates how to set the theme based on a query string value; however, this works equally well using cookies, session state, or other approaches.

```
'VB
Protected Sub Page_PreInit(ByVal sender As Object, ByVal e As System.EventArgs) _
  Handles Me.PreInit

  Select Case Request.QueryString("theme")
    Case "Blue"
      Page.Theme = "BlueTheme"
    Case "Pink"
      Page.Pink = "PinkTheme"
    End Select

End Sub

//C#
Protected void Page_PreInit(object sender, EventArgs e)
{
  switch (Request.QueryString["theme"])
  {
    case "Blue":
      Page.Theme = "BlueTheme";
      break;
    case "Pink":
      Page.Theme = "PinkTheme";
      break;
  }
}
```

To programmatically apply a style sheet theme (which works just like a theme but doesn't override control attributes), use the *Page.StyleSheetTheme* property.

Similarly, you can apply a theme to specific controls by setting the control's *SkinID* property in the *Page_PreInit* method. The following code shows how to set the skin for a control named *Calendar1*:

```
'VB
Sub Page_PreInit(ByVal sender As Object, ByVal e As System.EventArgs) _
  Handles Me.PreInit

  Calendar1.SkinID = "BlueTheme"

End Sub

//C#
void Page_PreInit(object sender, EventArgs e)
{
  Calendar1.SkinID = "BlueTheme";
}
```

LAB Creating and Applying Themes

In this lab, you create a new Web site and define two themes for that site.

If you encounter a problem completing an exercise, the completed projects are available in the samples installed from the companion CD.

EXERCISE 1 Create and Apply a Theme

In this exercise, you create two local themes, one for each vendor. You then apply and test the themes. Finally, you add code to allow the user to dynamically change the theme of the site.

1. Open Visual Studio and create a new ASP.NET Web site named **ThemesLab** using either C# or Visual Basic.
2. Add the App_Themes folder to your Web site. Right-click the site and choose Add ASP.NET Folder. Select Theme from the shortcut menu.
3. Create two theme folders. Name them **Contoso** and **Fabrikam**.
4. Inside the first theme folder, add a graphic file to represent the Contoso company. You can create one using the Paint utility or you can copy the graphic files from the samples installed from this book's CD. Name the file **Logo.png**.

   Repeat the same process for the second folder. In this folder, add a logo to represent Fabrikam. Again, name it **Logo.png**.
5. Add a .skin file to the Contoso theme. Define a named skin for the company logo; give it the *SkinId* of **Logo**. Add a skin for a *TextBox* control and a *Button* control. Your skin file for Contoso should look as follows:

```
<asp:Image ImageUrl="~/App_Themes/Contoso/logo.png"
  SkinId="Logo" runat="server" />
```

```
<asp:TextBox runat="server"
  BorderColor="Blue" BorderWidth="1pt" Font-Names="Arial" Font-Size="10pt"
  ForeColor="Brown" ></asp:TextBox>

<asp:Button runat="server"
  BorderColor="Blue" BorderWidth="1pt" Font-Bold="true"
  BackColor="White" ForeColor="DarkBlue" />
```

6. Repeat the same process for the Fabrikam theme. For this theme, modify the colors. Your skin file for Fabrikam should look as follows:

```
<asp:Image ImageUrl="~/App_Themes/Fabrikam/logo.png"
  SkinId="Logo" runat="server" />

<asp:TextBox runat="server"
  BorderColor="Orange" BorderWidth="1pt" Font-Names="Arial" Font-Size="10pt"
  ForeColor="Brown" ></asp:TextBox>

<asp:Button runat="server"
  BorderColor="DarkOrange" BorderWidth="1pt" Font-Bold="true"
  BackColor="DarkOrange" ForeColor="White" />
```

7. Add a style sheet file to your Contoso theme. Inside the style sheet add a style for the HTML body tag to set the default font and font size for the page. Also, define margins for the page.

   Next, add two classes to the style sheet: one for applying to the *Button* control and the other for the *TextBox* control. This will demonstrate the use of both skins and style sheets. Your style sheet should look as follows:

```
body
{
 font-family : Tahoma;
 font-size : 10pt;
 margin : 25px 25px 25px 25px;
}
.button
{
  margin-top : 5px;
  margin-left : 10px;
}
.textBox
{
 margin-bottom : 10px;
}
```

Copy this same style sheet to the Fabrikam folder.

8. Open the Default.aspx page in Source view. For now, set the *Theme* property in the @ *Page* directive to Fabrikam. Add the following controls to the page:

   - ***Image* control** Set the *SkinId* to **Logo**.
   - ***TextBox* control** Just above the *TextBox* control, add the text **User Name:**. Set the *CssClass* to **textBox**. This control will get part of its style from the skin and part from the style sheet.
   - ***TextBox* control** Add another *TextBox* control to the page. Just above it, add the text **Password:**. Set the *CssClass* to **textBox**. This control will also get part of its style from the skin and part from the style sheet.
   - ***Button* control** Add a *Button* control to the page. Set the *CssClass* to **button**. This control will also get part of its style from the skin and part from the style sheet.

   Your .aspx markup should look similar to the following (the Visual Basic @ *Page* directive is shown):

```
<%@ Page Language="VB" AutoEventWireup="false" CodeFile="Default.aspx.vb"
  Theme="Fabrikam" Inherits="_Default" %>

<!DOCTYPE html PUBLIC "-//W3C//DTD XHTML 1.0 Transitional//EN"
  "http://www.w3.org/TR/xhtml1/DTD/xhtml1-transitional.dtd">

<html xmlns="http://www.w3.org/1999/xhtml">
<head runat="server">
  <title>Login Page</title>
</head>
<body>
  <form id="form1" runat="server">
  <div>
    <asp:Image ID="Image1" SkinID="Logo" runat="server" />
    <br />
    User Name: <br />
    <asp:TextBox ID="TextBoxUname" runat="server"
      CssClass="textBox"></asp:TextBox>
    <br />
    Password: <br />
    <asp:TextBox ID="TextBoxPass" runat="server"
      CssClass="textBox"></asp:TextBox>
    <br />
    <asp:Button ID="ButtonSubmit" runat="server" Text="Login"
      CssClass="button" />
  </div>
  </form>
</body>
</html>
```

9. Run your Default.aspx page in a browser. You should see the full Fabrikam theme applied to the page. This includes the logo, skin, and style sheet. Figure 5-6 shows the page in a Web browser.

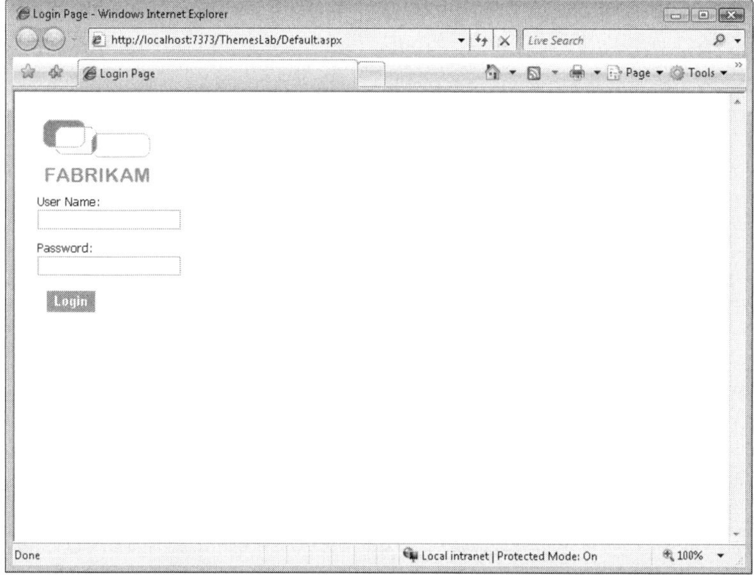

FIGURE 5-6 The theme applied to the Default.aspx page

10. Next, open Default.aspx in Source view. Clear the *Theme* attribute from the top of the page. Then, open the Web.config file. Find the *<pages>* element. Add the *Theme* attribute to the *<pages>* element and set the theme to Contoso as follows:

```
<pages theme="Contoso">
```

This should switch the site's theme. Run the application again. You should now see a new theme applied to the site as shown in Figure 5-7.

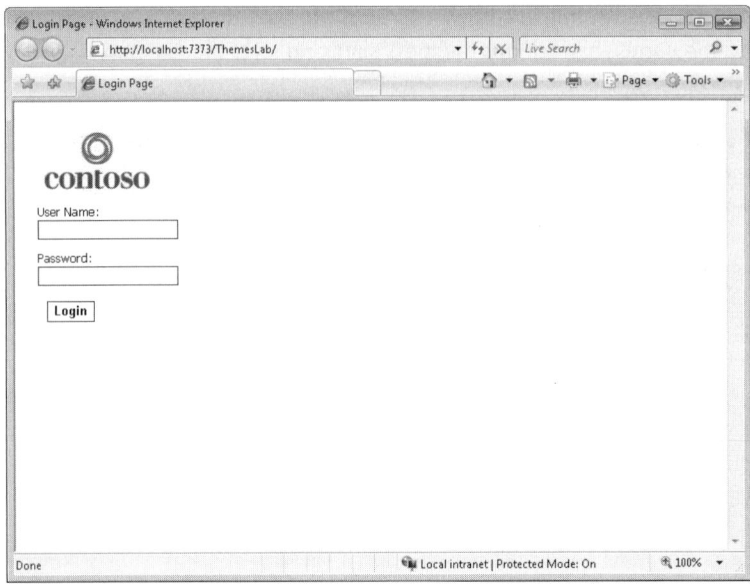

FIGURE 5-7 The second theme applied to the Default.aspx page via the Web.config file

11. Finally, you will simulate switching site themes based on the user's login. For this, add an event handler to the button's click event. Here change a session variable to the theme that is not currently active. Then, add a *PreInit* event to the page. Here, pull the theme from the session and then apply it to the page. Your code should look as follows:

```
'VB
Partial Class _Default
  Inherits System.Web.UI.Page

  Protected Sub Page_PreInit(ByVal sender As Object, _
      ByVal e As System.EventArgs) Handles Me.PreInit

    If Not Session("theme") Is Nothing Then
      Page.Theme = CType(Session("theme"), String)
    End If

  End Sub

  Protected Sub ButtonSubmit_Click(ByVal sender As Object, _
    ByVal e As System.EventArgs) Handles ButtonSubmit.Click

    Dim theme As String = Page.Theme

    'switch themes
```

```
    If theme = "Contoso" Then
      Session("theme") = "Fabrikam"
    Else
      Session("theme") = "Contoso"
    End If

  End Sub

End Class

//C#
public partial class _Default : System.Web.UI.Page
{
  protected void Page_PreInit(object sender, EventArgs e)
  {
    if (Session["theme"] != null)
    {
      Page.Theme = (string)Session["theme"];
    }
  }

  protected void ButtonSubmit_Click(object sender, EventArgs e)
  {
    string theme = Page.Theme;

    //switch themes
    if (theme == "Contoso")
    {
      Session["theme"] = "Fabrikam";
    }
    else
    {
      Session["theme"] = "Contoso";
    }
  }
}
```

Run the application and click Login a couple of times. Notice that after the first click the session is loaded; the next page refresh switches the page login. You would most likely switch pages after login and thus this session-setting refresh issue would not exist. In addition, you would most likely not want to set the theme on each page in your site. Rather, you might create a default page class from which the pages in your site derive or you might add this type of code to the master page.

Lesson Summary

- To create a theme, add an App_Themes subfolder to your application. Then, for each theme in your site, add a folder. The folder's name becomes the name of your theme.
- Themes contain skin files, a style sheet, graphics, and other resources.
- You can apply a theme at the page level, the site level (through the Web.config file), or at the individual control level.

Lesson Review

You can use the following questions to test your knowledge of the information in Lesson 2, "Using Themes." The questions are also available on the companion CD if you prefer to review them in electronic form.

> ***NOTE*** **ANSWERS**
>
> **Answers to these questions and explanations of why each answer choice is right or wrong are located in the "Answers" section at the end of the book.**

1. Which of the following theme applications will override an attribute that you specified directly on a control? (Choose all that apply.)
   - **A.** A theme specified using @ *Page Theme="MyTheme"*
   - **B.** A theme specified using @ *Page StyleSheetTheme="MyTheme"*
   - **C.** *<pages Theme="themeName">* element in the Web.config file
   - **D.** *<pages StyleSheetTheme="themeName">* element in the Web.config file
2. Which of the following is a valid skin definition inside a skin file?
   - **A.** `<asp:Label ID="Label1" BackColor="#FFE0C0" ForeColor="Red" Text="Label"></asp:Label>`
   - **B.** `<asp:Label ID="Label1" runat="server" BackColor="#FFE0C0" ForeColor="Red" Text="Label"></asp:Label>`
   - **C.** `<asp:Label runat="server" BackColor="#FFE0C0" ForeColor="Red"></asp:Label>`
   - **D.** `<asp:Label BackColor="#FFE0C0" ForeColor="Red"></asp:Label>`
3. You need to allow users to choose their own themes. In which page event should you specify the user-selected theme?
   - **A.** *Page_Load*
   - **B.** *Page_Render*
   - **C.** *Page_PreRender*
   - **D.** *Page_PreInit*

Lesson 3: Using Web Parts

Many Web pages are collections of components. These components work as self-contained bits of functionality. For example, examine your favorite news site—it probably has a navigation bar to the left, a title bar at the top, at least one column of news, and a footer. Additionally, many news and portal sites provide customized, optional components, such as weather reports and stock quotes.

ASP.NET Web Parts give you the ability to provide your users with control over the components that appear on a Web page. With Web Parts, users can minimize or completely close groups of controls. So, if they want to see the weather on your page, they can add a weather component—or they can close it to save room for other content. You can also provide a catalog of Web Parts to enable users to add groups of controls wherever they want on a page.

This lesson describes how to create and use ASP.NET Web Parts.

After this lesson, you will be able to:

- Describe what Web Parts are and how they can be used.
- Add Web Parts to a page.
- Create a Web page that allows users to edit and rearrange Web Parts.
- Connect Web Parts to each other to allow sharing of data.
- Enable personalization for Web Parts to enable customized settings to be persisted.

Estimated lesson time: 90 minutes

What Are Web Parts?

Web Parts are components of predefined functionality that can be embedded in a Web page. They have a centralized framework, management structure, and customization model. These components of functionality can be added and removed from pages by both a site designer and individual users. They can even be moved around on the page to fit the individual needs of users. Figure 5-8 shows an example of a Web Part page. Notice the individual Web Parts have client-side menus that enable users to control them.

You can also add a catalog to your Web Part page. A catalog allows users to add and remove Web Parts to the zones defined on your page. Figure 5-9 shows the same page in edit mode. Here users are given a list of Web Parts from which to choose. They can add these parts to the defined zones on the page.

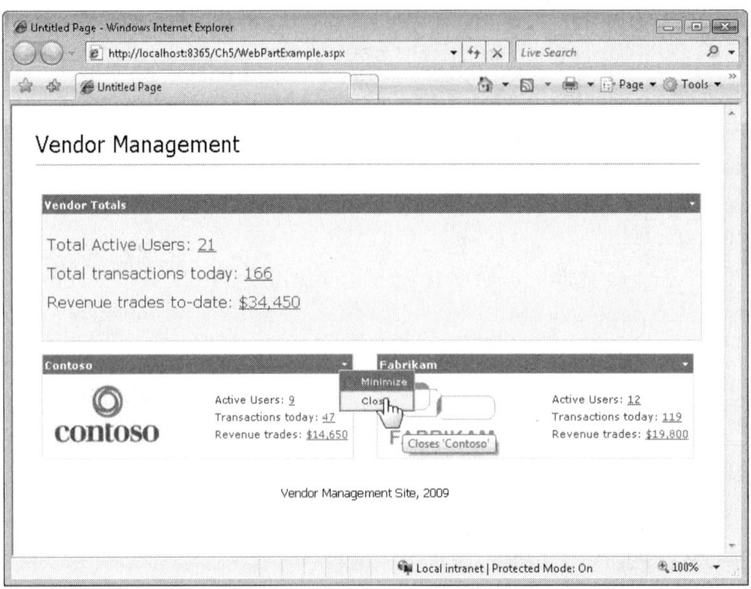

FIGURE 5-8 Web Parts generate client-side menus to enable customization

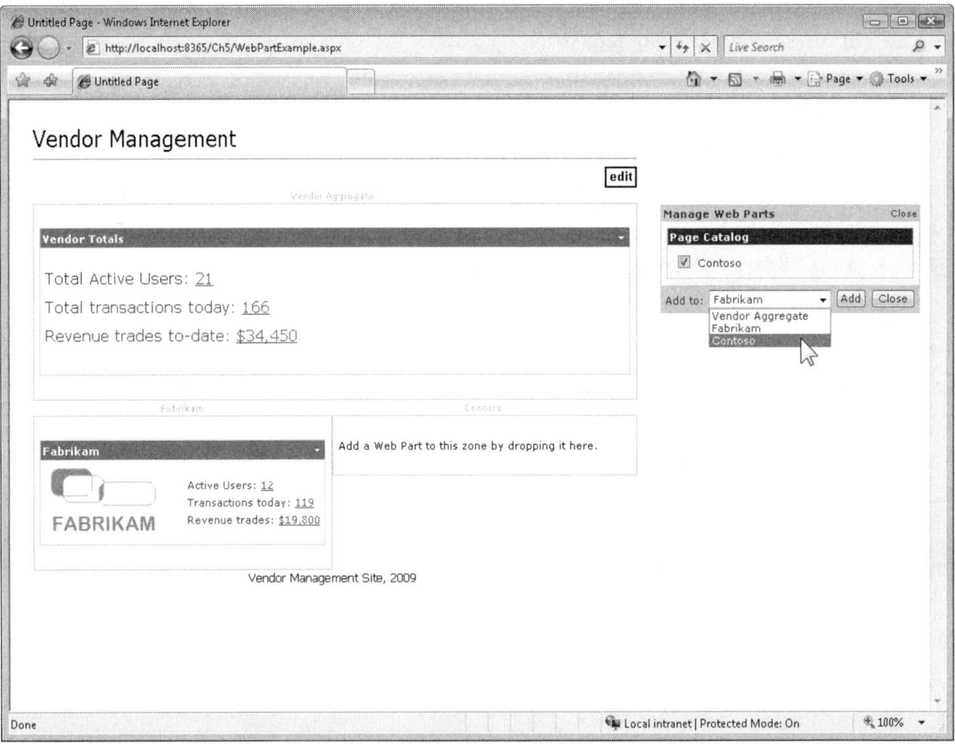

FIGURE 5-9 You can use a *CatalogZone* control to enable users to add Web Parts on demand, without writing any code

Web Part pages and sites can provide users with several customization options. This is great when developing bits of functionality that will be deployed to a wide audience. These bits of functionality come in a lot of flavors. Some common Web Parts you might create include the following:

- A list of recent news articles relating to your organization
- A calendar showing upcoming events
- A list of links to related Web sites
- A search box
- Picture thumbnails from a photo gallery
- Site navigation controls
- A blog
- News articles pulled from a Really Simple Syndication (RSS) feed
- Local weather retrieved from a Web service
- Stock market quotes and graphs

Any control can act as a Web Part, including standard controls and custom controls. Using Web Parts doesn't necessarily require writing any code, because you can do so entirely with the Visual Studio designer.

The *WebParts* Namespace

There are many Web Part classes and controls defined by ASP.NET. In fact, there are 13 controls in the designer Toolbox alone. These controls and classes can be found inside the namespace *System.Web.UI.WebControls.WebParts*. Figure 5-10 shows a number of the key classes you will find in this namespace.

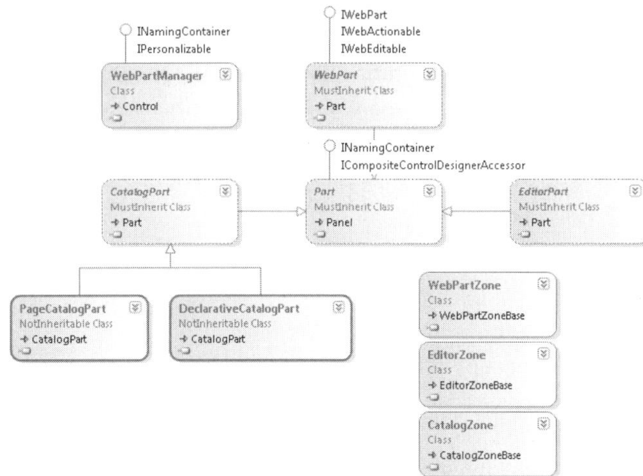

FIGURE 5-10 The major Web Part classes inside the *WebParts* namespace

Many of these classes are discussed in depth in the coming sections. The following, however, provides a high-level overview of most of the classes in Figure 5-10.

- ***WebPartManager*** The *WebPartManager* control is required on every page that includes Web Parts. It does not have a visual representation. Rather, it manages all the Web Part controls and their events on the given page.
- ***WebPart*** The *WebPart* class represents the base class for all Web Parts that you develop. It provides UI, personalization, and connection features.
- ***CatalogPart*** The *CatalogPart* provides the UI for managing a group of Web Parts that can be added to a Web Part page. This group is typically sitewide (and not just specific to a given page).
- ***PageCatalogPart*** The *PageCatalogPart* is similar to the *CatalogPart*. However, it only groups those Web Parts that are part of the given page. In this way, if a user closes certain Web parts on the page, he or she can use the *PageCatalogPart* to read them to the page.
- ***EditorPart*** The *EditorPart* control allows users to define customizations for the given Web Part, such as modifying property settings.
- ***DeclarativeCatalogPart*** The *DeclarativeCatalogPart* allows you to declare Web Parts that should be available to add to a page or the entire site.
- ***WebPartZone*** The *WebPartZone* control is used to define an area on your page in which Web Parts can be hosted.
- ***EditorZone*** The *EditorZone* control provides an area on the page where *EditorPart* controls can exist.
- ***CatalogZone*** The *CatalogZone* control defines an area in which a *CatalogPart* control can exist on the page.

IMPORTANT **WEB PARTS DATABASE**

The ASP.NET Web Parts require the ASP.NET personalization database. This allows the tracking of user customizations to specific Web Parts and Web Part pages. This database, ASPNETDB, will be installed for you by Visual Studio when you try to run your first Web Part page. By default, the database is SQL Express. You can, however, upgrade this to work with various editions of Microsoft SQL Server.

Defining Web Part Zones

Web Parts are added to a page using the concept of zones. Zones define areas on the page in which Web Parts can be placed by a user or added by a developer. Zones have a width, height, and placement on the page. You can add one, none, or many Web Parts to a single zone. Figure 5-11 shows the zones defined by the Web Part page shown in the previous two figures.

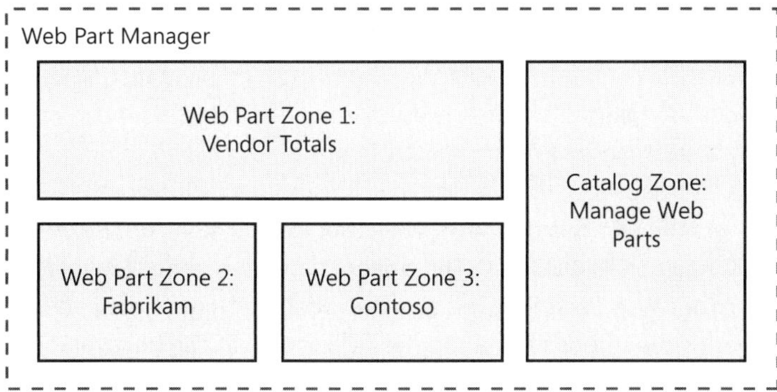

FIGURE 5-11 Define zones for your Web Parts using the *WebPartZone* control

Zones also allow you to set common styles for the Web Parts that are placed within the zone. This is called the Web Part's *chrome*. The chrome includes the Web Part's header style, the menu styles, outline borders, content styles, edit mode style, and more. Web parts added to a zone take on the styles defined by that zone's chrome. Of course, you can define the common zone style definitions using a skin (see Lesson 2 earlier in this chapter).

You create Web Part zones using the *WebPartZone* control. Again, this control defines an area on the page that contains (or can contain) Web Parts. This control also includes the attribute *HeaderText*. This attribute is used to define the text displayed to the user when the page (and zone) is in edit mode. Look closely at Figure 5-9 for an example of this text being displayed above the given zone.

As an example, consider the top zone in Figure 5-11. To define this zone, you add a *WebPartZone* control to your page. To place Web Parts inside this zone, you have to add the *ZoneTemplate* control inside the *WebPartZone*. The *ZoneTemplate* control lets you add other ASP.NET controls to the zone and have them turned into actual Web Parts (this is discussed later). The following markup shows an example:

```
<asp:WebPartManager ID="WebPartManager1" runat="server">
</asp:WebPartManager>

<asp:WebPartZone ID="WebPartZoneVendor" runat="server"
  HeaderText="Vendor Aggregate" style="width: 650px; height: auto">
  <ZoneTemplate>

    <!--Add  web parts to the zone-->

  </ZoneTemplate>
</asp:WebPartZone>
```

Notice that the markup also contains the definition for the *WebPartManager* control. This control is required of every Web Part page. It does not have a visual representation; it is used by ASP.NET to manage the Web Parts on the page.

Creating Web Parts

There are three principal methods for creating ASP.NET Web Parts that can be managed by the *WebPartManager* inside your Web pages. The first is by creating a standard user control; the second (and simplest) is by leveraging an existing ASP.NET control (like *Label*) to define your Web Part; and the third is to create your own custom control and derive it from the *WebPart* class. This section covers the first two methods. The latter, custom controls, is covered in Chapter 10, "Creating Custom Web Controls." The custom control method does offer the most granular control over your Web Parts, but it is also the most time-consuming and complicated method. The other two methods offer a simpler approach that can be leveraged for most Web Part scenarios.

Using User Controls as Web Parts

Web Parts are defined inside of zones on your page. They can be added to the zone at design time or run time, or they can be configured to be there by the user. To create a Web Part based on a user control, you simply need to add the user control to a Web Part zone. The ASP.NET Web Part model takes care of the rest. For example, notice that in Figure 5-8 the two bottom Web Parts (Contoso and Fabrikam) are similar. These could be defined by a single user control and thus this user control could have two instances on the page. To use a user control (on any ASP.NET page), you must first register it with the page. This is done by adding the @ *Register* directive for the control near the top of the page. The following line of code provides an example:

```
<%@ Register src="VendorWebPart.ascx" tagname="VendorWebPart" tagprefix="uc1" %>
```

Once registered, you then add the control to a Web Part zone. You can do so by nesting it inside the *ZoneTemplate* declaration. The following markup shows the *VendorWebPart* user control added to a Web Part zone:

```
<asp:WebPartZone ID="WebPartZone2" runat="server" HeaderText="Fabrikam"
  style="width: 350px; float: left; height: auto;">

  <ZoneTemplate>
    <uc1:VendorWebPart ID="VendorWebPart1" runat="server" title="Fabrikam" />
  </ZoneTemplate>

</asp:WebPartZone>
```

Notice the addition of the title attribute to the user control definition. This tells the Web Part the title to be displayed inside the Web Part's chrome.

Creating a Web Part Control from an Existing ASP.NET Control

You can also create a Web Part simply by inserting a standard ASP.NET control inside a *<ZoneTemplate>* element. The Web Part manager will take care of the rest. For example, the top section of Figure 5-8 shows a single Web Part titled Vendor Totals. This Web Part was created using a *Label* control. The *Label* control then nests other controls inside it. These controls define the actual contents of the Web Part, whereas the *Label* control is simply the container. The following code shows this example:

```
<asp:WebPartZone ID="WebPartZone1" runat="server"
  HeaderText="Vendor Aggregate" style="width: 700px; height: auto">
  <ZoneTemplate>
    <asp:Label ID="Label3" runat="server" Text="" title="Vendor Totals">
      <div style="margin-top: 12px; margin-bottom: 20px;
        line-height: 30px; font-size: 12pt">
        Total Active Users: <a href="#">21</a>
        <br />Total transactions today: <a href="#">166</a>
        <br />Revenue trades to-date: <a href="#">$34,450</a>
      </div>
    </asp:Label>
  </ZoneTemplate>
</asp:WebPartZone>
```

Enabling Users to Arrange and Edit Web Parts

The Web Parts on your page have a number of different displays to the user. These modes of display are dependent on what the user is doing with the Web Parts and the hosting page at any given time. For example, if the user is simply viewing the Web Parts on a given page, the display mode is browse and the user sees the Web Part as it appears in this mode. Of course, there are other modes and therefore other display properties for these modes.

You change the display mode of the Web Parts on a page through the *WebPartManager*. You do so by setting its *DisplayMode* property in your code-behind file. Table 5-1 shows the valid property values for *DisplayMode*.

TABLE 5-1 Web Part Display Modes

DISPLAY MODE	DESCRIPTION
BrowseDisplayMode	The standard way users browse Web pages. This is the default mode.
DesignDisplayMode	Enables users to drag and drop Web Parts into different locations.
EditDisplayMode	Like design mode, edit mode enables users to drag and drop Web Parts. Additionally, users can select Edit from the Web Parts menu to edit the title, size, direction, window appearance, and zone of Web Parts using *AppearanceEditorPart* and *LayoutEditorPart* controls. To use this mode, you must add an *EditorZone* control to your Web page, and then add either or both *AppearanceEditorPart* and *LayoutEditorPart*.

CatalogDisplayMode	Enables users to add additional Web Parts that you specify by using a *CatalogZone* control. This mode is available only after you add a *CatalogZone* to your Web page.
ConnectDisplayMode	Enables users to manually establish connections between controls by interacting with a *ConnectionZone* control. For example, Web Parts can be linked to show summary and detail information of the same report. This mode is only available after you add a *ConnectionZone* control to the page. For more information about Web Parts connections, see the section titled "Connecting Web Parts," later in this lesson.

As an example, consider the screen shot in Figure 5-9. You can see that the page is in a different display mode. Here the user has clicked the Edit button under the Vendor Management text to change the mode of the page. To enable this, the page had to first be set up with a *CatalogZone* control. The following code shows the markup of the layout of the *CatalogZone*:

```
<asp:CatalogZone ID="CatalogZone1" runat="server" HeaderText="Manage Web Parts">

  <ZoneTemplate>
    <asp:PageCatalogPart ID="PageCatalogPart1" runat="server">
    </asp:PageCatalogPart>
  </ZoneTemplate>

</asp:CatalogZone>
```

The next step is to put the page into this display mode when the user clicks the Edit button. This is done inside the code-behind class. Of course, you also need code to return the page from this mode back to the browse mode. The following shows the code for the button's click event:

```
'VB
Protected Sub ButtonEdit_Click(ByVal sender As Object, _
  ByVal e As System.EventArgs) Handles ButtonEdit.Click

  Dim mode As String = CType(ViewState("mode"), String)

  'switch modes
  If mode = "browse" Then
    ViewState("mode") = "edit"
    ButtonEdit.Text = "Done"
    WebPartManager1.DisplayMode = WebPartManager1.SupportedDisplayModes("Catalog")
  Else
    ViewState("mode") = "browse"
    ButtonEdit.Text = "Edit"
```

```
    WebPartManager1.DisplayMode = WebPartManager1.SupportedDisplayModes("Browse")
  End If

End Sub

//C#

protected void ButtonEdit_Click(object sender, EventArgs e)
{

  string mode = (string)ViewState["mode"];

  //switch modes
  if (mode == "browse")
  {
    ViewState["mode"] = "edit";
    ButtonEdit.Text = "Done";
    WebPartManager1.DisplayMode = WebPartManager1.SupportedDisplayModes["Catalog"];
  }
  else
  {
    ViewState["mode"] = "browse";
    ButtonEdit.Text = "Edit";
    WebPartManager1.DisplayMode = WebPartManager1.SupportedDisplayModes["Browse"];
  }

}
```

Notice that in the code, the display mode is set using the *SupportedDisplayModes* collection. Also notice that in this case, the display mode is being set inside of the *ViewState* (in *PageLoad*) and then passed to the page. Of course, there are other display modes defined in Table 5-1. This lesson's lab will walk you through creating a page that allows a user to switch between the various display modes.

Connecting Web Parts

One of the most powerful features of the Web Parts tool set is the ability to build connections between Web Parts. To understand the possibilities, imagine building an internal application to manage employee payroll. You could have:

- A main Web Part so you can browse employee data.
- A Web Part that displays a chart of the selected employee's overtime pay.
- A Web Part that shows a pie chart illustrating how payroll, benefits, stock options, and pension fit into the employee's overall compensation.
- A Web Part that compares the employee's pay to other employees in the same position.

With Web Parts connections, the user can select an employee file and have all the other Web Parts automatically update using that employee's information. Naturally, the user analyzing the data would have the ability to add, remove, and rearrange Web Parts.

Connections are also useful for consumer-oriented Web sites. For example, if you are building a portal site, you might have Web Parts that display localized information based on the user's postal code, including the weather, local news, and the phase of the moon. Rather than requiring the user to specify his or her postal code for each individual Web Part, all Web Parts can connect to a specialized Web Part that stores the users' postal codes.

Creating a Static Connection

Connections can be either static or dynamic. If a connection is static, you (as the developer) establish the connection during the development process, and it cannot be changed by the user. Static connections are permanent and cannot be deleted by users.

Static connections typically involve a provider and one or more consumer Web Parts. The provider provides the connection data. The consumer receives the provider data. You define providers and consumers using the attribute-based programming model of the .NET Framework. To create a static connection between Web Parts, you can follow these basic steps:

1. Create a provider Web Part. A provider Web Part can derive from the *WebPart* class or you can create it as a user control. You must create a public method inside your provider with the *ConnectionProvider* attribute attached to it. This method should return the value that the consumer will receive. The following code shows the code-behind file for a user control provider Web Part that contains a *TextBox* control and a *Button* control:

```
'VB
Partial Class Provider
  Inherits System.Web.UI.UserControl

  Dim _textBoxValue As String = ""

  <ConnectionProvider("TextBox provider", "GetTextBoxValue")> _
  Public Function GetTextBoxValue() As String
    Return _textBoxValue
  End Function

  Protected Sub Button1_Click(ByVal sender As Object, _
    ByVal e As System.EventArgs) Handles Button1.Click
    _textBoxValue = TextBoxProvider.Text
  End Sub

End Class

//C#
public partial class Provider : System.Web.UI.UserControl
```

```
{
  string _textBoxValue = "";

  [ConnectionProvider("TextBox provider", "GetTextBoxValue")]
  string GetTextBoxValue()
  {
    return _textBoxValue;
  }

  protected void Button1_Click(object sender, EventArgs e)
  {
    _textBoxValue = TextBoxProvider.Text;
  }

}
```

2. Create a consumer Web Part. A consumer Web Part can derive from the *WebPart* class or it can be a user control. You must create a public method with the *ConnectionConsumer* attribute that accepts the same type that the provider's *ConnectionProvider* method returns. The following code demonstrates a consumer Web Part user control:

```
'VB
Partial Class Consumer
  Inherits System.Web.UI.UserControl

  <ConnectionConsumer("TextBox consumer", "ShowTextBoxValue")> _
  Public Sub ShowTextBoxValue(ByVal textBoxValue As String)
    LabelConsumer.Text = textBoxValue
  End Sub

End Class

//C#
public partial class Consumer : System.Web.UI.UserControl
{
  [ConnectionConsumer("TextBox consumer", "ShowTextBoxValue")]
  void ShowTextBoxValue(string textBoxValue)
  {
    LabelConsumer.Text = textBoxValue;
  }
}
```

3. Create a Web page with a *WebPartManager* control. Add at least one *WebPartZone* container.
4. Add your provider and consumer Web Parts to *WebPartZone* containers. The following markup shows the preceding user controls added to the page:

```
<asp:WebPartZone ID="WebPartZoneProvider" runat="server"
  Height="400px" Width="300px">
  <ZoneTemplate>
    <uc1:Provider ID="Provider1" runat="server" title="Provider" />
    <uc2:Consumer ID="Consumer1" runat="server" title="Consumer" />
  </ZoneTemplate>
</asp:WebPartZone>
```

5. The next step is to add connection information to the *WebPartManager* markup. In this case you add a *<StaticConnections>* element that includes a *WebPartConnection* control to declare the connection between the provider and consumer.

   The *WebPartConnection* control must have an *ID* attribute, an attribute to identify the provider control (*ProviderID*), an attribute to identify the provider method (*Provider-ConnectionPointID*), an attribute to identify the consumer control (*ConsumerID*), and an attribute to identify the consumer method (*ConsumerConnectionPointID*). The following markup demonstrates this:

```
<asp:WebPartManager ID="WebPartManager1" runat="server">
  <StaticConnections>
    <asp:webPartConnection
      ID="conn1"
      ProviderID="Provider1"
      ProviderConnectionPointID="GetTextBoxValue"
      ConsumerID="Consumer1"
      ConsumerConnectionPointID="ShowTextBoxValue" />
  </StaticConnections>
</asp:WebPartManager>
```

   Note that you should have one *WebPartConnection* control for each pair of connected controls.

Exercise 3 in this lesson's lab walks you through the process of creating controls that connect to each other and configuring them in a Web page.

EXAM TIP

For the exam, know exactly how to establish a static connection, which attributes you must assign to each method, and what you must add to the .aspx page source.

Enabling Dynamic Connections

Dynamic connections can be established by users and are enabled by adding a *Connections-Zone* control to the Web page.

To enable dynamic connections that a user can create or break, follow these steps:

1. Create a page with a provider and consumer connection as described in the previous section.

2. Optionally, establish a static connection between the provider and consumer, as described in the previous section. This acts as a default connection that a user can break if desired.
3. Add a *ConnectionsZone* control to the Web page.
4. Add a control to enable a user to enter the Connect mode, as described in "Enabling Users to Arrange and Edit Web Parts," earlier in this lesson.

Establishing Dynamic Connections Among Web Parts

When a user views your page, he or she can enter connect mode and use the *ConnectionsZone* control to edit connections. To edit a connection as a user, follow these steps:

1. Switch the display mode of the page to Connect.
2. On the Web Parts menu for either the provider or the consumer, select Connect from the drop-down menu, as shown in Figure 5-12.

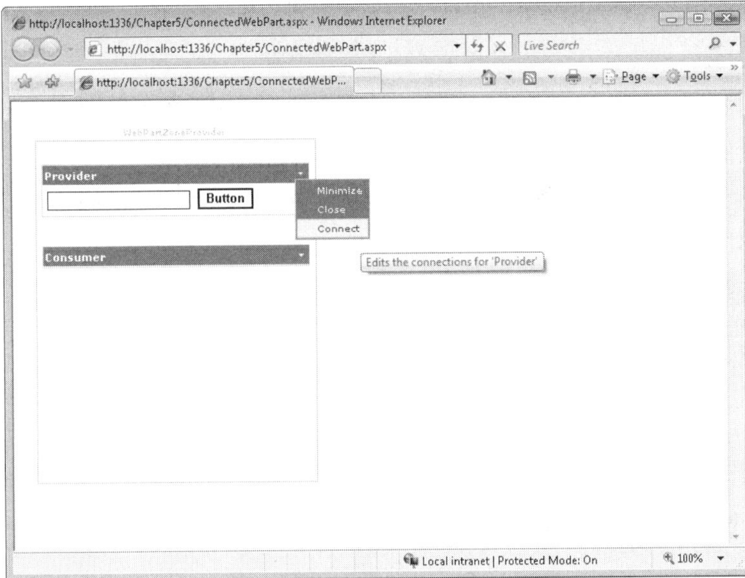

FIGURE 5-12 Select Connect from the Web Parts menu to edit the connection

3. The *ConnectionsZone* object appears, as shown in Figure 5-13.

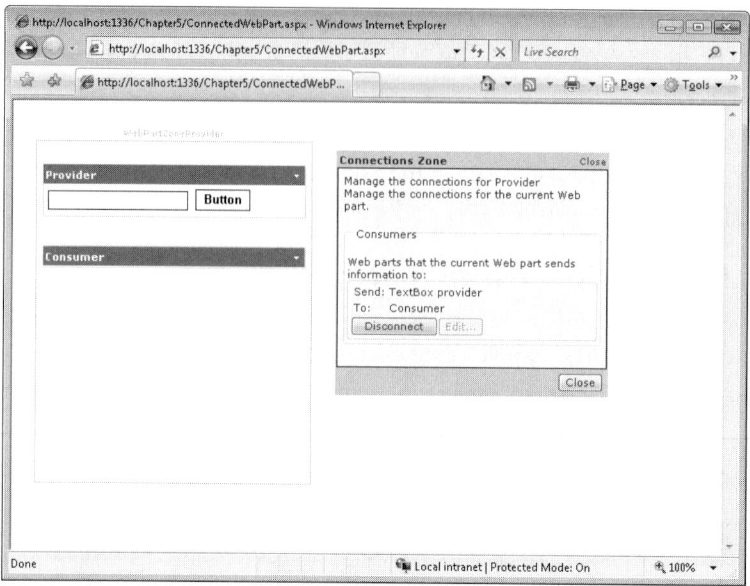

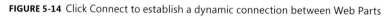

FIGURE 5-13 Use the *ConnectionsZone* control to dynamically establish a connection

4. If there is an existing connection, click Disconnect to break the current connection. Otherwise, click Create A Connection To A Consumer, select the consumer, and click Connect, as shown in Figure 5-14.

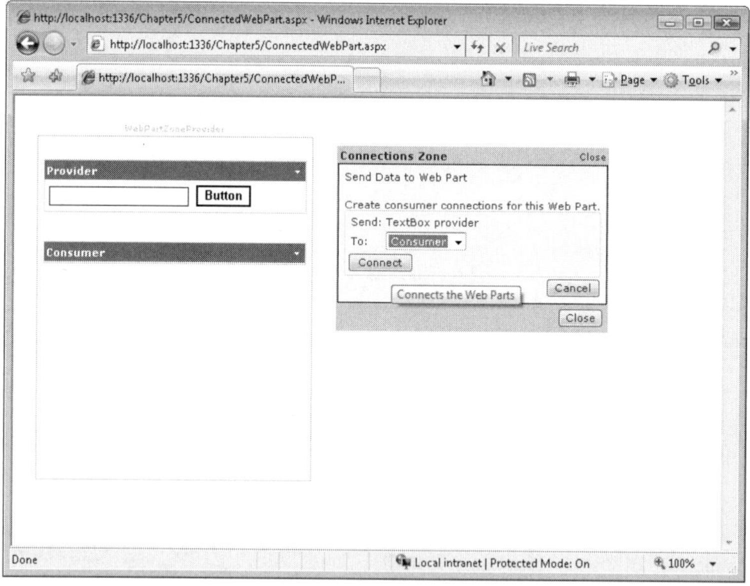

FIGURE 5-14 Click Connect to establish a dynamic connection between Web Parts

5. When you are done editing connections, click Close. The Web Parts are connected, just as if you had connected them statically.

Quick Check

1. **Why would you want to use Web Parts?**
2. **Which component is required for all pages that use Web Parts?**
3. **What component do you need to enable for a user to add new Web Parts to a page?**

Quick Check Answers

1. **Web Parts enable users to customize the components on a page and the layout of a page.**
2. **The *WebPartManager* control is required for all pages that use Web Parts.**
3. **The *CatalogZone* control enables a user to add new Web Parts to a page.**

Personalizing Web Parts

Web Parts support personalization. Personalization allows changes to the layout to be stored for each user so that the user sees the same layout the next time he or she visits the page. Web Parts personalization relies on client-side cookies. It uses these cookies to look up settings in the SQL Server database ASPNETDB. Typically, when you store personalized settings, you will also want to authenticate users using either Windows or Forms authentication. This is not required, however.

MORE INFO **USER AUTHENTICATION**

For more information about user authentication, refer to Chapter 14, "Implementing User Profiles, Authentication, and Authorization."

Enabling Personalization for Custom Controls

By default, personalization automatically remembers the location and other personalized Web Parts settings as described in the section "Enabling Users to Arrange and Edit Web Parts" earlier in this chapter. You can also store custom data in the personalization database to enable controls to remember information about users. To do so, you define a public property on the control. You then add the *Personalizable* attribute as the following simplified code demonstrates:

```
'VB
<Personalizable()> _
Property PostalCode() As String
  Get
    Return _postalCode
```

```
    End Get

    Set(ByVal value As String)
      _postalCode = value
    End Set
  End Property

//C#
[Personalizable]
public string PostalCode
{
  get
  {
    Return _postalCode;
  }

  set
  {
    _postalCode = value;
  }
}
```

Enabling Shared Personalization

Web Parts personalization is enabled by default, and authenticated users of a Web Parts page are able to personalize pages for themselves without any special configuration. However, individual or user-scoped personalization changes are visible only to the user who made them. If you want to provide Webmasters (or any user) the power to make personalization changes that affect how everyone sees Web Parts, you can enable shared personalization in your application's Web.config file.

Within the *<system.web>* section of the configuration file, add an *<authorization>* section, and within that, add an *<allow>* element to specify which user or users have access to shared personalization scope, as the following example shows:

```
<authorization>
  <allow verbs="enterSharedScope" users="SomeUserAccount"
    roles="admin"  />
</authorization>
```

The specified user or users now have the ability to edit a page in shared personalization scope so that the changes they make are visible to all users.

Disabling Personalization for a Page

You can also disable personalization for a page, which is useful if you want to take advantage of personalization on some pages but not on others. To disable personalization on a page, set the *WebPartManager.Personalization.Enabled* attribute to *False*. The following markup shows an example:

```
<asp:webPartManager ID="webPartManager1" runat="server">
  <Personalization Enabled="False" />
</asp:webPartManager>
```

LAB Using Web Parts

In this lab, you create a Web page that uses Web Parts. You then expand the page capabilities to enable users to customize the page, and then add controls that communicate with each other.

If you encounter a problem completing an exercise, the completed projects are available in the samples installed from the companion CD.

EXERCISE 1 Create a Web Page with Web Parts

In this exercise, you create a Web page that uses Web Parts and enables the user to arrange and modify the Web Parts.

1. Open Visual Studio and create a new ASP.NET Web site named **MyWebParts** using either C# or Visual Basic.
2. Open Default.aspx in Source view. From the Toolbox, on the WebParts tab, drag a *WebPartManager* control onto the page. This control isn't visible to users, but it must appear before any Web Part controls, or else the runtime throws an exception.
3. From the Toolbox, on the WebParts tab, drag four *WebPartZone* controls to the page. Set the *IDs* for these to ***WebPartZoneTop***, ***WebPartZoneLeft***, ***WebPartZoneCenter***, and ***WebPartZoneBottom***. Then set the *HeaderText* property for the zones to **Top Zone**, **Left Zone**, **Center Zone**, and **Bottom Zone**, respectively. Also, set their layout styles to display appropriately. Your markup code should look as follows:

```
<html xmlns="http://www.w3.org/1999/xhtml">
<head runat="server">
    <title>My Web Part Page</title>
</head>
<body>
    <form id="form1" runat="server">

    <asp:WebPartManager ID="WebPartManager1" runat="server">
    </asp:WebPartManager>

    <div style="width: 700px">

      <asp:WebPartZone ID="WebPartZoneTop" runat="server"
        HeaderText="Top Zone" style="width: 700px; height: auto">
      </asp:WebPartZone>
```

```
        <asp:WebPartZone ID="WebPartZoneLeft" runat="server"
          HeaderText="Left Zone" style="width: 300px; float: left; height: 300px">
        </asp:WebPartZone>

        <asp:WebPartZone ID="WebPartZoneCenter" runat="server"
          HeaderText="Center Zone"
          style="width: 400px; float: right; height: 300px">
        </asp:WebPartZone>

        <asp:WebPartZone ID="WebPartZoneBottom" runat="server"
          HeaderText="Bottom Zone" style="width: 700px; height: auto;">
        </asp:WebPartZone>

      </div>

      </form>
  </body>
  </html>
```

Your page, in Design view, should look similar to Figure 5-15.

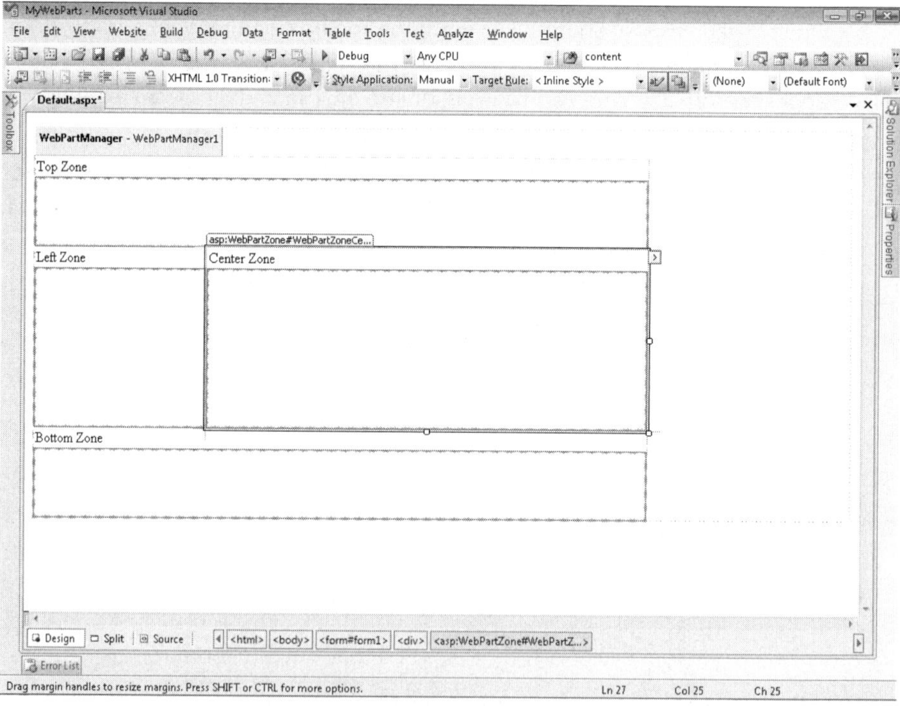

FIGURE 5-15 The Web page zones in Design view

5. Add two new user controls to your Web site by right-clicking the Web site and choosing Add New Item. Name them ***CalendarWebPart*** and ***LogoWebPart***. These will serve as simple Web Part examples. Add a *Calendar* control to the *CalendarWebPart* user control. Add an image to the *LogoWebPart*.

   These custom controls serve as examples only. A real Web Part would do something clever like display the weather or query a database. If you have created your own user controls, feel free to use those instead.

6. Open Default.aspx in Design view. Drag the *LogoWebPart* user control from the Solution Explorer to the Top Zone *WebPartZone* container. Next, drag *CalendarWebPart* to the Left Zone *WebPartZone* container.

7. Run your application in a browser. The first time it might take a minute to start because Visual Studio is adding the ASPNETDB to your project.

   Notice that your two controls appear on the page. Click the menu button in the upper-right corner of each control and experiment with minimizing and closing the Web Parts. Notice that if you close a control you cannot get it back without rerunning the site. Also notice that both Web Parts are currently labeled Untitled.

8. Return to Visual Studio and open Default.aspx in Design view. To give the Web Parts meaningful display names, you need to edit the *Title* property. Click the instance of *CalendarControl*, view the properties, and notice that the title is not displayed. To edit the *Title* property, you must manually add it to the source code, as shown here:

```
<asp:WebPartZone ID="WebPartZoneLeft" runat="server"
  HeaderText="Left Zone" style="width: 300px; float: left; height: 300px;">
  <ZoneTemplate>
    <uc2:CalendarWebPart ID="CalendarWebPart1" runat="server"
      title="Calendar" />
  </ZoneTemplate>
</asp:WebPartZone>
```

   Create a title for both the *CalendarControl* and *LogoControl* instances.

   Save the page and view it in a Web browser again to verify that the title appears.

EXERCISE 2 Enable Users to Customize Web Parts

In this exercise, you extend an existing Web Parts application to enable user customization.

1. Continue editing the project you created in the previous exercise. Alternatively, you can open the completed Lesson 3, Exercise 1 project in the samples installed from the CD.

2. Open the Default.aspx page in Source view. Inside the center zone add a *ZoneTemplate*. Next, create a simple Web Part by placing a *Label* control inside the *ZoneTemplate*. Finally, nest a *DropDownList* control inside the *Label* control. Set the *ID* property to ***DropDownListMode*** and set the *AutoPostBack* property to *true*. Your markup should look as follows:

```
<asp:WebPartZone ID="WebPartZoneCenter" runat="server"
  HeaderText="Center Zone" style="width: 400px; float: right; height: 300px;">
  <ZoneTemplate>
    <asp:Label ID="Label1" runat="server" Text="" title="Edit Page">
      <asp:DropDownList ID="DropDownListModes"
        runat="server" AutoPostBack="true">
      </asp:DropDownList>
    </asp:Label>
  </ZoneTemplate>
</asp:WebPartZone>
```

3. If you are using Visual Basic, edit the Default.aspx @ *Page* declaration to set the *AutoEventWireup* attribute to *true*. This is set to *true* by default in C#. This demonstrates the proper @ *Page* declaration:

```
<%@ Page Language="VB" AutoEventWireup="true" CodeFile="Default.aspx.vb"
  Inherits="_Default" %>
```

4. Create two methods inside your code-behind file: *Page_Init* and *GenerateModeList*. In the *Page_Init* method (which is automatically called when the page is created), add an event handler so that ASP.NET calls the *GenerateModeList* method during the *InitComplete* event. The following code demonstrates this:

```
'VB
Sub Page_Init(ByVal sender As Object, ByVal e As EventArgs)
 AddHandler Page.InitComplete, AddressOf GenerateModeList
End Sub

//C#
void Page_Init(object sender, EventArgs e)
{
 Page.InitComplete += new EventHandler(GenerateModeList);
}
```

5. Next, define the *GenerateModeList* method, which is called during the *InitComplete* event. Here, write code to populate the *DropDownListModes* control using the *SupportedDisplayModes* property of the *WebPartManager* control. Be sure to select the correct item in the list based on the current mode. The following sample code demonstrates this:

```
'VB
Protected Sub GenerateModeList(ByVal sender As Object, ByVal e As EventArgs)

  Dim _manager As WebPartManager = _
    WebPartManager.GetCurrentWebPartManager(Page)
```

```
  Dim browseModeName As String = webPartManager.BrowseDisplayMode.Name

  DropDownListModes.Items.Clear()

  'fill the drop-down list with the names of supported display modes.
  For Each mode As webPartDisplayMode In _manager.SupportedDisplayModes

    Dim modeName As String = mode.Name

    'make sure a mode is enabled before adding it.
    If mode.IsEnabled(_manager) Then
      Dim item As ListItem = New ListItem(modeName, modeName)
      DropDownListModes.Items.Add(item)
    End If

  Next

  'select the current mode
  Dim items As ListItemCollection = DropDownListModes.Items
  Dim selectedIndex As Integer = _
    items.IndexOf(items.FindByText(_manager.DisplayMode.Name))

  DropDownListModes.SelectedIndex = selectedIndex

End Sub
```

```
//C#
protected void GenerateModeList(object sender, EventArgs e)
{
  WebPartManager _manager = WebPartManager.GetCurrentWebPartManager(Page);
  String browseModeName = WebPartManager.BrowseDisplayMode.Name;
  DropDownListModes.Items.Clear();

  //fill the drop-down list with the names of supported display modes.
  foreach (WebPartDisplayMode mode in _manager.SupportedDisplayModes)
  {
    String modeName = mode.Name;
    //make sure a mode is enabled before adding it.
    if (mode.IsEnabled(_manager))
    {
      ListItem item = new ListItem(modeName, modeName);
      DropDownListModes.Items.Add(item);
    }
  }
```

```
  //select the current mode
  ListItemCollection items = DropDownListModes.Items;
  int selectedIndex = items.IndexOf(items.FindByText(_manager.DisplayMode.
Name));
  DropDownListModes.SelectedIndex = selectedIndex;
}
```

6. Add the event handler for the *DropDownListModes_SelectedIndexChanged* event. Then write code to set the current mode to the mode selected from the list, as the following code demonstrates:

```
'VB
Protected Sub DropDownListModes_SelectedIndexChanged(ByVal sender As Object, _
  ByVal e As EventArgs)

  Dim manager As WebPartManager = _
    WebPartManager.GetCurrentWebPartManager(Page)
  Dim mode As WebPartDisplayMode = _
    manager.SupportedDisplayModes(DropDownListModes.SelectedValue)

  If Not (mode Is Nothing) Then
    manager.DisplayMode = mode
  End If

End Sub

//C#
protected void DropDownListModes_SelectedIndexChanged(
  object sender, EventArgs e)
{
  WebPartManager manager =
    WebPartManager.GetCurrentWebPartManager(Page);

  WebPartDisplayMode mode =
    manager.SupportedDisplayModes[DropDownListModes.SelectedValue];

  if (mode != null)
    manager.DisplayMode = mode;
}
```

7. Run your Web site and open Default.aspx in Internet Explorer. Notice that your two controls appear on the page. Click the drop-down list and select Design. Then drag and drop your controls from one zone to another. Click the drop-down list again and return to Browse mode.

8. Return to Visual Studio and open Default.aspx in Design view. Remove the center zone control and replace it with a *<Div>* tag. Keep the drop-down control. Underneath it, add an *EditorZone* control. Then add an *AppearanceEditorPart* control and a *LayoutEditorPart* control to the *EditorZone* control. The following shows an example of the markup:

```
<div style="width: 395px; float: right; height: auto; padding-left: 5px">
  <asp:DropDownList ID="DropDownListModes" runat="server" AutoPostBack="true"
    OnSelectedIndexChanged="DropDownListModes_SelectedIndexChanged">
  </asp:DropDownList>

  <asp:EditorZone ID="EditorZone1" runat="server">
    <ZoneTemplate>
      <asp:AppearanceEditorPart ID="AppearanceEditorPart1" runat="server" />
      <asp:LayoutEditorPart ID="LayoutEditorPart1" runat="server" />
    </ZoneTemplate>
  </asp:EditorZone>

</div>
```

9. Run your application in Internet Explorer. Click the drop-down list and select the newly added item, Edit. Next, click the menu button in the upper-right corner of the calendar control and select Edit. Notice that the *EditorZone*, *AppearanceEditorPart*, and *LayoutEditorPart* controls appear.

   Experiment with the controls to change their appearance and layout. Notice that adding this capability doesn't require writing any other code; you simply need to add the controls to the page. The *WebPartManager* control detects the presence of the *EditorZone* and automatically enables the Edit mode.

10. Return to Visual Studio and open Default.aspx in Source view. Next, add a *CatalogZone* control below the *EditorZone* control. Now, add a *DeclarativeCatalogPart* control into the *CatalogZone* control.

   Add the *WebPartsTemplate* tag inside the *DeclarativeCatalogPart* control. This enables you to add controls to the catalog. Next, add your *LogoControl* and *CalendarControl* controls to the *CatalogZone* control. This adds the controls to the catalog. The following code provides an example:

```
<asp:CatalogZone ID="CatalogZone1" runat="server">
  <ZoneTemplate>
  <asp:DeclarativeCatalogPart ID="DeclarativeCatalogPart1" runat="server">
    <WebPartsTemplate>
      <uc1:LogoWebPart ID="LogoWebPart1" runat="server" title="Logo" />
      <uc2:CalendarWebPart ID="CalendarWebPart1" runat="server"
        title="Calendar" />
    </WebPartsTemplate>
```

```
    </asp:DeclarativeCatalogPart>
    </ZoneTemplate>
  </asp:CatalogZone>
```

11. Run your Web application in Internet Explorer. Click the drop-down list and select the newly added Catalog mode. The Catalog Zone you created appears and shows the available controls. Select the logo control, select a zone from the drop-down list, and then click Add. Continue experimenting with the control; switch back to Browse mode when you are done.

EXERCISE 3 Create Connected Web Parts

In this exercise, you extend an existing application to enable connected Web Parts.

1. Continue editing the project you created in the previous exercise. Alternatively, you can open the completed Lesson 3, Exercise 2 project in the samples installed from the CD.
2. Create three new Web user controls as follows:
   - **GetName** Add a *Label* control showing **Please type your name**. Add a *TextBox* control named **TextBoxName**. Then add a *Button* control named **ButtonSubmit** and labeled **Submit**.
   - **GreetUser** Add a *Label* control named ***LabelGreeting***.
   - **ShowNameBackwards** Add a *Label* control named ***LabelBackwards*** showing **Enter name to see it spelled backward**.
3. Open the code-behind file for the *GetName* control. Add code to capture the text the user types in the *TextBoxName* control when he or she clicks Submit.

   Next, create a public method named *GetUserName* and set the *ConnectionProvider* attribute. In this method, return the name the user typed. This control provides the user's name as data to the consumer controls. The following shows an example:

   ```
   'VB
   Partial Class GetName
     Inherits System.Web.UI.UserControl

     Private _name As String = String.Empty

     Protected Sub ButtonSubmit_Click(ByVal sender As Object, _
       ByVal e As System.EventArgs) Handles ButtonSubmit.Click

       _name = TextBoxName.Text

     End Sub

     <ConnectionProvider("User name provider", "GetUserName")> _
   ```

```
  Public Function GetUserName() As String
    Return _name
  End Function

End Class

//C#
public partial class GetName : System.Web.UI.UserControl
{
  private string _name = string.Empty;

  protected void ButtonSubmit_Click(object sender, EventArgs e)
  {
    _name = TextBoxName.Text;
  }

  [ConnectionProvider("User name provider", "GetUserName")]
  public string GetUserName()
  {
    return _name;
  }

}
```

4. Open the code-behind file for the *GreetUser* control. Here, create a public method named *GetName* and set the *ConnectionConsumer* attribute. This control reads the user's name from the *GetName* control (once connected) and displays it to the user as part of a greeting.

   Create the *GetName* method so that it accepts a string and uses it to create a greeting using the *Label* control as the following code demonstrates:

```
'VB
Partial Class GreetUser
    Inherits System.Web.UI.UserControl

  <ConnectionConsumer("User name consumer", "GetName")> _
  Public Sub GetName(ByVal Name As String)
    LabelGreeting.Text = "Welcome, " + Name + "!"
  End Sub

End Class

//C#
public partial class GreetUser : System.Web.UI.UserControl
```

```
{
  [ConnectionConsumer("User name consumer", "GetName")]
  public void GetName(string Name)
  {
    LabelGreeting.Text = "Welcome, " + Name + "!";
  }

}
```

5. Open the code-behind file for the *ShowNameBackwards* control. Create a public *GetName* method as you did for *GreetUser*. You can use a similar definition for the *ConnectionConsumer* attribute.

   Inside this method, write code to reverse the order of the user's name and display it in the *LabelBackwards* control as the following code demonstrates:

```
'VB
Partial Class ShowNameBackwards
    Inherits System.web.UI.UserControl

  <ConnectionConsumer("User name consumer", "GetName")> _
  Public Sub GetName(ByVal Name As String)

    Dim forwardsName As Char() = Name.ToCharArray
    Dim backwardsName As Char() = Name.ToCharArray
    Dim length As Integer = Name.Length - 1

    Dim x As Integer = 0
    While x <= length
      backwardsName(x) = forwardsName(length - x)
      x = x + 1
    End While

    LabelBackwards.Text = "Your name backward is: " + _
      New String(backwardsName)

  End Sub

End Class

//C#
public partial class ShowNameBackwards : System.Web.UI.UserControl
{
  [ConnectionConsumer("User name consumer", "GetName")]
  public void GetName(string Name)
```

```
  {
    char[] forwardsName = Name.ToCharArray();
    char[] backwardsName = Name.ToCharArray();
    int length = Name.Length - 1;

    for (int x = 0; x <= length; x++)
      backwardsName[x] = forwardsName[length - x];

    LabelBackwards.Text = "Your name backward is: " +
      new string(backwardsName);
  }
}
```

6. Open Default.aspx in Design view and add the *GetName*, *GreetUser*, and *ShowName-Backwards* controls to the bottom zone. Specify titles for each control as shown here:

```
<asp:WebPartZone ID="WebPartZoneBottom" runat="server"
  HeaderText="Bottom Zone" style="width: 700px; height: auto;">
  <ZoneTemplate>
    <uc3:GetName ID="GetName1" runat="server" title="Enter Name" />
    <uc4:GreetUser ID="GreetUser1" runat="server" title="Greeting" />
    <uc5:ShowNameBackwards ID="ShowNameBackwards1" runat="server"
      title="Backwards Name" />
  </ZoneTemplate>
</asp:WebPartZone>
```

7. Open Default.aspx in Source view. Within the *WebPartManager* control, add a *<StaticConnections>* element.

   Within the *<StaticConnections>* element, add two *WebPartConnection* controls that declare the connections between the *GetName* provider and the *GreetUser* and *ShowNameBackwards* consumers.

   The *WebPartConnection* control must have an *ID* attribute, an attribute to identify the provider control (*ProviderID*), an attribute to identify the provider method (*Provider-ConnectionPointID*), an attribute to identify the consumer control (*ConsumerID*), and an attribute to identify the consumer method (*ConsumerConnectionPointID*). The following markup demonstrates this:

```
<asp:webPartManager ID="webPartManager1" runat="server">
  <StaticConnections>
    <asp:webPartConnection
      ID="WebPartConnection1"
      ProviderID="GetName1"
      ProviderConnectionPointID="GetUserName"
      ConsumerID="GreetUser1"
```

```
        ConsumerConnectionPointID="GetName"
      />
      <asp:webPartConnection
        ID="WebPartConnection2"
        ProviderID="GetName1"
        ProviderConnectionPointID="GetUserName"
        ConsumerID="ShowNameBackwards1"
        ConsumerConnectionPointID="GetName"
      />
    </StaticConnections>
  </asp:webPartManager>
```

8. Run Default.aspx in your Web browser. In the *GetName* control, type your name and then click the button. Your name appears in the other two controls.

Lesson Summary

- Web Parts are controls that you create using custom controls that implement the Web Part class or standard user controls and ASP.NET controls. Web Parts are also managed by ASP.NET, which allows users to close, minimize, edit, and move them.
- To add Web Parts to a page, add a *WebPartManager* control to the top of the page, add *WebPartZone* containers to the page, and then add controls to the *WebPartZone* containers.
- To enable users to edit or rearrange Web Parts, you change the *DisplayMode* property of the *WebPartManager* control on your page.
- Web Parts can be connected to enable them to share data. You do so by defining both provider and consumer Web Parts using the attribute-based programming model. In addition, you configure the connections between Web Parts by adding a *<StaticConnections>* element to the *WebPartManager* control.

Lesson Review

You can use the following questions to test your knowledge of the information in Lesson 3, "Using Web Parts." The questions are also available on the companion CD if you prefer to review them in electronic form.

> ***NOTE*** **ANSWERS**
>
> **Answers to these questions and explanations of why each answer choice is right or wrong are located in the "Answers" section at the end of the book.**

1. Which of the following can be a Web Part? (Choose all that apply.)
   - A. A control based on the Web user control template
   - B. A standard *Label* control
   - C. A type derived from *WebPart*
   - D. A master page
2. Which of the following are required to enable users to change the title of a Web Part? (Choose all that apply.)
   - A. *LayoutEditorPart*
   - B. *EditorZone*
   - C. *CatalogZone*
   - D. *AppearanceEditorPart*
3. You have developed a Web page with many different Web Part components. Some Web Parts are enabled by default, and you want to give the user the ability to display others. Which classes should you use? (Choose all that apply.)
   - A. *LayoutEditorPart*
   - B. *DeclarativeCatalogPart*
   - C. *CatalogZone*
   - D. *AppearanceEditorPart*
4. You have created a Web Part control that prompts the user for personalization information, including his or her name, region, and preferences. You want other controls to be able to read information from this control to customize the information they display. How should you modify your Web Part to enable other Web Parts to connect to it?
   - A. Create a method that shares the user's information and add the *ConnectionConsumer* attribute to that method.
   - B. Create a method that shares the user's information and add the *ConnectionProvider* attribute to that method.
   - C. Create a public property that shares the user's information and add the *ConnectionConsumer* attribute to that method.
   - D. Create a public property that shares the user's information and add the *ConnectionProvider* attribute to that method.

Chapter Review

To further practice and reinforce the skills you learned in this chapter, you can perform the following tasks:

- Review the chapter summary.
- Complete the case scenarios. These scenarios set up real-world situations involving the topics of this chapter and ask you to create solutions.
- Complete the suggested practices.
- Take a practice test.

Chapter Summary

- Master pages enable you to have a consistent page structure and layout across all Web pages in your application. Any change to a master page can affect all pages that implement the given master page. You can create multiple master pages and allow users to select templates according to their preferences. You can even nest master pages.
- Themes, and specifically skins, can apply a set of attributes to all controls in a Web application. You should use themes to provide consistent, centrally managed appearances. To enable users to customize pages, you can dynamically change themes.
- Web Parts are components that contain Web controls and can be easily moved around a page. Users can have as much or as little control over Web Parts as you choose to grant them.

Case Scenarios

In the following case scenarios, you apply what you've learned about how to implement and apply customization and personalization. If you have difficulty completing this work, review the material in this chapter before beginning the next chapter. You can find answers to these questions in the "Answers" section at the end of this book.

Case Scenario 1: Meeting Customization Requirements for an Internal Insurance Application

You are an application developer for Fabrikam Insurance. Six months ago, you released version 1.0 of a new .NET Web application that internal staff uses to perform several critical tasks, including:

- Looking up customer information when a subscriber calls.
- Managing the list of in-network physicians.
- Identifying subscribers who are behind on payments.
- Analyzing claims to identify areas of high cost.

Since the release of your application, you've been focused on fixing bugs. However, the application is now very stable, and you are beginning discussions with users to determine future features. At this stage, your manager would like you to meet with some users, analyze their requests, and determine how feasible these features might be when using the .NET Framework.

INTERVIEWS

Following is a list of company personnel who were interviewed and their statements:

- **Accounts Receivable Manager** We have about two dozen employees in accounts receivable who are primarily responsible for chasing down subscribers who are behind on their payments. Your current application works great; however, it doesn't meet everyone's needs equally. To clarify, we have different groups for people responsible for corporate accounts, public sector accounts, small business accounts, and individual subscribers. Depending on the group, these employees want to see different information on the page. If possible, I'd like to enable users to customize pages and have those preferences remembered for each time they visit the page.
- **Underwriter** I'm responsible for analyzing claims and determining how we need to adjust prices to cover the cost of claims. I primarily use your application's reporting features. I love them—all I ask is that you make them more flexible. Right now, if I select a type of claim, I can see a chart of how the costs for that type of claim have changed over time. I'd like to be able to view that chart, but also view whether the claim is regional in nature, and whether specific types of organizations have more of that type of claim than others. Right now, I have to open different windows to see these different reports. I'd like them all to appear on a single page when I click a claim type.

QUESTIONS

Answer the following questions for your manager.

1. How can you provide the personalization capabilities requested by the Accounts Receivable Manager?
2. How can you enable different components to communicate with each other, as described by the underwriter?

Case Scenario 2: Provide Consistent Formatting for an External Web Application

You are an application developer working for Humongous Insurance. You are responsible for updating an external Web application based on user requests. Currently, the Web application's primary features are:

- Enabling subscribers to search and identify providers.
- Providing a reference for subscribers who need to know what is and isn't covered.
- Enabling subscribers to contact customer service representatives with questions.

- Providing portals to subscribers to enable them to read updates about Humongous Insurance and general health care topics.

You have a backlog of e-mails from users. Although you have quite a few positive e-mails, today you are reading through the negative e-mails to identify ways to update the application to better serve users.

E-MAILS

Following is the text of e-mails received from users:

- Awful. There are so many different fonts that it looks like a ransom note. Why does every page look different? Get an editor.
- I don't care about your stupid press releases. Take them off the page.
- Nice website, but the colors are awful.

QUESTIONS

Answer the following questions for your manager.

1. How can you address the concerns about the inconsistency of fonts?
2. How can you ensure a developer does not set the incorrect font on a control?
3. How can you allow users to remove the list of press releases from a Web page?
4. How can you enable users to change the colors of the Web site?

Suggested Practices

To help you successfully master the exam objectives presented in this chapter, complete the following tasks.

Implement a Consistent Page Design by Using Master Pages

For this task, you should complete Practices 1 and 2 to gain experience using master pages. Practice 3 shows you how to use master pages to change the layout of pages for different device types, and you should complete it if you are interested in client-specific rendering.

- **Practice 1** Using a copy of the last Web application you created, implement a master page model and convert your existing .aspx pages to content pages.
- **Practice 2** Using a copy of the last Web application you created, create multiple master pages and give users the option of switching between master pages based on their layout and color preferences.
- **Practice 3** Create a Web application that detects the client device and switches templates based on the client type. For traditional Web browsers, display a navigation bar on the left side of the screen. For mobile clients, consider displaying all content in a single column.

Customize a Web Page by Using Themes and User Profiles

For this task, you should complete at least Practices 1 and 2. If you want in-depth knowledge of how themes affect controls, complete Practice 3 as well.

- **Practice 1** Using a copy of the last Web application you created, add a theme to configure all controls with consistent colors.
- **Practice 2** Add authenticated user profiles to the last Web application you created. For example, you might use the user profile to track recent database queries and enable the user to select from a list of recent requests.
- **Practice 3** Create a custom control and experiment with setting the attributes using themes.

Implement Web Parts in a Web Application

For this task, you should complete all three practices to gain experience using Web Parts.

- **Practice 1** Using the Web Parts page you created in the Lesson 3 exercises, open the Web page using a non-Microsoft browser. Notice how ASP.NET renders the Web Part controls differently.
- **Practice 2** Using the Web Parts page you created in Lesson 3, Exercise 3, expand the connected control capabilities so that the user's name is stored persistently.
- **Practice 3** Using the Web Parts page you created in Lesson 3, Exercise 3, remove the static connections from Default.aspx. Then add a *ConnectionsZone* control to the page. View the page and use the *ConnectionsZone* control to manually establish the connections among the *GetName*, *GreetUser*, and *ShowNameBackwards* controls.

Take a Practice Test

The practice tests on this book's companion CD offer many options. For example, you can test yourself on just the content covered in this chapter, or you can test yourself on all the 70-562 certification exam content. You can set up the test so it closely simulates the experience of taking a certification exam, or you can set it up in study mode so you can look at the correct answers and explanations after you answer each question.

MORE INFO **PRACTICE TESTS**

For details about all the practice test options available, see the "How to Use the Practice Tests" section in this book's Introduction.

CHAPTER 6

Working with ASP.NET AJAX and Client-Side Scripting

Web applications are becoming more and more interactive and dynamic as the technology used to create them evolves. The latest generation of Web applications, often loosely referred to as Web 2.0, involve user interface (UI) enhancements that include functionality that was previously reserved for applications running on the desktop. This includes things like modal dialog boxes and pop-ups, partial screen (or page) updates, dynamically collapsing or sizing controls on a page, indicating application progress, and more. As these paradigms are adopted by some major Web applications, users are now demanding this same level of functionality on many more sites. This means the tools need to catch up with the demand.

The latest version of ASP.NET includes tools for building Web applications that provide this level of support. This includes controls for handling client-based interactivity, a rich library for working with client-side JavaScript, and a programming model for creating your own JavaScript-enabled controls. This chapter covers these scenarios and shows how you can enhance users' experiences with your Web applications.

Exam objectives in this chapter:

- Working with ASP.NET AJAX and Client-Side Scripting
    - Implement Web Forms by using ASP.NET AJAX.
    - Interact with the ASP.NET AJAX client-side library.
    - Create and register client script.

Lessons in this chapter:

Before You Begin

To complete the lessons in the chapter, you should be familiar with developing applications with Microsoft Visual Studio using Microsoft Visual Basic or C#. In addition, you should be comfortable with all of the following:

- The Visual Studio 2008 Integrated Development Environment (IDE).
- The basics of the JavaScript programming language and Dynamic HTML (DHTML).
- A basic understanding of Hypertext Markup Language (HTML) and client-side scripting with the JavaScript language.
- How to create a new Web site.
- Building a Web form by adding Web server controls to a Web page and programming against them on the server.

REAL WORLD

Mike Snell

I am fortunate enough to have been around when building Web applications first came into vogue. The early applications we built were nothing more than hyperlinked HTML and images. We quickly added server-side script and database connectivity to enable more meaningful scenarios.

The power of having a server-based, near-zero deployment, ubiquitous, cross-platform application environment has been (and still is) the driving force that pushes us to build Web applications. There has always been, however, a major gap with respect to the richness of the UI between a fat and a thin client. We've seen many attempts at closing this gap including Java, ActiveX, ActiveX Documents, DHTML, and others.

It remains to be seen if this gap will ever really be closed. However, AJAX does provide a nice compromise between a rich client and a Web-only application. It extends what is capable on the client without breaking the paradigm of a Web application. AJAX is rooted in the Web and, like its counterparts such as HTML and DHTML, it is standards-driven, cross-platform, and ubiquitous. This makes it a great choice for adding client interactivity to applications that must remain true to the concept of a Web site.

Lesson 1: Creating AJAX-Enabled Web Forms

Much of the increased client interactivity of Web 2.0 applications is provided by Asynchronous JavaScript and XML (AJAX). AJAX is a platform-independent technology that works with Web applications running inside Microsoft Internet Explorer, Firefox, Safari, and more. It is an ECMAScript-compliant technology. Therefore, it makes a logical choice for providing a richer UI for browser-based, cross-platform Web applications.

You can add AJAX to any Web application. Like other Web standards such as HTML, it is not specific to ASP.NET. However, ASP.NET does provide a number of items that make building AJAX-enabled Web forms easier. This includes controls to manage partial-page updates, a code library that enables object-oriented development on the client with JavaScript, the ability to call Web services from client code, the ability to create your own AJAX-enabled controls, and more.

This lesson covers building interactive Web forms using the AJAX controls built into ASP.NET. The JavaScript object library and building AJAX-enabled controls are covered in Lesson 2 of this chapter.

After this lesson, you will be able to:

- Understand and use the AJAX Extension controls built into ASP.NET.
- Create a Web form that performs partial-page updates to the server (without a full-page refresh).
- Display the progress of a request processing on the server.
- Periodically update portions of a Web form based on a time interval.

Estimated lesson time: 45 minutes

Introducing ASP.NET AJAX

There are many pieces that are part of (or related to) ASP.NET that are meant to enable AJAX features for developers. These items center on a common goal: improving user experiences by providing capabilities to create a more responsive Web application. These capabilities are many. Choosing the appropriate approach is dependent on your specific need. The following are the ASP.NET components related to AJAX capabilities:

- **Microsoft AJAX Library** The Microsoft AJAX Library is a set of JavaScript files that make programming client-side JavaScript easier. It provides an object-oriented model to the AJAX scripting language. This includes support for classes, namespaces, event handling, data types, and more. The library also has support for error handling, debugging, and globalization.

The library combines JavaScript features and DHTML. Like JavaScript, it works across browsers and across platforms. This library is used by ASP.NET and the AJAX Control Toolkit. However, you can also leverage this library to extend your own controls with AJAX behaviors.

- **ASP.NET AJAX server controls** ASP.NET ships with a set of AJAX server controls that can be embedded in your Web pages to enable partial-page updates, communicate with a server process to indicate progress, and periodically update portions of a page.
- **AJAX Control Toolkit** The AJAX Control Toolkit is a set of community-created and supported controls that show off the power of AJAX. These controls can be used in your Web pages to enable many client-side features typically reserved for applications running on the desktop, such as masked edit boxes, slider controls, filtered text boxes, modal pop-ups, and much more.

> ***NOTE*** **AJAX CONTROL TOOLKIT**
>
> **The AJAX Control Toolkit is an extension to Visual Studio and ASP.NET. It is therefore not covered in this book or on the exam. You can learn more by visiting *http://www.asp.net/ajax/*.**

- **Client-side web service support** ASP.NET provides support for calling Web services asynchronously from the client using JavaScript Object Notation (JSON) serialization and XML.

> ***NOTE*** **USING AJAX TO CALL A WEB SERVICE**
>
> **AJAX can be used to call a Web service from a client. This functionality is covered in Chapter 9, "Writing and Working with Services."**

Uses and Benefits of ASP.NET AJAX

The features built into ASP.NET AJAX provide a richer user experience than that of a standard, all server-side Web application. In addition, these features make programming AJAX a much easier task. As with any new technology, these benefits might not be readily apparent at first glance. The following lists some of the key usage scenarios and related benefits of building Web applications with ASP.NET AJAX.

- **Partial-page updates** This feature allows you to define an area of a page that should PostBack and update by itself. The rest of the page does get refreshed when the request finishes. This ensures the user stays in the context of the page and provides the user with the feeling he or she never left the application.
- **Client-side processing** This interactivity provides immediate feedback and responsiveness to users. With client script you can enable things like collapsible areas of a page, tabs on a Web page, sorting of data on the client, and much more.

- **Desktop-like UI** With AJAX, you can provide users with things like modal dialog boxes, progress indicators, masked edit boxes, ToolTips, and more. This helps blur the line between Web and rich desktop applications.
- **Progress indication** This allows you to track the progress of a server-side process and continuously update the user. This gives users the feeling that they are in control and the application is still processing (much like a desktop application).
- **Improved performance and higher scale** You get increased performance and scale by processing portions of a page on the client. You then leverage the user's machine, which takes load off the server. This results in a real and perceived performance increase.
- **Web service calls from the client** This allows you to call back to the server directly from client script running in a browser and then show the results.
- **Cross-browser cross-platform support** This feature allows you to maintain the benefits of a Web site in terms of its ability to run in more client environments than the average desktop application.

The AJAX Server Controls

The controls that ship with ASP.NET are meant to provide two basic AJAX features: partial-page updates and client-to-server progress updates. You work with these controls in a similar manner as other ASP.NET controls. You can drag them onto your page from the Toolbox, manipulate their properties, and code against them. Figure 6-1 shows a model of the AJAX Extension controls in ASP.NET.

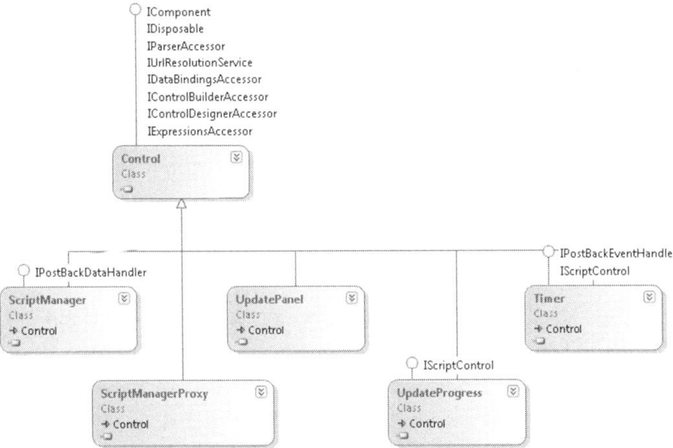

FIGURE 6-1 The AJAX Extensions controls

Each of these controls inherits from the *System.Web.UI.Control* class. This ensures they work in a similar manner as other ASP.NET Web controls. The sections that follow cover each of these controls in detail.

The *ScriptManager* and *ScriptManagerProxy* Controls

Each page you write that leverages ASP.NET AJAX requires one (and only one) instance of a *ScriptManager* control. The *ScriptManager* control is responsible for pushing the Microsoft AJAX Library down to the client when your page is requested. It also manages partial-page updates, progress indicators, and more.

You add the *ScriptManager* control to your page source. However, it does not have a visual representation. It is simply a control used to manage AJAX and other control processing. The basic page markup for a *ScriptManager* control in Source view looks as follows:

```
<asp:ScriptManager ID="ScriptManager1" runat="server">
</asp:ScriptManager>
```

By default, the *ScriptManager* control's *EnablePartialRending* property is set to *True*. This indicates that the page supports partial-page updates. You can use this property to turn this feature off if needed.

The *ScriptManager* is also used to register custom scripts with the Microsoft AJAX Library. In this way, if you write a script, it can be registered and managed with the Microsoft AJAX Library. This is covered in Lesson 2 of this chapter. Similarly, you can use the *ScriptManager* to register Web service method calls from the client. This is covered in Chapter 9.

USING AJAX WITH MASTER PAGES AND USER CONTROLS

You will often need to support AJAX inside a user control you write or directly in the master page of the site. This presents an issue, as a page can contain only a single *ScriptManager* control. Having one inside your user control and another inside the page that consumes the user control, for example, presents a problem. To overcome this issue, you can use the *Script-ManagerProxy* control.

The *ScriptManagerProxy* control can be used either by child pages that use a master page that already defines a *ScriptManager* control or by user and custom controls you write. You use it much the same way you would a *ScriptManager* control. You can register scripts that are specific to the child page or control you are writing. ASP.NET takes care of the rest.

The UpdatePanel Control

The *UpdatePanel* control allows you define areas of a page that should PostBack to the server independent of the rest of the page. This allows a different experience between the client and the server. Rather than the entire page being requested and thus refreshed on return, with partial-page updates you can post portions of a page to the server and only receive updates to those portions. In this way, the user does not see a full-screen refresh and does not lose context where he or she is on the page.

It is important to note that partial-page updates give the illusion of running client side. However, they do not run client side. Rather, they are smaller, asynchronous PostBacks to the server. The *ScriptManager* control manages the communication between this call and its return message.

The *UpdatePanel* control is a container for other controls. The controls you put inside the *UpdatePanel* control that cause a PostBack to the server will be managed as partial-page updates. As an example, consider a *GridView* control that allows users to page through data. By default, each time the user selects another page of data the entire Web page is refreshed and redisplayed. If you embed the *GridView* inside an *UpdatePanel* you can still process the data paging on the server. However, you now eliminate the full-page updates. The following shows the markup of an *UpdatePanel* that includes a *GridView* control:

```
<asp:UpdatePanel ID="UpdatePanel1" runat="server">
  <ContentTemplate>
    <asp:GridView ID="GridView1" runat="server" AllowPaging="True" Width="600"
      AutoGenerateColumns="False" DataKeyNames="id"
      DataSourceID="SqlDataSourceVendorDb" >
      <Columns>
        <asp:BoundField DataField="id" HeaderText="Id" InsertVisible="False"
          ReadOnly="True" SortExpression="id" />
        <asp:BoundField DataField="name" HeaderText="Name" SortExpression="name" />
        <asp:BoundField DataField="location" HeaderText="Location"
          SortExpression="location" />
        <asp:BoundField DataField="contact_name" HeaderText="Contact Name"
          SortExpression="contact_name" />
        <asp:BoundField DataField="contact_phone" HeaderText="Contact Phone"
          SortExpression="contact_phone" />
      </Columns>
    </asp:GridView>
  </ContentTemplate>
</asp:UpdatePanel>
```

CONTROLLING PARTIAL-PAGE UPDATES

You can combine multiple *UpdatePanel* controls on the same page. Each can update portions of the page independently or otherwise. You might also have controls that cause standard PostBacks on the same page as those that cause asynchronous PostBacks. In each of these cases, you need to be able to control how and when the page elements update. The *UpdatePanel* exposes the *UpdateMode* and *ChildrenAsTriggers* properties for controlling when a PostBack should occur to trigger an update of content contained in an *UpdatePanel*.

The first property, *UpdateMode*, has two possible settings: *Always* and *Conditional*. The *Always* value is used to indicate that the content of an *UpdatePanel* should be updated on every PostBack that originates from the page. This includes other, asynchronous updates that are the result of another *UpdatePanel* on the page as well as those that are simply standard PostBacks on the page.

The *Conditional* value of the *UpdatePanel.UpdateMode* property is more complex. It indicates that an update to the given *UpdatePanel* is conditional on something else on the page. For example, consider the case of nested *UpdatePanels*. If you set the nested *UpdatePanel* control's *UpdateMode* property to *Conditional,* it will only be updated when the parent *UpdatePanel* causes a PostBack.

Another way to trigger an update to an *UpdatePanel* with an *UpdateMode* set to *Conditional* is to explicitly call its *Update* method from server-side code. This might be done as the result of another asynchronous update on the page.

If you set the *UpdateMode* to the *Conditional* value, by default nested *UpdatePanel* controls will not cause an update to their parent. You can change this behavior by setting the outer *UpdatePanel* control's *ChildrenAsTriggers* property to *True.* In this case, any updates triggered by the nested *UpdatePanel* will also trigger an update to the parent *UpdatePanel.*

You can also explicitly define the controls that you wish to trigger an update to an *UpdatePanel.* These controls can be inside or outside the *UpdatePanel,* and the update happens for both *Conditional* and the *Always* mode. Adding a trigger to the *UpdatePanel* indicates that if a user triggers a PostBack from the given trigger control, the *UpdatePanel* content should also PostBack and be refreshed.

As an example, consider the *GridView* control discussed previously. This control is inside an *UpdatePanel* as shown in Figure 6-2. It updates itself when a user pages through the data. Now, consider that the page also supports a search function. In this case, the search is triggered based on a button named Search (also displayed in Figure 6-2).

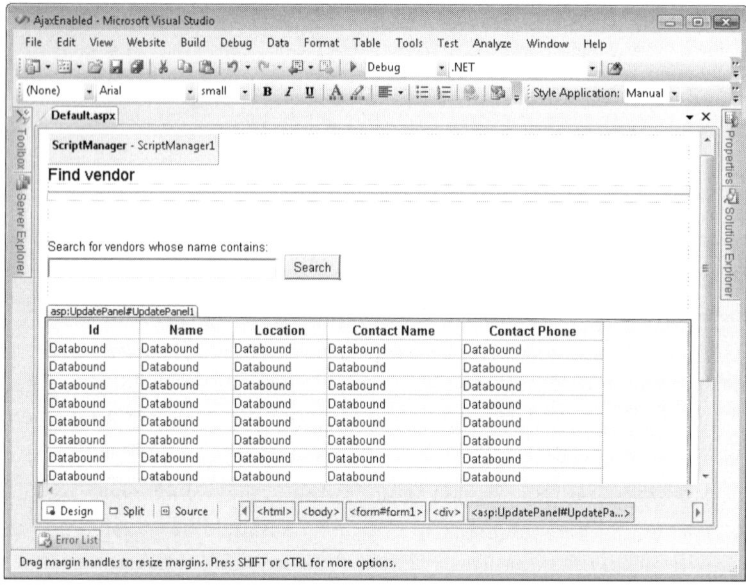

FIGURE 6-2 An .aspx page with a search button and *GridView* control

You might want the search to also result in a partial-page update to *GridView.* To do so, you can add a trigger to the *UpdatePanel* that contains the *GridView* control. A trigger can be defined directly in markup (or through the property window in Design view or in your code). The following markup shows an example:

```
<asp:UpdatePanel ID="UpdatePanel1" runat="server">
  <Triggers>
    <asp:AsyncPostBackTrigger ControlID="ButtonSearch" EventName="Click" />
  </Triggers>
  <ContentTemplate>

    ... Grid View markup ...

  </ContentTemplate>
</asp:UpdatePanel>
```

Notice that the trigger is of type *AsyncPostBackTrigger*. It contains both the ID of the control that causes the PostBack and the name of the trigger control's event that causes the PostBack. You can add more than one trigger to the *UpdatePanel* as well. In this example, clicking the Search button will update the *GridView* as a partial-page update.

PARTIAL-PAGE UPDATES AND ERROR HANDLING

You can handle errors that occur during a partial page update by writing a handler for the *AsyncPostBackError* event of the *ScriptManager* control. This event is raised on the server when an asynchronous PostBack throws an error. You can also set the *AsyncPostBackErrrorMessage* of the *ScriptManager* control to an error message you wish to display to the user when a partial-page update error occurs.

The *UpdateProgress* Control

The *UpdateProgress* control is used to provide information in the form of graphics or text that is displayed to the user during a partial-page update. For example, you might display an animated .gif image that shows the system is processing while you wait for the partial-page update to complete.

You can add an *UpdateProgress* control to an *UpdatePanel* control by nesting it inside the *UpdatePanel* control's *ContentTemplate* tag. This effectively associates the *UpdateProgress* control with the given *UpdatePanel*. You then define the information you wish to display to the user inside the *ProgressTemplate* tag of the *UpdateProgress* control. Content inside this element can be an image, text, or similar HTML content. The content will be rendered to the browser as a hidden *<div>* tag that gets shown when the partial-page update is executed. The following markup shows an example:

```
<asp:UpdatePanel ID="UpdatePanel1" runat="server">
  <ContentTemplate>
    <asp:GridView ID="GridView1" runat="server">
    </asp:GridView>
    <asp:UpdateProgress ID="UpdateProgress1" runat="server">
      <ProgressTemplate>
        <div style="font-size: large">Processing ...</div>
      </ProgressTemplate>
    </asp:UpdateProgress>
```

```
  </ContentTemplate>
</asp:UpdatePanel>
```

The *UpdateProgress* control can also be associated directly with an *UpdateProgress* control through the *AssociatedUpdatePanelId* property. You set this property to the ID value of the *UpdatePanel* to which you wish to associate.

If you do not set the *AssociatedUpdatePanelId* property of the *UpdateProgress* control, any *UpdatePanel* that causes an asynchronous PostBack will trigger the *UpdateProgress* control. In this way, you can use a single *UpdateProgress* control for multiple *UpdatePanels* on a single Web page.

By default, the *UpdateProgress* control is displayed a half-second after the partial-page update starts. You can set the *DisplayAfter* property to the number of milliseconds to wait before displaying the *UpdateProgress* content. This can prevent the control from showing for very quick operations and show it only for longer operations.

> ***MORE INFO*** **CANCELLING AN ASYNCHRONOUS POSTBACK**
>
> **You might need to allow a user to cancel an asynchronous PostBack. You could do so by providing a Cancel button inside the *UpdateProgress* control. The Microsoft AJAX Library supports this through the *abortPostBack* method of the *PageRequestManager* class. For more information and an example, lookup the *UpdateProgress* class inside the MSDN library.**

The *Timer* Control

The ASP.NET *Timer* control is an AJAX control that can be used to update portions of a page on a periodic, timed basis. This is useful if you need to update an image such as an advertisement on a Web page or perhaps a value like a stock or news ticker. The *Timer* control can also be used to simply run code on the server on a periodic basis.

You can add a *Timer* control directly to an *UpdatePanel* control. In this case, the *Timer* automatically triggers a partial-page update of the given *UpdatePanel* based on a time defined by the *Timer* control's *Interval* property (set to milliseconds). The following shows an example of a *Timer* control embedded in an *UpdatePanel*:

```
<asp:UpdatePanel ID="UpdatePanel1" runat="server">
  <ContentTemplate>
    <asp:Image ID="Image1" runat="server"
      ImageUrl="~/images/contoso.png" />
    <asp:Timer ID="Timer1" runat="server"
      Interval="5000" ontick="Timer1_Tick">
    </asp:Timer>
  </ContentTemplate>
</asp:UpdatePanel>
```

In this example, the *Timer* is set to fire every five seconds. When it does, the *Timer* control's *Tick* event is raised on the server and the content of the *UpdatePanel* gets refreshed. In this case, the *Tick* event simply cycles images to be displayed to the user. When you use a *Timer* with an *UpdatePanel*, the *Timer* starts again after the page has completed its PostBack to the server.

A *Timer* can also be used outside of an *UpdatePanel* control. It, too, requires the *ScriptManager* control. In this way, you can use the *Timer* control to update more than one *UpdatePanel* on the page or the entire page itself. To associate a *Timer* control that is outside an *UpdatePanel* to an *UpdatePanel* on the page you use a *Trigger* as discussed earlier.

Note that in the scenario where a trigger is outside an *UpdatePanel*, the timed interval resets as soon as it fires. It does not wait for the PostBack to complete. This can provide more exact timing of intervals. However, if a PostBack is still processing when the *Timer* fires, the first PostBack is cancelled.

Quick Check

1. **If you were building a user control that required ASP.NET AJAX functionality, which control would you add to the page?**
2. **How do you indicate that a control outside an *UpdatePanel* should trigger a partial-page update to the *UpdatePanel*?**

Quick Check Answers

1. **You would have to add a *ScriptManagerProxy* control to the page to ensure that the user control can work with pages that already contain a *ScriptManagerControl*.**
2. **To connect a control that is outside an *UpdatePanel* to an *UpdatePanel*, you register it as an *AsyncPostBackTrigger* in the *Triggers* section of the *UpdatePanel* markup.**

LAB Building an AJAX-Enabled Web Page

In this lab, you create a Web page and enable partial-page updates. You also add support for notifying the user when you connect to the server. Finally, you add a *Timer* control to periodically update a second portion of your page.

If you encounter a problem completing an exercise, the completed projects are available in the sample files installed from the companion CD in the Code folder.

EXERCISE 1 Enable Partial Page Update

In this exercise, you create a new ASP.NET Web site and define support for partial-page updates.

1. Open Visual Studio and create a new ASP.NET Web site named **AjaxExample** in either C# or Visual Basic.
2. Add the Vendors.mdf database file to the App_Data folder of the site. The database file can be found in the sample files installed from the CD inside the App_Data folder for this exercise. This database file is a SQL Express database that contains a single table called *vendor*.
3. Open Default.aspx in Source view. Add a *ScriptManager* control to the body of the page from the AJAX Extensions tab of the Toolbox.
4. Add text to the page to serve as a title followed by a horizontal line. Your code might look like this:

```
<div style="font-size: large;">Vendors</div>
<hr />
```

5. Add an AJAX *UpdatePanel* control to the page.
6. Switch to Design view and add a *GridView* control inside the *UpdatePanel*. Design view provides UI support for binding the *GridView* to the database table.
7. In this step you bind the *GridView* to the vendor table in the Vendors.mdf database. To start, click the smart tag in the upper right section of the *GridView* control to open the GridView Tasks window. From here, select the ChooseDataSource drop-down list and select New Data Source. This opens the Data Source Configuration Wizard.

   In the first step of the wizard, select Database and enter the ID for the data source as **SqlDataSourceVendors**. Click OK to open the Choose Your Data Connection page.

   Next, select Vendors.mdf from the Connection drop-down list and click Next.

   On the next page, choose to save the connection string and name it **Connection-StringVendors**. Click Next to continue.

   Next, configure the SQL statement to access all the data fields in the vendor table (select the * check box). Order the query by the vendor name (click ORDER BY and select Name in the Sort By list). Click Next to continue and then close the wizard by clicking Finish.
8. Again, open the GridView Tasks window using the smart tag. Select the Enable Paging check box.
9. Run the application and view the Default.aspx page in a browser. Click the data page numbers to move between data pages. Notice that only the grid is being updated and not the entire page; this is due to the *UpdatePanel* control.
10. Next, add a section at the top of the form (outside of the *UpdatePanel*) that allows a user to enter a new contact and have it added to the database. Your markup code might look as follows:

```
<div style="margin: 20px 0px 20px 40px">
  Name<br />
```

```
  <asp:TextBox ID="TextBoxName" runat="server" Width="200"></asp:TextBox>
  <br />
  Location<br />
  <asp:TextBox ID="TextBoxLocation" runat="server" Width="200"></asp:TextBox>
  <br />
  Contact Name<br />
  <asp:TextBox ID="TextBoxContact" runat="server" Width="200"></asp:TextBox>
  <br />
  Contact Phone<br />
  <asp:TextBox ID="TextBoxPhone" runat="server" Width="200"></asp:TextBox>
  <br />
  <asp:Button ID="ButtonEnter" runat="server" Text="Enter"
    style="margin-top: 15px" />
</div>
```

11. Next, add a *Click* event to the *ButtonEnter* button defined previously (*onclick= "ButtonEnter_Click"*). This *Click* event will call a stored procedure defined in the Vendors.mdf database. At the end of this event, rebind the *GridView* control. The following code shows an example (assuming you have imported the namespaces *System .Data* and *System.Data.SqlClient*):

```
'VB
Protected Sub ButtonEnter_Click(ByVal sender As Object, _
  ByVal e As System.EventArgs) Handles ButtonEnter.Click

  Dim cnnStr As String = _
    System.Web.Configuration.WebConfigurationManager.ConnectionStrings( _
      "ConnectionStringVendors").ConnectionString

  Dim cnn As New SqlConnection(cnnStr)
  Dim cmd As New SqlCommand("insert_vendor", cnn)
  cmd.CommandType = Data.CommandType.StoredProcedure

  Dim pName As New SqlParameter("@name", Data.SqlDbType.VarChar)
  pName.Value = TextBoxName.Text
  cmd.Parameters.Add(pName)

  Dim pLocation As New SqlParameter("@location", Data.SqlDbType.VarChar)
  pLocation.Value = TextBoxLocation.Text
  cmd.Parameters.Add(pLocation)

  Dim pContactName As New SqlParameter("@contact_name", _
    Data.SqlDbType.VarChar)
  pContactName.Value = TextBoxContact.Text
  cmd.Parameters.Add(pContactName)
```

```
    Dim pContactPhone As New SqlParameter("@contact_phone", _
      Data.SqlDbType.VarChar)
    pContactPhone.Value = TextBoxPhone.Text
    cmd.Parameters.Add(pContactPhone)

    cnn.Open()
    cmd.ExecuteNonQuery()

    'rebind the grid
    GridView1.DataBind()

End Sub
```

```
//C#
protected void ButtonEnter_Click(object sender, EventArgs e)
{

  string cnnStr =
    System.Web.Configuration.WebConfigurationManager.ConnectionStrings[
      "ConnectionStringVendors"].ConnectionString;

  SqlConnection cnn = new SqlConnection(cnnStr);
  SqlCommand cmd = new SqlCommand("insert_vendor", cnn);
  cmd.CommandType = CommandType.StoredProcedure;

  SqlParameter pName = new SqlParameter("@name", SqlDbType.VarChar);
  pName.Value = TextBoxName.Text;
  cmd.Parameters.Add(pName);

  SqlParameter pLocation = new SqlParameter("@location", SqlDbType.VarChar);
  pLocation.Value = TextBoxLocation.Text;
  cmd.Parameters.Add(pLocation);

  SqlParameter pContactName = new SqlParameter("@contact_name",
    SqlDbType.VarChar);
  pContactName.Value = TextBoxContact.Text;
  cmd.Parameters.Add(pContactName);

  SqlParameter pContactPhone = new SqlParameter("@contact_phone",
    SqlDbType.VarChar);
  pContactPhone.Value = TextBoxPhone.Text;
  cmd.Parameters.Add(pContactPhone);

  cnn.Open();
  cmd.ExecuteNonQuery();
```

```
    //rebind the grid
    GridView1.DataBind();
  }
```

Note that this code is very basic. It does not validate the data entered by the user and is therefore prone to error. It is simply an example.

12. Run the application and enter a row in the table. Notice that the entire page refreshes.

Add behavior to the page so that the Enter button triggers a partial-page update to the *GridView*. To do so, add a trigger to the *UpdatePanel* control and connect the trigger to the *ButtonEnter* control. The following markup shows an example:

```
<asp:UpdatePanel ID="UpdatePanelVendors" runat="server">
  <Triggers>
    <asp:AsyncPostBackTrigger ControlID="ButtonEnter" EventName="Click" />
  </Triggers>
  <ContentTemplate>
    <asp:GridView ...
```

Run the application again and notice that now only the *GridView* updates when a new row is added.

EXERCISE 2 Add a Progress Indicator

In this exercise, you add functionality that provides a notice to the user when the page is being partially updated on the server.

1. Continue editing the project you created in the previous exercise. Alternatively, you can open the completed Lesson 1, Exercise 1 project in the sample files installed from the CD.

2. Open Default.aspx in Source view. Add an *UpdateProgress* control to the *UpdatePanel*. Add the control to the bottom of the panel just inside the *ContentTemplate* element.

Add text inside the *ProgressTemplate* elements of the *UpdateProgress* control to notify the user that processing is happening on the server. The following shows a sample markup:

```
<asp:UpdateProgress ID="UpdateProgress1" runat="server">
<ProgressTemplate>
  <div style="margin-top: 20px; font-size: larger; color: Green">
  Processing, please wait ...
  </div>
</ProgressTemplate>
</asp:UpdateProgress>
```

3. The processing happens pretty fast. Therefore, add code to the *ButtonEnter* click event to pause the server-side processing. You can simply put the thread to sleep for a few seconds. The following code shows an example:

```
System.Threading.Thread.Sleep(2000)
```

4. Run the application and notice the notification is shown to the user when you enter a new record in the *GridView*.

EXERCISE 3 Use the *Timer* Control

In this exercise, you add functionality that demonstrates the use of the *Timer* control. You will add an area on the page that rotates through a series of graphics files at a timed interval.

1. Continue editing the project you created in the previous exercise. Alternatively, you can open the completed Lesson 1, Exercise 2 project in the sample files installed from the CD.
2. Open the Default.aspx page in Source view.
3. Add an *UpdatePanel* to appear to the right of the new vendor data entry form. This control will work like a rotating advertisement. It will periodically update and show a new image from the server.
4. Inside the *UpdatePanel* control's *ContentTemplate* element add a label with the text **Advertisement**.

   Under this text, add an image control. You can add a couple images to your project (or copy them from the sample files installed from the CD).
5. Under the image control (and still inside the *ContentTemplate* element) add a *Timer* control from the Ajax Extensions tab on the Toolbox.

   Set the *Timer* control's *Interval* attribute to 4,000 milliseconds (4 seconds).
6. Add an event handler for the *Timer* control's *Tick* event. Inside this event add code to cycle between images (a simple *if* statement should suffice).
7. Run the application and wait until the *Timer* event fires. Your application should look similar to Figure 6-3.

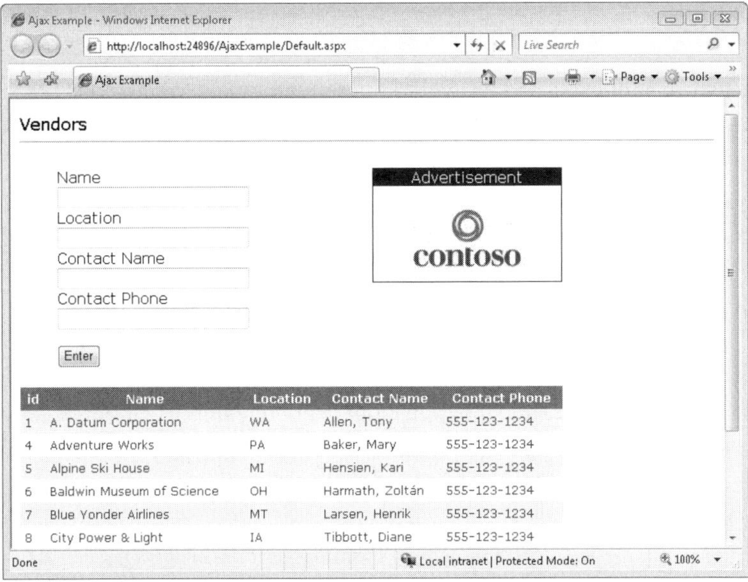

FIGURE 6-3 The Final Vendors form with an *UpdatePanel* that includes a *Timer* control

Lesson Summary

- AJAX is a platform-independent, ECMAScript-compliant technology for communicating between code running on the client and code running on the server.
- ASP.NET includes both a set of server controls for working with AJAX and a set of client-side JavaScript files called the Microsoft AJAX Library.
- The *ScriptManager* (or *ScriptManagerProxy*) control is required on all pages that work with the AJAX extensions for ASP.NET. It manages the JavaScript files sent to the client and the communication between the server and the client.
- The *UpdatePanel* control allows you to define an area within your page that can PostBack to the server and receive updates independent of the rest of the page.
- The *UpdateProgress* control is used to provide notice to the user that the page has initiated a call back to the server.
- The *Timer* control is used to periodically send a partial-page request (using an *UpdatePanel*) to the server at timed intervals.

Lesson Review

You can use the following questions to test your knowledge of the information in Lesson 1, "Creating AJAX-Enabled Web Forms." The questions are also available on the companion CD if you prefer to review them in electronic form.

> ***NOTE*** **ANSWERS**
>
> **Answers to these questions and explanations of why each answer choice is right or wrong are located in the "Answers" section at the end of the book.**

1. You need to write a page that contains a section that should be updated based on a user's action. This update should happen independently of the rest of the page to minimize screen refresh and maintain user context. Which controls must you add to the page to enable this scenario? (Choose all that apply.)
   - **A.** *UpdatePanel*
   - **B.** *AsyncPostBackTrigger*
   - **C.** *ScriptManagerProxy*
   - **D.** *ScriptManager*

2. You need to write a control that will be used across multiple pages. This control should contain updated sales figures. The control should update itself at various intervals if a containing page is left open. Which controls should you use to enable this scenario? (Choose all that apply.)
   - **A.** *UpdatePanel*
   - **B.** *Timer*
   - **C.** *ScriptManager*
   - **D.** *ScriptManagerProxy*

3. You have an *UpdatePanel* defined on a page. You need to indicate that a given *Button* control outside of the *UpdatePanel* should cause the *UpdatePanel* to execute an update. What steps should you take?
   - **A.** Set the *AsyncPostBackTrigger* attribute of the *UpdatePanel* to the ID of the *Button* control.
   - **B.** Set the *AsyncPostBackTrigger* attribute of the *Button* control to the ID of the *UpdatePanel.*
   - **C.** Add a *Trigger* control to the *AsyncPostBackTriggers* section of the *UpdatePanel.* Set the *ControlID* attribute of the *Trigger* control to the ID of the *Button* control.
   - **D.** Add an *AsyncPostBackTrigger* control to the *Triggers* section of the *UpdatePanel.* Set the *ControlID* attribute of the *AsyncPostBackTrigger* control to the ID of the *Button* control.

4. You are writing a page that contains an *UpdatePanel* for partial-page updates. You wish to notify the user that the update is processing only if the update takes longer than 5 seconds. Which actions should you take?

   A. Add a second *UpdatePanel* to the page. Set it to trigger based on the first *UpdatePanel*. Set the contents of this *UpdatePanel* to read "Processing, please wait."

   B. Add an *UpdateProgress* control to the *UpdatePanel*. Set its *DisplayAfter* attribute to 5,000. Set its *ProgressTemplate* contents to read "Processing, please wait."

   C. Add a *ProgressBar* control to the page. Write code on the server to call back to the client asynchronously to update the *ProgressBar* control after 5 seconds.

   D. Create a hidden *<div>* tag on your page that contains the text "Processing, please wait." Set the *<div>* tag's ID to match that of the *UpdatePanel*. Set the *UpdatePanel* control's *Interval* property to 5,000.

Lesson 2: Creating Client Scripts with the AJAX Client-Side Library

It is important to note that JavaScript is not new. It is also not really Java. It is a C-based scripting language invented by Netscape to add client scripting capabilities to a browser. It is now supported as part of every major browser on the market. The actual language is controlled and managed by a standards body, the European Computer Manufacturers Association (ECMA). Because it is widely deployed and offers developers the ability to write code on the client, it has become increasingly popular. This was especially true once features for communicating between the client script and server code using JSON and XML became prevalent.

However, the JavaScript language still lacks basic object-oriented concepts found in modern programming languages. It also lacks a standard framework for developers to program against. The Microsoft AJAX Library was written (in JavaScript) to provide these constructs. This library combined with the AJAX Server Controls, and the support for Visual Studio IntelliSense for JavaScript makes building AJAX-enabled applications more approachable.

This lesson covers the basics of client scripting with JavaScript. It then introduces the Microsoft AJAX Library and shows how you can use this library to add client-side functionality to your server controls.

After this lesson, you will be able to:

- Add client-side script blocks to your page and call them from client-side events.
- Use the *ClientScriptManager* class to add script to a page dynamically at run time.
- Register your client script with a page using the *ScriptManager* class.
- Understand the capabilities and use of the Microsoft AJAX Library.
- Add AJAX support for a client components and server controls.

Estimated lesson time: 90 minutes

Creating Your Own Client Scripts

Scripts that execute on the client have been around a lot longer than AJAX. Client scripts add a client-side, dynamic nature to a Web UI. It is AJAX, however, that has pushed a resurgence in JavaScript on the client. You will look at working with the Microsoft AJAX Library in the next section. First, however, you learn the ways in which you can define client script on your ASP.NET Web page. There are three basic patterns for doing so:

- Define a script block on your Web page. This script block may define client-side code or an *include* attribute that references a JavaScript (.js) file.
- Use the *ClientScriptManager* class to dynamically add JavaScript to a page at run time based on server-side processing.

- Leverage the *ScriptManager* server control to register JavaScript with your Web page.

These methods represent a more traditional approach to working with client-side script. Each is covered in the following sections.

Adding Script Blocks to Your ASP.NET Page

You can add client script to your page through a script block that includes code or through an *include* attribute that references a JavaScript (.js) file. Adding JavaScript to a Web page has been around for a long time. This is the traditional method of working with JavaScript on a Web page. It enables client-side functionality but it does not necessarily leverage the features built into the Microsoft AJAX library. The JavaScript elements are not created dynamically in this case and they do not require the advanced features provided by the Microsoft AJAX Library. However, this method can be useful when you need basic JavaScript functionality for your page.

As an example, suppose you wish to provide client-side functionality that hides an area of a Web page when the user toggles an open–close button. This provides the user with control over what is shown on his or her UI. To enable this scenario, you must first lay out the Web page.

The Web page should contain a titled area that includes a button for opening and closing an area on the page. This title area should always be shown so the user can reopen the area if required. Next, you need to define an area of the page that contains content to be shown or hidden. Both these areas are can be defined by *<div>* tags. The following markup shows an example:

```
<body style="font-family: Verdana;">
  <form id="form1" runat="server">
  <div>

    <div style="width: 200px; background-color: Blue; color: White;
      border-style: solid; border-width: thin; border-color: Blue">
      <div style="float: left; vertical-align: middle; margin-top: 3px;">
        Element Title
      </div>
      <div style="float: right; vertical-align: middle">
        <input id="ButtonCollapse" type="button" value="Close"
          onclick="Collapse()" />
      </div>
    </div>
    <div id="DivCollapse" style="width: 200px; height: 200px;
      border-style: solid; border-width: thin; border-color: Blue">
      <div style="margin-top: 20px; text-align: center;">
        Content area ...
      </div>
    </div>
```

```
    </div>
  </form>
</body>
```

In the preceding markup, the *onclick* event of the *input* button is set to call the method *Collapse*. This is a JavaScript method that will collapse (hide) the content *<div>* tag (called *DivCollapse*). You now need to write this function. You can do so inside the *head* section of the .aspx markup. Here you define a *script* block and a function. The following code shows an example:

```
<head id="Head1" runat="server">
  <title>Script Block</title>
  <script language="javascript" type="text/javascript">

    function Collapse()
    {
      if (DivCollapse.style.display == "")
      {
        DivCollapse.style.display = "none";
        document.forms[0].ButtonCollapse.value = "Open";
      }
      else
      {
        DivCollapse.style.display = "";
        document.forms[0].ButtonCollapse.value = "Close";
      }
    }

  </script>
</head>
```

When you run the code, the two areas defined by the *<div>* tags are shown along with the toggle button. Clicking this button executes the JavaScript on the client. Figure 6-4 shows an example of what the page looks like in the browser.

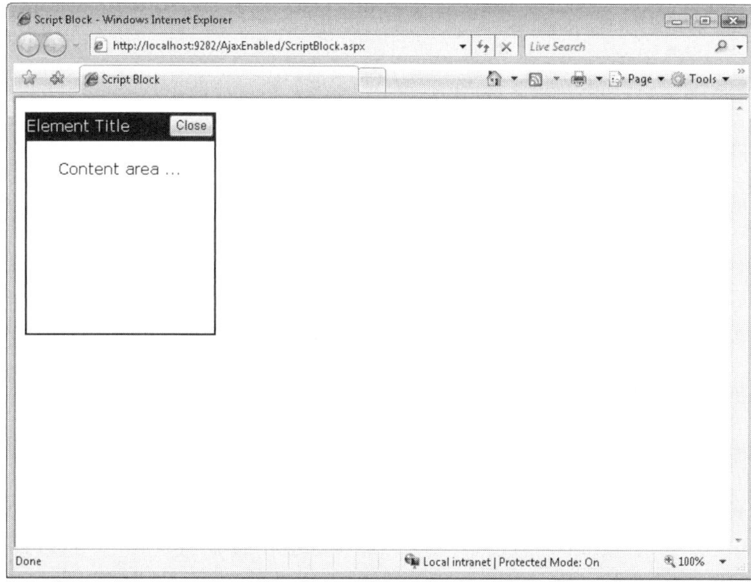

FIGURE 6-4 The JavaScript and HTML in the browser window

> ***NOTE*** **A BASIC EXAMPLE**
>
> **This is a basic example. This type of functionality is provided by the AJAX Control Toolkit and Web Parts in ASP.NET.**

In this example the JavaScript code is embedded directly in the page. If your JavaScript code is reused across multiple pages, you might want to externalize it into separate .js files. This allows both reuse and caching. The JavaScript files will be cached by browsers and thus improve the performance of your page. The following code shows how you can link to an external JavaScript file in your page:

```
<script type="text/javascript" src="SiteScripts.js"></script>
```

The preceding example does not leverage many ASP.NET controls. Instead, it uses the standard HTML *Input* tag to define a button. This tag's *onClick* event is wired to a JavaScript method. However, for an ASP.NET *Button* control, the *onClick* attribute is used to declaratively connect an ASP.NET *Button* control to its server-side event. Therefore, to connect an ASP.NET *Button* control to a client-side JavaScript method you must use the *onClientClick* attribute. In fact, you can set both the *onClick* and *onClientClick* attributes to respond to both a server- and a client-side event for the same control.

The following code shows an example of how you might replace the *Input* tag in the previous example with an ASP.NET *Button* control:

```
<asp:button id=" ButtonCollapse" runat="server" text="Close"
  onClientClick="Collapse();" />
```

It is also important to note that you can reference ASP.NET controls inside your client-side script. You reference them based on their rendering as HTML. Their IDs are set to the same ID you set in your code. The ASP.NET controls also have the *ClientId* property for changing the client ID from that of the server (by default it is set to match the server's ID).

Adding Script Dynamically to Your ASP.NET Page

There are times that you might need to generate your JavaScript and add it to your page at run time. This could be due to the fact that your controls are created at run time or there is information added to the page that determines the JavaScript that should be defined for the page. In either case, you can use the *ClientScriptManager* class to register JavaScript dynamically.

An instance of the *ClientScriptManager* class is exposed through the *Page* object's *ClientScript* property. You use this property to add JavaScript to the page at run time, determine if a script has already been registered, and other related tasks. To add a script, you define it inside a string or point to its file. You then call the *ClientScriptManager* object's *RegisterClientScriptBlock* method. This method takes a type (typically the instance of the page or control, a key that uniquely identifies the script (to help avoid collisions), the script itself, and a Boolean indicating if you need the registration to generate script tags or not.

As an example, suppose you have a *TextBox* that allows users to enter their password. Suppose you also want to give users the ability to check their password strength as they type their password. This feature is turned off by default but users can turn it on. When they do so, you need to register a client script with the page from your code. The following code shows the markup for this example page:

```
<body style="font-family: Verdana">
  <form id="form1" runat="server">
  <div>
    Enter Password<br />
    <asp:TextBox ID="TextBox1" runat="server" Width="250"></asp:TextBox>
      <span id="passwordStrength"></span>
    <br />
    <asp:CheckBox ID="CheckBox1" runat="server"
      Text="Turn on password strength checking" AutoPostBack="true" />
  </div>
  </form>
</body>
```

This markup includes a *CheckBox* control that is set to automatically PostBack when the user selects the check box. Therefore, you need to handle its *CheckedChanged* event in your code. Here you can check to see if the check box is selected and if so, register client script to verify the password. The following code listing shows an example:

```
'VB
Partial Class DynamicScript
    Inherits System.Web.UI.Page
```

```
  Protected Sub CheckBox1_CheckedChanged(ByVal sender As Object, _
    ByVal e As System.EventArgs) Handles CheckBox1.CheckedChanged

    If CheckBox1.Checked Then

      Dim passFunc As String = "function CheckPassword() {"
      passFunc &= "var passLen = document.forms[0].TextBox1.value.length;"
      passFunc &= " if (passLen < 4) {"
      passFunc &= " document.getElementById(""passwordStrength"")."
      passFunc &= "innerText = ""weak"";"
      passFunc &= " document.getElementById(""passwordStrength"")."
      passFunc &= "style.color = ""red"";}"
      passFunc &= " else if (passLen < 6) {"
      passFunc &= " document.getElementById(""passwordStrength"")."
      passFunc &= "innerText = ""medium"";"
      passFunc &= " document.getElementById(""passwordStrength"")."
      passFunc &= "style.color = ""blue"";}"
      passFunc &= " else if (passLen > 9) {"
      passFunc &= " document.getElementById(""passwordStrength"")."
      passFunc &= "innerText = ""strong"";"
      passFunc &= " document.getElementById(""passwordStrength"")."
      passFunc &= "style.color = ""green"";}}"

      'register the script
      Page.ClientScript.RegisterClientScriptBlock(Me.GetType(), _
        "CheckPasswordScript", passFunc, True)

      'add an event to the text box to call the script
      TextBox1.Attributes.Add("onkeyup", "CheckPassword()")

    Else
      'remove the event from the text box
      TextBox1.Attributes.Remove("onkeyup")
    End If

  End Sub

End Class

//C#
public partial class DynamicScriptC : System.Web.UI.Page
{
  protected void CheckBox1_CheckedChanged(object sender, EventArgs e)
    {
      if (CheckBox1.Checked)
      {
```

```
            string passFunc = "function CheckPassword() {";
            passFunc += @"var passLen = document.forms[0].TextBox1.value.length;";
            passFunc += @" if (passLen < 4) {";
            passFunc += @" document.getElementById(""passwordStrength"").";
            passFunc += @"innerText = ""weak"";";
            passFunc += @" document.getElementById(""passwordStrength"").";
            passFunc += @"style.color = ""red"";}";
            passFunc += @" else if (passLen < 6) {";
            passFunc += @" document.getElementById(""passwordStrength"").";
            passFunc += @"innerText = ""medium"";";
            passFunc += @" document.getElementById(""passwordStrength"").";
            passFunc += @"style.color = ""blue"";}";
            passFunc += @" else if (passLen > 9) {";
            passFunc += @" document.getElementById(""passwordStrength"").";
            passFunc += @"innerText = ""strong"";";
            passFunc += @" document.getElementById(""passwordStrength"").";
            passFunc += @"style.color = ""green"";}}";

            //register the script
            Page.ClientScript.RegisterClientScriptBlock(this.GetType(),
              "CheckPasswordScript", passFunc, true);

            //add an event to the text box to call the script
            TextBox1.Attributes.Add("onkeyup", "CheckPassword()");
          }
          else
          {
            //remove the event from the text box
            TextBox1.Attributes.Remove("onkeyup");
          }
        }
    }
```

When you run the page users have no indication of their password strength. However, if they select the check box the page posts to the server and a client script is added in the response. They now can verify their password strength as shown in Figure 6-5. Also, notice that in the preceding code listing that if the check box is not selected, you need to remove the event handler from the *TextBox* control or you will get an error as the script is removed after a PostBack (unless added back in).

You can also register client scripts to be executed only when the page submits. This allows you to know when the user has caused a page submission. You can then use your script code to validate the submission and cancel it if necessary. To register a client script to be executed only on page submission, you use the *RegisterOnSubmitStatement* method of the *ClientScript-Manager*. This method works in a similar fashion as *RegisterClientScriptBlock*. It takes a type, key, and the script as parameters.

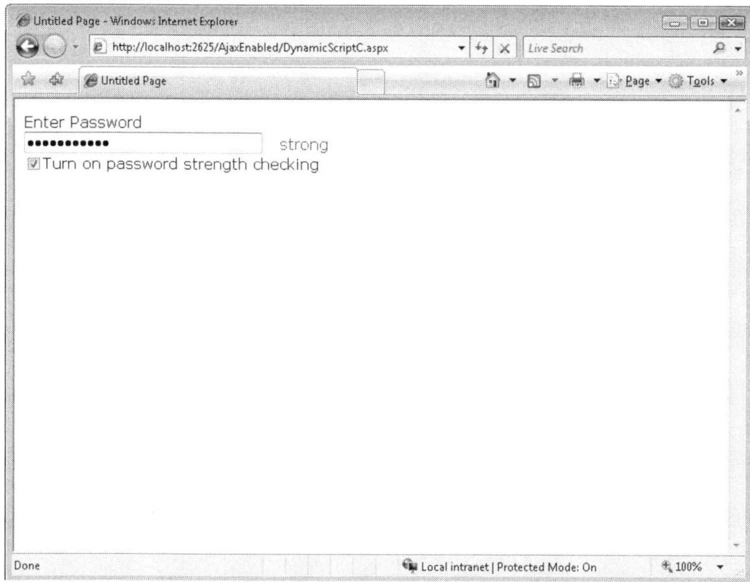

FIGURE 6-5 The dynamically added JavaScript running in a browser

Registering Client Scripts with the *ScriptManager* Control

The *ScriptManager* control, as discussed previously, is used by the ASP.NET AJAX Extension server controls. It automatically registers the appropriate script files defined by the Microsoft AJAX Library. If you are using a *ScriptManager* control, you can also leverage this library in your scripts (this is discussed in greater detail later).

In addition, you can use the *ScriptManager* to register your own scripts with the page. You can do so declaratively or programmatically. To add a script to the *ScriptManager* declaratively, you use the *<Scripts>* collection element of the *ScriptManager* control. The following markup shows an example:

```
<asp:ScriptManager ID="ScriptManager1" runat="server">
  <Scripts>
    <asp:ScriptReference Name="AppScripts.js" />
  </Scripts>
</asp:ScriptManager>
```

Note that if your JavaScript file is embedded in an assembly you can add the *Assembly* attribute to the *ScriptReference* tag and point to the .dll file. This is useful when you do not have full source code files or are working with precompiled objects.

You can also register scripts from your server code. You do so by creating an instance of the *ScriptReference* class. You then add this instance to the *Scripts* collection of the *Script-Manager* control as the following code illustrates:

```
'VB
Dim sr As New ScriptReference("AppScripts.js")
ScriptManager1.Scripts.Add(sr)

//C#
ScriptReference sr = new ScriptReference("AppScripts.js");
ScriptManager1.Scripts.Add(sr);
```

If you are using a *ScriptManager* control on your page already, you can use it to register client scripts. If you are not using AJAX features associated with a *ScriptManager* control, you are better off using the *ClientScriptManager* mentioned earlier, as it does not have the overhead of the *ScriptManager* server control.

IMPORTANT **SCRIPT REGISTRATION**

Only scripts registered with the *ScriptManager* are available for use in partial-page update scenarios. If you need your script in these scenarios you must register it with the *ScriptManager* class.

Quick Check

1. **Where should you place client script you intend to use across multiple pages of a site?**
2. **What property and method of the *Page* object do you use to register client script dynamically from code?**

Quick Check Answers

1. **You should place this code in a .js file. This allows you to easily share the code between pages. It also allows browsers to cache this code.**
2. **The *Page.ClientScript.RegisterClientScriptBlock* is used to dynamically register client script from code.**

Creating Your Own Client Callbacks

In the prior lesson you learned how to implement partial-page updates using the *UpdatePanel* and other features of the Microsoft AJAX controls. These controls make creating a client callback (a call to the server followed by a call back to the client from the server) a simple process. There may be times, however, when you need more control over how you call to the server from the client and vice versa. In these cases, you need to write your own asynchronous, client callbacks.

Creating a page with its own client callback code follows a standard set of steps. First, you must define the server-side code. To do so, you follow these steps:

- Implement the *System.Web.UI.ICallbackEventHandler* for your ASP.NET page. This server-side interface is used to set up both the receive call from the client (*RaiseCallbackEvent*) and the method that returns processing to the client (*GetCallbackResults*).
- Implement the *RaiseCallbackEvent* method for the *ICallbackEventHandler* interface. This method is called by the client. You can use it to receive parameter values from the client.
- Implement the *GetCallbackResult* method for the *ICallbackEventHandler* interface. This function is used to return the results of any server-side processing. The results are sent as a string back to the client code.

Once the server-side code is written, the next step is to create the client-side code. This also follows a standard set of steps:

- One client script that is necessary is the one that will be called by the server as the result of the server processing. You can use this function to process any results coming back from the server. This function's name gets registered with the *GetCallbackEventReference* inside your server-side code at the time of page load. This ensures the callback gets called after server-side processing.
- Another client script is a JavaScript function you create to call the server from the client. This function is typically created in your server-side code at the time of page load. Doing so allows you to register the client-side function using the *RegisterClientScriptBlock* method of the *ClientScriptManager*. This function is then used by one or more controls on your page to initiate the client-side call to the server.
- The final JavaScript function is actually generated for you by ASP.NET. This is the function that actually does the calling between the client and server. This function is generated when you use the *GetCallbackEventReference* method of the *ClientScriptManager* in your server-side code.

As an example, suppose you have a Web page that contains a *DropDownList* control. Imagine you want to call the server when the user selects an item from the *DropDownList* but you do not wish to do a full page post. Rather, you want to initiate an asynchronous client callback. You can then do some processing on the server and return the results to the client. The client page can then be updated without causing a refresh.

To get started creating this example, you need to implement the *ICallbackEventHandler* interface for the code-behind page. This code might look as follows:

```
'VB

Partial Class _Default
  Inherits System.Web.UI.Page
  Implements System.Web.UI.ICallbackEventHandler

//C#
public partial class Default2 :
  System.Web.UI.Page, System.Web.UI.ICallbackEventHandler
```

Next, you implement the *RaiseCallbackEvent*. This event is called by the client during a callback. It receives any event arguments from the client as a string. For this example, these event arguments represent the selected choice in the *DropDownList*. Suppose you wish to store these event arguments in a class-level variable. Your code should look as follows:

```
'VB
Dim _callbackArgs As String

Public Sub RaiseCallbackEvent(ByVal eventArgument As String) _
  Implements System.Web.UI.ICallbackEventHandler.RaiseCallbackEvent

  _callbackArgs = eventArgument

End Sub

//C#
string _callbackArgs;

public void RaiseCallbackEvent(string eventArgument)
{
  _callbackArgs = eventArgument;
}
```

You also have to implement the *GetCallbackResult* method. This method will return a result back to the client following the server-side processing. In our example, we simply return the user's selected item from the *DropDownList*. In a real-world scenario you might do some processing, call the database, and so forth. The code for this method looks as follows:

```
'VB
Public Function GetCallbackResult() As String _
  Implements System.Web.UI.ICallbackEventHandler.GetCallbackResult

  Return _callbackArgs

End Function

//C#
public string GetCallbackResult()
{
  return _callbackArgs;
}
```

You now need to add code to the page load event that registers the various client scripts. First, you register the client script that will be called by the server following the server-side processing. In this example, this script is called *ClientCallbackFunction*. This function is defined in the markup for the page. Next, you create a JavaScript function that is used to call the server-side code. In the example, this function is called, *MyServerCall*. It is referenced in the page markup to make the server-side call. You register this function with the *ClientScript-Manager* using the *RegisterClientScriptBlock* method as shown here:

```
'VB
Protected Sub Page_Load(ByVal sender As Object, _
  ByVal e As System.EventArgs) Handles Me.Load

  'register the name of the client-side function that will
  ' be called by the server
  Dim callbackRef As String = Page.ClientScript.GetCallbackEventReference( _
    Me, "args", "ClientCallbackFunction", "")

  'define a function used by the client to call the server
  Dim callbackScript As String = "function MyServerCall(args)" & _
      "{" & callbackRef & "; }"

  'register the client function with the page
  Page.ClientScript.RegisterClientScriptBlock(Me.GetType(), _
      "MyServerCall", callbackScript, True)

End Sub

//C#
protected void Page_Load(object sender, EventArgs e)
{
  //register the name of the client-side function that will
  // be called by the server
  string callbackRef = Page.ClientScript.GetCallbackEventReference(
    this, "args", "ClientCallbackFunction", "");

  //define a function used by the client to call the server
  string callbackScript = "function MyServerCall(args)" +
      "{" + callbackRef + "; }";

  //register the client function with the page
  Page.ClientScript.RegisterClientScriptBlock(this.GetType(),
      "MyServerCall", callbackScript, true);
}
```

The last step in this example is to write the page markup. Here you define a client script that receives the callback from the server. Recall this script is named, *ClientCallbackFunction* and takes a string (*args*) as a parameter. In this example, this function writes out the *args* value to a *Label* control. You also must initiate the call to the server from the client. For this, recall that you need to call the *MyServerCall* method. In the example, this method is called as a result of the *OnChange* event for the *DropDownList* control. The example passes the selected item as a parameter. These page markup items look as follows:

```
<script type="text/javascript">
function ClientCallbackFunction(args)
{
  LabelMessage.innerText = args;
}
</script>

  <asp:DropDownList ID="DropDownListChoice"
    runat="server"
    OnChange="MyServerCall(DropDownListChoice.value)">
    <asp:ListItem>Choice 1</asp:ListItem>
    <asp:ListItem>Choice 2</asp:ListItem>
    <asp:ListItem>Choice 3</asp:ListItem>
  </asp:DropDownList>
  <br /><br />
  <asp:Label ID="LabelMessage" runat="server"></asp:Label>
```

When the page is run, a user selects a choice from the drop-down list. This calls the *MyServerCall* client-side method, which initiates a call to the server. The *RaiseCallbackEvent* method is then called on the server; this accepts the event arguments (the user's choice). The server processes the request and calls the *GetCallbackResult* method. The results are then passed back to the client. Once back on the client, the *ClientCallbackFunction* JavaScript method is executed and the result (the user's choice) is shown to the user.

Working with the ASP.NET AJAX Library

As you have seen, you can create your own JavaScript and embed it in an ASP.NET page. However, JavaScript can be challenging to program with, especially if you are used to developing in an object-oriented world, having a strong type system, working with a framework, or having error handling and debugging support. The Microsoft AJAX Library helps solve these issues by bringing support for these items in the form of a wrapper library for the JavaScript language.

This section provides an overview of the Microsoft AJAX Library. It then covers how you can leverage this library to create AJAX-enabled server controls, client components, and behaviors that can be attached to client controls.

Features of the Microsoft AJAX Library

The Microsoft AJAX Library is actually written in JavaScript. It is a set of files that are output to the browser to provide a base of capabilities on which you can build. These files are automatically output by the *ScriptManager* on the page. The *ScriptManager* determines which files are required and manages their inclusion in the output. You do not get Microsoft AJAX Library support without a *ScriptManager* on your page or through explicitly including these files.

> ***NOTE*** **AJAX LIBRARY FILES**
>
> You can leverage the Microsoft AJAX Library outside of ASP.NET or examine the source code of the library. The files can be found at *www.asp.net/ajax* and include the file MicrosoftAjax.js (among others). There are also debug versions of the files like MicrosoftAjax.debug.js. The compiler and *ScriptManager* output the appropriate code depending on the mode of your application (release or debug).

The Microsoft AJAX Library is meant to make your JavaScript more robust, easier to write, and more reusable. The following are the core features and benefits of the library:

- **Object-oriented support** The library allows you to define namespaces; build classes that contain fields, properties, and methods; create event handlers; implement inheritance and interfaces; use data types and enumerations; and support reflection.
- **Base classes** The library includes a *Global* namespace that provides extensions to the JavaScript base types including *String*, *Number*, *Date*, *Boolean*, *Array*, and *Object*. It also adds the *Type* class to the language for registering namespaces, classes, and more.
- **A framework (or set of namespaces)** The Microsoft AJAX Library includes a root namespace called *Sys* that contains classes and other namespaces that make programming AJAX applications easier. Think of the *Sys* namespace as a client-side equivalent to *System* in the Microsoft .NET Framework (although obviously not as rich). Other namespaces include *Sys.Net*, *Sys.Services*, *Sys.UI*, *Sys.WebForms*, and *Sys.Serialization*.
- **Browser compatibility** JavaScript is a standards-driven language. However, there are multiple quirks to the implementations of that language across browsers just as there are for HTML. The Microsoft AJAX library takes these into account and has built-in support for browser compatibility with Internet Explorer, Firefox, and Safari.
- **Debugging and error handling** The Microsoft AJAX Library includes debugging extensions to make debugging easier. In fact, there are two versions of the library: a release version and a debug version. In addition, the library includes an extended *Error* object that provides more error information. It also includes tracing support with *Sys.Debug.trace*.
- **Globalization support** The Microsoft AJAX Library supports building global, localized client scripts for working across language and culture. Your single JavaScript code base can then provide localized UI support without posting back to the server. This is achieved through number and data format methods that work with the language and culture settings in the browser.

Next you will learn more about the contents of the *Sys* namespaces, how to code against the library, and how to work with client events. Following this, you will read about how you can use this information to add client-side capabilities to the page.

The Microsoft AJAX Library Namespaces

The Microsoft AJAX Library is about two things: extending the JavaScript language and providing a base framework for common AJAX tasks. There are many types, controls, enumerations, and members found in the library. The following provides an overview of how the library's namespaces are organized:

- ***Global*** The *Global* namespace represents an extension to JavaScript itself. It extends many of the core elements and capabilities of the language. For example, the *Number*, *String*, *Date*, *Array*, and other types are given new functionality when using the Microsoft AJAX Library. In addition, the *Global* namespace adds the *Type* class to JavaScript. The *Type* class is used to register object-oriented items in JavaScript like namespaces, classes, interfaces, and enumerations. The following line of JavaScript code shows an example usage of the *Type* class to register a namespace:

  ```
  Type.registerNamespace("MyCompany.MyApplication");
  ```

- ***Sys*** The *Sys* namespace is the root namespace of the AJAX Library. The *Global* namespace extends JavaScript, whereas the *Sys* namespace contains a framework for AJAX programming with JavaScript. There are a number of core classes in the *Sys* namespace. This includes the *Application* class, which is a run-time version of the library used for connecting to client-side events.

  The *Component* class is also in the *Sys* namespace. It is used for registering and creating instances of the components you create for use with the library. You do so by calling the *Component.create* method (also accessed via the shortcut *$create*). The *Component* class also serves as the base class for the *Control* and *Behavior* classes discussed later in this section.

  The *Sys* namespace includes other notable classes like *StringBuilder* for concatenating strings, *Debug* for debug and tracing support, *EventArgs* used as a base class for passing parameters to events, and more.

- ***Sys.Net*** The *Sys.Net* namespace contains classes focused on the communication between the browser and the server. This class represents the underpinnings for doing partial-page updates and calling Web services from the browser. This includes the *Sys .Net.WebRequest* class; this class is covered in Chapter 9 when discussing Web services.

- ***Sys.Serialization*** The *Sys.Serialization* namespace is also used to communicate between client and server. It contains a single class: *JavaScriptSerializer*. This class is used to serialize and deserialize data to be passed from browser and server in Web service calls.

- ***Sys.Services*** The *Sys.Services* namespace contains classes for working with the AJAX authentication and profile services from script.

- ***Sys.UI*** The *Sys.UI* namespace contains the classes used to add AJAX features to the UI. This includes the classes *Behavior*, *Control*, *DomElement*, and more. You use these classes when building your own AJAX UI features. These are covered in later sections.

- ***Sys.WebForms*** The *Sys.WebForms* namespace encapsulates the classes for partial-page updates. These classes are used by the *UpdatePanel* control. You can also use these to create your own partial-page scenarios. The *PageRequestManager* class is found here; it can be used to customize asynchronous PostBacks.

This number of namespaces can seem a little daunting at first. Like any library, however, there are some features you will end up using a lot and others you won't typically need. We cannot cover every class and method here. You will see, however, that much of the action takes place in the *Sys.UI* namespace; this is where you interact to write AJAX UI elements.

> ***MORE INFO*** **MICROSOFT AJAX LIBRARY REFERENCE**
>
> **If you get stuck with a specific class or method in the framework or in one of the following examples, you can look up the item in the complete library reference. This can be found inside of MSDN. You can also reference it on the Web at *http://msdn.microsoft.com/en-us/library/bb397702.aspx*.**

Object-Oriented AJAX Development

JavaScript has support for many basic features focused on simple classes, data types, operators, and the like. However, it is missing key object-oriented features. These include support for namespaces, inheritance, interfaces, fields, properties, enumerations, events, reflection, and more. The Microsoft AJAX Library tries to extend the language by providing support for these items.

A natural question to ask is why you need this type of support for JavaScript. The answer is that in many cases you do not. However, if you are building your own controls or need to enable very specific programming on the client, this library will help you. The best way to use the library is to define your requirements; create a JavaScript class definition in a .js file that will provide methods, properties, and the like to meet those requirements; and then register that file with your page. You can then create an instance of your class and work with it on the page. This includes associating the class items with the actions on controls.

This section covers the "create a class" step. You will read about how you connect to this class on your page in the sections that follow and in the lab.

NAMESPACES

The Microsoft AJAX Library adds the ability to work with namespaces to JavaScript. A namespace is a way to encapsulate code into a library for easier classification and reference. It also helps manage name collisions, as two classes cannot have the same name in a given namespace. In addition, namespaces that you create and register with the library are then available in IntelliSense in Visual Studio, making development a little easier.

The library provides an important class called *Type*. The *Type* class represents a typing system for JavaScript. It is the key class that enables you to have namespaces, classes, enumerations, and the like. The class sits inside the *Global* namespace.

You use the *registerNamespace* method of the *Type* class to define a namespace. This is typically done at the top of your class file. You then use the namespace you define here throughout your class definition to add classes and the like. The following line of code shows an example.

```
Type.registerNamespace("Contoso.Utilities");
```

In this example, the namespace *Contoso.Utilities* is being defined. Consider this a company-wide utility namespace that might include helper classes for a development team.

CLASSES (CONSTRUCTORS, FIELDS, PROPERTIES, AND METHODS)

The Microsoft AJAX Library also allows you to define class definitions. The syntax for creating a class with the library is *Namespace.ClassName*. You assign the class name to a function that also serves as your constructor. This function can also take parameters.

For example, suppose you wish to add a class to the *Contoso.Utilities* namespace defined earlier. The requirements for this class are to provide validation features (on the client) related to the process of a user changing his or her password. You might name this class *ChangePasswordValidator.* The following code shows a definition of this class:

```
//define class name (as function), create constructor, and
//  set class-level field values
Contoso.Utilities.ChangePasswordValidator =
  function(requirePasswordsNotMatch, requireNumber)
{
  Contoso.Utilities.ChangePasswordValidator.initializeBase(this);
  this.RequirePasswordsNotMatch = requirePasswordsNotMatch;
  this.RequireNumber = requireNumber;
  this._passwordRuleViolations = new Array();
}
```

Notice that the class is set to a function. This function serves as the constructor for the class. When a developer uses the *new* keyword to create an instance of your class he or she will be shown this constructor by *IntelliSense* and have to provide the two parameters defined by the function. These parameters are specific to the password scenario and facilitate how the password rules will process. The parameters are set to field-level items on the class inside the constructor. This is shown by the call `this.<FieldName> = <parameter>` (or in this example `this.RequireNumber = requireNumber`).

Also notice the call to *initializeBase*. This ensures that the base class from which your class derives gets its constructor called, too. You typically derive your classes from *Sys.Component* or one of its derivates. However, you do not have to. You derive from *Sys.Component*, *Sys.UI.Behavior*, or *Sys.UI.Control* if you intend to use the class as part of an AJAX control (more on this later).

After you define the class and its constructor, the next step is to define the fields, properties, methods, and the like that make up the actual class. You do so by defining a *prototype* for the class. You set the *prototype* definition to include fields, methods, and methods that act as properties.

For example, to define a prototype for the *ChangePasswordValidator* class you make a call to the JavaScript *prototype* property and set it equal to a class definition (enclosed in braces). To define fields for the class you simply declare variables at the class level and set their data type. Fields are essentially name–value pairs where the name is an element of the prototype (or class definition) and the value is set by the user of the class. The following code shows the start of a class definition that also defines two Boolean fields:

```
//define class contents (fields, properties, methods)
Contoso.Utilities.ChangePasswordValidator.prototype =
{

  //declare fields
  RequirePasswordsNotMatch: Boolean,
  RequireNumber: Boolean,

  ...
```

The next step is to add properties to the class definition just started. By default, JavaScript does not really support properties. Instead, you can define methods that act as properties by declaring two functions. One function returns the value of an internal member and the other function receives a value to be assigned to this internal member. The convention for naming properties in the Microsoft AJAX Library is using *set_propertyName* and *get_propertyName* for the setter and getter, respectively. The internal variables are defined with leading underscores ("_") as in *_privateMember*. This indicates to the library that these items should remain private to the class (even if JavaScript does not actually support private fields).

As an example, consider the class discussed earlier with respect to a user changing his or her password. You might want to define write-only properties for the current password and the password to which the user would like to change. You can do so by simply implementing a *set_* function (and not a *get_*). This is shown in the following code example along with a property to return all password violations that occur during validation:

```
//properties
set_currentPassword: function(value)
{
  this._currentPassword = value;
},

set_changeToPassword: function(value)
{
  this._changeToPassword = value;
},

get_passwordRuleViolations: function()
```

```
{
  return this._passwordRuleViolations;
},
```

You add methods to a class *prototype* in much the same way as a *function*. The following code shows two example functions. The first, *CheckPasswordStrength,* takes a string and returns an enumeration value, *Contoso.Utilities.PasswordStrength* (more on this in a moment). The second function definition, *AllowPasswordChange*, can be called to determine if a user's changed password meets the criteria for a change. If not, rules are added to an *Array* and the value *false* is returned by the function. These rules (or password error conditions) can then be accessed through the property defined previously.

```
//methods
CheckPasswordStrength: function(password)
{
  var strPass = new String(password.toString());
  if (strPass.length < 4)
  {
    return Contoso.Utilities.PasswordStrength.Weak;
  }
  else if (strPass.Length < 7)
  {
    return Contoso.Utilities.PasswordStrength.Medium;
  }
  else
  {
    return Contoso.Utilities.PasswordStrength.Strong;
  }
},

AllowPasswordChange: function()
{

  var pass1 = new String(this._currentPassword);
  var pass2 = new String(this._changeToPassword);

  //use new, extended Array type
  var ruleViolations = new Array();

  //min length rule
  if (pass2.length < 5)
  {
    Array.add(ruleViolations, 'Password too short.');
  }

  //check if passwords match
  if (this.RequirePasswordsNotMatch)
```

```
    {
      if (pass1 == pass2)
      {
        Array.add(ruleViolations, 'Passwords cannot match.');
      }
    }

    //contains numbers
    if (this.RequireNumber)
    {
      if (pass2.match(/\d+/) == null)
      {
        Array.add(ruleViolations, 'Password must include a number.');
      }
    }

    //reset rule violations property
    this._passwordRuleViolations = ruleViolations;

    //determine if change allowed
    if (ruleViolations.length > 0)
    {
      return false;
    }
    else
    {
      return true;
    }
  }

}
```

Like a namespace, you must also register a class with the Microsoft AJAX Library for it to be available with the *ScriptManager* at run time and through IntelliSense at design time. You register a class by calling the *registerClass* extension method of your object. This method has three parameters: *typeName*, *baseType*, and *interfaceTypes*. *TypeName* is the full name of the class you intend to register. *BaseType* is the class on which the new class builds. This is how inheritance is supported by the library. If your class should stand alone, you can pass *null* into this parameter. If your class is meant to be an AJAX control or a behavior, you pass in *Sys.UI.Control* or *Sys.UI.Behavior*, respectively. Finally, the *interfaceTypes* parameter indicates the interfaces that the class must implement. You can define your own interfaces with the library. You can also implement one or more framework interfaces. This parameter is an array, so you can pass multiple interfaces into it. The following code shows an example of the *registerClass* method:

```
//register code as an actual class
```

```
Contoso.Utilities.ChangePasswordValidator.registerClass(
  'Contoso.Utilities.ChangePasswordValidator', null, Sys.IDisposable);
```

ENUMERATIONS

The Microsoft AJAX Library provides support for enumerations. These enumerations are simply named integer values. Like enumerations in other languages (C# and Visual Basic included), enumerations provide a more readable and maintainable coding style.

You define an enumeration the same way you define a class, using the *prototype* property. You then define fields for the class and set their initial value. Finally, you call the *registerEnum* method of the *Type* class (used to extend the JavaScript library). The following is an example of an enumeration created to define a password's strength:

```
//create and register an enumeration
Contoso.Utilities.PasswordStrength = function(){};
Contoso.Utilities.PasswordStrength.prototype =
{
  Weak: 1,
  Medium: 2,
  Strong: 3
}
Contoso.Utilities.PasswordStrength.registerEnum(
  "Contoso.Utilities.PasswordStrength");
```

INHERITANCE

Support for inheritance is also available with the Microsoft AJAX Library. This allows a JavaScript class to inherit the properties and methods of a base class. Of course the inheriting class can also override those properties and methods. This is similar to inheritance in other object-oriented languages.

You implement inheritance through the *registerClass* method discussed earlier by setting the *baseType* property during registration. This enables single inheritance (similar to how the .NET Framework works). If you wish to override a function, you simply redefine it using the same name in the new class.

INTERFACES

You can also define and implement interfaces with the Microsoft AJAX Library. Interfaces here are again similar to those in the .NET Framework; they represent contracts that the class must implement. You can also implement multiple interfaces in a given class.

You indicate that a class should implement an interface through the *registerClass* method. This was shown earlier and is repeated in the following code. The third parameter of this method is the *interfaceTypes* that the class implements. You can pass a single interface here (as shown here with *Sys.IDisposable*) or multiple interfaces:

```
Contoso.Utilities.ChangePasswordValidator.registerClass(
  'Contoso.Utilities.ChangePasswordValidator', null, Sys.IDisposable);
```

The library also allows you to define and implement your own interfaces. To create an interface, you define it as you would a class. However, you do not add implementation to the interface, just method stubs. You then call the *registerInterface* method of the *Type* class. This registers your interface for use with the library. The following code shows an example of defining and registering an interface with the library:

```
//declare an interface
Contoso.Utilities.IValidationLogic = function() {}
Contoso.Utilities.IValidationLogic.prototype =
{
  get_isValid: function(){},
  get_validationRules: function() {},
  validate: function(){}
}
Contoso.Utilities.IValidationLogic.registerInterface(
  "Contoso.Utilities.IValidationLogic");
```

IMPORTANT **LOADED SCRIPT**

When you write JavaScript that is intended to be used by the Microsoft AJAX Library you need to tell the library once you have finished loading your script. You can do so by calling the *notifyScriptLoaded* method of the *Sys.Application* object. The following shows an example:

```
//notify the script manager this is the end of the class / script
if (typeof(Sys) !== 'undefined') Sys.Application.notifyScriptLoaded();
```

Using Custom Classes

Classes you create with the Microsoft AJAX Library can be used directly within your .aspx pages. To do so, you must first register the class with the *ScriptManager*. This tells the *ScriptManager* you have a class that is built with the library in mind. It also ensures you get IntelliSense in the IDE for your namespaces, classes, methods, and the like. The following page script shows an example of how you add the script defined in the prior section to the page:

```
<asp:ScriptManager ID="ScriptManager1" runat="server">
  <Scripts>
    <asp:ScriptReference path="ContosoUtilities.js" />
  </Scripts>
</asp:ScriptManager>
```

Once defined, you can use the class library as required in page-level script. For example, you can create a new instance of the *ChangePasswordValidator* control created earlier by using the *new* keyword and passing in the appropriate parameters to the constructor. The following code shows an example of creating an instance of the class, using the enumeration, calling properties, and calling methods.

```
<script language="javascript" type="text/javascript">

  //call constructor
  var validator =
    new Contoso.Utilities.ChangePasswordValidator(true, true, true);

  //check the password strength
  strength = validator.CheckPasswordStrength("password");
  switch (strength)
  {
    case Contoso.Utilities.PasswordStrength.Weak:
      alert("Weak");
      break;
    case Contoso.Utilities.PasswordStrength.Medium:
      alert("Medium");
      break;
    case Contoso.Utilities.PasswordStrength.Strong:
      alert("Strong");
      break;
  }

  //set properties
  validator.set_currentPassword("password");
  validator.set_changeToPassword("pas2");

  //call methods
  if (validator.AllowPasswordChange())
  {
    alert("Password may be changed");
  }
  else
  {
    var violations = validator.get_passwordRuleViolations();

    alert("Rule violations: " + violations.length);
    for (i = 0; i < violations.length; i++)
    {
      alert("Rule violation " + i + " = " + violations[i]);
    }
  }

</script>
```

AJAX Client-Side Life Cycle Events

The Microsoft AJAX Library also includes a client-based event life cycle. You can use this life cycle to intercept events when the page runs and load your code as required. Think of this as similar to how you work with code-behind files. For example, in a code-behind file you might write code in the *Page_Load* event. Similarly, in the code you write to run in the browser, you can implement the *Sys.Application.load* event.

Fortunately, the life cycle of your client code is very similar to that of your server code. This includes events for *init*, *load*, *unload*, and *disposing*. In this way, the *Application* client object works in a similar way as the *Page* object in your server code. To take advantage of this event model you must, of course, use a *ScriptManager* control on your page. You register an event in script using the *add_event* syntax. The following code shows how you would register code with the *Sys.Application.Load* event:

```
Sys.Application.add_load(PageLoad);
function PageLoad(sender)
{
  //page-load code goes here
}
```

The library also allows you to unregister (or remove) events. You do so in a similar manner but using the *remove_event* syntax. The following shows an example:

```
Sys.Application.remove_load(PageLoad);
```

You can follow this similar model to trap other events in the library. For example, another key class with events you might want to work with is the *PageRequestManager* class of the *Sys.WebForms* namespace. This class is used for partial-page updates and asynchronous PostBacks. It includes the following events:

- ***initializeRequest*** Raised before the async PostBack starts.
- ***beginRequest*** Raised as the async PostBack is sent to the server.
- ***pageLoading*** Raised when the async PostBack response first comes back from the server.
- ***pageLoaded*** Raised after the content has been loaded from the results of the async PostBack.
- ***endRequest*** Raised when the async PostBack has been completed.

As you might have guessed, the *UpdatePanel* relies heavily on these events. You can also use these events to cancel async PostBacks, provide custom information or animation to the user when these events are fired, or simply run your code at key times within the request.

Building Client Capabilities with AJAX

Thus far you've see how to program against the Microsoft AJAX Library. You can use these skills to create client-side controls. These controls are built on the Microsoft AJAX Library and thus are managed by it. It is important to remember that these are not server controls. Rather, they are controls that implement AJAX features on the client.

There are three types of client objects you can create with the AJAX Library: *component*, *control*, and *behavior*. The following provides a brief description of each:

- ***Sys.Component*** This object provides a base class for creating reusable AJAX components. Classes that derive from *Sys.Component* do not generate UI elements. Instead, they work as common controls that provide functionality across pages. For example, the *Timer* control in the AJAX Library implements *Sys.Component*.
- ***Sys.UI.Control*** This object provides a base class for creating reusable, AJAX-enabled client controls. These controls are typically related to a single Document Object Model (DOM) element (like an input box or button). They provide additional functionality to the DOM element with which they are meant to work.
- ***Sys.UI.Behavior*** This object represents a base class for creating behaviors that can be added to one or more DOM elements at design time. A behavior is not associated with a single DOM element. Rather, it can extend the DOM elements to which it is applied. For example, you might create a mouse-over pop-up window behavior. You could then apply this behavior to a button, input box, hyperlink, or otherwise.

Controls you create to work with the AJAX Library will each implement one of these controls as their base. Figure 6-6 shows an example of the object model of these three classes. Note that the figure does not show all the properties and methods of the classes. Rather, it represents their core.

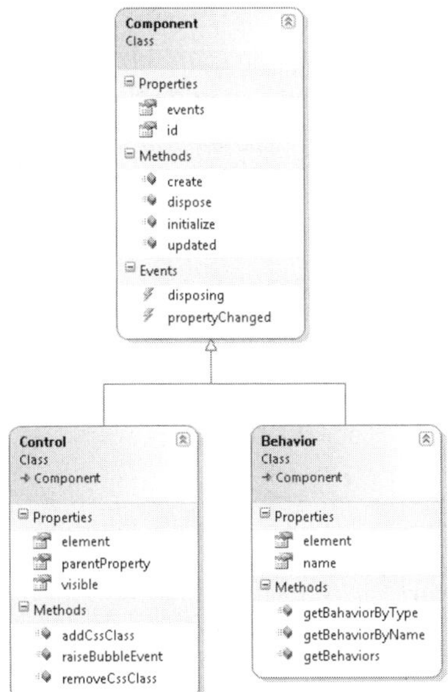

FIGURE 6-6 The AJAX Client Objects base classes

The sections that follow provide additional details on the three types of client objects you can create with the AJAX Library.

Creating an AJAX Client Component

An AJAX client component is a class you create that derives from the *Sys.Component* class. You derive from this class because you intend to create a class that gets managed by the AJAX Library but does not work directly with the UI. This is similar to the class we created in the previous section. However, in this case you inherit the *Sys.Component* base class. This ensures the library knows how to manage the lifetime of your object from initialize through dispose.

As an example (and sticking with the password theme), consider a class that you write as a component that provides methods for verifying the strength of a password on the client. You create this class in a similar way as discussed previously. However, you have a couple additional items to consider.

First, when you define the class constructor, you should make sure to initialize the base constructor in the base class. The following code shows an example:

```
Type.registerNamespace("AjaxEnabled");

//create constructor
AjaxEnabled.PasswordStrengthComponent = function() {
    AjaxEnabled.PasswordStrengthComponent.initializeBase(this);
}
```

Next, you might consider overriding the base class's methods. When you do so, you should also make sure to call the methods of the base class you are overriding. You can do so by calling the method *callBaseMethod* (of the *Type* class). As an example, if you override the *initialize* method of the base class, you should write the following code to call its *base init* method:

```
initialize: function() {
  AjaxEnabled.PasswordStrengthComponent.callBaseMethod(this, 'initialize');
  //add custom initialization here
}
```

Finally, when you register the actual component you must indicate that you are inheriting from the *Sys.Component* base class. The following shows an example of the *registerClass* method indicating inheritance of the *Component* class:

```
//register class as a Sys.Component
AjaxEnabled.PasswordStrengthComponent.registerClass(
  'AjaxEnabled.PasswordStrengthComponent', Sys.Component);
```

> ***NOTE*** **ADDING A REFERENCE TO THE AJAX LIBRARY**
>
> **When working with JavaScript files in the code editor, you can add a reference to the AJAX Library. This will ensure your coding gets IntelliSense for the library. This is similar to the *using* statement in C# and the *imports* statement in Visual Basic. You embed this reference in a comment at the top of your .js file. The following shows an example:**
>
> ```
> /// <reference name="MicrosoftAjax.js"/>
> ```

Using the client component is the same as using another AJAX Library class. You first register it with the *ScriptManager*. You can then create an instance of it in your page and work with it as you would any other AJAX class (as discussed earlier). The first lab at the end of this lesson walks through creating this component and working with it on an .aspx page.

Creating an AJAX Client Control

An AJAX client control is a control that you write that is meant to provide additional, client-side functionality to a DOM element (like a button or an input box). A client control is meant to work as a single, encapsulated control much the same way as the ASP.NET server controls or custom controls you would write. It is possible, however, to attach an AJAX client control to an existing DOM element or server control without creating a custom control. The more robust scenario is to create a custom server control that embeds the AJAX client control to provide additional features. This section explores both of these options.

NOTE AJAX TEMPLATES

Visual Studio ships with a few item templates that can help you get started with creating AJAX-enabled controls. This includes the templates *AJAX Client Control*, *AJAX Client Behavior*, and *AJAX Client Library*. Each of these stub out some code to get you started building a component, control, or behavior.

AJAX client controls extend the functionality of a DOM element. Therefore, you must provide a means to indicate the DOM element the AJAX control is meant to extend. This can be done in the constructor. For example, consider a password strength control that works with a text box to turn the text box different colors as the user types. These colors are based on the strength of the password after each key press. To start this control, you might define the following constructor:

```
//define the namespace
Type.registerNamespace('AjaxEnabled');

//create constructor
AjaxEnabled.PassTextBox = function(element) {
  AjaxEnabled.PassTextBox.initializeBase(this, [element]);

  this._weakCssClass = null;
  this._mediumCssClass = null;
  this._strongCssClass = null;

}
```

Notice that the constructor takes the parameter *element*. This represents the DOM element the control is meant to extend. The first line of the constructor calls the *initialize* method of the base class (*Sys.UI.Control*) and passes an instance of this class and a reference to the element being extended by this class.

The next step is to define the class itself. This is the same as creating AJAX classes, which we discussed previously. However, most client controls you write will intercept events fired from the given DOM element they intend to extend. They can also raise their own events to be used by the client. To enable this, you need to override the *initialize* method of the *Sys.UI.Control* base class. The following code shows an example of this function inside the class's *prototype*:

```
//initialize the UI control
initialize: function() {
  AjaxEnabled.PassTextBox.callBaseMethod(this, 'initialize');

  this._onKeyupHandler = Function.createDelegate(this, this._onKeyup);
  $addHandlers(this.get_element(), {'keyup' : this._onKeyup}, this);
},
```

Notice the first line in the code just given. Here you indicate that the *initialize* method should also call the base class's *initialize* method. The next line creates a delegate to the method *onKeyup* that you define in your class. You then register this method as a handler for the element. The *$addHandlers* method does this. The first parameter is the DOM element for which you wish to intercept events. You can call the method *get_element* to return the element associated with the class (from the constructor). The next parameter to the *$addHandlers* call is an array of the events you wish to intercept. Each event is referenced by name followed by the name of the method in your class you wish to have called when the event fires. In the final parameter you pass an instance of the running class.

In addition to the *initialize* event, you will also want to override *dispose* to clean things up. For example, you might want to remove the event handlers you added during *initialize*. Of course, here, too, you want to make sure to call the base class's *dispose* method. The following shows an example of doing both these things:

```
dispose: function() {
  $clearHandlers(this.get_element());
  AjaxEnabled.PassTextBox.callBaseMethod(this, 'dispose');
},
```

The next step is to define code for the events you intend to intercept. You do so by creating a function (named the same as the event you indicated in the *createDelegate* and *$addHandlers* calls) that takes a single parameter as the event arguments. Inside the event you have access to the DOM element the control extends through the call, *this.get_element()*. The following code shows an example of the intercepted *keypress* event to be called when a user types in a text box:

```
//define key press event
_onKeyup : function(e) {

  //get password text
  var pass = this.get_element().value;
  var strength = this.returnPasswordStrength(pass);

  switch (strength) {
    case "Weak":
      this.get_element().className = this._weakCssClass;
      break;
    case "Medium":
      this.get_element().className = this._mediumCssClass;
      break;
    case "Strong":
      this.get_element().className = this._strongCssClass;
      break;
  }
},
```

The next step is to finish out the class definition by creating your properties and methods. For the example, these items are covered in the Lab 2 of this lesson.

Finally, you register the class with the AJAX Library. When doing so, you indicate that the class inherits *Sys.UI.Control*. The following code shows an example:

```
//register class as a Sys.Control
AjaxEnabled.PassTextBox.registerClass('AjaxEnabled.PassTextBox', Sys.UI.Control);

//notify loaded
if (typeof(Sys) !== 'undefined') Sys.Application.notifyScriptLoaded();
```

Once complete (see Lab 2 later in this lesson for a complete class listing), you can use the class on a page. You have two options for doing so: registering the class on the page through JavaScript, or creating a custom control to encapsulate this client control. The following sections look at both options.

USING AN AJAX CLIENT CONTROL ON A PAGE

You can use the client control with existing ASP.NET controls and DOM elements by directly accessing it on your page. To do so, you must first add a *ScriptManager* control to your page. Inside it, you reference the script that contains your client control. The following code shows an example of this for the password strength control discussed earlier:

```
<asp:ScriptManager ID="ScriptManager1" runat="server">
  <Scripts>
    <asp:ScriptReference Path="PasswordStrength.js" />
  </Scripts>
</asp:ScriptManager>
```

You also need to add the DOM element you intend to extend to the page. This is as straightforward as adding a control to the page. The password strength example is meant to work with a text box. Therefore, you can add either an *<input />* box or an *<asp:TextBox />* control to the page. The following shows an example of the latter:

```
<asp:TextBox ID="TextBoxPass" runat="server" TextMode="Password"></asp:TextBox>
```

The final step is to create an instance of the client control and connect it to the DOM element. You will typically perform such actions inside the application *init* method of the AJAX Library. Therefore, you must create an override for this method. Inside the override, you use the *$create* method (a shortcut to *Sys.Component.create*) to both create an instance of your AJAX client control and connect that instance with the DOM element. The *$create* method has five parameters, as follows:

- ***type*** This parameter indicates the class instance you intend to create.
- ***properties*** This parameter is used to indicate properties and property values of the class instance that should be set when the item is created.
- ***events*** This parameter is used to indicate the events you intend to register from the client code to the client control.

- ***references*** This parameter indicates references to other components.
- ***element*** This parameter is used to indicate the DOM element to which your client control should be attached.

The following code shows a call to the *$create* method for the password strength control. Complete Lab 2 of this lesson to see the control in action.

```
<script language="javascript" type="text/javascript">

  var app = Sys.Application;
  app.add_init(appInit);

  function appInit(sender, args) {

    $create(AjaxEnabled.PassTextBox,
      {weakCssClass : 'weak', mediumCssClass : 'medium', strongCssClass : 'strong'},
      null, null, $get('TextBoxPass'));

  }

</script>
```

ENCAPSULATING AN AJAX CLIENT CONTROL INTO A CUSTOM SERVER CONTROL

A more robust solution for creating AJAX-enabled controls is to embed your client-side functionality into a custom control. Custom controls are covered in depth in Chapter 10, "Creating Custom Web Controls." You might want to skip ahead (and come back) if you need a quick overview of custom controls.

To create a custom control that embeds your client script, you must define a server-side class and use it to write the custom control. This class can be part of your Web site in the *App_Code* directory or can be embedded in its own assembly. The latter option allows you to isolate the control from the Web site and even use it across Web sites. The former option is great for dynamically compiling your control and deploying it on the code files associated with it (and not the .dll of a component).

The class itself must inherit from a control. This can be either an existing control you intend to extend or a base control (like *System.Web.UI.Control*). The control must also implement the interface *IScriptControl.* This interface is used to implement methods to embed your JavaScript in the control. The following code example shows the password strength example control inheriting from *TextBox* and implementing the *IScriptControl* interface:

```
'VB
Namespace AjaxEnabled

  Public Class PassTextBox
    Inherits TextBox
    Implements IScriptControl
    ...
```

```
//C#
namespace AjaxEnabled
{
  public class PassTextBoxCs : TextBox, IScriptControl
  {
    ...
```

The next step is to create a class-level variable to represent the *ScriptManager* that works with the control. You can declare this variable and then override the *OnPreRender* event of the control to set its value. You do so by calling the static method *ScriptManager.GetCurrent* and passing in the page containing the given control. The following shows an example:

```
'VB
Private _sMgr As ScriptManager
Protected Overrides Sub OnPreRender(ByVal e As EventArgs)
  If Not Me.DesignMode Then

    'test for the existence of a ScriptManager
    _sMgr = ScriptManager.GetCurrent(Page)

    If _sMgr Is Nothing Then _
        Throw New HttpException( _
        "A ScriptManager control must exist on the page.")

    _sMgr.RegisterScriptControl(Me)
  End If

  MyBase.OnPreRender(e)
End Sub

//C#
private ScriptManager sMgr;
protected override void OnPreRender(EventArgs e)
{
  if (!this.DesignMode)
  {
    //test for the existence of a ScriptManager
    sMgr = ScriptManager.GetCurrent(Page);

    if (sMgr == null)
      throw new HttpException(
        "A ScriptManager control must exist on the page.");

    sMgr.RegisterScriptControl(this);
  }
```

```
  base.OnPreRender(e);
}
```

Next, you define properties of the control that you intend users to set. In the password example, there are properties defined for the three style class names that should be set on the text box for each of the password strengths (weak, medium, and strong). You can add fields or properties to the server control to represent these items. You then create a *GetScript-Descriptors* method to map these properties or fields to properties of the control. The following shows an example:

```
'VB
Public WeakCssClass As String
Public MediumCssClass As String
Public StrongCssClass As String

Protected Overridable Function GetScriptDescriptors() _
  As IEnumerable(Of ScriptDescriptor)

  Dim descriptor As ScriptControlDescriptor = _
    New ScriptControlDescriptor("AjaxEnabled.PassTextBox", Me.ClientID)

  descriptor.AddProperty("weakCssClass", Me.WeakCssClass)
  descriptor.AddProperty("mediumCssClass", Me.MediumCssClass)
  descriptor.AddProperty("strongCssClass", Me.StrongCssClass)

  Return New ScriptDescriptor() {descriptor}

End Function

//C#
public string WeakCssClass;
public string MediumCssClass;
public string StrongCssClass;

protected virtual IEnumerable<ScriptDescriptor> GetScriptDescriptors()
{
  ScriptControlDescriptor descriptor =
    new ScriptControlDescriptor("AjaxEnabled.PassTextBox", this.ClientID);

  descriptor.AddProperty("weakCssClass", this.WeakCssClass);
  descriptor.AddProperty("mediumCssClass", this.MediumCssClass);
  descriptor.AddProperty("strongCssClass", this.StrongCssClass);

  return new ScriptDescriptor[] { descriptor };
}
```

You must also register the actual JavaScript code to be used by your control. You do so by writing a *GetScriptReferences* method. This method references the .js file that you intend to extend your custom control. There are two ways to implement this method: one for controls in the *App_Code* directory of the Web site and another for controls you create as stand-alone assemblies. The following code shows an example of the former, a custom control created in the Web site's *App_Code* directory and referencing a JavaScript file in the same Web site:

```
'VB
Protected Overridable Function GetScriptReferences() _
  As IEnumerable(Of ScriptReference)

  Dim reference As ScriptReference = New ScriptReference()
  reference.Path = ResolveClientUrl("PasswordStrength.js")

  Return New ScriptReference() {reference}

End Function

//C#
protected virtual IEnumerable<ScriptReference> GetScriptReferences()
{
  ScriptReference reference = new ScriptReference();
  reference.Path = ResolveClientUrl("PasswordStrength.js");

  return new ScriptReference[] { reference };
}
```

The latter method, embedding the control in its own assembly, is covered in Lab 3 at the end of this lesson.

To use the custom control, you register it with the page and then define its tag. For example, to use the password strength custom control created inside the *App_Code* directory, you add the following directive to the top of your Web page source:

```
<%@ Register Namespace="AjaxEnabled" TagPrefix="AjaxEnabled" %>
```

You then add a *ScriptManager* to your page. You can then define the control's markup as you would any other server control. The following shows the control in the example. Notice that the three properties of the control that manage the style of the text box are being set declaratively to style class names defined elsewhere on the page.

```
<asp:ScriptManager ID="ScriptManager1" runat="server">
</asp:ScriptManager>

<AjaxEnabled:PassTextBox ID="textbox1" runat="server"
  TextMode="Password" WeakCssClass="weak" MediumCssClass="medium"
  StrongCssClass="strong"></AjaxEnabled:PassTextBox>
```

Creating an AJAX Behavior for Client Controls

Fortunately, an AJAX behavior client control works in much the same way an AJAX client control does. The biggest distinction is that behaviors are meant to be more general and are created to extend one or more controls (and not to be embedded as their own, single UI control). Behaviors are meant to be applied to a DOM element at design time and thus extend the behavior of the controls to which it is applied.

For the most part, you write a behavior control as you would a client control. You write a JavaScript file that provides extensions to a control. However, you inherit from *Sys.UI.Behavior* instead of *Sys.UI.Control.*

ENCAPSULATING THE AJAX BEHAVIOR AS AN EXTENDER CONTROL

The bigger difference between client and behavior controls, although slight, comes in how you use the control. Rather than creating a custom control based on a single Web control (as discussed in the prior section), a custom behavior control inherits from the *ExtenderControl* class. In addition, when you define the class, you add the attribute *TargetControlType* to the class definition. This allows users of the control to set the control they want extended during design time. The following shows a basic class definition of a custom extender control.

```
'VB
<TargetControlType(GetType(Control))> _
Public Class MyExtender
  Inherits ExtenderControl

End Class

//C#
[TargetControlType(typeof(Control))]
public class MyExtender : ExtenderControl
{

}
```

From there, you use the same methods to build out the rest of the control as discussed when building out an AJAX custom server control previously. This includes a call to *GetScriptReferences* to set a reference to the AJAX behavior class used by the custom control.

USING THE AJAX BEHAVIOR

The AJAX behavior is encapsulated in a custom control that inherits from the *ExtenderControl* class. You therefore use the control as you would any other custom control (as discussed previously). You first register the control on the page using the @ *Register* directive. You then define an instance of the control in your markup. Because it is an extender control, however, you must also define the control it extends by setting the control's *TargetControlId* property to the ID of another control on the page. This indicates the control to which you wish to provide additional behavior. The following provides an example of what the markup looks like:

```
<asp:Button ID="Button1" runat="server" Text="Button" />

<ajaxEnabled: MyExtender runat="server"
    ID=" MyExtender1" TargetControlID="Button1"
    PropertyCssClass="MyCssClassName"/>
```

LAB 1 Create and Use an AJAX Component

In this lab, you create an AJAX client component. This component does not have a UI. Rather, it is meant to be used to provide additional functionality to the pages that leverage it. In the second exercise, you register and use the component on a page.

If you encounter a problem completing an exercise, the completed projects are available in the sample files installed from the companion CD in the Code folder.

EXERCISE 1 Create the AJAX Component

In this exercise, you create a new ASP.NET Web site and add a client component inside a JavaScript file. The client component defines a method for determining a password's strength.

1. Open Visual Studio and create a new ASP.NET Web site named **AjaxEnabled** in either C# or Visual Basic.
2. Add a new JavaScript file to the site. Right-click the Web site and select Add New Item. In the Add New Item dialog box, select AJAX Client Library. Name the file **PasswordStrengthComponent.js**.
3. Open the newly created JavaScript file. At the top of the file, add code to register a new namespace. The following shows an example:

   ```
   Type.registerNamespace("AjaxEnabled");
   ```

4. Next, define the constructor for your JavaScript class as a function. This is a simple AJAX component so not much happens here. The following shows an example:

   ```
   //create constructor
   AjaxEnabled.PasswordStrengthComponent = function() {
       AjaxEnabled.PasswordStrengthComponent.initializeBase(this);
   }
   ```

5. The next step is to define the inside of the class. You do so by creating its prototype. Inside the prototype, declare a function called *returnPasswordStrength* that takes a password, checks its value, and returns its strength. The following shows an example class definition that also includes the *dispose* method:

   ```
   //define class
   AjaxEnabled.PasswordStrengthComponent.prototype = {
     initialize: function() {
   ```

```
    //add custom initialization here
    AjaxEnabled.PasswordStrengthComponent.callBaseMethod(this, 'initialize');
  },

  returnPasswordStrength: function(password) {
    var strPass = new String(password.toString());
    if (strPass.length < 5) {
      return "Weak";
    }
    else {
      if (strPass.length < 8) {
        return "Medium";
      }
      else {
        return "Strong";
      }
    }
  },

  dispose: function() {
    //add custom dispose actions here
    AjaxEnabled.PasswordStrengthComponent.callBaseMethod(this, 'dispose');
  }
}
```

6. Finally, add code to the class to register it with the Microsoft AJAX Library by calling the *registerClass* method of the component. Be sure to indicate that the class inherits the *Sys.Component* class from the library. The following code shows an example that includes notification to the application that the script has been fully loaded:

```
//register class as a Sys.Component
AjaxEnabled.PasswordStrengthComponent.registerClass(
  'AjaxEnabled.PasswordStrengthComponent', Sys.Component);

//notify script loaded
if (typeof(Sys) !== 'undefined') Sys.Application.notifyScriptLoaded();
```

7. Save the file. You have completed creating the component. In the next exercise, you will see how you can use this component on a Web page.

EXERCISE 2 Call the AJAX Component from a Web Page

In this exercise, you add the AJAX component created in the previous exercise to a Web page.

1. Continue editing the project you created in the previous exercise. Alternatively, you can open the completed Lesson 2, Lab 1, Exercise 1 project in the sample files installed from the CD.
2. Open the Default.aspx page in Source view.
3. Add a *ScriptManager* control from the Toolbox to the page. Inside the *ScriptManager* control, set a reference to the PasswordStrengthComponent.js file created previously. The following shows an example:

```
<asp:ScriptManager ID="ScriptManager1" runat="server">
  <Scripts>
    <asp:ScriptReference Path="~/PasswordStrengthComponent.js" />
  </Scripts>
</asp:ScriptManager>
```

4. Next, add controls to the page that represents a user login form. This includes a text box control used for entering a password. Your UI controls might look as follows:

```
<div style="font-size: large; font-weight: bold">User Login</div>
<hr />
<br />
User Name:
<br />
<asp:TextBox ID="TextBoxUserName" runat="server" Width="200"></asp:TextBox>
<br />
Password:
<br />
<asp:TextBox ID="TextBoxPassword" runat="server"
  TextMode="Password" Width="200"></asp:TextBox>
<asp:Label ID="LabelStrength" runat="server" Text=""></asp:Label>
<br />
<input id="Button1" type="button" value="Submit" />
```

5. The next step is to define JavaScript on the page that works with your client component. In this example, you create an event that fires as the user presses a key inside the Password text box. Each time, you grab the contents of the text box and verify it using the custom library you wrote. You write the results out to the screen using a label control you define on the page (*LabelStrength*, defined in the prior step). The following code, which can be placed after the *ScriptManager*, shows an example:

```
<script language="javascript" type="text/javascript">

  function _OnKeypress() {
    var checker = new AjaxEnabled.PasswordStrengthComponent();
    var pass = document.getElementById("TextBoxPassword").value;
    var strength = checker.returnPasswordStrength(pass);
```

```
        document.getElementById("LabelStrength").innerText = strength;
    }

</script>
```

6. The last step is to make sure this event is registered for the Password text box. You can do so by adding the attribute *onkeyup="_OnKeypress()"* to the *TextBoxPassword* control defined previously.
7. Finally, run your page. Enter values in the Password text box and notice how the labels change as you type. Figure 6-7 shows an example of the page running.

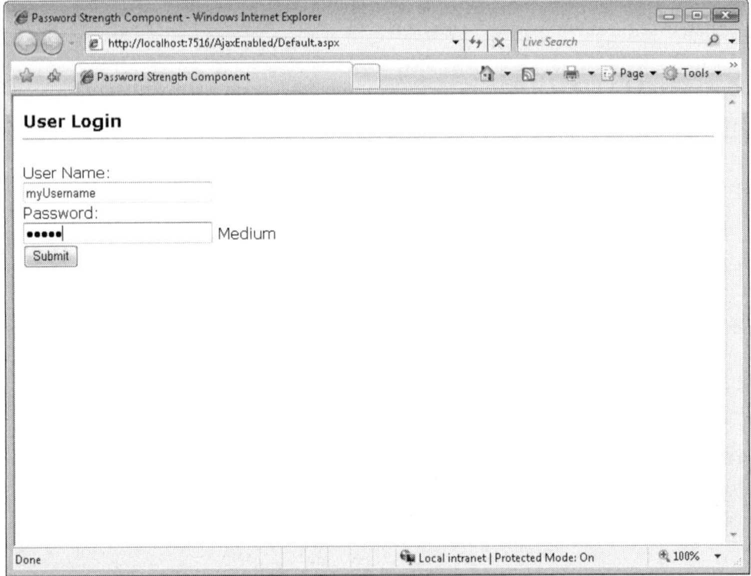

FIGURE 6-7 The AJAX password client component running in a browser

LAB 2 Create and Use an AJAX Client Control

In this lab, you create an AJAX client control that works with a text box DOM element to show users their password strength. In Exercise 2, you will add this control to a Web page and wire it to a text box. This same control is used in Lab 3, where you will wrap the control as a custom server control.

If you encounter a problem completing an exercise, the completed projects are available in the sample files installed from the companion CD in the Code folder.

EXERCISE 1 Create an AJAX Client Control

In this exercise, you create a JavaScript file for checking password strength.

1. Open Visual Studio and create a new ASP.NET Web site named **AjaxEnabled** (if you have a conflict with the Web site you created in Lab 1, place this project in a different folder) in either C# or Visual Basic.
2. Add a new JavaScript file to the site. Right-click the Web site and select Add New Item. In the Add New Item dialog box, select AJAX Client Control. Name the file **PassText-Box.js**.
3. Open the newly created JavaScript file. At the top of the file, modify the code to register a new namespace. The following shows an example:

```
Type.registerNamespace("AjaxEnabled");
```

4. Next, define the constructor for your JavaScript class as a function. In this case, the constructor takes the parameter *element*. This is meant to represent the DOM element that the control extends. Use this element to initialize the base class of *System.UI.Control*.

   This control will set the style of a text box based on the strength of the password. Therefore, it exposes three properties, one for each password strength. Inside the constructor, initialize the private fields used to represent these properties.

   The following shows an example of the constructor:

```
//create constructor
AjaxEnabled.PassTextBox = function(element) {
  AjaxEnabled.PassTextBox.initializeBase(this, [element]);

  this._weakCssClass = null;
  this._mediumCssClass = null;
  this._strongCssClass = null;

}
```

5. The next step is to define the inside of the class by creating its prototype. The prototype of this class will include both an *initialize* and a *dispose* method. It will also include event code called *onKeyup* that is wired to the text box *keyup* event. Finally, the code includes a number of properties for managing the setting and getting of the password style classes. The following shows an example of the prototype definition. Note: Most of this code was covered in the lesson. Refer back to the text if you have trouble following the code.

```
//define class
AjaxEnabled.PassTextBox.prototype = {

  //initialize the UI control
  initialize: function() {
    AjaxEnabled.PassTextBox.callBaseMethod(this, 'initialize');
```

```
    this._onKeyupHandler = Function.createDelegate(this, this._onKeyup);
    $addHandlers(this.get_element(), {'keyup' : this._onKeyup}, this);
  },

  dispose: function() {
    $clearHandlers(this.get_element());
    AjaxEnabled.PassTextBox.callBaseMethod(this, 'dispose');
  },

  //define key press event
  _onKeyup : function(e) {

    //get password text
    var pass = this.get_element().value;
    var strength = this.returnPasswordStrength(pass);

    switch (strength) {
      case "Weak":
        this.get_element().className = this._weakCssClass;
        break;
      case "Medium":
        this.get_element().className = this._mediumCssClass;
        break;
      case "Strong":
        this.get_element().className = this._strongCssClass;
        break;
    }
  },

  //define properties
  get_weakCssClass: function() {
    return this._weakCssClass;
  },
  set_weakCssClass: function(value) {
    this._weakCssClass = value;
  },
  get_mediumCssClass: function() {
    return this._mediumCssClass;
  },
  set_mediumCssClass: function(value) {
    this._mediumCssClass = value;
  },
  get_strongCssClass: function() {
    return this._strongCssClass;
  },
```

```
  set_strongCssClass: function(value) {
    this._strongCssClass = value;
  },

  returnPasswordStrength: function(password) {
    var strPass = new String(password.toString());
    if (strPass.length < 5) {
      return "Weak";
    }
    else {
      if (strPass.length < 8) {
        return "Medium";
      }
      else {
        return "Strong";
      }
    }
  }

}
```

6. Finally, add code to the class to register it with the Microsoft AJAX Library by calling the *registerClass* method of the component. Be sure to indicate that the class inherits the *Sys.UI.Control* class from the library. The following code shows an example that includes notification to the application that the script has been fully loaded:

```
//register class as a Sys.Control
AjaxEnabled.PassTextBox.registerClass('AjaxEnabled.PassTextBox',
  Sys.UI.Control);

//notify loaded
if (typeof(Sys) !== 'undefined') Sys.Application.notifyScriptLoaded();
```

7. Save the file. You have completed creating the AJAX UI portion of the control. In the next exercise, you will see how you can use this control on a Web page. In Lab 3, you will see how to wrap this script into a custom server control.

EXERCISE 2 Use the AJAX Client Control on a Web Page

In this exercise, you add the AJAX UI control created in the previous exercise to a Web page and connect it to a text box control.

1. Continue editing the project you created in the previous exercise. Alternatively, you can open the completed Lesson 2, Lab 2, Exercise 1 project in the sample files installed from the CD.
2. Open the Default.aspx page in Source view.

3. Add a *ScriptManager* control from the Toolbox to the page. Inside the *ScriptManager* control, set a reference to the PassTextBox.js file created previously. The following shows an example:

```
<asp:ScriptManager ID="ScriptManager1" runat="server">
  <Scripts>
    <asp:ScriptReference Path="PassTextBox.js" />
  </Scripts>
</asp:ScriptManager>
```

4. Next, add controls to the page that represents a user login form. This includes a text box control used for entering a password. Your UI controls might look as follows:

```
<div style="font-size: large; font-weight: bold">User Login</div>
<hr />
<br />
User Name:
<br />
<asp:TextBox ID="TextBoxUserName" runat="server" Width="200"></asp:TextBox>
<br />
Password:
<br />
<asp:TextBox ID="TextBoxPassword" runat="server"
  TextMode="Password" Width="200"></asp:TextBox>
<asp:Label ID="LabelStrength" runat="server" Text=""></asp:Label>
<br />
<input id="Button1" type="button" value="Submit" />
```

5. In addition, add style class definitions to the page for each of the password strengths. These will change the look of the text box based on the strength of the password. The following shows an example added to the *<head />* section of the page source:

```
<style type="text/css">
  .weak
  {
    border: thin solid #FF0000;
  }
  .medium
  {
    border: thin solid #FFFF00;
  }
  .strong
  {
    border: medium solid #008000;
  }
</style>
```

6. The next step is to define JavaScript on the page to create an instance of the AJAX UI control and connect it to the *TextBoxPassword* control. You can do so in the AJAX Library's application *initialize* event.

   When you create an instance of the control, you will want to pass in property definition settings and a reference to the text box. The following code shows an example:

```
<script language="javascript" type="text/javascript">

  var app = Sys.Application;
  app.add_init(appInit);

  function appInit(sender, args) {

    $create(AjaxEnabled.PassTextBox,
      {weakCssClass : 'weak', mediumCssClass : 'medium',
      strongCssClass : 'strong'},
      null, null, $get('TextBoxPassword'));
  }

</script>
```

7. Finally, run your page. Enter values in the Password text box and notice how the style of the text box changes as you type. Figure 6-8 shows an example of the page running. When the user enters a strong password, the text box turns green and has a thicker border.

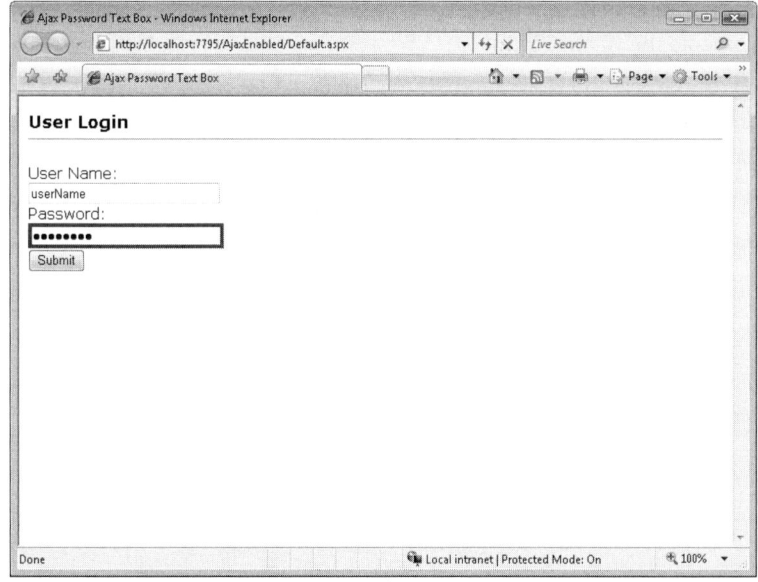

FIGURE 6-8 The AJAX password client UI control running in a browser

LAB 3 Encapsulate an AJAX Client Control as a Custom Control

In this lab, you encapsulate the AJAX UI control created in the previous example as a custom control. You then register and use it on the page.

If you encounter a problem completing an exercise, the completed projects are available in the sample files installed from the companion CD in the Code folder.

EXERCISE 1 Embed an AJAX Client Control as a Custom Control

In this exercise, you create a custom control that encapsulates the AJAX client control created in the prior lab.

Note that this lab uses the JavaScript file (PassTextBox.js) created in Lab 2.

1. Open Visual Studio and create a new ASP.NET Web site named **AjaxEnabled** (if you have a conflict, place the project in a separate folder) in either C# or Visual Basic.
2. Add a new class library to the solution (right-click the solution and choose Add New Project). Name this class library **PassTextBox**.
3. Add references to the project. Right-click the PassTextBox project and select Add Reference. On the .NET tab of the Add Reference dialog box, select the following references: *System.Drawing*, *System.Web*, and *System.Web.Extensions*. Close the dialog box.
4. Open the class file in the code editor. Set the root/default namespace of the class to **AjaxEnabled**. You can do so from the project Properties dialog box for the class library.

   Also, set the assembly name to **AjaxEnabled**. This is done through the project Properties dialog box.
5. Name the class *PassTextBox*. Indicate that the class inherits from the *TextBox* control and implements the *IScriptControl.*

   Add using (Imports in VB) statements for *System.Web.UI.WebControls*, *System.Web.UI*, and *System.Web.*

   Next, add a private variable to track a *ScriptManager* control at the class level.

   Also, add three fields to the control for managing the Password text box style properties based on password strength. The top portion of your control should now look as follows:

   ```
   'VB
   Public Class PassTextBox
     Inherits TextBox
     Implements IScriptControl

     Private _sMgr As ScriptManager


     Public WeakCssClass As String
     Public MediumCssClass As String
   ```

```
  Public StrongCssClass As String
...

//C#
public class PassTextBox : TextBox, IScriptControl
{

  private ScriptManager sMgr;

  public string WeakCssClass;
  public string MediumCssClass;
  public string StrongCssClass;
...
```

6. Next, add a method called *GetScriptDescriptors*. This method is meant to define the properties and events that work with the client control. Here, you want to add three property descriptors, one for each password strength style. The following code shows an example:

```
'VB
  Protected Overridable Function GetScriptDescriptors() _
    As IEnumerable(Of ScriptDescriptor)

    Dim descriptor As ScriptControlDescriptor = _
      New ScriptControlDescriptor("AjaxEnabled.PassTextBox", Me.ClientID)

    descriptor.AddProperty("weakCssClass", Me.WeakCssClass)
    descriptor.AddProperty("mediumCssClass", Me.MediumCssClass)
    descriptor.AddProperty("strongCssClass", Me.StrongCssClass)

    Return New ScriptDescriptor() {descriptor}

  End Function

//C#
  protected virtual IEnumerable<ScriptDescriptor> GetScriptDescriptors()
  {
    ScriptControlDescriptor descriptor =
      new ScriptControlDescriptor("AjaxEnabled.PassTextBox", this.ClientID);

    descriptor.AddProperty("weakCssClass", this.WeakCssClass);
    descriptor.AddProperty("mediumCssClass", this.MediumCssClass);
    descriptor.AddProperty("strongCssClass", this.StrongCssClass);
```

```
    return new ScriptDescriptor[] { descriptor };
  }
```

7. Now add a method called *GetScriptReference*. This method is meant to get a reference to the JavaScript that is used by this custom control. In this case, the JavaScript will be embedded in the same assembly. Therefore, add the following code:

```
'VB
  Protected Overridable Function GetScriptReferences() _
    As IEnumerable(Of ScriptReference)
    Dim reference As ScriptReference = New ScriptReference()

    reference.Assembly = "AjaxEnabled"
    reference.Name = "AjaxEnabled.PassTextBox.js"

    Return New ScriptReference() {reference}

  End Function

//C#
  protected virtual IEnumerable<ScriptReference> GetScriptReferences()
  {
    ScriptReference reference = new ScriptReference();
    reference.Assembly = "AjaxEnabled";
    reference.Name = "AjaxEnabled.PassTextBox.js";

    return new ScriptReference[] { reference };
  }
```

8. You now need to fill out the rest of this class. This code is straightforward and common to all controls of this nature. The rest of the class file reads as follows:

```
'VB

...
  Protected Overrides Sub OnPreRender(ByVal e As EventArgs)
    If Not Me.DesignMode Then

      'test for the existence of a ScriptManager
      _sMgr = ScriptManager.GetCurrent(Page)

      If _sMgr Is Nothing Then _
          Throw New HttpException( _
          "A ScriptManager control must exist on the page.")
```

```
      _sMgr.RegisterScriptControl(Me)
    End If

    MyBase.OnPreRender(e)
  End Sub

  Protected Overrides Sub Render(ByVal writer As HtmlTextWriter)
    If Not Me.DesignMode Then _
      _sMgr.RegisterScriptDescriptors(Me)
    MyBase.Render(writer)
  End Sub
  Function IScriptControlGetScriptReferences() _
    As IEnumerable(Of ScriptReference) _
    Implements IScriptControl.GetScriptReferences

    Return GetScriptReferences()

  End Function

  Function IScriptControlGetScriptDescriptors() _
    As IEnumerable(Of ScriptDescriptor) _
    Implements IScriptControl.GetScriptDescriptors

    Return GetScriptDescriptors()

  End Function

End Class

//C#

...
  protected override void OnPreRender(EventArgs e)
  {
    if (!this.DesignMode)
    {
      //test for the existence of a ScriptManager
      sMgr = ScriptManager.GetCurrent(Page);

      if (sMgr == null)
        throw new HttpException(
          "A ScriptManager control must exist on the page.");

      sMgr.RegisterScriptControl(this);
```

```
    }

    base.OnPreRender(e);
  }

  protected override void Render(HtmlTextWriter writer)
  {
    if (!this.DesignMode)
      sMgr.RegisterScriptDescriptors(this);

    base.Render(writer);
  }

  IEnumerable<ScriptReference> IScriptControl.GetScriptReferences()
  {
    return GetScriptReferences();
  }

  IEnumerable<ScriptDescriptor> IScriptControl.GetScriptDescriptors()
  {
    return GetScriptDescriptors();
  }
}
```

9. The final step is to embed your JavaScript file as a resource to this class.

First, copy the PassTextBox.js file created in the prior lab to your *PassTextBox* class library project (or get it from the sample files installed from the CD).

Second, in Solution Explorer, view properties for the PassTextBox.js file. In the Properties window, set the *Build Action* property to **Embedded Resource**.

Third, open the project's AssemblyInfo file. You might have to click the Show All Files toolbar button from Solution Explorer. In Visual Basic, you can then find this file under the My Project folder. In C# it is under a folder called Properties. Open this file and add the following Web resource assembly definition:

```
'VB
<Assembly: System.Web.UI.WebResource("AjaxEnabled.PassTextBox.js", "text/
javascript")>

//C#
[assembly: System.Web.UI.WebResource("AjaxEnabled.PassTextBox.js", "text/
javascript")]
```

10. Finally, build the project. You should now have a custom server control based on the *TextBox* class that also uses an embedded AJAX UI control targeted to work with the Microsoft AJAX Library. In the next exercise, you will see how you can use this control.

EXERCISE 2 Use the Custom AJAX Control on a Web Page

In this exercise, you add the custom AJAX control created in the previous exercise to a Web page.

1. Continue editing the project you created in the previous exercise. Alternatively, you can open the completed Lesson 2, Lab 3, Exercise 1 project in the sample files installed from the CD.
2. Open the Web site project.
3. Add a project reference to the *PassTextBox* control. Because both your Web site and your custom control are in the same solution, you can add a project reference from the Web site to the text box control by right-clicking the Web site project and choosing Add Reference. Select the Projects tab in the Add Reference dialog box and select the *PassTextBox* project.

   (If your projects are not in the same solution, you must copy the .dll files created by compiling the control in the prior exercise to the Bin directory of the Web site.)
4. Open the Default.aspx page in Source view.
5. Add a *ScriptManager* control from the Toolbox to the page. The following shows an example:

```
<asp:ScriptManager ID="ScriptManager1" runat="server">
</asp:ScriptManager>
```

6. At the top of the page, add a directive to register the custom control. This directive should point to the assembly that contains the custom control created previously.

   If you are following along closely, the name of this assembly is *AjaxEnabled*. If you went fast and perhaps missed Step 4 in Exercise 1 of this lab, your assembly might be named *PassTextBox*. You can check the Bin directory of the site to be sure.

```
<%@ Register Assembly="AjaxEnabled" Namespace="AjaxEnabled"
  TagPrefix="ajaxEnabled" %>
```

7. Next, add controls to the page that represents a user login form. These controls should be similar to those found at the end of the prior lab. This includes the style definitions set there as well.

   However, in this case, you do not define a text box and connect it to the AJAX UI control. Instead, you define an instance of the already embedded custom control as follows:

```
<ajaxEnabled:PassTextBox ID="textbox1" runat="server" width="200"
   TextMode="Password" WeakCssClass="weak" MediumCssClass="medium"
   StrongCssClass="strong"></ajaxEnabled:PassTextBox>
```

8. Finally, run your page. Enter values in the Password text box and notice how the style of the text box changes as you type.

> ***NOTE* POTENTIAL NAMESPACE CONFLICT**
>
> **If you are using C#, you might get an error due to a namespace conflict. The assembly name of the Web site and the assembly name of the control are set to the same value, *AjaxEnabled*. You can overcome this by changing the Web site's assembly name and namespace. To do so, right-click the Web site and choose Properties. Here you can set the values to these two items to *AjaxEnabled2*.**

Lesson Summary

- You can define client script for a page using the *Script* tag. You can write JavaScript inside this tag or you can use it to point to a .js file.
- The *ClientScriptManager* class is used to register client script dynamically from server-side code. An instance of this class is accessible from the *Page.ClientScript* property.
- The *ScriptManager* control can also be used to register your own custom client scripts. This is useful if you are already using this control for partial-page updates or to leverage the Microsoft AJAX Library.
- The Microsoft AJAX Library provides object-oriented support for building JavaScript code that extends the features of the client's browser. This includes a set of base classes and a framework (*Sys.*).
- There are typically three types of objects you create for use with the Microsoft Ajax Library: components, controls, and behaviors. A component is a class that has no UI. A control is typically a single control that provides AJAX capabilities. A behavior provides extended capabilities that can be attached to a control at design time.
- You can wrap an AJAX client control into a custom server control. To do so, you implement the *IScriptControl* interface.

Lesson Review

You can use the following questions to test your knowledge of the information in Lesson 2, "Creating Client Scripts with the AJAX Client-Side Library." The questions are also available on the companion CD if you prefer to review them in electronic form.

NOTE ANSWERS

Answers to these questions and explanations of why each answer choice is right or wrong are located in the "Answers" section at the end of the book.

1. Which of the following lines of JavaScript registers a new class you intend to use as an extension to a DOM element?
   - **A.** `MyNamespace.MyClass.registerClass('MyNamespace.MyClass ', Sys.UI.Control);`
   - **B.** `MyNamespace.MyClass.registerClass('MyNamespace.MyClass ', null, Sys.IDisposable);`
   - **C.** `MyNamespace.MyClass.registerClass('MyNamespace.MyClass ', null);`
   - **D.** `MyNamespace.MyClass.registerClass('MyNamespace.MyClass ', Sys.UI.Behavior);`
2. You are writing an AJAX component that does an asynchronous PostBack to the server for partial-page updates. You need your code to be notified when the partial-page response first comes back from the server. Which event should you intercept?
   - **A.** *endRequest*
   - **B.** *pageLoading*
   - **C.** *pageLoaded*
   - **D.** *beingRequest*
3. You write a JavaScript class that uses the Microsoft AJAX Library. You intend to use the class on a Web page. Which of the following actions should you take?
   - **A.** Add the following markup to the *<head />* section of the .aspx page:
     `<script src="ContosoUtilities.js" type="text/javascript"></script>`
   - **B.** Add a *ScriptManager* control to your page. It automatically finds your .js files in your solution. You can then work with them using IntelliSense.
   - **C.** Add a *ScriptManager* control to your page. Add a reference nested inside the *ScriptManager* control that points your JavaScript file.
   - **D.** Use the *ScriptReference* class in your code-behind file and set its path to the path of your .js file.
4. You wish to create a custom control that works as an AJAX client behavior. What action(s) should you take? (Choose all that apply.)
   - **A.** Create a custom, server-side class that inherits from a valid *System.Web.UI.Control.*
   - **B.** Create a custom, server-side class that inherits from *ExtenderControl.*
   - **C.** Create a custom, server-side class that implements the interface *IScriptControl.*
   - **D.** Create a custom, server-side class that is decorated with the attribute *TargetControlType.*

Chapter Review

To further practice and reinforce the skills you learned in this chapter, you can perform the following tasks:

- Review the chapter summary.
- Complete the case scenarios. These scenarios set up real-world situations involving the topics of this chapter and ask you to create solutions.
- Complete the suggested practices.
- Take a practice test.

Chapter Summary

- AJAX is a platform-independent, ECMAScript-compliant technology for communicating between code running on the client and code running on the server. ASP.NET includes both a set of server controls for working with AJAX and a set of client-side JavaScript files called the Microsoft AJAX Library.
- The *ScriptManager* (or *ScriptManagerProxy*) control is required on all pages that work with the AJAX extensions for ASP.NET and the Microsoft AJAX Library.
- ASP.NET includes a set of AJAX extension controls. These include the *UpdatePanel* control, the *UpdateProgress* control, and the *Timer* control. All of these controls are used for defining partial-page, asynchronous updates.
- The Microsoft AJAX Library allows you to build JavaScript code that extends the features of controls hosted in a browser. This includes creating components, controls, and behaviors.

Case Scenarios

In the following case scenarios, you apply what you've learned about AJAX in ASP.NET. You can find answers to these questions in the "Answers" section at the end of this book.

Case Scenario 1: Using the ASP.NET AJAX Extensions

You are an application developer for Contoso Pharmacy. You have recently converted your internal data analysis application over to an ASP.NET Web site. This has provided additional access to the application and easier deployment. However, users are trying to get used to having to search and page through data rather than having a more direct connection to it.

One complaint has been lodged about a particularly feature-rich page. This page contains multiple data grids and a number of user actions. The page can take five to ten seconds to fully load. However, once in the page, users typically work on the same page for many minutes.

In addition, the page contains a grid of data near the bottom. This grid is searchable and can only show 25 records at a time. Each search or request for an additional page of data requires a refresh of the page. Users complain they then lose the context of the page and have to scroll back down to the area in which they were working (in addition to waiting another five to ten seconds for the page to load).

You have been asked to take a look at these issues and come up with a plan.

QUESTIONS

1. What ASP.NET AJAX control could you use to stop the page from fully refreshing when users search for new data in the grid?
2. You decide to use ASP.NET AJAX to help solve some of these issues. What control must you add to the page?
3. When the page executes an asynchronous PostBack, you want to notify the user as to the progress of the PostBack. What ASP.NET control can you use to do so?

Case Scenario 2: Using the Microsoft AJAX Library

You are a developer at Fabrikam Manufacturing. Your new product that you put in the field will be Web-based. You know that users need a highly interactive client so you decide to implement ASP.NET AJAX. You have identified and plan to write the following components for the site:

- A clock that shows how long any given page on the site has been opened in the browser window
- The ability to highlight the control that has the current focus on the page
- Logic that can be used by the client to validate data including part numbers, vendor codes, and more

QUESTIONS

1. Using the Microsoft AJAX Library, how would you implement each of these in terms of component, control, or behavior?
2. Which of these features would you wrap as a custom server control and what class would you use to implement it?

Suggested Practices

To help you successfully master the exam objectives presented in this chapter, complete the following tasks.

Add Partial-Page Update Support to a Page

For this task, you should complete Practice 1 to gain experience with partial-page updates. Practice 2 shows you how you can leverage the *Timer* control. Practice 3 demonstrates the *UpdateProgress* control.

- **Practice 1** Find a page in your current Web application that uses a data grid to display data. Put this data grid into an *UpdatePanel* to enable partial-page updates when paging through the data.
- **Practice 2** Create a Web page that allows a user to cycle through a series of pictures. Use the *Timer* control to automatically update the graphic on display at periodic intervals.
- **Practice 3** Find a page in your current application that takes a long time to load and provides a lot of user interaction. Add partial-page update to this page. When the page updates, use the *UpdateProgress* control to notify the user.

Create Client Code Using the Microsoft AJAX Library

For this task, you should complete Practice 1 to learn the basics of building a control with the AJAX library. Practice 2 will give you insight into building a client behavior control.

- **Practice 1** Create an AJAX client control that extends an ASP.NET button with a confirmation alert window. Wrap the control as a custom server control using the *IScriptControl* interface.
- **Practice 2** Create an AJAX client behavior control that highlights a control as it receives focus. Wrap the control as a custom server control using the *ExtenderControl* class.

Take a Practice Test

The practice tests on this book's companion CD offer many options. For example, you can test yourself on just the content covered in this chapter, or you can test yourself on all the 70-562 certification exam content. You can set up the test so it closely simulates the experience of taking a certification exam, or you can set it up in study mode so you can look at the correct answers and explanations after you answer each question.

> ***MORE INFO*** **PRACTICE TESTS**
>
> **For details about all the practice test options available, see the "How to Use the Practice Tests" section in this book's Introduction.**

CHAPTER 7

Using ADO.NET, XML, and LINQ with ASP.NET

Probably the most important facet of any business application is the retrieval and storage of data. Virtually all business applications exist for the purpose of data retrieval, manipulation, and storage. Not surprisingly, this is a big topic and a big section of the Microsoft .NET Framework. The topic spans accessing and working with both connected and disconnected data using ADO.NET. This includes querying this data using the language-integrated query engine (or LINQ) built into the .NET Framework.

The first two lessons of this chapter cover ADO.NET in first disconnected and then connected scenarios. These lessons provide in-depth coverage of the core classes in ADO.NET. They also cover how you can use LINQ to work directly with this data. Figure 7-1 shows the major items covered by these lessons.

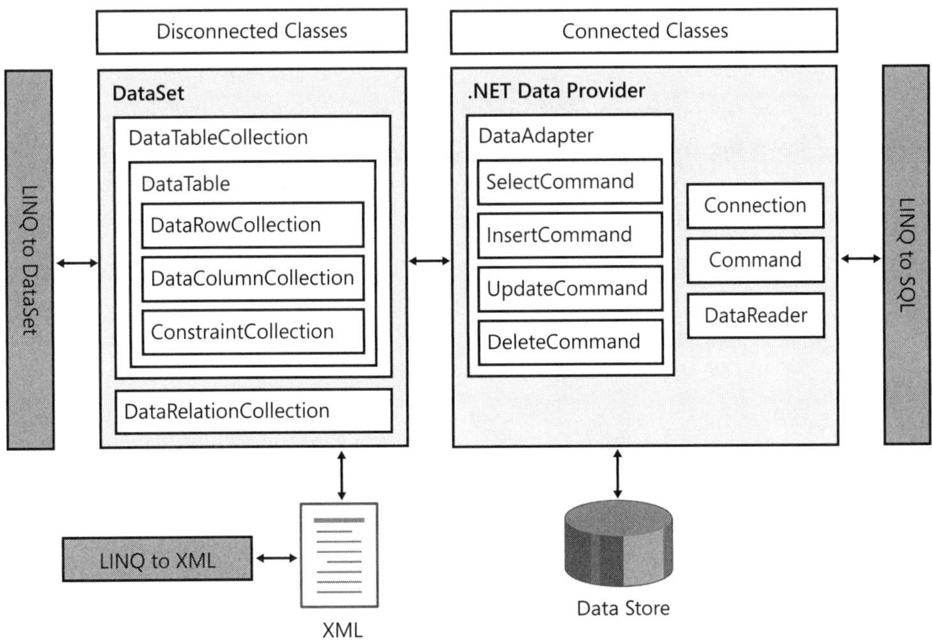

FIGURE 7-1 The major disconnected and connected classes

The final lesson of this chapter covers working with data stored as Extensible Markup Language (XML). This includes coverage of the classes that are available in the framework related to XML and their roles in providing data storage and retrieval.

Exam objectives in this chapter:

- Working with Data and Services
  - Manipulate data by using *DataSet* and *DataReader* objects.
  - Read and write XML data.

Lessons in this chapter:

Before You Begin

To complete the lessons in this chapter, you should be familiar with developing applications with Microsoft Visual Studio using Visual Basic or C#. In addition, you should be comfortable with all of the following:

- The Visual Studio 2008 Integrated Development Environment (IDE).
- Having Microsoft SQL Server Express Edition installed.
- SQL Server.
- A basic understanding of Hypertext Markup Language (HTML) and client-side scripting with the JavaScript language.
- Building a Web form by adding Web server controls to a Web page and programming against them on the server.

Lesson 1: Using the ADO.NET Disconnected Classes

This lesson covers using the disconnected data access classes like *DataTable* and *DataSet* within a Web application. These classes can be created from data stored inside a database or another data store. The key is that once created, they are disconnected from the underlying data store that was used to create them. You can also use these disconnected classes without actually connecting to a data store. However, this is not a common scenario.

This lesson starts by covering the *DataTable* object, as it is a core class when working with disconnected data. From there, you examine the *DataSet* and the *DataTableReader classes.* Finally, you will see how you can use LINQ to *DataSet* to write queries against disconnected data.

After this lesson, you will be able to:

- Work with the following disconnected data classes in your Web application:
  - *DataTable*
  - *DataColumn*
  - *DataRow*
  - *DataView*
  - *DataSet*
- Serialize (and deserialize) *DataSets* to and from XML.
- Use LINQ to *DataSet* to query against disconnected data using Visual Basic or C#.

Estimated lesson time: 60 minutes

Getting Started with the *DataTable* Object

The *DataTable* object represents tabular data as rows, columns, and constraints. Use the *DataTable* object to hold data in memory while performing disconnected data operations. You typically get a *DataTable* object by connecting to the database and returning table data (more on this in the next lesson).

However, the *DataTable* object can be explicitly created by instantiating the *DataTable* class. You then add *DataColumn* objects to the class to define the type of data to be held by the class instance. The *DataColumn* objects also contain *constraints,* which maintain data integrity by limiting the data that can be placed into a column.

Once the *DataTable* is defined with columns, you can add *DataRow* objects that contain data for the table. These rows must meet any constraints you define on the table. The following code is a function that creates and returns an empty employee *DataTable* that includes *DataColumn* objects:

```
'VB
Private Function GetDataTable() As DataTable
  'Create the DataTable named "Employee"
  Dim employee As New DataTable("Employee")

  'Add the DataColumn using all properties
  Dim eid As New DataColumn("Eid")
  eid.DataType = GetType(String)
  eid.MaxLength = 10
  eid.Unique = True
  eid.AllowDBNull = False
  eid.Caption = "EID"
  employee.Columns.Add(eid)

  'Add the DataColumn using defaults
  Dim firstName As New DataColumn("FirstName")
  firstName.MaxLength = 35
  firstName.AllowDBNull = False
  employee.Columns.Add(firstName)
  Dim lastName As New DataColumn("LastName")
  lastName.AllowDBNull = False
  employee.Columns.Add(lastName)

  'Add the decimal DataColumn using defaults
  Dim salary As New DataColumn("Salary", GetType(Decimal))
  salary.DefaultValue = 0.0
  employee.Columns.Add(salary)

  'Derived column using expression
  Dim lastNameFirstName As New DataColumn("LastName and FirstName")
  lastNameFirstName.DataType = GetType(String)
  lastNameFirstName.MaxLength = 70
  lastNameFirstName.Expression = "lastName + ', ' + firstName"
  employee.Columns.Add(lastNameFirstName)

  Return employee
End Function

//C#
private DataTable GetDataTable()
{
  //Create the DataTable named "employee"
  DataTable employee = new DataTable("Employee");

  //Add the DataColumn using all properties
  DataColumn eid = new DataColumn("Eid");
```

```
    eid.DataType = typeof(string);
    eid.MaxLength = 10;
    eid.Unique = true;
    eid.AllowDBNull = false;
    eid.Caption = "EID";
    employee.Columns.Add(eid);

    //Add the DataColumn using defaults
    DataColumn firstName = new DataColumn("FirstName");
    firstName.MaxLength = 35;
    firstName.AllowDBNull = false;
    employee.Columns.Add(firstName);
    DataColumn lastName = new DataColumn("LastName");
    lastName.AllowDBNull = false;
    employee.Columns.Add(lastName);

    //Add the decimal DataColumn using defaults
    DataColumn salary = new DataColumn("Salary", typeof(decimal));
    salary.DefaultValue = 0.00m;
    employee.Columns.Add(salary);

    //Derived column using expression
    DataColumn lastNameFirstName = new DataColumn("LastName and FirstName");
    lastNameFirstName.DataType = typeof(string);
    lastNameFirstName.MaxLength = 70;
    lastNameFirstName.Expression = "lastName + ', ' + firstName";
    employee.Columns.Add(lastNameFirstName);

    return employee;
}
```

In this example, each *DataColumn* object is defined as a *DataType* of *string*, except *salary*, which is a *decimal* object for containing currency values. The *MaxLength* property constrains the length of the string data. The string data is truncated if you exceed this length and no exception will be thrown.

There are a number of other *DataColumn* properties set in this example. If the *Unique* property of the *DataColumn* is set to *True*, an index is created to prevent duplication of entries in the *DataTable*. The *AllowDBNull* property is set to *False* to mandate the population of the column with data. The *Caption* property is a string that holds the column heading that is to be displayed when this *DataTable* object is used with Web server controls.

The *lastNameFirstName DataColumn* object shows how an expression column is created. In this case, it does so by assigning an expression. *Expression columns* are also known as calculated or derived columns. Adding a derived column is especially beneficial when data is available but not in the correct format.

The following is a list of the default values for *DataColumn* properties if you create a *DataColumn* without specifying a value for a given property:

- ***DataType*** *String*
- ***MaxLength*** –1, which means that no maximum length check is performed
- ***Unique*** *False*, which allows duplicate values
- ***AllowDBNull*** *True*, which means that the *DataColumn* does not need to have a value
- ***Caption*** The *DataColumn* object, which is the *ColumnName* property value

Creating Primary Key Columns

The *primary key* of a *DataTable* object consists of one or more columns that define data that represent a unique identity for each row in the data. In the employee example, the employee identification (*Eid*) is considered to be a unique key that can be used to retrieve the data for a given employee. The following code shows how to set the *PrimaryKey* property for the employee *DataTable* object:

```
'VB
'Set the Primary Key
employee.PrimaryKey = new DataColumn(){eid}

//C#
//Set the Primary Key
employee.PrimaryKey = new DataColumn[] {eid};
```

In some scenarios, a unique key might require combining two or more fields to achieve uniqueness. For example, a sales order typically contains line items. The primary key for each of the line item rows would typically be a combination of the order number and the line number. The *PrimaryKey* property must be set to an array of *DataColumn* objects to accommodate composite (multiple) keys.

Adding Data with *DataRow* Objects

After the *DataTable* is created with its schema, the *DataTable* is populated by adding *DataRow* objects. You create a *DataRow* object by using a *DataTable* instance. This ensures the *DataRow* conforms to the constraints of the given *DataTable* object's columns.

ADDING DATA TO THE *DATATABLE*

The *DataTable* object contains a *Rows* collection, which contains a collection of *DataRow* objects. You can insert data into the *Rows* collection by using the *Add* method on the *Rows* collection or by using the *Load* method on the *DataTable* object.

The *Add* method contains an overload that accepts an array of objects instead of a *DataRow* object. The array of objects must match the quantity and data types of *DataColumn* objects in the *DataTable*.

The *Load* method can be used to update existing *DataRow* objects or load new *DataRow* objects. The *PrimaryKey* property must be set so the *DataTable* object can locate the *DataRow* that is to be updated. The *Load* method expects an array of objects and a *LoadOption* enumeration value that has one of the following values:

- ***OverwriteChanges*** Overwrites the original *DataRowVersion* and the current *DataRowVersion* and changes the *RowState* to *Unchanged*. New rows also have the *RowState* of *Unchanged*.
- ***PreserveChanges* (default)** Overwrites the original *DataRowVersion*, but does not modify the current *DataRowVersion*. New rows have the *RowState* of *Unchanged* as well.
- ***Upsert*** Overwrites the current *DataRowVersion*, but does not modify the original *DataRowVersion*. New rows have the *RowState* of *Added*. Rows that had a *RowState* of *Unchanged* have the *RowState* of *Unchanged* if the current *DataRowVersion* is the same as the original *DataRowVersion*, but if they are different, the *RowState* is *Modified*.

The following code demonstrates the methods of creating and adding data to the employee *DataTable*:

```
'VB
'Add New DataRow by creating the DataRow first
Dim newemployee As DataRow = employee.NewRow()
newemployee("Eid") = "123456789A"
newemployee("FirstName") = "Nancy"
newemployee("LastName") = "Davolio"
newemployee("Salary") = 10.0
employee.Rows.Add(newemployee)

'Add New DataRow by simply adding the values
employee.Rows.Add("987654321X", "Andrew", "Fuller", 15.0)

'Load DataRow, replacing existing contents, if existing
employee.LoadDataRow( _
  New Object() {"987654321X", "Janet", "Leverling", 20.0}, _
  LoadOption.OverwriteChanges)

//C#
//Add New DataRow by creating the DataRow first
DataRow newemployee = employee.NewRow();
newemployee["Eid"] = "123456789A";
newemployee["FirstName"] = "Nancy";
newemployee["LastName"] = "Davolio";
newemployee["Salary"] = 10.00m;
employee.Rows.Add(newemployee);

//Add New DataRow by simply adding the values
```

```
employee.Rows.Add("987654321X", "Andrew", "Fuller", 15.00m);

//Load DataRow, replacing existing contents, if existing
employee.LoadDataRow(
  new object[] { "987654321X", "Janet", "Leverling", 20.00m },
  LoadOption.OverwriteChanges);
```

This code adds new *DataRow* objects to the employee *DataTable*. The first example explicitly creates a new *DataRow* using the *NewRow* method on the employee *DataTable*. The next example adds a new *DataRow* by simply passing the values into the *employee.Rows.Add* method. Remember that nothing has been permanently stored to a database. We cover that scenario in the next lesson.

BINDING TO THE *DATATABLE*

A *DataTable* object can be bound to any data-bound control by assigning it to the *DataSource* property of the data-bound control and executing the *DataBind* method of the control. Data binding is covered in Chapter 8, "Working with Data Source and Data-Bound Controls." Figure 7-2 shows the employee *DataTable* rendered in a browser.

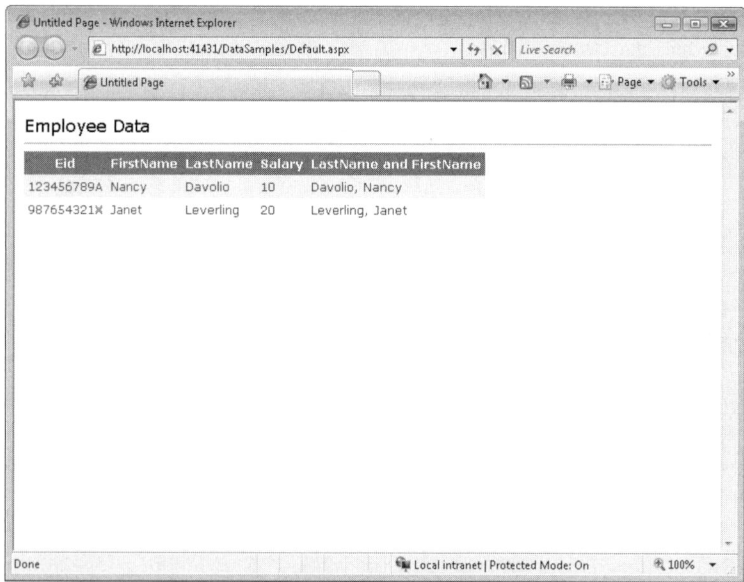

FIGURE 7-2 The employee *DataTable* object is bound to a *GridView* control

USING *DATAROWSTATE* WITH THE *DATAROW* OBJECT

The DataRow has a RowState property that can be viewed and filtered at any time and can be any of the following DataRowState enumeration values:

- ***Detached*** *DataRow* is created but not added to a *DataTable*.
- ***Added*** *DataRow* is added to a *DataTable*.

- ***Unchanged*** *DataRow* has not changed since the last call to the *AcceptChanges* method. The *DataRow* changes to this state when the *AcceptChanges* method is called.
- ***Modified*** *DataRow* has been modified since the last time the AcceptChanges method was called.
- ***Deleted*** *DataRow* is deleted using the *Delete* method of the *DataRow.*

Figure 7-3 shows the *RowState* transitions at different times in the *DataRow* object's life.

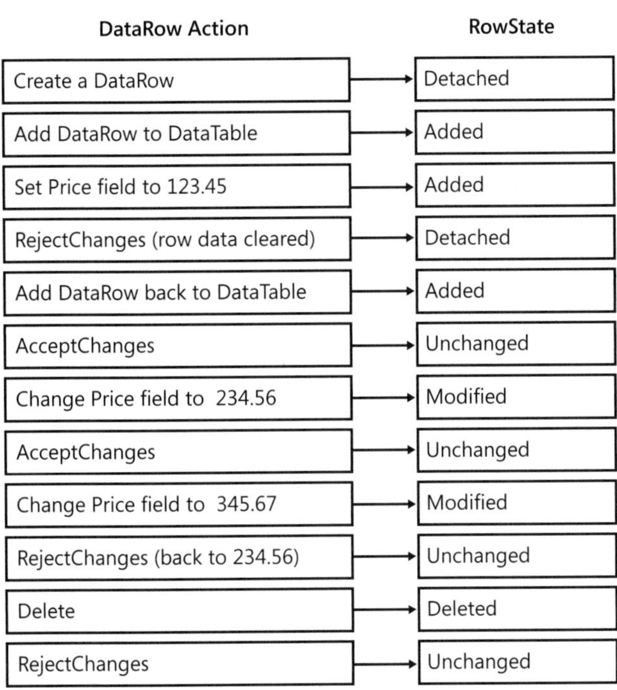

FIGURE 7-3 The *RowState* changes during the lifetime of a *DataRow* object

Notice that, after the *Price* is assigned a value of 123.45, the *RowState* does not change to *Modified.* The *RowState* is still *Added* because *RowState* is an indicator of an action required to send an update of this data to the database. The fact that 123.45 was placed into the *Price* field is not as important as the fact that a *DataRow* needs to be added to the database.

HOLDING MULTIPLE COPIES OF DATA WITH THE *DATAROWVERSION*

The *DataRow* object can hold up to three versions, or copies, of the data: Original, Current, and Proposed. When the *DataRow* is created, it contains a single copy of the data, which is the Current version. When the *DataRow* is placed into edit mode by executing its *BeginEdit* method, changes to the data are placed in a second version of the data, called the Proposed version. When the *EndEdit* method is executed, the Current version becomes the Original version, the Proposed version becomes the Current version, and the Proposed version no longer exists. After *EndEdit* has completed its execution, there are two versions of the *DataRow* data: Original and Current. If the *BeginEdit* method is called again, the Current version of the data is copied to a third version of the data, which is the Proposed version. Calling *EndEdit* again causes the Proposed version to become the Current version and the Proposed version to no longer exist.

When you retrieve data from the *DataRow*, the *DataRowVersion* you want to retrieve can also be specified as follows:

- ***Current*** This is the current value of the *DataRow*, even after changes have been made. This version exists in all situations, except when the *RowState* property is *Deleted*. If you attempt to retrieve the *Current* version and the *RowState* is *Deleted*, an exception is thrown.
- ***Default*** If the *RowState* is *Added* or *Modified*, the default version is *Current*. If the *RowState* is *Deleted*, an exception is thrown. If the *BeginEdit* method has been executed, the default version is *Proposed*.
- ***Original*** This is the value at the time the last *AcceptChanges* method was executed. If the *AcceptChanges* method was never executed, the Original version is the value that was originally loaded into the *DataRow*. Note that this version is not populated until the *RowState* becomes *Modified*, *Unchanged*, or *Deleted*. If the *RowState* is *Deleted*, this information is still retrievable. If the *RowState* is *Added*, a *VersionNotFoundException* is thrown.
- ***Proposed*** This is the value at the time of editing the *DataRow*. If the *RowState* is *Deleted*, an exception is thrown. If the *BeginEdit* method has not been explicitly executed, or if *BeginEdit* was implicitly executed via editing a detached *DataRow* (an orphaned *DataRow* object that has not been added to a *DataTable* object), a *VersionNotFoundException* is thrown.

You can also query the *HasVersion* method on the *DataRow* object to test for the existence of a particular *DataRowVersion*. You can use this method to test for the existence of a *DataRowVersion* before attempting to retrieve a version that does not exist. The following code snippet demonstrates how to retrieve a string using the *RowState* and the *DataRowVersion*:

```
'VB
Private Function GetDataRowInfo( _
  ByVal row As DataRow, ByVal columnName As String) As String

  Dim retVal As String = String.Format( _
  "RowState: {0} <br />", row.RowState)

  Dim versionString As String
  For Each versionString In [Enum].GetNames( _
    GetType(DataRowVersion))
    Dim version As DataRowVersion = _
     CType([Enum].Parse(GetType(DataRowVersion), _
      versionString), DataRowVersion)
    If (row.HasVersion(version)) Then
```

```
      retVal += String.Format( _
      "Version: {0} Value: {1} <br />", _
      version, row(columnName, version))
    Else
      retVal += String.Format( _
        "Version: {0} does not exist.<br />", version)
    End If
  Next
  Return retVal
End Function
```

```
//C#
private string GetDataRowInfo(DataRow row, string columnName)
{
  string retVal = string.Format(
  "RowState: {0}<br />", row.RowState);

  foreach (string versionString in
  Enum.GetNames(typeof(DataRowVersion)))
  {
    DataRowVersion version = (DataRowVersion)Enum.Parse(
      typeof(DataRowVersion), versionString);

    if (row.HasVersion(version))
    {
      retVal += string.Format("Version: {0} Value: {1}<br />",
      version, row[columnName, version]);
    }
    else
    {
      retVal += string.Format("Version: {0} does not exist.<br />",
        version);
    }
  }
  return retVal;
}
```

RESETTING THE *ROWSTATE* WITH *ACCEPTCHANGES* AND *REJECTCHANGES*

The *AcceptChanges* method is used to reset the *DataRow* state to *Unchanged*. This method exists on the *DataRow*, *DataTable*, and *DataSet* objects. (We cover *DataSet* later in this chapter.) After data has been loaded from the database, the *RowState* property of the loaded rows is set to *Added*. Calling *AcceptChanges* on the *DataTable* resets the *RowState* of all of the *DataRow* objects to *Unchanged*. If you modify the *DataRow* objects, their *RowState* changes to *Modified*. When you are ready to save the data, you can easily query the *DataTable* object for its changes by using the *GetChanges* method on the *DataTable* object, which returns a

DataTable that is populated only with the *DataRow* objects that have changed since the last time *AcceptChanges* was executed. Only the changes need to be sent to the data store.

After the changes have been successfully sent to the data store, change the state of the *DataRow* objects to *Unchanged* by calling the *AcceptChanges* method, which indicates that the *DataRow* objects are synchronized with the data store. Note that executing the *AcceptChanges* method also causes the *DataRow* object's Current *DataRowVersion* to be copied to the *DataRow* object's Original version. Consider the following code snippet:

'VB

```
Protected Sub Button2_Click(ByVal sender As Object, _
  ByVal e As System.EventArgs) Handles Button2.Click

  'add label to form
  Dim lbl As New Label()
  lbl.Style.Add("position", "absolute")
  lbl.Style.Add("left", "275px")
  lbl.Style.Add("top", "20px")
  lbl.EnableViewState = false
  form1.Controls.Add(lbl)

  'get the first row to play with
  Dim dr As DataRow = GetDataTable().Rows(0)

  'clear the rowstate
  dr.AcceptChanges()

  'make change in a single statement
  dr("FirstName") = "Marie"

  'start making changes that may span multiple statements
  dr.BeginEdit()
  dr("FirstName") = "Marge"
  lbl.Text = GetDataRowInfo(dr, "FirstName")
  dr.EndEdit()

End Sub
```

//C#

```
protected void Button2_Click(object sender, EventArgs e)
{
  //add label to form
  Label lbl = new Label();
  lbl.Style.Add("position", "absolute");
  lbl.Style.Add("left", "275px");
  lbl.Style.Add("top", "20px");
  lbl.EnableViewState = false;
```

```
    form1.Controls.Add(lbl);

    //get the first row to play with
    DataRow dr = GetDataTable().Rows[0];

    //clear the rowstate
    dr.AcceptChanges();

    //make change in a single statement
    dr["FirstName"] = "Marie";

    //start making changes that may span multiple statements
    dr.BeginEdit();
    dr["FirstName"] = "Marge";
    lbl.Text = GetDataRowInfo(dr, "FirstName");
    dr.EndEdit();
}
```

This code starts by adding a *Label* control to the Web page that holds the results of this test. Next, the first *DataRow* object in the employee *DataTable* is retrieved. The *DataRow* has an initial *RowState* of *Added*, and the *AcceptChanges* method clears the *RowState* to *Unchanged*. Next, the *FirstName* is modified in a single statement, which causes the *RowState* to become *Modified*. At this time, the Current version contains the modified data and the Original version contains the data values that exist after the *AcceptChanges* method is executed. Next, the *BeginEdit* method is executed to place the *DataRow* in an edit mode and the *FirstName* is changed again. At this time, the Proposed version contains the current data and executing the *GetDataRowInfo* method displays the results shown in Figure 7-4.

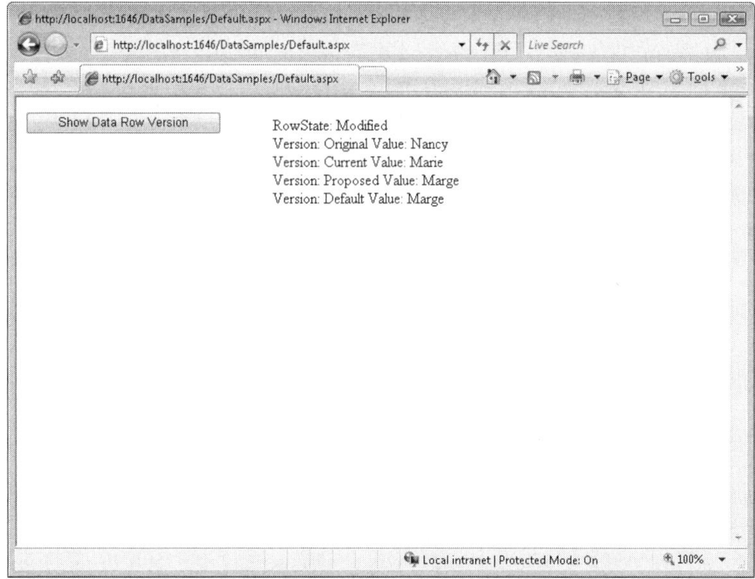

FIGURE 7-4 The *DataRow* information after making changes

The *RejectChanges* method is used to roll back the *DataRow* to the point in time when you last called the *AcceptChanges* method. The *AcceptChanges* method overwrites the Original *DataRowVersion*, which means that you cannot roll back to a point in time that is earlier than the last time *AcceptChanges* was called.

EXPLICITLY CHANGING *ROWSTATE* WITH THE *SETADDED* AND *SETMODIFIED* METHODS

The *SetAdded* and *SetModified* methods on the *DataRow* allow you to explicitly set the *RowState*. This is useful when you want to force a *DataRow* to be stored in a data store that is different from the data store from which the *DataRow* was originally loaded.

DELETING AND UNDELETING THE *DATAROW*

The *Delete* method on the *DataRow* is used to set the *RowState* of the *DataRow* to *Deleted.* A *DataRow* object that has a *RowState* of *Deleted* indicates that the row needs to be deleted from the data store.

There are many scenarios where you need to undelete a *DataRow.* The *DataRow* object doesn't have an undelete method, but you can use the *RejectChanges* method to perform an undelete that may satisfy some scenarios. The problem is that executing the *RejectChanges* method copies the Original *DataRowVersion* to the Current *DataRowVersion,* which effectively restores the *DataRow* object to its state at the time the last *AcceptChanges* method was executed. This means that any changes that were made to the data prior to deleting are lost.

Copying and Cloning the *DataTable*

You often need to create a full copy of a *DataTable* in your application, possibly to pass it to another application, or to use it as a scratch pad for operations that may be thrown out later. For example, you might want to assign a *DataTable* object to a *GridView* control to allow a user to edit the data, but you also might want to provide a cancel button that aborts all changes on the Web page. A simple way to implement this functionality is to create a copy of your *DataTable* object and use the copy for editing. If the user clicks the cancel button, the *DataTable* copy is thrown out. If the user decides to keep the changes, you can replace the original *DataTable* object with the edited copy.

To create a copy of a *DataTable* object, use the *Copy* method on the *DataTable,* which copies the *DataTable* object's schema and data. The following code snippet shows how to invoke the *Copy* method:

```
'VB
Dim copy as DataTable = employee.Copy()

//C#
DataTable copy = employee.Copy();
```

You often require a copy of the *DataTable* schema without the data. You can accomplish this by invoking the *Clone* method on the *DataTable.* Use this method when an empty copy of the *DataTable* is required and to which *DataRow* objects will be added at a later time. The following code shows the *Clone* method:

```
'VB
Dim clone as DataTable = employee.Clone()

//C#
DataTable clone = employee.Clone();
```

Importing *DataRow* Objects into a *DataTable*

The *ImportRow* method on the *DataTable* object copies a *DataRow* from a *DataTable* that has the same schema. The *ImportRow* method also imports Current and Original version data. If you attempt to import a *DataRow* that has a primary key value that already exists in the *DataTable* object, a *ConstraintException* is thrown. The following code snippet shows the process for cloning the *DataTable* and then copying a single *DataRow* to the cloned copy:

```
'VB
Dim clone as DataTable = employee.Clone()
clone.ImportRow(employee.Rows(0))

//C#
DataTable clone = employee.Clone();
clone.ImportRow(employee.Rows[0]);
```

Using the *DataTable* with XML Data

You can use the *WriteXml* method of a *DataTable* to write the contents of the *DataTable* to an XML file or stream. This method should be used with the *Server.MapPath* method to convert a simple file name to the Web site path, as shown in the following code snippet:

```
'VB
Protected Sub Button3_Click(ByVal sender As Object, _
  ByVal e As System.EventArgs) Handles Button3.Click

  Dim employee As DataTable = GetDataTable()
  employee.WriteXml(Server.MapPath("employee.xml"))
  Response.Redirect("employee.xml")

End Sub

//C#
protected void Button3_Click(object sender, EventArgs e)
{
  DataTable employee = GetDataTable();
  employee.WriteXml(Server.MapPath("employee.xml"));
  Response.Redirect("employee.xml");
}
```

When this method is executed, the Employee.xml file is produced, which looks like the following:

```
<?xml version="1.0" standalone="yes"?>
<DocumentElement>
  <Employee>
   <Eid>123456789A</Eid>
   <FirstName>Nancy</FirstName>
   <LastName>Davolio</LastName>
   <Salary>10</Salary>
   <LastName_x0020_and_x0020_FirstName>
    Davolio, Nancy
   </LastName_x0020_and_x0020_FirstName>
  </Employee>
  <Employee>
   <Eid>987654321X</Eid>
   <FirstName>Janet</FirstName>
   <LastName>Leverling</LastName>
   <Salary>20</Salary>
   <LastName_x0020_and_x0020_FirstName>
    Leverling, Janet
   </LastName_x0020_and_x0020_FirstName>
  </Employee>
</DocumentElement>
```

This example uses *DocumentElement* as the root element and uses repeating *Employee* elements for each *DataRow*. The data for each *DataRow* is nested as an element within each *Employee* element. Also, notice that an XML element name cannot have spaces, so *LastName and FirstName* is automatically encoded as (converted to) *LastName_x0020_and_x0020_FirstName*.

You can fine-tune the XML output by providing an XML schema or by setting properties on the *DataTable* and its objects. To change the name of the repeating element for the *DataRow* objects from *Employee* to *Person*, you can change the *DataTable* object's *TableName*. The *DataColumn* has a *ColumnMapping* property you can use to configure the output of each column by assigning one of the following *MappingType* enumeration values:

- ***Attribute*** Places the column data into an XML attribute.
- ***Element*** The default; places the column data into an XML element.
- ***Hidden*** The column data is not sent to the XML file.
- ***SimpleContent*** The column data is stored as text within the row's element tags and does not include element tags for the column.

To change the *Eid*, *LastName*, *FirstName*, and *Salary* to XML attributes, you can set each *DataColumn* object's *ColumnMapping* property to *MappingType.Attribute*. The *LastName and FirstName* column is an expression column, so its data does not need to be stored. Therefore, its *ColumnMapping* property can be set to *MappingType.Hidden*. The following snippets show the necessary code and the resulting XML file contents:

```
'VB
Protected Sub Button4_Click(ByVal sender As Object, _
   ByVal e As System.EventArgs) Handles Button4.Click
  Dim employee As DataTable = GetDataTable()
  employee.TableName = "Person"
  employee.Columns("Eid").ColumnMapping = MappingType.Attribute
  employee.Columns("FirstName").ColumnMapping = MappingType.Attribute
  employee.Columns("LastName").ColumnMapping = MappingType.Attribute
  employee.Columns("Salary").ColumnMapping = MappingType.Attribute
  employee.Columns("LastName and FirstName").ColumnMapping = _
    MappingType.Hidden
  employee.WriteXml(Server.MapPath("Person.xml"))
  Response.Redirect("Person.xml")
End Sub
```

```
//C#
protected void Button4_Click(object sender, EventArgs e)
{
  DataTable employee = GetDataTable();
  employee.TableName = "Person";
  employee.Columns["Eid"].ColumnMapping = MappingType.Attribute;
  employee.Columns["FirstName"].ColumnMapping = MappingType.Attribute;
  employee.Columns["LastName"].ColumnMapping = MappingType.Attribute;
  employee.Columns["Salary"].ColumnMapping = MappingType.Attribute;
  employee.Columns["LastName and FirstName"].ColumnMapping =
    MappingType.Hidden;
  employee.WriteXml(Server.MapPath("Person.xml"));
  Response.Redirect("Person.xml");
}
```

```
XML
<?xml version="1.0" standalone="yes"?>
<DocumentElement>
  <Person Eid="123456789A" FirstName="Nancy" LastName="Davolio" Salary="10" />
  <Person Eid="987654321X" FirstName="Janet" LastName="Leverling" Salary="20" />
</DocumentElement>
```

Although the resulting XML file is compact, the data types aren't saved, so all data is considered to be string data. You can use the *XmlWriteMode.WriteSchema* enumeration value to store the XML schema with the data, as shown here in bold, along with the resulting XML:

```
'VB
Protected Sub Button5_Click(ByVal sender As Object, _
  ByVal e As System.EventArgs) Handles Button5.Click
```

```
  Dim employee As DataTable = GetDataTable()
  employee.TableName = "Person"
  employee.Columns("Eid").ColumnMapping = MappingType.Attribute
  employee.Columns("FirstName").ColumnMapping = MappingType.Attribute
  employee.Columns("LastName").ColumnMapping = MappingType.Attribute
  employee.Columns("Salary").ColumnMapping = MappingType.Attribute
  employee.Columns("LastName and FirstName").ColumnMapping = _
    MappingType.Hidden
  employee.WriteXml(Server.MapPath("PersonWithSchema.xml"), _
    XmlWriteMode.WriteSchema)

  Response.Redirect("PersonWithSchema.xml")

End Sub

//C#
protected void Button5_Click(object sender, EventArgs e)
{
  DataTable employee = GetDataTable();
  employee.TableName = "Person";
  employee.Columns["Eid"].ColumnMapping = MappingType.Attribute;
  employee.Columns["FirstName"].ColumnMapping = MappingType.Attribute;
  employee.Columns["LastName"].ColumnMapping = MappingType.Attribute;
  employee.Columns["Salary"].ColumnMapping = MappingType.Attribute;
  employee.Columns["LastName and FirstName"].ColumnMapping =
    MappingType.Hidden;
  employee.WriteXml(Server.MapPath("PersonWithSchema.xml"),
    XmlWriteMode.WriteSchema);
  Response.Redirect("PersonWithSchema.xml");
}
```

XML

```
<?xml version="1.0" standalone="yes"?>
<NewDataSet>
  <xs:schema id="NewDataSet" xmlns="" xmlns:xs="http://www.w3.org/2001/XMLSchema"
xmlns:msdata="urn:schemas-microsoft-com:xml-msdata">
  <xs:element name="NewDataSet" msdata:IsDataSet="true"
    msdata:MainDataTable="Person" msdata:UseCurrentLocale="true">
   <xs:complexType>
    <xs:choice minOccurs="0" maxOccurs="unbounded">
     <xs:element name="Person">
      <xs:complexType>
       <xs:attribute name="Eid" msdata:Caption="EID" use="required">
        <xs:simpleType>
        <xs:restriction base="xs:string">
```

```
          <xs:maxLength value="10" />
        </xs:restriction>
        </xs:simpleType>
      </xs:attribute>
      <xs:attribute name="FirstName" use="required">
        <xs:simpleType>
        <xs:restriction base="xs:string">
          <xs:maxLength value="35" />
        </xs:restriction>
        </xs:simpleType>
      </xs:attribute>
      <xs:attribute name="LastName" type="xs:string" use="required" />
      <xs:attribute name="Salary" type="xs:decimal" default="0.00" />
      <xs:attribute name="LastName_x0020_and_x0020_FirstName"
        msdata:ReadOnly="true"
        msdata:Expression="lastName + ', ' + firstName"
        use="prohibited">
        <xs:simpleType>
        <xs:restriction base="xs:string">
          <xs:maxLength value="70" />
        </xs:restriction>
        </xs:simpleType>
      </xs:attribute>
     </xs:complexType>
    </xs:element>
   </xs:choice>
  </xs:complexType>
  <xs:unique name="Constraint1" msdata:PrimaryKey="true">
   <xs:selector xpath=".//Person" />
   <xs:field xpath="@Eid" />
  </xs:unique>
 </xs:element>
 </xs:schema>
 <Person Eid="123456789A" FirstName="Nancy" LastName="Davolio"
  Salary="10.00" />
 <Person Eid="987654321X" FirstName="Janet" LastName="Leverling"
  Salary="20.00" />
</NewDataSet>
```

With the XML schema included in the file, the data types are defined. Notice that the XML schema also includes the maximum length settings for *Eid* and *FirstName*. A *DataTable* can be loaded with this XML file, and the resulting *DataTable* is the same as the *DataTable* that was saved to the file. The following code snippet reads the XML file into a new *DataTable* object:

```
'VB
Protected Sub Button6_Click(ByVal sender As Object, _
  ByVal e As System.EventArgs) Handles Button6.Click
```

```
    'add grid to form
    Dim gv As New GridView()
    gv.Style.Add("position", "absolute")
    gv.Style.Add("left", "275px")
    gv.Style.Add("top", "20px")
    gv.EnableViewState = False
    form1.Controls.Add(gv)

    'get the table and display
    Dim xmlTable as New DataTable()
    xmlTable.ReadXml(Server.MapPath("PersonWithSchema.xml"))

    gv.DataSource = xmlTable
    gv.DataBind()

End Sub

//C#
protected void Button6_Click(object sender, EventArgs e)
{
    //add grid to form
    GridView gv = new GridView();
    gv.Style.Add("position", "absolute");
    gv.Style.Add("left", "275px");
    gv.Style.Add("top", "20px");
    gv.EnableViewState = false;
    form1.Controls.Add(gv);

    //get the table and display
    DataTable xmlTable = new DataTable();
    xmlTable.ReadXml(Server.MapPath("PersonWithSchema.xml"));

    gv.DataSource = xmlTable;
    gv.DataBind();
}
```

Although the data for the *LastName and FirstName* column was not saved, the column data is populated because this column is derived and the schema contains the expression to re-create this column data.

Opening a *DataView* Window in a *DataTable*

The *DataView* object provides a window into a *DataTable* that can be sorted and filtered using the *Sort*, *RowFilter*, and *RowStateFilter* properties. A *DataTable* can have many *DataView* objects assigned to it, allowing the data to be viewed in many different ways without requiring the data to be reread from the database. The *DataView* object also contains the *AllowDelete*, *AllowEdit*, and *AllowNew* properties to constrain user input as needed.

If you look at the *DataView* object's internal structure, you will find that it is essentially an index. You can provide a sort definition to sort the index in a certain order, and you can provide a filter to filter the index entries.

ORDERING DATA USING THE *SORT* PROPERTY

The *Sort* property requires a sort expression. The default order for the sort is ascending, but you can specify *ASC* or *DESC* with a comma-separated list of columns to be sorted. In the following code snippet, the *employee DataTable* is retrieved (with some additional rows added) and a *DataView* is created on the *employee DataTable* with a compound sort on the *LastName* column and the *FirstName* column in ascending order and on the *Salary* column in descending order.

```
'VB
Protected Sub Button7_Click(ByVal sender As Object, _
  ByVal e As System.EventArgs) Handles Button7.Click

  'get datatable
  Dim employee As DataTable = GetDataTable()

  'sort and display
  Dim view As New DataView(employee)
  view.Sort = "LastName ASC, FirstName ASC, Salary  DESC"

  GridView1.DataSource = view
  GridView1.DataBind()

End Sub

//C#
protected void Button7_Click(object sender, EventArgs e)
{
  //get datatable
  DataTable employee = GetDataTable();

  //sort and display
  DataView view = new DataView(employee);
  view.Sort = "LastName ASC, FirstName ASC, Salary  DESC";

  GridView1.DataSource = view;
  GridView1.DataBind();
}
```

Figure 7-5 shows the sorted *DataView* when the Web page is run.

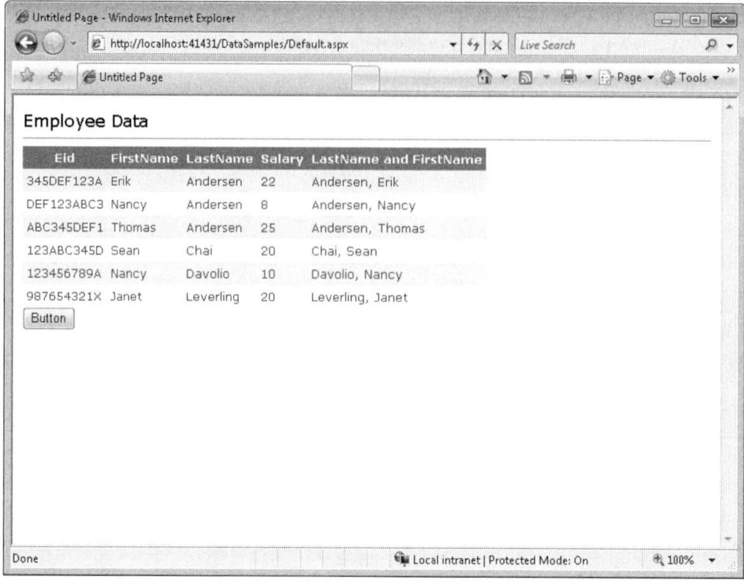

FIGURE 7-5 The sorted employee *DataView* object

NARROWING THE SEARCH WITH THE *ROWFILTER* AND *ROWSTATEFILTER* PROPERTIES

The *DataView* filters comprise a *RowFilter* and a *RowStateFilter*. The *RowFilter* is set to a SQL *WHERE* clause without the word *"WHERE."* The following code shows a filter on the *LastName* column for employees whose names begin with the letter A and on the *Salary* column for employees whose salaries are greater than 15.

```
'VB
view.RowFilter = "LastName like 'A%' and Salary > 15"

//C#
view.RowFilter = "LastName like 'A%' and Salary > 15";
```

The *RowStateFilter* provides a filter based on the *DataRow* object's *RowState* property. This filter provides an easy way to retrieve specific version information within the *DataTable* using one of the *DataViewRowState* enumeration values, which are as follows:

- ***Added*** Retrieves the Current *DataRowVersion* of *DataRow* objects that have a *RowState* of *Added.*
- ***CurrentRows*** Retrieves all *DataRow* objects that have a Current *DataRowVersion.*
- ***Deleted*** Retrieves the Original *DataRowVersion* of *DataRow* objects that have a *RowState* of *Deleted.*
- ***ModifiedCurrent*** Retrieves the Current *DataRowVersion* of *DataRow* objects that have a *RowState* of *Modified.*

- ***ModifiedOriginal*** Retrieves the Original *DataRowVersion* of *DataRow* objects that have a *RowState* of *Modified.*
- ***None*** Clears the *RowStateFilter* property.
- ***OriginalRows*** Retrieves the *DataRow* objects that have an Original *DataRowVersion.*
- ***Unchanged*** Retrieves *DataRow* objects that have a *RowState* of *Unchanged.*

Using a *DataSet* Object

The *DataSet* is a memory-based relational representation of data and the primary disconnected data object. The *DataSet* contains a collection of *DataTable* and *DataRelation* objects, as shown in Figure 7-6 (built using the DataSet designer in Visual Studio). The *DataTable* objects can contain unique and foreign key constraints to enforce data integrity. The *DataSet* also provides methods for cloning the *DataSet* schema, copying the *DataSet*, merging with other *DataSet* objects, and retrieving changes from the *DataSet.*

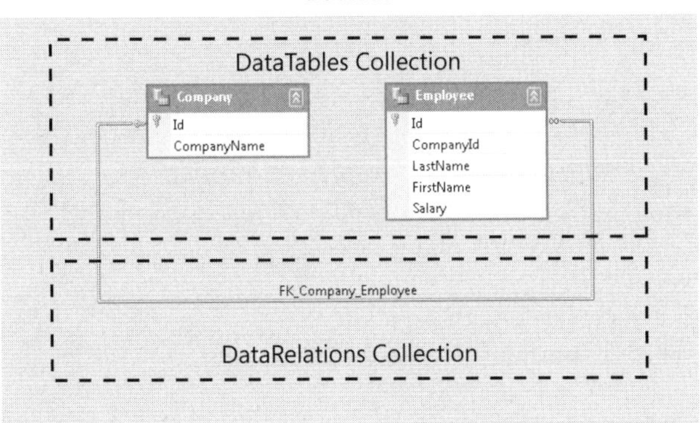

FIGURE 7-6 The *DataSet* object contains a collection of *DataTable* and *DataRelation* objects

You can create the *DataSet* schema programmatically or by providing an XML schema definition. The following code demonstrates the creation of a simple *DataSet* containing a *DataTable* for companies and a *DataTable* for employees. The two *DataTable* objects are joined using a *DataRelation* named *Company_Employee.* The *DataRelation* is discussed in more detail in the next section of this chapter.

```
'VB
Private Function GetDataSet() As DataSet

  Dim companyData As New DataSet("CompanyList")

  Dim company As DataTable = companyData.Tables.Add("company")
  company.Columns.Add("Id", GetType(Guid))
  company.Columns.Add("CompanyName", GetType(String))
```

```
    company.PrimaryKey = New DataColumn() {company.Columns("Id")}

    Dim employee As DataTable = companyData.Tables.Add("employee")
    employee.Columns.Add("Id", GetType(Guid))
    employee.Columns.Add("companyId", GetType(Guid))
    employee.Columns.Add("LastName", GetType(String))
    employee.Columns.Add("FirstName", GetType(String))
    employee.Columns.Add("Salary", GetType(Decimal))
    employee.PrimaryKey = New DataColumn() {employee.Columns("Id")}

    companyData.Relations.Add( _
      "Company_Employee", _
      company.Columns("Id"), _
      employee.Columns("CompanyId"))

    Return companyData
  End Function

//C#
private DataSet GetDataSet()
{
  DataSet companyData = new DataSet("CompanyList");

  DataTable company = companyData.Tables.Add("company");
  company.Columns.Add("Id", typeof(Guid));
  company.Columns.Add("CompanyName", typeof(string));
  company.PrimaryKey = new DataColumn[] { company.Columns["Id"] };

  DataTable employee = companyData.Tables.Add("employee");
  employee.Columns.Add("Id", typeof(Guid));
  employee.Columns.Add("companyId", typeof(Guid));
  employee.Columns.Add("LastName", typeof(string));
  employee.Columns.Add("FirstName", typeof(string));
  employee.Columns.Add("Salary", typeof(decimal));
  employee.PrimaryKey = new DataColumn[] { employee.Columns["Id"] };

  companyData.Relations.Add(
    "Company_Employee",
    company.Columns["Id"],
    employee.Columns["CompanyId"]);
  return companyData;
}
```

After the *DataSet* is created, the *DataTable* objects can be populated with data, as shown in the following code sample. This code populates the *Id* columns by creating a new globally unique identifier (GUID). After a company is created and added to the company *DataTable*, the employee names for that company are created and added.

```
'VB
Dim company As DataTable = companyData.Tables("Company")
Dim employee As DataTable = companyData.Tables("Employee")

Dim coId, empId As Guid
coId = Guid.NewGuid()
company.Rows.Add(coId, "Northwind Traders")
empId = Guid.NewGuid()
employee.Rows.Add(empId, coId, "JoeLast", "JoeFirst", 40.00)
empId = Guid.NewGuid()
employee.Rows.Add(empId, coId, "MaryLast", "MaryFirst", 70.00)
empId = Guid.NewGuid()
employee.Rows.Add(empId, coId, "SamLast", "SamFirst", 12.00)

coId = Guid.NewGuid()
company.Rows.Add(coId, "Contoso")
empId = Guid.NewGuid()
employee.Rows.Add(empId, coId, "SueLast", "SueFirst", 20.00)
empId = Guid.NewGuid()
employee.Rows.Add(empId, coId, "TomLast", "TomFirst", 68.00)
empId = Guid.NewGuid()
employee.Rows.Add(empId, coId, "MikeLast", "MikeFirst", 18.99)


//C#
DataTable company = companyData.Tables["Company"];
DataTable employee = companyData.Tables["Employee"];

Guid coId, empId;
coId = Guid.NewGuid();
company.Rows.Add(coId, "Northwind Traders");
empId = Guid.NewGuid();
employee.Rows.Add(empId, coId, "JoeLast", "JoeFirst", 40.00);
empId = Guid.NewGuid();
employee.Rows.Add(empId, coId, "MaryLast", "MaryFirst", 70.00);
empId = Guid.NewGuid();
employee.Rows.Add(empId, coId, "SamLast", "SamFirst", 12.00);

coId = Guid.NewGuid();
company.Rows.Add(coId, "Contoso");
empId = Guid.NewGuid();
employee.Rows.Add(empId, coId, "SueLast", "SueFirst", 20.00);
```

```
empId = Guid.NewGuid();
employee.Rows.Add(empId, coId, "TomLast", "TomFirst", 68.00);
empId = Guid.NewGuid();
employee.Rows.Add(empId, coId, "MikeLast", "MikeFirst", 18.99);
```

Using the GUID as a Primary Key

The previous code sample creates and populates a *DataSet*. Notice the use of the *Guid* data type for the *Id* columns. Although this option is not mandatory, you should consider implementing this option, especially when working with disconnected data. This can help you deal with the following issues:

- If you use an auto-number *Id* column and if many people are creating new *DataRow* objects, it will be difficult for you to merge data later because there may be many duplicate keys.
- The *Guid* data type is a "surrogate" key, meaning that its only purpose is to define uniqueness of the row and aid in connecting multiple tables together via relationships. This means that there is no reason for a user to see and change this value, which simplifies maintenance of the *DataSet*. If you allow the user to change the primary key on a row, you have to propagate the change down to all of the related tables. For example, changing a *CompanyId* value in the *company* table requires the update of the *CompanyId* value in the *employee* table.
- The use of the *Guid* can simplify the joining of tables, which is better than the scenarios in which you use compound keys that are based on the actual data. Compound keys typically result in smaller data footprints because the key is based on actual data, whereas joining tables is usually more difficult because compound joins are required. Remember that if you are using compound keys that are based on the actual data, you inevitably need to deal with recursive updates.

Using Typed *DataSets*

You can access a *DataTable* object by using its table name. For example, if you have a *DataSet* called *salesData* that includes a company table, you can access this table as follows:

```
'VB
Dim companyTable as DataTable = salesData.Tables("Company")

//C#
DataTable companyTable = salesData.Tables["Company"];
```

If the name of the table is misspelled, however, an exception is thrown at run time. This can be problematic. The same is true for fields on the table. Each is typically accessed through a string value. In addition, each field is only type-checked at run time. You can overcome these issues at compile time by creating a specialized *DataSet* class called a typed *DataSet*. A typed *DataSet* inherits from the *DataSet object*. You define a property for each of the tables in the

DataSet. You do the same for each field in the table. For example, a typed *DataSet* class might contain a property called *Company* that can be accessed as follows:

```
'VB
Dim companyTable as DataTable = vendorData.Company

//C#
DataTable companyTable = vendorData.Company;
```

In this example, a compile-time error is generated if *Company* is not spelled correctly. (Keep in mind that you probably won't misspell the *Company* property because Visual Studio's IntelliSense displays the *Company* property for quick selection when the line of code is being typed.)

You can provide an XML Schema Definition (XSD) file to generate a typed *DataSet* class. You can use the *DataSet* Editor to graphically create and modify an XSD file, which, in turn, can be used to generate the typed *DataSet* class. Figure 7-7 shows the CompanyList *DataSet* that is loaded into the *DataSet* Editor.

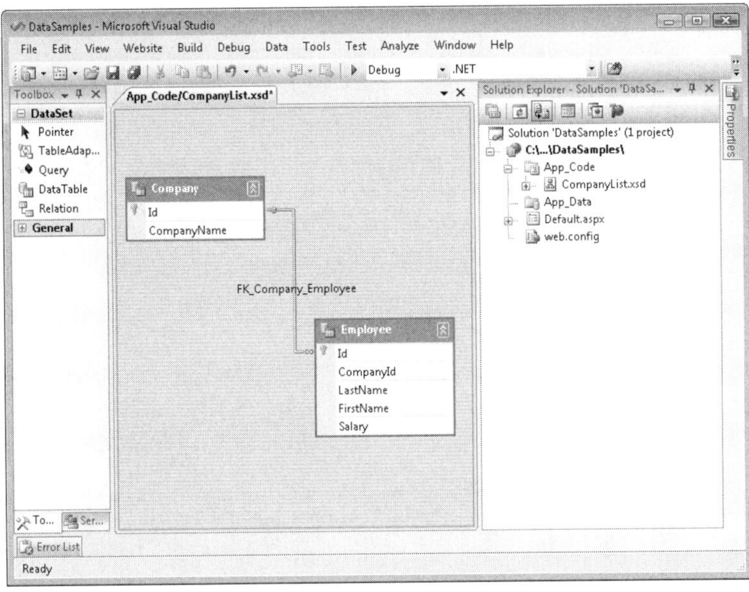

FIGURE 7-7 The *DataSet* template contains an XML schema definition and generates source code to create a typed *DataSet*

Navigating *DataTable* Objects with *DataRelation* Objects

The *DataRelation* object is used to join two *DataTable* objects that are in the same *DataSet*, thus providing a navigable path between the two *DataTable* objects. The *DataRelation* can be traversed from parent *DataTable* to child *DataTable* or from child *DataTable* to parent

DataTable. The following code example populates the *company* and *employee DataTable* objects and then performs *DataRelation* object navigation.

Note that in the following code, the method *GetLabel* is called but the code has been omitted. This method is used throughout this chapter to define a *Label* control, set its left and top position, and add it to the form collection.

'VB

```
Protected Sub Button8_Click(ByVal sender As Object, _
  ByVal e As System.EventArgs) Handles Button8.Click
  'add a label to the form
  Dim lbl As Label = GetLabel(275, 20)

  'get the dataset and populate
  Dim companyList As DataSet = GetDataSet()

  'get the relationship
  Dim dr As DataRelation = companyList.Relations("Company_Employee")

  'display second company
  Dim companyParent As DataRow = companyList.Tables("company").Rows(1)
  lbl.Text = companyParent("CompanyName") + "<br />"

  'display employees
  For Each employeeChild As DataRow In companyParent.GetChildRows(dr)
    lbl.Text += "   " + employeeChild("Id").ToString() + " " _
      + employeeChild("LastName") + " " _
      + employeeChild("FirstName") + " " _
      + String.Format("{0:C}", employeeChild("Salary")) + "<br />"
  Next

  lbl.Text += "<br /><br />"

  'display second employee
  Dim employeeParent As DataRow = companyList.Tables("employee").Rows(1)
  lbl.Text += employeeParent("Id").ToString() + " " _
    + employeeParent("LastName") + " " _
    + employeeParent("FirstName") + " " _
    + String.Format("{0:C}", employeeParent("Salary")) + "<br />"

  'display company
  Dim companyChild As DataRow = employeeParent.GetParentRow(dr)
  lbl.Text += "   " + companyChild("CompanyName") + "<br />"
End Sub
```

//C#

```
protected void Button8_Click(object sender, EventArgs e)
```

```
{
  //add a label to the form
  Label lbl = GetLabel(275, 20);

  //get the dataset and populate
  DataSet companyList = GetDataSet();

  //get the relationship
  DataRelation dr = companyList.Relations["Company_Employee"];

  //display second company
  DataRow companyParent = companyList.Tables["company"].Rows[1];
  lbl.Text = companyParent["CompanyName"] + "<br />";

  //display employees
  foreach (DataRow employeeChild in companyParent.GetChildRows(dr))
  {
    lbl.Text += "   " + employeeChild["Id"] + " "
      + employeeChild["LastName"] + " "
      + employeeChild["FirstName"] + " "
      + string.Format("{0:C}", employeeChild["Salary"]) + "<br />";
  }

  lbl.Text += "<br /><br />";

  //display second employee
  DataRow employeeParent = companyList.Tables["employee"].Rows[1];
  lbl.Text += employeeParent["Id"] + " "
    + employeeParent["LastName"] + " "
    + employeeParent["FirstName"] + " "
    + string.Format("{0:C}", employeeParent["Salary"]) + "<br />";

  //display company
  DataRow companyChild = employeeParent.GetParentRow(dr);
  lbl.Text += "   " + companyChild["CompanyName"] + "<br />";
}
```

In this code example, the previously declared *Company_Employee DataRelation* allows navigation from parent to child as well as from child to parent. The results are shown in a *Label* control.

PRIMARY AND FOREIGN KEY CONSTRAINT CREATION

When you create a *DataRelation* object without unique and foreign key constraints, its sole purpose is to navigate between parent and child *DataTable* objects. The *DataRelation* constructor allows for the creation of a unique constraint on the parent *DataTable* object and a foreign key constraint on the child *DataTable* object.

CASCADING UPDATES AND DELETES

There are many scenarios where you want the deletion of a parent *DataRow* object to force the deletion of child *DataRow* objects. You can accomplish this by setting the *DeleteRule* on the *ForeignKeyConstraint* to *Cascade* (the default). The following is a list of the *Rule* enumeration members:

- ***Cascade*** This is the default. It deletes or updates the child *DataRow* objects when the *DataRow* object is deleted or its unique key is changed.
- ***None*** This throws an *InvalidConstraintException* if the parent *DataRow* object is deleted or its unique key is changed.
- ***SetDefault*** This sets the foreign key column(s) value to the default value of the *DataColumn* object(s) if the parent *DataRow* object is deleted or its unique key is changed.
- ***SetNull*** This sets the foreign key column(s) value to *DbNull* if the parent *DataRow* object is deleted or its unique key is changed.

As with deleting, on some occasions, you'll want to cascade changes to a unique key in the parent *DataRow* object to the child *DataRow* object's foreign key. You can set the *ChangeRule* to a member of the *Rule* enumeration to get the appropriate behavior.

Serializing and Deserializing *DataSet* Objects

A *DataSet* can be serialized as XML or as binary data to a stream or file. The *DataSet* can also be deserialized from XML or binary data from a stream or file. The serialized data can be transferred across a network via many protocols, including HTTP. This section looks at the various methods of transferring data.

SERIALIZING THE *DATASET* OBJECT AS XML

You can serialize a *DataSet* to an XML file by executing the *DataSet* object's *WriteXml* method. The following code uses the populated CompanyList *DataSet* that was created earlier in this chapter and writes the contents to an XML file. A portion of the resulting XML file contents are also shown.

```
'VB
Protected Sub Button9_Click(ByVal sender As Object, _
  ByVal e As System.EventArgs) Handles Button9.Click

  'get dataset and populate
  Dim companyList As DataSet = GetDataSet()

  'write to xml file
  companyList.WriteXml(MapPath("CompanyList.xml"))

  'display file
  Response.Redirect("CompanyList.xml")
```

```
End Sub

//C#
protected void Button9_Click(object sender, EventArgs e)
{
  //get the dataset and populate
  DataSet companyList = GetDataSet();

  //write to xml file
  companyList.WriteXml(MapPath("CompanyList.xml"));

  //display file
  Response.Redirect("CompanyList.xml");
}
```

XML

```
<?xml version="1.0" standalone="yes"?>
<CompanyList>
  <company>
    <Id>c2a464fb-bdce-498a-a216-fb844dfb05a5</Id>
    <CompanyName>Northwind Traders</CompanyName>
  </company>
  <company>
    <Id>aa40966c-18b7-451b-acea-237eaa5e08af</Id>
    <CompanyName>Contoso</CompanyName>
  </company>
  <employee>
    <Id>7ad2a59c-dd3a-483b-877c-b4fe0d0c9bbe</Id>
    <coId>c2a464fb-bdce-498a-a216-fb844dfb05a5</coId>
    <LastName>JoeLast</LastName>
    <FirstName>JoeFirst</FirstName>
    <Salary>40</Salary>
  </employee>
  <employee>
    <Id>343d98b0-e6aa-432d-9755-2c9501cd1ace</Id>
    <coId>c2a464fb-bdce-498a-a216-fb844dfb05a5</coId>
    <LastName>MaryLast</LastName>
    <FirstName>MaryFirst</FirstName>
    <Salary>70</Salary>
  </employee>
  ...
</CompanyList>
```

The XML document is well formed and its root node is called *CompanyList*. You can change this by changing the *DataSetName* property.

Notice that the single *Company DataRow* object is represented in the XML file by the single *Company* element, and the *Employee DataRow* objects are represented in the XML file by the repeating *Employee* elements. The column data is represented as elements within the element for the *DataRow*, but you can change this by changing the *ColumnMapping* property of the *DataColumn* objects.

You can nest the *Employee* elements inside the *Company* object that has the employees by setting the *Nested* property of the *DataRelation* object to *True*. In the following code, the XML format is changed substantially by nesting the data and setting all of the *DataColumn* objects to *Attribute*. The resulting XML file is also shown.

```
'VB
Protected Sub Button10_Click(ByVal sender As Object, _
  ByVal e As System.EventArgs) Handles Button10.Click

  'get the dataset and populate
  Dim companyList As DataSet = GetDataSet()

  'format xml
  companyList.Relations("Company_Employee").Nested = True
  For Each dt As DataTable In companyList.Tables
    For Each dc As DataColumn In dt.Columns
      dc.ColumnMapping = MappingType.Attribute
    Next
  Next

  'write to xml file
  companyList.WriteXml(MapPath("CompanyListNested.xml"))

  'display file
  Response.Redirect("CompanyListNested.xml")
End Sub

//C#
protected void Button10_Click(object sender, EventArgs e)
{
  //get the dataset and populate
  DataSet companyList = GetDataSet();

  //format xml
  companyList.Relations["Company_Employee"].Nested = true;
  foreach (DataTable dt in companyList.Tables)
  {
    foreach (DataColumn dc in dt.Columns)
    {
      dc.ColumnMapping = MappingType.Attribute;
    }
```

```
  }

  //write to xml file
  companyList.WriteXml(MapPath("CompanyListNested.xml"));

  //display file
  Response.Redirect("CompanyListNested.xml");
}
```

XML


```
<?xml version="1.0" standalone="yes"?>
<CompanyList>
  <company Id="63cd2a1e-c578-4f21-a826-c5dfb50258b0"
   CompanyName="Northwind Traders">
  <employee Id="a2e7bbba-20ba-4b73-86b3-2d0cca4f1bbb"
    coId="63cd2a1e-c578-4f21-a826-c5dfb50258b0"
    LastName="JoeLast" FirstName="JoeFirst" Salary="40" />
  <employee Id="5cf475e8-1d97-4784-b72f-84bfbf4a8e14"
    coId="63cd2a1e-c578-4f21-a826-c5dfb50258b0"
    LastName="MaryLast" FirstName="MaryFirst" Salary="70" />
  <employee Id="55ff1a2b-8956-4ded-99a4-68610134b774"
    coId="63cd2a1e-c578-4f21-a826-c5dfb50258b0"
    LastName="SamLast" FirstName="SamFirst" Salary="12" />
  </company>
  <company Id="0adcf278-ccd3-4c3d-a78a-27aa35dc2756"
   CompanyName="Contoso">
  <employee Id="bc431c32-5397-47b6-9a16-0667be455f02"
    coId="0adcf278-ccd3-4c3d-a78a-27aa35dc2756"
    LastName="SueLast" FirstName="SueFirst" Salary="20" />
  <employee Id="5822bf9f-49c1-42dd-95e0-5bb728c5ac60"
    coId="0adcf278-ccd3-4c3d-a78a-27aa35dc2756"
    LastName="TomLast" FirstName="TomFirst" Salary="68" />
  <employee Id="1b2334a4-e339-4255-b826-c0453fda7e61"
    coId="0adcf278-ccd3-4c3d-a78a-27aa35dc2756"
    LastName="MikeLast" FirstName="MikeFirst" Salary="18.99" />
  </company>
</CompanyList>
```


In the example, the XML file is written, but the XML file contains no information that describes the data types of the data. When not specified, the default data type for all data is *string*. If the XML file is read into a new *DataSet*, all data, including *DateTime* data and numeric data, is loaded as string data. Use the *XmlWriteMode.WriteSchema* enumeration value when saving because it stores the data type information with the XML file.

The resulting XML file is substantially larger. Instead of embedding the schema in the XML file, you can create a separate XSD file to load before loading the data. You can use the

DataSet object's *WriteXmlSchema* method to extract the XML schema definition to a separate file, as shown here:

```
'VB
'write to xsd file
companyList.WriteXmlSchema( _
  MapPath("CompanyListSchema.xsd"))

//C#
//write to xsd file
companyList.WriteXmlSchema(
  MapPath("CompanyListSchema.xsd"));
```

SERIALIZING A CHANGED *DATASET* OBJECT AS A DIFFGRAM

A *DiffGram* is an XML document that contains all of the data from your *DataSet* object, including the original *DataRow* object information. To save as a DiffGram, use the *XmlWriteMode.DiffGram* enumeration value when serializing a *DataSet* object. The following code shows the creation of company rows with changes that make it so that one is inserted, one is updated, one is deleted, and one is unchanged. Then the *DataSet* is written as a DiffGram.

```
'VB
Protected Sub Button11_Click(ByVal sender As Object, _
  ByVal e As System.EventArgs) Handles Button11.Click

  'get the dataset and populate
  Dim companyList As DataSet = GetDataSet()
  Dim company as DataTable = companyList.Tables("company")

  company.Rows.Add(Guid.NewGuid(), "UnchangedCompany")
  company.Rows.Add(Guid.NewGuid(), "ModifiedCompany")
  company.Rows.Add(Guid.NewGuid(), "DeletedCompany")
  companyList.AcceptChanges()
  company.Rows(1)("CompanyName") = "ModifiedCompany1"
  company.Rows(2).Delete()
  company.Rows.Add(Guid.NewGuid(), "AddedCompany")

  'format xml
  companyList.Relations("Company_Employee").Nested = True
  For Each dt As DataTable In companyList.Tables
    For Each dc As DataColumn In dt.Columns
      dc.ColumnMapping = MappingType.Attribute
    Next
  Next

  'write to xml diffgram file
  companyList.WriteXml( _
```

```
    MapPath("companyListDiffGram.xml"), XmlWriteMode.DiffGram)

  'display file
  Response.Redirect("companyListDiffGram.xml")
End Sub

//C#
protected void Button11_Click(object sender, EventArgs e)
{
  //get the dataset and populate
  DataSet companyList = GetDataSet();
  DataTable company = companyList.Tables["company"];
  company.Rows.Add(Guid.NewGuid(), "UnchangedCompany");
  company.Rows.Add(Guid.NewGuid(), "ModifiedCompany");
  company.Rows.Add(Guid.NewGuid(), "DeletedCompany");
  companyList.AcceptChanges();
  company.Rows[1]["CompanyName"] = "ModifiedCompany1";
  company.Rows[2].Delete();
  company.Rows.Add(Guid.NewGuid(), "AddedCompany");

  //format xml
  companyList.Relations["Company_Employee"].Nested = true;
  foreach (DataTable dt in companyList.Tables)
  {
    foreach (DataColumn dc in dt.Columns)
    {
      dc.ColumnMapping = MappingType.Attribute;
    }
  }

  //write to xml diffgram file
  companyList.WriteXml(
    MapPath("CompanyListDiffGram.xml"), XmlWriteMode.DiffGram);

  //display file
  Response.Redirect("CompanyListDiffGram.xml");
}
```

The DiffGram is mostly used in an environment where a user occasionally connects to a database to synchronize a disconnected *DataSet* object with the current information that is contained in the database. When the user is not connected to the database, the *DataSet* object is stored locally as a DiffGram to ensure that you still have the original data, because the original data is needed when it's time to send your changes back to the database.

The DiffGram contains all of the *DataRowVersion* information, as shown in the following XML document. Company1 has not been modified. Notice that Company2 has been modified, and its status is indicated as such. Also notice that the bottom of the XML document contains the original information for *DataRow* objects that have been modified or deleted. This XML document also shows Company3 as deleted because Company3 has "before" information but not current information. Company4 is an inserted *DataRow* object as indicated, so this *DataRow* object has no "before" information.

```
<?xml version="1.0" standalone="yes"?>
<diffgr:diffgram xmlns:msdata="urn:schemas-microsoft-com:xml-msdata"
   xmlns:diffgr="urn:schemas-microsoft-com:xml-diffgram-v1">
  <CompanyList>
  <company diffgr:id="company1" msdata:rowOrder="0"
    Id="09b8482c-e801-4c63-82f6-0f5527b3768b"
    CompanyName="UnchangedCompany" />
  <company diffgr:id="company2" msdata:rowOrder="1"
    diffgr:hasChanges="modified"
    Id="8f9eceb3-b6de-4da7-84dd-d99a278a23ee"
    CompanyName="ModifiedCompany1" />
  <company diffgr:id="company4" msdata:rowOrder="3"
    diffgr:hasChanges="inserted"
    Id="65d28892-b8af-4392-8b64-718a612f6aa7"
    CompanyName="AddedCompany" />
  </CompanyList>
  <diffgr:before>
  <company diffgr:id="company2" msdata:rowOrder="1"
    Id="8f9eceb3-b6de-4da7-84dd-d99a278a23ee"
    CompanyName="ModifiedCompany" />
  <company diffgr:id="company3" msdata:rowOrder="2"
    Id="89b576d2-60ae-4c36-ba96-c4a7a8966a6f"
    CompanyName="DeletedCompany" />
  </diffgr:before>
</diffgr:diffgram>
```

DESERIALIZING A *DATASET* FROM XML

You can deserialize an XML file or stream into a *DataSet* object by loading the schema and reading the stream. You can use the following code to read the schema file and load the XML file:

```
'VB
Protected Sub Button12_Click(ByVal sender As Object, _
  ByVal e As System.EventArgs) Handles Button12.Click

  'get the dataset and populate schema
  Dim companyList as new DataSet()
  companyList.ReadXmlSchema(MapPath("CompanyListSchema.xsd"))

  'populate from file
  companyList.ReadXml(MapPath("CompanyListNested.xml"))
```

```
    'display
    GridViewCompany.DataSource = companyList
    GridViewCompany.DataMember = "Company"

    GridViewEmployee.DataSource = companyList
    GridViewEmployee.DataMember = "Employee"

    GridViewCompany.DataBind()
    GridViewEmployee.DataBind()

End Sub

//C#
protected void Button12_Click(object sender, EventArgs e)
{
    //get the dataset and populate schema
    DataSet companyList = new DataSet();
    companyList.ReadXmlSchema(MapPath("CompanyListSchema.xsd"));

    //populate from file
    companyList.ReadXml(MapPath("CompanyListNested.xml"));

    //display
    GridViewCompany.DataSource = companyList;
    GridViewCompany.DataMember = "Company";
    GridViewEmployee.DataSource = companyList;
    GridViewEmployee.DataMember = "Employee";

    GridViewCompany.DataBind();
    GridViewEmployee.DataBind();
}
```

When reading an XML file, you can optionally pass an *XmlReadMode* enumeration value. If this value is not passed, the default is *XmlReadMode.IgnoreSchema*. This means that if the XML data file contains an XSD, it is ignored. Listed here are the other options of the *XmlReadMode* enumeration:

- ***Auto*** The XML source is examined by the *ReadXml* method and the appropriate mode is selected.
- ***DiffGram*** If the *XmlFile* contains a DiffGram, the changes are applied to the *DataSet* using the same semantics that the *Merge* method uses. (*Merge* is covered in more detail in the section "Using *Merge* to Combine *DataSet* Data.")
- ***Fragment*** This option causes the XML to be read as a fragment. Fragments can contain multiple root elements. *FOR XML* in SQL Server is an example of something that produces fragments.

- ***IgnoreSchema*** This causes any schema that is defined within the XML data file to be ignored.
- ***InferSchema*** Using this option, the XML file is read, and the *DataTable* objects and *DataColumn* objects are created based on the data. If the *DataSet* currently has *DataTable* objects and *DataColumn* objects, they are used and extended to accommodate new tables and columns that exist in the XML document, but don't exist in the *DataSet* object. All data types of all *DataColumn* objects are a string.
- ***InferTypedSchema*** Using this option, the XML file is read, and the schema is created based on the data. An attempt is made to identify the data type of each column, but if the data type cannot be identified, it is a string.
- ***ReadSchema*** Using this option, the XML file is read, and then an embedded schema is searched for. If the *DataSet* already has *DataTable* objects with the same name, an exception is thrown. All other existing tables remain.

Inferring a schema simply means that the *DataSet* attempts to create a schema for the data based on looking for patterns of XML elements and attributes.

SERIALIZING THE *DATASET* OBJECT AS BINARY DATA

The size of an XML file that is produced when serializing a *DataSet* object can cause problems with resources, such as memory and drive space or bandwidth when you move this data across the network. If XML is not required and you want the best performance, the *DataSet* can be serialized as a binary file. The following code writes the contents of the *vendorData DataSet* that we previously defined and populated to a binary file:

```
'VB
'Add the following Imports statements to the top of the file
Imports System.Runtime.Serialization.Formatters.Binary
Imports System.IO

Protected Sub Button13_Click(ByVal sender As Object, _
  ByVal e As System.EventArgs) Handles Button13.Click

  'get the dataset and populate
  Dim companyList As DataSet = GetDataSet()

  'set output to binary else this will be xml
  companyList.RemotingFormat = SerializationFormat.Binary

  'write to binary file
  Using fs As New FileStream( _
    MapPath("CompanyList.bin"), FileMode.Create)

    Dim fmt As New BinaryFormatter()
    fmt.Serialize(fs, companyList)
```

```
  End Using

  'feedback
  Label1.Text = "File Saved."

End Sub

//C#
//Add the following using statements to the top of the file
using System.Runtime.Serialization.Formatters.Binary;
using System.IO;

protected void Button13_Click(object sender, EventArgs e)
{
  //get the dataset and populate
  DataSet companyList = GetDataSet();

  //set output to binary else this will be xml
  companyList.RemotingFormat = SerializationFormat.Binary;

  //write to binary file
  using (FileStream fs =
    new FileStream(MapPath("CompanyList.bin"), FileMode.Create))
  {
    BinaryFormatter fmt = new BinaryFormatter();
    fmt.Serialize(fs, companyList);
  }

  //feedback
  Label1.Text = "File Saved.";
}
```

The *DataSet* object's *RemotingFormat* property must be set to ensure binary serialization. This property is also available on the *DataTable* object for scenarios where only a single *DataTable* is to be binary serialized. Be careful when making the choice to serialize as XML or binary, because binary files contain more initial overhead (about 20 kilobytes) than XML files. For large *DataSet* objects, binary serialization always produces a smaller file, but for small *DataSet* objects, binary serialization might not produce smaller output.

DESERIALIZING A *DATASET* FROM BINARY DATA

You can easily deserialize the binary data file that we created in the previous example into a *DataSet* from a file or stream. The *BinaryFormatter* stores the schema automatically, so there is no need to load a schema first. The *BinaryFormatter* automatically identifies the file as having been saved as *BinaryXml*. You can use the following code to load the binary file and display the *companyList*:

```
'VB
Protected Sub Button14_Click(ByVal sender As Object, _
  ByVal e As System.EventArgs) Handles Button14.Click

  'get the dataset from the file
  Dim companyList As DataSet
  Using fs As New FileStream( _
    MapPath("CompanyList.bin"), FileMode.Open)
    Dim fmt As New BinaryFormatter()
    companyList = CType(fmt.Deserialize(fs), DataSet)
  End Using

  'display
  GridViewCompany.DataSource = companyList
  GridViewCompany.DataMember = "Company"
  GridViewEmployee.DataSource = companyList
  GridViewEmployee.DataMember = "Employee"

  GridViewCompany.DataBind()
  GridViewEmployee.DataBind()
End Sub

//C#
protected void Button14_Click(object sender, EventArgs e)
{
  //get the dataset from the file
  DataSet companyList;
  using (FileStream fs = new FileStream(
    MapPath("CompanyList.bin"), FileMode.Open))
  {
    BinaryFormatter fmt = new BinaryFormatter();
    companyList = (DataSet)fmt.Deserialize(fs);
  }

  //display
  GridViewCompany.DataSource = companyList;
  GridViewCompany.DataMember = "Company";
  GridViewEmployee.DataSource = companyList;
  GridViewEmployee.DataMember = "Employee";

  GridViewCompany.DataBind();
  GridViewEmployee.DataBind();
}
```

USING *MERGE* TO COMBINE *DATASET* DATA

On many occasions, data available in one *DataSet* must be combined with another *DataSet*. For example, an expense application might need to combine serialized *DataSet* objects (expense reports) received by e-mail from a number of people. It's also common within an application (based on the user clicking Update) to merge a modified version back to the original *DataSet*.

The *Merge* method on the *DataSet* is used to combine data from multiple *DataSet* objects. The *Merge* method has several overloads that allow data to be merged from *DataSet*, *DataTable*, or *DataRow* objects. The following code example demonstrates how to use the *Merge* method to combine changes from one *DataSet* into another *DataSet*:

```
'VB
Protected Sub Button15_Click(ByVal sender As Object, _
  ByVal e As System.EventArgs) Handles Button15.Click

  'get the dataset
  Dim original As DataSet = GetDataSet()

  'add AdventureWorks
  original.Tables("Company").Rows.Add( _
    Guid.NewGuid(), "AdventureWorks")

  'copy the dataset
  Dim copy as DataSet = original.Copy()

  'modify the copy
  Dim aw as DataRow = copy.Tables("Company").Rows(0)
  aw("CompanyName") = "AdventureWorks Changed"
  Dim empId as Guid
  empId = Guid.NewGuid()
  copy.Tables("Employee").Rows.Add(empId, aw("Id"), _
    "MarkLast", "MarkFirst", 90.00)
  empId = Guid.NewGuid()
  copy.Tables("Employee").Rows.Add(empId, aw("Id"), _
    "SueLast", "SueFirst", 41.00)

  'merge changes back to the original
  original.Merge(copy, False, MissingSchemaAction.AddWithKey)

  'display
  GridViewCompany.DataSource = original
  GridViewCompany.DataMember = "company"
  GridViewEmployee.DataSource = original
```

```
    GridViewEmployee.DataMember = "employee"
    GridViewCompany.DataBind()
    GridViewEmployee.DataBind()
End Sub

//C#
protected void Button15_Click(object sender, EventArgs e)
{
    //get the dataset
    DataSet original = GetDataSet();
    //add AdventureWorks
    original.Tables["Company"].Rows.Add(
      Guid.NewGuid(), "AdventureWorks");

    //copy the dataset
    DataSet copy = original.Copy();

    //modify the copy
    DataRow aw = copy.Tables["Company"].Rows[0];
    aw["CompanyName"] = "AdventureWorks Changed";
    Guid empId;
    empId = Guid.NewGuid();
    copy.Tables["Employee"].Rows.Add(empId, aw["Id"],
      "MarkLast", "MarkFirst", 90.00m);
    empId = Guid.NewGuid();
    copy.Tables["employee"].Rows.Add(empId, aw["Id"],
      "SueLast", "SueFirst", 41.00m);

    //merge changes back to the original
    original.Merge(copy, false, MissingSchemaAction.AddWithKey);

    //display
    GridViewCompany.DataSource = original;
    GridViewCompany.DataMember = "Company";
    GridViewEmployee.DataSource = original;
    GridViewEmployee.DataMember = "Employee";
    GridViewCompany.DataBind();
    GridViewEmployee.DataBind();
}
```

The *Merge* method is always called on the original *DataSet (*that you will merge into); it takes three parameters. The first parameter is the object to be merged. The second parameter is a Boolean that specifies whether updates from the *DataSet* to be merged should overwrite changes made in the original object. The last parameter is a *MissingSchemaAction* enumeration member. If *AddWithKey* is specified, as in this example, a new *DataTable* has been added to the object to be merged, and the new *DataTable* and its data are added to the original *DataSet* object. The following is a list of the *MissingSchemaAction* enumeration members:

- ***Add*** This adds the necessary *DataTable* and *DataColumn* objects to complete the schema.
- ***AddWithKey*** This adds the necessary *DataTable*, *DataColumn*, and *PrimaryKey* objects to complete the schema.
- ***Error*** This throws an exception if a *DataColumn* does not exist in the DataSet that is being updated.
- ***Ignore*** This ignores data that resides in *DataColumns* that are not in the *DataSet* being updated.

When you use the *Merge* method, make sure each of the *DataTable* objects has a primary key. Failure to set the *PrimaryKey* property of the *DataTable* object results in a *DataRow* object being appended rather than an existing *DataRow* object being modified.

Quick Check

1. **When working with disconnected data, what primary data object must you always have at least one of?**
2. **You have a *DataSet* with *Order* and *OrderDetail DataTable* objects. You want to be able to retrieve the *OrderDetail* rows for a specific *Order*. What data object can you use to navigate from an *Order* row to the related *OrderDetail* rows?**
3. **You want to save a *DataSet* object to an XML file, but you are concerned that you might lose the original version of the *DataRow* object. How should you save the DataSet object?**

Quick Check Answers

1. **You must have at least one *DataTable* object.**
2. **Use the *DataRelation* object.**
3. **Save it as a DiffGram.**

Using LINQ to *DataSet* to Query Data

LINQ is a language feature built into the latest editions of C# and Visual Basic. LINQ provides a consistent model for querying data no matter where that data comes from. This allows you to write .NET Framework code (in lieu of SQL) when working with data. LINQ gives you compile-time syntax checking against your data, static typing, and IntelliSense in the code editor. All of these features make programming data easier and more consistent, regardless of the origin of the data.

There are three features of LINQ covered in this chapter: LINQ to *DataSet*, LINQ to SQL, and LINQ to XML. Each is covered in the appropriate lesson. This lesson focuses on using the features of LINQ to *DataSet*.

> ***NOTE*** **LINQ LANGUAGE FEATURES**
>
> **LINQ is an extension to the development languages of C# and Visual Basic. This is not a language book. For more information on the LINQ language extensions, you can review the MSDN topic, "Getting Started with LINQ in C# (or Visual Basic)."**

The *DataSet* and *DataTable* objects allow you to store a lot of data in memory and even share that data between requests (through caching). However, these objects have limited data query functionality. That is, you cannot query a *DataSet* the same way you would query a database. LINQ to *DataSet* changes this. It allows you to use the standard query features of LINQ to query data stored in a *DataSet*.

As an example, imagine you have a large *DataTable* that contains employee records. This *DataTable* may exist in memory and you might therefore need to query against it. You can do so using LINQ. You first define your query as a variable of a type that implements the *IEnumerable(T)* interface. This ensures that the query can execute and enumerate over the data. You define this variable using the LINQ syntax of `From <element> In <collection>`. You can then define a *Where* clause, *Order By* clause, and more. The following code shows an example of defining a query against employee data in a *DataTable* object.

```
'VB
Protected Sub Page_Load(ByVal sender As Object, _
  ByVal e As System.EventArgs) Handles Me.Load

  Dim employees As DataTable = _
    MyDataProvider.GetEmployeeData()

    Dim query As EnumerableRowCollection(Of DataRow) = _
      From employee In employees.AsEnumerable() _
      Where employee.Field(Of Decimal)("salary") > 20 _
      Order By employee.Field(Of Decimal)("salary") _
      Select employee

    For Each emp As DataRow In query
      Response.Write(emp.Field(Of String)("LastName") & ": ")
      Response.Write(emp.Field(Of Decimal)("salary") & "<br />")
    Next

End Sub

//C#
protected void Page_Load(object sender, EventArgs e)
```

```
{
  DataTable employees =
    MyDataProvider.GetEmployeeData();

    EnumerableRowCollection<DataRow> query =
      from employee in employees.AsEnumerable()
      where employee.Field<Decimal>("salary") > 20
      orderby employee.Field<Decimal>("salary")
      select employee;

  foreach (DataRow emp in query)
  {
    Response.Write(emp.Field<String>("LastName") + ": ");
    Response.Write(emp.Field<Decimal>("salary") + "<br />");
  }
}
```

The query in the example is referred to as a *deferred query*. This means that the query does not actually execute until it is iterated over using *for-each*. Instead, the query definition is just a variable with a value. This allows you to define your query and then store it until execution. You can force a query to execute independent of *for-each* using the *ToList* and *ToArray* methods.

You can use LINQ to perform a number of different queries against your data. This includes adding calculated fields to the data based on data groupings. As an example, suppose you wish to calculate the average salary in the employee *DataSet*. You can group the *DataSet* as a single group (and thus return a single row). You then use the construct *Select New* to define new fields. You can then use the group definition to calculate the average of a given field. The following code shows an example:

```
'VB
Dim queryAvg = _
  From employee In employees.AsEnumerable() _
  Group employee By empId = "" Into g = Group _
  Select New With _
  { _
    .AvgSalary = g.Average(Function(employee) _
      employee.Field(Of Decimal)("Salary")) _
  }

For Each emp In queryAvg
  Response.Write(emp.AvgSalary & "<br />")
Next

//C#
var queryAvg =
  from employee in employees.AsEnumerable()
```

```
  group employee by "" into g
  select new
  {
    AvgSalary = g.Average(employee =>
      employee.Field<Decimal>("Salary"))
  };

foreach (var emp in queryAvg)
{
  Response.Write(emp.AvgSalary.ToString() + "<br />");
}
```

LINQ provides an easier way to get at this same data. You can use the methods of the enumerator to get at counts, max values, averages, and more. This type of query is also called a singleton query, as it returns a single value.

```
'VB
Dim avgSalary As Decimal = _
    employees.AsEnumerable.Average(Function(employee) _
    employee.Field(Of Decimal)("Salary"))

Response.Write(avgSalary.ToString())

//C#
Decimal avgSalary =
    employees.AsEnumerable().Average(
    employee => employee.Field<Decimal>("Salary"));

Response.Write(avgSalary.ToString());
```

This section provided an overview of what is possible with LINQ to *DataSet*. There are many more query scenarios that are possible with LINQ. We look at more in the upcoming lessons.

LAB Working with Disconnected Data

In this lab, you create and use a typed *DataSet* that you add graphically to your Web site. This *DataSet* populates a *GridView* control with *Customer* rows.

If you encounter a problem completing an exercise, the completed projects are available in the samples installed from the companion CD in the Code folder.

EXERCISE 1 Create the Web Site and the Typed *DataSet*

In this exercise, you create the Web site and add the controls to the site.

1. Open Visual Studio and create a new Web site called **DisconnectedData**, using your preferred programming language.

2. In Solution Explorer, add a typed *DataSet* graphically by right-clicking the Web site project and selecting Add New Item. Select *DataSet*, and name the *DataSet* **Sales.xsd**.
3. Drag a *DataTable* from the ToolBox and drop it onto the DataSet Editor surface.
4. Select the *DataTable*. In the Properties window, set the name of the *DataTable* to **Customer**.
5. Add the following columns to the Customer table by right-clicking the *DataTable*, selecting Add, and selecting Column. You can set the data type for each column in the Properties dialog box.

COLUMN NAME	DATA TYPE
Id	*System.Guid*
CustomerName	*System.String*

6. Save the *DataSet* and close the data set editor.
7. Open Default.aspx and add a *GridView* control to the page. The *GridView* should be named **GridView1**.
8. Open the code-behind file for the page. In the code-behind file, add code to create and populate an instance of the **Sales** typed *DataSet*. Assign the *DataSet* object to the *GridView*. This code only needs to execute when the page is not being posted back and should look like the following:

```
'VB
Protected Sub Page_Load(ByVal sender As Object, _
  ByVal e As System.EventArgs) Handles Me.Load

  If Not IsPostBack Then

    Dim salesDataSet As New Sales()

    salesDataSet.Customer.Rows.Add(Guid.NewGuid(), "A. Datum Corporation")
    salesDataSet.Customer.Rows.Add(Guid.NewGuid(), "Northwind Traders")
    salesDataSet.Customer.Rows.Add(Guid.NewGuid(), "Alpine Ski House")
    salesDataSet.Customer.Rows.Add(Guid.NewGuid(), "Coho Winery")
    salesDataSet.Customer.Rows.Add(Guid.NewGuid(), "Litware, Inc.")

    GridView1.DataSource = salesDataSet
    DataBind()

  End If

End Sub
```

```
//C#
protected void Page_Load(object sender, EventArgs e)
{
  if (!IsPostBack)
  {
    Sales salesDataSet = new Sales();

    salesDataSet.Customer.Rows.Add(Guid.NewGuid(), "A. Datum Corporation");
    salesDataSet.Customer.Rows.Add(Guid.NewGuid(), "Northwind Traders");
    salesDataSet.Customer.Rows.Add(Guid.NewGuid(), "Alpine Ski House");
    salesDataSet.Customer.Rows.Add(Guid.NewGuid(), "Coho Winery");
    salesDataSet.Customer.Rows.Add(Guid.NewGuid(), "Litware, Inc.");

    GridView1.DataSource = salesDataSet;
    DataBind();

  }
}
```

9. Run the Web page. Figure 7-8 shows the results.

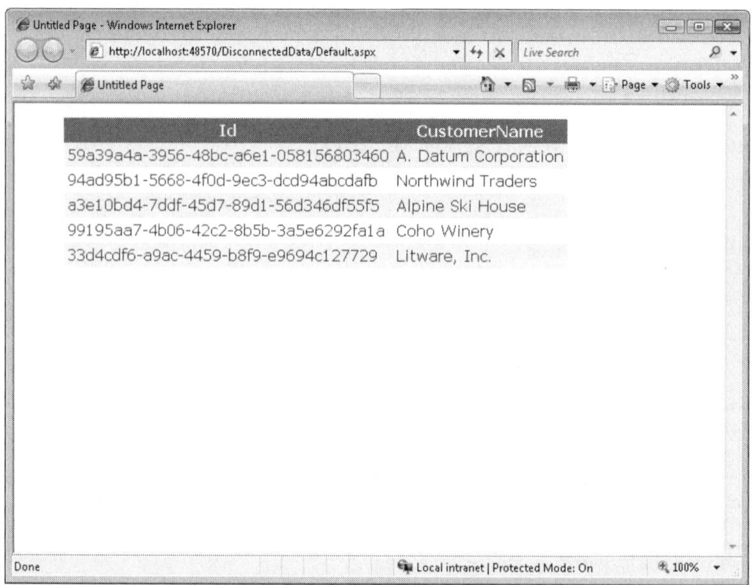

FIGURE 7-8 The typed *DataSet* populated and bound to the *GridView* control

Lesson Summary

- This lesson covers ADO.NET's disconnected classes. When you work with disconnected data, a *DataTable* object is always required.
- The *DataTable* object contains *DataColumn* objects, which define the schema, and *DataRow* objects, which contain the data. *DataRow* objects have *RowState* and *DataRowVersion* properties.
- You use the *RowState* property to indicate whether the *DataRow* should be inserted, updated, or deleted from the data store when the data is persisted to a database.
- The *DataRow* object can contain up to three copies of its data, based on the *DataRow-Version*. This feature allows the data to be rolled back to its original state, and you can use it when you write code to handle conflict resolution.
- The *DataSet* object is an in-memory, relational data representation. The *DataSet* object contains a collection of *DataTable* objects and a collection of *DataRelation* objects.
- *DataSet* and *DataTable* objects can be serialized and deserialized to and from a binary or XML file or stream. Data from other *DataSet*, *DataTable*, and *DataRow* objects can be merged into a *DataSet* object.
- LINQ to *DataSet* provides a mechanism for writing complex queries against in-memory data using C# or Visual Basic.

Lesson Review

You can use the following questions to test your knowledge of the information in Lesson 1, "Using the ADO.NET Disconnected Classes." The questions are also available on the companion CD if you prefer to review them in electronic form.

> ***NOTE*** **ANSWERS**
>
> **Answers to these questions and explanations of why each answer choice is right or wrong are located in the "Answers" section at the end of the book.**

1. You have a *DataSet* containing a *Customer DataTable* and an *Order DataTable*. You want to easily navigate from an *Order DataRow* to the *Customer* who placed the order. What object will allow you to easily navigate from the *Order* to the *Customer*?
   - **A.** The *DataColumn* object
   - **B.** The *DataTable* object
   - **C.** The *DataRow* object
   - **D.** The *DataRelation* object

2. Which of the following is a requirement when merging modified data into a *DataSet*?
   A. A primary key must be defined on the *DataTable* objects.
   B. The *DataSet* schemas must match.
   C. The destination *DataSet* must be empty prior to merging.
   D. A *DataSet* must be merged into the same *DataSet* that created it.
3. You are working with a *DataSet* and want to be able to display data, sorted different ways. How do you do so?
   A. Use the *Sort* method on the *DataTable* object.
   B. Use the *DataSet* object's *Sort* method.
   C. Use a *DataView* object for each sort.
   D. Create a *DataTable* for each sort, using the *DataTable* object's *Copy* method, and then *Sort* the result.
4. You have a large *DataSet* that is stored in memory on your Web server. The *DataSet* represents vendor records. You need to write a query against that *DataSet* to return a subset of the data based on active vendors sorted by highest to lowest in terms of the business that your company does with them. You intend to use LINQ for the query. How will you build the query? (Choose all that apply.)
   A. Use the *AsEnumerable* method of the vendor *DataTable* inside the *DataSet*.
   B. Use a *Where* clause in your code to restrict vendors to only those that are active.
   C. Use an *Order By* clause in your code to sort the vendors.
   D. Use the *Group By* clause in your code to group by active vendors.

Lesson 2: Using the ADO.NET Connected Classes

The ADO.NET libraries contain *provider classes*, which are classes that you can use to transfer data between a data store and the client application. There are many different kinds of data stores, meaning that there is a need for specialized code to provide the necessary bridge between the disconnected data access classes and a particular data store. The provider classes fulfill this need.

This lesson focuses on these specialized classes, starting with the most essential, such as *DbConnection* and *DbCommand*. The lesson then covers more elaborate classes such as *DbProviderFactory* and *DbProviderFactories*. The chapter concludes with a discussion on using LINQ to SQL to leverage the power of LINQ against connected data.

After this lesson, you will be able to:

- Identify and use the following connected data classes in your Web application:
  - *DbConnection*
  - *DbCommand*
  - *DbDataAdapter*
  - *DbProviderFactory*
  - *DbProviderFactories*
- Use LINQ to SQL to work with connected data using LINQ in Visual Basic and C#.

Estimated lesson time: 90 minutes

Using Provider Classes to Move Data

The classes that are responsible for working with the database for connecting, retrieving, updating, inserting, and deleting data are referred to as provider classes in the framework. There is a provider framework on which these classes are built. This ensures that each provider is written in a similar manner and only the implementation code changes. These provider classes represent the bridge between the database and the disconnected data classes discussed in the prior lesson.

The Microsoft .NET Framework contains the following data access providers:

- ***OleDb*** This contains classes that provide general-purpose data access to many data sources. You can use this provider to access Microsoft SQL Server 6.5 (and earlier versions), SyBase, DB2/400, and Microsoft Access.
- ***Odbc*** This contains classes for general-purpose data access to many data sources. This provider is typically used when no newer provider is available.

- **SQL Server** This contains classes that provide functionality similar to the generic *OleDb* provider. The difference is that these classes are tuned for SQL Server 7.0 and later versions (SQL Server 2005 and SQL Server 2008).
- **Oracle** Contains classes for accessing Oracle 8i and later versions. This provider is similar to the *OleDb* provider but provides better performance.

There are also many third-party providers available for the .NET Framework. This includes an Oracle provider written and supported by Oracle, *DB2,* and *MySql*. Each of these additional providers can be downloaded from the Internet.

Table 7-1 lists the primary base provider classes and interfaces. These classes are sub-classed by the given provider implementation. An implementation typically replaces the base class's *Db* prefix with a provider prefix, such as *Sql*, *Oracle*, *Odbc*, or *OleDb*. The SQLClient classes are shown in the second column as an example.

TABLE 7-1 Primary Provider Classes and Interfaces in ADO.NET

BASE CLASSES	*SQLCLIENT* CLASSES	GENERIC INTERFACE
DbConnection	*SqlConnection*	*IDbConnection*
DbCommand	*SqlCommand*	*IDbCommand*
DbDataReader	*SqlDataReader*	*IDataReader/IDataRecord*
DbTransaction	*SqlTransaction*	*IDbTransaction*
DbParameter	*SqlParameter*	*IDbDataParameter*
DbParameterCollection	*SqlParameterCollection*	*IDataParameterCollection*
DbDataAdapter	*SqlDataAdapter*	*IDbDataAdapter*
DbCommandBuilder	*SqlCommandBuilder*	
DbConnectionStringBuilder	*SqlConnectionStringBuilder*	
DBDataPermission	*SqlPermission*	

You can also use the base classes with factory classes to create client code that is not tied to a specific provider. The following sections describe these classes.

Getting Started with the *DbConnection* Object

To access a data store, you need a valid, open connection object. The *DbConnection* class is an abstract class from which the provider-specific connection classes inherit. The connection class hierarchy is shown in Figure 7-9.

To create a connection, you must have a valid connection string. The following code snippet shows how to create the connection object and then assign the connection string. When you are finished working with the connection object, you must close the connection to free up the resources being held. The *pubs* sample database is used in this example. The *pubs* and

Northwind sample databases are available from the Microsoft download site and are also included in the samples installed from the CD.

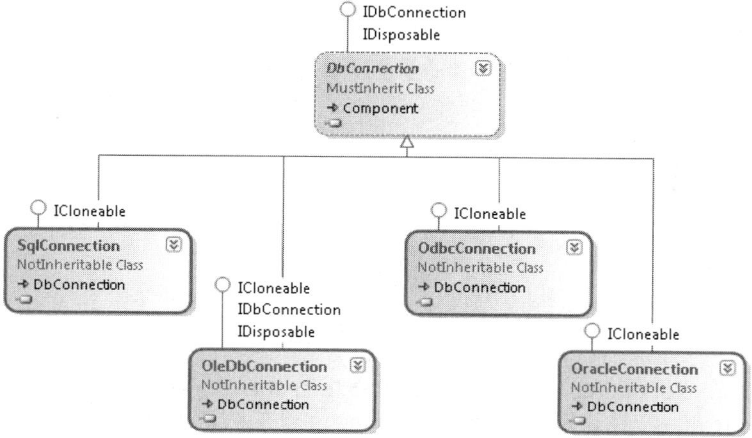

FIGURE 7-9 The *DbConnection* class hierarchy

```
'VB
Dim connection as DbConnection = new SqlConnection()
connection.ConnectionString = _
  "Server=.;Database=pubs;Trusted_Connection=true"
connection.Open()

'do work here
connection.Close()

//C#
DbConnection connection = new SqlConnection();
connection.ConnectionString =
  "Server=.;Database=pubs;Trusted_Connection=true";
connection.Open();

//do work here
connection.Close();
```

Creating an instance of the *SqlConnection* class using the SQL Server .NET provider creates the *DbConnection*. The *ConnectionString* property is initialized to use the local machine (".") and the database is set to *pubs*. Finally, the connection uses a trusted connection for authentication when connecting to SQL Server.

The connection must be opened before you can send commands to the data store, and you must always close the connection when you're done to prevent orphaned connections to the data store. You can close the connection by executing the *Close* method or by executing the *Dispose* method. It's common to create a *Using* block to force the *Dispose* method to execute, as shown in the following code:

```
'VB
Using (connection)
  connection.Open()
  'database commands here
End Using

//C#
using (connection)
{
  connection.Open();
  //database commands here
}
```

You can place the *Using* block inside a *Try-Catch* block to force the connection to be disposed, which typically provides a cleaner implementation than the *Try-Catch-Finally* block.

Regardless of the programming language used, the connection string is the same. The following sections explain how to configure a connection string using each of the .NET Framework providers.

CONFIGURING AN ODBC CONNECTION STRING

Open Database Connectivity (ODBC) is one of the older technologies that the .NET Framework supports, primarily because there are still many scenarios in which the .NET Framework is required to connect to older database products that have ODBC drivers. Table 7-2 describes the most common ODBC connection string settings.

TABLE 7-2 ODBC Connection String Keywords

KEYWORD	DESCRIPTION
Driver	The ODBC driver to use for the connection
DSN	A data source name, which can be configured via the ODBC Data Source Administrator (Control Panel | Administrative Tools | Data Sources (ODBC))
Server	The name of the server to which to connect
Trusted_Connection	A description that specifies what security is based on using the domain account of the currently logged-on user
Database	The database to which to connect
DBQ	Typically, the physical path to a data source

WORKING WITH SAMPLE ODBC CONNECTION STRINGS

The following connection string instructs the text driver to treat the files that are located in the C:\Sample\MySampleFolder subdirectory as tables in a database:

```
Driver={Microsoft Text Driver (*.txt; *.csv)};
  DBQ=C:\\Sample\\MySampleFolder;
```

The following connection string instructs the Access driver to open the *Northwind* database file that is located in the C:\Code\mySampleFolder folder:

```
Driver={Microsoft Access Driver (*.mdb)};
  DBQ=C:\\Code\\mySampleFolder\\northwind.mdb
```

The following connection string uses the settings that have been configured as a data source name (DSN) on the current machine:

```
DSN=My Application DataSource
```

The following is a connection to an Oracle database. The name and password are passed in as well:

```
Driver={Microsoft ODBC for Oracle};
  Server=ORACLE8i7;
  UID=john;
  PWD=s3$W%1Xz
```

The following connection string uses the Microsoft Excel driver to open the MyBook.xls file:

```
Driver={Microsoft Excel Driver (*.xls)};
  DBQ=C:\\Samples\\MyBook.xls
```

The following connection string uses the SQL Server driver to open the *Northwind* database on MyServer using the specified user name and password:

```
DRIVER={SQL Server};
  SERVER=MyServer;
  UID=AppUserAccount;
  PWD=Zx%7$ha;
  DATABASE=northwind;
```

This connection string uses the SQL Server driver to open the *Northwind* database on MyServer using SQL Server's trusted security:

```
DRIVER={SQL Server};
  SERVER=MyServer;
  Trusted_Connection=yes
  DATABASE=northwind;
```

CONFIGURING AN OLEDB CONNECTION STRING

Another common, but older, technology that is used to access databases is Object Linking and Embedding for Databases (OLEDB). Table 7-3 describes the most common OLEDB connection string settings.

TABLE 7-3 OLEDB Connection String Keywords

KEYWORD	DESCRIPTION
Data Source	The name of the database or physical location of the database file.
File Name	The physical location of a file that contains the real connection string.
Persist Security Info	A setting that, if set to *True*, retrieves the connection string and returns the complete connection string that was originally provided. If set to *False*, the connection string contains the information that was originally provided, minus the security information.
Provider	The vendor-specific driver to use for connecting to the data store.

WORKING WITH SAMPLE OLEDB CONNECTION STRINGS

This connection string uses the settings stored in the MyAppData.udl file (the .udl extension stands for universal data link):

```
FILE NAME=C:\Program Files\MyApp\MyAppData.udl
```

This connection string uses the Jet driver, which is the Access driver, and opens the demo.mdb database file. Retrieving the connection string from the connection returns the connection that was originally passed in, minus the security information.

```
Provider=Microsoft.Jet.OLEDB.4.0;
  Data Source=C:\Program Files\myApp\demo.mdb;
  Persist Security Info=False
```

CONFIGURING A SQL SERVER CONNECTION STRING

The SQL Server provider allows you to access SQL Server 7.0 and later. If you need to connect to SQL Server 6.5 and earlier, use the OLEDB provider. Table 7-4 describes the most common SQL Server connection string settings.

TABLE 7-4 SQL Server Connection String Keywords

KEYWORD	DESCRIPTION
Data Source, addr, address, network address, server	The name or IP address of the database server.
Failover Partner	A support provider for database mirroring in SQL Server.

KEYWORD	DESCRIPTION
AttachDbFilename, extended properties, initial file name	The full or relative path and name of a file containing the database to be attached to. The path supports the keyword string |*DataDirectory*|, which points to the application's data directory. The database must reside on a local drive. The log file name must be in the format <database-File-Name>_log.ldf or it will not be found. If the log file is not found, a new log file is created.
Initial Catalog, database	The name of the database to use.
Integrated Security, trusted_connection	A secure connection to SQL Server, in which authentication is via the user's domain account. Can be set to *True*, *False*, or *sspi*. The default is *False*.
Persist Security Info, persistsecurityinfo	A setting that, if set to *True*, causes a retrieval of the connection string to return the complete connection string that was originally provided. If set to *False*, the connection string contains the information that was originally provided, minus the security information. The default is *False*.
User ID, uid, user	The user name to use to connect to the SQL Server when not using a trusted connection.
Password, pwd	The password to use to log on to the SQL Server when not using a trusted connection.
Enlist	When set to *True*, the pooler automatically enlists the connection into the caller thread's ongoing transaction context.
Pooling	A setting that, when set to *True*, causes the request for a new connection to be drawn from the pool. If the pool does not exist, one is created.
Max Pool Size	A setting that specifies the maximum allowed connections in the connection pool. The default is 100.
Min Pool Size	A setting that specifies the minimum number of connections to keep in the pool. The default is 0.
Asynchronous Processing, async	A setting that, when set to *True*, enables execution of asynchronous commands on the connection. (Synchronous commands should use a different connection to minimize resource usage.) The default is *False*.
Connection Reset	A setting that, when set to *True*, indicates that the database connection is reset when the connection is removed from the pool. The default is *True*. A setting of *False* results in fewer round-trips to the server when creating a connection, but the connection state is not updated.

KEYWORD	DESCRIPTION
MultipleActiveResultSets	A setting that, when set to *True*, allows for the retrieval of multiple forward-only, read-only result sets on the same connection. The default is *False*.
Replication	A setting that is used by SQL Server for replication.
Connect Timeout, connection timeout, timeout	The time in seconds to wait while an attempt is made to connect to the data store. The default is 15 seconds.
Encrypt	A setting in which, if *Encrypt* is set to *True* and SQL Server has a certificate installed, all communication between the client and server is SSL encrypted.
Load Balance Timeout, connection lifetime	The maximum time in seconds that a pooled connection should live. The maximum time is checked only when the connection is returned to the pool. This setting is useful in getting load-balanced cluster configurations to force a balance between a server that is online and a server that has just started. The default is 0.
Network Library, net, network	The network dynamic-link library (DLL) to use when connecting to SQL Server. Allowed libraries include dbmssocn (TCP/IP), dbnmpntw (Named Pipes), dbmsrpcn (Multiprotocol), dbmsadsn (Apple Talk), dbmsgnet (VIA), dbmsipcn (Shared Memory), and dbmsspxn (IPX/SPX). The default is dbmssocn (TCP/IP), but if a network is not specified and either "." or "(local)" is specified for the server, shared memory is used as the default.
Packet Size	The size in bytes for each packet that is sent to SQL Server. The default is 8192.
Application Name, app	The name of the application. If not set, this defaults to .NET SQL Client Data Provider.
Current Language, language	The SQL Server language record name.
Workstation ID, wsid	The name of the client computer that is connecting to SQL Server.

Working with Sample SQL Server Connection Strings

The following connection string connects to the *Northwind* database on the current computer (localhost) using integrated security. This connection must be made within 30 seconds or an exception is thrown. The security information is not persisted.

```
Persist Security Info=False;
  Integrated Security=SSPI;
  database=northwind;
```

```
  server=localhost;
  Connect Timeout=30
```

This next connection string uses the Transmission Control Protocol (TCP) sockets library (DBMSSOCN) and connects to the *MyDbName* database on the computer located at Internet Protocol (IP) address 192.168.1.5, using port 1433. Authentication is based on using MyUsername as the user name and u$2hJq@1 as the password.

```
Network Library=DBMSSOCN;
  Data Source=192.168.1.5,1433;
  Initial Catalog=MyDbName;
  User ID=myUsername;
  Password= u$2hJq@1
```

Attaching to a Local SQL Database File with SQL Express

Microsoft SQL Server Express Edition is installed as part of the default Visual Studio installation, which makes it an excellent database to use when you're developing applications that are destined to be used on SQL Server Express Edition or SQL Server. When you're building small Web sites and single-user applications, SQL Server Express Edition is a natural choice due to its XCOPY deployment capabilities, reliability, and high-performance engine. In addition, SQL Server Express Edition databases can easily be attached to SQL Server. To attach a local database file, you can use the following connection string:

```
Data Source=.\SQLEXPRESS;
  AttachDbFilename=C:\MyApplication\PUBS.MDF;
  Integrated Security=True;
  User Instance=True
```

In this example, the Data Source is set to an instance of SQL Server Express Edition called .\SQLEXPRESS. The database file name is set to the database file located at C:\MyApplication \PUBS.MDF. Integrated security is used to authenticate with SQL Server Express Edition; setting *User Instance* to *True* starts an instance of SQL Server Express Edition using the current user's account.

Although you can use SQL Server Express Edition to attach to a local file, SQL Server does not work with the *User Instance=True* setting. Also, SQL Server keeps the database attached when your application ends, so the next time you run SQL Server, an exception will be thrown because the data file is already attached.

AttachDBFilename can also understand the keyword *|DataDirectory|* to use the application's data directory. Here is the revised connection string:

```
Data Source=.\SQLEXPRESS;
  AttachDbFilename=|DataDirectory|\PUBS.MDF;
  Integrated Security=True;
  User Instance=True
```

For a Web application, the *|DataDirectory|* keyword resolves to the App_Data folder.

STORING THE CONNECTION STRING IN THE WEB CONFIGURATION FILE

Connection strings should always be located outside your source code to simplify changes without requiring a recompile of your application. You can store connection strings in the machine or Web configuration file. You place the *connectionStrings* element under the *configuration* root element. This section supports the *<add>*, *<remove>*, and *<clear>* tags, as shown here:

```
<connectionStrings>
  <add name="PubsData"
   providerName="System.Data.SqlClient"
   connectionString=
   "Data Source=.\SQLEXPRESS;
    AttachDbFilename=|DataDirectory|PUBS.MDF;
    Integrated Security=True;
    User Instance=True"/>
</connectionStrings>
```

This example adds a new connection string setting called *PubsData*. The *connectionStrings* element can be accessed in code by using the static *ConnectionStrings* collection of the *ConfigurationManager* class. In the following code sample, a connection string is read from the Web.config file, and a connection object is created using the connection information.

```
'VB
Dim pubs As ConnectionStringSettings
pubs = ConfigurationManager.ConnectionStrings("PubsData")
Dim connection as DbConnection = new SqlConnection(pubs.ConnectionString)

//C#
ConnectionStringSettings pubs =
  ConfigurationManager.ConnectionStrings["PubsData"];
DbConnection connection = new SqlConnection(pubs.ConnectionString);
```

WORKING WITH CONNECTION POOLS

Creating and opening a connection to a data store can be a time-consuming and resource-intensive proposition, especially on Web-based systems, if you require separate connections to the data store on a user-by-user basis. It's easy to get into a situation where every user has one or more open connections to the database and the database server is consuming too many resources just managing connections. Ideally, the data store should be spending most of its time delivering data and as little time as possible maintaining connections. This is where connection pooling can help.

Connection pooling is the process of reusing existing active connections instead of creating new connections when a request is made to the database. It involves the use of a connection manager that is responsible for maintaining a list, or pool, of available connections. When the connection manager receives a request for a new connection, it checks its pool for available connections. If a connection is available, it is returned. If no connections are available, and the maximum pool size has not been reached, a new connection is created and returned. If the maximum pool size has been reached, the connection request is added to the queue and the next available connection is returned, as long as the connection timeout has not been reached.

Connection pooling is controlled by parameters placed into the connection string. The following is a list of parameters that affect pooling:

- ***Connection Timeout*** The time in seconds to wait while a connection to the data store is attempted. The default is 15 seconds.
- ***Min Pool Size*** The minimum amount of pooled connections to keep in the pool. The default is 0. It's usually good to set this to a low number, such as 5, when your application requires consistent, fast response, even if the application is inactive for long periods of time.
- ***Max Pool Size*** The maximum allowed number of connections in the connection pool. The default is 100, which is usually more than enough for most Web site applications.
- ***Pooling*** A setting in which a value of *True* causes the request for a new connection to be drawn from the pool. If the pool does not exist, it is created. The default is *True*.
- ***Connection Reset*** An indicator that the database connection is reset when the connection is removed from the pool. The default is *True*. A value of *False* results in fewer round-trips to the server when creating a connection, but the connection state is not updated.
- ***Load Balancing Timeout, Connection Lifetime*** The maximum time in seconds that a pooled connection should live. The maximum time is checked only when the connection is returned to the pool. This setting is useful in load-balanced cluster configurations to force a balance between a server that is online and a server that has just started. The default is 0.
- ***Enlist*** When this value is *True*, the connection is automatically enlisted into the creation thread's current transaction context. The default is *True*.

To implement connection pooling, you must follow a few rules:

- The connection string must be exactly the same, character by character, for every user or service that participates in the pool. Remember that each character must match in terms of lowercase and uppercase as well.
- The user ID must be the same for every user or service that participates in the pool. Even if you specify *Integrated Security=true*, the Windows user account of the process is used to determine pool membership.
- The process ID must be the same. It has never been possible to share connections across processes, and this limitation extends to pooling.

Where is the Pool Located?

Connection pooling is a client-side technology, which means that the connection pool exists on the machine that initiates the *DbConnection* object's *Open* statement. The database server has no idea that there might be one or more connection pools involved in your application.

When is the Pool Created?

A connection pool group is an object that manages the connection pools for a specific ADO.NET provider. When the first connection is instantiated, a connection pool group is created, but the first connection pool is not created until the first connection is opened.

Do Connections Stay in the Pool?

A connection is removed from the pool of available connections for use and then returned to the pool of available connections. When a connection is returned to the connection pool, it has a default idle lifetime of four to eight minutes, which is an intentionally random time span to ensure that idle connections are not held indefinitely. You can set the connection string's *Min Pool Size* to 1 or greater when you want to make sure that at least one connection is available when your application is idle for long periods.

Using the Load Balancing Timeout

The connection string has a setting called the *Load Balancing Timeout*, which is also known as the *Connection Lifetime*. *Connection Lifetime* still exists for backward compatibility, but the new name better describes this setting's intended use. Use this setting only in an environment with clustered servers, because it is meant to aid in load-balancing database connections. This setting is only examined on closed connections. If the connection stays open longer than its *Load Balancing Timeout* setting, the connection is destroyed. Otherwise, the connection is added back into the pool.

The *Load Balancing Timeout* setting can be used to ensure that new connections are being created when you are using a database server cluster. If two database servers are clustered together and they appear heavily loaded, you might choose to add a third database server. After adding the third database server, you might notice that the original databases still seem overloaded and the new server has few or no connections.

The problem is that connection pooling is doing its job by maintaining connections to the existing database servers. Specify a *Load Balancing Timeout* setting that throws out some of the good connections so a new connection can go to the newly added database server. You lose a bit of performance because you destroy good connections, but the new connections potentially go to a new database server, which improves performance.

USING VISUAL STUDIO TO ADD A CONNECTION

If you need to perform database management tasks, you can add a connection to the database using the Server Explorer window and the Connection Wizard. A connection is automatically created for each database file that is added to your project, and you can also add connections manually. Figure 7-10 shows the Server Explorer window after the Pubs.mdf and Northwind.mdf files were added to the project, and after a connection was manually added to the *Northwind* database on the local copy of SQL Server by right-clicking the *Connections* node and selecting New Connection to start the Connection Wizard.

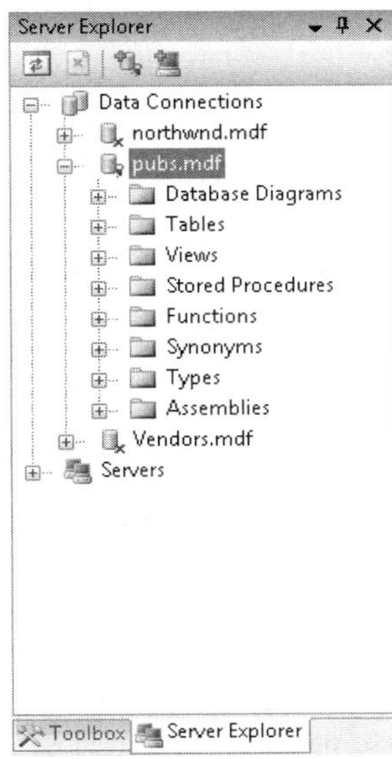

FIGURE 7-10 The Server Explorer window shows the connections that were added

You can use the connection to perform maintenance, modify the database schema and data, and run queries. Also, controls such as the *SqlDataSource* allow you to select one of these connections when you add the control to the Web page.

SECURING CONNECTION STRINGS WITH ENCRYPTION

You store connection strings in your configuration files to make it easy to change the connection string without requiring a recompile of the application. The problem is that connection strings might contain login information such as user names and passwords.

The solution is to encrypt the connection string section of your configuration file by using the Aspnet_regiis.exe utility. You can use the /? option to get help on the utility.

You encrypt and decrypt the contents of a Web.config file by using the *System.Configuration.DPAPIProtectedConfigurationProvider*, which uses the Windows Data Protection API (DPAPI) to encrypt and decrypt data, or the *System.Configuration.RSAProtectedConfigurationProvider*, which uses the Rivest–Shamir–Adleman (RSA) encryption algorithm to encrypt and decrypt data.

When you need to use the same encrypted configuration file on many computers in a Web farm, you must use the *System.Configuration.RSAProtectedConfigurationProvider*, which allows you to export the encryption keys used to encrypt the data. The encryption keys can be imported into another server. This is the default setting. A typical Web.config file might look like the following:

```
<?xml version="1.0"?>
<configuration xmlns="http://schemas.microsoft.com/.NetConfiguration/v2.0">
  <appSettings/>
  <connectionStrings>
    <add name="ConnectionString"
      connectionString="Data Source=.\SQLEXPRESS;
      AttachDbFilename=|DataDirectory|\northwnd.mdf;
      Integrated Security=True;User Instance=True"
      providerName="System.Data.SqlClient" />
  </connectionStrings>
  <system.web>
   ...
  </system.web>
</configuration>
```

The *connectionStrings* element can be encrypted by running the Visual Studio command prompt, executing the following command, and specifying the full path to your Web site folder:

```
aspnet_regiis -pef "connectionStrings" "C:\...\EncryptWebSite"
```

Note that the *–pef* switch requires you to pass the physical Web site path, which is the last parameter. Be sure to verify the path to your Web.config file. The encrypted Web.config file will look like the following:

```
<?xml version="1.0"?>
<configuration xmlns="http://schemas.microsoft.com/.NetConfiguration/v2.0">
  <protectedData>
   <protectedDataSections>
    <add name="connectionStrings"
      provider="RsaProtectedConfigurationProvider"
      inheritedByChildren="false" />
   </protectedDataSections>
  </protectedData>
  <appSettings/>
  <connectionStrings>
   <EncryptedData Type="http://www.w3.org/2001/04/xmlenc#Element"
    xmlns="http://www.w3.org/2001/04/xmlenc#">
    <EncryptionMethod
      Algorithm="http://www.w3.org/2001/04/xmlenc#tripledes-cbc" />
    <KeyInfo xmlns="http://www.w3.org/2000/09/xmldsig#">
      <EncryptedKey Recipient=""
       xmlns="http://www.w3.org/2001/04/xmlenc#">
       <EncryptionMethod
        Algorithm="http://www.w3.org/2001/04/xmlenc#rsa-1_5" />
       <KeyInfo xmlns="http://www.w3.org/2000/09/xmldsig#">
        <KeyName>Rsa Key</KeyName>
```

```
        </KeyInfo>
        <CipherData>
<CipherValue>PPWA1TkWxs2i698Dj07iLUberpFYIj6wBhbmqfmNK/plarau4i1k+xq5bZzB4VJW8
OkhwzcIIdZIXff6INJ1wlZz76ZV1DIbRzbH71t6d/L/qJtuOexXxTi2LrepreK/q3svMLpsJycnDPa
t9xaGoaLq4Cg3P19Z1J6HquFILeo=</CipherValue>
        </CipherData>
       </EncryptedKey>
     </KeyInfo>
     <CipherData>
<CipherValue>Q1re8ntDDv7/dHsvWbnIKdZF6COA1y3S91hmnhUN3nxYfrjSc7FrjEVyJfJhl5EDX
4kXd8ukAjrqwuBNnQbsh1PAXNFDflzB4FF+jyPKP/jm1Q9mDnmiq+NCuo3KpKj8F4vcHbcj+f3GYqq
B4pYbblAvYnjPyPrrPmxLNT9KDtDr8pDbtGnKqAfcMnQPvA8l5w3BzPM4a73Vtt2kL/z9QJRu3Svd9
33taxOO/HufRJEnE2/hcBq3OWcBmEuXx3LFNjV+xVmuebrInhhxQgM2froBKYxgjwWiWNjIIjIeTI2
FQ8nZ8V8kzAVohmDYkZpCj4NQGdrjD996h97phI6NnHZYZHJ7oPRz</CipherValue>
     </CipherData>
    </EncryptedData>
  </connectionStrings>
  <system.web>
   ...
  </system.web>
</configuration>
```

If changes are made to the *connectionStrings* section using the graphical user interface (GUI) tools, the new connection is encrypted, which means that you won't have to run the aspnet_regiis utility again.

You can decrypt the *connectionStrings* section by using the following command:

```
aspnet_regiis -pdf "connectionStrings" "C:\...\EncryptWebSite"
```

After the *connectionStrings* section is decrypted, it looks just as it did before it was encrypted.

Using the *DbCommand* Object

The *DbCommand* object is used to send one or more Structured Query Language (SQL) statements to the data store. The *DbCommand* can be any of the following types:

- **Data Manipulation Language (DML)** Commands that retrieve, insert, update, or delete data
- **Data Definition Language (DDL)** Commands that create tables or other database objects, or modify the database schema
- **Data Control Language (DCL)** Commands that grant, deny, or revoke permissions

The *DbCommand* object requires a valid open connection to issue the command to the data store. A *DbConnection* object can be passed into the *DbCommand* object's constructor or attached to the *DbCommand* object's *Connection* property after the *DbCommand* is created, but you should always consider using the *CreateCommand* method on the

DbConnection object to limit the amount of provider-specific code in your application. The *DbConnection* automatically creates the appropriate provider-specific *DbCommand*.

The *DbCommand* also requires a valid value for its *CommandText* and *CommandType* properties. The following code shows how to create and initialize (but not execute) a *DbCommand* that calls a stored procedure:

```
'VB
Dim pubs As ConnectionStringSettings
pubs = ConfigurationManager.ConnectionStrings("PubsData")

Dim connection As DbConnection = New SqlConnection()
connection.ConnectionString = pubs.ConnectionString

Dim cmd As DbCommand = connection.CreateCommand()
cmd.CommandType = CommandType.StoredProcedure
cmd.CommandText = "uspGetCustomerById"

//C#
ConnectionStringSettings pubs =
  ConfigurationManager.ConnectionStrings["PubsData"];
DbConnection connection =
  new SqlConnection(pubs.ConnectionString);

DbCommand cmd = connection.CreateCommand();
cmd.CommandType = CommandType.StoredProcedure;
cmd.CommandText = "uspGetCustomerById";
```

This code creates a *SqlConnection* object and assigns it to the connection variable that has the data type of *DbConnection*. The *DbConnection* object is then used to create a *SqlCommand*, which is assigned to the *cmd* variable. The *DbConnection* must be opened before the command can be executed. To execute a stored procedure as shown, the *CommandText* property contains the name of the stored procedure, and the *CommandType* indicates that this is a call to a stored procedure.

USING *DBPARAMETER* OBJECTS TO PASS DATA

When you need to pass data to a stored procedure, you should use *DbParameter* objects. For example, a user-defined stored procedure called *uspGetCustomerById* might require a customer ID to retrieve the appropriate customer. You can create *DbParameter* objects by using the *Parameters.Add* method of the *Command* object, as shown here:

```
'VB
Dim pubs As ConnectionStringSettings
pubs = ConfigurationManager.ConnectionStrings("PubsData")

Dim connection As DbConnection = New SqlConnection()
connection.ConnectionString = pubs.ConnectionString
```

```
Dim cmd As DbCommand = connection.CreateCommand()
cmd.CommandType = CommandType.StoredProcedure
cmd.CommandText = "uspGetCustomerById"

Dim parm As DbParameter = cmd.CreateParameter()
parm.ParameterName = "@Id"
parm.Value = "AROUT"
cmd.Parameters.Add(parm)

//C#
ConnectionStringSettings pubs =
  ConfigurationManager.ConnectionStrings["PubsData"];

DbConnection connection =
  new SqlConnection(pubs.ConnectionString);

DbCommand cmd = connection.CreateCommand();
cmd.CommandType = CommandType.StoredProcedure;
cmd.CommandText = "uspGetCustomerById";

DbParameter parm = cmd.CreateParameter();
parm.ParameterName = "@Id";
parm.Value = "AROUT";
cmd.Parameters.Add(parm);
```

This code creates and configures a *DbConnection* object and a *DbCommand* object. A single parameter called *@Id* is created and assigned the value *AROUT*.

> ***NOTE*** **BE CAREFUL WITH PARAMETER NAMES AND PARAMETER ORDER**
>
> **The SQL provider requires that the parameter names match the parameter names defined in the stored procedure. The creation of the parameters is, therefore, not order-dependent.**
>
> **The *OleDb* provider, on the other hand, requires the parameters to be defined in the same order that they are defined in the stored procedure. This means the name assigned to the parameter need not match the name defined in the stored procedure.**

Use the name assigned to the *DbParameter* object to access the parameter through code. For example, to retrieve the value that is currently in the *SqlParameter* called *@Id*, use the following code:

```
'VB
Dim id as String = cmd.Parameters("@Id").Value

//C#
string id = (string)((DbParameter)cmd.Parameters["@Id"]).Value;
```

BUILDING SQL COMMANDS USING SERVER EXPLORER

The Server Explorer window can be used to create SQL commands by right-clicking a connection and selecting New Query. This opens a four-pane window and prompts you to select tables, views, functions, and synonyms to be added to the query. The window provides the following four panes:

- **Diagram pane** This pane usually shows the tables and views that have been selected, and also shows the relationships between them.
- **Criteria pane** This tabular pane allows you to select the columns and specify attributes for each column, such as alias, sort, and filters.
- **SQL pane** This textual pane shows the actual SQL statement that is being built.
- **Results pane** This tabular pane shows the results after the query has been executed.

USING THE *EXECUTENONQUERY* METHOD

When you want to execute a *DbCommand* object and you don't expect a tabular result to be returned, you should use the *ExecuteNonQuery* method. Examples of SQL statements that don't return any rows are an insert, an update, or a delete query. The *ExecuteNonQuery* method returns an integer that represents the number of rows affected by the operation. The following example executes a SQL statement to increment the *qty* field in the Sales table for sales with *qty* greater than 50; it returns the number of rows that were updated.

```
'VB
Dim pubs As ConnectionStringSettings
pubs = ConfigurationManager.ConnectionStrings("PubsData")

Dim connection As DbConnection = New SqlConnection()
connection.ConnectionString = pubs.ConnectionString
Dim cmd As DbCommand = connection.CreateCommand()
cmd.CommandType = CommandType.Text
cmd.CommandText = _
 "UPDATE SALES SET qty = qty + 1 WHERE qty > 50"

connection.Open()
Dim count As Integer = cmd.ExecuteNonQuery()
connection.Close()

//C#
ConnectionStringSettings pubs =
  ConfigurationManager.ConnectionStrings["PubsData"];

DbConnection connection = new SqlConnection(pubs.ConnectionString);

DbCommand cmd = connection.CreateCommand();
cmd.CommandType = CommandType.Text;
cmd.CommandText = "UPDATE SALES SET qty = qty + 1 WHERE qty > 50";
```

```
connection.Open();
int count = cmd.ExecuteNonQuery();
connection.Close();
```

USING THE *EXECUTESCALAR* METHOD

You might execute a query that is expected to return a tabular result containing a single row and column, such as a query that retrieves the total sales for the day. In situations such as this, the results can be treated as a single return value. For example, the following SQL statement returns a result that consists of a single row with a single column:

```
SELECT COUNT(*) FROM Sales
```

If you use the *ExecuteScalar* method, the .NET runtime does not create an instance of a *DataTable* to hold the result (which means less resource usage and better performance). The following code shows how to use the *ExecuteScalar* method to easily retrieve the number of rows in the Sales table into a variable called *count*:

```
'VB
Dim pubs As ConnectionStringSettings
pubs = ConfigurationManager.ConnectionStrings("PubsData")

Dim connection As DbConnection = New SqlConnection()
connection.ConnectionString = pubs.ConnectionString

Dim cmd As DbCommand = connection.CreateCommand()
cmd.CommandType = CommandType.Text
cmd.CommandText = "SELECT COUNT(*) FROM Sales"
connection.Open()

Dim count As Integer = cmd.ExecuteScalar()
connection.Close()

//C#
ConnectionStringSettings pubs =
  ConfigurationManager.ConnectionStrings["PubsData"];

DbConnection connection = new SqlConnection(pubs.ConnectionString);

DbCommand cmd = connection.CreateCommand();
cmd.CommandType = CommandType.Text;
cmd.CommandText = "SELECT COUNT(*) FROM Sales";
connection.Open();

int count = (int)cmd.ExecuteScalar();
connection.Close();
```

USING THE *EXECUTEREADER* METHOD

The *ExecuteReader* method returns a *DbDataReader* instance that represents a forward-only, read-only, server-side cursor. *DbDataReader* objects can be created only by executing one of the *ExecuteReader* methods on the *DbCommand* object. (See the next section for more information on the *DbDataReader*.) The following example uses the *ExecuteReader* method to create a *DbDataReader* object with the query results, then continuously loops through the results and writes them out to a Web page. Once the end of the data has been reached (when the *Read* method returns *False*), the connection to the database is closed.

```
'VB
Dim pubs As ConnectionStringSettings
pubs = ConfigurationManager.ConnectionStrings("PubsData")

Dim connection As DbConnection = New SqlConnection()
connection.ConnectionString = pubs.ConnectionString

Dim cmd As DbCommand = connection.CreateCommand()
cmd.CommandType = CommandType.Text
cmd.CommandText = "SELECT stor_id, ord_num FROM Sales"

connection.Open()
Dim rdr As DbDataReader = cmd.ExecuteReader()

While (rdr.Read())
  Response.Write(rdr("stor_id") + ": " + rdr("ord_num") + "<br />")
End While
connection.Close()

//C#
ConnectionStringSettings pubs =
  ConfigurationManager.ConnectionStrings["PubsData"];

DbConnection connection = new SqlConnection(pubs.ConnectionString);

DbCommand cmd = connection.CreateCommand();
cmd.CommandType = CommandType.Text;
cmd.CommandText = "SELECT stor_id, ord_num FROM Sales";

connection.Open();
DbDataReader rdr = cmd.ExecuteReader();

while (rdr.Read())
{
  Response.Write(rdr["stor_id"] + ": " + rdr["ord_num"] + "<br />");
}
connection.Close();
```

Using the *DbDataReader* Object

A *DbDataReader* object provides a high-performance method of retrieving data from the data store. It delivers a forward-only, read-only, server-side cursor. This makes the *DbDataReader* object an ideal choice for populating *ListBox* controls, *DropDownList* controls, and even *GridView* controls that display read-only data. When you run reports, you can use the *DbDataReader* object to retrieve the data from the data store. The *DbDataReader* might not be a good choice when you are coding an operation that modifies data and needs to send the changes back to the database. For data modifications, the *DbDataAdapter* object, which is discussed in the next section, might be a better choice.

The *DbDataReader* contains a *Read* method that retrieves data into its buffer. Only one row of data is ever available at a time, which means that the data does not need to be completely read into the application before it is processed. The following code uses the *Load* method of the *DataTable* object to populate a *DataTable* directly from a *DataReader* object connected to the database:

```
'VB
Dim pubs As ConnectionStringSettings
pubs = ConfigurationManager.ConnectionStrings("PubsData")

Dim connection As DbConnection = New SqlConnection()
connection.ConnectionString = pubs.ConnectionString

Dim cmd As DbCommand = connection.CreateCommand()
cmd.CommandType = CommandType.Text
cmd.CommandText = "SELECT pub_id, pub_name FROM publishers"

connection.Open()

Dim rdr As DbDataReader = cmd.ExecuteReader()
Dim publishers As New DataTable()

publishers.Load(rdr, LoadOption.Upsert)
connection.Close()

GridView1.DataSource = publishers
GridView1.DataBind()

//C#
ConnectionStringSettings pubs =
  ConfigurationManager.ConnectionStrings["PubsData"];

DbConnection connection = new SqlConnection(pubs.ConnectionString);

DbCommand cmd = connection.CreateCommand();
cmd.CommandType = CommandType.Text;
```

```
cmd.CommandText = "SELECT pub_id, pub_name FROM Publishers";

connection.Open();

DbDataReader rdr = cmd.ExecuteReader();
DataTable publishers = new DataTable();
publishers.Load(rdr, LoadOption.Upsert);

connection.Close();

GridView1.DataSource = publishers;
GridView1.DataBind();
```

Notice that the *DataTable* object's *Load* method contains a *LoadOption* parameter. The *LoadOption* gives you the option of deciding which *DataRowVersion* should get the incoming data. For example, if you load a *DataTable* object, modify the data, and then save the changes back to the database, you might encounter concurrency errors if someone else has modified the data between the time you got the data and the time you attempted to save it. One option is to load the *DataTable* object again, using the default *PreserveCurrentValues* enumeration value, which loads the original *DataRowVersion* with the data from the database, leaving the current *DataRowVersion* untouched. Next, you can execute the *Update* method again and the update will check for conflicts.

For this to work properly, the *DataTable* must have a *PrimaryKey* defined. Failure to define a *PrimaryKey* results in duplicate *DataRow* objects being added to the *DataTable* object. The *LoadOption* enumeration members are as follows:

- ***OverwriteChanges*** This setting overwrites the original DataRowVersion and the current DataRowVersion and changes the RowState to Unchanged. New rows have a RowState of Unchanged as well.
- ***PreserveChanges* (default)** This setting overwrites the original DataRowVersion but does not modify the current DataRowVersion. New rows have a RowState of Unchanged as well.
- ***Upsert*** This setting overwrites the current DataRowVersion but does not modify the original DataRowVersion. New rows have a RowState of Added. Rows that had a RowState of Unchanged have a RowState of Unchanged if the current DataRowVersion is the same as the original DataRowVersion; if they are different, the RowState is Modified.

USING MULTIPLE ACTIVE RESULT SETS (MARS) TO EXECUTE MULTIPLE COMMANDS ON A CONNECTION

One of the problems with the *DbDataReader* is that it keeps an open server-side cursor while you are looping through the results of your query. If you try to execute another command while the first command is still executing, you receive an *InvalidOperationException* stating

"There is already an open DataReader associated with this Connection which must be closed first." You can avoid this exception by setting the *MultipleActiveResultSets* connection string option to *True* when connecting to MARS-enabled hosts, such as SQL Server. For example, the following connection string shows in bold how this setting is added into a new connection string called *PubsDataMars*:

```
<connectionStrings>
  <add name="PubsData"
   providerName="System.Data.SqlClient"
   connectionString=
   "Data Source=.\SQLEXPRESS;
    AttachDbFilename=|DataDirectory|PUBS.MDF;
    Integrated Security=True;
    User Instance=True"/>
  <add name="PubsDataMars"
   providerName="System.Data.SqlClient"
   connectionString=
   "Data Source=.\SQLEXPRESS;
    AttachDbFilename=|DataDirectory|PUBS.MDF;
    Integrated Security=True;
    User Instance=True;
    MultipleActiveResultSets=True"/>
</connectionStrings>
```

NOTE **MARS PERFORMANCE**

MARS does not provide any performance gains, but it does simplify your coding efforts. As a matter of fact, setting *MultipleActiveResultSets=True* in the connection string has a negative performance impact, so you should not turn on MARS arbitrarily.

MARS is something that you can live without. It simply makes your programming easier. Think of a scenario in which you execute a query to get a list of authors and, while you are looping through a list of the authors that are returned, you want to execute a second query to get the total royalties for each author.

On a database server without MARS, you could first read the list of authors into a collection and close the connection. After that, you could loop through the collection to get each author's ID and execute a query to get the total royalties for the author. This means that you would loop through the authors twice: once to populate the collection, and again to get each author's ID and execute a query to get the author's total royalties. A MARS solution is to simply create two commands: one for the author list and one for the total royalties query.

MARS is also beneficial for a situation in which you have purchased database client licenses that are based on the quantity of connections to the database. Without MARS, you would have to open a separate connection to the database for each command that needs to run at the same time, which means that you might need to purchase more client licenses.

Performing Bulk Copy Operations with the *SqlBulkCopy* Object

The *SqlBulkCopy* class provides a high-performance method for copying data to a table in a SQL Server database. The source of the copy is constrained to the overloads of the *WriteToServer* method, which can accept an array of *DataRow* objects, an object that implements the *IDbDataReader* interface, a *DataTable* object, or a *DataTable* and *DataRowState*, as shown in Figure 7-11. This variety of parameters means that you can retrieve data from most locations.

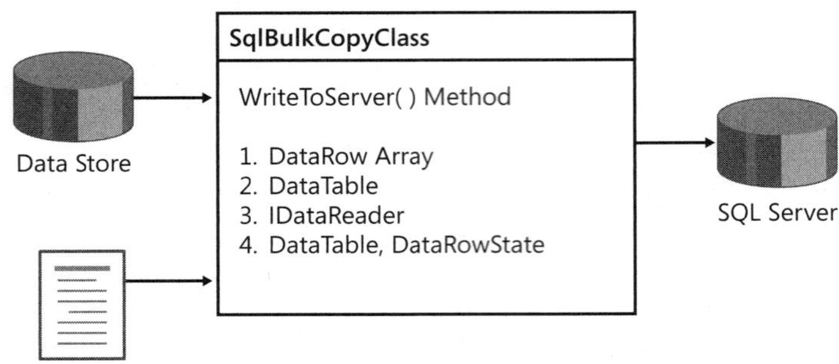

FIGURE 7-11 The *SqlBulkCopy* object can copy from a variety of sources to a SQL Server table

The following code shows how you can use a *SqlBulkCopy* object to copy data from the Store table in the *pubs* database to the StoreList table:

```
'VB
Dim pubs As ConnectionStringSettings
pubs = ConfigurationManager.ConnectionStrings("PubsData")
Dim connection As DbConnection = New SqlConnection()
connection.ConnectionString = pubs.ConnectionString
Dim bulkCopy As ConnectionStringSettings
bulkCopy = ConfigurationManager.ConnectionStrings("PubsData")
Dim bulkCopyConnection As DbConnection = New SqlConnection()
bulkCopyConnection.ConnectionString = bulkCopy.ConnectionString
Dim cmd As DbCommand = connection.CreateCommand()
cmd.CommandType = CommandType.Text
cmd.CommandText = "SELECT stor_name FROM Stores"
connection.Open()
bulkCopyConnection.Open()

'make sure that table exists and is empty
'in case button is clicked more than once
Dim cleanup as SqlCommand = bulkCopyConnection.CreateCommand()
cleanup.CommandText = _
  "IF EXISTS ( SELECT * FROM sys.objects " _
  + " WHERE object_id = OBJECT_ID('dbo.StoreList')  " _
  + " AND type in ('U')) " _
  + "DROP TABLE dbo.StoreList " _
```

```
  + "CREATE TABLE dbo.StoreList(stor_name varchar(40) NOT NULL )"
cleanup.ExecuteNonQuery()

'do the bulkcopy
Dim rdr As DbDataReader = cmd.ExecuteReader()
Dim bc As New SqlBulkCopy(bulkCopyConnection)
bc.DestinationTableName = "StoreList"
bc.WriteToServer(rdr)
connection.Close()
bulkCopyConnection.Close()

//C#
ConnectionStringSettings pubs =
  ConfigurationManager.ConnectionStrings["PubsData"];
DbConnection connection =
  new SqlConnection(pubs.ConnectionString);
ConnectionStringSettings bulkCopy =
  ConfigurationManager.ConnectionStrings["PubsData"];
SqlConnection bulkCopyConnection =
  new SqlConnection(bulkCopy.ConnectionString);
DbCommand cmd = connection.CreateCommand();
cmd.CommandType = CommandType.Text;
cmd.CommandText = "SELECT stor_name FROM Stores";
connection.Open();
bulkCopyConnection.Open();

//make sure that table exists and is empty
//in case button is clicked more than once
SqlCommand cleanup = bulkCopyConnection.CreateCommand();
cleanup.CommandText =
  "IF EXISTS ( SELECT * FROM sys.objects "
  + " WHERE object_id = OBJECT_ID('dbo.StoreList')  "
  + " AND type in ('U')) "
  + "DROP TABLE dbo.StoreList "
  + "CREATE TABLE dbo.StoreList(stor_name varchar(40) NOT NULL )";
cleanup.ExecuteNonQuery();

//do the bulkcopy
DbDataReader rdr = cmd.ExecuteReader();
SqlBulkCopy bc = new SqlBulkCopy(bulkCopyConnection);
bc.DestinationTableName = "StoreList";
bc.WriteToServer(rdr);
connection.Close();
bulkCopyConnection.Close();
```

You should consider using the *IDbDataReader* parameter whenever possible to get the best performance with the fewest resources used. You can decide how much data should be copied based on the query that you use. For example, the preceding code sample retrieved only the store names and could have had a WHERE clause to further limit the data.

Using the *DbDataAdapter* Object

The *DbDataAdapter* object is used to retrieve and update data between a *DataTable* and a data store. The *DbDataAdapter* is derived from the *DataAdapter* class and is the base class of the provider-specific *DbDataAdapter* classes, as shown in Figure 7-12.

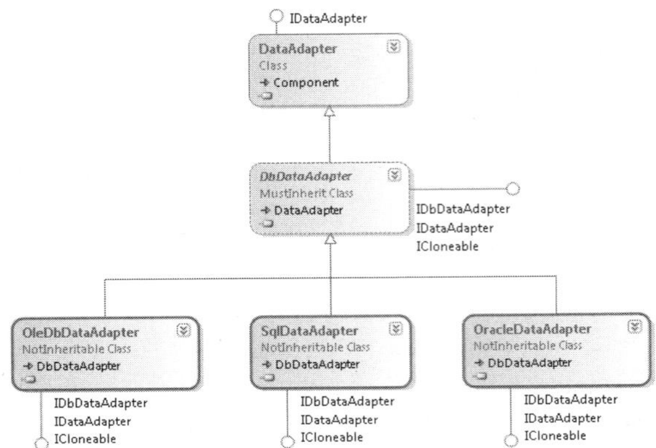

FIGURE 7-12 The *DbDataAdapter* hierarchy, showing the *DataAdapter* base class and the provider-specific derived classes

The *DbDataAdapter* has a *SelectCommand* property that you use when retrieving the data. The *SelectCommand* must contain a valid *DbCommand* object, which must have a valid connection.

The *DbDataAdapter* also has *InsertCommand*, *UpdateCommand*, and *DeleteCommand* properties, which can optionally contain *DbCommand* objects to send *DataTable* changes to the data store. You don't need to create these command objects if you only need to read data from the data store, but if you create one of these latter three commands, you must create all four of them.

USING THE *FILL* METHOD

The *Fill* method moves data from the data store to the *DataTable* object that you pass into this method. The *Fill* method has several overloads, some of which accept only a *DataSet* as a parameter. When a *DataSet* is passed to the *Fill* method, a new *DataTable* object is created in the *DataSet* if a source *DataTable* object is not specified.

The following code shows how a *DataTable* can be loaded using the *Fill* method:

```
'VB
Dim pubs As ConnectionStringSettings
pubs = ConfigurationManager.ConnectionStrings("PubsData")
```

```
Dim connection As DbConnection = New SqlConnection()
connection.ConnectionString = pubs.ConnectionString

Dim cmd As SqlCommand = CType(connection.CreateCommand(), SqlCommand)
cmd.CommandType = CommandType.Text
cmd.CommandText = "SELECT pub_id, pub_name FROM publishers"

Dim pubsDataSet As New DataSet("Pubs")
Dim da As New SqlDataAdapter(cmd)
da.Fill(pubsDataSet, "publishers")

GridView1.DataSource = pubsDataSet
GridView1.DataBind()

//C#
ConnectionStringSettings pubs =
  ConfigurationManager.ConnectionStrings["PubsData"];
DbConnection connection = new SqlConnection(pubs.ConnectionString);

SqlCommand cmd = (SqlCommand)connection.CreateCommand();
cmd.CommandType = CommandType.Text;
cmd.CommandText = "SELECT pub_id, pub_name FROM Publishers";

SqlDataAdapter da = new SqlDataAdapter(cmd);
DataSet pubsDataSet = new DataSet("Pubs");
da.Fill(pubsDataSet, "publishers");

GridView1.DataSource = pubsDataSet;
GridView1.DataBind();
```

SAVING CHANGES TO THE DATABASE USING THE *UPDATE* METHOD

The *Update* method retrieves the changes from a *DataTable* object and executes the appropriate *InsertCommand*, *UpdateCommand*, or *DeleteCommand* to send each change to the data store on a row-by-row basis. The *Update* method retrieves the *DataRow* objects that have been changed by looking at the *RowState* property of each row. If the *RowState* is anything but *Unchanged*, the *Update* method sends the change to the database.

For the *Update* method to work, all four commands must be assigned to the *DbDataAdapter*. Normally, this means creating individual *DbCommand* objects for each command. You can easily create the commands by using the *DbDataAdapter* configuration wizard, which starts when a *DbDataAdapter* is dropped onto the form. The wizard can generate stored procedures for all four commands.

Another way to populate the *DbDataAdapter* object's commands is to use the *DbCommandBuilder* object. This object creates the *InsertCommand*, *UpdateCommand*, and *DeleteCommand* as long as a valid *SelectCommand* exists.

SAVING CHANGES TO THE DATABASE IN BATCHES

One way to increase update performance is to send the changes to the database server in batches instead of sending changes on a row-by-row basis. You can do this by assigning a value to the *DbDataAdapter* object's *UpdateBatchSize* property. This property defaults to 1, which causes each change to be sent to the server on a row-by-row basis. Setting the value to 0 instructs the *DbDataAdapter* object to create the largest possible batch size for changes, or you can set the value to the number of changes you want to send to the server in each batch. Setting the *UpdateBatchSize* to a number greater than the number of changes that need to be sent is equivalent to setting it to 0.

You can confirm that the changes are being sent to the database server in batches by adding a *RowUpdated* event to the *DbDataAdapter* object. The event handler method exposes the number of rows affected in the last batch. When the *UpdateBatchSize* is set to 1, the *RecordsAffected* property is always 1. In the following code, the Publishers table contains eight rows. The *pubsDataSet* is filled, and then the *pub_name* field is modified on all eight rows. Before the *Update* method is executed, the *UpdateBatchSize* is changed to 3. When the *Update* method is executed, the changes are sent to the database as a batch of three changes, another batch of three changes, and finally, a batch of two changes. This code contains a *RowUpdated* event handler to collect batch information, which is displayed after the *Update* method is executed.

```
'VB
Public WithEvents da As New SqlDataAdapter()
Public sb As New System.Text.StringBuilder()

Private Sub rowUpdated(ByVal sender As Object, _
   ByVal e As SqlRowUpdatedEventArgs) Handles da.RowUpdated
  sb.Append("Rows: " & e.RecordsAffected.ToString() & vbCrLf)
End Sub

Protected Sub Button14_Click(ByVal sender As Object, _
   ByVal e As System.EventArgs) Handles Button14.Click

  Dim pubs As ConnectionStringSettings
  pubs = ConfigurationManager.ConnectionStrings("PubsData")
  Dim connection As DbConnection = New SqlConnection()
  connection.ConnectionString = pubs.ConnectionString
  Dim cmd As SqlCommand = _
    CType(connection.CreateCommand(), SqlCommand)
  cmd.CommandType = CommandType.Text
  cmd.CommandText = "SELECT * FROM publishers"
  Dim pubsDataSet As New DataSet("Pubs")
  da.SelectCommand = cmd
  Dim bldr As New SqlCommandBuilder(da)
  da.Fill(pubsDataSet, "publishers")
```

```
    'Modify data here
    For Each dr As DataRow In pubsDataSet.Tables("publishers").Rows
     dr("pub_name") = "Updated Toys " _
       + DateTime.Now.Minute.ToString() _
       + DateTime.Now.Second.ToString()
    Next
    da.UpdateBatchSize = 3
    da.Update(pubsDataSet, "publishers")

    Dim lbl As Label = GetLabel(275, 20)
    lbl.Text = sb.ToString()

End Sub

//C#
public SqlDataAdapter da = new SqlDataAdapter();
public System.Text.StringBuilder sb = new System.Text.StringBuilder();

private void rowUpdated(object sender, SqlRowUpdatedEventArgs e)
{
  sb.Append("Rows: " + e.RecordsAffected.ToString() + "\r\n");
}

protected void Button14_Click(object sender, EventArgs e)
{
  //event subscription is normally placed in constructor but is here
  //to encapsulate the sample
  da.RowUpdated += new SqlRowUpdatedEventHandler(rowUpdated);
  ConnectionStringSettings pubs =
    ConfigurationManager.ConnectionStrings["PubsData"];
  DbConnection connection = new SqlConnection(pubs.ConnectionString);
  SqlCommand cmd = (SqlCommand)connection.CreateCommand();
  cmd.CommandType = CommandType.Text;
  cmd.CommandText = "SELECT * FROM Publishers";
  da.SelectCommand = cmd;
  DataSet pubsDataSet = new DataSet("Pubs");
  SqlCommandBuilder bldr = new SqlCommandBuilder(da);
  da.Fill(pubsDataSet, "publishers");
  //Modify data here
  foreach (DataRow dr in pubsDataSet.Tables["publishers"].Rows)
  {
    dr["pub_name"] = "Updated Toys "
      + DateTime.Now.Minute.ToString()
      + DateTime.Now.Second.ToString();
  }
  da.UpdateBatchSize = 3;
```

```
  da.Update(pubsDataSet, "publishers");

  //if event subscription is in the contructor, no need to
  //remove it here. . ..
  da.RowUpdated -= new SqlRowUpdatedEventHandler(rowUpdated);

  Label lbl = GetLabel(275, 20);
  lbl.Text = sb.ToString();
}
```

USING THE *OLEDBDATAADAPTER* OBJECT TO ACCESS ADO RECORDSET OR RECORD

The *OleDbDataAdapter* is similar to the *SqlDataAdapter*; however, the *OleDbDataAdapter* provides a unique feature: the ability to read a legacy ADO recordset or record into a *DataSet*. Consider the following code:

```
'VB
Dim da as  new OleDbDataAdapter()
Dim ds as new DataSet()

' set reference to adodb.dll and
' add Imports ADODB
Dim adoCn as new ADODB.Connection()
Dim adoRs as new ADODB.Recordset()
adoCn.Open( _
  "Provider=Microsoft.Jet.OLEDB.4.0;" _
  + "Data Source=" _
  + MapPath("App_Data/MyDatabase.mdb") + ";" _
  + "Persist Security Info=False", "", "", -1)

adoRs.Open("SELECT * FROM Customers", _
  adoCn, ADODB.CursorTypeEnum.adOpenForwardOnly, _
  ADODB.LockTypeEnum.adLockReadOnly, 1)
da.Fill(ds, adoRs, "Customers")
adoCn.Close()

GridView1.DataSource = ds
GridView1.DataMember = "Customers"
GridView1.DataBind()

//C#
OleDbDataAdapter da = new OleDbDataAdapter();
DataSet ds = new DataSet();

// set reference to adodb.dll and
// add using ADODB
```

```
ADODB.Connection adoCn = new ADODB.Connection();
ADODB.Recordset adoRs = new ADODB.Recordset();

adoCn.Open(
  "Provider=Microsoft.Jet.OLEDB.4.0;"
  + "Data Source="
  + MapPath("App_Data/MyDatabase.mdb") + ";"
  + "Persist Security Info=False", "", "", -1);

adoRs.Open("SELECT * FROM Customers",
  adoCn, ADODB.CursorTypeEnum.adOpenForwardOnly,
  ADODB.LockTypeEnum.adLockReadOnly, 1);
da.Fill(ds, adoRs, "Customers");
adoCn.Close();

GridView1.DataSource = ds;
GridView1.DataMember = "Customers";
GridView1.DataBind();
```

This code sample is opening a connection to a Microsoft Access database called *Northwind.mdb* and retrieving the Customers table into an ADODB.Recordset. The recordset is passed to the *Fill* method on the *OleDbDataAdapter*, which uses the recordset as the source when filling the *DataSet* object.

The primary purpose of this feature is to support legacy data, which can be useful in situations where you have a legacy ADODB.Recordset and you want to display it using one of the .NET Framework GUI controls, or if you want to save the data to a data store using one of the .NET Framework providers.

Using the *DbProviderFactory* Classes

There are many reasons for writing an application that does not require database provider-specific code. A company might want the flexibility to upgrade from one database product to another, such as moving from Microsoft Access to SQL Server. A company might have a retail application that must allow connectivity to any data source.

ADO.NET provides base classes that the provider-specific classes inherit from, as shown earlier in Table 7-1. The .NET Framework supports only single inheritance, so this approach has limitations if you want to create your own base class, but for classes that will expand, providing base class inheritance is better than providing interface implementation. Note that interfaces are still provided for backward compatibility.

The *DbProviderFactory* lets you create a factory object that is responsible for creating the appropriate provider objects. Each provider must supply a subclass of *DbProviderFactory* that can be used to create instances of its provider classes. For example, you can use the *SqlClientFactory* to create instances of any of the SQL Server classes. Figure 7-13 shows the *DbProviderFactory* class hierarchy.

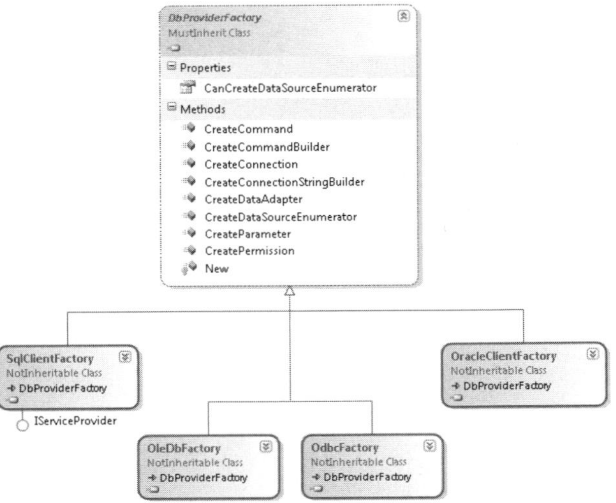

FIGURE 7-13 The *DbProviderFactory* and the *SqlClientFactory* classes

The provider factory classes are implemented as singletons, where each class provides an *Instance* property that is used to access the methods and properties shown in Figure 7-13. For example, you can use the following code to create a new connection using the *SqlClientFactory*:

```
'VB
'Get the singleton instance
Dim factory As DbProviderFactory = SqlClientFactory.Instance

Public Function GetProviderConnection() As DbConnection
  Dim connection As DbConnection = factory.CreateConnection()
  connection.ConnectionString = "Data Source=.\SQLEXPRESS;" _
    & "AttachDbFilename=|DataDirectory|PUBS.MDF;" _
    & "Integrated Security=True;User Instance=True"
  Return connection
End Function

//C#
//Get the singleton instance
DbProviderFactory factory = SqlClientFactory.Instance;

public DbConnection GetProviderConnection()
{
  DbConnection connection = factory.CreateConnection();
  connection.ConnectionString = @"Data Source=.\SQLEXPRESS;"
    + "AttachDbFilename=|DataDirectory|PUBS.MDF;"
    + "Integrated Security=True;User Instance=True";
```

```
  return connection;
}
```

Using the *DbProviderFactories* Class

To query for the list of available factories, you can use the *DbProviderFactories* class. This class is a factory for obtaining factories. It contains a method called *GetFactoryClasses* that returns a *DataTable* that is populated with information describing all available providers. Retrieving the list of providers can be easily demonstrated by using the following code:

```
'VB
Dim providersList As DataTable = Nothing

providersList = _
  System.Data.Common.DbProviderFactories.GetFactoryClasses()
GridView1.DataSource = providersList
GridView1.DataBind()

//C#
DataTable providersList = null;
providersList =
  System.Data.Common.DbProviderFactories.GetFactoryClasses();
GridView1.DataSource = providersList;
GridView1.DataBind();
```

When this code is run, the screen shown in Figure 7-14 is displayed.

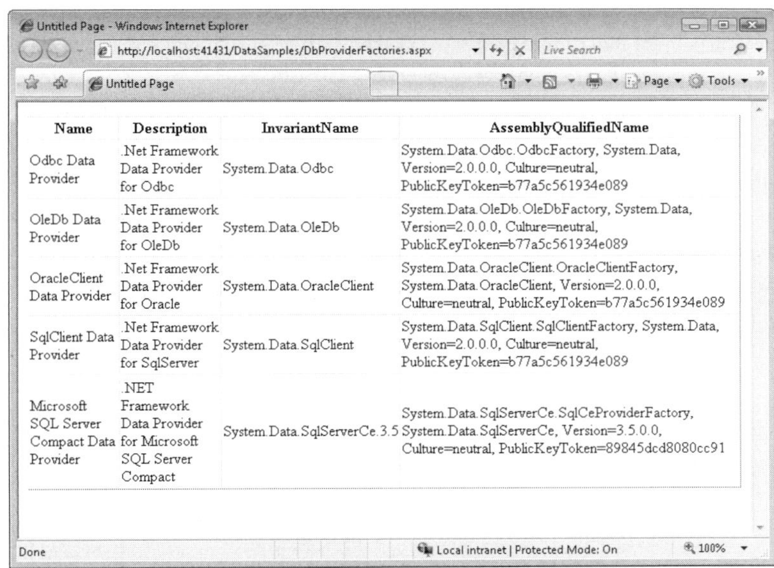

Name	Description	InvariantName	AssemblyQualifiedName
Odbc Data Provider	.Net Framework Data Provider for Odbc	System.Data.Odbc	System.Data.Odbc.OdbcFactory, System.Data, Version=2.0.0.0, Culture=neutral, PublicKeyToken=b77a5c561934e089
OleDb Data Provider	.Net Framework Data Provider for OleDb	System.Data.OleDb	System.Data.OleDb.OleDbFactory, System.Data, Version=2.0.0.0, Culture=neutral, PublicKeyToken=b77a5c561934e089
OracleClient Data Provider	.Net Framework Data Provider for Oracle	System.Data.OracleClient	System.Data.OracleClient.OracleClientFactory, System.Data.OracleClient, Version=2.0.0.0, Culture=neutral, PublicKeyToken=b77a5c561934e089
SqlClient Data Provider	.Net Framework Data Provider for SqlServer	System.Data.SqlClient	System.Data.SqlClient.SqlClientFactory, System.Data, Version=2.0.0.0, Culture=neutral, PublicKeyToken=b77a5c561934e089
Microsoft SQL Server Compact Data Provider	.NET Framework Data Provider for Microsoft SQL Server Compact	System.Data.SqlServerCe.3.5	System.Data.SqlServerCe.SqlCeProviderFactory, System.Data.SqlServerCe, Version=3.5.0.0, Culture=neutral, PublicKeyToken=89845dcd8080cc91

FIGURE 7-14 The available provider factory classes on an example computer

The invariant column contains a string that you can use to retrieve a specific provider. The name and description provide information that you can use to display a friendly provider list to an application user. The listed assembly names are fully qualified. Any provider on the list must be located within the application's probing path. This means that the .NET runtime must be able to locate the provider. In most situations, the provider library is installed in the global assembly cache (GAC) or the application folder.

The provider list shown in Figure 7-14 is from the Machine.config file, which, by default, contains the following provider information within the *configuration* root element:

```
<system.data>
  <DbProviderFactories>
    <add name="Odbc Data Provider" invariant="System.Data.Odbc"
      description=".Net Framework Data Provider for Odbc"
      type="System.Data.Odbc.OdbcFactory, System.Data,
      Version=2.0.0.0, Culture=neutral, PublicKeyToken=b77a5c561934e089"/>
    <add name="OleDb Data Provider" invariant="System.Data.OleDb"
      description=".Net Framework Data Provider for OleDb"
      type="System.Data.OleDb.OleDbFactory, System.Data, Version=2.0.0.0,
      Culture=neutral, PublicKeyToken=b77a5c561934e089"/>
    <add name="OracleClient Data Provider" invariant="System.Data.OracleClient"
      description=".Net Framework Data Provider for Oracle"
      type="System.Data.OracleClient.OracleClientFactory,
      System.Data.OracleClient, Version=2.0.0.0,
      Culture=neutral, PublicKeyToken=b77a5c561934e089"/>
    <add name="SqlClient Data Provider" invariant="System.Data.SqlClient"
      description=".Net Framework Data Provider for SqlServer"
      type="System.Data.SqlClient.SqlClientFactory, System.Data,
      Version=2.0.0.0, Culture=neutral, PublicKeyToken=b77a5c561934e089"/>
  </DbProviderFactories>
</system.data>
```

Notice that *DbDatabaseProviderFactories* uses the *add* element. By using the *add* element, you can add more providers to the Machine.config file or the application's configuration file. You can also use a *remove* element to remove providers from the default Machine.config list. For example, the following is a sample App.config file that removes the ODBC provider from the defaults defined in Machine.config:

```
<configuration>
  <system.data>
  <DbProviderFactories>
    <remove invariant="System.Data.Odbc" />
  </DbProviderFactories>
  </system.data>
</configuration>
```

If very few specific providers (such as SQL Server and Oracle) are required, you can use the *clear* element to remove all of the providers in the Machine.config file and then use the *add* element to add the desired providers back into the list. The following example clears the provider list and adds the SQL Server provider back into the list:

```
<configuration>
  <system.data>
  <DbProviderFactories>
    <clear/>
    <add name="SqlClient Data Provider"
     invariant="System.Data.SqlClient"
     description=".Net Framework Data Provider for SqlServer"
     type="System.Data.SqlClient.SqlClientFactory, System.Data,
     Version=2.0.0.0, Culture=neutral,
     PublicKeyToken=b77a5c561934e089" />
  </DbProviderFactories>
  </system.data>
</configuration>
```

Enumerating Data Sources

Sometimes you want to display a list of the available data sources for a given provider. For example, if an application allows data to be read from one SQL Server and written to a different SQL Server, it might require a dialog box for selecting from a list of available SQL Servers for the source and destination servers. The following code shows how to enumerate the data sources:

```
'VB
Dim factory as DbProviderFactory  = _
  DbProviderFactories.GetFactory("System.Data.SqlClient")

'get SQL Server instances
Dim sources as DataTable = _
  factory.CreateDataSourceEnumerator().GetDataSources()

GridView1.DataSource = sources
GridView1.DataBind()

//C#
DbProviderFactory factory =
  DbProviderFactories.GetFactory("System.Data.SqlClient");

//get SQL Server instances
DataTable sources =
  factory.CreateDataSourceEnumerator().GetDataSources();

GridView1.DataSource = sources;
GridView1.DataBind();
```

Catching Provider Exceptions

All provider-specific exceptions inherit from a common base class called *DbException*. When working with a provider-neutral coding model, your *Try-Catch* block can simply catch *DbException* generically instead of trying to catch each provider-specific exception. The *DbException* object contains a *Data* collection property that contains information about the error; you can also use the *Message* property to retrieve information about the error. In the following example, a loop is created to show how you might want to retry a command on error. This code also demonstrates the use of the *Try-Catch* block and the *using* block.

```
'VB
Protected Sub Button19_Click(ByVal sender As Object, _
   ByVal e As System.EventArgs) Handles Button19.Click

  Dim lbl As Label = GetLabel(275, 20)
  Dim maxTries As Integer = 3

  For i As Integer = 1 To maxTries
    Dim pubs As ConnectionStringSettings = _
     ConfigurationManager.ConnectionStrings("PubsData")
    Dim connection As DbConnection = _
     New SqlConnection(pubs.ConnectionString)
    Dim cmd As DbCommand = connection.CreateCommand()

    Try
      Using (connection)
        Using (cmd)
          cmd.CommandType = CommandType.Text
          'choose the SQL statement; one causes error, other does not.
          cmd.CommandText = "RaisError('Custom Error',19,1) With Log"
          'cmd.CommandText = "Select @@Version"
          connection.Open()
          cmd.ExecuteNonQuery()
        End Using
      End Using
      lbl.Text += "Command Executed Successfully<br />"
      Return
    Catch xcp As DbException
      lbl.Text += xcp.Message + "<br />"
      for each item as DictionaryEntry in  xcp.Data
        lbl.Text += "  " + item.Key.ToString()
        lbl.Text += " = " + item.Value.ToString()
        lbl.Text += "<br />"
      Next
    End Try
  Next
```

```
  lbl.Text += "Max Tries Exceeded<br />"
End Sub
```

```
//C#
protected void Button19_Click(object sender, EventArgs e)
{
  Label lbl = GetLabel(275, 20);
  int maxTries = 3;
  for (int i = 0; i < maxTries; i++)
  {
    ConnectionStringSettings pubs =
      ConfigurationManager.ConnectionStrings["PubsData"];
    DbConnection connection =
      new SqlConnection(pubs.ConnectionString);
    DbCommand cmd = connection.CreateCommand();

    try
    {
      using (connection)
      {
        using (cmd)
        {
          cmd.CommandType = CommandType.Text;
          //choose the SQL statement; one causes error, other does not.
          cmd.CommandText = "RaisError('Custom Error',19,1) With Log";
          //cmd.CommandText = "Select @@Version";
          connection.Open();
          cmd.ExecuteNonQuery();
        }
      }
      lbl.Text += "Command Executed Successfully<br />";
      return;
    }
    catch (DbException xcp)
    {
      lbl.Text += xcp.Message + "<br />";
      foreach (DictionaryEntry item in xcp.Data)
      {
        lbl.Text += "  " + item.Key.ToString();
        lbl.Text += " = " + item.Value.ToString();
        lbl.Text += "<br />";
      }
    }
  }
  lbl.Text += "Max Tries Exceeded<br />";
}
```

DETECTING INFORMATION WITH THE *CONNECTION* EVENT

The connection classes contain an event called *InfoMessage* that can be used to retrieve general and error information from the database. You can use the *InfoMessage* event to view the results of SQL *Print* statements and any messages that are available as a result of the SQL *RaiseError* statement, regardless of the error level.

The following code shows how this can be used to display information by subscribing to the *InfoMessage* event when running a query that has informational messages:

```
'VB
Private errMessage As String = String.Empty
Private errCollection As New List(Of SqlError)

Protected Sub Page_Load(ByVal sender As Object, _
  ByVal e As System.EventArgs) Handles Me.Load

  Dim pubs As ConnectionStringSettings = _
   ConfigurationManager.ConnectionStrings("PubsData")

  Dim connection As New SqlConnection(pubs.ConnectionString)
  AddHandler connection.InfoMessage, AddressOf connection_InfoMessage

  Dim cmd As DbCommand = connection.CreateCommand()
  cmd.CommandType = CommandType.Text
  cmd.CommandText = "SELECT job_id, job_desc FROM Jobs;" _
    + "Print 'Hello Everyone';" _
    + "Raiserror('Info Error Occured', 10,1 )" _
    + "Print GetDate()"

  connection.Open()
  Dim rdr As DbDataReader = cmd.ExecuteReader()
  Dim publishers As New DataTable()
  publishers.Load(rdr, LoadOption.Upsert)
  connection.Close()

  GridView1.DataSource = publishers
  GridView1.DataBind()

  LabelError.Text = errMessage
  GridViewError.DataSource = errCollection
  GridViewError.DataBind()

End Sub

Private Sub connection_InfoMessage(ByVal sender As Object, _
  ByVal e As SqlInfoMessageEventArgs)
```

```
    errMessage += "Message: " + e.Message + "<br />"

    For Each err As SqlError In e.Errors
      errCollection.Add(err)
    Next

End Sub

//C#
private string errMessage = string.Empty;
private List<SqlError> errCollection = new List<SqlError>();

protected void Page_Load(object sender, EventArgs e)
{
  ConnectionStringSettings pubs =
   ConfigurationManager.ConnectionStrings["PubsData"];

  SqlConnection connection = new SqlConnection(pubs.ConnectionString);
  connection.InfoMessage +=
   new SqlInfoMessageEventHandler(connection_InfoMessage);

  DbCommand cmd = connection.CreateCommand();
  cmd.CommandType = CommandType.Text;
  cmd.CommandText = "SELECT job_id, job_desc FROM Jobs;"
    + "Print 'Hello Everyone';"
    + "Raiserror('Info Error Occured', 10,1 )"
    + "Print GetDate()";

  connection.Open();
  DbDataReader rdr = cmd.ExecuteReader();
  DataTable publishers = new DataTable();
  publishers.Load(rdr, LoadOption.Upsert);
  connection.Close();

  GridView1.DataSource = publishers;
  GridView1.DataBind();
  LabelError.Text = errMessage;
  GridViewError.DataSource = errCollection;
  GridViewError.DataBind();
}

void connection_InfoMessage(object sender, SqlInfoMessageEventArgs e)
{
  errMessage += "Message: " + e.Message + "<br />";
  foreach(SqlError err in e.Errors) errCollection.Add(err);
}
```

Using the ADO.NET *Transaction* Object

A *transaction* is an atomic unit of work that must be completed in its entirety. The transaction succeeds if it is committed and fails if it is aborted. Transactions have four essential properties: atomicity, consistency, isolation, and durability (known as the *ACID properties*).

- **Atomicity** The work cannot be broken into smaller parts. Although a transaction might contain many SQL statements, it must be run as an all-or-nothing proposition, which means that if a transaction is only partially complete when an error occurs, the work reverts to its state prior to the start of the transaction.
- **Consistency** A transaction must operate on a consistent view of the data and must also leave the data in a consistent state. Any work in progress must not be visible to other transactions until the transaction has been committed.
- **Isolation** A transaction should appear to be running by itself, the effects of other ongoing transactions must be invisible to this transaction, and the effects of this transaction must be invisible to other ongoing transactions.
- **Durability** When a transaction is committed, it must be persisted so it is not lost in the event of a power failure or other system failure. Only committed transactions are recovered during power-up and crash recovery; uncommitted work is rolled back.

You can use the *DbConnection* object with the *BeginTransaction* method, which creates a *DbTransaction* object. The following code shows how this is done:

```
'VB
Dim cnSetting As ConnectionStringSettings = _
  ConfigurationManager.ConnectionStrings("PubsData")

Using cn As New SqlConnection()
  cn.ConnectionString = cnSetting.ConnectionString
  cn.Open()

  Using tran As SqlTransaction = cn.BeginTransaction()
    Try
      Using cmd As SqlCommand = cn.CreateCommand()
        cmd.Transaction = tran
        cmd.CommandText = "UPDATE jobs SET min_lvl=min_lvl * 1.1"
        cmd.ExecuteNonQuery()
      End Using
      tran.Commit()
    Catch xcp As Exception
      tran.Rollback()
    End Try
  End Using
End Using

//C#
ConnectionStringSettings cnSetting =
```

```
  ConfigurationManager.ConnectionStrings["PubsData"];
using (SqlConnection cn = new SqlConnection())
{
  cn.ConnectionString = cnSetting.ConnectionString;
  cn.Open();
  using (SqlTransaction tran = cn.BeginTransaction())
  {
    try
    {
      //work code here
      using (SqlCommand cmd = cn.CreateCommand())
      {
        cmd.Transaction = tran;
        cmd.CommandText = "UPDATE jobs SET min_lvl=min_lvl * 1.1";
        cmd.ExecuteNonQuery();
      }
      tran.Commit();
    }
    catch (Exception xcp)
    {
      tran.Rollback();
    }
  }
}
```

In this code, a *SqlConnection* object is created and opened, and the connection object is used to create a transaction object by executing the *BeginTransaction* method. The *Try* block does the work and commits the transaction. If an exception is thrown, the *Catch* block rolls back the transaction. Also, notice that the *SqlCommand* object must have its *Transaction* property assigned to the connection's transaction.

The scope of the transaction is limited to the code within the *Try* block, but the transaction was created by a specific connection object, so the transaction cannot span to a different *Connection* object.

Asynchronous Data Access

Asynchronous access to data can greatly improve the performance or perceived performance (responsiveness) of your application. With asynchronous access, multiple commands can be executed simultaneously and notification of command completion can be accomplished by polling, using *WaitHandles*, or delegating.

Synchronous vs. Asynchronous Access

Commands are normally executed synchronously, which causes the command to "block" program execution until the command has completed. Blocking execution keeps the program from continuing until the command has finished executing. This simplifies the writing of the code because the developer simply thinks about code execution in a rather procedural, step-by-step fashion, as shown in Figure 7-15. The problem arises with long-running commands, because blocking inhibits the program's ability to do other work such as performing additional commands or, more important, allowing the user to abort the command.

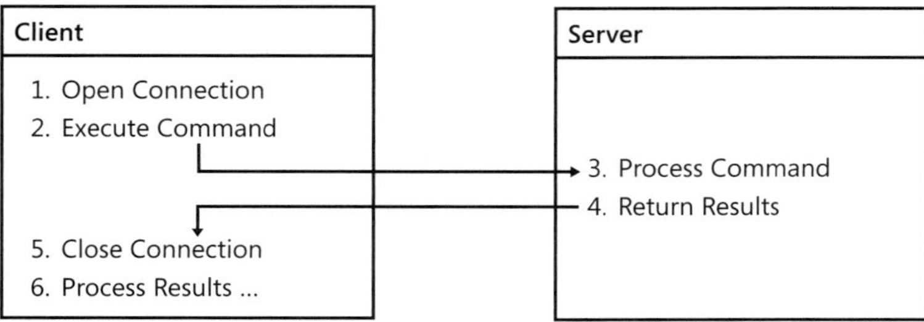

FIGURE 7-15 Synchronous data access

Asynchronous command execution does not block program execution because it takes place on a new thread, which is another path of execution for your code. This means the original thread can continue executing while the new thread is waiting for its command to complete, as shown in Figure 7-16. The original thread is free to repaint the screen or listen for other events, such as button clicks.

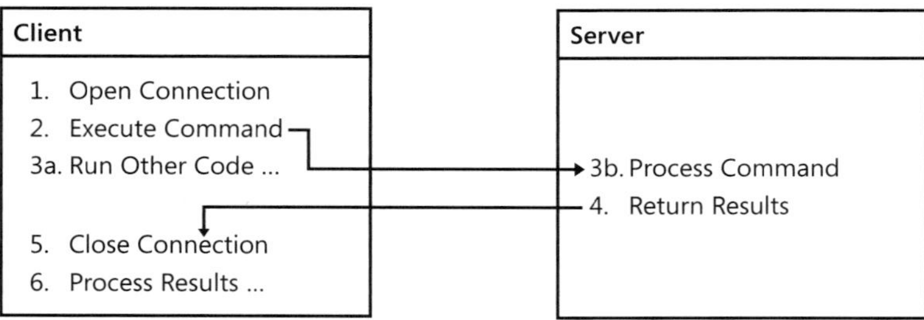

FIGURE 7-16 Asynchronous data access

To demonstrate the difference between synchronous and asynchronous data access, the following code uses synchronous data access. This code simulates three long-running queries and then places a message in a label on the form.

```
'VB
Protected Sub Button21_Click(ByVal sender As Object, _
   ByVal e As System.EventArgs) Handles Button21.Click
  Dim lbl As Label = GetLabel(275, 20)
  Dim dtStart as DateTime = DateTime.Now
  Dim ver As String = string.Empty
  Dim cnSettings As SqlConnectionStringBuilder
  cnSettings = New SqlConnectionStringBuilder( _
   "Data Source=.;" _
```

```
  + "Database=PUBS;" _
  + "Integrated Security=True;" _
  + "Max Pool Size=5")
Using cn1 As SqlConnection = _
  New SqlConnection(cnSettings.ConnectionString)
Using cn2 As SqlConnection = _
  New SqlConnection(cnSettings.ConnectionString)
Using cn3 As SqlConnection = _
  New SqlConnection(cnSettings.ConnectionString)
  Using cmd1 As SqlCommand = cn1.CreateCommand()
  Using cmd2 As SqlCommand = cn2.CreateCommand()
  Using cmd3 As SqlCommand = cn3.CreateCommand()
    cmd1.CommandText = _
      "WaitFor Delay '00:00:10' Select '1st Query<br />'"
    cmd2.CommandText = _
      "WaitFor Delay '00:00:10' Select '2nd Query<br />'"
    cmd3.CommandText = _
      "WaitFor Delay '00:00:10' Select '3rd Query<br />'"

    cn1.Open()
    Dim dr1 as SqlDataReader = cmd1.ExecuteReader()
    While dr1.Read()
      ver += dr1(0).ToString()
    End While
    dr1.Close()

    cn2.Open()
    Dim dr2 as SqlDataReader = cmd2.ExecuteReader()
    While dr2.Read()
      ver += dr2(0).ToString()
    End While
    dr2.Close()

    cn3.Open()
    Dim dr3 as SqlDataReader = cmd3.ExecuteReader()
    While dr3.Read()
      ver += dr3(0).ToString()
    End While
    dr3.Close()

  End Using
  End Using
  End Using
End Using
End Using
End Using
```

```
  Dim dtEnd as DateTime = DateTime.Now
  ver += "Running Time: " _
   + (dtEnd - dtStart).ToString() + " Seconds<br />"
  lbl.Text = ver
End Sub

//C#
protected void Button21_Click(object sender, EventArgs e)
{
  Label lbl = GetLabel(275, 20);
  DateTime dtStart = DateTime.Now;
  string ver = string.Empty;
  SqlConnectionStringBuilder cnSettings =
   new SqlConnectionStringBuilder(
  "Data Source=.;"
   + "Database=PUBS;"
   + "Integrated Security=True;"
   + "Max Pool Size=5");
  using (SqlConnection cn1 =
    new SqlConnection(cnSettings.ConnectionString))
  {
  using (SqlConnection cn2 =
    new SqlConnection(cnSettings.ConnectionString))
  {
  using (SqlConnection cn3 =
    new SqlConnection(cnSettings.ConnectionString))
  {
    using (SqlCommand cmd1 = cn1.CreateCommand())
    {
    using (SqlCommand cmd2 = cn2.CreateCommand())
    {
    using (SqlCommand cmd3 = cn3.CreateCommand())
    {
      cmd1.CommandText =
        "WaitFor Delay '00:00:10' Select '1st Query<br />'";
      cmd2.CommandText =
        "WaitFor Delay '00:00:10' Select '2nd Query<br />'";
      cmd3.CommandText =
        "WaitFor Delay '00:00:10' Select '3rd Query<br />'";

      cn1.Open();
      SqlDataReader dr1 = cmd1.ExecuteReader();
      while (dr1.Read())
      {
        ver += dr1[0].ToString();
      }
```

```
        dr1.Close();

        cn2.Open();
        SqlDataReader dr2 = cmd2.ExecuteReader();
        while (dr2.Read())
        {
          ver += dr2[0].ToString();
        }
        dr2.Close();

        cn3.Open();
        SqlDataReader dr3 = cmd3.ExecuteReader();
        while (dr3.Read())
        {
          ver += dr3[0].ToString();
        }
        dr3.Close();

      }
      }
      }
    }
    }
    }

    DateTime dtEnd = DateTime.Now;
    ver += "Running Time: "
      + (dtEnd - dtStart).ToString() + " Seconds<br />";
    lbl.Text = ver;
}
```

In this code, each of the three queries is run, one at a time. The running time displayed is approximately 30 seconds.

To use asynchronous code to run these queries, you must set the connection string to have *Asynchronous Processing=true* and *async=true,* or an exception is thrown. Next, one of the command object's *Begin* methods must be executed. The *SqlCommand* object provides the *BeginExecuteNonQuery*, *BeginExecuteReader*, and *BeginExecuteXmlReader* methods. The following code shows the asynchronous implementation:

```
'VB
Protected Sub Button22_Click(ByVal sender As Object, _
   ByVal e As System.EventArgs) Handles Button22.Click
   Dim lbl As Label = GetLabel(275, 20)
  Dim dtStart as DateTime = DateTime.Now
  Dim ver As String = string.Empty
  Dim cnSettings As SqlConnectionStringBuilder
```

```
cnSettings = New SqlConnectionStringBuilder( _
 "Data Source=.;" _
  + "Database=PUBS;" _
  + "Asynchronous Processing=true;" _
  + "Integrated Security=True;" _
  + "Max Pool Size=5")
Using cn1 As SqlConnection = _
  New SqlConnection(cnSettings.ConnectionString)
Using cn2 As SqlConnection = _
  New SqlConnection(cnSettings.ConnectionString)
Using cn3 As SqlConnection = _
  New SqlConnection(cnSettings.ConnectionString)
  Using cmd1 As SqlCommand = cn1.CreateCommand()
  Using cmd2 As SqlCommand = cn2.CreateCommand()
  Using cmd3 As SqlCommand = cn3.CreateCommand()
    cmd1.CommandText = _
      "WaitFor Delay '00:00:10' Select '1st Query<br />'"
    cmd2.CommandText = _
      "WaitFor Delay '00:00:10' Select '2nd Query<br />'"
    cmd3.CommandText = _
      "WaitFor Delay '00:00:10' Select '3rd Query<br />'"

    cn1.Open()
    cn2.Open()
    cn3.Open()
    Dim ar1 as IAsyncResult = cmd1.BeginExecuteReader()
    Dim ar2 as IAsyncResult = cmd2.BeginExecuteReader()
    Dim ar3 as IAsyncResult = cmd3.BeginExecuteReader()

    ar1.AsyncWaitHandle.WaitOne()
    Dim dr1 as SqlDataReader = cmd1.EndExecuteReader(ar1)
    While dr1.Read()
      ver += dr1(0).ToString()
    End While
    dr1.Close()

    ar2.AsyncWaitHandle.WaitOne()
    Dim dr2 as SqlDataReader = cmd2.EndExecuteReader(ar2)
    While dr2.Read()
      ver += dr2(0).ToString()
    End While
    dr2.Close()

    ar3.AsyncWaitHandle.WaitOne()
    Dim dr3 as SqlDataReader = cmd3.EndExecuteReader(ar3)
    While dr3.Read()
```

```
        ver += dr3(0).ToString()
      End While
      dr3.Close()

    End Using
    End Using
    End Using
  End Using
  End Using
  End Using

  Dim dtEnd as DateTime = DateTime.Now
  ver += "Running Time: " _
   + (dtEnd - dtStart).ToString() + " Seconds<br />"
  lbl.Text = ver
End Sub
```

```
//C#
protected void Button22_Click(object sender, EventArgs e)
{
  Label lbl = GetLabel(275, 20);
  DateTime dtStart = DateTime.Now;
  string ver = string.Empty;
  SqlConnectionStringBuilder cnSettings =
   new SqlConnectionStringBuilder(
  "Data Source=.;"
   + "Database=PUBS;"
   + "Asynchronous Processing=true;"
   + "Integrated Security=True;"
   + "Max Pool Size=5");
  using (SqlConnection cn1 =
    new SqlConnection(cnSettings.ConnectionString))
  {
  using (SqlConnection cn2 =
    new SqlConnection(cnSettings.ConnectionString))
  {
  using (SqlConnection cn3 =
    new SqlConnection(cnSettings.ConnectionString))
  {
    using (SqlCommand cmd1 = cn1.CreateCommand())
    {
    using (SqlCommand cmd2 = cn2.CreateCommand())
    {
    using (SqlCommand cmd3 = cn3.CreateCommand())
    {
      cmd1.CommandText =
```

```
      "WaitFor Delay '00:00:10' Select '1st Query<br />'";
    cmd2.CommandText =
      "WaitFor Delay '00:00:10' Select '2nd Query<br />'";
    cmd3.CommandText =
      "WaitFor Delay '00:00:10' Select '3rd Query<br />'";

    cn1.Open();
    cn2.Open();
    cn3.Open();
    IAsyncResult ar1 = cmd1.BeginExecuteReader();
    IAsyncResult ar2 = cmd2.BeginExecuteReader();
    IAsyncResult ar3 = cmd3.BeginExecuteReader();

    ar1.AsyncWaitHandle.WaitOne();
    SqlDataReader dr1 = cmd1.EndExecuteReader(ar1);
    while (dr1.Read())
    {
      ver += dr1[0].ToString();
    }
    dr1.Close();

    ar2.AsyncWaitHandle.WaitOne();
    SqlDataReader dr2 = cmd2.EndExecuteReader(ar2);
    while (dr2.Read())
    {
      ver += dr2[0].ToString();
    }
    dr2.Close();

    ar3.AsyncWaitHandle.WaitOne();
    SqlDataReader dr3 = cmd3.EndExecuteReader(ar3);
    while (dr3.Read())
    {
      ver += dr3[0].ToString();
    }
    dr3.Close();

  }
  }
  }
}
}
}

DateTime dtEnd = DateTime.Now;
ver += "Running Time: "
```

```
    + (dtEnd - dtStart).ToString() + " Seconds<br />";
  lbl.Text = ver;
}
```

In this example, the label is populated with the result of the queries, and the running time is only about 10 seconds. The *BeginExecuteReader* method was used to spawn each of the new threads. After the threads were spawned, the *IAsyncResult* object's *AsyncWaitHandle* property was used to wait until the command finished executing.

Storing and Retrieving Binary Large Object Data

When working with data, one challenge is to move large objects between the client application and the database server. In some scenarios, you might be able to treat large-object data just like any other data, but in many cases, you might be forced to look at alternative approaches.

In ADO.NET you can work with binary large objects (BLOBs) by using a *SqlDataReader* object to return a result set, by using a *SqlDataAdapter* object to fill a *DataTable* object, or by using a *SqlParameter* configured as an output parameter. If an object is so large that you can't load it without running out of memory, you must deal with it by reading and processing it a chunk at a time.

READING BLOB DATA

The normal operation of the *DataReader* object is to read one row at a time. When the row is available, all of the columns are buffered and available for you to access in any order.

To access the *DataReader* object in a stream fashion, you can change the *DbCommand* object's behavior to a sequential stream when you execute the *ExecuteReader* method. In this mode, you must get the bytes from the stream in the order of each column that is being returned, and you can't retrieve the data more than once. You essentially have access to the underlying *DataReader* object's stream.

To work with chunks of data, you should understand the operation of a stream object. When you read from a stream, you pass a byte array buffer that the stream populates. The stream does not have an obligation to populate the buffer, however. The stream's only obligation is to populate the buffer with at least one byte if the stream is not at its end. If the end has been reached, no bytes are read. When you use slow streams, such as a slow Internet network stream, data might not be available when you attempt to read the stream. In this case, the stream is not at its end, but no bytes are available, and the thread will block (wait) until one byte has been received. Based on the stream operation described, you should always perform stream reading in a loop that continues until no more bytes are read.

The following code sample reads all of the logos from the pub_info table in the *pubs* database and stores the logos to a .gif file:

```
'VB
Protected Sub Button23_Click(ByVal sender As Object, _
    ByVal e As System.EventArgs) Handles Button23.Click
```

```
Const pubIdColumn As Integer = 0
Const pubLogoColumn As Integer = 1
'bufferSize must be bigger than oleOffset
Const bufferSize As Integer = 100
Dim buffer(bufferSize) As Byte
Dim byteCountRead As Integer
Dim currentIndex As Long = 0

Dim pubSetting As ConnectionStringSettings = _
 ConfigurationManager.ConnectionStrings("PubsData")
Using cn As New SqlConnection()
  cn.ConnectionString = pubSetting.ConnectionString
  cn.Open()

  Using cmd As SqlCommand = cn.CreateCommand()
   cmd.CommandText = _
     "SELECT pub_id, logo FROM pub_info"
   Dim rdr As SqlDataReader = cmd.ExecuteReader( _
     CommandBehavior.SequentialAccess)
    While (rdr.Read())

      Dim pubId As String = _
        rdr.GetString(pubIdColumn)
      Dim fileName As String = MapPath(pubId + ".gif")

      ' Create a file to hold the output.
      Using fs As New FileStream( _
        fileName, FileMode.OpenOrCreate, _
        FileAccess.Write)
        currentIndex = 0
        byteCountRead = _
          CInt(rdr.GetBytes(pubLogoColumn, _
          currentIndex, buffer, 0, bufferSize))
        While (byteCountRead <> 0)
          fs.Write(buffer, 0, byteCountRead)
          currentIndex += byteCountRead
          byteCountRead = _
            CInt(rdr.GetBytes(pubLogoColumn, _
            currentIndex, buffer, 0, bufferSize))
        End While
      End Using
    End While
  End Using
End Using
Dim lbl as Label = GetLabel(275,20)
```

```
  lbl.Text = "Done Writing Logos To Disk"
End Sub

//C#
protected void Button23_Click(object sender, EventArgs e)
{
  const int pubIdColumn = 0;
  const int pubLogoColumn = 1;
  //bufferSize must be bigger than oleOffset
  const int bufferSize = 100;
  byte[] buffer = new byte[bufferSize];
  int byteCountRead;
  long currentIndex = 0;

  ConnectionStringSettings pubSetting =
   ConfigurationManager.ConnectionStrings["PubsData"];
  using (SqlConnection cn = new SqlConnection())
  {
    cn.ConnectionString = pubSetting.ConnectionString;
    cn.Open();

    using (SqlCommand cmd = cn.CreateCommand())
    {
      cmd.CommandText =
        "SELECT pub_id, logo FROM pub_info";
      SqlDataReader rdr = cmd.ExecuteReader(
        CommandBehavior.SequentialAccess);
      while (rdr.Read())
      {
        string pubId =
          rdr.GetString(pubIdColumn);
        string fileName = MapPath(pubId + ".gif");

        //Create a file to hold the output.
        using (FileStream fs = new FileStream(
          fileName, FileMode.OpenOrCreate,
          FileAccess.Write))
        {
          currentIndex = 0;
          byteCountRead =
            (int)rdr.GetBytes(pubLogoColumn,
            currentIndex, buffer, 0, bufferSize);
          while (byteCountRead != 0)
          {
            fs.Write(buffer, 0, byteCountRead);
```

```
                currentIndex += byteCountRead;
                byteCountRead =
                  (int)rdr.GetBytes(pubLogoColumn,
                  currentIndex, buffer, 0, bufferSize);
              }
            }
          }
        }
      }
      Label lbl = GetLabel(275, 20);
      lbl.Text = "Done Writing Logos To Disk";
    }
```

This code gives you the pattern for reading a BLOB and writing it to a file. The *Execute-Reader* method is executed with the *CommandBehavior.SequentialAccess* parameter. Next, a loop runs to read row data, and within the loop and for each row, the *pub_id* is read to create the file name. A new *FileStream* object is created, which opens the file for writing.

Next, a loop reads bytes into a byte array buffer and then writes the bytes to the file. The buffer size is set to 100 bytes, which keeps the amount of data in memory to a minimum.

WRITING BLOB DATA

You can write BLOB data to a database by issuing the appropriate *INSERT* or *UPDATE* statement and passing the BLOB value as an input parameter. You can use the SQL Server *UPDATETEXT* function to write the BLOB data in chunks of a specified size. The *UPDATETEXT* function requires a pointer to the BLOB field being updated, so the SQL Server *TEXTPTR* function is first called to get a pointer to the field of the record to be updated.

The following code example updates the pub_info table, replacing the logo for pub_id 9999 with a new logo from a file:

```
'VB
Protected Sub Button24_Click(ByVal sender As Object, _
   ByVal e As System.EventArgs) Handles Button24.Click
  Const bufferSize As Integer = 100
  Dim buffer(bufferSize) As Byte
  Dim currentIndex As Long = 0
  Dim logoPtr() As Byte

  Dim pubString As ConnectionStringSettings = _
   ConfigurationManager.ConnectionStrings("PubsData")
  Using cn As New SqlConnection()
    cn.ConnectionString = pubString.ConnectionString
    cn.Open()

    Using cmd As SqlCommand = cn.CreateCommand()
      cmd.CommandText = _
```

```
        "SELECT TEXTPTR(Logo) FROM pub_info WHERE pub_id = '9999'"
      logoPtr = CType(cmd.ExecuteScalar(), Byte())
    End Using
    Using cmd As SqlCommand = cn.CreateCommand()
      cmd.CommandText = _
        "UPDATETEXT pub_info.Logo @Pointer @Offset null @Data"
      Dim ptrParm As SqlParameter = _
        cmd.Parameters.Add("@Pointer", SqlDbType.Binary, 16)
      ptrParm.Value = logoPtr
      Dim logoParm As SqlParameter = _
        cmd.Parameters.Add("@Data", SqlDbType.Image)
      Dim offsetParm As SqlParameter = _
        cmd.Parameters.Add("@Offset", SqlDbType.Int)
      offsetParm.Value = 0
      Using fs As New FileStream(MapPath("Logo.gif"), _
          FileMode.Open, FileAccess.Read)
        Dim count As Integer = fs.Read(buffer, 0, bufferSize)
        While (count <> 0)
          logoParm.Value = buffer
          logoParm.Size = count
          cmd.ExecuteNonQuery()
          currentIndex += count
          offsetParm.Value = currentIndex
          count = fs.Read(buffer, 0, bufferSize)
        End While
      End Using
    End Using
  End Using
  Dim lbl As Label = GetLabel(275, 20)
  lbl.Text = "Done Writing Logos To DB"
End Sub

//C#
protected void Button24_Click(object sender, EventArgs e)
{
  const int bufferSize = 100;
  byte[] buffer = new byte[bufferSize];
  long currentIndex = 0;
  byte[] logoPtr;

  ConnectionStringSettings pubString =
   ConfigurationManager.ConnectionStrings["PubsData"];
  using (SqlConnection cn = new SqlConnection())
  {
    cn.ConnectionString = pubString.ConnectionString;
```

```
      cn.Open();

      using (SqlCommand cmd = cn.CreateCommand())
      {
        cmd.CommandText =
          "SELECT TEXTPTR(Logo) FROM pub_info WHERE pub_id = '9999'";
        logoPtr = (byte[])cmd.ExecuteScalar();
      }
      using (SqlCommand cmd = cn.CreateCommand())
      {
        cmd.CommandText =
          "UPDATETEXT pub_info.Logo @Pointer @Offset null @Data";
        SqlParameter ptrParm =
          cmd.Parameters.Add("@Pointer", SqlDbType.Binary, 16);
        ptrParm.Value = logoPtr;
        SqlParameter logoParm =
          cmd.Parameters.Add("@Data", SqlDbType.Image);
        SqlParameter offsetParm =
          cmd.Parameters.Add("@Offset", SqlDbType.Int);
        offsetParm.Value = 0;
        using (FileStream fs = new FileStream(MapPath("Logo.gif"),
          FileMode.Open, FileAccess.Read))
        {
          int count = fs.Read(buffer, 0, bufferSize);
          while (count != 0)
          {
           logoParm.Value = buffer;
           logoParm.Size = count;
           cmd.ExecuteNonQuery();
           currentIndex += count;
           offsetParm.Value = currentIndex;
           count = fs.Read(buffer, 0, bufferSize);
          }
        }
      }
    }
    Label lbl = GetLabel(275, 20);
    lbl.Text = "Done Writing Logos To DB";
  }
```

This code opens a connection and retrieves a pointer to the logo that is to be updated by calling the *TEXTPTR* function using a *SqlCommand* object. Then, a new *SqlCommand* object is created, and its *CommandText* property is set to the following:

```
"UPDATETEXT pub_info.logo @Pointer @Offset null @Data "
```

Note that the *null* parameter defines the quantity of bytes to delete. Passing *null* indicates that all existing data should be deleted. Passing a 0 (zero) indicates that no data should be deleted; the new data simply overwrites the existing data. (You pass a number other than 0 if you want to delete some of the data.) The other parameters represent the pointer to the start of the logo, the current offset to insert data, and the data being sent to the database.

After the file is opened, a loop starts that reads chunks of the file into the buffer and then sends the chunks to the database.

Quick Check

1. **What two objects are required to send instructions to a SQL Server database?**
2. **What connected object is used to obtain the fastest access to SQL Server data?**
3. **When you need to copy large amounts of data to SQL Server, what object should you use?**

Quick Check Answers

1. ***SqlConnection* and *SqlCommand* objects are required.**
2. **The *SqlDataReader* object is used to obtain the fastest access to SQL Server data.**
3. **The *SqlBulkCopy* object should be used.**

Using LINQ to SQL to Work with Data

Lesson 1 demonstrated the powerful query capabilities of LINQ when working with a *DataSet*. This feature represents a great method for writing queries against static data in a *DataSet*. However, it does not fulfill one of the key promises of LINQ: strong type-checking at design time, including IntelliSense against your database. Instead, you access data by defining field names inside of method calls. In addition, with a *DataSet*, you work against static data and have to use an adapter (or similar) to update, insert, and delete data. This is fine, but LINQ promises object development against the database. These features are enabled with LINQ to SQL.

LINQ to SQL is a technology inside of ADO.NET built to work directly with a SQL Server database to enable LINQ-style programming against it. With LINQ to SQL, you build an object-relational (O/R) map that connects .NET classes to database elements. This O/R map can be built in a number of ways (we look at these momentarily). Once the map is built, you are able to program against your database as if you were writing code against objects (because you are). This greatly simplifies and accelerates database development. Instead of writing SQL script and code that is not strongly typed, you are able to write .NET, object-oriented code to work with your database.

You enable LINQ to SQL programming by following a few basic steps. These steps are required to get started writing LINQ code against your database. The following is an overview:

1. Add a reference to the *System.Data.Linq* namespace to your project. This namespace contains the *DataContext* object, which is the core object that connects the database to the O/R map.
2. Create an O/R map that connects objects to data tables, columns, and more. There are multiple ways to create an O/R map in the .NET Framework. We look at three of them in the coming section.
3. Connect to your database using the *DataContext* object of LINQ to SQL. Again, this object represents the pipeline between the database and your objects.
4. Use the features of LINQ and LINQ to SQL to work with your database. This includes writing queries using strongly typed objects. In addition, you can use the features of LINQ to SQL to insert, update, and delete data.

It is important to note that LINQ to SQL is part of ADO.NET. Therefore, you can use it with other ADO.NET components such as transactions. This allows you to build LINQ to SQL items but still leverage any existing objects you've written against ADO.NET. In addition, LINQ to SQL allows you to leverage your existing database code such as stored procedures.

Mapping Objects to Relational Data

To program against objects that represent your database, you have to create them. The good news is that the Visual Studio tools provide two automated code generators that help you create the O/R map objects. In addition, you can hand-code your own O/R map for full control over the mapping for specific scenarios. This section shows how to use all three options.

MAPPING WITH THE VISUAL STUDIO DESIGNER TOOL

The easiest way to build your O/R map is through the Visual Studio LINQ to SQL designer. This provides a design surface on which you can build your classes. To get started, you add a LINQ to SQL Classes file to your project. You can do so through the Add New Item dialog box.

The LINQ to SQL Classes file is of type .dbml, which stands for database markup language. The file contains XML that defines the metadata of your database. Behind this XML file you will find a layout file for use by the designer and a code file (.vb or .cs). The code file represents the actual objects against which you write your database code.

You build your map by dragging and dropping database entities from Server Explorer onto the design surface. Visual Studio does the rest by generating code relating these entities. The designer also understands foreign key relationships in the database. It implements these same relationships in the class model. In addition, you can drag stored procedures from the database into a method window and code will be generated that allows these stored procedures to act as .NET methods.

As an example, suppose you are working with the pubs database and want to generate an O/R map for the author and title database tables. You can do so by opening the .dbml file in the designer, opening the database in Server Explorer, and then dragging entities from Server Explorer onto the design surface. Figure 7-17 shows an example. Notice the *byroyalty* stored procedure (in the upper right) added to the method window of the .dbml design surface.

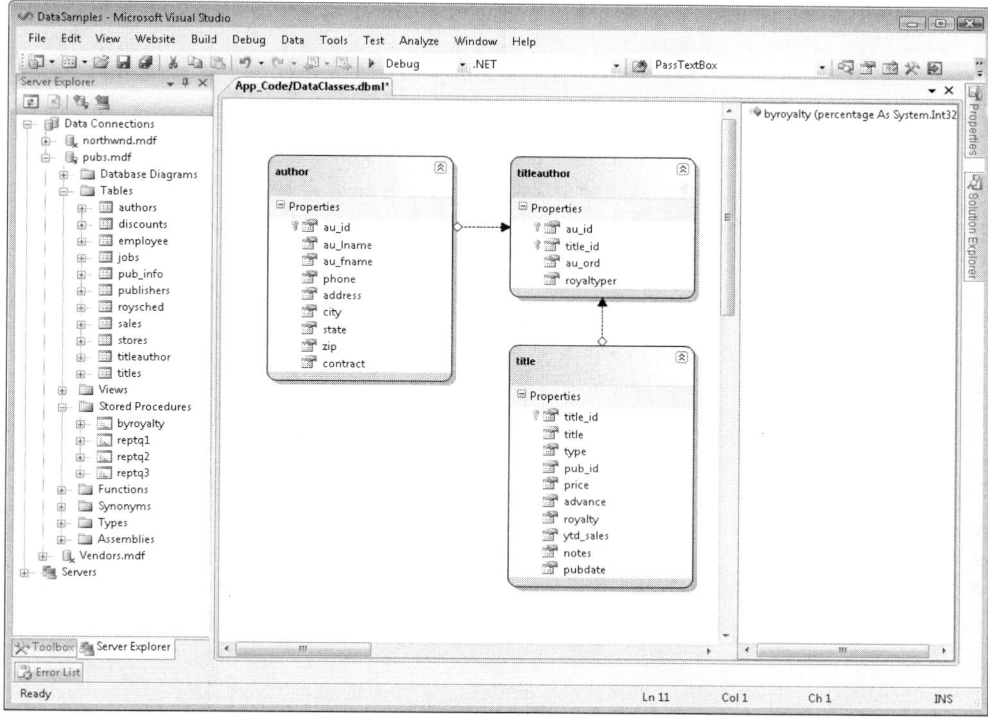

FIGURE 7-17 The LINQ to SQL O/R mapping tool

What gets generated by this designer is XML representing the metadata of the database (including the stored procedure) and code that allows a developer to work with the databases using objects. For example, the XML for the author table (found in the .dbml file) looks as follows:

```
<Table Name="dbo.authors" Member="authors">
  <Type Name="author">
    <Column Name="au_id" Type="System.String" DbType="VarChar(11) NOT NULL"
      IsPrimaryKey="true" CanBeNull="false" />
    <Column Name="au_lname" Type="System.String" DbType="VarChar(40) NOT NULL"
      CanBeNull="false" />
    <Column Name="au_fname" Type="System.String" DbType="VarChar(20) NOT NULL"
      CanBeNull="false" />
    <Column Name="phone" Type="System.String" DbType="Char(12) NOT NULL"
      CanBeNull="false" />
    <Column Name="address" Type="System.String" DbType="VarChar(40)" CanBeNull="true" />
    <Column Name="city" Type="System.String" DbType="VarChar(20)" CanBeNull="true" />
```

```
    <Column Name="state" Type="System.String" DbType="Char(2)" CanBeNull="true" />
    <Column Name="zip" Type="System.String" DbType="Char(5)" CanBeNull="true" />
    <Column Name="contract" Type="System.Boolean" DbType="Bit NOT NULL"
CanBeNull="false" />
    <Association Name="author_titleauthor" Member="titleauthors" OtherKey="au_id"
      Type="titleauthor" />
  </Type>
</Table>
```

The code generated by the tool is generated in either Visual Basic or C# depending on your preference. The code defines an object for each table and properties within the object for each field of the table. This code is very readable and easy enough to understand. You will see an example of writing some of this code yourself in the coming section.

MAPPING WITH THE COMMAND LINE TOOL

You can use the command line tool SqlMetal.exe to generate both .dbml files and O/R code for a given database. This tool is very useful for larger databases where it might not be practical to drag and drop objects onto a designer. The files it generates, however, are the same: a .dbml file and a code file (.vb or .cs).

There are many options available from this tool, but there are a few key ones. First, you can simply point to an .mdf file as the basis of the generation. If you are using a SQL database server, you can instead define the */server*, */database*, */user*, and */password* options to set connection information. Alternatively, you can use */conn* to define a connection string. Another option is */language* for setting the language of the file you want to generate (options are *vb* or *cs*).

To use the file, you typically first generate a .dbml file. You can indicate the type of file through the */dbml* option or the */code* option. The following command line shows an example of generating a .dbml file (for C#, swap the language parameter to *cs*):

```
sqlmetal "C:\Code\Northwind and Pubs Dbs\pubs.mdf" /language:vb /dbml:Pubs.dbml
```

To create the code, you simply indicate the */code* option as follows:

```
sqlmetal "C:\Code\Northwind and Pubs Dbs\pubs.mdf" /language:vb /code:Pubs.vb
```

MAPPING OBJECTS TO ENTITIES IN THE CODE EDITOR

The third option for connecting classes to database objects is to code it yourself. This can provide granular control, but it can also be a lot of work. It is recommended that you use an automated tool, but this section demonstrates how you can define your own O/R map.

To get started, you first create a class file. At the top of the class file, you should define an *Imports* (*using* in C#) statement to include the following namespaces:

```
'VB
Imports System.Data.Linq
Imports System.Data.Linq.Mapping
```

```
//C#
using System.Data.Linq;
using System.Data.Linq.Mapping;
```

The next step is to link your class to a table in the database through the *Table* attribute. The following code shows an example:

```
'VB
<Table(Name:="Authors")> _
Public Class Author

//C#
[Table(Name="Authors")]
public class Author
{
```

The next step is to create properties on the object that map to the database table columns with the *Column* attribute class. This class lets you set the name of the database field (if different from the name of the property), the variable you intend to use to store the field's value, the data type, whether the item is a primary key, and more. The following code shows an example of two properties mapped to columns in the authors table of the *pubs* database:

```
'VB
 Private _authorId As String
 <Column(IsPrimaryKey:=True, Storage:="_authorId", name:="au_id")> _
 Public Property Id() As String
   Get
     Return _authorId
   End Get
   Set(ByVal value As String)
     _authorId = value
   End Set
 End Property

 Private _lastName As String
 <Column(Storage:="_lastName", name:="au_lname")> _
 Public Property LastName() As String
   Get
     Return _lastName
   End Get
   Set(ByVal value As String)
     _lastName = value
   End Set
 End Property

//C#
private string _authorId;
```

```
[Column(IsPrimaryKey=true, Storage="_authorId", Name="au_id")]
public string Id
{
  get
  {
    return _authorId;
  }
  set
  {
    _authorId = value;
  }
}

private string _lastName;
[Column(Storage = "_lastName", Name = "au_lname")]
public string LastName
{
  get
  {
    return _lastName;
  }
  set
  {
    _lastName = value;
  }
}
```

Once complete, you can use your custom O/R map class as you would use one that was generated from a code generator. If you add additional (nonmapped) properties, fields, and methods, they are ignored at run time. In this way, you control the logic you intend to put in your classes when you write your O/R map.

Query Data with LINQ to SQL

You query data using LINQ to SQL in a similar manner as you would write any LINQ query. The big difference is how you connect to the actual data and the fact that you can write your queries using the O/R mapped objects.

To create a connection to a database with LINQ to SQL, you define a *DataContext* object. This object acts as the go-between for your database and your objects. A best practice is to create an object that inherits from *DataContext*. This allows you to expose your database and its tables without having *DataContext* calls spread throughout your code. When you create an instance of *DataContext*, you pass a database connection string to it. The following example shows doing so in the constructor of the class:

```
'VB
Public Class PubsDb
```

```
  Inherits DataContext

  Public Authors As Table(Of Author)
  Public Titles As Table(Of Title)

  Public Sub New(ByVal connection As String)
    MyBase.New(connection)
  End Sub

End Class

//C#
public class PubsDb: DataContext
{
  public Table<Author> Authors;
  public Table<Title> Titles;

  public PubsDb(string connection) : base(connection)
  {
  }
}
```

The next step is to create an instance of your class that inherits from *DataContext* and pass it a valid connection string. You then have access to write queries against the tables the class exposes. Again, with LINQ, the queries execute when you iterate over them. The following code shows defining a query against the Authors table and then using the *ToArray* method to execute the query and bind the results to a grid of data:

```
'VB
Dim pubString As ConnectionStringSettings = _
  ConfigurationManager.ConnectionStrings("PubsData")

Dim pubs As New PubsDb(pubString.ConnectionString)

Dim query = _
  From author In pubs.Authors _
  Where author.state = "CA" _
  Order By author.au_lname _
  Select author

GridView1.DataSource = query.ToArray()
GridView1.DataBind()

//C#
ConnectionStringSettings pubString =
  ConfigurationManager.ConnectionStrings["PubsData"];
```

```
PubsDb pubs = new PubsDb(pubString.ConnectionString);

var query =
  from author in pubs.Authors
  where author.state == "CA"
  orderby author.au_lname
  select author;

GridView1.DataSource = query.ToArray();
GridView1.DataBind();
```

Notice in this example that you are using the strong types for tables, collections, and fields. This makes the programming easier, faster, and more readable.

Inserting, Updating, and Deleting with LINQ to SQL

LINQ to SQL makes inserting, updating, and deleting data in your database a very simple process. It creates the connections between your O/R map and your database. You simply need to make a modification to object instances and then save the changes. You work with your object model to add a new instance to a collection, modify a given object, or remove an object from the collection. Once complete, you call the *SubmitChanges* method of the *Data-Context* object to write the results back to the database.

For example, if you wish to add a new author to the database, you start by creating a new *author* object. You then add it to the Authors table using the method *InsertOnSubmit*. When you are ready to submit all changes, you call *SubmitChanges*. The following code shows this example:

```
'VB
Dim pubString As ConnectionStringSettings = _
  ConfigurationManager.ConnectionStrings("PubsData")

Dim pubs As New PubsDb(pubString.ConnectionString)

Dim newAuthor As New author
newAuthor.au_id = "000-00-0001"
newAuthor.au_fname = "Michael"
newAuthor.au_lname = "Allen"
newAuthor.address = "555 Some St."
newAuthor.state = "WA"
newAuthor.city = "Redmond"
newAuthor.contract = False
newAuthor.phone = "555-1212"
newAuthor.zip = "12345"

pubs.Authors.InsertOnSubmit(newAuthor)
pubs.SubmitChanges()
```

```
//C#
ConnectionStringSettings pubString =
  ConfigurationManager.ConnectionStrings["PubsData"];

PubsDb pubs = new PubsDb(pubString.ConnectionString);

author newAuthor = new author();
newAuthor.au_id = "000-00-0001";
newAuthor.au_fname = "Michael";
newAuthor.au_lname = "Allen";
newAuthor.address = "555 Some St.";
newAuthor.state = "WA";
newAuthor.city = "Redmond";
newAuthor.contract = false;
newAuthor.phone = "555-1212";
newAuthor.zip = "12345";

pubs.Authors.InsertOnSubmit(newAuthor);
pubs.SubmitChanges();
```

Deleting data works much the same way. You call the *DeleteOnSubmit* method instead, however. You can pass the instance you wish to delete to this method. You can then call *SubmitChanges*.

To update data, you first retrieve the data using a query (or use the *GetTable* method of the *DataContext* object). You can then update the data and call *SubmitChanges* to save your changes to the database. The following code shows an example. In this case, a single row is returned from the query. Therefore the *First* method is used to return the first element only.

```
'VB
Dim pubString As ConnectionStringSettings = _
  ConfigurationManager.ConnectionStrings("PubsData")

Dim pubs As New PubsDb(pubString.ConnectionString)

Dim query = _
  From author In pubs.Authors _
  Where author.au_id = "213-46-8915" _
  Select author

Dim updateAuthor As author = query.First()
updateAuthor.phone = "123-1234"

pubs.SubmitChanges()

//C#
ConnectionStringSettings pubString =
```

```
  ConfigurationManager.ConnectionStrings["PubsData"];

PubsDb pubs = new PubsDb(pubString.ConnectionString);

var query =
  from author in pubs.authors
  where author.au_id == "213-46-8915"
  select author;

author updateAuthor = query.First();
updateAuthor.phone = "123-1234";

pubs.SubmitChanges();
```

LAB Working with Connected Data

In this lab, you work with Visual Studio to create a Web site and work with data in the *Northwind* database.

If you encounter a problem completing an exercise, the completed projects are available in the samples installed from the companion CD in the Code folder.

EXERCISE 1 Create a Web Site and Connect to the *Northwind* Database

In this exercise, you create the Web site and add a connection to the *Northwind* database using a *DetailsView* control.

1. Open Visual Studio and create a new Web site called **ConnectedData** using your preferred programming language.
2. In Solution Explorer, right-click the App_Data folder and select Add Existing Item. Navigate to the Northwind.mdf file in the samples installed from the CD and select it.
3. Open Default.aspx in Design view. From the Toolbox, drag a *DetailsView* control from the Data section onto the page.

   Click the smart tag in the upper right corner of the *DetailsView* control to display the DetailsView Tasks window. Inside the window, click the Auto Format link and select Classic. Also, stretch the width of the control to approximately 250 pixels.
4. Click the smart tag again. This time select the Choose Data Source drop-down list and select New Data Source. This starts the Data Source Configuration Wizard. For the data source type, select Database and click OK.
5. Next, on the Choose Your Data Connection page, select Northwind.mdf from the drop-down list. If it is not in your drop-down list, click New Connection and follow these steps:
   a. In the Add Connection window, set the DataSource by clicking Change and selecting the Microsoft SQL Server Database File (SqlClient).

   b. In the Database File Name property, select the Northwind.mdf file that you just added to the App_Data folder and click Open.
   c. Click OK to accept the changes and go back to the Choose Your Data Connection page.
6. Click Next to go to the Save The Connection String To The Application Configuration File page. Here, select the Yes check box. Change the connection string name to **NorthwindConnectionString** and click Next.
7. On the Configure Select Statement page, select the Shippers table from the Name drop-down list box and click the asterisk (*) to select all rows and columns.

   While still on the Configure Select Statement page, click Advanced and select the Generate Insert, Update, And Delete Statements and Use Optimistic Concurrency options. Click OK to close the Advanced window and click Next.
8. On the Test Query page, click Test Query to see the data. Click Finish to return to the DetailsView Tasks window.
9. Click the DetailsView smart tag again and select the Enable Paging, Enable Inserting, Enable Editing, and Enable Deleting options. The configuration of the *DetailsView* is complete.
10. Run the Web site. Notice that the data was retrieved and displayed.

    Add a new shipper. Notice that the *CompanyName* and the *Phone* fields are displayed, but the *ShipperID* field is an autonumber field, so it is not a field on the insert form.
11. Open the Source view of the Web page and examine the markup. This provides a good demonstration of declarative data access with markup (as opposed to code).

EXERCISE 2 **Create a LINQ to SQL O/R Map and Display Data**

In this exercise, you create an O/R map and use the code generated by it to connect to data using LINQ and display that data on a Web form.

1. For this exercise, continue working with the project you created in the prior exercise. Alternatively, you can open the completed Exercise 1 lab from the CD and start there.
2. Add a LINQ to SQL Classes file to your project: Right-click the project and select Add New Item. Select the LINQ to SQL Classes template from the list. Name your file **NorthwindClasses.dbml**. Set the language to either Visual Basic or C#. This serves as your O/R map.
3. Open the Northwind.dmbl file. Expand the *Northwind.mdf* database in Server Explorer. Expand the Tables folder of the database.
4. Drag the Orders and Order_Details tables from Server Explorer onto the O/R map design surface. Notice how the two tables are linked by their foreign key relationship.

   Expand the Stored Procedures folder for the database. Drag the first three stored procedures onto the method area of the O/R map. Notice how these stored procedures become methods.

Save and close the O/R map.

5. Navigate to the NorthwindClasses.dbml file in Solution Explorer. Expand the file to view its code-behind file. Open the NorthwindClasses.designer.vb (or .cs) file. Review the generated code and notice how the tables, fields, and functions are mapped to code using attributes. Close the file after you have reviewed it.
6. Add a new page to your site. Name the page **LinqToSql.aspx**.
7. In Design view, add a *GridView* control to the page. Set its *AutoFormat* property to *Professional*.
8. Add a reference to your Web site by right-clicking it and choosing Add Reference. In the Add Reference dialog box, select *System.Data.Linq*. Click OK.
9. Open the code-behind file for the LinqToSql.aspx page. At the top of the page, add an *Imports* (*using* in C#) statement to include the *System.Data.Linq* namespace.
10. Inside the *Page Load* event, add code to do the following:
    - Get the database connection string from the configuration file.
    - Create an instance of the *DataContext* object associated with the O/R map you created earlier. Pass the connection string to this instance.
    - Write a LINQ query to return orders whose *ShipRegion* is set to "OR". Order the results by *ShippedDate*.
    - Bind the results to the *GridView* control using the *ToArray* method.

    The following code shows an example:

```
'VB
Imports System.Data.Linq

Partial Class LinqToSql
  Inherits System.Web.UI.Page

  Protected Sub Page_Load(ByVal sender As Object, _
    ByVal e As System.EventArgs) Handles Me.Load

    If Not IsPostBack Then

      Dim nwConnect As ConnectionStringSettings = _
        ConfigurationManager.ConnectionStrings( _
        "NorthwindConnectionString")

      Dim nw As New NorthwindClassesDataContext _
        (nwConnect.ConnectionString)

      Dim query = _
        From order In nw.Orders _
        Where order.ShipRegion = "OR" _
```

```
            Order By order.ShippedDate _
            Select order

        GridView1.DataSource = query.ToArray()
        GridView1.DataBind()

      End If

    End Sub

End Class

//C#
using System;
using System.Linq;
using System.Configuration;
using System.Data.Linq;

public partial class LinqToSql : System.Web.UI.Page
{
    protected void Page_Load(object sender, EventArgs e)
    {
      if (!IsPostBack)
      {
        ConnectionStringSettings nwConnect =
          ConfigurationManager.ConnectionStrings[
          "NorthwindConnectionString"];

        NorthwindClassesDataContext nw = new
          NorthwindClassesDataContext(nwConnect.ConnectionString);

        var query =
          from order in nw.Orders
          where order.ShipRegion == "OR"
          orderby order.ShippedDate
          select order;

        GridView1.DataSource = query.ToArray();
        GridView1.DataBind();
      }
    }
}
```

11. Run your page and view the results.

Lesson Summary

- Connected classes, also known as provider classes, are responsible for movement of data between the data store and the disconnected classes. A valid *DbConnection* object is required to use most of the primary provider classes.
- You use the *DbCommand* object to send a SQL command to a data store. You can also create parameters and pass them to the *DbCommand* object.
- The *DbDataReader* object provides a high-performance method of retrieving data from a data store by delivering a forward-only, read-only, server-side cursor.
- The *SqlBulkCopy* object can be used to copy data from a number of sources to a SQL Server table.
- You can use the *DbDataAdapter* object to retrieve and update data between a *Data-Table* and a data store. The *DbDataAdapter* can contain a single *SelectCommand* for read-only data, or it can contain a *SelectCommand*, *InsertCommand*, *UpdateCommand*, and *DeleteCommand* for fully updatable data.
- The *DbProviderFactory* object helps you create provider-independent code, which might be necessary when the data store needs to be quickly changeable.
- Use the *Using* statement to ensure that the *Dispose* method is called on the connection and command objects to avoid connection leaks.
- You can use the *DbProviderFactories* object to obtain a list of the provider factories that are available on a computer.
- You can work with BLOBs using the same techniques you use for smaller data types, unless the objects are too large to fit into memory. When a BLOB is too large to fit into memory, you must use streaming techniques to move the data.
- You can use LINQ to SQL to create an O/R map of your database. Programming against an automatically generated O/R map makes database programming faster and easier by providing design-time type checking and IntelliSense against your data tables and their columns.

Lesson Review

You can use the following questions to test your knowledge of the information in Lesson 2, "Using the ADO.NET Connected Classes." The questions are also available on the companion CD if you prefer to review them in electronic form.

> ***NOTE*** **ANSWERS**
>
> **Answers to these questions and explanations of why each answer choice is right or wrong are located in the "Answers" section at the end of the book.**

1. Which of the following ways can you proactively clean up a database connection's resources? (Choose two.)
   - **A.** Execute the *DbConnection* object's *Cleanup* method.
   - **B.** Execute the *DbConnection* object's *Close* method.
   - **C.** Assign *Nothing* (C# *null*) to the variable that references the *DbConnection* object.
   - **D.** Create a *Using* block for the *DbConnection* object.
2. What event of the *SqlConnection* class can you subscribe to if you want to display information from SQL Print statements?
   - **A.** *InfoMessage*
   - **B.** *MessageReceived*
   - **C.** *PostedMessage*
   - **D.** *NewInfo*
3. To perform asynchronous data access, what must be added to the connection string?
   - **A.** *BeginExecute=true*
   - **B.** *MultiThreaded=true*
   - **C.** *MultipleActiveResultSets=true*
   - **D.** *Asynchronous Processing=true*
4. Which of the following steps must you take to write code using LINQ to SQL? (Choose all that apply.)
   - **A.** Generate an O/R map of your database.
   - **B.** Reference the *System.Data.Linq* namespace.
   - **C.** Connect to your database through a *DataContext* object.
   - **D.** Use a *GridView* control to map your database to LINQ.

Lesson 3: Working with XML Data

The .NET Framework provides vast support for XML. The implementation of XML is focused on performance, reliability, and scalability. The integration of XML with ADO.NET offers the ability to use XML documents as a data source. This lesson covers many of the XML objects that are included in the .NET Framework.

After this lesson, you will be able to:

- Use the Document Object Model (DOM) to manage XML data.
- Use the XmlNamedNodeMap object.
- Use the XmlNodeList object.
- Use the XmlReader and XmlWriter objects.
- Use the XmlNodeReader to read node trees.
- Validate data with the XmlValidatingReader.

Estimated lesson time: 45 minutes

The XML Classes

The World Wide Web Consortium (W3C) has provided standards that define the structure and provide a standard programming interface that can be used in a wide variety of environments and applications for XML documents. This is called the *Document Object Model* (*DOM*). Classes that support the DOM are typically capable of random access navigation and modification of the XML document.

The XML classes are accessible by setting a reference to the System.Xml.dll file and adding the *Imports System.Xml* (C# *using System.Xml;*) directive to the code. The System.Data.dll file also extends the *System.Xml* namespace. This is the location of the *XmlDataDocument* class. If this class is required, a reference must also be set to the System.Data.dll file.

This section covers the primary XML classes in the .NET Framework. Each of these classes offers varying degrees of functionality. It is important to look at each of the classes in detail to make the correct decision on which classes should be used. Figure 7-18 shows a high-level view of the objects that are covered.

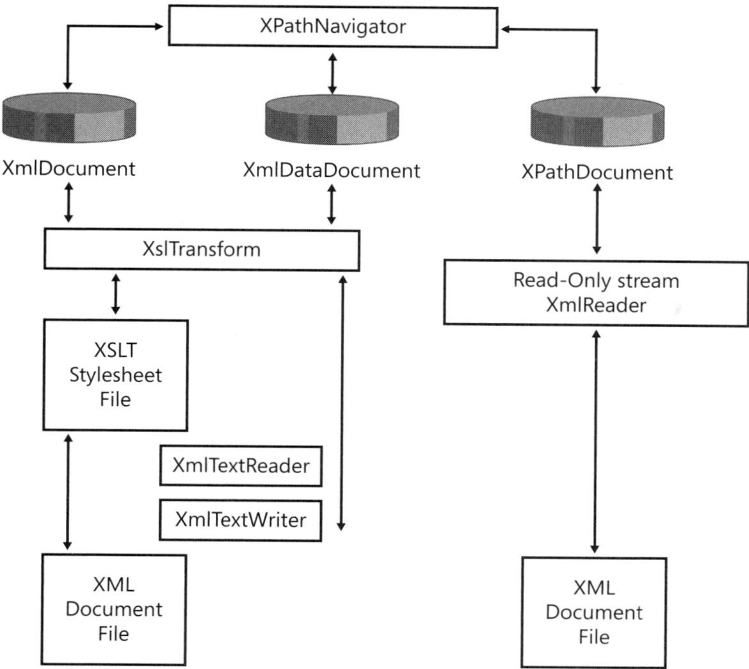

FIGURE 7-18 The primary XML objects covered in this lesson

XmlDocument and *XmlDataDocument*

The *XmlDocument* and *XmlDataDocument* objects are in-memory representations of XML that use the DOM Level 1 and Level 2. These classes can be used to navigate and edit the XML nodes.

The *XmlDataDocument* inherits from the *XmlDocument* and also represents relational data. The *XmlDataDocument* can expose its data as a *DataSet* to provide relational and nonrelational views of the data. The *XmlDataDocument* is in the *System.Data.dll* assembly.

These classes provide many methods to implement the Level 2 specifications, and also contain methods to facilitate common operations. The methods are summarized in Table 7-5. The *XmlDocument* contains all of the methods for creating *XmlElements* and *XmlAttributes*.

TABLE 7-5 *XmlDocument* and *XmlDataDocument* Methods

METHOD	DESCRIPTION
Create<NodeType>	Creates an XML node in the document. There are *Create* methods for each node type.

METHOD	DESCRIPTION
CloneNode	Creates a duplicate of an XML node. This method takes a Boolean argument called *deep*. If *deep* is *False*, only the node is copied. If *deep* is *True*, all child nodes are recursively copied as well.
GetElementByID	Locates and returns a single node based on its *ID* attribute. Note that this requires a Document Type Definition (DTD) that identifies an attribute as being an *ID* type. An attribute that has the name of *ID* is not an *ID* type by default.
GetElementsByTagName	Locates and returns an *XmlNodeList* containing all of the descendant elements based on the element name.
ImportNode	Imports a node from a different *XmlDocument* into this document. The source node remains unmodified in the original *XmlDocument*. This method takes a Boolean argument called *deep*. If *deep* is *False*, only the node is copied. If *deep* is *True*, all child nodes are recursively copied as well.
InsertBefore	Inserts an *XmlNode* immediately before the referenced node. If the referenced node is *Nothing*, then the new node is inserted at the end of the child list. If the new node already exists in the tree, the original node is removed before the new node is inserted.
InsertAfter	Inserts an XmlNode immediately after the referenced node. If the referenced node is *Nothing*, then the new node is inserted at the beginning of the child list. If the new node already exists in the tree, the original node is removed before the new node is inserted.
Load	Loads an XML document from a disk file, Uniform Resource Locator (URL), or stream.
LoadXml	Loads an XML document from a string.
Normalize	Assures that there are no adjacent text nodes in the document. This is like saving the document and reloading it. This method might be desirable when text nodes are being programmatically added to an *XmlDocument*, and the text nodes are side by side. Normalizing combines the adjacent text nodes to produce a single text node.
PrependChild	Inserts a node at the beginning of the child node list. If the new node is already in the tree, the original node is removed before the new node is inserted. If the node is an *XmlDocumentFragment*, the complete fragment is added.

METHOD	DESCRIPTION
ReadNode	Loads a node from an XML document using an *XmlTextReader* or *XmlNodeReader* object. The reader must be on a valid node before executing this method. The reader reads the opening tag, all child nodes, and the closing tag of the current element. This repositions the reader to the next node.
RemoveAll	Removes all children and attributes from the current node.
RemoveChild	Removes the referenced child.
ReplaceChild	Replaces the referenced child with a new node. If the new node is already in the tree, it is removed first.
Save	Saves the XML document to a disk, file, URL, or stream.
SelectNodes	Selects a list of nodes that match the XPath expression.
SelectSingleNode	Selects the first node that matches the XPath expression.
WriteTo	Writes a node to another XML document using an *XmlTextWriter.*
WriteContentsTo	Writes a node and all of its descendants to another XML document using an *XmlTextWriter.*

XPathDocument

The *XPathDocument* provides a cached read-only *XmlDocument* that can be used for performing quick XPath queries. The constructor for this class requires a stream object to create an instance of this object. The only useful method that this class exposes is the *CreateNavigator* method.

XmlConvert

The *XmlConvert* class has many static methods for converting between XSD data types and common language runtime (CLR) data types. This class is especially important when working with data sources that allow names that are not valid XML names. If a column in a database table is called List Price, trying to create an element or attribute with a space character throws an exception. Using *XmlConvert* to encode the name converts the space to *_0x0020_*, so the XML element name becomes *List_x0020_Price*. Later, this name can be decoded using the *XmlConvert.DecodeName* method.

XmlConvert also provides many static methods for converting strings to numeric values.

XPathNavigator

DocumentNavigator provides efficient navigation of an *XmlDocument* by providing XPath support for navigation. *XPathNavigator* uses a cursor model and XPath queries to provide read-only random access to the data. *XPathNavigator* supports Extensible Stylesheet Language Transformations (XSLT) and can be used as the input to a transform.

XmlNodeReader

The *XmlNodeReader* provides forward-only access to data in an *XmlDocument* or *XmlDataDocument*. It provides the ability to start at a given node in the *XmlDocument* and sequentially read each node.

XmlTextReader

The *XmlTextReader* provides noncached, forward-only access to XML data. It parses XML tokens but makes no attempt to represent the XML document as a DOM. The *XmlTextReader* does not perform document validation, but it checks the XML data to ensure that it is well formed.

XmlTextWriter

The *XmlTextWriter* provides noncached, forward-only writing of XML data to a stream of files, ensuring that the data conforms to the W3C XML 1.0 standard. The *XmlTextWriter* contains logic for working with namespaces and resolving namespace conflicts.

XmlReader

The *XmlReader* provides an object for reading and validating against DTD, XML Schema Reduced (XDR), or XSD. The constructor expects a reader or a string as the source of the XML to be validated.

XslTransform

The *XslTransform* can transform an XML document using an Extensible Stylesheet Language (XSL) stylesheet. The *XslTransform* supports XSLT 1.0 syntax and provides two methods: *Load* and *Transform*.

The *Load* method is used to load an XSLT stylesheet from a file or a stream. The *Transform* method is used to perform the transformation. The *Transform* method has several overloads but essentially expects an *XmlDocument* or *XmlNode* as the first argument, an *XsltArgumentList*, and an output stream.

Working with XML Documents

There are certainly many ways of working with XML data in the .NET Framework. This section covers some of the methods, such as creating a new XML file from scratch, reading and writing XML files, searching XML data, and transforming XML data.

Creating a New *XmlDocument* from Scratch

To create a new *XmlDocument*, start by creating an *XmlDocument* object. The *XmlDocument* object contains *CreateElement* and *CreateAttribute* methods that are used to add nodes to the *XmlDocument* object. The *XmlElement* contains the *Attributes* property, which is an *XmlAttributeCollection*. The *XmlAttributeCollection* inherits from the *XmlNamedNodeMap* class, which is a collection of names with corresponding values.

The following code shows how an *XmlDocument* can be created from scratch and saved to a file, and also uses the same *GetLabel* method that is used elsewhere in this chapter.

```
'VB
Protected Sub Button1_Click(ByVal sender As Object, _
   ByVal e As System.EventArgs) Handles Button1.Click
  'Declare and create new XmlDocument
  Dim xmlDoc As New XmlDocument()

  Dim el As XmlElement
  Dim childCounter As Integer
  Dim grandChildCounter As Integer

  'Create the xml declaration first
  xmlDoc.AppendChild( _
    xmlDoc.CreateXmlDeclaration("1.0", "utf-8", Nothing))

  'Create the root node and append into doc
  el = xmlDoc.CreateElement("myRoot")
  xmlDoc.AppendChild(el)

  'Child Loop
  For childCounter = 1 To 4
    Dim childelmt As XmlElement
    Dim childattr As XmlAttribute

    'Create child with ID attribute
    childelmt = xmlDoc.CreateElement("myChild")
    childattr = xmlDoc.CreateAttribute("ID")
    childattr.Value = childCounter.ToString()
    childelmt.Attributes.Append(childattr)

    'Append element into the root element
    el.AppendChild(childelmt)
    For grandChildCounter = 1 To 3
      'Create grandchildren
      childelmt.AppendChild(xmlDoc.CreateElement("GrandChild"))
    Next
  Next
```

```
  'Save to file
  xmlDoc.Save(MapPath("XmlDocumentTest.xml"))
  Dim lbl as Label = GetLabel(275, 20)
  lbl.Text = "XmlDocumentTest.xml Created"
End Sub

//C#
protected void Button1_Click(object sender, EventArgs e)
{
  //Declare and create new XmlDocument
  XmlDocument xmlDoc = new XmlDocument();

  XmlElement el;
  int childCounter;
  int grandChildCounter;

  //Create the xml declaration first
  xmlDoc.AppendChild(
  xmlDoc.CreateXmlDeclaration("1.0", "utf-8", null));

  //Create the root node and append into doc
  el = xmlDoc.CreateElement("myRoot");
  xmlDoc.AppendChild(el);

  //Child Loop
  for (childCounter = 1; childCounter <= 4; childCounter++)
  {
    XmlElement childelmt;
    XmlAttribute childattr;

    //Create child with ID attribute
    childelmt = xmlDoc.CreateElement("myChild");
    childattr = xmlDoc.CreateAttribute("ID");
    childattr.Value = childCounter.ToString();
    childelmt.Attributes.Append(childattr);

    //Append element into the root element
    el.AppendChild(childelmt);
    for (grandChildCounter = 1; grandChildCounter <= 3; grandChildCounter++)
    {
      //Create grandchildren
      childelmt.AppendChild(xmlDoc.CreateElement("GrandChild"));
    }
  }

  //Save to file
```

```
  xmlDoc.Save(MapPath("XmlDocumentTest.xml"));
  Label lbl = GetLabel(275, 20);
  lbl.Text = "XmlDocumentTest.xml Created";
}
```

This code starts by creating an instance of an *XmlDocument*. Next, the XML declaration is created and placed inside the child collection. An exception is thrown if this is not the first child of the *XmlDocument*. The following is the XML file that was produced by running the code sample:

```
<?xml version="1.0" encoding="utf-8"?>
<myRoot>
  <myChild ID="1">
  <GrandChild />
  <GrandChild />
  <GrandChild />
  </myChild>
  <myChild ID="2">
  <GrandChild />
  <GrandChild />
  <GrandChild />
  </myChild>
  <myChild ID="3">
  <GrandChild />
  <GrandChild />
  <GrandChild />
  </myChild>
  <myChild ID="4">
  <GrandChild />
  <GrandChild />
  <GrandChild />
  </myChild>
</myRoot>
```

The previous code also works with the *XmlDataDocument*, but the *XmlDataDocument* has more features for working with relational data. These features are explored later in this lesson.

Parsing *XmlDocuments* Using the DOM

An *XmlDocument* can be parsed by using a recursive routine to loop through all elements. The following code is an example of parsing an *XmlDocument*:

```
'VB

Dim lbl as New Label

Protected Sub Button2_Click(ByVal sender As Object, _
   ByVal e As System.EventArgs) Handles Button2.Click
```

```
  lbl = GetLabel(275, 20)
  Dim xmlDoc As New XmlDocument()
  xmlDoc.Load(MapPath("XmlDocumentTest.xml"))
  RecurseNodes(xmlDoc.DocumentElement)
End Sub

Public Sub RecurseNodes(ByVal node As XmlNode)
  'start recursive loop with level 0
  RecurseNodes(node, 0)
End Sub

Public Sub RecurseNodes(ByVal node As XmlNode, ByVal level As Integer)
  Dim s As String
  Dim n As XmlNode
  Dim attr As XmlAttribute

  s = String.Format("{0} <b>Type:</b>{1} <b>Name:</b>{2} <b>Attr:</b> ", _
    New String("-", level), node.NodeType, node.Name)
  For Each attr In node.Attributes
    s &= String.Format("{0}={1} ", attr.Name, attr.Value)
  Next
  lbl.Text += s & "<br>"
  For Each n In node.ChildNodes
    RecurseNodes(n, level + 1)
  Next
End Sub
```

//C#

```
Label lbl = new Label();

protected void Button2_Click(object sender, EventArgs e)
{
  lbl = GetLabel(275, 20);
  XmlDocument xmlDoc = new XmlDocument();
  xmlDoc.Load(MapPath("XmlDocumentTest.xml"));
  RecurseNodes(xmlDoc.DocumentElement);
}

public void RecurseNodes(XmlNode node)
{
  //start recursive loop with level 0
  RecurseNodes(node, 0);
}

public void RecurseNodes(XmlNode node, int level)
```

```
{
  string s;
  s = string.Format("{0} <b>Type:</b>{1} <b>Name:</b>{2} <b>Attr:</b> ",
    new string('-', level), node.NodeType, node.Name);
  foreach (XmlAttribute attr in node.Attributes)
  {
    s += string.Format("{0}={1} ", attr.Name, attr.Value);
  }
  lbl.Text += s + "<br>";
  foreach (XmlNode n in node.ChildNodes)
  {
    RecurseNodes(n, level + 1);
  }
}
```

This code starts by loading an XML file and then calling a procedure called *RecurseNodes*. The *RecurseNodes* procedure is overloaded. The first call simply passes the *xmlDoc* object's root node. The recursive calls pass the recursion level. Each time the *RecurseNodes* procedure executes, the node information is printed, and for each child that the node has, a recursive call is made.

Parsing XmlDocuments Using the *XPathNavigator*

The *XPathNavigator* provides an alternate method of walking the XML document recursively. This object does not use the methods that are defined in the DOM. Instead, it uses XPath queries to navigate the data and is in the *System.Xml.XPath* namespace. It offers many methods and properties that can be used, as shown in the following code:

```
'VB
Protected Sub Button3_Click(ByVal sender As Object, _
  ByVal e As System.EventArgs) Handles Button3.Click

  lbl = GetLabel(275, 20)
  Dim xmlDoc As New XmlDocument()
  xmlDoc.Load(MapPath("XmlDocumentTest.xml"))

  Dim xpathNav As XPathNavigator = xmlDoc.CreateNavigator()
  xpathNav.MoveToRoot()
  RecurseNavNodes(xpathNav)
End Sub

Public Sub RecurseNavNodes(ByVal node As XPathNavigator)
  'start recursive loop with level 0
  RecurseNavNodes(node, 0)
End Sub

Public Sub RecurseNavNodes(ByVal node As XPathNavigator, _
```

```
    ByVal level As Integer)
  Dim s As String

  s = string.Format("{0} <b>Type:</b>{1} <b>Name:</b>{2} <b>Attr:</b> ", _
    New String("-", level), node.NodeType, node.Name)

  If node.HasAttributes Then
    node.MoveToFirstAttribute()
    Do
      s += string.Format("{0}={1} ", node.Name, node.Value)
    Loop While node.MoveToNextAttribute()
    node.MoveToParent()
  End If

  lbl.Text += s + "<br>"

  If node.HasChildren Then
    node.MoveToFirstChild()
    Do
      RecurseNavNodes(node, level + 1)
    Loop While node.MoveToNext()
    node.MoveToParent()
  End If
End Sub

//C#
protected void Button3_Click(object sender, EventArgs e)
{
  lbl = GetLabel(275, 20);
  XmlDocument xmlDoc = new XmlDocument();
  xmlDoc.Load(MapPath("XmlDocumentTest.xml"));

  XPathNavigator xpathNav = xmlDoc.CreateNavigator();
  xpathNav.MoveToRoot();
  RecurseNavNodes(xpathNav);
}

public void RecurseNavNodes(XPathNavigator node)
{
  //start recursive loop with level 0
  RecurseNavNodes(node, 0);
}

public void RecurseNavNodes(XPathNavigator node, int level)
{
  string s = null;
```

```
    s = string.Format("{0} <b>Type:</b>{1} <b>Name:</b>{2} <b>Attr:</b> ",
      new string('-', level), node.NodeType, node.Name);

    if (node.HasAttributes)
    {
      node.MoveToFirstAttribute();
      do
      {
        s += string.Format("{0}={1} ", node.Name, node.Value);
      } while (node.MoveToNextAttribute());
      node.MoveToParent();
    }

    lbl.Text += s + "<br>";

    if (node.HasChildren)
    {
      node.MoveToFirstChild();
      do
      {
        RecurseNavNodes(node, level + 1);
      } while (node.MoveToNext());
      node.MoveToParent();
    }
  }
```

This is recursive code that works in a similar fashion to the DOM example previously covered. The difference is in the methods that are used to get access to each node.

To get access to the attributes, there is a *HasAttributes* property that is *True* if the current node has attributes. The *MoveToFirstAttribute* and *MoveToNextAttribute* methods are used to navigate the attributes. After the attribute list has been navigated, the *MoveToParent* method moves back to the element.

The *HasChildren* property returns *True* if the current node has child nodes. The *MoveToFirstChild* and *MoveToNext* are used to navigate the child nodes. After the children have been navigated, the *MoveToParent* method moves back to the parent element.

Depending on the task at hand, it might be preferable to use the *XPathNavigator* instead of the DOM. In this example, other than syntax, there is little difference between the two methods.

Searching the *XmlDocument* Using the DOM

The DOM provides *GetElementByID* and the *GetElementsByTagName* methods for searching an *XmlDocument*. The *GetElementByID* method locates an element based on its ID. The ID refers to an ID type that has been defined in a DTD document. To demonstrate this, the following XML is used in many of the examples:

XML File: XmlSample.xml

```
<?xml version="1.0" encoding="utf-8"?>
<!DOCTYPE myRoot [
<!ELEMENT myRoot ANY>
<!ELEMENT myChild ANY>
<!ELEMENT myGrandChild EMPTY>
<!ATTLIST myChild
ChildID ID #REQUIRED
>
]>
<myRoot>
<myChild ChildID="ref-1">
<myGrandChild/>
<myGrandChild/>
<myGrandChild/>
</myChild>
<myChild ChildID="ref-2">
<myGrandChild/>
<myGrandChild/>
<myGrandChild/>
</myChild>
<myChild ChildID="ref-3">
<myGrandChild/>
<myGrandChild/>
<myGrandChild/>
</myChild>
<myChild ChildID="ref-4">
<myGrandChild/>
<myGrandChild/>
<myGrandChild/>
</myChild>
</myRoot>
```

The *ChildID* has been defined as an *ID* data type, and an ID must begin with a character, underscore, or colon. The following code performs a lookup of the element with an *ID* of *ref-3*:

```
'VB
Protected Sub Button4_Click(ByVal sender As Object, _
   ByVal e As System.EventArgs) Handles Button4.Click
  lbl = GetLabel(275, 20)
  Dim s As String
  'Declare and create new XmlDocument
  Dim xmlDoc As New XmlDocument()
  xmlDoc.Load(MapPath("XmlSample.xml"))
```

```
  Dim node As XmlNode
  node = xmlDoc.GetElementById("ref-3")

  s = string.Format("<b>Type:</b>{0} <b>Name:</b>{1} <b>Attr:</b>", _
    node.NodeType, node.Name)

  Dim a As XmlAttribute
  For Each a In node.Attributes
    s += string.Format("{0}={1} ", a.Name, a.Value)
  Next
  lbl.Text = s + "<br>"
End Sub

//C#
protected void Button4_Click(object sender, EventArgs e)
{
  lbl = GetLabel(275, 20);
  string s;
  //Declare and create new XmlDocument
  XmlDocument xmlDoc = new XmlDocument();
  xmlDoc.Load(MapPath("XmlSample.xml"));

  XmlNode node;
  node = xmlDoc.GetElementById("ref-3");

  s = string.Format("<b>Type:</b>{0} <b>Name:</b>{1} <b>Attr:</b>",
    node.NodeType, node.Name);

  foreach (XmlAttribute a in node.Attributes)
  {
    s += string.Format("{0}={1} ", a.Name, a.Value);
  }
  lbl.Text = s + "<br>";
}
```

When an *ID* data type is defined, the ID must be unique. This code locates *ref-3* and displays the node and attributes information.

The *SelectSingleNode* method can also be used to locate an element. The *SelectSingleNode* method requires an XPath query to be passed into the method. The previous code sample has been modified to call the *SelectSingleNode* method to achieve the same result using an XPath query. The sample code, with changes in bold, is as follows:

```
'VB
Protected Sub Button5_Click(ByVal sender As Object, _
   ByVal e As System.EventArgs) Handles Button5.Click
```

```
    lbl = GetLabel(275, 20)
    Dim s As String
    'Declare and create new XmlDocument
    Dim xmlDoc As New XmlDocument()
    xmlDoc.Load(MapPath("XmlSample.xml"))

    Dim node As XmlNode
    node = xmlDoc.SelectSingleNode("//myChild[@ChildID='ref-3']")

    s = String.Format("<b>Type:</b>{0} <b>Name:</b>{1} <b>Attr:</b>", _
      node.NodeType, node.Name)

    Dim a As XmlAttribute
    For Each a In node.Attributes
      s += String.Format("{0}={1} ", a.Name, a.Value)
    Next
    lbl.Text = s + "<br>"
End Sub

//C#
protected void Button5_Click(object sender, EventArgs e)
{
    lbl = GetLabel(275, 20);
    string s;
    //Declare and create new XmlDocument
    XmlDocument xmlDoc = new XmlDocument();
    xmlDoc.Load(MapPath("XmlSample.xml"));

    XmlNode node;
    node = xmlDoc.SelectSingleNode("//myChild[@ChildID='ref-3']");

    s = string.Format("<b>Type:</b>{0} <b>Name:</b>{1} <b>Attr:</b>",
      node.NodeType, node.Name);

    foreach (XmlAttribute a in node.Attributes)
    {
      s += string.Format("{0}={1} ", a.Name, a.Value);
    }
    lbl.Text = s + "<br>";
}
```

The *SelectSingleNode* method does not require a DTD to be provided and can perform an XPath lookup on any element or attribute where the *SelectSingleNode* requires an *ID* data type and a DTD.

The *GetElementsByTagName* method returns an *XmlNodeList* containing all matched elements. This code returns a list of nodes that have the tag name of *myGrandChild*:

```
'VB
Protected Sub Button6_Click(ByVal sender As Object, _
   ByVal e As System.EventArgs) Handles Button6.Click

  lbl = GetLabel(275, 20)
  Dim s As String

  'Declare and create new XmlDocument
  Dim xmlDoc As New XmlDocument()
  xmlDoc.Load(MapPath("XmlSample.xml"))

  Dim elmts As XmlNodeList
  elmts = xmlDoc.GetElementsByTagName("myGrandChild")

  For Each node as XmlNode In elmts
    s = string.Format("<b>Type:</b>{0} <b>Name:</b>{1}", _
      node.NodeType, node.Name)
    lbl.Text += s + "<br>"
  Next
End Sub

//C#
protected void Button6_Click(object sender, EventArgs e)
{
  lbl = GetLabel(275, 20);
  string s;

  //Declare and create new XmlDocument
  XmlDocument xmlDoc = new XmlDocument();
  xmlDoc.Load(MapPath("XmlSample.xml"));

  XmlNodeList elmts;
  elmts = xmlDoc.GetElementsByTagName("myGrandChild");

  foreach (XmlNode node in elmts)
  {
    s = string.Format("<b>Type:</b>{0} <b>Name:</b>{1}",
      node.NodeType, node.Name);
    lbl.Text += s + "<br>";
  }
}
```

This code retrieves the list of elements that have the tag names of *myGrandChild*. This method does not require a DTD to be included, which makes this method preferred, even for a single-node lookup when searching by tag name.

The *SelectNodes* method can also be used to locate an *XmlNodeList*. The *SelectNodes* method requires an XPath query to be passed into the method. The previous code sample has been modified to call the *SelectNodes* method to achieve the same result. The code, with changes in bold, is as follows:

```
'VB
Protected Sub Button7_Click(ByVal sender As Object, _
   ByVal e As System.EventArgs) Handles Button7.Click

    lbl = GetLabel(275, 20)
  Dim s As String

  'Declare and create new XmlDocument
  Dim xmlDoc As New XmlDocument()
  xmlDoc.Load(MapPath("XmlSample.xml"))

  Dim elmts As XmlNodeList
  elmts = xmlDoc.SelectNodes("//myGrandChild")
  For Each node As XmlNode In elmts
    s = String.Format("<b>Type:</b>{0} <b>Name:</b>{1}", _
      node.NodeType, node.Name)
    lbl.Text += s + "<br>"
  Next
End Sub

//C#
protected void Button7_Click(object sender, EventArgs e)
{
  lbl = GetLabel(275, 20);
  string s;

  //Declare and create new XmlDocument
  XmlDocument xmlDoc = new XmlDocument();
  xmlDoc.Load(MapPath("XmlSample.xml"));

  XmlNodeList elmts;
  elmts = xmlDoc.SelectNodes("//myGrandChild");
  foreach (XmlNode node in elmts)
  {
    s = string.Format("<b>Type:</b>{0} <b>Name:</b>{1}",
      node.NodeType, node.Name);
    lbl.Text += s + "<br>";
  }
}
```

Note that this method can perform an XPath lookup on any element or attribute, with much more querying flexibility, whereas the *GetElementsByTagName* is limited to a tag name.

Using the *XPathNavigator* to Search XPath Documents

The *XPathNavigator* offers much more flexibility for performing searches than the DOM. The *XPathNavigator* has many methods that are focused around XPath queries using a cursor model. The *XPathNavigator* works with the *XmlDocument*, but the *XPathDocument* object is tuned for the *XPathNavigator* and uses fewer resources than the *XmlDocument*. If the DOM is not required, use the *XPathDocument* instead of the *XmlDocument*. The following code performs a search for the *myChild* element, where the *ChildID* attribute is equal to *ref-3*:

```
'VB
Protected Sub Button8_Click(ByVal sender As Object, _
   ByVal e As System.EventArgs) Handles Button8.Click
  lbl = GetLabel(275, 20)
  Dim s As String
  Dim xmlDoc As New XPathDocument(MapPath("XmlSample.xml"))
  Dim nav As XPathNavigator = xmlDoc.CreateNavigator()

  Dim expr As String = "//myChild[@ChildID='ref-3']"

  'Display the selection.
  Dim iterator As XPathNodeIterator = nav.Select(expr)
  Dim navResult As XPathNavigator = iterator.Current
  While (iterator.MoveNext())

    s = string.Format("<b>Type:</b>{0} <b>Name:</b>{1} ", _
     navResult.NodeType, navResult.Name)

    If navResult.HasAttributes Then
      navResult.MoveToFirstAttribute()
      s += "<b>Attr:</b> "
      Do
        s += string.Format("{0}={1} ", _
        navResult.Name, navResult.Value)
      Loop While navResult.MoveToNextAttribute()
    End If

    lbl.Text += s + "<br>"
  End While
End Sub

//C#
protected void Button8_Click(object sender, EventArgs e)
{
  lbl = GetLabel(275, 20);
  string s;
  XPathDocument xmlDoc = new XPathDocument(MapPath("XmlSample.xml"));
  XPathNavigator nav = xmlDoc.CreateNavigator();
```

```
  string expr = "//myChild[@ChildID='ref-3']";

  //Display the selection.
  XPathNodeIterator iterator = nav.Select(expr);
  XPathNavigator navResult = iterator.Current;
  while (iterator.MoveNext())
  {
    s = String.Format("<b>Type:</b>{0} <b>Name:</b>{1} ",
     navResult.NodeType, navResult.Name);

    if (navResult.HasAttributes)
    {
      navResult.MoveToFirstAttribute();
      s += "<b>Attr:</b> ";
      do
      {
        s += String.Format("{0}={1} ",
        navResult.Name, navResult.Value);
      } while (navResult.MoveToNextAttribute());
    }

    lbl.Text += s + "<br>";
  }
}
```

This code uses an XPath query to locate the *myChild* element for which the *ChildID* attribute is equal to *ref-3*. The *Select* method is called with the query string. The *Select* method returns an *XPathNodeIterator* object, which allows navigation over the node or nodes that are returned. The *XPathNodeIterator* has a property called *Current*, which represents the current node, and is in itself an *XPathNavigator* data type. Rather than using *iterator.Current* throughout the code, a variable called *navResult* is created and assigned a reference to *iterator.Current*. Note that the call to *MoveToParent* is not required when finishing the loop through the attributes. This is because *iterator.MoveNext* doesn't care what the current location is, because it is simply going to the next node in its list.

Some of the real power of the *XPathNavigator* starts to show when the requirement is to retrieve a list of nodes and sort the output. Sorting involves compiling an XPath query string to an *XPathExpression* object, and then adding a sort to the compiled expressions. The following is an example of compiling and sorting:

```
'VB
Protected Sub Button9_Click(ByVal sender As Object, _
   ByVal e As System.EventArgs) Handles Button9.Click
  lbl = GetLabel(275, 20)
  Dim s As String
  Dim xmlDoc As New XPathDocument(MapPath("XmlSample.xml"))
  Dim nav As XPathNavigator = xmlDoc.CreateNavigator()
```

```
  'Select all myChild elements
  Dim expr As XPathExpression
  expr = nav.Compile("//myChild")

  'Sort the selected books by title.
  expr.AddSort("@ChildID", _
    XmlSortOrder.Descending, _
    XmlCaseOrder.None, "", _
    XmlDataType.Text)

  'Display the selection.
  Dim iterator As XPathNodeIterator = nav.Select(expr)
  Dim navResult As XPathNavigator = iterator.Current
  While (iterator.MoveNext())

    s = String.Format("<b>Type:</b>{0} <b>Name:</b>{1} ", _
      navResult.NodeType, navResult.Name)

    If navResult.HasAttributes Then
      navResult.MoveToFirstAttribute()
      s += "<b>Attr:</b> "
      Do
        s += String.Format("{0}={1} ", _
          navResult.Name, navResult.Value)
      Loop While navResult.MoveToNextAttribute()
    End If

    lbl.Text += s + "<br>"
  End While
End Sub
```

//C#

```
protected void Button9_Click(object sender, EventArgs e)
{
  lbl = GetLabel(275, 20);
  string s;
  XPathDocument xmlDoc = new XPathDocument(MapPath("XmlSample.xml"));
  XPathNavigator nav = xmlDoc.CreateNavigator();

  //Select all myChild elements
  XPathExpression expr;
  expr = nav.Compile("//myChild");

  //Sort the selected books by title.
  expr.AddSort("@ChildID",
    XmlSortOrder.Descending,
```

```
      XmlCaseOrder.None, "",
      XmlDataType.Text);

    //Display the selection.
    XPathNodeIterator iterator = nav.Select(expr);
    XPathNavigator navResult = iterator.Current;
    while (iterator.MoveNext())
    {
      s = String.Format("<b>Type:</b>{0} <b>Name:</b>{1} ",
       navResult.NodeType, navResult.Name);

      if (navResult.HasAttributes)
      {
        navResult.MoveToFirstAttribute();
        s += "<b>Attr:</b> ";
        do
        {
          s += String.Format("{0}={1} ",
            navResult.Name, navResult.Value);
        } while (navResult.MoveToNextAttribute());
      }
      lbl.Text += s + "<br>";
    }
  }
```

This code is similar to the previous example, with the exception of the creation of the *expr* variable. The *expr* variable is created by compiling the query string to an *XPathExpression*. After that, the *AddSort* method is used to sort the output in descending order, based on the *ChildID* attribute.

When working with XML, it might seem easier to use the *DOM* methods to access data, but there are limits to the search capabilities that could require walking the tree to get the desired output. On the surface, the *XPathNavigator* might appear to be more difficult to use, but having the ability to perform XPath queries and sorting make this the object of choice for more complex XML problem solving.

Writing a File Using the *XmlTextWriter*

The *XmlTextWriter* can be used to create an XML file from scratch. This class has many properties that aid in the creation of XML nodes. The following sample creates an XML file called EmployeeList.xml and writes two employees to the file:

```
'VB
Protected Sub Button10_Click(ByVal sender As Object, _
   ByVal e As System.EventArgs) Handles Button10.Click
  Dim xmlWriter As New _
    XmlTextWriter(MapPath("EmployeeList.xml"), _
```

```
    System.Text.Encoding.UTF8)

  With xmlWriter
   .Formatting = Formatting.Indented
   .Indentation = 5

   .WriteStartDocument()
   .WriteComment("XmlTextWriter Test Date: " & _
    DateTime.Now.ToShortDateString())

   .WriteStartElement("EmployeeList")

   'New Employee
   .WriteStartElement("Employee")
   .WriteAttributeString("EmpID", "1")
   .WriteAttributeString("LastName", "JoeLast")
   .WriteAttributeString("FirstName", "Joe")
   .WriteAttributeString("Salary", XmlConvert.ToString(50000))

   .WriteElementString("HireDate", _
      XmlConvert.ToString(#1/1/2003#, _
      XmlDateTimeSerializationMode.Unspecified))

   .WriteStartElement("Address")
   .WriteElementString("Street1", "123 MyStreet")
   .WriteElementString("Street2", "")
   .WriteElementString("City", "MyCity")
   .WriteElementString("State", "OH")
   .WriteElementString("ZipCode", "12345")

   'Address
   .WriteEndElement()
   'Employee
   .WriteEndElement()

   'New Employee
   .WriteStartElement("Employee")
   .WriteAttributeString("EmpID", "2")
   .WriteAttributeString("LastName", "MaryLast")
   .WriteAttributeString("FirstName", "Mary")
   .WriteAttributeString("Salary", XmlConvert.ToString(40000))

   .WriteElementString("HireDate", _
      XmlConvert.ToString(#1/2/2003#, _
      XmlDateTimeSerializationMode.Unspecified))
```

```
    .WriteStartElement("Address")
    .WriteElementString("Street1", "234 MyStreet")
    .WriteElementString("Street2", "")
    .WriteElementString("City", "MyCity")
    .WriteElementString("State", "OH")
    .WriteElementString("ZipCode", "23456")

    'Address
    .WriteEndElement()
    'Employee
    .WriteEndElement()

    'EmployeeList
    .WriteEndElement()
    .Close()
  End With
  Response.Redirect("EmployeeList.xml")
End Sub

//C#
protected void Button10_Click(object sender, EventArgs e)
{
  XmlTextWriter xmlWriter  = new
    XmlTextWriter(MapPath("EmployeeList.xml"),
    System.Text.Encoding.UTF8);

  xmlWriter.Formatting = Formatting.Indented;
  xmlWriter.Indentation = 5;

  xmlWriter.WriteStartDocument();
  xmlWriter.WriteComment("XmlTextWriter Test Date: " +
    DateTime.Now.ToShortDateString());

  xmlWriter.WriteStartElement("EmployeeList");

  //New Employee
  xmlWriter.WriteStartElement("Employee");
  xmlWriter.WriteAttributeString("EmpID", "1");
  xmlWriter.WriteAttributeString("LastName", "JoeLast");
  xmlWriter.WriteAttributeString("FirstName", "Joe");
  xmlWriter.WriteAttributeString("Salary", XmlConvert.ToString(50000));

  xmlWriter.WriteElementString("HireDate",
    XmlConvert.ToString(DateTime.Parse("1/1/2003"),
    XmlDateTimeSerializationMode.Unspecified));
```

```
    xmlWriter.WriteStartElement("Address");
    xmlWriter.WriteElementString("Street1", "123 MyStreet");
    xmlWriter.WriteElementString("Street2", "");
    xmlWriter.WriteElementString("City", "MyCity");
    xmlWriter.WriteElementString("State", "OH");
    xmlWriter.WriteElementString("ZipCode", "12345");

    //Address
    xmlWriter.WriteEndElement();
    //Employee
    xmlWriter.WriteEndElement();

    //New Employee
    xmlWriter.WriteStartElement("Employee");
    xmlWriter.WriteAttributeString("EmpID", "2");
    xmlWriter.WriteAttributeString("LastName", "MaryLast");
    xmlWriter.WriteAttributeString("FirstName", "Mary");
    xmlWriter.WriteAttributeString("Salary", XmlConvert.ToString(40000));

    xmlWriter.WriteElementString("HireDate",
      XmlConvert.ToString(DateTime.Parse("1/2/2003"),
      XmlDateTimeSerializationMode.Unspecified));

    xmlWriter.WriteStartElement("Address");
    xmlWriter.WriteElementString("Street1", "234 MyStreet");
    xmlWriter.WriteElementString("Street2", "");
    xmlWriter.WriteElementString("City", "MyCity");
    xmlWriter.WriteElementString("State", "OH");
    xmlWriter.WriteElementString("ZipCode", "23456");

    //Address
    xmlWriter.WriteEndElement();
    //Employee
    xmlWriter.WriteEndElement();

    //EmployeeList
    xmlWriter.WriteEndElement();
    xmlWriter.Close();

    Response.Redirect("EmployeeList.xml");
}
```

This code starts by opening the file as part of the constructor for the *XmlTextWriter*. The constructor also expects an encoding type. Because an argument is required, passing *Nothing* causes the encoding type to be UTF-8, which is the same as the value that is explicitly being passed. The following is the EmployeeList.xml file that is created:

```xml
<?xml version="1.0" encoding="utf-8"?>
<!--XmlTextWriter Test Date: 8/16/2006-->
<EmployeeList>
  <Employee EmpID="1" LastName="JoeLast" FirstName="Joe" Salary="50000">
    <HireDate>2003-01-01T00:00:00</HireDate>
    <Address>
      <Street1>123 MyStreet</Street1>
      <Street2 />
      <City>MyCity</City>
      <State>OH</State>
      <ZipCode>12345</ZipCode>
    </Address>
  </Employee>
  <Employee EmpID="2" LastName="MaryLast" FirstName="Mary" Salary="40000">
    <HireDate>2003-01-02T00:00:00</HireDate>
    <Address>
      <Street1>234 MyStreet</Street1>
      <Street2 />
      <City>MyCity</City>
      <State>OH</State>
      <ZipCode>23456</ZipCode>
    </Address>
  </Employee>
</EmployeeList>
```

There are many statements that are doing nothing more than writing to the *xmlWriter*. Typing time is saved in the Visual Basic code by the use of the *With xmlWriter* statement, which allows a simple dot to be typed to represent the *xmlWriter* object.

The *XmlTextWriter* handles the formatting of the document by setting the *Formatting* and *Indentation* properties.

The *WriteStartDocument* method writes the XML declaration to the file. The *WriteComment* method writes a comment to the file.

When writing elements, you can use either the *WriteStartElement* method or the *Write-ElementString* method. The *WriteStartElement* method only writes the starting element but keeps track of the nesting level and adds new elements inside this element. The element is completed when a call is made to the *WriteEndElement* method. The *WriteElementString* method simply writes a closed element to the file.

The *WriteAttribute* method takes a name and value pair and writes the attribute into the current open element.

When writing is complete, the *Close* method must be called to avoid losing data. The file is then saved.

Reading a File Using the *XmlTextReader*

The *XmlTextReader* is used to read an XML file node by node. The reader provides forward-only, noncaching access to an XML data stream. The reader is ideal for use when there is a possibility that the information that is desired is near the top of the XML file and the file is large. If random access is required, use the *XPathNavigator* class or the *XmlDocument* class. The following code reads the XML file that was created in the previous example and displays information about each node:

```
'VB
Protected Sub Button11_Click(ByVal sender As Object, _
   ByVal e As System.EventArgs) Handles Button11.Click
  lbl = GetLabel(275, 20)
  Dim xmlReader As New _
    XmlTextReader(MapPath("EmployeeList.xml"))

  Do While xmlReader.Read()

    Select Case xmlReader.NodeType
      Case XmlNodeType.XmlDeclaration, _
           XmlNodeType.Element, _
           XmlNodeType.Comment
        Dim s As String
        s = String.Format("{0}: {1} = {2}<br>", _
          xmlReader.NodeType, _
          xmlReader.Name, _
          xmlReader.Value)
        lbl.Text += s
      Case XmlNodeType.Text
        Dim s As String
        s = String.Format(" - Value: {0}<br>", _
          xmlReader.Value)
        lbl.Text += s
    End Select

    If xmlReader.HasAttributes Then
      Do While xmlReader.MoveToNextAttribute()
        Dim s As String
        s = String.Format(" - Attribute: {0} = {1}<br>", _
          xmlReader.Name, xmlReader.Value)
        lbl.Text += s
      Loop
    End If
  Loop
  xmlReader.Close()
End Sub
```

```
//C#
protected void Button11_Click(object sender, EventArgs e)
{
  lbl = GetLabel(275, 20);
  XmlTextReader xmlReader = new
   XmlTextReader(MapPath("EmployeeList.xml"));

  while (xmlReader.Read())
  {
    switch( xmlReader.NodeType)
    {
      case XmlNodeType.XmlDeclaration:
      case XmlNodeType.Element:
      case XmlNodeType.Comment:
      {
        string s;
        s = String.Format("{0}: {1} = {2}<br>",
          xmlReader.NodeType,
          xmlReader.Name,
          xmlReader.Value);
        lbl.Text += s;
        break;
      }
      case XmlNodeType.Text:
      {
        string s;
        s = String.Format(" - Value: {0}<br>",
          xmlReader.Value);
        lbl.Text += s;
        break;
      }
    }

    if (xmlReader.HasAttributes)
    {
      while (xmlReader.MoveToNextAttribute())
      {
        string s;
        s = String.Format(" - Attribute: {0} = {1}<br>",
        xmlReader.Name, xmlReader.Value);
        lbl.Text += s;
      }
    }
  }
  xmlReader.Close();
}
```

This code opens the EmployeeList file, and then performs a simple loop, reading one element at a time until finished. For each node that is read, a check is made on the *NodeType*, and the node information is printed. When a node is read, its corresponding attributes are read as well. A check is made to see if the node has attributes, and they are displayed.

Modifying an XML Document

Once the *XmlDocument* object is loaded, you can easily add and remove nodes. When removing a node, you simply need to locate the node and delete it from its parent. When adding a node, you need to create the node, search for the appropriate location into which to insert the node, and insert the node. The following code deletes an existing node and adds a new node:

```
'VB
Protected Sub Button12_Click(ByVal sender As Object, _
   ByVal e As System.EventArgs) Handles Button12.Click

  lbl = GetLabel(275, 20)

  'Declare and load new XmlDocument
  Dim xmlDoc As New XmlDocument()
  xmlDoc.Load(MapPath("XmlSample.xml"))

  'delete a node
  Dim node As XmlNode
  node = xmlDoc.SelectSingleNode("//myChild[@ChildID='ref-3']")
  node.ParentNode.RemoveChild(node)

  'create a node and add it
  Dim newElement as XmlElement = _
    xmlDoc.CreateElement("myNewElement")
  node = xmlDoc.SelectSingleNode("//myChild[@ChildID='ref-1']")
  node.ParentNode.InsertAfter(newElement, node)
  xmlDoc.Save(MapPath("XmlSampleModified.xml"))
  Response.Redirect("XmlSampleModified.xml")
End Sub

//C#
protected void Button12_Click(object sender, EventArgs e)
{
  lbl = GetLabel(275, 20);

  //Declare and load new XmlDocument
  XmlDocument xmlDoc = new XmlDocument();
  xmlDoc.Load(MapPath("XmlSample.xml"));
```

```
  //delete a node
  XmlNode node;
  node = xmlDoc.SelectSingleNode("//myChild[@ChildID='ref-3']");
  node.ParentNode.RemoveChild(node);

  //create a node and add it
  XmlElement newElement =
    xmlDoc.CreateElement("myNewElement");
  node = xmlDoc.SelectSingleNode("//myChild[@ChildID='ref-1']");
  node.ParentNode.InsertAfter(newElement, node);
  xmlDoc.Save(MapPath("XmlSampleModified.xml"));
  Response.Redirect("XmlSampleModified.xml");
}
```

To delete a node, use the *SelectSingleNode* method to locate the node to delete. After the node is located, the node can be removed from its parent by using the *ParentNode* property's *RemoveChild* method.

To add a node, execute the *CreateElement* method on the *XmlDocument* object. Next, the insert location is searched and the *ParentNode* property's *InsertAfter* method is used to insert the new node.

Validating XML Documents

An important element to exchanging documents between disparate systems is the ability to define the structure of an XML document and then validate the XML document against its defined structure. The .NET Framework offers the ability to perform validation against a DTD or schema. Earlier versions of the .NET Framework used the *XmlValidatingReader* object to perform validation, but this object is now obsolete. Instead, this section explores XML document validation using the *XmlReader* class.

The *XmlReader* class performs forward-only reading and validation of a stream of XML. The *XmlReader* class contains a *Create* method that can be passed as a string or a stream, as well as an *XmlReaderSettings* object. To perform validation, the *XmlReaderSettings* object must be created and its properties set to perform validation. In the next example, the files XmlSample.xml and XmlBadSample.xml are validated using the following code:

```
'VB
Protected Sub Button13_Click(ByVal sender As Object, _
   ByVal e As System.EventArgs) Handles Button13.Click
  lbl = GetLabel(275, 20)
  If ValidateDocument(MapPath("XmlSample.xml")) Then
    lbl.Text += "Valid Document<br />"
  Else
    lbl.Text += "Invalid Document<br />"
  End If
End Sub
```

```
Protected Sub Button14_Click(ByVal sender As Object, _
   ByVal e As System.EventArgs) Handles Button14.Click
  lbl = GetLabel(275, 20)
  If ValidateDocument(MapPath("XmlBadSample.xml")) Then
    lbl.Text += "Valid Document<br />"
  Else
    lbl.Text += "Invalid Document<br />"
  End If
End Sub

Public Function ValidateDocument(ByVal fileName As String) _
   As Boolean
  Dim xmlSet As New XmlReaderSettings()
  xmlSet.ValidationType = ValidationType.DTD
  xmlSet.ProhibitDtd = False
  Dim vr As XmlReader = XmlReader.Create( _
     fileName, xmlSet)

  Dim xd As New XmlDocument()
  Try
    xd.Load(vr)
    Return True
  Catch ex As Exception
    lbl.Text += ex.Message + "<br />"
    Return False
  Finally
    vr.Close()
  End Try
End Function

//C#
protected void Button13_Click(object sender, EventArgs e)
{
  lbl = GetLabel(275, 20);
  if (ValidateDocument(MapPath("XmlSample.xml")))
  {
    lbl.Text += "Valid Document<br />";
  }
  else
  {
    lbl.Text += "Invalid Document<br />";
  }
}

protected void Button14_Click(object sender, EventArgs e)
{
```

```
    lbl = GetLabel(275, 20);
    if (ValidateDocument(MapPath("XmlBadSample.xml")))
    {
      lbl.Text += "Valid Document<br />";
    }
    else
    {
      lbl.Text += "Invalid Document<br />";
    }
  }

  private bool ValidateDocument(string fileName)
  {
    XmlReaderSettings xmlSet = new XmlReaderSettings();
    xmlSet.ValidationType = ValidationType.DTD;
    xmlSet.ProhibitDtd = false;
    XmlReader vr = XmlReader.Create(fileName, xmlSet);
    XmlDocument xd = new XmlDocument();
    try
    {
      xd.Load(vr);
      return true;
    }
    catch (Exception ex)
    {
      lbl.Text += ex.Message + "<br />";
      return false;
    }
    finally
    {
      vr.Close();
    }
  }
```

The XmlBadSample.xml file is as follows:

XML File: XmlBadSample.xml

```
<?xml version="1.0" encoding="utf-8"?>
<!DOCTYPE myRoot [
  <!ELEMENT myRoot ANY>
  <!ELEMENT myChild ANY>
  <!ELEMENT myGrandChild EMPTY>
  <!ATTLIST myChild
ChildID ID #REQUIRED
>
]>
<myRoot>
```

```
  <myChild ChildID="ref-1">
   <myGrandChild/>
   <myGrandChild/>
   <myGrandChild/>
  </myChild>
  <myChild ChildID="ref-2">
   <myGrandChild/>
   <myGrandChild/>
   <myGrandChild>this is malformed</myGrandChild>
  </myChild>
  <myChild ChildID="ref-3">
   <myGrandChild/>
   <myGrandChild/>
   <myGrandChild/>
  </myChild>
  <myChild ChildID="ref-4">
   <myGrandChild/>
   <myGrandChild/>
   <myGrandChild/>
  </myChild>
</myRoot>
```

This code simply opens the XML file with an *XmlReader,* and, while the *XmlDocument* is being read, the document is being validated. Because this code has an embedded DTD, the document is validated.

The DTD states that the *myGrandChild* element must be empty, but one of the *myGrandChild* elements of *myChild ref-1* has a *myGrandChild* element containing the words, *this is malformed*. This causes an error. Attempts to read from the *XmlReader* when valid should always be within a *Try-Catch* block to catch possible validation exceptions.

Quick Check

1. **What method can you execute to locate a single XML node by its tag name?**
2. **What method can you use to search for all elements that have a specific tag name and retrieve the results as an *XmlNodeList*?**
3. **What object should you use to perform XPath queries on large XML documents?**

Quick Check Answers

1. **You can execute *SelectSingleNode*.**
2. **You can use *GetElementsByTagName* or *SelectNodes*.**
3. **You should use *XPathNavigator*.**

Using LINQ to XML

Another way to work with XML in the .NET Framework is through the LINQ to XML classes found inside the *System.Xml.Linq* namespace. These classes provide an easier, faster, and richer experience when working with XML data. In addition, they leverage LINQ to ensure a consistent query model when searching for data embedded in XML. With LINQ to XML, you can do everything you've seen thus far, including loading XML from a file, serializing it to streams and files, querying against it, validating, manipulating it in memory, and much more. In fact, many of the LINQ to XML classes use the other objects discussed previously as their internal means of working with data (such as the *XmlReader* class used to read XML).

The LINQ to XML Classes

The LINQ to XML classes are accessible through the *System.Xml.Linq* namespace. There are many classes here. However, the key class with which you will work is the *XElement* class, which provides the ability to easily create XML elements, load them from files, query against them, and write them back out or send them across the wire. Figure 7-19 shows a high-level view of the objects that are defined inside the *Xml.Linq* namespace.

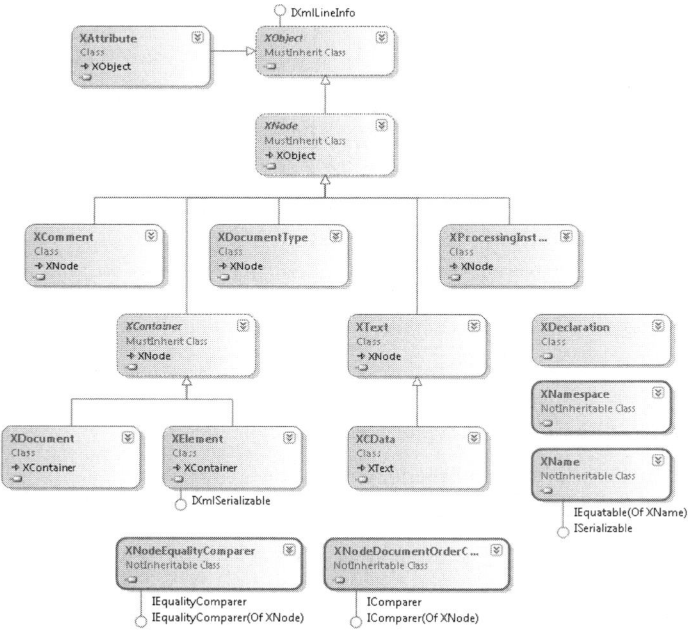

FIGURE 7-19 The classes of LINQ to XML (*System.Xml.Linq* namespace)

The sections that follow provide an overview of working with *XElement*. However, it is important to have an understanding of the other classes that make up LINQ to XML. Table 7-6 presents the classes shown in Figure 7-19 and provides a description of each.

TABLE 7-6 The LINQ to XML Classes Inside the *System.Xml.Linq* Namespace

CLASS	DESCRIPTION
XAttribute	Represents a class for working with XML attributes. You can create a new instance of this class that includes a name and value. You can use the *XAttribute* class to add attributes to an *XElement*. The *XAttribute* class is also used for functional XML programming (described later) when defining trees.
XCData	Represents a CDATA string section of an XML element or document. This class derives from *XText*.
XComment	Represents a comment in an XML structure. The *XComment* class can be a child of an *XElement* or a sibling of the root node in an *XDocument*.
XContainer	Represents the base class for *XElement* and *XDocument*.
XDeclaration	Represents an XML declaration including XML version and encoding information.
XDocument	Represents a valid XML document. This class contains the full document. Many times you only need to work with elements of a document. In this case, the *XElement* is the preferred class. The *XDocument* exists for when you need to work with an entire structure of an XML document (including elements, comments, declarations, and so on).
XDocumentType	Represents an XML DTD used for validating XML trees and supplying default attributes.
XElement	Represents an XML element. This is the core class of LINQ to XML. You can use this class to declare, load, and work with portions of an XML structure.
XName	Represents names of elements and attributes.
XNamespace	Represents a namespace for *XElement* or *XAttribute*. Namespaces are part of *XName*.
XNode	Represents the nodes of an XML tree. This is a base class for *XText*, *XContainer*, *XComment*, *XProcessingInstruction*, and *XDocumentType*.
XNodeDocumentOrder-Compare	Represents features used to compare nodes for document order.
XNodeEqualityComparer	Represents features used to compare nodes for equality.
XObject	Represents a base class used by *XNode* and *XAttribute*. Provides base event functionality for these classes.

CLASS	DESCRIPTION
XObjectChange	Represents the event type for events raised by classes that use *XObject*.
XObjectChangeEventArgs	Represents the data for the *Changing* and *Changed* events.
XProcessingInstruction	Represents an XML processing instruction.
XText	Represents a text node in XML.

Loading an XML Tree

To work with LINQ to XML, you need to get XML into memory. This means loading (or parsing) it from a file, string, or *XmlReader*. You parse XML data into an *XElement* (or *XDocument*). As an example, if you have a file that contains employee data, you can read that file by calling the *Load* method of *XElement*. The following code shows this feature. Notice the call to *Server.MapPath* to get the path to the Employee.xml file stored in the root of the Web site.

```
'VB
Dim xmlFile As String = Server.MapPath("/DataSamples") & "\employee.xml"
Dim employees As XElement = XElement.Load(xmlFile)

//C#
string xmlFile = Server.MapPath(@"/DataSamples") + @"\employee.xml";
XElement employees = XElement.Load(xmlFile);
```

The *XElement* class also contains the *Parse* method, which is used to load XML from a string. You simply pass the string as a parameter to the static *Parse* method. This is great if your XML is already in a string. However, if you are defining XML in your code, you should do so functionally and not as a string, as using the functional approach is faster. This is discussed further in the section "Creating an XML Tree with *XElement*" later in this lesson.

Writing LINQ Queries Against XML Trees

The queries you write with LINQ to XML can be seen as similar to XPath and XQuery. However, they use the standard LINQ notation. This ensures a single, consistent query model across different types of data. You write LINQ to XML queries in a similar way as querying against a *DataSet*. This is because the XML data, like the *DataSet*, is an in-memory store. In addition, there is not an O/R map as in LINQ to SQL.

As an example, suppose you have an XML file that contains employees. The XML file might look like this:

```
<?xml version="1.0" standalone="yes"?>
<Employees>
  <Employee>
    <id>A-C71970F</id>
    <FirstName>Aria</FirstName>
```

```
    <LastName>Cruz</LastName>
    <Salary>15</Salary>
  </Employee>
  <Employee>
    <id>A-R89858F</id>
    <FirstName>Annette</FirstName>
    <LastName>Roulet</LastName>
    <Salary>24</Salary>
  </Employee>
  <Employee>
    <id>CFH28514M</id>
    <FirstName>Carlos</FirstName>
    <LastName>Hernadez</LastName>
    <Salary>18</Salary>
  </Employee>
  <Employee>
    <id>M-L67958F</id>
    <FirstName>Maria</FirstName>
    <LastName>Larsson</LastName>
    <Salary>17</Salary>
  </Employee>
  <Employee>
    <id>VPA30890F</id>
    <FirstName>Victoria</FirstName>
    <LastName>Ashworth</LastName>
    <Salary>21</Salary>
  </Employee>
</Employees>
```

Suppose you need to write a query against this XML that returns all employees whose salary is greater than 20. You would start by first loading the XML into memory as an *XElement* instance. You could then define a LINQ query against the *XElement* to return employee elements that contain a *Salary* element with a value greater than 20. The following code demonstrates this query and writes the results out to a Web page:

```
'VB
Dim xmlFile As String = Server.MapPath("/DataSamples") & "\employee.xml"
Dim employees As XElement = XElement.Load(xmlFile)

Dim query As IEnumerable(Of XElement) = _
    From emp In employees.<Employee> _
    Where CType(emp.Element("Salary"), Integer) > 20 _
    Select emp

For Each emp As XElement In query
  Response.Write(emp.Element("FirstName").ToString() & ", ")
  Response.Write(emp.Element("LastName").ToString() & "<br />")
```

```
  Response.Write(emp.Element("Salary").ToString() & "<br /><br />")
Next

//C#
string xmlFile = Server.MapPath(@"/DataSamples") + @"\employee.xml";
XElement employees = XElement.Load(xmlFile);

IEnumerable<XElement> query =
  from emp in employees.Elements("Employee")
  where (int)emp.Element("Salary") > 20
  select emp;

foreach (XElement emp in query)
{
  Response.Write(emp.Element("FirstName").ToString() + ", ");
  Response.Write(emp.Element("LastName").ToString() + "<br />");
  Response.Write(emp.Element("Salary").ToString() + "<br /><br />");
}
```

Creating an XML Tree with *XElement*

LINQ to XML also adds the ability to functionally define XML in your code. This means creating an XML *XElement* object tree in code (and not just as a parsed string). This can make your code easier to read and easier to write. In fact, Visual Basic developers can actually write the XML as angle-bracketed items with intelligent coloring in the IDE. C# developers, on the other hand, still have to call object constructors. However, they also have an easy way to build XML trees in code.

As an example, suppose you wish to define an *XElement* that represents a list of employees. You might also want to define a few child elements that represent actual employees and their data. You could do so by simply nesting calls to the new *XElement* constructor, which takes a parameter array as a value. For Visual Basic developers, this is abstracted further and you can simply write XML in your code. The following shows an example:

```
'VB
Dim employees As XElement = _
  <Employees>
    <Employee>
      <id>MFS52347M</id>
      <FirstName>Martin</FirstName>
      <LastName>Sommer</LastName>
      <Salary>15</Salary>
    </Employee>
  </Employees>

//C#
XElement employees =
```

```
  new XElement("Employees",
    new XElement("Employee",
      new XElement("id", "MFS52347M"),
      new XElement("FirstName", "Martin"),
      new XElement("LastName", "Sommer"),
      new XElement("Salary", 15)
    )
  );
```

To add further power to defining XML, you can also embed queries as one of the parameters to building *XElements*. The result of these queries will get added to the XML stream.

For example, consider the previous employees definition. Suppose you wish to add all the employees from the Employee.xml file to this list. You could do so in the *XElement* definition by adding a query at the end of the first employee definition. The following code shows an example. Notice the statement `from emp in empFile.Elements()`; this is the call to the query.

```
'VB
Dim xmlFile As String = Server.MapPath("/DataSamples") & "\employee.xml"
Dim empFile As XElement = XElement.Load(xmlFile)

Dim employees As XElement = _
  <Employees>
    <Employee>
      <id>MFS52347M</id>
      <FirstName>Martin</FirstName>
      <LastName>Sommer</LastName>
      <Salary>15</Salary>
    </Employee>
    <%= From emp In empFile.Elements() _
      Select emp %>
  </Employees>

For Each emp As XElement In employees.Elements
  Response.Write(emp.Element("FirstName").ToString() & ", ")
  Response.Write(emp.Element("LastName").ToString() & "<br />")
  Response.Write(emp.Element("Salary").ToString() & "<br /><br />")
Next

//C#
string xmlFile = Server.MapPath(@"/DataSamples") + @"\employee.xml";
XElement empFile = XElement.Load(xmlFile);

XElement employees =
  new XElement("Employees",
    new XElement("Employee",
      new XElement("id", "MFS52347M"),
```

```
        new XElement("FirstName", "Martin"),
        new XElement("LastName", "Sommer"),
        new XElement("Salary", 15)
      ),
        from emp in empFile.Elements()
        select emp
  );

foreach (XElement emp in employees.Elements())
{
  Response.Write(emp.Element("FirstName").ToString() + ", ");
  Response.Write(emp.Element("LastName").ToString() + "<br />");
  Response.Write(emp.Element("Salary").ToString() + "<br /><br />");
}
```

LAB Working with XML Data

In this lab, you work with XML data to display a subset of an XML file in a *GridView* control, using the *XmlDataSource* and an XSLT file.

If you encounter a problem completing an exercise, the completed projects are available in the samples installed from the companion CD in the Code folder.

EXERCISE 1 Create the Web Site and the XML Files

In this exercise, you create the Web site and XML file.

1. Open Visual Studio; create a new Web site called **XmlData** using your preferred programming language.
2. In Solution Explorer, right-click the App_Data folder and select Add New Item. Select XML File, name the file **ProductList.xml**, and click Add.
3. In the XML file, add the following:

```
<?xml version="1.0" encoding="utf-8" ?>
<ProductList>
  <Product Id="1A59B" Department="Sporting Goods" Name="Baseball" Price="3.00"
/>
  <Product Id="9B25T" Department="Sporting Goods" Name="Tennis Racket"
Price="40.00" />
  <Product Id="3H13R" Department="Sporting Goods" Name="Golf Clubs"
Price="179.00" />
  <Product Id="7D67A" Department="Clothing" Name="Shirt" Price="12.00" />
  <Product Id="4T21N" Department="Clothing" Name="Jacket" Price="45.00" />
</ProductList>
```

4. Open the Default.aspx page. In Design view, drag a *DetailsView* control onto the page and size it wide enough to display the car information.
5. Click the smart tag in the upper right corner of the *DetailsView* control to display the *DetailsView* Tasks window.

   Click the Auto Format link and select Professional.
6. Click the Choose Data Source drop-down list and select New Data Source to start the Data Source Configuration Wizard. For the data source type, select XML File and click OK.
7. On the Configure Data Source page, click Browse next to the Data File text box and browse to the ProductList.xml file in the App_Data folder.
8. Click OK.
9. Select the Enable Paging option in the *DetailsView* tasks window. Configuration of the *DetailsView* is complete.
10. Run the Web page. Notice that the data is retrieved and displayed.

Lesson Summary

- XML documents can be accessed using the DOM.
- The *XPathNavigator* uses a cursor model and XPath queries to provide read-only, random access to the data.
- The *XmlReader* provides an object for validating against DTD, XDR, or XSD by setting the *XmlReaderSettings* object properties.
- LINQ to XML uses the *XElement* class to load XML data, write LINQ queries against it, and write the data back if need be. You can also functionally define XML in your code using LINQ to XML.

Lesson Review

You can use the following questions to test your knowledge of the information in Lesson 3, "Working with XML Data." The questions are also available on the companion CD if you prefer to review them in electronic form.

> ***NOTE*** **ANSWERS**
>
> **Answers to these questions and explanations of why each answer choice is right or wrong are located in the "Answers" section at the end of the book.**

1. Which class can be used to create an XML document from scratch?
   A. *XmlConvert*
   B. *XmlDocument*
   C. *XmlNew*
   D. *XmlSettings*
2. Which class can be used to perform data type conversion between .NET Framework data types and XML types?
   A. *XmlType*
   B. *XmlCast*
   C. *XmlConvert*
   D. *XmlSettings*
3. You are writing a function that accepts a string as a parameter. The string data will be sent to the function in the form of XML. You need to write LINQ to XML code to query this XML and process it. What steps should you take? (Choose all that apply.)
   A. Use the *XElement.Load* method to load the XML data into a new *XElement*.
   B. Use the *XElement.Parse* method to load the XML data into a new *XElement*.
   C. Define a query variable of type *IEnumerable*<> where the generic type is set to *XElement*.
   D. Define a query variable of type *IEnumerable*<> where the generic type is set to the value of the string parameter passed to the function.

Chapter Review

To further practice and reinforce the skills you learned in this chapter, you can perform the following tasks:

- Review the chapter summary.
- Complete the case scenarios. These scenarios set up real-world situations involving the topics of this chapter and ask you to create solutions.
- Complete the suggested practices.
- Take a practice test.

Chapter Summary

- ADO.NET provides disconnected objects like the *DataTable* and *DataSet* that can be used independently from a database connection. In addition, LINQ to *DataSet* provides a query processing engine for data represented in the disconnected objects *DataSet* and *DataTable*.
- ADO.NET provides connected objects that are provider-specific for SQL, Oracle, OLEDB, and ODBC. In addition, LINQ to SQL provides a powerful set of features for programming against SQL Server databases with O/R mapping.
- ADO.NET provides access to XML files using the classes in the *System.Xml* namespace. The LINQ to XML technology allows you to work with XML data using the query features of LINQ.

Case Scenarios

In the following case scenarios, you will apply what you've learned in this chapter. If you have difficulty completing this work, review the material in this chapter before beginning the next chapter. You can find answers to these questions in the "Answers" section at the end of this book.

Case Scenario 1: Determining Ways to Update the Database

You are creating a new Web page that allows users to upload expense reports (as XML data). The expense report data contains general information about the expense report, such as the employee name and ID, the branch office number, and the week-ending date. The expense report file also contains information that describes each specific expense. For mileage, this data includes the date and the mileage amount, and the to and from locations. For entertainment, the data includes the location, the expense amount, and a description of the entertainment expense.

You need to import this data into a SQL database and are looking for options.

QUESTIONS

1. What are some methods of importing this data into the SQL Server database?

Case Scenario 2: Storing a *DataSet* to a Binary File

Your code populates a *DataSet* with more than 200,000 *DataRows* in several related *DataTables*. You want to store this *DataSet* object to a file, but you want the file to be as small as possible.

QUESTIONS

1. What object would you use to store the data?
2. What settings would you set to serialize the data properly?

Suggested Practices

To help you successfully master the exam objectives presented in this chapter, complete the following tasks.

Create a Web Page for Updating Database Data

For this task, you should complete all three practices.

- **Practice 1** Create a Web page and add Web server controls to prompt the user for a percentage increase (or decrease) for the price of the products in your database. Use the *Northwind* database, which has a *Products* table.
- **Practice 2** Add code to open a connection to the database and execute a SQL query to increase or decrease the UnitPrice of all products based on the value submitted by the user.
- **Practice 3** Add code to perform the update of the *Products* table within a *SqlTransaction*.

Create a Web Page for Editing Disconnected Data

For this task, you should complete the first practice for working with the *DataTable* objects. The second practice helps you with LINQ to *DataSet*.

- **Practice 1** Create a Web page and add a button to create a *DataTable* that contains a schema for employees, a button that adds a *DataRow* into the employees *DataTable*, a button that modifies an existing *DataRow*, and a button that deletes a *DataRow*.

- **Practice 2** Read the employee data from the *pubs* database into a *DataTable* object and disconnect from the database. Write a LINQ to *DataSet* query against the *DataTable* to show all employee records where the hire date is greater than 1991. Order the data by hire date. Bind the results to a *GridView* control.

Create a Web Page for Editing Connected Data

For this task, you should complete both practices.

- **Practice 1** Create a Web page and add a *SqlDataSource* configured to read data from a SQL Server or SQL Server Express Edition database and display the data in a *GridView* control.
- **Practice 2** Modify the Web page to enable inserts, updates, and deletions.

Create a Web Page for Working with XML Data

For this task, you should complete the first two practices for working with the standard XML classes. The third practice can be used for learning more about LINQ to XML.

- **Practice 1** Create a Web page that uses an *XmlDataSource* to read data from an XML file and display the data in a *GridView* control.
- **Practice 2** Modify the Web page to enable inserts, updates, and deletions.
- **Practice 3** Create an XML file using one of the tables in the *Pubs* database as source data. You can read this data in as a *DataSet* and serialize it out as XML. Write a Web page to load this XML data into an *XElement* class. Write a LINQ query against this data and display the results on a Web page.

Create a Web Page for Reading, Modifying, and Writing XML Data

For this task, you should complete all three practices.

- **Practice 1** Create an XML file that contains a list of products and their prices.
- **Practice 2** Create a Web page and add Web server controls to prompt the user for a percentage increase (or decrease) for the price of the products in your XML file.
- **Practice 3** Add code to use the *XmlReader* to read the products file, modify the price, and then use the *XmlWriter* to write the data to a file.

Take a Practice Test

The practice tests on this book's companion CD offer many options. For example, you can test yourself on just the content covered in this chapter, or you can test yourself on all the 70-562 certification exam content. You can set up the test so it closely simulates the experience of taking a certification exam, or you can set it up in study mode so you can look at the correct answers and explanations after you answer each question.

MORE INFO **PRACTICE TESTS**

For details about all the practice test options available, see the "How to Use the Practice Tests" section in this book's Introduction.

CHAPTER 8

Working with Data Source and Data-Bound Controls

In the previous chapter, you learned about using ADO.NET for accessing data in your business applications. ASP.NET also provides a number of server controls that build on top of the features of ADO.NET. These controls simplify the development of data-driven Web applications. They make it easier to build Web pages that access, display, manipulate, and save data. Using these controls can provide development efficiency when building Web-based business applications that rely heavily on data.

This chapter first presents the ASP.NET data source controls. You use these controls to configure access to data that you intend to use on a Web page. A data source can be a relational database, data stored inside of in-memory objects, Extensible Markup Language (XML)-based data, or data you retrieve via language-integrated query engine (LINQ). The second lesson in this chapter demonstrates how you can bind to data to allow users to interact with it. This includes using Web server controls like *GridView*, *Repeater*, *DetailsView*, and many more.

Exam objectives in this chapter:

- Consuming and Creating Server Controls
  - Implement data-bound controls.
- Working with Data and Services
  - Implement a *DataSource* control.
  - Bind controls to data by using data binding syntax.

Lessons in this chapter:

Before You Begin

To complete the lessons in this chapter, you should be familiar with developing applications with Microsoft Visual Studio using Visual Basic or C#. In addition, you should be comfortable with all of the following:

- The Visual Studio 2008 Integrated Development Environment (IDE)
- A basic understanding of Hypertext Markup Language (HTML) and client-side scripting
- How to create a new Web site
- Adding Web server controls to a Web page
- Working with ADO.NET, XML, and LINQ

REAL WORLD

Mike Snell

Not all applications require abstracted data layers and re-usable frameworks. I've seen many simple business applications that suffered from overengineering. Many of these smaller applications can take advantage of the simple data-binding techniques built into the Visual Studio ASP.NET tools. These applications can be created quickly, typically do not require as much testing, and allow developers to focus on solving business problems rather than building frameworks and reusable components. Applications that can benefit from this approach often have a common profile: They typically have a compressed schedule, are meant as Web applications from beginning to end, and might fill a somewhat temporary need. When optimizing for these considerations, you might find that building data-bound applications using the server controls in ASP.NET is faster, easier, and cheaper.

Lesson 1: Connecting to Data with Data Source Controls

In the previous chapter, you saw how to write code that leverages the features of ADO.NET to connect and work with data that was disconnected or stored in an XML file or a database. This code is useful when writing database code to build an abstracted layer such as a data access or business object tier. However, there are many scenarios in which you simply need to build Web pages that know how to connect and work with data, without writing all the ADO.NET code. For these scenarios, ASP.NET includes the data source controls.

Data source controls are server controls that you can drag onto your page at design time. They do not have a direct visual component (you use data-bound controls for this, as discussed in the next lesson). Instead, they allow you to declaratively define access to data found in objects, XML, and databases. This lesson examines how you can use data source controls to make connecting to and working with data in an ASP.NET page a faster and easier development process.

After this lesson, you will be able to:

- Use the data source controls (*LinqDataSource*, *ObjectDataSource*, *SqlDataSource*, *AccessDataSource*, *XmlDataSource*, and *SiteMapDataSource*) to select data and bind it to a data-bound control.
- Pass parameter values to data source controls to allow data filtering.
- Enable data sorting with data source controls.
- Modify data and save the changes to a data store using data source controls.

Estimated lesson time: 30 minutes

Understanding the Data Source Controls

The data source controls in ASP.NET manage the tasks of selecting, updating, inserting, and deleting data on a Web page. They do so in combination with data-bound controls. The data-bound controls provide the user interface (UI) elements that allow a user to interact with the data by triggering events that call the data source controls.

There are multiple data source controls in ASP.NET. Each is meant to provide specialized access to a certain type of data such as direct access to a database, objects, XML, or LINQ-based queries. These controls can be found in the *System.Web.UI.WebControls* namespace. Figure 8-1 shows an overview of the data source controls in ASP.NET.

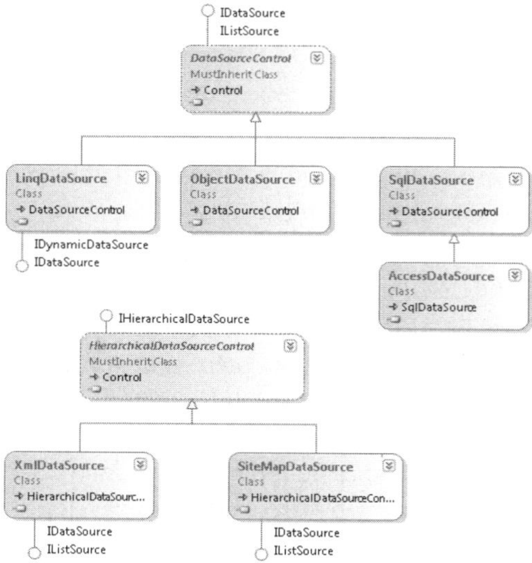

FIGURE 8-1 The *DataSource* Web control classes

Each data source control is used in a similar manner. You can drag the control onto your Web page from the Toolbox in Visual Studio. You can then use the Configre Data Source Wizard to connect to your data and generate markup for the data source. Connecting to data with markup (instead of code) is referred to as declarative data binding, as you are declaring your data access rather than writing ADO.NET code. Figure 8-2 shows the step to select data in this wizard.

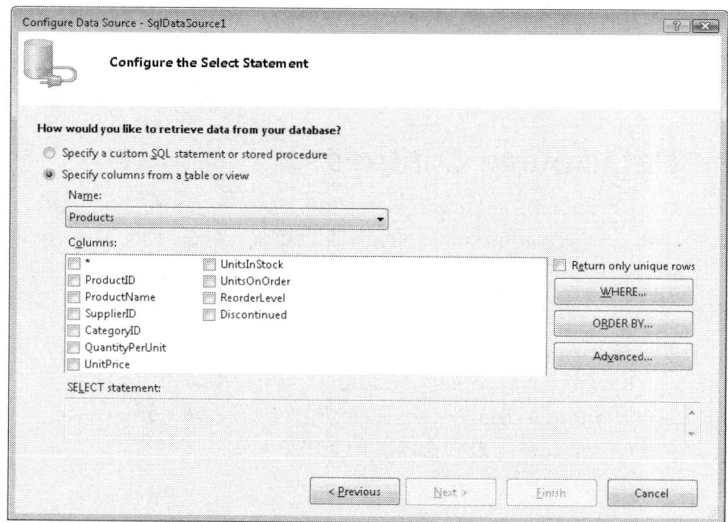

FIGURE 8-2 The step to select data in the Configure Data Source Wizard in Visual Studio

This wizard creates the declarative markup used to define the data source connection information. This markup can contain connection information, data manipulation statements (such as SQL), and more. The following shows an example of the *SqlDataSource* control's markup for connecting to the Products table in the *Northwind* database.

```
<asp:SqlDataSource ID="SqlDataSource1" runat="server"
  ConnectionString="<%$ ConnectionStrings:NorthwindConnectionString %>"
  SelectCommand="SELECT * FROM [Products]"></asp:SqlDataSource>
```

EXAM TIP

The wizard-based UI is a great tool for defining many of your data source declarations. However, it is important you know the markup syntax for working with these controls. This will help with both programming against the controls and taking the exam. Therefore, the rest of this lesson focuses on the markup (and not the wizard-based UI).

Each data source control is specialized for the type of data with which it is meant to work. The following sections provide an overview of what makes each of these controls unique. This includes some of the more common uses of data source controls such as binding, filtering, sorting, modifying data, and more.

Using Objects as Data Sources with *ObjectDataSource*

Many Web applications work with a middle tier, or business layer, for retrieving and working with application data. This middle tier encapsulates database code inside of classes. Web developers can then call methods on these classes to select, insert, modify, and delete data. In this way, they do not have to write direct, ADO.NET code, as this is written by whoever wrote the middle tier. In addition, this middle tier is often reusable across different applications.

You can use the *ObjectDataSource* control in ASP.NET to connect to and work with middle-tier objects in a similar manner as working with the other data source objects. This control can be added to a page and configured to create an instance of a middle-tier object and call its methods to retrieve, insert, update, and delete data. The *ObjectDataSource* control is responsible for the lifetime of the object. It creates it and disposes of it. Therefore, the business layer code should be written in a stateless manner. Alternatively, if the business layer uses *static* (*shared* in Visual Basic) methods, the *ObjectDataSource* can use these methods without creating an instance of the actual business object.

You configure an *ObjectDataSource* to connect to a class by setting its *TypeName* attribute to a string that represents a valid type to which the Web application has access. This class might be inside your *App_Code* directory or inside a .dll file to which the Web application has a reference (it should not be in your page's code-behind file). You then set the *SelectMethod* attribute to a valid method name on the class. The *ObjectDataSource* control will then call this method when the data is requested.

As an example, imagine you need to write an interface to allow a user to manage the shipper table inside the *Northwind* database. You might have a business object that knows how to return all the shippers in the database that looks as follows:

```
'VB
Public Class Shipper

  Private Shared _cnnString As String = _
      ConfigurationManager.ConnectionStrings("NorthwindConnectionString").ToString

  Public Shared Function GetAllShippers() As DataTable
    Dim adp As New SqlDataAdapter( _
      "SELECT * FROM shippers", _cnnString)

    Dim ds As New DataSet("shippers")
    adp.Fill(ds, "shippers")

    Return ds.Tables("shippers")
  End Function

End Class

//C#
public class Shipper
{
  private static string _cnnString =
    ConfigurationManager.ConnectionStrings["NorthwindConnectionString"].ToString();

  public static DataTable GetAllShippers()
  {
    SqlDataAdapter adp = new SqlDataAdapter(
      "SELECT * FROM shippers", _cnnString);

    DataSet ds = new DataSet("shippers");
    adp.Fill(ds, "shippers");

    return ds.Tables["shippers"];
  }
}
```

The *Shipper* class just listed returns a *DataTable* as a result of a call to *GetAllShippers*. You can configure an *ObjectDataSource* control to provide this data by setting the *TypeName* and *SelectMethod* attributes as in the following code:

```
<asp:ObjectDataSource
  ID="ObjectDataSource1"
  runat="server"
```

```
  TypeName="Shipper"
  SelectMethod="GetAllShippers">
</asp:ObjectDataSource>

<asp:DetailsView
  ID="DetailsView1"
  runat="server"
  DataSourceID="ObjectDataSource1"
  AllowPaging="true">
</asp:DetailsView>
```

This code also binds the *ObjectDataSource* to a *DetailsView* control to display the information to the user. Figure 8-3 shows an example of the output.

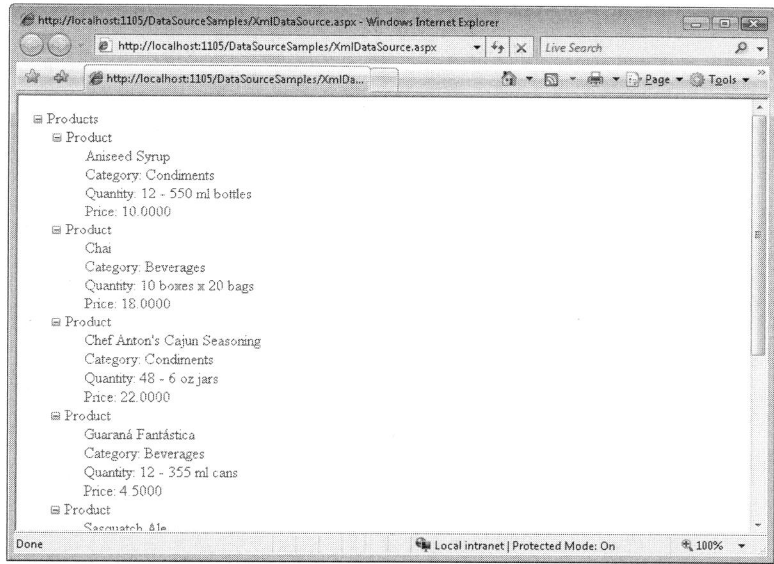

FIGURE 8-3 An *ObjectDataSource* bound to a *DetailsView* control

Notice that the *Shipper.GetAllShippers* method returns a *DataTable*. An *ObjectDataSource* class can work with any data that implements any of the following interfaces: *IEnumerable*, *IListSource*, *IDataSource*, or *IHierarchicalDatasource*. This means as long as your business object class returns data as a *DataTable*, a *DataSet*, or some form of a collection, you can be sure this data can be used with an *ObjectDataSource* control.

Passing Parameters

The business objects with which you work will undoubtedly define methods that take parameter values. These parameters might define a filter on the data or indicate values to be used when inserting or updating data. Fortunately, you can use the *ObjectDataSource* to map various page-level elements to parameters to be passed to your objects.

There are multiple sets of parameters you can define for a given *ObjectDataSource*. These sets include *Select*, *Insert*, *Update*, *Delete*, and *Filter* parameters. These parameters work in conjunction with the given method of the same name. For example, the *<SelectParameters>* set works with the method defined by the *SelectMethod* attribute.

The source of the given parameter's value can come from multiple places in your page or site. This includes a *Cookie*, *Control*, *Session*, *QueryString*, *Form*, or *Profile* object. These options make defining and mapping a data source an easier task. You can also define the source value in code.

As an example, imagine you have a business object name *Customer*. Assume this object contains the method *GetCustomersByCity*, which takes a city value as string. The method then returns a list of customers for the given city parameter. Now imagine you need to create a data source control to map to this class. The *ObjectDataSource* should pass the value for city to the method from the query string. In this case, you would create a *SelectParameters* set that includes a *QueryStringParameter* definition. The *QueryStringParameter* definition would map between the name of the query string parameter and the name of the method's parameter. The following code shows an example:

```
<asp:ObjectDataSource
  ID="ObjectDataSource1"
  runat="server"
  TypeName="Customer"
  SelectMethod="GetCustomersByCity">
  <SelectParameters>
    <asp:QueryStringParameter
      Name="city"
      QueryStringField="city"
      Type="String" />
  </SelectParameters>
</asp:ObjectDataSource>
```

You might then attach this data source to a *GridView* or similar control. You can then call the page by passing in the appropriate query string value as follows:

```
http://localhost:5652/DataSourceSamples/CustomersObjectDs.aspx?city=London
```

You can use this same technique to pass multiple parameters of various types and from various sources. You can also use this same technique to pass parameters meant for handling inserting, updating, and deleting, as discussed in the next section.

Inserting, Updating, and Deleting

You can also use an *ObjectDataSource* control to define how data should be inserted, updated, and deleted. The attributes *InsertMethod*, *UpdateMethod*, and *DeleteMethod* can be mapped directly to an object's methods that are to be called when these activities are invoked. You then use parameter definitions to map values to these method calls.

As an example, recall the *Shipper* class discussed previously. Now imagine that additional methods have been added to this object. These method signatures might look as follows:

```
'VB
Public Shared Function GetAllShippers() As DataTable
Public Shared Sub InsertShipper(ByVal companyName As String, ByVal phone As String)
Public Shared Sub UpdateShipper(ByVal shipperId As Integer, _
  ByVal companyName As String, ByVal phone As String)
Public Shared Sub DeleteShipper(ByVal shipperId As Integer)

//C#
public static DataTable GetAllShippers()
public static void InsertShipper(string companyName, string phone)
public static void UpdateShipper(int shipperId, string companyName, string phone)
public static void DeleteShipper(int shipperId)
```

You can map an *ObjectDataSource* control to each of these methods. In doing so, you need to define the parameters each method expects. The following markup shows an example:

```
<asp:ObjectDataSource
  ID="ObjectDataSource1"
  runat="server"
  TypeName="Shipper"
  SelectMethod="GetAllShippers"
  InsertMethod="InsertShipper"
  UpdateMethod="UpdateShipper"
  DeleteMethod="DeleteShipper">
  <DeleteParameters>
    <asp:Parameter
      Name="ShipperId"
      Type="Int32" />
  </DeleteParameters>
  <UpdateParameters>
    <asp:Parameter
      Name="shipperId" Type="Int32" />
    <asp:Parameter
      Name="companyName" Type="String" />
    <asp:Parameter Name="phone"
      Type="String" />
  </UpdateParameters>
  <InsertParameters>
    <asp:Parameter
      Name="companyName"
      Type="String" />
    <asp:Parameter
      Name="phone"
```

```
      Type="String" />
  </InsertParameters>
</asp:ObjectDataSource>
```

You can then use this *ObjectDataSource* control with a data-bound control such as a *DetailsView*. The following markup is an example. In this case, the fields are bound individually. This allows granular control over the *ShipperId* field as it is an auto-generated primary key (identity) in a SQL Server database. Therefore, you set the *InsertVisible* property to *False* to make sure the *DetailsView* does not try to pass a value for *ShipperId* to the *InsertMethod* of the *ObjectDataSource*. You also set the *ReadOnly* attribute of the same field to *True* to indicate the value should not be available to change during an edit operation.

```
<asp:DetailsView
  ID="DetailsView1"
  runat="server"
  AllowPaging="True"
  DataSourceID="ObjectDataSource1"
  AutoGenerateRows="False"
  Width="450px"
  DataKeyNames="ShipperID">
  <Fields>
    <asp:BoundField DataField="ShipperID" HeaderText="ShipperId"
      ReadOnly="true" InsertVisible="false" />
    <asp:BoundField DataField="CompanyName" HeaderText="CompanyName" />
    <asp:BoundField DataField="Phone" HeaderText="Phone" />
    <asp:CommandField
      ShowInsertButton="True"
      ShowDeleteButton="True"
      ShowEditButton="True" />
  </Fields>
</asp:DetailsView>
```

Defining a Filter

You can also apply filters to an *ObjectDataSource*. Filters apply to data returned from the given object's methods as a *DataSet* or *DataTable*. This is because the filter is a valid filter expression as defined by the ADO.NET *DataColumn* class.

To define a filter for an *ObjectDataSource* control, you set the *FilterExpression* attribute to a valid filter. This filter will be applied after the data is retrieved from the database. You can also use *FilterParameters* to map values from the page to the filter expression by defining a filter expression that contains parameter mappings as numbers enclosed in braces. You then add the appropriate filter parameters.

The following code shows an example. Here, the *Customer.GetAllCustomers* method is bound to an *ObjectDataSource* control. When the data is returned, the filter expression *city='{0}'* is applied to the result. The query string value for *city* is then passed as the *{0}* parameter to the filter expression.

```
<asp:ObjectDataSource
  ID="ObjectDataSource1"
  runat="server"
  TypeName="Customer"
  SelectMethod="GetAllCustomers"
  FilterExpression="city='{0}'">
  <FilterParameters>
    <asp:QueryStringParameter
      Name="city"
      QueryStringField="city"
      Type="String" />
  </FilterParameters>
</asp:ObjectDataSource>
```

Sorting and Paging

The data-bound controls that work with an object data source control can be configured to page and sort the data returned by the data source control. However, it is often better to sort and page this data when the data is requested from the database. Doing so can reduce the consumption of resources on your server.

The *ObjectDataSource* control defines specific attributes for managing sorting and paging. You set these attributes to parameters of your *SelectMethod*. The *SelectMethod* must also define these properties and use them for sorting and paging. In addition, by using these specific properties, data-bound controls such as *GridView* can automatically work with your data source to provide inputs for sorting and paging.

As an example, imagine you wish to provide a business object method to control how customer data is sorted and paged as it is retrieved and not after the fact. You could define a business method as follows:

```
'VB
Public Shared Function GetPagedCustomersSorted( _
  ByVal sortCol As String, ByVal pageStart As Integer, _
  ByVal numRecords As Integer) As DataTable

  If numRecords <= 0 Then numRecords = 10

  Dim cnn As New SqlConnection(_cnnString)

  Dim sql As String = "SELECT * FROM customers"
  If sortCol <> "" Then sql = sql & " order by " & sortCol

  Dim cmd As New SqlCommand(sql, cnn)
```

```
  Dim adp As New SqlDataAdapter(cmd)

  cnn.Open()
  Dim ds As New DataSet("customers")

  adp.Fill(ds, pageStart, numRecords, "customers")

  Return ds.Tables("customers")
End Function

//C#
public static DataTable GetPagedCustomersSorted(
  string sortCol, int pageStart, int numRecords)
{
    if (numRecords <= 0)
      numRecords = 10;

    SqlConnection cnn = new SqlConnection(_cnnString);

    string sql = "SELECT * FROM customers";
    if (sortCol != "")
      sql = sql + " order by " + sortCol;

    SqlCommand cmd = new SqlCommand(sql, cnn);

    SqlDataAdapter adp = new SqlDataAdapter(cmd);

    DataSet ds = new DataSet("customers");

    cnn.Open();
    adp.Fill(ds, pageStart, numRecords, "customers");

    return ds.Tables["customers"];
}
```

Notice this business method defines a parameter for sorting the data, setting the starting record (or page), and setting the number of records in a given page. You can then use these parameters when defining an *ObjectDataSource*. You set the control's *SortParameterName* attribute to the parameter of your business object that is used for sorting data. You set the *StartRowIndexParameterName* to the parameter that defines the row number at which you wish to start retrieving data. You then set the *MaximumRowsParameterName* to the parameter that is used to define the number of rows you wish to include in a given data page. The following markup shows an example:

```
<asp:ObjectDataSource
  ID="ObjectDataSource1"
```

```
  runat="server"
  TypeName="Customer"
  SelectMethod="GetPagedCustomersSorted"
  SortParameterName="sortCol"
  EnablePaging="true"
  StartRowIndexParameterName="pageStart"
  MaximumRowsParameterName="numRecords">
</asp:ObjectDataSource>
```

You can then bind this data source to a control such as a *GridView*. The following markup shows an example:

```
<asp:GridView ID="GridView1" runat="server"
  DataSourceID="ObjectDataSource1"
  AllowPaging="True" PageSize="10" AllowSorting="true">
</asp:GridView>
```

When the page is run, the *GridView* control passes sort and paging information to the data source. However, because the paging is happening before the *GridView* is bound, the *GridView* does not know the number of pages to display. Therefore, you need to implement your own custom paging in this scenario to advance the *PageIndex* property of the *GridView* control on user request. Once you reset this value, the *GridView* will pass the value on to the *ObjectDataSource*.

Caching Data

You can tell ASP.NET to cache your *ObjectDataSource* control. This will keep the data in memory between page calls. This can increase performance and scalability of your application if the data is shared and accessed often.

To indicate caching of an *ObjectDataSource*, you set the *EnableCaching* attribute to *True*. You then set the *CacheDuration* property to the number of seconds you wish to have ASP.NET cache the data. The following shows an example of these settings:

```
<asp:ObjectDataSource
  ID="ObjectDataSource1"
  runat="server"
  TypeName="Shipper"
  SelectMethod="GetAllShippers"
  EnableCaching="true"
  CacheDuration="30">
</asp:ObjectDataSource>
```

The first call to this page will call the object and return its data. Subsequent calls within the same 30 seconds (such as moving through data pages) will use the cached data (and not call the underlying object).

Creating a *DataObject* Class

There are not too many restrictions on which objects you can use as the source of *ObjectDataSource* controls. If you know your business object will be used as an *ObjectDataSource,* you can define attributes on your class that make consuming your class inside an *ObjectDataSource* easier inside the designer. These attributes are used to predefine which methods you intend as *Select*, *Insert*, *Update*, and *Delete*.

To get started, you set the *DataObject* attribute at the top of your class. This simply indicates that your class is meant to be a *DataObject*. Again, this is not required for use with *ObjectDataSource* controls, but simply makes things easier. The following shows an example of the class declaration and attribute:

```
'VB
<System.ComponentModel.DataObject()> _
Public Class Shipper

//C#
[DataObject()]
public class Shipper
```

You then add the attribute *DataObjectMethod* to the top of each method you intend as a data object method. You pass a *DataObjectMethodType* enum value to this attribute to indicate *Delete*, *Insert*, *Update*, or *Select*. The following code shows an example of the method signature and attribute:

```
'VB
<System.ComponentModel.DataObjectMethod(ComponentModel.DataObjectMethodType.Select)> _
Public Shared Function GetAllShippers() As DataTable

//C#
[DataObjectMethod(DataObjectMethodType.Select)]
public static DataTable GetAllShippers()
```

By defining these attributes, you make the designer aware of your business object's intentions. This can ease the burden of configuring an *ObjectDataSource* control when using large business objects with many methods.

Connecting to Relational Databases with *SqlDataSource*

The *SqlDataSource* control is used to configure access to relational databases such as SQL Server and Oracle. It can also be configured to work with Open Database Connectivity (ODBC) and Object Linking and Embedding (OLE) Db data connections. You configure the control to connect to one of these database types. The code inside the control will then use the appropriate provider based on your configuration settings. These are the same ADO.NET provider classes discussed in Chapter 7, "Using ADO.NET, XML, and LINQ with ASP.NET," such as *SqlClient*, *OracleClient*, *OleDb*, and *Odbc*.

You configure the *SqlDataSource* control by first setting its *ID* property to a unique identifying string value. This property is similar to any other Web control *ID* property. However, the value is used when referring to the data source during data binding (discussed momentarily). You then set the *ConnectionString* property either to a valid connection string or to page script that reads the connection string from the Web.config file (as shown in the next code example).

You then set various command properties. This includes commands for selecting, inserting, updating, and deleting data. The command properties you set are based on how you intend to use the control. For example, you use the *SelectCommand* to define a SQL statement that can be used to retrieve data from a database. In this case, you would use the *SelectCommandType* of *Text* (the default). You can also set the *SelectCommandType* to *StoredProcedure* and then provide a stored procedure name for the *SelectCommand* attribute.

The *DataSourceMode* attribute is used to define how you want the *SqlDataSource* control to retrieve your data. You have two options: *DataSet* and *DataReader*. The former connects to the database and returns all records as a *DataSet* instance. It then closes the database connection before continuing to process the page. The latter, *DataReader*, keeps an open connection to the database while it reads each row into the data source control.

The following markup shows an example of connecting to a SQL Server Express database by first reading the connection string from the Web.config file. It uses a text-based SQL statement and a *DataReader*. It then binds the data source to a *GridView* control for display.

```
<asp:SqlDataSource
  ID="SqlDataSource1"
  runat="server"
  ConnectionString="<%$ ConnectionStrings:NorthwindConnectionString %>"
  SelectCommandType="Text"
  SelectCommand="SELECT * FROM [products]"
  DataSourceMode="DataReader">
</asp:SqlDataSource>

<asp:GridView
  ID="GridView1"
  runat="server"
  DataSourceID="SqlDataSource1">
</asp:GridView>
```

You can also work with the data source controls from code. When doing so, you replace the markup attribute settings with object property settings. You first create the data source control inside the *Page_Init* method. You then add the data source control to the page to ensure it is available to be bound to other controls. The following code shows the preceding markup example translated as code in a code-behind page:

```
'VB
Partial Class _Default
  Inherits System.Web.UI.Page
```

```
  Protected Sub Page_Init(ByVal sender As Object, _
    ByVal e As System.EventArgs) Handles Me.Init

    Dim sqlDs As New SqlDataSource
    sqlDs.ConnectionString = _
      ConfigurationManager.ConnectionStrings("NorthwindConnectionString").ToString
    sqlDs.ID = "SqlDataSource1"
    sqlDs.SelectCommandType = SqlDataSourceCommandType.Text
    sqlDs.SelectCommand = "SELECT * FROM [products]"
    sqlDs.DataSourceMode = SqlDataSourceMode.DataReader
    Me.Controls.Add(sqlDs)
  End Sub

  Protected Sub Page_Load(ByVal sender As Object, _
    ByVal e As System.EventArgs) Handles Me.Load
    GridView1.DataSourceID = "SqlDataSource1"
  End Sub

End Class

//C#
public partial class DefaultCs : System.Web.UI.Page
{
  protected void Page_Init(object sender, EventArgs e)
  {
    SqlDataSource sqlDs = new SqlDataSource();
    sqlDs.ConnectionString =
      ConfigurationManager.ConnectionStrings["NorthwindConnectionString"].ToString();
    sqlDs.ID = "SqlDataSource1";
    sqlDs.SelectCommandType = SqlDataSourceCommandType.Text;
    sqlDs.SelectCommand = "SELECT * FROM [products]";
    sqlDs.DataSourceMode = SqlDataSourceMode.DataReader;
    this.Controls.Add(sqlDs);
  }

  protected void Page_Load(object sender, EventArgs e)
  {
    GridView1.DataSourceID = "SqlDataSource1";
  }
}
```

Working with data source controls in code is less common than working with them in markup. It is also very straightforward, as you set the same properties in code as you would define attributes in markup. Therefore, the majority of this lesson assumes you are working with markup only instead of providing examples in both markup and code.

Using Parameters

The *SqlDataSource* control can also be configured to use parameters for *Select*, *Insert*, *Update*, *Filter*, and *Delete* commands. You do so by defining parameters inside your SQL statements using the *@param* syntax. You then map parameter values to these parameter definitions using parameter declarations.

As an example, imagine you are creating a *SqlDataSource* control to return products based on their category ID. The category ID will be passed to the page as a value from the query string. You can define this parameter inside the *SelectParameters* collection as a *QueryStringParameter*. The following shows the markup of this example:

```
<asp:SqlDataSource
  ID="SqlDataSource1"
  runat="server"
  ConnectionString="<%$ ConnectionStrings:NorthwindConnectionString %>"
  SelectCommandType="Text"
  SelectCommand="SELECT * FROM [products] WHERE CategoryID=@CategoryId"
  DataSourceMode="DataSet">
  <SelectParameters>
    <asp:QueryStringParameter
      Name="CategoryId"
      QueryStringField="catId"
      Type="Int16" />
  </SelectParameters>
</asp:SqlDataSource>
```

You can then bind this control to a *GridView* (or similar control). When the page is accessed, the data is filtered based on the query string parameter. The following shows an example Uniform Resource Locator (URL) for this call:

```
http://localhost:5652/DataSourceSamples/MySqlDsExample.aspx?catId=2
```

You use this same method for defining *InsertParameters*, *UpdateParameters*, and *DeleteParameters*. These parameters are mapped to the respective *InsertCommand*, *UpdateCommand*, and *DeleteCommand*. Controls such as *GridView* and *DetailsView* work to trigger update, insert, and delete actions and in doing so, pass parameter values to the appropriate command. This is similar to what was demonstrated in the *ObjectDataSource* section.

Filtering Data with *SqlDataSource*

Like the *ObjectDataSource*, you can also filter data inside a *SqlDataSource* control. Again, the data must be a *DataSet* because the filter is applied to the ADO.NET *DataColumn* or *DataView.RowFilter* property.

To define a filter, you set the *FilterExpression* attribute to a valid filter. This filter will be applied after the data is retrieved from the database. You can also use *FilterParameters* to map values from the page to the filter expression by defining a filter expression that contains parameter mappings as numbers enclosed in braces. You then add the appropriate filter parameters.

The following code shows an example of a *SqlDataSource* control that first selects all products from the database. It then applies a *FilterExpression* to show only those products that have been discontinued.

```
<asp:SqlDataSource
  ID="SqlDataSource1"
  runat="server"
  ConnectionString="<%$ ConnectionStrings:NorthwindConnectionString %>"
  SelectCommandType="Text"
  SelectCommand="SELECT * FROM [products]"
  DataSourceMode="DataSet"
  FilterExpression="Discontinued=true">
</asp:SqlDataSource>
```

Caching *SqlDataSource* Data

Like an *ObjectDataSource*, you can also configure a *SqlDataSource* control to be cached by the server. When doing so, however, you must set the *DataSourceMode* property to *DataSet*. *DataReader* sources cannot be cached, as they would hold open a connection to the server.

You indicate caching of a *SqlDataSource* control the same way you would an *ObjectDataSource* control: by setting the *EnableCaching* and *CacheDuration* attributes. The following shows an example:

```
<asp:SqlDataSource
  ID="SqlDataSource1"
  runat="server"
  ConnectionString="<%$ ConnectionStrings:NorthwindConnectionString %>"
  SelectCommandType="Text"
  SelectCommand="SELECT * FROM [products]"
  DataSourceMode="DataSet"
  EnableCaching="True"
  CacheDuration="30">
</asp:SqlDataSource>
```

Working with Microsoft Access Data Files and *AccessDataSource* Controls

The *AccessDataSource* control is meant to connect to and work with Microsoft Access file-based databases (.mdb files). This control is very similar to the *SqlDataSource* control. In fact, it derives from the class *SqlDataSource*. Therefore, you can expect to work with the *AccessDataSource* control in a very similar manner. This includes passing parameters, caching, filtering data, and calling Access stored procedures.

NOTE THE NEW ACCESS DATABASE ENGINE

The Access database engine has been changed in recent versions from Jet to one based on SQL Server. The *AccessDataSource* control is used to work with Jet-based databases. These can be identified by the .mdf file extension. Newer Access files have the .accdb extension. You can connect to these database files using the *SqlDataSource* control (not the *AccessDataSource* control).

One of the main differences between the controls is how you connect to the database. The *AccessDataSource* control replaces the *SqlDataSource.ConnectionString* property with the *DataFile* property. You pass a path to a database file to this property to define a connection to an Access database. The following markup shows how you configure the *AccessDataSource* control to connect to an .mdb file in the *App_Data* folder:

```
<asp:AccessDataSource
  ID="AccessDataSource1" runat="server"
  DataFile="~/App_Data/AccessNorthwind.mdb"
  SelectCommand="SELECT * FROM [Products]">
</asp:AccessDataSource>
```

The code inside this data source control uses the ADO.NET *System.Data.OleDb* provider for connecting to an Access data file. You should be familiar with this provider from Chapter 7. Of course, this code is abstracted for you by the control itself. You need only define the markup to begin accessing and working with data in the Access file.

NOTE CONFIGURE ACCESS TO A FILE-BASED DATABASE

To ensure the Web page has access to this file, the ASP.NET process identity should be configured to allow file-based access to the .mdb file.

Connecting to XML Data Using *XmlDataSource*

The *XmlDataSource* control provides a means to create a binding connection between controls on your page and an XML file. The XML data source control is best used when you wish to bind to XML data that is represented as hierarchical. In these cases, the outer elements of the XML represent data records. The child elements can themselves be subrecords related to the outer records. In addition, the child elements and attributes of these outer "record" elements are typically bound to as fields. You can think of these fields as columns of data on the given record. Due to this hierarchical nature, the *XmlDataSource* control is typically bound to controls that show data in a hierarchical manner such as the *TreeView* control. However, they can be used to display data as tabular, too.

You configure the *XmlDataSource* control at design time to point to an .xml file. XML data in your project is typically stored in your project's *App_Data* folder. To bind to a file, you set the *DataFile* attribute on the data source control to point to the path of the .xml file. The following code shows an example of defining an *XmlDataSource* control that points to a file containing product data:

```
<asp:XmlDataSource
  ID="XmlDataSource1"
  runat="server"
  DataFile="~/App_Data/products.xml" >
</asp:XmlDataSource>
```

You can also bind directly to a string value that represents XML. The *XmlDataSource* class provides the *Data* property for connecting to a string value in your code-behind page.

Transforming XML with the *XmlDataSource* Control

You can use the *XmlDataSource* control to define an Extensible Stylesheet Language (XSL) transformation to change the shape and content of your XML data. You do so by setting the *TransformFile* attribute to a valid .xsl file. The XSL file will be applied to your .xml data after your XML is loaded into memory and prior to the XML being bound for output.

As an example, consider the following XML file that defines a set of products across varied categories:

```
<?xml version="1.0" standalone="yes"?>
<Products>
  <Product>
    <Category>Beverages</Category>
    <Name>Chai</Name>
    <QuantityPerUnit>10 boxes x 20 bags</QuantityPerUnit>
    <UnitPrice>18.0000</UnitPrice>
  </Product>
  <Product>
    <Category>Condiments</Category>
    <Name>Aniseed Syrup</Name>
    <QuantityPerUnit>12 - 550 ml bottles</QuantityPerUnit>
    <UnitPrice>10.0000</UnitPrice>
  </Product>
  <Product>
    <Category>Condiments</Category>
    <Name>Chef Anton's Cajun Seasoning</Name>
    <QuantityPerUnit>48 - 6 oz jars</QuantityPerUnit>
    <UnitPrice>22.0000</UnitPrice>
  </Product>
  <Product>
    <Category>Produce</Category>
    <Name>Uncle Bob's Organic Dried Pears</Name>
    <QuantityPerUnit>12 - 1 lb pkgs.</QuantityPerUnit>
    <UnitPrice>30.0000</UnitPrice>
```

```
  </Product>
  <Product>
    <Category>Beverages</Category>
    <Name>Guaraná Fantástica</Name>
    <QuantityPerUnit>12 - 355 ml cans</QuantityPerUnit>
    <UnitPrice>4.5000</UnitPrice>
  </Product>
  <Product>
    <Category>Beverages</Category>
    <Name>Sasquatch Ale</Name>
    <QuantityPerUnit>24 - 12 oz bottles</QuantityPerUnit>
    <UnitPrice>14.0000</UnitPrice>
  </Product>
  <Product>
    <Category>Beverages</Category>
    <Name>Steeleye Stout</Name>
    <QuantityPerUnit>24 - 12 oz bottles</QuantityPerUnit>
    <UnitPrice>18.0000</UnitPrice>
  </Product>
</Products>
```

Imagine that you have to transform this data by first sorting it and then adding descriptive text to each field to help a user when viewing the data in a *TreeView* control. In this case, you can write an XSL transform file. The following code represents an example:

```
<xsl:stylesheet version="1.0"
  xmlns:xsl="http://www.w3.org/1999/XSL/Transform">
  <xsl:template match="Products">
    <Products>
      <xsl:for-each select="Product">
        <xsl:sort select="Name" order="ascending" />
        <Product>
          <Name>
            <xsl:value-of select="Name"/>
          </Name>
          <Category>
            <xsl:text>Category: </xsl:text>
            <xsl:value-of select="Category"/>
          </Category>
          <QuantityPerUnit>
            <xsl:text>Quantity: </xsl:text>
            <xsl:value-of select="QuantityPerUnit"/>
          </QuantityPerUnit>
          <UnitPrice>
            <xsl:text>Price: </xsl:text>
            <xsl:value-of select="UnitPrice"/>
```

```
          </UnitPrice>
        </Product>
      </xsl:for-each>
    </Products>
  </xsl:template>
</xsl:stylesheet>
```

Next, you set the *TransformFile* attribute of the *XmlDataSource* control to point to the .xsl file. The following shows an example of how the configured data source control would read in your markup, followed by an example of how the *XmlDataSource* control is bound to a *TreeView* control in markup:

```
<asp:XmlDataSource
  ID="XmlDataSource1"
  runat="server"
  DataFile="~/App_Data/products.xml"
  TransformFile="~/App_Data/ProductTransform.xsl" >
</asp:XmlDataSource>

<asp:TreeView
  id="TreeView1"
  runat="server"
  DataSourceID="XmlDataSource1">
  <DataBindings>
    <asp:TreeNodeBinding DataMember="Name" TextField="#InnerText" />
    <asp:TreeNodeBinding DataMember="Category" TextField="#InnerText" />
    <asp:TreeNodeBinding DataMember="QuantityPerUnit" TextField="#InnerText" />
    <asp:TreeNodeBinding DataMember="UnitPrice" TextField="#InnerText" />
  </DataBindings>
</asp:TreeView>
```

When the page is rendered, ASP.NET loads the .xml file into memory. It then applies the .xsl file to the XML data. Finally, the result is bound to the *TreeView* and embedded in the HTTP response. Figure 8-4 shows this data as it would look in a browser window. Notice how the data is sorted and the additional descriptive text has been added to a number of the nodes.

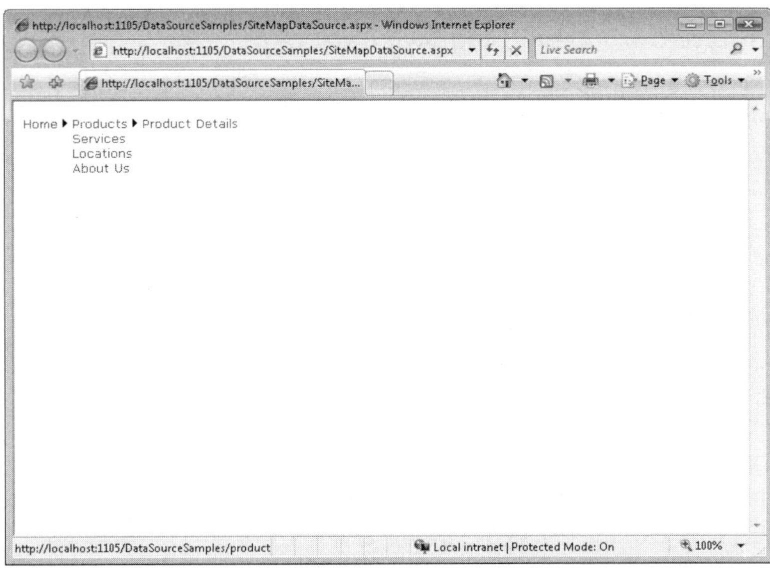

FIGURE 8-4 The transformed file displayed in a browser window

Filtering XML with the *XmlDataSource* Control

The *XmlDataSource* control also allows you to define a data filter to define a subset of your XML. This is done via the *XPath* attribute. You set this attribute to a valid XPath expression that represents a filter expression. For example, to retrieve a subset of the product data in the XML file defined in the previous section, you could set the *XPath* attribute as in the following markup:

```
<asp:XmlDataSource
  ID="XmlDataSource1"
  runat="server"
  DataFile="~/App_Data/products.xml"
  TransformFile="~/App_Data/ProductTransform.xsl"
  XPath="/Products/Product[Category='Category: Beverages']" >
</asp:XmlDataSource>
```

In this example, the data is filtered for only those products with a category value set to *"Beverages"*. Notice that the value is actually set to *"Category: Beverages"*. This is because the XPath expression is applied following any XSL transformations. Recall that in the prior example, the text *"Category: "* was added to data. Therefore, you have to account for it in the XPath expression.

NOTE **INSERTING, DELETING, MODIFYING, AND SAVING XML DATA**

The *XmlDataSource* control is typically used when reading XML data. Unlike many of the other data source controls, it does not provide automatic attributes for inserting, deleting, updating, and saving XML data. Instead, you have to write your own custom code if you require this behavior. Please see Chapter 7 for more information on working with XML data in this manner.

Connecting to LINQ-Based Data with *LinqDataSource*

You can use the *LinqDataSource* control to easily connect to data supplied by an object-relational (O/R) map. Recall that you can generate data classes using the O/R designer (Linq to Sql .dbml file) or SqlMetal.exe code generation tool as discussed in Chapter 7. Doing so creates a set of classes that represent your database. You can then program directly against those classes using LINQ. You can also bind to those classes using the *LinqDataSource* control.

The *LinqDataSource* control uses the *ContextTypeName* attribute to define the database context of your LINQ-based data. This can be set to point to the name of the class that represents your database context. As an example, imagine you have created a file to represent the *Northwind* database. This file might define the class *NorthwindDataContext*. The following markup shows how you would connect to this class using the *LinqDataSource* control:

```
<asp:LinqDataSource
  ID="LinqDataSource1"
  runat="server"
  ContextTypeName="NorthwindDataContext"
  EnableDelete="True"
  EnableInsert="True"
  EnableUpdate="True"
  OrderBy="CompanyName"
  TableName="Suppliers"
  Where="Country == @Country">
  <WhereParameters>
    <asp:QueryStringParameter
      DefaultValue="USA"
      Name="Country"
      QueryStringField="country"
      Type="String" />
  </WhereParameters>
</asp:LinqDataSource>
```

The *LinqDataSource* control is similar to other data source controls. It allows you to define parameters, indicate sorting, enable paging, and more. However, its LINQ-style declarative syntax makes it unique. Consider the preceding markup. Notice that the *TableName* attribute is set to *Suppliers*. You then define a query that indicates both a *Where* clause and an *OrderBy* clause using attributes. The *Where* clause uses the *WhereParameters*. This parameter represents a query string that filters the data based on the value of *country* on the query string.

You can also bind a *LinqDataSource* control to a data-bound control as you would any other data source. You can set values on the *LinqDataSource* to indicate whether you allow deleting, inserting, and updating of data. The data-bound control will then work with the *LinqDataSource* as appropriate.

Connecting to Site Navigation Data with *SiteMapDataSource*

The *SiteMapDataSource* control is used to connect to site navigation data for your Web site. The data for this control is defined in a special XML file called a web.sitemap. You can define one sitemap file in the root of your Web application. The file includes information about the pages in your site and their hierarchy. It also includes page names, navigational information, and a description of the page. It is meant as a central place for managing the navigational data of your site; it is used by controls such as *Menu* and *TreeView* to allow users to easily navigate your application.

As an example, imagine the following web.sitemap file is defined at the root of your Web application:

```
<?xml version="1.0" encoding="utf-8" ?>
<siteMap xmlns="http://schemas.microsoft.com/AspNet/SiteMap-File-1.0" >
  <siteMapNode url="" title="Home"  description="">
    <siteMapNode url="products.aspx" title="Products"  description="">
      <siteMapNode url="productDetails.aspx" title="Product Details"  description="" />
    </siteMapNode>
    <siteMapNode url="services.aspx" title="Services"  description="" />
    <siteMapNode url="locations.aspx" title="Locations"  description="" />
    <siteMapNode url="about.aspx" title="About Us"  description="" />
  </siteMapNode>
</siteMap>
```

You can connect to this data using a *SiteMapDataSource* control. You simply add it to your page. You cannot configure it to point to a specific file. Instead, it automatically picks up the web.sitemap file defined at the root of your Web application. The following markup shows an example. You bind to this data in a similar manner as you bind to the other data source controls. The following code also demonstrates binding to a *Menu* control:

```
<asp:SiteMapDataSource
  ID="SiteMapDataSource1"
  runat="server" />

<asp:Menu ID="Menu1"
```

```
  runat="server"
  DataSourceID="SiteMapDataSource1">
</asp:Menu>
```

The results of this binding are shown in Figure 8-5.

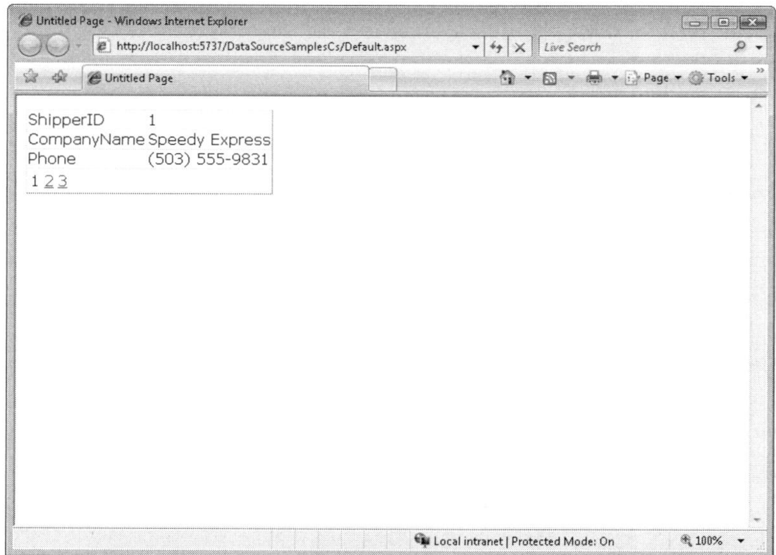

FIGURE 8-5 The site map data bound to a Menu control and displayed in a browser

Filtering the Data Shown in the *SiteMapDataSource*

Sometimes, you might wish to show only a portion of the data in your sitemap data file. The *SiteMapDataSource* control provides a couple attributes you can use to control the data that is shown. The first, *StartingNodeUrl,* is used to indicate the node in the sitemap file that should be used as the root of the data source.

As an example, consider the sitemap file discussed previously. Suppose you need to display only the *Products* node and its subnodes. You can do so by setting the *SiteMapDataSource* control's *StartingNodeUrl* property to product.aspx as shown in the following sample markup:

```
<asp:SiteMapDataSource
  ID="SiteMapDataSource1"
  runat="server"
  StartingNodeUrl="products.aspx" />
```

You can also use the attribute *ShowStartingNode* to indicate whether or not you wish to display the node where the *SiteMapDataSource* control is set to start. You set this value to *False* if you wish to hide the starting node. This property works with the other properties of the *SiteMapDataSource* control such as *StartingNodeUrl.*

You might find that you want your navigation controls to display navigation data based on the current active page in the browser. You can do so by setting the *StartFromCurrentNode* attribute to *True*. This evaluates the name of the current page, finds it in the sitemap, and uses it as the start node for any bound controls on that page. This setting is especially useful if you embed your navigation and *SiteMapDataSource* controls inside a master page.

Finally, the *StartingNodeOffset* attribute is used to move the starting node up or down the sitemap data tree. You set the value to a negative number to move the start node up the tree from its current evaluated position. A positive number moves it deeper in the tree hierarchy.

Quick Check

1. **Which attribute of the *SqlDataSource* control do you use to define a connection to the database?**
2. **How do you define an *ObjectDataSource* to connect to a business object?**
3. **Which attribute of the *LinqDataSource* control do you use to indicate the O/R class used for connecting to and working with LINQ-based data?**

Quick Check Answers

1. **You use the *ConnectionString* attribute.**
2. **You use the *TypeName* attribute.**
3. **You use the *ContextTypeName* attribute.**

LAB Using a Data Source Control on a Web Page

In this lab, you work with Visual Studio to create a Web page to work with an *ObjectDataSource* control that connects to the *Northwind* database.

If you encounter a problem completing an exercise, the completed projects are available in the samples installed from the companion CD.

EXERCISE 1 Create a Web Site and Define the Shipper Business Object

In this exercise, you create a Web site and add a business object to work with the *Shipper* class in the *Northwind* database.

1. Open Visual Studio and create a new Web site called **DataSourceLab** using your preferred programming language.
2. Add the Northwind.mdf file to your App_Data directory. You can copy the file from the installed sample files.
3. Open the Web.config file. Find the *<connectionStrings/>* element. Replace it with connection information for the *Northwind* database. Your setting should look as follows:

```
<connectionStrings>
  <add name="NorthwindConnectionString"
```

```
    connectionString="Data Source=.\SQLEXPRESS;
      AttachDbFilename=|DataDirectory|\northwnd.mdf;
      Integrated Security=True;User Instance=True"
    providerName="System.Data.SqlClient"/>
</connectionStrings>
```

4. Add a new class file to your site. Name the file **Shipper.vb** (or .cs). When prompted to create the App_Code directory, respond in the affirmative.
5. Inside the *Shipper* class, add an *Imports* statement (*using* in C#) at the top of the file for the *System.ComponentModel*, *System.Data*, and *System.Data.SqlClient* namespaces.
6. Add the *DataObject* attribute at the class level to indicate the class is a data source object class. Recall that these attributes are optional but make the design experience a better one.
7. At the class level, add a *static* (*shared* in Visual Basic) variable that is set to the connection string from the Web.config file.
8. Next, add methods to the *Shipper* class for selecting, inserting, updating, and deleting records from the shippers table in the Northwind.mdf database file. You can use basic ADO.NET code to fill out the contents of the methods. Be sure to mark each method using the *DataObjectMethod* attribute and set the appropriate enum (*Select*, *Insert*, *Delete*, *Update*).

   The following code represents how your *Shipper* class should look when complete (minus the *Imports/using* statements):

```
'VB
<DataObject()> _
Public Class Shipper

  Private Shared _cnnString As String = _
    ConfigurationManager.ConnectionStrings( _
    "NorthwindConnectionString").ToString

  <DataObjectMethod(DataObjectMethodType.Select)> _
  Public Shared Function GetAllShippers() As DataTable

    Dim adp As New SqlDataAdapter( _
      "SELECT * FROM shippers", _cnnString)

    Dim ds As New DataSet("shippers")
    adp.Fill(ds, "shippers")

    Return ds.Tables("shippers")

  End Function
```

```
<DataObjectMethod(DataObjectMethodType.Insert)> _
Public Shared Sub InsertShipper(ByVal companyName As String, _
  ByVal phone As String)

  Dim cnn As New SqlConnection(_cnnString)
  Dim cmd As New SqlCommand( _
    "INSERT INTO shippers (CompanyName, Phone) " & _
    "values(@CompanyName, @Phone)", cnn)

  cmd.Parameters.Add("@CompanyName", SqlDbType.VarChar, 40).Value = _
    companyName
  cmd.Parameters.Add("@Phone", SqlDbType.VarChar, 24).Value = phone

  cnn.Open()
  cmd.ExecuteNonQuery()

End Sub

<DataObjectMethod(DataObjectMethodType.Update)> _
Public Shared Sub UpdateShipper(ByVal shipperId As Integer, _
  ByVal companyName As String, ByVal phone As String)

  Dim cnn As New SqlConnection(_cnnString)
  Dim cmd As New SqlCommand( _
    "UPDATE shippers SET CompanyName=@CompanyName, phone=@Phone " & _
    "WHERE ShipperId=@ShipperId", cnn)

  cmd.Parameters.Add("@ShipperId", SqlDbType.Int, 0).Value = shipperId
  cmd.Parameters.Add("@CompanyName", SqlDbType.VarChar, 40).Value = _
    companyName
  cmd.Parameters.Add("@Phone", SqlDbType.VarChar, 24).Value = phone

  cnn.Open()
  cmd.ExecuteNonQuery()

End Sub

<DataObjectMethod(DataObjectMethodType.Delete)> _
Public Shared Sub DeleteShipper(ByVal shipperId As Integer)

  Dim cnn As New SqlConnection(_cnnString)
  Dim cmd As New SqlCommand( _
    "DELETE shippers WHERE ShipperId=@ShipperId", cnn)

  cmd.Parameters.Add("@ShipperId", SqlDbType.Int, 0).Value = shipperId
```

```
    cnn.Open()
    cmd.ExecuteNonQuery()

  End Sub

End Class

//C#
[DataObject]
public static class Shipper
{

  private static string _cnnString =
    ConfigurationManager.ConnectionStrings[
    "NorthwindConnectionString"].ToString();

  [DataObjectMethod(DataObjectMethodType.Select)]
  public static DataTable GetAllShippers()
  {
    SqlDataAdapter adp = new SqlDataAdapter(
      "SELECT * FROM shippers", _cnnString);

    DataSet ds = new DataSet("shippers");
    adp.Fill(ds, "shippers");

    return ds.Tables["shippers"];
  }

  [DataObjectMethod(DataObjectMethodType.Insert)]
  public static void InsertShipper(
    string companyName, string phone)
  {
    SqlConnection cnn = new SqlConnection(_cnnString);
    SqlCommand cmd = new SqlCommand(
      "INSERT INTO shippers (CompanyName, Phone) values(@CompanyName, @Phone)",
      cnn);

    cmd.Parameters.Add("@CompanyName", SqlDbType.VarChar, 40).Value =
      companyName;
    cmd.Parameters.Add("@Phone", SqlDbType.VarChar, 24).Value = phone;

    cnn.Open();
    cmd.ExecuteNonQuery();
  }
```

```
    [DataObjectMethod(DataObjectMethodType.Update)]
    public static void UpdateShipper(int shipperId,
      string companyName, string phone)
    {
      SqlConnection cnn = new SqlConnection(_cnnString);
      SqlCommand cmd = new SqlCommand(
        "UPDATE shippers SET CompanyName=@CompanyName, phone=@Phone " +
        "WHERE ShipperId=@ShipperId", cnn);

      cmd.Parameters.Add("@ShipperId", SqlDbType.Int, 0).Value = shipperId;
      cmd.Parameters.Add("@CompanyName", SqlDbType.VarChar, 40).Value =
        companyName;
      cmd.Parameters.Add("@Phone", SqlDbType.VarChar, 24).Value = phone;

      cnn.Open();
      cmd.ExecuteNonQuery();
    }

    [DataObjectMethod(DataObjectMethodType.Delete)]
    public static void DeleteShipper(int shipperId)
    {
      SqlConnection cnn = new SqlConnection(_cnnString);
      SqlCommand cmd = new SqlCommand(
        "DELETE shippers WHERE ShipperId=@ShipperId", cnn);

      cmd.Parameters.Add("@ShipperId", SqlDbType.Int, 0).Value = shipperId;

      cnn.Open();
      cmd.ExecuteNonQuery();
    }
  }
```

EXERCISE 2 Bind to the Shipper Business Object

In this exercise, you add functionality to a Web page to bind to the *Shipper* object created in the previous exercise.

1. Continue editing the project you created in the previous exercise. Alternatively, you can open the completed Lesson 1, Exercise 1 project in the samples installed from the CD.
2. Open the Default.aspx page in Design view. Drag an *ObjectDataSource* control onto the page from the Data tab of the Toolbox.

3. Click the smart tag in the upper right corner of the *ObjectDataSource* control to open the *ObjectDataSource* Tasks. Select Configure Data Source to open the Configure Data Source Wizard.

   Walk through the steps of the wizard to configure the control to work with your *Shipper* class. Notice how the select, update, insert, and delete methods are mapped based on their attributes and are available only on the appropriate tab of the Define Data Methods wizard page.

   Finish the wizard and switch to Source view for your page. Your markup should look similar to the following:

```
<asp:ObjectDataSource runat="server"
  ID="ObjectDataSource1"
  TypeName="Shipper"
  SelectMethod="GetAllShippers"
  InsertMethod="InsertShipper"
  DeleteMethod="DeleteShipper"
  UpdateMethod="UpdateShipper">
  <DeleteParameters>
    <asp:Parameter Name="shipperId" Type="Int32" />
  </DeleteParameters>
  <UpdateParameters>
    <asp:Parameter Name="shipperId" Type="Int32" />
    <asp:Parameter Name="companyName" Type="String" />
    <asp:Parameter Name="phone" Type="String" />
  </UpdateParameters>
  <InsertParameters>
    <asp:Parameter Name="companyName" Type="String" />
    <asp:Parameter Name="phone" Type="String" />
  </InsertParameters>
</asp:ObjectDataSource>
```

4. Next, add a *DetailsView* to the page (again from the Data tab of the Toolbox). You can configure the *DetailsView* in markup or inside the Design mode.

   Set the control to work with your *ObjectDataSource* control. In addition, enable paging, inserting, editing, and deleting.

   Next, set the *AutoGenerateRows* attribute to *False* and the *DataKeyNames* to *ShipperID*. Then, declare the fields as *BoundField* objects. Set the *ShipperID* file to read-only and set *InsertVisible* to *False*. Your markup should look as follows:

```
<asp:DetailsView
  ID="DetailsView1"
  runat="server"
  AllowPaging="True"
  DataSourceID="ObjectDataSource1"
  AutoGenerateRows="False"
```

```
  Width="450px"
  DataKeyNames="ShipperID">
  <Fields>
    <asp:BoundField DataField="ShipperID" HeaderText="ShipperId"
      ReadOnly="true" InsertVisible="false" />
    <asp:BoundField DataField="CompanyName" HeaderText="CompanyName" />
    <asp:BoundField DataField="Phone" HeaderText="Phone" />
    <asp:CommandField
      ShowInsertButton="True"
      ShowDeleteButton="True"
      ShowEditButton="True" />
  </Fields>
</asp:DetailsView>
```

5. Now run your application. Select different records using the data pager. Insert a new record. Update a record. Delete a record (note that you can only delete records you add; existing records might have a foreign-key relationship you would have to manage).

Lesson Summary

- ASP.NET provides a number of data source controls (*LinqDataSource*, *ObjectDataSource*, *SqlDataSource*, *AccessDataSource*, *XmlDataSource*, and *SiteMapDataSource*) that allow you to easily work with various types of data. This includes binding to data using data-bound Web server controls.
- You can pass parameters to most data source controls. A parameter can be bound to a value in a cookie, the session, a form field, the query string, or similar object.
- You can cache data using many of the data source controls. This includes the *ObjectDataSource*, *SqlDataSource*, and *AccessDataSource* controls.

Lesson Review

You can use the following questions to test your knowledge of the information in Lesson 1, "Connecting to Data with *DataSource* Controls." The questions are also available on the companion CD if you prefer to review them in electronic form.

> ***NOTE* ANSWERS**
>
> **Answers to these questions and explanations of why each answer choice is right or wrong are located in the "Answers" section at the end of the book.**

1. You have a data context map for your SQL Server database defined inside a class file. You need to connect to this data using a data source control. Which data source control should you use?

A. *ObjectDataSource*

B. *SqlDataSource*

C. *SiteMapDataSource*

D. *LinqDataSource*

2. You are using an *ObjectDataSource* control to connect to a business object. Which attributes of the control must you set to return data for the given data source? (Choose all that apply.)

A. *TypeName*

B. *SelectMethod*

C. *DataSourceId*

D. *SelectParameters*

3. You wish to apply caching to your data source control to increase your scalability for frequently used data. You wish to set the cache to expire every 60 seconds. Which attributes of your data source control should you set to do so? (Choose all that apply.)

A. *CacheTimeout*

B. *CacheDuration*

C. *EnableCaching*

D. *DisableCaching*

Lesson 2: Working with Data-Bound Web Server Controls

Chapter 7 and Lesson 1 showed how you connect to various data sources using ADO.NET and the data source controls. Once accessed, the data needs to be displayed to users for them to interact with it. ASP.NET provides a large set of controls for doing so. These controls are referred to as data-bound controls. Data-bound controls are controls that provide Web-based UI output (HTML and JavaScript) and also bind to data on the server.

This lesson presents an overview of data binding in ASP.NET. It then presents the many data-bound controls found inside ASP.NET.

After this lesson, you will be able to:

- Understand the basics of how data-bound controls operate.
- Use simple data-bound controls such as *DropDownList*, *ListBox*, *CheckBoxList*, *RadioButtonList*, and *BulletedList*.
- Use composite data-bound controls such as *GridView*, *DetailsView*, *FormView*, *DataList*, *Repeater*, *ListView*, and *DataPager*.
- Use hierarchical data-bound controls such as *TreeView* and *Menu*.

Estimated lesson time: 60 minutes

Introducing Data-Bound Controls

The data-bound controls in ASP.NET can be classified as simple, composite, or hierarchical controls. Simple data-bound controls are the controls that inherit from the *ListControl*. Composite data-bound controls are classes that inherit from *CompositeDataBoundControl*, such as the *GridView*, *DetailsView*, *FormsView*, and the like. Hierarchical data-bound controls are the *Menu* and *TreeView* controls.

The Microsoft .NET Framework provides several base classes that are used to provide common properties and behavior for the concrete data-bound controls. These classes form the basis of many of the data-bound controls. In this way, each data-bound control works in a similar manner to the next. Figure 8-6 shows the hierarchy of the base classes used for data-bound controls in ASP.NET.

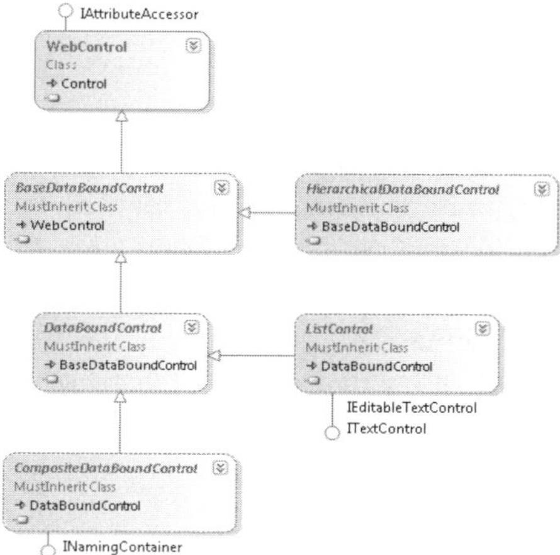

FIGURE 8-6 The base data-bound class hierarchy

The *BaseDataBoundControl* is the first control in the hierarchy (inheriting from *WebControl*). This class contains the *DataSource* and *DataSourceID* properties used in data binding. The *DataSource* property gets or sets the object that the data-bound control uses to retrieve its data items. This property is most often used when binding to data in code. It was the default binding property in early versions of ASP.NET. However, the *DataSourceID* property was introduced later to provide a declarative means of binding to data. You use the *DataSourceID* property to get or set the ID of a data source control that contains the source of the data, such as the *data source controls discussed in Lesson 1*. You typically set either the *DataSource* or the *DataSourceID* property (and not both). If both properties are set, the *DataSourceID* takes precedence.

You can bind a data-bound Web control to any data that implements *IEnumerable, IListSource, IDataSource*, or *IHierarchicalDatasource*. The data-bound control will automatically connect to the data source at run time by calling the *DataBind* method (which also raises the *DataBound* event). You can also call this method yourself in code to force a rebinding of data to the given control.

The next control in Figure 8-6, *HierarchicalDataBoundControl*, inherits from the *BaseDataBoundControl*. It is the parent class for controls that display hierarchical data such as the *Menu* and *TreeView* controls.

The *DataBoundControl* inherits from the *BaseDataBoundControl* and is the parent class to the *CompositeDataBoundControl* and the *ListControl*. These classes are the parent classes to controls that display tabular data such as the *GridView* and *DropDownList*. The *DataBoundControl* control's *DataMember* property is a string data type that is used when the *DataSource* contains more than one tabular result set. In this scenario, the *DataMember* property is set to the name of the tabular result set that is to be displayed.

Mapping Fields to Templates

Templated binding can be used on controls that support templates. A template control is a control that has no default UI. The control simply provides the mechanism for binding to data. The developer supplies the UI in the form of inline templates. The template can contain declarative elements such as HTML and Dynamic Hypertext Markup Language (DHTML). The template can also contain ASP.NET data-binding syntax to insert data from the data source. Controls that support templates include *GridView*, *DetailsView*, and *FormView* among others. A typical control might allow the following templates to be programmed:

- ***HeaderTemplate*** This is an optional header, which is rendered at the top of the control.
- ***FooterTemplate*** This is an optional footer, which is rendered at the bottom of the control.
- ***ItemTemplate*** The item template is rendered for each row in the data source.
- ***AlternatingItemTemplate*** This is an optional alternating item template; if implemented, every other row is rendered using this template.
- ***SelectedItemTemplate*** This is an optional selected item template; if implemented, the template is used to render a row that has been selected.
- ***SeparatorTemplate*** This is an optional separator template that defines the separation of each item and alternate item.
- ***EditItemTemplate*** This is an optional edit item template that is used to render a row that is in edit mode. This usually involves displaying the data in a *TextBox* instead of a *Label* control.

Some of the upcoming examples look at defining these templates for specific controls. For the most part, this process is similar regardless of the control with which you are working.

Using the *DataBinder* Class

In addition to automatically binding data with data-bound controls, you sometimes will need to have more granular control over which fields get bound to which controls on your page. For this, ASP.NET provides the *DataBinder* class. This class can be used to define code inside your script that controls how a given data source is bound.

The *DataBinder* class provides the static *Eval* method to help bind data in this manner. The *Eval* method uses reflection to perform a lookup of a *DataItem* property's underlying type by looking at the type metadata that is stored in the type's assembly. After the metadata is retrieved, the *Eval* method determines how to connect to the given field. This makes writing data binding syntax on your page an easy task. For example, the following shows binding to the *Vin* property of a *Car* object:

```
<%# Eval("Vin") %>
```

The *Eval* method also provides an overloaded method that allows a format string to be assigned as part of the data binding. As an example, if you were to bind to a field called *Price,* you can modify the display of this field by providing currency formatting as shown here:

```
<%# Eval("Price", "{0:C}") %>
```

The *Eval* method is great for one-way (or read-only) data binding. However, it does not support read-write data binding and thus cannot be used for insert and edit scenarios. The *Bind* method of the *DataBinder* class, however, can be used for two-way data binding. This makes *Bind* desirable when editing or inserting records.

Just like the *Eval* method, the *Bind* method has two overloads: one without a format and one with the *format* parameter. The code for the *Bind* method looks the same as that of the *Eval* method. However, the *Bind* method does not work with all bound controls. It only works with those that support read, insert, update, and delete scenarios such as *GridView, Details-View,* and *FormView.*

Simple Data-Bound Controls

There are a number of controls in ASP.NET that provide basic, list-based data binding. These controls are not meant to work with pages of data or provide elaborate editing scenarios. Instead, they allow you to provide a list of data items with which a user can operate. Figure 8-7 shows these simple data-bound controls, including their common base class, *ListControl.*

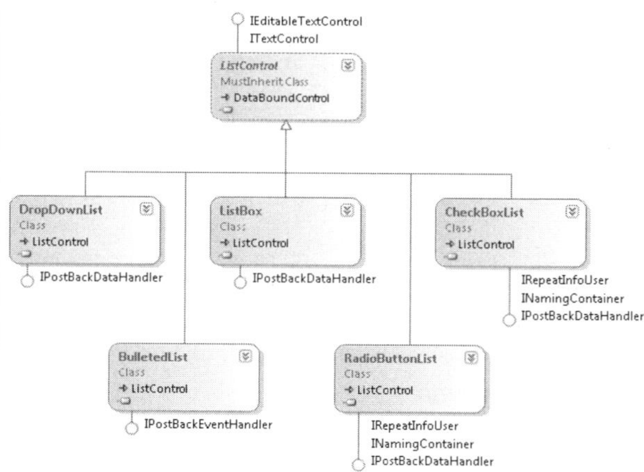

FIGURE 8-7 The *ListControl* class hierarchy

The *ListControl* class is an abstract base class that provides common functionality for the classes that derive from it. This includes an *Items* collection, which is a collection of *ListItem* data objects. Each *ListItem* object contains a *Text* property that is displayed to the user and a *Value* property that is posted back to the Web server.

You can add items to the *ListItems* collection in code or declaratively in markup. You can also bind data to the controls that inherit from *ListControl* by setting the *DataSource* property or the *DataMember* property if the source data has more than one table. You can also declaratively data-bind a *ListControl* derived object by setting the *DataSourceID* property to the ID of a valid data source control on your page.

You can also choose the fields in your results that you will bind to the *ListItem.Text* and *ListItem.Value* properties. You can do so in code or through declarative markup by using the *DataTextField* and *DataValueField* properties, respectively. The text displayed for each item in the list control can also be formatted by setting the *DataTextFormatString* property. As an example, the following shows the declarative syntax for a *ListBox* bound to a *SqlDataSource* that provides the *Northwind* shipper table data:

```
<asp:ListBox
  ID="ListBox1"
  runat="server"
  DataSourceID="SqlDataSource1"
  DataTextField="CompanyName"
  DataValueField="ShipperID">
</asp:ListBox>
```

The *SelectedIndex* property lets you get or set the index of the selected item in the given *ListControl*. Using the *SelectedItem* property, you can access the selected *ListItem* object's properties. If you only need to access the value of the selected *ListItem*, use the *SelectedValue* property.

The *ListControl* also contains the property called *AppendDataBoundItems* that can be set to *True* to keep all items that are currently in the *ListControl* in addition to appending the items from the data binding. Setting this property to *False* clears the *Items* property prior to binding the data.

The *ListControl* also provides the *SelectedIndexChanged* event, which is raised when the selection in the list control changes between posts to the server. Recall that you need to set a control's *AutoPostback* property to *True* if you intend that it post back to the server for this type of event.

The *DropDownList* Control

The *DropDownList* control is used to display a list of items to users to allow them to make a single selection. The *Items* collection contains the collection of *ListItem* objects contained in the *DropDownList* control. To determine the item that is selected, you can retrieve the *SelectedValue*, *SelectedItem*, or *SelectedIndex* property.

In the following example, a *DropDownList* control is bound to a *SqlDataSource* that returns data from the *Territories* database table in the *Northwind* database. Notice that the *DataTextField* and *DataValueField* attributes are set to fields in the database table.

```
<asp:DropDownList runat="server" Width="250px"
  ID="DropDownList1"
  DataSourceID="SqlDataSource1"
  DataTextField="TerritoryDescription"
```

```
  DataValueField="TerritoryID" >
</asp:DropDownList>
```

Imagine this page also contains a button with an event that captures the selected item from the *DropDownList* and displays it on a label. This button control's event code might look as follows:

```
'VB
Label1.Text = "You selected TerritoryID: " & DropDownList1.SelectedValue

//C#
Label1.Text = "You selected TerritoryID: " + DropDownList1.SelectedValue;
```

When the page is run and the user makes a selection in the *DropDownList* control and then presses the button, the results are displayed in the label. Figure 8-8 shows an example.

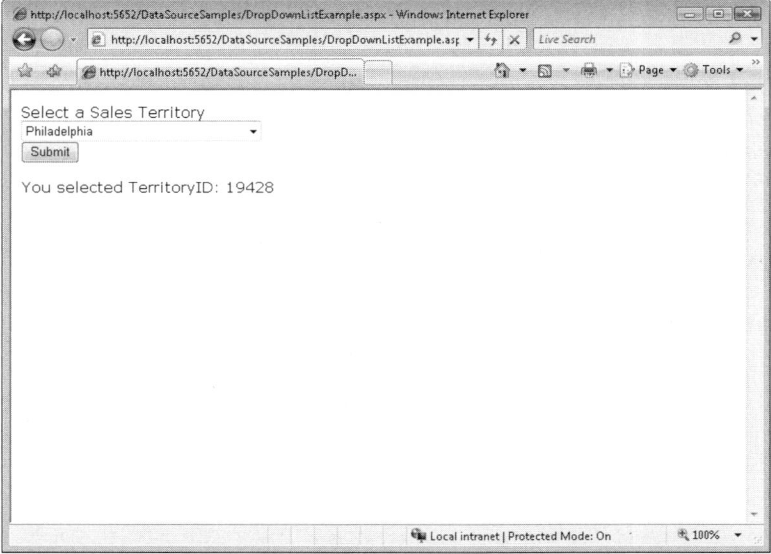

FIGURE 8-8 The *DropDownList* control with an item selected and output to a label

The *ListBox* Control

The *ListBox* control is used to display items in a longer list rather than one at a time like the *DropDownList*. Users can see more data at a given time. The control can also be configured to allow the selection of a single item or multiple items. To do so, you set the *SelectionMode* property. The *ListBox* control also has the *Rows* property, which is used to specify the number of items displayed on the screen at any given time. The following shows an example of a *ListBox* that is set to allow multiple selections and show up to 13 rows:

```
<asp:ListBox runat="server" Height="225px" Width="275px"
  ID="ListBox1"
```

```
    Rows="13"
    DataSourceID="SqlDataSource1"
    DataTextField="TerritoryDescription"
    DataValueField="TerritoryID"
    SelectionMode="Multiple">
</asp:ListBox>
```

The *Items* collection contains the collection of *ListItem* objects in the *ListBox* control. To determine the items that are selected, you can enumerate the *ListItem* objects in the *Items* collection by examining the *Selected* value for each *ListItem* element. The following code shows an example of processing the selected items and displaying them inside a *Label* control:

```
'VB
For Each i As ListItem In ListBox1.Items
  If i.Selected Then
    Label1.Text = Label1.Text & "You selected TerritoryID: " & i.Value & "<br />"
  End If
Next

//C#
foreach (ListItem i in ListBox1.Items)
{
  if(i.Selected)
    Label1.Text = Label1.Text + "You selected TerritoryID: " + i.Value + "<br />";
}
```

The results of this example are shown in Figure 8-9.

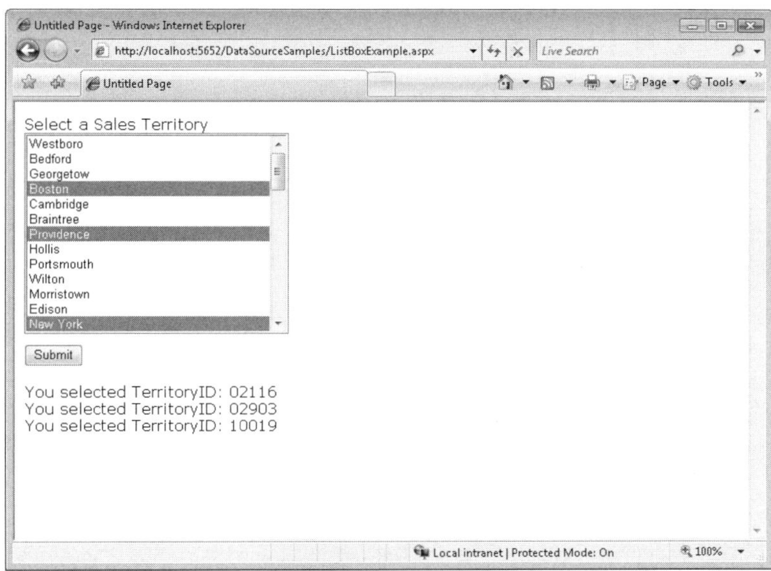

FIGURE 8-9 The *ListBox* control with items selected and output to the *Label* control

The *CheckBoxList* and *RadioButtonList* Controls

The *CheckBoxList* and *RadioButtonList* controls are very similar. They are both used to display lists of items to users to allow them to make selections. The *RadioButtonList* control is used to make a single selection. The *CheckBoxList* control allows users to make multiple selections.

These controls contain a *RepeatColumns* property that is used to indicate the number of columns to be displayed horizontally. In addition, the *RepeatDirection* can be set to *Horizontal* or *Vertical* (the default) to indicate if the data should be rendered across and down by rows or down and then up across columns.

The following shows a *CheckBoxList* control configured to work with the *Territory* data and show data across five columns:

```
<asp:CheckBoxList runat="server"
  ID="CheckBoxList1"
  DataSourceID="SqlDataSource1"
  DataTextField="TerritoryDescription"
  DataValueField="TerritoryID" RepeatColumns="5">
</asp:CheckBoxList>
```

The *Items* collection contains the collection of *ListItem* objects, which are inside the *CheckBoxList* and the *RadioButtonList* controls. Use the *SelectedValue* property to determine the item that has been selected for the *RadioButtonList*. To find the selected *CheckBoxList* items, you can enumerate the *ListItem* objects in the *Items* collection by examining the value of the *Selected* property for each *ListItem* element (as shown in the *ListBox* example).

Figure 8-10 shows an example of the sales territories displayed as check boxes. When the user clicks the Submit button, the value of each selected check box is displayed in a *Label* control.

FIGURE 8-10 The *CheckBoxList* control showing the use of *RepeatColumns*

The *BulletedList* Control

The *BulletedList* control displays an unordered or ordered list of items that renders as HTML *ul* or *ol* elements, respectively. The *BulletedList* control inherits from the *ListControl* control. This control renders as either bullets or numbers based on the *BulletStyle* property.

If the control is set to render as bullets, you can select the bullet style of *Disc*, *Circle*, or *Square*. Note that the *BulletStyle* settings are not compatible with all browsers. A custom image can also be displayed instead of the bullet.

If the *BulletList* control is set to render numbers, you can set the *BulletStyle* to *LowerAlpha*, *UpperAlpha*, *LowerRoman*, and *UpperRoman* fields. You can also set the *FirstBulletNumber* property to specify the starting number for the sequence.

The *DisplayMode* property can be set to *Text*, *LinkButton*, or *HyperLink*. If set to *LinkButton* or *HyperLink*, the control performs a PostBack when a user clicks an item to raise the *Click* event.

The following example shows a data-bound *BulletedList* control. The control is bound to a data source control that selects the *Shippers* table data from the *Northwind* database.

```
<asp:BulletedList runat="server"
  ID="BulletedList1"
  DataSourceID="SqlDataSource1"
  DataTextField="CompanyName"
  DataValueField="ShipperID" BulletStyle="Circle">
</asp:BulletedList>
```

Composite Data-Bound Controls

There are a number of data-bound controls that use other ASP.NET controls to display bound data to the user. For this reason, these controls are referred to as composite data-bound controls. These controls inherit from the base class, *CompositeDataBoundControl*. This class implements the *INamingContainer* interface, which means that an inheritor of this class is a naming container for child controls.

The classes that inherit from *CompositeDataBoundControl* directly are *FormsView*, *DetailsView*, and *GridView*, as shown in Figure 8-11. These controls are covered in this section along with the related data-bound controls of *ListView*, *DataPager*, *Repeater*, and *DataList*.

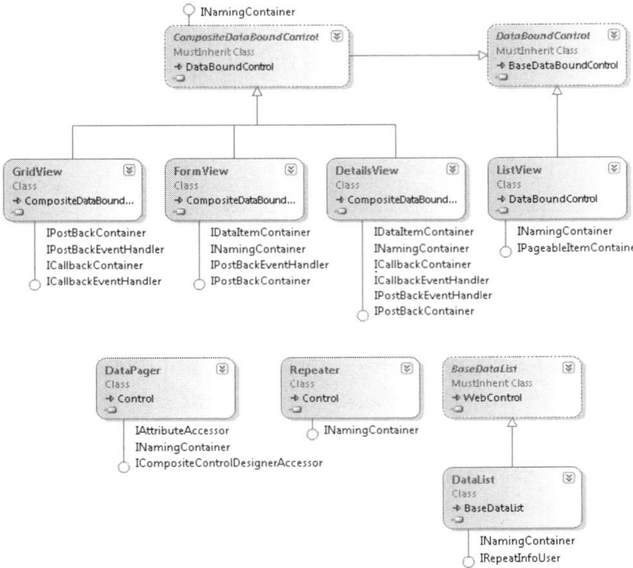

FIGURE 8-11 The *CompositeDataBoundControl* classes (and related)

The *GridView* Control

The *GridView* control is used to display data in a tabular (rows-and-columns) format. The control renders in the browser as an HTML table. The *GridView* control makes it easy to configure features such as paging, sorting, and editing data without having to write much code.

The basic structure of the *GridView* is shown in Figure 8-12. The *GridView* control consists of a collection of *GridViewRow* (row) objects and a collection of *DataControlField* (column) objects. The *GridViewRow* object inherits from the *TableRow* object, which contains the *Cells* property. This property is a collection of *DataControlFieldCell* objects.

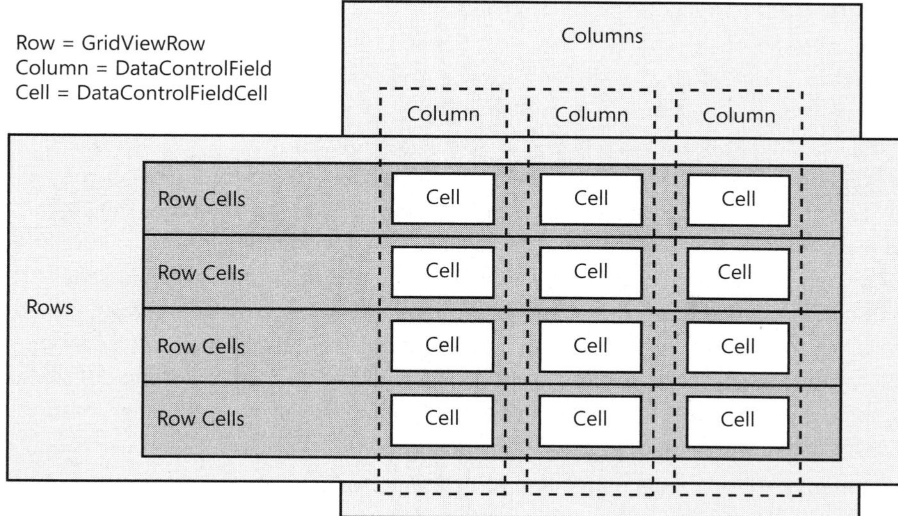

FIGURE 8-12 The basic *GridView* control structure

Although the *GridViewRow* object holds the collection of cells, each *DataControlField* (column) object provides the behavior to initialize cells of a specific type in the *DataControlField* object's *InitializeCell* method. The column classes that inherit from *DataControlField* override the *InitializeCell* method. The *GridView* control has an *InitializeRow* method that is responsible for creating a new *GridViewRow* and the row's cells by making calls to the overridden *InitializeCell* method when the row is being created.

The *DataControlField* class hierarchy is shown in Figure 8-13. The derived classes are used to create a *DataControlFieldCell* with the proper contents. Remember that you don't define cell types for your *GridView* control; you define column types and your column object supplies a cell object to the row using the *InitializeCell* method. The *DataControlField* class hierarchy shows the different column types that are available in a *GridView* control.

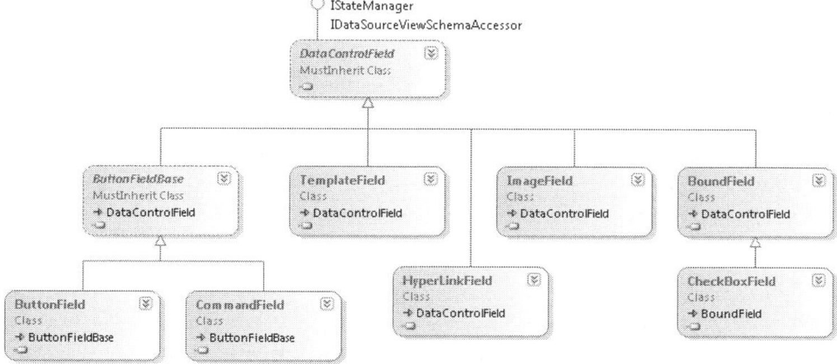

FIGURE 8-13 The *DataControlField* class hierarchy

USING STYLES TO FORMAT THE *GRIDVIEW* CONTROL

You use styles to format the *GridView*. There are a number of styles available for you to manage, including an overall *GridViewStyle*, *HeaderStyle*, *FooterStyle*, *RowStyle*, *AlternatingRowStyle*, *SelectedRowStyle*, *EditRowStyle*, and more. You can set these styles declaratively at design time. In addition, the *RowCreated* and *RowDataBound* events can also be used to control the style programmatically. In these event handlers, the *Cells* collection on the newly created row can be used to apply a style to a single cell in the row. The difference between the two events is that the *RowCreated* event takes place first, but the data is not available at this time. You can use the *RowDataBound* event when you need to apply a different style to a cell based on the data in the cell. These events fire after the styles are applied, which means you can override any existing styles. Applying a different style to a cell based on the data in the cell allows you to apply business rules to determine whether a cell should stand out from other cells (such as making negative "quantity on hand" numbers red, but only when an item is shipped more than once per month).

As an example, consider a page that contains a *SqlDataSource* control bound to the *Products* table in the *Northwind* database. Suppose this data source control provides SQL statements for selecting, updating, inserting, and deleting data. You can use this data source control to configure a *GridView* control that allows for this editing. The following markup shows an example of how the *GridView* would look in Source view:

```
<asp:GridView ID="GridView1" runat="server"
  AllowPaging="True"
  AllowSorting="True"
  AutoGenerateColumns="False"
  DataKeyNames="ProductID"
  DataSourceID="SqlDataSource1">
  <Columns>
    <asp:CommandField ShowDeleteButton="True" ShowEditButton="True"
      ShowSelectButton="True" />
    <asp:BoundField DataField="ProductID" HeaderText="ProductID"
      InsertVisible="False" ReadOnly="True" SortExpression="ProductID" />
    <asp:BoundField DataField="ProductName" HeaderText="ProductName"
      SortExpression="ProductName" />
    <asp:BoundField DataField="SupplierID" HeaderText="SupplierID"
      SortExpression="SupplierID" />
    <asp:BoundField DataField="CategoryID" HeaderText="CategoryID"
      SortExpression="CategoryID" />
    <asp:BoundField DataField="QuantityPerUnit" HeaderText="QuantityPerUnit"
      SortExpression="QuantityPerUnit" />
    <asp:BoundField DataField="UnitPrice" HeaderText="UnitPrice"
      SortExpression="UnitPrice" />
    <asp:BoundField DataField="UnitsInStock" HeaderText="UnitsInStock"
      SortExpression="UnitsInStock" />
    <asp:BoundField DataField="UnitsOnOrder" HeaderText="UnitsOnOrder"
      SortExpression="UnitsOnOrder" />
```

```
    <asp:BoundField DataField="ReorderLevel" HeaderText="ReorderLevel"
      SortExpression="ReorderLevel" />
    <asp:CheckBoxField DataField="Discontinued" HeaderText="Discontinued"
      SortExpression="Discontinued" />
  </Columns>
</asp:GridView>
```

Notice the *Columns* collection in the markup. Each column is defined along with the *DataField* and the text to be displayed as the column header (*HeaderText*). When this Web page is executed and displayed, each row is shown to the user along with action buttons for editing, deleting, and selecting the row. A user can click the Edit link on one of the rows to place the row into edit mode. Figure 8-14 shows an example.

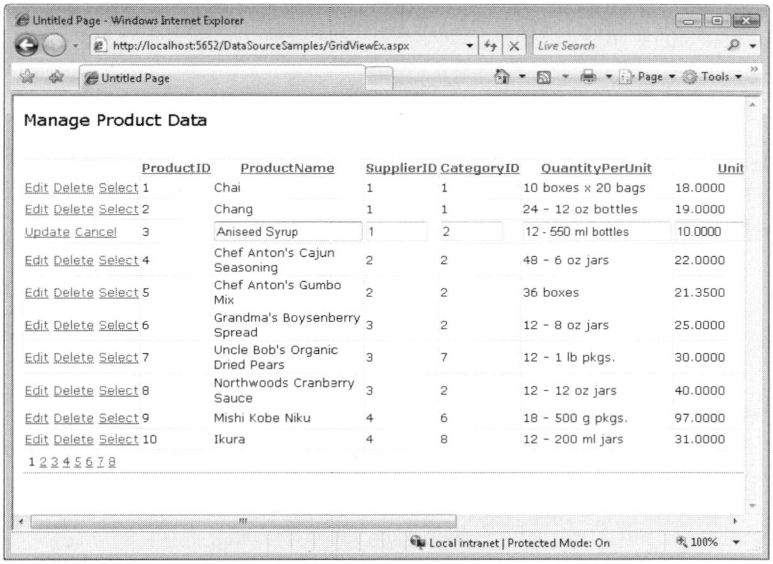

FIGURE 8-14 The *GridView* control in edit mode

The *DetailsView* Control

The *DetailsView* control is used to display the values of a single record at a time from a data source in an HTML table. The *DetailsView* control allows you to edit, delete, and insert records. If the *AllowPaging* property is set to *True,* the *DetailsView* can be used by itself to navigate the data source. However, the *DetailsView* can also be used in combination with other controls such as the *GridView*, *ListBox*, or *DropDownList* for scenarios in which you want to display a master-detail form.

The *DetailsView* does not directly support sorting, whereas the *GridView* does. However, you can use the data source, as discussed in Lesson 1, to manage data sorting. You should also note that the *GridView* does not automatically support inserting new records, whereas the *DetailsView* does support this feature.

The *DetailsView* supports the same formatting options that are available with the *GridView* control. You can format the *DetailsView* control using the *HeaderStyle*, *RowStyle*, *Alternating-RowStyle*, *CommandRowStyle*, *FooterStyle*, *PagerStyle*, and *EmptyDataRowStyle* properties.

As an example, again consider a page that has a *SqlDataSource* control used for defining selection, insertion, updates, and deletion of product data in the *Northwind* database. You can configure a *DetailsView* to show this product data as pages and allow users to edit this data, insert new records, and delete existing ones. The following markup shows an example:

```
<asp:DetailsView runat="server" Width="300px"
  ID="DetailsView1"
  AllowPaging="True"
  AutoGenerateRows="False"
  DataKeyNames="ProductID"
  DataSourceID="SqlDataSource1">
  <Fields>
    <asp:BoundField DataField="ProductID" HeaderText="ProductID"
      InsertVisible="False" ReadOnly="True" SortExpression="ProductID" />
    <asp:BoundField DataField="ProductName" HeaderText="ProductName"
      SortExpression="ProductName" />
    <asp:BoundField DataField="SupplierID" HeaderText="SupplierID"
      SortExpression="SupplierID" />
    <asp:BoundField DataField="CategoryID" HeaderText="CategoryID"
      SortExpression="CategoryID" />
    <asp:BoundField DataField="QuantityPerUnit" HeaderText="QuantityPerUnit"
      SortExpression="QuantityPerUnit" />
    <asp:BoundField DataField="UnitPrice" HeaderText="UnitPrice"
      SortExpression="UnitPrice" />
    <asp:BoundField DataField="UnitsInStock" HeaderText="UnitsInStock"
      SortExpression="UnitsInStock" />
    <asp:BoundField DataField="UnitsOnOrder" HeaderText="UnitsOnOrder"
      SortExpression="UnitsOnOrder" />
    <asp:BoundField DataField="ReorderLevel" HeaderText="ReorderLevel"
      SortExpression="ReorderLevel" />
    <asp:CheckBoxField DataField="Discontinued" HeaderText="Discontinued"
      SortExpression="Discontinued" />
    <asp:CommandField ShowDeleteButton="True" ShowEditButton="True"
      ShowInsertButton="True" />
  </Fields>
</asp:DetailsView>
```

Notice that each column in the data table is set inside the *Fields* collection. The *DataField* attribute maps to the name of the column in the data source. The *HeaderText* property is used as the label that describes the given data field. When the page is executed and displayed, the *DetailsView* shows Edit, Delete, and New buttons. When users click the Edit button, they are taken to edit mode for the selected record as shown in Figure 8-15.

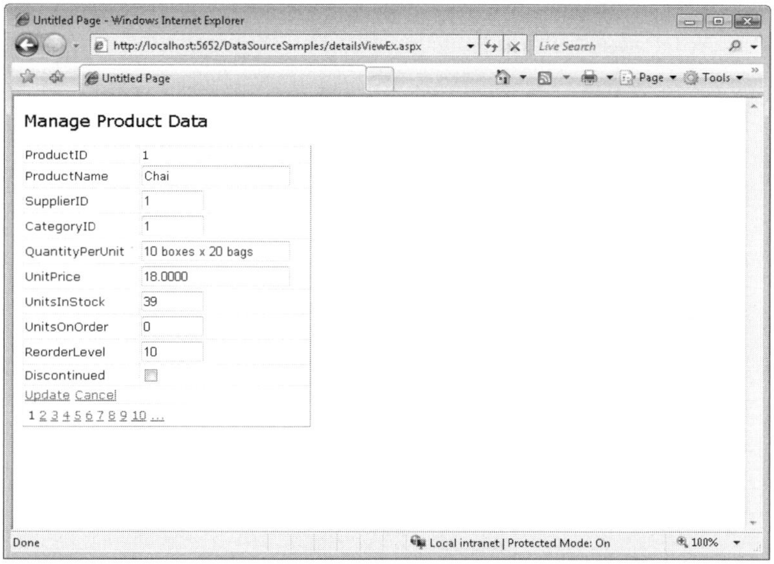

FIGURE 8-15 The *DetailsView* control in edit mode after clicking the Edit button

The *FormView* Control

Like the *DetailsView*, the *FormView* control is used to display a single record from a data source. However, the *FormView* control does not automatically output the data in a predefined HTML table. Instead, it allows developers to create templates that define how the data should be displayed. You can define different templates for viewing, editing, and updating records. Creating your own templates gives you the greatest flexibility in controlling how data is displayed.

The *FormView* contains the following template definitions: *ItemTemplate*, *EditItemTemplate*, *InsertItemTemplate*, *EmptyDataTemplate*, *FooterTemplate*, *HeaderTemplate*, and *PagerTemplate*. You define these templates by placing markup inside the template and adding binding code within this markup. You then set the appropriate mode of the *FormView* control to switch to the given template.

As an example, consider a page that defines a data source control for selecting the shipper data from the *Northwind* database. You can configure a *FormView* control to work with this data. For display, you can define the *<ItemTemplate>*. Here you set the controls and HTML used to lay out this data. You use the binding syntax (*Eval* and *Bind*) to connect data from the *SqlDataSource* to the *FormView*. The following markup shows an example:

```
<asp:FormView runat="server"
  ID="FormView1"
  AllowPaging="True"
  DataSourceID="SqlDataSource1">
  <ItemTemplate>
```

```
      Shipper Identification:
      <asp:Label runat="server" Font-Bold="True"
        ID="Label1"
        Text='<%# Eval("ShipperID") %>'>
      </asp:Label>
      <br />
      <br />
      Company Name<br />
      <asp:TextBox runat="server" Width="250px"
        ID="TextBox1"
        Text='<%# Bind("CompanyName") %>'>
      </asp:TextBox>
      <br />
      Phone Number<br />
      <asp:TextBox runat="server" Width="250px"
        ID="TextBox2"
        Text='<%# Bind("Phone") %>'>
      </asp:TextBox>
    </ItemTemplate>
  </asp:FormView>
```

When you run the page, the custom template is used with the *FormView* to display data as defined. Figure 8-16 shows the results in a browser window.

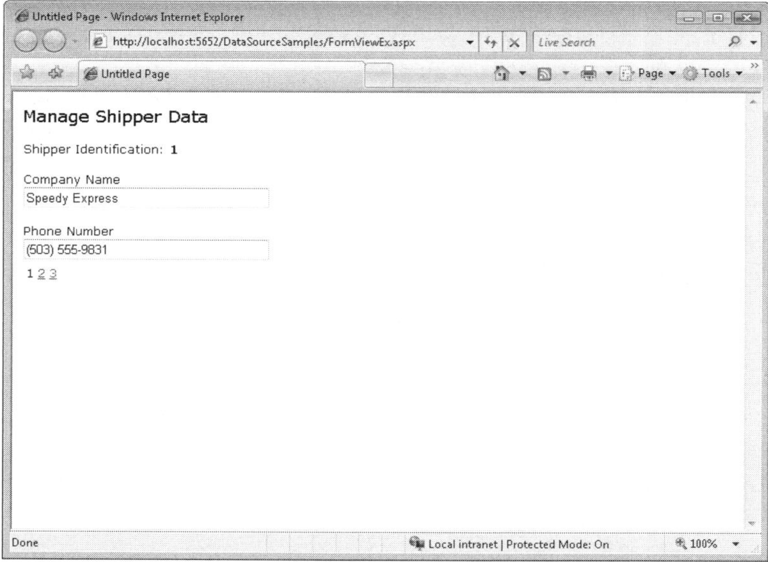

FIGURE 8-16 The *FormView* control showing the *ItemTemplate* in a browser

The *Repeater* Control

The *Repeater* control also uses templates to define custom binding. However, it does not show data as individual records. Instead, it repeats the data rows as you define in your template. This allows you to create a single row of data and have it repeat across your page.

The *Repeater* control is a read-only template. That is, it only supports the *ItemTemplate*. It does not implicitly support editing, insertion, and deletion. You should consider one of the other controls if you need this functionality or you will have to code this yourself for the *Repeater* control.

The following markup is similar to that of the *FormView*. It displays shipper data from the *Northwind* database as bound to a *Label* and two *TextBox* controls.

```
<asp:Repeater runat="server"
  ID="Repeater1"
  DataSourceID="SqlDataSource1">
  <ItemTemplate>
    <br /><br />
    Shipper Identification:
    <asp:Label runat="server" Font-Bold="True"
      ID="Label1"
      Text='<%# Eval("ShipperID") %>'>
    </asp:Label>
    <br />
    <br />
    Company Name<br />
    <asp:TextBox runat="server" Width="250px"
      ID="TextBox1"
      Text='<%# Bind("CompanyName") %>'>
    </asp:TextBox>
    <br />
    Phone Number<br />
    <asp:TextBox runat="server" Width="250px"
      ID="TextBox2"
      Text='<%# Bind("Phone") %>'>
    </asp:TextBox>
  </ItemTemplate>
</asp:Repeater>
```

When this data is displayed, however, it is repeated down the page. Figure 8-17 shows the results in a browser window.

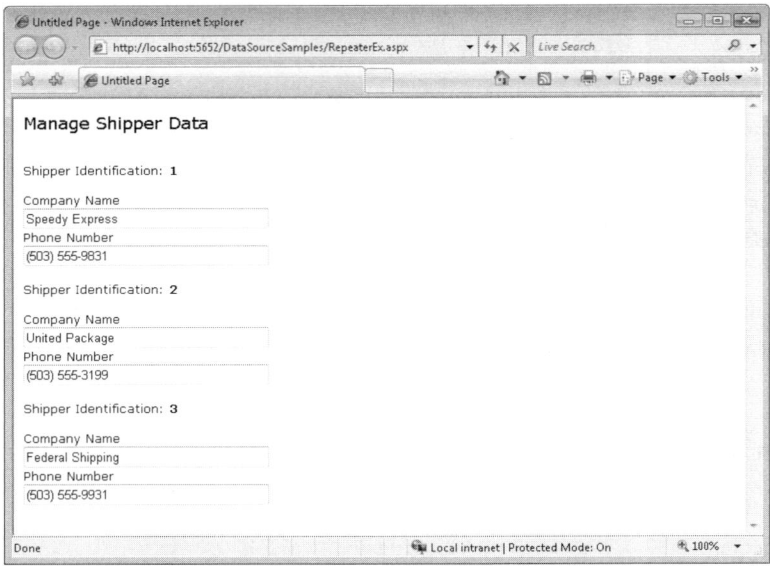

FIGURE 8-17 The *Repeater* control showing the *ItemTemplate* in a browser

THE *LISTVIEW* CONTROL

The *ListView* control also uses templates for the display of data. However, it supports many additional templates that allow for more scenarios when working with your data. This includes the *LayoutTemplate*. The *LayoutTemplate* allows you to indicate an overall layout inside which rows of your data should be displayed. The rows themselves are defined using the *ItemTemplate*. At run time, rows are placed within the *LayoutTemplate* placeholder as identified by a control that has its *ID* attribute set to *itemPlaceholder*.

Another template is the *GroupTemplate*. This template allows you to define groups of data. You can then set the *GroupItemCount* value to indicate the number of items in a group. You can then set the control to lay out groups of data and allow users to page through them.

The *ItemSeparatorTemplate* allows you to define content that should be placed in between rows of items. This allows you to put graphic separators in place or other data in between rows.

The *ListView* control also implicitly supports the ability to edit, insert, and delete data using a data source control (unlike *DataList* and *Repeater*). You can define individual templates for each of these scenarios. You can then change the mode of the *ListView* control through a server-side call and thus invoke the template for the user.

As an example, consider a page that includes a data source control that exposes the *Product* table from the *Northwind* database. You can create a *ListView* control to work with this data. The following markup shows such an example. Here there is a *LayoutTemplate* that defines a *Div* tag that includes the *itemPlaceholder* setting. The *ItemTemplate* is then defined by a *Div* tag. At run time, each row will be added as a *Div* tag in the placeholder.

```
<asp:ListView runat="server"
  ID="ListView1"
  DataKeyNames="ProductID"
  DataSourceID="SqlDataSource1">
  <LayoutTemplate>
    <div id="itemPlaceholder" runat="server"></div>
    <br />
    <div style="text-align: center">
      <asp:DataPager ID="DataPager1" runat="server" PageSize="4">
        <Fields>
          <asp:NextPreviousPagerField
            ButtonType="Button"
            ShowFirstPageButton="True"
            ShowLastPageButton="True" />
        </Fields>
      </asp:DataPager>
    </div>
  </LayoutTemplate>
  <ItemTemplate>
    <div style="text-align: center">
      <b>ProductName:</b>
      <asp:Label ID="ProductNameLabel" runat="server"
        Text='<%# Eval("ProductName") %>' />
      <br />
      <b>QuantityPerUnit:</b>
      <asp:Label ID="QuantityPerUnitLabel" runat="server"
        Text='<%# Eval("QuantityPerUnit") %>' />
      <br />
      <b>UnitPrice:</b>
      <asp:Label ID="UnitPriceLabel" runat="server"
        Text='<%# Eval("UnitPrice") %>' />
      <br />
    </div>
  </ItemTemplate>
  <ItemSeparatorTemplate>
    <hr />
  </ItemSeparatorTemplate>
</asp:ListView>
```

Notice also that the *ListView* control uses the ASP.NET *DataPager* control. This control allows you to provide custom data pagers for your data lists. Here the control is embedded at the end of the *LayoutTemplate*. The *ListView* control automatically uses the *DataPager* to move the user through data.

Finally, notice the use of the *ItemSeparatorTemplate*. This is used to put a horizontal rule between data rows. Figure 8-18 shows the results in a browser window.

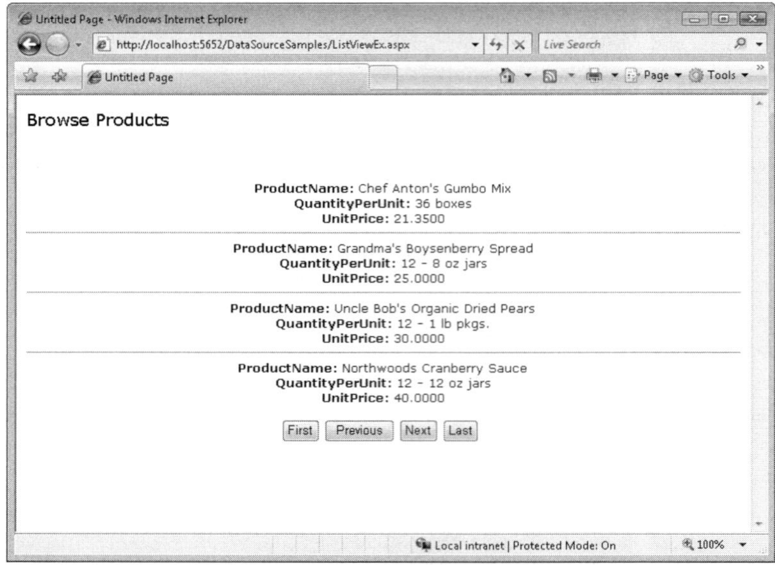

FIGURE 8-18 The *ListView* control rendered in the browser

The *DataList* Control

The *DataList* control works like the *Repeater* control. It repeats data for each row in your data set. It also shows this data per your defined template. However, it lays out the data defined in the template within various HTML structures. This includes the options for horizontal or vertical layout. It also allows you to set how the data should be repeated, as flow or table layout.

The *DataList* control does not automatically take advantage of editing data using a data source control. Instead, it provides a number of command events in which you can write your own code for these scenarios. To enable these events, you add a *Button* control to one of the templates and set the button's *CommandName* property to the keywords of edit, delete, update, or cancel. The appropriate event is then raised by the *DataList* control.

The following markup shows an example of a *DataList* control configured to show product data from the *Northwind* database. This control's *RepeatDirection* is set to show data vertically using a *RepeatLayout* of flow.

```
<asp:DataList runat="server"
  DataSourceID="SqlDataSource1"
  RepeatDirection="Vertical"
  ID="DataList1"
  RepeatLayout="flow">
  <ItemTemplate>
    <asp:Label ID="Label1" runat="server"
      Text='<%# Eval("ProductName") %>'
      Font-Bold="True">
```

```
    </asp:Label>
    <asp:Label ID="Label2" runat="server"
      Text='<%# Eval("UnitPrice", "{0:C}") %>'>
    </asp:Label>
    <br />
  </ItemTemplate>
</asp:DataList>
```

The product data is bound to the *DataList* control inside the *ItemTemplate* code. Figure 8-19 shows the results in a browser window.

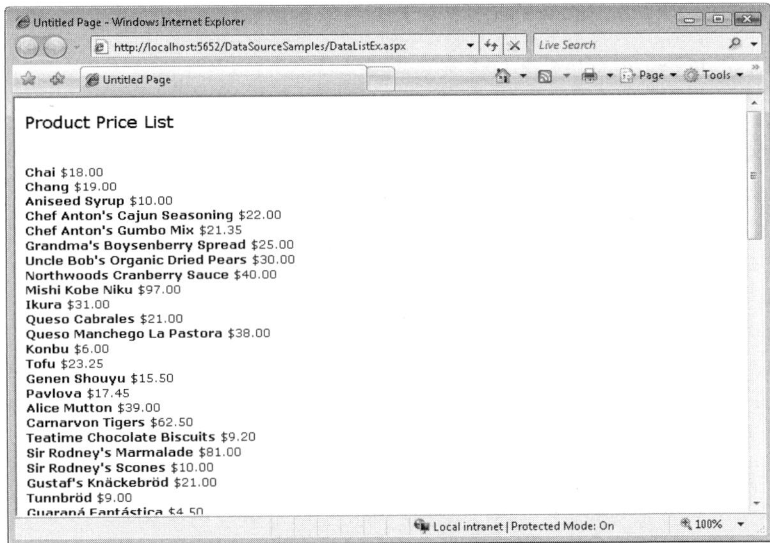

FIGURE 8-19 The *DataList* control rendered in the browser

Hierarchical Data-Bound Controls

The *HierarchicalDataBoundControl* control serves as a base class for controls that render data in a hierarchical fashion. The classes that inherit from *HierarchicalDataBoundControl* are *TreeView* and *Menu,* as shown in Figure 8-20.

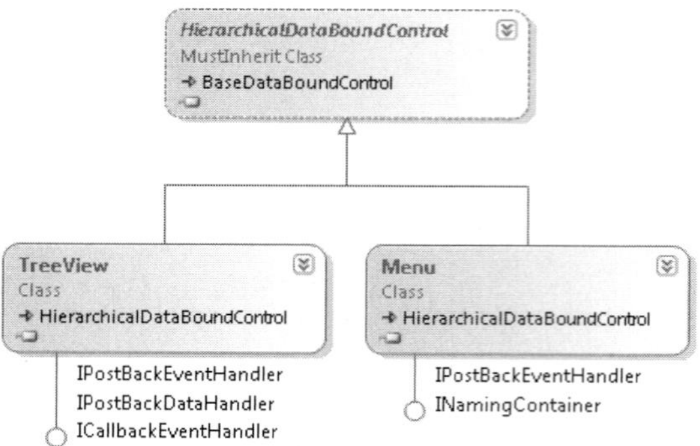

FIGURE 8-20 The *HierarchicalDataBoundControl* class hierarchy

The *TreeView* Control

The *TreeView* control is a data-bound control that is used to display hierarchical data, such as a listing of files and folders, or a table of contents in a tree structure. The nodes of this control can be bound to XML, tabular, or relational data. This control can also provide site navigation when used with the *SiteMapDataSource* control.

You can programmatically access and control the properties of the *TreeView* control. The *TreeView* can also be populated via client-side script using modern browsers. In addition, nodes can be displayed as either plaintext or hyperlinks, and you can optionally display a check box next to each node.

Each entry in the tree is called a node and is represented by a *TreeNode* object. A node that contains other nodes is called a *parent node*. A node that is contained by another node is called a *child node*. A node can be a parent node and a child node. A node that has no children is called a *leaf node*. A node that is not contained by any other node but is the ancestor to all the other nodes is the *root node*.

The typical *TreeView* tree structure has only one root node, but you can add multiple root nodes to the tree structure. This means that you can display a tree hierarchy without being forced to have a single root node.

The *TreeNode* has a *Text* property that is populated with the data that is to be displayed. The *TreeNode* also has a *Value* property that is used to store the data that is posted back to the Web server.

A node can be configured to be a selection node or a navigation node by setting the *NavigateUrl* property. If the *NavigateUrl* property is set to an empty string (*string.Empty*), it is a selection node, where clicking the node simply selects it. If the *NavigateUrl* property is not set to an empty string, it is a navigation node, where clicking the node attempts to navigate to the location that is specified by the *NavigateUrl* property.

POPULATING THE *TREEVIEW* CONTROL

The *TreeView* control can be populated using static data or by data binding to the control. To populate the *TreeView* control with static data, you can use declarative syntax by placing opening and closing *<Nodes>* tags in the *TreeView* element, and then creating a structure of nested *<asp:TreeNode>* elements within the *<Nodes>* element. Each *<asp:TreeNode>* has properties that you can set by adding attributes to the *<asp:TreeNode>* element.

To use data binding to populate the *TreeView* control, you can use any data source that implements the *IHierarchicalDataSource* interface, such as an *XmlDataSource* control or a *SiteMapDataSource* control. Simply set the *DataSourceID* property of the *TreeView* control to the ID value of the data source control, and the *TreeView* control automatically binds to the specified data source control.

You can also bind to an *XmlDocument* object or a *DataSet* object that contains *DataRelation* objects by setting the *DataSource* property of the *TreeView* control to the data source, and then calling the *DataBind* method.

The *TreeView* control contains a *DataBindings* property that is a collection of *TreeNodeBinding* objects that define the binding between a data item and the *TreeNode*. You can specify the criteria for binding and the data item property to display in the node. This is useful when binding to XML elements where you are interested in binding to an attribute of the element.

Assume you want to use a *TreeView* control to display customer data from a file called Customers.xml, which contains a list of customers, their orders and invoices, and the items for each order. This data is stored in a hierarchical format in the XML file. The Customers.xml file looks like the following:

```
<?xml version="1.0" encoding="utf-8" ?>
<Customers>
  <Customer CustomerId="1" Name="Northwind Traders">
    <Orders>
      <Order OrderId="1" ShipDate="06-22-2006">
        <OrderItems>
          <OrderItem OrderItemId="1" PartNumber="123"
             PartDescription="Large Widget" Quantity="5"
             Price="22.00" />
          <OrderItem OrderItemId="2" PartNumber="234"
             PartDescription="Medium Widget" Quantity="2"
             Price="12.50" />
        </OrderItems>
      </Order>
      <Order OrderId="2" ShipDate="06-25-2006">
        <OrderItems>
          <OrderItem OrderItemId="5" PartNumber="432"
             PartDescription="Small Widget" Quantity="30"
```

```
            Price="8.99" />
          <OrderItem OrderItemId="4" PartNumber="234"
            PartDescription="Medium Widget" Quantity="2"
            Price="12.50" />
        </OrderItems>
      </Order>
    </Orders>
    <Invoices>
      <Invoice InvoiceId="6" Amount="99.37" />
      <Invoice InvoiceId="7" Amount="147.50" />
    </Invoices>
  </Customer>
  <Customer CustomerId="2" Name="Tailspin Toys">
    <Orders>
      <Order OrderId="8" ShipDate="07-11-2006">
        <OrderItems>
          <OrderItem OrderItemId="9" PartNumber="987"
            PartDescription="Combo Widget" Quantity="2"
            Price="87.25" />
          <OrderItem OrderItemId="10" PartNumber="654"
            PartDescription="Ugly Widget" Quantity="1"
            Price="2.00" />
        </OrderItems>
      </Order>
      <Order OrderId="11" ShipDate="08-21-2006">
        <OrderItems>
          <OrderItem OrderItemId="12" PartNumber="999"
            PartDescription="Pretty Widget" Quantity="50"
            Price="78.99" />
          <OrderItem OrderItemId="14" PartNumber="575"
            PartDescription="Tiny Widget" Quantity="100"
            Price="1.20" />
        </OrderItems>
      </Order>
    </Orders>
    <Invoices>
      <Invoice InvoiceId="26" Amount="46.58" />
      <Invoice InvoiceId="27" Amount="279.15" />
    </Invoices>
  </Customer>
</Customers>
```

An *XmlDataSource* and a *TreeView* control are added to the Web page and configured. The following shows the markup for the *TreeView* control:

```
<asp:TreeView ID="TreeView1" runat="server"
   DataSourceID="XmlDataSource1"
   ShowLines="True" ExpandDepth="0">
   <DataBindings>
     <asp:TreeNodeBinding DataMember="Customer"
      TextField="Name" ValueField="CustomerId" />
     <asp:TreeNodeBinding DataMember="Order"
      TextField="ShipDate" ValueField="OrderId" />
     <asp:TreeNodeBinding DataMember="OrderItem"
      TextField="PartDescription" ValueField="OrderItemId" />
     <asp:TreeNodeBinding DataMember="Invoice"
      TextField="Amount" ValueField="InvoiceId"
      FormatString="{0:C}" />
   </DataBindings>
</asp:TreeView>
```

In this example, the configuration is kept to a minimum, but configuration is required to display information that is more important than the XML element name, such as the customer's name instead of the XML element name (*Customer*). The following code is added to the code-behind page to simply display the value of the selected node:

```
'VB
Partial Class TreeView_Control
  Inherits System.Web.UI.Page

  Protected Sub TreeView1_SelectedNodeChanged(ByVal sender As Object, _
    ByVal e As System.EventArgs) Handles TreeView1.SelectedNodeChanged
      Response.Write("Value:" + TreeView1.SelectedNode.Value)
  End Sub

End Class

//C#
public partial class TreeView_Control : System.Web.UI.Page
{
  protected void TreeView1_SelectedNodeChanged(object sender, EventArgs e)
  {
    Response.Write("Value:" + TreeView1.SelectedNode.Value);
  }
}
```

When the Web page is displayed, the *Customers* node is visible. You can also click the plus (+) sign to expand the nodes as shown in Figure 8-21.

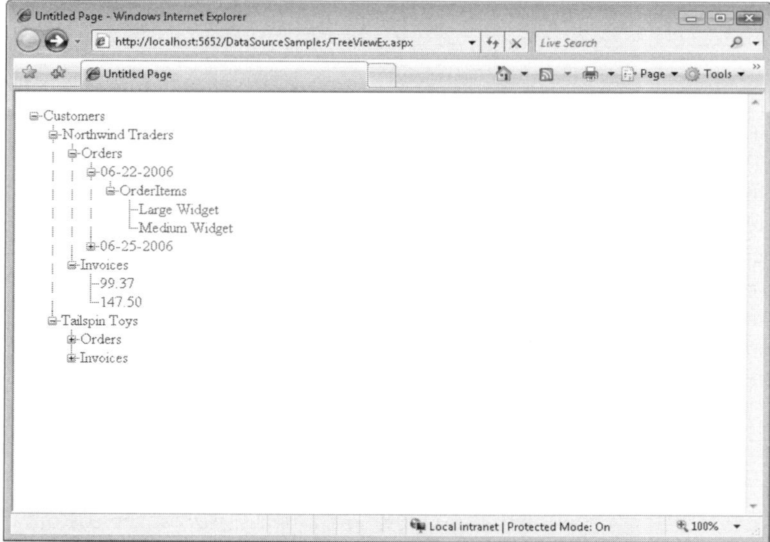

FIGURE 8-21 The *TreeView* displays the nodes as configured

The *Menu* Control

The *Menu* control is a data-bound control that is used to display hierarchical data in the form of a menu system. The *Menu* control is often used in combination with a *SiteMapDataSource* control for navigating a Web site.

The *Menu* control can be populated using static data or by data binding to the control. To populate the *Menu* control with static data, you can use declarative syntax by placing opening and closing *<Items>* tags in the *Menu* element, and then you can create a structure of nested *<asp:MenuItem>* elements within the *<Items>* element. Each *<asp:MenuItem>* has properties that you can set by adding attributes to the *<asp:MenuItem>* element.

To use data binding to populate the *Menu* control, you can use any data source that implements the *IHierarchicalDataSource* interface, such as an *XmlDataSource* control or a *SiteMapDataSource* control. Simply set the *DataSourceID* property of the *Menu* control to the ID value of the data source control, and the *Menu* control automatically binds to the specified data source control.

You can also bind to an *XmlDocument* object or a *DataSet* object that contains *DataRelation* objects by setting the *DataSource* property of the *Menu* control to the data source, and then calling the *DataBind* method.

The *Menu* control contains a *DataBindings* property that is a collection of *MenuItemBinding* objects that define the binding between a data item and the menu item it is binding to in a *Menu* control. You can specify the criteria for binding and the data item properties to display in the items. This is useful when binding to XML elements where you are interested in binding to an attribute of the element.

Assume you want to use a *Menu* control to display menu data from a file called MenuItems.xml, which contains a list of the menu items to be displayed. The data is stored in a hierarchical format in the XML file. The MenuItems.xml file looks like this:

```
<?xml version="1.0" encoding="utf-8" ?>
<MenuItems>
   <Home display="Home"  url="~/" />
   <Products display="Products" url="~/products/">
      <SmallWidgets display="Small Widgets"
         url="~/products/smallwidgets.aspx" />
      <MediumWidgets display="Medium Widgets"
         url="~/products/mediumwidgets.aspx" />
      <BigWidgets display="Big Widgets"
         url="~/products/bigwidgets.aspx" />
   </Products>
   <Support display="Support"  url="~/Support/">
      <Downloads display="Downloads"
         url="~/support/downloads.aspx" />
      <FAQs display="FAQs"
         url="~/support/faqs.aspx" />
   </Support>
   <AboutUs display="About Us" url="~/aboutus/">
      <Company display="Company"
         url="~/aboutus/company.aspx" />
      <Locations display="Location"
         url="~/aboutus/locations.aspx" />
   </AboutUs>
</MenuItems>
```

An *XmlDataSource*, a *Menu*, and a *Label* control are added to the Web page. The *XmlDataSource* is configured to use the XML file. The *Menu* control is configured to use the *XmlDataSource*. The following is the Web page markup:

```
<asp:Menu runat="server"
  ID="Menu1"
  DataSourceID="XmlDataSource1"
  OnMenuItemClick="Menu1_MenuItemClick">
</asp:Menu>
```

In this example, showing the *MenuItems* root node in the XML file is not desirable, so an XPath expression is supplied to retrieve the nodes that exist under the *MenuItems* element. The following code is added to the code-behind page to simply display the *ValuePath* property of the selected *MenuItem*:

```
'VB
Partial Class Menu_Control
  Inherits System.Web.UI.Page

  Protected Sub Menu1_MenuItemClick(ByVal sender As Object, _
    ByVal e As System.Web.UI.WebControls.MenuEventArgs) _
    Handles Menu1.MenuItemClick
      Label1.Text = e.Item.ValuePath
  End Sub
End Class

//C#
public partial class Menu_Control : System.Web.UI.Page
{
  protected void Menu1_MenuItemClick(object sender, MenuEventArgs e)
  {
    Label1.Text = e.Item.ValuePath;
  }
}
```

When the Web page is displayed, the *Menu* displays and you can hover above a menu item to see its child menu items, as shown in Figure 8-22.

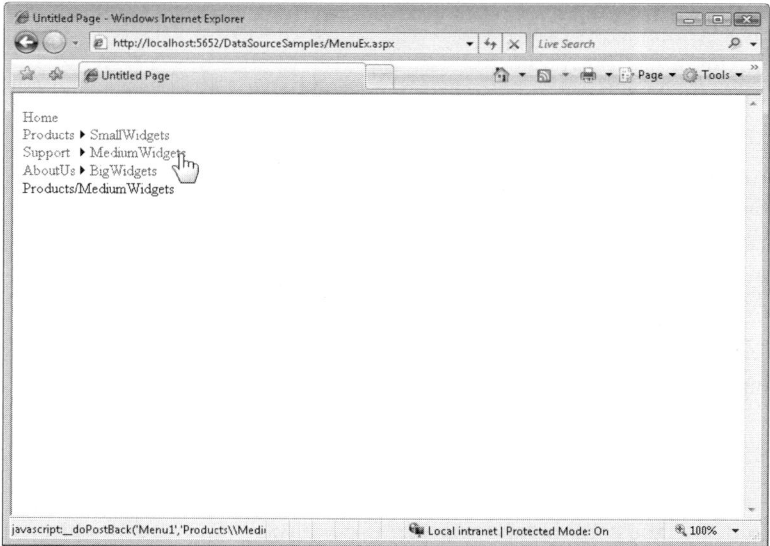

FIGURE 8-22 The *Menu* displays the nodes as configured

Quick Check

1. What method should you call on a data-bound control when the data is ready to be read from the data source?
2. What method is used in a *FormView* to perform two-way data binding?
3. What GUI object can provide a data source that allows you to connect middle-tier objects to data-bound controls?

Quick Check Answers

1. You should call the *DataBind* method.
2. The *Bind* method is used to perform two-way data binding.
3. The *ObjectDataSource* control can provide a data source that allows you to connect middle-tier objects to data-bound controls.

LAB Using the *GridView* and *DetailsView* Controls

In this lab, you use the *GridView* and *DetailsView* data-bound controls together to create a master-detail page.

If you encounter a problem completing an exercise, the completed projects are available in the sample files installed from the companion CD.

EXERCISE 1 Create the Web Site, Add Controls to the Page, and Configure the Controls

In this exercise, you create a new Web site and add the database and data source control. You then add the data-bound controls and configure them accordingly.

1. Open Visual Studio and create a new Web site called **UsingDataBoundControls** using your preferred programming language.
2. Add the Northwind.mdf file to your App_Data directory. You can copy the file from the samples installed from the CD.
3. Add a *SqlDataSource* control to the Default.aspx page and name it **SqlDataSource-ReadList**. This control will simply read data for display by the *GridView* control.
4. In Design view of the Default.aspx page, click the smart tag in the upper right corner of the *SqlDataSource* control to launch the Configure Data Source Wizard. On the first page, set the connection to the Northwind.mdf file in the App_Code directory and click Next. When prompted, save the connection string as **ConnectionStringNorth-wind** and click Next again.
5. On the Configure Select Statement page, select the Customers table from the Name drop-down list box. Select the fields *CustomerID*, *CompanyName*, *ContactName*, *City*, *Country*, and *Phone*. Click Next, and then click Finish to close the wizard.
6. Drag and drop a *GridView* control onto the Default.aspx page.

7. Using either Design or Source view, configure the *GridView* control as follows: Set *AllowPaging* to *True*, set *AllowSorting* to *True*, and set the *DataSourceId* to *SqlDataSourceReadList* created previously. Also, set *AutoGenerateColumns* to *False* and configure the *CustomerID*, *CompanyName*, *ContactName*, *City*, *Country*, and *Phone* fields to display. Also, add a *CommandField* for allowing a user to select a row of data. Your markup should look similar to the following:

```
<asp:GridView runat="server"
  ID="GridView1"
  AllowPaging="True"
  AllowSorting="True"
  DataSourceID="SqlDataSourceReadList"
  DataKeyNames="CustomerID"
  Width="700px"
  AutoGenerateColumns="False">
  <Columns>
    <asp:CommandField ShowSelectButton="True" />
    <asp:BoundField DataField="CustomerID" HeaderText="ID" ReadOnly="True"
      SortExpression="CustomerID" />
    <asp:BoundField DataField="CompanyName" HeaderText="Company"
      SortExpression="CompanyName" />
    <asp:BoundField DataField="ContactName" HeaderText="Contact"
      SortExpression="ContactName" />
    <asp:BoundField DataField="City" HeaderText="City"
      SortExpression="City" />
    <asp:BoundField DataField="Country" HeaderText="Country"
      SortExpression="Country" />
    <asp:BoundField DataField="Phone" HeaderText="Phone"
      SortExpression="Phone" />
  </Columns>
</asp:GridView>
```

8. Optionally, select the *GridView* in Design view and click the AutoFormat link on the task pane (from the smart tag). Select Colorful or another formatting option.

   Run the Web application. Page through data, sort data, and select a row.

9. Next, add another *SqlDataSource* control to the Default.aspx page; name it **SqlDataSourceUpdate**. Configure this control as before, using the Configure Data Source Wizard. On the first page, select the *ConnectionStringNorthwind* and click Next.

   The next step is to configure the *SELECT* statement to pick up the *CustomerID* parameter from the selected row on the *GridView* control. On the Configure The Select Statement page, select the Customers table. This time, select each field in the table. Then, click Where to launch the Add WHERE Clause dialog box. Set the column to CustomerID. Set the Operator to "=". Set the Source to Control. Under Parameter Properties, set the Control ID to *GridView1*. Click Add and click OK to close the dialog box.

Click Advanced. In the Advanced Sql Generation Options dialog box, select the Generate Insert, Update, And Delete Statements option. Close this dialog box. Click Next, and then click Finish to close the wizard.

10. Add a *DetailsView* control to the page. In Design view, set the control's data source to *SqlDataSourceUpdate*. Enable inserting and editing (deleting requires managing a foreign key constraint so leave that cleared for this example). Click Edit Templates and select the EmptyData Template. In the template in Design view, type **"No customers currently selected"** and add a *LinkButton* control to the template. Set the *LinkButton* control's *CausesValidation* property to *False*. Set its *CommandName* property to **New**. Set its *Text* property to **New**. In the *DetailView* Tasks window, click End Template Editing.

11. Next, you need to add code to update the *GridView* when a record has been inserted or edited in the *DetailsView* control. To do so, add event handlers for both the *ItemUpdated* and *ItemInserted* events of the *DetailsView* control. Inside each event, rebind the *GridView* control. The following code shows an example:

```
'VB
Protected Sub DetailsView1_ItemInserted(ByVal sender As Object, _
  ByVal e As System.Web.UI.WebControls.DetailsViewInsertedEventArgs) _
  Handles DetailsView1.ItemInserted

  GridView1.DataBind()

End Sub

Protected Sub DetailsView1_ItemUpdated(ByVal sender As Object, _
  ByVal e As System.Web.UI.WebControls.DetailsViewUpdatedEventArgs) _
  Handles DetailsView1.ItemUpdated

  GridView1.DataBind()

End Sub

//C#
protected void DetailsView1_ItemUpdated(object sender,
  DetailsViewUpdatedEventArgs e)
  {
    GridView1.DataBind();
  }

protected void DetailsView1_ItemInserted(object sender,
  DetailsViewInsertedEventArgs e)
  {
    GridView1.DataBind();
  }
```

12. Optionally, select the *DetailsView* control in Design view and click the AutoFormat link in the task pane (from the smart tag). Select Colorful or another formatting option.

    Run the Web page. Notice that the empty *DetailsView* control allows you to add a new record. Select a row from the *GridView*. Notice how it appears in the *DetailsView* section, as shown in Figure 8-23. Click the Edit link and edit a record.

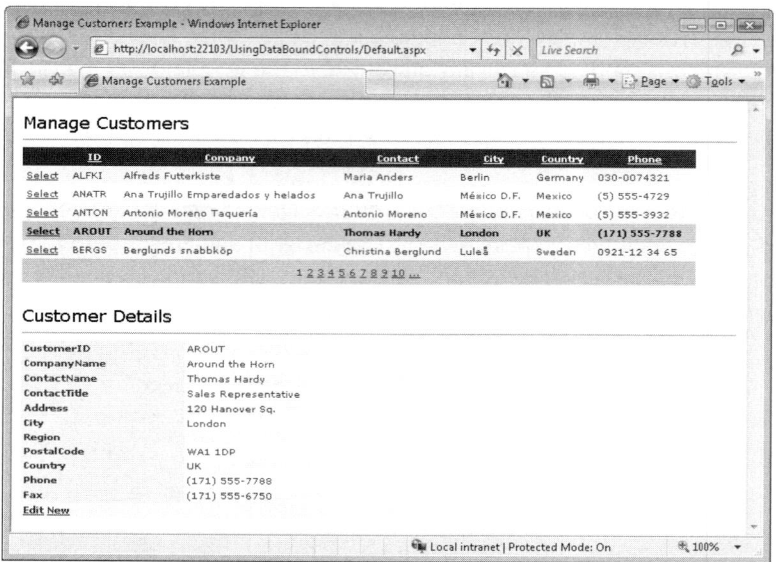

FIGURE 8-23 The master-detail form shown in the browser window

Lesson Summary

- Simple data-bound controls consist of controls that inherit from the *ListControl* such as *DropDownList*, *ListBox*, *CheckBoxList*, *BulletedList*, and *RadioButtonList*. For these controls, you set the *DataTextField* to the name of the column that contains the data you wish to display to the user. You set the *DataValueField* to the column that contains the value(s) you wish to return to the server for a selected item.
- Composite data-bound controls consist of the *GridView*, *DetailsView*, *FormView*, *Repeater*, *ListView*, and *DataList* controls. The *GridView* and *DetailsView* controls show data as tables. The other controls allow you to define templates for laying out your data.
- Hierarchical data-bound controls consist of the *Menu* and *TreeView* controls. These controls are used for displaying data that contains parent–child relationships.

Lesson Review

You can use the following questions to test your knowledge of the information in Lesson 2, "Working with Data-Bound Controls." The questions are also available on the companion CD if you prefer to review them in electronic form.

> ***NOTE*** **ANSWERS**
>
> **Answers to these questions and explanations of why each answer choice is right or wrong are located in the "Answers" section at the end of the book.**

1. You are creating a data-bound *CheckBoxList* control that allows a user to select options for configuring a vehicle. When the data is displayed to the user, you want the *OptionName* column to display. When the data is posted back to the server, you need the *OptionId* column value for all selected items. Which of the following attribute definitions would you set? (Choose all that apply.)
   - **A.** *DataTextField=OptionId*
   - **B.** *DataTextField=OptionName*
   - **C.** *DataValueField=OptionId*
   - **D.** *DataValueField =OptionName*
2. You wish to display a list of suppliers on a Web page. The supplier list must display 10 suppliers at a time, and you require the ability to edit individual suppliers. Which Web control is the best choice for this scenario? (Choose all that apply.)
   - **A.** The *DetailsView* control
   - **B.** The *Repeater* control
   - **C.** The *GridView* control
   - **D.** The *ListView* control
3. You want to display a list of parts in a master-detail scenario where users can select a part number from a list that takes a minimum amount of space on the Web page. When the part is selected, a *DetailsView* control displays all the information about the part and allows users to edit the part. Which Web control is the best choice to display the part number list for this scenario?
   - **A.** The *DropDownList* control
   - **B.** The *RadioButtonList* control
   - **C.** The *FormView* control
   - **D.** The *TextBox* control

Chapter Review

To further practice and reinforce the skills you learned in this chapter, you can perform the following tasks:

- Review the chapter summary.
- Complete the case scenarios. These scenarios set up real-world situations involving the topics of this chapter and ask you to create solutions.
- Complete the suggested practices.
- Take a practice test.

Chapter Summary

- You can use the data source controls in ASP.NET to easily work with various types of data. You can configure these controls declaratively through markup or in your code. Most data source controls support selecting, inserting, updating, deleting, filtering, and caching data.
- The data source controls in ASP.NET include *LinqDataSource*, *ObjectDataSource*, *SqlDataSource*, *AccessDataSource*, *XmlDataSource*, and *SiteMapDataSource*.
- There are many data-bound controls in ASP.NET. Simple controls allow the display and selection of data typically from a single source and two fields (text and value). Other data-bound controls such as *GridView* allow for the display of data in a tabular mode. You can use the *DetailsView* control to edit records in a form-like layout. The *ListView*, *DataList*, *Repeater*, and *FormView* controls allow users to define templates for the layout of their data.

Case Scenarios

In the following case scenarios, you will apply what you've learned in this chapter. If you have difficulty completing this work, review the material in this chapter before beginning the next chapter. You can find answers to these questions in the "Answers" section at the end of this book.

Case Scenario 1: Determining Data Source Controls

You are a developer at Contoso, a car insurance company. You have been asked to write an application that allows a customer service agent to provide an insurance quote to a customer over the phone. However, there are many factors that go into pricing the insurance policy. Each of these factors contains data from different sources. This data is displayed to the customer for selection. Based on his or her selection, a price is generated.

You identify most of the data sources as follows:

- **Location premium markup data** Provided as XML from a Web service.

- **Year, make, and model rates** Provided inside a SQL Server database.
- **Driver history** Provided through an XML Web service.
- **Existing customer information** Provided through a shared customer object to which the application has a reference.

QUESTIONS

1. Which data source control would you use for accessing the data returned by the location and driver history Web services? How would you configure the data source control to receive this data?
2. Which data source control would you use for accessing the year, make, and model rate data?
3. How would you access the data provided by the customer object?

Case Scenario 2: Implementing a Master-Detail Solution

You are a developer who is creating a Web page for displaying customers and their orders in a master-detail scenario. The top of the Web page will provide a list of customers that contains the customer numbers and names. The bottom of the Web page will provide a list of the orders containing the order numbers, the order dates, the order amounts, and the ship dates. The orders will be displayed for the customer that is selected.

QUESTIONS

1. What controls would you use to display the customer and orders?
2. If you want to use this Web page to add customers and orders, what are some ways that you can provide this functionality?

Suggested Practices

To help you successfully master the exam objectives presented in this chapter, complete the following tasks.

Create Pages Using Each of the Controls

For this task, you should complete Practice 1 for the data source controls. Practice 2 should be completed for additional use of the data-bound Web controls. If completing Practice 2, you should complete Practice 1 first.

- **Practice 1** Create a new Web site and add a new page for each of the data source controls in this chapter, especially those not defined in the lab for Lesson 1. Configure these controls to access data.
- **Practice 2** Add the ability to display the data defined in the pages in Practice 1. For each data source, select a different display control. Use the *Menu* control for XML data. Also, be sure to define a layout control that uses templates.

Create a Master-Detail Solution Using the Data-Bound Server Controls

For this task, you should complete Practice 1.

- **Practice 1** Create a new Web site that uses a domain familiar to you, such as customers and orders, owners and vehicles, employees and sick days, or albums and songs. Add a Web page that is configurable as a master-detail page to provide access to related data.

Take a Practice Test

The practice tests on this book's companion CD offer many options. For example, you can test yourself on just the content covered in this chapter, or you can test yourself on all the 70-562 certification exam content. You can set up the test so it closely simulates the experience of taking a certification exam, or you can set it up in study mode so you can look at the correct answers and explanations after you answer each question.

MORE INFO **PRACTICE TESTS**

For details about all the practice test options available, see the "How to Use the Practice Tests" section in this book's Introduction.

CHAPTER 9

Writing and Working with Services

Developers are using services to make better use of legacy code across applications. Web services enable system integration, business process workflow across boundaries, business logic reuse, and more. There are two primary ways to create services in ASP.NET. You can create Web services based on the ASP.NET (.asmx) model. This is a familiar ASP.NET programming experience for services that are meant to be exclusively bound to Hypertext Transfer Protocol (HTTP) and hosted by Microsoft Internet Information Services (IIS) and ASP.NET. You can also use Microsoft Windows Communication Foundation (WCF) to create Web services. This model allows developers to write services that can be configured to work with a variety of hosts, protocols, and clients. Of course, this includes hosting in IIS and communicating through HTTP.

This chapter first covers the ASP.NET Extensible Markup Language (XML) Web service model. This includes building, hosting, and consuming Web services with Microsoft Visual Studio and ASP.NET. The first lesson in the chapter introduces ASP.NET developers to working with WCF-based services. This second lesson covers creating WCF services to be hosted inside IIS and ASP.NET. It also walks through calling WCF services from an ASP.NET Web page.

Exam objectives in this chapter:

- Working with Data and Services
  - Call a Windows Communication Foundation (WCF) service or a Web service from an ASP.NET Web page.
- Working with ASP.NET AJAX and Client-Side Scripting
  - Consume services from client scripts.

Lessons in this chapter:

Before You Begin

To complete the lessons in this chapter, you should be familiar with developing applications with Visual Studio using Visual Basic or C#. In addition, you should be comfortable with all of the following:

- The Visual Studio 2008 Integrated Development Environment (IDE)
- A basic understanding of Hypertext Markup Language (HTML) and client-side scripting with the JavaScript language
- How to create a new Web site
- The basics of the JavaScript programming language and Dynamic HTML (DHTML)

Lesson 1: Creating and Consuming XML Web Services

Web services have become the common programming model for implementing interoperability between systems that have little or no real connectivity. Prior to Web services, connecting applications in meaningful ways was a difficult challenge. This challenge was exacerbated by having to cross application domains, servers, networks, data structures, security boundaries, and the like. However, with the prominence of the Internet, Web services have become a common model for accessing data, performing distributed transactions, and exposing business process workflow.

The Internet and its supported standards around HTTP and XML make Web services possible. However, having to program directly against HTTP, XML, and Simple Object Access Protocol (SOAP) is a challenging (and time-consuming) proposition. Thankfully, ASP.NET provides a model for building and consuming XML Web services. With it, you can define a Web service as code (an .asmx file and related class). ASP.NET will then wrap this code as a Web service object. This object will know how to expose your Web service. This includes deserializing SOAP requests, executing your .NET Framework code, and serializing your response to be sent back to the requesting client as a SOAP message.

Additionally, ASP.NET provides a simple client model for consuming Web services. A proxy object is generated for you when you reference a Web service. You can then program against this proxy object as if you were calling in-process code. The proxy object takes care of serialization, SOAP messaging, and the related processes.

Figure 9-1 provides a high-level overview of the XML Web service model in ASP.NET.

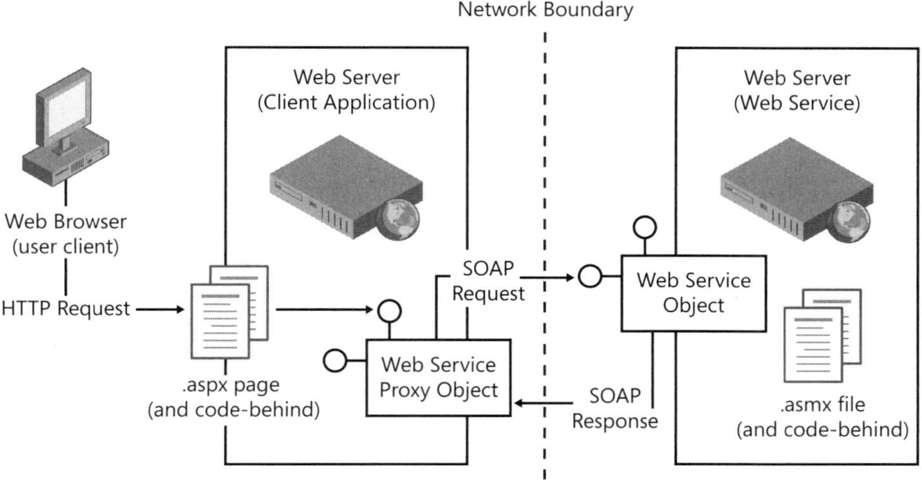

FIGURE 9-1 The XML Web service model in ASP.NET

This lesson starts by covering the basics of an XML Web service. This includes defining Web service projects and the Web services themselves. You then see how to consume XML Web services with ASP.NET.

After this lesson, you will be able to:

- Understand how ASP.NET uses Internet standards to allow you to build XML Web services.
- Create XML Web services.
- Consume XML Web services inside an ASP.NET page.
- Call an XML Web service from client-side script.

Estimated lesson time: 45 minutes

REAL WORLD

Mike Snell

I have really seen Web services take off over the last few years. This technology had been making big promises, but few were making big bets on it. Now, organizations are using Web services to expose and consume all kinds of legacy data that was difficult to get at previously. I have seen projects that expose billing data, customer data, reporting information, business workflow, and much more. In addition, software vendors have added services as part of their base offering. It used to be commonplace to provide an application programming interface (API) with your application. Now, this includes a base set of services that the application uses and that you can use to extend the application. Some great examples include Microsoft Office SharePoint Server and Microsoft Team Foundation Server. Thankfully, Web services is one technology that has really lived up to its original promise.

Creating an ASP.NET Web Service

An ASP.NET XML Web service is a class you write that inherits from the class *System.Web.Services.WebService*. This class provides a wrapper for your service code. In this way, you are free to write a Web service in pretty much the same way you would write any other class and method. The *WebService* class and ASP.NET take care of the rest. Figure 9-2 shows the objects leveraged by most ASP.NET Web services.

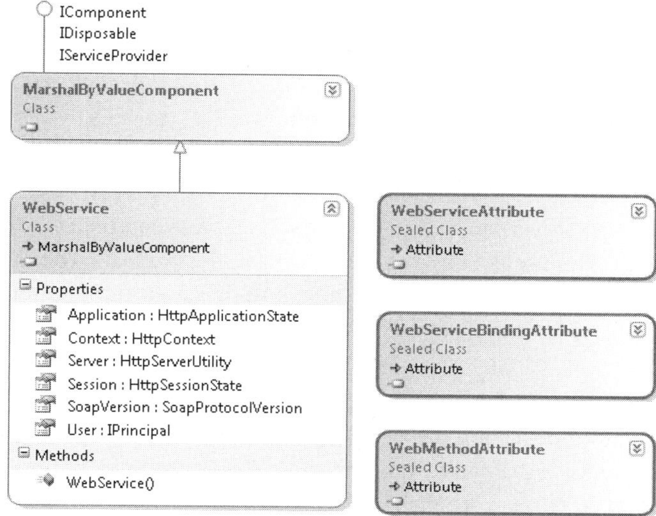

FIGURE 9-2 Classes related to creating ASP.NET Web services

Each of these classes controls how your Web service works and how ASP.NET and the compiler view your service code. You can inherit from the *WebService* class to get access to standard ASP.NET features. The attribute classes allow you to mark parts of your code as related to XML Web services. Items marked for use as Web services are identified by ASP.NET. It then knows how to deserialize requests for your service, call your service, and serialize the response. It also handles working with SOAP, XML, Web Services Description Language (WSDL), and the related Web service standards. You will see how each of these classes is used for creating Web services in the coming sections.

NOTE **WEB SERVICE DESIGN CONSIDERATIONS**

When you write a class that contains a Web service, it is important to remember that this class's calls will be across a network and across application domains. Calls to XML Web service calls are sent as messages through HTTP. These messages must be packaged (serialized) and unpackaged (deserialized) for transport in both directions. These types of calls, although powerful, can be expensive in terms of processing time. Therefore, you want to make the most of these calls. For this reason, you should define your methods to do a large amount of work and then return processing. You do not want, on the other hand, Web services that maintain state on the server and require a lot of smaller calls to access and set class data. These calls should be saved for working with in-process objects only.

ASP.NET Web Service Projects

Web services in ASP.NET are defined by an .asmx file. This file can be added directly to an existing Web site. This is useful if you intend for your Web site to expose Web services in addition to Web pages. Of course, you can also create a simple Web site and use it for only .asmx Web service files.

Another scenario is to create a Web service project through the Add New Project dialog box. Here, you select the ASP.NET Web service application. This generates a separate project for your Web service application. This project has a structure similar to a Web site. This includes a folder for App_Data, a Web.config file, and related elements. It is important to note that in both scenarios, your Web service is hosted within ASP.NET and therefore has access to its features (session state, security model, configuration, and so on).

Like a Web page, Web services are exposed through Uniform Resource Locators (URLs). This means your domain name followed by a page name, as in *http://MyDomain/MyService.asmx*. The page for an XML Web service is defined by the .asmx file. This file is nothing more than a simple text file that is used as a pointer to the code of your Web service.

You add an .asmx file to your site for each Web service you wish to expose. In this case, think of a Web service like a class that only exposes methods. Therefore, each Web service can expose multiple methods. As an example, suppose you wish to write an XML Web service that exposes methods related to working with the author data in Microsoft's sample database called *Pubs*. You might start by creating an .asmx file called Authors.asmx. This file would contain an *@ WebService* directive that points to the actual code for the Web service. The following is an example:

```
'VB
<%@ WebService Language="VB" CodeBehind="Authors.asmx.vb" Class="PubsServices.Authors"
%>

//C#
<%@ WebService Language="C#" CodeBehind="Authors.asmx.cs" Class="PubsServices.Authors"
%>
```

This markup is similar to what you would see for a Web page. However, there is no additional markup included inside a Web service. Instead, the Web service is defined entirely in code.

The *WebServiceAttribute* Class

Creating an .asmx file and exposing public methods marked as *WebMethod* (see later) is sufficient for defining Web services in ASP.NET. However, there are a number of other classes that can be used to provide additional functionality. One such class is the *WebServiceAttribute* class (recall that attribute classes can be used with or without the *Attribute* suffix). This class can be used to provide information about your Web service. This information is used by clients that wish to reference the Web service.

You can provide both a namespace and a description of your Web service by applying the *WebService* attribute and parameters to your class. The description parameter is simply text you write to identify the high-level intent of your Web service. The namespace parameter sets the namespace of your Web service. This should be a domain name under your control. Visual Studio uses the *tempuri.org* namespace as filler until you define your actual namespace.

As an example, imagine again that you are creating a Web service centered on exposing author information. You would define your class inside the code-behind file for the .asmx file. You could then add the *WebService* attribute to the class, as shown here:

```
'VB
<System.Web.Services.WebService(Description:="Services related to published authors",
  Namespace:="http://tempuri.org/")> _
Public Class Authors

//C#
[WebService(Description = "Services related to published authors",
  Namespace = "http://tempuri.org/")]
public class Authors
```

The *WebService* Class

The *WebService* class represents a base class for creating XML Web services in ASP.NET. This class is similar to the *Page* class for Web pages. It provides access to ASP.NET objects like *Application* and *Session*.

It is important to note that this class is optional: You do not need to inherit from this class to create XML Web services. Instead, you use this class as a base class only when you wish to access and use the features of an ASP.NET application. You might, for example, need to leverage session state between service calls. You could do so easily by first inheriting from this class and then accessing the session object as if you were coding an ASP.NET Web page.

The following code shows the authors example Web service. Here, the *Authors* class inherits directly from the *WebService* base class.

```
'VB
<System.Web.Services.WebService(Description:="Services related to published authors", _
  Namespace:="http://tempuri.org/")> _
Public Class Authors
  Inherits System.Web.Services.WebService

//C#
[WebService(Description = "Services related to published authors",
  Namespace = "http://tempuri.org/")]
public class Authors : System.Web.Services.WebService
```

The *WebMethodAttribute* Class

Your Web service exposes Web methods. Each of these methods provides some sort of functionality encapsulated by the Web service. Your class can identify these methods through the use of the *WebMethod* attribute. You apply this attribute to any public method in your Web service class you wish to expose as part of your service.

You can assign the *WebMethod* attribute to a class without setting any of the parameters of the *WebMethod* class. This simply identifies your method as a Web service method. However, the *WebMethod* attribute class also has a number of constructors used for various groups of parameter values. The parameters include the following:

- ***enableSessionState*** This parameter is used to indicate whether the given method should be able to work with session state. You set this value to *false* to disable the use of session state for the given Web method.
- ***transactionOption*** This parameter is used to indicate if your Web method supports transactions. The parameter is of the type *System.EnterpriseServices.TransactionOption*. Web services are stateless HTTP calls. Therefore, you can only use an XML Web service as the root of a transaction. This means the *TransactionOptions* that indicate a root transaction are equivalent (*Required*, *RequiresNew*). All other transaction options indicate no transaction support for the given service (*Disabled*, *NotSupported*, *Supported*).
- ***cacheDuration*** This parameter is used to define the number of seconds for which the response should be cached by the server. This is useful if your service has a high volume of access and the data is relatively static. In this case, you can cache results between calls to increase performance.
- ***bufferResponse*** This parameter is used to indicate whether the Web service response should be buffered back to the client.

Consider the author example. Imagine you have a public method called *GetAuthorTitles* that returns a list of titles based on the ID of a given author. Because this data only changes when an author publishes a new book, it is also a good candidate for caching. The following shows the *WebMethod* attribute applied to this method. Here, the *cacheDuration* parameter is set to 5 minutes (300 seconds).

```
'VB
<WebMethod(CacheDuration:=300)> _
Public Function GetAuthorTitles(ByVal authorId As String) As DataTable
  ...
End Function

//C#
[WebMethod(CacheDuration=300)]
public DataTable GetAuthorTitles(string authorId)
{ ... }
```

WEB SERVICES AND DATA TYPES

Notice that the previous example method, *GetAuthorTitles*, returns a *DataTable* object. This is possible as the object supports serialization. It can serialize itself into XML. Provided the calling client is also .NET, it can pick this XML up and deserialize it back into a strongly typed *DataTable*. In this case, ASP.NET does this for you without you having to really think about it.

You might also wish to provide instances of your own classes as return values of your functions or as parameters. You can do so by creating the object inside the Web service application. In this case, the compiler will take care of making the objects you expose serializable. These objects simply need a default constructor that does not accept parameters. You can also use the *Serializable* attribute class to tag class outside your Web service. This ensures any public members of the class can be serialized by ASP.NET.

Consuming an ASP.NET Web Service

You can consume an ASP.NET Web service in any application capable of making an HTTP call. This means most .NET application types can call Web services, including console applications, Windows-based applications, and ASP.NET. This section focuses on calling an XML Web service from an ASP.NET application.

Referencing a Web Service

To get started, you need to have access to a published Web service. This Web service can be published on a server or can be another project in your same solution. Either way, as long as it is a valid Web service, you will be able to subscribe to it.

The first step is setting a Web reference from your Web site to the given service. You do this by right-clicking your project file and choosing Set Web Reference. This opens the Add Web Reference dialog box. Here, you define the URL of your service, select the given service (.asmx file), and set a name for the reference. This name will be used by the generated proxy class to define the namespace for accessing your service. Figure 9-3 shows an example of connecting to the Authors.asmx service.

Once you have set the reference, Visual Studio and ASP.NET work to generate a *Proxy* class for working with the service. This allows you to write code against the service as if the service was just another class in your application. This proxy class does all the work of communicating to and from the Web service, serializing and deserializing data, and more.

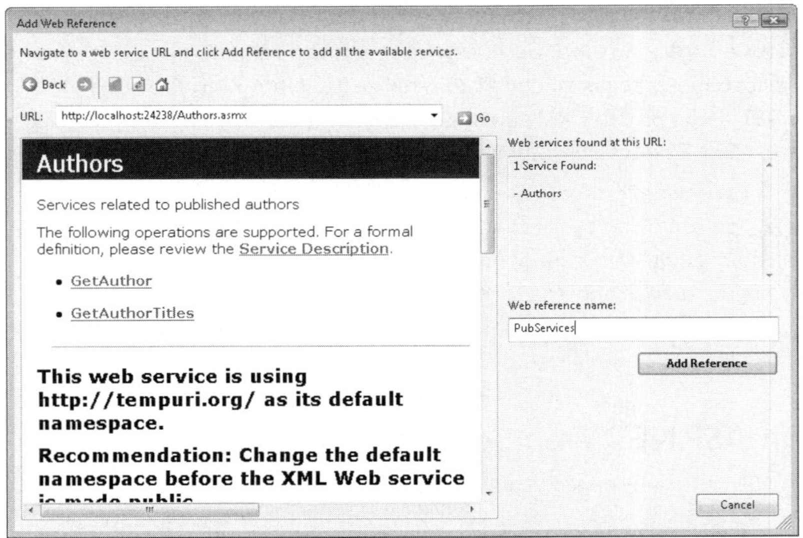

FIGURE 9-3 The Add Web Reference dialog box

As an example, the Authors.asmx file has two Web methods: *GetAuthor* and *GetAuthorTitles*. The first returns an instance of the *Author* class as embedded in the service class. The second returns a *DataTable*. To work with the *Author* class (of which the Web application knows nothing), Visual Studio generates this type from the WSDL of the Web service and puts it inside the proxy's namespace. Figure 9-4 shows an example of the contents inside the proxy namespace for the Author.asmx Web service reference.

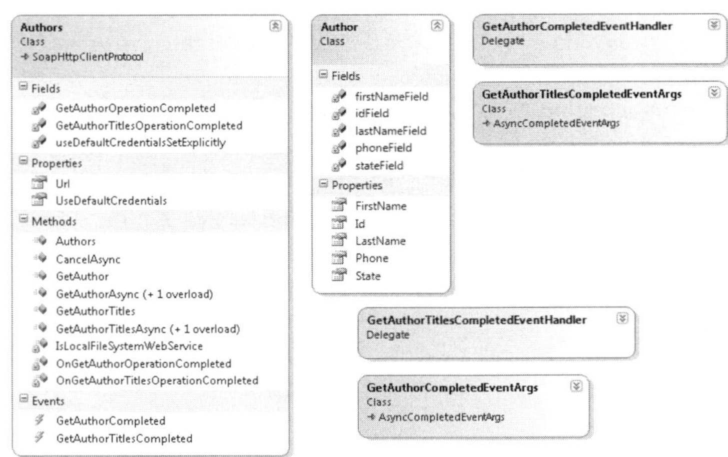

FIGURE 9-4 A Web service proxy for the *Authors* service

NOTE **WSDL.EXE**

Visual Studio includes the command-line tool WSDL.exe. You can use this tool to create a proxy class from an existing Web service. You specify the language of the proxy class and a URL to the Web service. The tool will use this information to generate a proxy class file.

Calling a Web Service

You call the Web service through the proxy. This is as simple as writing code to call a method. For example, the following code shows how you call the *GetAuthor* method from the Authors .asmx Web service discussed previously:

```
'VB
Dim pubs As New PubsServices.Authors()
Dim auth As PubsServices.Author = pubs.GetAuthor("213-46-8915")

Label1.Text = auth.FirstName + " " + auth.LastName

//C#
PubServices.Authors pubs = new PubServices.Authors();
PubServices.Author auth = pubs.GetAuthor();

Label1.Text = auth.FirstName + " " + auth.LastName;
```

Note that in the preceding example code, only the call to *GetAuthor* actually hits the Web service. The object creation and property gets are simply calls to the proxy object and are thus in-process calls.

You can also bind to the Web service call. Remember, the Web service is exposed through a local proxy object. Therefore, you can use object data binding to bind to the given Web service (via the proxy). As an example, recall the *GetAuthorTitles* Web service. This service is accessed via a proxy object method of the same name. You can set this method as the *SelectMethod* of an object data source as shown in the following code. You can then bind the results to a *GridView* control.

```
<asp:ObjectDataSource runat="server"
  ID="ObjectDataSourceAuthors"
  TypeName="PubsServices.Authors">
  SelectMethod="GetAuthorTitles"
  <SelectParameters>
    <asp:QueryStringParameter
      Name="authorId"
      QueryStringField="auId"
      Type="String" />
  </SelectParameters>
</asp:ObjectDataSource>
```

```
<asp:GridView ID="GridView1" runat="server"
  DataSourceID="ObjectDataSourceAuthors">
</asp:GridView>
```

Calling a Web Service from Client Script Using AJAX

You can use the AJAX functionality built into ASP.NET to call a Web service directly from client-side JavaScript. This is useful if you wish to kick off an operation on the server from the user's browser. When the results are returned, the user's browser can then be updated. Of course, this all takes place asynchronously and without a browser refresh. Refer back to Chapter 6, "Working with ASP.NET AJAX and Client-Side Scripting," if you need a quick review of ASP.NET and AJAX.

There are a number of steps required to set up your Web service and an AJAX client page. First, your client-side page and your XML Web service (.asmx file) must be in the same domain. From there, you should be sure to perform all of the following steps:

- Mark your Web service class with the *ScriptServiceAttribute* class. This indicates that the Web methods inside the Web service can be called from client script.
- Register the HTTP handler *ScriptHandlerFactory* with your Web site. You can do so inside the *<system.Web><httpHandlers>* element in the Web.config file. Depending on your project, this handler might already be set.
- Add a *ScriptManager* control to your client page. The *ScriptManager* control is required for all AJAX-enabled pages. However, inside it you need to set a *ServiceReference*. This reference should point to the XML Web service (.asmx file). Doing so will tell ASP.NET to generate a JavaScript client proxy to your Web service.
- Add a JavaScript method to your page. You can add code inside this method to call your Web service through the client-side proxy generated by ASP.NET. Your Web method can be referenced through the class name of the Web service and the method name of the Web method. Of course, you can, optionally, pass parameters to the Web service.
- Optionally, you can add another JavaScript method to your client page to serve as the callback handler. This method will be called by the JavaScript proxy and receive the results of the Web service call. You can use this method to update the user.

As an example, imagine you have a simple Web service that takes a Fahrenheit value and returns its Celsius equivalent. For starters, you would mark the Web service with the *ScriptService* attribute. The following shows an example:

```
'VB
<System.Web.Script.Services.ScriptService()> _
<WebService(Namespace:="http://tempuri.org/")> _
Public Class TempConversion
  Inherits System.Web.Services.WebService

  <WebMethod()> _
```

```
  Public Function GetCelsius(ByVal temperature As Single) As Single
    Return (5 / 9) * (temperature - 32)
  End Function

End Class
```

```
//C#
[System.Web.Script.Services.ScriptService]
[WebService(Namespace = "http://tempuri.org/")]
public class TempConversion : System.Web.Services.WebService
{
  [WebMethod]
  public float GetCelsius(float temperature)
  {
    return (5 / 9) * (temperature - 32);
  }
}
```

Next, you need to make sure the HTTP handler *ScriptHandlerFactory* is registered with your site inside the Web.config file. The following shows an example:

```
<httpHandlers>
  <remove verb="*" path="*.asmx" />
  <add verb="*" path="*.asmx" validate="false"
    type="System.Web.Script.Services.ScriptHandlerFactory" />
</httpHandlers>
```

You now need to create a client Web page. Remember, this Web page must be in the same domain as the Web service. Inside the Web page markup, you add a *ScriptManager* control. This control should be set to reference the actual Web service (.asmx file). The following shows an example of this markup:

```
<asp:ScriptManager runat="server" ID="ScriptManager1">
  <Services>
    <asp:ServiceReference
       path="TempConversion.asmx" />
  </Services>
</asp:ScriptManager>
```

The next step would be to add JavaScript functionality to call the Web service, passing the user's input. In addition, you need to write a simple callback function that takes the results and displays them to the user. The following code demonstrates this. The user input is inside the *TextBoxTemp* and the results are shown using *LabelResults*.

```
<script type="text/javascript">
  function GetCelsius()
  {
    var val = document.getElementById("TextBoxTemp");
```

```
    TempConversion.GetCelsius(val.value, FinishCallback);
  }

  function FinishCallback(result)
  {
    var results = document.getElementById("LabelResults");
    results.innerHTML = result;
  }
</script>
```

Finally, you need to add the remaining markup to the page. This simply consists of the user input information. The following shows an example:

```
Enter Fahrenheit Temperature:<br />
<asp:TextBox ID="TextBoxTemp" runat="server"></asp:TextBox> 
<asp:Label ID="LabelResults" runat="server" Text=""></asp:Label>
<br />
<input id="Button1" type="button" value="Calculate" onclick="GetCelsius()" />
```

Notice that in this markup, the *GetCelsius* JavaScript method defined earlier is called when the user clicks the Calculate button. This triggers the Web service. The results are returned to the *FinishCallback* JavaScript method and then displayed in the *Label* control. Figure 9-5 shows the call in action.

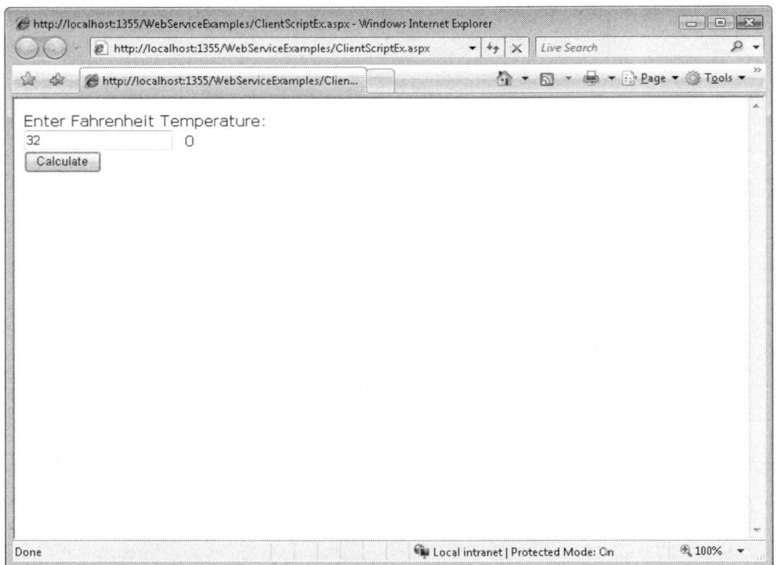

FIGURE 9-5 The Web service call from a Web browser

Security and XML Web Services

You have two primary options for securing XML Web services written as .asmx files and hosted by ASP.NET. The first is to use one of the standard ASP.NET security methods to authenticate and authorize users. This option is similar to securing any ASP.NET resources such as a Web page, directory, or other file. The second approach is to write a custom security model using SOAP headers. This option can be useful if your calling clients cannot participate in the standard, Windows-based security models used by ASP.NET.

ASP.NET Security

There a number of ways you can use the authentication and authorization methods of ASP.NET to secure your XML Web services. Thankfully, these options are not much different from securing other ASP.NET resources. This is a result of the Web service working much like a Web page. They both have a URL that points to a file. You can therefore lock down this file like you would any ASP.NET resource.

Each ASP.NET security option comes with performance versus security trade-offs. As an example, if you are processing sensitive information such as social security numbers, credit cards, and the like, you will want to encrypt this data as it travels over the network. However, this encryption will decrease performance as the calls have to be encrypted and decrypted, and the messages themselves will be larger. On the other hand, if you are sending basic information to and from the Web service (such as a part numbers, category identifiers, or similar details), you can relax the need for encryption and focus instead on authenticating and authorizing a user. This will help increase your performance and throughput. If your Web service is meant to be public (either inside or outside the firewall), you can always provide anonymous access to your Web service.

The first step in setting up your security model is determining a method for authentication. This means determining who the user actually is. The second is to decide if the user has authorization rights to actually access the Web service or the features the Web service exposes. The following list describes the basic ASP.NET security methods and a brief description of how they can be applied to Web services for both authentication and authorization.

- **Windows Basic Authentication** You use basic authentication to restrict rights to authorized users. In this case, the users are defined on the Web server and are given file-based access rights to the site or the service. When a user hits your service, they are challenged to provide credentials. Of course, these credentials can be provided by the calling client (and not the actual user). However, basic authentication sends the user and password information from the client to the server in clear text. This can be helpful if your clients are non-Windows clients. However, as the information is encoded (and not encrypted), it can be intercepted by network monitoring tools and compromised.
- **Windows Basic Authentication over SSL** This version of basic authentication encrypts the calls over Secure Sockets Layer (SSL). This adds additional security to this type of authentication as the name and password are encrypted. However, the entire

communication, in this scenario, is also encrypted. Therefore, while you gain in security, you lose in performance.

- **Client certificates** You can use client certificates to identify both the caller and the Web service. Certificates, in this case, are obtained from a trusted, third-party certificate authority. The client's certificate is presented with the service call and verified as trusted. You can then use Windows to map the certificate to an actual user account. You then use the user account to define access to the given service resource.
- **Windows digest** This is similar to Windows Basic. However, digest sends the user's password in a hashed, encrypted format so it cannot be compromised. This option does not require SSL and will often work through default firewalls. However, platforms outside of Windows do not support Windows digest security.
- **Forms-based authentication** Forms-based authentication is not supported for Web service scenarios.
- **Windows Integrated** You can use Windows Integrated security to securely pass encrypted credentials from the client to the server. However, this option requires that both the client and the server are running Windows.

If you are accessing a secured service from the user's browser, it can pass the credentials on to the Web server where they will be evaluated for authentication. In the case of Windows Integrated security, you must be using Microsoft Internet Explorer on the client. That said, user client calls to a Web service is an unlikely scenario with Web services. It is more likely that you will be calling a Web service from code inside your Web site (running server-side).

To pass basic authentication credentials from your Web server to a Web service, you first create a *NetworkCredentials* class. This class contains the user name, password, and domain information. You can then create a *CredentialCache* object to which you add the *NetworkCredentials* instance. You then set the Web service's generated client proxy's *Credentials* property to the newly created *CredentialCache* object.

If you are using integrated security between the Web server and the Web service, you set the *Credentials* property of the Web service proxy class to *System.Net.CredentialCache.DefaultCredentials*. The Web server running your Web page will then pass credentials to the Web service.

> ***NOTE*** **SETTING UP ASP.NET SECURITY**
>
> **Configuring and setting up ASP.NET security is similar for both Web services and ASP.NET pages. Therefore, it is covered in Chapter 14, "Implementing User Profiles, Authentication, and Authorization." You can also review the section "How to: Configure an XML Web Service for Windows Authentication" on MSDN for additional context.**

Custom Security with SOAP Headers

You can also use SOAP headers to write a custom mechanism for passing user information into a Web service. Because this option uses Web service standards and not Windows, you can use it to work in scenarios where you require access to your service from other platforms besides Windows.

Custom SOAP headers can be used in a secure, encrypted manner. However, the encryption is optional and up to you to write (using the .NET Framework, of course). You can also use SOAP headers to send information to the service as plaintext (unencrypted). This is useful if you need to pass along information or you are behind a trusted firewall. It is not, however, a best practice to send unencrypted user information (name and password) using a SOAP header.

There are no default, built-in features for working with custom SOAP headers in authentication scenarios. Instead, both the client and the service need to be aware of how to format and pass the header information. In addition, on the server, you need to implement the *IHttpModule* interface to intercept the SOAP request, get the SOAP header, and parse (and decrypt) the user information. If the operation fails, you throw a *SoapException* instance.

MORE INFO **USING CUSTOM SOAP HEADERS**

For more information on implementing custom SOAP headers in ASP.NET, see the topic "Perform Custom Authentication Using SOAP Headers" on MSDN.

Quick Check

1. What type of file do you use to create an XML Web service?
2. What is the name of the attribute class you apply to your Web service?
3. How do you identify a method as exposed as part of a Web service?

Quick Check Answers

1. You add a new .asmx file to a Web site to create an XML Web service.
2. You use the *WebServiceAttribute* class to mark a class as an XML Web service.
3. You use the *WebMethodAttribute* class to tag a method as a Web method.

LAB Creating and Consuming ASP.NET Web Services

In this lab, you create a Web service that works with information in the *Pubs* database. You then create a Web client interface to call that Web service.

If you encounter a problem completing an exercise, the completed projects are available in the samples installed from the companion CD.

EXERCISE 1 Creating an ASP.NET Web Service

In this exercise, you create the Web Service application project and define a Web service.

1. Open Visual Studio and create a new ASP.NET Web Service Application project using either C# or Visual Basic. Name the project **PubsServices**.
2. Add the Pubs.mdf file to the App_Data directory of the Web Service application. You can get the database file in the samples installed from this book's companion CD.
3. Delete Service.asmx (and its code-behind file) from your project. Add a new service file called **Authors.asmx** by right-clicking the project and choosing Add New Item. Select the Web Service template from the Add New Item dialog box.
4. Open the code-behind file for Authors.asmx in the code editor. Delete the default code in the service file template. Add a new class definition for the Authors service. There is no need to inherit from the *WebService* class as this service does not use the features of ASP.NET. Tag the class with the *WebServiceAttribute* class and pass a default namespace. Your class definition should look similar to the following:

```
'VB
<WebService(Namespace:="http://tempuri.org/")> _
Public Class Authors

End Class

//C#
namespace PubsServices
{
  [WebService(Namespace = "http://tempuri.org/")]
  public class Authors
  {

  }
}
```

5. Open the Web.config file. Find the *<connectionStrings />* element. Add markup to define a connection to the *pubs.mdf* database. The following shows an example (formatted to fit on the printed page):

```
<connectionStrings>
  <add name="PubsConnectionString" connectionString="Data Source=.\SQLEXPRESS;
    AttachDbFilename=|DataDirectory|\pubs.mdf;Integrated Security=True;
    User Instance=True" providerName="System.Data.SqlClient"/>
</connectionStrings>
```

6. Return to the .asmx service file. Add *using* (*Imports* in Visual Basic) statements to the class file for *System.Data*, *System.Data.SqlClient*, and *System.Configuration*.

7. Add a private variable at the class level to store the connection string to the *Pubs* database. Name this variable *_cnnString*, as shown in the following code:

```
'VB
Private _cnnString As String = _
  ConfigurationManager.ConnectionStrings("PubsConnectionString").ToString

//C#
private string _cnnString =
  ConfigurationManager.ConnectionStrings["PubsConnectionString"].ToString();
```

8. Add a method to the class to return all titles for a given author based on their *authorId*. These authors can be returned as a *DataTable* instance. Name this method *GetAuthorTitles*.

9. Tag the *GetAuthorTitles* method with the *WebMethodAttribute* class. Set the *CacheDuration* to 300 seconds. Your method should look as follows:

```
'VB
<WebMethod(CacheDuration:=300)> _
Public Function GetAuthorTitles(ByVal authorId As String) As DataTable

  Dim sql As String = "SELECT titles.title, titles.type, titles.price, " & _
    "titles.pubdate FROM titleauthor INNER JOIN titles ON " & _
    "titleauthor.title_id = titles.title_id "
  If authorId <> "0" Then sql = sql & " WHERE (titleauthor.au_id = @AuthorId)"

  Dim cnn As New SqlConnection(_cnnString)
  Dim cmd As New SqlCommand(sql, cnn)
  cmd.Parameters.Add("AuthorId", SqlDbType.VarChar, 11).Value = authorId

  Dim adp As New SqlDataAdapter(cmd)
  Dim ds As New DataSet()

  adp.Fill(ds)

  Return ds.Tables(0)

End Function

//C#
[WebMethod(CacheDuration = 300)]
public DataTable GetAuthorTitles(string authorId)
{
  string sql = "SELECT titles.title, titles.type, titles.price, " +
    "titles.pubdate FROM titleauthor INNER JOIN titles ON " +
```

```
        "titleauthor.title_id = titles.title_id ";
        if(authorId != "0")
          sql = sql + " WHERE (titleauthor.au_id = @AuthorId) ";

      SqlConnection cnn = new SqlConnection(_cnnString);
      SqlCommand cmd = new SqlCommand(sql, cnn);
      cmd.Parameters.Add("AuthorId", SqlDbType.VarChar, 11).Value = authorId;

      SqlDataAdapter adp = new SqlDataAdapter(cmd);
      DataSet ds = new DataSet();

      adp.Fill(ds);

      return ds.Tables[0];
    }
```

10. Compile your application and make sure there are no errors.

EXERCISE 2 Consuming an ASP.NET Web Service

In this exercise, you create a client for accessing an ASP.NET Web service.

1. Continue editing the project you created in the previous exercise. Alternatively, you can open the completed Lesson 1, Exercise 1 project in the samples installed from the CD.
2. Add a new Web site to the solution: Right-click the solution and choose Add | New Web Site. Select the ASP.NET Web Site template. Name the Web site **PubsClient**. Right-click the Web site and choose Set As StartUp Project.
3. Add a Web reference to the Web service created in Exercise 1. Start by right-clicking the Web site; choose Add Web Reference. In the Add Web Reference dialog box, select Web Services In This Solution. This should display the Authors service; click it. On the right side of the dialog box, change the Web reference name to **PubsService**. Finish by clicking Add Reference.

> ***NOTE*** **VIEWING THE GENERATED PROXY CLASS**
>
> **If you want to see the generated proxy class, you should change your project type from Web Site to Web Application. In this case, your code is compiled as .dll files and the generated code is exposed. For Web sites, Visual Studio generates code and compiles it on demand.**

4. Open the Default.aspx page in your Web site. Add an object data source control to the page. Configure it to use the Web service proxy class. Set the *authorId* parameter to be set via the query string value *auId*.

Add a *GridView* control to the page and set its *DataSourceId* property to the object data source. Your markup should look as follows:

```
<asp:ObjectDataSource runat="server"
  ID="ObjectDataSourceAuthors"
  TypeName="PubsService.Authors"
  SelectMethod="GetAuthorTitles">
  <SelectParameters>
    <asp:QueryStringParameter
      Name="authorId"
      QueryStringField="auId"
      Type="String"
      DefaultValue="0" />
  </SelectParameters>
</asp:ObjectDataSource>

<asp:GridView ID="GridView1" runat="server"
  DataSourceID="ObjectDataSourceAuthors">
</asp:GridView>
```

5. Run the application to see the results.

Lesson Summary

- You create an XML Web service in ASP.NET by defining an .asmx file. You use the attribute class *WebServiceAttribute* to mark a class as a Web service. You use the *WebMethod* attribute class to define the methods on that class that should be exposed as Web services. You can also inherit from *WebService* if you intend to use the features of ASP.NET (like session) inside your service.
- You can consume an XML Web service in an ASP.NET Web site by setting a Web reference to it. This generates a proxy class for you. You can program against the proxy as if the Web service were actually running on the same server. The proxy class handles the rest.
- You can call a Web service from the client using ASP.NET AJAX extensions. You use the *ScriptManager* class to reference a Web service that is in the same domain as the given Web page. A JavaScript client proxy is then generated for you. You can use this proxy to call your Web service. ASP.NET AJAX takes care of the rest.
- You secure a Web service in ASP.NET as you would any other ASP.NET resource. You can also define custom Web service security through custom SOAP headers.

Lesson Review

You can use the following questions to test your knowledge of the information in Lesson 1, "Creating and Consuming XML Web Services." The questions are also available on the companion CD if you prefer to review them in electronic form.

> ***NOTE*** **ANSWERS**
>
> **Answers to these questions and explanations of why each answer choice is right or wrong are located in the "Answers" section at the end of the book.**

1. You wish to create a new Web service that will expose multiple methods that are meant to work with user-specific data through a transaction. You decide to use ASP.NET session state to manage the user's context on the server between Web service requests. How shoul d you define your Web service?
   - **A.** Define a class that inherits from *WebServiceAttribute*.
   - **B.** Define a class that inherits from *WebService*.
   - **C.** Define a class that inherits from *WebMethodAttribute*.
   - **D.** Do not inherit from a base class. Hosting the Web service in ASP.NET is sufficient.
2. You wish to consume an existing Web service from your ASP.NET Web site. What actions should you take? (Choose all that apply.)
   - **A.** Use the Add Reference dialog box to set a reference to the .wsdl file that contains the Web service.
   - **B.** Use the Add Web Reference dialog box to point to the URL of the given Web service.
   - **C.** Write a method in your Web site that has the same function signature as your Web service. Do not implement this method. Instead, mark it with the *WebMethod* attribute.
   - **D.** Call a proxy class that represents calling your Web service.
3. You need to secure your Web service. The service will be accessed over the Internet by multiple, different systems. Authentication information should be secured. You wish to trust only those callers that have been verified as trusted. What type of security should you consider?
   - **A.** Windows Basic
   - **B.** Windows digest
   - **C.** Client certificates
   - **D.** Custom SOAP headers

4. You wish to write a Web service and call it from client-side script. What actions should you take? (Choose all that apply.)

   A. Add the *ScriptService* attribute to the Web service class.

   B. Make sure the *ScriptHandlerFactory* is registered for your Web site inside the Web .config file.

   C. Add a *ScriptManager* class to your Web page. Set the *ServiceReference* to point to the .asmx Web service.

   D. Make sure your Web page and service are in the same domain.

Lesson 2: Creating and Consuming WCF Services

In the previous lesson, you learned about creating XML Web services with ASP.NET. This is a very useful, straightforward way to create Web services that you intend to host in IIS and call over HTTP. However, the service model can be extended beyond HTTP. For example, you might want to write a service that is accessed inside the firewall over Transmission Control Protocol (TCP) instead of HTTP. This can provide increased performance in this scenario. In earlier versions of the .NET Framework, this meant you wrote the service using Remoting. However, if that same service code needed to be called over both HTTP and TCP, you had to write and host it twice. This is one of the many problems WCF is meant to solve.

WCF is a unifying programming model. It is meant to define a singular way for writing services and thereby unify things like Web services (.asmx), .NET Remoting, Message Queue (MSMQ), Enterprise Services (COM+), and Web Services Enhancements (WSE). It does not replace these technologies on an individual basis. Instead, it provides a single programming model that you can use to take advantage of all of these items at once. With WCF, you can create a single service that can be exposed as HTTP, TCP, named pipes, and so on. You also have multiple hosting options.

This lesson covers the basics of WCF to give you a solid footing when working with this technology. This lesson is not all-encompassing on WCF. Rather, it focuses on those areas inside WCF that are specific to an ASP.NET developer: writing, hosting, and calling WCF services with ASP.NET Web sites.

After this lesson, you will be able to:

- Understand the architecture of WCF.
- Create a WCF service in ASP.NET and host it.
- Call a WCF service from an ASP.NET Web page.

Estimated lesson time: 45 minutes

Presenting Windows Communication Foundation (WCF)

Before you build your first WCF service application, it is important to get an overview of how the technology works. WCF enables message-based communication to and from endpoints. You write your service and then attach, or configure, endpoints. A given service can have one or more endpoints attached to it. Each WCF *endpoint* defines a location to which messages are sent and received. This location includes an address, a binding, and a contract. This address, binding, and contract concept is often referred to as the ABCs of WCF. The following list describes each of these items in detail:

- **A is for address** The endpoint's address is the location of the service as a Uniform Resource Identifier (URI). Each endpoint of a given service is meant to have a unique address. Therefore, if you have a service that exposes more than one endpoint (or transport protocol), you will uniquely identify the address based on the endpoint's transport protocol. This might mean changing a port number, defining the address as HTTPS, or taking a similar action.
- **B is for binding** The binding defines how the service is meant to communicate, such as HTTP, TCP, MSMQ, Binary HTTP, and so on. This is referred to as the binding's *transport*. You can add multiple bindings to a single service. Bindings can include other information, too, like encoding and security. Each binding must, at a minimum, define a transport.
- **C is for contract** The contract represents the public definition, or interface, of the service. It defines things like the namespace of the service, how messages should be sent, callbacks, and related contract items. There are multiple contract types in WCF, including service contract, operation contract, message contract, fault contract (for error handling), and data contract. These contracts work together to indicate to the client code consuming the WCF service how it should define communication messages.

Once you define your WCF service and configure at least one endpoint, you must host it. There are a few options here, which are discussed in a moment. However, the one host this lesson focuses on is IIS and ASP.NET. To call the service, a client generates a compatible endpoint. This endpoint indicates where the service is, how communication should work, and the format of that communication. At run time, clients typically initiate requests to a listening, hosted service. Like a Web service, the WCF service processes the request and returns results—all using the defined endpoint information.

The good news is that there are multiple tools and configuration support for creating WCF services. Again, it is still important to understand how this works. As an additional overview, the following section presents the layers of the WCF architecture.

The Layers of the WCF Architecture

A WCF application has multiple layers that work together to provide a wide range of functionality and options for building a service-oriented application (SOA). For the most part, these layers are behind the scenes and the configuration of services is done for you or through configuration tools that make it easier. Figure 9-6 shows an overview of the core layers of a WCF application.

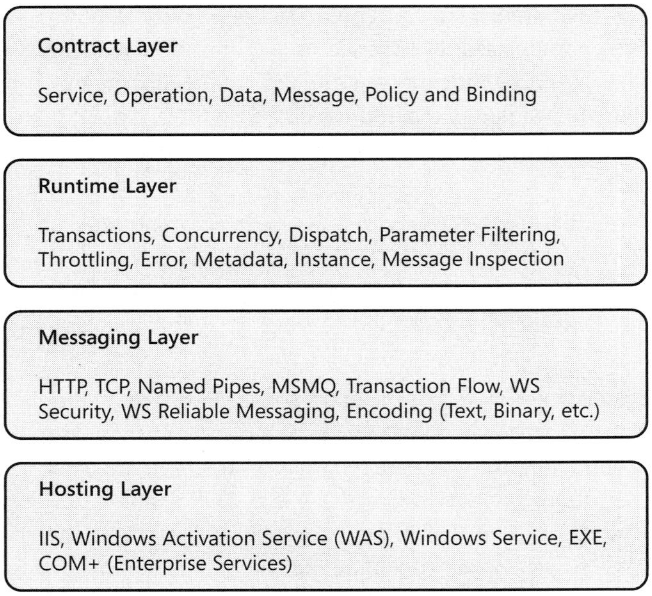

Contract Layer

Service, Operation, Data, Message, Policy and Binding

Runtime Layer

Transactions, Concurrency, Dispatch, Parameter Filtering, Throttling, Error, Metadata, Instance, Message Inspection

Messaging Layer

HTTP, TCP, Named Pipes, MSMQ, Transaction Flow, WS Security, WS Reliable Messaging, Encoding (Text, Binary, etc.)

Hosting Layer

IIS, Windows Activation Service (WAS), Windows Service, EXE, COM+ (Enterprise Services)

FIGURE 9-6 The layers of the WCF architecture

It is important to understand these layers and the many options they provide you as a service developer. The following list provides an overview of each layer.

- **Contract layer** The contract layer is meant to define the contract your service exposes to end clients. This includes the message the service supports for calling operations, receiving results, and managing errors. In addition, the contract includes the endpoint information of policy and binding. For example, the contract might indicate that the service requires HTTP with a binary encoding.
- **Runtime layer** The service runtime layer controls how your service is executed and how the message body is processed. You can configure this layer to support transactions, handle concurrency, and emit error information. For example, you can use throttling to indicate the number of messages your service can process; you can use the instance functionality to indicate how many instances of your service should be created to manage requests.
- **Messaging layer** The messaging layer represents the WCF channel stack in terms of transport and protocol. Transport channels work to convert messages to work across HTTP, named pipes, TCP, and related protocols. Protocol channels work to process messages for things like reliability and security.
- **Hosting layer** The hosting layer defines the host, or executable, that runs the service in process. Services can be self-hosted (run in an executable), hosted by IIS, Windows Activation Service (WAS), a Windows Service, or COM+. Picking a host for your service depends on a number of factors like client access, scalability, reliability, and the need

for other services of the host (like ASP.NET). In most enterprise application cases, you will want to use an existing host for your service rather than writing your own.

You can see there are many options for creating, configuring, and hosting a wide array of services. Again, this chapter covers building, hosting, and calling WCF services with respect to ASP.NET (HTTP transport and IIS hosting).

Creating a WCF Service with ASP.NET

Creating and consuming WCF services follow a standard set of programming tasks. You follow these steps every time you wish to create and consume a new WCF service:

1. Define the service contract.
2. Implement (or write) the service contract.
3. Configure a service endpoint(s).
4. Host the service in an application.
5. Reference and call the service from a client application.

As you can see, a WCF service application starts with the contract. This contract indicates the features and functionality your service will offer to calling clients. In WCF programming, you create this contract by first defining an interface and decorating that interface with a number of attributes. Figure 9-7 shows an overview of the key WCF attribute classes.

FIGURE 9-7 The attribute classes used by WCF services

These WCF attribute classes are found in the *System.ServiceModel* namespace. These classes are used to define the details of the contract that your service will have with calling clients. For example, you can indicate if your service contract is one-way, request-reply, or duplex. These attributes also define your service operations and the data that define these operations. The following list provides a description for each of these classes.

- ***ServiceContract*** The *ServiceContract* attribute class is used to indicate that a given interface (or class) is a WCF service. The *ServiceContract* attribute class has parameters for setting things like whether the service requires a session (*SessionMode*), the namespace, the name of the contract, the return contract on a two-way contract (*CallbackContract*), and more.

- ***OperationContract*** The *OperationContract* attribute class is used to mark methods inside an interface (or class) as service operations. Methods marked with *OperationContract* represent those exposed by the service to clients. You can use the parameters of the *OperationContract* attribute class to set things like whether the contract does not return a reply (*IsOneWay*), the message-level security (*ProtectionLevel*), or whether the method supports asynchronous calls (AsyncPattern).
- ***DataContract*** The *DataContract* attribute class is used to mark types you write (classes, enumerations, structures) as participating in WCF serialization via the *DataContractSerializer.* Marking your classes with this attribute ensures they can be sent to and from disparate clients in an efficient manner.
- ***DataMember*** The *DataMember* attribute class is used to mark individual fields and properties that you want to serialize. You use this class in conjunction with the *DataContract* class.

The WCF Service Application

Visual Studio and ASP.NET define the WCF Service Application project template. This template defines a Web project that serves to host the WCF service. This project contains a reference to *System.ServiceModel.dll,* which contains the WCF classes. Creating a new instance of this project template will also generate a default service (Service1.svc) and a related contract file (IService1.vb or .cs).

The contract file is a regular .NET Framework interface that includes the service attribute classes tagging the service (class), the operations (methods), and the data members (types, fields, properties). The .svc file is a class that implements this interface. Like other ASP.NET templates, you can use these classes to create your own service.

Finally, a WCF Service application is automatically configured to be hosted in IIS and expose a standard HTTP endpoint. This information can be found inside the *<system.servicemodel>* section of the Web.config file. The following code shows an example:

```
<system.serviceModel>
  <services>
    <service name="NorthwindServices.Service1"
      behaviorConfiguration="NorthwindServices.Service1Behavior">
      <endpoint address="" binding="wsHttpBinding"
        contract="NorthwindServices.IService1">
        <identity>
          <dns value="localhost"/>
        </identity>
      </endpoint>
      <endpoint address="mex" binding="mexHttpBinding" contract="IMetadataExchange"/>
    </service>
  </services>
```

```
  <behaviors>
    <serviceBehaviors>
      <behavior name="NorthwindServices.Service1Behavior">
        <!-- to avoid disclosing metadata information, set the value below to false
             and remove the metadata endpoint above before deployment -->
        <serviceMetadata httpGetEnabled="true"/>
        <!-- To receive exception details in faults for debugging purposes, set the
             value below to true.  Set to false before deployment to avoid disclosing
             exception information -->
        <serviceDebug includeExceptionDetailInFaults="false"/>
      </behavior>
    </serviceBehaviors>
  </behaviors>
</system.serviceModel>
```

As you can see, the WCF Service application in ASP.NET takes care of many of the common steps to a WCF service. In fact, steps 1, 3, and 4, as discussed previously, are taken care of by default. That leaves step 2, implement the service, and step 5, call the service from a client application.

Implementing the WCF Service

To implement the service, you start by defining the contract via the interface. For example, suppose you wish to create a service that exposes methods that work with the Shippers table in the *Northwind* database. You might start by creating a *Shipper* class and marking it as a *DataContract* and marking its members as *DataMembers*. This allows you to pass the *Shipper* class in and out of the service. The following code shows an example:

```
'VB
<DataContract()> _
Public Class Shipper

  Private _shipperId As Integer

  <DataMember()> _
  Public Property ShipperId() As Integer
    'implement property (see lab)
  End Property

  'implement remaining properties (see lab)

End Class

//C#
[DataContract]
public class Shipper
{
```

```
    [DataMember]
    public int ShipperId { get; set; }

    //implement remaining properties (see lab)
}
```

The next step is to define the methods of your interface. You need to mark those with the *OperationContract* attribute. You need to mark the interface with the *ServiceContract* attribute. For example, suppose the shipping service exposes operations for retrieving a single shipper and saving a single shipper. In this case, your interface should look as follows:

```
'VB
<ServiceContract()> _
Public Interface IShipperService

    <OperationContract()> _
    Function GetShipper(ByVal shipperId As Integer) As Shipper

    <OperationContract()> _
    Sub SaveShipper(ByVal shipper As Shipper)

End Interface

//C#
[ServiceContract]
public interface IShipperService
{
    [OperationContract]
    Shipper GetShipper(int shipperId);

    [OperationContract]
    Shipper SaveShipper(Shipper shipper);
}
```

This interface will be used by WCF to expose a service. Of course, the service will be configured based on the information inside the Web.config file. The service interface also still needs to be implemented. To do so, you implement the service interface inside an .svc file. For example, if you were to implement the interface contract defined previously for working with the Shipper data, you would do so as the following code demonstrates:

```
'VB
Public Class ShipperService
    Implements IShipperService

    Public Function GetShipper(ByVal shipperId As Integer) As Shipper _
        Implements IShipperService.GetShipper

        'code to get the shipper from the db and return it (see lab)
```

```
  End Function

  Public Sub SaveShipper(ByVal shipper As Shipper) _
    Implements IShipperService.SaveShipper

    'code to save the shipper to the db (see lab)

  End Sub

End Class

//C#
public class ShipperService : IShipperService
{
  private string _cnnString =
    ConfigurationManager.ConnectionStrings["NwConnectionString"].ToString();

  public Shipper GetShipper(int shipperId)
  {
    //code to get the shipper from the db and return it (see lab)
  }

  public void SaveShipper(Shipper shipper)
  {
    //code to save the shipper to the db (see lab)
  }
}
```

Consuming a WCF Service in an ASP.NET Page

You are now ready to call the WCF service created previously. The contract is defined via the *IShipperService* interface. The contract is implemented inside the *ShipperService.svc* file. An endpoint is configured via the default HTTP endpoint set up inside the Web.config file. The service is hosted by IIS and ASP.NET (or your local Web server). The final step is to set a client to call the service. In this case, we assume the client is another ASP.NET Web site. However, it could easily be a Windows application or another application on a different platform.

To start, you need to generate a proxy class for calling the WCF service. This can be done using Visual Studio. You right-click your Web site and select Add Service Reference. This opens the Add Service Reference dialog box, as shown in Figure 9-8.

This dialog box allows you to define an address to your service. Again, this is based on the endpoint that your service exposes. In this example, a connection is being made to the ShipperService.svc created in the prior section. Notice how the contract is shown via the service's interface.

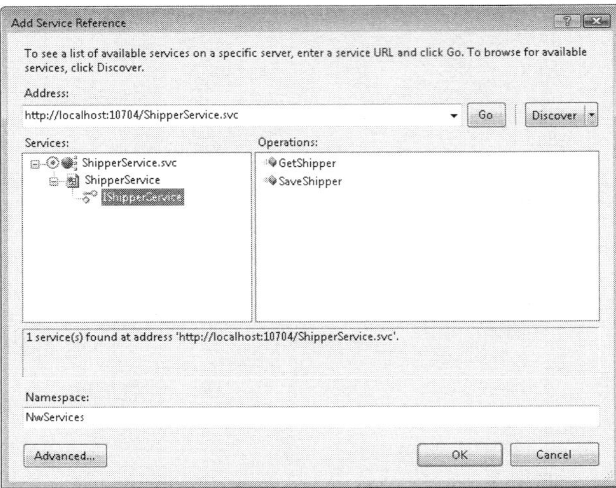

FIGURE 9-8 The Add Service Reference dialog box for generating a WCF service client

Notice in Figure 9-8 that a namespace was set. The namespace defines the name for the proxy class that is generated by Visual Studio. This proxy class is a WCF service client that allows you to program against the service without having to deal with the intricacies of WCF. This is similar to how you worked with Web services in the prior lesson.

You can view the contents of the service reference by selecting Show All Files from Solution Explorer. Of course, this only works with a Web application (and not a Web site). Figure 9-9 shows the many files of this service reference.

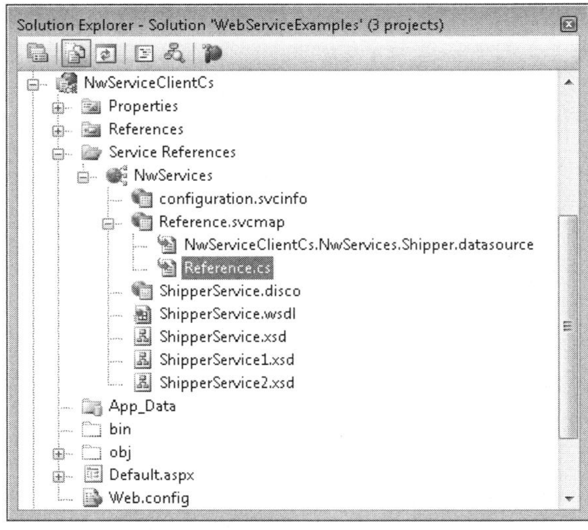

FIGURE 9-9 The Service Reference expanded inside of Solution Explorer

The file Reference.cs (or .vb) contains the actual proxy class. The other files are used by this proxy class when working with the service. This proxy class communicates with the Web service. In fact, it contains classes and methods that look just like those of the service, thanks to the service contract. Figure 9-10 shows an overview of the types found inside Reference .cs (or .vb). Notice you can call the *ShipperServiceClient* code and even pass a local type called *Shipper* that contains the same properties defined by the service contract.

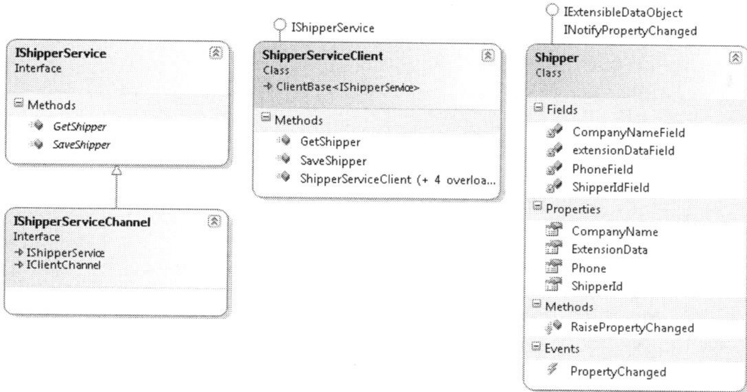

FIGURE 9-10 The generated service client proxy types

Your client code must also define binding and endpoint information. The Add Service Reference task generates the appropriate endpoint information automatically when you add the service reference. This information can be found inside the Web.config file of the service client Web site. The following shows an example:

```
<system.serviceModel>
  <bindings>
    <wsHttpBinding>
      <binding name="WSHttpBinding_IShipperService" closeTimeout="00:01:00"
          openTimeout="00:01:00" receiveTimeout="00:10:00" sendTimeout="00:01:00"
          bypassProxyOnLocal="false" transactionFlow="false"
          hostNameComparisonMode="StrongWildcard" maxBufferPoolSize="524288"
          maxReceivedMessageSize="65536" messageEncoding="Text"
          textEncoding="utf-8" useDefaultWebProxy="true" allowCookies="false">
        <readerQuotas maxDepth="32" maxStringContentLength="8192"
            maxArrayLength="16384" maxBytesPerRead="4096"
            maxNameTableCharCount="16384" />
        <reliableSession ordered="true" inactivityTimeout="00:10:00"
            enabled="false" />
        <security mode="Message">
          <transport clientCredentialType="Windows" proxyCredentialType="None"
              realm="" />
          <message clientCredentialType="Windows" negotiateServiceCredential="true"
              algorithmSuite="Default" establishSecurityContext="true" />
        </security>
```

```
      </binding>
    </wsHttpBinding>
  </bindings>
  <client>
    <endpoint address="http://localhost:4392/ShipperService.svc"
        binding="wsHttpBinding"
        bindingConfiguration="WSHttpBinding_IShipperService"
        contract="NwServices.IShipperService"
        name="WSHttpBinding_IShipperService">
      <identity>
        <dns value="localhost" />
      </identity>
    </endpoint>
  </client>
</system.serviceModel>
```

You can edit the WCF configuration information directly in Web.config. Alternatively, you can use the Service Configuration Editor to manage your endpoints (for both clients and the services you create). To do so, right-click the Web.config file and choose Edit Wcf Configuration. This will launch the dialog box shown in Figure 9-11.

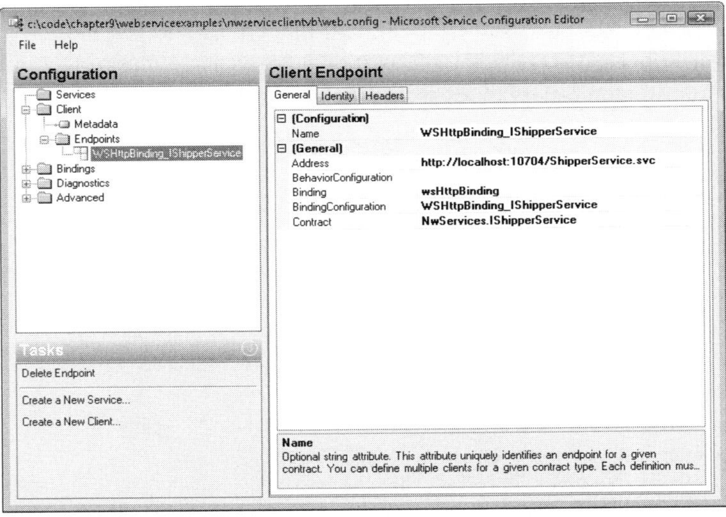

FIGURE 9-11 Editing a WCF endpoint stored in the Web.config file using the Service Configuration Editor

All that remains is to write a Web page that works with the proxy class to call the service. You will look at an example of doing just that in the coming lab.

Calling a WCF Service from Client Script Using AJAX (REST and JSON)

WCF allows you to create and work with a number of different types of services. Remember, it is a technology used to define service endpoints that have an address, binding, and contract. This level of flexibility built into the framework allows it to support various message types and communication protocols.

One such service type is based on representational state transfer (REST) and JavaScript Object Notation (JSON). Services based on these concepts have become very popular as the result of AJAX programming. AJAX becomes easier with a simple service (REST) based on a simple message format (JSON). WCF and the .NET Framework have built-in support for both.

A REST service is a Web service you write that responds to HTTP GET requests. Clients can therefore call a REST service the same way they would access a page: using a URL and a query string. The server then responds with a text document as it would for any HTTP GET request. This way, a REST service does not require knowledge of the XML schema used to call the service. Instead, it simply sends the request and processes the text-based response (usually JSON formatted data).

> ***NOTE*** **SECURING A REST-BASED SERVICE**
>
> **REST-based services do not use SOAP. Many service-based security models are based on SOAP. Therefore, if the security of the data being passed is a concern, you should use HTTPS between the client and server for all RESTful services.**

The response of a REST service is typically in the form of JSON data. JSON is a message data format that evolved out of the heavy use of AJAX. The message format is not XML-based (as are most services). Instead, it is simple, lightweight, and text-based. A JSON message can be processed easily by the JavaScript engine that exists inside nearly all Web browsers. This makes it ideal when calling services from JavaScript. In fact, a JSON message can be parsed using the JavaScript *eval* function because basically it is syntactically formatted JavaScript. The following is an example of a JSON-formatted message:

```
{
  "proudctName": "Computer Monitor",
  "price": "229.00",
  "specifications": {
    "size": 22,
    "type": "LCD",
    "colors": ["black", "red", "white"]
  }
}
```

Writing a WCF Service Based on REST and JSON

Creating a WCF service based on REST and JSON is somewhat simplified in ASP.NET. This is due in part to the AJAX support built into ASP.NET. Because of this, there is a WCF template that you can use to quickly create a service that leverages the REST calling mechanism and the JSON data format.

This AJAX-WCF item template is the AJAX-enabled WCF Service template. It can be found in the Add New Item dialog box for a Web site project. The template defines a class that can be used to create a WCF service for use with AJAX.

As an example, suppose you were creating a service to calculate a product's full price based on the item ID and the postal code to which you are shipping the item. The following code shows an example of an AJAX-enabled WCF Service that simulates such a method:

```
'VB
<ServiceContract(Namespace:="PricingServices")> _
<AspNetCompatibilityRequirements( _
  RequirementsMode:=AspNetCompatibilityRequirementsMode.Allowed)> _
Public Class PricingService

  <OperationContract()> _
  <WebInvoke()> _
  Public Function CalculatePrice(ByVal itemId As String, _
    ByVal shipToPostalCode As String) As Double

    Dim price As Double

    'simulate product price lookup based on item id
    price = 45

    'simulate calculation of sales tax based on shipping postal code
    price = price * 1.06

    'simulate calculation of shipping based on shipping postal code
    price = price * 1.1

    Return price

  End Function

End Class

//C#
namespace PricingServices
{
  [ServiceContract(Namespace = "PricingServices")]
```

```
[AspNetCompatibilityRequirements(RequirementsMode =
  AspNetCompatibilityRequirementsMode.Allowed)]
public class PricingService
{
  [OperationContract]
  [WebInvoke]
  public double CalculatePrice(string itemId, string shipToPostalCode)
  {
    double price;

    //simulate product price lookup based on item id
    price = 45;

    //simulate calculation of sales tax based on shipping postal code
    price = price * 1.06;

    //simulate calculation of shipping based on shipping postal code
    price = price * 1.1;

    return price;
  }
}
}
```

Notice that the service method is marked with the *WebInvoke* attribute. This indicates that the method can be called by an HTTP request. Methods marked with *WebInvoke* are called using HTTP POST. This can be important if you are sending data to the server to be written or do not wish your request to be cached by a browser or the server. If, however, your service typically returns data that is somewhat static, you might mark the method with the *WebGet* attribute. This indicates an HTTP GET request with results that can be cached. This is the only reason to use the *WebGet* attribute. The ASP.NET AJAX *ScriptManager* control can work with both HTTP GET and POST services.

Visual Studio also updates the site's Web.config file when the AJAX-enabled WCF Service is added to the project. The following shows an example. Notice the element *<enableWebScript />*. This indicates that the endpoint is a RESTful service that uses the JSON data format and can therefore be consumed by AJAX. Also notice that the binding is set to *webHttpBinding* indicating again that this service is called via HTTP (and not SOAP).

```
<system.serviceModel>
  <behaviors>
    <endpointBehaviors>
      <behavior name="PricingServices.PricingServiceAspNetAjaxBehavior">
        <enableWebScript/>
      </behavior>
    </endpointBehaviors>
```

```
  </behaviors>
  <serviceHostingEnvironment aspNetCompatibilityEnabled="true"/>
    <services>
      <service name="PricingServices.PricingService">
        <endpoint address=""
          behaviorConfiguration="PricingServices.PricingServiceAspNetAjaxBehavior"
          binding="webHttpBinding" contract="PricingServices.PricingService"/>
      </service>
    </services>
</system.serviceModel>
```

As you can see, ASP.NET simplifies creating WCF services based on REST and JSON. You can also use the features of WCF and the .NET Framework to define REST services and JSON-based messages outside of ASP.NET. In fact, the .NET Framework supports serializing between .NET types and JSON data structures.

Calling a JSON-Based WCF Service from AJAX

The AJAX support in ASP.NET also makes calling a REST-based service from AJAX a relatively straightforward process. The *ScriptManager* control allows you to set a service reference to the given RESTful WCF service. It then defines a JavaScript proxy class for you to call. This proxy class manages the call from the AJAX-enabled page to the WCF service.

For example, to call the service defined previously, you start by adding a *ScriptManager* control to your page. You then define a *ServiceReference* to the actual service. The following markup shows an example:

```
<asp:ScriptManager ID="ScriptManager1" runat="server">
  <Services>
    <asp:ServiceReference Path="PricingService.svc" />
  </Services>
</asp:ScriptManager>
```

You can then define a script block on your page to call the proxy class generated for you based on this service reference. In the example, the service takes a product ID and a postal code. The following JavaScript assumes these values are entered by a user in a couple of text box controls. The code also responds to a user clicking a button on the page.

```
<script language="javascript" type="text/javascript">
  function ButtonCalculate_onclick() {
    var service = new PricingServices.PricingService();
    service.CalculatePrice(document.forms[0].TextBoxProduct.value,
      document.forms[0].TextBoxPostCode.value, onSuccess, onFail, null);
  }

  function onSuccess(result){
    LabelPrice.innerText = result;
```

```
    }

    function onFail(result){
      alert(result);
    }
</script>
```

Notice that in the previous code, the call to the *CalculatePrice* method goes through a proxy that defines some additional parameters. This allows you to pass in a JavaScript method name to be called by the *ScriptManager* after the service is called. You can define a method both for success and for failure. In this case, a successful call writes the results to a *Label* control.

The following code shows the markup for the page's controls to round out the example:

```
<div>
  Product:<br />
  <asp:TextBox ID="TextBoxProduct" runat="server"></asp:TextBox>
  <br />
  Ship to (postal code):<br />
  <asp:TextBox ID="TextBoxPostCode" runat="server"></asp:TextBox>
  <br />

  <input name="ButtonCalculate" type="button" value="Get Price"
    onclick="ButtonCalculate_onclick()" />

  <br />
  <asp:Label ID="LabelPrice" runat="server"></asp:Label>
</div>
```

> ***NOTE*** **COMPLEX TYPES, WCF, AND AJAX**
>
> **There are times when you want to pass complex types between the server and a JavaScript function. Fortunately, the *ScriptManager* control already supports this. It converts your complex type into a JSON message structure. After the call completes, you can access the individual values of the complex type using the syntax *result.member,* where *result* is the name of your complex type and *member* is a property name of the complex type.**

Quick Check

1. How do you mark a class or interface as a WCF service?
2. How do you mark methods in an interface or class so they are exposed as part of the class's service contract?

Quick Check Answers

1. You use the *ServiceContractAttribute* class to tag an interface or class as a WCF service.
2. You use the *OperationContractAttribute* class to tag a method as a service method.

LAB Creating and Consuming a WCF Service

In this lab, you create a WCF service that works with information in the *Northwind* database. You then create a Web page to call that WCF service.

If you encounter a problem completing an exercise, the completed projects are available in the samples installed from the companion CD.

EXERCISE Creating a WCF Service Application

In this exercise, you create the WCF Service application project and define the WCF service.

1. Open Visual Studio and create a new WCF Service Application project using either C# or Visual Basic. Name the project **NorthwindServices**.
2. Copy the *Northwind* database (*Northwnd.mdf*) into the App_Data directory of your project. You can find the file in the samples installed from the CD.
3. Delete the IService1.cs (or .vb) and Service1.svc files from the project.
4. Add a new WCF service to the application: Right-click the project and choose Add | New Item. Select the WCF Service template. Name the service **ShipperService.svc**.

   Notice that both an interface file (*IShipperService*) and an .svc file are created.
5. Open Web.config. Navigate to *<system.serviceModel>*. Delete both the *<service>* and *<behavior>* nodes for *Service1*.

   Navigate to the *<connectionStrings>* node in Web.config. Add a connection string for the *Northwind* database. This connection string should read as follows (formatted to fit on the printed page):

```
<connectionStrings>
  <add name="NwConnectionString" connectionString="Data Source=.\SQLEXPRESS;
    AttachDbFilename=|DataDirectory|\northwnd.mdf;Integrated Security=True;
    User Instance=True" providerName="System.Data.SqlClient"/>
</connectionStrings>
```

6. Open IShipperService.vb (or .cs). Define a data contract class that represents a *Shipper* object. Remember to use the *DataContract* and *DataMember* attributes. Your code should read as follows:

```
'VB
<DataContract()> _
Public Class Shipper

  Private _shipperId As Integer
  <DataMember()> _
  Public Property ShipperId() As Integer
    Get
      Return _shipperId
    End Get
    Set(ByVal value As Integer)
      _shipperId = value
    End Set
  End Property

  Private _companyName As String
  <DataMember()> _
  Public Property CompanyName() As String
    Get
      Return _companyName
    End Get
    Set(ByVal value As String)
      _companyName = value
    End Set
  End Property

  Private _phone As String
  <DataMember()> _
  Public Property Phone() As String
    Get
      Return _phone
    End Get
    Set(ByVal value As String)
      _phone = value
    End Set
  End Property

End Class
//C#
namespace NorthwindServices
{
  [DataContract]
  public class Shipper
  {
    [DataMember]
```

```
        public int ShipperId { get; set; }

        [DataMember]
        public string CompanyName { get; set; }

        [DataMember]
        public string Phone { get; set; }
    }
}
```

7. Next, define the interface for the *Shipper* class. Create one method for returning a *Shipper* instance and another for accepting a *Shipper* instance for updating. Remember to use the *ServiceContract* and *OperationContract* attributes. Your code should look as follows:

```
'VB
<ServiceContract()> _
Public Interface IShipperService

  <OperationContract()> _
  Function GetShipper(ByVal shipperId As Integer) As Shipper

  <OperationContract()> _
  Sub SaveShipper(ByVal shipper As Shipper)

End Interface

//C#
[ServiceContract]
public interface IShipperService
{
  [OperationContract]
  Shipper GetShipper(int shipperId);

  [OperationContract]
  Shipper SaveShipper(Shipper shipper);
}
```

8. Open the ShipperService.svc code by double-clicking the file. Add *using* (*Imports* in Visual Basic) statements for *System.Data*, *System.Data.SqlClient*, and *System.Configuration*. Add code to get the connection string from the database.

   Implement the *GetShipper* method by calling the database to retrieve a record from the Shipper table. Copy this data into a *Shipper* instance and return it as a result of the function.

Implement the *SaveShipper* method by updating a shipping record with data inside a *Shipper* instance. Your code for the service implementation should read as follows:

```
'VB
Public Class ShipperService
  Implements IShipperService

  Private _cnnString As String = _
      ConfigurationManager.ConnectionStrings("NwConnectionString").ToString

  Public Function GetShipper(ByVal shipperId As Integer) As Shipper _
    Implements IShipperService.GetShipper

    Dim sql As String = "SELECT shipperId, companyName, phone " & _
      "FROM shippers WHERE (shipperId = @ShipperId) "

    Dim cnn As New SqlConnection(_cnnString)
    Dim cmd As New SqlCommand(sql, cnn)
    cmd.Parameters.Add("ShipperId", SqlDbType.Int, 0).Value = shipperId

    Dim adp As New SqlDataAdapter(cmd)
    Dim ds As New DataSet()

    adp.Fill(ds)

    Dim s As New Shipper()
    s.ShipperId = shipperId
    s.CompanyName = ds.Tables(0).Rows(0)("companyName").ToString()
    s.Phone = ds.Tables(0).Rows(0)("phone").ToString()

    Return s

  End Function

  Public Sub SaveShipper(ByVal shipper As Shipper) _
    Implements IShipperService.SaveShipper

    Dim sql As String = "UPDATE Shippers SET phone=@Phone, " & _
      "companyName=@CompanyName WHERE shipperId = @ShipperId "

    Dim cnn As New SqlConnection(_cnnString)
    Dim cmd As New SqlCommand(sql, cnn)
    cmd.Parameters.Add("Phone", SqlDbType.NVarChar, 24).Value = shipper.Phone
    cmd.Parameters.Add("CompanyName", SqlDbType.NVarChar, 40).Value = _
      shipper.CompanyName
    cmd.Parameters.Add("ShipperId", SqlDbType.Int, 0).Value = shipper.ShipperId
```

```
    cnn.Open()
    cmd.ExecuteNonQuery()
    cnn.Close()

  End Sub

End Class

//C#
namespace NorthwindServices
{
  public class ShipperService : IShipperService
  {
    private string _cnnString =
      ConfigurationManager.ConnectionStrings["NwConnectionString"].ToString();

    public Shipper GetShipper(int shipperId)
    {
      string sql = "SELECT shipperId, companyName, phone " +
        "FROM shippers WHERE (shipperId = @ShipperId) ";

      SqlConnection cnn = new SqlConnection(_cnnString);

      SqlCommand cmd = new SqlCommand(sql, cnn);
      cmd.Parameters.Add("ShipperId", SqlDbType.Int, 0).Value = shipperId;

      SqlDataAdapter adp = new SqlDataAdapter(cmd);
      DataSet ds = new DataSet();

      adp.Fill(ds);

      Shipper s = new Shipper();
      s.ShipperId = shipperId;
      s.CompanyName = ds.Tables[0].Rows[0]["companyName"].ToString();
      s.Phone = ds.Tables[0].Rows[0]["phone"].ToString();

      return s;
    }

    public void SaveShipper(Shipper shipper)
    {
      string sql = "UPDATE Shippers set phone=@Phone, " +
        "companyName=@CompanyName WHERE shipperId = @ShipperId ";

      SqlConnection cnn = new SqlConnection(_cnnString);
```

```
            SqlCommand cmd = new SqlCommand(sql, cnn);
            cmd.Parameters.Add("Phone", SqlDbType.NVarChar, 24).Value = shipper.Phone;
            cmd.Parameters.Add("CompanyName", SqlDbType.NVarChar, 40).Value =
              shipper.CompanyName;
            cmd.Parameters.Add("ShipperId", SqlDbType.Int, 0).Value = shipper.
ShipperId;

            cnn.Open();
            cmd.ExecuteNonQuery();
            cnn.Close();
        }
    }
}
```

9. Compile and run your Service application. Doing so should launch the service in a Web browser. Here, you will see details on how your WCF service should be called. Figure 9-12 shows an example.

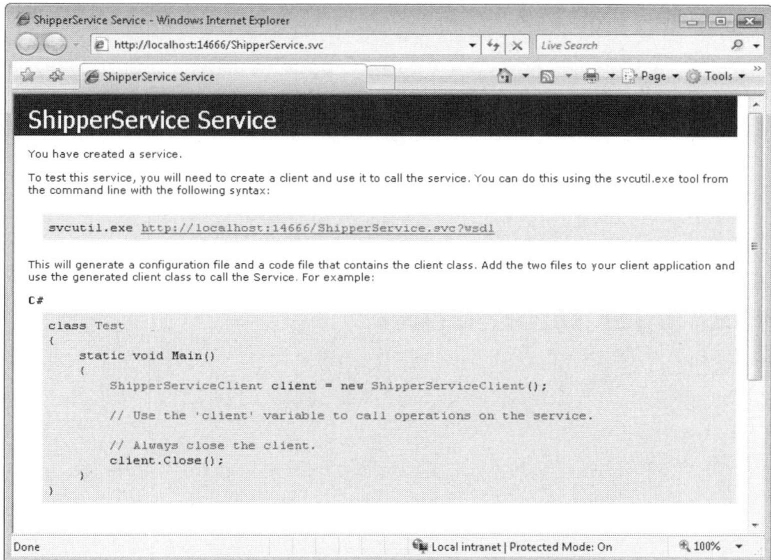

FIGURE 9-12 The WCF service in a Web browser

10. Click the link at the top of the Web page to see the WSDL for your WCF service.
11. Generate a test client for your WCF service using Svcutil.exe. Start by opening a Visual Studio command prompt (Start | All Programs | Microsoft Visual Studio 2008 | Visual Studio Tools). Navigate to a directory to which you wish to generate the test client. Copy the command from the top of the Web page into the command window and press Enter. Exit the command prompt.

12. Navigate to the files you generated. Open these files and examine them. There should be a configuration file that defines an endpoint for communicating with the service. There should also be a code file that shows how to call the WCF service. This is the proxy class you can use to write an actual client. These are also the same files that get generated when you set a service reference to a WCF service.

EXERCISE 2 Consuming a WCF Service

In this exercise, you create a Web client for accessing the WCF service created in the previous exercise.

1. Continue editing the project you created in the previous exercise. Alternatively, you can open the completed Lesson 2, Exercise 1 project in the samples installed from the CD.
2. Add a new Web site to the solution: Right-click the solution and choose Add | New Web Site. Select ASP.NET Web Site. Name the Web site **ShipperClient**. Right-click the Web site and choose Set As StartUp Project.
3. Right-click the newly added Web site and choose Add Service Reference. Click Discover in the Add Service Reference dialog box. Select the *ShipperService*. Set the namespace to **NwServices**. Click OK to close the dialog box.
4. Open the Default.aspx page. Add controls to the page to allow a user to select a shipper based on their ID, display the details of that shipper, edit them, and save them back to the WCF service. Your form layout should be similar to that shown in Figure 9-13.

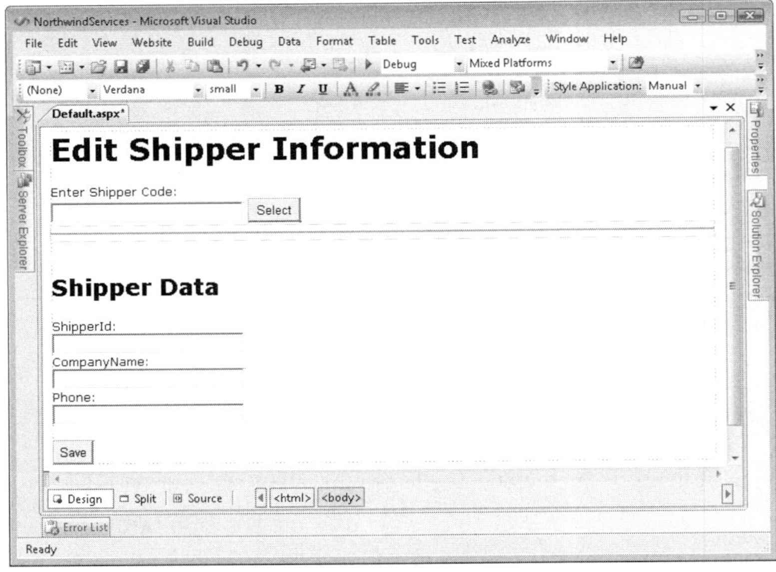

FIGURE 9-13 The WCF service in a Web browser

5. Add code to the Select button's click event to call the WCF service and put the results into the Shipper Data form. Your code should look as follows:

```
'VB
Protected Sub ButtonGetShipper_Click(ByVal sender As Object, _
  ByVal e As System.EventArgs) Handles ButtonGetShipper.Click

  'todo: add validation & error handling
  Dim shipperId As Integer = Integer.Parse(TextBoxGetId.Text)

  Dim nwShipper As New NwServices.ShipperServiceClient()

  Dim shipper As NwServices.Shipper
  shipper = nwShipper.GetShipper(shipperId)

  TextBoxShipperId.Text = shipper.ShipperId.ToString()
  TextBoxCompany.Text = shipper.CompanyName
  TextBoxPhone.Text = shipper.Phone

End Sub

//C#
protected void ButtonGetShipper_Click(object sender, EventArgs e)
{
  //todo: add validation & error handling
  int shipperId = int.Parse(TextBoxGetId.Text);

  NwServices.ShipperServiceClient nwShipper  =
    new NwServices.ShipperServiceClient();

  NwServices.Shipper shipper = new NwServices.Shipper();
  shipper = nwShipper.GetShipper(shipperId);

  TextBoxShipperId.Text = shipper.ShipperId.ToString();
  TextBoxCompany.Text = shipper.CompanyName;
  TextBoxPhone.Text = shipper.Phone;
}
```

6. Add code to the Save button's click event to call the WCF service with the values from the various *TextBox* controls. Your code should look as follows:

```
'VB
Protected Sub ButtonSave_Click(ByVal sender As Object, _
  ByVal e As System.EventArgs) Handles ButtonSave.Click

  'todo: add validation & error handling
  Dim shipper As New NwServices.Shipper()
```

```
    shipper.ShipperId = Integer.Parse(TextBoxShipperId.Text)
    shipper.CompanyName = TextBoxCompany.Text
    shipper.Phone = TextBoxPhone.Text

    Dim nwShipper As New NwServices.ShipperServiceClient()
    nwShipper.SaveShipper(shipper)

End Sub

//C#
protected void ButtonSave_Click(object sender, EventArgs e)
{
    //todo: add validation & error handling
    NwServices.Shipper shipper = new NwServices.Shipper();
    shipper.ShipperId = int.Parse(TextBoxShipperId.Text);
    shipper.CompanyName = TextBoxCompany.Text;
    shipper.Phone = TextBoxPhone.Text;

    NwServices.ShipperServiceClient nwShipper = new NwServices.
ShipperServiceClient();
    nwShipper.SaveShipper(shipper);
}
```

7. Run the application. Enter a Shipper ID (1, 2, or 3). Edit the data and save it back to the database.

Lesson Summary

- WCF is a unifying programming model for creating service-oriented applications. With WCF, you can create services that work with HTTP, TCP, MSMQ, and named pipes.
- ASP.NET and IIS allow you to host WCF services that you wish to expose as HTTP. You can use this model to write services that take advantage of ASP.NET features such as session state and security.
- You write a WCF service by first defining a contract (typically as an interface). The contract uses the attribute classes *ServiceContract* and *OperationContract* to define the service and its methods, respectively.

Lesson Review

You can use the following questions to test your knowledge of the information in Lesson 2, "Creating and Consuming WCF Services." The questions are also available on the companion CD if you prefer to review them in electronic form.

NOTE ANSWERS

Answers to these questions and explanations of why each answer choice is right or wrong are located in the "Answers" section at the end of the book.

1. You wish to write a WCF service application. You intend to host the service in IIS and leverage ASP.NET to build the service. What type of project should you create?
   - **A.** A WCF Service library
   - **B.** A WCF Service application
   - **C.** An ASP.NET Web Service application
   - **D.** A Windows Service
2. You define your own custom type to be used with your WCF service. This type represents a product at your company. It contains a number of public properties. You wish to expose this type in such a way as to be serialized and defined by an XSD schema. What actions should you take? (Choose all that apply.)
   - **A.** Mark your product class with the *DataContract* attribute.
   - **B.** Mark your product class with the *ServiceContract* attribute.
   - **C.** Mark the public members of your product class with the *OperationContract* attribute.
   - **D.** Mark the public members of your product class with the *DataMember* attribute.
3. You write a WCF service. You wish to indicate that a method of the service never returns a message. Rather, it is meant to be called with the assumption that no message will be returned. Which parameter of the *OperationContract* class should you use?
   - **A.** *IsOneWay*
   - **B.** *AsyncPattern*
   - **C.** *IsInitiating*
   - **D.** *ReplyAction*

Chapter Review

To further practice and reinforce the skills you learned in this chapter, you can perform the following tasks:

- Review the chapter summary.
- Complete the case scenario. This scenario sets up real-world situations involving the topics of this chapter and asks you to create solutions.
- Complete the suggested practices.
- Take a practice test.

Chapter Summary

- ASP.NET allows you to create XML Web services through the .asmx file format. You use the *WebServiceAttribute* class to indicate a Web service. The *WebMethodAttribute* class is used to define the methods exposed by a Web service.
- You can create WCF services with ASP.NET and host them inside of IIS. A WCF service defines a contract with clients. The contract is defined by the attribute classes *ServiceContract* and *OperationContract*.

Case Scenario

In the following case scenario, you apply what you've learned about writing and working with services. You can find answers to these questions in the "Answers" section at the end of this book.

Case Scenario: Selecting a Service Model

You are an application developer for Contoso specialty retail. You have been asked to write a set of services that allow your partners to view your product catalog and inventory. This information updates daily and is shared across partners.

You and your partners work exclusively over the Web and have no special communication infrastructure outside of the Internet.

You should also expose services that allow these partners to process a user through the shopping experience: cart, checkout, shipping, order history, and so on. You need to be able to track users through the process without committing their details to the transaction system until they submit their order.

QUESTIONS

Thinking about how you will build these services, answer the following questions:

1. What type of service programming model should you implement?
2. Where should you host your service application?

3. How might you manage access to common data such as catalog and product information?
4. How might you handle user information through the checkout process?

Suggested Practices

To help you successfully master the exam objectives presented in this chapter, complete the following tasks.

Working with XML Web Services

For this task, you should complete Practices 1 and 2. Complete Practice 3 to get experience with ASP.NET security. Complete Practice 4 for more work with AJAX.

- **Practice 1** Return to the lab code created from Lesson 1. Extend the Authors.asmx service by adding support for returning a single author as a serialized, custom class you write. Also, add support for receiving an instance of this class through a service and updating the database.
- **Practice 2** Use the code created in Practice 1 to add client support for working with the custom object returned from the service. Notice how Visual Studio generates a version of the *Author* class as part of the *Proxy* reference class.
- **Practice 3** Add security to the Web service defined in the lab for Lesson 1. Set the service to use Windows Integrated security. Change the calling client to pass credentials to the service using the *NetworkCredentials* class.
- **Practice 4** Use the example code in Lesson 1 for calling a Web service using AJAX to create your own Web service and client-side call.

Working with WCF Services and ASP.NET

For this task, you should complete Practice 1. Complete Practice 2 for more work with AJAX.

- **Practice 1** Return to the lab code for Lesson 2. Add another WCF service for returning all shippers in a single call to be displayed in a list. Change the WCF client code to show all shippers and change the search feature to one of selection.
- **Practice 2** Call a WCF service from client script using ASP.NET AJAX. Follow the pattern discussed in Lesson 1 and apply it to WCF.

Take a Practice Test

The practice tests on this book's companion CD offer many options. For example, you can test yourself on just the content covered in this chapter, or you can test yourself on all the 70-562 certification exam content. You can set up the test so it closely simulates the experience of taking a certification exam, or you can set it up in study mode so you can look at the correct answers and explanations after you answer each question.

> ***MORE INFO*** **PRACTICE TESTS**
>
> **For details about all the practice test options available, see the "How to Use the Practice Tests" section in this book's Introduction.**

CHAPTER 10

Creating Custom Web Controls

The controls that ship with ASP.NET are meant to save you development time and make you a more efficient, productive developer. There is no doubt that trying to build a modern Web application without controls would be a costly endeavor. Even with all its controls, however, ASP.NET does not have all the encapsulated features that you might need for applications built for your given business domain. For example, you might have a common need to show user data across multiple applications. In this case, you would want to encapsulate this functionality and provide it to each application as a control.

Fortunately, ASP.NET provides the capability to take the existing controls and group them together in what are called user controls. You can also take the additional step of encapsulating controls as Web server controls. These controls work on the same framework as the ASP.NET controls and therefore take advantage of design-time support in the Integrated Development Environment (IDE). This chapter covers how you create and use these two primary custom Web controls.

Exam objectives in this chapter:

- Consuming and Creating Server Controls
  - Load user controls dynamically.
  - Create and consume custom controls.

Lessons in this chapter:

Before You Begin

To complete the lessons in this chapter, you should be familiar with developing applications in Microsoft Visual Studio using Visual Basic or C#. In addition, you should be comfortable with all of the following:

- The Visual Studio 2008 IDE.
- A basic understanding of Hypertext Markup Language (HTML) and client-side scripting.
- How to create a new Web site.
- Adding Web server controls to a Web page.
- Working with ADO.NET, Extensible Markup Language (XML), and language-integrated query engine (LINQ).

REAL WORLD

Mike Snell

Code reuse still remains elusive in many development teams. I have the opportunity to speak with a lot of developers about this exact issue. I find a common theme: Developers feel they do not have the time, process, or support to make code reuse a reality in their organization. They want to do it. They know there is duplicate code in their applications. However, they are often unable to achieve much code reuse.

The solution to this common issue seems to be twofold: understanding the technology and creating a culture that values reuse. The technology issue is a question of training. If developers learn how to write code that lends itself to reuse, they will be better positioned to get more out of the code they write. This includes understanding how to build code that works well as custom controls. The culture issue is multifaceted. You need management to value (and incentivize) reusable code over faster development. This means spending time now to save time later. Another facet is the culture of collaboration, communication, and sharing. Developers will often take extra steps when writing their code provided they know other team members will benefit from this code. This can be done through peer reviews, internal demonstrations, and related activities. Hopefully, with these approaches, the goal of code reuse will be within reach of more and more development teams.

Lesson 1: Working with User Controls

A *user control* is a file you create that contains a set of other ASP.NET controls and code grouped together to provide common functionality. The user control can then be used on different pages within a Web site.

User controls in ASP.NET are created as .ascx files. An .ascx file is similar to the Web page's .aspx file and can have its own code-behind page. To enable reuse, the .ascx and code-behind files must be included in each project that requires the user control. For this reason, user controls are typically reserved for reuse within a given site. If you need reuse between sites, you should consider abstracting the functionality as a Web server control.

In this lesson, you learn how to create a standard user control and use it on a Web page. You then see how you can create a user control that defines different templates for layout.

After this lesson, you will be able to:

- Create a user control.
- Add a user control to a Web page.
- Handle events within the user control code-declaration block or code-behind file.
- Create and use a templated user control.

Estimated lesson time: 40 minutes

Creating User Controls

A user control provides an easy way to combine several controls into a single unit of functionality that can be dragged onto multiple Web pages. Pages within a site often contain common functionality using similar sets of controls. In these cases, encapsulating this functionality allows for reuse and helps define a consistent user interface (UI). As an example, imagine a site that needs to prompt users for address information such as during billing and again during shipping. You might encapsulate several built-in controls to input the name, address, city, state, and zip code into a single user control. This user control can be reused when address input is required.

The user controls you create inherit from the *UserControl* class. This class inherits from the *TemplateControl* class. The full class hierarchy is shown in Figure 10-1.

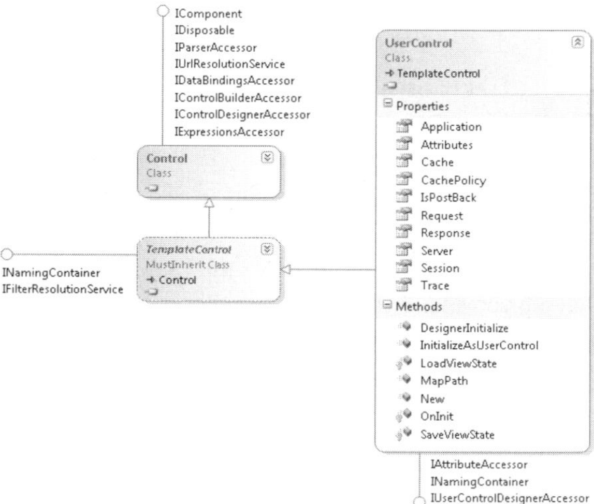

FIGURE 10-1 The *UserControl* class hierarchy

User controls are created using a procedure similar to building a standard Web page. You create a user control in Visual Studio from the Add New Item dialog box. From here, you select Web User Control. This adds a file with the .ascx extension to your application. The user control has both a Design and Source view similar to that of an .aspx page. However, a quick glance at the markup reveals the @ *Control* directive instead of the @ *Page* directive of an .aspx page. The following markup shows an example:

```
'VB
<%@ Control Language="VB"
  AutoEventWireup="false"
  CodeFile="MyWebUserControl.ascx.vb"
  Inherits="MyWebUserControl" %>

//C#
<%@ Control Language="C#"
   AutoEventWireup="true"
   CodeFile=" MyWebUserControl.ascx.cs"
   Inherits=" MyWebUserControl" %>
```

You drag and drop controls onto a user control like you would onto a page. For example, if you were developing the address control discussed previously, you might add text, *TextBox* controls, and layout information to the user control. Of course, the resulting user control needs to be added to a Web page for it to work. However, the design experience when building a user control is very similar to that of building a page. Figure 10-2 shows the Address user control from this chapter in the Visual Studio designer.

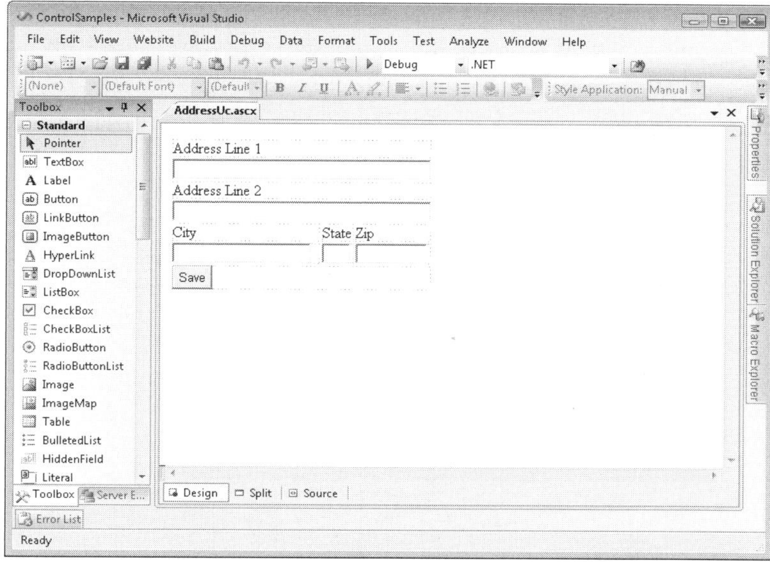

FIGURE 10-2 The Address user control inside the Visual Studio designer

> ***NOTE*** **SEPARATE YOUR CONTROLS FROM THEIR DESIGN**
>
> **Generally, it is wise to refrain from putting much style information beyond layout inside a user control. This allows a user control to take on the styles and themes defined by the pages and site to which it is added.**

Defining User Control Events

User controls can have their own encapsulated events. This includes life cycle events such as *Init* and *Load*. These events are called in sync with the events on the page. For example, after the page *Init* event is called, the control's *Init* event is called in turn. Processing then returns to the page for the *Load* event; following this the control's *Load* event is called. This continues throughout the life cycle. This model allows you to develop user controls in a manner similar to developing a Web page.

User controls can also cause PostBack for the Web page to which they belong. When doing so, the user control's events are raised accordingly along with the events of the page. The event handlers for a user control, however, are typically encapsulated in the given user control. This ensures the code for these events can be maintained independent of the pages that use the user controls.

Consider the Address user control example. This control has a Save button. When the user clicks this button, you might wish to trigger an event that saves the address information for the given user and the address type (billing, shipping, and so on). To do so, you add a button click event handler to the user control and put your code there. When the user control is added to a page and the page is executed, a click of the Save button executes the code on the user control. The following code shows a simple example of the Address user control's *Save* button click event calling out to a custom class called *UserProfile*:

```
'VB
Protected Sub ButtonSave_Click(ByVal sender As Object, _
  ByVal e As System.EventArgs) Handles ButtonSave.Click

  'to do: validate user input

  'save new address for user
  UserProfile.AddNewAddress(Me.UserId, Me.AddressType, _
    TextBoxAddress1.Text, TextBoxAddress2.Text, _
    TextBoxCity.Text, TextBoxState.Text, TextBoxZip.Text)

End Sub

//C#
protected void ButtonSave_Click(object sender, EventArgs e)
{
  //to do: validate user input

  //save new address for user
  UserProfile.AddNewAddress(this.UserId, this.AddressType,
    TextBoxAddress1.Text, TextBoxAddress2.Text,
    TextBoxCity.Text, TextBoxState.Text, TextBoxZip.Text);
}
```

Notice that in the preceding code , the calls to the *AddNewAddress* method also include access to properties on the user control (*UserId* and *AddressType*). The properties were added to the user control definition and are discussed next.

Passing Events Up to the Page

Often, you do not know the actual implementation of a given control's event at design time. Instead, you need to add the control, such as a *Button* control, to your user control and allow the developer who uses the user control to implement the event handler for the *Button* control's click event. You can do so by defining an event on your user control and passing this event to the Web page when the *Button* control's click event fires.

As an example, consider the Address user control's Save button. You might need to define an event that is passed to the page when this button is clicked. This event would most likely pass the values from the user control's subcontrols back to the page (unless they are exposed as properties, as discussed in the next section). Therefore, you would modify the Address user control to expose an event and raise that event in response to a Save button click.

The following steps you through sample code for this example. First, you should define the event arguments class as follows. Notice this class inherits *EventArgs*. It will be used by the event to pass the address information from the user control to the page.

```
'VB
Public Class AddressEventArgs
  Inherits EventArgs

  Public Sub New(ByVal addressLine1 As String, _
    ByVal addressLine2 As String, ByVal city As String, _
    ByVal state As String, ByVal zip As String)

    Me._addressLine1 = addressLine1
    Me._addressLine2 = addressLine2
    Me._city = city
    Me._state = state
    Me._zip = zip
  End Sub

  Private _addressLine1 As String
  Public ReadOnly Property AddressLine1() As String
    Get
      Return _addressLine1
    End Get
  End Property

  Private _addressLine2 As String
  Public ReadOnly Property AddressLine2() As String
    Get
      Return _addressLine2
    End Get
  End Property

  Private _city As String
  Public ReadOnly Property City() As String
    Get
      Return _city
    End Get
  End Property

  Private _state As String
  Public ReadOnly Property State() As String
    Get
      Return _state
    End Get
```

```
  End Property

  Private _zip As String
  Public ReadOnly Property Zip() As String
    Get
      Return _zip
    End Get
  End Property

End Class
```

```
//C#
public class AddressEventArgs : EventArgs
{

  public AddressEventArgs(string addressLine1, string addressLine2,
    string city, string state, string zip)
  {
    this.AddressLine1 = addressLine1;
    this.AddressLine2 = addressLine2;
    this.City = city;
    this.State = state;
    this.Zip = zip;
  }

  public string AddressLine1 { get; private set; }
  public string AddressLine2 { get; private set; }
  public string City { get; private set; }
  public string State { get; private set; }
  public string Zip { get; private set; }

}
```

Next, you should declare a delegate if you are using C#. The delegate can be put in the same class file that contains both the event arguments and the user control class. However, the delegate does not go into one of those classes. Note that if you are using Visual Basic, you can rely on the event model to handle this step for you.

```
//C#
public delegate void SaveButtonClickHandler(object sender, AddressEventArgs e);
```

The next step is to add code to the user control that defines an event and raises that event when the user clicks the button. This event will be trapped by the page that consumes the user control. The following code shows an example. Notice that the C# version of the code defines the event as the delegate type created in the prior step.

```
'VB
Public Event SaveButtonClick(ByVal sender As Object, ByVal e As AddressEventArgs)

Protected Sub ButtonSave_Click(ByVal sender As Object, _
  ByVal e As System.EventArgs) Handles ButtonSave.Click

  Dim addArgs As New AddressEventArgs(TextBoxAddress1.Text, _
    TextBoxAddress2.Text, TextBoxCity.Text, _
    TextBoxState.Text, TextBoxZip.Text)

  RaiseEvent SaveButtonClick(Me, addArgs)

End Sub

//C#
public event SaveButtonClickHandler SaveButtonClick;

protected void ButtonSave_Click(object sender, EventArgs e)
{
  if (SaveButtonClick != null)
  {
    SaveButtonClick(this, new AddressEventArgs(TextBoxAddress1.Text,
      TextBoxAddress2.Text, TextBoxCity.Text, TextBoxState.Text,
      TextBoxZip.Text));
  }
}
```

Finally, you add code to the page that contains the user control (you will see how to add a user control to a page in an upcoming section). This code should trap the event exposed by the user control. In Visual Basic, you can add a handler for the user control's exposed event in the code editor. In C#, you wire up a handler using the += syntax inside the *Page_Init* method. Inside your handler, you use *AddressEventArgs* as required. In the following example, these event arguments are used to save the address information.

```
'VB
Protected Sub AddressUc1_SaveButtonClick( _
  ByVal sender As Object, ByVal e As AddressEventArgs) _
  Handles AddressUc1.SaveButtonClick

  UserProfile.AddNewAddress(Me._userId, AddressUc1.AddressType, _
    e.AddressLine1, e.AddressLine2, e.City, e.State, e.Zip)

End Sub

//C#
protected void Page_Init(object sender, EventArgs e)
```

```
{
  AddressUc1.SaveButtonClick += this.AddressUc_SaveButtonClick;
}

private void AddressUc_SaveButtonClick(
  object sender, AddressEventArgs e)
{
  UserProfile.AddNewAddress(this._userId, AddressUc1.AddressType,
    e.AddressLine1, e.AddressLine2, e.City, e.State, e.Zip);
}
```

Defining Properties in User Controls

The user controls you create will often need configuration data. You can define this configuration data through properties. Properties added to user controls can then be configured in the page markup that uses the control. When developers use the user control, they can set the properties declaratively through markup. In fact, these properties are also available through IntelliSense.

Properties that are configured by a developer when using a user control can be set at design time or at run time, and are available in PostBack. This is the same experience you get with other controls in ASP.NET. Properties set through code need to be reset on PostBack or they are lost. Again, this is the same experience you get with other ASP.NET controls.

You define user control properties as you would any other class-level property in the .NET Framework. For example, to add the *UserId* and *AddressType* properties to the Address user control, you would add code as follows:

```
'VB
Private _userId As Integer
Public Property UserId() As Integer
  Get
    Return Integer.Parse(ViewState("userId"))
  End Get
  Set(ByVal value As Integer)
    _userId = value
  End Set
End Property

Private _addressType As UserProfile.AddressType
Public Property AddressType() As UserProfile.AddressType
  Get
    Return Integer.Parse(ViewState("addressType"))
  End Get
  Set(ByVal value As UserProfile.AddressType)
    _addressType = value
  End Set
```

```
End Property
```

```
//C#
public int UserId { get; set; }
public UserProfile.AddressType AddressType { get; set; }
```

Again, you can set these properties on the page to which you add the user control. The next section covers adding controls to a page and defining its properties.

Accessing Control Values

Another common scenario is the need to access the values of the controls contained by a user control. Controls on a user control are declared as protected members of the control. This means they are not directly accessible outside the user control class. Therefore, to access a control, you can return a reference to it through a property setting. However, this exposes the entire control. A more common scenario is to define a property that allows a user to set and get the values of a control. This allows you to contain the user control but provide access to the enclosed controls.

As an example, imagine the Address user control needs to allow users to preset values of the controls contained by the user control. In this case, you can expose the *TextBox.Text* properties as properties of the user control. The following shows one of the user control's *TextBox.Text* properties (*TextBoxAddress1*) exposed as a value from the user control. You could repeat this code for the other controls inside the Address user control.

```
'VB
Public Property AddressLine1() As String
  Get
    Return TextBoxAddress1.Text
  End Get
  Set(ByVal value As String)
    TextBoxAddress1.Text = value
  End Set
End Property

//C#
public string AddressLine1
{
  get
  {
    return TextBoxAddress1.Text;
  }
  set
  {
    TextBoxAddress1.Text = value;
  }
}
```

Adding a User Control to a Page

You can add a user control to a Web page by simply dragging it from Solution Explorer and dropping it on a Web page. When you add the user control to a page, you can see the control contents in Design view. If you switch to Source view, you can see the markup information that Visual Studio added to your page. The following shows an example of the Address user control added to a Web page:

```
<%@ Page Language="VB" AutoEventWireup="false"
  CodeFile="UserProfilePage.aspx.vb" Inherits="UserProfilePage" %>

<%@ Register src="AddressUc.ascx" tagname="AddressUc" tagprefix="uc1" %>

<!DOCTYPE html PUBLIC "-//W3C//DTD XHTML 1.0 Transitional//EN"
  "http://www.w3.org/TR/xhtml1/DTD/xhtml1-transitional.dtd">

<html xmlns="http://www.w3.org/1999/xhtml">
<head runat="server">
    <title>User Profile Settings</title>
</head>
<body style="font-family: Verdana; font-size: small">
  <form id="form1" runat="server">
    <div>
      <uc1:AddressUc ID="AddressUc1" runat="server" AddressType="Home" />
    </div>
  </form>
</body>
</html>
```

Notice the @ *Register* directive at the top of the page. This directive is required to register the user control on the page. The *TagPrefix* attribute is a namespace identifier for the control. Your markup uses this prefix to define the control. The default *TagPrefix* is *uc1* (as in User Control 1). Of course, you can change this value. The *TagName* attribute is the name of the control. The *Src* attribute is the location of the user control file. The actual instance definition for the control is nested within the form tag. Notice that the ID is automatically created as *AddressUc1*. Also, notice that the custom property *AddressType* is defined as an attribute of the control. The other property, *UserId*, is meant to indicate a unique ID of the user whose address values are being modified. Therefore, this property would most likely be set in code (from a query string value, session, cookie, or similar).

Dynamically Loading User Controls

Like other server controls, user controls can be loaded dynamically. Loading controls dynamically can be useful in situations in which you wish to add a variable quantity of a given control to a page.

To dynamically load a user control, you use the *LoadControl* method of the *Page* class. This method takes the name and path to a file that contains the user control's definition. The method also returns a reference to the control class it creates. You can set this to a variable by casting the returned object to a strong type. For this to work, the control must already be registered with the page.

For example, suppose you need to add multiple instances of the Address user control discussed previously. You might need to add a variable number based on the number of stored addresses for a given user. The following code shows an example of how you would dynamically load the control:

```
'VB
Dim addressControl As AddressUc = _
  CType(LoadControl("AddressUc.ascx"), AddressUc)

form1.Controls.Add(addressControl)


//C#
AddressUc addressControl =
  (AddressUc)LoadControl("AddressUc.ascx");

form1.Controls.Add(addressControl);
```

Notice the second line of code. Once the control has been loaded, it needs to be added to the form object for display and use.

Creating a Templated User Control

A templated user control provides separation of control data from the presentation of that data. A templated user control does not provide a default UI layout. Instead, this layout is provided by the developer who uses the user control on his or her page. This provides increased flexibility in terms of layout while keeping the encapsulation and reuse benefits of a user control.

There are a number of steps to creating a templated user control. The following outlines these steps:

1. You start by adding a user control file to your Web application.
2. Inside the user control file, you place an ASP.NET *Placeholder* control. This defines a placeholder for the template. You will expose this template as a property. The users of your control will then define their code inside this template.
3. Next, you define a class file in your application to serve as a naming container. This class file will contain a reference to the data for your user control. This data will be bound to when a user of your control creates his or her own layout template.

   This class inherits from *Control* and implements the *INamingContainer* interface. The class should also contain public properties for any data elements it is meant to contain.

4. You then return to your user control. In its code-behind file, you implement a property of type *ITemplate*. This property will serve as the template for users of your control. The name you give this property is the name of the template tag in any consuming page's markup.

   You apply the attribute *TemplateContainerAttribute* to the *ITemplate* property, which marks it as a template. To this attribute, you pass the type of the naming container class as an argument of the constructor. This serves to allow binding between the container and the template definition markup when the user control is added to a page.

   You also apply the attribute *PersistenceModeAttribute* to the *ITemplate* property. You pass the enumeration value of *PersistenceMode.InnerProperty* into the attribute's constructor.

5. Next, you add code to the *Page_Init* method of the user control. Here you test for the *ITemplate* property. If the *ITemplate* property is set, you create an instance of the naming container class and create an instance of the template in the naming container. You then add the naming container instance to the *Controls* collection of the *PlaceHolder* server control.

6. You might also need to pass data from your user control to the naming container. This allows users to set properties of your user control and store and use them in the container. In this case, you have to define this data in your user control as properties that a user of the user control can set. You then must pass a reference to this data to the naming container. This ensures the naming container is updated when the property values change on the user control.

As an example, suppose you wish to implement the address control discussed previously as a templated user control. You start by adding a *PlaceHolder* control to the page as shown in the following markup:

The Address User Control Markup

```
'VB
<%@ Control Language="VB" AutoEventWireup="false"
  CodeFile="AddressUcTemplated.ascx.vb" Inherits="AddressUcTemplated" %>

<asp:PlaceHolder runat="server"
  ID="PlaceHolderAddressTemplate">
</asp:PlaceHolder>

//C#
<%@ Control Language="C#" AutoEventWireup="true"
  CodeFile="AddressUcTemplated.ascx.cs" Inherits="AddressUcTemplated" %>

<asp:PlaceHolder runat="server"
  ID="PlaceHolderAddressTemplate">
</asp:PlaceHolder>
```

You then add code to the code-behind file for the user control. This includes the *ITemplate* property and the *Page_Init* code. The *ITemplate* property is used to define the layout area for users of the user control. The *Page_Init* code is meant to instantiate the naming container and connect it to the layout template.

In addition, the code-behind file should contain any properties you wish the user to be able to access from the user control. In our example, this is defined as an *Address* property that is defined as a custom *Address* class (not shown). This class contains the address properties discussed previously. The following shows an example of the code-behind file for the Address user control:

The Address User Control's Code-Behind File

```
'VB
Partial Class AddressUcTemplated
    Inherits System.Web.UI.UserControl

  Public Sub Page_Init(ByVal sender As Object, _
      ByVal e As EventArgs) Handles Me.Init

    'clear the controls from the placeholder
    PlaceHolderAddressTemplate.Controls.Clear()

    If LayoutTemplate Is Nothing Then
      PlaceHolderAddressTemplate.Controls.Add( _
        New LiteralControl("No template defined."))
    Else

      Dim container As New AddressUcContainer(Me.Address)

      Me.LayoutTemplate.InstantiateIn(container)

      'add the controls to the placeholder
      PlaceHolderAddressTemplate.Controls.Add(container)
    End If

  End Sub

  Private _layout As ITemplate
  <PersistenceMode(PersistenceMode.InnerProperty)> _
  <TemplateContainer(GetType(AddressUcContainer))> _
  Public Property LayoutTemplate() As ITemplate
    Get
      Return _layout
    End Get
    Set(ByVal value As ITemplate)
      _layout = value
    End Set
```

```
  End Property

  Private _address As New Address()
  Public Property Address() As Address
    Get
      Return _address
    End Get
    Set(ByVal value As Address)
      _address = value
    End Set
  End Property

End Class

//C#
public partial class AddressUcTemplated :
  System.Web.UI.UserControl
{
    protected void Page_Init(object sender, EventArgs e)
    {
      //clear the controls from the placeholder
      PlaceHolderAddressTemplate.Controls.Clear();

      if (LayoutTemplate == null)
      {
        PlaceHolderAddressTemplate.Controls.Add(
          new LiteralControl("No template defined."));
      }
      else
      {
        AddressUcContainer container = new
          AddressUcContainer(this.Address);

        this.LayoutTemplate.InstantiateIn(container);

        //add the controls to the placeholder
        PlaceHolderAddressTemplate.Controls.Add(container);
      }
    }

    [PersistenceMode(PersistenceMode.InnerProperty)]
    [TemplateContainer(typeof(AddressUcContainer))]
    public ITemplate LayoutTemplate { get; set; }

    public Address Address { get; set; }
}
```

The final step is to define the naming container. Note that the previous code actually used the naming container as if it were already defined. Recall that the naming container must inherit from *Control* and implement the *INamingContainer* interface. Property values passed from the user control to the naming container should be passed in the constructor. If you need to be able to set properties of the user control and have those property values reflected in the naming container, you must set the properties as an object reference. The following code shows an example of exposing the *Address* object through the naming container:

The Naming Container Class

```
'VB
Public Class AddressUcContainer
  Inherits Control
  Implements INamingContainer

  Public Sub New(ByVal address As Address)
    Me.Address = address
  End Sub

  Private _address As Address
  Public Property Address() As Address
    Get
      Return _address
    End Get
    Set(ByVal value As Address)
      _address = value
    End Set
  End Property

End Class

//C#
public class AddressUcContainer : Control, INamingContainer
{
  public AddressUcContainer(Address address)
  {
    this.Address = address;
  }

  public Address Address { get; set; }
}
```

Using a Templated User Control

Like any user control, a templated user control must be used within the same project and can be added to a page by dragging it from Solution Explorer onto a Web page. Recall that this registers the control with the page as follows:

```
<%@ Register src="AddressUcTemplated.ascx"
  tagname="AddressUcTemplated" tagprefix="uc1" %>
```

You then define the template for the user control's layout. In the address example, this means nesting layout and code within the *<LayoutTemplate>* tag that was defined with the *ITemplate* property. Inside the template you can reference data by calling the *Container* object. This object is an instance of the naming container class created as part of the templated user control process. The following markup shows the definition of the user control on a page:

```
<uc1:AddressUcTemplated ID="AddressUcTemplated1"
  runat="server" AddressType="Home">
  <LayoutTemplate>
      <h1>Edit Home Address</h1>
      <table>
        <tr>
          <td>Address Line 1:</td>
          <td>
            <asp:TextBox ID="TextBoxAddress" runat="server"
              Text="<%#Container.Address.AddressLine1%>"></asp:TextBox>
          </td>
        </tr>
        <tr>
          <td>Address Line 2:</td>
          <td>
            <asp:TextBox ID="TextBoxAddressLine2" runat="server"
              Text="<%#Container.Address.AddressLine2%>"></asp:TextBox>
          </td>
        </tr>
        <tr>
          <td>City:</td>
          <td>
            <asp:TextBox ID="TextBoxCity" runat="server"
              Text="<%#Container.Address.City%>"></asp:TextBox>
          </td>
        </tr>
        <tr>
          <td>State:</td>
          <td>
            <asp:TextBox ID="TextBoxState" runat="server"
              Text="<%#Container.Address.State%>"></asp:TextBox>
          </td>
        </tr>
        <tr>
          <td>Zip:</td>
          <td>
```

```
            <asp:TextBox ID="TextBoxZip" runat="server"
              Text="<%#Container.Address.Zip%>"></asp:TextBox>
          </td>
        </tr>
        <tr>
          <td></td>
          <td>
            <asp:Button ID="ButtonSave" runat="server" Text="Save" />
          </td>
        </tr>
      </table>
  </LayoutTemplate>
</uc1:AddressUcTemplated>
```

You must also add code to the consuming page's code-behind file. This code should call the *Page.DataBind* method to ensure the container is bound to the templated layout. The following code shows an example:

```
'VB
Protected Sub Page_Load(ByVal sender As Object, _
  ByVal e As System.EventArgs) Handles Me.Load

  'simulate getting a user and loading his or her profile
  AddressUcTemplated1.Address.AddressLine1 = "1234 Some St."
  AddressUcTemplated1.Address.City = "Pontiac"
  AddressUcTemplated1.Address.State = "MI"
  AddressUcTemplated1.Address.Zip = "48340"

  'bind data to controls
  Page.DataBind()

End Sub

//C#
protected void Page_Load(object sender, EventArgs e)
{
  //simulate getting a user and loading his or her profile
  AddressUcTemplated1.Address.AddressLine1 = "1234 Some St.";
  AddressUcTemplated1.Address.City = "Ann Arbor";
  AddressUcTemplated1.Address.State = "MI";
  AddressUcTemplated1.Address.Zip = "48888";

  //bind data to controls
  Page.DataBind();
}
```

Note that the templated user control does not display in Design view. You need to create a custom Web control for that to work. However, when you run the Web page, it displays as designed. Figure 10-3 shows an example of the control running in a browser.

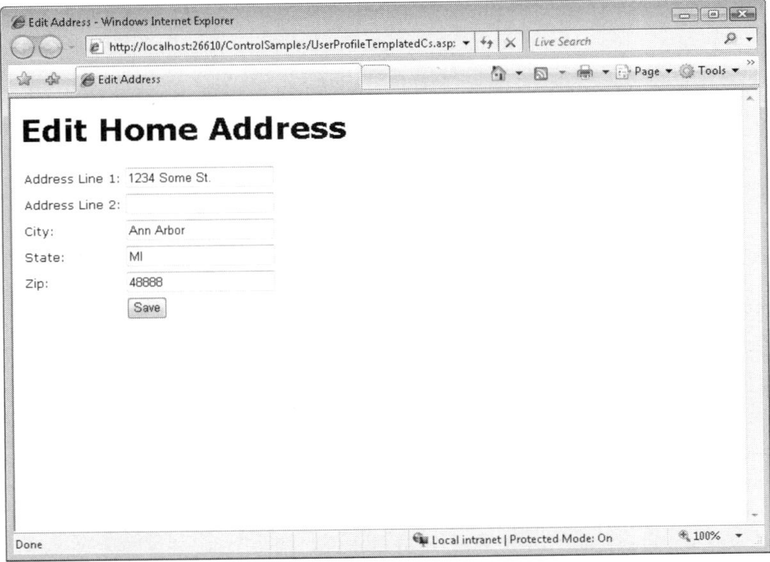

FIGURE 10-3 The templated Address user control

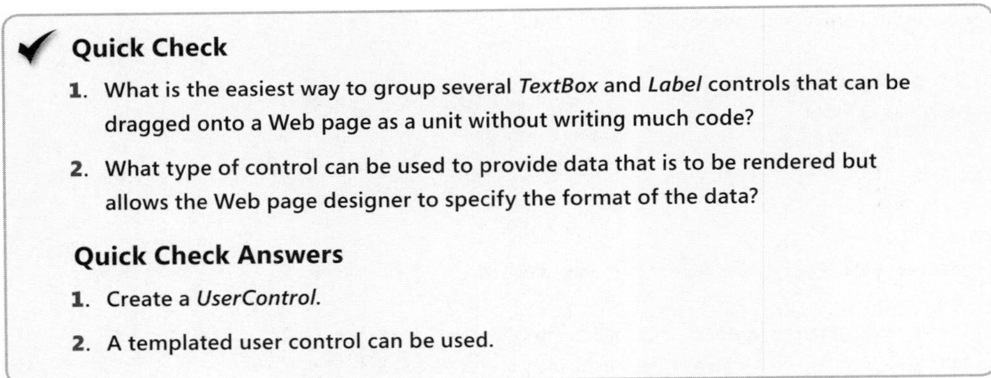

Quick Check

1. What is the easiest way to group several *TextBox* and *Label* controls that can be dragged onto a Web page as a unit without writing much code?
2. What type of control can be used to provide data that is to be rendered but allows the Web page designer to specify the format of the data?

Quick Check Answers

1. Create a *UserControl*.
2. A templated user control can be used.

LAB Working with User Controls

In this lab, you create a version of the Address user control discussed in the text.

If you encounter a problem completing an exercise, the completed projects are available in the samples installed from the companion CD.

EXERCISE 1 Create the Web Site and the User Control

In this exercise, you create the Web site and create the user control.

1. Create a new Web site called **UserControlLab** using your preferred programming language.
2. Add a user control to the site: Right-click the Web site and choose Add New Item. In the Add New Item dialog box, select Web User Control. Name the user control **AddressUserControl.ascx**.
3. Open the user control and add input elements for address, city, state, and zip code. Your control markup should look similar to the following:

```
<div>
  Address
  <br />
  <asp:TextBox ID="TextBoxAddress" runat="server" Width="275px"
    Height="80px" TextMode="MultiLine"></asp:TextBox>
  <div style="width: 280px">
    <div style="float: left; margin-right: 3px">
      City
      <br />
      <asp:TextBox ID="TextBoxCity" runat="server" Width="150"></asp:TextBox>
    </div>
    <div style="float: left; margin-right: 3px">
      State
      <br />
      <asp:TextBox ID="TextBoxState" runat="server" Width="30"></asp:TextBox>
    </div>
    <div style="float: left">
      Zip
      <br />
      <asp:TextBox ID="TextBoxZip" runat="server" Width="70"></asp:TextBox>
    </div>
  </div>
  <asp:Button ID="ButtonSave" runat="server" Text="Save" />
</div>
```

4. Open the code-behind file and add properties to expose the *Text* property of the user control's *TextBox* controls. Your code should look similar to the following:

```
'VB
Public Property Address() As String
  Get
    Return TextBoxAddress.Text
  End Get
  Set(ByVal value As String)
    TextBoxAddress.Text = value
```

```
  End Set
End Property

Public Property City() As String
  Get
    Return TextBoxCity.Text
  End Get
  Set(ByVal value As String)
    TextBoxCity.Text = value
  End Set
End Property

Public Property State() As String
  Get
    Return TextBoxState.Text
  End Get
  Set(ByVal value As String)
    TextBoxState.Text = value
  End Set
End Property

Public Property Zip() As String
  Get
    Return TextBoxZip.Text
  End Get
  Set(ByVal value As String)
    TextBoxZip.Text = value
  End Set
End Property

//C#
public string Address
{
  get { return TextBoxAddress.Text; }
  set { TextBoxAddress.Text = value; }
}
public string City
{
  get { return TextBoxCity.Text; }
  set { TextBoxCity.Text = value; }
}
public string State
{
  get { return TextBoxState.Text; }
  set { TextBoxState.Text = value; }
}
```

```
public string Zip
{
  get { return TextBoxZip.Text; }
  set { TextBoxZip.Text = value; }
}
```

5. Next, you will define the event handler for the Save button. This event will raise an event to the host of the user control. Given that the user control already exposes properties for reading its values, the event will not pass them as an argument; it will simply raise a generic event.

   If using C#, start by adding a delegate to the user control. Add the delegate to the code-behind file but outside the class. Your delegate should look as follows:

   ```
   public delegate void SaveButtonClickHandler(object sender, EventArgs e);
   ```

   Next, add the event declaration to the user control's code-behind class file. This code should read as follows:

   ```
   'VB
   Public Event SaveButtonClick(ByVal sender As Object, ByVal e As EventArgs)

   //C#
   public event SaveButtonClickHandler SaveButtonClick;
   ```

   Finally, add code to the button's click event that raises this event. The following is an example:

   ```
   'VB
   Protected Sub ButtonSave_Click(ByVal sender As Object, _
     ByVal e As System.EventArgs) Handles ButtonSave.Click

     RaiseEvent SaveButtonClick(Me, New EventArgs())

   End Sub

   //C#
   protected void ButtonSave_Click(object sender, EventArgs e)
   {
     if (SaveButtonClick != null)
     {
       SaveButtonClick(this, new EventArgs());
     }
   }
   ```

6. Compile your code and make sure there are no errors.

EXERCISE 2 Host the User Control on a Web Page

In this exercise, you consume the user control created in the prior exercise.

1. Continue editing the project you created in the previous exercise. Alternatively, you can copy the completed Lesson 1, Exercise 1 project from the CD to your hard drive and begin from there.

2. Open the Default.aspx page in Design view. While in Design view, drag AddressUser-Control.ascx to the page from Solution Explorer.

   Review the page's source. Notice that you can initialize the control's custom properties through markup. The properties are also available in the Properties window when in Design view.

3. Add an event handler to trap the event fired by the user control when a user clicks the Save button. Open the Default.aspx page's code-behind file.

   In Visual Basic, use the drop-down control at the top left of the code editor to select the user control (*AddressControl1*). Then, use the drop-down list on the right to select the *SaveButtonClick* event handler. This should generate your event handler stub as follows:

```
Protected Sub AddressUserControl1_SaveButtonClick(ByVal sender As Object, _
  ByVal e As System.EventArgs) Handles AddressUserControl1.SaveButtonClick

End Sub
```

   In C#, you need to first add a method to the page. This method should have the same signature as the event exposed by the user control. You then need to wire up the event from the user control to the newly defined method. You can do this inside the page's *Init* method. The following code shows an example:

```
protected void Page_Init(object sender, EventArgs e)
{
  AddressUserControl1.SaveButtonClick += this.AddressSave_Click;
}
protected void AddressSave_Click(object sender, EventArgs e)
{
}
```

4. You now need to add code to the intercepted event. For this example, this code will simply take the user's input and write it out to the debug window. The following shows an example:

```
'VB
Protected Sub AddressUserControl1_SaveButtonClick(ByVal sender As Object, _
  ByVal e As System.EventArgs) Handles AddressUserControl1.SaveButtonClick
```

```
    System.Diagnostics.Debug.WriteLine("Address: " & _
      AddressUserControl1.Address & _
      " City: " & AddressUserControl1.City & _
      " State: " & AddressUserControl1.State & _
      " Zip: " & AddressUserControl1.Zip)
End Sub

//C#
protected void AddressSave_Click(object sender, EventArgs e)
{
  System.Diagnostics.Debug.WriteLine("Address: " +
    AddressUserControl1.Address +
    " City: " + AddressUserControl1.City +
    " State: " + AddressUserControl1.State +
    " Zip: " + AddressUserControl1.Zip);
}
```

5. Finally, run the application in debug mode to view the results. (You must enable script debugging in your browser.) Enter address information in the user control. Click the Save button. Return to Visual Studio and view the Output window to see the results of the trapped Save button's event.

Lesson Summary

- A user control enables a Web developer to easily combine ASP.NET controls into a single control for encapsulating common functionality.
- A user control cannot be compiled to its own .dll and shared. It can only be shared within a single Web site (without copy and paste, of course).
- A user control follows the same life cycle as a page.
- You can expose properties, events, and methods in a user control.
- You can dynamically load a user control at run time by using the *LoadControl* method.
- You can create templated user controls, which allow the Web page designer to specify the formatting of data that the user control provides.

Lesson Review

You can use the following questions to test your knowledge of the information in Lesson 1, "Working with User Controls."

The questions are also available on the companion CD if you prefer to review them in electronic form.

NOTE ANSWERS

Answers to these questions and explanations of why each answer choice is right or wrong are located in the "Answers" section at the end of the book.

1. You wish to consume a user control on a page. However, you do not know the number of instances you wish to create. This information will be available at run time. Therefore, you wish to dynamically create these controls. Which actions should you take? (Choose all that apply.)
   - **A.** Add the controls using the *Controls.Add* method of the page instance.
   - **B.** Add the controls using the *Controls.Add* method of the form instance.
   - **C.** Call the form's *LoadControl* method for each control you wish to add to the page.
   - **D.** Call the page's *LoadControl* method for each control you wish to add to the page.
2. You want to create a user control to display data, but you are concerned that you don't know how the Web page designers want to format the data. Also, some of the page designers mention that the format of the data might be different, depending on the Web page. How can you best create a user control to solve this problem?
   - **A.** Create a separate user control for each Web page and get each Web page designer to tell you the format to implement in each user control.
   - **B.** Create a separate user control for each variation of the format once the Web page designers give you the desired formatting options.
   - **C.** Create a templated user control that exposes the data to the Web page designers so they can specify their desired format.
   - **D.** Create a user control that simply renders the data and let the Web page designers specify the style properties for the user control.
3. You have two *TextBox* controls inside your user control. You wish to allow a user of the user control to initialize, read, and modify the *Text* property of these controls. What step should you take?
   - **A.** Add a constructor to the user control. The constructor should take parameters for each of the *TextBox.Text* properties. It will then set these parameter values appropriately.
   - **B.** Create properties on the user control that allow users to get and set the *Text* property of each *TextBox* control.
   - **C.** Controls added to a user control, by default, expose their default property.
   - **D.** Add code to the *Init* method of the user control. This code should raise an event. The page that hosts the control can then use this event to set the *TextBox.Text* properties accordingly.

Lesson 2: Working with Custom Web Server Controls

Sometimes you wish to encapsulate functionality into a complete Web server control that can be deployed as a .dll file and used across sites. Doing so will give you more use and control over the given control. It will also allow you to define a better design-time experience for the consumers of your control. This includes Toolbox and designer functionality. This lesson explores how you create custom Web server controls targeted at ASP.NET developers.

After this lesson, you will be able to:

- Create a custom Web server control.
- Add custom Web server controls to a Web page.
- Individualize a custom Web server control.
- Create a custom designer for a custom Web server control.
- Consume a custom Web server control in a Web site.

Estimated lesson time: 60 minutes

Creating a Custom Web Server Control

A *custom Web control* is a control that inherits from a *WebServer* control. The custom Web control contains the code necessary to render the control (or inherits it from another control). A custom Web control can be compiled into a separate .dll file that can be shared among applications and can optionally be installed in the global assembly cache (GAC).

There are two common approaches to creating a custom Web server control. The first approach is to create a Web server control that inherits directly from *WebControl*. The *WebControl* class provides a base set of functionality. This includes handling styles with UI-related properties such as *BackColor*, *ForeColor*, *Font*, *Height*, and *Width*. However, this leaves a lot of work to develop the control. The second approach is to inherit from an existing Web control that already provides the core features of your control. This can give you a jump start and allow you to focus on what makes your control different. This is the more common scenario. This section explores both approaches.

Regardless of the approach, you should consider the reusability of the control. If the custom Web server control is targeted to multiple Web sites, you should place the new custom Web server control class into a class library project to create a .dll file that can be shared. If the custom Web server control is only meant for the current Web site, you can add the custom Web server control's class file to the Web site.

Inheriting from Existing Web Server Controls

A common scenario is to create a custom Web server control by inheriting from an existing control to add additional functionality. This method ensures that you get a lot of base functionality from the inherited control. You then extend this functionality with your custom control.

For example, suppose you wish to create a custom version of the *TextBox* control. This custom version will include text that labels the given *TextBox* (such as "User Name" or "Password"). You create this control by first inheriting from *TextBox*. If you are externalizing your control into a separate .dll file, you must also set a reference to the *System.Web* namespace.

In this example, you want to allow consumers for your control to set the value for the *TextBox* description or prompt. You might also wish to allow them to set the width of this prompt text to help with alignment. There are no other properties that you need to set, as the control inherits form *TextBox* and thus exposes its properties already.

The final step is to render the display of your user control. For this you must override the *Render* method of the *TextBox* control. This will use an *HtmlTextWriter* to output your display information (the *TextBox* prompt) and the base rendering of the *TextBox* control. The following code shows an example of the complete, custom *LabeledTextBox* Web user control.

```
'VB
Imports System.Web.UI
Imports System.Web.UI.WebControls

Public Class LabeledTextBox
  Inherits TextBox

  Private _promptText As String
  Public Property PromptText() As String
    Get
      Return _promptText
    End Get
    Set(ByVal value As String)
      _promptText = value
    End Set
  End Property

  Private _promptWidth As Integer
  Public Property PromptWidth() As Integer
    Get
      Return _promptWidth
    End Get
    Set(ByVal value As Integer)
      _promptWidth = value
```

```
    End Set
  End Property

  Protected Ov-errides Sub Render(ByVal writer As HtmlTextWriter)
    writer.Write( _
      "<span style=""display:inline-block;width:{0}px"">{1} </span>", _
      PromptWidth, PromptText)
    MyBase.Render(writer)
  End Sub

End Class
```

```
//C#
using System;
using System.Web.UI;
using System.Web.UI.WebControls;

public class LabeledTextBox : TextBox
{
  public string PromptText { get; set; }
  public int PromptWidth { get; set; }

  protected override void Render(HtmlTextWriter writer)
  {
    writer.Write(
      @"<span style=""display:inline-block;width:{0}px"">{1} </span>",
      PromptWidth, PromptText);
    base.Render(writer);
  }
}
```

Note that this control does not, at present, provide design-time support. However, the control can still be used as a control on a Web page as long as it is created through code. If the control is externalized into its own project, you need to set a reference to it from the Web site. You can then create it as you would any other control. The following code shows an example of a Web page's code-behind file that does just that:

```
'VB
Protected Sub Page_Init(ByVal sender As Object, ByVal e As System.EventArgs) _
  Handles Me.Init

  Dim width As Integer = 150
  Dim prompt1 As New MyUserControls.LabeledTextBox()

  prompt1.PromptText = "Enter Name:"
```

```
  prompt1.PromptWidth = width
  form1.Controls.Add(prompt1)

  Dim br As New LiteralControl("<br />")
  form1.Controls.Add(br)

  Dim prompt2 As New MyUserControls.LabeledTextBox()
  prompt2.PromptText = "Enter Address:"
  prompt2.PromptWidth = width
  form1.Controls.Add(prompt2)

End Sub

//C#
protected void Page_Init(object sender, EventArgs e)
{
  int width = 150;
  MyUserControls.LabeledTextBox prompt1 = new
    MyUserControls.LabeledTextBox();

  prompt1.PromptText = "Enter Name:";
  prompt1.PromptWidth = width;
  form1.Controls.Add(prompt1);

  LiteralControl br = new LiteralControl("<br />");
  form1.Controls.Add(br);

  MyUserControls.LabeledTextBox prompt2 = new
    MyUserControls.LabeledTextBox();
  prompt2.PromptText = "Enter Address:";
  prompt2.PromptWidth = width;
  form1.Controls.Add(prompt2);
}
```

Figure 10-4 shows the rendered Web page. When this Web page is run, the two *Labeled-TextBox* control instances have their *TextBox* controls lined up vertically because the *LabelWidth* property is set for these controls.

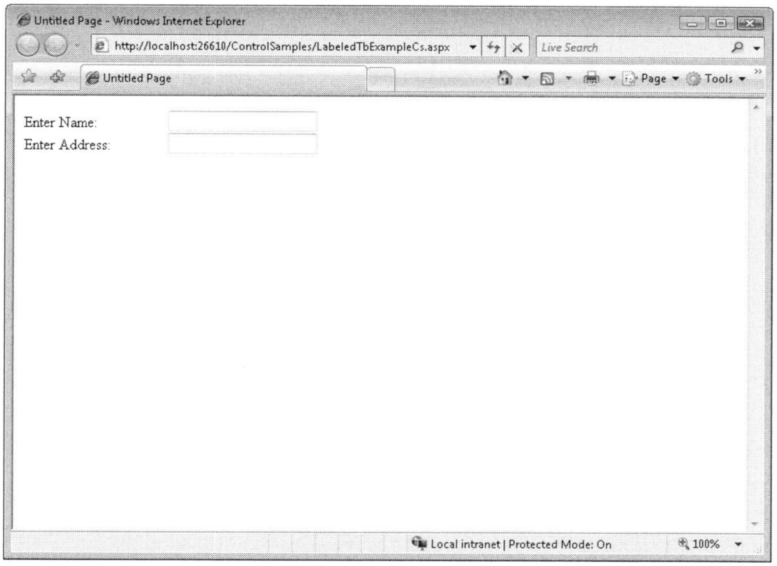

FIGURE 10-4 The rendered *LabeledTextBox* control

Inheriting Directly from the *WebControl* Class

Another approach to creating a custom Web control is to inherit directly from the *WebControl* class. This approach is desirable when there is no control that currently provides default behavior similar to the control you wish to implement. When inheriting from the *WebControl* class, you must override the *Render* method to provide the desired output.

For example, suppose you wish to create a custom control that allows a user to display a logo and an associated company name for the logo. For this, you might create two properties: *LogoUrl* and *CompanyName*. You would then add code to the *Render* method to output the display of your control. The following code shows an example:

```
'VB
Imports System.Web.UI
Imports System.Web.UI.WebControls

Public Class LogoControl
  Inherits WebControl

  Private _logoUrl As String
  Public Property LogoUrl() As String
    Get
      Return _logoUrl
    End Get
    Set(ByVal value As String)
```

```
      _logoUrl = value
    End Set
  End Property

  Private _companyName As String
  Public Property CompanyName() As String
    Get
      Return _companyName
    End Get
    Set(ByVal value As String)
      _companyName = value
    End Set
  End Property

  Protected Overrides Sub Render( _
        ByVal writer As System.Web.UI.HtmlTextWriter)
    writer.WriteFullBeginTag("div")
    writer.Write("<img src=""{0}"" /><br />", LogoUrl)
    writer.Write(CompanyName + "<br />")
    writer.WriteEndTag("div")
  End Sub

End Class

//C#
using System;
using System.Web.UI;
using System.Web.UI.WebControls;

public class LogoControl : WebControl
{
  public LogoControl()
  {
  }

  public string LogoUrl
  {
    get { return _logoUrl; }
    set { _logoUrl = value; }
  }
  private string _logoUrl;

  public string CompanyName
  {
    get { return _companyName; }
```

```
    set { _companyName = value; }
  }
  private string _companyName;

  protected override void Render(HtmlTextWriter writer)
  {
    writer.WriteFullBeginTag("div");
    writer.Write(@"<img src=""{0}"" /><br />", LogoUrl);
    writer.Write(CompanyName + "<br />");
    writer.WriteEndTag("div");
  }
}
```

When this control is rendered, a *<div>* tag is output to the browser. The *div* tag contains a nested *img* tag with the *src* set to the *LogoUrl*. Also in the *div* tag is the *CompanyName* as text on the line that follows the image.

You can create an instance of this control and use it on a page the same way you would with the first custom Web control (in the prior section). Again, there is still no Toolbox or designer support. We look at those options in the coming sections.

Adding Toolbox Support for a Custom Web Server Control

In the previous examples, the custom Web controls were added to a Web page dynamically by placing code in the code-behind page. However, developers are used to working with controls that originate from the Visual Studio Toolbox and provide design-time, declarative markup support. Web server control developers will want to take this capacity.

The primary requirement to allow a custom Web control to be added to the Toolbox is that the Web control be placed into a separate .dll file. In this case, you can right-click the Toolbox and select Choose Items. You can then browse to the given user control's .dll file to add the controls that are contained in the file to the Toolbox.

As an example, suppose the controls created previously are in their own class library called *MyUserControls.dll*. You can set a reference to this .dll file to add the .dll to the Bin folder of your project. You can then use the Choose Toolbox Items dialog box to select any controls within the library and add them to the Toolbox. You can then drag these controls from the Toolbox to a Web page to set them declaratively.

Figure 10-5 shows an example. Notice that the controls are defined in their own grouping at the top of the Toolbox. When you drag a control to the page, the control must be registered. This markup is shown at the top of the page. The bottom of the page shows the control defined declaratively (including custom properties).

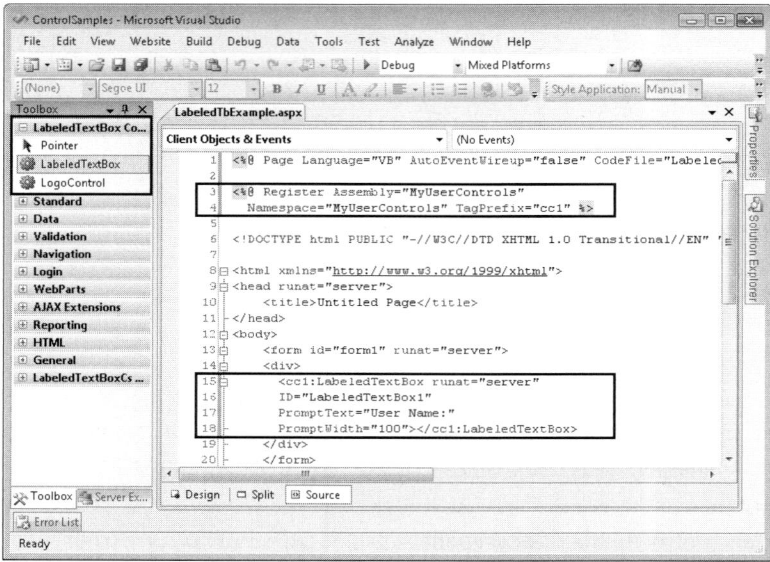

FIGURE 10-5 The custom Web controls in the Toolbox used declaratively

Adding a Custom Icon for Your Control

Notice in Figure 10-5 that the control uses a default icon. You can add your own custom icon through an attribute called *ToolboxBitmap of the System.Drawing namespace*. This attribute specifies a bitmap that is 16 × 16 pixels in size.

The path to the icon must either be an absolute path with a drive letter specified or an embedded bitmap stored in the control as a resource. Clearly the second option is more practical, as you can deploy your control as a single file. When doing so, you need to define your .bmp file as having the same name as the class (classname.bmp). You must also select the file in Solution Explorer and view its properties window. From here, you set the *Build Action* property to *Embedded Resource* to ensure the file is embedded in the .dll.

As an example, suppose you wish to create a custom icon for the *LabeledTextBox* control. You must first set a reference from your control project to *System.Drawing*. You then add a 16 × 16 bitmap to the root of your project. You can then set the *ToolBoxBitmapAttribute* for the class. The following code shows an example:

```
'VB
<ToolboxBitmap(GetType(LabeledTextBox), _
  "MyUserControls.LabeledTextBox.bmp")> _
Public Class LabeledTextBox
  Inherits TextBox
```

```
//C#
[ToolboxBitmap(typeof(LabeledTextBox),
  "MyUserControls.LabeledTextBox.bmp")]
  public class LabeledTextBox : TextBox
```

Figure 10-6 shows the results in the Toolbox window. You can see the custom *LabeledTextBox* control has a specialized icon.

FIGURE 10-6 A custom icon for the *LabeledTextBox* control in the Toolbox

Setting a Default Property for Your Custom Control

You can also set the default property for your control. A default property is accessed without actually specifying a property. For example, the *Text* property of the *TextBox* control is a default property. This means calls to an instance of *TextBox* will return this property if no other property is requested.

You set the default property for your control through the *DefaultProperty* attribute class in the *System.ComponentModel* namespace. You apply this attribute at the class level. You simply pass the name of one of your properties to this attribute. The following code shows an example:

```
'VB
<DefaultProperty("PromptText")> _
Public Class LabeledTextBox
  Inherits TextBox

//C#
[DefaultProperty("PromptText")]
public class LabeledTextBox : TextBox
```

Control the Markup Generated for Your Custom Control

You can further change the way your custom server control behaves when it is dropped onto the Web page by setting the *ToolboxDataAttribute* in your control class. This attribute is used to change the markup that gets generated by Visual Studio. A common scenario is to set default values for properties on the control inside the generated markup.

The following code shows an implementation of the *ToolboxDataAttribute* for the *LabeledTextBox* control created earlier:

```
'VB
<ToolboxData( _
   "<{0}:LabeledTextBox runat=""server"" PromptText="""" PromptWidth=""100""  />")> _
Public Class LabeledTextBox
  Inherits TextBox

//C#
[ToolboxData(
  @"<{0}:LabeledTextBox runat=""server"" PromptText="""" PromptWidth=""100"" />")]
public class LabeledTextBox : TextBox
```

In this example, the placeholder {0} contains the namespace prefix as defined by the Web page designer. Notice that the *PromptText* and *PromptWidth* attributes are inserted automatically. *PromptWidth* is assigned the default value of 100. When added to a page, the following markup is generated:

```
<cc1:LabeledTextBox ID="LabeledTextBox1" runat="server" PromptText="" PromptWidth="100">
</cc1:LabeledTextBox>
```

You can also change the namespace prefix that is assigned by the Web page designer by assigning the *TagPrefixAttribute* of the *System.Web.UI* namespace to the assembly that contains your custom control. The following code shows the namespace prefix being changed to "muc" (my user controls) for the controls in the *MyUserControls* project:

```
'VB
<Assembly: TagPrefix("MyUserControls", "muc")>

//C#
[assembly: TagPrefix("MyUserControls", "muc")]
```

With the previous change to the *LabeledTextBox* control, the *Register* directive will change as follows when a user drags the control onto a page:

```
<%@ Register Assembly="MyUserControls" Namespace="MyUserControls" TagPrefix="muc" %>
```

The control will also change to use the new prefix as displayed here:

```
<muc:LabeledTextBox ID="LabeledTextBox1" runat="server" PromptText="" PromptWidth="100">
</muc:LabeledTextBox>
```

Creating a Custom Designer for a Custom Control

Controls added from the Toolbox already have design-time support; that is, you can see them in Design view of the page and work with their properties in the Properties window. However, you might wish to alter the default rendering of the control in design mode. In addition, some controls might not be visible due to code that needs to run to populate specific properties. In these cases you can specify a custom designer for your control.

To do so, you start by adding a reference to the *System.Design.dll* assembly in your user control. You then create a new class in your user control that inherits from the *ControlDesigner* class. This class will override the *GetDesignTimeHtml* method of the *ControlDesigner* class to render separate design-time HTML that can be set based on the property settings of the control instance. You then apply the *Designer* attribute to your control. To this, you pass an instance of your *ControlDesigner* class.

For example, suppose you wish to customize the design-time view of the *LabelTextBox* control. You might set the control to display a reminder to users when they have yet to set the *PromptText* property. To get started, you create a new class that inherits from *ControlDesigner* and overrides the *GetDesignTimeHtml* method. This override should get an instance of the control and check it to see if the *PromptText* value has been set. If not, it should display an alternate view. The following code shows an example (this code requires a project reference to *System.Design*):

```
'VB
Imports System.ComponentModel

Public Class LabeledTextBoxDesigner
  Inherits System.Web.UI.Design.ControlDesigner

  Private _labeledTextBoxControl As LabeledTextBox

  Public Overrides Function GetDesignTimeHtml() As String

    _labeledTextBoxControl = CType(Component, LabeledTextBox)
    If (_labeledTextBoxControl.PromptText.Length = 0) Then
      Return "<div style='color: Gray'>[Define PromptText]</div>"
    Else
      Return MyBase.GetDesignTimeHtml()
    End If

  End Function

End Class

//C#
using System;
```

```
using System.ComponentModel;
using System.Web.UI.Design;

namespace MyUserControls
{
  public class LabeledTextBoxDesigner : ControlDesigner
  {
    private LabeledTextBox _labeledTextBoxControl;

    public override string GetDesignTimeHtml()
    {
      if (_labeledTextBoxControl.PromptText.Trim().Length == 0)
        return "<div style='color: Gray'>[Define PromptText]</div>";
      else
        return base.GetDesignTimeHtml();
    }

    public override void Initialize(IComponent component)
    {
      _labeledTextBoxControl = (LabeledTextBox)component;
      base.Initialize(component);
      return;
    }
  }
}
```

After the class is created, you can assign the *DesignerAttribute* to the *user control* class, as shown in the following code:

```
'VB
<Designer("MyUserControls.LabeledTextBoxDesigner, MyUserControls")> _
Public Class LabeledTextBox
  Inherits TextBox

//C#
[Designer("MyUserControls.LabeledTextBoxDesigner, MyUserControls")]
public class LabeledTextBox : TextBox
```

Now, when the control is dragged and dropped onto a Web page, the designer code executes and determines the layout (custom or base). If the *PromptText* property is not set, the control is displayed as shown in Figure 10-7. When the property is set, the control displays as before.

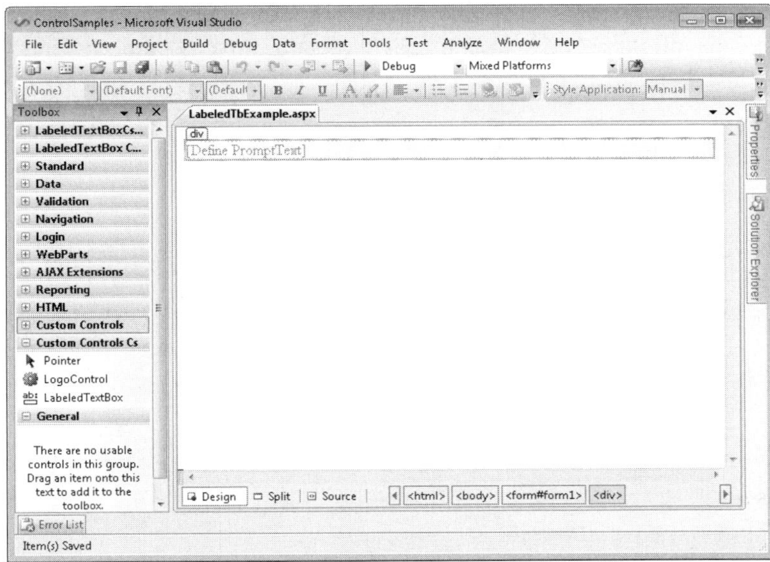

FIGURE 10-7 The *LabeledTextBox* control shown with a custom Design view

Creating a Composite Control

A composite control is a custom Web control that contains other controls. This sounds like a user control, but the composite control doesn't provide a designer screen for creating the control, nor an .ascx file that lets you drag and drop controls on it at design time. Instead, you create a custom control that inherits from the *CompositeControl* class. You then add constituent controls to this control. The composite control then handles events raised by its child controls.

A composite control is rendered out as a tree of constituent controls, each having its own life cycle. Together, these constituent controls form a new control. Because each of the child controls knows how to handle its own *ViewState* and *PostBack* data, you don't need to write extra code to deal with this.

To create a composite control, you start by creating a class that inherits from the *CompositeControl* class and overrides the *CreateChildControls* method. The *CreateChild-Controls* method contains the code to instantiate the child controls and set their properties. If you want to be able to assign styles to the composite control, you should create an instance of the *Panel* class to provide a container that can have attributes assigned to it. In this case, you add it to the *Controls* collection of your composite control, and then add your controls to the *Panel* control.

As an example, you wish to create a composite control that prompts users for their user name and password. You might also include a submit button with a click event that can be subscribed to. You start by defining a class that inherits from *CompositeControl* and implements the *INamingContainer* interface. The following code shows the implementation of this control:

```
'VB
Imports System.Web.UI
Imports System.Web.UI.WebControls

Public Class UserPasswordControl
  Inherits CompositeControl
  Implements INamingContainer

  Public Event Submitted As System.EventHandler

  Public Property UserName() As String
    Get
      Dim txt As TextBox
      txt = CType(Me.FindControl("UserName"), TextBox)
      Return txt.Text
    End Get
    Set(ByVal Value As String)
      Dim txt As TextBox
      txt = CType(Me.FindControl("UserName"), TextBox)
      txt.Text = Value
    End Set
  End Property

  Public Property Password() As String
    Get
      Dim txt As TextBox
      txt = CType(Me.FindControl("Password"), TextBox)
      Return txt.Text
    End Get
    Set(ByVal Value As String)
      Dim txt As TextBox
      txt = CType(Me.FindControl("Password"), TextBox)
      txt.Text = Value
    End Set
  End Property

  Protected Overrides Sub CreateChildControls()
    Dim pnl As New Panel()
    Dim txtUserName As New TextBox()
    Dim txtPassword As New TextBox()
    Dim btnSubmit As New Button()
```

```
    AddHandler btnSubmit.Click, Addressof btnSubmit_Click

    'start control buildup
    Controls.Add(pnl)
    'add user name row
    pnl.Controls.Add(New LiteralControl("<table><tr><td>"))
    pnl.Controls.Add(New LiteralControl("User Name:"))
    pnl.Controls.Add(New LiteralControl("</td><td>"))
    pnl.Controls.Add(txtUserName)
    pnl.Controls.Add(New LiteralControl("</td></tr>"))
    'add password row
    pnl.Controls.Add(New LiteralControl("<tr><td>"))
    pnl.Controls.Add(New LiteralControl("Password:"))
    pnl.Controls.Add(New LiteralControl("</td><td>"))
    pnl.Controls.Add(txtPassword)
    pnl.Controls.Add(New LiteralControl("</td></tr>"))
    'add submit button row
    pnl.Controls.Add(New LiteralControl( _
      "<tr><td colspan=""2"" align=""center"" >"))
    pnl.Controls.Add(btnSubmit)
    pnl.Controls.Add(New LiteralControl("</td></tr></table>"))

    'set up control properties
    pnl.Style.Add("background-color", "silver")
    pnl.Style.Add("width", "275px")
    txtUserName.ID = "UserName"
    txtUserName.Style.Add("width", "170px")
    txtPassword.ID = "Password"
    txtPassword.TextMode = TextBoxMode.Password
    txtPassword.Style.Add("width", "170px")
    btnSubmit.Text = "Submit"

  End Sub

  Public Sub btnSubmit_Click(ByVal sender As Object, ByVal e As EventArgs)
    RaiseEvent Submitted(Me, e)
  End Sub
End Class
```

```
//C#
using System;
using System.ComponentModel;
using System.Web.UI;
using System.Web.UI.WebControls;
using System.Drawing;
```

```
public class UserPasswordControl : CompositeControl
{

  public event System.EventHandler Submitted;

  public string UserName
  {
    get
    {
      TextBox txt = (TextBox)FindControl("UserName");
      return txt.Text;
    }
    set
    {
      TextBox txt = (TextBox)FindControl("UserName");
      txt.Text = value;
    }
  }

  public string Password
  {
    get
    {
      TextBox pwd = (TextBox)FindControl("Password");
      return pwd.Text;
    }
    set
    {
      TextBox pwd = (TextBox)FindControl("Password");
      pwd.Text = value;
    }
  }

  protected override void CreateChildControls()
  {
    Panel pnl = new Panel();
    TextBox txtUserName = new TextBox();
    TextBox txtPassword = new TextBox();
    Button btnSubmit = new Button();
    btnSubmit.Click += new EventHandler(btnSubmit_Click);

    //start control buildup
    Controls.Add(pnl);
    //add user name row
    pnl.Controls.Add(new LiteralControl("<table><tr><td>"));
```

```
    pnl.Controls.Add(new LiteralControl("User Name:"));
    pnl.Controls.Add(new LiteralControl("</td><td>"));
    pnl.Controls.Add(txtUserName);
    pnl.Controls.Add(new LiteralControl("</td></tr>"));
    //add password row
    pnl.Controls.Add(new LiteralControl("<tr><td>"));
    pnl.Controls.Add(new LiteralControl("Password:"));
    pnl.Controls.Add(new LiteralControl("</td><td>"));
    pnl.Controls.Add(txtPassword);
    pnl.Controls.Add(new LiteralControl("</td></tr>"));
    //add submit button row
    pnl.Controls.Add(new LiteralControl(
      @"<tr><td colspan=""2"" align=""center"" >"));
    pnl.Controls.Add(btnSubmit);
    pnl.Controls.Add(new LiteralControl("</td></tr></table>"));

    //set up control properties
    pnl.Style.Add("background-color", "silver");
    pnl.Style.Add("width", "275px");
    txtUserName.ID = "UserName";
    txtUserName.Style.Add("width", "170px");
    txtPassword.ID = "Password";
    txtPassword.TextMode = TextBoxMode.Password;
    txtPassword.Style.Add("width", "170px");
    btnSubmit.Text = "Submit";
  }

  void btnSubmit_Click(object sender, EventArgs e)
  {
    if (Submitted != null) Submitted(this, e);
  }
}
```

In this code, the *UserName* and *Password* properties are exposed to give users of the control access to this data. Notice these properties have to use the *FindControl* method to expose the properties of the constituent controls. An event called *Submitted* is also created so users can receive notification when the submit button's *Click* event fires. The *CreateChildControls* method performs the work to instantiate the child controls for this composite control.

This control can be tested by adding it to a Web page using the same techniques described for the other custom Web controls. In the following code example, code is added in the code-behind file of the UserPassControlTest.aspx page to create a *UserPasswordControl* dynamically and set its properties. The *Submitted* event is used simply to display the user name and password.

```
'VB
Partial Class UserPasswordControlTest
  Inherits System.Web.UI.Page

  Protected Sub Page_Init(ByVal sender As Object, _
      ByVal e As System.EventArgs) Handles Me.Init
    Dim p As New MyUserControls.UserPasswordControl()
    p.Style.Add("position", "absolute")
    p.Style.Add("left", "25px")
    p.Style.Add("top", "50px")
    form1.Controls.Add(p)
    AddHandler p.Submitted, AddressOf p_Submitted
  End Sub

  Public Sub p_Submitted(ByVal sender As Object, ByVal e As EventArgs)
    Dim p As UserPasswordControl = CType(sender, UserPasswordControl)
    Response.Write("User: " + p.UserName + "  Pass: " + p.Password)
  End Sub
End Class

//C#
using System;
using System.Web.UI;
using System.Web.UI.WebControls;

public partial class UserPasswordControlTest : System.Web.UI.Page
{
  protected void Page_Init(object sender, EventArgs e)
  {
    UserPasswordControl p = new MyUserControls.UserPasswordControl();
    p.Style.Add("position", "absolute");
    p.Style.Add("left", "25px");
    p.Style.Add("top", "50px");
    form1.Controls.Add(p);
    p.Submitted += new EventHandler(p_Submitted);
  }

  void p_Submitted(object sender, EventArgs e)
  {
    UserPasswordControl p = (UserPasswordControl)sender;
    Response.Write("User: " + p.UserName + "  Pass: " + p.Password);
  }
}
```

When this Web page is run, the *UserPasswordControl* displays at the location determined by the *Style* property. After typing a user name and password, click Submit to display that user name and password. Figure 10-8 shows an example.

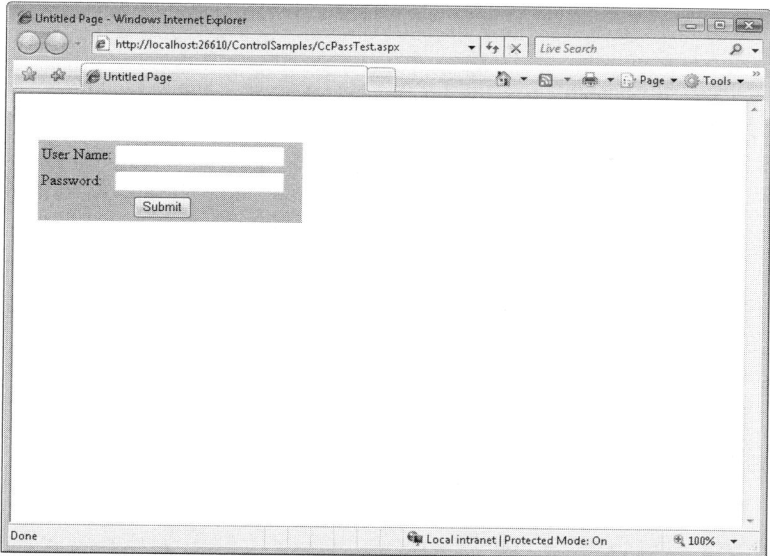

FIGURE 10-8 The *UserPasswordControl* collects the user name and password and exposes the *Submitted* event for processing the data

Creating a Templated Custom Web Control

A templated custom Web control provides separation of control data from its presentation. This means that a templated control does not provide a default UI. For example, if you know that you need to display product data, but you don't know how the developer who intends to use your control wants to format the product data, you could create a templated control called *ProductControl* that allows the page designer to supply the format for the product data as a template.

A templated control must provide a naming container and a class with properties and methods that are accessible to the host page. The template contains the UI for the templated user control and is supplied by the page developer at design time. The templates can contain controls and markup. You can create a templated control using the following steps:

1. Create a *ClassLibrary* (.dll) project for your templated control.
2. Add a reference to the *System.Web.dll* library.
3. To your project, add a container class that has public properties for the data that you wish to be able to access via the *Container* object in your template.
4. In the container class file, add an *Imports* (*using* in C#) statement for the *System.Web.UI* namespace.

5. Code your container class to inherit from the *System.Web.UI.Control* class and implement the *INamingContainer* interface.
6. Add a class to the project for your templated control.
7. In the class file, add an *Imports* (*using* in C#) statement for the *System.Web.UI* namespace.
8. Code your templated control to inherit from the *System.Web.UI.Control* class and implement the *INamingContainer* interface.
9. Add the *ParseChildren(true)* attribute to the class. This attribute provides direction to the page parser to indicate that the nested content contained within the server control is parsed as a control and not used to set properties of the templated control.
10. Create one or more properties in the templated control class with the data type of *ITemplate*. These properties will be used by the page developer to define the actual layout of the control. These properties need to have the *TemplateContainer* attribute set to the data type of the container, which might be the templated control. Alternatively, you can create a subcontainer if you have repeating items to display in the template. Also, these properties have to have the *PersistenceMode* attribute set to *PersistenceMode.InnerProperty*, which allows page designers to add inner HTML elements to the HTML source of the templated control.
11. Add the desired properties to the template container that are to be accessible by the template.
12. The *DataBind* method must be overridden to call the *EnsureChildControls* method on the base *Control* class.
13. The *CreateChildControls* method must be overridden to provide the code to instantiate the template using the *InstantiateIn* method of the *ITemplate* interface. Code should also be provided for a default implementation if no template is provided.

As you can see, many of the steps to create a templated custom Web server control are similar to those for creating a templated user control. The primary differences are in how you actually create the custom Web server control versus creating a user control.

Quick Check

1. **You wish to create a new, custom Web server control that does not rely on any one existing ASP.NET control. From what class should you inherit?**
2. **You want to create a control that can be distributed as a .dll. The control contains several *TextBox*, *Label*, and *Button* controls and you want to be able to add the control to the Toolbox. What is the best choice of control to create?**
3. **You wish to create a new, custom control that extends from the *CheckBox* control. From which class should you inherit?**

Quick Check Answers

1. Inherit from the *WebControl* class.
2. Create a composite control.
3. You should inherit directly from the *CheckBox* class.

LAB Working with Custom Web Server Controls

In this lab, you create a custom Web server control called *StateControl* that displays a list of states in the United States. Of course, you can repurpose this control to display a static list of almost anything.

EXERCISE 1 Create the Visual Studio Projects and Define the Custom Control

In this exercise, you create the projects used by this lab. You also write the code for the custom server control.

1. Open Visual Studio and create a new Web site called **CustomControlLab** using your preferred programming language. This Web site will serve to host the custom control on a page.
2. Add a class library project to your solution. Name this library **MyCustomControls**.
3. Rename *Class1* to ***StateListControl***.
4. Add references to the custom control project to both *System.Web.dll* and the *System.Drawing.dll* assemblies.
5. Open the *StateListControl* class file. Add code at the top of the page to import the *System.Web.UI.Webcontrols* and *System.Drawing* namespaces.
6. Define the *StateListControl* as inheriting from *DropDownList*.
7. Add code to the constructor of the *StateControl class* to create an empty *ListItem* and a *ListItem* for each state. Add the *ListItems* to the *Items* collection of the *StateControl*. The *ListItem* for each state displays the full name of the state, but the posted value is the two-character state abbreviation. The following is an example:

```
'VB
Imports System.Web.UI.WebControls
Imports System.Drawing

Public Class StateListControl
  Inherits DropDownList

  Public Sub New()
    Items.Add(New ListItem("", ""))
    Items.Add(New ListItem("Alabama", "AL"))
```

```
    '-- add code for additional states (see code on CD)

    SelectedIndex = 0
  End Sub

End Class

//C#
using System;
using System.Web.UI.WebControls;
using System.Drawing;

namespace MyCustomControls
{
  public class StateListControl : DropDownList
  {
    public StateListControl()
    {
      Items.Add(new ListItem("", ""));
      Items.Add(new ListItem("Alabama", "AL"));

      //-- add code for additional states (see code on CD)

      SelectedIndex = 0;
    }
  }
}
```

8. Build the *MyCustomControls* project.

EXERCISE 2 Add the Custom Control to a Web Page

In this exercise, you add the *StateListControl* created in the prior exercise to the Toolbox and to a Web page.

1. Continue editing the project you created in the previous exercise. Alternatively, you can open the completed Lesson 1, Exercise 1 project from the sample files installed from the CD and begin from there.
2. Add the *StateListControl* to the Toolbox by right-clicking the Toolbox and selecting Choose Items. Click Browse and locate the *MyCustomControls.dll* assembly. Select the *MyCustomControls.dll* assembly, and the *StateListControl* is displayed in the Toolbox.
3. Open the Default.aspx page and drag the *StateListControl* from the Toolbox onto the page. This will register the control with the page (see the @ *Register* directive). It will also create the following markup for the control on your page:

```
<cc1:StateListControl ID="StateListControl1" runat="server">
</cc1:StateListControl>
```

4. Run the Web site in a browser to test the user control.

Lesson Summary

- You can build a custom Web control by inheriting from the *WebControl* class or through inheriting directly from an existing ASP.NET control's class provided you wish to extend the features of that control.
- You create a composite Web control when you need to base your control on multiple ASP.NET controls. You do so by inheriting from the *CompositeControl* class.
- You can add Toolbox support to your custom control to control the icon, the generated markup, and the display of the control in the designer.
- You can create a templated custom Web server control to allow users to define the layout of the given control at design time.

Lesson Review

You can use the following questions to test your knowledge of the information in Lesson 2, "Working with Custom Web Server Controls."

The questions are also available on the companion CD if you prefer to review them in electronic form.

> ***NOTE*** **ANSWERS**
>
> **Answers to these questions and explanations of why each answer choice is right or wrong are located in the "Answers" section at the end of the book.**

1. You wish to define a custom image to be displayed in the Toolbox for your custom Web server control. Which actions do you take? (Choose all that apply.)
   - **A.** Set a reference to the *System.Design* namespace.
   - **B.** Set a reference to the *System.Drawing* namespace.
   - **C.** Add the *ToolboxBitmap* attribute to the class.
   - **D.** Add the *ToolboxData* attribute to the class.
2. You are going to create a custom Web server control that inherits directly from the *WebControl* class. Which method do you need to override to get your control to display in the browser window?

A. *OnInit*

B. *Finalize*

C. *ToString*

D. *Render*

3. You are creating a composite control. You create a class that inherits from the *CompositeControl* class. What method must be overridden so you can provide code to instantiate the child controls and set their properties?

   A. *CreateChildControls*

   B. *DataBindChildren*

   C. *CreateControlStyle*

   D. *BuildProfileTree*

Chapter Review

To further practice and reinforce the skills you learned in this chapter, you can perform the following tasks:

- Review the chapter summary.
- Complete the case scenarios. These scenarios set up real-world situations involving the topics of this chapter and ask you to create solutions.
- Complete the suggested practices.
- Take a practice test.

Chapter Summary

- You create user controls by combining ASP.NET controls onto a single control. User controls encapsulate common functionality. User controls are not compiled into their own .dll files. Instead, they are shared within a single Web site. When a user control runs, it executes following the same life cycle as that of a Web page.
- You create custom Web controls by defining a class that inherits either from *WebControl* or from another ASP.NET control. You use attributes to change how your custom controls work within the Toolbox, generate markup, and display in the designer.

Case Scenarios

In the following case scenarios, you apply what you've learned in this chapter. If you have difficulty completing this work, review the material in this chapter before beginning the next chapter. You can find answers to these questions in the "Answers" section at the end of this book.

Case Scenario 1: Sharing Controls Between Applications

You are creating a new Web site and find that you need to have a group of controls on many pages. These controls are used jointly to collect data from the user. On further investigation, you realize that your company uses these controls to collect user data on several other Web sites. Also, the company wants to standardize the layout and behavior of the user data collection controls.

QUESTIONS

1. What type of control should you create?
2. Based on your answer to Question 1, why have you excluded other types of controls?

Case Scenario 2: Providing Layout Flexibility

You are a Web developer at Contoso Pharmacy. You are working on an existing Web site and you notice that there are several areas where customer information is displayed throughout the site. After additional investigation, you notice that the custom information needs to be rendered uniquely in many of the areas where it is defined. You wish to provide a common control that can be used within this site to display this customer information.

QUESTIONS

1. Should you create a custom control or a user control?
2. How should you lay out the control?
3. From what class should your control inherit?

Suggested Practices

To help you successfully master the exam objectives presented in this chapter, complete the following tasks.

Create a New Custom User Control

For this task, you should complete both practices.

- **Practice 1** Consider a common feature of some of the sites you've developed. Take that feature and create a user control. The user control should contain other ASP.NET controls and expose them as properties. Practice adding the user control to several Web pages and write code to access the properties of the user control.
- **Practice 2** Add one or more custom events to the user control. Subscribe to this event from the hosting page.

Create a New Custom Web Server Control

For this task, you should complete Practice 1 to get an overview of creating controls that inherit from *WebControl*. Practices 2 and 3 extend Practice 1 and help develop additional skills.

- **Practice 1** Consider a feature that is common across different sites you've developed; try to think of a feature that does not involve a specific, existing control. Use this feature to develop a new custom Web server control that inherits from the *WebControl* class.
- **Practice 2** Create a custom bitmap for your control created in Practice 1. Add the file to your project. Embed the bitmap as a resource to the project and apply it to the class. Compile the application and use it on a Web page. Be sure to add the control to the Toolbox.

- **Practice 3** Return to your control. Add a custom designer layout to be displayed when the control is in a certain state.

Create a New Composite Web Server Control

For this task, you should complete both practices.

- **Practice 1** Create a class library project that contains a new class that inherits from the *System.Web.UI.CompositeControl* class. Implement code to add constituent controls to your composite control and add properties to the composite control. Compile and add the custom Web control to the ToolBox.
- **Practice 2** Practice adding the composite control to several Web pages and write code to access the composite control properties.

Create a New Templated Control

For this task, you should complete both practices.

- **Practice 1** Return to the *LabeledTextbox* control created earlier in this chapter. Convert this control to a custom Web server control with a layout that is based on templates.
- **Practice 2** Practice adding the templated control to several Web pages and defining different layouts.

Take a Practice Test

The practice tests on this book's companion CD offer many options. For example, you can test yourself on just the content covered in this chapter, or you can test yourself on all the 70-562 certification exam content. You can set up the test so it closely simulates the experience of taking a certification exam, or you can set it up in study mode so you can look at the correct answers and explanations after you answer each question.

> ***MORE INFO*** **PRACTICE TESTS**
>
> **For details about all the practice test options available, see the "How to Use the Practice Tests" section in this book's Introduction.**

CHAPTER 11

Programming the Web Application

The tools in Microsoft Visual Studio and ASP.NET allow you to easily create Web pages and push them to a server without giving much thought to the underlying architecture of the application server itself. This can be beneficial, but it is important to know when, why, and how you might interact with the application server. In fact, to write more efficient and reliable Web applications, you should understand where you can leverage the many components of your Web application server.

Fortunately, ASP.NET provides you access to a great deal of information related to the server platform and the browser-to-server communication. It allows you to examine information about the server using a set of intrinsic objects. It also allows you to intercept messages on the server to program against the server's features. This chapter explores both programming against the Web site and using the ASP.NET objects to get more information from the application server.

Exam objectives in this chapter:

- Programming Web Applications
  - Implement the Generic Handler.
  - Work with ASP.NET intrinsic objects.

Lessons in this chapter:

Before You Begin

To complete the lessons in this chapter, you should be familiar with developing applications with Visual Studio using Visual Basic or C#. In addition, you should be comfortable with all of the following:

- The Visual Studio 2008 Integrated Development Environment (IDE).
- A basic understanding of Hypertext Markup Language (HTML) and client-side scripting.
- How to create a new Web site.
- Adding Web server controls to a Web page.

Lesson 1: Using Web Site Programmability

There are certain Web programming tasks that are outside the bounds of the basic page request–response scenario. This includes catching otherwise unhandled exceptions, running tasks asynchronously, creating custom Hypertext Transfer Protocol (HTTP) handlers, and more. In these cases, you need to be able to write code that directly interacts with ASP.NET and Microsoft Internet Information Services (IIS). This lesson describes many of these ASP.NET programming tasks.

After this lesson, you will be able to:

- Catch unhandled exceptions at the page or application level.
- Read and modify settings in different configuration files.
- Enable asynchronous communication inside Web pages.
- Create a custom HTTP handler to respond to requests for nonstandard file types.

Estimated lesson time: 30 minutes

Page and Application Exception Handling

Exception handling is most effective when you catch exceptions for small blocks of code. For example, you should surround code that establishes a database connection with a *try-catch* block so that you can present very specific error information to the user. However, unhandled exceptions can still occur. In most cases, if you are not expecting to handle an exception, your code often does not have a *try-catch* block. In these cases, you can still capture these errors without sending the user to an ASP.NET error page.

There are two options for catching unhandled errors: catch them at the page level or catch them at the application level. To catch errors at the page level, you create a *Page_Error* event handler inside the code for each page for which you wish to catch unhandled errors. The event handler must accept an *Object* parameter and an *EventArgs* parameter. Typically, you do not need to examine either of these parameters within the event handler. Instead, you access the *Server.GetLastError* method to retrieve the last error, and then call *Server.ClearError* to remove the error from the queue. The following code sample demonstrates this by writing out the error message using *Trace.Write* (for information on tracing, see Chapter, 12, "Monitoring, Troubleshooting, and Debugging").

```
'VB
Protected Sub Page_Error(ByVal sender As Object, _
  ByVal e As System.EventArgs) Handles Me.Error

  Trace.Write("ERROR: " & Server.GetLastError().Message)
  Server.ClearError()
```

```
End Sub

//C#
private void Page_Error(object sender, EventArgs e)
{
  Trace.Write("ERROR: " + Server.GetLastError().Message);
  Server.ClearError();
}
```

Note that you cannot display error messages in controls. Controls are not accessible from within *Page_Error*.

EXAM TIP

Know that you retrieve the last error by calling *Server.GetLastError* and then clear the last error by calling *Server.ClearError*.

You can also catch unhandled exceptions at the application level. This allows you to have an application-wide, generic error handler. It also saves you from having to add *Page_Error* event handlers to each page in your site. You define an application-wide handler by adding the *Application_Error* method to your application's Global.asax file. Here you typically pass the error handling onto another page that might log the error and display troubleshooting information to the user. You can do so using the *Server.Transfer* method. This redirects the request to a different Web page for handling the error. The following shows code added to a Global .asax file for just this purpose:

```
'VB
Sub Application_Error(ByVal sender As Object, ByVal e As EventArgs)
  'code that runs when an unhandled error occurs
  Server.Transfer("HandleError.aspx")
End Sub

//C#
void Application_Error(object sender, EventArgs e)
{
  //code that runs when an unhandled error occurs
  Server.Transfer("HandleError.aspx");
}
```

Visual Studio automatically generates the *Application_Error* event handler for you when you add an item to your project using the Global Application Class template. In the page that handles the error, you should call *Server.GetLastError* to retrieve the error, and then clear the error by calling *Server.ClearError* (just as you would do for a *Page_Error* event handler).

SECURITY ALERT An attacker can potentially use any details about the inner workings of your application to which he or she gains access to identify a vulnerability. For this reason, attackers commonly use port scanning and system profiling to gain information about a target computer. Often, one of the most detailed sources of information for attackers is the error message.

To facilitate troubleshooting, good developers often provide very detailed error messages. Although this is a very good practice, it can also weaken the security of your application. Therefore, you should display general error information to end users. Save the details for administrators and developers to view using logging and tracing.

Programming the Web.config File Settings

You (or a systems administrator) can make many standard configuration changes using the ASP.NET Web Site Administration tool (Website | ASP.NET Configuration). For other changes, you need to edit the Web.config file. That works well when you need to make changes manually, but there are other times when you might want to programmatically edit configuration settings, such as in the following scenarios:

- During initial configuration of the Web.config file during setup, based on user input
- As part of a custom application administration tool to simplify management for systems administrators
- To automatically adjust the Web site configuration based on network conditions

Fortunately, ASP.NET provides the ASP.NET Configuration application programming interface (API) for this purpose. It is the same API that the ASP.NET Microsoft Management Console (MMC) snap-in and the ASP.NET Web Site Administration tool use to make configuration changes.

You use a *System.Configuration.Configuration* class to read the Web.config file and write any changes you might make. To create a *Configuration* object for the current application, you can use the static class *WebConfigurationManager* (found inside the *System.Web.Configuration* namespace).

With this class, you can read configuration sections by calling the *GetSection* and *GetSectionGroup* methods. The current user or process must have read permissions to all configuration files in the hierarchy. If you make any changes, call the *Save* method to persist those changes to the Web.config file (which requires permission to modify the file), or call the *SaveAs* method to save those changes to a new configuration file (which requires permission to create a new file). You might use *SaveAs* if you want to create new configuration settings that apply only to a subfolder.

For example, the following code sample displays the current authentication mode as defined in the *<system.web><authentication>* section, and then displays it in the *Label1* control:

```
'VB
Dim section As AuthenticationSection = _
  WebConfigurationManager.GetSection("system.web/authentication")
Label1.Text = section.Mode.ToString()

//C#
AuthenticationSection section =
  (AuthenticationSection) WebConfigurationManager.GetSection("system.web/
authentication");
Label1.Text = section.Mode.ToString();
```

Each standard element in the Web.config file has its own class, and you must use that class to access the configuration information. In C#, this requires an explicit conversion after calling the *GetSection* method (as the prior code sample demonstrated). Table 11-1 lists the .NET classes and their related configuration sections.

TABLE 11-1 Classes Used to Access Configuration Sections

CLASS	CONFIGURATION SECTION
AuthenticationSection	*<system.web><authentication>*
AnonymousIdentificationSection	*<system.web><anonymousIdentification>*
AuthorizationSection	*<system.web><authorization>*
CacheSection	*<system.web><cache>*
CompilationSection	*<system.web><compilation>*
CustomErrorsSection	*<system.web><customErrors>*
DeploymentSection	*<system.web><deployment>*
GlobalizationSection	*<system.web><globalization>*
HealthMonitoringSection	*<system.web><healthMonitoring>*
HostingEnvironmentSection	*<system.web><hostingEnvironment>*
HttpCookiesSection	*<system.web><httpCookies>*
HttpHandlersSection	*<system.web><httpHandlers>*
HttpRuntimeSection	*<system.web><httpRuntime>*
IdentitySection	*<system.web><identity>*
MachineKeySection	*<system.web><machineKey>*
MembershipSection	*<system.web><membership>*
OutputCacheSection	*<system.web><outputCache>*
PagesSection	*<system.web><pages>*
ProcessModeSection	*<system.web><processMode>*

ProfileSection	*<system.web><profile>*
RolesManagerSection	*<system.web><rolesManager>*
SecurityPolicySection	*<system.web><securityPolicy>*
SessionPageStateSection	*<system.web><sessionPageState>*
SessionStateSection	*<system.web><sessionState>*
SiteMapSection	*<system.web><siteMap>*
SqlCacheDependencySection	*<system.web><sqlCacheDependency>*
TraceSection	*<system.web><trace>*
TrustSection	*<system.web><trust>*
WebControlsSection	*<system.web><webControls>*
WebPartsSection	*<system.web><webParts>*
XhtmlConformanceSection	*<system.web><xhtmlConformance>*

Once you have created an instance of one of these classes, you can use the class's methods and properties to read or write configuration settings information.

Reading Application Settings

Besides accessing the *<system.web>* section, you can access custom application settings using the *WebConfigurationManager.AppSettings* collection. The following code sample demonstrates how to display the *MyAppSetting* custom application setting (which you could add using the ASP.NET Web Site Configuration tool) in a *Label* control:

```
'VB
Label1.Text = WebConfigurationManager.AppSettings("MyAppSetting")

//C#
Label1.Text = WebConfigurationManager.AppSettings["MyAppSetting"];
```

Reading Connection Strings

Similarly, you can programmatically access connection strings using the *WebConfigurationManager.ConnectionStrings* collection:

```
'VB
Label1.Text = WebConfigurationManager.ConnectionStrings("Northwind").ConnectionString

//C#
Label1.Text = WebConfigurationManager.ConnectionStrings["Northwind"].ConnectionString;
```

Writing Configuration Data

Accessing the static *WebConfigurationManager* methods is the most efficient way to read configuration settings because it takes into account the entire hierarchy of system and application configuration settings and indicates your effective settings. If you want to make changes, however, you must choose a specific configuration location. To do this, create an instance of a *Configuration* object. To create an instance of the root Web.config file that applies to all applications, call the static *WebConfigurationManager.OpenWebConfiguration* method and pass a *null* parameter to create a *Configuration* object. Then, use the *Configuration* object to create objects for individual sections. Edit values in those sections and save the changes by calling *Configuration.Save*.

The following code sample demonstrates how to enable tracing in the root Web.config file through code. This example assumes the application has the necessary security permissions.

> ***NOTE*** **PROVIDING ADMINISTRATIVE CREDENTIALS**
>
> **The *OpenWebConfiguration* method has overloads that allow you to specify a different server and to provide credentials.**

```
'VB
Dim rootConfig As Configuration = WebConfigurationManager.OpenWebConfiguration(Nothing)
Dim section As TraceSection = rootConfig.GetSection("system.web/trace")
section.Enabled = True
rootConfig.Save()

//C#
Configuration rootConfig = WebConfigurationManager.OpenWebConfiguration(null);
TraceSection section = (TraceSection)rootConfig.GetSection("system.web/trace");
section.Enabled = true;
rootConfig.Save();
```

You can open other configuration files by passing the application path (but not the full file name). For example, if you want to edit the Web.config file for the MyApp application on the current Web server to enable tracing, you can use the following code sample (notice that only the parameter for the first line has changed):

```
'VB
Dim rootConfig As Configuration = WebConfigurationManager.OpenWebConfiguration("/MyApp")
Dim section As TraceSection = rootConfig.GetSection("system.web/trace")
section.Enabled = True
rootConfig.Save()

//C#
Configuration rootConfig = WebConfigurationManager.OpenWebConfiguration("/MyApp");
TraceSection section = (TraceSection)rootConfig.GetSection("system.web/trace");
section.Enabled = true;
rootConfig.Save();
```

This code adds the following line to the /MyApp/Web.config file (assuming the line does not yet exist):

```
<trace enabled="true" />
```

> ***NOTE*** **FINDING THE APPLICATION PATH**
>
> **To retrieve the application path at run time, use the *Request.ApplicationPath* property. This property is described in more detail in Lesson 2 of this chapter.**

Because there is a hierarchy of configuration files, there are different ways to handle saving settings. The *ConfigurationSaveMode* enumeration allows you to specify the save technique using one of these values:

- **Full** Causes all properties to be written to the configuration file. This is useful mostly for creating information configuration files or moving configuration values from one machine to another.
- **Minimal** Causes only properties that differ from inherited values to be written to the configuration file.
- **Modified** Causes only modified properties to be written to the configuration file, even when the value is the same as the inherited value.

Creating a New Configuration File

To create a new configuration file, call the *Configuration.SaveAs* method and provide a location. The following code sample demonstrates how to call *Configuration.SaveAs* using the *ConfigurationSaveMode* enumeration:

```
'VB
Dim config As Configuration = WebConfigurationManager.OpenWebConfiguration("/MyApp")
config.SaveAs("c:\MyApp.web.config", ConfigurationSaveMode.Full, True)

//C#
Configuration config = WebConfigurationManager.OpenWebConfiguration("/MyApp");
config.SaveAs(@"c:\MyApp.web.config", ConfigurationSaveMode.Full, true);
```

Asynchronous Web Page Programming

Asynchronous programming allows a request to execute on a different thread. This stops the current thread from waiting and enables it to perform additional actions while the other thread executes. This can dramatically improve performance in situations where a request would otherwise need to wait (or block) for a relatively long action such as accessing a network resource.

If you have done asynchronous programming in Windows Forms applications, you can also use those techniques in ASP.NET Web forms. However, ASP.NET provides a different technique as well. Additionally, because ASP.NET Web pages can have dozens of users simultaneously, the considerations and benefits of asynchronous programming are slightly different.

Improving Performance with Asynchronous Web Page Programming

In a Windows Forms application, you often use asynchronous programming to allow the application to respond to user input while a long-running process executes. In Web pages, the user cannot interact with the page until page rendering is complete, so responding to user input isn't a valid reason for using asynchronous programming. Instead, you should use asynchronous programming to improve the efficiency of long-running Web pages. This is true even if each page only needs to perform one task at a time. In this case, the Web application becomes much more efficient during busy times when multiple pages are requested simultaneously because the thread pool responding to user requests is used more efficiently.

For example, if you are creating a Web page that must query a network resource (such as a Web service), IIS and ASP.NET can only render a limited number of pages simultaneously. Therefore, the thread pool can become completely consumed, creating a performance bottleneck. Once the thread pool is consumed, your server waits for pages to finish rendering before beginning to process other pages. Even though the server might have available processor cycles, requests are queued. By enabling asynchronous Web page programming, the server can begin rendering more pages simultaneously, improving efficiency and reducing page rendering time.

> ***NOTE*** **IMPROVING PERFORMANCE WITH THREAD POOLING**
>
> **Thread pooling can be tricky. When implementing asynchronous Web pages, use a performance testing tool such as the Web Capacity Analysis Tool or the Web Application Stress Tool to verify that performance improves under heavy load. Often, the overhead introduced by asynchronous programming can offset the benefits. Whether performance improves depends on many aspects of the application and Web server configuration. For more information about stress testing tools, read Microsoft Knowledge Base article 231282 at *http://support.microsoft.com/kb/231282*.**

Enabling an Asynchronous Web Page

To enable asynchronous Web page programming, follow these steps:

1. Add the *Async="true"* attribute to the *@ Page* directive, as the following example shows:

```
'VB
<%@ Page Language="VB" Async="true" AutoEventWireup="false" %>

//C#
<%@ Page Language="C#" Async="true" AutoEventWireup="true" %>
```

2. Create events to start and end your asynchronous code that implements *System.Web.IHttpAsyncHandler.BeingProcessRequest* and *System.Web.IHttpAsyncHandler.EndProcessRequest*. These events must match the following signatures:

```
'VB
Function BeginGetAsyncData(ByVal src As Object, ByVal args As EventArgs, _
  ByVal cb As AsyncCallback, ByVal state As Object) As IAsyncResult
End Function

Sub EndGetAsyncData(ByVal ar As IAsyncResult)
End Sub

//C#
IAsyncResult BeginGetAsyncData(Object src, EventArgs args,
  AsyncCallback cb, Object state)
  { }

void EndGetAsyncData(IAsyncResult ar)
  { }
```

3. Call the *AddOnPreRenderCompleteAsync* method to declare your event handlers, as demonstrated by the following code:

```
'VB
Dim bh As New BeginEventHandler(AddressOf Me.BeginGetAsyncData)
Dim eh As New EndEventHandler(AddressOf Me.EndGetAsyncData)
Me.AddOnPreRenderCompleteAsync(bh, eh)

//C#
BeginEventHandler bh = new BeginEventHandler(this.BeginGetAsyncData);
EndEventHandler eh = new EndEventHandler(this.EndGetAsyncData);
AddOnPreRenderCompleteAsync(bh, eh);
```

Creating a Custom HTTP Handler

An HTTP handler is code that executes when an HTTP request for a specific resource is made to the server. For example, when a user requests an .aspx page from IIS, the ASP.NET page handler is executed. When an .asmx file is accessed, the ASP.NET service handler is called. You can create your own custom HTTP handlers, register them with IIS, and receive notice when a specific request has been made. This allows you to interact with the request and write your own custom output to the browser.

To create a custom Hypertext Transfer Protocol (HTTP) handler, you first create a class that implements the *IHttpHandler* interface (to create a synchronous handler) or the *IHttpAsyncHandler* (to create an asynchronous handler). Both handler interfaces require you to implement the *IsReusable* property and the *ProcessRequest* method. The *IsReusable* property specifies whether the *IHttpHandlerFactory* object (the object that actually calls the appropriate handler) can place your handlers in a pool and reuse them to increase performance or whether it must create new instances every time the handler is needed. The *ProcessRequest* method is responsible for actually processing the individual HTTP requests. Once it is created, you then register and configure your HTTP handler with IIS.

As an example, consider the processing of image requests in ASP.NET. Each image in an HTML page requires a separate browser request and a separate response from the Web server. By default, IIS does not pass requests for images to ASP.NET. Instead, IIS simply reads the image file from the file system and sends it directly to the Web browser.

Now, imagine you want to handle requests for images in ASP.NET instead of them just being passed back by IIS. You might need to dynamically generate a chart displaying performance information over a period of time or you might want to dynamically create thumbnails in a photo album application. In these circumstances, you either periodically generate the images in advance or you can create a custom HTTP handler to receive the image requests. It is the latter action on which this example focuses. The following outlines how you can configure ASP.NET (and your custom HTTP handler code) to receive requests for images:

1. Write code to dynamically generate the images.
2. Configure IIS to pass requests for the required image types to ASP.NET.
3. Configure ASP.NET to process requests for files with the required file extensions.

Dynamically Generating Images

The following code demonstrates how you can write an HTTP handler for generating images. You will get a chance to work with this example in the upcoming lab.

```
'VB
Public Class ImageHandler
  Implements IHttpHandler

  Public ReadOnly Property IsReusable() As Boolean _
    Implements System.Web.IHttpHandler.IsReusable
    Get
      Return False
    End Get
  End Property

  Public Sub ProcessRequest(ByVal context As System.Web.HttpContext) Implements _
    System.Web.IHttpHandler.ProcessRequest
    'set the MIME type
    context.Response.ContentType = "image/jpeg"
    'TODO: Generate the image file using the System.Drawing namespace
    '  and then use Context.Response to transmit the image
  End Sub

End Class
```

```
//C#
public class ImageHandler : IHttpHandler
{
  public ImageHandler()
  { }

  public bool IsReusable
  {
    get { return false; }
  }

  public void ProcessRequest(HttpContext context)
  {
    //set the MIME type
    context.Response.ContentType = "image/jpeg";
    //TODO: Generate the image file using the System.Drawing namespace
    //  and then use Context.Response to transmit the image
  }
}
```

Configuring IIS to Forward Requests to ASP.NET

For performance reasons, IIS passes only requests for specific file types to ASP.NET. For example, IIS passes requests for .aspx, .axd, .ascx, and .asmx to the Aspnet_Isapi.dll file that performs the ASP.NET processing. For all other file types, including .htm, .jpg, and .gif, ASP.NET simply passes the file from the file system directly to the client browser.

Therefore, to handle image requests using ASP.NET, you must configure an IIS application mapping from the image file extension you need to the Aspnet_Isapi.dll file. The process of configuring this information is different for IIS 6 and IIS 7. The following steps outline the process for configuring with IIS 7:

1. Open IIS Manager.
2. Expand the nodes until you get to your site or Default Web Site. Select the node for your application.
3. Double-click the Handler Mappings icon in the center pane of IIS Manager.
4. In the Actions pane (right side), select Add Managed Handler.
5. In the Add Managed Handler dialog box, shown in Figure 11-1, set the Request path to the file name or extension you wish to map, in this case, .jpg. The Type name is the class name of the HTTP handler. If your HTTP handler is inside the App_Code directory, it will appear in the drop-down list. The *Name* field is simply a descriptive name.

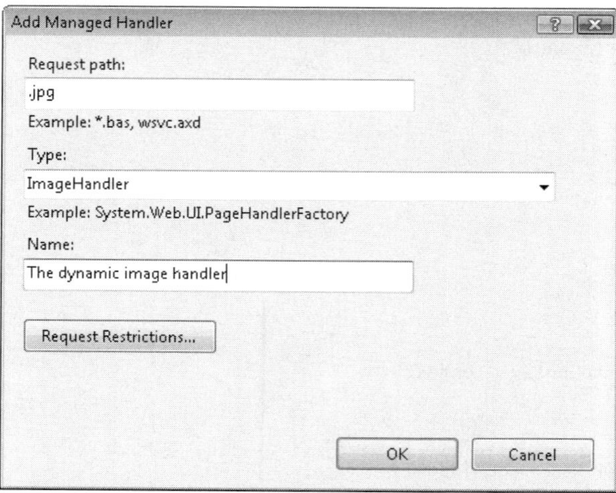

FIGURE 11-1 Configure an application mapping to process image requests in ASP.NET

Once you configure the application extension mapping, all requests for that file type are forwarded to ASP.NET and to your handler. To enable normal image processing in most areas of your Web site, create a separate virtual directory just for dynamically generated images.

Configuring the Handler in Web.config

Alternatively, if you are using IIS 7, you can simply configure the handler for the file extension in your Web.config file. You do not, then, need to use IIS Manager. For each file extension or file name you want to register, create an *<add>* element in the *<configuration><system.web><httpHandlers>* section of your Web.config file, as the following example demonstrates:

```
<configuration>
  <system.web>
    <httpHandlers>
      <add verb="*" path="*.jpg" type="ImageHandler"/>
      <add verb="*" path="*.gif" type="ImageHandler"/>
    </httpHandlers>
  </system.web>
</configuration>
```

In this example, ASP.NET handles requests for files ending in .jpg or .gif by forwarding them to the *ImageHandler* class. For this to work properly, the *ImageHandler* assembly must be available in the application's Bin folder or the source code must be in the App_Code folder.

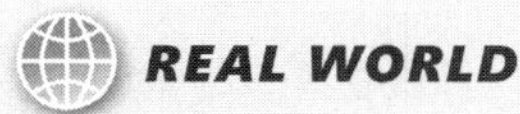

Tony Northrup

Dynamically generating images can be slow. If you plan to dynamically generate images, do performance testing on your Web site to ensure you can keep up with incoming requests. If the same image will be requested repeatedly, store the image file in the *Cache* object. In some circumstances, it might be more efficient to generate images using a service or a scheduled console application. On my personal photo album Web application, I pregenerate the most frequently accessed images, and only dynamically generate pictures when users need an unusual resolution.

Quick Check

1. What type does *WebConfigurationManager.GetSection* return, and how should you handle it?
2. How can you programmatically update a connection string stored in the Web .config file?

Quick Check Answers

1. *WebConfigurationManager.GetSection* returns an *Object* type. You must cast it to a type specific to the configuration section.
2. Create a *Configuration* object. Then, update the connection string using the *ConnectionStrings* collection. Finally, call *Configuration.Save*.

LAB Creating a Custom Handler

In this lab, you create a custom image handler to dynamically generate images that are part of ASP.NET Web pages. If you get stuck with an exercise, you can find the completed project in the samples installed from the CD.

EXERCISE 1 Create a Custom Image Handler

In this exercise, you create an ASP.NET Web application that dynamically generates images.

1. Open Visual Studio. Create a new, file-based Web site called **LabPictures**.
2. Add a new class to your project. Name the class **ImageHandler**. When prompted, choose to place the class in the App_Code folder.
3. Edit the automatically generated class declaration so that it implements the *IHttpHandler* interface, as the following shows:

```
'VB
Public Class ImageHandler
  Implements IHttpHandler

End Class

//C#
public class ImageHandler : IHttpHandler
```

4. Use Visual Studio to automatically generate the required *IHttpHandler* members *IsReusable* and *ProcessRequest*.
5. Implement the *IsReusable* property by returning *False*. If you want to enable pooling, return *True* instead.

```
'VB
Public ReadOnly Property IsReusable() As Boolean _
  Implements System.Web.IHttpHandler.IsReusable
  Get
    Return False
  End Get
End Property

//C#
public bool IsReusable
{
  get { return false; }
}
```

6. Implement the *ProcessRequest* method to return an image file using the *HttpContext.Response* object (passed to the method as a parameter). You can dynamically generate the image using the *System.Drawing* namespace. For simplicity, the following example demonstrates how to transmit an existing file located elsewhere on the file system (you might need to edit the path to a picture that exists on your Web server or machine):

```
'VB
Public Sub ProcessRequest(ByVal context As System.Web.HttpContext) _
  Implements System.Web.IHttpHandler.ProcessRequest

  context.Response.ContentType = "image/jpeg"
  context.Response.TransmitFile("C:\Users\Public\Pictures\Sample Pictures\" & _
    "dock.jpg")

End Sub
```

```
//C#
public void ProcessRequest(HttpContext context)
{
  context.Response.ContentType = "image/jpeg";
  context.Response.TransmitFile(@"C:\Users\Public\Pictures\Sample Pictures\" +
    "dock.jpg");
}
```

> ***NOTE*** **DEFINING THE MIME TYPE**
>
> **Note that this code sample sets the *context.Response.ContentType* property to *"image/jpeg."* You should use this property to define the correct Multipurpose Internet Mail Extensions (MIME) type so that the browser knows how to handle the file you send it. Otherwise, the browser might try to display it as text.**

7. Open the Web.config file. Navigate to the *<httpHandlers>* node. Add a handler that maps the .jpg file extension to your *ImageHandler* class. The following markup demonstrates this:

```
<configuration>
  <system.web>
    <httpHandlers>
      <add verb="*" path="*.jpg" type="ImageHandler"/>
    </httpHandlers>
  </system.web>
</configuration>
```

8. Open Default.aspx in the designer. Drag an *Image* control to the page. Change the *ImageUrl* property to **Test.jpg**. This file does not exist, so a placeholder is displayed in the designer. However, this is a request for a .jpg file. Your *HttpHandler* will intercept this request and display the image as defined in the *ProcessRequest* code (it will display Dock.jpg).
9. Run your application using the local Web application server (and not IIS). The local Web server will simulate the custom handler. You can verify the results in a browser window.

Lesson Summary

- You can catch unhandled exceptions at the page level by responding to *Page_Error*, or at the application level by responding to *Application_Error*. In either event handler, you read the last error by calling *Server.GetLastError*. Then, you must remove it from the queue by calling *Server.ClearError*.

- You can call *WebConfigurationManager.GetSection* to return a configuration section from the Web.config file. You cast the returned object to the section-specific type. If you make an update to the configuration settings, write the changes by calling *Configuration.Save* or *Configuration.SaveAs*.
- Asynchronous Web pages can improve performance in scenarios where the thread pool might be limiting performance. To enable asynchronous pages, first add the *Async="true"* attribute to the *@ Page* directive. Then, create events to start and end your asynchronous code.
- By default, ASP.NET handles a limited number of file types, including .aspx, .ascx, and .axd. You can configure ASP.NET to handle any file type, which is useful if you need to dynamically generate normally static files, such as images. To configure ASP.NET to receive requests for other types, you create a custom *HttpHandler* class and add the type to the Web.config file in the *httpHandlers* section.

Lesson Review

You can use the following questions to test your knowledge of the information in Lesson 1, "Using Web Site Programmability." The questions are also available on the companion CD if you prefer to review them in electronic form.

> ***NOTE* ANSWERS**
>
> **Answers to these questions and explanations of why each answer choice is right or wrong are located in the "Answers" section at the end of the book.**

1. You catch an unhandled exception in a *Page_Error* handler. How can you access the last error?
   - **A.** *Server.GetLastError*
   - **B.** *Server.ClearError*
   - **C.** *Request.GetLastError*
   - **D.** *Application.GetLastError*
2. Which of the following can you use to catch unhandled exceptions in an application? (Choose all that apply.)
   - **A.** *Response_Error*
   - **B.** *Page_Error*
   - **C.** *Application_Error*
   - **D.** *Server_Error*
3. Which of the following code samples correctly retrieves the current cookie configuration settings?

A. 'VB

```
Dim section As String = WebConfigurationManager.GetSection _
    ("system.web/httpCookies")
```

//C#

```
string section = WebConfigurationManager.GetSection("system.web/httpCookies");
```

B. 'VB

```
Dim section As HttpCookiesSection = _
    WebConfigurationManager.GetSection("httpCookies")
```

//C#

```
HttpCookiesSection section =
    (HttpCookiesSection) WebConfigurationManager.GetSection("httpCookies");
```

C. 'VB

```
Dim section As String = WebConfigurationManager.GetSection("httpCookies")
```

//C#

```
string section = WebConfigurationManager.GetSection("httpCookies");
```

D. 'VB

```
Dim section As HttpCookiesSection = _
    WebConfigurationManager.GetSection("system.web/httpCookies")
```

//C#

```
HttpCookiesSection section = (HttpCookiesSection)
    WebConfigurationManager.GetSection("system.web/httpCookies");
```

4. You need to have ASP.NET dynamically generate Word documents when a Web browser requests a file ending in a .doc extension. How can you do this?

A. Implement the *IPartitionResolver* interface.

B. Implement the *IHttpModule* interface.

C. Implement the *IHttpHandler* interface.

D. Implement the *IHttpHandlerFactory* interface.

Lesson 2: Using the ASP.NET Intrinsic Objects

You can use the objects inside of ASP.NET to gain access to a lot of useful information about your application, the server hosting the application, and the client requesting resources on the server. These objects are referred to as the ASP.NET intrinsic objects. They are exposed through objects like *Page*, *Browser*, *Server*, and *Context*. Together, these objects provide you a great deal of useful information like the user's Internet Protocol (IP) address, the type of browser making the request, errors generated during a response, the title of a given page, and much more.

This lesson describes how you can use objects like *Page*, *Browser*, *Response*, *Request*, *Server*, and *Context* to program specific scenarios on your Web site.

After this lesson, you will be able to:

- Use the *Browser* object to identify client capabilities.
- Use *Page* and *Application* context to examine and update information, such as the details of the client request and the communications being sent back to the client.
- Access Web page headers to dynamically define the page title or the style sheet.

Estimated lesson time: 30 minutes

Page and Application Context Overview

You can access the many ASP.NET objects to examine almost any detail of the current request and response. These objects are exposed as properties of the *Page* object. You can reference them through the *Page* object (*Page.Response*, for example) or you can reference them directly, without the qualifying namespace. Many of these objects have been with ASP since the first version. Referencing them without the object qualifier provides the same experience that ASP developers are used to.

Table 11-2 lists the objects (exposed as properties of the *Page* object) that you can use to examine information relating to page and application context.

TABLE 11-2 ASP.NET Intrinsic Objects

OBJECT	DESCRIPTION
Response	An instance of the *System.Web.HttpResponse* class. Provides access to the HTTP response sent from the server to the client after receiving an incoming Web request. You can use this class to inject text into the page, to write cookies, redirect the user, add cache dependencies, and other tasks related to the HTTP response. You can edit most aspects of the *Response*.

Request	An instance of the *System.Web.HttpRequest* class. Provides access to information that is part of the current page request as sent from the Web browser, including the request headers, cookies, client certificate, and query string. You can use this class to read what the browser sent to the Web server. These properties cannot be updated.
Server	An instance of the *System.Web.HttpServerUtility* class. Exposes utility methods that you can use to transfer control between pages, get information about the most recent error, and encode and decode HTML text. Most of the useful *Server* methods are static.
Context	An instance of the *System.Web.HttpContext* class. Provides access to the entire current context (including the *Request* object). Most of the methods and properties provided by *Context* are also provided by other more frequently used objects, such as *Request* and *Server.*
Session	An instance of the *System.Web.HttpSessionState* class. Provides information to the current user session. Also provides access to a session-wide cache you can use to store information, along with the means to control how the session is managed. For detailed information about the *Session* object, read Chapter 4, "ASP.NET State Management."
Application	An instance of the *System.Web.HttpApplicationState* class. Provides access to application-wide methods and events for all sessions. Also provides access to an application-wide cache you can use to store information. For detailed information about the *Application* object, read Chapter 4.
Trace	An instance of the *System.Web.TraceContext* class. Provides a way to display both system and custom trace diagnostic messages in the HTTP page output. For more information about the *Trace* object, read Chapter 12, "Monitoring, Troubleshooting, and Debugging."

The *Response* Object

The *Page.Response* property is an *HttpResponse* object that allows you to add data to the HTTP response being sent back to the client who requested a Web page. The *Response* object includes the following useful methods:

- ***BinaryWrite*** Writes binary characters to the HTTP response. To write a text string instead, call Write.
- ***AppendHeader*** Adds an HTTP header to the response stream. You only need to use this if you need to provide a special directive to the Web browser that IIS does not add.
- ***Clear*** Removes everything from the HTTP response stream.
- ***ClearContent*** Removes the content from the response stream, not including the HTTP headers.
- ***ClearHeaders*** Removes the headers from the response stream, not including the content.

- ***End*** Completes the response and returns the page to the user.
- ***Flush*** Sends the current output to the client without ending the request. This is useful if you want to return a partial page to the user; for example, if you had to perform a time-consuming database query or submit information to a credit card processing service, you could display, "Processing your transaction" using *Response.Write*, call *Response.Flush* to send this message immediately to the user, process the transaction, and then display the transaction information when it is ready.
- ***Redirect*** Instructs the Web browser to open a different page by returning an HTTP/302 code with the new Uniform Resource Locator (URL). This is an alternative to the *Server.Transfer* method, which causes ASP.NET to process a different page without the Web browser submitting a new request.
- ***TransmitFile*** Writes a file to the HTTP response without buffering it.
- ***Write*** Writes information to the HTTP response with buffering.
- ***WriteFile*** Writes a file to the HTTP response with buffering.
- ***WriteSubstitution*** Replaces strings in the response. This is useful if you are returning cached output, but you want to dynamically update that cached output. To initiate the replacement, call the *WriteSubstitution* method, passing it the callback method. On the first request to the page, *WriteSubstitution* calls the *HttpResponseSubstitutionCallback* delegate to produce the output. Then, it adds a substitution buffer to the response, which retains the delegate to call on future requests. Finally, it degrades client-side cachability from public to server-only, ensuring future requests to the page reinvoke the delegate by not caching on the client. As an alternative to using *WriteSubstitution*, you can use the *Substitution* control.

The *Response* object also includes the following useful properties:

- ***Cookies*** Enables you to add cookies that are sent back to the Web browser. If the Web browser supports cookies, it returns the exact same cookie to you using the Request object. For more information about cookies, read Chapter 7, "Using ADO.NET, XML, and LINQ with ASP.NET."
- ***Buffer*** If *True*, the response is buffered before sending it back to the user. If *False*, the response is sent back to the user in chunks. Typically, you should buffer the response, unless you are sending back a very large response, or the response will take a long time to generate.
- ***Cache*** Gets the caching policy of the Web page, such as the expiration time and privacy policy.
- ***Expires*** The number of minutes after which the browser should stop caching the page. Set this to the time period for which the page will be valid. If the page is constantly updated, set it to a very short period of time. If the page is static and rarely changes, you can increase this time to reduce the number of unnecessary page requests and improve the performance of your server.

- ***ExpiresAbsolute*** Similar to the *Expires* property, *ExpiresAbsolute* sets an absolute date and time after which the page cache is no longer valid.
- ***Status and StatusCode*** Gets or sets the HTTP status code that indicates whether the response was successful. For example, the status code 200 indicates a successful response, 404 indicates a file not found, and 500 indicates a server error.

The *Request* Object

The *Page.Request* property is an *HttpRequest* object that allows you to add data to the HTTP response being sent back to the client who requested a Web page. The *Request* object includes the following useful methods:

- ***MapPath*** Maps the virtual path to a physical path, allowing you to determine where on the file system a virtual path is. For example, this allows you to convert /about.htm to C:\Inetpub\Wwwroot\About.htm.
- ***SaveAs*** Saves the request to a file.
- ***ValidateInput*** Throws an exception if the user input contains potentially dangerous input, such as HTML input, or input that might be part of a database attack. ASP.NET does this automatically by default, so you only need to manually call this method if you have disabled ASP.NET security features.

The *Request* object also includes several useful properties:

- ***ApplicationPath*** Gets the ASP.NET application's virtual application root path on the server.
- ***AppRelativeCurrentExecutionFilePath*** Gets the virtual path of the application root and makes it relative by using the tilde (~) notation for the application root (as in ~/page.aspx).
- ***Browser*** Allows you to examine details of the browser's capabilities (see "Determining the Browser Type" later in this lesson).
- ***ClientCertificate*** Gets the client's security certificate, if the client provided one.
- ***Cookies*** Enables you to read cookies sent from the Web browser that you have previously provided in a *Response* object. For more information about cookies, read Chapter 4.
- ***FilePath*** Gets the virtual path of the current request.
- ***Files*** If the client has uploaded files, this gets the collection of files uploaded by the client.
- ***Headers*** Gets the collection of HTTP headers.
- ***HttpMethod*** Gets the HTTP data transfer method (such as *GET*, *POST*, or *HEAD*) used by the client.
- ***IsAuthenticated*** A Boolean value that is *True* if the client is authenticated.
- ***IsLocal*** A Boolean value that is *True* if the client is from the local computer.

- ***IsSecureConnection*** A Boolean value that is *True* if the connection uses secure HTTP (HTTPS).
- ***LogonUserIdentity*** Gets the *WindowsIdentity* object that represents the current user.
- ***Params*** A combined collection that includes the *QueryString*, *Form*, *ServerVariables*, and *Cookies* items. For more information about query strings and cookies, read Chapter 4.
- ***Path*** The virtual path of the current request.
- ***PhysicalApplicationPath*** The physical path of the application root directory.
- ***PhysicalPath*** The physical path of the current request.
- ***QueryString*** A collection of query string variables. For more information about query strings, read Chapter 4.
- ***RawUrl* and *Url*** The URL of the current request.
- ***TotalBytes*** The length of the request.
- ***UrlReferrer*** Gets information about the URL of the client's previous request that linked to the current URL. You can use this to determine which page within your site or which external Web site brought the user to the current page.
- ***UserAgent*** Gets the user agent string, which describes the browser the user has. Some non-Microsoft browsers indicate that they are Internet Explorer for compatibility.
- ***UserHostAddress*** The client's IP address.
- ***UserHostName*** The Domain Name System (DNS) name of the remote client.
- ***UserLanguages*** A sorted string array of languages the client browser has been configured to prefer. ASP.NET can automatically display the correct language for a user. For more information, read Chapter 13, "Globalization and Accessibility."

The *Server* Object

The *Page.Server* property is an *HttpServerUtil* object that provides static methods useful for processing URLs, paths, and HTML. The most useful methods are the following:

- ***ClearError*** Clears the last error.
- ***GetLastError*** Returns the previous exception, as described in Lesson 1 of this chapter.
- ***HtmlDecode*** Removes HTML markup from a string. You should call *HtmlDecode* on user input before displaying it again to remove potentially malicious code.
- ***HtmlEncode*** Converts a string to be displayed in a browser. For example, if the string contains a "<" character, *Server.HtmlEncode* converts it to the "<" phrase, which the browser displays as a less-than sign rather than treating it as HTML markup.
- ***MapPath*** Returns the physical file path that corresponds to the specified virtual path on the Web server.
- ***Transfer*** Stops processing the current page and starts processing the specified page. The URL is not changed in the user's browser.

- ***UrlDecode*** Decodes a string encoded for HTTP transmission and sent to the server in a URL.
- ***UrlEncode*** Encodes a string for reliable HTTP transmission from the Web server to a client through the URL.
- ***UrlPathEncode*** URL encodes the path portion of a URL string and returns the encoded string.
- ***UrlTokenDecode*** Decodes a URL string token to its equivalent byte array using base 64 digits.
- ***UrlTokenEncode*** Encodes a byte array into its equivalent string representation using base 64 digits suitable for transmission on the URL.

The *Context* Object

The *Page.Context* property is an *HttpContext* object that provides access to a variety of objects related to the HTTP request and response. Many of these objects are redundant, providing access to *Page* members including *Cache*, *Request*, *Response*, *Server*, and *Session*. However, the *Context* object includes several unique methods:

- ***AddError*** Adds an exception to the page, which can later be retrieved by calling *Server.GetLastError* or cleared by calling *Server.ClearError* or *Context.ClearError*.
- ***ClearError*** Clears the last error, exactly the same way as *Server.ClearError*.
- ***RewritePath*** Assigns an internal rewrite path and allows for the URL that is requested to differ from the internal path to the resource. *RewritePath* is used in cookieless session state to remove the session state value from the path Uniform Resource Identifier (URI).

The *Context* object also includes several unique properties:

- ***AllErrors*** A collection of unhandled exceptions that have occurred on the page.
- ***IsCustomErrorEnabled*** A Boolean value that is *true* if custom errors are enabled.
- ***IsDebuggingEnabled*** A Boolean value that is true if debugging is enabled.
- ***Timestamp*** The timestamp of the HTTP request.

Determining the Browser Type

HTML has a defined, controlled standard. However, not all Web browsers implement that standard in the same way. There are many differences among the many browser versions and brands. In addition, browsers often have different capabilities. Sometimes, this is because two competing browsers interpret standards differently. Other times, the browser might have restrictions imposed for security reasons or to better suit a mobile device.

To make sure your Web pages are displayed properly, it's important to test Web pages in every type of browser that your users might have. If you primarily rely on ASP.NET controls, your chances of running into a compatibility issue are greatly reduced. ASP.NET controls automatically adapt to different browser types and capabilities. However, if you use a lot of

Dynamic Hypertext Markup Language (DHTML), JavaScript, and Cascading Style Sheets (CSS), you are bound to come across more than one browser compatibility issue.

When you do run into an issue, you will want to adjust your Web page so that a single version of the page renders correctly for your supported browser types. To display different versions of Web pages for different browsers, you will need to write code that examines the *HttpBrowserCapabilities* object. This object is exposed through *Request.Browser*. *Request.Browser* has many members that you can use to examine individual browser capabilities.

There are two primary methods exposed by *HttpBrowserCapabilities*. Table 11-3 lists these methods.

TABLE 11-3 *Request.Browser* Methods

METHOD	DESCRIPTION
GetClrVersions	Returns all versions of the .NET Framework common language runtime that are installed on the client.
IsBrowser	Gets a value indicating whether the client browser is the same as the specified browser.

The *HttpBrowserCapabilities* object also exposes a number of properties. These properties provide information about the browser making the request such as the browser type, if it supports cookies, if it is a mobile device, if it supports ActiveX, if it allows frames, and other browser-related options. Table 11-4 lists many of the more important *Request.Browser* properties.

TABLE 11-4 *Request.Browser* Properties

PROPERTY	DESCRIPTION
ActiveXControls	Gets a value indicating whether the browser supports ActiveX controls.
AOL	Gets a value indicating whether the client is an America Online (AOL) browser.
BackgroundSounds	Gets a value indicating whether the browser supports playing background sounds using the <*bgsounds*> HTML element.
Browser	Gets the browser string (if any) that was sent by the browser in the User-Agent request header. Note that some non-Microsoft browsers incorrectly identify themselves as Internet Explorer to improve compatibility. Therefore, this string is not always accurate.
ClrVersion	Gets the version of the .NET Framework that is installed on the client.
Cookies	Gets a value indicating whether the browser supports cookies.

PROPERTY	DESCRIPTION
Crawler	Gets a value indicating whether the browser is a search engine Web crawler (or bot).
Frames	Gets a value indicating whether the browser supports HTML frames.
IsColor	Gets a value indicating whether the browser has a color display. *False* indicates that the browser has a grayscale display, which typically indicates a mobile device.
IsMobileDevice	Gets a value indicating whether the browser is a recognized mobile device.
JavaApplets	Gets a value indicating whether the browser supports Java.
JavaScript	Gets a value indicating whether the browser supports JavaScript.
JScriptVersion	Gets the JScript version that the browser supports.
MobileDeviceManufacturer	Returns the name of the manufacturer of a mobile device, if known.
MobileDeviceModel	Gets the model name of a mobile device, if known.
MSDomVersion	Gets the version of Microsoft HTML (MSHTML) Document Object Model (DOM) that the browser supports.
Tables	Gets a value indicating whether the browser supports HTML <*table*> elements.
VBScript	Gets a value indicating whether the browser supports Visual Basic Scripting edition (VBScript).
Version	Gets the full version number (integer and decimal) of the browser as a string.
W3CDomVersion	Gets the version of the World Wide Web Consortium (W3C) XML DOM that the browser supports.
Win16	Gets a value indicating whether the client is a Win16-based computer.
Win32	Gets a value indicating whether the client is a Win32-based computer.

The properties exposed by the *Request.Browser* object indicate inherent capabilities of the browser but do not necessarily reflect current browser settings. For example, the *Cookies* property indicates whether a browser inherently supports cookies, but it does not indicate whether the browser that made the request has cookies enabled. People often disable cookies for security reasons, but the *Request.Browser* object still indicates that the browser supports cookies. For this reason, ASP.NET session state can be configured to test the client browser for cookie support.

MORE INFO ASP.NET SESSION SUPPORT FOR COOKIES

For more information about ASP.NET sessions, refer to Chapter 4.

Quick Check

1. Which of the following browser capabilities can you *not* check using *Request.Browser*?
   - Frames support
   - Support for embedded images
   - Tables support
   - Cookies support
   - JavaScript support
2. How can you determine if the client is a bot indexing your site for a search engine?

Quick Check Answers

1. Of the capabilities listed, the only one not provided by *Request.Browser* is support for embedded images.
2. Check *Request.Browser.Crawler.*

Accessing Web Page Headers

The header information of a rendered HTML page contains important information that helps describe the page. This includes the name of the style sheet, the title of the page, and metadata used by search engines. ASP.NET allows you to edit this information programmatically using the *System.Web.Ui.HtmlControls.HtmlHead* control. This control is exposed via the *Page.Header* property. For example, you might use this to set the title of a page dynamically at run time based on the page's content.

Table 11-5 lists the most important members of the *HtmlHead* control.

TABLE 11-5 *Page.Header* Properties

PROPERTY	DESCRIPTION
StyleSheet	The *StyleSheet* object that enables you to call the *CreateStyleRule* and *RegisterStyle* methods.
Title	The title of the page. This is used in the window title bar, in the Favorite name, and by search engines.

To set a page's title programmatically, access *Page.Header.Title*, as the following code sample demonstrates:

```
'VB
Page.Header.Title = "Current time: " & DateTime.Now

//C#
Page.Header.Title = "Current time: " + DateTime.Now;
```

To set style information for the page (using the *<head><style>* HTML tag), access *Page.Header.StyleSheet*. The following code sample demonstrates how to use the *Page.Header.StyleSheet.CreateStyleRule* method to programmatically set the background color for a page to light gray and the default text color to blue:

```
'VB
'create a style object for the body of the page.
Dim bodyStyle As New Style()

bodyStyle.ForeColor = System.Drawing.Color.Blue
bodyStyle.BackColor = System.Drawing.Color.LightGray

'add the style rule named bodyStyle to the header
'  of the current page. The rule is for the body HTML element.
Page.Header.StyleSheet.CreateStyleRule(bodyStyle, Nothing, "body")

//C#
//create a style object for the body of the page.
Style bodyStyle = new Style();

bodyStyle.ForeColor = System.Drawing.Color.Blue;
bodyStyle.BackColor = System.Drawing.Color.LightGray;

//add the style rule named bodyStyle to the header
//  of the current page. The rule is for the body HTML element.
Page.Header.StyleSheet.CreateStyleRule(bodyStyle, null, "body");
```

The previous two code samples generate an HTML page with the following header:

```
<head>
  <title>Current time: 6/30/2006 4:00:05 PM</title>
  <style type="text/css">
    body { color:Blue;background-color:LightGrey; }
  </style>
</head>
```

Note that you need to access *Page.Header.StyleSheet* only if you need to set the style dynamically. Typically, you will set the style for a specific page by using the Visual Studio designer to edit the document's *Style* property with the Style Builder.

LAB Examine Page and Application Context

In this lab, you create a Web site that includes a Web page that displays information about the request, response, and page context. If you get stuck with an exercise, you can open the completed project in the samples installed from the CD.

EXERCISE 1 Display Page and Application Context Information

In this exercise, you create the Web site and Web page. You then add information to the Web page to display context information.

1. Open Visual Studio. Create a new Web site called **IntrinsicObjects**.
2. Open the Default.aspx page. In the *Page_Load* event handler, write code to display the HTTP status code and description using the *Response* object, as the following code sample demonstrates:

```
'VB
Response.Write(Response.StatusCode & ": " & _
  Response.StatusDescription)

//C#
Response.Write(Response.StatusCode + ": " +
  Response.StatusDescription);
```

3. Next, write code to display the timestamp using the *Context* object, as the following code sample demonstrates:

```
'VB
Response.Write(Context.Timestamp.ToString)

//C#
Response.Write(Context.Timestamp.ToString());
```

4. Write code to display the URL referrer if it exists. If this is the user's first request, the *Request.UrlReferrer* object will be null, so you must check to determine if it is null before displaying it. This code sample demonstrates this:

```
'VB
If Not (Request.UrlReferrer Is Nothing) Then
  Response.Write(Request.UrlReferrer.ToString)
Else
  Response.Write("No referrer")
End If

//C#
if (Request.UrlReferrer != null)
```

```
  Response.Write(Request.UrlReferrer.ToString());
else
  Response.Write("No referrer");
```

5. Write code to display the user languages. The *Request.UserLanguages* object is a collection of strings, so you must iterate through the strings to display them. The following code sample demonstrates this:

```
'VB
For Each s As String In Request.UserLanguages
  Response.Write(s & "<br>")
Next

//C#
foreach (string s in Request.UserLanguages)
  Response.Write(s + "<br>");
```

6. Write code to output data from the *Request* object. You can use *Server.MapPath* to translate the virtual path to the physical path and use *Server.UrlDecode* to display HTTP headers in more readable text. This code sample demonstrates this:

```
'VB
Response.Write(Request.ApplicationPath)
Response.Write(Request.FilePath)
Response.Write(Server.MapPath(Request.FilePath))
Response.Write(Server.UrlDecode(Request.Headers.ToString).Replace("&", "<br>"))
Response.Write(Request.HttpMethod)
Response.Write(Request.IsAuthenticated.ToString)
Response.Write(Request.IsLocal.ToString)
Response.Write(Request.IsSecureConnection.ToString)
Response.Write(Request.LogonUserIdentity.ToString)
Response.Write(Request.TotalBytes.ToString)
Response.Write(Request.UserAgent)
Response.Write(Request.UserHostAddress)

//C#
Response.Write(Request.ApplicationPath);
Response.Write(Request.FilePath);
Response.Write(Server.MapPath(Request.FilePath));
Response.Write(Server.UrlDecode(Request.Headers.ToString()).Replace("&",
"<br>"));
Response.Write(Request.HttpMethod);
Response.Write(Request.IsAuthenticated.ToString());
Response.Write(Request.IsLocal.ToString());
Response.Write(Request.IsSecureConnection.ToString());
```

```
Response.Write(Request.LogonUserIdentity.ToString());
Response.Write(Request.TotalBytes.ToString());
Response.Write(Request.UserAgent);
Response.Write(Request.UserHostAddress);
```

7. Run the application and examine the values displayed. Next, run the application from a different computer with a different Web browser and notice how the values change. Think about how this information can be useful in real-world applications.

Lesson Summary

- You can use the *Request* object to examine details of the client Web browser's request to the Web server, including the request headers, cookies, client certificate, query string, and more. You can use the *Response* object to send data directly to the client without using standard ASP.NET server controls. You can use the *Server* object's static methods to perform processing of HTML and URL data. The *Context* object provides several unique methods for adding errors and enabling debugging.
- You can use the *Browser* object to determine the client Web browser type and whether it supports cookies, ActiveX, JavaScript, and other capabilities that can affect its ability to render your Web pages correctly.
- Use the *Page.Header.StyleSheet* object to dynamically set the page's style sheet (including information such as the background color), and use the *Page.Header.Title* object to dynamically set the page title.

Lesson Review

You can use the following questions to test your knowledge of the information in Lesson 2, "Using the ASP.NET Intrinsic Objects." The questions are also available on the companion CD if you prefer to review them in electronic form.

> ***NOTE*** **ANSWERS**
>
> **Answers to these questions and explanations of why each answer choice is right or wrong are located in the "Answers" section at the end of the book.**

1. Which of the following bits of information can you determine from the *Request.Browser* object? (Choose all that apply.)
   - **A.** Whether the client has the .NET Framework common language runtime installed
   - **B.** Whether the user is logged on as an administrator
   - **C.** The user's e-mail address
   - **D.** Whether the browser supports ActiveX
   - **E.** Whether the browser supports JavaScript

2. You have created an ASP.NET search page and want to set the page title to "Search results: <*Query*>". How can you dynamically set the page title?

   A. *Page.Title*

   B. *Page.Header.Title*

   C. *Response.Header.Title*

   D. *Response.Title*

3. Which of the following *Response* methods causes ASP.NET to send the current response to the browser while allowing you to add to the response later?

   A. *Flush*

   B. *Clear*

   C. *End*

   D. *ClearContent*

Chapter Review

To further practice and reinforce the skills you learned in this chapter, you can perform the following tasks:

- Review the chapter summary.
- Complete the case scenarios. These scenarios set up real-world situations involving the topics of this chapter and ask you to create solutions.
- Complete the suggested practices.
- Take a practice test.

Chapter Summary

- ASP.NET provides features for programming against your Web site. For one, you can catch unhandled exceptions at both the page and application level. You can do so by responding to the *Page_Error* or the *Application_Error* methods. You can also use the *WebConfigurationManager.GetSection* to work with configuration information in your Web.config file. In addition, ASP.NET supports asynchronous Web pages and custom HTTP handlers.
- The ASP.NET intrinsic objects allow you to work with data about the server and the request processing on the server. This includes the *Request*, *Response*, and *Context* objects. The *Request.Browser* object can be used to determine information about the client's browser requesting a page on your server. The *Page.Header* property can be used to set information contained in the HTML header such as the style sheet, title, and search metadata.

Case Scenarios

In the following case scenarios, you apply what you've learned about how to implement and apply serialization, as well as how to upgrade applications that make use of serialization. You can find answers to these questions in the "Answers" section at the end of this book.

Case Scenario 1: Dynamically Generating Charts

You are an application developer for Fabrikam, Inc., a financial services company. You have been asked to write an ASP.NET application that enables users with Web browsers to view financial data graphically. For example, users should be able to visit the Web site to view a Web page displaying line charts comparing several different stock prices, or to view a comparison of home sales and mortgage rates.

QUESTIONS

Answer the following questions for your manager.

1. I'd like to display the charts as .gif images. How can you generate the charts?

2. The charts need to be dynamically generated. However, we cannot save the charts to disk. How can you display a dynamically generated .gif file in an ASP.NET Web page?
3. What configuration changes are required?

Case Scenario 2: Dynamically Adjusting Pages Based on Browser Capabilities

You are an application developer for Fabrikam, Inc., a financial services company. The application you created in the previous scenario has been very successful. However, the IT group has received several user requests for improvements to your application. Users have requested the following:

- An ActiveX chart that enables users to adjust the scale dynamically
- Scaled-down images for mobile clients
- More contrast for charts created for grayscale clients

QUESTIONS

Answer the following questions for your manager.

1. What specific property can you examine to determine whether the client supports ActiveX?
2. What property can you examine to determine whether the browser is running on a mobile client?
3. What property can you examine to determine whether the browser supports color or uses monochrome only?

Suggested Practices

To help you successfully master the exam objectives presented in this chapter, complete the following tasks.

Using Web Site Programmability

For this task, you should complete Practices 1 and 2 for practice working with Web.config programming. Complete Practice 3 for experience with application exception handling. Complete Practice 4 for practice writing asynchronous pages. Practice 5 helps in understanding custom HTTP handlers.

- **Practice 1** Create a Web page that enables you to browse and edit the Web application's settings.
- **Practice 2** Create a Web setup project that prompts the user for input and configures the application's configuration file based on that user input.
- **Practice 3** Using the last production ASP.NET Web site you created, add application-level error handling to catch unhandled exceptions. Log exceptions to a file

or database and let the application run for several days. Make note of whether any unhandled exceptions are occurring without your knowledge.

- **Practice 4** Create a synchronous ASP.NET Web page that displays the output from a Web service located on a different server. Test the performance of the Web page when 10 requests are issued simultaneously. Rewrite the Web page to be asynchronous. Retest the Web page and note whether performance changes.
- **Practice 5** Create an application that enables you to browse pictures on the Web server's local file system and view the pictures at different resolutions. Within the ASP.NET page's HTML, reference the images using query parameters that specify the file names and resolutions. Generate the pictures dynamically.

Using the ASP.NET Intrinsic Objects

For this task, you should complete all three practices for experience working with the *Request.Browser* object.

- **Practice 1** Download and install a non-Microsoft Web browser. Then, use the browser to open the last several Web applications you have created. Note how different ASP.NET controls behave when viewed with different browsers. In particular, notice how Web Parts behave differently. Web Parts are described in Chapter 5, "Customizing and Personalizing a Web Application."
- **Practice 2** If you have a production ASP.NET Web site available, add code that creates a log of browser types and capabilities for each new user. Examine the variety of browsers and capabilities in your user base and think about how you might adjust your Web application to provide a better experience for all types of browsers.
- **Practice 3** Download one or two non-Microsoft browsers. Use those browsers to visit different Web sites and compare them side by side with Internet Explorer. Note how some Web sites display pages differently.

Take a Practice Test

The practice tests on this book's companion CD offer many options. For example, you can test yourself on just the content covered in this chapter, or you can test yourself on all the 70-562 certification exam content. You can set up the test so it closely simulates the experience of taking a certification exam, or you can set it up in study mode so you can look at the correct answers and explanations after you answer each question.

> ***MORE INFO*** **PRACTICE TESTS**
>
> **For details about all the practice test options available, see the "How to Use the Practice Tests" section in this book's Introduction.**

CHAPTER 12

Monitoring, Troubleshooting, and Debugging

A large part of the development process involves removing bugs and other issues from your application. Microsoft Visual Studio and ASP.NET provide a number of tools to support this task. This includes the ability to set breakpoints in code, to step through your code inside the Integrated Development Environment (IDE), to view variable values in watch windows, to execute code in the command window, and more. These debugging tools work for all the applications you create with Visual Studio, not just Web applications. Web applications do, however, present their own set of challenges. They run in a distributed environment where the network, database, and client are all running on separate processes. This can make it difficult just to get debugging set up and to get the right troubleshooting information out of your application and its environment.

This chapter explores how you debug, monitor, and troubleshoot Web applications. The first lesson covers setting up debugging, creating custom errors, debugging on a remote server, and debugging client script. The second lesson is about troubleshooting and monitoring a running ASP.NET site.

Exam objectives in this chapter:

- Troubleshooting and Debugging Web Applications
    - Configure debugging and custom errors.
    - Set up an environment to perform remote debugging.
    - Debug unhandled exceptions when using ASP.NET AJAX.
    - Implement tracing of a Web application.
    - Debug deployment issues.
    - Monitor Web applications.

Lessons in this chapter:

Before You Begin

To complete the lessons in this chapter, you should be familiar with developing applications with Visual Studio using Microsoft Visual Basic or C#. In addition, you should be comfortable with all of the following:

- Working with the Visual Studio 2008 IDE.
- Using Hypertext Markup Language (HTML) and client-side scripting.
- Creating ASP.NET Web sites and forms.

Lesson 1: Debugging an ASP.NET Application

Debugging an ASP.NET Web site can be complicated, as the client and server are typically distributed across different machines. In addition, the state that the application uses is also distributed among database, Web server, cache, session, cookie, and so on. Thankfully, Visual Studio and ASP.NET have a number of tools that allow you to get debugging information from your site during development.

This lesson covers setup and configuration of the ASP.NET debugging features. This includes remote debugging and client-side script debugging.

> ***NOTE*** **CHAPTER CONTENTS**
>
> **This lesson covers the configuration and setup of debugging with ASP.NET and Visual Studio. It does not cover using the basics of the Visual Studio debugger such as setting breakpoints and viewing variables in watch windows. Rather, it is focused on managing debugging of an ASP.NET Web site.**

After this lesson, you will be able to:

- Configure a Web site for debugging with Visual Studio.
- Set up remote debugging between a development machine and a server.
- Redirect users to a default error page or custom error pages based on Hypertext Transfer Protocol (HTTP) status codes.
- Debug client-side script.

Estimated lesson time: 20 minutes

Configuring ASP.NET for Debugging

You can debug an ASP.NET application using the standard features of the Visual Studio debugger like breakpoints, watch windows, code step-through, error information, and the like. To do so, you must first configure ASP.NET for debugging. There are two areas where you set this information: the project's property page and the Web.config file.

Activate the ASP.NET Debugger

The first step is to enable the ASP.NET debugger in your project's Property Pages dialog box. For sites created through Visual Studio, this is enabled by default. However, if you need to set or modify this setting, you can do so by following these steps:

1. Right-click the Web site in Solution Explorer to open the shortcut menu.
2. Select Property Pages from the shortcut menu. This will open the Property Pages dialog box for the given Web site, as shown in Figure 12-1.

3. Select Start Options from the left side of the dialog box.
4. In the Debuggers section, at the bottom of the dialog box, select (or clear) the ASP.NET check box to enable (or disable) the ASP.NET debugger for Visual Studio.

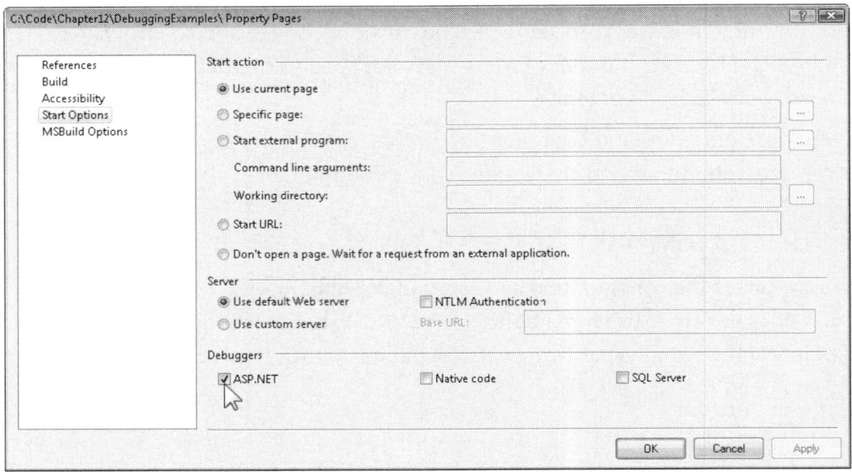

FIGURE 12-1 The project Property Pages dialog box for an ASP.NET Web site

Configure Debugging

The second step is to enable debugging either for your entire site or on a page-by-page basis. By default, debugging is not enabled for Web sites created with Visual Studio. Doing so will add debug symbols into the compiled code. Visual Studio uses these symbols to provide debugging support. However, this can slow the performance of your Web application. In addition, turning on debugging will output error information to the Web browser when you run the page outside of Visual Studio. This can present a security risk, as error information provides potential attackers with a lot of information about how your site works. For these reasons, you only want to turn debugging on during development.

You enable debugging for your entire site through the Web.config file by setting the *debug* attribute of the *compilation* element to *true*. The following markup shows an example that includes the nesting level of the *compilation* element:

```
<configuration>
  <system.web>
    <compilation debug="true">
    </compilation>
  <system.web>
</configuration>
```

It might not always be desirable to turn on debugging for your entire site. In these cases, you can switch debugging on and off at the individual page level. This will compile only that page with the debug symbols. The rest of the site will be compiled without debugging. To enable page-level debugging, set the *Debug* attribute of the *@ Page* directive (found at the top of the markup for an .aspx page). The following shows an example:

```
<%@ Page Debug="true" ... %>
```

Once you have debugging enabled you can use the many features of the Visual Studio debugger. When you run your application, Visual Studio automatically attaches to the running ASP.NET Web server process (unless doing remote development, which is discussed later in this lesson). You can then set breakpoints in your code, step through line-by-line, and view variable values in the watch window. In addition, if debugging is enabled, you can get error information output to the browser Window even when not running your application through Visual Studio.

Defining Custom Errors

In your production environment it is likely that you do not want to show users the default, ASP.NET error page if your site happens to break. This holds true for the default, Microsoft Internet Information Services (IIS) errors as well. Rather, you most likely want users to see a page that instructs them on how they can contact support to resolve the problem. In the previous chapter you saw how you can catch unhandled errors and respond accordingly. However, you can also configure your site to display a generic error page if users happen to encounter an unhandled error. You can set this page at the site level. You can also set individual pages for specific error types.

Configuring a Custom Site-Level Error Page

You configure custom errors inside the Web.config file using the *<customErrors>* element nested inside *<system.web>*. This element has the attributes *mode* and *defaultRedirect*. The *mode* attribute can be set to *on* to turn custom errors on, *off* to turn them off, or *RemoteOnly* to turn custom errors on for remote clients only. With *RemoteOnly*, if a user (typically an administrator) is on the server, he or she will not get the custom error, but instead will get the real error message.

The *defaultRedirect* attribute is used to indicate the path to a default error page. This page will be hit when an unhandled exception occurs on the site. The only exception is when a specific custom error page is added to the *<error>* child elements of *<customErrors>* (as discussed in the next section). The following example shows markup for a custom error definition inside Web.config:

```
<configuration>
  <system.web>
    <customErrors defaultRedirect="SiteErrorPage.aspx" mode="RemoteOnly">
    </customErrors>
  <system.web>
</configuration>
```

Notice that in the previous markup, the page is set to an .aspx page. You can set this to an .htm, .aspx, or other resource to which the Web server can redirect.

On redirection, the server passes the path of the page that caused the error. This path is provided as part of the query string using the named parameter aspxErrorPath. For example, the following shows the browser's Uniform Resource Locator (URL) when the SiteErrorPage .aspx is hit based on an error thrown on Default.aspx:

```
http://localhost/examples/SiteErrorPage.aspx?aspxerrorpath=/examples/Default.aspx
```

Configuring Error-Specific Error Pages

It is also possible to define specific pages for various HTTP status codes. This allows you to provide more specific information to users when they hit a given status code. For example, if users do not have access to a given page or resource, they will be shown the HTTP error 403. This status code indicates they are denied access to the resource. You can then write a custom page that explains the process for obtaining access to a given resource. Use the *<error>* element to redirect to that custom page. The following markup shows an example:

```
<configuration>
  <system.web>
    <customErrors defaultRedirect="SiteErrorPage.aspx" mode="RemoteOnly">
      <error statusCode="403" redirect="RestrictedAccess.aspx" />
    </customErrors>
  <system.web>
</configuration>
```

There are many HTTP status codes. However, errors fall in the range from 400 to 600. Codes with numbers 400 to 499 are reserved for request errors. Codes of 500 to 599 are set aside for server errors. Table 12-1 lists some common HTTP status codes for errors.

TABLE 12-1 Common HTTP Status Codes

CODE	DESCRIPTION
400	Request is not understood (unintelligible)
403	User does not have access to requested resource
404	File not found at requested URL
405	The request method is not supported
406	The requested Multipurpose Internet Mail Extensions (MIME) type is not accepted
408	The request has timed out
500	An internal server error has occurred
503	The capacity of the server has been reached

MORE INFO IIS 7 HTTP STATUS CODES

The HTTP status codes inside IIS 7 have been extended to provide some additional information on a given status. They now include decimal point values. For example, the 403 code that indicates access is forbidden includes 403.1 to 403.19 to provide details on why access was forbidden. For more information, see "The HTTP status codes in IIS 7.0" in the MSDN Knowledge Base.

Debugging Remotely

In most scenarios you debug a Web site by running it locally, on your development machine. This puts the client browser, the development environment (Visual Studio), and the Web server on a single machine. In this case, Visual Studio automatically connects to the running site's process and allows you to debug your Web site. However, there might be occasions when your development server is not local or you wish to debug an issue against a test server. In these scenarios, you will need to enable remote debugging.

Some of the details of enabling remote debugging are specific to a given environment. There are slight modifications to the process depending on your domain, credentials, and the operating systems in use by the developer and the server. However, the process of enabling remote debugging is made easier through the Remote Debugging Monitor (Msvsmon.exe). You run this tool on the server you intend to debug. The tool can be found inside your development environment installation folder (for example, Program Files\Microsoft Visual Studio 9.0\Common7\IDE\Remote Debugger\x64). You can copy the .exe to a file share or over to the server. You can also install the tool from the Visual Studio DVD set.

When you run the tool, it displays a remote debugging monitor user interface. This interface shows debugging events. It also allows you to configure the remote debugging options. Figure 12-2 shows an example of the application running on a server.

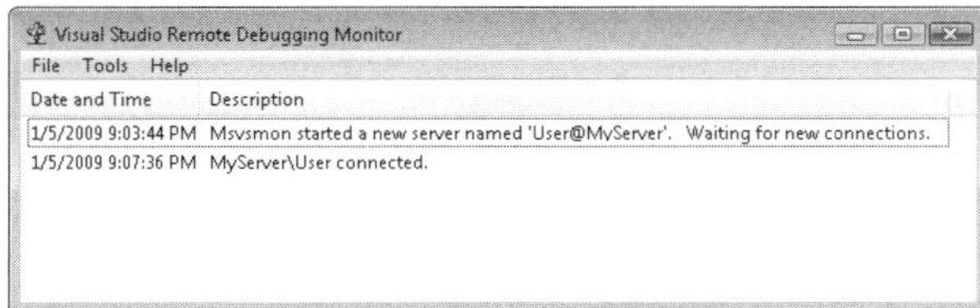

FIGURE 12-2 The Remote Debugging Monitor user interface

You can use the Remote Debugging Monitor tool to set remote debugging security options on the server. To do so, from the Tools menu, select Options. This opens the Options dialog box as shown in Figure 12-3. Here you set the server name to a user and a server. Each instance of the remote debugger running on a single server has a unique server name. You typically run an instance of the remote debugger for each developer who is doing remote debugging on the server. The Options dialog box also allows you to set the user authentication mode and permissions. Typically this is set to Windows Authentication. You then give the appropriate user in the Active Directory access rights to remotely debug.

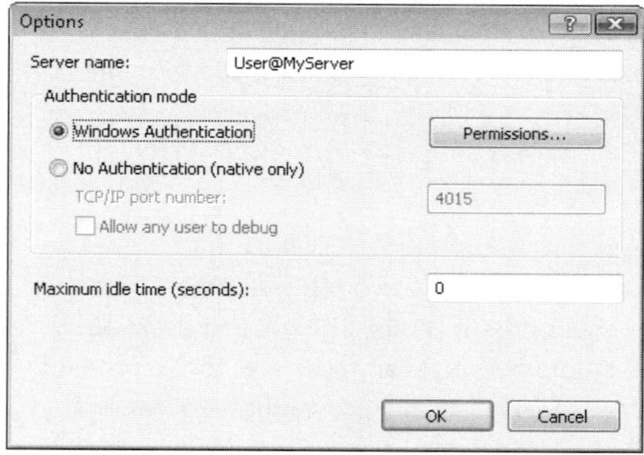

FIGURE 12-3 The Options dialog box for the Remote Debugging Monitor

Depending on your environment, you might also need to enable remote debugging through your firewall. Both the Remote Debugging Monitor and Visual Studio will do this for you. However, if you are running Microsoft Windows Vista, you might be prompted by the User Account Control (UAC) dialog box. If you are not on the server, you might not notice this message. Therefore, you should consider manually configuring firewall access in this case by allowing communication through port 135. You can find a detailed walkthrough of this process inside the MSDN documentation (under the title "How to: Manually Configure the Windows Vista Firewall for Remote Debugging").

You begin a remote debugging session by opening Visual Studio and a solution that includes the code you intend to debug. You can then attach to the server running the Remote Debugging Monitor application from the Debug menu by selecting Attach To Process. This opens the Attach To Process dialog box shown in Figure 12-4.

In this dialog box, you set the Qualifier to the name of the server running the Remote Debugging Monitor. Recall that this is the server name set in the Options dialog box for the Remote Debugging Monitor and typically is defined as *User@Server*. You will then see a list of running processes on the server. Select the ASP.NET Web server process and click Attach to start remote debugging. You can then hit the server through a browser to cause a breakpoint to fire or an error to occur. Doing so will send you into debug mode inside of Visual Studio.

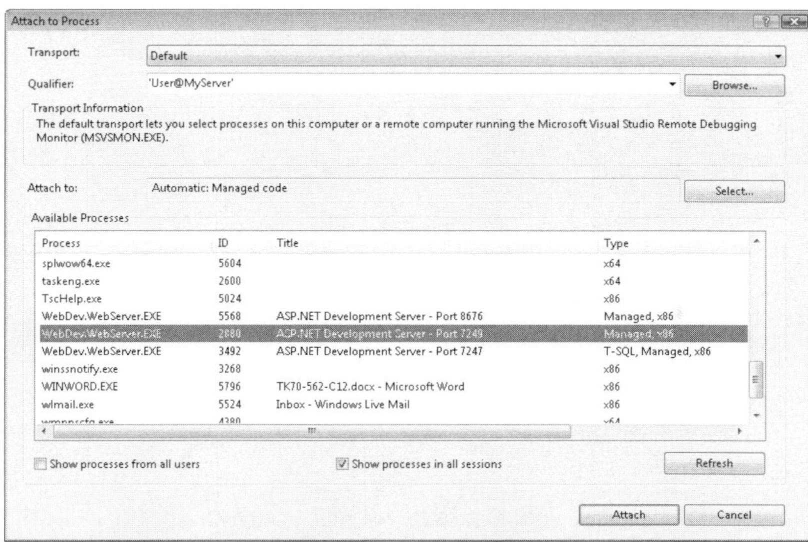

FIGURE 12-4 The Attach To Process dialog box inside Visual Studio

Debugging Client-Side Script

Visual Studio also allows you to debug client script running inside a browser. This is useful if you write a lot of JavaScript and need to walk through the code line by line and use the other features of the debugging toolset.

To get started, you need to enable script debugging support inside the browser. To do so, you open Microsoft Internet Explorer and select Tools | Internet Options. This opens the Internet Options dialog box shown in Figure 12-5. Click the Advanced tab. Find the *Browsing* node in the Settings tree and clear the Disable Script Debugging (Internet Explorer) check box.

You can then begin debugging client script. You can get started by setting a breakpoint in your client script and running the site through Visual Studio. You can also manually attach to code running in a browser. You do this by first opening the source code in Visual Studio and then using the Attach To Process dialog box discussed in the prior section to attach to the browser's process. Any error will give you the option to debug.

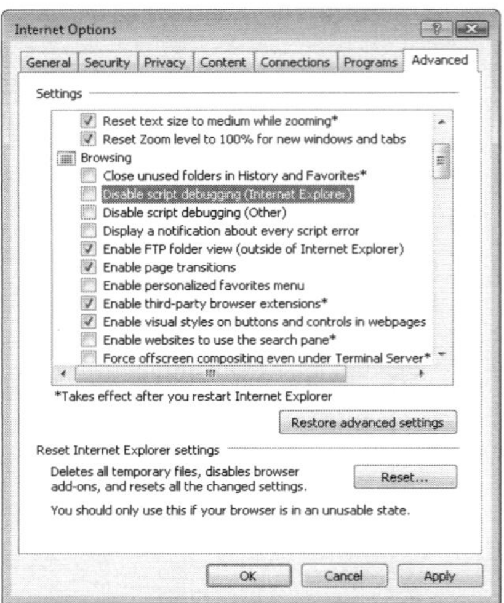

FIGURE 12-5 Using the Internet Options dialog box to enable script debugging for Internet Explorer

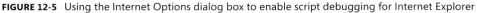

> ***NOTE*** **DEBUGGING AJAX**
>
> **For more information on debugging client script that uses the Microsoft AJAX Library, see "Tracing AJAX Applications" in Lesson 2 of this chapter.**

Quick Check

1. **In which dialog box do you enable the ASP.NET debugger for your project?**
2. **What is the name of the element in the Web.config file that you use to define the *debug* attribute to turn on debugging for your site?**

Quick Check Answers

1. **You can enable the ASP.NET debugger from your project's Property Pages dialog box.**
2. **You can turn on debugging using the *debug* attribute of the *compilation* element.**

LAB Configuring Debugging in ASP.NET

In this lab, you configure a Web site to support debugging and custom errors. You also set up Internet Explorer to support script debugging.

If you encounter a problem completing an exercise, you can find the completed projects in the samples installed from the companion CD.

EXERCISE 1 Configure a Web Site for Debugging

In this exercise, you create a Web site and configure it for debugging.

1. Open Visual Studio. Create a new, file-based Web site called **Debugging**.
2. Open the Web.config file and navigate to the *compilation* node. Set the *debug* attribute to *true* as follows:

```
<compilation debug="true">
```

3. Open the code-behind file for Default.aspx. Add a *Page_Load* event handler. Inside this event throw an exception. The following code shows an example:

```
'VB
Protected Sub Page_Load(ByVal sender As Object, _
  ByVal e As System.EventArgs) Handles Me.Load

  Throw New ApplicationException("Example exception.")

End Sub

//C#
protected void Page_Load(object sender, EventArgs e)
{
  throw new ApplicationException("Example exception.");
}
```

4. Run the Default.aspx page in a browser by right-clicking the page in Solution Explorer and choosing View in Browser. This should display the debugging error information as shown in Figure 12-6.

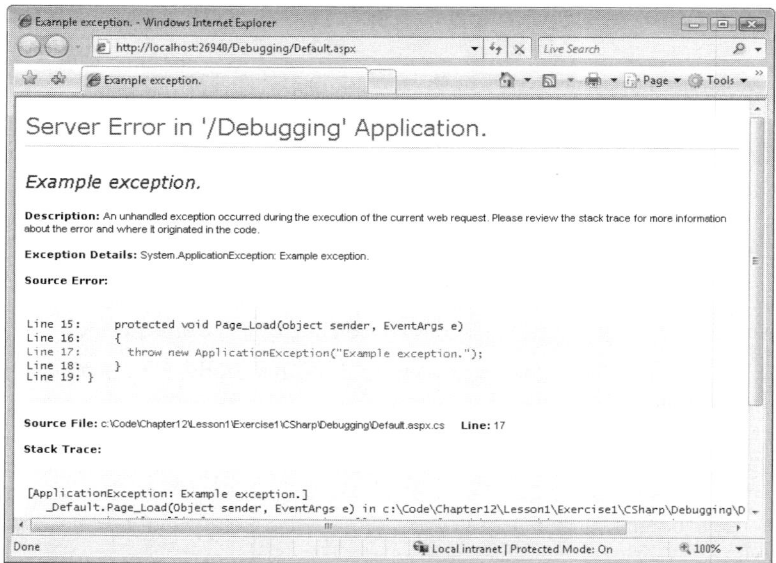

FIGURE 12-6 The ASP.NET debugging error information in a Web browser

EXERCISE 2 Add a Custom Error Page

In this exercise, you create a custom error page and configure your site to redirect to it for a specific HTTP status code.

1. Open the project you created in the previous exercise. Alternatively, you can open the completed Lesson 1, Exercise 1 project in the samples installed from the CD.
2. Add a new Web form to the site. Name this form **ResourceNotFound.aspx**.

   Add text to the body of this page to display a custom error message to users when they try to access a resource that is not on the Web server. You can use the *aspxerror-path* query string parameter to display the path of the requested resource inside the message.
3. Open the Web.config file again. Navigate to the *customErrors* section (commented out by default). Turn on custom errors. Add an *error* element for HTTP status code 404 (resource not found). The following markup shows an example:

```
<customErrors mode="On">
  <error statusCode="404" redirect="ResourceNotFound.aspx" />
</customErrors>
```

4. View Default.aspx in a browser again. Notice that the debugging error message is no longer shown. This is because the *on* setting in the *customErrors* node indicates that the site should only display custom errors.

Next, change the URL in your browser to request Default2.aspx (which should not exist in your site). This will redirect the browser to the ResourceNotFound.aspx page.

EXERCISE 3 Enable Script Debugging

In this exercise, you enable client script debugging for a Web site.

1. Open the project you created in the previous exercise. Alternatively, you can open the completed Lesson 1, Exercise 2 project in the samples installed from the CD.
2. Add a new Web page to your site. Name the page **ScriptDebug.aspx**.
3. Add a JavaScript function to the markup. This can be a simple script as follows:

```
<script language="javascript" type="text/jscript">

  function buttonClick() {
    alert('Button clicked.');
  }

</script>
```

4. Add an HTML button to the page. Set the *OnClick* event to call the JavaScript function as follows:

```
<input id="Button1" type="button" value="button" onclick="buttonClick()" />
```

5. Open Internet Explorer and select Tools | Internet Options. Click the Advanced tab and clear the Disable Script Debugging (Internet Explorer) check box. Click OK.
6. Return to Visual Studio. Set a breakpoint on the *buttonClick* function inside the markup. You can do so by clicking the margin area in the code editor (on the left side).
7. Run the application from Visual Studio by choosing Start Debugging from the Debug menu (or simply press F5). Navigate to the ScriptDebug.aspx page. Click the button to break into the script debugger.

Lesson Summary

- You turn on debugging for your Web application inside the Web.config file by setting the *debug* attribute of the *compilation* element to *true*. You can also turn on debugging at the individual page level using the *Debug* attribute of the @ *Page* directive.
- You can set a custom error page for your entire site by setting the *defaultRedirect* attribute of the *customErrors* element. You can also map specific pages to HTTP status codes using the *errors* child element.
- The Remote Debugging Monitor (Msvsmon.exe) allows you to configure debugging on a remote server. Once it is configured, you need to attach to your site's ASP.NET process from Visual Studio.

- You can set an option in Internet Explorer to allow you to debug client script from Visual Studio. This allows you to use the debugging features of Visual Studio with client-side JavaScript.

Lesson Review

You can use the following questions to test your knowledge of the information in Lesson 1, "Debugging an ASP.NET Application." The questions are also available on the companion CD if you prefer to review them in electronic form.

> ***NOTE*** **ANSWERS**
>
> **Answers to these questions and explanations of why each answer choice is right or wrong are located in the "Answers" section at the end of the book.**

1. You are debugging an application on a test server. You have an issue on a particular page and need to get the error details. You do not want to turn on debugging for the entire site. What action should you take? (Choose all that apply.)
   - **A.** In the Web.config file, set the *debug* attribute of the compilation element to *true*.
   - **B.** In the Web.config file, set the *debug* attribute of the compilation element to *false*.
   - **C.** On the page that throws the error, set the *debug* attribute of the @ *Page* directive to *true*.
   - **D.** On the page that throws the error, set the *debug* attribute of the @ *Page* directive to *false*.
2. You are deploying your application to a production environment. You wish to redirect users to a default error page if they hit any unhandled exceptions or HTTP errors within the site. You also wish to indicate the user's requested resource on the error page to help with support calls. What action should you take? (Choose all that apply.)
   - **A.** Set the *redirect* attribute of the *error* element to an error page within your site.
   - **B.** Set the *defaultRedirect* attribute of the *customErrors* element to an error page within your site.
   - **C.** Use the *statusCode* query string parameter to get the requested resource to display on the error page.
   - **D.** Use the *aspxerrorpath* query string parameter to get the requested resource to display on the error page.
3. You have an error that is only occurring when the application is deployed to the development or test server. You need to debug this error remotely. What action should you take? (Choose all that apply.)

A. Run the Remote Debugging Monitor (Msvsmon.exe) on the development computer doing the debugging. Use the tool to define connection rights to the server you wish to debug.

B. Run the Remote Debugging Monitor (Msvsmon.exe) on the server you wish to debug. Use the tool to define connection rights for the developer doing the debugging.

C. In Visual Studio, use the Attach To Process dialog box to attach to the ASP.NET process on the server you wish to debug.

D. In Visual Studio, use the Attach To Process dialog box to attach to the browser's process that is running the application you wish to debug.

Lesson 2: Troubleshooting a Running ASP.NET Application

Not all issues can be found using Visual Studio. Therefore, ASP.NET provides the ability to trace and monitor your code as it executes in a test or production environment. These facilities of ASP.NET can be used to troubleshoot and diagnose problems that might otherwise prove impossible to re-create. In addition, these features allow you to examine statistics and usage on your Web site.

This lesson first covers enabling and configuring tracing in ASP.NET. It then explores how you can monitor a running Web site.

After this lesson, you will be able to:

- Enable and configure ASP.NET tracing.
- Understand the data that is available through ASP.NET tracing.
- Work with monitoring tools to evaluate a running ASP.NET site.

Estimated lesson time: 20 minutes

REAL WORLD

Mike Snell

Many issues that developers encounter only happen in the wild. That is, they occur only in a deployed, production-like setting. In fact, most of us have heard (or recited) the common developer mantra, "Works on my machine." In these cases there is often something very specific to the environment that is causing the issue. I have seen issues that involve bad configuration settings, security, a different service pack on the server, and many other things that only seem to happen when you are in a production setting. Of course, this includes issues that only present themselves under user load, like issues with state management, caching, locking, and concurrency. Fortunately, there are tools and support inside of ASP.NET that allow you to instrument your code with tracing and monitor your application. These are very valuable skills for developers. After all, even if you didn't write the code, that won't stop someone from asking you to support it.

Implementing Tracing

Tracing is the process of emitting data about a running application. In ASP.NET, this data is logged to a trace log file that you can access through a Web browser. The data provides important information about your site, such as who accessed the site, what the results were, what the various HTTP data looked like, and much more. You can also inject your own tracing calls into your code. This data will be emitted alongside the ASP.NET data. The following data is collected by ASP.NET tracing by default:

- **Request details** This includes session ID, the type of request (*GET/POST*), and the status of the request.
- **Trace information** This provides the timings for the various stages of your requests. This section also shows unhandled exceptions (in red) if there are any.
- **Controls** This indicates the controls on your page, their view state, and their rendered bytes.
- **Session/application state** This indicates the session and application variables and their current values for the given request.
- **Request/response cookies** Indicates the value and size of any cookies that are part of the request or response.
- **Headers** This indicates the HTTP header information such as the type of browser making the request.
- **Form data** This indicates the name and value of any posted form fields.
- **Query string values** This indicates the name and value of query string parameters sent as part of the request.
- **Server variables** This is used to view each server variable and its value at the time of the request.

You enable tracing through the Web.config file. You can edit this file manually or you can use the Web Site Administration Tool (WSAT) to provide a user-friendly interface to enable and configure tracing.

Enabling Trace Using the Web Site Administration Tool

The following steps identify how to enable and configure the trace facility using the WSAT:

1. Open the WSAT by selecting Website | ASP.NET Configuration from the Visual Studio menu.
2. On the home page, click the Application tab of the WSAT. This will bring up settings for your application.
3. On the Application tab, click Configure Debugging And Tracing (bottom right). This will display the configuration options for debugging and tracing as shown in Figure 12-7.
4. Select the Capture Tracing Information check box. This enables the tracing features to be changed as necessary.

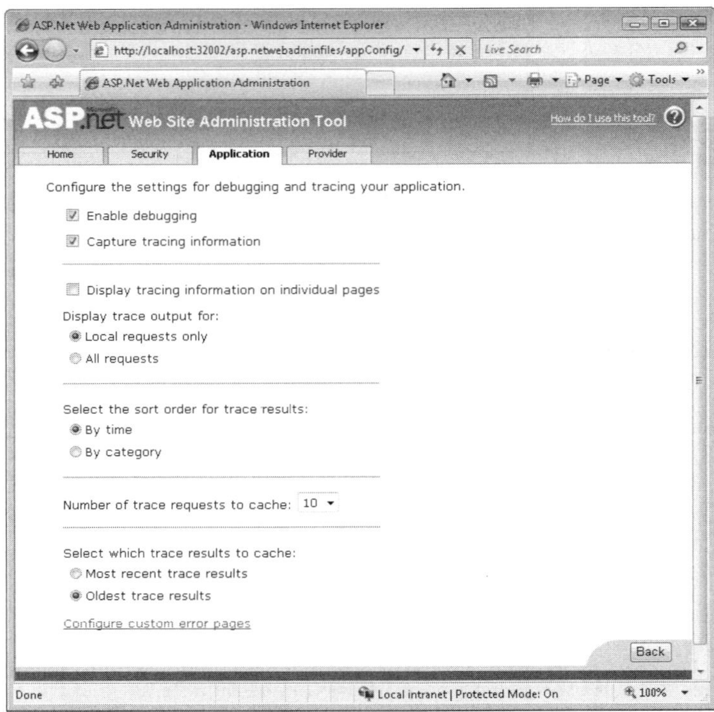

FIGURE 12-7 The debugging and tracing options inside the WSAT

As you can see from Figure 12-7, there are many options for you to configure with respect to tracing. These options also map to Web.config settings (as that is what the WSAT administers). Table 12-2 describes each of the options both from the perspective of the WSAT and Web.config.

TABLE 12-2 ASP.NET Trace Settings

WEB SITE ADMINISTRATION TOOL SETTING	WEB.CONFIG SETTING	DESCRIPTION
Capture Tracing Information	enabled	Enables tracing for your application. When this is set to *true*, the other trace options are also made available.
Display Tracing Information On Individual Pages	pageOutput	Displays the trace information directly on the Web page that is being traced. Depending on the page content, the trace information displays either at the bottom of the Web page or behind the regular Web page content.

WEB SITE ADMINISTRATION TOOL SETTING	WEB.CONFIG SETTING	DESCRIPTION
Display Trace Output For	localOnly	Designates whether you intend to display tracing for just local requests or for all requests. When set to Local Requests Only, the trace facility only operates with requests from the computer on which the Web server is running. The All Requests setting enables tracing for all requests from any computer to the Web site.
Select The Sort Order For Trace Results	traceMode	Enables sorting of the trace output either by time or by category.
Number Of Trace Requests To Cache	requestLimit	Sets the number of records to hold in the cache (or trace log).
Select Which Trace Results To Cache	mostRecent	Designates whether you intend to store the most recent trace result or the oldest. When set to Most Recent Trace Results, the cache continues to update, only holding the latest results. When set to Oldest Trace Results, as soon as the number of requests has been met, the cache no longer updates until after the Web application is restarted or the log is cleared.

Enabling Trace Using the Web.Config File

You can enable tracing manually through editing the Web.config file of an ASP.NET site. You do so by editing attributes (listed in Table 12-2) of the *<trace>* element. This element is nested under *<configuration><system.web>*. The following markup shows an example:

```
<configuration>
  <system.web>
    <trace enabled="true"
      requestLimit="100"
      pageOutput="false"
      traceMode="SortByTime"
      localOnly="false"
      mostRecent="true" />
  <system.web>
</configuration>
```

In the preceding markup, tracing is enabled (*enabled="true"*) for all requests to the server (*localOnly="false"*). The trace log will cache the most recent 100 requests (*"requestLimit=100" and mostRecent="true"*). The trace log will be sorted by time (*"traceMode=SortyByTime"*). The data will only be viewable through the trace log and not on each individual page (*pageOutput="false"*).

Enabling Tracing at the Page Level

You can also enable tracing for specific pages only. This is useful if you do not wish to turn on tracing at the site level, but instead enable it only on a page you are troubleshooting. You enable tracing at the page level by setting the *trace* attribute of the *@ Page* directive to *true*. This is found at the top of the page's markup. The following shows an example:

```
<@Page trace="true" ... />
```

Viewing Trace Data

Once it is configured and turned on, you can view the ASP.NET trace data on each Web page (*pageOutput="true"*) or view the trace output by navigating to the Trace.axd page on the current Web application (*http://server/application/trace.axd*). When viewing on the same page, the trace information is appended to the bottom of the page (for pages that use flow layout). Figure 12-8 shows an example.

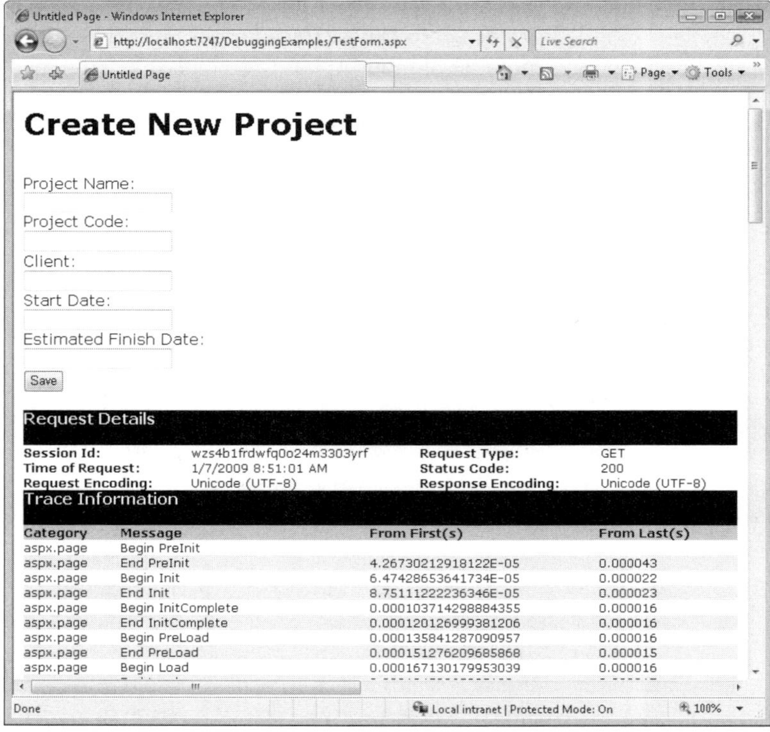

FIGURE 12-8 Tracing information output on an ASP.NET page

To view your entire log, you navigate to the Trace.axd page for your site. This page will show a log event if *pageOutput* is set to *true*. The first page of the log is a summary page. This page contains a list of trace results that are in the cache. Figure 12-9 shows an example.

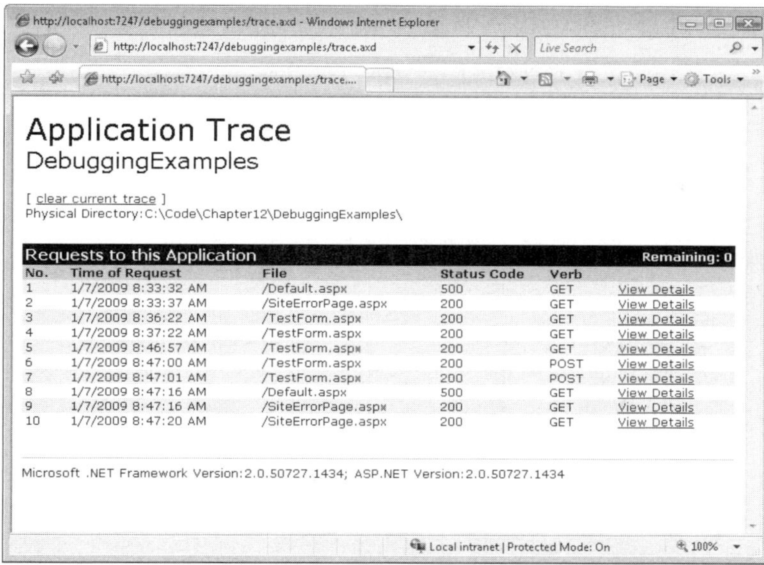

FIGURE 12-9 The Trace.axd page

You can click one of the cached results to view the details of the trace record for a single page request. These details are similar to the information that is shown on each Web page (as shown in Figure 12-8).

SECURITY ALERT **If you opt to display the trace information on individual pages, the trace information can be displayed on any browser that makes a request. This is a potential security threat because sensitive information such as server variables will display. Be sure to disable page tracing on production Web servers.**

The trace result page is separated into sections, as described in Table 12-3. This information can be very useful when you are trying to identify performance issues and resource usage.

TABLE 12-3 Trace Result Sections

TRACE RESULT SECTION	DESCRIPTION
Request Details	Provides general details about the page request.
Trace Information	Displays performance information related to the Web page's life-cycle events. The From First(s) column displays the running time from when the page request started. The From Last(s) column shows the elapsed time since the previous event.

TRACE RESULT SECTION	DESCRIPTION
Control Tree	Displays information about each control on the Web page, such as the size of the rendered controls.
Session State	Displays all session variables and their values.
Application State	Displays all application variables and their states.
Request Cookies Collection	Displays the list of cookies that are passed to the server as part of the request.
Response Cookies Collection	Displays the list of cookies that are passed to the browser as part of the response.
Headers Collection	Displays the list of HTTP headers that are sent to the Web server as part of the request.
Form Collection	Displays the list of values that are posted back to the Web server.
QueryString Collection	Displays the list of values that are included in the query string.
Server Variables	Displays all server variables.

Emitting Custom Trace Data

You can add your own trace messages to the data that is output by ASP.NET tracing through the *Trace* class in the *System.Diagnostics* namespace. This class is exposed as a member of the *Page* object. This allows you to call *Page.Trace* (or just *Trace*). You use the *Write* method of this object to output a message to the trace log. When doing so, you can provide a category and the message.

The following shows an example of writing to the trace log. Here a message is being added to the log when the page is loaded and when a user clicks the button on the page. The category of the message is set at Custom Category. This category allows you to find your message easily. Custom messages are output in the Trace Information section of the trace details.

```
'VB
Protected Sub Page_Load(ByVal sender As Object, _
  ByVal e As System.EventArgs) Handles Me.Load

  Trace.Write("Custom Category", "Page_Load called")

End Sub

Protected Sub Button1_Click(ByVal sender As Object, _
  ByVal e As System.EventArgs) Handles Button1.Click

  Trace.Write("Custom Category", "Button1_Click called")
```

```
End Sub

//C#
protected void Page_Load(object sender, EventArgs e)
{
  Trace.Write("Custom Category", "Page_Load called");
}
protected void Button1_Click(object sender, EventArgs e)
{
  Trace.Write("Custom Category", "Button1_Click called");
}
```

Tracing AJAX Applications

Debugging an AJAX application presents its own issues. You do not have a server process on which to rely. Instead, you have to try to debug the code as it executes in the browser. In the previous section you saw how you can do this. However, AJAX-enabled applications tend to have a lot of client code. Therefore, they can present even more issues when debugging. For this reason, the Microsoft AJAX Library provides the *Sys.Debug* client-side namespace.

The tracing you enable on the server is not fired for AJAX partial-page requests. Therefore, you will see nothing in the Trace.axd log for these types of requests. Instead, you have to use the features of *Sys.Debug* to write out trace messages. The *Debug* class includes the *assert*, *trace*, *clearTrace*, *traceDump*, and *fail* methods. These methods can be used to output and manage messages to a trace log based on your needs.

As an example, you write out a message using *Sys.Debug.trace*. Of course, your page must include the Microsoft AJAX Library JavaScript file. This is done by adding a *ScriptManager* control to your page. Refer to Chapter 6, "Working with ASP.NET AJAX and Client-Side Scripting," for more details on working with AJAX. The following markup shows part of an .aspx page that includes a *ScriptManager* control and a JavaScript function named *button1_onclick*. When this function is fired (from the user clicking *button1*), the *trace* method is called.

```
<html xmlns="http://www.w3.org/1999/xhtml">
<head id="Head1" runat="server">
  <title>AJAX Trace Example</title>

  <script language="javascript" type="text/javascript">
    function button1_onclick() {
      Sys.Debug.trace("Button1 clicked");
    }
  </script>

</head>
<body>
  <form id="form1" runat="server">
```

```
    <div>

    <asp:ScriptManager ID="ScriptManager1" runat="server">
    </asp:ScriptManager>

    <input id="Button1" type="button" value="button"
      onclick="button1_onclick()" />

  </div>
  </form>
</body>
</html>
```

You can view the trace messages output by the AJAX library in the Visual Studio Output window. This works if you are using Internet Explorer and Visual Studio and debugging on the same machine. However, you can also create a *TextArea* control on the page that includes your JavaScript. You set the *TextArea* control's ID to *TraceConsole*. This will tell the Microsoft AJAX library to output its trace messages to this *TextArea* for you to view. If the browser you are debugging has a debugging console (as do the Apple Safari and Opera Software Opera browsers), it can also be used to view the trace messages. Figure 12-10 shows the result of the preceding markup as output to the Visual Studio Output window (bottom of the image).

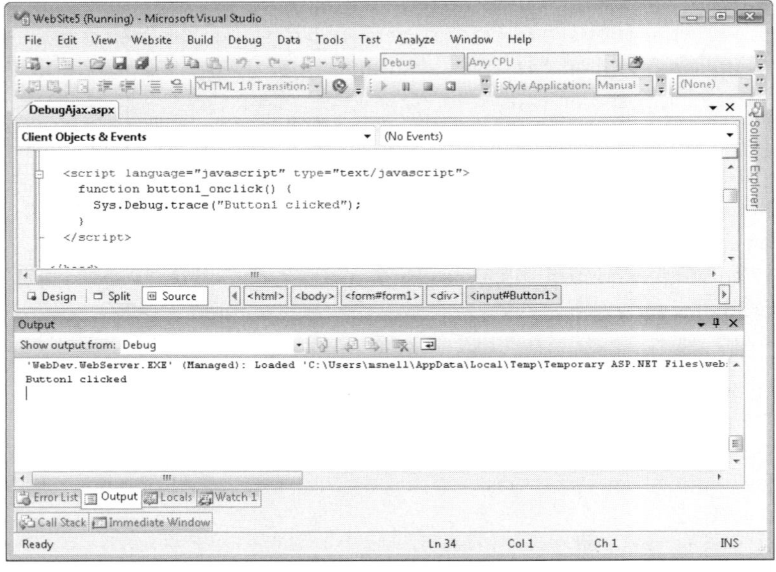

FIGURE 12-10 The *Sys.Debug.trace* message in the Output window

Quick Check

1. How can you make trace data display on your Web page?
2. What is the name of the virtual page that you can request to view trace data when the trace data is not displayed on its corresponding Web page?

Quick Check Answers

1. Set *pageOutput="true"*.
2. The virtual page is called Trace.axd.

Monitoring a Running Web Application

Tracing helps provide diagnostic information about a page. This can be very useful to troubleshoot problems with pages in a test environment. However, you often need information about the overall health of your application. You want to be able to monitor the application and be notified of various events such as error conditions, security issues, and request failures. You can do so using the features of ASP.NET health monitoring.

ASP.NET health monitoring provides a set of classes in the *System.Web.Management* namespace for tracking the health of your application. You can use these classes to create your own events and your own custom event listeners (and viewers). You can also use the default features exposed by these classes to monitor most aspects of any running Web application. This section focuses on the latter option.

The Health Monitoring Classes

The health monitoring system works by raising and logging ASP.NET events based on your configuration. You enable these events based on what you wish to monitor with respect to your application's performance and health. The monitoring happens in a deployed environment. You can use the features of health monitoring to receive e-mails about important activities, to log information to the event log, and to log information to SQL Server.

The first step in health monitoring is determining for which events you intend to listen. These events are defined as classes. The classes are based on a class hierarchy that defines the data that gets logged with the event. For example, a given Web health monitoring event class might contain information about the process executing your code, the HTTP request, the HTTP response, and error conditions.

You can also use the base Web event classes in the *System.Web.Management* namespace to write your own Web events for health monitoring purposes. Table 12-4 lists the key Web event classes and their basic use.

TABLE 12-4 The Web Event Classes in the .NET Framework

CLASS NAME	DESCRIPTION
WebBaseEvent	Base class to create your own Web events
WebManagementEvent	Base class for creating Web events that contain application process information
WebHeartbeatEvent	Serves as a periodic event that raises information about your application at set intervals
WebRequestEvent	Base class that contains Web-request information
WebApplicationLifetimeEvent	Raised when a significant application event occurs, such as application start or shutdown
WebBaseErrorEvent	Base class for creating error-based events
WebErrorEvent	Used to provide information about an error when it occurs inside your application
WebRequestErrorEvent	Contains request data for request errors
WebAuditEvent	Base class for creating audit (security) events
WebSuccessAuditEvent	Raised when a successful security operation occurs for your application
WebAuthenticationSuccessAuditEvent	Used to provide information when a successful user authentication occurs on the site
WebFailureAuditEvent	Raised when a failed security operation occurs
WebAuthenticationFailureAuditEvent	Used to provide information when a failed attempt at user authentication occurs on the site
WebViewStateFailureAuditEvent	Fires when the view state fails to load (typically as a result of tampering)

Once you know for which events you intend to listen, the second step is to enable a listener (or log). The ASP.NET health monitoring system defines a set of providers (or listeners) that are used to collect the Web event information. These listeners consume the Web health events and typically log the given event details. You can leverage the default listeners or write your own by extending the existing *WebEventProvider* class. The default providers include *EventLogWebEventProvider*, *WmiWebEventProvider*, and *SqlWebEventProvider*. You configure Web events and Web providers in ASP.NET configuration files, discussed next.

Configuring Health Monitoring

You turn on Web events and connect them to listeners inside the Web.config file. To do so, you configure the *<healthMonitoring>* element of the Web.config file. The *healthMonitoring* element contains the *enabled* attribute, which you set to *true* to enable health monitoring. It also contains the attribute *heartbeatInterval*. You can set this to the number of seconds to wait between raising the *WebHeartbeatEvent*. The individual events themselves also contain the *minInterval* attribute that works in a similar fashion.

The process of configuring a Web event and provider is as follows:

1. Add an *eventMappings* child element to *healthMonitoring*. You use the *add* element to add the Web event class you wish to use.
2. Add a *providers* child element to *healthMonitoring*. This indicates your health monitoring listener(s).
3. Finally, add a *rules* element to *healthMonitoring*. You use the *add* child element of *rules* to indicate an association between a registered Web event and registered listener.

Fortunately, you do not need to register the default Web events and providers. Instead, these are already registered for you by the overall configuration file on your server. Therefore, you need only add rules to your Web.config file to turn these events on. As an example, the following configuration turns on the heartbeat and application lifetime events. These events are written to the *EventLogProvider*.

```
<configuration>
  <system.web>
    <healthMonitoring enabled="true" heartbeatInterval="1">

      <rules>
        <add name="Heart Beat"
          eventName="Heartbeats"
          provider="EventLogProvider"
          profile="Default"/>
        <add name="App Lifetime"
          eventName="Application Lifetime Events"
          provider="EventLogProvider"
          profile="Default"
          minInstances="1" minInterval=""
          maxLimit="Infinite"/>
      </rules>

    </healthMonitoring>
  <system.web>
<configuration>
```

Notice that this configuration requires you to know the configured name of the event class and the provider. You can look up these names in your root configuration file. You can also find them on MSDN under the topic titled "*healthMonitoring* Element (ASP.NET Settings Schema)." The default configuration markup is listed there.

Figure 12-11 shows a logged event in Event Viewer. Notice this event fired when the application unexpectedly shut down. This was the result of the application lifetime event (*WebApplicationLifetimeEvent*) firing.

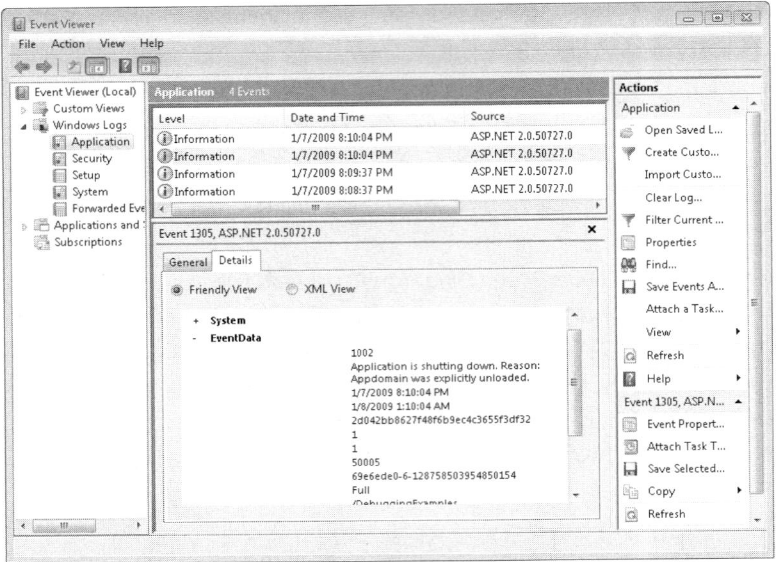

FIGURE 12-11 The Web event data output to the Event Log

LAB Using the ASP.NET Trace Facility

In this lab, you create a basic Web site and enable ASP.NET tracing. You then execute the site and view the trace details both at the page level and using the ASP.NET trace listener.

If you encounter a problem completing an exercise, you can find the completed projects in the samples installed from the companion CD.

EXERCISE 1 Enable ASP.NET Tracing

In this exercise, you work with ASP.NET tracing to view details about a running page in your site.

1. Open Visual Studio. Create a new, file-based Web site called **TracingCode**.
2. Open the Web Site Administration Tool from the Visual Studio menu by selecting Website | ASP.NET Configuration.
3. Click the Application tab to display the application settings. Click Configure Debugging And Tracing.
4. Select the Capture Tracing Information check box. This enables tracing for your site.

   Make the following additional changes using this page:

   - Ensure the Display Tracing Information On Individual Pages check box is cleared.
   - Set the Display Trace Output For option to Local Requests Only.
   - Set the Select The Sort Order For Trace Results option to By Time.

- Set the Number Of Trace Requests To Cache drop-down list to 50.
- Set the Select Which Trace Results To Cache option to Most Recent Trace Results.

Close the Web Site Administration Tool when finished.

5. Open the Web.config file. Navigate to the *trace* element. The *trace* element should look as follows (notice defaults are not listed, only the items that had to be overridden):

```
<trace
  enabled="true"
  mostRecent="true"
  requestLimit="50" />
```

6. Run the Web application. Although the Default.aspx page is blank, tracing still logs the request. Refresh the Web page a few times to write more results to the log.
7. In the Address bar of the browser, change the URL to access Trace.axd for the site. This will bring up the trace log. You should see entries for each time you requested the page.

   Click one of the View Details links to open a given record. Notice that Trace Information contains the timings for the events in the Web page life cycle.

   Close the Web browser.
8. Open Default.aspx in Visual Studio. Add the attribute *trace="true"* to the *@ Page* directive at the top of the page. Run the site again; notice that the page now includes the trace information written out.

   Close the Web browser.
9. Open the code-behind file for Default.aspx in Visual Studio. Add an event handler for the *Page_Load* event. Inside the event handler use *Page.Trace* to write out a tracing message. Your code should look as follows:

```
'VB
Protected Sub Page_Load(ByVal sender As Object, _
  ByVal e As System.EventArgs) Handles Me.Load

  Trace.Write("Custom Category", "Page_Load called")

End Sub

//C#
protected void Page_Load(object sender, EventArgs e)
{
  Trace.Write("Custom Category", "Page_Load called");
}
```

10. Run the application again. Notice your custom tracing message inside the Trace Information section of the page's trace output.

Lesson Summary

- You can use ASP.NET tracing to troubleshoot and diagnose problems with a page in your Web site. It outputs information about the request, response, and the environment.
- You can use the *trace* method to output custom trace messages to the trace log.
- An AJAX-enabled page can use the client-side *Sys.Debug.trace* method to output tracing information to a Web page (using a *TextArea* control), the Visual Studio Output window, or a browser's debug console.
- ASP.NET provides health monitoring tools (*System.Web.Management*) to enable you to monitor a running Web application. You can configure Web events with listeners through *rule* child elements of the *healthMonitoring* element inside Web.config.

Lesson Review

You can use the following questions to test your knowledge of the information in Lesson 2, "Troubleshooting a Running ASP.NET Application." The questions are also available on the companion CD if you prefer to review them in electronic form.

> ***NOTE* ANSWERS**
>
> **Answers to these questions and explanations of why each answer choice is right or wrong are located in the "Answers" section at the end of the book.**

1. You want to identify which event in the Web page life cycle takes the longest time to execute. How can you accomplish this?
   - **A.** Turn on ASP.NET tracing and run the Web application. After that, review the trace results.
   - **B.** Add a line of code to each of the life-cycle events that will print the current time.
   - **C.** In the Web.config file, add the *monitorTimings* attribute and set it to *true*.
   - **D.** In the Web site properties, turn on the performance monitor and run the Web application. After that, open the performance monitor to see the timings.
2. You want to run the trace continuously to enable you to quickly look at the 10 most recent traces from anyone using your Web site, but you are concerned about filling your hard drive with excessive data. Which of the following settings will accomplish your objective?
   - **A.**
   ```
   <trace
       enabled="false"
       requestLimit="10"
   ```

```
        pageOutput="false"
        traceMode="SortByTime"
        localOnly="true"
        mostRecent="true"
    />
```

B.
```
    <trace
        enabled="true"
        requestLimit="10"
        pageOutput="true"
        traceMode="SortByTime"
        localOnly="true"
        mostRecent="true"
    />
```

C.
```
    <trace
        enabled="true"
        requestLimit="10"
        pageOutput="false"
        traceMode="SortByTime"
        localOnly="true"
        mostRecent="false"
    />
```

D.
```
    <trace
        enabled="true"
        requestLimit="10"
        pageOutput="false"
        traceMode="SortByTime"
        localOnly="false"
        mostRecent="true"
    />
```

3. You are interested in examining the data that is posted to the Web server. What trace result section can you use to see this information?

- **A.** Control Tree section
- **B.** Headers Collection section
- **C.** Form Collection section
- **D.** Server Variables section

4. You wish to configure ASP.NET health monitoring to log information every time a user fails to log in to the server. Which Web event class should you use?

- **A.** *WebRequestEvent*
- **B.** *WebAuditEvent*
- **C.** *WebApplicationLifetimeEvent*
- **D.** *WebAuthenticationSuccessAuditEvent*

Chapter Review

To further practice and reinforce the skills you learned in this chapter, you can perform the following tasks:

- Review the chapter summary.
- Complete the case scenarios. These scenarios set up real-world situations involving the topics of this chapter and ask you to create solutions.
- Complete the suggested practices.
- Take a practice test.

Chapter Summary

- You can use debugging in ASP.NET to debug a site running locally or a site running on a remote server. You can enable debugging at the site level through Web.config or at the page level using the @ *Page* directive. You can also attach to your browser's process to debug client-side script.
- ASP.NET provides tools for troubleshooting and monitoring a running Web site. You can use the default ASP.NET tracing to get key data about a requested page. You can emit your own server-side trace messages with *Page.Trace*. You can also use the *Sys .Debug* namespace of the Microsoft AJAX Library to trace client-side script. Finally, you can enable health monitoring for your site to log and monitor key events on the site.

Case Scenarios

In the following case scenarios, you apply what you've learned in this chapter. If you have difficulty completing this work, review the material in this chapter before beginning the next chapter. You can find answers to these questions in the "Answers" section at the end of this book.

Case Scenario 1: Debugging

You are an application developer for Fabrikam, Inc., a financial services company. You have been told that users are receiving hard errors on certain pages in the site. You need to turn off the hard errors in production and direct users to a default error page. However, administrators executing code directly on the server should still be able to see the hard errors.

You also need to debug these errors. You cannot reproduce them on your machine. Therefore, you need to debug them against the staging server.

QUESTIONS

Answer the following questions based on the scenario just defined.

1. How will you turn off hard errors for users of the site?
2. How will you implement a default error page for users?
3. How will you ensure hard errors are still on for administrators?
4. How can you debug against the staging environment?

Case Scenario 2: Troubleshooting

You are an application developer for Fabrikam, Inc., a financial services company. The configuration changes you made to your application in the previous scenario have been very successful. However, you still have one persistent issue that you cannot seem to solve in development or staging. Therefore, you wish to turn tracing on for the given page and view the results by hitting the page from the server. In addition, your manager has asked you to begin monitoring key events in the system to verify the application's health.

QUESTIONS

Answer the following questions based on the scenario just defined.

1. How should you configure tracing for the given issue?
2. How should you enable health monitoring for your application?

Suggested Practices

To help you successfully master the exam objectives presented in this chapter, complete the following tasks.

Debugging a Web Site

For this task, you should complete the first practice to gain experience working with remote debugging. Practice 2 helps with client script debugging.

- **Practice 1** Find some ASP.NET code that matches code deployed on a development server. Deploy the remote debugging tool to the development server. Run the remote debugging tool from the server. Use Visual Studio to open the code, attach to the running server process, and step into code based on a request.
- **Practice 2** Find (or write) some code that contains client-side JavaScript. You can also get such code from this book's CD (in the samples for Chapter 6). Open the code in Visual Studio. Run the Web page in a browser. Configure Internet Explorer to allow script debugging. Use Visual Studio to connect to the browser's process and step into the client-side code.

Troubleshooting a Web Site

For this task, you should complete the first item for practice with tracing. The second practice should help with health monitoring.

- **Practice 1** Turn on tracing for one of your existing Web applications. Be sure to do so only in a test environment. Review the trace data about your pages. Look carefully and determine if there are unexpected results.
- **Practice 2** Turn on health monitoring for one of your existing Web applications. Again, be sure to do so only in a test environment. Review the data logged over a few days and assess the results.

Take a Practice Test

The practice tests on this book's companion CD offer many options. For example, you can test yourself on just the content covered in this chapter, or you can test yourself on all the 70-562 certification exam content. You can set up the test so it closely simulates the experience of taking a certification exam, or you can set it up in study mode so you can look at the correct answers and explanations after you answer each question.

MORE INFO **PRACTICE TESTS**

For details about all the practice test options available, see the "How to Use the Practice Tests" section in this book's Introduction.

CHAPTER 13

Globalization and Accessibility

Given the ubiquitous nature of the Web, it is not surprising that many sites are accessed by a wide variety of people who often live in different countries and speak a variety of languages. To effectively reach these people, your site should adapt to their language and culture. In addition, accessing a wide array of users must include support for accessibility. This means supporting the many different display types and input devices that can be used to access your site. Thankfully, ASP.NET provides a number of features to help you with both globalization and accessibility. This chapter covers these important topics from the perspective of an ASP.NET Web developer.

Exam objectives in this chapter:

- Programming Web Applications
  - Implement globalization and accessibility.

Lessons in this chapter:

Before You Begin

To complete the lessons in this chapter, you should be familiar with developing applications with Microsoft Visual Studio using Microsoft Visual Basic or C#. In addition, you should be comfortable with all of the following:

- Working with the Visual Studio 2008 Integrated Development Environment (IDE).
- Using Hypertext Markup Language (HTML) and client-side scripting.
- Creating ASP.NET Web sites and forms.

Mike Snell

Most Web applications I have written, seen, or been a part of were written for a single-language, single-culture audience. In nearly all cases, globalization was either an afterthought or never even a consideration. I have seen many of these same applications exist just fine for years, until they need to support another language. Companies are bought; others merge; new markets are explored. If you have had a similar experience, you know that converting a single-language application to one that supports globalization requires no small amount of tedious work.

It's also true that implementing globalization at the start is much easier than it is after the application has been around for a while. Given this fact, and the ease with which ASP.NET applications can support globalization, I suggest that nearly all enterprise solutions consider globalization from the start. Even if you have no current plans to translate an application, this step will pay off in the future. If you are writing an enterprise, mission-critical application, globalization should be assumed; if you are writing commercial software, it is an absolute imperative.

Lesson 1: Configuring Globalization and Localization

Many Web application developers are asked to support users in different cultures who speak different languages. These developers might be writing intranet applications for a multinational company, public Web sites for global audiences, or other Web applications that need to reach a wide audience. For these reasons, ASP.NET provides the infrastructure to create Web applications that automatically adjust formatting and languages according to the user's preferred language and culture.

This lesson describes how you use these features to create Web applications suitable for a broad audience.

> **After this lesson, you will be able to:**
>
> - Support multiple languages in your Web site with resource files.
> - Create a Web page layout that is flexible to accommodate different languages.
> - Programmatically set the language and culture of a Web page.
>
> **Estimated lesson time: 30 minutes**

About ASP.NET Resources

To display an ASP.NET page in one of several different languages, you could prompt the user for his or her preferred language, and then write *if-then* statements to update the text of your page. However, that would be a complex, time-consuming chore that would require the person translating the Web site to know how to write code. Clearly this is not an effective solution. Instead, you need to externalize the items requiring translation and look these items up at run time. This allows a nontechnical translator to work independent of the code. It also saves you from compiling your application when adding another language.

ASP.NET uses resource files to support multiple languages. A resource file contains a language-specific set of text for a page or the entire site. Your code accesses a resource file based on the user's requested language. If a resource file exists for that language, ASP.NET uses it and thus shows your site in the requested language. If no resource file exists for the given request, ASP.NET uses the default language setting for the site.

There are two types of resources in ASP.NET: local and global. The sections that follow elaborate on each of these types of resources.

Using Local Resource Files

Local resources are specific to a single Web page and should be used for providing versions of a Web page in different languages. Local resources must be stored in the special folder App_LocalResources. This is either a subfolder of your site or a subfolder inside any folder containing Web pages. If your site contains many folders, you might have an App_Local-Resources subfolder in each folder of your site.

Each local resource file is page-specific. Therefore, it is named using the page name as in <*PageName*>.aspx.resx. For example, to create a resource file for the Default.aspx page, you would create a file called Default.aspx.resx. This becomes the default base resource file for the page. ASP.NET uses this file if it cannot find a match for the user's requested language-culture setting.

You create language-specific versions by copying the resource file and renaming it to include the given language information as in <*PageName*>.aspx.<*languageId*>.resx. For example, a Spanish version of a page would be named Default.aspx.es.resx ("es" is the abbreviation for Spanish). A German file would be named Default.aspx.de.resx ("de" represents German).

Culture-Specific Local Resources

In ASP.NET development, the term *culture* refers to regional language and formatting differences. For example, English spoken in the United States is slightly different than the English spoken in England, Australia, or other parts of the world. Each country might also have different standards for currency, date, and number formatting. For example, in the United States, numbers are written as 12,345.67. In parts of Europe, the comma and period are used differently, and the same number is written as 12.345,67.

When a request specifies a culture, the .NET Framework will adjust formatting as needed. That is, if you are formatting data as a date and the request defines both language and culture, the .NET Framework will know to format the data according to the request. You do not have to do anything additional in your code or resource files.

If, however, you need to translate differently based on culture, you should add a culture designation to your resource file. This is useful if there are different dialects you need to support, such as the difference between English in the United States and Great Britain or Spanish in Mexico and Spain.

You add a culture designation to your resource by naming the file as follows: <*PageName*>.aspx.<*languageId*>-<*cultureId*>.resx. As an example, a Spanish (es) resource file designated for Mexico (mx) would be named as follows: Default.aspx.es-mx.resx. If you have defined resource files for both es and es-mx, ASP.NET uses the es-mx file for users requesting from Mexico; all other Spanish-speaking cultures receive the Default.aspx.es.resx file.

Generating Local Resources

You can use Visual Studio to automatically generate the default version of your local resource file. Doing so extracts the key page and control elements into a resource file, which can save you time and effort. To automatically generate a resource file using Visual Studio, follow these steps:

1. Open your page in Visual Studio. Be sure you are in Design mode.
2. From the Tools menu, select Generate Local Resource.

   This causes Visual Studio to perform the following tasks:

   - Create the App_LocalResources folder (if necessary).
   - Generate an Extensible Markup Language (XML)-based local resource file for the Web page in the App_LocalResources folder. This file will contain resource settings for page and control properties like *Text*, *ToolTip*, *Title*, *Caption*, and other string-based properties.

As an example, consider the example form shown in Figure 13-1. This page contains *Label*, *TextBox*, *Calendar*, and *Button* controls.

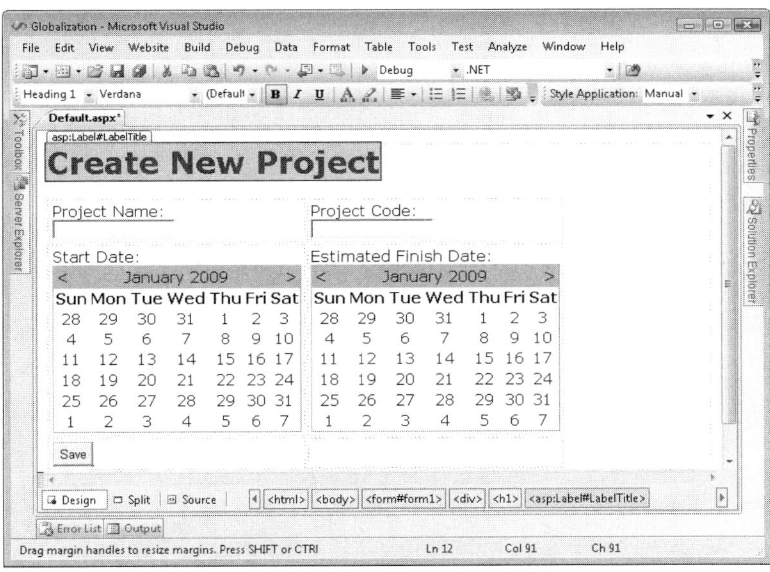

FIGURE 13-1 A sample .aspx page to demonstrate generation of resource files

Generating a resource file for the page shown in Figure 13-1 will externalize the key string properties of these controls into a .resx file. This file can be opened and edited using Visual Studio's resource file editor. Figure 13-2 shows the generated file open inside Visual Studio. Notice many of the string values were set already based on the values that were defined in the markup.

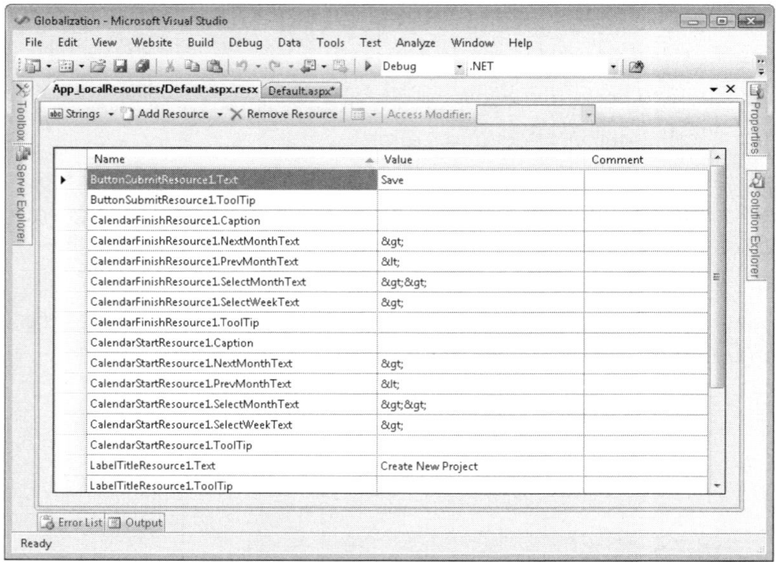

FIGURE 13-2 The generated resource file opened in the Visual Studio resource editor

You can also open the .resx file in an XML editor. Here you will notice that the file consists mostly of name–value pairs. Each pair is an XML *<data>* element with a name that matches the named element on the page. The following shows an example of the elements defined for the *Button* control inside the XML:

```
<data name="ButtonSubmitResource1.Text" xml:space="preserve">
  <value>Save</value>
</data>
<data name="ButtonSubmitResource1.ToolTip" xml:space="preserve">
  <value />
</data>
```

When the resource file was generated, it did not generate resources for all the text on the page. Rather, it only generated a resource for those items that are controls. In the example, the text above the controls (Project Name, Project Code, and so on) was not created using *Label* controls. Therefore, no resources were defined for these items. This is something you need to consider when creating your pages. If the text on your page requires resource-based localization, it is best to encapsulate that text inside a control.

Attaching Controls to a Resource

When Visual Studio generates a resource file, it also automatically changes your markup to attach page elements to the given resource. To do so, it adds the markup *meta:resourcekey* as an attribute of a given control. This tells ASP.NET to look up the value for this item from the resource file using the specified resource key (name of the data element in the .resx XML).

The following markup shows an example of the *Label* used to show the page title to the user. Notice this markup still has a value defined for the *Text* property. This is to aid you at design time when laying out the page. Notice this markup also contains the *meta:resourcekey* set to *LabelTitleResource1*.

```
<asp:Label id="LabelTitle" runat="server" Text="Create New Project"
  meta:resourcekey="LabelTitleResource1"></asp:Label>
```

The *meta:resourcekey* is then mapped to the .resx file. ASP.NET then uses this key to find any properties that might be set inside the resource file as *meta:resourcekey.<propertyName>*. The following markup shows the *<data>* element for the *LabelTitleResource1.Text* property:

```
<data name="LabelTitleResource1.Text" xml:space="preserve">
  <value>Create New Project</value>
</data>
```

You use this same method and naming convention when manually defining resources and attaching them to your markup. This is important as you often will add or change controls on a Web page after generating the resource file. In this case, Visual Studio does not automatically modify the resource file. Therefore, you typically generate resource files as one of the last steps of the development process. This becomes even more important as you build up different resource files for different languages and cultures. A change to your page in this case results in a change to each of the many resource files associated with the page.

Creating Language-Specific Local Resources

You typically create culture- and language-specific resource files by first creating a default resource file. You can use this default file as a base. You copy and paste it to create a new resource file for the target language or culture and name the file accordingly. You then need to modify the resource values for the new language or culture. To copy the default resource file, follow these steps:

1. In Solution Explorer, right-click your default resource file and select Copy.
2. Right-click the App_LocalResources folder, and then select Paste.
3. Right-click the new resource file, and then select Rename. Type a new name for the resource file that includes the language and culture code before the file extension. For example, you might name the file **Default.aspx.fr.resx** to create a French-language version of the Default.aspx page (the abbreviation for French is "fr").
4. Double-click the new resource file to open it in Visual Studio. Visual Studio displays a table containing values and comments for each resource. Update the values for the new culture, and then save the resource file.

You repeat these steps to create resource files for every language and culture that you want to support. Although Visual Studio provides a convenient interface for developers, translators can use any standard XML editor to update the resource files.

Testing Resource Files for Other Cultures

ASP.NET automatically determines the user's preferred culture based on information provided by the Web browser. The browser's language preferences are set during installation. However, they can be modified by users. You can also modify them to help test your site. To test other cultures, you need to update the preferred language in your Web browser by following these steps:

1. Open Microsoft Internet Explorer. From the Tools menu, select Internet Options to launch the Internet Options dialog box.
2. On the General tab, click Languages in the Appearance group. This opens the Language Preference dialog box.
3. In the Language Preference dialog box, click Add.
4. In the Add Language dialog box, under Language, select the language you want to test, and then click OK.
5. Figure 13-3 shows the English (Belize) (en-BZ) setting added to the Language Preferences. From here, you select the language you want to test, then click Move Up to move the language you wish to test to the top of the list. Finally, click OK twice to close the open dialog boxes.

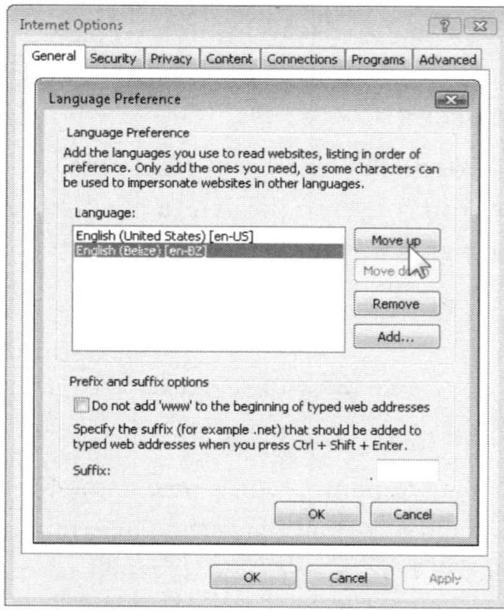

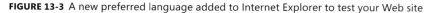

FIGURE 13-3 A new preferred language added to Internet Explorer to test your Web site

You can now visit the Web page and view the selected culture's resource file. When you are done testing, remember to reset your browser to your actual preferred language and culture.

Using Global Resources

A *global resource* is one that is defined to be read from any page or code that is in the Web site. These are not page-specific resources like a local resource. Rather, global resources are designed for when you need to access a single resource from multiple Web pages in your site. In this way you can define the resource once and share its value across pages.

Global resources are still .resx files. You still create a default version and one for each language and culture you intend to support. The file naming scheme remains the same as for local resource files. However, global resource files are stored in the App_GlobalResources folder at the root of an application. In addition, to use a global resource, you must do so explicitly.

The use of the *meta:resourcekey* markup on controls for local resources is referred to as implicit localization. ASP.NET picks up the localization implicitly based on this markup. It maps the key to the data element and given control's property (attribute). However, for global resources, you must use *explicit localization*. For this, you associate individual control properties (attributes) directly to a resource in the global resource file. There is no implicit lookup of the control's text-based properties. Instead, the control's property is mapped directly, one-to-one, with a resource in the global .resx file.

Creating a Global Resource File

To use explicit localization, you start by creating a default global resource file. This file should externalize all the resources you intend to share across pages. You can then map individual control properties across pages to the resource of choice. Finally, you can create separate versions of the global resource file for each language and culture you intend to support. ASP.NET will automatically pick up the right version of the global resource file based on the user's defined language and culture setting (just like local resources).

To create a global resource file, follow these steps:

1. In Solution Explorer, right-click the root of your Web site. Select Add ASP.NET Folder, and then select the App_GlobalResources suboption. This will add a folder of the same name to the root of your site.
2. Next, right-click the App_GlobalResources folder and select Add New Item.
3. In the Add New Item dialog box, select Resource File. In the Name text box, type any file name with a .resx extension. For example, you could name your global resource file LocalizedText.resx. Click Add to add the resource file to your site.
4. Open the new resource file in Visual Studio. Visual Studio displays a table-like format for adding and editing resources. From here you can add strings, images, icons, audio, files, and other resources. Remember, this is your default resource file. Therefore, you add items here that are meant to be the default language and culture (when no language-specific resource file version is found).

5. Once you have defined your default resource file, you copy and paste it to create resource files for different languages. You name these files the same way you would local resource files. For example, you might name a French global resource file LocalizedText.fr.resx. You then open each language-specific version and edit it to provide the resource translation.

Attaching Control Properties to Global Resources

Once you have defined a global resource file, you can associate control properties (such as *Label.Text*) from different pages to the global resource. In this way, you can share the given resource file across pages. ASP.NET will automatically display the correct text from your resource file based on the user's defined culture. Therefore, if you have a *Label* that displays a greeting message on every page, you only need to define the message once for each culture (rather than defining it in separate resource files for each Web page).

In Design mode, you can associate a control's property value with a global resource through the *(Expressions)* property. To do so, follow these steps:

1. Open your page in Design view in Visual Studio. View the given control's Property tab. Select the *(Expressions)* property (in the Data category). Click the ellipsis (…) button next to the property to launch the control's Expressions dialog box.
2. From the Bindable Properties list, select a property that you want to bind to a resource.
3. From the Expression type list, select Resources.
4. In the Expression Properties list, set *ClassKey* to the name of your global resource file (without the extension). Under that, set *ResourceKey* to the name of the resource within the resource file. Figure 13-4 shows an example.

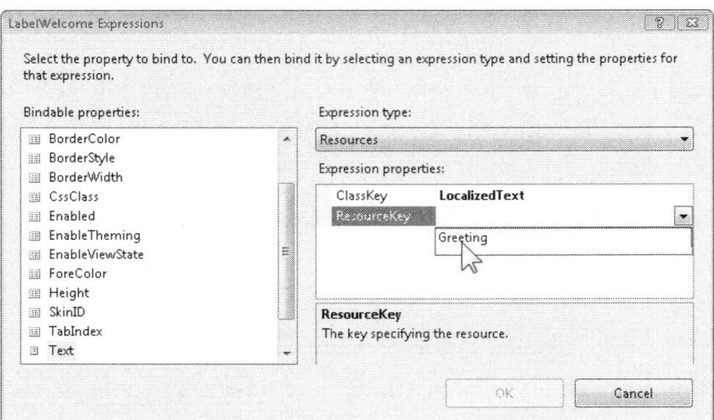

FIGURE 13-4 Use expressions to bind controls to global resources

5. Click OK to close the dialog box.

NOTE IMPLICITLY BOUND PROPERTIES

Implicitly bound control properties are shown in the property window with a red note icon. To explicitly bind them, you must first remove the *meta:resourcekey* from the control's markup.

Once set, Visual Studio displays the default resource value for the given control in Design view. Of course, this will be changed to display the language-specific resource when a user visits the Web page.

Within the page markup, Visual Studio updates the control's *Text* property to call the resource. For example, if binding a *Label* control's *Text* property to a message named *Greeting* in the LocalizedText.resx global resource, the markup looks as follows:

```
<asp:Label id="LabelWelcome" runat="server"
  Text="<%$ Resources:LocalizedText, Greeting %>"></asp:Label>
```

EXAM TIP

You should be sure to know the *<%$ Resources:ResourceFile, Name %>* format for the exam.

Accessing Resource Values Programmatically

You can also access resource values programmatically using the syntax *Resources.ResourceFile.Resource*. After saving global resources, Visual Studio creates a strongly typed class of the *Resources.Resource* object for each resource file. You access the class through the file name of the global resource file. Each resource in the file is a member of the class. For example, if you add a value named *Greeting* to the resource file, *LocalizedText*, you can assign the value to a *Label* control's *Text* property inside your page's code-behind using the following syntax:

```
'VB
Label1.Text = Resources.LocalizedText.Greeting

//C#
Label1.Text = Resources.LocalizedText.Greeting;
```

NOTE THE *LOCALIZE* CONTROL

To localize static text that is not part of a control, you can either convert it to a control or use the *Localize* control. It functions much like the *Literal* control.

The preceding syntax assumes your resources are available at design time. If they are, Visual Studio can generate the matching class files. If, however, your resource files are not available at design time, Visual Studio cannot generate these classes. In this case, you must use the *GetLocalResourceObject* and *GetGlobalResourceObject* methods.

To use the *GetLocalResourceObject* method, simply provide the name of the resource. To use *GetGlobalResourceObject*, provide both the file name (without the extension) and the resource name. For example, the following code uses these methods to get resources for two different controls:

```
'VB
Button1.Text = GetLocalResourceObject("Button1.Text").ToString()
Image1.ImageUrl = CType(GetGlobalResourceObject("WebResourcesGlobal", "LogoUrl"),
String)

//C#
Button1.Text = GetLocalResourceObject("Button1.Text").ToString();
Image1.ImageUrl = (String)GetGlobalResourceObject("WebResourcesGlobal", "LogoUrl");
```

Quick Check

1. In which folder should you store global resource files?
2. In which folder should you store local resource files?

Quick Check Answers

1. Global resources should be stored in the App_GlobalResources folder.
2. Store local resources in the App_LocalResources folder.

HTML Layout Best Practices

Globalization can be as simple as replacing text with text from another language and reformatting numbers and symbols. However, some languages, such as Arabic languages, require different layouts because text flows from right to left. To allow Web pages to be used by the widest variety of cultures, follow these guidelines:

- **Avoid using absolute positioning and sizes for controls** Rather than specifying control locations in pixels, allow the Web browser to position them automatically. You can do this by simply not specifying a size or location. The easiest way to determine if any controls have absolute positions is to view the source for a Web page. For example, the following illustrates a control that uses absolute positioning (which should be avoided):

  ```
  <div id = idLabel style = "position: absolute; left: 0.98em; top: 1.21em;
    width: 4.8em; height: 1.21em;">
  ```

- **Use the entire width and height of forms** Although many Web sites specify a number of pixels for the width of a form or table column, this can cause formatting problems for languages that use more letters or a different text layout. Instead of indicating a specific width, use 100 percent of the width of the Web browser, as the following sample demonstrates:

```
<table width=100%>
```

- **Size elements relative to the overall size of the form** When you do need to provide a specific size for a control, use relative proportions to allow the entire form to be easily resized. You can achieve this using style sheet expressions, as the following sample demonstrates:

```
<div style='
  height: expression(document.body.clientHeight / 2);
  width: expression(document.body.clientWidth / 2); '>
```

- **Use a separate table cell for each control** This allows text to wrap independently and ensures correct alignment for cultures in which text layout flows from right to left.
- **Avoid enabling the *NoWrap* property in tables** Setting *HtmlTableCell.NoWrap* to *true* disables word wrapping. Although word wrapping might work well in your native language, other languages can require more space and might not display correctly.
- **Avoid specifying the *Align* property in tables** Setting a left or right alignment in a cell can override layout in cultures that use right-to-left text. Therefore, avoid them.

In summary, the less explicitly you configure layout, the better your page can be localized, because you leave layout decisions to the client's browser.

Setting the Culture

Often, Web browsers are configured with the user's language preferences. However, many times a user's Web browser is not configured correctly. For example, an American tourist in Mexico might use a Web browser at an Internet café that has been configured for Spanish. Of course, it is likely the American would prefer to read your site in English. For this reason, you should use the browser's setting as the default but allow users to override that default setting in your application. This is often done by providing a setting value of the home page that includes text in multiple languages describing how to change the language setting. When a user changes the setting, you execute code to use this new setting (stored in a cookie, session variable, or similar element).

In an ASP.NET Web page, you use two different *Page* properties to set language and culture:

- ***Culture*** This object determines the results of culture-dependent functions, such as the date, number, and currency formatting. You can only define the *Culture* object with *specific cultures* that define both language and regional formatting requirements, such as "es-MX" or "fr-FR." You cannot define the *Culture* object with *neutral cultures* that define only a language, such as "es" or "fr."

- ***UICulture*** This property determines which global or local resources are loaded for the page. You can define *UICulture* with either neutral or specific cultures.

You define the *Culture* and *UICulture* properties by overriding the page's *InitializeCulture* method. From this method, define the *Culture* and *UICulture* properties, and then call the page's base *InitializeCulture* method. The following code sample demonstrates this, assuming that *DropDownList1* contains a list of cultures:

```
'VB
Protected Overloads Overrides Sub InitializeCulture()
  If Not (Request.Form("DropDownList1") Is Nothing) Then
    'define the language
    UICulture = Request.Form("DropDownList1")
    'define the formatting (requires a specific culture)
    Culture = Request.Form("DropDownList1")
  End If
  MyBase.InitializeCulture()
End Sub

//C#
protected override void InitializeCulture()
{
  if (Request.Form["DropDownList1"] != null)
  {
    //define the language
    UICulture = Request.Form["DropDownList1"];

    //define the formatting (requires a specific culture)
    Culture = Request.Form["DropDownList1"];
  }
  base.InitializeCulture();
}
```

Normally, you should provide users with a list of cultures and languages for which you have configured resources. For example, if you have configured resources for English, Spanish, and French, you should only allow users to choose from one of those three options. However, you can also retrieve an array of all available cultures by calling the *System.Globalization.CultureInfo.GetCultures* method. Pass this method a *CultureTypes* enumeration that specifies which subset of available cultures you want to list. The most useful *CultureTypes* values are the following:

- ***AllCultures*** This represents all cultures included with the .NET Framework, including both neutral and specific cultures. If you use *AllCultures* in your code, be sure to verify that a selected culture is a specific culture before assigning it to the *Culture* object.
- ***NeutralCultures*** Neutral cultures provide only a language and not regional formatting definitions.

- ***SpecificCultures*** Specific cultures provide both language and regional formatting definitions.

You can also declaratively set the culture for a Web site or Web page. To define the culture for an entire Web site, add a *<globalization>* section to the Web.config file, and then set the *UICulture* and *Culture* attributes, as the following sample demonstrates:

```
<globalization uiculture="es" culture="es-MX" />
```

To declare a culture for a Web page, define the *UICulture* and *Culture* attributes of the @ *Page* directive, as shown here:

```
<%@ Page uiculture="es" culture="es-MX" %>
```

By default, Visual Studio defines the *UICulture* and *Culture* page attributes as *auto*.

LAB Creating a Web Page That Supports Multiple Cultures

In this lab, you create a site that uses resource files for different languages.

If you encounter a problem completing an exercise, the completed projects are available in the sample files installed from the companion CD in the Code folder.

EXERCISE Create a Web Page for Both English and Spanish

In this exercise, you create a Web page that displays language-specific text based on the user's browser preference, while allowing users to overwrite the default setting.

1. Open Visual Studio. Create a new file-based Web site called **GlobalSite**.
2. Open the Default.aspx form. Add a *Label* and a *DropDownList* control to the page. Name the controls **LabelWelcome** and **DropDownListLanguage**, respectively.

   You will use the *Label* control to display a culture-specific greeting to the user. The *DropDownList* control allows a user to choose a specific language.

   Set the *DropDownList.AutoPostBack* property to *True*.

   Your markup should look similar to the following:

   ```
   <h1>
     <asp:Label ID="LabelWelcome" runat="server"
       Text="Welcome"></asp:Label>
   </h1>
   <br />
   <asp:DropDownList ID="DropDownListLanguage" runat="server"
     AutoPostBack="true">
   </asp:DropDownList>
   ```

3. Make sure you are in Design view for Default.aspx. From the Tools menu, select Generate Local Resource. This will create the App_LocalResources folder and the Default.aspx.resx file.

4. In Solution Explorer, double-click Default.aspx.resx.

   For the *LabelWelcomeResource1.Text* value, type **Hello**.

   For the *PageResource1.Title* value, type **English**.

   Close and save the Default.aspx.resx file.

5. In Solution Explorer, right-click Default.aspx.resx, and then click Copy. Right-click App_LocalResources and click Paste. Next, rename the new resource file **Default .aspx.es.resx**.

6. Double-click Default.aspx.es.resx. For the *LabelWelcomeResource1.Text* value, type **Hola**. For the *PageResource1.Title* value, type **Español**. Then close and save the Default. aspx.es.resx file.

7. Run your page in a Web browser. Notice that the *Label* control displays Hello even though you never directly set the *LabelWelcome.Text* property to this value. Also notice that the page title (shown in the Internet Explorer title bar) displays English.

8. In Internet Explorer, follow these steps:

   a. From the Tools menu, select Internet Options.

   b. In the Internet Options dialog box, click Languages.

   c. In the Language Preference dialog box, click Add.

   d. In the Add Language dialog box, under Language, select Spanish (Mexico) [es-mx]. Click OK.

   e. In the Language list, select Spanish, and then click Move Up to make it your preferred language.

   f. Click OK twice to return to Internet Explorer.

   Reload the Web page and verify that the page displays the Spanish resources you provided.

9. Return to Visual Studio and open the code-behind file for Default.aspx. Add the *System.Globalization* namespace to the page (with an *Imports* or *using* statement) to allow you to use the *CultureInfo* object.

10. Add a *Page_Load* event handler to the code. Write code to populate the *DropDownListLanguage* control with a list of cultures. The following code sample illustrates this:

```
'VB
For Each ci As CultureInfo In CultureInfo.GetCultures(CultureTypes.
NeutralCultures)
  DropDownListLanguage.Items.Add(New ListItem(ci.NativeName, ci.Name))
Next

//C#
foreach (CultureInfo ci in CultureInfo.GetCultures(CultureTypes.
NeutralCultures))
```

```
{
  DropDownListLanguage.Items.Add(new ListItem(ci.NativeName, ci.Name));
}
```

> ***NOTE*** **NEUTRAL VS. SPECIFIC CULTURES**
>
> **This code sample uses *CultureTypes.Neutral Cultures* to get a list of cultures that provide both language and culture information (for example "en-us" instead of just "en"). You can use *CultureTypes.SpecificCultures* instead if you want the user to pick both language and country. You can use neutral cultures to define the *UICulture* object, but you can only use specific cultures to define the *Culture* object.**

11. Now create a method that overrides the *InitializeCulture* method for the page. This method should include code that sets the page's culture based on the item selected from the *DropDownList* control. Because you are defining only language, use the *UICulture* object, rather than the *Culture* object. Call the base *InitializeCulture* event after you have defined *UICulture*. The following code sample demonstrates this:

```
'VB
Protected Overloads Overrides Sub InitializeCulture()
  If Not (Request.Form("DropDownListLanguage") Is Nothing) Then
    UICulture = Request.Form("DropDownListLanguage")
  End If
  MyBase.InitializeCulture()
End Sub

//C#
protected override void InitializeCulture()
{
  if (Request.Form["DropDownListLanguage"] != null)
  {
    UICulture = Request.Form["DropDownListLanguage"];
  }
  base.InitializeCulture();
}
```

12. Run the page in a Web browser. From the drop-down list, select English as shown in Figure 13-5.

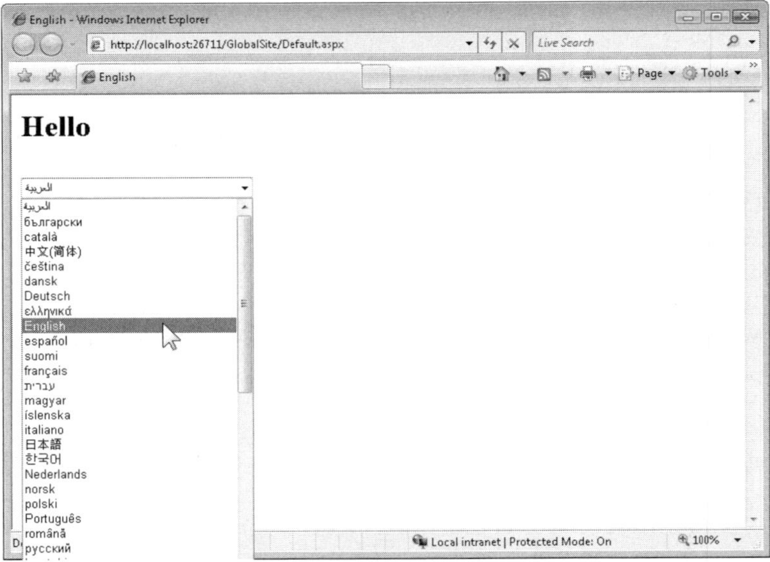

FIGURE 13-5 Use expressions to bind controls to global resources

The page should reload and display the English greeting. Select Espanol and notice that the page changes back to Spanish.

The drop-down list and your implementation of *InitializeCulture* allow ASP.NET to automatically select the browser's preferred language, yet still giving users the option of overriding the default choice.

13. Repeat Step 8 to reconfigure Internet Explorer to your normal language settings.

Lesson Summary

- Local resource files allow you to provide translations for controls on a single Web page. Local resource files are named using the format <*PageName*>.[*language*].resx.
- Global resources provide translations for phrases that can be assigned to any control in the Web application and should be placed in the App_GlobalResources folder at the root of the application.
- To make your page as easy to globalize as possible, follow these best practices:
  - Avoid using absolute positioning and sizes for controls.
  - Use the entire width and height of forms.
  - Size elements relative to the overall size of the form.
  - Use a separate table cell for each control.
  - Avoid enabling the *NoWrap* property in tables.
  - Avoid specifying the *Align* property in tables.

- To programmatically set the language, set the *UICulture* object to the neutral or specific culture abbreviation. To programmatically set the regional formatting preferences, set the *Culture* object to the specific culture abbreviation.

Lesson Review

You can use the following questions to test your knowledge of the information in Lesson 1, "Configuring Globalization and Localization." The questions are also available on the companion CD if you prefer to review them in electronic form.

> ***NOTE*** **ANSWERS**
>
> **Answers to these questions and explanations of why each answer choice is right or wrong are located in the "Answers" section at the end of the book.**

1. You need to create a Web page that is available in both the default language of English and in German. Which of the following resource files should you create? (Choose all that apply.)

   A. App_LocalResources/Page.aspx.resx.de

   B. App_LocalResources/Page.aspx.resx

   C. App_LocalResources/Page.aspx.de.resx

   D. App_LocalResources/Page.aspx.en.resx

2. What must you do to enable users to select their own language preferences? (Choose all that apply.)

   A. Define the *Page.Culture* property.

   B. Define the *Page.UICulture* property.

   C. Override the *Page.InitializeCulture* method.

   D. Override the *Page.ReadStringResource* method.

3. How can you define a control property using a global resource at design time?

   A. In Visual Studio, define the *DataValueField* property.

   B. In Visual Studio, define the *DataSourceID* property.

   C. In Visual Studio, edit the *Text* property.

   D. In Visual Studio, edit the *(Expressions)* property.

4. You add a global resource with the name *Login* by using Visual Studio. How can you access that global resource programmatically?

   A. *Resources.Resource.Login*

   B. *Resources.Resource("Login")*

   C. *Resources("Login")*

   D. *Resources.Login*

Lesson 2: Configuring Accessibility

Whether you are creating a public Web site for millions to use, or a small intranet Web application, you should recognize the need to make it usable for those that need large text and nontraditional input devices. For example, many users do not use a conventional mouse. Others use screen readers to read the text on Web sites rather than displaying it on a monitor. This lesson provides best practices for making your Web application more accessible to these users and their devices.

After this lesson, you will be able to:

- Describe public accessibility standards.
- Explain how ASP.NET controls provide accessibility by default.
- Create Web pages that support visual accessibility tools.
- Create Web pages that support accessibility tools for user input.
- Test the accessibility of individual Web pages or entire Web applications.

Estimated lesson time: 30 minutes

Public Accessibility Guidelines

Many people are working to make technology accessible to the widest audience possible. One of the most prominent groups is the World Wide Web Consortium (W3C), a Web standards organization. Through the Web Accessibility Initiative (WAI), the W3C has created the Web Content Accessibility Guidelines (WCAG).

MORE INFO **WCAG**

The WCAG is very thorough; this book only attempts to cover the key points as they relate to ASP.NET development. For more information about WCAG, visit *http://www.w3.org/WAI/*.

The U.S. government has also created accessibility standards in Section 508 of the Rehabilitation Act. Depending on the organization for which you are developing a Web application, you might be required to conform your application to these standards. The Section 508 guidelines are conceptually similar to the WCAG guidelines.

MORE INFO **SECTION 508 GUIDELINES**

For more information about Section 508 guidelines, visit *http://www.section508./gov/*.

How ASP.NET Controls Support Accessibility

ASP.NET controls are designed to be accessible by default. For example, login controls such as *Login*, *ChangePassword*, *PasswordRecovery*, and *CreateUserWizard* use text boxes with associated labels to help a user who uses a screen reader or who does not use a mouse. These controls also use input controls with tab index settings to make data entry without a mouse easier.

Another way some ASP.NET controls support accessibility is by allowing users to skip link text. *Screen readers* typically read the text of links from the top to the bottom of a page, enabling users to choose a specific link. ASP.NET controls that include navigation links provide the *SkipLinkText* property, which is enabled by default and allows users to skip past the link text. The *CreateUserWizard*, *Menu*, *SiteMapPath*, *TreeView*, and *Wizard* controls each support skipping links. These links are not visible to users viewing the page with a traditional Web browser. For example, the following HTML source code (which has been slightly simplified) is generated by default when you add a *Menu* control to a Web page:

```
<a href="#Menu1_SkipLink">
  <img alt="Skip Navigation Links" src="/WebResource.axd?d=_9Q2Lm" width="0" height="0"
/>
</a>
… menu links …
<a id="Menu1_SkipLink"></a>
```

As the HTML demonstrates, a zero-pixel image file with the alt text "Skip Navigation Links" links to a location on the page immediately after the menu. Whereas traditional browsers do not display the zero-pixel image, screen readers read the alt text and allow users to skip past the menu. The simplest way to follow this best practice is to use one of the ASP.NET controls that provides the *SkipLinkText* property. However, if you implement custom controls with navigation links, you can provide similar functionality.

Although ASP.NET controls are designed to be as accessible as possible, you, as the developer, must take advantage of these features by providing text descriptions for certain controls. The next sections provide more detailed information.

Improving Visual Accessibility

Many users have tools to supplement or replace a traditional monitor, including screen readers, magnifiers, and high-contrast display settings. To make your application as accessible as possible using these tools, follow these guidelines:

- **Describe every image by providing alt text using the *AlternateText* property** This is useful for users who have images disabled in browsers or otherwise cannot see the pictures. Screen readers, which use speech synthesis to verbally read text on a Web page, can read alt text descriptions. You can also set the *Image.DescriptionUrl* property to specify an HTML page that further describes an image, but you should only configure it if you want to provide a longer description than is possible with *AlternateText*. If an image is not important (such as an image that forms a border), set the *GenerateEmpty-AlternateText* property to *True* to cause screen readers to ignore it.

- **Use solid colors for background and use contrasting colors for text** All users appreciate easy-to-read text, especially users who might not be able to perceive low-contrast text. Therefore, you should avoid text that is a similar shade to the background color.
- **Create a flexible page layout that scales correctly when text size is increased** Internet Explorer and other browsers support the ability to increase text size, which makes text easier to read. This is useful for both users who have specialized accessibility settings and those with high-resolution displays.
- **Set the *Table.Caption* property to a description of the table** Screen readers can read the *Table.Caption* property to describe the purpose of the data contained in a table to users. This allows the user to quickly determine whether he or she wants to hear the contents of the table or skip past it.
- **Provide a way to identify column headers** You can create table headers by using the *TableHeaderRow* class and setting the *TableSection* property to the *TableHeader* enumeration of the *TableRowSection* class. This causes the table to render a *thead* element. When you create cells with the *TableCell* control, you can set each *Associated-HeaderCellID* property for the cell to the ID of a table header cell. This causes the cell to render a header attribute that associates the cell with the corresponding column heading, simplifying table navigation for users with screen readers. The *Calendar*, *DetailsView*, *FormView*, and *GridView* ASP.NET server controls render HTML tables with these features.
- **Avoid defining specific font sizes** Use heading tags (such as <H1> or <H3>) instead of font sizes to support the user's formatting options. Heading tags are available on the Visual Studio Formatting toolbar.
- **Avoid requiring client scripts** Assistive technologies often cannot render client scripts, so you should use client script only for nonessential effects, such as mouse rollovers. For example, validator controls use client scripts to determine whether input meets specified requirements, and then to dynamically display error messages. However, screen readers and other assistive technologies might not render this correctly. Therefore, you should set the *EnableClientScript* property to *false* to improve accessibility. WCAG standards do not allow controls that require client scripts, so if you must comply with these standards, you should also avoid using the *LinkButton*, *ImageButton*, and *Calendar* controls.

NOTE **WCAG STANDARDS AND CLIENT SCRIPTS**

In practice, your users might not have problems with the client scripts included with ASP.NET server controls. These client scripts have been developed to comply with WCAG accessibility guidelines. However, total WCAG compliance does require you to avoid insisting on client script support.

If you cannot meet accessibility goals, consider providing alternative text-only Web pages. You can use global resources to allow both accessible and nonaccessible versions of a Web page to share the same text content.

Quick Check

1. What can you do to make a Web page more useful to users who use special displays or screen readers to make text more readable?
2. What can you do to make a Web page more useful to a user who does not use a mouse?

Quick Check Answers

1. First, avoid specifying font sizes or using colors that might be difficult to read. Second, provide descriptions for images, tables, and forms that screen readers can use.
2. Provide access keys for all controls that require user input and underline the access keys in associated labels. Define a logical tab order that allows the user to progress through the form using the Tab key. Additionally, specify default buttons for forms and *Panel* controls.

Improving the Accessibility of Forms Requiring User Input

Many users prefer not to use a mouse or have difficulties using pointing devices. For these users, it's critical that you make your Web application usable by keyboard alone. Although providing keyboard shortcuts is common in Windows Forms applications, it's fairly uncommon in Web applications.

To make your application as accessible as possible using a keyboard, follow these guidelines:

- **Set the *DefaultFocus* property for a form to place the cursor in a logical location where data entry normally begins** *DefaultFocus* defines where the cursor starts when a user opens a Web page. Typically, you set the default focus to the topmost editable field on a page.
- **Define the tab order in a logical way so that a user can complete forms without using a mouse** Ideally, a user should be able to complete one text box, and then press the Tab key to jump to the next text box.
- **Specify default buttons for forms and *Panel* controls by setting the *DefaultButton* property** Default buttons can be accessed simply by pressing Enter. Not only does this make user input simpler for a user who doesn't use a mouse, but it can speed data entry.

- **Provide useful link text** Screen readers enable users to choose links by speaking hyperlinked text. Therefore, all hyperlinked text should describe the link. Avoid adding hyperlinks to text such as "Click here," because users with a screen reader will not be able to distinguish it from other links. Instead, provide the name of the link destination with the hyperlink, such as "Directions to Contoso headquarters."
- **Define access keys for button controls by setting the *AccessKey* property** You can use access keys for Web controls just like you would for a Windows Forms application. When you set the *AccessKey* property for a control, the user can hold down the Alt key and press the specified letter to immediately move the cursor to that control. The standard method of indicating a shortcut key is to underline a letter in the control. The next guideline describes how to provide shortcut keys for *TextBox* controls.
- **Use *Label* controls to define access keys for text boxes** *TextBox* controls do not have descriptions that can be easily read by screen readers. Therefore, you should associate a descriptive *Label* control with a *TextBox* control and use the *Label* control to define the *TextBox* control's shortcut key. To associate the *Label* with another control, define both the *AccessKey* and *AssociatedControlID* properties. Also, underline the access key in the *Label's* text using the underline HTML element (*<u>* and *</u>*). The following source demonstrates a *Label* control and an associated *TextBox* control:

```
<asp:Label
  AccessKey="N"
  AssociatedControlID="TextBox1"
  ID="Label1"
  runat="server"
  Text="<u>N</u>ame:">
</asp:Label>
 
<asp:TextBox ID="TextBox1" runat="server" />
```

- **Use the *Panel* control to create subdivisions in a form and define the *Panel .GroupingText* property with a description of the controls in that panel** ASP.NET uses the *GroupingText* property to create *<fieldset>* and *<legend>* HTML elements, which can make forms easier for users to navigate. For example, you might define separate *Panel* controls to collect a user's shipping, billing, and credit card information on a checkout page. The following HTML demonstrates how ASP.NET renders the *Panel.GroupingText* property as a *<legend>* element:

```
<form  method="post" action="Default.aspx" id="form1">
<div id="Panel1" style="height:50px;width:125px;">
  <fieldset>
    <legend>
      Shipping Information
    </legend>
    <input name="TextBox2" type="text" id="TextBox2" />
```

```
    </fieldset>
  </div>
  <div id="Panel2" style="height:50px;width:125px;">
    <fieldset>
      <legend>
        Billing Information
      </legend>
      <input name="TextBox1" type="text" id="TextBox1" />
    </fieldset>
  </div>
  </form>
```

- **Specify meaningful error messages in the *Text* and *ErrorMessage* properties of validator controls** Although the default asterisk (*) is sufficient to identify input controls that need to be completed for some users, it is not useful to users with screen readers. Instead, provide descriptive error messages, such as "You must provide your e-mail address."

REAL WORLD

Tony Northrup

Making a Web site accessible takes only a few extra minutes and usually doesn't have a negative impact on users with traditional Web browsers. Contrary to popular belief, you don't need to use huge font sizes or black-and-white text. People with accessibility requirements typically already have their computers configured to meet their requirements.

The first key to accessibility is to avoid forcing small font sizes and difficult-to-read colors on users in such a way that it overrides their font size and color settings. Often, that's as easy as not specifying special formatting or colors, and just letting the Web browser make display choices based on user settings.

The second key to accessibility is providing multiple techniques for viewing and selecting objects. Provide hidden text descriptions for tables, forms, and images. Provide keyboard shortcuts for buttons and text boxes. A user who doesn't use a mouse will appreciate it, and others won't notice.

Testing Accessibility

Visual Studio can test Web pages or entire Web applications for compliance with WCAG and Section 508 standards. The sections that follow describe how to use Visual Studio to automatically test your work.

Checking the Accessibility of a Single Page

To use Visual Studio to test the accessibility of a Web page, follow these steps:

1. In Visual Studio, open the page you wish to check.
2. From the View menu, select Error List to display the Error List window.
3. From the Tools menu, select Check Accessibility. The Accessibility Validation dialog box appears, as shown in Figure 13-6.

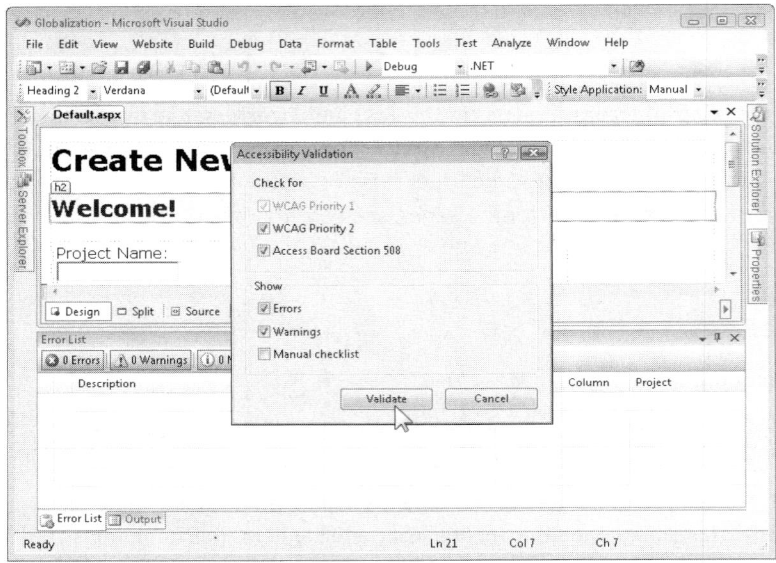

FIGURE 13-6 The Accessibility Validation dialog box in Visual Studio

4. Select the check boxes for the type and level of accessibility checking that you want to perform, and then click Validate. The results of the check are displayed in the Error List window.

Automatically Checking the Accessibility of a Web Application

You can use Visual Studio to automatically test the accessibility of an entire Web application when you build it. To do so, follow these steps:

1. In Solution Explorer, right-click your Web site and select Property Pages.
2. Click the *Accessibility* node. Figure 13-7 shows an example.

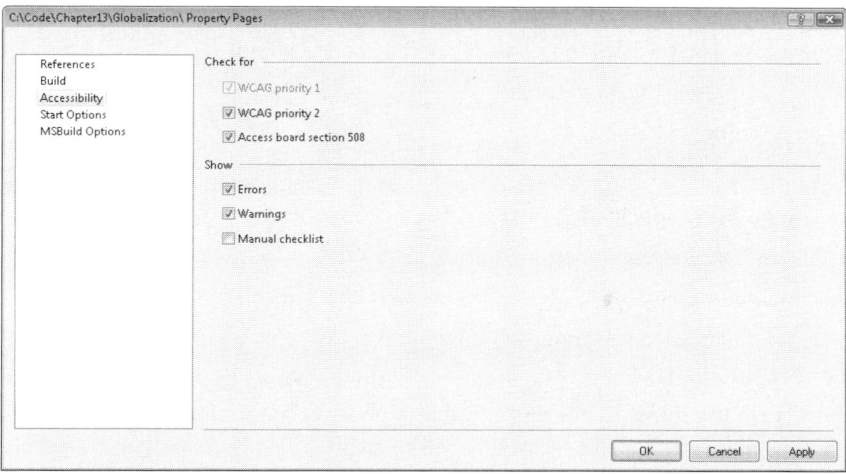

FIGURE 13-7 The *Accessibility* node in the project Property Pages in Visual Studio

3. Select the check boxes for the type and level of accessibility checking that you want to perform, and then click Apply.
4. Next, select the *Build* node of the Property Pages dialog box.
5. In the Accessibility Validation group, select one or both of the following check boxes, depending on whether you want to check individual pages, the entire Web site, or both, when building the Web site:
   - Include Accessibility Validation When Building Page
   - Include Accessibility Validation When Building Web
6. Click OK to close the Property Pages dialog box.

Now, when you build your Web application, Visual Studio automatically generates a list of accessibility warnings. Accessibility warnings won't prevent a successful build. You will have to manually view the Error List to examine any accessibility issues.

LAB Improving the Accessibility of a Web Page

In this lab, you improve the accessibility of an ASP.NET Web application.

If you encounter a problem completing an exercise, the completed projects are available in the samples installed from the companion CD.

EXERCISE 1 Make an Accessible Checkout Page

In this exercise, you update an existing e-commerce checkout page to make it more accessible by following accessibility best practices.

1. Open the Lesson2, Exercise1 - Partial project in the samples installed from the companion CD.

2. Run the application and view the Default.aspx page in a browser. Make note of the nonaccessible aspects of the page, including the following:
   - Lack of panels to divide the form
   - Noncontrasting colors
   - Lack of alt text for images
   - No tab order specified
   - Labels not associated with text boxes
   - No default focus
   - No default button configured
3. To fix these problems, in Visual Studio first add two *Panel* controls to the form, and then move the shipping address and billing address images and tables into their respective panels.

   Then, set the *GroupingText* property for the new *Panel* controls to ***Shipping Address*** and ***Billing Address***. Panel controls help with accessibility by enabling users to easily navigate to different parts of a form, and the *GroupingText* property replaces the Shipping Address and Billing Address images, which screen readers cannot read.
4. Using the image editor of your choice, replace the Contoso-Logo.gif file with a logo that has colors with more contrast. The existing foreground and background colors are too similar and are not easily readable. You can also change the page background color to match the logo.

> ***NOTE*** **COMPLYING WITH LOGO REQUIREMENTS**
>
> **Many organizations have very strict logo requirements that specify the colors that must be used when displaying the logo. However, most organizations also have a high-contrast version of their logo. For more information, contact the public relations group within your organization.**

5. Provide alt text for the logo by setting the *Image1.AlternateText* property to ***Contoso, Inc. logo***.
6. Specify a tab order for the text boxes by setting the *TextBox.TabIndex* property for each text box. Make the top text box ***1*** and number the rest sequentially as you work down the page. Also, set the *TabIndex* properties for the two buttons at the bottom of the page.
7. Replace the text that is currently labeling the text boxes with *Label* controls. For each *Label* control, define a unique *AccessKey* property and underline that letter in the label. Note that the access keys you define should not interfere with those defined by the browser.

Also, define the *AssociatedControlID* property to associate each label with the correct *TextBox* control.

8. Finally, configure a default button and default focus. Switch to Source view (if you are not already there) and click the Form ASP.NET element. Then view the Properties window and set the *DefaultButton* property to ***Button1*** and set the *DefaultFocus* property to ***TextBox1***.
9. Run the application in a Web browser. Use the shortcut keys to navigate between fields. View the alt text for the logo by hovering your cursor over the logo.
10. Return to Visual Studio. From the Tools menu, select Check Accessibility. Examine the errors that are output in the Error list.

Lesson Summary

- Two of the most prominent accessibility standards are the W3C's WCAG standards and the U.S. government's Section 508 standards.
- ASP.NET controls support accessibility whenever possible. For example, controls that provide multiple navigation links give users with screen readers the opportunity to skip the links.
- To make Web pages as visually accessible as possible, follow these guidelines:
    - Provide good alternative (alt) text for all graphics.
    - Write useful link text.
    - Use tables and their alternatives correctly.
    - Avoid requiring client scripts.
- To make Web pages accessible for users with different input tools, design good keyboard navigation by providing keyboard shortcuts, default buttons, and logical tab orders.
- Visual Studio can test your Web page or an entire Web application for WCAG or Section 508 compliance.

Lesson Review

You can use the following questions to test your knowledge of the information in Lesson 2, "Configuring Accessibility." The questions are also available on the companion CD if you prefer to review them in electronic form.

> ***NOTE* ANSWERS**
>
> **Answers to these questions and explanations of why each answer choice is right or wrong are located in the "Answers" section at the end of the book.**

1. Which *Image* properties can you define to enable screen readers to describe a picture on a Web page? (Choose all that apply.)
   - A. *AccessKey*
   - B. *AlternateText*
   - C. *DescriptionUrl*
   - D. *ToolTip*
2. Which of the following are accessibility features provided by ASP.NET? (Choose all that apply.)
   - A. Controls provide properties that enable you to provide hidden descriptions that are available to screen readers.
   - B. Controls are displayed in high contrast by default.
   - C. Controls that include a list of links at the top provide hidden links to skip over the links.
   - D. Controls display text in large font sizes by default.
3. For which of the following guidelines does ASP.NET provide automated testing? (Choose all that apply.)
   - A. WCAG Priority 1
   - B. WCAG Priority 2
   - C. ADA
   - D. Access Board Section 508

Chapter Review

To further practice and reinforce the skills you learned in this chapter, you can perform the following tasks:

- Review the chapter summary.
- Complete the case scenarios. These scenarios set up real-world situations involving the topics of this chapter and ask you to create solutions.
- Complete the suggested practices.
- Take a practice test.

Chapter Summary

- Globalization enables users who speak other languages and have different formatting standards to use your Web application. ASP.NET provides local and global resources to simplify the process of providing translations for controls. Local resources enable you to translate single pages, and global resources provide translations that can be shared among multiple pages. Besides providing translations, you should also follow HTML layout best practices to improve the likelihood that your Web application is rendered correctly in other languages. Web browsers automatically provide the user's language and regional preferences to the Web server, but you should also allow a user to override that preference by choosing options from a list that specifies the *UICulture* and *Culture* objects.
- Accessibility enables users with different input and display devices to interact with your Web application. ASP.NET controls are designed with accessibility in mind. However, you, as a developer, must still define specific properties to improve the accessibility of Web pages. For example, you should always define the *Image.AlternateText* property, because screen readers verbally speak the image's description, helping users without conventional monitors to navigate the site.

Case Scenarios

In the following case scenarios, you apply what you've learned in this chapter. If you have difficulty completing this work, review the material in this chapter before beginning the next chapter. You can find answers to these questions in the "Answers" section at the end of this book.

Case Scenario 1: Upgrade an Application for Multiple Languages

You are an application developer for Contoso, Inc., which manufactures shelving and display units that are used by retail outlets. Traditionally, Contoso's sales staff has been focused entirely within the United States. Typically, a sales staff develops a relationship with a retail chain, and then provides access to the Contoso Web application for new orders and support. You are responsible for developing that Web application.

Contoso has decided to expand globally. First the company plans to expand into Canada, and, later, into Mexico. The sales staff is struggling, however, because Contoso's identity is too focused around the English-speaking United States. Sales staff members in Canada complain that although parts of Canada prefer to speak French, the Web site is English-only. Similarly, Mexican sales staff members have requested a Spanish Web site with regional settings aligned with those commonly used in Mexico.

QUESTIONS

Answer the following questions for your manager.

1. How can we provide a French version of our Web site?
2. How can translators provide updated text for the Web site?
3. How can users choose between the French and English versions of our Web site?
4. How can we distinguish between Mexican regional requirements and those of other Spanish-speaking countries, such as Spain?

Case Scenario 2: Making a Web Application Accessible

You are an application developer working for Humongous Insurance. Recently, management has begun an initiative to make all facilities and other resources usable with alternative input and display devices, using the U.S. government's Rehabilitation Act, Section 508, as a guideline. Your intranet Web application is included within the scope of this initiative.

QUESTIONS

Answer the following questions for your manager.

1. How can we determine if any aspects of your Web application are not compliant with Section 508?
2. What does it mean for an application to be accessible?
3. Will the updated Web application be awkward to use with a traditional keyboard, mouse, and monitor if we make it accessible?
4. What types of things do you need to do to make your Web application compliant with Section 508?

Suggested Practices

To successfully master the exam objective presented in this chapter, complete the following tasks.

Implement Globalization and Accessibility

For this task, you should complete at least Practices 1, 2, and 3 for a better understanding of how to provide Web applications for multiple languages and cultures. If you want an understanding of the real-world complexity of providing Web application translations, complete Practice 4 as well. Then, complete Practices 5, 6, and 7 to gain an understanding of how to best develop accessible Web applications.

- **Practice 1** Update the Web application you created in Lesson 1 to also display French and German languages.
- **Practice 2** Update the Web application you created in Lesson 1 to display a list of specific cultures, and add resources for multiple specific cultures.
- **Practice 3** Configure Internet Explorer to use a different preferred language. Then, visit your favorite Web sites to see which ones provide alternate languages. Make note of which elements of the page have changed.
- **Practice 4** Create an application to enable nondeveloper translators to create local and global resource files. Then, use the tool to provide an alternate language version of the last Web application you created.
- **Practice 5** Experiment with the Microsoft Windows Vista accessibility tools. To use these accessibility tools, click Start, click Control Panel, click Ease Of Access, and then click Ease Of Access Center.
- **Practice 6** Visit this screen reader simulation to experience how screen readers can be used to interact with Web pages: *http://www.webaim.org/simulations/screenreader.php*.
- **Practice 7** Using the last production Web application you created, use the Check Accessibility tool to identify any accessibility problems. Then, address as many of the accessibility problems as possible.

Take a Practice Test

The practice tests on this book's companion CD offer many options. For example, you can test yourself on just the content covered in this chapter, or you can test yourself on all the 70-562 certification exam content. You can set up the test so it closely simulates the experience of taking a certification exam, or you can set it up in study mode so you can look at the correct answers and explanations after you answer each question.

> ***MORE INFO*** **PRACTICE TESTS**
>
> **For details about all the practice test options available, see the "How to Use the Practice Tests" section in this book's Introduction.**

CHAPTER 14

Implementing User Profiles, Authentication, and Authorization

Most Web applications require users to authenticate to gain access to private information, custom settings, and role-based features. Developers need to be able to securely authenticate a user, determine his or her authorization, and manage his or her site membership information. This is true for internal Web applications that you write that use role-based security. It is also true for public sites looking to allow user-level customizations, data storage, security, and basic user profile information.

ASP.NET includes a number of components, classes, and controls that allow you to manage the security and authorization of your sites. You can use these features to implement security based on a Windows or form-driven account. You can then identify user information through profiles. You can also use the ASP.NET membership features to help manage users. Finally, there is a set of controls that work with the security, profile, and membership features. These include *Login*, *LoginStatus*, *ChangePassword*, *PasswordRecovery*, and more. These controls allow developers to quickly add basic security, profile, and membership features to their site.

This chapter explores how developers can leverage the many features of ASP.NET user management, including profiles, membership, and security.

Exam objectives in this chapter:

- Configuring and Deploying Web Applications
  - Configure providers.
  - Configure authentication, authorization, and impersonation.

Lessons in this chapter:

Before You Begin

To complete the lessons in this chapter, you should be familiar with developing applications with Microsoft Visual Studio using Microsoft Visual Basic or C#. In addition, you should be comfortable with all of the following:

- Working with the Visual Studio 2008 Integrated Development Environment (IDE).
- Using Hypertext Markup Language (HTML) and client-side scripting.
- Creating ASP.NET Web sites and forms.

REAL WORLD

Mike Snell

User management and site security can consume a large portion of a project's budget. You have to create a security system and define data storage. You often have to create an entire back-end user administration system for managing user roles and their authorization. You have to provide for sign-up, login, password recovery, profile management, and the like.

What's worse is that this process is often repeated from project to project. This is a waste, as enterprise developers are typically hired to add actual business value through their applications and not to write (and rewrite) basic security. For this reason, I implore developers to use the ASP.NET features for managing their site authentication, authorization, and membership. This will save them time and often result in a better security model than one built from scratch.

Lesson 1: Working with User Profiles

A user profile in ASP.NET is a set of properties that you define on a per-user basis for your site. This might include color preferences, address information, or other information you wish to track on a per-user basis. Users set up a profile with your site. You store their profile information between site visits. ASP.NET will then automatically load a user's profile information based on his or her identification. You can then use this profile information in your application to make decisions, prefill data entry boxes, set customizations, and the like.

This lesson describes how you set up, define, configure, and use ASP.NET *user profiles*.

> **After this lesson, you will be able to:**
>
> - Define a custom user profile.
> - Retrieve and use user profile information to make decisions in your code.
> - Configure user profile data storage.
> - Enable and use both authenticated and anonymous user profiles.
>
> **Estimated lesson time: 20 minutes**

User Profile Basics

The ASP.NET user profile feature allows you to quickly and easily create a means to define, store, retrieve, and use user profile information in your site. You can configure most of the setup inside of Web.config. This includes defining a storage mechanism and the actual fields you wish to use to define a user profile. ASP.NET and the related user profile classes will then take care of storing your data (without you creating a specific schema), retrieving it, and providing it to you in a strongly typed class.

The following list gives the steps involved with setting up user profiles for an ASP.NET Web site:

1. **Configure a user profile provider** This class is used to store and retrieve user profile information to and from a database. There is a default provider for SQL Server. You can also create your own custom profile providers.
2. **Define the user profile** Set up the fields of a user profile you wish to track using the Web.config file. These fields are used by ASP.NET to store data and return it to you in a strongly typed class.
3. **Uniquely identify users** You can identify both anonymous and authenticated users of your site. You use a unique value to return their profile from the data storage.
4. **Set and save a user profile** You must provide a means that allows users to set their profile information. This information will then be saved by the configured profile provider.

5. **Recognize a returning visitor** When a user revisits your site, you can retrieve his or her user profile information as a strongly typed class. Your code can then use the profile information to set customizations, prefill data entry fields, and make other decisions related to the application.

These steps represent the basic elements you need to set up to use the ASP.NET profile feature. Each step is covered in detail in the following sections.

Configuring a User Profile Provider

User profiles are stored and retrieved in a database using a provider class. This class abstracts the storage and retrieval from the actual profile itself. In this way, you can always configure a new provider (and data store) without having to change any of your code.

ASP.NET provides a default, configured provider for use with user profiles. This provider is the *SqlProfileProvider* class found in the *System.Web.Profile* namespace. When ASP.NET is installed, a setting is added to the Machine.config file that connects the *SqlProfileProvider* class to an instance of a SQL Server database on the local machine. This setting is *AspNetSqlProfileProvider* and is set to work with a local configured version of SQL Server. By default, this is SQL Server Express. However, you can change this. The following shows an example of the provider's configuration:

```
<profile>
  <providers>
    <add name="AspNetSqlProfileProvider"
      connectionStringName="LocalSqlServer" applicationName="/"
      type="System.Web.Profile.SqlProfileProvider, System.Web, Version=2.0.0.0,
        Culture=neutral, PublicKeyToken=b03f5f7f11d50a3a"/>
  </providers>
</profile>
```

Notice that in the preceding markup, the provider is configured to use the connection string *LocalSqlServer*. This is also found inside of Machine.config. By default, it points to a SQL Server Express edition of a database named aspnetdb. The following markup shows an example:

```
<connectionStrings>
  <add name="LocalSqlServer" connectionString="data source=.\SQLEXPRESS;
      Integrated Security=SSPI;AttachDBFilename=|DataDirectory|aspnetdb.mdf;
      User Instance=true" providerName="System.Data.SqlClient"/>
</connectionStrings>
```

In fact, if your Web server includes SQL Server Express, ASP.NET will automatically create the profile database when this feature is used. It does so inside the configured DataDirectory (or App_Data). You can, of course, override these settings.

Configuring a New Profile Database

In most cases, you can rely on this database to exist in your development environment and therefore need to do nothing to configure a user profile provider or database. However, you might wish to configure a provider to use a standard version of SQL Server. To do so, you must first generate the database schema on the given database server. ASP.NET provides the Aspnet_regsql.exe tool to help.

The Aspnet_regsql.exe tool can be found on your development machine at the following path:

```
%windows%\Microsoft.NET\Framework\%version%
```

For example, on a standard install of a Windows Vista development machine, you can find this tool at the following path:

```
C:\Windows\Microsoft.NET\Framework\v2.0.50727
```

When you run the tool, you have the option of running it in command-line mode or using the user interface to walk you through a wizard that allows you to set up the profile schema database. In command-line mode, you have the option to set the database name (*-d*), the server name (*-S*), and other important information such as login (*-U*) and password (*-P*).

This tool can be used to set up more than just the profile table. It is used to define the role, membership, profile, and Web part tables. To define the tables you wish to set up, you use the *-A* command and append another letter(s) based on the table you wish to set up. For example, *-Aall* sets up all the tables, whereas *-Ap* only sets up the Profile table.

The following example configures the profile table (*-Ap*) for the server (*-S*) of localhost using Windows credentials (*-E*):

```
aspnet_regsql.exe -E -S localhost -Ap
```

The Setup Wizard will walk you through the process of both configuring ASP.NET application services and removing them. Figure 14-1 shows the main page in the wizard. By default, the profile database is named aspnetdb.

Once executed, the tool will update the configuration information (Machine.config) to use this new provider. You might have to make this same change when you move your application to another server. You can, of course, override these settings in your Web.config file for your individual site by adding a new connection string setting to your Web.config file. You then define a provider element that points to this connection string.

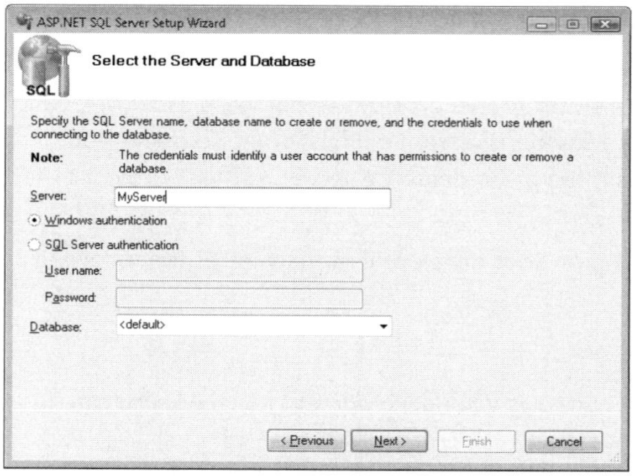

FIGURE 14-1 Defining an ASP.NET Application Services database

> ***NOTE*** **CUSTOM PROVIDERS**
>
> **You can create your own custom provider classes by implementing the base class *ProfileProvider*. You then build this provider and configure it inside your Web.config file. For more information, see the MSDN topic titled "Implementing a Profile Provider."**

Defining the User Profile

You define a user profile by determining the individual fields you wish to track for each user in your site. For instance, you might want to track the user's first and last name, the date and time of his or her last visit, preferred font and color settings, and so on. Each value you wish to track is defined as a profile property. Profile properties can be of any type, such as *string*, *DateTime*, and even custom types you create.

You define user profile fields inside the Web.config file by adding a *<profile>* element to the configuration file followed by a *<properties>* element. Inside the *<properties>* element, you use the *<add>* child element to indicate a new field. You name the field using the *name* attribute. Unless otherwise specified, property fields are of type *string*. However, you can use the *type* attribute to specify another specific type. The following is an example of a user profile defined inside of a Web.config file:

```
<configuration>
  <system.web>
    <profile>
      <properties>
        <add name="FirstName" />
        <add name="LastName" />
        <add name="LastVisit" type="System.DateTime" />
      </properties>
```

```
    </profile>
  </system.web>
</configuration>
```

Anonymous User Profiles

By default, a user profile and its properties are enabled only for authenticated users, those users you ask to provide login credentials for your site and then authenticate against a user data store. However, you might want to allow anonymous users (those who do not have login credentials to your site) to use features of a user profile. To do so, you start by defining properties as anonymous using the *allowAnonymous* attribute. You set this attribute value to *true* for each property for which you want to allow anonymous profiles.

Next, you must add the *<anonymousIdentification>* element to your Web.config file and set the *enabled* attribute to *true*. The *<anonymousIdentification>* element has several other attributes that you can define to control how cookies are used. However, the default settings are typically sufficient.

The following shows an example of both the *anonymousIdentification* element and the *allowAnonymous* attribute:

```
<anonymousIdentification enabled="true" />

<profile>
  <properties>
    <add name="FirstName" allowAnonymous="true" />
    <add name="LastName" allowAnonymous="true" />
    <add name="LastVisit" type="System.DateTime" allowAnonymous="true" />
  </properties>
</profile>
```

In this case, anonymous profiles are enabled and ASP.NET creates a unique identification for each user the first time he or she visits your site. This value is stored and tracked with a browser cookie. By default, this cookie is set to expire 70 days after the user last visited your site. If a browser does not support cookies, user profiles can also function without them by storing unique identifiers in the Uniform Resource Locator (URL) of the page request; however, the profile is lost when the user closes his or her browser.

Profile Property Groups

You can group profile properties together under a group name. For example, you might want to define an *Address* group that contains properties of *Street, City,* and *PostalCode.* Adding these items to a group allows you to access them through the profile class in a similar way you would encapsulate data in a class (*Profile.Address.Street*).

The following markup demonstrates defining a grouped profile property in a Web.config file:

```
<profile enabled="true">
  <properties>
    <group name="Address">
      <add name="Street" />
      <add name="City" />
      <add name="PostalCode" />
    </group>
  </properties>
</profile>
```

Custom Profile Property Types

You can create your own custom class and use it as a profile property. For example, you might have a class that defines a user's position in your organization, that user's reports-to information, and his or her direct reports. You could use this type as a profile property. To do so, you need to make sure your custom class is marked as serializable using the *Serializable* attribute. You then reference the custom type using the *type* attribute of the *<add>* element. The following markup shows an example of adding a custom type called *OrgPosition*:

```
<profile>
  <properties>
    <add name="Position" type="MyNamespace.OrgPosition" serializeAs="Binary" />
  </properties>
</profile>
```

Identifying Users

As discussed, user profiles can be used with either authenticated or anonymous users. If your Web application requires and implements user authentication, you can immediately begin using profiles as they are automatically enabled for authenticated users. For more information on implementing user authentication, see Lesson 3, "Securing Your Site," later in this chapter.

If your site does not authenticate users, you must explicitly enable user profiles through the Web.config setting *<anonymousIdentification enabled="true" />* as discussed previously. In this case, users are identified by either a cookie setting or a URL value.

You might also want to implement a scenario whereby users of your site have anonymous profiles to start. However, at some point they might wish to create an account and thus make their anonymous profile one that requires authentication. Thankfully, ASP.NET supports this scenario.

Migrating Anonymous User Profiles

If you enable anonymous user profiles but later wish to allow a user to create authentication credentials, ASP.NET creates a new profile for the user. To avoid losing the user's anonymous profile information, you respond to the *MigrateAnonymous* event that ASP.NET raises when a user logs on to your site. The following code demonstrates how to migrate information when a user is first authenticated with his or her new credentials:

```
'VB
Public Sub Profile_OnMigrateAnonymous(sender As Object, args As ProfileMigrateEventArgs)
  Dim anonymousProfile As ProfileCommon = Profile.GetProfile(args.AnonymousID)

  Profile.ZipCode = anonymousProfile.ZipCode
  Profile.CityAndState = anonymousProfile.CityAndState
  Profile.StockSymbols = anonymousProfile.StockSymbols

  'delete the anonymous profile. If the anonymous ID is not
  'needed in the rest of the site, remove the anonymous cookie.
  ProfileManager.DeleteProfile(args.AnonymousID)
  AnonymousIdentificationModule.ClearAnonymousIdentifier()
End Sub

//C#
public void Profile_OnMigrateAnonymous(object sender, ProfileMigrateEventArgs args)
{
  ProfileCommon anonymousProfile = Profile.GetProfile(args.AnonymousID);

  Profile.ZipCode = anonymousProfile.ZipCode;
  Profile.CityAndState = anonymousProfile.CityAndState;
  Profile.StockSymbols = anonymousProfile.StockSymbols;

  //delete the anonymous profile. If the anonymous ID is not
  //needed in the rest of the site, remove the anonymous cookie.
  ProfileManager.DeleteProfile(args.AnonymousID);
  AnonymousIdentificationModule.ClearAnonymousIdentifier();
}
```

Notice that in this code, the user's anonymous profile information is actually copied into his or her new profile. After this action, the user's anonymous profile is deleted from the system.

Set and Save a User Profile

You can save a user profile by simply setting the values of individual properties and then calling the *Profile.Save* method. This method will use the configured profile provider to write the profile data out to the configured database.

Typically, you set user profile information in response to a user's selection, such as his or her preferred color or font size for your Web site. You might also allow users to enter and edit their profile information using a Web form. You do so in a way similar to how you might code any Web form. You add controls to the page, validation, a save button, and an event in your code-behind file to write the data to the data store.

For example, imagine you have a user profile that contains both first and last name along with the last time a user visited your site. In this case, you might start by creating a form to allow users to edit their name information. This form would contain a couple *TextBox* controls, a *Button* control, and perhaps some validation controls. When the user clicks the save button, you simply set the profile information and call the *Save* method. The following code shows an example:

```
'VB
Protected Sub Button1_Click(ByVal sender As Object,
  ByVal e As System.EventArgs) Handles Button1.Click

  Profile.FirstName = TextBoxFirst.Text
  Profile.LastName = TextBoxLast.Text
  Profile.Save()

End Sub

//C#
protected void Button1_Click(object sender, EventArgs e)
{
  Profile.FirstName = TextBoxFirst.Text;
  Profile.LastName = TextBoxLast.Text;
  Profile.Save();
}
```

To set the time of the user's last visit, you could add code to the Global.asax file. Here you might override the *Session_End* event. The following shows an example:

```
'VB
Sub Session_End(ByVal sender As Object, ByVal e As EventArgs)

  Profile.LastVisit = DateTime.Now
  Profile.Save()

End Sub

//C#
void Session_End(object sender, EventArgs e)
{
  Profile.LastVisit = DateTime.Now;
  Profile.Save();
}
```

Recognize a Returning Visitor

ASP.NET will automatically load a user's profile based on his or her identification. Again, if you allow anonymous authentication, this identification is passed as a cookie setting. Otherwise, identification happens at the time of authorization. Either way, once the profile is loaded, you can access the data to make decisions such as setting color and font preferences.

In the previous example, a Web form was used to allow a user to set his or her profile information. You could add code to the *Load* method of this form to initialize the form fields with any profile data. This code would look as follows:

```
'VB
Protected Sub Page_Load(ByVal sender As Object, ByVal e As System.EventArgs) _
  Handles Me.Load
  If Not IsPostBack Then
    TextBoxFirst.Text = Profile.FirstName
    TextBoxLast.Text = Profile.LastName
    LabelLastVisit.Text = Profile.LastVisit.ToString()
  End If
End Sub

//C#
protected void Page_Load(object sender, EventArgs e)
{
  if (!IsPostBack)
  {
    TextBoxFirst.Text = Profile.FirstName;
    TextBoxLast.Text = Profile.LastName;
    LabelLastVisit.Text = Profile.LastVisit.ToString();
  }
}
```

Using profiles in this way is extremely easy compared to the alternatives, as you do not need to explicitly determine who the user is or perform any database lookups. Simply referring to a profile property value causes ASP.NET to perform the necessary actions to identify the current user and look up the value in the persistent profile store.

LAB Applying User Profiles

In this lab, you define and configure user profiles. You also create a form that allows a user to modify his or her profile information.

If you encounter a problem completing an exercise, the completed projects are available in the sample files installed from the companion CD in the Code folder.

EXERCISE 1 Working with ASP.NET User Profiles

In this exercise, you enable user profiles for anonymous users and track information for Web site visitors.

1. Open Visual Studio. Create a new, file-based Web site called **UserProfile**.
2. Open the Web.config file for your project. Navigate to the *<system.web>* element. Inside this element, add markup to configure anonymous user profiles. The following shows an example:

```
<anonymousIdentification enabled="true" />
```

3. Add user profile information to the Web.config file under *<system.web>*. Add fields for name, postal code, and color preference, as in the following:

```
<profile>
  <properties>
    <add name="Name" allowAnonymous="true" />
    <add name="PostalCode" type="System.Int16" allowAnonymous="true" />
    <add name="ColorPreference" allowAnonymous="true" />
  </properties>
</profile>
```

4. Add a master page to your site. Right-click the site and choose Add New Item. Use the default page name of MasterPage.master.
5. Add markup to the master page to include a *HyperLink* control to both show the name of the user and link to the user profile edit page you will create in a later step.

   Surround your markup with a *Panel* control. This control will be used to set the user's preferred color for the site. The contents of the *<body>* element for your page should look similar to the following:

```
<body style="font-family: Verdana">
  <form id="form1" runat="server">
  <asp:Panel ID="Panel1" runat="server">
    <h1>My Site</h1>
    <hr />
    <div style="float: right">
      <asp:HyperLink ID="HyperLinkUserProfile" runat="server"
        NavigateUrl="UserProfile.aspx"></asp:HyperLink>
    </div>
    <asp:ContentPlaceHolder id="ContentPlaceHolderMain" runat="server">
    </asp:ContentPlaceHolder>
  </asp:Panel>
  </form>
</body>
```

6. Add a *Page_Load* event handler to the master page's code-behind file. In this handler, add code to set the *HyperLink* control's text and the *Panel* control's background based on the user's profile. Your code should look similar to the following:

```
'VB
Protected Sub Page_Load(ByVal sender As Object, _
  ByVal e As System.EventArgs) Handles Me.Load

  If Profile.Name.Length > 0 Then
    HyperLinkUserProfile.Text = "Welcome, " & Profile.Name
  Else
    HyperLinkUserProfile.Text = "Set Profile"
  End If

  If Profile.ColorPreference.Length > 0 Then
    Panel1.BackColor = _
      System.Drawing.Color.FromName(Profile.ColorPreference)
  End If

End Sub

//C#
protected void Page_Load(object sender, EventArgs e)
{
  if (Profile.Name.Length > 0)
  {
    HyperLinkUserProfile.Text = "Welcome, " + Profile.Name;
  }
  else
  {
    HyperLinkUserProfile.Text = "Set Profile";
  }

  if (Profile.ColorPreference.Length > 0)
  {
    Panel1.BackColor =
      System.Drawing.Color.FromName(Profile.ColorPreference);
  }
}
```

7. Delete the Default.aspx page from your Web site.

   Add a new Web form called Default.aspx. When doing so, select the Select Master Page check box in the Add New Item dialog box. Click OK; select MasterPage.master in the Select A Master Page dialog box, then click OK. In Solution Explorer, right-click the page to set it as the startup page for the solution.

Inside the new Default.aspx page, add text within the second *asp:Content* control to indicate the user is on the home page. Your markup might look as follows:

```
<asp:Content ID="Content1" ContentPlaceHolderID="head" Runat="Server">
  <title>Home</title>
</asp:Content>

<asp:Content ID="Content2" ContentPlaceHolderID="ContentPlaceHolderMain"
Runat="Server">
  <h2>Home</h2>
</asp:Content>
```

8. Add another new form to your page. Name it **UserProfile.aspx**. Be sure to select MasterPage.master as its master page.
9. Edit the markup of the UserProfile.aspx page to include form fields to allow a user to manage his or her profile. Your markup might look similar to the following:

```
<asp:Content ID="Content1" ContentPlaceHolderID="head" Runat="Server">
  <title>User Profile</title>
</asp:Content>

<asp:Content ID="Content2"
  ContentPlaceHolderID="ContentPlaceHolderMain" Runat="Server">

  <h2>User Profile</h2>

  Name<br />
  <asp:TextBox ID="TextBoxName" runat="server"></asp:TextBox>
  <br /><br />
  Postal Code<br />
  <asp:TextBox ID="TextBoxPostal" runat="server"></asp:TextBox>
  <br /><br />
  Background Preference<br />
  <asp:DropDownList ID="DropDownListColors" runat="server">
    <asp:ListItem Text="White" Value="White"></asp:ListItem>
    <asp:ListItem Text="Yellow" Value="Yellow"></asp:ListItem>
    <asp:ListItem Text="Green" Value="Green"></asp:ListItem>
  </asp:DropDownList>
  <br /><br />

  <asp:Button ID="ButtonSave" runat="server" Text="Save" />

</asp:Content>
```

10. Add an event handler for the UserProfile.aspx page's *ButtonSave* click event. (You might need to build your project before you are able to view the page in Design view.)

Add code to this event handler to set the user's profile, save it, and redirect the user back to the home page (Default.aspx). Your code should look similar to the following:

```
'VB
Protected Sub ButtonSave_Click(ByVal sender As Object, _
  ByVal e As System.EventArgs) Handles ButtonSave.Click

  Profile.Name = TextBoxName.Text
  Profile.PostalCode = TextBoxPostal.Text
  Profile.ColorPreference = DropDownListColors.SelectedValue.ToString()

  Profile.Save()

  Response.Redirect("Default.aspx")

End Sub

//C#
protected void ButtonSave_Click(object sender, EventArgs e)
{
  Profile.Name = TextBoxName.Text;
  Profile.PostalCode = short.Parse(TextBoxPostal.Text);
  Profile.ColorPreference = DropDownListColors.SelectedValue.ToString();

  Profile.Save();

  Response.Redirect("Default.aspx");
}
```

11. Add another event handler to the UserProfile.aspx page for the *Page.Load* event. Add code to this event to initialize the form fields if user profile values exist. Your code should look as follows:

```
'VB
Protected Sub Page_Load(ByVal sender As Object, _
  ByVal e As System.EventArgs) Handles Me.Load

  If Not IsPostBack Then
    TextBoxName.Text = Profile.Name
    If Profile.PostalCode > 0 Then
      TextBoxPostal.Text = Profile.PostalCode
    End If
    If Profile.ColorPreference.Length > 0 Then
      DropDownListColors.SelectedValue = Profile.ColorPreference.ToString()
    End If
  End If
```

```
End Sub

//C#
protected void Page_Load(object sender, EventArgs e)
{
  if (!IsPostBack)
  {
    TextBoxName.Text = Profile.Name;
    if (Profile.PostalCode > 0)
    {
      TextBoxPostal.Text = Profile.PostalCode.ToString();
    }
    if (Profile.ColorPreference.Length > 0)
    {
      DropDownListColors.SelectedValue = Profile.ColorPreference.ToString();
    }
  }
}
```

12. Run the application and visit the Default.aspx page. Notice that the first time you run the application it takes a little time, as ASP.NET generates the ASPNETDB file for your site.

    Click the Set Profile link to edit your profile and view the results. Close the application and run it again to notice how ASP.NET stores your information between requests.

13. In Solution Explorer, click the refresh button. Notice that the App_Data subdirectory now contains an ASPNETDB.mdf database file.

Lesson Summary

- You can configure user profiles using the Web.config file and the *<profile>* element. You add fields to this element based on which data elements you intend to track for users of your site.
- ASP.NET automatically creates a strongly typed object based on your profile field settings in the Web.config file. You can access this class and its properties through the *Profile.<FieldName>* syntax in your code.
- You call the *Profile.Save* method to save a user's profile to a database.
- By default, ASP.NET uses the *SqlProfileProvider* to store and retrieve user profile information to a SQL Server Express database called ASPNETDB.mdf. You can change the provider and the database using configuration files.

Lesson Review

You can use the following questions to test your knowledge of the information in Lesson 1, "Working with User Profiles." The questions are also available on the companion CD if you prefer to review them in electronic form.

> ***NOTE*** **ANSWERS**
>
> **Answers to these questions and explanations of why each answer choice is right or wrong are located in the "Answers" section at the end of the book.**

1. Which of the following Web.config files correctly enables the Web application to track the age of anonymous users in a variable of type *Int32*?

   A.
   ```
   <anonymousIdentification enabled="true" />
   <profile>
     <properties>
       <add name="Age" type="System.Int32" allowAnonymous="true" />
     </properties>
   </profile>
   ```

   B.
   ```
   <anonymousIdentification enabled="true" />
   <profile>
     <properties>
       <add name="Age" allowAnonymous="true" />
     </properties>
   </profile>
   ```

   C.
   ```
   <anonymousIdentification enabled="true" />
   <profile>
     <properties>
       <add name="Age" type="System.Int32" />
     </properties>
   </profile>
   ```

   D.
   ```
   <profile>
     <properties>
       <add name="Age" type="System.Int32" />
     </properties>
   </profile>
   ```

2. You wish to create a user profile that uses a custom type as one of the profile properties. What actions must you take? (Choose all that apply.)

A. Mark your class as serializable.

B. Set the type attribute of the given profile property to the fully qualified name of your custom type.

C. Add the group element to your profile property. Add one element to the group element for each property in your custom type. Set each element's name to match that of a property in your custom type.

D. Add your custom type in the Machine.config file in the *<customTypes>* element.

Lesson 2: Using ASP.NET Membership

One key feature of nearly every enterprise Web application is the ability to manage users and their access to the features of a site. This includes creating and editing users, managing their passwords, authenticating users based on role, and much more. In the past, this code was written by nearly every Web application team out there (sometimes more than once). Thankfully, ASP.NET now includes membership features that reduce the amount of code you have to write. ASP.NET membership features include all of the following:

- Wizard-based configuration of user management capabilities
- Browser-based user management and access control configuration
- A set of ASP.NET controls that provides users with the ability to log in, log out, create new accounts, and recover lost passwords
- The *Membership* and *Roles* classes, which you can use to access user management capabilities within your code

ASP.NET membership is related to user profiles that you read about in Lesson 1. User profiles store data about unique users. Membership is meant to uniquely identify users. This lesson describes how you leverage the ASP.NET membership features in your own Web applications to manage user accounts and authorization. Lesson 3 of this chapter discusses how you use ASP.NET to authenticate users.

MORE INFO **PROTECTING WEB SERVERS**

This chapter strives to provide the information that you need to maximize the security of your Web applications. The topic of improving security for Web servers is massive, and most of the burden of protection falls on the shoulders of system administrators. For more information about protecting servers, read the MSDN topic titled "Securing Your Web Server." For more information about protecting ASP.NET applications, read the MSDN topic titled "Building Secure ASP.NET Applications: Authentication, Authorization, and Secure Communication."

After this lesson, you will be able to:

- Understand the features of the ASP.NET login controls and use them in a site.
- Configure an ASP.NET Web application to support user management.
- Use the *Membership* class to manage user information.
- Use the *Roles* class to define authentication groups for your site.

Estimated lesson time: 45 minutes

Using WSAT to Configure Security

You can use the Web Site Administration Tool (WSAT) to define and manage users, roles, and security on your site. Administrators and developers can use the tool to manage security settings from a Web browser. This tool allows you to configure authentication, create and manage users, and create and manage role-based authorization.

Creating Users

Recall that you launch this tool in Visual Studio by choosing ASP.NET Configuration from the Website menu. This takes you to the administration page for your site. The user configuration information is found on the Security tab. The first step is to click the Select Authentication Type link. Here you choose Windows-based, local Active Directory security authentication (From A Local Network) or Web-based forms using a database authentication (From The Internet). Once the type of authentication is selected, you can create users, manage users, define their roles, and control their access. Figure 14-2 shows an example of creating a new user with the WSAT.

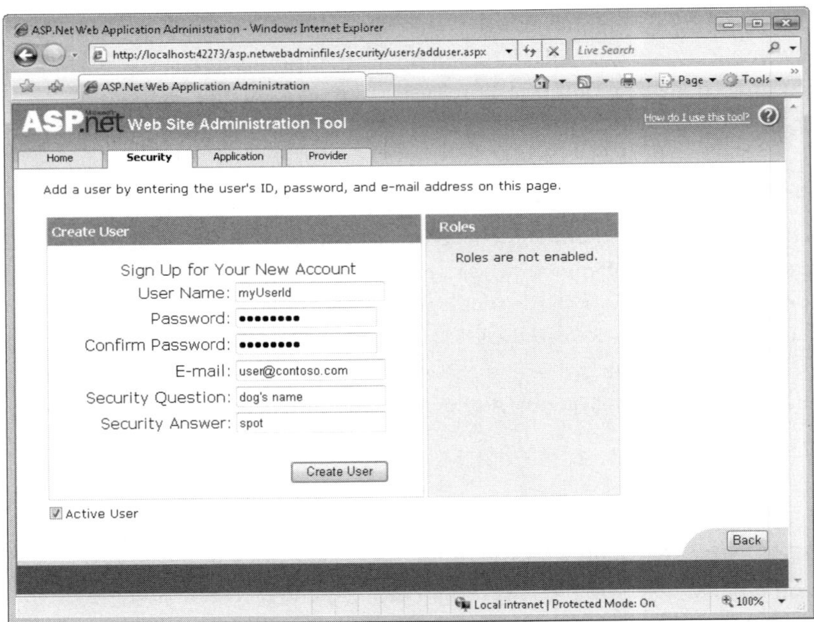

FIGURE 14-2 Creating a user using the WSAT

When you select Web-based security using the WSAT, ASP.NET automatically creates the ASPNETDB.mdf file for your site and stores it in the App_Data directory (see Lesson 1 for configuring a different database). It also updates your site's Web.config file to enable this security feature. It adds the authentication element as shown here:

```
<configuration>
  <system.web>
    <authentication mode="Forms" />
  </system.web>
</configuration>
```

The WSAT is a great tool for administrators and developers. You can use it to edit configuration settings and manage the data found inside ASPNETDB. However, it does not allow user-provisioning of accounts or other related, user-based management. For this, you need to use the login controls to create pages for users to set up and manage their information.

Creating Roles

You can also use the WSAT to create, configure, and manage user roles, which are simply groups of users that you define. You can then apply authorization at the role level rather than at the individual user level. This makes management easier as roles do not change, just the users assigned to them do.

To enable roles using the WSAT, on the Security tab, click the Enable Roles link. This will edit your Web.config file to enable roles as shown in the following:

```
<configuration>
  <system.web>
    <roleManager enabled="true" />
  </system.web>
</configuration>
```

On the Security tab, you can now use the Create Or Manage Roles link. To create a new role, you start by assigning it a name. You then click Manage for the given role to assign or remove users from the role.

Roles, by themselves, do not enforce security on your site. Instead, you need to do one of two things (or both). First, you can use the *Roles* class in your code to determine if a user has access to a given page or feature. You can query the *IsUserInRole* method to do so (described later in this lesson). Second, you can use the WSAT to create role-based access rules for your site.

Creating Access Rules

You create role-based access rules on the Security tab in the WSAT. An access rule allows you to define folder-level access to items in your site on either a per-user or role basis. You start by clicking the Create Access Rules link. This takes you to the Add New Access Rule page, as shown in Figure 14-3. From here, you can apply a rule to a role, an individual user, all users, or anonymous users. You select a folder for the rule, to whom the rule applies, and if you intend to allow or deny permission.

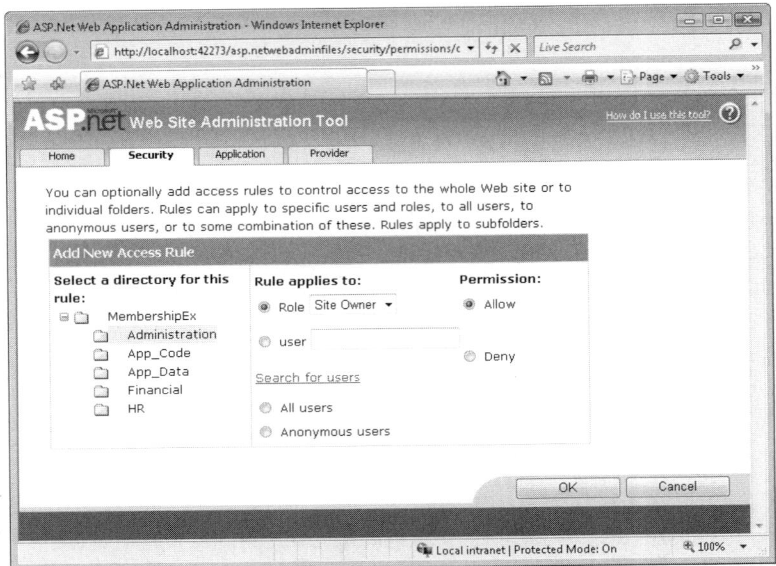

FIGURE 14-3 Managing access rules using the WSAT

The WSAT adds (or edits) a Web.config file to any folder to which you apply an access rule. This configuration file applies only to the content of that folder. In the example shown in Figure 14-3, the role of Site Owner is being allowed for the Administration folder. The following represents the content of the Web.config file found inside the Administration folder after this operation:

```
<?xml version="1.0" encoding="utf-8"?>
<configuration>
  <system.web>
    <authorization>
      <allow roles="Site Owner" />
    </authorization>
  </system.web>
</configuration>
```

Login Controls

ASP.NET provides a set of controls, classes, and management tools for authenticating users with Web forms and storing user information in a database. These controls allow you to track, manage, and authenticate users without creating your own schema, relying on Active Directory, or managing users by other means. Prior to version 2.0 of the .NET Framework, custom user *authentication* required creation from scratch of many complex components, such as user database schemas, login pages, password management pages, and user administration. Creating these components yourself is time-consuming and risky to your application's security. ASP.NET helps you minimize this risk.

The Login Control Classes

There are seven controls inside of ASP.NET for managing the login information of a user. These seven controls are grouped together as the login controls. They provide user interface elements for managing the login features related to users. Like the profile features, these controls are configured to work with the ASPNETDB SQL Server Express database by default. You can, of course, create your own custom providers or migrate to a higher version of SQL Server.

Figure 14-4 shows an overview of the login controls class hierarchy.

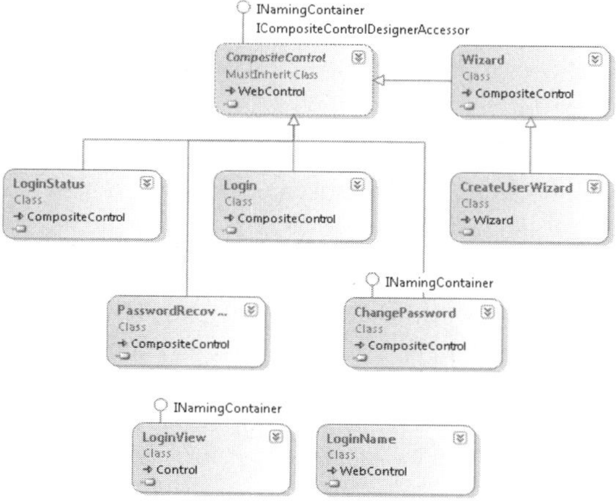

FIGURE 14-4 The ASP.NET login controls

Each of these controls provides a specific feature required of most user-driven Web sites. The following is a list of each of these controls and their purpose:

- ***CreateUserWizard*** This control gathers information from a new user such as user name and password and creates a new user account. You can use the user profile features in conjunction with the *CreateUserWizard*.
- ***Login*** This control defines a user interface for prompting users for their user name and password and enables users to select whether they wish to be automatically authenticated the next time they visit your site. You can use the *Login* control with ASP.NET membership without writing any code, or you can write your own authentication code by adding a handler for the *Authenticate* event.
- ***LoginView*** This control is used to display different information if a user is logged into your site. For example, you could use this control to provide links to features that are available only to authenticated users.
- ***LoginStatus*** You use this control to allow users to link to your login page if they haven't been authenticated. It displays a link to log out for users who are currently logged in.
- ***LoginName*** This control displays the current user's user name (if logged in).

- ***PasswordRecovery*** This control enables password retrieval or reset for a user by sending an e-mail message or by having the user answer a security question.
- ***ChangePassword*** This control enables a user who is logged in to change his or her password.

With the functionality built into these controls, you can create without writing any code a Web site that enables users to create their own accounts, change and reset their passwords, and log on and log off.

Creating a User Account Creation Page

Most public Web sites allow users to create their own accounts. This simplifies user creation and takes the burden off of an administrator. However, to enable this functionality, you must create a page that allows users to define an account.

You use the *CreateUserWizard* control to create a page that allows users to create their own accounts using the standard ASP.NET membership. This control can be added to a page and will automatically work with the provider talking to ASPNETDB.

The *CreateUserWizard* control, by default, prompts a user for user name, password, e-mail, security question, and security answer. Figure 14-5 shows an example of the control on a page inside Visual Studio. Note that the *CreateUserWizard* control also includes features for validating required fields, ensuring a strong password, and confirming a password.

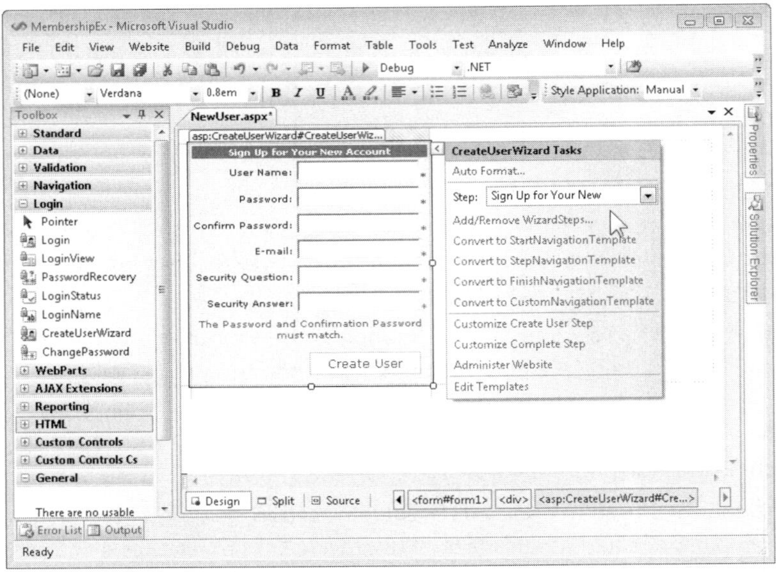

FIGURE 14-5 The ASP.NET *CreateUserWizard* control in Visual Studio

There is nothing additional that you need to do to configure, set up, or use a *CreateUserWizard* control. However, you will most likely wish to set the *ContinueDestinationPageUrl* property. This property should be set to the page to which you wish users to go once they have completed their account creation process. In addition, you can add your own code to the *ContinueButtonClick* event to add additional processing when the user clicks the final step in the Wizard.

The *CreateUserWizard* control is a composite, template-driven control. Therefore, you have access to edit the templates that are defined by the control. You can even change and add to the steps defined by the wizard. These features are useful if you wish to add additional information to the user registration process or change the layout of the interface.

As an example, suppose you wish to add controls to allow a user to define additional profile information as part of the account creation process. You can do so by clicking the Customize Create User Step link from the CreateUserWizard Tasks pane (refer back to Figure 14-5). This will render the entire markup to create a user form inside your page. You can then edit this markup to include your own controls as necessary. Figure 14-6 shows an example of a *CheckBox* control added to the page.

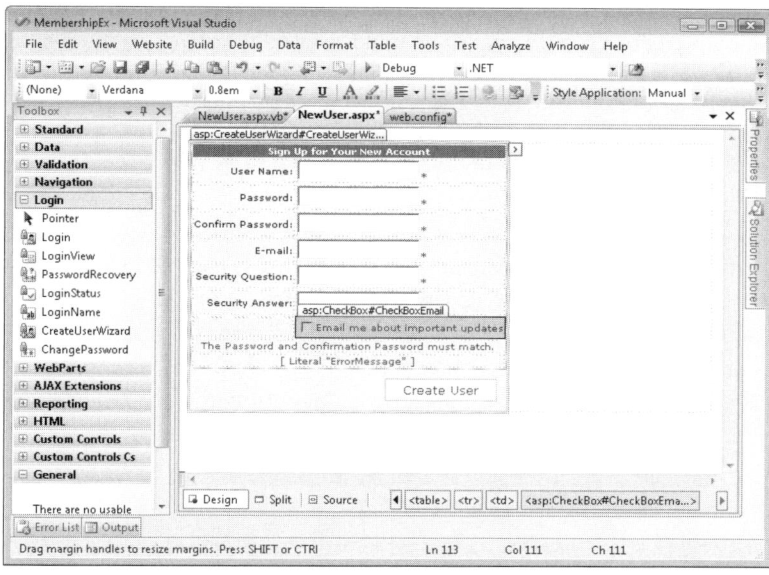

FIGURE 14-6 A customized version of the *CreateUserWizard* control

You can store this additional information by handling the *CreatedUser* event. In this event, you use the *Membership* class (discussed later in this lesson) to get the user and update the *Comment* property of the *MembershipUser* class. This property is used to store custom values for a user. However, a better method is to use the user *Profile* object as discussed in Lesson 1.

Unfortunately, you cannot easily set the user's profile information inside the *CreatedUser* event because the user is not considered identified and authenticated to the site until after this event completes. To help with this issue, the *CreateUserWizard* control exposes the properties *EditProfileText* and *EditProfileUrl*. You can use these properties to create a link that appears on the final page for the created user. This link can take users to a page that allows them to edit their profile (as discussed in Lesson 1). This profile will be associated with the newly created user. However, without deeper customizations, you will have to maintain both a profile page and a create user page.

By default, new user accounts do not belong to any roles. To add a new user to a role (such as a default Users role), add a handler for the *CreateUserWizard.CreatedUser* event, and then call the *Roles.AddUserToRole* method as described later in this lesson.

Creating a Login Page

A login page allows a user to present his or her credentials to your site and then be authenticated. In most cases, a login page will include login information, a link to create a new account, and a link to retrieve a password for an existing account. Users expect to see these features grouped together on a page.

To get started, you should create a login page. You should then edit the Web.config file to point nonauthenticated requests to your login page by adding the *loginUrl* attribute to the *<forms>* element as follows:

```
<authentication mode="Forms">
  <forms loginUrl="Login.aspx" />
</authentication>
```

On the login page, you start by adding a *Login* control. This control is used to prompt a user for his or her credentials. The *Login* control also includes features for validation to ensure the user types a user name and password. However, to get the actual error messages to the page (instead of just asterisks), you should add a *ValidationSummary* control to your login page. You configure this control to work with the *Login* control by setting the *ValidationGroup* property to the ID of your *Login* control. Figure 14-7 shows an example of both controls added to a page.

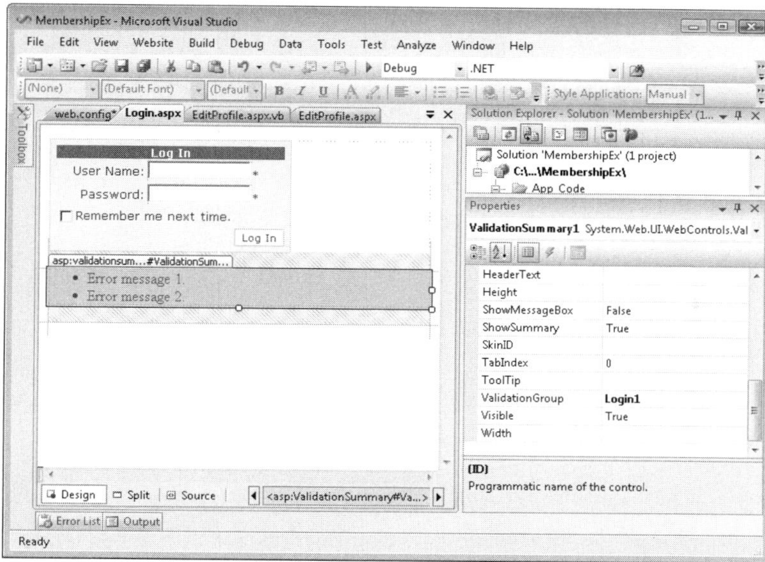

FIGURE 14-7 The *Login* control prompts the user for credentials

You do not need to write any code to use the login control. It works automatically with the site configuration to authenticate users using forms-based authentication.

Adding Password Recovery

To complete your login page, you might wish to add a *PasswordRecovery* control. This control assists users if they forget their password. This control enables users to type their user name and receive a new, random password via e-mail. E-mails are sent based on the configured e-mail provider in Web.config. Optionally, users can also be required to answer a security question before their password is sent.

> ***MORE INFO*** **CONFIGURING AN E-MAIL SERVER**
>
> **You can configure an e-mail server for your site manually inside of the Web.config file. You can also use the WSAT. You set up a Simple Mail Transfer Protocol (SMTP) server using WSAT on the Application tab.**

Figure 14-8 shows an example of the control in Visual Studio. Notice that there are three template views: UserName, Question, and Success. The UserName view allows a user to enter his or her user name, the Question view allows you to ask and validate the user's secret question, and the Success view indicates a successful lookup.

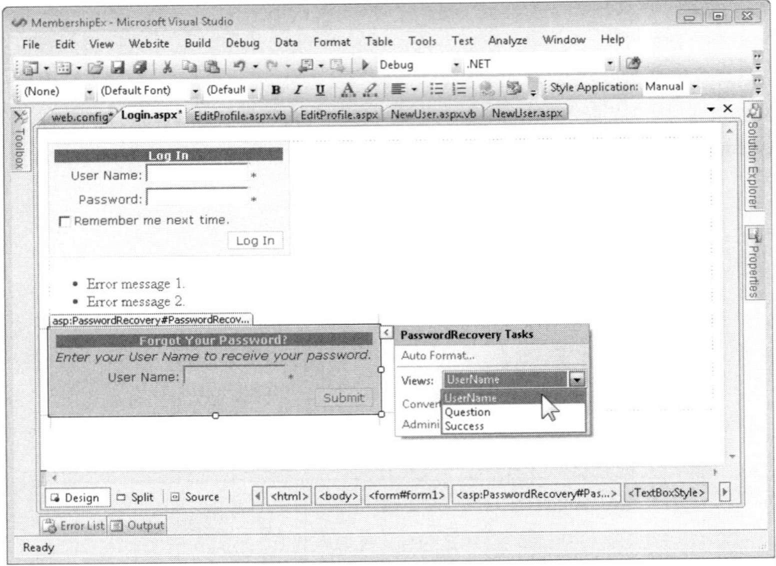

FIGURE 14-8 The *PasswordRecovery* control can send e-mail to users who request their passwords

If the user provides valid credentials, the user is logged in to your site. The membership controls such as *LoginStatus* will then automatically reflect that. If the user does not provide valid credentials, the *Login* control prompts the user to retype his or her password. You should create a handler for the *Login.LoginError* event and perform security auditing by adding an event to the Security event log. Similarly, you should handle (log) the *PasswordRecovery.UserLookupError* and *PasswordRecovery.AnswerLookupError* events. This ensures that administrators can discover excessive attempts to look up and recover a user account.

Creating a Password Change Page

Another important form is the change password form. This allows users to enter their current password and create a new one. You create a change password form using the *ChangePassword* control. Figure 14-9 shows an example.

On completion, you can either show a success message or automatically navigate to another page. To enable the latter scenario, set the *SuccessPageUrl* property of the *ChangePassword* control to the name of the page to which you wish to redirect the user following a successful password change. The control also exposes other useful properties such as *EditProfileUrl* and *EditProfileText* to create a link to allow the user to edit other portions of his or her profile if required.

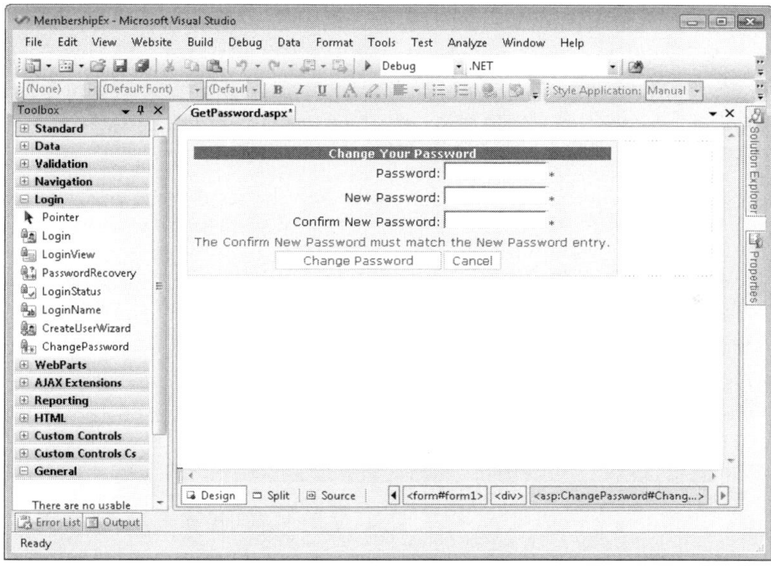

FIGURE 14-9 The *ChangePassword* control allows users to change their passwords

The *Membership* Class

The login controls discussed previously use the methods of the *System.Web.Security.Membership* class to implement their functionality. This is, for the most part, abstracted from developers. However, there are many cases in which you might want to use these methods yourself. These include creating your own custom user interface outside of the login controls, intercepting login control events, and implementing other security-related code on your site. In each case, you use the *Membership* class. It provides capabilities to add, remove, and find users. The following are the important, static methods in this class, along with each method's capability:

- ***CreateUser*** This method adds a user to the database. Use this method if you create a custom page to enable users or administrators to add new accounts.
- ***DeleteUser*** This method removes a user from the data store. Use this method if you create custom user management tools.
- ***FindUsersByEmail*** This method gets a collection of membership users with the specified e-mail addresses.
- ***FindUsersByName*** This method gets a collection of membership users with the specified user names.
- ***GeneratePassword*** This method creates a random password of the specified length. Use this if you are implementing custom controls to generate or reset passwords.
- ***GetAllUsers*** This method returns a collection of all users in the database.

- ***GetNumberOfUsersOnline*** This method returns the number of users currently logged on.
- ***GetUser*** This method returns a *MembershipUser* object representing the current logged-on user. Call this method any time you need to access the current user's account.
- ***GetUserNameByEmail*** This method gets a user name with the specified e-mail address.
- ***UpdateUser*** This method updates the database with the information for the specified user. Use this method if you create a page to enable users or administrators to modify existing accounts.
- ***ValidateUser*** This method verifies that the supplied user name and password are valid. Use this method to check a user's credentials if you create your own custom login controls.

The *Roles* Class

Role management consists of a set of classes and interfaces that establish roles for the current user and manage role information. In ASP.NET user management, roles function as user groups, enabling you to assign access rights to all users who are part of a specific role. The most useful of these classes is *System.Web.Security.Roles*, which provides capabilities to add users to or remove users from roles, create new roles, and determine to which roles a user belongs.

The Roles class provides many static methods, including the following:

- ***AddUserToRole*, *AddUsersToRole*, and *AddUsersToRoles*** These methods add a user to a role.
- ***CreateRole*** This method creates a new role.
- ***DeleteRole*** This method deletes an existing role.
- ***FindUsersInRole*** This method returns a collection of users in a role.
- ***GetAllRoles*** This method returns a collection of all roles that currently exist.
- ***GetRolesForUser*** This method returns a collection of roles for the current user.
- ***IsUserInRole*** This method returns true if the user is a member of a specified role.
- ***RemoveUserFromRole*, *RemoveUsersFromRole*, *RemoveUserFromRoles*, and *RemoveUsersFromRoles*** These methods remove a user from a role.

For example, if you want to assign the user being created as part of the *CreateUserWizard* control to a role named *Users*, you could use the following code:

```
'VB
Roles.AddUserToRole(CreateUserWizard1.UserName, "Users")

//C#
Roles.AddUserToRole(CreateUserWizard1.UserName, "Users");
```

You cannot use the *Roles* class to manage Windows user groups when using Windows authentication. Windows authentication is discussed in more detail in Lesson 3 of this chapter.

Quick Check

1. Which control would you use to provide a login link?
2. Which login controls are useful only to authenticated users?

Quick Check Answers

1. Use the *LoginStatus* control to provide a login link.
2. The *LoginName*, *ChangePassword*, and *LoginView* controls are useful only to authenticated users.

LAB Configuring Authentication in ASP.NET Applications

In these exercises, you create an ASP.NET Web application and then configure it to restrict access using roles.

If you encounter a problem completing an exercise, the completed projects are available in the sample files installed from the companion CD in the Code folder.

EXERCISE 1 Create and Configure an ASP.NET Site to Use Membership Features

In this exercise, you create a new ASP.NET Web site and add support for ASP.NET memberships.

1. Open Visual Studio. Create a new, file-based Web site called **UserMembership**.
2. Create two subfolders in your site. Name one **Members** and the other **Admin**. You can do so by right-clicking the project and choosing New Folder.
3. To each subfolder, add a blank ASP.NET Web form named Default.aspx. Later, you'll access these pages to verify that ASP.NET requires proper authentication.
4. From the Website menu, in Visual Studio, select ASP.NET Configuration. This should launch the WSAT in a browser.
5. Click the Security tab to get started. In the Users section, click the Select Authentication Type link. On the next screen, select From The Internet and click Done. This enables forms-based authentication.
6. On the Security tab, click the Enable Roles link to enable roles for the site.
7. Next, in the Roles section, click the Create Or Manage Roles link. On the next screen, add a role called **Users**. Repeat this process to add another role called **Administrators**.

8. Click the Security tab to return to the main security page. Use the Create User link to add two users. First, create a user named **StandardUser**. In the Roles section, select the Users role.

   Add another user named **Admin**. In the Roles section, select the Administrators role.

   For both users, you can set the password, security question, and e-mail address as you like. (The code provided in the samples installed from the CD uses the password *password!*.)

9. Click the Security tab to return to the main security page. In the Access Rules section, click the Create Access Rules link. Create the following rules:
   - Create a rule that denies all anonymous users access to the root of the site.
   - Create a rule that grants all users (outside of anonymous) access to the root of the site.
   - Create a rule that grants users in the Administrators role access to the Admin directory.
   - Create a rule that denies all users access to the Admin directory.

   Note that the order of the rule creation is important, as each rule is processed in order. You can move rules up or down in the WSAT interface.

10. Return to Visual Studio. Click the refresh button at the top of Solution Explorer. Notice the inclusion of the ASPNETDB.mdf file in your site. Also notice the additional Web.config file inside the Admin folder.

    Open both Web.config files for your site and examine the new settings.

The Web site is ready to use ASP.NET membership; you have created users, roles, and access rules. Continue working with this Web site for the next exercise.

EXERCISE 2 Create Web Forms That Use *Login* Controls

In this exercise, you create Web forms using *Login* controls to take advantage of ASP.NET membership.

1. Continue working with the Web site you created in the previous exercise. This site is configured to support ASP.NET membership and has users and roles added to the database. Alternatively, you can open the completed Lesson 2, Exercise 1 project in the samples installed from the CD.
2. Create a new ASP.NET Web form named **Login.aspx**. Add a *Login* control to the page.
3. Open the Default.aspx page in the site root. Add the following controls:
   - A *LoginStatus* control
   - A *HyperLink* control with the *text* set to **Members only** and *NavigateUrl* set to **Members/Default.aspx**
   - A *HyperLink* control with the *text* set to **Administrators only** and *NavigateUrl* set to **Admin/Default.aspx**

4. Run Default.aspx in a Web browser. Notice that you are redirected to the Login.aspx page. Log in as StandardUser. (The code provided in the samples installed from the CD uses the password *password!*.) You should now be able to view the page.

   Click the Members Only link. You should have full access.

   Click the Administrators Only link. You should be redirected to the Login page. Notice that the URL includes a parameter named *ReturnUrl* that contains the page you were attempting to access.

   Log in as Admin and notice you are redirected to the Administrators Only page.

Lesson Summary

- ASP.NET provides several login controls to enable you to easily build pages that support creating user accounts, logging in, logging out, and resetting passwords. These controls include *Login*, *LoginView*, *LoginStatus*, *LoginName*, *PasswordRecovery*, *CreateUserWizard*, and *ChangePassword*.
- Use the *Membership* class when you need to perform user management tasks from within your code, such as creating, deleting, or modifying user accounts. This class enables you to create custom forms that provide similar functionality to that provided by the standard ASP.NET login controls.
- Use the *Roles* class when you need to perform role management tasks from within your code, such as adding users to roles, removing users from roles, creating new roles, or examining to which roles a user belongs.

Lesson Review

You can use the following questions to test your knowledge of the information in Lesson 2, "Using ASP.NET Membership." The questions are also available on the companion CD if you prefer to review them in electronic form.

> ***NOTE* ANSWERS**
>
> **Answers to these questions and explanations of why each answer choice is right or wrong are located in the "Answers" section at the end of the book.**

1. Which of the following controls provides a link for unauthenticated users to log on?

   A. *Login*

   B. *LoginView*

   C. *LoginStatus*

   D. *LoginName*

2. You use the ASP.NET Web Site Administration Tool to configure ASP.NET membership with forms authentication. What should you name your login form so that you do not have to modify the Web.config file?

   A. Login.aspx

   B. LoginPage.aspx

   C. Default.aspx

   D. Auth.aspx

3. You are creating a Web form that enables users to log in to your Web site. Which of the following ASP.NET controls should you add to the page? (Choose two answers.)

   A. *Login*

   B. *CreateUserWizard*

   C. *LoginName*

   D. *PasswordRecovery*

4. You have created an ASP.NET Web form that enables users to create accounts with a *CreateUserWizard* control. After a new user creates an account, you want to redirect the user to a page listing the rules for your Web site. To which of the following events should you respond?

   A. *CreateUserWizard.Unload*

   B. *CreateUserWizard.ContinueButtonClick*

   C. *CreateUserWizard.CreatedUser*

   D. *CreateUserWizard.Init*

Lesson 3: Securing Your Site

Thus far you've looked at user profiles, the WSAT tool, the login controls, and the basic configuration of ASP.NET membership. These items will serve you well for most Web applications you build. However, ASP supports at least four types of authentication:

- Windows authentication
- Forms authentication (which ASP.NET membership uses)
- Passport authentication
- Anonymous access

This lesson describes how to configure both Microsoft Internet Information Services (IIS) and your applications for each of the standard Web authentication types.

After this lesson, you will be able to:

- Configure an ASP.NET Web application to require Windows authentication.
- Create an ASP.NET Web application that uses custom forms for user authentication.
- Configure an ASP.NET Web application to require Passport authentication.
- Configure Web applications for anonymous access.
- Configure impersonation so that ASP.NET uses nondefault user credentials.
- Restrict access to Web applications, files, and folders by manually editing Web.config files.

Estimated lesson time: 45 minutes

REAL WORLD

Tony Northrup

I've spent time as both a developer and a systems administrator. Each role has different responsibilities. Typically, systems administrators should be responsible for configuring Windows security for a Web application. This doesn't require them to write any code, because they can configure it using the IIS Manager and the ASP.NET Web Site Administration Tool.

So, if you're creating an application that should use Windows authentication, it's okay to leave it up to the systems administrator to configure. Not all systems administrators know how to properly configure it, however, so you should be familiar with the process and be able to demonstrate how it's done when you hand off

application support. You do need to configure forms authentication and Passport authentication, however, because those require application-specific configuration settings, such as specifying the login page. Typically, you would provide all the configuration information as part of your Web.config file.

Configuring Web Applications to Require Windows Authentication

If your application is targeted for use inside an organization where users accessing the application have existing user accounts within a local user database or Active Directory, then you should authenticate users with Windows authentication. You can configure Windows authentication in two ways: within IIS and within your ASP.NET application. To provide stronger security, you should configure your site to use both techniques.

When a Web application requires Windows authentication, the application rejects any request that does not include a valid user name and password in the request header. The user's browser then prompts the user for a user name and password. Because the browser prompts the user for credentials, you do not have to create a page to request the user's user name and password. Some browsers, such as Microsoft Internet Explorer, automatically provide the user's current user name and password when the server is located on the intranet. This seamlessly authenticates the user, eliminating the need to retype the password for intranet site visits.

Additionally, because users are authenticated against the server's local user database or Active Directory domain, using Windows authentication saves you from creating a database to store user credentials. Leveraging the Windows authentication mechanism is, therefore, the simplest way to authenticate users. To configure IIS to require all users to authenticate on computers running Microsoft Windows Server 2003, for example, follow these steps:

1. In the Administrative Tools program group, open IIS Manager.
2. In the IIS Manager console, click to expand your server name, expand Web Sites, and then to expand your Web site.
3. Right-click the site or folder name for which you are configuring authentication and select Properties.
4. Click the Directory Security tab. In the Authentication And Access Control group, click Edit.
5. Clear the Enable Anonymous Access check box, which is selected by default.
6. Select the Integrated Windows Authentication check box. Optionally, select Digest Windows Authentication For Windows Domain Servers to enable authentication across proxy servers.
7. Click OK twice to return to the IIS Manager console.

At this point, all Web requests to the virtual directory will require Windows authentication, even if ASP.NET is configured for anonymous access only. Even though configuring IIS is sufficient to require users to present Windows credentials, it is good practice to edit the application's Web.config file to also require Windows authentication.

To configure an ASP.NET application for Windows Authentication, edit the *<authentication>* section of the Web.config file. This section, like most sections related to ASP.NET application configuration, must be defined within the *<system.web>* section. The *<system.web>* section, in turn, must exist within the *<configuration>* section. This example shows the *<authentication>* section of the Web.config file configured to use Windows authentication:

```
<configuration>
  <system.web>
    <authentication mode="Windows" />
      <authorization>
        <deny users="?" />
      </authorization>
   </system.web>
</configuration>
```

The *<authorization>* section simply requires all users to be successfully authenticated. Specifying *<deny users="?" />* within *<authorization>* requires users to be authenticated, whereas specifying *<allow users="*" />* within *<authorization>* bypasses authentication entirely. The question mark (?) represents unauthenticated users, and the asterisk (*) represents all users, both authenticated and unauthenticated.

You can also configure Windows authentication in your application's Web.config file by following these steps, which are more user-friendly:

1. Create an ASP.NET Web application using Visual Studio.
2. From the Website menu, select ASP.NET Configuration.
3. Click the Security tab, and then click Select Authentication Type.
4. Under How Will Your Users Access The Site, select From A Local Network, and then click Done.

Creating Custom ASP.NET Forms to Authenticate Web Users

Windows authentication presents the end user with a browser-generated dialog box. Although giving the browser the responsibility of gathering the user's user name and password enables automatic authentication on intranet sites, it gives you, as a developer, very little flexibility. Web applications developed for external sites commonly use form-based authentication instead. Form-based authentication presents the user with an HTML-based Web page that prompts the user for credentials.

Once authenticated via forms authentication, ASP.NET generates a cookie to serve as an authentication token. The browser presents this cookie with all future requests to the Web site, allowing the ASP.NET application to validate requests. This cookie can, optionally, be encrypted by a private key located on the Web server, enabling the Web server to detect an attacker who attempts to present a cookie that the Web server did not generate.

ASP.NET membership allows you to quickly add forms authentication to your Web application. Because Microsoft thoroughly tests the controls and classes involved in authenticating and storing the user information, these controls are probably more secure than controls that any developer might make. Therefore, you should use ASP.NET membership whenever possible.

However, if you need complete control over how users are authenticated and managed, you can also create custom forms authentication controls and pages. In the sections that follow, you will learn how to configure an ASP.NET configuration file to require forms authentication, how to add user credentials to a Web.config file, and how to create an ASP.NET Web form to authenticate users.

Configuring a Web.Config File for Forms Authentication

To configure forms authentication, you have to create an authentication page that uses an HTML form to prompt the user for credentials. Therefore, forms authentication can be used on only those ASP.NET Web applications developed with this authentication method in mind. Although you can choose to rely on administrators to configure Windows or on anonymous authentication, you *must* distribute a Web.config file if your application uses forms authentication.

Administrators deploying your application should not need to modify the Web.config file, but they can control some aspects of how forms authentication behaves. This might include configuring the timeout period after which a user will need to log in again. A simple Web.config file requiring forms authentication is shown here:

```
<configuration>
  <system.web>
    <authentication mode="Forms">
      <forms loginURL="Login.aspx" />
    </authentication>
    <authorization>
      <deny users="?" />
    </authentication>
  </system.web>
</configuration>
```

In the preceding example, all users who have not yet signed in are redirected to the Login.aspx page when they attempt to access any ASP.NET file. Typically, the form prompts the user for a user name and password and handles authentication within the application itself.

Regardless of the way the application handles the user's input, the user's credentials are sent to the server as a *Hypertext Transfer Protocol (HTTP)* request—without any automatic encryption. HTTP is the protocol Web browsers and Web servers use to communicate. The best way to ensure privacy of user credentials submitted by using forms authentication is to configure a Secure Sockets Layer (SSL) certificate within IIS and require *Hypertext Transfer Protocol Secure (HTTPS)* for the login form. HTTPS is an encrypted form of HTTP, which is used by virtually every e-commerce Web site on the Internet to protect private information about end users and to protect end users from submitting private information to a rogue server impersonating another server.

The user name and password can be checked against a database, a list contained in the Web.config file, an Extensible Markup Language (XML) file, or any other mechanism you create. Forms authentication is tremendously flexible; however, you are entirely responsible for protecting your authentication mechanism from attackers. Because proof of authentication is stored in a cookie provided by the Web server (by default), and that cookie generally contains only the user's user name, an attacker can potentially create a fake cookie to trick the Web server into considering the user as authenticated. ASP.NET includes the ability to encrypt and validate authentication cookies, but naturally this protection includes some overhead for the Web server.

The type of encryption and validation used is controlled by the *protection* attribute of the *<authentication>* section. If the *protection* attribute is not set, it defaults to *All*. If the *protection* attribute is set to *Encryption*, the cookie is encrypted with the Triple Data Encryption Standard (3DES). This encryption protects the privacy of the data contained in the cookie but performs no validation. If the *protection* attribute is set to *Validation*, as the following example demonstrates, the server verifies the data in the cookie on each transaction to reduce the likelihood of it being modified between the time it is sent from the browser and the time it is received by the server. If the *protection* attribute is set to *None*, neither encryption nor validation is performed. This setting reduces the overhead on the server, but it is suitable only in situations in which privacy is not a concern, such as Web site personalization.

```
<authentication mode="Forms" protection="Validation" >
  <forms loginURL="Login.aspx" />
</authentication>
```

> ***IMPORTANT*** **OPTIMIZING SECURITY FOR FORMS AUTHENTICATION**
>
> **For optimal security (with a slight performance cost), leave protection at the default setting of All.**

By default, ASP.NET stores the authentication token in a cookie for most devices. However, if the browser does not support cookies, ASP.NET will store the authentication information as part of the URL. You can control this behavior by setting the *cookieless* attribute of the *<forms>* element to one of the following settings:

- ***UseCookies*** This setting always attempts to send a cookie to the client, even if the client indicates it cannot support cookies.

- ***UseUri*** This setting always stores the authentication token as part of the URL rather than a cookie. Technically, the token is stored in the Uniform Resource Identifier (URI), which is the last portion of the URL.
- ***AutoDetect*** If a browser indicates that it supports cookies, the *AutoDetect* setting causes ASP.NET to test whether the browser actually does support cookies. If it does not, or if the browser indicates that it does not support cookies, ASP.NET uses cookieless authentication instead.
- ***UseDeviceProfile*** The default setting, *UseDeviceProfile*, uses a cookie to prove authentication if the browser profile indicates that it supports cookies. You might find that some users have changed the default setting to not allow cookies. In this case, forms authentication does not work properly unless you change the *cookieless* setting to *AutoDetect*.

For example, the following section of a Web.config file enables cookieless forms authentication for all clients. This works well, but it causes the authentication token to be included in bookmarks and whenever the user sends a URL to another user:

```
<authentication mode="Forms" >
  <forms Cookieless="UseUri" loginURL="Login.aspx" />
</authentication>
```

Another important attribute of the *<forms>* section is *timeout,* which defines, in minutes, the amount of idle time allowed between requests before the user is forced to log in again. If the *<forms>* section is *<forms loginUrl="YourLogin.aspx" timeout="10">,* the user is forced to log in again if he or she does not send any requests to the ASP.NET application within 10 minutes. This number should be decreased to reduce the risk of the browser being misused while the user is away from the computer. The *<forms>* section has other attributes, but *LoginUrl, protection,* and *timeout* are the most important.

Quick Check

1. **By default, under what circumstances does forms authentication provide cookies to the browser?**
2. **If you have users who have disabled cookies in their browsers, what can you do to enable them to use forms authentication?**

Quick Check Answers

1. **By default, cookies are provided to browser types that support cookies, whether or not the browser has cookies enabled.**
2. **Use the *AutoDetect* setting of the *cookieless* attribute.**

Configuring User Accounts in the Web.Config File

To avoid creating a database to store user credentials, you can store the user credentials directly in the Web.config file. The passwords can be stored in one of three formats: clear text, encrypted with the Message-Digest 5 (MD5) one-way *hash algorithm,* or encrypted with the Secure Hash Algorithm 1 (SHA1) one-way hash algorithm. Using one of the two hash algorithms to mask the user credentials reduces the likelihood that a malicious user with read access to the Web.config file will gather another user's login information. Define the hashing method used within the *<forms>* section in the *<credentials>* section. An example is shown here:

```
<authentication mode="Forms">
  <forms loginUrl="login.aspx" protection="Encryption" timeout="30" >
    <credentials passwordFormat="SHA1" >
      <user name="Eric" password="07B7F3EE06F278DB966BE960E7CBBD103DF30CA6"/>
      <user name="Sam" password="5753A498F025464D72E088A9D5D6E872592D5F91"/>
    </credentials>
  </forms>
</authentication>
```

To enable administrators to use hashed password information in the Web.config file, your ASP.NET application must include a page or tool to generate these passwords. The passwords are stored in hexadecimal format and hashed with the specified hashing protocol. You can use the *System.Security.Cryptography* namespace to generate such a hash. The following console application demonstrates this by accepting a password as a command-line parameter and displaying the hash of the password. The resulting hash can be pasted directly into the Web.config file.

```
'VB
Imports System.Security.Cryptography
Imports System.Text

Module Module1
  Sub Main(ByVal args As String())
    Dim myHash As SHA1CryptoServiceProvider = New SHA1CryptoServiceProvider
    Dim password As Byte() = Encoding.ASCII.GetBytes(args(0))
    myHash.ComputeHash(password)
    For Each thisByte As Byte In myHash.Hash
      Console.Write(thisByte.ToString("X2"))
    Next
    Console.WriteLine()
  End Sub
End Module

//C#
using System;
```

```
using System.Security.Cryptography;
using System.Text;

namespace HashExample
{
  class Program
  {
    static void Main(string[] args)
    {
      SHA1CryptoServiceProvider myHash=new SHA1CryptoServiceProvider();

      byte[] password  = Encoding.ASCII.GetBytes(args[0]);
      myHash.ComputeHash(password);

      foreach (byte thisByte in myHash.Hash)
        Console.Write(thisByte.ToString("X2"));
      Console.WriteLine();
    }
  }
}
```

Alternatively, you can call the *FormsAuthentication.HashPasswordForStoringInConfigFile* method to generate a password hash. This method is described in the next section.

> ***IMPORTANT*** **STORING CREDENTIALS IN A WEB.CONFIG FILE**
>
> **You should store credentials in a Web.config file only during testing. Protecting passwords with a hash is not much deterrent to an attacker who can read the contents of the Web.config file because hashed password databases exist that can quickly identify common passwords.**

The *FormsAuthentication* Class

The *FormsAuthentication* class is the basis for all forms authentication in ASP.NET. The class includes the following read-only properties, which you can use to programmatically examine the current configuration:

- ***FormsCookieName*** This property returns the configured cookie name used for the current application.
- ***FormsCookiePath*** This property returns the configured cookie path used for the current application.
- ***RequireSSL*** This property gets a value indicating whether the cookie must be transmitted using SSL (that is, over HTTPS only).

IMPORTANT IMPROVING SECURITY IF THE WEB SERVER HAS AN SSL CERTIFICATE

Enable *RequireSSL* for best security. This will ensure that forms authentication is encrypted.

- ***SlidingExpiration*** This property gets a value indicating whether sliding expiration is enabled. Enabling sliding expiration resets the user's authentication timeout with every Web request.

IMPORTANT IMPROVING SECURITY (AT THE COST OF CONVENIENCE)

Disable *SlidingExpiration* for the highest level of security. This prevents a session from remaining open indefinitely.

Additionally, you can call the following methods:

- ***Authenticate*** This method attempts to validate the given credentials against those contained in the configured credential store.
- ***Decrypt*** This method returns an instance of a *FormsAuthenticationTicket* class, given a valid encrypted authentication ticket obtained from an HTTP cookie.
- ***Encrypt*** This method produces a string containing an encrypted authentication ticket suitable for use in an HTTP cookie, given a *FormsAuthenticationTicket* object.
- ***GetAuthCookie*** This method creates an authentication cookie for a given user name.
- ***GetRedirectUrl*** This method returns the redirect URL for the original request that caused the redirect to the login page.
- ***HashPasswordForStoringInConfigFile*** Given a password and a string identifying the hash type, this routine produces a hash password suitable for storing in a configuration file. If your application stores user credentials in the Web.config file and hashes the password, build this method into a management tool to enable administrators to add users and reset passwords.
- ***RedirectFromLoginPage*** This method redirects an authenticated user back to the originally requested URL. Call this method after verifying a user's credentials with the *Authenticate* method. You must pass this method a string and a Boolean value. The string should uniquely identify the user, and the method uses the string to generate a cookie. The Boolean value, if true, allows the browser to use the same cookie across multiple browser sessions. Generally, this unique piece of information should be the user's user name.
- ***RenewTicketIfOld*** This method conditionally updates the sliding expiration on a *FormsAuthenticationTicket* object.

- ***SetAuthCookie*** This method creates an authentication ticket and attaches it to the cookie's collection of the outgoing response. It does not perform a redirect.
- ***SignOut*** This method removes the authentication ticket, essentially logging the user off.

Creating a Custom Forms Authentication Page

When using forms authentication, you must include two sections at a minimum:

- A forms authentication page
- A method for users to log off and close their current sessions

To create a forms authentication page, create an ASP.NET Web form to prompt the user for credentials and call members of the *System.Web.Security.FormsAuthentication* class to authenticate the user and redirect him or her to a protected page. The following code sample demonstrates an overly simple authentication mechanism that just verifies that the contents of *usernameTextBox* and *passwordTextBox* are the same, and then calls the *RedirectFromLoginPage* method to redirect the user to the page originally requested. Notice that the Boolean value passed to *RedirectFromLoginPage* is *true*, indicating that the browser saves the cookie after the browser is closed, enabling the user to remain authenticated if the user closes and reopens his or her browser before the authentication cookie expires.

```
'VB
If usernameTextBox.Text = passwordTextBox.Text Then
  FormsAuthentication.RedirectFromLoginPage(usernameTextBox.Text, True)
End If

//C#
if (usernameTextBox.Text == passwordTextBox.Text)
  FormsAuthentication.RedirectFromLoginPage(usernameTextBox.Text, true);
```

Although the authentication mechanism demonstrated in the previous code sample (verifying that the user name and password are equal) can never provide adequate protection for a Web application, it demonstrates the flexibility of forms authentication. You can check the user's credentials using any mechanism required by your application. Most often, the user name and a hash of the user's password is looked up in a database.

If user credentials are stored in the Web.config file, or you have configured them using ASP.NET membership, call the *FormsAuthentication.Authenticate* method to check the credentials. Simply pass to the method the user's user name and password. The method returns *true* if the user's credentials match a value in the Web.config file. Otherwise, it returns *false*. The following code sample demonstrates the use of this method to redirect an authenticated user. Notice that the Boolean value passed to *RedirectFromLoginPage* is *false*, indicating that the browser does not save the cookie after the browser is closed, requiring the user to reauthenticate if he or she closes and reopens the browser, thus improving security.

```
'VB
If FormsAuthentication.Authenticate(username.Text, password.Text) Then
  'user is authenticated. Redirect user to the page requested.
  FormsAuthentication.RedirectFromLoginPage(usernameTextBox.Text, False)
End If

//C#
if (FormsAuthentication.Authenticate(username.Text,
password.Text))
{
  //user is authenticated. Redirect user to the page requested.
  FormsAuthentication.RedirectFromLoginPage(usernameTextBox.Text, false);
}
```

In addition to creating a page to authenticate users, provide a method for users to log off of the application. Generally, this is a simple Log Out hyperlink that calls the *FormsAuthentication.SignOut* static method to remove the user's authentication cookie.

Configuring Web Applications to Require Passport Authentication

You can also authenticate users using a service from Microsoft called Passport. Passport is a centralized directory of user information that Web sites can use, in exchange for a fee, to authenticate users. Users can choose to allow the Web site access to personal information stored on Passport, such as their addresses, ages, and interests. Storing information about users worldwide within the Passport service relieves end users from maintaining separate user names and passwords on different sites. Further, it saves the user time by eliminating the need to provide personal information to multiple Web sites.

> ***MORE INFO*** **PASSPORT SOFTWARE DEVELOPMENT KIT**
>
> **For more detailed information about the requirements for building a Web application that uses Passport, you can download and review the free Microsoft .NET Passport Software Development Kit from *http://support.microsoft.com/?kbid=816418*.**

Configuring Web Applications for Anonymous Access Only

You can explicitly disable authentication for your application if you know that it will be used only by anonymous users. However, in most cases where your application does not require authentication, you should simply not provide an authentication configuration setting in the Web.config file and allow the system administrator to configure authentication with IIS.

This example shows a simple Web.config file that allows only anonymous access to an ASP.NET application:

```
<configuration>
  <system.web>
    <authentication mode="None" />
  </system.web>
</configuration>
```

Configuring Impersonation by Using .config Files

By default, ASP.NET applications make all requests for system resources from the ASPNET account (IIS 5.0) or the Network Service account (IIS 6.0 and later). This setting is configurable and is defined in the *<processModel>* item of the *<system.web>* section of the Machine.config file. The default setting for this section is:

```
<processModel autoConfig="true" />
```

Setting *autoConfig* to *true* causes ASP.NET to automatically handle *impersonation*. However, you can change *autoConfig* to *false* and set the *userName* and *password* attribute to define the account ASP.NET impersonates when requesting system resources on behalf of a Web user.

Automatic configuration is sufficient for most ASP.NET implementations. However, in many cases, administrators need to configure ASP.NET to impersonate the client's authenticated user account, IIS's anonymous user account, or a specific user account. This configuration is done by setting the *impersonate* attribute of the *<identity>* element of the Machine.config (for server-wide settings) or Web.config (for application- or directory-specific settings) files. To enable impersonation of the client's authenticated Windows account, or the IIS IUSR_*MachineName* account for anonymous access, add the following line to the *<system.web>* section of the Web.config file:

```
<identity impersonate="true" />
```

When IIS is configured for anonymous access, ASP.NET makes requests for system resources using the IUSR_*MachineName* account. When a user authenticates directly to IIS using a Windows logon, ASP.NET impersonates that user account. To enable ASP.NET to impersonate a specific user account, regardless of how IIS authentication is handled, add the following line to the *<system.web>* section of the Web.config file and replace the *DOMAIN*, *UserName*, and *Password* placeholders with the account logon credentials:

```
<identity impersonate="true" userName="DOMAIN\UserName" password="Password"/>
```

Restricting Access to ASP.NET Web Applications, Files, and Folders

Authentication determines a user's identity, whereas authorization defines what the user might access. Before the .NET Framework, administrators controlled Web user authorization entirely with NTFS permissions. Although NTFS permissions are still a key part of configuring security for ASP.NET applications, these permissions are now complemented by ASP.NET's authorization capabilities. Authorization is now controlled with Web.config files, just like authentication. This enables authorization to work with any type of authentication—even if the authorization doesn't use the local user database or Active Directory directory service on which NTFS permissions are based. The use of Web.config files also makes copying file permissions between multiple Web servers as easy as copying files.

In the sections that follow, you will learn how to restrict access according to user and group names, how to restrict access to specific files and folders using either a .config file or file permissions, and how to use impersonation in an ASP.NET application.

Restricting Access to Users and Groups

The default Machine.config file contains the following authorization information:

```
<authorization>
  <allow users="*"/>
</authorization>
```

Unless you modify this section of the Machine.config file, or override the Machine.config file by adding this section to your application's Web.config file, all users permitted by your authentication configuration are allowed to interact with all parts of your ASP.NET Web application. The *<allow users="*">* subsection of the *<authorization>* section tells ASP.NET that all users who pass the authentication requirements are allowed access to all ASP.NET content.

To configure an ASP.NET application to provide access only to the users Eric and Sam, override the Machine.config security settings by editing the Web.config file in the root of the ASP.NET application and add the following lines within the *<system.web>* section:

```
<authorization>
  <allow users="Eric, Sam"/>
  <deny users="*"/>
</authorization>
```

The *<allow>* and *<deny>* subsections contain *users* and *roles* attributes. The *users* attribute should be set to a list of user names separated by commas, an asterisk (*) to indicate all authenticated or unauthenticated users, or a question mark (?) to indicate anonymous users. If Windows authentication is used, the user names should match names in the local user database or Active Directory service and need to include a domain name (that is, *DOMAIN\user* for domain accounts or *COMPUTERNAME\user* for local user accounts).

The *roles* element contains a comma-separated list of roles. When Windows authentication is used, roles correspond to Windows user groups. In this case, the names must exactly match group names in the local user database or Active Directory. Provide the domain name for groups in the Active Directory, but do not specify the computer name for local groups. For example, to specify the IT group in the CONTOSO domain, use **CONTOSO\IT**. To specify the local users group, use **Users**.

If you are using Windows authentication, you must disable the *roleManager* element in your Web.config file to use role security to authorize Windows user groups. The *roleManager* element is disabled by default, so removing it from your Web.config file is sufficient to disable it. You can authorize Windows users with *roleManager* enabled, but it must be disabled to authorize Windows groups.

Controlling Authorization for Folders and Files by Using .config Files

The previous techniques are useful for controlling user access to an entire ASP.NET application. To restrict access to specific files or folders, add a *<location>* section to the *<configuration>* section of the Web.config file. The *<location>* section contains its own *<system.web>* subsection, so do not place it within an existing *<system.web>* section.

To configure access restrictions for a specific file or folder, add the *<location>* section to your Web.config file with a single *path* section. The *path* section must be set to the relative path of a file or folder; absolute paths are not allowed. Within the *<location>* section, include a *<system.web>* subsection and any configuration information that is unique to the specified file or folder. For example, to require forms authentication for the file ListUsers.aspx and restrict access to the user named admin, add the following text to the *<configuration>* section of the Web.config file:

```
<location path="ListUsers.aspx">
  <system.web>
    <authentication mode="forms">
      <forms loginUrl="AdminLogin.aspx" protection="All"/>
    </authentication>
    <authorization>
      <allow users="admin"/>
      <deny users="*"/>
    </authorization>
  </system.web>
</location>
```

When using multiple *<location>* sections, files and subfolders automatically inherit all settings from their parents. Therefore, you do not need to repeat settings that are identical to the parents' configurations. When configuring authorization, inheritance has the potential to lead to security vulnerabilities. Consider the following Web.config file:

```
<configuration>
  <system.web>
  <authentication mode="Windows" />
  <authorization>
    <deny users="?" />
  </authorization>
  </system.web>

  <location path="Protected">
```

```
  <system.web>
    <authorization>
    <allow roles="CONTOSO\IT" />
    </authorization>
  </system.web>
  </location>
</configuration>
```

In this example, there are actually *three* layers of inheritance. The first is the Machine .config file, which specifies the default *<allow users="*"/>*. The second layer is the first *<system.web>* section in the example, which applies to the entire application. This setting, *<deny users="?"/>*, denies access to all unauthenticated users. By itself, this second layer denies access to any user. However, combined with the Machine.config file, this layer allows access to all authenticated users and denies access to everyone else.

The third layer is the *<location>* section, which grants access to the CONTOSO\IT group. However, this section also inherits the *<deny users="?"/>* and *<allow users="*"/>* settings. Therefore, the effective settings for the Protected subfolder are the same as for the parent folder: All authenticated users have access. To restrict access to *only* users in the CONTOSO\IT group, you must explicitly deny access to users who are not specifically granted access, as the following code demonstrates:

```
<location path="Protected">
  <system.web>
  <authorization>
    <allow roles="CONTOSO\IT" />
    <deny users="*" />
  </authorization>
  </system.web>
</location>
```

> ***NOTE*** **USING FILE PERMISSIONS**
>
> **You can also control access to files and folders by setting NTFS file permissions. However, file permissions are typically managed by system administrators. Additionally, because file permissions cannot be distributed as easily as a Web.config file and they can only be used with Windows security, they should not be relied on as the primary method of file authorization for developers.**

LAB Controlling Authorization in ASP.NET Applications

In this lab, you modify an ASP.NET Web application to use Windows authentication.

If you encounter a problem completing an exercise, the completed projects are available in the sample files installed from the companion CD in the Code folder.

EXERCISE 1 **Create a Web Site That Uses ASP.NET Memberships**

In this exercise, you update a previously created ASP.NET Web site to disable role manager and use Windows authentication instead.

1. Continue working with the Web site you created in Lesson 2, Exercise 2, which has been configured to support ASP.NET membership and has users and roles added to the database. Alternatively, you can open the completed Lesson 2, Exercise 2 project in the samples installed from the CD.
2. From the Website menu, select ASP.NET Configuration.
3. Click the Security tab. In the Users section, click the Select Authentication Type link.

   On the next page, select the From A Local Network option. Click Done.
4. In Visual Studio, examine the Web.config file in the Web site root. Notice that the *authentication* element has been removed, which means forms authentication is no longer enabled. Now remove the *<roleManager>* element so that the *roles* element refers to Windows groups instead of the roles you added using Role Manager.
5. In Visual Studio, add a *LoginName* control to the root Default.aspx page. This enables you to see the user account you are using to access the Web site.
6. Run the site and visit the Default.aspx page. Notice that the *LoginName* control shows that you are automatically logged in using your Windows user account.
7. Click the Members Only link. If your current account is a member of the local Users group, you are allowed to access the page. Otherwise, ASP.NET denies you access.
8. Click the Administrators Only link. If your current account is a member of the local Administrators group, you are allowed to access the page. Otherwise, ASP.NET denies you access.

   Note that in Windows Vista, if you are running the page from Visual Studio, you must also be running Visual Studio as an Administrator.
9. From the Website menu of Visual Studio, select ASP.NET Configuration. Click the Security tab. Notice that you can no longer use the Web Site Administration Tool to manage roles. When Role Manager is disabled, ASP.NET uses Windows groups as roles. Therefore, you must manage the groups using tools built into Windows, such as the Computer Management console.
10. On the Security tab of the Web Site Administration Tool, click Manage Access Rules. Then, select the Admin subfolder. Notice that it displays the existing rules. Click Add New Access Rule and notice that you can add a rule for specific users, all users, or anonymous users. You cannot, however, add rules to grant access to roles, because Role Manager has been disabled. To add access rules for Windows Groups using roles, you must manually edit the *<authorization>* section of the Web.config files.

This exercise worked because the role names you created in Lesson 2 are exactly the same as the default group names in the local Windows user database. Typically, you would not use the ASP.NET Web Site Administration Tool to create access rules. Instead, you would manually edit the Web.config files, as described earlier in this lesson.

Lesson Summary

- You can configure an application to require Windows credentials from a user by either configuring IIS, configuring the Web.config file, or both.
- To create custom ASP.NET forms for user authentication, first configure your Web.config file to specify the authentication form. Then, create an ASP.NET Web form to prompt the user for credentials and write code to verify the credentials and authenticate the user. You should also provide a way for users to log off.
- ASP.NET Web applications support Passport, which uses a centralized authentication service provided by Microsoft for a fee.
- If an application does not require authentication, you can explicitly configure it for anonymous access.
- By default, ASP.NET accesses resources using ASP.NET credentials. If you need to access resources from the user's account or from a specific user account, you can use impersonation, either from within your code or by configuring the Web.config file.
- To control which users can access folders and files in a Web application, you can use either NTFS file permissions or Web.config files.

Lesson Review

You can use the following questions to test your knowledge of the information in Lesson 3, "Securing Your Site." The questions are also available on the companion CD if you prefer to review them in electronic form.

> ***NOTE* ANSWERS**
>
> **Answers to these questions and explanations of why each answer choice is right or wrong are located in the "Answers" section at the end of the book.**

1. Which of the following Web.config segments correctly requires that all users be authenticated using a Windows user account?

   A.
   ```
   <authentication mode="Windows" />
   <authorization>
       <deny users="*" />
   </authorization>
   ```

   B.
   ```
   <authentication mode="Windows" />
   <authorization>
       <allow users="*" />
   </authorization>
   ```

C.
```
<authentication mode="Windows" />
<authorization>
    <deny users="?" />
</authorization>
```

D.
```
<authentication mode="Windows" />
<authorization>
    <allow users="*" />
</authorization>
```

2. By default, how does ASP.NET track which users have successfully authenticated using forms authentication?

   A. It provides an authentication token in the form of a cookie.

   B. It provides an authentication token in the URI.

   C. It provides an authentication token in the form of a cookie if the client's browser proves that it can store and return a cookie. Otherwise, it stores the authentication token in the URI.

   D. It provides an authentication token in the form of a cookie if the client's browser type supports cookies. Otherwise, it stores the authentication token in the URI.

3. Given the following Web.config file, what permissions do users have to the Marketing folder?

```
<configuration>
  <system.web>
    <authentication mode="Windows" />
    <authorization>
      <deny users="?" />
    </authorization>
  </system.web>

  <location path="Marketing">
    <system.web>
      <authorization>
        <allow roles="FABRIKAM\Marketing" />
        <deny users="*" />
      </authorization>
    </system.web>
  </location>
</configuration>
```

   A. Authenticated users and members of the FABRIKAM\Marketing group have access. All other users are denied access.

   B. Members of the FABRIKAM\Marketing group have access. All other users are denied access.

C. All users, authenticated and unauthenticated, have access.

D. All users are denied access.

4. You are configuring NTFS file permissions for a Web application with the following Web.config file:

```
<configuration>
  <system.web>
    <authentication mode="Windows" />
    <authorization>
      <deny users="?" />
    </authorization>
  </system.web>

  <location path="Marketing">
    <system.web>
      <authorization>
        <allow roles="FABRIKAM\Marketing" />
        <deny users="*" />
      </authorization>
    </system.web>
  </location>
</configuration>
```

For the Marketing folder, you remove all file permissions, and then grant read access to the FABRIKAM\John and FABRIKAM\Sam user accounts. John is a member of the FABRIKAM\Domain Users and FABRIKAM\Marketing groups. Sam is only a member of the FABRIKAM\Domain Users group. Which of the following users can access Web forms located in the Marketing folder?

A. Unauthenticated users

B. Authenticated users

C. Members of the FABRIKAM\Domain Users group

D. FABRIKAM\John

E. FABRIKAM\Sam

Chapter Review

To further practice and reinforce the skills you learned in this chapter, you can perform the following tasks:

- Review the chapter summary.
- Complete the case scenarios. These scenarios set up real-world situations involving the topics of this chapter and ask you to create solutions.
- Complete the suggested practices.
- Take a practice test.

Chapter Summary

- Many Web sites identify individual users to personalize the Web sites, to enable users to view account information such as past orders, or to provide unique identities to individual users for communicating on a forum. ASP.NET provides membership capabilities to enable you to identify users with a user name and password without writing any code. Once you've added membership capabilities to your site, you can use a wide variety of controls in your ASP.NET Web pages to enable users to create accounts, reset their passwords, log on, and log off.
- Authentication verifies a user's identity, and can grant the user access to protected areas of your Web site. ASP.NET provides several different authentication mechanisms to meet different requirements:
  - Windows authentication enables you to identify users without creating a custom page. Credentials are stored in the Web server's local user database or an Active Directory domain. Once identified, you can use the user's credentials to gain access to resources that are protected by Windows authorization.
  - Forms authentication enables you to identify users with a custom database, such as an ASP.NET membership database. Alternatively, you can implement your own custom database. Once authenticated, you can reference the roles the user is in to restrict access to portions of your Web site.
  - Passport authentication relies on a centralized service provided by Microsoft. Passport authentication identifies a user using his or her e-mail address and a password, and a single Passport account can be used with many different Web sites. Passport authentication is primarily used for public Web sites with thousands of users.
  - Anonymous authentication does not require the user to provide credentials.

Case Scenarios

In the following case scenarios, you apply what you've learned about how to authenticate users and control access using authorization. You can find answers to these questions in the "Answers" section at the end of this book.

Case Scenario 1: Configuring Web Application Authorization

You are a developer for Southridge Video, a business that creates instructional videos. The business is deploying a new ASP.NET intranet application, and the administrators need some help configuring the security. The Web application has several subfolders, and each subfolder is managed by a different organization within Southridge. You meet with each of the managers and review the technical requirements to determine how you should configure security for each organization's subfolder.

INTERVIEWS

Following is a list of company personnel interviewed and their statements:

- **Wendy Richardson, IT Manager** My Web experts have created an ASP.NET intranet application in the /Southridge/ virtual folder of our Web server's default Web site. The application should be accessible only to users who have valid accounts in the SOUTHRIDGE Active Directory domain. Several of the internal groups have their own subfolders in the application, including IT. Check with each of the managers to determine how he or she wants security configured. For the IT subfolder, I just want members of the IT group in the SOUTHRIDGE domain to be able to access it.
- **Arif Rizaldy, Systems Administrator** Hey, I hear you're configuring a new Web application. Can you do me a favor and put all the configuration in a single Web.config file? I had to troubleshoot a security problem the other day and spent hours trying to figure out what it was because I forgot that there might be a Web.config file in any of the folders. One Web.config file is just easier for me to manage.
- **Anders Riis, Production Manager** For now, I'd like our Production subfolder to be accessible to members of the Production group. Oh, also, give Thomas access to it. Thomas is the Sales Manager. I don't know what his user account name is.
- **Catherine Boeger, Customer Service Manager** Anyone who is an employee should be able to open the CustServ folder.
- **Thomas Jensen, Sales Manager** For now, only I should have access to the Sales folder. I'll probably change this later, but there's confidential information in there now. My user account is TJensen. Sometimes I have to enter it as Southridge-backslash-TJensen.

TECHNICAL REQUIREMENTS

Create a single Web.config file for the application that configures permissions for each of the subfolders according to the requirements outlined in Table 14-1. Require Windows authentication for every file in the application.

TABLE 14-1 Application Authorization Requirements for Southridge Video

FOLDER	AUTHORIZED USERS
/Southridge/	All authenticated users
/Southridge/IT/	All members of the SOUTHRIDGE\IT group
/Southridge/Production/	All members of the SOUTHRIDGE\Production group plus the SOUTHRIDGE\TJensen user account
/Southridge/CustServ/	All authenticated users
/Southridge/Sales/	Only the SOUTHRIDGE\TJensen user account

QUESTIONS

Configure security for Southridge Video, and then answer the following questions.

1. What does the Web.config file that you created look like?
2. Besides creating a Web.config file, how can you further protect the folders?

Case Scenario 2: Configuring Web Application Authentication

You are a developer for Northwind Traders. Your manager has asked you to create a simple ASP.NET Web page to display the contents of a text file. The text files are generated by a legacy system to report on various aspects of your company's financial status, so they are protected using NTFS file permissions. The IT Manager, Nino Olivotto, describes the problem:

"The financial people want to be able to view these text reports from our intranet, so it would be nice if you could create an ASP.NET Web form to allow that. Here's the catch, though. I don't want to change the permissions on the file so that just anyone can read it. The Web server doesn't have the file permissions to access the files by default, and I don't want it to. Instead, I'd like to have the user provide Windows credentials, and have your application use those credentials to show the file. Oh—and name the project ShowReport. You can place it in the C:\Inetpub\Wwwroot\ShowReport\ folder."

You review the company's technical requirements before creating the ASP.NET Web application.

TECHNICAL REQUIREMENTS

Create an ASP.NET Web application in the C:\Inetpub\Wwwroot\ShowReport\ folder using either C# or Visual Basic .NET. Create several text files in the ShowReport folder, remove all default NTFS permissions, and then add permissions so that only specific users can access the files. Use impersonation to take advantage of the user's Windows credentials to display the contents of the files.

QUESTIONS

Create the ASP.NET Web application and then answer the following questions to explain to the IT manager how you created the application and why you did what you did.

1. What authentication method did you use? Why?
2. How did you implement impersonation? Why?
3. What XML code did you add to the Web.config file?
4. What code did you write to display the text files?

Suggested Practices

To successfully master the exam objectives presented in this chapter, complete the following tasks.

Establish a User's Identity by Using Forms Authentication

For this task, you should complete at least Practices 1 and 3 to get a solid understanding of how forms authentication behaves. If you want a better understanding of how to implement custom user databases, complete Practice 2 as well.

- **Practice 1** Create an ASP.NET Web application and implement custom forms authentication. For simplicity, store user names and passwords in a collection. Use the Web.config files to restrict access to specific files and folders and verify that the authorization features work properly.
- **Practice 2** Extend the Web application you created in the previous practice to store user credentials in a database. Store the passwords using hashes so that they are less vulnerable to attack.
- **Practice 3** Use a browser that supports cookies to visit an ASP.NET Web site you created that uses forms authentication. Then, disable cookies in the browser and attempt to visit the site. Change the *cookieless* attribute of the *<forms>* element to *AutoDetect* and test the Web site again.

Use Authorization to Establish the Rights of an Authenticated User

For this task, you should complete all three practices to gain experience using authorization to protect portions of a Web application.

- **Practice 1** Create a custom Web form that provides common user management features, such as displaying a list of users, allowing you to delete users, and adding users to roles.
- **Practice 2** Using the Web application you created in Lessons 2 and 3, delete the Web .config files in the Admin and Members folders. Then, use *<location>* elements in the root Web.config file to configure identical access rules in a single file.
- **Practice 3** Create an ASP.NET Web application that uses Windows authentication. Then, create several different groups and user accounts on the Web server. Experiment with NTFS file permissions and Web.config access rules to determine how ASP.NET behaves when one or both denies access to a user.

Implement Microsoft Windows Authentication and Impersonation

For this task, you should complete both practices to gain an understanding of how ASP.NET uses Windows authentication and impersonation.

- **Practice 1** Create an ASP.NET Web application that uses Windows authentication. Then, create several different groups and user accounts on the Web server. Write code that examines the user's account and displays the user name and whether the user is a member of built-in groups such as Users and Administrators.
- **Practice 2** Enable object access auditing on your development computer (or a development Web server) as described in the Microsoft Knowledge Base article at *http://support.microsoft.com/?kbid=310399*. Create a folder on your computer and add a text file to it. Then, enable success and failure auditing on the folder. Using the Web application you created in the previous practice, write code to read the text file and display it on a Web page. Note whether the code succeeds or fails. Then, view the Security event log to examine the auditing events and identify which user account ASP.NET used to access the file. Next, enable impersonation in your Web application and repeat the process to determine whether the user account changed.

Use Login Controls to Control Access to a Web Application

For this task, you should complete at least Practices 1 and 2. If you want experience with sending e-mail messages to new users, complete Practice 3 as well.

- **Practice 1** Using the ASP.NET Web application you created in the labs for Lessons 2 and 3, create a template to modify the colors and fonts used by the controls.

- **Practice 2** Using the ASP.NET Web application you created in the labs for Lessons 2 and 3, modify the text displayed by each of the controls to display messages in a different language.
- **Practice 3** Respond to the *CreateUserWizard.CreatedUser* event to automatically send an e-mail to the new user welcoming him or her to your Web site.

Take a Practice Test

The practice tests on this book's companion CD offer many options. For example, you can test yourself on just the content covered in this chapter, or you can test yourself on all the 70-562 certification exam content. You can set up the test so it closely simulates the experience of taking a certification exam, or you can set it up in study mode so you can look at the correct answers and explanations after you answer each question.

> ***MORE INFO*** **PRACTICE TESTS**
>
> **For details about all the practice test options available, see the "How to Use the Practice Tests" section in this book's Introduction.**

CHAPTER 15

Creating ASP.NET Mobile Web Applications

Handheld devices, mobile phones, and computers all now include Internet browsers. The power of these devices comes from their ability to connect people to the Web from untethered locations. People are using these devices to shop, look up information, and do work. In fact, enterprises are increasingly leveraging these tools to keep their work force connected to the office when they are traveling or out of the office. This means ASP.NET developers need to be able to use their skills to create mobile versions of key enterprise applications.

This chapter presents mobile Web applications for ASP.NET developers. This includes the unique challenges of building Web applications that need to be displayed on compact screens across a vast array of devices.

Exam objectives in this chapter:

- Targeting Mobile Devices
    - Access device capabilities.
    - Control device-specific rendering.
    - Add mobile Web controls to a Web page.
    - Implement control adapters.

Lessons in this chapter:

Before You Begin

To complete the lesson in this chapter, you should be familiar with developing applications with Microsoft Visual Studio using Visual Basic or C#. In addition, you should be comfortable with all of the following:

- Working with the Visual Studio 2008 Integrated Development Environment (IDE).
- Using Hypertext Markup Language (HTML) and client-side scripting.
- Creating ASP.NET Web sites and forms.

Lesson 1: Building Mobile Applications

This lesson covers the basics of ASP.NET Mobile applications. You will learn how to use the controls built into ASP.NET, how to set up an emulator, and how to create a mobile application that can be rendered on a variety of devices.

After this lesson, you will be able to:

- Create a mobile Web application.
- Use device-specific rendering to display controls on a variety of devices.
- Use adaptive rendering to modify the appearance of Web server controls.
- Use the mobile Web controls to display content on a device.

Estimated lesson time: 60 minutes

The ASP.NET Mobile Web Application Roadmap

Since their initial release with .NET Framework 1.0, there have been multiple versions of mobile controls and varied levels of support within Visual Studio. Mobile Web controls were first introduced in ASP.NET 1.0. These controls used to be known as the Microsoft Mobile Internet Toolkit. However, they are now referred to as ASP.NET Mobile and consist of the mobile Web controls that ship with ASP.NET inside *System.Web.UI.MobileControls* and the features exposed by *System.Web.Mobile*.

Starting with ASP.NET 2.0, the mobile Web controls were updated to allow the controls to use a new adapter-based architecture. This architecture allows the controls to be adapted to different device types. This helps ensure support for different browsers on these devices. At the same time, Microsoft began creating device-specific adapter files. However, two things happened: The number of devices increased and these devices began standardizing on their browser support. Although Microsoft still has device-specific adapters, their stated direction is to move to a broader, standards-driven approach focused on markup-compliant rendering of HTML, Compact HTML (cHTML), Wireless Markup Language (WML), and Extensible Hypertext Markup Language (XHTML).

MORE INFO **ROADMAP**

You can read more about the Microsoft mobile Web story, roadmap, and FAQ by visiting *http://www.asp.net/mobile/road-map/*.

Early .NET Framework versions of Visual Studio had built-in support for mobile Web applications. There were application templates for mobile Web applications and item templates for mobile Web forms, mobile Web user controls, and more. These versions also allowed you to build mobile Web applications using a designer. This gave developers toolbox and design-time layout support. If you've used these tools in the past, you will undoubtedly notice they are missing from Visual Studio 2008. You can still create mobile Web applications with Visual Studio 2008, there are just not out-of-the-box templates for doing so. Instead, you use the standard ASP.NET templates and modify them accordingly. It is unclear why this support was dropped from the tool or if it will return. If you cannot live without these templates, see the following note.

> ***NOTE*** **CUSTOM MOBILE TEMPLATES**
>
> **The Visual Web Developer team at Microsoft has posted templates for use with Visual Studio 2008 and ASP.NET Mobile Web forms and controls. These templates make it easier to build mobile Web applications. However, there is still no designer support. You can download these templates at *http://www.asp.net/mobile/road-map/* or search for "ASP.NET Mobile Development with Visual Studio 2008."**

Creating a Mobile Web Application

A mobile Web application has a similar programming model to that of any ASP.NET Web site. You create forms, code-behind classes, style sheets, configuration files, and more. The mobile Web application also uses the same server-side architecture for connecting to databases, managing state, and caching data. You can, of course, also use the same techniques for troubleshooting and debugging a mobile Web application. The primary difference is in the classes you use to create your forms and the controls you place on a page.

Therefore, to start creating a mobile Web application, you simply create an ASP.NET Web site as you would any other. You can even mix mobile pages with nonmobile pages.

Creating Mobile Web Forms

Like standard Web forms, the mobile Web form is an .aspx page that is accessible by a Uniform Resource Locator (URL) and can optionally have a code-behind page. The difference is that a mobile Web form inherits from *System.Web.UI.MobileControls.MobilePage* instead of *System.Web.UI.Page.*

In Visual Studio 2008, you create a mobile Web form by starting with a standard Web form. You then open the code-behind file and change the inheritance to use the *MobilePage* class. The following code shows an example:

```
'VB
Partial Class Default
  Inherits System.Web.UI.MobileControls.MobilePage

End Class

//C#
public partial class Default : System.Web.UI.MobileControls.MobilePage
```

```
{
  protected void Page_Load(object sender, EventArgs e)
  {

  }
}
```

Next, you register the *MobileControls* namespace and assembly with your page. Doing so will give you IntelliSense access to the mobile controls inside Source view for your Web page. The following markup should be added to your page after the @ *Page* directive to accomplish this:

```
<%@ Register TagPrefix="mobile"
  Namespace="System.Web.UI.MobileControls"
  Assembly="System.Web.Mobile" %>
```

The last step is to replace the markup with mobile-like markup. This means adding a *<mobile:Form>* control to the *<body>* tag. The following shows an example:

```
<html xmlns="http://www.w3.org/1999/xhtml" >
<body>
    <mobile:Form id="Form1" runat="server">

    </mobile:Form>
</body>
</html>
```

At this point, you can begin adding other mobile controls to your page. However, you have to do so through markup. Visual Studio 2008 does not provide designer support for mobile forms. This is in part due to the way pages render differently on each mobile device. You therefore must mark up your form in Source view and then view it in a browser or device to see how it will look to a user.

Mobile Web forms have the same application life cycle as an ASP.NET page. Therefore, you can expect to see *Load* events, button events, and the like.

The Form Control

Unlike the standard Web form that can only contain one form declaration, the mobile Web form can contain many *<mobile:Form>* controls. The *<mobile:Form>* control is actually a group or container for other mobile controls. The *<mobile:Form>* control is of the type *MobileControls.Form.*

By default, the first *<mobile:Form>* control on the page is visible. You can switch from one *<mobile:Form>* to another by setting the *ActiveForm* property of the mobile Web form in code.

When creating a mobile form, you typically place all the forms for a user activity on a single page. Each form represents a step in the user's process. For example, you might have a single page for a user to look up travel information. You would create a form to enter the request, another to show a list of results, and another to show details of a selected item in the results. Each of these forms would typically be added to a single page and made active at the appropriate time.

You should split forms, however, when transferring the user to a different major feature of the application, when a different URL is required, or when performance of your form is suffering. It is important to know that every time a page is instantiated, all of the controls on the mobile Web form are instantiated. This might hurt performance and resource usage if you have too much on a single form. If you have too many *<mobile:Form>* controls on a mobile Web form, you can move seldom-used *<mobile:Form>* controls to a different page and redirect users accordingly.

Adding Controls

You add mobile controls to a mobile form through markup. There is no real Toolbox support. However, if you have the *MobileControls* namespace registered, you will get IntelliSense support in Source view.

There are a number of mobile controls you can add to a page. These controls output less information to the page, as mobile devices typically have slower connections. You can add many mobile controls to the *<mobile:Form>* control, but for performance reasons, the number of mobile controls should be kept to a small number of organized controls. The majority of these controls are covered in a coming section.

Controls added to a mobile Web form must all have a unique ID regardless of their form grouping. If you have two *<mobile:TextBox>* controls on a page, for example, you must give them unique ID values even if they are in different form controls. In addition, all controls in all *<mobile:Form>* controls are programmatically accessible from within the code-behind file based on their ID value (just like ASP.NET controls).

Viewing and Testing Mobile Web Applications

You can view a mobile Web form using a Web browser as you would any ASP.NET page. However, you typically create mobile Web forms because you expect them to be used on various mobile devices. This is problematic if you do not have access to all of these target devices or you wish to be able to test your code without having to always deploy it and access it from a targeted device. This is where device emulators can help.

Many of the mobile device manufacturers provide emulators that can be used to test mobile Web applications. Emulators display the mobile Web application as it would appear on the hardware device. In fact, if you are doing a lot of mobile Web development, you can set an emulator as the default browser. In this way, when you run your application, it will open the emulator to help debug the mobile application.

The OpenWave Emulator

There are multiple device emulators out there. You can find a list of some of the more common ones at *http://www.asp.net/mobile/device-simulators/*. One of the more common cell phone emulator providers is OpenWave; you can download the latest phone emulators from *http://developer.openwave.com*. Figure 15-1 shows the generic phone emulator. In addition, OpenWave also provides skins for many popular phones.

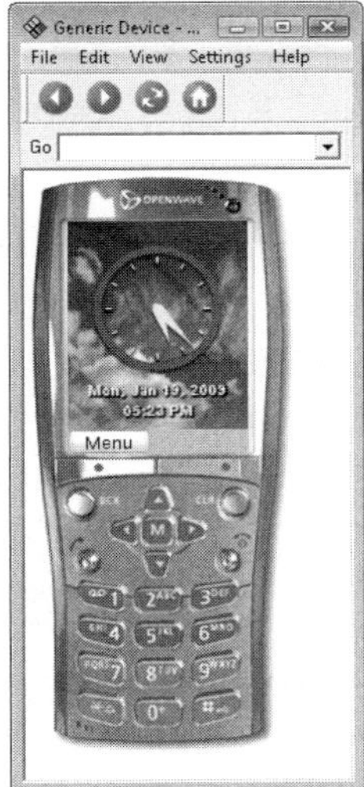

FIGURE 15-1 The OpenWave generic phone emulator (Image courtesy Openwave Systems Inc.)

When the generic phone is displayed, the Simulator Console window is also displayed, as shown in Figure 15-2. The Simulator Console window displays the raw Hypertext Transfer Protocol (HTTP) and header information, which can be helpful when attempting to diagnose problems.

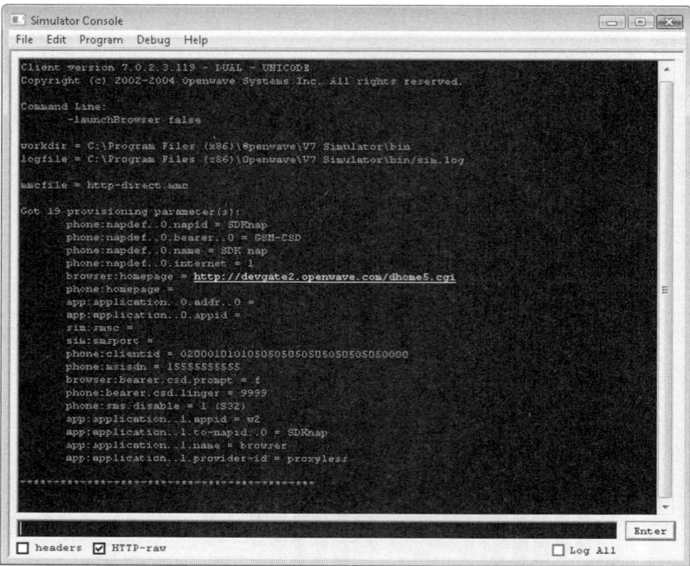

FIGURE 15-2 The OpenWave Simulator Console window (Image courtesy Openwave Systems Inc.)

The Microsoft Device Emulator

The Microsoft device emulator installs with Microsoft Visual Studio and is intended to be used primarily when testing applications developed for use with the Compact Framework (CF). However, it can also be used to test mobile Web applications as all the device simulators have a browser.

To access the emulator, in Visual Studio, from the Tools menu, select Device Emulator Manager. This launches the Device Emulator Manager, as shown in Figure 15-3. Here you can see the emulators that are installed. You can also select an emulator, right-click it, and select Connect to launch it. Figure 15-4 shows the Pocket PC Square Emulator in action.

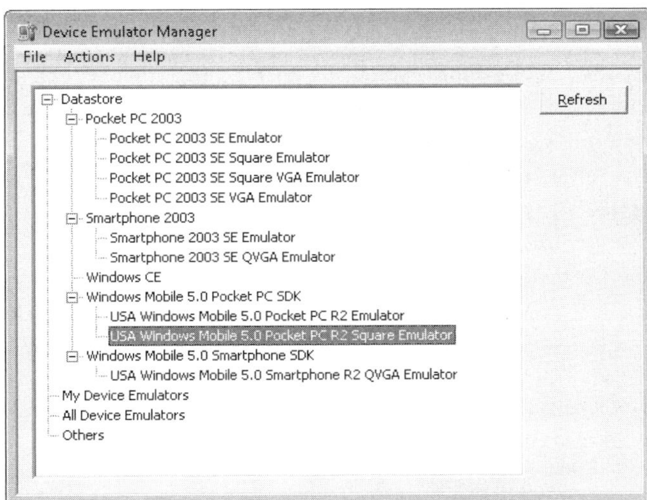

FIGURE 15-3 The Device Emulator Manager in Visual Studio

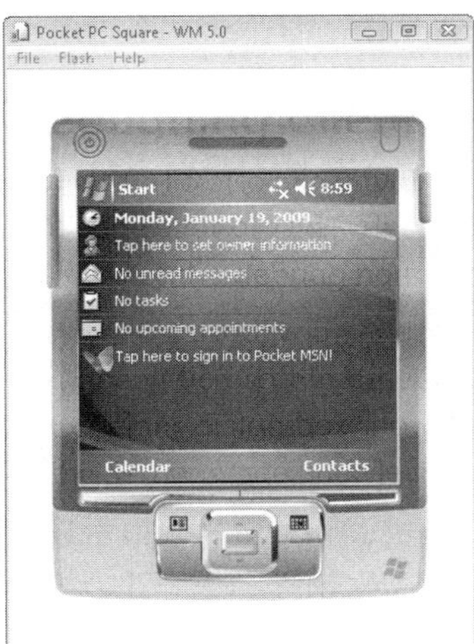

FIGURE 15-4 The Pocket PC Square emulator

> ***NOTE*** **CONNECTING TO YOUR PROJECT**
>
> Setting up a network connection through the emulator can be a small challenge. It depends on your environment and chosen emulator. However, for the most part, you need to set up either Virtual Machine Network Services (typically installed as part of Virtual PC) or Microsoft Windows Mobile Device Center (Windows Vista only), formerly known as Active Sync. Both require environment-specific steps to set up. There is a lot of help available on the Web (blogs, MSDN, newsgroups, and so on) on this topic. One such site is the Windows Mobile Developer Center at *http://msdn.microsoft.com/en-us/windowsmobile/default.aspx*.

For example, to use Microsoft Windows Mobile Device Center, you first must download and install it. You then select the Connection Settings option and enable direct memory access (DMA) under the allowed connections. You then launch the emulator. On the emulator you need to modify the connection settings (Start, Settings, Connections tab, Connections icon, Advanced tab). You then click Select Networks and set both options to My ISP. Finally, from the device's browser, you navigate to your local server by Internet Protocol (IP) address and protocol as in the following: *http://192.168.1.102:7357/WebSite1/Default.aspx*. If you do not have an IP address, you can install the Microsoft Loopback Connector and set a static IP address.

If you have an actual physical device, you can also use that from Visual Studio. You first connect the device to your computer, typically a Universal Serial Bus (USB) connection. You can then choose Connect To A Device from the Visual Studio Tool menu to connect to your actual device.

Using Mobile Controls

The mobile control set should be familiar to ASP.NET developers. There are basic controls for user input such as *Calendar*, *TextBox*, *Image*, *Label*, *Command* (button-like behavior), and *List*. There are also a set of validation controls that work in a manner similar to those used by regular Web forms.

In addition to control familiarity, developers should expect a similar event model. The mobile controls each provide *Init*, *Load*, *Prerender*, and *Unload* events. There are also control-specific events such as *OnClick* for *Command*. You intercept these events in your code-behind file for any server-side event. The data-binding techniques are similar, too.

You should adhere to the following guidelines when working with mobile controls:

- Always place mobile controls inside a *<mobile:Form>* control.
- Do not add standard Web server controls or HTML server controls anywhere on a mobile page other than in an HTML template.
- Follow the cardinality and containment rules for each control. You can find these rules in the help function for each control. Be careful not to add a control when its cardinality rules dictate that the number of controls has reached the maximum.

All controls have a *BreakAfter* property that is set to *true* by default. This means that all controls default to having one control per line; that is, they have a linear layout behavior. The linear behavior is typically desirable, as many devices are capable of displaying only a single control on a line.

The following sections describe many of the mobile controls that are included in ASP.NET.

Label Control

The *Label* control can be used to display a string to the user that cannot be edited by the user. You use a *Label* control when you need access to the control from code at run time. In addition, the *Label* control has properties for various styles as well as *Alignment* and *Wrapping* properties.

When working with long strings, it is preferable to use the *TextView* control, because the *Label* control might not render as nicely.

TextBox Control

The *TextBox* control provides the user the ability to input a string. The *TextBox* control contains several style settings to allow customization of the *TextBox* view. This includes a *Size* property to limit the width of the *TextBox* to the number of characters to which *Size* is set. The *TextBox* also contains a *MaxLength* property that limits the number of characters that can be entered into the *TextBox*.

You can restrict entry in the *TextBox* control, too. For example, the *TextBox* can be configured to only accept numeric input by setting the *Numeric* property to *true*. The *TextBox* can also be used to enter passwords by setting the *Password* property to *true*.

TextView Control

The *TextView* control provides the ability to display many lines of text. This control allows the use of some HTML formatting tags to control the output, such as *a* (hyperlink), *b* (bold), *br* (break), *i* (italic), and *p* (paragraph).

Command Control

The *Command* control represents a programmable button. On some devices, the *Command* button renders as a button, whereas on other devices, such as cell phones, it renders as a soft key that can be pressed. The *Text* property of the button is displayed on the control or in the soft key layout.

The *Command* control raises the *OnClick* event when the button is clicked and has an *ItemCommand* that propagates to the container when the button is clicked.

Image Control

The *Image* control displays an image based on the capabilities of the device. The image also supports the ability to have device filters assigned, which means that each type of device can have a different image. The *AlternateText* property should always be set on the *Image* control, because some devices might not support images, and some devices might not support the type of image that is being provided. For example, if a .gif file is being provided and the device only works with .wbmp files, the *AlternateText* is displayed.

List Control

The *List* control displays a static list of items. List items can be added to the *Items* property of the control or by binding data to the control. This list is paginated as required.

The *List* control supports data binding using the *DataSource*, *DataMember*, *DataTextField*, and *DataValueField* properties. Whereas this list is primarily used to display static data with links, the *SelectionList* control (which we describe next) is intended to provide a selection list with options that are more similar to the menu type.

SelectionList Control

The *SelectionList* is very similar to the *List* control, except the *SelectionList* does not post back to the server. This means that a command button must be provided on the form.

The *SelectionList* also allows multiple selections, whereas the *List* control allows only a single selection. The *SelectionList* does not offer pagination, although the *List* control does.

By default, this control renders on most devices as a drop-down list box, which means that only one selection is visible. The *SelectType* property of the *SelectionList* control can be set to *CheckBox* or *MultiSelectListBox* to allow multiple selections.

This control also supports data binding using the *DataSource*, *DataMember*, *DataTextField*, and *DataValueField* properties.

ObjectList Control

One might refer to the *ObjectList* control as being the *mobile grid*. This control is used to display tabular data. The *ObjectList* control is bound to data using the *DataSource* and *DataMember* properties and contains a property called *LabelField,* which displays when the control is initially rendered. The *LabelField* is typically set to the primary key field, and when rendered, produces a list of primary key values as hyperlinks that can be clicked to see the rest of the data.

As an example, suppose you wish to display the Customers table from the *Northwind* database on a mobile device. You could create a simple mobile form that included an *ObjectList* control as follows:

```
<html xmlns="http://www.w3.org/1999/xhtml" >
<body>
  <mobile:Form id="Form1" runat="server">
    <mobile:ObjectList Runat="server" ID="ObjectList1">
    </mobile:ObjectList>
  </mobile:Form>
</body>
</html>
```

In the code-behind file, you need to add code to connect to your database, fill a data table, and then bind it to your list control. The following code shows the binding operations inside the *MobilePage* load event (for details on connecting to data, refer to Chapter 8, "Working with Data Source and Data-Bound Controls").

```
'VB
Protected Sub Page_Load(ByVal sender As Object, _
  ByVal e As System.EventArgs) Handles Me.Load

  If Not IsPostBack Then
    ObjectList1.DataSource = GetCustomerData()
    ObjectList1.LabelField = "CustomerID"
    ObjectList1.DataBind()
  End If

End Sub

//C#
protected void Page_Load(object sender, EventArgs e)
{
  if (!IsPostBack)
  {
    ObjectList1.DataSource = GetCustomerData();
    ObjectList1.LabelField = "CustomerID";
    ObjectList1.DataBind();
  }
}
```

In the preceding code, notice that the *LabelField* is set to the CustomerID column. This tells the *ObjectList* control to show this data first for user selection. Figure 15-5 shows an example of the output.

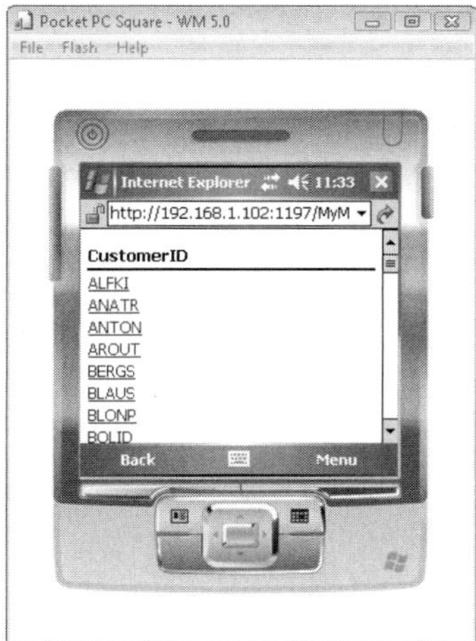

FIGURE 15-5 The *ObjectList* control when bound to the Customers table

In Figure 15-5, notice that a list of *CustomerID* values are initially displayed. Selecting a value brings up a new screen that shows the details for the selected item. Figure 15-6 shows an example of a selected item from the list.

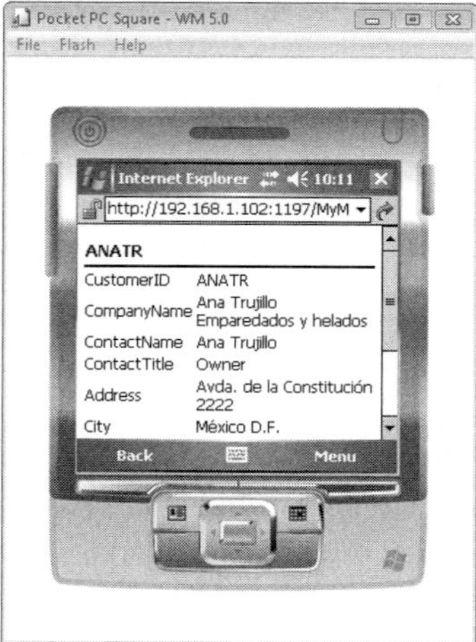

FIGURE 15-6 The *ObjectList* control bound to the Customers table and showing customer details

Calendar Control

The *Calendar* control allows the user to specify a date. The presentation of the date selection might be very different, depending on the type of device. The *Calendar* control renders as a series of forms, in which the user can drill down to a specific date. The user also has the ability to manually enter a date.

AdRotator Control

The *AdRotator* control can be used to place an advertisement on a device. This control is similar to ASP.NET's *AdRotator* control, except that the rendering adapts to the device.

The *AdRotator* control can be assigned a series of images. The *AdRotator* control does not require a specific image type. The image can be assigned, based on the device type, by assigning device filters (discussed later in this lesson).

The *AdRotator* control requires an .xml file to configure the advertisements. This file can be the same file that is used by the standard *AdRotator* Web server control, in which the root element of the .xml file is called *Advertisements*. The *Advertisements* element can contain many *Ad* elements. Each *Ad* element contains elements for each advertisement property.

PhoneCall Control

The *PhoneCall* control provides a simple method of dialing a phone number on devices that support placing calls. The *PhoneCall* control has a *PhoneNumber* property that can be set to the phone number that is to be dialed. The phone number is displayed on the device as a hyperlink, but if the *Text* property is set, the *Text* is displayed as the hyperlink text instead of the actual phone number. The *SoftKeyLabel* property can be set to a custom string, such as *Call* for the function key, if the device supports function keys.

The *PhoneCall* control displays the contents of the *AlternateText* property if the device does not support phone calls. The *AlternateText* property defaults to {0} {1}, where {0} is the *Text* property and {1} is the *PhoneNumber* property.

Validation Controls

Validation controls are a very important part of standard ASP.NET Web pages, and they are included as mobile controls as well. The following is a list of mobile validation controls:

- ***RequiredFieldValidator*** An entry is required in this field.
- ***RangeValidator*** The entry must be within the specified range.
- ***CompareValidator*** The entry is compared to another value.
- ***CustomValidator*** A custom validation function validates the entry.
- ***RegularExpressionValidator*** The entry must match the specified pattern.
- ***ValidationSummary*** This displays a summary of all input errors.

These controls are essentially the same as the controls that are available in the nonmobile version of ASP.NET except that the mobile validator controls do not provide client-side validation. You can combine these controls as necessary. For example, a *TextBox* can have both the *RequiredFieldValidator* and the *RegularExpressionValidator*.

Data Binding

Data binding with mobile controls is essentially the same as data binding in ASP.NET. Most controls support the *DataSource* and *DataMember* properties and some controls support the *DataTextField* and the *DataValue* fields as well. It is important to use the *IsPostBack* property and load data into the cache. Rather than binding all controls, only the controls for the current form should be bound.

Maintaining Session State

In a typical ASP.NET Web site, session state is maintained by issuing a session cookie to the browser. When the browser communicates to the Web server, the session cookie is passed to the Web server, and the Web server retrieves the session ID value from the session cookie to look up the session state data for your session.

Many mobile devices, such as most cell phones, don't accept cookies. This causes problems with maintaining session state. The solution is to enable cookieless sessions. This can be accomplished by adding the following element to the Web.config file inside the *system.web* element:

```
<sessionState cookieless="true" />
```

With cookieless sessions, the session ID value is placed into the URL for the Web site instead of a cookie. You should plan on implementing cookieless sessions on all mobile applications to ensure that your mobile Web site is compatible with the majority of mobile devices.

If you are using forms-based authentication for your mobile application, you also need to configure the cookieless data dictionary. This can be done by adding the following to your configuration file:

```
<mobileControls cookielessDataDictionaryType="System.Web.Mobile.CookielessData" />
```

Control Grouping for User Input

Mobile Web developers understand that mobile users input data differently from traditional computer users. Cell phones are typically more difficult to input data into. Many cell phones display only a few lines of text and some cell phones are able to display only one text box for user input at a time. This means that a *mobile form* with many controls can be displayed broken apart, so it's important to focus on grouping controls that should be kept together. Mobile controls are organized by placing them into containers. Each container holds a logical group of controls, which helps the runtime render each mobile device page.

Pagination

You can separate the *mobile form* content into smaller chunks by using pagination. Enabling pagination causes the runtime to format the output to the target device. Pagination is disabled by default but can be enabled by setting the *Paginate* property of each *mobile form* control to *true*.

For inputting data, pagination is typically not required, because many devices already contain mechanisms for allowing input of one item at a time. Pagination is best suited for mobile form controls that display lots of read-only data to keep a device from running out of memory.

In addition to enabling and disabling the pagination, custom pagination is also supported by the *List*, *ObjectList*, and *TextView* controls. These controls support internal pagination, which means that these controls provide pagination of their own items. These controls provide the ability to set the items per page and can raise the *LoadItems* event to load data.

Panels

Panels are container controls that can be used to provide further grouping of controls for the purpose of enabling, disabling, hiding, and showing controls as a single group. Panels cannot be navigated to in the same way that forms can. You can use panels as a placeholder for dynamically created controls. The runtime attempts to display all controls that are with the panel on the same screen.

Styles

Styles can be used to change the visual appearance of a control. You can group styles and assign them to controls to provide a consistent appearance across your application. Implement styles by using the *StyleSheet* control or by using the *<style>* tag. Only one *StyleSheet* control can be assigned to a mobile Web form.

Styles are treated as hints. If the device supports the assigned style, the runtime attempts to assign the style to the controls as required. If the device does not support the assigned style, the runtime ignores the style.

A control inherits styles that are assigned to the container that the control is in. You can override a style by assigning a style directly to the control. When assigning styles, you can assign them directly to a property of the control, or assign the *StyleReference* property to a control.

Understanding Adaptive Rendering

Adaptive rendering is the act of rendering a control differently based on the browser that requested the Web page. In the following example, a mobile *Calendar* control is placed on a mobile Web form, and a cell phone requests the mobile Web form. The *Calendar* control renders as shown in Figure 15-7.

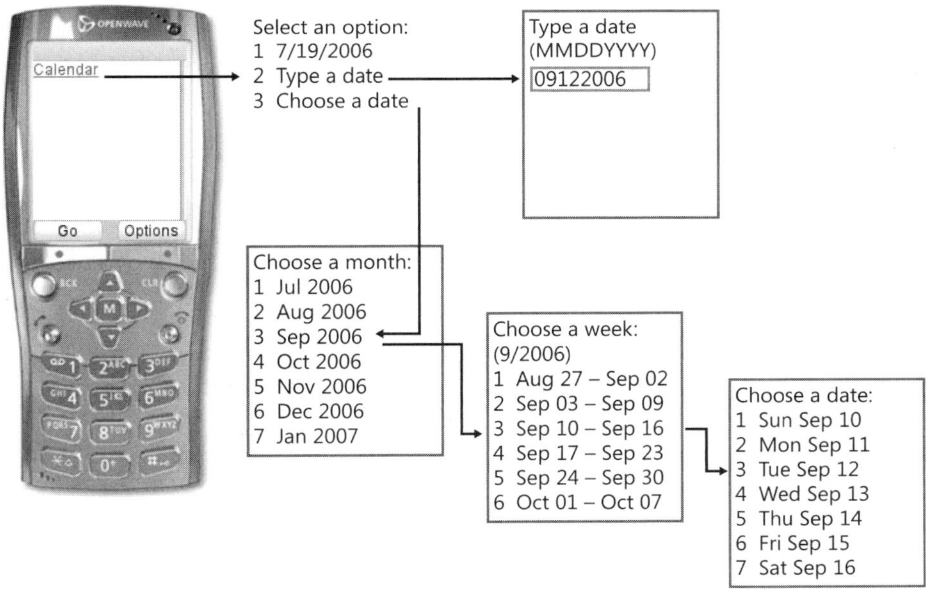

FIGURE 15-7 The mobile *Calendar* control rendered on a cell phone

Notice that there is not enough space on the cell phone to render the current month, so the control is rendered as a hyperlink that simply states Calendar. If the user clicks this link, a menu is presented to give the user some options for entering the date. The user can simply select the current date, type in a date, or go through more menu screens to select a date.

If the same Web page is selected using a SmartPhone, the calendar renders full size as shown in Figure 15-8.

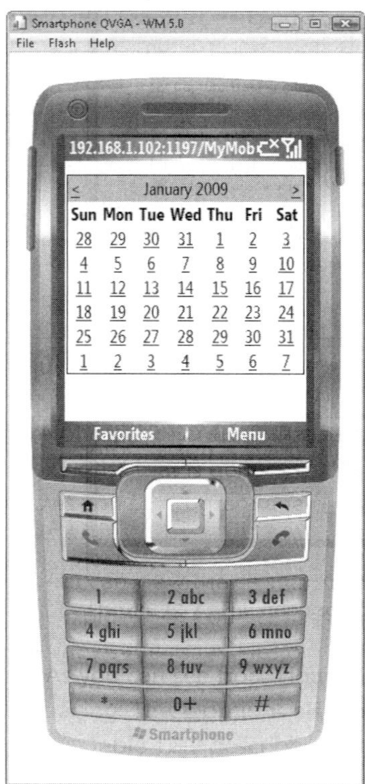

FIGURE 15-8 The mobile *Calendar* control rendered on a SmartPhone

When a browser requests a Web page, it sends an HTTP header called the *User-Agent*, which is a string that is used to identify the browser. The runtime uses the *User-Agent* string to look up the browser's capabilities. The capability settings for each browser can be viewed and set in the *browserCaps* element in the config files.

In ASP.NET, *browserCaps* relies on XML files that contain a hierarchal structure of browser definitions. The default location of the XML files is as follows:

```
C:\WINDOWS\Microsoft.NET\Framework\v2.0.50727\CONFIG\Browsers\
```

Each of the XML files has a .browser extension; these files are used to build a class called *HttpBrowserCapabilities*, which is a factory class that creates an instance of *HttpBrowser-Capabilities* and populates its properties based on the browser type. You can modify the existing .browser files and create new .browser files. The *HttpBrowserCapabilities* class is in an assembly called *ASP.BrowserCapsFactory.dll* that is installed in the global assembly cache.

To regenerate the *ASP.BrowserCapsFactory.dll* assembly and its *HttpBrowserCapabilities* class based on changes to the .browser files, run the aspnet_regbrowsers command-line tool in the .NET Command Prompt window using the *–i* switch (install).

Implementing Device-Specific Rendering

Device-specific rendering is the ability to specify rendering for a control based on a device type. One way to use device-specific rendering is to query the various *Request.Browser* properties and perform actions based on the browser type. For example, a mobile *Label* control has been added to a mobile Web form. The following code has been added to the code-behind file to display a different message based on whether the browser is a mobile device:

```
'VB
Partial Class LabelTest
  Inherits System.Web.UI.MobileControls.MobilePage

  Protected Sub Page_Load(ByVal sender As Object, _
    ByVal e As System.EventArgs) Handles Me.Load

    If (Request.Browser.IsMobileDevice) Then
      Label1.Text = "A mobile device"
    Else
      Label1.Text = "Not a mobile device"
    End If

  End Sub
End Class

//C#
public partial class LabelTest :
  System.Web.UI.MobileControls.MobilePage
{
  protected void Page_Load(object sender, EventArgs e)
  {
    if (Request.Browser.IsMobileDevice)
    {
      Label1.Text = "A mobile device";
    }
    else
    {
      Label1.Text = "Not a mobile device";
    }
  }
}
```

Another way to perform device-specific rendering is to use the *DeviceSpecific* control. A single *DeviceSpecific* control can be nested inside any mobile control or in the *<mobile:Form>* element to provide custom behavior based on a filter.

You add entries in the Web.config file for your site to define filters. A filter simply identifies a device. Once configured, a filter is available to show adaptive rendering based on the given device. The following are all filters that you might define in a Web.config file inside the *<system.web>* element:

```
<deviceFilters>
  <filter name="isJPhone" compare="Type" argument="J-Phone" />
  <filter name="isHTML32" compare="PreferredRenderingType" argument="html32" />
  <filter name="isWML11" compare="PreferredRenderingType" argument="wml11" />
  <filter name="isCHTML10" compare="PreferredRenderingType" argument="chtml10" />
  <filter name="isGoAmerica" compare="Browser" argument="Go.Web" />
  <filter name="isMME" compare="Browser" argument="Microsoft Mobile Explorer" />
  <filter name="isMyPalm" compare="Browser" argument="MyPalm" />
  <filter name="isPocketIE" compare="Browser" argument="Pocket IE" />
  <filter name="isUP3x" compare="Type" argument="Phone.com 3.x Browser" />
  <filter name="isUP4x" compare="Type" argument="Phone.com 4.x Browser" />
  <filter name="isEricssonR380" compare="Type" argument="Ericsson R380" />
  <filter name="isNokia7110" compare="Type" argument="Nokia 7110" />
  <filter name="prefersGIF" compare="PreferredImageMIME" argument="image/gif" />
  <filter name="prefersWBMP" compare="PreferredImageMIME"
    argument="image/vnd.wap.wbmp" />
  <filter name="supportsColor" compare="IsColor" argument="true" />
  <filter name="supportsCookies" compare="Cookies" argument="true" />
  <filter name="supportsJavaScript" compare="Javascript" argument="true" />
  <filter name="supportsVoiceCalls" compare="CanInitiateVoiceCall" argument="true" />
</deviceFilters>
```

Once configured, you can then use the filter as a choice inside the *DeviceSpecific* control. When a request is made by a device, it passes its type to ASP.NET. This type is then looked up based on the filter. If the control to be rendered has a *DeviceSpecific* filter, the filter gets applied before the response is sent back to the device. The following markup shows a *DeviceSpecific* control added to the *Label* control.

```
<html xmlns="http://www.w3.org/1999/xhtml" >
<body>
  <mobile:Form id="Form1" runat="server">
    <mobile:Label Runat="server" ID="Label1">
      <DeviceSpecific>
        <Choice Filter="IsMobile" Font-Italic="True" />
        <Choice Filter="IsIE" Font-Name="Arial Black" Font-Size="Large" />
      </DeviceSpecific>
    </mobile:Label>
  </mobile:Form>
```

```
</body>
</html>
```

If this page is run in Microsoft Internet Explorer, the IsIE filter choice rendering applies. This changes the text to large, Arial Black, as shown in Figure 15-9.

FIGURE 15-9 The filter applied to Internet Explorer

If, however, this page is run on a mobile device, the IsMobile filter choice rendering applies. This changes the text to italics, as shown in Figure 15-10.

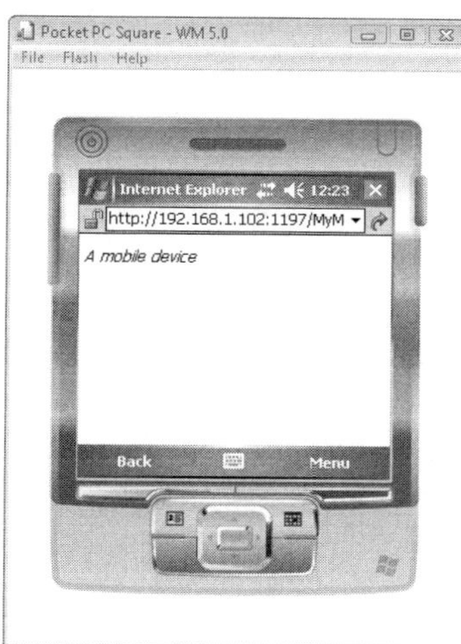

FIGURE 15-10 The filter applied to a mobile device

Applying Best Practices to Mobile Applications

In many respects, writing applications for mobile use can be a challenging endeavor. The following list identifies some guidelines and best practices that you should consider.

- **Provide a separate desktop presentation** Although many devices are adaptive, desktop users want and expect a much richer presentation. It's usually best to provide two presentations: one for the desktop and one for the mobile devices.
- **Page content** Keep page content as simple as possible.
- **Data access** Instead of sending a complete result set to the user, only send the data record that the user is interested in. Only bind the required controls.
- **Adaptive controls** Test adaptive controls with several devices, including devices that display a few lines.
- **Default values** Present the user with default values whenever possible.
- **Evaluate *ViewState*** In many applications, better performance can be obtained by turning off *ViewState,* because this reduces the amount of data that is being transferred to a slow mobile device. Turning off *ViewState* might require the server to rebuild the data each time the user posts back to the server.
- **Use caching** Whenever possible, cache data access results to keep from retrieving data each time the user accesses the server.
- **Combine many forms on a page** It is much easier to share data between forms on a page than it is to share data between pages. However, there is a point at which performance suffers. Look for places where it is easy to pass a few items to a new page.
- **Use cookieless sessions** Many mobile devices do not support cookies, so it is important to use cookieless sessions.
- **Using hyperlinks to a form** A hyperlink can be created to a form by using the syntax, *#form2* (where *form2* represents the name of the form). If the page has a user control called *myControl*, which has forms, a hyperlink can be created using the *#myControl:form2* syntax.
- **Minimize image usage** Use of images should be kept to a minimum due to the low bandwidth and screen resolution that is available on most mobile devices. Some mobile devices might not support images, and others might not support the image type that is being supplied, such as when a .gif file is used on a mobile device that only supports .wbmp files. Be sure to assign a value to the *AlternateText* property of all graphics.

✔ **Quick Check**

1. **What is a primary difference between the standard validator controls and the mobile validator controls?**
2. **What can you do to ensure that session state is maintained when mobile devices that don't accept cookies are accessing your mobile Web site?**

Quick Check Answers

1. **The mobile validator controls don't provide client-side validation.**
2. **You should enable cookieless sessions in the Web.config file.**

LAB Working with Mobile Web Applications

In this lab, you create a mobile Web site application. This application demonstrates the use of mobile controls to access and display data on a cell phone or browser. This application presents the user with the option of searching products by name, by product ID, or by drilling down through categories to get to products.

If you encounter a problem completing an exercise, the completed projects are available in the sample files installed from the companion CD in the Code folder.

EXERCISE 1 Create the Web Site and Define the Mobile Page

In this exercise, you create the mobile Web site, define the mobile forms on a given page, and add controls to that page.

1. Open Visual Studio and create a new Web site called **MobileSite** using your preferred programming language.
2. Open the code-behind file for the Default.aspx page. Change the class inheritance to use the *MobilePage* class. Your code should look as follows:

```
'VB
Partial Class _Default
  Inherits System.Web.UI.MobileControls.MobilePage

End Class

//C#
public partial class _Default : System.Web.UI.MobileControls.MobilePage
{
}
```

3. Open the markup for Default.aspx in Source view. Remove the *<!DOCTYPE>* element from the page. Under the *@ Page* directive, add the *@ Register* directive to register the *MobileControls* namespace. This markup looks as follows:

```
<%@ Register TagPrefix="mobile"
  Namespace="System.Web.UI.MobileControls"
  Assembly="System.Web.Mobile" %>
```

4. Next, you define the mobile form controls used by the page. The page is meant to walk a user through a search process on a mobile device. Create a mobile form for each of the following:
   - ID = **FormMain** and Title = **Select a Search Method**.
   - ID = **FormSearchName** and Title = **Enter a Name**.
   - ID = **FormSearchId** and Title = **Enter ID**.
   - ID = **FormSearchCategory** and Title = **Select a Category**.
   - ID = **FormResult** and Title = **Search Results**.
5. Next, you need to define the controls used by each form.
   - **FormMain** Add a mobile *List* control. Set the ID to **ListMainMenu**. Add the following to the *Items* collection: *By Name* (value=1), *By ID* (value=2), and *By Category* (value=3).
   - **FormSearchName** Add a *Label* control and set its *ID* to **LabelSearchName** and its *Text* to **Enter Name**. Add a mobile *TextBox* control and set its *ID* to **TextBoxSearchName**. Add a mobile *Command* control and set its *ID* to **CommandSearchName** and its *CommandName* to **Search**.
   - **FormSearchId** Add a *Label* control and set its *ID* to **LabelSearchId** and its *Text* to **Enter ID**. Add a mobile *TextBox* control and set its *ID* to **TextBoxSearchId**. Add a mobile *Command* control and set its *ID* to **CommandSearchId** and its *CommandName* to **Search**.
   - **FormSearchCategory** Add a mobile *List* control. Set its *ID* to **ListCategory**.
   - **FormResults** Add an *ObjectList* control. Set its *ID* to **ObjectListResults**.

   Your markup should now look as follows:

```
<html xmlns="http://www.w3.org/1999/xhtml" >
<body>

  <mobile:Form id="FormMain" runat="server"
    Title="Select a Search Method">
    <mobile:List ID="ListMainMenu" Runat="server">
      <Item Text="By Name" Value="1" />
      <Item Text="By ID" Value="2" />
      <Item Text="By Category" Value="3" />
    </mobile:List>
  </mobile:Form>

  <mobile:Form id="FormSearchName" runat="server"
    Title="Enter Name">
    <mobile:Label ID="LabelSearchName" Runat="server">Enter Name</mobile:Label>
    <mobile:TextBox ID="TextBoxSearchName" Runat="server"></mobile:TextBox>
    <mobile:Command ID="CommandSearchName" Runat="server" CommandName="Search">
    </mobile:Command>
```

```
    </mobile:Form>

    <mobile:Form id="FormSearchId" runat="server"
      Title="Enter ID">
      <mobile:Label ID="LabelSearchId" Runat="server">Enter ID</mobile:Label>
      <mobile:TextBox ID="TextBoxSearchId" Runat="server"></mobile:TextBox>
      <mobile:Command ID="CommandSearchId" Runat="server" CommandName="Search">
      </mobile:Command>
    </mobile:Form>


    <mobile:Form id="FormSearchCategory" runat="server"
      Title="Select a Category">
      <mobile:List Runat="server" ID="ListCategory"></mobile:List>
    </mobile:Form>

    <mobile:Form id="FormResults" runat="server"
      Title="Search Results">
      <mobile:ObjectList Runat="server" ID="ObjectListResults">
      </mobile:ObjectList>
    </mobile:Form>

  </body>
  </html>
```

EXERCISE 2 Add Code to the Mobile Form

In this exercise, you continue working with the page you created in the prior exercise by adding code to complete the page.

1. Continue working with the Web site you created in the previous exercise. Alternatively, you can open the completed Lesson 1, Exercise 1 project in the samples installed from the CD.

2. Add the *Northwind* database to the App_Data folder. You can copy this database from the installed samples.

3. Open your site's Web.config file. Navigate to the *<connectionStrings>* element. Add markup to connect to the *Northwind* database. Your markup should look as follows:

```
<connectionStrings>
  <add name="NorthwindConnectionString"
    connectionString="Data Source=.\SQLEXPRESS;
      AttachDbFilename=|DataDirectory|\northwnd.mdf;
      Integrated Security=True;User Instance=True"
    providerName="System.Data.SqlClient"/>
</connectionStrings>
```

4. Open the code-behind file for the Default.aspx page. Add the following bits of code:
   - A private, class-level variable called **_cnnString** for getting the database connection string
   - A private function called **GetProducts** that loads product data from the database and returns a *DataTable* object
   - A private function called **GetCategories** that loads category data from the database and returns a *DataTable* object

   Your code should look similar to the following:

```
'VB
Imports System.Data
Imports System.Data.SqlClient

Partial Class _Default
  Inherits System.Web.UI.MobileControls.MobilePage

  Private _cnnString As String = _
    ConfigurationManager.ConnectionStrings("NorthwindConnectionString").ToString

  Private Function GetProducts() As DataTable
    Dim adp As New SqlDataAdapter( _
      "select * from products", _cnnString)

    Dim ds As New DataSet("products")
    adp.Fill(ds, "products")

    Return ds.Tables("products")
  End Function

  Private Function GetCategories() As DataTable
    Dim adp As New SqlDataAdapter( _
      "SELECT * FROM categories", _cnnString)

    Dim ds As New DataSet("categories")
    adp.Fill(ds, "categories")

    Return ds.Tables("categories")
  End Function

End Class

//C#
using System;
using System.Data;
using System.Data.SqlClient;
```

```
using System.Configuration;

public partial class _Default : System.Web.UI.MobileControls.MobilePage
{
  private string _cnnString =
    ConfigurationManager.ConnectionStrings[
    "NorthwindConnectionString"].ToString();

  private DataTable GetProducts()
  {
    SqlDataAdapter adp = new SqlDataAdapter(
      "select * from products", _cnnString);

    DataSet ds = new DataSet("products");
    adp.Fill(ds, "products");

    return ds.Tables["products"];
  }

  private DataTable GetCategories()
  {
    SqlDataAdapter adp = new SqlDataAdapter(
      "SELECT * FROM categories", _cnnString);

    DataSet ds = new DataSet("categories");
    adp.Fill(ds, "categories");

    return ds.Tables["categories"];
  }
}
```

5. Add an event handler for the *ListMainMenu* control's *ItemCommand* to the code-behind page. In Visual Basic, you can add the event handler as you would normally. However, in C#, you might not get the event button on the Properties window. Therefore, you might need to add the attribute setting, *OnItemCommand="ListMainMenu_ItemCommand"* to the markup for the *ListMainMenu* control.

   This control's event is used to set the active form based on the user's search selection (by name, by ID, by category). If category is selected, bind the *ListCategory* control to the Categories table using the *GetCategories* method. Your code should look similar to the following:

   ```
   'VB
   Protected Sub ListMainMenu_ItemCommand(ByVal sender As Object, _
   ```

```
  ByVal e As System.Web.UI.MobileControls.ListCommandEventArgs) _
  Handles ListMainMenu.ItemCommand

  If e.ListItem.Value = "1" Then
    'search by name
    Me.ActiveForm = FormSearchName
  ElseIf e.ListItem.Value = "2" Then
    'search by ID
    Me.ActiveForm = FormSearchId
  ElseIf e.ListItem.Value = "3" Then
    'search by category
    Me.ActiveForm = FormSearchCategory
    ListCategory.DataSource = GetCategories()
    ListCategory.DataTextField = "CategoryName"
    ListCategory.DataValueField = "CategoryID"
    ListCategory.DataBind()
  End If

End Sub

//C#
protected void ListMainMenu_ItemCommand(object sender ,
  System.Web.UI.MobileControls.ListCommandEventArgs e)
{
  if (e.ListItem.Value == "1")
  {
    //search by name
    this.ActiveForm = FormSearchName;
  }
  else if (e.ListItem.Value == "2")
  {
    //search by ID
    this.ActiveForm = FormSearchId;
  }
  else if (e.ListItem.Value == "3")
  {
    //search by category
    this.ActiveForm = FormSearchCategory;
    ListCategory.DataSource = GetCategories();
    ListCategory.DataTextField = "CategoryName";
    ListCategory.DataValueField = "CategoryID";
    ListCategory.DataBind();
  }
}
```

6. The next step is to do the actual search based on user selection. In this case, you will return all the product data from the database and filter it on the server. This simplifies the lab. In a real scenario, you would either create separate search methods to get only the data you need or retrieve and cache this data on the server.

   To respond to search requests, you need to add the following event handlers to your code.

   - ***CommandSearchId Click* handler** Here you get the product data but filter it based on the user-entered ID value.
   - ***CommandSearchName Click* handler** Again, you get the product data and filter the results. This time you do so based on the product name.
   - ***ListCategory ItemCommand* handler** This time you get the product data and filter it based on the selected product category.

   In addition, you need to add a method called *ShowResults* to your code-behind file. This method should be called at the end of each of the preceding events to display the results in the *ObjectListResults* control and set the active form to *FormResults*.

   The code for these three event handlers and *ShowResults* should look as follows:

```
'VB
Protected Sub CommandSearchId_Click(ByVal sender As Object, _
  ByVal e As System.EventArgs) Handles CommandSearchId.Click

  Dim products As DataTable = GetProducts()
  products.DefaultView.RowFilter = _
    String.Format("ProductID = {0}", TextBoxSearchId.Text)

  ShowResults(products)

End Sub

Protected Sub CommandSearchName_Click(ByVal sender As Object, _
  ByVal e As System.EventArgs) Handles CommandSearchName.Click

  Dim products As DataTable = GetProducts()
  products.DefaultView.RowFilter = _
    String.Format("ProductName like '{0}%'", TextBoxSearchName.Text)

  ShowResults(products)

End Sub

Protected Sub ListCategory_ItemCommand(ByVal sender As Object, _
  ByVal e As System.Web.UI.MobileControls.ListCommandEventArgs) _
  Handles ListCategory.ItemCommand
```

```
  Dim products As DataTable = GetProducts()
  products.DefaultView.RowFilter = _
    String.Format("CategoryID = {0}", e.ListItem.Value)

  ShowResults(products)

End Sub

Private Sub ShowResults(ByVal data As DataTable)
  ObjectListResults.DataSource = data.DefaultView
  ObjectListResults.LabelField = "ProductName"
  ObjectListResults.DataBind()
  Me.ActiveForm = FormResults
End Sub

//C#
protected void CommandSearchId_Click(object sender, EventArgs e)
{
  DataTable products = GetProducts();
  products.DefaultView.RowFilter =
    String.Format("ProductID = {0}", TextBoxSearchId.Text);

  ShowResults(products);
}

protected void CommandSearchName_Click(object sender, EventArgs e)
{
  DataTable products = GetProducts();
  products.DefaultView.RowFilter =
    String.Format("ProductName like '{0}%'", TextBoxSearchName.Text);

  ShowResults(products);
}

protected void ListCategory_ItemCommand(object sender,
  System.Web.UI.MobileControls.ListCommandEventArgs e)
{
  DataTable products = GetProducts();
  products.DefaultView.RowFilter =
    String.Format("CategoryID = {0}", e.ListItem.Value);

  ShowResults(products);
}

private void ShowResults(DataTable data)
```

```
{
    ObjectListResults.DataSource = data.DefaultView;
    ObjectListResults.LabelField = "ProductName";
    ObjectListResults.DataBind();
    this.ActiveForm = FormResults;
}
```

Depending on how you add these events to your code, you might have to wire them up to their controls. There are multiple ways to do so. An easy way is to use the markup for the given control's event, for example, *OnClick="CommandSearchName_Click"* for the *CommandSearchName Click* event and *OnItemCommand="ListCategory_ItemCommand"* for the *ListCategory* control.

7. Run the mobile Web form in both Internet Explorer and a mobile emulator. Test each option by entering data or selecting a value.

Figure 15-11 shows each form in the application running on a Windows device emulator.

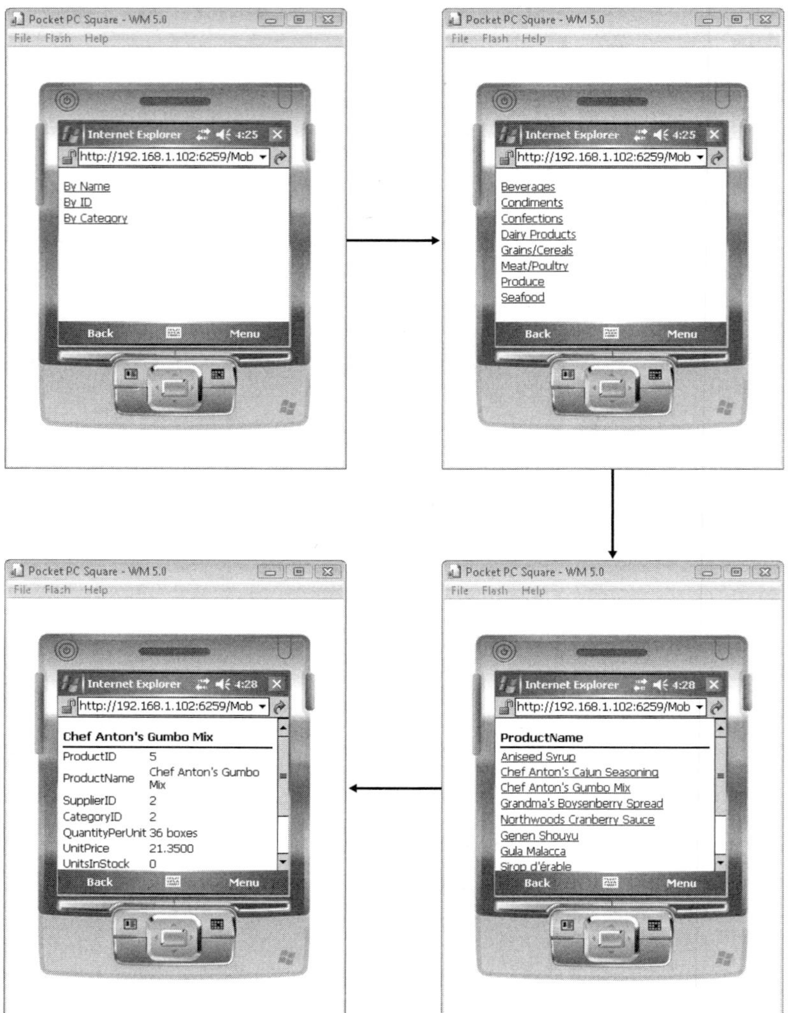

FIGURE 15-11 The mobile Web application running on a mobile device emulator

Lesson Summary

- A mobile Web application has the ability to render to a wide variety of mobile devices.
- You can test your mobile application using Internet Explorer, various physical devices, or device emulators.
- To create a mobile Web application, create a standard ASP.NET Web site using your preferred programming language. You then modify regular Web forms to inherit from *MobilePage*. You should also register the mobile Web controls in your markup.
- You can enable state to a wide variety of mobile devices by using cookieless sessions.

- The mobile Web controls provide adaptive rendering for various device types. You also have the ability to provide device-specific rendering, which allows you to override the default rendering.

Lesson Review

You can use the following questions to test your knowledge of the information in Lesson 1, "Building Mobile Applications." The questions are also available on the companion CD if you prefer to review them in electronic form.

> ***NOTE*** **ANSWERS**
>
> **Answers to these questions and explanations of why each answer choice is right or wrong are located in the "Answers" section at the end of the book.**

1. You need to create a mobile Web site application. What steps should you take? (Choose all that apply).

A. Create a standard ASP.NET Web site.

B. Use standard ASP.NET Web forms. Change these forms to inherit from *System.Web.UI.MobileControls.MobilePage*.

C. Add an @ *Register* directive to your page to register the *System.Web.Mobile* assembly.

D. Add one or more *<mobile:Form>* controls to your page.

2. You have a mobile *Label* control on your mobile Web form. You want the text to be different based on whether the browser is Internet Explorer or a mobile device. How can you perform this task? (Choose two answers.)

A. In your code, add a test for *Request.Browser.IsMobileDevice*, and then set the *Text* property accordingly.

B. In your code, call the *IsDevice* method on the mobile Web form and pass the *Device.Mobile* enumeration value, and then set the *Text* property accordingly.

C. Read the *UserAgent* property on the *Request* object, and if the *UserAgent* is equal to *mobile*, set the *Text* property accordingly.

D. Set the default *Text* value, and then define a mobile device in the *AppliedDeviceFilters,* and use this to set the *Text* property using the *PropertyOverrides* property of the mobile *Label* control.

3. You created a mobile Web site that appears to be working properly for your users. Joe just purchased a new state-of-the-art mobile device. When he attempted to view a *Calendar* control on your Web site, the control attempted to render a month view, but Joe's mobile device screen wasn't big enough to display the calendar. You decide to create a new .browser file that represents Joe's mobile device and the settings will cause the calendar to render appropriately. How can you get the runtime to recognize the new .browser file settings?

A. Add the name of the .browser file to the Machine.config file in the *Browsers* element.

B. Add the .browser file name to the Web.config file for your Web site in the *Browsers* element.

C. Run the aspnet_regbrowsers command-line tool in the .NET Command Prompt window using the *–i* switch.

D. Run the aspnet_regiis command-line tool in the .NET Command Prompt window using the *–registerbrowsers* switch.

Chapter Review

To further practice and reinforce the skills you learned in this chapter, you can perform the following tasks:

- Review the chapter summary.
- Complete the case scenarios. These scenarios set up real-world situations involving the topics of this chapter and ask you to create solutions.
- Complete the suggested practices.
- Take a practice test.

Chapter Summary

- Mobile Web applications can be built using the ASP.NET mobile controls. This allows you to create sites that are better suited for display on small devices with limited connectivity.
- A mobile Web application has the ability to render to a wide variety of mobile devices. The mobile Web controls provide adaptive rendering for various device types. You have the ability to provide device-specific rendering, which allows you to override the default rendering.

Case Scenarios

In the following case scenarios, you apply what you've learned in this chapter. You can find answers to these questions in the "Answers" section at the end of this book.

Case Scenario 1: Determining the Mobile Control to Use

You are creating a mobile Web application that will be used by real estate agents to enter search criteria into their mobile devices. These criteria include price range, quantity of rooms, lot size, and city. After entering the criteria, the data is sent to the Web server and the Web server responds with a list of houses that meet the search criteria.

QUESTIONS

1. What control would you use to display the results?

Case Scenario 2: Determining How Many Web Pages to Create

You are creating a mobile Web application that will be accessible using desktop computers, notebook computers, PDAs, Smart Phones with Windows Mobile, and cell phones with mobile browsers. Your boss is concerned that for every Web page you might need to provide a device-specific Web page.

QUESTIONS

1. How can you implement the Web site with a minimum amount of Web pages?
2. How should you implement the Web site?

Suggested Practices

To successfully master the exam objectives presented in this chapter, complete the following tasks.

Creating a Mobile Web Application

For this task, you should complete Practice 1 if you wish to create a mobile Web application from an ASP.NET template. Practice 2 uses community-supplied templates for mobile Web applications.

- **Practice 1** Create a new mobile Web application by converting a new ASP.NET Web site.
- **Practice 2** Download the community-supplied templates for mobile Web applications from *http://www.asp.net/mobile/road-map/* or search for "ASP.NET Mobile Development with Visual Studio 2008." Follow the instructions to install these templates. Create a new ASP.NET site. Add each of the new mobile item templates to your site: mobile form, mobile user control, and mobile config file. Open each file and review its contents.

Implement Device-Specific Rendering

- **Practice 1** Create a new mobile Web form and add a calendar mobile control to the form. Add device-specific rendering based on two or more devices. Each rendering should show the calendar differently. Run the form on multiple device emulators and view the results.

Create a Data-Collection Page with Validation

- **Practice 1** Create a new mobile Web form that collects data from a user such as his or her profile information. Add mobile validator controls to the form to restrict data entry.

Take a Practice Test

The practice tests on this book's companion CD offer many options. For example, you can test yourself on just the content covered in this chapter, or you can test yourself on all the 70-562 certification exam content. You can set up the test so it closely simulates the experience of taking a certification exam, or you can set it up in study mode so you can look at the correct answers and explanations after you answer each question.

MORE INFO **PRACTICE TESTS**

For details about all the practice test options available, see the "How to Use the Practice Tests" section in this book's Introduction.

CHAPTER 16

Deploying, Configuring, and Caching Applications

After you've developed and tested your application, it's time to deploy it to a production environment. In most real-world scenarios, deployment involves moving an application from a staged area where users have reviewed and tested functionality to one or more production servers. The deployment process can be automated with tools and scripts, managed and governed by IT departments, or deployed directly by developers through Microsoft Visual Studio. How your application gets built, verified, and deployed really depends on your scenarios, type of application, and environment. This chapter explores those tools and features of Visual Studio that make deploying Web applications easier.

Once an application is deployed, you might encounter the occasional performance issue that limits scalability or blocks access to shared data. Often, the solution can be to cache certain elements of your site to increase performance and throughput. This chapter also looks at how you can leverage the caching features of ASP.NET to increase the responsiveness and scalability of your application.

Exam objectives in this chapter:

- Configuring and Deploying Web Applications
  - Publish Web applications.
  - Configure application pools.
  - Compile an application by using Visual Studio or command-line tools.

Lessons in this chapter:

Before You Begin

To complete the lessons in this chapter, you should be familiar with developing applications with Visual Studio using Microsoft Visual Basic or C#. In addition, you should be comfortable with all of the following:

- Working with the Visual Studio 2008 Integrated Development Environment (IDE)
- Using Hypertext Markup Language (HTML) and client-side scripting
- Creating ASP.NET Web sites and forms

Mike Snell

One of the biggest challenges that modern development teams face is the build and deployment process, especially as it relates to continued releases against existing code. In fact, I have seen developers introduce many errors into a system as the result of faulty, human-driven, manual build processes. For some reason, getting the code from development to stage to production seems to introduce complexities and errors that should never occur. We often work with teams to help them automate their build and deployment process. This takes the human-error factor out of the process and allows for better management and tracking (and fewer bugs). We've also noticed that once you set up an automated process, the team is free to do more build and deployments on a regular basis, as they do not have the burden of an error-prone, manual process.

Lesson 1: Deploying Web Applications

Application build and deployment is an afterthought for most developers. Perhaps it is because they are not asked to deploy on a regular basis. Instead, they run their application with the simple click of a button in the IDE. Everything is deployed and executed locally. However, if they have to push that code to a server on a regular basis, they soon think of automation. Getting the build right on the server can be tedious.

In addition, only the simplest of production environments run on a single Web server. Highly available and highly scalable applications often run on multiple Web servers simultaneously. These same environments often have environments for development, staging, and production. Additionally, many Web developers must release their applications commercially; this means other people need to be able to deploy them in environments that the developer knows nothing about.

In each of these scenarios, you must create a plan to deploy your application and any updates that you release in the future. This lesson describes the different techniques available to deploy Web applications.

After this lesson, you will be able to:

- Create a Web Setup Project and use the resulting files to deploy your application.
- Update and deploy Web applications in environments with multiple developers and servers using the Copy Web tool.
- Precompile Web applications using the Publish Web Site tool.

Estimated lesson time: 40 minutes

About Web Setup Projects

Depending on the scenario, a .NET Framework Web application can be extremely easy to deploy. Web sites, by default, are entirely file-based. This means you typically deploy the source code to the server. The server then compiles that code as pages are requested. In this scenario, you can deploy a Web application to a Web server by simply copying the files to the correct directory on the server.

Even if you are deploying a new version of your site, in most cases you can simply overwrite the old files with the new ones. In addition, if you are writing a Web application that works on a single server and is file-based, there is often no real need to run any type of setup process, edit the registry, or add items to the start menu. The copy and paste (or a tool-based push) should be sufficient).

This simplicity provides a great deal of flexibility in other scenarios, too. If your Web application is to be deployed to an array of Web servers (in which multiple Web servers host the same Web site for scalability and availability), you can use any file-synchronization tool to copy the files between the servers. This allows you to deploy to a master server and have the deployment synchronized across the Web farm.

There are times, however, when you might need more control over how your application gets deployed. You might need to configure the Web server as part of deployment, deploy files to other locations on the server, add registry entries for your application, download and install prerequisites, set security, add dependent dynamic-link libraries (DLLs), and so on.

You might also not have direct control over the deployment process; rather, you might be reliant on a system administrator to manage deployment. In this case you might have to create a Windows Installer (.msi) file and even use tools for distribution like Microsoft Systems Management Server (SMS).

The sections that follow describe how to create a Web Setup Project, how to configure deployment properties, how to configure deployment conditions, and how to deploy Web applications that meet the requirements of the aforementioned scenarios.

Creating a Web Setup Project

A Web Setup Project is very similar to a standard Setup Project that you might make for a Windows Forms application; however, it provides specialized capabilities required by Web applications. To add a Web Setup Project to a Web site, follow these steps:

1. Open your Web site in Visual Studio.
2. From the File menu (or by right-clicking your solution in Solution Explorer), select Add, and then select New Project to launch the Add New Project dialog box.
3. Under Project Types, expand Other Project Types and select Setup And Deployment. Under Templates, select Web Setup Project. In the Name text box, type a name for your project. An example of the Add New Project dialog box is shown in Figure 16-1.

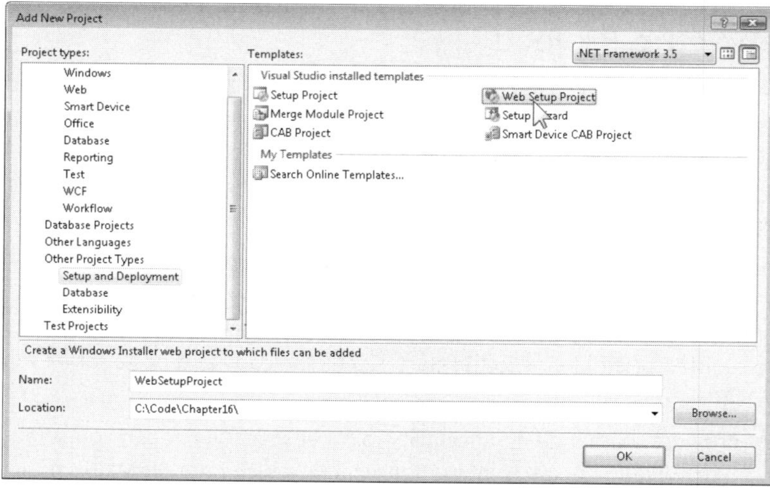

FIGURE 16-1 Add a new project to your Web site to create a Web Setup Project

4. After creating a new Web Setup Project, Visual Studio adds the project to your solution and displays the File System editor. The next common step is to create a project output group by right-clicking the Web Application Folder and selecting Add and then Project Output.

   In the Add Project Output Group dialog box, you select the project to output, the content files option, and the configuration (Active by default). This ensures that your setup project will output the contents of the selected project.

   Figure 16-2 shows an example of the configured Web Setup Project in Visual Studio.

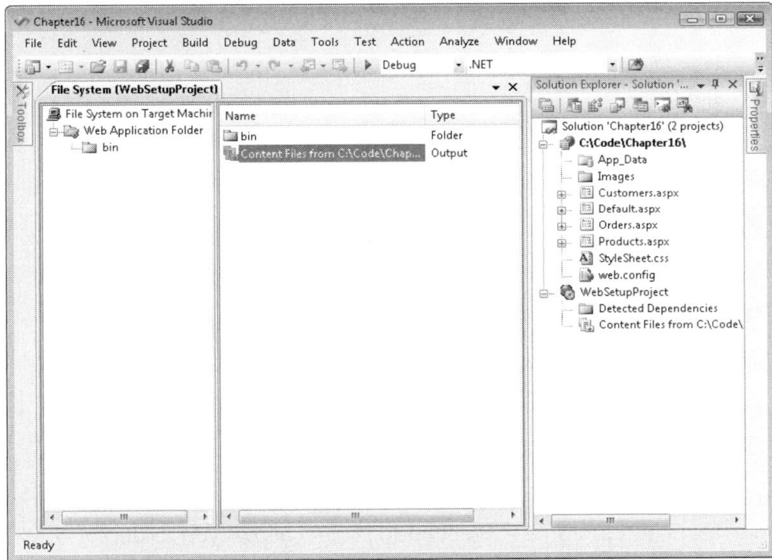

FIGURE 16-2 The File System editor for your Web Setup Project

Once you've created a Web Setup Project, you can add additional folders, files, and assemblies that are not part of your project output to the Web Setup Project. This might be necessary if, for example, you had a separate folder containing images that you have not added to your Web site project. You do so by again right-clicking the Web Application Folder in the File System editor.

Building a Web Setup Project

Web Setup Projects are not automatically built when you build or run your Web application. Instead, you must manually select the Web Setup Project in Solution Explorer and choose Build. You can do so by right-clicking the given project or through the Build menu.

When you build the setup project, Visual Studio validates your code in the Web site. It then builds an .msi file and packages each element of your site in the .msi. You can follow the build process in Visual Studio through the Output window (View | Output). This script shows you each step and where the .msi file is generated. By default, it is placed in the same folder that contains your solution file. Figure 16-3 shows an example.

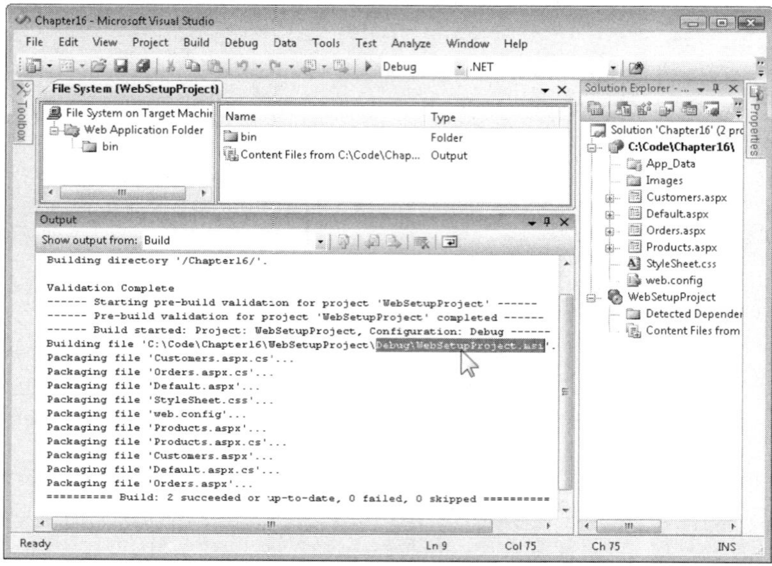

FIGURE 16-3 The .msi build in the Output window of Visual Studio

Many Web applications do not require custom configuration. In these cases, you can simply build your .msi file and be ready to deploy. However, more complex scenarios include dependencies (such as particular operating system versions or service packs), custom registry entries, or administrator configuration. A Web Setup Project allows you to deploy Web applications that meet these requirements. The sections that follow help you with each of these specific scenarios.

Creating Launch Conditions

A launch condition is used to restrict the server requirements for your application installation. For example, you can check for specific versions of Windows or verify that specific service packs are present before you allow an install. The Web setup template includes the IIS Launch condition. This searches for the presence of the right version of Microsoft Internet Information Services (IIS) and displays an error message to users if this version is not present, as shown in Figure 16-4.

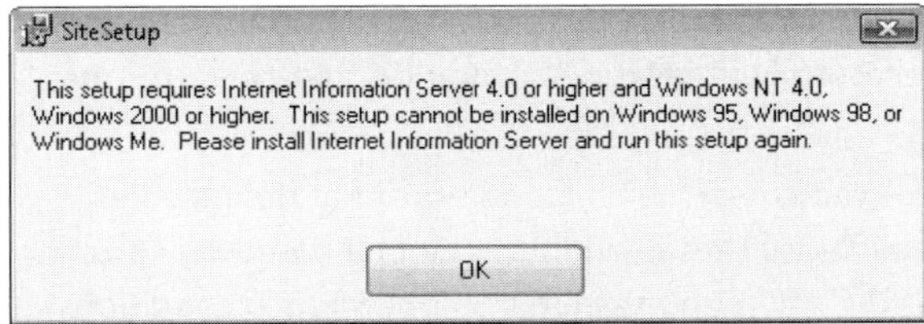

FIGURE 16-4 The Launch Conditions error message

To create and manage new launch conditions, you use the Launch Conditions editor in Visual Studio. This tool can be accessed by selecting your project in Visual Studio and then clicking the View menu. You will see an Editor submenu that contains a number of setup editors, including Registry, File System, File Types, User Interface, Custom Actions, and Launch Conditions.

Selecting the Launch Conditions submenu opens the Launch Conditions editor, shown in Figure 16-5. Notice that you right-click the Launch Conditions folder to add a new condition (more on this in a moment).

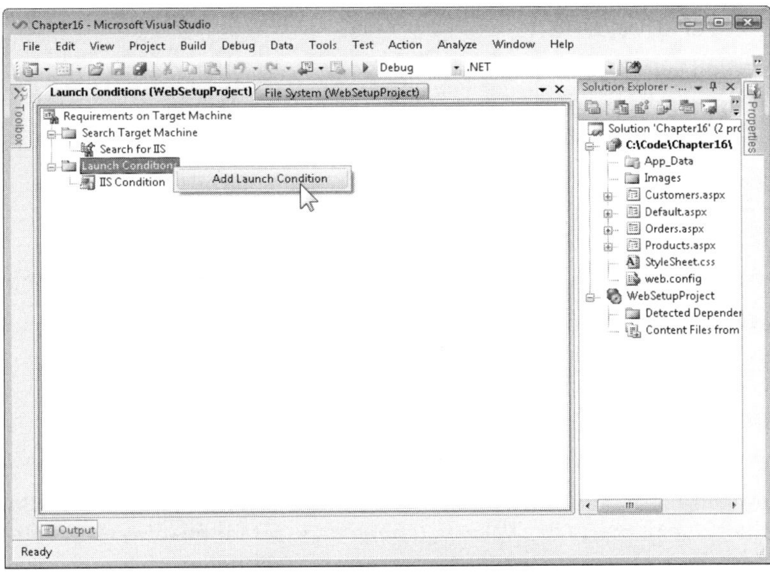

FIGURE 16-5 Use the Launch Conditions editor to configure requirements for your target computer

There are two main branches of the Launch Conditions editor: Search Target Machine and Launch Conditions. Each is described here:

- **Search Target Machine** This branch allows you to define criteria to search for prior to installation. By default, this node contains Search For IIS. You can add file, registry, and Windows Installer search conditions. Typically, you pair a search condition that determines whether a change is necessary with a launch condition that performs the change.

- **Launch Conditions** Allows you to create new launch conditions that define conditions that must be met prior to installation. These conditions can be based on search conditions or other criteria (such as the operating system version). Launch conditions can provide a useful message to the user if a requirement is missing. It can then automatically retrieve a Web page. By default, Web Setup Projects include conditions for ensuring the presence of the right version of IIS (such as greater than version 4).

Typically, you must add an item to each of these two nodes to require a single component as part of your install. For example, if you want to verify that a specific DLL is present, you must create a search condition under Search Target Machine and store the result of the search in a property. You then create a launch condition that uses the search condition's property. If the required condition is not met (file is missing), you specify an error message to be displayed to the user. You can also optionally add a Uniform Resource Locator (URL) to the required component for download.

Adding a Simple Search Condition

You can add both search and launch conditions manually by right-clicking the respective folder and choosing the appropriate item to add. This allows you to create both search and launch conditions at a granular level and manually decide how to connect them.

To add a basic search condition, start by right-clicking the *Search Target Machine* node in the Launch Conditions editor. You will have three search condition types to choose from: Add File Search, Add Registry Search, and Add Windows Installer Search. Each is a different search type. Depending on your selection, you will get different property values to set. The following provides an overview of each search type's options:

- **File Search** This search type allows you to define a search for a file. You set the *FileName* to the name of the file you are searching for, the *Folder* to search, and the *Property* to a variable name you use for tracking the results of the search.
- **Registry Search** This search type allows you to specify a registry search. You set the *Root* property to a place to start looking in the registry, the *RegKey* to a registry key to search for, and the *Value* property to a value you hope to be set for the given key. You store the results of your search in the *Property* property as a variable name that can be used in a related launch condition.
- **Windows Installer Search** This search type allows you to search for a registered component. You set the *ComponentId* to a GUID of the component for which you are searching. You set the *Property* property to a variable that indicates the results of your search.

You can also rename your search and launch conditions to something that makes sense to your specific scenario.

Adding a Simple Launch Condition

You can manually add a launch condition that must be met prior to installing your Web application. To do so, you right-click the Launch Conditions folder, and then select Add Launch Condition.

With the new launch condition selected, view the Properties window to configure your launch condition. You can set the *Condition* property to match the *Property* value of a search condition or specify a different condition. To download software to resolve the missing launch condition, provide a URL in the *InstallUrl* property. In the *Message* property, type a message to be displayed to the person installing your Web application if a condition is not met.

You can configure launch conditions to require specific operating system versions, specific service pack levels, and other criteria by setting the *Condition* property to an environment variable or key word and using both an operand and a value. Table 16-1 lists some commonly used conditions.

TABLE 16-1 Windows Installer Conditions

CONDITION	DESCRIPTION
VersionNT	Version number for Microsoft Windows NT–based operating systems, including Microsoft Windows 2000, Microsoft Windows XP, and Microsoft Windows Server 2003
Version9X	Version number for early Windows consumer operating systems, including Microsoft Windows 95, Microsoft Windows 98, and Microsoft Windows Me
ServicePackLevel	Version number of the operating system service pack
WindowsBuild	Build number of the operating system
SystemLanguageID	Default language identifier for the system
AdminUser	Tool that determines whether the user has administrative privileges
PhysicalMemory	Size of the installed RAM in megabytes
IISVERSION	Version of IIS, if installed

To evaluate environment variables, preface the variable name with a % symbol, as this example illustrates:

```
%HOMEDRIVE = "C:" (verify that the home drive is C:\)
```

To simply check a property for a specific value, you can use the = operator, as the following example shows:

```
IISVERSION = "#6" (check for IIS 6.0)
VersionNT = 500 (check for Windows 2000)
```

You can also check for ranges:

```
IISVERSION >= "#4" (check for IIS 4.0 or later)
Version9X <= 490 (check for Windows Me or earlier)
```

You can also check for multiple conditions using Boolean operators: *Not, And* (*True* if both values are *True*), *Or* (*True* if either value is *True*), *Xor* (*True* if exactly one value is *True*), *Eqv* (*True* if both values are the same), and *Imp* (*True* if the left term is *False* or the right term is *True*). The following example demonstrates these Boolean operators:

```
WindowsBuild=2600 AND ServicePackLevel=1 (check for Windows XP with Service Pack 1)
```

Creating Pregrouped Launch Conditions

You can also create pregrouped search and launch condition sets for common scenarios. Doing so simply creates both a search and a launch condition. However, these items are preconfigured to work together. You simply need to tweak their properties according to your needs. To create a grouped launch condition, you right-click the root node, *Requirements On Target Machine*, and select one of the following:

- Add File Launch Condition
- Add Registry Launch Condition
- Add Windows Installer Launch Condition
- Add .NET Framework Launch Condition
- Add Internet Information Services Launch Condition

As an example, adding file-based (such as a .dll) conditions is a common practice. To that end, the following provides a step-by-step walkthrough of creating a file-based, pregrouped launch condition:

1. In the Launch Conditions editor window, right-click the *Requirements On Target Machine* root node. Select Add File Launch Condition to get started.

   The Launch Conditions editor adds a search condition (Search For File1) to the *Search Target Machine* node and a launch condition (Condition1) to the *Launch Conditions* node. The new search condition's *Property* property value has a default name of *FILE-EXISTS1*. This value links it to the *Condition* property of the launch condition.

2. You can rename both the new search condition and the new launch condition so that the names indicate the file you are searching for.

   Figure 16-6 shows an example of both conditions added to the Launch Conditions editor. Notice that the Search For Customer.dll condition is selected along with its Properties window. Notice that the *Property* property is set to *FILEEXISTS1*.

LAB Deploying Web Applications

In this lab, you deploy applications using two techniques: a Web Setup Project and the Copy Web tool.

If you encounter a problem completing an exercise, the completed projects are available in the sample files installed from the companion CD in the Code folder.

EXERCISE 1 Create a Web Setup Project

In this exercise, you create a new ASP.NET Web site and a related Web Setup Project.

1. Open Visual Studio and create a new Web site called **MyNewWebSite** using the language of your preference. This site will serve as the basis for your setup project.
2. Add a number of simple pages to the site. This will give you something to set up and deploy. These pages could include order.aspx, product.aspx, customer.aspx, and vendor.aspx.
3. Add a Web Setup Project to your solution. To do so, from the File menu, select Add, and then select New Project. Under Project Types, expand Other Project Types, and then select Setup And Deployment. Under Templates (right side), select Web Setup Project. Name the project **MyWebSetup** and click OK.

   You should see a new project added to Visual Studio Solution Explorer. You should also see the File System editor for the setup project.
4. Next, you need to connect the setup project to your Web site. Within the left pane of the editor, right-click Web Application Folder, select Add, and then select Project Output. In the Add Project Output Group dialog box, select Content Files and click OK.

   If you were to build and install your project at this point, it would copy the site pages and code-behind files to the location specified by a user during setup.
5. In the File System editor, expand the Web Application Folder. Notice there is a Bin directory. This is where you would embed any .dll files that might need to be included by your solution. You would do so by right-clicking Bin and selecting Add to add a file. For this lab, there are no dependent .dll files so you can skip this.
6. Next, add a folder and a file that should be included with the build. To do so, right-click the Web Application Folder in the File System editor. Select Add, and then select Web Folder. Name the folder **Images**.

   Right-click the Images folder, select Add, and then select File. Navigate to the Pictures folder on your machine. Select a few sample pictures and click Open.
7. Now add a launch condition. From the View menu, select Editor, and then select Launch Conditions. In the Launch Conditions editor, right-click Requirements On Target Machine, and then select Add File Launch Condition.

   Rename the new search condition (currently named Search For File1) to **Search for Browscap**. Select the new search condition and view the Properties window.

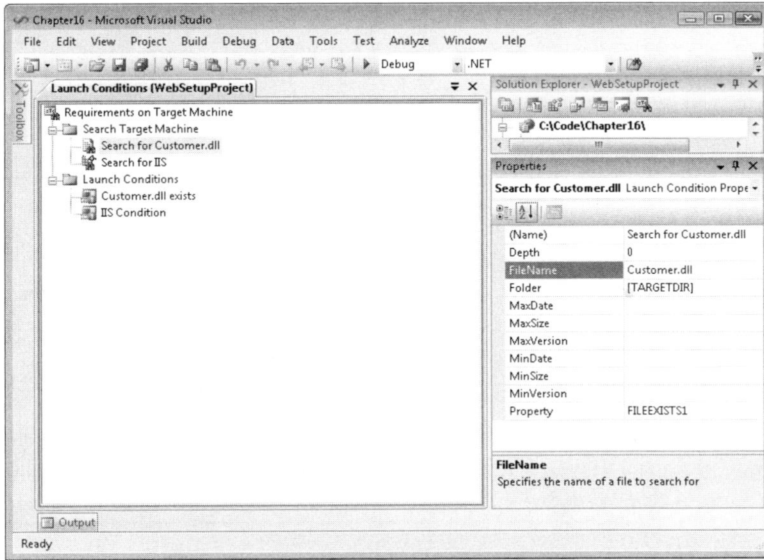

FIGURE 16-6 The file search criteria and related condition

3. Notice that in Figure 16-6, there are a number of search condition properties in the Properties window. For a file search, you typically configure these properties as described in Table 16-2.

TABLE 16-2 File Search Condition Properties

PROPERTY	DESCRIPTION
FileName	The name of the file to look for. Just specify the file name with extension, and not the folder.
Folder	The folder in which to search for the file. Here you can select a special folder such as [CommonFilesFolder] or [WindowsFolder]. You can also hard-code a direct path to the file. You can search subfolders by specifying the *Depth* field.
Depth	The number of nested folders within the specified folder to search.
MinDate, MaxDate	The minimum and maximum last modified date of the file.
MinSize, MaxSize	The minimum and maximum size of the file.
MinVersion, MaxVersion	The minimum and maximum version of the file.
Property	The name of the property that stores the results of this search. You specify this property name in the corresponding launch condition.

4. Next, you select the new launch condition and view its Properties window. The properties are typically configured as described in Table 16-3.

TABLE 16-3 Launch Condition Properties

PROPERTY	DESCRIPTION
Condition	The condition that must evaluate to *true* for installation to continue. By default, this is the name of a property assigned to a search condition, and if the search does find the required file or other object, the launch condition is fulfilled. You can specify more complex conditions to check for operating system version, service pack levels, and other criteria.
InstallUrl	If the *Condition* is not met, the setup project retrieves this URL to install the required component. This is an optional setting.
Message	The message that is displayed to the user if the launch condition is not met.

Those are the steps involved in adding a new file-based, pregrouped launch condition. Your setup will now look for the dependent file as configured in the search condition. Your launch condition will then execute and throw an error if the file is not found.

Writing to the Registry as Part of Deployment

Storing information in the registry used to be the preferred way of storing application settings. The best practice for configuring .NET Framework applications is to store settings in configuration files. Although rare, there might still be times when you need to add registry entries during setup. For example, you might need to configure an aspect of the operating system or another application.

To configure a Web Setup Project to add a registry entry during setup, follow these steps:

1. In Solution Explorer, select your setup project.
2. From the View menu, select Editor, and then select Registry. The Registry Settings editor appears.
3. The core folders of the registry are shown by default. To add a registry setting in a nested key, you need to add each nested key to the editor. For example, to add a setting to HKEY_LOCAL_MACHINE\SOFTWARE\Microsoft\ASP.NET\, you need to add the SOFTWARE, Microsoft, and ASP.NET keys to the HKEY_LOCAL_MACHINE hive in the Registry Settings editor.
4. Right-click the key to which you want to add a setting, select New, and then select String Value, Environment String Value, Binary Value, or DWORD Value. Type the name of the value, and then press Enter.

5. To define the value, select the registry value, view the Properties window, and set the *Value* property. To make the installation of the value conditional, define the *Condition* property.

   Figure 16-7 shows an example of the Registry editor in Visual Studio.

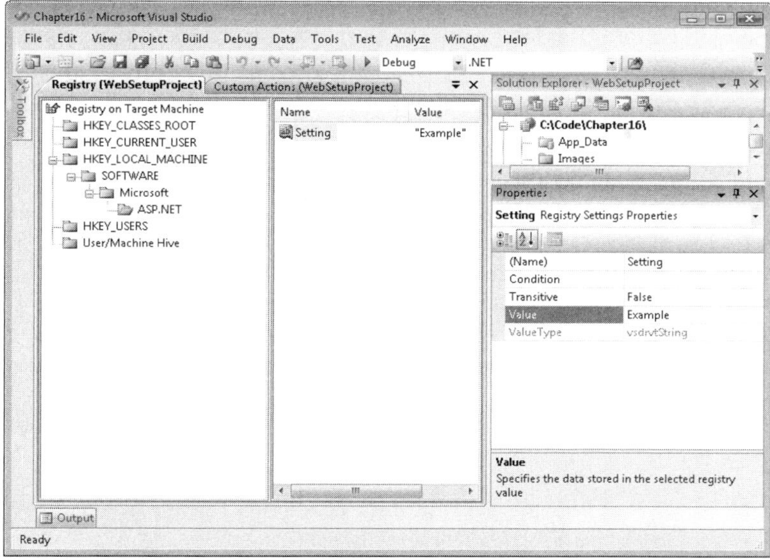

FIGURE 16-7 Adding a Registry entry to the deployment process

By default, registry keys are not removed when an application is uninstalled. To automatically remove a registry key during uninstallation, select the key and view the Properties window. Then, set the *DeleteAtUninstall* property to *True*.

Adding a Custom Setup Page

Administrators responsible for deploying and managing your Web applications can customize settings by editing your Web.config file. To enable simpler configuration at setup time, you can add custom setup wizard pages. With these pages, you can prompt users to custom-configure information, and then provide that information as parameters for custom actions. Combined, custom setup wizard pages and custom actions enable you to perform the following types of tasks at setup time:

- **Display a license agreement** A Web Setup Project provides a dialog box template for requiring the user to accept a license agreement.
- **Modify settings in the Web.config file** You can use user input to modify configuration settings without requiring administrators to know how to configure an Extensible Markup Language (XML) file.

- **Perform custom configuration** You can use a custom configuration to prompt the user for information that might be stored in the registry or in another unusual location.
- **Activate or register your application** You can prompt the user for a product key or registration information. Prompts can be either required or optional.

To add a custom setup wizard page to your Web deployment project, you use the User Interface Editor (View | Editor | User Interface). The User Interface editor displays the different setup phases for both standard and administrative installs of your application. Figure 16-8 shows the default view of the User Interface editor.

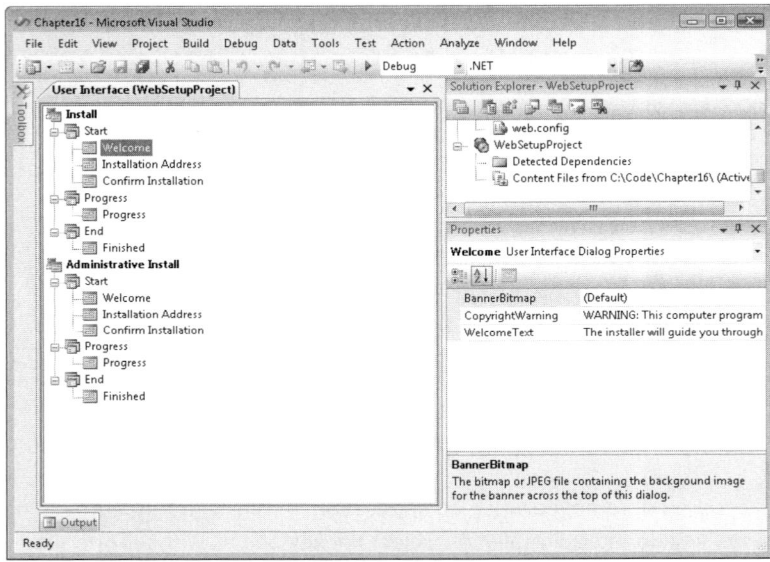

FIGURE 16-8 Use the User Interface editor to add pages to the setup wizard

To add a custom setup page, you right-click the setup phase to which you want to add and then select Add Dialog. Normally, you add dialog boxes to the Start phase under the *Install* node. The Add Dialog box, shown in Figure 16-9, shows you the dialog boxes that can be added to the selected install setup.

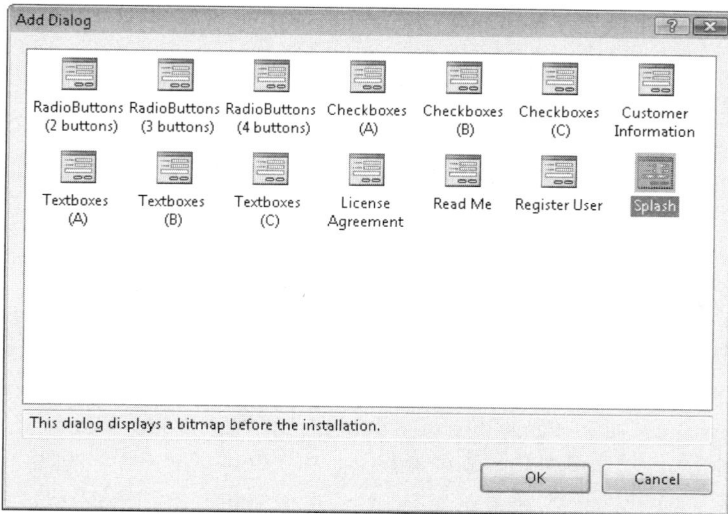

FIGURE 16-9 The Add Dialog setup pages

The *Administrative Install* node is more restrictive. There, you can add only a splash page, a license agreement page, or a Read Me page.

The different dialog box templates allow for collecting different types of information during setup. You can only customize these dialog boxes by hiding some controls and displaying different labels.

You customize these controls through the Properties window. There, you configure all aspects of the dialog box; Visual Studio does not provide a designer. To control the information for which the dialog box prompts the user, edit the labels and property names for the dialog box. For the text box and radio button series of dialog boxes, you can configure the label for each field (for example, *Edit1Label* or *Button1Label*), the name in which the value is to be stored (for example, *Edit1Property* or *ButtonProperty*), and the default value (for example, *Edit1Value* or *DefaultValue*). The License Agreement template allows you to specify a license agreement file, and the Splash template allows you to display a bitmap file.

You can also control the order in which your dialog boxes are shown to a user during setup. To do so, right-click a dialog box, and then click Move Up or Move Down. You can also delete a step in the process by right-clicking and selecting Delete.

When you run the Web Setup Project, your custom dialog boxes appear as setup wizard pages. If you configured pages to collect custom information from users, you can reference that data in custom actions, as described in the next section.

Adding Custom Actions to Your Deployment

Web Setup Projects provide a great deal of flexibility and can meet most setup requirements. If you have more demanding requirements, such as submitting registration information to a Web service or validating a product key, you can add a custom action to your setup project. Custom actions can run in any of the four phases of setup:

- **Install** This phase performs the bulk of the work done during setup by adding files and creating configuration settings required by your application to run.
- **Commit** After the Install phase is complete and all changes required to run your application have been made, the Commit phase finalizes these changes. After the Commit phase, setup cannot be rolled back and the application should be uninstalled with Add or Remove Programs.
- **Rollback** The Rollback phase runs only if setup fails or is cancelled. In such a case, the Rollback phase occurs instead of the Commit phase and removes any new files or settings.
- **Uninstall** This phase removes files and settings from the computer when the application is removed with Add or Remove Programs. Often, uninstall routines leave settings and databases in place so that they can be restored if the application is later reinstalled.

You add a custom action to your setup project through the Custom Actions editor. You can access this editor by first selecting your setup project in Solution Explorer and then selecting View | Editor | Custom Actions.

The Custom Actions editor displays the four setup phases. You can right-click the phase to which you want to add a custom action. You then select Add Custom Action. Doing so launches the Select Item In Project dialog box. From here you can select to add a custom .exe or script file to execute at the appropriate phase of deployment. You can select files from your current project or elsewhere. Figure 16-10 shows an example of this dialog box.

If you add more than one custom action to a single phase, you can rearrange the custom actions by right-clicking them and then clicking Move Up or Move Down.

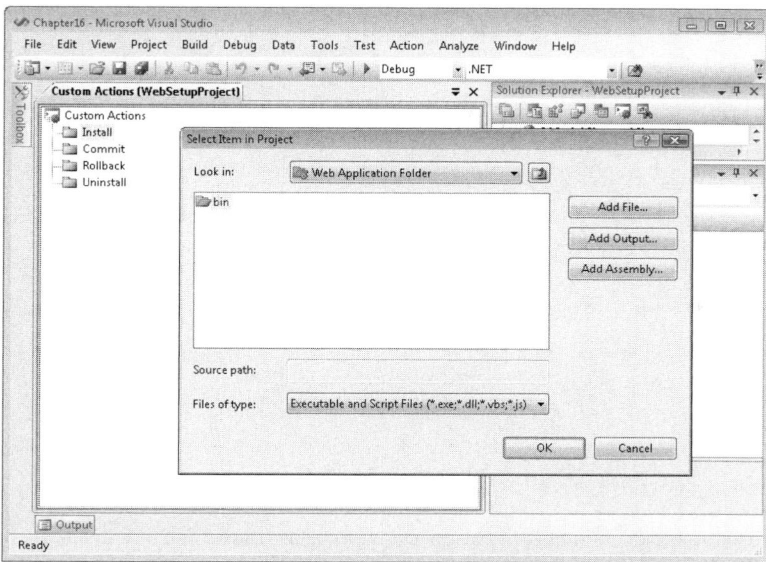

FIGURE 16-10 Adding a custom action to the deployment process

Deploying Web Applications Using a Web Setup Project

After you configure your Web Setup Project and build it using Visual Studio, you are ready to deploy it to an application server. To do so, you need to use the files generated as part of the build process. There are typically two generated to the target build directory for Web Setup Projects: an .exe and an .msi. These files are described in more detail here:

- **Setup.exe** This is an executable file that installs the files and settings you added to your Web Setup Project. When it is being run, the setup wizard guides a user through the installation process and prompts him or her for any required configuration settings, such as the Web site, virtual directory, and application pool (or process). Figure 16-11 shows an example.

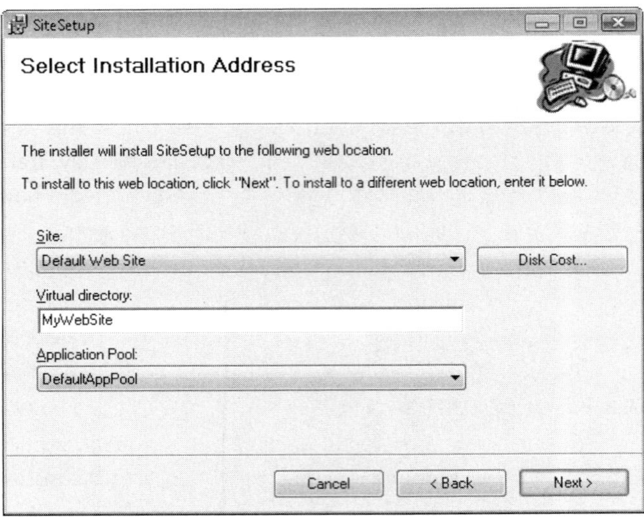

FIGURE 16-11 Web Setup Projects enable a Web application to be installed using a setup wizard

- **<WebSetupProjectName>.msi** This is the Windows Installer file containing any files you added to your Web Setup Project. A user can install this file by double-clicking it and launching the setup wizard. This is equivalent to running the Setup.exe file. Alternatively, network administrators can distribute the .msi file using Active Directory software distribution or Microsoft Systems Management Server (SMS).

Although users are more familiar with using Setup.exe to install an application, the Windows Installer file is smaller, far more versatile, and familiar to most systems administrators. The only disadvantage to deploying the application with the .msi file is that the target Web server must have Windows Installer. Most Web servers already have this component, however.

About Windows Installer (MSI)

Windows Installer, also known as *Microsoft Installer* or *MSI*, is a technology and file format for installing applications on computers running Windows. Most new applications, including almost all new Microsoft applications, include Windows Installer files. The inclusion of a Windows Installer package (.msi) file with an application greatly simplifies deployment in enterprise environments by enabling administrators to automatically install the application in a variety of ways.

> ***NOTE*** **WINDOWS INSTALLER BEHAVIOR**
>
> **Windows Installer packages (.msi) are not executable files, even though they behave exactly like Setup.exe files. When you launch an .msi file, the operating system opens the file with Windows Installer (Msiexec.exe).**

Windows Installer packages provide the following features to enable flexible application deployment:

- **Transforms** A transform is a collection of changes that administrators deploying your application can apply to a base Windows Installer package. They can do this without your assistance and without accessing your Web Setup Project files directly. Transforms for Windows Installer package files are similar to answer files that you might have used to automate the installation of an operating system such as Windows XP.
- **Properties can be defined on the command line** Properties are variables that Windows Installer uses during an installation. A subset of these, called public properties, can be set on the command line. This enables you to allow administrators to pass nonstandard parameters to your setup procedure, and enables automated installations even when you have custom requirements.
- **Standardized command-line options** Command-line options are used to specify variables, switches, and file and path names and control the actions of the installation at run time.

Table 16-4 displays the most important Windows Installer command-line options and related capabilities such as reinstalling, repairing, and removing applications. For example, for every application installed using MSI, you can use the command-line option */qn* to perform an installation without displaying a user interface (UI). The command-line option to create verbose log files is */lv**. Table 16-4 shows most of the other options.

TABLE 16-4 Windows Installer Command-Line Options

OPTION	PARAMETERS	DEFINITION
/i	*{package| ProductCode}*	Installs or configures a product. For example, to install a product from A:\Example.msi, use the following command: *msiexec /i A:\Example.msi*
/a	*package*	Performs an administrative installation.

/f	*[p][o][e][d][c] [a][u][m][s][v]* *{package|ProductCode}*	Repairs a product. This option ignores any property values entered on the command line. *p*: Reinstall only if file is missing. *o*: Reinstall if file is missing or if an older version is installed. *e*: Reinstall if file is missing or an equal or older version is installed. *d*: Reinstall if file is missing or a different version is installed. *c*: Reinstall if file is missing or the stored checksum does not match the calculated value. *a*: Force all files to be reinstalled. *u*: Rewrite all required user-specific registry entries. *m*: Rewrite all required computer-specific registry entries. *s*: Overwrite all existing shortcuts. *v*: Run from source and recache the local package. For example, you can repair the installation package using the following command: *msiexec /fpecms Example.msi*
/x	*{package|ProductCode}*	Uninstalls a product. For example, you can remove or uninstall a package using the following command: *msiexec /x Example.msi*

/L	*[i][w][e][a][r]* *[u][c][m][p][v]* *[+][!]logfile*	Specifies the path to the log file. The following flags indicate which information to log: *i*: Status messages. *w*: Nonfatal warnings. *e*: All error messages. *i*: Startup of actions. *r*: Action-specific records. *i*: User requests. *c*: Initial UI parameters. *m*: Out-of-memory. *p*: Terminal properties. *v*: Verbose output. +: Append to existing file. *!*: Flush each line to the log. *: Wildcard; log all information except for the *v* option. To include the *v* option, specify */L*v*. For example, to install a package and create a log file that contains the information related to the status, out-of-memory, and error messages, use the following command: *msiexec /i Example.msi /Lime logfile.txt*
/p	*PatchPackage*	Applies a patch. To apply a patch to an installed administrative image, you must combine options as follows: */p: PatchPackage* */a: package* For example, to apply a patch to an administrative installation package, use the following syntax: *msiexec /p <PatchPackage> /a Example.msi*

/q	*{n|b|r|f}*	Sets UI level. *qn*: No UI. *qb*: Basic UI. *qr*: Reduced UI with a modal dialog box displayed at the end of the installation. *qf*: Full UI with a modal dialog box displayed at the end. *qn+*: No UI except for a modal dialog box displayed at the end. *qb+*: Basic UI with a modal dialog box displayed at the end. *qb-*: Basic UI with no modal dialog boxes. For example, to display the basic UI options during the package installation, use the following command: *msiexec /qb Example.msi*
/? or */h*	None	Displays the Windows Installer version and copyright information. For example, to display the version and copyright information, use the following command: *msiexec /?*

Deploying Web Applications Using the Copy Web Tool

Web Setup Projects are useful if you are providing a Web application to many users or to an administrative team. However, if you are responsible for updating a specific Web site, it might be impractical to log on to the Web server, copy over an install, and run the Windows Installer package each time you make an update to the site. This is especially true if you deploy a lot to a development or test server.

For some development scenarios, you might be able to edit the Web application directly on the Web server. However, changes you make are immediately implemented on that server. Of course, this includes any bugs that might be lurking in the new code.

There are many scenarios in which you simply need to copy changes between two servers. This might be changes from your development environment up to staging or even from staging to production in some limited scenarios. In these cases, you can use the Copy Web tool to publish changes between any two Web servers.

The Copy Web tool can copy individual files or an entire Web site. You can select a source and a remote site and move files between them. You can also use the tool to synchronize files. This involves copying only changed files and detecting possible versioning conflicts in which the same file on both the source and remote site have been separately edited. The Copy Web tool, however, does not merge changes within a single file; it only does complete file copies.

You launch the Copy Web tool from Visual Studio. To do so, you typically open the Web site you intend as the source (copy from). You can then right-click the site in Solution Explorer and choose Copy Web Site. This launches the Copy Web tool, as shown in Figure 16-12.

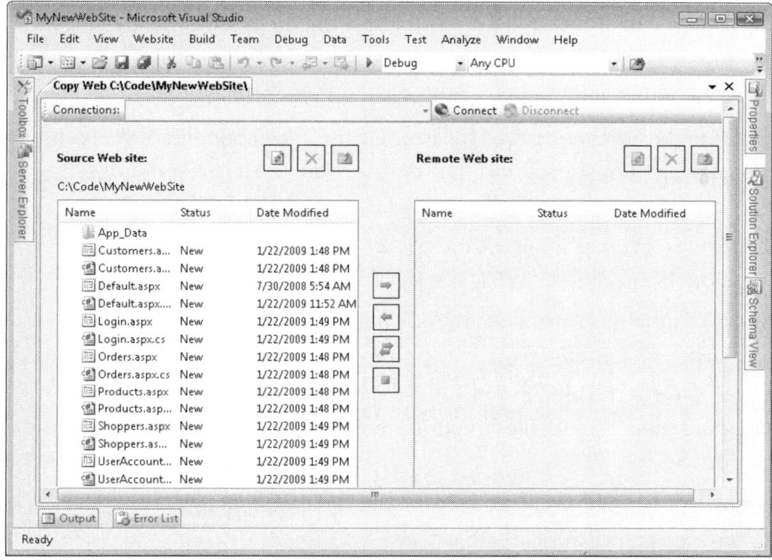

FIGURE 16-12 Use the Copy Web tool to synchronize two Web sites

The Copy Web tool displays two panes: Source Web Site and Remote Web Site. The source Web site is the site from which you wish to copy. The remote Web site is the copy-to site or destination. To set up a remote Web site, you must create a connection by clicking Connect at the top of the tool. This launches the Open Web Site dialog box, which allows you to find a Web site. There are four options for navigating to a remote Web site:

- **File system** This option provides a destination Web site on a local hard drive or a shared folder. A network drive connected to a shared folder on the remote Web server is the fastest way to transfer a Web site to a server on your intranet. You must have previously configured the Web application on the server and shared the Web application folder. This technique transfers your source code across the network in clear text.
- **Local IIS** This provides a destination Web application running within IIS on your local computer. You can use this interface to create a new Web application on your local server.
- **FTP site** This provides a destination remote Web site where the server is configured to run a File Transfer Protocol (FTP) server and allow uploads and downloads to the Web application folder. You must have previously configured the Web application on the server and shared the Web application folder. This technique transfers your user credentials and your source code across the network in clear text, and therefore is not recommended.

- **Remote site** This provides an interface where you can transfer files to and from a remote Web application using Microsoft FrontPage extensions, provided you have configured the Web server to allow this type of update. You can use this interface to create a new Web application on your server. To prevent your source code from being sent across the network in clear text, configure the Web site with a Secure Sockets Layer (SSL) certificate and select the Connect Using Secure Sockets Layer check box in the Open Web Site dialog box.

Visual Studio will save configured connections for future use. Once connected, you can copy or synchronize files between the source and the remote Web site in several different ways:

- **Copy individual files** Select files in either the source or the remote Web site, and then click the directional Copy Selected Files buttons.
- **Copy the entire site** Right-click the Source Web Site pane, and then select Copy Site To Remote. To copy the Remote Web Site to the source Web site, right-click the Remote Web Site pane, and then select Copy Site To Source.
- **Synchronize individual files** Select files in either the source or remote Web site, and then click Synchronize Selected Files.
- **Synchronize the entire site** Right-click the Source Web Site pane, and then select Synchronize Site.

When copying or synchronizing files, versioning conflicts are possible if another developer modifies the remote copy of a file that you edited. Visual Studio doesn't have the capability to merge or analyze these changes. Therefore, the Copy Web tool simply notifies you of the conflict and lets you choose whether to overwrite the remote file with your local file, overwrite your local file, or not overwrite either file. Unless you know exactly what changed on a file, you should never overwrite it. Instead, you should analyze the file, determine what changed, and attempt to manually merge the changes. Otherwise, you might overwrite a coworker's development effort.

Precompiling Web Applications

The first time a page is requested from a new or updated Web application, ASP.NET compiles the application. Compiling doesn't typically take long (often less than a second or two), but the first few Web page requests are delayed while the application is compiled. To avoid this delay, you can precompile your Web application before you publish it to a server.

To precompile and publish a Web application, follow these steps:

1. Open the Web site you wish to precompile and publish. Next, you can right-click your Web application in Solution Explorer and select Publish Web Site. Alternatively, you can select the Build menu and then choose Publish Web Site.
2. In the Publish Web Site dialog box, specify a location to which to publish. If you click the ellipsis button (...), you can browse the file system, local IIS, an FTP site, or a remote site, exactly as you would using the Copy Web tool.

3. In the Publish Web Site dialog box, select your options:
   - **Allow This Precompiled Site To Be Updatable** This check box, when selected, specifies that the content of .aspx pages are not compiled into an assembly; instead, the markup is left as is, allowing you to change HTML and client-side functionality after precompiling the Web site. Selecting this check box is equivalent to adding the *-u* option to the *aspnet_compiler.exe* command.
   - **Use Fixed Naming And Single Page Assemblies** This option specifies that batch builds are turned off during precompilation to generate assemblies with fixed names. Themes and skin files continue to be compiled to a single assembly. This option is not available for in-place compilation.
   - **Enable Strong Naming On Precompiled Assemblies** This check box, when selected, specifies that the generated assemblies are strongly named by using a key file or key container to encode the assemblies and to ensure that they have not been tampered with. After you select this check box, you can do the following:
     - Specify the location of a key file to use to sign the assemblies. If you use a key file, you can select Delay Signing, which signs the assembly in two stages: first with the public key file, and then with a private key file that is specified later during a call to the *aspnet_compiler.exe* command.
     - Specify the location of a key container from the system's cryptographic service provider (CSP) to use to name the assemblies.
     - Specify whether to mark the assembly with the *AllowPartiallyTrustedCallers* property, which allows strongly named assemblies to be called by partially trusted code. Without this declaration, only fully trusted code can use such assemblies.
4. The last step is to click OK to compile and publish the precompiled Web site.

Publishing a Web site can be an easy way to move a Web site from a development server to a staging or production server.

Quick Check

1. **What launch condition does a Web Setup Project include by default?**
2. **What are the four phases of a Web Setup Project deployment?**

Quick Check Answers

1. **By default, a Web Setup Project checks for an IIS version later than 4.**
2. **Install, Commit, Rollback, and Uninstall are the four phases of Web Setup Project deployment.**

- Set the *FileName* property to **Nothing.ini** (this file doesn't exist, but you'll fix the error later).
- Set the *Folder* property to [WindowsFolder] (for Vista) and set the *Depth* property to **4**. This tells setup to search the system folder and all subfolders four levels deep for a file named Browscap.ini (which should be present on any Web server). Note that the *Property* value is set to *FILEEXISTS1*.

Rename the new launch condition (currently named Condition1) to **Browscap Condition**. Select the new launch condition and view the Properties window.

- Set the *InstallUrl* property to **http://support.microsoft.com/kb/826905**, which contains information about the Browscap.ini file. In the real world, you would provide a link with instructions on how to fulfill the requirement.
- Set the *Message* property to **You must have a Browscap.ini file to complete installation. Would you like more information?**. Notice that the *Condition* property is already set to *FILEEXISTS1*, which corresponds to the search condition *Property* value.

8. Build the Web Setup Project. Right-click your setup project In Solution Explorer, and then select Build. In the Output window, make note of the folder containing the output files.

   Open the output folder in Windows Explorer and examine the files that are present. You should see both an .msi and a setup.exe file.

In the next exercise, you install the Web application.

EXERCISE 2 Deploy a Web Setup Project

In this exercise, you install a Web application using a Windows Installer file.

1. Start with the project created in Exercise 1. Alternatively, you can copy the completed project for Lesson 1, Exercise 1 from the CD to your hard drive.
2. Open the folder that contains the .msi file you created in Exercise 1. Double-click the .msi file to launch setup. After a few seconds, you should see an error indicating that the Browscap.ini file does not exist, as shown in Figure 16-13.

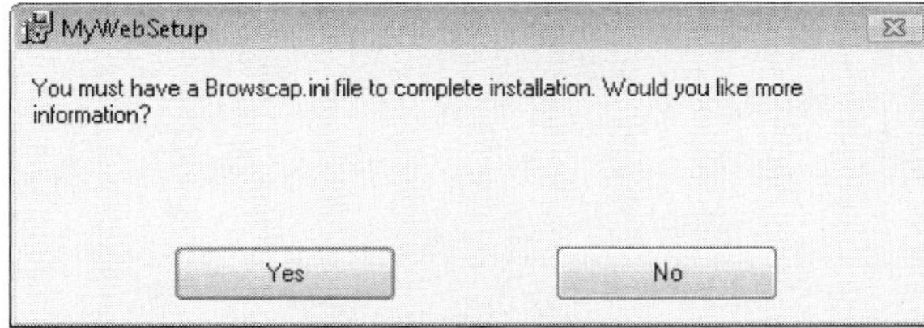

FIGURE 16-13 The .msi file error message

Recall that we added this condition in Exercise 1. We also set the *FileName* property of the search condition to *Nothing.ini*, which is why this error is being thrown.

Click Yes. You will be taken to the *InstallUrl* set as part of the condition.

3. Return to Visual Studio. Open the Launch Conditions editor for the Web Setup Project.

   Select Search For Browscap under Search Target Machine. View the Properties window. Change the *FileName* property to look for the file **Browscap.ini**.

4. Rebuild the Web Setup Project (right-click and select Rebuild).

5. Return to the directory where the .msi file exists. Rerun the .msi file. This time, the computer should meet the setup requirements because the Browscap.ini file exists in the Windows folder.

NOTE INSTALLATION ISSUES

Depending on your environment, you might run into additional issues. If, for example, you are running Windows Vista and IIS 7.0, you need an IIS 6-compatible metabase for the IIS condition to validate. You can tweak the condition or add the IIS 6 metabase to IIS 7.0 from Control Panel (classic view), Programs And Features, Turn Windows Feature On Or Off, Internet Information Services, Web Management Tools, IIS 6 Management Compatibility. Another issue is security in Vista. You might have to run the Setup.exe (and not the .msi) file by right-clicking Setup.exe and selecting Run As Administrator.

6. On the Select Installation Address page, notice that you have the opportunity to select the Web site, virtual directory, and application pool. Choose a unique virtual directory name and make note of it. Click Next.

   Finish walking through the installation steps.

7. Open the Internet Information Services console (Control Panel | Administrative Tools | Internet Information Services [IIS] Manager). Find the virtual directory in which you installed the Web application. Verify that the pages, code-behind files, and images exist. Figure 16-14 shows an example.

FIGURE 16-14 The installed site in IIS Manager

As you can see, deploying a Web application can be as easy as installing a Windows Forms application. Although this process takes you through a manual installation of a Windows Installer package, you can also deploy the .msi file in an automated manner.

Lesson Summary

- Web Setup Projects allow you to create executable Setup.exe files and Windows Installer packages (.msi files) that administrators can use to easily deploy your applications to a Web server.
- The Copy Web tool can synchronize a Web site between a remote server and your local computer. This is useful if you want to do deployment and testing on your local computer and then upload the Web site to a remote Web server. The Copy Web tool can also be useful in environments with multiple developers because it detects versioning conflicts.
- Precompiling a Web application removes the delay that occurs when ASP.NET compiles an application after the first user request. To precompile a Web application, use the Publish Web Site tool.

Lesson Review

You can use the following questions to test your knowledge of the information in Lesson 1, "Deploying Web Applications." The questions are also available on the companion CD if you prefer to review them in electronic form.

> ***NOTE*** **ANSWERS**
>
> **Answers to these questions and explanations of why each answer choice is right or wrong are located in the "Answers" section at the end of the book.**

1. You need to add a registry entry to make your application function. In which phase of the Web Setup Project should you add the registry entry?
   - **A.** Install
   - **B.** Commit
   - **C.** Rollback
   - **D.** Uninstall
2. You need to make a change to an operating system–related registry entry to make your application function. You want to ensure you remove this change if setup is cancelled or the application is removed from the computer. In which phases should you undo your registry modification? (Choose all that apply.)
   - **A.** Install
   - **B.** Commit
   - **C.** Rollback
   - **D.** Uninstall
3. Which of the following deployment tools enable multiple developers to work on a site simultaneously while detecting potential versioning conflicts?
   - **A.** Setup Project
   - **B.** Web Setup Project
   - **C.** Copy Web tool
   - **D.** Publish Web Site tool
4. Which of the following deployment tools has the potential to improve responsiveness of the Web site to end users?
   - **A.** Setup Project
   - **B.** Web Setup Project
   - **C.** Copy Web tool
   - **D.** Publish Web Site tool

Lesson 2: Using Caching to Improve Performance

ASP.NET caching stores frequently accessed data or whole Web pages in memory where they can be retrieved faster than they could be from a file or database. This helps to improve performance and increase scalability (in terms of number of users serviced) of a Web application. As an example, if you have a product catalog in an e-commerce application, you might consider putting a lot of the catalog data into cache. Data that changes infrequently and is accessed by a lot of users is a good candidate for caching. The first access of this data would load it into the cache; subsequent requests would be served from the cache until the cache expires.

ASP.NET and the .NET Framework enable you to take advantage of caching without requiring you to write a lot of code to deal with the complexities of caching such as cache expiration, updates, and memory management. There are two different types of caching in ASP.NET:

- **Application caching** This represents a collection that can store any object in memory and automatically remove the object based on memory limitations, time limits, or other dependencies.
- **Page output caching** This is ASP.NET's ability to store a rendered page, portion of a page, or version of a page in memory to reduce the time required to render the page in future requests.

This lesson covers both application caching and page output caching.

After this lesson, you will be able to:

- Use application caching to store frequently accessed data that is expensive to obtain.
- Use page output caching to improve the response time of page requests.

Estimated lesson time: 40 minutes

Application Caching

Application caching (also called application data caching) is the process of storing data (and not pages) in a cache object. The cache object is available as a property of the *Page* object. It represents a collection class of type *System.Web.Caching.Cache*. The *Page.Cache* property actually uses an application-wide cache (and not just a page-specific cache). This means that a single *Cache* object exists for your entire application; items in the *Cache* can be shared between user sessions and requests. This application cache object is managed by ASP.NET for you. Figure 16-15 shows the *Cache* object.

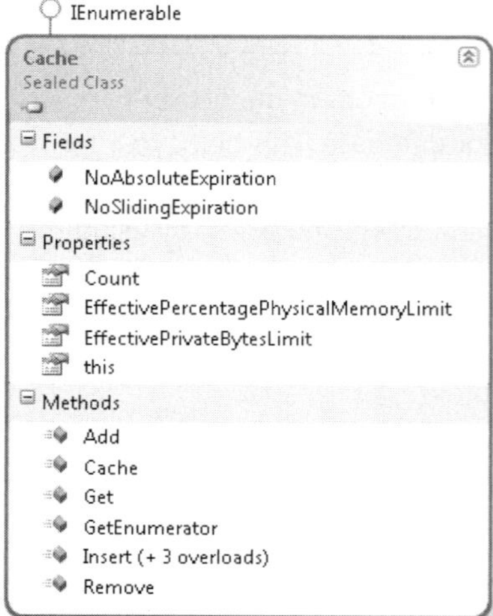

FIGURE 16-15 The *Cache* object in *System.Web.Caching*

Using the *Cache* Object

You work with the *Cache* object like you would *Session* or similar objects. You can assign items directly to the cache by giving them a name (key) and assigning them an object (value). You retrieve objects from the cache by checking for the given key. It is always wise to verify that the item is not null. If a value is null, that value either hasn't been cached or it has expired from the cache. If an item is null in the cache, you should have a means to reset it back to the cache (more on this to come). The following code sample demonstrates how to cache and retrieve a *String* object with the *Cache* collection:

```
'VB
Cache("Greeting") = "Hello, world!"
If Not (Cache("Greeting") Is Nothing) Then
  value = CType(Cache("Greeting"), String)
Else
  value = "Hello, world!"
End If

//C#
Cache["Greeting"] = "Hello, world!";
if (Cache["Greeting"] != null)
  value = (string)Cache["Greeting"];
else
  value = "Hello, world!";
```

You wouldn't normally cache a static string in your application; you'd more likely cache a file, a database query result, or other data that is shared and expensive to obtain. You can cache any object type, including your own custom types. However, you must cast the object back to the correct type when you access it from the cache.

Inserting Items into the Cache

The previous example demonstrates that you can use the *Cache* object like you would *Session* or *Application*. You can access much more sophisticated functionality, however, by using the *Add* and *Insert* methods. Each of these methods enables you to add an item to the cache and control how that item gets removed from the cache. This includes automatic removal based on a specific period of time, when a file changes, or another cache object expires.

The *Cache* object has both the *Add* and *Insert* methods. The *Add* method exists to satisfy the collection interface and therefore returns the item added to the cache as a result of the call. This *Add* method is meant to comply with the collection interface. The *Insert* method, however, has been the preferred method for adding items to the cache. Both define the same set of parameters and do the same thing behind the scenes. However, *Insert* has a number of overloads based on the many parameters you can set when adding an item to the cache. The following list outlines the parameters of the *Cache.Insert* method:

- ***key*** This is the name (as a *String*) that you'll use to access the cached object in the *Cache* collection. The *key* must be unique in the cache.
- ***value*** This is the data (as an *Object*) that you want to cache.
- ***dependencies*** A *CacheDependency* object identifies a file or a key to another item in the cache. When the file or related cached item is changed, this will trigger this cached object to be removed from the cache.

  If you cache a file, you should configure a dependency for the file so that it is removed from the cache after being modified. This helps ensure that your cache never becomes stale. You might also call the parameter *onRemoveCallback* to reload the cached item.
- ***absoluteExpiration*** This is the time (as a *DateTime* object) at which the object should be removed from the cache. This is absolute and therefore does not take into consideration whether the item has been recently accessed by a user. If you do not wish to use absolute expiration, you can set this property to *System.Web.Caching.Cache .NoAbsoluteExpiration*.
- ***slidingExpiration*** This is the time (as a *TimeSpan* object) after which the object should be removed from the cache if it has not been accessed by a user. Set this to *System.Web.Caching.Cache.NoSlidingExpiration* if you don't want to use it.
- ***priority*** This is a *CacheItemPriority* enumeration value that you can use to determine which objects are removed first when memory starts to run low (this process is called scavenging). Lower priority objects are removed sooner. The values for priority, from lowest (most likely to be removed) to highest (least likely to be removed) include the following:
  - *Low*
  - *BelowNormal*

- *Normal* (Default is equivalent to *Normal*)
- *AboveNormal*
- *High*
- *NotRemovable*

- ***onRemoveCallback*** This is an event handler that is called when the object is removed from the cache. This can be null if you don't want to specify a callback method.

Defining a Cache Dependency

A cache dependency links a cached item to something else such as a file or another item in the cache. ASP.NET monitors the dependency and invalidates the cache if the dependent item changes. The following code sample demonstrates how to make a cache dependency based on a file. If the dependent file changes, the object is removed from the cache.

```
'VB
Cache.Insert("FileCache", "CacheContents", New System.Web.Caching.CacheDependency( _
  Server.MapPath("SourceFile.xml")))

//C#
Cache.Insert("FileCache", "CacheContents", new System.Web.Caching.CacheDependency(
  Server.MapPath("SourceFile.xml")));
```

You can also create multiple dependencies for a single cached item. The following example demonstrates how to use an *AggregateCacheDependency* object to add an item to the cache that is dependent on both an item named *CacheItem1* and a file named *SourceFile.xml*.

```
'VB
Dim dep1 As CacheDependency = New CacheDependency(Server.MapPath("SourceFile.xml"))
Dim keyDependencies2 As String() = {"CacheItem1"}
Dim dep2 As CacheDependency = New System.Web.Caching.CacheDependency(Nothing, _
  keyDependencies2)
Dim aggDep As AggregateCacheDependency = New System.Web.Caching.
AggregateCacheDependency()
aggDep.Add(dep1)
aggDep.Add(dep2)
Cache.Insert("FileCache", "CacheContents", aggDep)

//C#
System.Web.Caching.CacheDependency dep1 =
  new System.Web.Caching.CacheDependency(Server.MapPath("SourceFile.xml"));
string[] keyDependencies2 = { "CacheItem1" };
System.Web.Caching.CacheDependency dep2 =
  new System.Web.Caching.CacheDependency(null, keyDependencies2);
System.Web.Caching.AggregateCacheDependency aggDep =
```

```
  new System.Web.Caching.AggregateCacheDependency();
aggDep.Add(dep1);
aggDep.Add(dep2);
Cache.Insert("FileCache", "CacheContents", aggDep);
```

Setting an Absolute Cache Expiration

Many times you want to cache data for a specific amount of time. This allows you to limit the amount of time between cache refresh. To do so, you pass the *absoluteExpiration* parameter to the *Cache.Insert* method. This parameter takes a time in the future at which your data should expire. The *DateTime.Now* object has a variety of methods for adding a specific number of minutes to the current time. The following example demonstrates this:

```
'VB
Cache.Insert("FileCache", "CacheContents", Nothing, DateTime.Now.AddMinutes(10), _
  Cache.NoSlidingExpiration)

//C#
Cache.Insert("FileCache", "CacheContents", null, DateTime.Now.AddMinutes(10),
  Cache.NoSlidingExpiration);
```

Setting a Sliding Cache Expiration

If you want your most frequently used cached objects to stay in your cache longer, you can specify a sliding expiration. A sliding expiration indicates the amount of time that must elapse between subsequent requests before an item is removed from the cache. Each time a new request comes in for a given item, the sliding scale restarts.

You set a sliding expiration by passing a *TimeSpan* to the *slidingExpiration* parameter of the *Insert* method. The *TimeSpan* is the time after the last read request that the cached object will be retained. This example shows you how to keep an object in cache for 10 minutes after the last request:

```
'VB
Cache.Insert("CacheItem7", "Cached Item 7", _
  Nothing, System.Web.Caching.Cache.NoAbsoluteExpiration, New TimeSpan(0, 10, 0))

//C#
Cache.Insert("CacheItem7", "Cached Item 7",
  null, System.Web.Caching.Cache.NoAbsoluteExpiration, new TimeSpan(0, 10, 0));
```

You have to be careful with these settings. For example, if you set no absolute expiration but just a sliding expiration, it is possible that heavy usage will result in an item never being removed from the cache (or not for a very long time). It might be wise to use both these properties; the *absoluteExpiration* can be a fallback if the *slidingExpiration* never transpires.

✔ Quick Check

1. How can you cause a cached object to be automatically invalidated after a specific amount of time?
2. Where is *Cache* data stored—in memory, on the hard disk, in a database, or on a state server?
3. What types of data can you store in the *Cache* collection?
4. What must you do before you retrieve an object from the *Cache* collection?

Quick Check Answers

1. Call the *Cache.Add* or *Cache.Insert* methods and provide a dependency.
2. The *Cache* object is stored in memory on the server.
3. You can store any type of data in the *Cache* collection. However, when you retrieve it, you must cast it to the correct type.
4. You must verify that the object is not null. If it is null, you must retrieve it from the original source rather than from *Cache*.

Page Output Caching

After a Web browser retrieves a page, the browser often keeps a copy of the page on the local computer. The next time the user requests the page, the browser simply verifies that the cached version is still valid, and then displays the cached page to the user. This improves the responsiveness of the site by decreasing the time required to load the page. It also reduces the load on the server because the server is not required to render a page.

Client-side caching requires that each individual user retrieve a dynamically generated version of your page. If one user visits your Web site 100 times, your Web server only has to generate the page once. If 100 users visit your Web site once, your Web server needs to generate the page 100 times.

To improve performance and reduce rendering time, ASP.NET also supports page output caching. With page output caching, ASP.NET can keep a copy of a rendered ASP.NET Web page in memory on the server. The next time a user requests it—even if it's a different user—ASP.NET can return the page almost instantly. If a page takes a long time to render (for example, if the page makes multiple queries), this can significantly improve performance. If you have a lot of activity on your server, it can also increase your scalability, as resources used to retrieve data can be freed.

If your page shows dynamic information or is customized for individual users, you don't want the same version of the page sent from the cache to every user. Fortunately, ASP.NET gives you flexible configuration options to meet almost any requirement. You can even implement user controls to do partial-page caching while generating other portions of the page dynamically.

Declaratively Configuring Caching for a Single Page

You can configure each ASP.NET page in your site to be cached independently. This gives you granular control over which pages get cached and how they get cached. You manage this by adding the @ *OutputCache* directive to the top of a page's markup. You can configure this directive using the attributes shown in Table 16-5.

TABLE 16-5 *OutputCache* Attributes

ATTRIBUTE	DESCRIPTION
Duration	The number of seconds to cache the page. This is the only required parameter.
Location	One of the *OutputCacheLocation* enumeration values, such as *Any*, *Client*, *Downstream*, *Server*, *None*, or *ServerAndClient*. The default is *Any*.
CacheProfile	The name of the cache settings to associate with the page. The default is an empty string ("").
NoStore	A Boolean value that determines whether to prevent secondary storage of sensitive information.
Shared	A Boolean value that determines whether user control output can be shared with multiple pages. The default is *False*.
VaryByParam	A semicolon-separated list of strings used to vary the output cache. By default, these strings correspond to a query string value sent with *Get* method attributes, or a parameter sent using the *Post* method. When this attribute is set to multiple parameters, the output cache contains a different version of the requested document for each combination of specified parameters. Possible values include *none*, an asterisk (*), and any valid query string or *Post* parameter name. Either this attribute or the *VaryByControl* attribute is required when you use the @ *OutputCache* directive on ASP.NET pages and user controls. A parser error occurs if you fail to include it. If you do not want to specify a parameter to vary cached content, set the value to *none*. If you want to vary the output cache by all parameter values, set the attribute to an asterisk (*).
VaryByControl	A semicolon-separated list of strings used to vary a user control's output cache. These strings represent the ID property values of ASP.NET server controls declared in the user control.

SqlDependency	A string value that identifies a set of database and table name pairs on which a page or control's output cache depends. Note that the *SqlCacheDependency* class monitors the table in a database that the output cache depends on, so that when items in a table are updated, those items are removed from the cache when using table-based polling. When using notifications (in Microsoft SQL Server) with the value *CommandNotification*, ultimately a *SqlDependency* class is used to register for query notifications with the SQL Server.
VaryByCustom	Any text that represents custom output caching requirements. If this attribute is given a value of *browser*, the cache is varied by browser name and major version information. If a custom string is entered, you must override the *GetVaryByCustomString* method in your application's Global.asax file.
VaryByHeader	A semicolon-separated list of Hypertext Transfer Protocol (HTTP) headers used to vary the output cache. When this attribute is set to multiple headers, the output cache contains a different version of the requested document for each combination of specified headers.

The *Location*, *CacheProfile*, and *NoStore* attributes cannot be used in user controls (.ascx files). The *Shared* attribute cannot be used in ASP.NET pages (.aspx files).

The following example demonstrates how to cache a page for 15 minutes, regardless of the parameters passed to the page:

```
<%@ OutputCache Duration="15" VaryByParam="none" %>
```

If the page might display differently based on parameters, provide the names of those query string parameters in the *VaryByParam* attribute. The following example caches a different copy of the page for different values provided in the location or count query string parameters:

```
<%@ OutputCache Duration="15" VaryByParam="location;count" %>
```

Partial-Page Caching

To cache a portion of an ASP.NET Web page, move the portion of the page that you want to cache into an .ascx user control. Then, add the @ *OutputCache* directive to the user control. That user control will be cached separately from the parent page.

Programmatically Configuring Caching for a Single Page

If you need to make run-time decisions about output caching, you can do so using the *Response.Cache* object. The available programmatic methods do not correspond directly to the attributes provided by the @ *OutputCache* directive, but they provide basic functionality:

- ***Response.Cache.SetExpires*** Use this method to specify the number of seconds that the page is to be cached.

- ***Response.Cache.SetCacheability*** Use this method to specify an *HttpCacheability* enumeration value, such as *HttpCacheability.Public* (which enables caching at both the client and the server) or *HttpCacheability.Server* (which enables caching at the server but disables caching at the client).
- ***Response.Cache.SetValidUntilExpires*** Pass this method a *True* value to configure the cache to ignore cache-invalidation headers.

Using Substitution to Update Caches

Some pages might not be eligible for caching because they have simple elements that must be dynamically generated. As an alternative to creating separate user controls for the dynamic element and configuring different a caching policy for those user controls, you can use substitution. ASP.NET provides two cache substitution techniques:

- **The *Response.WriteSubstitution* method** You add static placeholders to your page in places where dynamic content is required, and then use the *Response.WriteSubstitution* method to specify a method that replaces portions of a cached page with dynamically generated content. To specify the substitution method, call *WriteSubstitution* and pass a callback method with an *HttpResponseSubstitutionCallback* signature.

> ***NOTE*** **SUBSTITUTION WITH CACHED USER CONTROLS**
>
> **You can't use substitution to update cached user controls where output caching is applied at the user control level.**

- **The *Substitution* control** *Substitution* controls are similar to *Label* controls, but *Substitution* controls are exempt from output caching. The only useful property is *Substitution.MethodName*, which you use to specify the method that generates the content that is inserted at the location of the *Substitution* control. The method specified by *MethodName* must accept an *HttpContext* parameter and return a *String*. The *String* value is inserted into the response at the *Substitution* control location when the cached page is returned to the user. The following code demonstrates how to specify a substitution method that displays the current time in a *Substitution* control named *Substitution1*:

```
'VB
Sub Page_Load(ByVal sender As Object, ByVal e As System.EventArgs)
  'Specify the callback method.
  Substitution1.MethodName = "GetCurrentDateTime"
End Sub

'the Substitution control calls this method to retrieve the current date and time.
'this section of the page is exempt from output caching.
Shared Function GetCurrentDateTime(ByVal context As HttpContext) As String
  Return DateTime.Now.ToString()
```

```
End Function

//C#
void Page_Load(object sender, System.EventArgs e)
{
  //specify the callback method.
  Substitution1.MethodName = "GetCurrentDateTime";
}

//the Substitution control calls this method to retrieve the current date and
time.
//this section of the page is exempt from output caching.
public static string GetCurrentDateTime (HttpContext context)
{
  return DateTime.Now.ToString();
}
```

The *AdRotator* control also performs postcache substitution, by default, to constantly display new ads.

Programmatically Invalidating Cached Pages

Often, you want to cache pages, but specific events might require you to stop using the cached page. For example, a page that displays results from a database query should only be cached until the results of the database query change. Similarly, a page that processes a file should be cached until the file is changed. Fortunately, ASP.NET gives you several ways to invalidate cached pages.

Determining Whether to Return a Cached Page Prior to Rendering

To directly control whether a cached version of a page is used or whether the page is dynamically regenerated, respond to the *ValidateCacheOutput* event and set a valid value for the *HttpValidationStatus* attribute. Then, from the *Page.Load* event handler, call the *AddValidationCallback* method and pass an *HttpCacheValidateHandler* object with your method.

The following example demonstrates how to create a method to handle the *ValidatePage* event:

```
'VB
Public Shared Sub ValidatePage(ByVal context As HttpContext, _
  ByVal data As [Object], ByRef status As HttpValidationStatus)

  If Not (context.Request.QueryString("Status") Is Nothing) Then
    Dim pageStatus As String = context.Request.QueryString("Status")

    If pageStatus = "invalid" Then
      status = HttpValidationStatus.Invalid
```

```
    ElseIf pageStatus = "ignore" Then
      status = HttpValidationStatus.IgnoreThisRequest
    Else
      status = HttpValidationStatus.Valid
    End If
  Else
    status = HttpValidationStatus.Valid
  End If

End Sub
```

```
//C#
public static void ValidateCacheOutput(HttpContext context, Object data,
  ref HttpValidationStatus status)
{
  if (context.Request.QueryString["Status"] != null)
  {
    string pageStatus = context.Request.QueryString["Status"];

    if (pageStatus == "invalid")
      status = HttpValidationStatus.Invalid;
    else if (pageStatus == "ignore")
      status = HttpValidationStatus.IgnoreThisRequest;
    else
      status = HttpValidationStatus.Valid;
  }
  else
    status = HttpValidationStatus.Valid;
}
```

Notice that this code sample uses logic to specify one of the *HttpValidationStatus* values to control how the page is cached:

- ***HttpValidationStatus.Invalid*** This causes the cache to be invalidated so that the page is dynamically generated. The newly generated page is stored in the cache, replacing the earlier cached version.
- ***HttpValidationStatus.IgnoreThisRequest*** This causes the current page request to be dynamically generated without invalidating the previously cached version of the page. The dynamically generated page output is not cached, and future requests might receive the previously cached output.
- ***HttpValidationStatus.Valid*** This causes ASP.NET to return the cached page.

The following sample demonstrates how to configure your event handler so that it is called when ASP.NET determines whether to use the cached version of the page:

```
'VB
Protected Sub Page_Load(ByVal sender As Object, _
```

```
  ByVal e As System.EventArgs) Handles Me.Load

  Response.Cache.AddValidationCallback( _
    New HttpCacheValidateHandler(AddressOf ValidatePage), Nothing)

End Sub

//C#
protected void Page_Load(object sender, EventArgs e)
{
  Response.Cache.AddValidationCallback(
    new HttpCacheValidateHandler(ValidateCacheOutput), null);
}
```

ASP.NET calls the method you specify when it determines whether to use the cached version of the page. Depending on how you set the *HttpValidationStatus* in your handler, ASP.NET will use a cached page or a new, dynamically generated version.

Creating a Cache Page Output Dependency

To create a cache page output dependency, call one of the following *Response* methods:

- ***Response.AddCacheDependency*** This makes the validity of a cached response dependent on a CacheDependency object.
- ***Response.AddCacheItemDependency* and *Response.AddCacheItemDependencies*** These make the validity of a cached response dependent on one or more other items in the cache.
- ***Response.AddFileDependency* and Response.AddFileDependencies** These make the validity of a cached response dependent on one or more files.

Configuring Caching for an Entire Application

You can also configure output caching profiles that you can easily reference from pages in your application. This provides centralized configuration of output caching. To create a cache profile, add the *<caching><outputCacheSettings><outputCacheProfiles>* section to your Web .config file's *<system.web>* element, as the following sample demonstrates:

```
<caching>
  <outputCacheSettings>
    <outputCacheProfiles>
      <add name="OneMinuteProfile" enabled="true" duration="60"/>
    </outputCacheProfiles>
  </outputCacheSettings>
</caching>
```

Caching profiles support most of the same attributes as the @ *OutputCache* directive, including *Duration*, *VaryByParameter*, *VaryByHeader*, *VaryByCustom*, *VaryByControl*,

SqlDependency, *NoStore*, and *Location*. Additionally, you must provide a *Name* attribute to identify the profile, and you can use the *Enabled* attribute to disable a profile if necessary.

Once you create a cache profile, reference it from within a page using the *CacheProfile* attribute of the @ *OutputCache* directive, as the following example demonstrates. You can override specific attributes on a per-page basis.

```
<%@ OutputCache CacheProfile="OneMinuteProfile" VaryByParam="none" %>
```

LAB Using Page Output Caching to Improve Performance

In this lab, you configure page output caching for a simple ASP.NET Web application.

If you encounter a problem completing an exercise, the completed projects are available in the sample files installed from the companion CD in the Code folder.

EXERCISE 1 Enable Page Output Caching

In this exercise, you enable page output caching for an ASP.NET Web page.

1. Open Visual Studio and create a new Web site called **CachedSite** using the language of your preference.
2. Next, you will add controls to a page and enable output caching. To get started, open Default.aspx.

   Add a *Label* control and call it **LabelChosen**.

   Add a *DropDownList* control and name it **DropDownListChoice**. Add three *ListItem* controls to the *DropDownList* (one for each choice).

   Add a *Button* control called **ButtonSubmit**.

   Your markup should look similar to the following:

```
<body style="font-family: Verdana">
    <form id="form1" runat="server">
    <div>
        <asp:Label ID="LabelChosen" runat="server" Font-Size="XX-Large"
          Text="nothing chosen"></asp:Label><br />
        <br />Make a choice: <br />
        <asp:DropDownList ID="DropDownListChoice" runat="server">
            <asp:ListItem>Choice One</asp:ListItem>
            <asp:ListItem>Choice Two</asp:ListItem>
            <asp:ListItem>Choice Three</asp:ListItem>
        </asp:DropDownList>
        <br /><br />
        <asp:Button ID="ButtonSubmit" runat="server" Text="Submit" />
    </div>
    </form>
</body>
```

3. Add an event handler for the *Button* control's click event. Add code to display the user's selected choice and the current time in the *LabelChosen* control. The following code shows an example:

```
'VB
Protected Sub ButtonSubmit_Click(ByVal sender As Object, _
  ByVal e As System.EventArgs) Handles ButtonSubmit.Click

  LabelChosen.Text = DropDownListChoice.Text & " at " & _
    DateTime.Now.TimeOfDay.ToString()

End Sub

//C#
protected void ButtonSubmit_Click(object sender, EventArgs e)
{
  LabelChosen.Text = DropDownListChoice.Text + " at " +
    DateTime.Now.TimeOfDay.ToString();
}
```

4. Run the project from Visual Studio. Note that each time you choose a different item from the list and click Submit, the name of the chosen item and the current time are displayed at the top of the page.

5. Return to Visual Studio and open the Default.aspx page in Source view. Add a page output cache directive to the top of the page so that the page is automatically cached for 10 seconds. Do not specify any dependencies. The following code sample demonstrates how to do this:

```
<%@ OutputCache Duration="10" VaryByParam="none" %>
```

6. Run the page again in a Web browser. Make a choice from the list and notice that the page updates correctly. Immediately make another choice from the list and notice that the page name does not change and that it continues to display the previous time.

   Make note of the time and repeatedly choose different pages from the list until 10 seconds have passed. After 10 seconds, notice that the page updates correctly and again shows the current time. This demonstrates that page output caching is working correctly; however, the caching prevents the form from functioning as intended.

7. Return to Visual Studio and open the Default.aspx page in Source view. Modify the page output cache to vary the cache based on the *DropDownList* control. The following code sample demonstrates how to do this:

```
<%@ OutputCache Duration="10" VaryByParam="DropDownListChoice" %>
```

8. Run the page again in a Web browser. Choose an item from the list and notice the time displayed. Immediately choose another item from the list and notice that the page updates correctly. Quickly choose the previous item from the list again. If you chose it within 10 seconds of the first time you chose it, you will see the previous time. You might have to extend your caching to 20 seconds to give you time to click around.

   Because of the change you made to the *OutputCache* declaration, ASP.NET caches a separate version of the page for each value of the *DropDownList* control that you choose, and each expires 10 seconds after it is generated.

Lesson Summary

- You can use the *Cache* object to store data of any type. You can then access the cached data from other Web pages in your application. The *Cache* object is an excellent way to reduce the number of database calls and file reads. Use the *Cache.Add* and *Cache.Insert* methods to add an object to the cache with a dependency to ensure the cached object does not become stale.
- Page output caching stores a copy of a rendered page (or user control) in the server's memory. Subsequent requests for the given resources are served from memory. Page output caching practically eliminates rendering time.

Lesson Review

You can use the following questions to test your knowledge of the information in Lesson 2, "Using Caching to Improve Performance." The questions are also available on the companion CD if you prefer to review them in electronic form.

> ***NOTE*** **ANSWERS**
>
> **Answers to these questions and explanations of why each answer choice is right or wrong are located in the "Answers" section at the end of the book.**

1. You are creating an ASP.NET Web page that displays a list of customers generated by a database query. The user can filter the list so that only customers within a specific state are displayed. You want to maximize the performance of your Web application by using page output caching. You want to ensure users can filter by state, but you are not concerned about displaying updates to the list of customers because the customer list doesn't change very frequently. Which declarative @ *OutputCache* attribute should you configure?

   A. *VaryByParam*

   B. *VaryByHeader*

   C. *SqlDependency*

   D. *VaryByCustom*

2. You need to programmatically configure page output caching. Which object would you use?
   A. *Request*
   B. *Response*
   C. *Application*
   D. *Server*
3. You want to cache an object but have it automatically expire in 10 minutes. How can you do this? (Choose all that apply.)
   A. Directly define the *Cache* item.
   B. Call *Cache.Get*.
   C. Call *Cache.Insert*.
   D. Call *Cache.Add*.
4. Which tool can you use to create performance counters? (Choose all that apply.)
   A. An HTTP header
   B. A file
   C. A time span
   D. A registry key
   E. Another object in the *Cache*

Chapter Review

To further practice and reinforce the skills you learned in this chapter, you can perform the following tasks:

- Review the chapter summary.
- Complete the case scenarios. These scenarios set up real-world situations involving the topics of this chapter and ask you to create solutions.
- Complete the suggested practices.
- Take a practice test.

Chapter Summary

- You can deploy Web applications in a variety of ways. The simplest way to deploy a Web application is to simply copy the files. Alternatively, you can use the Copy Web tool to synchronize the files between two Web sites, enabling you to keep separate development and staging servers. The Copy Web tool also works well in environments with multiple developers, because it can detect versioning conflicts. The Publish Web Site tool is capable of precompiling a Web site, which reduces the delay that occurs when a user requests the first page from a Web site. If you have more complex setup requirements, you can create a Web Setup Project and deploy the Setup.exe file or the Windows Installer file to Web servers.
- Caching is one of the most effective ways to improve performance. ASP.NET provides two different types of caching: application caching (implemented using the *Cache* object) and page output caching. Application caching requires writing code, but it gives you detailed control over how objects are cached. Page output caching keeps a copy of rendered HTML from an ASP.NET page or user control. Both types of caching are extremely useful for reducing the time required to submit redundant database queries and access files.

Case Scenarios

In the following case scenarios, you will apply what you've learned about optimizing and deploying Web applications. You can find answers to these questions in the "Answers" section at the end of this book.

Case Scenario 1: Deploying a Web Application

You are a developer for Contoso Video. You are the sole developer of the company's external Web site, which allows customers to rent videos online. The reliability of the application is critical, so the quality assurance team must test any changes you make on a staging server before you make changes to the production Web server.

You frequently work from your home. Unfortunately, Contoso's virtual private network (VPN) is unreliable, so you must do your development on your laptop computer. You can only access the staging and production Web servers from the internal network or the VPN, but that's not a problem because you don't need to make updates to those servers very frequently. Additionally, you don't have a broadband connection, so you need to avoid sending large updates across the connection when it is working.

QUESTIONS

Answer the following questions.

1. Which tool would you use to update the staging server?
2. Which tool should the quality assurance people use to update the production server?

Case Scenario 2: Improving the Performance of a Public Web Site

You are a developer for Contoso Video. Fortunately, the site has been getting busier and busier. Currently, both the Web server and the back-end database are hosted on a single computer. Unfortunately, you've discovered that the server that runs the site and database isn't powerful enough to meet peak demand. During the busiest hours, you discover that processor utilization is very high.

You discuss the problems with other people at your organization. Following is a list of company personnel interviewed and their statements:

- **Arif Rizaldy, Database Administrator** I did some analysis on the SQL Server database performance like you asked. The biggest problem is that when a user clicks on a movie genre on the Web site, such as comedy or drama, your application performs a very processor-intensive query to find the appropriate movies. I've optimized the indexes already, so there's nothing we can do besides upgrading the server or querying the database less often.
- **Wendy Richardson, IT Manager** The company is doing well, but we don't have any budget to upgrade the server. So, find a way to make the application more efficient.

QUESTIONS

Answer the following questions for your manager.

1. Is there a way you can use the application *Cache* object to improve performance?
2. How can you make sure stale cache information isn't sent to users after the company adds new movies?
3. Each page on the Web site is personalized with the current users' preferences. Is there a way you can use page output caching to improve performance?

Suggested Practices

To help you successfully master the exam objectives presented in this chapter, complete the following tasks.

Use a Web Setup Project

For this task, you should complete at least Practices 1 and 2 to get a solid understanding of how to use Web Setup Projects. If you want a better understanding of how applications are distributed in enterprises and you have sufficient lab equipment, complete Practice 3 as well.

- **Practice 1** Create a Web Setup Project that prompts the user to provide database connection information, and then stores the connection information as part of a connection string in the Web.config file.
- **Practice 2** Using the last real-world application you created or one of the applications you created for an exercise in this book, create a Web Setup Project for it. Deploy it to different operating systems, including Windows 2000, Windows XP, Windows Server 2003, and Windows Server 2008. Verify that the deployed application works on all platforms. If it does not work, modify your Web Setup Project to make it work properly. Make note of how the Web Setup Project handles computers that lack the .NET Framework 3.5.
- **Practice 3** Create a Web Setup Project and generate a Windows Installer file. If you have sufficient lab equipment, use Active Directory software distribution to distribute the Web application automatically to multiple servers.

Using the Copy Web Tool

For this task, you should complete both practices to gain experience using the Copy Web tool.

- **Practice 1** Use the Copy Web tool to create a local copy of your last real-world Web application. With your computer disconnected from the network, make an update to the Web site. Then, use the Copy Web tool to update that single file on the remote Web server.
- **Practice 2** Using a local copy of a Web site, make an update to different files on both your local copy and the remote Web site. Then, use the Copy Web tool to synchronize the local and remote Web site.

Precompile and Publish a Web Application

For this task, you should complete Practice 1 to gain an understanding of the performance gains that can be realized by precompiling an application.

- **Practice 1** Enable tracing in a Web application. Then, modify the Web.config file and save it to force the application to restart. Open a page several times, and then view the Trace.axd file to determine how long the first and subsequent requests took. Next, use the Publish Web Site tool to precompile the application. Open a page several times, and then view the Trace.axd file to determine how long the first and subsequent requests took with the precompiled application.

Optimize and Troubleshoot a Web Application

For this task, you should complete Practice 1 to learn more about application caching.

- **Practice 1** Using the last real-world ASP.NET Web application you created that accesses a database, use the *Cache* object to store a copy of database results. View the Trace.axd page before and after the change to determine whether caching improves performance.

Take a Practice Test

The practice tests on this book's companion CD offer many options. For example, you can test yourself on just the content covered in this chapter, or you can test yourself on all the 70-562 certification exam content. You can set up the test so that it closely simulates the experience of taking a certification exam, or you can set it up in study mode so that you can look at the correct answers and explanations after you answer each question.

> ***MORE INFO*** **PRACTICE TESTS**
>
> **For details about all the practice test options available, see the "How to Use the Practice Tests" section in this book's Introduction.**

Answers

Chapter 1: Lesson Review Answers

Lesson 1

1. Correct Answer: D
   - **A. Incorrect:** The *IsCallback* property indicates if the page is the result of a callback.
   - **B. Incorrect:** The *IsReusable* property indicates to ASP.NET if the *Page* object can be reused.
   - **C. Incorrect:** The *IsValid* property indicates if an ASP.NET page passed validation.
   - **D. Correct:** The *IsPostBack* property indicates if the client is sending data as part of its request (*true*) or the page is simply being requested for display (*false*).
2. Correct Answer: A
   - **A. Correct:** The *PUT* verb allows a client to create a file on the Web server and copy the message body to the file.
   - **B. Incorrect:** The *CONNECT* verb is used to work with a proxy server and SSL.
   - **C. Incorrect:** The *POST* verb is used to send data back to the server for processing.
   - **D. Incorrect:** The *GET* verb is used to retrieve the contents of a file on the Web server.

Lesson 2

1. Correct Answer: C
   - **A. Incorrect:** You can connect to a remote HTTP server with Visual Studio provided it has Front Page Server Extensions installed and enabled.
   - **B. Incorrect:** A file system Web site type will run locally on the development machine (and not a remote server).
   - **C. Correct:** You can communicate with a remote server that does not have Front Page Server Extensions installed using FTP. Of course the server must have FTP enabled.
   - **D. Incorrect:** A local HTTP server (*http://localhost*) will run locally on the development machine.
2. Correct Answer: D
   - **A. Incorrect:** Local HTTP is used to connect to a local version of IIS and not a remote server.
   - **B. Incorrect:** The file system project runs locally using the ASP.NET Web server and not an IIS instance.

   C. **Incorrect:** FTP is useful when your hosting provider does not have Front Page Server Extensions enabled on the server.

   D. **Correct:** Remote HTTP can be used for remote servers with Front Page Server Extensions installed and enabled.

3. **Correct Answer: B**

   A. **Incorrect:** This model puts both layout markup and code in a single file.

   B. **Correct:** The code-behind model is used to separate code and user interface markup.

   C. **Incorrect:** The single-file model is sometimes referred to as an inline model. This model combines code and markup in a single file.

   D. **Incorrect:** The client-server model is not a mode for ASP page definition.

4. **Correct Answer: A**

   A. **Correct:** You can combine both C# and Visual Basic pages in a single Web site.

   B. **Incorrect:** This will work. However, Joe will waste his effort rewriting this code, as it is not required.

   C. **Incorrect:** The files do not need to be rewritten. They can be used as is.

   D. **Incorrect:** You cannot reference one site from another site in ASP.NET.

Lesson 3

1. **Correct Answer: C**

   A. **Incorrect:** The Global.asax file is used to define application-level events (and not settings).

   B. **Incorrect:** The Web.config file will only set settings for Web applications and not Windows applications.

   C. **Correct:** You can use the Machine.config file to manage settings for both Web and Windows applications at the machine level.

   D. **Incorrect:** The Global.asa file was used by classic ASP applications for application-level event handling.

2. **Correct Answer: B**

   A. **Incorrect:** The Web.config files in the same folder as Machine.config will apply to all Web sites on the machine, not just the current Web application.

   B. **Correct:** The Web.config file at the Web application root will apply only to that Web application.

   C. **Incorrect:** The Machine.config file is used to set global settings on the machine.

   D. **Incorrect:** The Global.asax file is used to define application-wide events.

3. Correct Answer: D
   - **A. Incorrect:** You can edit the XML in Notepad. However, it will not provide a user-friendly GUI.
   - **B. Incorrect:** Microsoft Word will not provide a good editing experience for this XML file.
   - **C. Incorrect:** This will open the XML file for text-based editing (and not a GUI).
   - **D. Correct:** The WSAT tool will allow you to manage the settings for a single Web application. In addition, you can do so through its Web-based interface.
4. Correct Answer: A
   - **A. Correct:** You can combine both C# and Visual Basic pages in a single Web site.
   - **B. Incorrect:** This will work. However, Joe will waste his effort rewriting this code, as it is not required.
   - **C. Incorrect:** The files do not need to be rewritten. They can be used as is.
   - **D. Incorrect:** You cannot reference one site from another site in ASP.NET.

Chapter 1: Case Scenario Answers

Case Scenario 1: Creating a New Web Site

1. The Web site type will be file system. The following list describes how the file-based Web site type fulfills the requirements:
   - File system Web sites do not require IIS to be installed on the developer machines.
   - Each developer can debug independently with the file system web site. If you attempt to use a centralized server with IIS installed, you will run into problems when multiple developers attempt to debug at the same time.

Case Scenario 2: Placing Files in the Proper Folders

1. You will place the ShoppingCart.dll file in the Bin folder. You will place the database files in the App_Data folder. The wrapper file (ShoppingCartWrapper.cs or .vb) will be placed in the site's App_Code directory.

   A primary benefit to adhering to the ASP.NET folder structure is that these folders are secured. A user who attempts to browse to any of these folders will receive an HTTP 403 Forbidden error.

Chapter 2: Lesson Review Answers

Lesson 1

1. Correct Answer: C

   A. **Incorrect:** The correct attribute to indicate an HTML server control should be run on the server is the *runat* attribute (not *run*).

   B. **Incorrect:** Double-clicking an HTML control will not convert it to run on the server. Instead, it will generate a client-side event handler (in JavaScript) for the control.

   C. **Correct:** To convert an HTML element into a server control you add the *runat="server"* attribute and value to the element.

   D. **Incorrect:** Visual Studio does not allow you to modify this attribute from the Properties window. You must set this value in Source view.

2. Correct Answer: A

   A. **Correct:** To indicate that a control's default event should cause a PostBack, you set the *AutoPostBack* property of the control to *true*.

   B. **Incorrect:** ASP.NET does not define a method called *ForcePostBack*.

   C. **Incorrect:** An ASP.NET Web page does not have a property called *PostBackAll*.

   D. **Incorrect:** The client makes no attempt to communicate with the server for the *CheckBox* click event until you set the *AutoPostBack* property to *true*.

3. Correct Answer: A

   A. **Correct:** The *PreInit* event is where you want to create (and re-create) your dynamically generated controls. This ensures they will be available for initialization, *ViewState* connection, and code inside other events such as *Load*.

   B. **Incorrect:** The *Init* event is meant to be raised after all controls have been initialized. You can also use this event to initialize additional control properties. Adding a control here will technically work, but it will not follow the prescribed life cycle.

   C. **Incorrect:** Prior to the *Load* event, ASP.NET ensures there is an instance of each control and each control's view state has been connected. Adding your controls here will result in undesirable behavior during PostBack such as their view state not being properly set.

   D. **Incorrect:** The *PreRender* event is used to make final changes to the page prior to its rendering. Adding your controls here will result in undesirable behavior.

4. Correct Answer: D

   A. **Incorrect:** The *TextBox* control does not define a *ShowControl* method.

   B. **Incorrect:** The *Visible* property of a control is by default *true*. However, the control will not show on the page until it has been added to a form.

C. **Incorrect:** The page class does not expose an *Add* method for adding controls.

D. **Correct:** A dynamically created control must be added to a form element associated with the page. The form element must also be set to *runat="server"*.

Lesson 2

1. Correct Answer: D

   A. **Incorrect:** The *RadioButton* control does not implement an *Exclusive* property.

   B. **Incorrect:** The *RadioButton* control does not implement a *MutuallyExclusive* property.

   C. **Incorrect:** The *RadioButton* control does not implement a *Grouped* property.

   D. **Correct:** The *RadioButton* control's *GroupName* property is used to group two or more mutually exclusive radio buttons.

2. Correct Answer: B

   A. **Incorrect:** There is no such button type in ASP.NET.

   B. **Correct:** You create a command button by setting the *CommandName* property of the button and responding to the *Command* event for the button.

   C. **Incorrect:** There is no such button type in ASP.NET.

   D. **Incorrect:** There is no such button type in ASP.NET.

3. Correct Answer: D

   A. **Incorrect:** This method will work. However, it is more difficult than simply double-clicking the control.

   B. **Incorrect:** Visual Studio does not have a Create Handler menu option.

   C. **Incorrect:** Visual Studio does not allow you to drag event handlers from the Toolbox.

   D. **Correct:** The easiest way to create an event handler for the default event of a control is to double-click the control in Design view.

Lesson 3

1. Correct Answer: B

   A. **Incorrect:** Unless you intend to use the *Table* control on the server, you should consider using a standard HTML table.

   B. **Correct:** In this case you will spend a lot of time manipulating the *Table* control on the server.

   C. **Incorrect:** In this case a standard HTML table will work as the data is static. No server-side processing is required.

   D. **Incorrect:** A tabular result set of data should be displayed using a *GridView* control and not a *Table* control.

2. Correct Answer: D
   - **A. Incorrect:** Although you could employ this method, it could be difficult to execute and certainly is not the best way to accomplish this task.
   - **B. Incorrect:** The product lines are not rectangular, so this would not be an option.
   - **C. Incorrect:** The *MultiView* only shows one *View* at a time, so this would not be a solution.
   - **D. Correct:** The *ImageMap* provides the ability to define hot spot areas and the *PostBack-Value* can be used to determine the area that was clicked.
3. Correct Answer: C
   - **A. Incorrect:** The *View* control requires a *MultiView* to work properly. In either case, this would not be the easiest solution to the problem.
   - **B. Incorrect:** The *TextBox* control will not provide multiple page data collection.
   - **C. Correct:** The *Wizard* control will solve this issue by providing an easy-to-implement solution for collecting multiple pages of data from users.
   - **D. Incorrect:** Visual Studio does not implement a *DataCollection* control.

Chapter 2: Case Scenario Answers

Case Scenario 1: Determining the Type of Controls to Use

1. For this application, consider using Web server controls. These controls provide a more consistent programming model for developers and often provide a better user experience for users.
   - Use *TextBox* controls to capture the customer names and addresses. The text associated with these controls can be simple HTML text.
   - Use a *CheckBox* control for the active indicator.
   - Use multiple *CheckBox* controls for the vertical market categories. This allows the user to select multiple categories.
   - Use *RadioButton* controls to allow the user to select a single, mutually exclusive quantity of computers.

Case Scenario 2: Selecting the Proper Events to Use

1. You should place the code to dynamically create the controls in the *Page_PreInit* event handler. After the *Page_PreInit* event handler has been executed, all dynamically created controls should be instantiated. Following the *Page_Init* event, all controls on the page should be initialized.

2. You should place the code to set the control properties in the *Page_Load* event handler. When the *Page_Load* event handler fires, all controls should already be instantiated. Here you can check whether the page is a PostBack and set control properties appropriately. The controls should already have been initialized in the *Page_PreInit* event.

Case Scenario 3: Determining How to Prompt for Data

1. You could divide the prompts by category and create a separate Web page for each category. This solution splits your code and data over several pages and can add to the overall complexity of the Web site.

   Alternatively, you could implement a solution using the *MultiView* control and create a separate View for each category. The *MultiView* and *View* controls do not have a user interface, so you have complete flexibility with regard to the graphical interface of the Web page.

   As a third alternative, you could implement the *Wizard* control and create a *WizardStep* control for each category. The *Wizard* contains the behavior for moving between steps and offers a more complete solution.

Case Scenario 4: Implementing a Calendar Solution

1. This solution can use the *Calendar* control in every situation where a date or dates are required to be entered by the user and in every situation where a schedule is being displayed to a user. The following list describes some of the situations in which you can use the *Calendar* control:
   - Prompt for class start date
   - Prompt for class end date
   - Display training provider's class schedule
   - Display contractor's schedule
2. Although you could use the *Table* control in these situations, you would need to write lots of code to get the functionality that the *Calendar* control provides natively, so the *Calendar* control is the best solution.

Chapter 3: Lesson Review Answers

Lesson 1

1. **Correct Answer: C**
   - **A. Incorrect:** The *RegularExpressionValidator* does string pattern matching. It should not be used to look up database values.
   - **B. Incorrect:** The *RangeValidator* validates data in a given range. In addition, the control does not define a *DbLookup* operation.

- **C.** **Correct:** The *CustomValidator* control can be used to call server-side code to validate the vendor ID.
- **D.** **Incorrect:** The *CompareValidator* does not define a feature as described. It is used to compare two values.

2. Correct Answer: A
   - **A.** **Correct:** You need to test the *IsValid* property of the Web page before executing code in your event handler methods.
   - **B.** **Incorrect:** The *IsValid* property is not set yet; exiting the *Load* event handler method still allows the event handler methods to execute.
   - **C.** **Incorrect:** Although this will appear to correct the problem, a would-be hacker could disable client-side validation and the server-side problem would still exist.
   - **D.** **Incorrect:** This is the default setting and does not correct the problem.
3. Correct Answer: B
   - **A.** **Incorrect:** The *Text* property should be an asterisk and the *ErrorMessage* should be the detailed error message.
   - **B.** **Correct:** Setting the *Text* property to an asterisk places the asterisk next to the control and setting the *ErrorMessage* to the detailed error message causes the detailed errors to be placed into the *ValidationSummary* control at the top of the Web page.
   - **C.** **Incorrect:** The *Text* property should be an asterisk and the *ErrorMessage* should be the detailed error message.
   - **D.** **Incorrect:** The *Text* property should be an asterisk and the *ErrorMessage* should be the detailed error message.

Lesson 2

1. Correct Answer: C
   - **A.** **Incorrect:** The *Redirect* method is available on the *HttpResponse* class and it causes a round trip back to the client.
   - **B.** **Incorrect:** The *MapPath* method returns the physical path of a given virtual path.
   - **C.** **Correct:** The *Page.Server.Transfer* method transfers the page processing to another page without calling back to the client.
   - **D.** **Incorrect:** The *UrlDecode* method decides a string that was encoded before being transmitted over HTTP.
2. Correct Answer: D
   - **A.** **Incorrect:** The *Menu* control requires a data source.
   - **B.** **Incorrect:** The *TreeView* control requires a data source.

C. **Incorrect:** The *SiteMapDataSource* control is a data source and does not have a visual display for a user.

D. **Correct:** The *SiteMapPath* will automatically pick up a site map file and display its contents to a user.

3. Correct Answer: C

   A. **Incorrect:** The *SiteMapPath* control connects to the site map file and displays the user's current, bread-crumb-like navigation path.

   B. **Incorrect:** The *SiteMapDataSource* is used to provide data binding from a site map file to a navigation control.

   C. **Correct:** The *SiteMap* class will allow you to load the given site map file and work with the data contained inside.

   D. **Incorrect:** The *HttpServerUtility* class does not provide such functionality.

Chapter 3: Case Scenario Answers

Case Scenario 1: Determining the Proper Validation Controls to Implement on a User Name

1. The *RequiredFieldValidator* ensures that non-whitespace has been entered.

   - The *RegularExpressionValidator* can be used, and the *ValidationExpression* can be set to Internet e-mail address.

Case Scenario 2: Determining the Proper Password Validation Controls to Implement

1. Use a *RequiredFieldValidator* to ensure that data has been entered.

   - Use a *CustomValidator* and write code to check for the character types and length as specified by the requirements.

Case Scenario 3: Implementing a Site Map

1. You can use the *TreeView* control with the *SiteMapDataSource*, and a *SiteMapPath* control to display the breadcrumb path.

Chapter 4: Lesson Review Answers

Lesson 1

1. Correct Answer: B
   - **A.** **Incorrect:** Client-side state management requires the client to transmit the user name and password with each request. It also requires the client to store the information locally where it might be compromised. This is not a secure solution.
   - **B.** **Correct:** Server-side state management provides better security for confidential information by reducing the number of times the information is transmitted across the network.
2. Correct Answer: A
   - **A.** **Correct:** Client-side state management is an excellent choice for storing nonconfidential information. It is much easier to implement than server-side state management when multiple Web servers are involved, and it minimizes load on the servers.
   - **B.** **Incorrect:** You could use server-side state management; however, it would require a back-end database to synchronize information among multiple Web servers. This would increase the load on your servers.
3. Correct Answer: A
   - **A.** **Correct:** View state is the simplest way to store this information. Because it is enabled by default, you might not need to write any code to support state management for your form.
   - **B.** **Incorrect:** You can use control state; however, it requires extra coding and is only necessary if you are creating a control that might be used in a Web page that has view state disabled.
   - **C.** **Incorrect:** You can store the information in hidden fields; however, that requires writing extra code. View state supports your requirements with little or no additional code.
   - **D.** **Incorrect:** Cookies require extra coding and are only required if you need to share information between multiple Web forms.
   - **E.** **Incorrect:** You can use query strings to store user preferences. However, you need to update every link on the page that the user might click. This is very time-consuming to implement.
4. Correct Answer: D
   - **A.** **Incorrect:** View state can only store information for a single Web form.
   - **B.** **Incorrect:** Control state can only store information for a single control.
   - **C.** **Incorrect:** Hidden fields can only store information for a single Web form.
   - **D.** **Correct:** Unless you specifically narrow the scope, the user's browser submits information stored in a cookie to every page on your site. Therefore, each page processes the user

preference information. If you configure the cookie expiration to make it persistent, the browser submits the cookie the next time the user visits your site.

- **E.** **Incorrect:** You can use query strings to store user preferences. However, you need to update every link on the page that the user might click. This is very time-consuming to implement.

5. Correct Answer: E
   - **A.** **Incorrect:** View state information is not stored in the URL, and therefore is lost if the URL is bookmarked.
   - **B.** **Incorrect:** Control state information is not stored in the URL, and therefore is lost if the URL is bookmarked.
   - **C.** **Incorrect:** Hidden fields are not stored in the URL, and therefore are lost if the URL is bookmarked.
   - **D.** **Incorrect:** Cookies are not stored in the URL, and therefore are lost if the URL is bookmarked.
   - **E.** **Correct:** Query strings are stored in the URL. Although they are not the easiest type of client-side state management to implement, they are the only way to enable state management data to be easily bookmarked and e-mailed.

Lesson 2

1. Correct Answer: C
   - **A.** **Incorrect:** You cannot respond to the *Application_Start* event within a Web page.
   - **B.** **Incorrect:** You cannot write code to respond to any event inside the Web.config file.
   - **C.** **Correct:** The Global.asax file allows you to trap special events such as the *Application_Start* event.
   - **D.** **Incorrect:** These pages represent code-behind files to Web pages. You cannot respond to application-level events from a Web page.
2. Correct Answer: B
   - **A.** **Incorrect:** The *Session* object is user-specific and therefore not available to all users and pages in the site.
   - **B.** **Correct:** The *Application* object allows you to store data that is scoped at the application level and therefore available to all users.
   - **C.** **Incorrect:** The *Cookies* collection is client and user specific.
   - **D.** **Incorrect:** The *ViewState* collection is client and user specific.
3. Correct Answer: A
   - **A.** **Correct:** Storing this value in the *Session* object will prevent the client from tampering with the value. It will also ensure this user-specific data is only available for the given session and user.

B. **Incorrect:** The *Application* collection represents global data available to all users.

C. **Incorrect:** Storing authentication information in the user's cookie file exposes the site to a potential security risk.

D. **Incorrect:** The *ViewState* is sent to the client and therefore would pose a security risk.

4. **Correct Answer: D**

   A. **Incorrect:** *Application_Start* is called when the application loads. You cannot access the *Session* object from the *Application_Start* event handler.

   B. **Incorrect:** *Application_End* is called when the application shuts down. You cannot access the *Session* object from the *Application_End* event handler.

   C. **Incorrect:** *Session_Start* is called when a user first connects.

   D. **Correct:** The *Session_End* event handler is called when a user's session times out. However, this event will not fire in the event of the server being shut off unexpectedly or if the *SessionState* mode is not set to *InProc*.

5. **Correct Answer: A and D**

   A. **Correct:** You must manage session state on a central server in this case. *StateServer* allows you to do so.

   B. **Incorrect:** You cannot set the *SessionState* mode attribute to *InProc* as this would store each user's session on the individual Web servers. The load balancer might then route different requests to different servers and thus break your application.

   C. **Incorrect:** Turning sessions off for your application will break the application in this case.

   D. **Correct:** You must manage session state on a central server in this case. *SqlServer* allows you to do so.

Chapter 4: Case Scenario Answers

Case Scenario 1: Remembering User Credentials

1. You should use client-side state management in the form of cookies. You should not, however, store the user's credentials in this cookie (see question 2). Cookies, however, will allow you to identify the user between requests and between sessions as they can be persisted on the client.

2. First, you should not store the users' actual credentials in the cookie. Instead, you should store a token that proves the user has authenticated. Second, you can require Secure Sockets Layer (SSL) for your Web application so that all communications are encrypted. Third, you can narrow the scope of the cookies so that the browser only submits them to the SSL-protected portion of your Web site. Finally, you should remember the user. However, if you are relying on a cookie, you should ask the user to reauthenticate before doing anything of consequence on the site like making a purchase or accessing private information.

3. You should not use state management techniques to store previous orders. Instead, you should retrieve that information directly from the database.

Case Scenario 2: Analyzing Information for Individual Users and for All Users

1. You can use the *Application* object to log data related to all users. You can update a collection that tracks the number of users currently viewing certain pages in your site. Of course, you would want to periodically reset this collection, as it should be a snapshot of a certain time period.
2. You can use the *Session* object to track where a user has gone on the site and in what navigational path. For each page view, you could add the page that the user visits to a custom collection in the *Session* object. You can log this information and allow the marketing department to watch and analyze this information to make advertisement decisions.

Chapter 5: Lesson Review Answers

Lesson 1

1. Correct Answer: B, C, and D
   - **A. Incorrect:** Content pages cannot reference private properties or methods in the master page.
   - **B. Correct:** Content pages can reference public properties in the master page.
   - **C. Correct:** Content pages can reference public methods in the master page.
   - **D. Correct:** Content pages can use the *Master.FindControl* method to reference controls in the master page.
2. Correct Answer: A and C
   - **A. Correct:** The @ *MasterType* declaration is required to access the properties in the master page.
   - **B. Incorrect:** You only need to add the @ *Master* declarations to the master page, not the content pages.
   - **C. Correct:** Content pages must have a *MasterPageFile* attribute in the @ *Page* declaration that points to the master page.
   - **D. Incorrect:** The master page, not the content pages, has the *ContentPlaceHolder* control.
3. Correct Answer: D
   - **A. Incorrect:** *Page_Load* occurs after the content page has bound to the master page. If you attempt to change the master page, the runtime throws an exception.

B. **Incorrect:** *Page_Render* occurs after the content page has bound to the master page. If you attempt to change the master page, the runtime throws an exception.

C. **Incorrect:** *Page_PreRender* occurs after the content page has bound to the master page. If you attempt to change the master page, the runtime throws an exception.

D. **Correct:** *Page_PreInit* is the last opportunity to change the master page. After this event, the page binds with the master page, preventing you from changing it.

Lesson 2

1. **Correct Answer: A and C**

   A. **Correct:** Themes specified using the page's *Theme* attribute override control attributes.

   B. **Incorrect:** Themes specified using the *StyleSheetTheme* attribute do not override control attributes.

   C. **Correct:** Themes specified using the *Theme* attribute override control attributes.

   D. **Incorrect:** Themes specified using the *StyleSheetTheme* attribute do not override control attributes.

2. **Correct Answer: C**

   A. **Incorrect:** Skin files should not include the *ID* attribute, and skin files must include the *runat="server"* attribute.

   B. **Incorrect:** Skin files should not include the *ID* attribute.

   C. **Correct:** Skin files must include the *runat="server"* attribute but should not include the *ID* attribute.

   D. **Incorrect:** Skin files must include the *runat="server"* attribute.

3. **Correct Answer: D**

   A. **Incorrect:** *Page_Load* occurs too late in the rendering process to change the theme.

   B. **Incorrect:** *Page_Render* occurs too late in the rendering process to change the theme.

   C. **Incorrect:** *Page_PreRender* occurs too late in the rendering process to change the theme.

   D. **Correct:** *Page_PreInit* is the proper method in which to specify the theme.

Lesson 3

1. **Correct Answer: A, B, and C**

   A. **Correct:** A user control can be leveraged as a Web Part by placing it into a Web Part zone.

   B. **Correct:** ASP.NET will automatically define a Web Part when you place a standard control, such as a *Label*, into a Web Part zone.

   C. **Correct:** You can create Web Parts by defining custom controls based on the *WebPart* class.

D. **Incorrect:** A master page defines a common interface for your application and is not used as a Web Part.

2. **Correct Answer: B and D**

   A. **Incorrect:** The *LayoutEditorPart* control enables users to change the chrome state and zone of a control. It does not provide the ability to change the Web Part's title.

   B. **Correct:** You must add an *EditorZone* container to the Web page. Then, add an *AppearanceEditorPart* control to the *EditorZone*.

   C. **Incorrect:** *CatalogZone* enables users to add new Web Parts to a page, but it does not enable them to change Web Part titles.

   D. **Correct:** The *AppearanceEditorPart* control enables users to set the titles of Web Parts.

3. **Correct Answer: B and C**

   A. **Incorrect:** The *LayoutEditorPart* control enables a user to change the chrome state and zone of a control. It does not provide the ability to add Web Parts.

   B. **Correct:** The *DeclarativeCatalogPart* control enables a user to add Web Parts when the page is in Catalog mode.

   C. **Correct:** The *CatalogZone* container is required to hold the *DeclarativeCatalogPart* control, which enables a user to add Web Parts.

   D. **Incorrect:** The *AppearanceEditorPart* control enables the user to edit the appearance of existing Web Parts, but does not enable a user to add new Web Parts.

4. **Correct Answer: B**

   A. **Incorrect:** The *ConnectionConsumer* attribute should be applied to the method that receives the provider Web Part's data.

   B. **Correct:** You should apply the *ConnectionProvider* attribute to a public method to allow consumers to access the method.

   C. **Incorrect:** You cannot use properties for connections between Web Parts.

   D. **Incorrect:** You cannot use properties for connections between Web Parts.

Chapter 5: Case Scenario Answers

Case Scenario 1: Meeting Customization Requirements for an Internal Insurance Application

1. You can use a combination of user profiles and customizable Web Parts to meet their requirements.
2. Connected Web Parts can provide what you need. You can have a provider Web Part that enables the underwriter to choose a claim type, and consumer Web Parts that retrieve the currently selected claim type and display related statistics.

Case Scenario 2: Provide Consistent Formatting for an External Web Application

1. You can use themes and add a .skin file that defines fonts for different controls.
2. If you apply a theme using the *<pages Theme="themeName">* element in the Web.config file, it overrides control attributes.
3. You can use customizable Web Parts to enable users to remove unwanted controls.
4. To enable users to change colors on a Web site, use programmatically applied themes and user profiles. Then, users can customize their profiles and ASP.NET remembers their preferences for future visits.

Chapter 6: Lesson Review Answers

Lesson 1

1. **Correct Answer: A and D**
   - **A. Correct:** The *UpdatePanel* control will enable the portion contained inside the panel to update independently of the rest of the page.
   - **B. Incorrect:** The *AsyncPostBackTrigger* control is used to have a control outside the *UpdatePanel* trigger an update to the *UpdatePanel*. This is not a requirement of this scenario.
   - **C. Incorrect:** The *ScriptManagerProxy* control is used for creating AJAX-enabled child pages of a master page or user controls. Neither is a requirement of this scenario.
   - **D. Correct:** The *ScriptManager* control is required of every AJAX page to manage the JavaScript files sent to the client and the communication between client and server.
2. **Correct Answer: A, B, and D**
   - **A. Correct:** An *UpdatePanel* control can be used to update only the portion of the page.
   - **B. Correct:** A *Timer* control can be used to retrieve updates from the server on a periodic basis.
   - **C. Incorrect:** Using a *ScriptManager* control on a user control prevents the user control from being added to a page already containing a *ScriptManager* control.
   - **D. Correct:** The *ScriptManagerProxy* control is used so as not to conflict with a *ScriptManager* control already on a containing page.
3. **Correct Answer: D**
   - **A. Incorrect:** The *UpdatePanel* does not have an *AsyncPostBackTrigger* attribute.
   - **B. Incorrect:** A *Button* control does not have an *AsyncPostBackTrigger* attribute.

C. **Incorrect:** An *AsyncPostBackTrigger* control should be added to the *Triggers* collection and not the other way around.

D. **Correct:** An *AsyncPostBackTrigger* control should be added to the *Triggers* collection of the *UpdatePanel*. You then set the *ControlID* property to the *Button* control's ID.

4. Correct Answer: B

A. **Incorrect:** A nested *UpdatePanel* will be shown to the user at all times. It will not be simply a part of the progress indicator.

B. **Correct:** An *UpdateProgress* control is used to display text or graphics during a partial-page update. The *DisplayAfter* attribute controls how long the page waits from the start of the request until it displays the progress indicator. If the request returns during this time, the progress indicator is not shown.

C. **Incorrect:** A *ProgressBar* is a Windows (not Web) control.

D. **Incorrect:** You cannot set two controls to have the same ID on the page. This will cause an error. In addition, the *UpdatePanel* does not have an *Interval* property.

Lesson 2

1. Correct Answer: A

A. **Correct:** You must derive from the *Sys.UI.Control* class to create an AJAX UI control.

B. **Incorrect:** This call simply indicates that you intend to implement the interface *IDisposable*. It does not indicate inheritance of the *Sys.UI.Control,* which is required to extend a DOM element.

C. **Incorrect:** This call creates your class without inheritance. To extend a DOM element, you should inherit from *Sys.UI.Control.*

D. **Incorrect:** In this case, you create a control that is meant to work as a behavior and not just a UI control.

2. Correct Answer: B

A. **Incorrect:** The *endRequest* event fires when the PostBack has completed (and is over).

B. **Correct:** The *pageLoading* event fires when the PostBack first comes back from the server.

C. **Incorrect:** The *pageLoaded* event fires when the PostBack comes back from the server and the content has been updated in the browser (after *pageLoading*).

D. **Incorrect:** The *beginRequest* event fires as the PostBack is being sent to the server.

3. Correct Answer: C

A. **Incorrect:** You need a *ScriptManager* control on the page to use the Microsoft AJAX Library. In addition, your scripts must be registered with the *ScriptManager* control.

B. **Incorrect:** You must explicitly register your .js files with the *ScriptManager.*

C. **Correct:** To use a .js file that targets the Microsoft AJAX Library you set a reference to it inside a *ScriptManager* control. You do so through the *<asp:ScriptReference />* element.

D. **Incorrect:** The *ScriptReference* class is used from a custom control (and not a page) to reference and embed a .js file.

4. **Correct Answer: B and D**

   A. **Incorrect:** A behavior is meant to extend multiple controls. Therefore, it is not specific to a single control as this would imply.

   B. **Correct:** A behavior is implemented by inheriting the *ExtenderControl* class.

   C. **Incorrect:** The *IScriptControl* interface is implemented for custom UI controls. It is not used for a behavior control.

   D. **Correct:** The *TargetControlType* attribute is used by a behavior control to allow users to attach a behavior to a control.

Chapter 6: Case Scenario Answers

Case Scenario 1: Using the ASP.NET AJAX Extensions

1. The *UpdatePanel* control will allow you to encapsulate the grid control and execute its updates independent of the rest of the page. This will speed these updates and keep the user's context within the page.
2. You must add a *ScriptManager* control to the page to use ASP.NET AJAX.
3. The *UpdateProgress* control can be used to notify the user as to the progress of the partial-page update.

Case Scenario 2: Using the Microsoft AJAX Library

1. The clock should be implemented as a *Sys.UI.Control* class so it could be used across pages of the site and provide a UI for a single control.

   The highlight object should be written as a *Sys.UI.Behavior* class as it extends the behavior of multiple controls.

   The validation logic does not have a UI. Therefore, you can implement it as a *Sys.Component* class.

2. The highlight control should be implemented as a custom server control. In doing so, you would inherit the *ExtenderControl* class.

   You could also consider wrapping the clock control as a custom server control. In doing so you would inherit from a control like the *Label* control (or similar). You would also implement the interface *IScriptControl*.

Chapter 7: Lesson Review Answers

Lesson 1

1. **Correct Answer: D**
   - **A. Incorrect:** The *DataColumn* object represents a column definition in a table and does not directly impact navigation.
   - **B. Incorrect:** The *DataTable* represents an entire table and does not explicity help with the navigation.
   - **C. Incorrect:** The *DataRow* object represents a row of data and won't directly help with the navigation.
   - **D. Correct:** You can use the *DataRelation* object to navigate from a child to the parent or from the parent to a child.
2. **Correct Answer: A**
   - **A. Correct:** Primary keys must be defined or the changed data will be appended into the destination *DataSet* instead of being merged.
   - **B. Incorrect:** The *DataSet* schemas do not need to match, and you can specify what to do about the differences.
   - **C. Incorrect:** The destination *DataSet* does not need to be empty.
   - **D. Incorrect:** The *DataSet* does not need to be merged back to the same *DataSet* that created it.
3. **Correct Answer: C**
   - **A. Incorrect:** The *DataTable* object does not have a *Sort* method.
   - **B. Incorrect:** The *DataSet* object does not have a *Sort* method.
   - **C. Correct:** The *DataView* can be used for each sort.
   - **D. Incorrect:** The *DataTable* object does not have a *Sort* method.
4. **Correct Answer: A, B, and C**
   - **A. Correct:** The *AsEnumerable* method of the *DataTable* is used to define a LINQ query.
   - **B. Correct:** The *Where* clause can be set to select only those vendors that are active.
   - **C. Correct:** The *Order By* clause will sort the vendors by a given field.
   - **D. Incorrect:** The *Group By* clause will group vendors into sets but will not filter them.

Lesson 2

1. **Correct Answer: B and D**
   - **A. Incorrect:** There is no *Cleanup* method on the *DbConnection* class.
   - **B. Correct:** The *Close* method of the *DbConnection* class will clean up the connection.
   - **C. Incorrect:** This will not necessarily clean up connections. Instead, it might orphan them and waste resources.
   - **D. Correct:** The *Using* block ensures the *Dispose* method is called (which cleans up connections).
2. **Correct Answer: A**
   - **A. Correct:** The *InfoMessage* event displays informational messages as well as the output of the SQL Print statement.
   - **B. Incorrect:** There is no such event on the *SqlConnection* class.
   - **C. Incorrect:** There is no such event on the *SqlConnection* class.
   - **D. Incorrect:** There is no such event on the *SqlConnection* class.
3. **Correct Answer: D**
   - **A. Incorrect:** The connection string does not have such a key.
   - **B. Incorrect:** The connection string does not have such a key.
   - **C. Incorrect:** The *MultipleActiveResultSets* setting is used to reuse a connection with an open data reader.
   - **D. Correct:** Setting the key *Asynchronous Processing =true* for the connection string will allow you to access data asynchronously.
4. **Correct Answer: A, B, and C**
   - **A. Correct:** You need to generate an O/R map to use LINQ to SQL. You can do so with SqlMetal. You can also use the O/R designer or hand-code your map.
   - **B. Correct:** You must reference the *System.Data.Linq* namespace to use the features of LINQ to SQL.
   - **C. Correct:** The *DataContext* object is the connection between your O/R map and the actual database.
   - **D. Incorrect:** A *GridView* control shows data. It can be bound to most .NET Framework data sources but is not required by LINQ to SQL.

Lesson 3

1. **Correct Answer: B**
   - **A. Incorrect:** The *XmlConvert* class cannot be used to create a new XML document.
   - **B. Correct:** Use the *XmlDocument* class to create a new XML document from scratch.

   - **C.** **Incorrect:** There is no class called *XmlNew* inside the *System.XML* namespace.
   - **D.** **Incorrect:** There is no class called *XmlSettings* inside the *System.XML* namespace.
2. **Correct Answer: C**
   - **A.** **Incorrect:** There is not a class called *XmlType* inside the *System.XML* namespace.
   - **B.** **Incorrect:** There is not a class called *XmlCast* inside the *System.XML* namespace.
   - **C.** **Correct:** The *XmlConvert* class is used for data conversions between XML and .NET Framework data types.
   - **D.** **Incorrect:** There is not a class called *XmlSettings* inside the *System.XML* namespace.
3. **Correct Answer: B and C**
   - **A.** **Incorrect:** The *Load* method is used to load an XML file (not a string).
   - **B.** **Correct:** The *Parse* method parses a string into an *XElement*.
   - **C.** **Correct:** To write your query, you define an *IEnumerable<XElement>* variable.
   - **D.** **Incorrect:** The *IEnumerable<>* takes a generic type (and not a variable). In this case, you need an *XElement* type to query against the XML.

Chapter 7: Case Scenario Answers

Case Scenario 1: Determining Ways to Update the Database

1. You can load the XML file into a *DataSet* and then use a *SqlDataAdapter* to retrieve all changes and send the changes to the database.

   You can read the XML file into an *XmlDocument* object and use the DOM to parse the data and write code to send the changes to the database.

   You can use the *XmlTextReader* to read the XML file node by node, capturing the data and sending it to the database.

   You can use LINQ to XML to load the data into an *XElement* object. You can then read this XML data and use ADO.NET code to send the data to the database.

Case Scenario 2: Storing a *DataSet* to a Binary File

1. Store the *DataSet* as a binary file by using the *BinaryFormatter* object.
2. You must set the *RemotingFormat* property of the *DataSet* to *SerializationFormat.Binary* to force the *DataSet* to be serialized as binary.

Chapter 8: Lesson Review Answers

Lesson 1

1. Correct Answer: D
   - **A. Incorrect:** The *ObjectDataSource* control is used to connect data defined in a middle-tier business object and not an O/R map.
   - **B. Incorrect:** The *SqlDataSource* control can be used to connect to a SQL Server database. However, in this case it would ignore the O/R map.
   - **C. Incorrect:** The *SiteMapDataSource* control is used to connect to data found in a .sitemap file.
   - **D. Correct:** The *LinqDataSource* can be used to connect to a context map defined for your database.
2. Correct Answer: A and B
   - **A. Correct:** *TypeName* is used to indicate the name of the class you intend to use for your object-based data source control.
   - **B. Correct:** *SelectMethod* is used to indicate a method on your object used for selecting data.
   - **C. Incorrect:** The *DataSourceId* property is not part of the *ObjectDataSource* control. Instead, it is used by a data-bound control to connect to a data source control.
   - **D. Incorrect:** The *SelectParameters* attribute is used to define parameters for your *ObjectDataSource* select method. These are optional and not mentioned in the question.
3. Correct Answer: B and C
   - **A. Incorrect:** There is not a *CacheTimeout* attribute defined for data source controls.
   - **B. Correct:** The *CacheDuration* attribute defines for how long the data of the control should be cached.
   - **C. Correct:** The *EnableCaching* attribute is used to turn on caching for the given data source control.
   - **D. Incorrect:** There is not a *DisableCaching* attribute defined for data source controls.

Lesson 2

1. Correct Answer: B and C
   - **A. Incorrect:** The *DataTextField* is used to set the data displayed to the user. This would display IDs to the user (and not names).
   - **B. Correct:** The *DataTextField* is used to display text to the user.

C. **Correct:** The *DataValueField* is used to return values for selected items.

D. **Incorrect:** The *DataValueField* is used to set the value returned for checked items. This would return names and not IDs.

2. Correct Answer: C and D

   A. **Incorrect:** The *DetailsView* control is used to show only a single record at a given time.

   B. **Incorrect:** The *Repeater* control does not implicitly support the ability to edit data with a data source control.

   C. **Correct:** The *GridView* control allows for the display of multiple rows of data and allows users to update that data.

   D. **Correct:** The *ListView* implicitly supports displaying data in a list and updating that data.

3. Correct Answer: A

   A. **Correct:** The *DropDownList* control can display a list that uses a minimum amount of space.

   B. **Incorrect:** The *RadioButtonList* control does not provide a list in a minimum amount of space.

   C. **Incorrect:** The *FormView* control does not provide a list in a minimum amount of space.

   D. **Incorrect:** The *TextBox* control does not provide a list.

Chapter 8: Case Scenario Answers

Case Scenario 1: Determining Data Source Controls

1. The data is returned as XML. You could therefore configure an XML data source control to work with this data. You can also use the *Data* property for setting the data based on a string value.
2. A *SqlDataSource* control can be configured to provide access to this data.
3. You can configure an *ObjectDataSource* control to access the customer data.

Case Scenario 2: Implementing a Master-Detail Solution

1. A *GridView* is probably best suited to display the customers and orders because the ability to display this data as a list is a requirement.
2. The *GridView* does not natively support the abiltiy to add new data records, but you can modify the *GridView* to provide this functionality. You can also supply a *Button* control that simply adds an empty data record and then places the record in edit mode.

   Another solution is to provide a *DetailsView* control in addition to the *GridView* control for the customers and orders. The *DetailsView* provides the ability to add new rows, and you can edit all of the fields.

Chapter 9: Lesson Review Answers

Lesson 1

1. Correct Answer: B
   - **A. Incorrect:** The *WebServiceAttribute* class is used to mark a class as a Web service. It does not provide a base class and does not allow for access to ASP.NET features.
   - **B. Correct:** The *WebService* class is a base class that will allow your Web service to have access to session state and more.
   - **C. Incorrect:** The *WebMethodAttribute* class is used to tag public methods as Web services.
   - **D. Incorrect:** To get easy access to the ASP.NET objects you should inherit from *WebService*. This will give you similar access as inheriting from the *Page* object does for Web pages.
2. Correct Answer: B and D
   - **A. Incorrect:** The Add Reference dialog box is used for referencing .dll files.
   - **B. Correct:** The Add Web Reference dialog box will find the Web service and its description and generate a proxy for use by your Web site.
   - **C. Incorrect:** To call a Web service, you simply call the generated proxy class.
   - **D. Correct:** The proxy class will provide access to the Web service.
3. Correct Answer: C
   - **A. Incorrect:** Windows Basic would send unencrypted passwords over the wire. This would invite tampering.
   - **B. Incorrect:** Windows digest works only with Windows-based systems.
   - **C. Correct:** Client certificates can be secured and verified by a third party.
   - **D. Incorrect:** A custom SOAP header might be a viable option. However, it is not, by default, verifiable as trusted.
4. Correct Answer: A, B, C, and D
   - **A. Correct:** The *ScriptService* class indicates that the given Web service can be called from client script.
   - **B. Correct:** The *ScriptHandlerFactory* configuration is required for managing communication between the client and the server.
   - **C. Correct:** You set a reference to the .asmx service from the *ScriptManager*. This tells the *ScriptManager* to generate a client proxy for calling the Web service.
   - **D. Correct:** To use ASP.NET AJAX for calling a Web service from client script, both the client and the service need to be in the same domain.

Lesson 2

1. **Correct Answer: B**

   A. Incorrect: The WCF Service library creates a .dll for your service. You can still reference this from a Web site and therefore host in IIS. However, you are not taking advantage of the ASP.NET programming model in this case.

   B. Correct: A WCF Service application is an ASP.NET Web site that is set up to define and expose WCF services.

   C. Incorrect: The ASP.NET Web Service application project is used for creating XML Web services with ASP.NET (and not WCF services).

   D. Incorrect: A Windows Service application is used to create a Windows service (and not a WCF service). A Windows service can, however, host a WCF service outside of IIS.

2. **Correct Answer: A and D**

   A. Correct: The *DataContract* attribute class indicates your class can be serialized with WCF.

   B. Incorrect: *ServiceContract* is used to define a WCF service class.

   C. Incorrect: *OperationContract* is used to define a service method.

   D. Correct: The *DataMember* attribute indicates public members that should be serialized as part of the *DataContract*.

3. **Correct Answer: A**

   A. Correct: Setting the *IsOneWay* parameter to *true* indicates that the operation does not return a response.

   B. Incorrect: The *AsyncPattern* parameter is used to indicate that the operation supports asynchronous callers.

   C. Incorrect: The *IsInitiating* parameter is used to indicate if an operation can be the first operation in a session.

   D. Incorrect: The *ReplyAction* parameter is used to indicate the SOAP action for the reply message of an operation.

Chapter 9: Case Scenario Answers

Case Scenario: Selecting a Service Model

1. Both .asmx and WCF services can be configured to work. The current requirements do not dictate that you need the features of WCF (multiple endpoints for communicating across multiple channels). Therefore, you might lean toward building these services with .asmx over WCF.

2. All access to the services is done over the Web. In addition, the application would benefit greatly from the scalability of IIS, the caching in ASP.NET, session state management, and more. Therefore, you should consider hosting the services in IIS.
3. You should cache this information, as it is not updated that often. Use the *CacheDuration* option of the *WebMethod* class to do so.
4. The user information can be stored using ASP.NET sessions (in memory, a proxy caching server, or inside a SQL Server database).

Chapter 10: Lesson Review Answers

Lesson 1

1. **Correct Answer: B and D**
   - **A. Incorrect:** This will not add the controls to the form. User controls must be added to a form to operate.
   - **B. Correct:** Each control must be added to the form.
   - **C. Incorrect:** The form object does not support a *LoadControl* method.
   - **D. Correct:** You can load a user control dynamically with the *LoadControl* method of the page object.
2. **Correct Answer: C**
   - **A. Incorrect:** Although you could use this method, it would be difficult to do and certainly is not the best way to accomplish this task.
   - **B. Incorrect:** Although you could use this method, it would be difficult to do and certainly is not the best way to accomplish this task.
   - **C. Correct:** The templated user control exposes the data to the Web page designer, who can then specify the format of the data in a template.
   - **D. Incorrect:** This user control does not natively expose the style property, and if you choose to expose the property, you can only set an overall format for the user control, not a format for each of the data elements that is being exposed.
3. **Correct Answer: B**
   - **A. Incorrect:** This will not allow a user to read and modify the user control's *TextBox* control's *Text* properties as required.
   - **B. Correct:** This will ensure a user is able to read and modify the values stored in the *TextBox* control.
   - **C. Incorrect:** Controls inside a user control are, by default, private to the user control.
   - **D. Incorrect:** This will not allow a user to read and modify the user control's *TextBox* control's *Text* properties as required.

Lesson 2

1. Correct Answer: B and C

   A. **Incorrect:** There is no need to set a reference to this namespace.

   B. **Correct:** This namespace is required for the *ToolboxBitmap* class.

   C. **Correct:** The *ToolboxBitmap* attribute allows you to define an image for your custom control inside the Toolbox.

   D. **Incorrect:** The *ToolboxData* attribute is used to influence the markup when your control is added to the page.

2. Correct Answer: D

   A. **Incorrect:** This method does not output display to the browser.

   B. **Incorrect:** This method does not output display to the browser.

   C. **Incorrect:** This method does not output display to the browser.

   D. **Correct:** The *Render* method must be overridden and you must provide code to display your control.

3. Correct Answer: A

   A. **Correct:** The *CreateChildControls* method must be overridden with code to create the child controls and set their properties.

   B. **Incorrect:** This method is not used for creating child control properties.

   C. **Incorrect:** This method is not used for creating child control properties.

   D. **Incorrect:** This method is not used for creating child control properties.

Chapter 10: Case Scenario Answers

Case Scenario 1: Sharing Controls Between Applications

1. You should consider developing a custom Web control. You should also make this a composite control as these types of controls can easily contain other controls and the layout of the control is always the same.
2. A user control will not be compiled into a .dll file that you can share.

   A templated control is ruled out, as the goal of the requirements is to keep the layout of the control consistent.

Case Scenario 2: Providing Layout Flexibility

1. You should consider creating a user control, as this control is only within the one site. This can provide easier development and additional flexibility in change and deployment.

2. You should consider creating the control as a templated control. This will allow the users of the control to manage the many layouts required by the site.
3. A user control inherits from the *System.Web.UI.UserControl* class.

Chapter 11: Lesson Review Answers

Lesson 1

1. Correct Answer: A
   - **A. Correct:** *Server.GetLastError* retrieves the most recent error message. After processing it, you call *Server.ClearError* to remove the error from the queue.
   - **B. Incorrect:** You should call *Server.ClearError* to remove an error from the queue after processing it. However, you must first call *Server.GetLastError* to handle the error.
   - **C. Incorrect:** The *GetLastError* method is a member of the *Server* object, not the *Request* object.
   - **D. Incorrect:** The *GetLastError* method is a member of the *Server* object, not the *Application* object.
2. Correct Answer: B and C
   - **A. Incorrect:** Errors are not trapped at the *Response* object level.
   - **B. Correct:** You can catch errors at the page level by trapping the *Page_Error* method.
   - **C. Correct:** You can catch application-wide, unhandled errors by trapping the *Application_Error* method inside the Global.asax file.
   - **D. Incorrect:** Errors are not trapped at the *Server* object level.
3. Correct Answer: D
   - **A. Incorrect:** The *WebConfigurationManager.GetSection* method returns an object that must be cast to a section-specific type. It does not return a string.
   - **B. Incorrect:** To identify the *<httpCookies>* section, you must reference *system.web/httpCookies* because *<httpCookies>* exists within *<system.web>*.
   - **C. Incorrect:** The *WebConfigurationManager.GetSection* method returns an object that must be cast to a section-specific type. It does not return a string. Additionally, to identify the *<httpCookies>* section, you must reference *system.web/httpCookies* because *<httpCookies>* exists within *<system.web>*.
   - **D. Correct:** To retrieve a section from the master Web.config file, call *WebConfigurationManager.GetSection*. This method returns an object that must be cast to the correct type. In Visual Basic, the casting happens automatically. However, it must be done explicitly in C#.

4. **Correct Answer: C**
   - **A. Incorrect:** *IPartitionResolver* defines methods that must be implemented for custom session state partition resolution, and does not relate to handling custom file types.
   - **B. Incorrect:** *IHttpModule* provides module initialization and disposal events, enabling you to respond to *BeginRequest* and *EndRequest* HTTP events before and after a Web page is generated. You would not use it to handle a custom file type.
   - **C. Correct:** Implement the *IHttpHandler* interface to generate custom file types. Additionally, you must configure IIS to forward requests for .doc files to ASP.NET.
   - **D. Incorrect:** *IHttpHandlerFactory* is used as part of *IHttpHandler*, but it has no functionality itself.

Lesson 2

1. **Correct Answer: A, D, and E**
   - **A. Correct:** The *ClrVersion* property is used to get the version of the .NET Framework installed on the client.
   - **B. Incorrect:** The *Browser* object does not expose user security information.
   - **C. Incorrect:** The *Browser* object does not expose the user's e-mail address.
   - **D. Correct:** The *ActiveXControls* property is used to indicate whether the browser supports ActiveX controls.
   - **E. Correct:** The *JavaScript* property is used to indicate if the browser supports JavaScript.
2. **Correct Answer: B**
   - **A. Incorrect:** The *Page* object does not expose the *Title* property.
   - **B. Correct:** The *Page.Header* property exposes an *HtmlHeader* control. You can use this control instance to set the *Title* property for the page.
   - **C. Incorrect:** The *Response* object does not expose the *Header* property.
   - **D. Incorrect:** The *Response* object does not expose the *Title* property.
3. **Correct Answer: A**
   - **A. Correct:** The *Flush* method sends the current output to the client without ending the response.
   - **B. Incorrect:** The *Clear* method removes everything from the HTTP response stream.
   - **C. Incorrect:** The *End* method finishes the response and returns the page.
   - **D. Incorrect:** The *ClearContent* method removes the content from the response stream, not including the HTTP headers.

Chapter 11: Case Scenario Answers

Case Scenario 1: Dynamically Generating Charts

1. The charts can be dynamically generated using the features of the *System.Drawing* namespace. You can then output them to the client using the *Context.Response* object.
2. Create a custom HTTP handler that implements the *IHttpHandler* interface. Inside the *ProcessRequest* method, call the code that generates the image. Send the output as part of the response.
3. You need to configure IIS to call your custom HTTP handler for requests of type .gif. You can do so using IIS 7 directly inside the Web.config file. Add a node to the *httpHandler* section.

Case Scenario 2: Dynamically Adjusting Pages Based on Browser Capabilities

1. You can check the *Request.Browser.ActiveXControls* property to determine if the browser supports ActiveX.
2. You can check the *Request.Browser.IsMobileDevice* property to determine if the request came from a mobile device.
3. You can use the *IsColor* property of the *Request.Browser* object to determine if the browser is using a color display.

Chapter 12: Lesson Review Answers

Lesson 1

1. Correct Answer: B and C
   - **A. Incorrect:** This will turn on debugging for the entire site.
   - **B. Correct:** Setting *debug* to *false* inside the *compilation* element of Web.config will turn off debugging for the entire site.
   - **C. Correct:** Setting the *debug* attribute of the @ *Page* directive to *true* will turn on debugging just for the selected page.
   - **D. Incorrect:** This will turn off debugging for the given page.
2. Correct Answer: B and D
   - **A. Incorrect:** This action is used to define error-specific pages (and not a sitewide default error page).
   - **B. Correct:** The *defaultRedirect* attribute of the *customErrors* element will set a default sitewide error page.

C. **Incorrect:** You use *statusCode* to define an attribute of the *error* element to set specific error pages based on HTTP status codes.
D. **Correct:** You can use the *aspxerrorpath* query string parameter to retrieve the requested page to display on the default error page.

3. Correct Answer: B and C

A. **Incorrect:** You need to run the Remote Debugging Monitor on the server and not the debug host computer.
B. **Correct:** Running the Remote Debugging Monitor on the server will allow remote debugging for a given user with the appropriate rights.
C. **Correct:** You need to attach to the process on the server that is hosting the application.
D. **Incorrect:** Attaching to the browser's process is valid only if you are debugging client-side script. To debug the server-side code you need to attach to the server process running your application.

Lesson 2

1. Correct Answer: A

A. **Correct:** You can use ASP.NET tracing to view page life cycle timings.
B. **Incorrect:** This might get the results, but it is a time-consuming effort and will not be as accurate or easy to maintain.
C. **Incorrect:** This attribute does not exist in the Web.config file.
D. **Incorrect:** There is no such setting in the Web site properties.

2. Correct Answer: D

A. **Incorrect:** In this option, tracing is disabled. The *localOnly* attribute is also set wrong.
B. **Incorrect:** This option has the wrong values for *pageOutput* and *localOnly*.
C. **Incorrect:** This option has the wrong value for *mostRecent*.
D. **Correct:** This option matches the requirements defined in the question.

3. Correct Answer: C

A. **Incorrect:** The Control Tree section shows information about each control on the Web page, but not the posted data.
B. **Incorrect:** The Headers Collection section does not contain the posted data.
C. **Correct:** The Form Collection section contains the posted data.
D. **Incorrect:** The Server Variables section doesn't contain the posted data.

4. Correct Answer: D

A. **Incorrect:** This is a base Web event class that includes request data.
B. **Incorrect:** This is a base Web event class for logging audit events.

C. **Incorrect:** This class sends an event when the Web application starts, stops, or processes another significant event.

D. **Correct:** This class will send an event when a user successfully authenticates with the Web application.

Chapter 12: Case Scenario Answers

Case Scenario 1: Debugging

1. Edit the Web.config file and set *debug* to *false* for the *compilation* element.
2. Create a default error page. Add a *customErrors* element to the Web.config file. Set the *defaultRedirect* attribute to the name of the default error page.
3. Set the *mode* attribute of the *customErrors* element to *RemoteOnly*.
4. Run the Remote Debugging tool (Msvsmon.exe) on the staging server. Connect to the ASP.NET process on the staging server from Visual Studio.

Case Scenario 2: Troubleshooting

1. Turn tracing on for the site by setting the *enabled* attribute of the *trace* element to *true* inside the Web.config file. In addition, set the *localOnly* attribute to *true* to enable tracing only for local users.

   Note that you cannot set tracing on at the page level in this scenario. This will override any settings in the Web.config file and output trace information on the page for any users that hit the page.
2. Add child *rule* elements to the *healthMonitoring* element in the Web.config file. Also set the *healthMonitoring* element's *enabled* attribute to *true*.

Chapter 13: Lesson Review Answers

Lesson 1

1. **Correct Answer: B and C**

   A. **Incorrect:** The language abbreviation must precede the .resx extension.

   B. **Correct:** The default language file should not have a language extension.

   C. **Correct:** To create a German language file, add the language extension (de) between the page file name and the .resx extension.

   D. **Incorrect:** You do not need to add a language abbreviation to the resource name for the default language.

2. **Correct Answer: B and C**

   A. **Incorrect:** The *Page.Culture* property defines cultural formatting, such as how numbers are formatted. It is not required for defining a language.

   B. **Correct:** The *Page.UICulture* property defines the language resource file that is used.

   C. **Correct:** ASP.NET pages initialize the culture in the *InitializeCulture* method. You should override this method, set the *UICulture* property, and then call the base *Page.InitializeCulture* method.

   D. **Incorrect:** The *Page.ReadStringResource* method is not related to defining language.

3. **Correct Answer: D**

   A. **Incorrect:** The *DataValueField* property is only used when a control is linked to a *DataSource.*

   B. **Incorrect:** The *DataSourceID* property is only used when a control is linked to a *DataSource.*

   C. **Incorrect:** Although you could programmatically define the *Text* property using a global resource, at design time, you should use the *(Expressions)* property.

   D. **Correct:** Visual Studio provides an editor for the *(Expressions)* property that enables you to link any other property to a global resource.

4. **Correct Answer: A**

   A. **Correct:** Visual Studio automatically creates strongly named objects within *Resources .Resource* for every value you create.

   B. **Incorrect:** Although you can access global resources using strings, you need to call the *GetGlobalResourceObject* method.

   C. **Incorrect:** Although you can access global resources using strings, you need to call the *GetGlobalResourceObject* method.

   D. **Incorrect:** Visual Studio does not create strongly typed objects under *Resources* directly. Instead, they are within *Resources.Resource.*

Lesson 2

1. **Correct Answer: B and C**

   A. **Incorrect:** ASP.NET uses the *Image.AccessKey* parameter to provide a keyboard shortcut for an image.

   B. **Correct:** ASP.NET uses the *Image.AlternateText* parameter to create the alt text for an image. Screen readers typically describe images using the alt text.

   C. **Correct:** *DescriptionUrl* links to an HTML page that provides a long description of an image. ASP.NET uses this link to create the *longdesc* HTML attribute.

   D. **Incorrect:** *ToolTip* is not related to accessibility. *ToolTip* defines data that Internet Explorer displays when you hover your pointer over an image.

2. **Correct Answer: A and C**

   A. **Correct:** Controls such as *Image* provide properties that you can use to provide a description for those who cannot see the image.

   B. **Incorrect:** ASP.NET controls are not displayed in high contrast by default. However, they are designed to support high-contrast mode by default.

   C. **Correct:** Controls such as *CreateUserWizard*, *Menu*, *SiteMapPath*, *TreeView*, and *Wizard* support skipping links.

   D. **Incorrect:** ASP.NET controls do not display text in large font sizes by default. However, they are designed to support browsers configured to display large font sizes.

3. **Correct Answer: A, B, and D**

   A. **Correct:** Visual Studio can automatically test Web applications for compliance with WCAG Priority 1 guidelines.

   B. **Correct:** Visual Studio can automatically test Web applications for compliance with WCAG Priority 2 guidelines.

   C. **Incorrect:** ADA, the Americans with Disabilities Act, provides accessibility guidelines for facilities, transportation, and more. However, it does not provide Web application accessibility guidelines.

   D. **Correct:** Visual Studio automatically tests Web applications for compliance with Section 508 guidelines.

Chapter 13: Case Scenario Answers

Case Scenario 1: Upgrade an Application for Multiple Languages

1. You can use local and global resources to provide translations for your Web site. Use local resources to provide page-specific translations, and use global resources to provide phrases that are used on multiple pages.
2. Translators need to update the local and global resource files. These are standard XML files, so any XML editor can be used. You can also create an application to facilitate the translations.
3. Web browsers often are configured for language preferences. ASP.NET can automatically detect this preference and use the preferred language if the resource is available. Additionally, you should allow a user to specify a language.
4. Specific cultures distinguish both languages and regional requirements, as opposed to neutral cultures, which only distinguish the language.

Case Scenario 2: Making a Web Application Accessible

1. Visual Studio includes tools to test individual Web pages. Additionally, you can configure Visual Studio to automatically test an entire Web application for Section 508 compliance during the build process.
2. Accessible applications can be used with alternative input and display devices.
3. No, accessible applications do not require users with traditional input and display devices to make any sacrifices. Most accessibility features take the form of hidden textual descriptions and access keys, which users who do not need them will probably not notice.
4. You need to provide textual descriptions for all visual elements, such as forms, tables, and images. Additionally, you should make the Web application usable without a mouse.

Chapter 14: Lesson Review Answers

Lesson 1

1. Correct Answer: A
   - **A. Correct:** User profiles are disabled by default for anonymous users. To enable anonymous user profiles, add the *<anonymousIdentification enabled="true" />* element to the *<system.Web>* section of the Web.config file. Then in the *<profile><properties>* section, add the variables you want to track and set *allowAnonymous="true"* for each variable.
   - **B. Incorrect:** You must specify the type of all variables except strings.
   - **C. Incorrect:** You must set *allowAnonymous="true"* for each variable that anonymous users will access.
   - **D. Incorrect:** You must add the *<anonymousIdentification enabled="true" />* element to the *<system.Web>* section of the Web.config file. Additionally, you need to set *allowAnonymous="true"* for each variable that anonymous users will access.
2. Correct Answer: A and B
   - **A. Correct:** Custom types that you wish to use as profile properties must be marked serializable.
   - **B. Correct:** When you use a custom type, you must qualify it by namespace and class in the *type* attribute of the profile property.
   - **C. Incorrect:** A profile property group is created with the group element. It has nothing to do with custom types.
   - **D. Incorrect:** You do not need to register a custom type with the Machine.config file in any way.

Lesson 2

1. Correct Answer: C
   - **A. Incorrect:** The *Login* control prompts the user for a user name and password.
   - **B. Incorrect:** The *LoginView* control enables you to display custom content for authenticated or unauthenticated users.
   - **C. Correct:** The *LoginStatus* control displays "Login," with a link to log in if the user is unauthenticated, or "Logout" to authenticated users.
   - **D. Incorrect:** The *LoginName* control displays the user's name when he or she is authenticated. The control is not visible when a user is not authenticated.
2. Correct Answer: A
   - **A. Correct:** If no filename is specified in the Web.config file, ASP.NET redirects unauthenticated users to the Login.aspx page, regardless of whether the page exists.
   - **B. Incorrect:** ASP.NET directs users who need to log in to the page named Login.aspx by default.
   - **C. Incorrect:** ASP.NET directs users who need to log in to the page named Login.aspx by default.
   - **D. Incorrect:** ASP.NET directs users who need to log in to the page named Login.aspx by default.
4. Correct Answer: A and D
   - **A. Correct:** The *Login* control is required on a login page, because it prompts the user for a user name and password.
   - **B. Incorrect:** The *CreateUserWizard* control enables a user to create an account for himself or herself. However, it is a very large control, and a user should only need to access it once. Therefore, it should be placed on its own page.
   - **C. Incorrect:** The *LoginName* control is not a good choice for a login page because it displays an authenticated user's name. Because the user is not yet logged on when accessing the login page, there would not be a user name to display, and the control would not be visible.
   - **D. Correct:** The *PasswordRecovery* control is a good choice for a login page because it can be used to recover a password in the event the user forgets his or her password.
5. Correct Answer: B
   - **A. Incorrect:** The *Unload* event is called when the control is unloaded and does not allow you to redirect the user after a successful account creation.
   - **B. Correct:** After a user creates an account, he or she is notified of the successful account creation and prompted to click Continue. The *ContinueButtonClick* event is called when the user clicks that button.

- **C.** **Incorrect:** The *CreatedUser* event is called when a user account is successfully created. However, it is called before the user has been notified of the account creation. Therefore, you should respond to *ContinueButtonClick* instead.
- **D.** **Incorrect:** The *Init* event is called when the page is initialized, which would occur before the user account had been created. Therefore, redirecting the user in response to this event prevents him or her from being able to create an account.

Lesson 3

1. **Correct Answer: C**
   - **A.** **Incorrect:** The asterisk (*) refers to all users, authenticated or unauthenticated. Therefore, this Web.config file blocks all users.
   - **B.** **Incorrect:** The asterisk (*) refers to all users, authenticated or unauthenticated. Therefore, this Web.config file grants access to all users without prompting them for credentials.
   - **C.** **Correct:** The question mark (?) refers to all unauthenticated users. Therefore, this Web.config file correctly blocks unauthenticated access.
   - **D.** **Incorrect:** The question mark (?) refers to all unauthenticated users. Therefore, this Web.config file grants access to unauthenticated users without prompting them for credentials.
2. **Correct Answer: D**
   - **A.** **Incorrect:** By default, cookies are used for browsers that support them. For browsers that do not support them, the authentication token is stored in the URI. You can configure cookies to always be used by setting the *cookieless* attribute of the *<forms>* element to *UseCookies*.
   - **B.** **Incorrect:** By default, the authentication token is only stored in the URI if the browser does not support cookies. You can configure cookies to never be used by setting the *cookieless* attribute of the *<forms>* element to *UseUri*.
   - **C.** **Incorrect:** This behavior is useful, but it is not the default setting. To configure this behavior, set the *cookieless* attribute of the *<forms>* element to *AutoDetect*.
   - **D.** **Correct:** This is the default behavior, and is equivalent to setting the *cookieless* attribute of the *<forms>* element to *UseDeviceProfile*.
3. **Correct Answer: B**
   - **A.** **Incorrect:** Authenticated users who are not members of the FABRIKAM\Marketing group are denied access, because the *<deny users="*" />* element overrides the *<allow users ="?" />* default element in the Machine.config file.
   - **B.** **Correct:** Only members of the FABRIKAM\Marketing group are allowed access, because the settings in the *<location>* element override the settings in the parent folders.

   C. Incorrect: The *<deny users="*">* element in the *<location>* element blocks users who are not members of the FABRIKAM\Marketing group.
   D. Incorrect: The *<allow roles="FABRIKAM\Marketing" />* element takes precedence over the *<deny users="*">* element, granting members of the FABRIKAM\Marketing group access.

4. **Correct Answer: D**
   A. Incorrect: Unauthenticated users do not have access because the Web.config file denies them access. Additionally, NTFS permissions also deny them access.
   B. Incorrect: Authenticated users do not have access because the Web.config file denies them access to the Marketing folder. Additionally, NTFS permissions deny them access, because the NTFS permissions grant access only to John and Sam.
   C. Incorrect: Members of the Domain Users group do not have access because the Web.config file denies them access to the Marketing folder. Additionally, NTFS permissions also deny them access, because the NTFS permissions grant access only to John and Sam.
   D. Correct: John has access because he is granted permissions through ASP.NET because of his membership in the FABRIKAM\Marketing group. Additionally, he is granted NTFS permission to access the folder.
   E. Incorrect: Sam does not have access because the Web.config file denies him access to the Marketing folder. However, he can access the Web pages from a shared folder, because NTFS permissions grant him access. Only ASP.NET blocks access.

Chapter 14: Case Scenario Answers

Case Scenario 1: Configuring Web Application Authorization

1. Your Web.config file should resemble the following:

```
Code View: Scroll / Show All
<?xml version="1.0" encoding="utf-8" ?>
<configuration>

  <system.web>
    <authentication mode="Windows" />
    <authorization>
        <deny users="?" />
    </authorization>
  </system.web>

  <location path="IT">
    <system.web>
      <authorization>
        <allow roles="SOUTHRIDGE\IT" />
```

```
      <deny users="*" />
    </authorization>
  </system.web>
</location>

<location path="Production">
  <system.web>
    <authorization>
      <allow roles="SOUTHRIDGE\Production" />
      <allow users="SOUTHRIDGE\TJensen" />
      <deny users="*" />
    </authorization>
  </system.web>
</location>

<location path="Sales">
  <system.web>
    <authorization>
      <allow users="SOUTHRIDGE\TJensen" />
      <deny users="*" />
    </authorization>
  </system.web>
</location>
</configuration>
```

You also could have explicitly created a <location> section for the CustServ folder. However, because its permissions are identical to those of the parent folder, creating the <location> section is unnecessary.

2. You can use NTFS file permissions to further restrict access to the folders. This would provide defense-in-depth protection.

Case Scenario 2: Configuring Web Application Authentication

1. You should use Windows authentication, because you need the user to provide Windows credentials that the application can use to access the file.
2. Although you could configure impersonation in the application's Web.config file, that would grant the application unnecessary privileges and would give all users the same rights to the files. Instead, you should leave impersonation disabled in the Web.config file and implement impersonation only for the section of code that requires the user's elevated privileges.
3. You should configure the *<authentication>* and *<authorization>* sections as follows:

```
<configuration>
     <system.web>
          <authentication mode="Windows" />
          <authorization>
```

```
            <deny users="?" />
        </authentication>
    </system.web>
</configuration>
```

4. The following code works if added to the *Page_Load* method, assuming you create *TextBox* objects named *filenameTextBox* and *reportTextBox*:

```
'VB
Imports System.Security.Principal
Imports System.IO
...
' Impersonate the user with the account used to authenticate.
Dim realUser As WindowsImpersonationContext
realUser = CType(User.Identity, WindowsIdentity).Impersonate

' Perform tasks that require user permissions.
' Read the requested file.

Dim reader As StreamReader = File.OpenText(filenameTextBox.Text)
reportTextBox.Text = reader.ReadToEnd
reader.Close()

' Undo the impersonation, reverting to the normal user context.
realUser.Undo()


//C#
using System.Security.Principal;
using System.IO;
...
// Impersonate the user with the account used to authenticate.
WindowsImpersonationContext realUser;
realUser = ((WindowsIdentity)User.Identity).Impersonate();

// Perform tasks that require user permissions.
// Read the requested file.
StreamReader reader = File.OpenText(filenameTextBox.Text);
reportTextBox.Text = reader.ReadToEnd();
reader.Close();

// Undo the impersonation, reverting to the normal user context.
realUser.Undo();
```

Chapter 15: Lesson Review Answers

Lesson 1

1. **Correct Answer: A, B, C, and D**
   - **A. Correct:** There is not a site template for mobile Web applications by default in Visual Studio 2008.
   - **B. Correct:** The standard Default.aspx page inherits from *System.Web.UI.Page* but a mobile form inherits from *System.Web.UI.MobileControls.MobilePage*.
   - **C. Correct:** You must register the *MobileControls* inside the *Mobile* assembly to use them on your page.
   - **D. Correct:** You add mobile controls to mobile form controls.
2. **Correct Answer: A and D**
   - **A. Correct:** You can add a test for *Request.Browser.IsMobileDevice* and set the *Text* property based on the value returned from the test.
   - **B. Incorrect:** The mobile Web form does not contain an *IsDevice* method.
   - **C. Incorrect:** The *UserAgent* property on the *Request* object will not be set to *mobile* for mobile devices.
   - **D. Correct:** You can set the default *Text* value, and then define a mobile device in the *AppliedDeviceFilters*, and use this to set the *Text* property using the *PropertyOverrides* property of the mobile *Label* control.
3. **Correct Answer: C**
   - **A. Incorrect:** This is not a valid operation.
   - **B. Incorrect:** This is not a valid operation.
   - **C. Correct:** You must run the aspnet_regbrowsers command-line tool in the .NET Command Prompt window using the *–i* switch.
   - **D. Incorrect:** No such switch exists for the aspnet_regiis tool.

Chapter 15: Case Scenario Answers

Case Scenario 1: Determining the Mobile Control to Use

1. Use the *ObjectList* control to display the search results. This control is capable of displaying tabular data to a mobile device.

Case Scenario 2: Determining How Many Web Pages to Create

1. To create a Web site with the minimum number of Web pages, you can produce a single set of Web pages that are compatible with all devices by using mobile controls exclusively.
2. You should consider creating two sets of Web pages. One set would be for the desktop and notebook computers that have more processing power and have hardware that can render richer Web pages with more animation. The other set of Web pages would be for all other devices and would use the mobile controls that can render device-specific Web pages.

Chapter 16: Lesson Review Answers

Lesson 1

1. **Correct Answer: A**
   - **A. Correct:** Any installation changes you make should occur in the Install phase.
   - **B. Incorrect:** If you can divide an aspect of setup into separate installation and commit phases, you should do that. However, registry entries are simple changes and you can make them entirely in the Install phase.
   - **C. Incorrect:** The Rollback phase is used to remove changes made during the Install phase if setup is cancelled or otherwise fails.
   - **D. Incorrect:** The Uninstall phase is called when a user removes an application from Add or Remove Programs.
2. **Correct Answer: C and D**
   - **A. Incorrect:** You would perform the initial change in the Install phase and record the previous value so that it could be removed later. However, you do not undo your registry modification in this phase.
   - **B. Incorrect:** The Commit phase finalizes setup changes and should not be used for undoing setup modifications.
   - **C. Correct:** The Rollback phase is used to remove changes made during the Install phase if setup is cancelled or otherwise fails. Therefore, you should undo your registry modification here if the change has already taken place.
   - **D. Correct:** The Uninstall phase is called when a user removes an application from Add or Remove Programs. Therefore, you should undo your registry modification here.
3. **Correct Answer: C**
   - **A. Incorrect:** Setup Projects are used to deploy Windows Forms applications, not Web applications.
   - **B. Incorrect:** Web Setup Projects package Web sites in executable setups and Windows Installer files. You can use a Web Setup Project to deploy a Web application to a Web

server. However, it does not assist the development process by detecting versioning conflicts.

C. Correct: The Copy Web tool detects when a version of a file has been modified on the Web server after it is synchronized with the local copy of a file. Therefore, it can detect versioning conflicts when multiple developers work on a single site.

D. Incorrect: The Publish Web Site tool is used to precompile and deploy Web sites. However, it does not have the ability to detect versioning conflicts.

4. Correct Answer: D

A. Incorrect: Setup Projects are used to deploy Windows Forms applications, not Web applications.

B. Incorrect: Web Setup Projects package Web sites in executable setups and Windows Installer files. You can use a Web Setup Project to deploy a Web application to a Web server; however, it does not precompile the Web site.

C. Incorrect: The Copy Web tool detects when a version of a file has been modified on the Web server after it was synchronized with the local copy of a file. It does not enable you to precompile the Web site, however.

D. Correct: The Publish Web Site tool is used to precompile and deploy Web sites. Precompiling reduces the delay when the first user requests a Web page, improving initial responsiveness of a site.

Lesson 2

1. Correct Answer: A

A. Correct: In this example, your primary concern is that a different copy of the page is cached for each state that the user might select. The state would be provided as a parameter; therefore, configuring the *VaryByParam* attribute with the name of the control containing the state input provides optimal caching.

B. Incorrect: The *VaryByHeader* attribute is used to dynamically generate the page if an item in the page's header varies. In this case, the header is not unique for different states, and you cannot use the attribute to configure the correct type of caching.

C. Incorrect: The *SqlDependency* attribute might seem like the correct attribute because the Web page is based on a SQL query. However, in this scenario, you are not concerned about updating the page if the database is updated. You are only concerned with updating the page output if the user chooses to filter the customer list, which is provided by a parameter, not the database.

D. Incorrect: The *VaryByCustom* attribute enables you to implement custom control over how pages are cached. Although you could implement a custom method to meet your requirements, this would be time-consuming and inefficient. The capability you need is provided by the *VaryByParam* attribute.

2. Correct Answer: B

   A. **Incorrect:** The *Request* object contains methods and parameters that describe the user's request. To configure page output caching, you must use the *Response* object instead.

   B. **Correct:** The *Response* object contains methods such as *Response.Cache.SetExpires* and *Response.AddCacheDependency* that enable you to configure page output caching programmatically.

   C. **Incorrect:** The *Application* collection allows you to share data across all pages and processes in your application. Page output caching is configured on a per-page basis using the *Response* object.

   D. **Incorrect:** The *Server* object contains methods such as *UrlDecode* and *UrlEncode* that are useful for processing server file paths. To configure page output caching, you must use the *Response* object instead.

3. Correct Answer: C and D

   A. **Incorrect:** You can directly define *Cache* items. However, this technique does not provide for automatic expiration. When you directly define a *Cache* item, it stays cached until you remove it manually.

   B. **Incorrect:** The *Cache.Get* method allows you to retrieve cached items, not define them.

   C. **Correct:** You can use the *Cache.Insert* method to add an object to the cache and specify one or more dependencies, including an expiration time span.

   D. **Correct:** You can use the *Cache.Add* method to add an object to the cache and specify one or more dependencies, including an expiration time span. Unlike *Cache.Insert, Cache .Add* also returns the cached value, which might make it easier to use in your code.

4. Correct Answer: B, C, and E

   A. **Incorrect:** You can configure page output caching to vary with an HTTP header. However, the *Cache* object cannot use HTTP headers as dependencies.

   B. **Correct:** You can create file dependencies for *Cache* objects.

   C. **Correct:** You can make a *Cache* object expire after a specific time span or at a specific time.

   D. **Incorrect:** You cannot configure a *Cache* object to expire when a registry key is changed.

   E. **Correct:** You can configure a *Cache* object to expire when a different cached object expires.

Chapter 16: Case Scenario Answers

Case Scenario 1: Deploying a Web Application

1. You can use either the Copy Web tool or the Publish Web Site tool to update the staging server. However, the Copy Web tool is more bandwidth-efficient because it only copies changed files.
2. The Publish Web Site tool is the best way for the quality assurance people to update the production Web server. That tool enables the site to be precompiled, which can improve performance.

Case Scenario 2: Improving the Performance of a Public Web Site

1. Yes. You can use the *Cache* object to store a copy of database query results, and then quickly retrieve those results the next time they are required.
2. The database administrator mentioned that you are using SQL Server, so you could configure a dependency on the database table that contains the list of movies.
3. Yes. If you create user controls for cacheable components, such as the portion of the page that displays a list of movies, that user control can be cached while the rest of the page is dynamically generated.

Index

Symbols and Numbers

A

B

C

D

E

F

I

J

K

L

M

N

O

P

Q

R

S

T

U

V

W

X

Z

About the Author

MIKE SNELL has close to 20 years of experience writing software and consulting with clients looking to build their next generation of software products. Mike runs the delivery division of CEI (*www.ceiamerica.com*) in Pittsburgh, Pennsylvania. There, with a team of architects and developers, he helps CEI's clients build enterprise-ready software solutions.

Mike is also recognized as a Microsoft Regional Director. Regional Directors are members of a worldwide group of technology thought leaders known for their national and international speaking tours; their authorship of books, articles, and blogs; and their business acumen. For more information you can visit *www.theRegion.com*.

Mike blogs at *www.visualstudiounleashed.com*.